AF835347

Democracy and International Law

The Library of Essays in International Law
Series Editor: Robert McCorquodale

Titles in the Series:

International Law of Human Rights
Michael K. Addo

International Law and Indigenous Peoples
S. James Anaya

The International Criminal Court
Olympia Bekou and Robert Cryer

Democracy and International Law
Richard Burchill

Law of the Sea
Hugo Caminos

The Law of Treaties
Scott Davidson

Humanitarian Law
Judith Gardam

International Economic Regulation
Jane Kelsey

International Organizations
Jan Klabbers

International Peacekeeping
Boris Kondoch

Sources of International Law
Martti Koskenniemi

Space Law
Francis Lyall and Paul B. Larsen

Self-Determination in International Law
Robert McCorquodale

International Dispute Settlement
Mary Ellen O'Connell

International Crimes
Nikos Passas

International Environmental Law Volumes I and II
Paula M. Pevato

State Responsibility in International Law
René Provost

Jurisdiction in International Law
Michael Reisman

Title to Territory
Malcolm N. Shaw

The Nature of International Law
Gerry Simpson

Collective Security Law
Nigel D. White

Democracy and International Law

Edited by

Richard Burchill

University of Hull, UK

Routledge
Taylor & Francis Group
LONDON AND NEW YORK

First published 2006 by Ashgate Publishing

Published 2016 by Routledge
2 Park Square, Milton Park, Abingdon, Oxon OX14 4RN
711 Third Avenue, New York, NY 10017, USA

Routledge is an imprint of the Taylor & Francis Group, an informa business

Copyright © 2006 Richard Burchill. For copyright of individual articles please refer to the Acknowledgements.

All rights reserved. No part of this book may be reprinted or reproduced or utilised in any form or by any electronic, mechanical, or other means, now known or hereafter invented, including photocopying and recording, or in any information storage or retrieval system, without permission in writing from the publishers.

Notice:
Product or corporate names may be trademarks or registered trademarks, and are used only for identification and explanation without intent to infringe.

British Library Cataloguing in Publication Data
Democracy and international law. – (The library of essays in international law)
1. Democracy 2. International Law
I. Burchill, Richard
340.1'1

Library of Congress Control Number: 2006926340

ISBN 9780754624226 (hbk)

Contents

Acknowledgements vii
Series Preface ix
Introduction xi

PART I DEMOCRACY AND INTERNATIONAL LAW

1 Thomas M. Franck (1992), 'The Emerging Right to Democratic Governance', *American Journal of International Law*, **86**, pp. 46–91. 3
2 James Crawford (1993), 'Democracy and International Law', *British Yearbook of International Law*, **64**, pp. 113–33. 49
3 Gregory H. Fox and Brad R. Roth (2001), 'Democracy and International Law', *Review of International Studies*, **27**, pp. 327–52. 71

PART II DEFINITION(S) OF DEMOCRACY IN INTERNATIONAL LAW

4 Steven Wheatley (2002), 'Democracy in International Law: A European Perspective', *International and Comparative Law Quarterly*, **51**, pp. 225–48. 99
5 Molly Beutz (2003), 'Functional Democracy: Responding to Failures of Accountability', *Harvard International Law Journal*, **44**, pp. 387–431. 123
6 Reginald Ezetah (1997), 'The Right to Democracy: A Qualitative Inquiry', *Brooklyn Journal of International Law*, **22**, pp. 495–534. 169

PART III DEMOCRACY AND THE INTERNATIONAL SYSTEM

7 Fernando R. Tesón (1992), 'The Kantian Theory of International Law', *Columbia Law Review*, **92**, pp. 53–102. 211
8 Anne-Marie Slaughter (1995), 'International Law in a World of Liberal States', *European Journal of International Law*, **6**, pp. 503–38. 261
9 Eric Stein (2001), 'International Integration and Democracy: No Love at First Sight', *American Journal of International Law*, **95**, pp. 489–534. 297

PART IV INTERNATIONAL INSTITUTIONS AND THE PROMOTION AND PROTECTION OF DEMOCRACY

10 Christopher C. Joyner (1999), 'The United Nations and Democracy', *Global Governance*, **5**, pp. 333–57. 345

11 Richard Burchill (2001), 'The Promotion and Protection of Democracy by Regional Organizations in Europe: The Case of Austria', *European Public Law*, **7**, pp. 79–102. 371

12 Dexter S. Boniface (2002), 'Is There a Democratic Norm in the Americas? An Analysis of the Organization of American States', *Global Governance*, **8**, pp. 365–81. 395

13 Kofi Oteng Kufuor (2002), 'The OAU and the Recognition of Governments in Africa: Analyzing its Practice and Proposals for the Future', *American University International Law Review*, **17**, pp. 369–401. 413

14 Carlos Santiso (2001), 'Good Governance and Aid Effectiveness: The World Bank and Conditionality', *Georgetown Public Policy Review*, **7**, pp. 1–22. 447

PART V CRITICAL/SCEPTICAL VOICES ON DEMOCRACY AND INTERNATIONAL LAW

15 Susan Marks (1997), 'The End of History? Reflections on Some International Legal Theses', *European Journal of International Law*, **3**, pp. 449–77. 471

16 Gerry J. Simpson (1994), 'Imagined Consent: Democratic Liberalism in International Legal Theory', *Australian Yearbook of International Law*, **15**, pp. 103–28. 501

17 Dianne Otto (1993), 'Challenging the "New World Order": International Law, Global Democracy and the Possibilities for Women', *Transnational Law and Contemporary Problems*, **3**, pp. 371–415. 527

18 Yash Ghai (1994), 'Human Rights and Governance: The Asia Debate', *Australian Year Book of International Law*, **15**, pp. 1–34. 573

19 Larbi Sadiki (1995), 'Al-La Nidam: An Arab View of the New World (Dis)Order', *Arab Studies Quarterly*, **17**, pp. 1–22. 607

Name Index 629

Acknowledgements

The editor and publishers wish to thank the following for permission to use copyright material.

American Society of International Law for the essays: Thomas M. Franck (1992), 'The Emerging Right to Democratic Governance', *American Journal of International Law*, **86**, pp. 46–91. Copyright © 1992 American Society of International Law; Eric Stein (2001), 'International Integration and Democracy: No Love at First Sight', *American Journal of International Law*, **95**, pp. 489–534. Copyright © 2001 American Society of International Law.

Association of Arab American University for the essay: Larbi Sadiki (1995), 'Al-La Nidam: An Arab View of the New World (Dis)Order', *Arab Studies Quarterly*, **17**, pp. 1–22.

Australian Year Book of International Law for the essay: Yash Ghai (1994), 'Human Rights and Governance: The Asia Debate', *Australian Year Book of International Law*, **15**, pp. 1–34.

Molly Beutz (2003), 'Functional Democracy: Responding to Failures of Accountability', *Harvard International Law Journal*, **44**, pp. 387–431. Copyright © 2003 Molly Beutz.

Brooklyn Journal of International Law for the essay: Reginald Ezetah (1997), 'The Right to Democracy: A Qualitative Inquiry', *Brooklyn Journal of International Law*, **22**, pp. 495–534. Copyright © 1997 Brooklyn Law School.

Cambridge University Press for the essays: Gregory H. Fox and Brad R. Roth (2001), 'Democracy and International Law', *Review of International Studies*, **27**, pp. 327–52. Copyright © 2001 British International Studies Association; Steven Wheatley (2002), 'Democracy in International Law: A European Perspective', *International and Comparative Law Quarterly*, **51**, pp. 225–48; Anne-Marie Slaughter (1995), 'International Law in a World of Liberal States', *European Journal of International Law*, **6**, pp. 503–38; Susan Marks (1997), 'The End of History? Reflections on Some International Legal Theses', *European Journal of International Law*, **3**, pp. 449–77.

Georgetown Public Policy Review for the essay: Carlos Santiso (2001), 'Good Governance and Aid Effectiveness: The World Bank and Conditionality', *Georgetown Public Policy Review*, **7**, pp. 1–22. Copyright © 2001 Georgetown Public Policy Review.

Kluwer Law International for the essay: Richard Burchill (2001), 'The Promotion and Protection of Democracy by Regional Organizations in Europe: The Case of Austria', *European Public Law*, **7**, pp. 79–102. Copyright © 2001 Kluwer Law International.

Lynne Rienner Publishers for the essays: Christopher C. Joyner (1999), 'The United Nations and Democracy', *Global Governance*, **5**, pp. 333–57. Copyright © 1999 Lynne Rienner Publishers; Dexter S. Boniface (2002), 'Is There a Democratic Norm in the Americas? An Analysis of the Organization of American States', *Global Governance*, **8**, pp. 365–81. Copyright © 2002 Lynne Rienner Publishers.

Oxford University Press for the essay: James Crawford (1993), 'Democracy and International Law', *British Yearbook of International Law*, **64**, pp. 113–33. Copyright © 1993 James Crawford.

Fernando R. Tesón (1992), 'The Kantian Theory of International Law', *Columbia Law Review*, **92**, pp. 53–102. Copyright © 1991 Fernando R. Tesón.

Transnational Law and Contemporary Problems for the essay: Dianne Otto (1993), 'Challenging the "New World Order": International Law, Global Democracy and the Possibilities for Women', *Transnational Law and Contemporary Problems*, **3**, pp. 371–415. Copyright © 1993 Transnational Law and Contemporary Problems, University of Iowa College of Law.

Every effort has been made to trace all the copyright holders, but if any have been inadvertently overlooked the publishers will be pleased to make the necessary arrangement at the first opportunity.

Series Preface

Open a newspaper, listen to the radio or watch television any day of the week and you will read or hear of some matter concerning international law. The range of matters include the extent to which issues of trade and human rights should be linked, concerns about refugees and labour conditions, negotiations of treaties and the settlement of disputes, and decisions by the United Nations Security Council concerning actions to ensure compliance with international law. International legal issues have impact on governments, corporations, organisations and people around the world and the process of globalisation has increased this impact. In the global legal environment, knowledge of international law is an indispensable tool for all scholars, legal practitioners, decision-makers and citizens of the 21st century.

The Library of Essays in International Law is designed to provide the essential elements for the development of this knowledge. Each volume contains essays of central importance in the development of international law in a subject area. The proliferation of legal and other specialist journals, the increase in international materials and the use of the internet, has meant that it is increasingly difficult for legal scholars to have access to all the relevant articles on international law and many valuable older articles are now unable to be obtained readily. These problems are addressed by this series, which makes available an extensive range of materials in a manner that is of immeasurable value for both teaching and research at all levels.

Each volume is written by a leading authority in the subject area who selects the articles and provides an informative introduction, which analyses the context of the articles and comments on their significance within the developments in that area. The volumes complement each other to give a clear view of the burgeoning area of international law. It is not an easy task to select, order and place in context essays from the enormous quantity of academic legal writing prublished in journals – in many languages – throughout the world. This task requires professional scholarly judgment and difficult choices. The editors in this series have done an excellent job, for which I thank and congratulate them. It has been a pleasure working with them.

ROBERT MCCORQUODALE
General Series Editor
School of Law
University of Nottingham

Introduction

Speaking before the American Society of International Law in 1917 Elihu Root set out a vigorous defence of the need for the promotion and protection of democracy in international law. Root saw events around the world demonstrating strong support for democracy and, as a further consequence, he believed that international law's embrace of democracy would help to remedy the wrongs of the international system at the time. He pointedly declared that there was no room for any other ideology or system of government in the world if international law was to survive. Root's position was based on two main concerns. The first was that the existence of what he termed 'autocratic' governments was detrimental to the effectiveness of international law since these governments acted in secrecy, with no respect for rules or law and only in the self-interested pursuit of power. On the other hand, he believed, democracies obeyed and understood the importance of rules and acted within the limits set out by a legal system with the result that international law was respected. His second concern involved the importance of democracy for individuals. Root posited the belief that governments accountable to the people would not pursue policies or actions that would place the people under threat. In a democracy, power was exercised for the good of the people and not in the pursuit of aggressive power. Root felt that these two factors meant that international law had to promote and protect democracy in a proactive fashion. He even went so far as to say that conflict between democratic and non-democratic forms of government was inevitable but democracy had to prevail even if it meant that it had to 'kill its enemy when it can and where it can' (Root, 1917, p. 10).

Almost 90 years later, discussions about democracy and international law have been revived following the end of the Cold War. The downfall of communist regimes around the world from the mid-1980s into the 1990s led to claims that the world was experiencing a new wave of democracy and also that these events demonstrated an international victory for democracy as the only credible ideology remaining.[1] For international lawyers this quickly led to assertions that there existed a right to democracy in international law and that the promotion of democracy was essential to international peace. More recently there has been the practical manifestation of Root's (and others') belief that the enemies of democracy must be removed, as has been demonstrated by the interventions in Afghanistan and Iraq justified on, among other things, bringing democracy to these states in order, it is asserted, to ensure a more peaceful world.[2] Claims and assertions that democracy has become an integral feature of international law and relations have quickly proliferated, and democracy has a well accepted, if disputed, position in the international legal discourse.

1 The idea of the 'Third Wave' is attributable to Samuel P. Huntington's book, *The Third Wave* (1991). The victory for democracy was famously claimed by Francis Fukuyama in *The End of History and the Last Man* (1992).

2 For example. see George W. Bush's 'State of the Union Address' (2004); also Ledeen (2004).

Democracy and International Law

The movement towards democracy in the international system from the 1990s is not a unique event, as the international system has seen similar developments in the past (Huntington, 1991, pp.13–26). However, this 'Third Wave' of democratization has been different on account of its breadth, depth and the actual impact it has had on international law. The academic debate about democracy in international law truly took off with Thomas Franck's 1992 essay 'The Emerging Right to Democratic Governance' (Chapter 1). Franck made grand claims concerning democracy, but his initial belief was that a right to democratic governance is only emerging in international law. Franck views democracy as the key factor for determining the legitimacy of states in the international system. His approach to legitimacy is twofold: a government achieves domestic legitimacy through the existence of democratic processes, and in turn the international system will bestow legitimacy upon a government that respects democracy. Franck's thesis relies on the developments associated with the new wave of democracy leading to the emergence of normative expectations in the international system that states will be organized as democracies. He also undertakes a historical view to show that these normative expectations have a substantial pedigree in international relations. Franck's essay has been subjected to a number of substantial criticisms from various angles, but it is truly a seminal piece in this field.

Many international legal scholars quickly embraced the idea that there was a definitive right or entitlement to democracy in the international system, with some claims even postdating this existence to the adoption of the UDHR in 1948 (Cerna, 1995). As James Crawford demonstrates in his essay concisely titled 'Democracy and International Law' (Chapter 2), the influence of democracy on international law is far-reaching. But Crawford also explains that international law has had very little substantive interest in democracy until very recently and that significant aspects of international law were, and remain, clearly undemocratic. He views the adoption of the UN Charter as marking a new system for the ordering of international relations with international law moving from a primarily descriptive system to one that attempted to be more proscriptive, even in relation to domestic issues such as the nature of a government. This shift mainly occurred through the evolution of international human rights law but remained limited in its effect because international law maintained a number of undemocratic features as primary rules of the international system. Crawford goes on to note a range of areas where democracy clearly has had an influence on the actions of states, such as justifying the use of force against non-democratic regimes, the use of democratic criteria in the process of recognition, an increasing emphasis on minority rights, and the importance of democratic principles for intergovernmental organizations. His essay goes beyond the relatively narrow scope of Franck's right to democratic governance to show the extent to which democracy has, or has not, had an influence on the development of international law.

As international practice explicitly in support of democracy grows, is it possible, as Crawford points out (p. 58), to claim that a 'new stress on democracy as a value, even a dominant value, in national and international relations' had taken hold in the international system? Gregory Fox's and Brad Roth's essay (Chapter 3), under the same title as Crawford's work, provides an important update and expansion on the points raised by Crawford, demonstrating this 'new stress' on democracy as a dominant value in the international system. Fox and Roth examine the growth of action and attention within international law in support of democracy and further engage in discussions about the major justifications that can be put forth in support of democracy's increased importance. They identify four primary considerations: first, the importance of democracy for the protection of human rights; second, democracy as a means of preventing internal armed conflict; third, democracy as a means of promoting peace among states; and, fourth, the use of democratic processes in the formulation of emerging international norms. By setting out justifications for democracy, the authors make a significant contribution to the controversial debate about international law shedding its claimed neutrality and its movement towards an explicitly normative position in support of democracy.

All of the essays in Part I of this volume demonstrate that international law generally is increasingly promoting and protecting democracy. Although democracy may not as yet have become the leading ideology of the international system, Fox and Roth provide a persuasive case as to why it should be. They also demonstrate, whether one favours the idea of democracy or not, that the time has come for the issue of democracy to be addressed as a legal question.

Definition(s) of Democracy in International Law

A key issue in the development of democracy in international law is determining what is meant by the term. Democracy has a long history but its meaning is highly contested.[3] As a result, democracy is commonly viewed as a term with no determinate content, a definitional difficulty which international law has yet to overcome. However, as international law begins to address democracy as a legal question, the definitional issue must be directly addressed. Each of the essays in Part II makes the point that the dominant understanding of what democracy means in international law is limited to the undertaking of basic procedures, such as voting. All the authors feel that confining democracy to basic procedural norms is unhelpful and not consistent with the true meaning of democracy as an emancipatory project. Undeniably, a minimalist conception of democracy does perhaps provide the easiest way of verifying the existence of what is understood to be a democracy and, in Franck's view, represents the maximum level of agreement possible in the international system. The authors included here do not all agree on how we should define democracy, but all agree that there is a need to look beyond procedural norms to fully understand the relevance and importance of democracy for the international system.

Even though Steven Wheatley's essay 'Democracy in International Law: A European Perspective' (Chapter 4) is focused on a 'European perspective' of democracy, he deals with the definition question as part of general international law in this area. Wheatley very rightly explains that, when it comes to efforts at establishing democracy as a legal requirement, some attempt at defining democracy in theory and in practice is required. In the international legal literature there is a tendency to adopt a minimalist understanding of democracy, limiting it to the existence of certain procedures and institutions, primarily based around elections (Marks, 2000, pp. 30–49). But, as Wheatley shows, there is a good deal of material beyond elections to draw upon in working out a definition of democracy in international law. While this material does not provide an exact definition of democracy, if such a thing is even possible or desirable, it does point in specific directions allowing for a greater understanding of what democracy

[3] The literature on the history and meaning of democracy is voluminous, but David Held (1996) provides a useful overview.

entails. From this material Wheatley distils two cardinal principles – popular sovereignty and political equality. He also emphasizes the importance of tolerance and broadmindedness: democracy is not just about majority rule for there must be equal respect for all members of society. Wheatley's view is that democracy means individuals participating in the decision-making process and government being obliged to take into account the interests expressed. In his survey of international law he finds that these principles are well articulated in relation to the political, social and economic spheres of society, demonstrating that democracy means more than just elections.

Molly Beutz addresses a similar definition of democracy in the essay 'Functional Democracy: Responses to Failures of Accountability' (Chapter 5). Buetz's main focus is the issue of accountability which, in a democratic sense, involves ensuring that decision-makers face the consequences of their actions through the existence of some form of sanction available to the people. This, in turn, ensures that the interests of the people will be accounted for in the decision-making process and that they will be able to participate in this process as well. Buetz also emphasizes the existence of dispute settlement mechanisms that allow for conflicts to be dealt with peacefully and provide a means for determining how various functions, such as the allocation of resources, are carried out. She believes that defining democracy in this way helps to overcome the emptiness of minimalist definitions while at the same time avoiding the problematic issue of defining democracy in terms of achieving particular ends. This approach is valuable because, as Beutz shows, international law is hesitant to address values and ends and, while its embrace of democracy is an adoption of certain values, there remains a good deal of dispute as to how those values should be manifested. By addressing the issue of functionality – democracy's ability to respond to the needs of the people – Buetz feels that international law will be in a much better position to support democracy. She notes that, so far, responses to failures of democracy have been ad hoc and opportunistic with no clear determination as to meaning. Her definition, she believes, will work to improve international law's response by viewing democracy as more than a procedure but not becoming bogged down in disputes about what sort of ends democracy should be producing.

In Reginald Ezetah's essay, 'The Right to Democracy: A Qualitative Inquiry' (Chapter 6), the author views democracy as a crucial part of human development so his definition focuses on issues such as participation, consent, accountability, resolving disputes through non-violent means and providing for the welfare of the people. Ezetah emphasizes the need for democracy to be understood as a 'context dependent idea' as there is no one single definition applicable to all situations. But, at the same time, he argues that democracy does contain a core understanding in terms of human development (p. 170). He traces this core through the main international legal instruments, which in turn help him to formulate the Convention on Democratic Governance grounded in Articles 21–28 of the Universal Declaration on Human Rights. As Ezetah notes, there will never be a solution to the 'riddle of immense proportion' that defining democracy represents, but satisfaction with a minimalist conception of democracy remains one of the key shortcomings in international law's embrace of the idea.

Democracy originated as a revolutionary concept that directly challenges those who hold power to share that power and be more accountable as to how power is exercised. International law's embrace of democracy is built along these lines as the origins of the democratic entitlement is commonly seen as originating in international human rights law, another area that directly challenges those who hold and exercise power. However, the minimalist conceptions of democracy fail to realize democracy's full potential as an emancipatory force. Democracy is about participation in the processes of government and governance allowing for the development of the individual and society. Elections at regular intervals do not do enough to ensure this, as it has been clearly demonstrated that increased election activity in the world has not necessarily brought conditions conducive to the development of the individual and society (Zakaria, 1997, 2004). In discussing what is meant by democracy there is much potential for disagreement, but international law should not shy away from messy situations. Whether one agrees or not with the views of democracy put forth in Part II of this volume is not the point. The key factor is that these authors have engaged with a difficult area, setting an example that needs to be emulated. The authors further demonstrate that international law already possesses significant resources for dealing with quandaries about definition. The wide range of international legal instruments, declarations and resolutions that address the place of individuals and groups in relation to the exercise of power provide details as to what democracy can be, both in terms of theory and practice. Many of these sources existed long before the current attention to democracy became a concern for international law but they share common goals with democracy since they are all concerned with the development and well-being of individuals and groups in the world. International law's ongoing quest to define and understand what is meant by democracy is not a venture into the unknown or unattainable, but is instead grounded in a range of values and practices international law has already proclaimed itself to be pursuing.[4]

Democracy and the International System

The end of the ideological divide that was the Cold War has allowed international law to promote actively democracy and has also opened the way for democracy to become a major factor in how international relations are conducted and ultimately how the international system is organized (see Fox and Roth, 2000). The idea of a world based on democratic governments has its origins in the eighteenth-century writings of Immanuel Kant. Kant's view of the ideal international system was a world of republics – states based on constitutional principles that provided for a separation of powers and manifested the general will – where there was a direct link between the government and the governed based both on the consent of the people and the fact that the government would only act to serve the interests of the people.[5] For Kant, the international system was best ordered if all sovereigns were republics since they would carry out their relations through peaceful means and not have recourse to force with one another.

A Kantian vision of the international system is once again being discussed in detail. Fernando Tesón's essay, 'The Kantian Theory of International Law' (Chapter 7), provides an extensive treatment of what a Kantian vision of international law would look like and how it influences the development of international law. As Tesón explains, international law's primary purpose should be to ensure the respect and protection of individual human beings.

---

4 For example, see UN Commission on Human Rights Resolution 2003/36, 'Interdependence between Democracy and Human Rights' (23 April 2003), para. 7.

5 Kant did not favour democracy, which he viewed as a form of despotism as each individual strives for ultimate executive power, making government impossible. See Kant (1795), Section II, 'First Definitive Article for Perpetual Peace'.

International law should not be wholly based on the idea of state sovereignty whereby a sovereign is able to control society through any means possible. Instead there is the need for domestic legitimacy based on whether or not the state actually represents the interests of those it governs. This Kantian view of international law also leads to the classifying of states according to their domestic political structures, disregarding the classical international law view of sovereign equals, and this in turn impacts on how international law is utilized in the conduct of international relations. The primary justification for making these distinctions lies in the idea of the 'democratic' peace. Tesón uses Kant's original view of the democratic peace to assert that, if democracies do not go to war with one another and a key feature of current international law is the maintenance of international peace and security, then this stands as a clear reason for pursuing a world of democratic states.

The idea of the democratic peace lies at the heart of Anne-Marie Slaughter's view of the international system as set out in her essay 'International Law in a World of Liberal States' (Chapter 8). Slaughter has been one of the principal proponents of the idea of an international system based on democratic states, and this piece encapsulates her views and explains how they would influence the nature and structure of international law. Slaughter believes that states constituted on a liberal democratic basis – that is, states that have some form of representative government, a free-market economy based on personal property rights, and protection for civil and political rights – will engage in closer forms of cooperation through transnational networks that will develop between domestic institutions and individuals, ensuring a more peaceful world. Slaughter believes that this cooperation will be based on shared core principles that are central to democracy and that these principles will spread in the international system as more states adopt democracy. The model of interstate relations she proposes allows for the formulation of expectations about the relations between liberal and non-liberal states and the generation of what she views to be a universal set of norms, based on liberal democracy and applicable to all states in the international system. Slaughter admits that her view of an international system of liberal states does not yet exist and that it is unlikely to come into being in the near future. Other studies (for example, Alvarez, 2001) have raised serious questions concerning the extent to which liberal states do cooperate in the way Slaughter perceives. She also recognizes that the distinction between regime types is 'distasteful' for some (p. 264), but her views have had a noticeable influence on academics and policy-makers (Alvarez, 2001, p. 190).

Moving away from Kantian views of international law, Eric Stein's essay, 'International Integration and Democracy: No Love at First Sight' (Chapter 9) discusses another major development in the international system that influences the promotion and protection of democracy: increased integration through intergovernmental organizations as states have realized that it is through greater cooperation that common goals can be achieved. Slaughter discounts this area of state action believing that substantive action concerning the spread of democracy will occur through transnational networks rather than through interstate relations in intergovernmental organizations. But Eric Stein's research (Chapter 9) shows that increased integration is certainly on the rise and cannot be ignored. Stein goes on to discuss how this increased integration activity raises serious questions about democracy and the extent to which individuals affected by decisions from intergovernmental organizations have been able to participate in the formulation of those decisions and how accountability is maintained. At a simple level of understanding, increased integration leads to less democracy, understood as the ability of individuals to participate in decision-making and to hold decision-makers accountable. As intergovernmental organizations become more involved in processes that were traditionally carried out at the state level, the basic issue of democracy – the ability of individuals and groups to be part of the processes that impact on them – becomes strained.

Stein identifies a paradox developing from current trends in the international system: there is an increase in modes of integration but also increased attention given to what are considered to be core democratic values such as participation and accountability, something for which intergovernmental organizations often lack the structure. The prime example of increased integration accompanied by increased disillusionment with integration structures that do not appear to adhere to core values of democracy is the EU which has increasingly become an active promoter and protector of democracy among its member states and potential members. Yet, at the same time as the EU's activities have been expanding, the organization itself has been subject to criticisms about its own lack of democracy (Burchill, 2004). Stein makes some suggestions as to how it is possible to 'inject the voice of individual citizens into the exclusively state-based structures' (p. 341). He suggests two broad areas of action: recognizing the rights of individuals in the constituent treaties that can be enforced at either the domestic or supranational level and the creation of an assembly that is directly elected and has real power in the law-making process. Stein recognizes that his suggestions may be considered radical, and that no single solution will be widely applicable. In his study, however, he does find enough evidence that various idiosyncratic arrangements based on the level of integration already achieved have produced favourable results. From this it is possible to examine and assess the extent to which intergovernmental organizations are adhering to democratic principles.

International Institutions and the Promotion and Protection of Democracy

Stein's work shows that intergovernmental organizations present a number of problems with regard to democratic principles and practices in international law. At the same time, it is recognized that intergovernmental organizations, especially regional organizations, have made significant contributions to the development of democracy in international law. As the essays dealing with definitions of democracy have shown, intergovernmental organizations have been at the forefront of developing international legal obligations directly requiring democracy or obligations strongly supporting democracy, such as human rights. Intergovernmental organizations, as traditionally understood in international law, are not autonomous units able to create international law obligating states without their direct consent (Sands and Klein 2001, ch. 15). As the essays in Part IV demonstrate, intergovernmental organizations have been able to build on the values and obligations concerning democracy that states have come to agree upon in order to create legally defined obligations.

Agreement on the promotion and protection of democracy has been most prominent in the regional organizations of Europe, and the Western hemisphere. Organizations in these regions have explicitly set out membership requirements based on democracy that, combined with other efforts in support of democracy, have resulted in democracy becoming an international legal obligation for the states of these regions (see Wheatley, Chapter 4; Boniface, Chapter 12). As a universal organization with global membership, the UN might seem to be an unlikely place for the promotion and protection of democracy given that membership to the UN does not depend on democratic credentials (Charter of the United Nations, Chapter II). The UN did exclude the South African government during the apartheid regime,[6] but the UN Charter only mentions 'peace-loving' states as a requirement for membership. As democracy is not an explicit objective of the organization, support for democracy in the UN has remained conditioned on respect for state sovereignty and the right of a state to determine its own social and political system (Charter of the United Nations, Article 2(7)), which makes the UN's support for democracy uneven at best.[7] Despite this, Christopher Joyner's essay on 'The United Nations and Democracy' (Chapter 10) demonstrates that the UN has been actively involved in the promotion of democracy in a wide range of areas. Joyner emphasizes the importance of the UN as a universal body in the promotion of democracy as an important aspect of international law and relations. As the activities of the UN involve states from all over the globe and not just certain regions, this helps creates the perception that the organization possesses impartiality and universal legitimacy, giving greater credibility to its support of democracy. Joyner's essay clearly demonstrates that the UN has an active role to play in the promotion and protection of democracy in international law. It further demonstrates that the idea of democracy has become a dominant value in guiding the organization's work.

While intergovernmental organizations have shown a great deal of support for the promotion of democracy, the legal enforcement of democracy becomes very tricky, even where there exist legal obligations upon states directly calling for the existence of democratic systems. Richard Burchill's contribution, 'The Promotion and Protection of Democracy by Regional Organizations in Europe: The Case of Austria' (Chapter 11) demonstrates that, even where a requirement of democracy is set out in a treaty, there is still plenty of scope for discussion and debate over the meaning of the concept, which in turn impacts on the ability of an organization to act. When the 1999 elections in Austria brought the far-right Freedom Party into a government coalition, European intergovernmental organizations were faced with a difficult dilemma. Austria had undertaken free and fair elections, but the policies and the views of the Freedom Party and their leader were seen as contrary to the democratic values of Europe as set out in the various membership treaties for the organizations of the region. Within the EU there were calls for Austria's exclusion from the organization on the basis that it was in violation of the treaty requirements of democracy as set out in Article 6 of the Treaty of European Union. In the circumstances, I argue, Austria did not act contrary to the values of democracy as it had held a free and fair election where over 20 per cent of the electorate had expressed a preference for the Freedom Party. If Austria had refused to recognize the result of this election that would have been clearly contrary to democracy, but it was difficult to see how Austria could be acting in breach of any legal requirements of democracy by including a certain political party in the government. The Austrian situation demonstrates that, even though democracy is being understood in legal terms, views on democracy and on

---

[6] See Report of the UN Credentials Committee, 29th Session of the General Assembly, UN Doc. A/9779 (1974) and UN Doc. A/PV 2248 (1974).

[7] As demonstrated by the statements from the President of the UN General Assembly during the 52nd Session in 1997. Razali Ismail expressed his view that there was a politicalization of liberal global values such as human rights, democracy and free markets which are being promoted as the answer to all of humankind's problems. In his view the UN was an inappropriate forum for the development of democracy as the notion is not widely accepted in Asia and in a great number of other states in the world. See *UN Chronicle* **4**(3), 1997, p. 13.

action to be taken in order to protect democracy continue to be tempered heavily by political preferences.

Even where there are relatively clear details as to what a treaty-based requirement of democracy entails and how action is to be taken, the enforcement of those obligations remains indeterminate and heavily tempered by non-legal considerations, as Dexter Boniface sets out in his essay 'Is There a Democratic Norm in the Americas: An Analysis of the Organization of American States' (Chapter 12). He examines the strong normative position on democracy developed over a long period of time by the OAS, paying particular attention to the recently approved instruments that detail what the democratic obligation entails and how the organization will react if those obligations are not met. Boniface shows that, even where a good deal of elaboration on the meaning of democracy has been undertaken, the ability of an organization to react to disruptions of democracy will depend heavily on the attitude of member states at the time. Boniface's study helps further an understanding of the complexities involved with the protection of democracy by an intergovernmental organization as actual action is based more on non-legal strategic interests at the time, which will determine the form and intensity of the action taken to protect democracy. This, of course, leads to accusations of selectivity and indeterminacy with regard to the determinacy of legal obligations concerning democracy.

The problems of indeterminacy and selectivity are also highlighted in Kofi Oteng Kufuor's essay 'The OAU and the Recognition of Governments in Africa: Analyzing its Practice and Proposals for the Future' (Chapter13). Very little work has been done on the role of regional organizations in Africa in the promotion and protection of democracy, primarily because of the lack of any developed normative framework in support of democracy, and Kufuor's research is important for understanding the problems they face. He shows that the overall context in Africa is dramatically different from the situation with the OAS or Europe as African intergovernmental organizations have not developed a strong normative position on democracy, with traditional international law rules on non-intervention in domestic affairs taking primacy over any developments in support of democracy. Even though the former Organization of African Unity (now the African Union) has worked to develop norms of democracy, such actions face significant obstacles due to the political, social and economic conditions in the region, which are not always conducive to the promotion of democracy. Kufuor discusses a number of case studies that demonstrate the indeterminacy of intergovernmental organizations when dealing with the promotion and protection of democracy among the member states. He also utilizes more recent proclamations in the region that support the promotion and protection of democracy to suggest means for improving the institutional infrastructure. He calls for clear obligations of democracy to be applicable to all states in the region and for any sort of organizational response to be transparent and clearly based on existing normative declarations. Kufuor's essay highlights the tensions that exist between recent developments in support of democracy and more well-established rules of sovereignty and non-intervention in domestic affairs that are of much greater prominence and determinacy in international law.

The most contentious area in the debate over selectivity is perhaps the use of democracy in aid and development policies. This is commonly known as conditionality, where international institutions, especially international financial institutions, condition the delivery of aid and support programmes on the existence of certain criteria such as the promotion and protection of democracy or human rights. This area is contentious because, as Carlos Santiso discusses in 'Good Governance and Aid Effectiveness: The World Bank and Conditionality' (Chapter 14), it is easily subjected to criticisms of imperialism because it entails more developed states requiring from other states certain forms of normative behaviour that have not necessarily been consented or agreed to. In the past, international financial institutions have tried to remain detached from debates about the nature of government in a recipient state. But, as Santiso argues, international financial institutions cannot, and should not, ignore the nature of the government in the states that are receiving aid. The policies and practices of international financial institutions deal directly with the structure of government and the process of governance, making it necessary to give greater considerations to the existence of democracy. This is a significant departure from the dominant view of development aid, which has focused solely on open trade, fiscal restraint and less state regulation and control over economic matters in favour of free market-based mechanisms. Santiso shows how research in this field has demonstrated that the political context is crucial for economic performance, with poverty reduction strategies dependent on some form of democratic system as this will ensure policies conducive to development and will put the institutional structures in place to deliver and, importantly, be able to resolve conflicts peacefully and mediate interests and changes. Given the high levels of expenditure and international activity that occur in this field, Santiso's views need to be seriously considered.

Critical/Sceptical Voices on Democracy and International Law

The sudden emergence and apparent widespread acceptance of democratic norms in the international legal discourse has been extraordinary. In an extremely short period of time, and based on sparse and inconsistent evidence, it is claimed that international law has gone from a system of supposed ideological neutrality, with little to no attention given to how government was structured, to a full embrace of the idea that democracy is now the standard of legitimacy in the international system (Cerna, 1995; Franck, Chapter 1; Reisman, 1990). It is remarkable how an indeterminate political concept, which had been ravaged by Cold War ideological struggles, has seemingly become a hard and fast rule of international law. The essays in Part V all take issue with the grand claims that have been made about the victory of democracy and international law's embrace of it. All of the authors question the extent to which the type of democracy being celebrated is truly changing the nature and structure of international law or just working to solidify and legitimize the unequal power arrangements that already exist. In short, the essays included here provide a good dose of healthy scepticism by asking whether international law's promotion and protection of democracy lives up to the emancipatory ideals that underlie the term.

In 'The End of History? Reflections on Some International Legal Theses' (Chapter 15) Susan Marks explains that a good deal of the international legal scholarship on democracy adopts a position that actually works to 'attenuate the emancipatory and critical force that democracy might have' (p. 472). She describes how scholars looked to a selected range of events to draw strong conclusions posited as universal developments and goes on to show how they were quick to validate the victory for democracy in the early 1990s at the expense of giving adequate attention to whether or not the developments they were citing in fact contributed to the promotion of democracy understood as an emancipatory project. Marks discusses how international law's embrace of democracy has not necessarily helped to lessen uneven or oppressive power structures and how it has not provided for the freedom and participation it claims to embody. She feels that international law emphasizes form over substance in determining the existence of democracy, which is not beneficial to the development of democracy in international law. The end result is that democracy fails to become a liberating force because individuals and groups fail to benefit from the full potential it offers.

Marks also takes issue with the emphasis some scholars place on international law's role in the promotion and protection of democracy as primarily concerned just with the level of the state. There is a need to address the issue of multiple sources of power if international law's development of democracy is to remain credible. With more and more action being taken beyond the state, questions about democratic legitimacy need to be directed at these sites of power. Marks shows that a failure on the part of international law to understand and address the implications of democracy beyond the state will not only discredit the emancipatory nature of the democracy project, but will also lead to a bizarre paradox in which intergovernmental organizations strive to promote democracy among their members but fail in themselves to uphold the very same principles and practices.

Gerry Simpson's essay 'Imagined Consent: Democratic Liberalism in International Legal Theory' (Chapter 16) is concerned with theoretical views of the nature of international law with an emphasis on the impact of Kantian views and the democratic norm thesis as set out by Franck. Simpson's treatment of the various strains of thought in democratic liberalism provides an illuminating study of the changes that international law is undergoing in trying to place the individual as one of its substantive subjects. Simpson outlines and critiques Tesón's views on the Kantian vision of international law and Franck's work on democratic governance. He makes the point that, in both cases, there is a tendency to overlook the various contexts and conditions that will influence the nature of democracy. Like that of Marks, Simpson's critique focuses on the lack of attention paid to the way in which international law's support for democracy actually works to support the problems inherent in the existing power relations. The value of this essay lies in the way in which it demonstrates how the embrace of democracy in international law by scholars has not necessarily been thought through adequately and is too often based on limited evidence. More crucially, he also shows the necessity of caution in making grand claims based upon 'a series of largely indeterminate and formless legal principles' (p. 521). Simpson's essay fits well with this collection as it provides the reader with a critical perspective of two of the leading proponents of democratic developments in international law – Franck and Tesón – who are also included in this collection.

Diane Otto's contribution, 'Challenging the "New World Order": International Law, Global Democracy and the Possibilities for Women' (Chapter 17), discusses how international law's emphasis on form over substance in the promotion and protection of democracy erases any appeals to diversity or dissent that are inherent in the democratic project. Otto's essay connects well with the views set out by Marks and Simpson in that it demonstrates how international law's support of democracy is not necessarily inclusive and empowering, as evidenced by the role of women. Otto highlights how international law's discourse on democracy provides the potential for a truly inclusive process but, due to what she views as the liberal roots of international system, democracy remains confined with a greater emphasis on minimalist conceptions that allow international law to concern itself with enforcing or controlling democratic processes. She provides a strong critique of the dominate views of liberal democracy, demonstrating how the emphasis on creating 'homogeneous, autonomous, abstract, male individuals motivated by private self-interest' (p. 553) and set in relations of formal equality, works to undermine any forms of resistance and dissent by upholding a single dominant model. She undertakes a study of alternative forms of democracy that move beyond the formalism of minimalist conceptions, engage with more than just the political sphere of society, emphasize participation, and recognize diversity as a value for empowerment and not as a threat to the status quo. Otto's contribution demonstrates that international law has the potential for either reinforcing existing power relationships and undermining the emancipatory value of democracy or working to support and reinforce democratic diversity in the international system and challenging any attempt at exclusionary practices.

In examining international law's support for the promotion and protection of democracy not only is the type of democracy being supported subject to critical analysis, but the project itself has been brought into question. Yash Ghai's essay, 'Human Rights and Governance: The Asia Debate' (Chapter 18) provides a well-balanced and insightful discussion with regard to the issue of the applicability of ideas and values of democracy and human rights that are commonly associated with the West and claimed to be of limited value to Asian societies. Ghai makes an essential observation in this regard demonstrating how there is no single 'Asian view' on the nature and applicability of democracy, due to the diversity of the region. His essay explores a range of official government positions which assert that the international promotion of democracy is 'connected with the desire for Western global hegemony' (p. 591). It also brings to light a different set of Asian voices, those of 'the oppressed and the marginalised', 'the passionate voices of indigenous peoples whose cultures are destroyed by governments who claim to be the custodians of Asian culture' (p. 597). These voices attempt to engage with the international promotion of democracy in order to challenge the monopoly on power possessed by governments. Ghai rightly demonstrates that issues of democracy and human rights have to be understood in the context of the political, social and economic conditions of society. But he also explains that this cannot be used as an excuse or justification for the denial of human rights and democracy. Ghai's essay is extremely useful in helping to foster constructive debate about the cultural cleavages that are said to exist between Western and Asian views of democracy and human rights.

Resistance to the international promotion of democracy has also come from Arab commentators, as shown in Larbi Sadiki's essay, 'Al-La Nidam: An Arab View of the New World (Dis)Order' (Chapter 19). Sadiki demonstrates that the issue is not necessarily the inapplicability of democracy to Arab society, but more the way in which international law is being manipulated by powerful states to achieve their own political goals, justified on the basis of promoting democracy. The essay was written in the wake of events in the Gulf region during the early 1990s and in the context of the claims for the international victory of democracy. Sadiki points out that this supposed new world order did not herald the actual promotion and protection of democracy, but instead brought about a range of double standards that were applied not only in relation to the involvement of the USA in the Middle East but also in respect of the UN's position in the promotion and protection of democracy. Sadiki's critique remains relevant with regard to events in the Arab world early in this century, as there continues to be a great deal of apprehension concerning the way democracy is being promoted in the region.[8] Significantly, however, as Sadiki notes, there is no full-scale rejection

[8] For a useful survey of recent opinions see Wickham, (2004).

of the principles and practices of democracy as these, he believes, continue to be of crucial importance to Arab states. Instead, attention needs to be given as to how the international system promotes and protects democracy so that it can live up to its emancipatory value for all and not become just a tool for the powerful.

An Agenda for the Future

The essays in this volume demonstrate that there can be no doubt that an 'infiltration of concerns for democratic legitimacy into virtually every aspect of international legal discourse' has taken place (Fox and Roth, this volume, p. 75). Whether one favours the growth of democracy in international law or not, it must be recognized that international law speaks the language of democracy in most aspects, and therefore international lawyers have to at least acknowledge it, if not actively engage with it. International law still cannot claim any rule requiring democracy from all members of the international system, but democracy has come to influence a plethora of international activities.

Marks has identified a worrying tendency in the international legal literature to uncritically accept an international legal principle of democracy based on minimalist conceptions through rather weak evidence. This has quickly turned into a belief that democracy is a well-established principle of international law and that therefore there is little left to discuss on the matter (Marks, p. 493). International lawyers continue to vigorously debate long-established legal principles such as sovereignty and custom, refusing to accept that these are clearly established principles. Why, then, has there appeared to such a quick acceptance of democracy as a principle of international law? Clearly there is no straightforward answer to this issue. Democracy is a difficult and controversial concept, both in theory and practice. It is even possible that, as a political concept subject to substantial disagreement, democracy cannot be treated as a determinate legal concept. So far, international law has addressed this point by offering a very basic minimalist understanding of democracy. This allows for the avoidance of more intense controversy and prevents the embarrassing emergence of any sort of credibility gap exhibiting a wide difference between what the law professes and what actually happens in reality. By relying on a minimalist conception international law can rightly claim widespread support for the existence of what is understood to be democracy. But, in many respects, this is a self-defeating strategy as the current understanding of democracy only serves to entrench dominance and exclusion: the very things democracy sets outs to resist. A key feature of democracy is ongoing debate and discussion about what is to be achieved and how best to achieve it. International law has to remain active in this discussion and not accept a rather static understanding of democracy for the sake of simplicity.

The essays in this volume address the wide parameters of the debate about democracy and international law. Each essay draws on a number of specific areas in international law where democracy has had significant influence, such as international human rights, membership of intergovernmental organizations, various forms of assistance with elections, the law of recognition, trade conditionality and the use of force. International practice within these various areas demonstrates that democracy in international law is more than just a vague entitlement or right in the international system. In the same way that recognized bodies of laws, declarations and practice are conceptualized as a single body of law in areas such as international human rights law or international environmental law, the international system is now witnessing the development of an 'international law of democracy' (Burchill, 2001). However, this development is far from a natural progression. Almost 100 years ago Elihu Root was praising developments in the international system that demonstrated that democracy was taking hold as an international legal principle. Root's vision was put on hold until the 1990s and has still not necessarily taken hold in the international system in this century. The current embrace of democracy in international law is more complex and contested than is generally recognized in the international legal literature, making the ongoing process of probing and critical research imperative.

References

Alvarez, José (2001), 'Do Liberal States Behave Better? A Critique of Slaughter's Liberal Theory', *European Journal of International Law*, **12,** pp. 183–246.

Burchill, Richard (2001), 'The Developing International Law of Democracy', *Modern Law Review*, **64**, pp. 123–34.

Burchill, Richard (2004), 'The European Union and European Democracy: Social Democracy or Democracy with a Social Dimension?', *Canadian Journal of Law and Jurisprudence*, **17**, pp. 185–207.

Bush, George W. (2004), 'State of the Union Address', 20 January, available at: http://www.whitehouse.gov/news/releases/2004/01/20040120-7.html.

Cerna, Christina (1995), 'Universal Democracy: An International Legal Right or the Pipe Dream of the West?', *New York University Journal of International Law and Politics*, **27**, pp. 289–330.

Fox, Gregory and Roth, Brad (eds) (2000), *Democratic Governance and International Law*, Cambridge: Cambridge University Press.

Fukuyama, Francis (1992), *The End of History and the Last Man*, New York: Free Press.

Held, David (1996), *Models of Democracy* (2nd edn), Cambridge: Polity Press.

Huntington, Samuel P. (1991), *The Third Wave: Democratization in the Late Twentieth Century*, Norman, OK: University of Oklahoma Press.

Kant, Immanuel (1795), *Perpetual Peace: A Philosophical Sketch*, available at: http://www.mtholyoke.edu/acad/intrel/kant/kant1.htm.

Ledeen, Michael A (2004), 'From Tyranny to Freedom', *National Review Online*, **7**, April, available at http://www.nationalreview.com/ledeen/ledeen200404070843.asp.

Marks, Susan (2000), *The Riddle of All Constitutions: International Law, Democracy and the Critique of Ideology*, Oxford: Oxford University Press.

Reisman, Michael (1990), 'Sovereignty and Human Rights in Contemporary International Law', *American Journal of International Law*, **84**, pp. 866–76.

Root, Elihu (1917), *The Effect of Democracy on International Law* (Pamphlet 30), Washington DC: Carneige Endowment for International Peace.

Sands, Philippe and Klein, Pierre (2001), *Bowett's Law of International Institutions* (5th edn), London: Sweet and Maxwell.

Wickham, Carrie (2004), 'The Problem with Coercive Democratization: The Islamist Response to U.S. Democracy Reform Initiative', *Muslim World Journal of Human Rights*, 1, Article 6, available at: http://www.bepress.com/mwjhr.

Zakaria, Fareed (1997), 'The Rise of Illiberal Democracy', *Foreign Affairs*, **76**, pp. 22–43.

Zakaria, Fareed (2004), *The Future of Freedom: Illiberal Democracy at Home and Abroad*, New York, NY: W.W. Norton Publishers.

Further Reading

Allott, Philip (1990), *Eunomia: A New Order for a New World*, Oxford: Oxford University Press.

Barnes, Samuel (2001), 'The Contribution of Democracy to Rebuilding Postconflict Societies', *American Journal of International Law*, **95,** pp. 86–101.

Burchill, Richard (2003), 'The Role of Democracy in the Protection of Human Rights: Lessons from the European and Inter-American Human Rights Systems', in David Forsythe and Patrice McMahon (eds), *Human Rights and Diversity: Area Studies Revisited*, Lincoln, NE: University of Nebraska Press, pp. 137–56.

Burley, Anne-Marie (1992), 'Toward an Age of Liberal Nations', *Harvard International Law Journal*, **33,** pp. 393–405.

Cahn, Jonathan (1993), 'Challenging the New Imperial Authority: The World Bank and the Democratization of Development', *Harvard Human Rights Journal*, **6**, pp. 159–94.

Crawford, James and Marks, Susan (1998), 'The Global Democracy Deficit: An Essay in International Law and its Limits', in D. Archibugi, D. Held and M. Kohler (eds), *Re-imagining Political Community: Studies in Cosmopolitan Democracy*, Cambridge: Polity Press, pp. 72–90.

Donnelly, Jack (1999), 'Human Rights, Democracy and Development', *Human Rights Quarterly*, **21**, pp. 608–32.

Donoho, Douglas Lee (1996), 'Evolution of Expediency: The United Nations Response to the Disruption of Democracy', *Cornell International Law Journal*, **29**, pp. 329–82.

Farer, Tom (1993), 'Collectively Defending Democracy in a World of Sovereign States', *Human Rights Quarterly*, **15**, pp. 716–50.

Fox, Gregory (1992), 'The Right to Political Participation in International Law', *Yale Journal of International Law*, **17**, pp. 539–607.

Fox, Gregory and Nolte, Georg (1995), 'Intolerant Democracies', *Harvard International Law Journal*, **36**, pp. 1–70.

Gassama, Ibrahim (1997), 'Safeguarding the Democratic Entitlement: A Proposal for United Nations Involvement in National Politics', *Cornell International Law Journal*, **30**, pp. 287–333.

Held, David (1995), *Democracy and the Global Order*, Oxford: Polity Press.

Kennedy, David (1991), 'Turning to Market Democracy: A Tale of Two Architectures', *Harvard International Law Journal*, **32**, pp. 373–96.

Koskenniemi, Martti (1996), '"Intolerant Democracies": A Reaction', *Harvard International Law Journal*, **37**, pp. 231–35.

Macpherson, C.B. (1966), *The Real World of Democracy*, Oxford: Clarendon Press.

Macpherson, C.B. (1967), *The Life and Times of Liberal Democracy*, Oxford: Oxford University Press.

Moore, John Norton (2004), 'Beyond the Democratic Peace: Solving the War Puzzle', *Virginia Journal of International Law*, **44**, pp. 341–429.

Murphy, Sean (1999), 'Democratic Legitimacy and the Recognition of States and Governments', *International and Comparative Law Quarterly*, **48**, pp. 545–81.

Panel (1997) 'Implementing Democratization: What Role for International Organizations?', *Proceedings of the American Society of International Law*, **91**, pp. 356–76.

Pevehouse, Jon C. (2002), 'Democracy from the Outside-In? Intergovernmental Organizations and Democratization', *International Organization*, **56**, pp. 515–49.

Rich, Roland (2001), 'Bringing Democracy into International Law', *Journal of Democracy*, **12**, pp. 20–34.

Roth, Brad (1996), 'Democratic Intolerance: Observations on Fox and Nolte', *Harvard International Law Journal*, **37**, pp. 235–38.

Roth, Brad (1999), *Governmental Illegitimacy in International Law*, Oxford: Oxford University Press.

Simpson, Gerry (2001), 'Two Liberalisms', *European Journal of International Law*, **12**, pp. 537–72.

Steiner, Henry (1988), 'Political Participation as a Human Right', *Harvard Human Rights Yearbook*, **1**, pp. 77–134.

Udombana, Nsongurua (2003), 'Articulating the Right to Democratic Governance in Africa', *Michigan Journal of International Law*, **24**, pp. 1209–87.

Wheatley, Steven (2003), 'Deliberative Democracy and Minorities', *European Journal of International Law*, **14**, pp. 507–27.

White, Nigel D. (1997), 'Accountability and Democracy within the United Nations: A Legal Perspective', *International Relations*, **13**, pp. 1–18.

White, Nigel D. (2000), 'The United Nations and Democracy Assistance: Development Practice within a Constitutional Framework', in P. Burnell (ed.), *Democracy Assistance: International Co-operation for Democratization*, (London: Frank Cass) pp. 67–89.

Part I
Democracy and International Law

[1]

THE EMERGING RIGHT TO DEMOCRATIC GOVERNANCE

*By Thomas M. Franck**

> Legitimacy in 1991 flows not from the barrel of a gun but from the will of the people.
>
> *U.S. Secretary of State James A. Baker III*

> I know what real democracy is, what democracy is worth.
>
> *A thirty-seven-year-old Soviet lieutenant colonel who early on sided with anticoup forces*†

I. Introduction: The Power of Democratic Legitimacy

More than two centuries have elapsed since the signatories of the U.S. Declaration of Independence sought to manifest two radical propositions. The first is that governments, instituted to secure the "unalienable rights" of their citizens, derive "their just powers from the consent of the governed." We may call this the "democratic entitlement." The second proposition, perhaps less noted by commentators, is that a nation earns "separate and equal station" in the community of states by demonstrating "a decent respect to the opinions of mankind." The authors of the Declaration apparently believed that the legitimacy of the new Confederation of American States was not made evident solely by the transfer of power from Britain but also needed to be acknowledged by "mankind." This we may perceive as a prescient glimpse of the legitimating power of the community of nations.

For two hundred years, these two notions have remained a radical vision. The purpose of this essay is to demonstrate that the radical vision, while not yet fully word made law, is rapidly becoming, in our time, a normative rule of the international system. In the process, the two notions have merged. Increasingly, governments recognize that their legitimacy depends on meeting a normative expectation of the community of states. This recognition has led to the emergence of a community expectation: that those who seek the validation of their empowerment patently govern with the consent of the governed. Democracy, thus, is on the way to becoming a global entitlement, one that increasingly will be promoted and protected by collective international processes.

II. The Validation of Governance

Two recent events underscore this trend. The failure of the August coup in the Soviet Union, an event of inestimable human, political and historic import, demonstrates—for those sensitive to trends—that democracy is beginning to be seen as the *sine qua non* for validating governance. While President Boris Yeltsin of the Russian Republic and many Soviet citizens deserve primary credit for this

* Editor in Chief. The author wishes to express warm appreciation to many members of the Board of Editors for their helpful comments, as well as Paul Szasz, Robert Crouse, Gregory Fox, Dennis Sughrue, and the members of my honors seminar at the NYU Center for International Studies. Special thanks are due to the Filomen D'Agostino and Max E. Greenberg Research Fund of New York University School of Law.

† N.Y. Times, Aug. 22, 1991, at A15, col. 6; and *id.*, Aug. 21, 1991, at A9, col. 1.

triumph, it also derived considerable impetus from the new global climate, as evidenced by the vigor with which leaders of other democracies around the world aligned themselves against the coup's leaders. Equally significant is the reaction of governments in the Organization of American States and the United Nations General Assembly to the overthrow, in September 1991, of the elected President of Haiti, Jean-Bertrand Aristide, by a military coup. On October 11, the Assembly unanimously, without vote, approved a ground-breaking resolution demanding the return of Aristide to office, full application of the Haitian Constitution and full observance of human rights in Haiti.[1] The OAS, a week earlier, had unanimously recommended that its member states take "action to bring about the diplomatic isolation of those who hold power illegally in Haiti" and "suspend their economic, financial, and commercial ties" with the country until constitutional rule is restored.[2]

In both the Soviet and the Haitian cases, the leaders of states constituting the international community vigorously asserted that *only* democracy validates governance. This dramatic statement attains even more potency if, as in the Haitian case, it is transposed from political philosophy, where it is "mere" moral prescription, to law, where a newly recognized "democratic entitlement" was used in both the OAS and the UN General Assembly to impose new and important legal obligations on states. The OAS resolution, for one, stated that "the solidarity of the American states and the high aims which are sought through it require the political organization of those states on the basis of the effective exercise of representative democracy."[3] Undeniably, a new legal entitlement is being created, based in part on custom and in part on the collective interpretation of treaties.

This newly emerging "law"—which requires democracy to validate governance—is not merely the law of a particular state that, like the United States under its Constitution, has imposed such a precondition on national governance. It is also becoming a requirement of international law, applicable to all and implemented through global standards, with the help of regional and international organizations.

The transformation of the democratic entitlement from moral prescription to international legal obligation has evolved gradually. In the past decade, however, the tendency has accelerated. Most remarkable is the extent to which an international law-based entitlement is now urged by governments themselves. This is a cosmic, but unmysterious, change. For nations surfacing from long, tragic submergence beneath bogus "people's democracy" or outright dictatorship, the legitimation of power is a basic, but elusive, move in the direction of reform. As of late 1991, there are more than 110 governments, almost all represented in the United Nations, that are legally committed to permitting open, multiparty, secret-ballot elections with a universal franchise. Most joined the trend in the past five years.[4] While a few, arguably, are democracies more in form than in substance,

[1] UN Doc. A/46/L.8/Rev.1 (1991).

[2] Support to the Democratic Government of Haiti, OEA/Ser.F/V.1/MRE/RES.1/91, corr.1, paras. 5, 6 (1991).

[3] *Id.*, preamble.

[4] This enumeration was compiled by reference to reports in the *New York Times* and the *Country Reports on Human Rights Practices for 1990*, *infra* note 10, submitted by the Department of State to the appropriate committees of Congress. States that currently make legal provision for determining their governments by recourse to multiparty, secret-ballot elections are: Albania, Angola, Antigua and Barbuda, Argentina, Australia, Austria, the Bahamas, Bangladesh, Barbados, Belgium, Belize, Benin, Byelorussia, Bolivia, Botswana, Brazil, Bulgaria, Canada, Cape Verde, Chile, Colombia, the Comoros,

most are, or are becoming, genuinely open to meaningful political choice. Many of these new regimes want, indeed need, to be validated by being seen to comply with global standards for free and open elections.

That governments themselves now argue for the entitlement merely indicates their long-overdue recognition of an immutable fact of life: government cannot govern by force alone. To be effective, pace Austin,[5] law needs to secure the habitual, *voluntary* compliance of its subjects; it cannot rely entirely, or even primarily, upon the commanding power of a sovereign to compel obedience. Consequently, governments no longer blinded by the totalitarian miasma seek to validate themselves in such a way as to secure a high degree of voluntary public acquiescence in the governing process. Consent benefits the governing as much as the governed: that sociological truism is at last becoming a political axiom. In western industrialized nations, at least since the middle of the nineteenth century, such validation has increasingly been sought and achieved by governments. This is the hard-won tradition most of the world now seeks to emulate.

Since the beginning of the twentieth century, however, there has also been a countertendency. The notion of democracy as validation has been challenged, quite powerfully, first, by the notion of the "dictatorship of the proletariat" and, more recently, by a related theory of forced-march "modernization."

The doctrine of the dictatorship of the proletariat argued, with considerable force, that governing, especially in an industrial society, should not be an art but a science. It postulated, at least in theory, a dictatorship of trained and doctrinally correct economists, administrators, sociologists and political scientists capable of implementing correct policies. The complexities of governance were thought to be too great to be left to amateurs selected by the vagaries of popular passion.[6]

Congo, the Cook Islands, Costa Rica, the Côte d'Ivoire, Cyprus, Czechoslovakia, Denmark, Dominica, the Dominican Republic, Ecuador, Egypt, El Salvador, Estonia, Finland, France, Gabon, Gambia, Germany, Greece, Grenada, Guatemala, Guyana, Hungary, Honduras, Iceland, India, Ireland, Israel, Italy, Jamaica, Japan, Kiribati, Korea (Republic of), Latvia, Liberia, Liechtenstein, Lithuania, Luxembourg, Madagascar, Malaysia, Mali, Malta, the Marshall Islands, Mauritius, Mexico, the Micronesian Federation, Mongolia, Morocco, Mozambique, Namibia, Nauru, Nepal, the Netherlands, New Zealand, Nicaragua, Niger, Norway, Pakistan, Panama, Papua New Guinea, Paraguay, Peru, the Philippines, Poland, Portugal, Romania, São Tomé, Senegal, Singapore, the Solomon Islands, the Soviet Union, Spain, Sri Lanka, St. Kitts, St. Lucia, St. Vincent, Sweden, Switzerland, Tonga, Trinidad, Tunisia, Turkey, the Ukraine, the United Kingdom, Uruguay, Vanuatu, Venezuela, Western Samoa, Zambia and Zimbabwe. Several more states, such as Nigeria and Ethiopia, are committed to free, multiparty elections but have not yet enacted the necessary constitutional or legislative fiat. It must also be conceded that there are borderline cases, such as Morocco (included) and Jordan (not included), in which the elections are not necessarily decisive, depending on various factors, including the disposition of a monarch with substantial residual powers. In the large majority of cases, however, the decision to include or exclude is not seriously in doubt—though it should be recalled that the test for inclusion is whether the legal system establishes free and secret elections. Whether these are conducted fairly is another question.

[5] Austin defined law as the enforced command of a sovereign to a subject. J. AUSTIN, THE PROVINCE OF JURISPRUDENCE DETERMINED 201 (I. Berlin, S. Hampshire & R. Wollheim eds. 1954) (1832).

[6] *See, e.g.*, Theses on the Role of the Communist Party in the Proletarian Revolution Adopted by the Second Congress, in 1 THE COMMUNIST INTERNATIONAL: 1919–1943 DOCUMENTS 127 (J. Degras ed. 1971).

In 1920 Trotsky offered this response to a suggestion that the dictatorship of the Communist Party and the dictatorship of the proletariat were not identical:

> Today we received peace proposals from the Polish Government. Who decides this question? We have the Council of People's Commissars, but that too must be subject to a certain control. Whose

The contemporary theory of "modernization," which originated in the European fascist-charterist dictatorships of the 1930s, found new respectability among leaders of postcolonial Latin America, Africa and Asia, as well as some western friends of the Third World.[7] In the Third World, it was argued, the task of modern nation building—melding disparate tribes and clans to create new economies of scale—was said to warrant suspending imported bourgeois democratic values which, at any rate, were virtually meaningless in a largely rural, communal and illiterate society. The model was not a pompous Mussolini making Italian trains run punctually but Oliver Cromwell dismissing Parliament and getting Britain organized. In a few countries—Singapore, South Korea and Taiwan—the model seemed to work for a time, in the sense that much social and economic progress was achieved. In most instances, however, the implied promise was not kept.

Since the middle of the 1980s, both the "dictatorship of the proletariat" and the theory of "modernization" have collapsed under the weight of their evident failure. Throughout socialist Eastern Europe and in most of the dictatorships of Africa and Asia, the people have rejected both theories, together with the espousing governments, beginning with the televised popular revolution against Ferdinand Marcos in the Philippines. Instead, people almost everywhere now demand that government be validated by western-style parliamentary, multiparty democratic process. Only a few, usually military or theocratic, regimes still resist the trend. Very few argue that parliamentary democracy is a western illusion and a neocolonialist trap for unwary Third World peoples.

This almost-complete triumph of the democratic notions of Hume, Locke, Jefferson and Madison—in Latin America, Africa, Eastern Europe and, to a lesser extent, Asia—may well prove to be the most profound event of the twentieth century and, in all likelihood, the fulcrum on which the future development of global society will turn. It is the unanswerable response to those who have said that free, open, multiparty, electoral parliamentary democracy is neither desired nor desirable outside a small enclave of western industrial states.

The question is not whether democracy has swept the boards, but whether global society is ready for an era in which *only* democracy and the rule of law will be capable of validating governance. This may be a venerable philosophical issue known to Plato,[8] but it is also a functional question that can be, and now is being, stated in global legal terms. Are we witnessing the evolution of an international rule system that defines the minimal requisites of a democratic process capable of validating the exercise of power? What norms will such a rule system encompass? Is the international community capable of developing, consensually, an institutional and normative framework for monitoring compliance with those requisites? Is the community of nations able to define and manage appropriate consequences of noncompliance?

> control? That of the working class as a formless, chaotic mass? No. So we convened the central committee of the party to discuss the proposal and decide on the answer. . . . The same is true of the agrarian question, the food question, and all other questions.

Id. at 127–28.

[7] *Cf.* D. Apter, The Politics of Modernization (1965).

[8] Plato's effort, in the *Statesman*, the *Laws* and the *Republic*, to define the extent to which a ruler's legitimacy is validated by wisdom, on the one hand, and by his subordination to the laws, on the other, is analyzed in G. Sabine, A History of Political Theory 67–105 (rev. ed. 1953).

III. LEGITIMACY AND THE INTERNATIONAL SYSTEM OF RULES

These questions, in turn, raise two separate issues of legitimacy that are related but should not be confused: first, the legitimacy of national governments and, second, the legitimacy of the emerging international rules and processes by which the governance of nations is increasingly being monitored and validated. The latter issue is of primary interest to the international lawyer, but its importance is due to its manifest connection with the former. We are witnessing a sea change in international law, as a result of which the legitimacy of each government someday will be measured definitively by international rules and processes. We are not quite there, but we can see the outlines of this new world in which the citizens of each state will look to international law and organization to guarantee their democratic entitlement. For some states, that process will merely embellish rights already protected by their existing domestic constitutional order. For others, it could be the realization of a cherished dream.

Citizens, however, will not be the only beneficiaries. We have observed that the engine pulling the democratic entitlement is the craving of governments for validation. Without validation, the task of governance becomes fraught with difficulty. Regimes prize validation, then, as evidence of their legitimacy. Legitimacy, in turn, is the quality of a rule, or a system of rules, or a process for making or interpreting rules that pulls both the rule makers and those addressed by the rules toward voluntary compliance.

Western democracies have achieved legitimacy largely by subjecting the political process to rules, often immutably entrenched in an intrepid constitution. These lucky few nations have succeeded in evolving their own legitimate means of validating the process by which the people choose those they entrust with the exercise of power. To achieve such a system of autochthonous validation (and thus to facilitate governing), those who hold or seek political power have made a far-sighted bargain comparable to John Locke's social compact;[9] they have surrendered control over the nation's validation process to various others: national electoral commissions, judges, an inquisitive press and, above all, the citizenry acting at the ballot box. This collectivity decides whether the standards of the democratic entitlement have been met by those who claim the right to govern. In return, the legitimacy bestowed by that process gives back far more power to those who govern than they surrendered.

In many nations, unfortunately, no such bargain was struck. Those who claim to govern cannot demonstrate that they have fulfilled the requirements of the democratic entitlement, even if they purport to recognize that entitlement. Senegal, for example, is a multiparty state with universal franchise and a secret ballot, but the results of the 1988 national elections were rejected as fraudulent both by opposition parties and by other social institutions. The other parties subsequently boycotted the 1990 local elections and refused to accept the Government's legitimacy.[10] Increasingly, as will be demonstrated later in this essay, governments whose legitimacy is questioned are turning to the international system for that

[9] *See* J. LOCKE, TWO TREATISES OF GOVERNMENT 119–20, 164–66 (W. Carpenter ed. 1955) (1690).

[10] U.S. DEPARTMENT OF STATE, 102D CONG., 1ST SESS., COUNTRY REPORTS ON HUMAN RIGHTS PRACTICES FOR 1990: REPORT SUBMITTED TO THE COMMITTEE ON FOREIGN RELATIONS, U.S. SENATE AND THE COMMITTEE ON FOREIGN AFFAIRS, HOUSE OF REPRESENTATIVES 322–23 (Comm. Print 1991).

validation which their national *polis* is as yet unable to give. They do so to avoid the alternative—persistent challenge to authority by coups, countercoups, instability and stasis—and to enable themselves to govern with essential societal acquiescence. What they seek is legitimation by a global standard monitored by processes of the international system.

The capacity of the international community to extend legitimacy to national governments, however, depends not only on its capacity to monitor an election or to recognize the credentials of a regime's delegates to the UN General Assembly, but also on the extent to which such international activity has evolved from the ad hoc to the normative: that is, the degree to which the process of legitimation itself has become legitimate.

In any rule system, national or international, legitimacy has its own modalities. It is to the latter that the international lawyer's creative perspective must turn. Do the global requisites for democratic validation of governments now include, or are they evolving into, rules and procedures that are perceived as legitimate by those to whom they are addressed? In the international context,[11] legitimacy is achieved if—or to the extent that—those addressed by a rule, or by a rule-making institution, perceive the rule or institution to have come into being and to be operating in accordance with generally accepted principles of right process.[12]

Empirically, legitimacy can be demonstrated by observing rules, and the decisions of rule-making or rule-applying institutions. Some are habitually obeyed, without recourse to police enforcement, while others are largely ignored. Different rules exhibit varying degrees of compliance pull, which is the measure of a rule's legitimacy. However, the degree of a rule's pull to compliance cannot be measured solely by observing actual compliance. A more sensitive measure would have to take into account, additionally, the degree to which a violator exhibits deference to a rule even while violating it: for example, by lying about, or covering up, the violation or the circumstances in which the violation occurred.

Purely deductive research on rule legitimacy—pulse taking in the form of large-scale empirical investigation of compliance pull—is difficult to structure. Abstract/inductive reasoning about the nature of legitimacy is more feasible. Thus, one may postulate four indicators: *pedigree, determinacy, coherence* and *adherence.*[13] The content of these four indicators of legitimacy will be defined in ensuing sections of this essay. For this general overview, it is sufficient to summarize as follows: pedigree refers to the depth of the rule's roots in a historical process; determinacy refers to the rule's ability to communicate content; coherence refers to the rule's internal consistency and lateral connectedness to the principles underlying other rules; and adherence refers to the rule's vertical connectedness to a normative hierarchy, culminating in an ultimate rule of recognition, which embodies the principled purposes and values that define the community of states. A hypothesis may now be ventured: the degree to which a rule, or a rule-making process, exhibits these four qualities will determine the degree to which the rule or the process has matured and is perceived to be legitimate.

Those indicators provide a conceptual map with which to approach the previously posed questions. They afford a convenient way of sorting through the welter

[11] Legitimacy, in this as in all other contexts, is a matter of degree. Some rules and institutions enjoy more legitimacy than others.

[12] T. Franck, The Power of Legitimacy Among Nations 19 (1990).

[13] *Id.* at 50–194.

of data to reach some estimate as to whether the global system is evolving legitimate rules and institutions capable of validating national governance. That estimate, in turn, will help us understand and react appropriately to the inevitable counterindicative challenges: recidivist tendencies and totalitarian holdouts.

In seeking to assess whether an international democratic order is emerging, data will be marshaled from three related generations of rule making and implementation. The oldest and most highly developed is that subset of democratic norms which emerged under the heading of "self-determination." The second subset—freedom of expression—developed as part of the exponential growth of human rights since the mid-1950s and focuses on maintaining an open marketplace of ideas. The third and newest subset seeks to establish, define and monitor a right to free and open elections.

These three subsets somewhat overlap, both chronologically and normatively. Collectively, they do not necessarily penetrate every nook and cranny of democratic theory. For example, the three subsets do not yet address normatively the thorny issue of the right of a disaffected portion of an independent state to secede; nor, as we shall see, is it conceptually or strategically helpful—at least at this stage of its evolution—to treat the democratic entitlement as inextricably linked to the claim of minorities to secession. Still, these three increasingly normative subsets are large building stones, gradually reinforcing each other and assuming the shape of a coherent normative edifice. Moreover, regional subsets are adding some supernumerary buttresses, cornices and lintels to the new structure that dovetail with, and enrich, the emerging global architecture. Some examples of these will be included in our inventory.

IV. Pedigree: The Case of Self-Determination

Self-determination is the historic root from which the democratic entitlement grew. Its deep-rootedness continues to confer important elements of legitimacy on self-determination, as well as on the entitlement's two newer branches, freedom of expression and the electoral right.

Symbolic validation and pedigree provide legitimacy's cultural and anthropological dimension.[14] As with any rule, the capacity of the democratic entitlement to pull toward voluntary compliance depends, in part, on the strength of what W. Michael Reisman refers to as "the authority signal."[15] Specifically, the legitimacy of a rule reflects the durability, as well as the consistency, of its acknowledgment and application in practice.

Since self-determination is the oldest aspect of the democratic entitlement, its pedigree is the best established. Self-determination postulates the right of a people organized in an established territory to determine its collective political destiny in a democratic fashion and is therefore at the core of the democratic entitlement. Symbolically, it is signified by a long-evolving tradition of maintaining observers, on behalf of international and regional organizations, at elections in colonies and trust territories. Early observer missions developed operational procedures. They sent reports to their sponsoring international agency or committee, which helped the community's political organs and individual member governments make deductions about the legitimacy of the decolonization process. Gradually, with many variations, the observer missions' methods became the standard operating proce-

[14] *Id.* at 91.

[15] Reisman, *International Lawmaking: A Process of Communication*, 75 ASIL Proc. 101, 110 (1981).

dure for validating an exercise of self-determination. Later in this essay, we will recapitulate these rules and procedures. Here, however, we are concerned with the pedigree, the time frame within which those processes took root and matured.

The aspiration that underpins the principle of self-determination is of an antiquity traceable, in the West, at least to the Hebrews' exodus from Egypt,[16] estimated to have been approximately in 1000 B.C.[17] Its modern rise to the status of universal entitlement began when the Versailles Peace Conference[18] undid, or brought into line with late nineteenth-century European nationalist sensibilities, the work of the Congress of Vienna, which had utterly disregarded ethnic sensibilities in redrawing the map of post-Napoleonic Europe. Embarking on another redesign of Europe after the First World War, President Woodrow Wilson made self-determination his lodestar. To this end, firmly overriding the doubts of Secretary of State Robert Lansing,[19] he reinforced the U.S. team of negotiators with an unusual contingent of historians, geographers and ethnologists,[20] the more effectively to argue for the norm's supremacy over power politics and strategic or economic considerations. Consequently, the American delegation summoned up extensive data on demographics and evidence of ethnicity in advocating free choice by "peoples."[21]

Thus prodded, the conference authorized twenty-six on-site consultations with different European groups seeking self-determination.[22] The Danes of Schleswig, annexed to Prussia in 1864, were able to secure agreement that "the frontier between Germany and Denmark shall be fixed in conformity with the wishes of the population."[23] Wilson also prevailed in the view "that all branches of the Slav race" in what was to become Czechoslovakia "should be completely freed from German and Austrian rule"[24] in full consultation with Slavic representatives.[25] He resisted efforts by France's Premier Clemenceau to establish an independent Rhenish buffer state consisting of unwilling Germans.[26] Although the Versailles settlement also brought self-determination to Poland,[27] as regards the Upper Silesian and Czech boundary settlements, as well as Fiume, Wilson reluctantly came to concede that sometimes one had to consider "other principles"—strategic, economic and logistic—that could "clash with the requirements of self-determination."[28]

[16] *Exodus* 1:2.

[17] The author is indebted to Fr. Robert Crouse, Professor of Classics at Dalhousie University and King's College, for this approximation, one carefully hedged with caveats appropriate to so risky an enterprise.

[18] *See* H. HANNUM, AUTONOMY, SOVEREIGNTY, AND SELF-DETERMINATION 20–31 (1990). The use of self-determination at Versailles and subsequently is also discussed more fully in Franck, *Legitimacy in the International System*, 82 AJIL 705, 743–48 (1988).

[19] "[T]he phrase [self-determination] is simply loaded with dynamite. It will raise hopes which can never be realized." R. LANSING, THE PEACE NEGOTIATIONS, A PERSONAL NARRATIVE 97 (1921). *See* Brilmayer, *Secession and Self-Determination: A Territorial Interpretation*, 16 YALE J. INT'L L. 177 (1991).

[20] 1 R. S. BAKER, WOODROW WILSON AND WORLD SETTLEMENT 109 (1922).

[21] 1 S. WAMBAUGH, PLEBISCITES SINCE THE WORLD WAR 13 (1933).

[22] 1 R. S. BAKER, *supra* note 20, at 188.

[23] 2 A HISTORY OF THE PEACE CONFERENCE OF PARIS 203 (H. W. V. Temperley ed. 1920).

[24] 4 *id.* at 261.

[25] *Id.* at 262.

[26] 4 THE INTIMATE PAPERS OF COLONEL HOUSE 334–35, 345 (C. Seymour ed. 1928).

[27] 1 S. WAMBAUGH, *supra* note 21, at 16.

[28] M. POMERANCE, SELF-DETERMINATION IN LAW AND PRACTICE 4 (1982); D. FLEMING, THE UNITED STATES AND WORLD ORGANIZATION 152–55 (1938). For example, Czechoslovakia ended up with defensible boundaries only by denying self-determination to a large Sudeten-German minority.

Nevertheless, the principle of self-determination, as championed by Wilson and the minorities released from the embrace of the German, Russian and Austro-Hungarian Empires, was applied vigorously, if sometimes imperfectly, to the vanquished lands of postwar Europe. In the rest of Europe, however, it was applied only in Ireland. In denying self-determination to the Aaland Islands—which sought to join Sweden by breaking away from Finland, itself newly emancipated from Russia—a Versailles-created international commission of jurists observed that the Covenant of the League of Nations did not even mention the principle and that it had not yet attained the status of a positive rule of law.[29] More important, self-determination played little part in the disposition of the vast overseas lands and peoples of the former German Empire, which were doled out to Australia, Belgium, Britain, France, Japan, New Zealand and South Africa. It was applied badly, if at all, to the former Turkish dependencies in Asia. The League's mandate system evinced only muted concern for the wishes of those territories' inhabitants.

Remarkably, after the Second World War the principle of self-determination became the most dynamic concept in international relations. Former German, Japanese and Italian colonies were placed under the trusteeship of the victors (and, in one case, the vanquished), with the clear obligation "to promote . . . progressive development towards self-government or independence" in accordance with "the freely expressed wishes of the peoples concerned."[30] Conceptual evolution, however, did not stop there. Soon not only was self-determination recognized as a writ for obtaining decolonization but, by the terms of the very first article of the UN Charter, it achieved the status of a fundamental right of all "peoples" as a necessary prerequisite to the development of "friendly relations among nations." At least potentially, the concept was thus both universalized and internationalized, for it could now be said to portend a duty owed by all governments to their peoples and by each government to all members of the international community.

This was no random theoretical happenstance. In the postwar world of rising nationalisms, denials of self-determination were palpably no mere domestic matter. Repression tended to generate friction with neighboring states where liberation movements habitually sought sanctuary and succor. As in Bangladesh, Eritrea and the Southern Sudan, self-determination, denied, precipitated the flight of hordes of refugees, placing onerous economic, social and political strains on the neighboring states of refuge. Thus was self-determination firmly linked in theory and fact to the main UN task of preventing conflict among nations, a link that carries far-reaching, but ambiguous, implications for its future normative development (as this essay later seeks to demonstrate).

In the thirty-five years following the surrender of the Axis powers, self-determination transformed the world's political landscape. At this stage, the norm had clear, though limited, secessionist overtones, in the sense that it legitimated the secession of colonies from empires. Concurrently, the norm also evolved in a way that did not legitimate self-determination of minorities *within* a colony. The General Assembly warned against efforts to compromise a colony's "territorial integrity" by those—like Nigeria's Ibos—seeking to secede.[31] Beginning with India,

[29] L. Buchheit, Secession: The Legitimacy of Self-Determination 71 (1978).

[30] UN Charter Art. 76(b).

[31] Note, however, the decision of the political leaders of imperial India to partition the country, in effect permitting Pakistan to secede. On "territorial integrity," see Declaration on the Granting of

Burma and West Africa's Gold Coast, Britain acted in compliance with the norm's evolving requirements; it was followed, with more or less enthusiasm, by France, the Netherlands, Belgium, Spain, Portugal and South Africa. Imperial powers complained about the General Assembly's use of Charter Article 73(c) to monitor political developments in their colonies, but the resistance gradually abated. As a result of the impetus of decolonization, UN membership almost tripled. That this remarkable devolution could have been accomplished, for the most part, without recourse to war or revolution is a tribute to the normative legitimacy and primacy accorded self-determination by the consistent practice—despite lapses—of the community of states.[32] As we shall see, the growth of this process was facilitated by UN reporting requirements, the Organization's close scrutiny of the work of colonial administrations and the active involvement of the United Nations in monitoring elections and plebiscites in territories advancing toward independence. Self-determination was seen to require democratic consultation with colonial peoples, legitimated by an international presence at elections immediately preceding the creative moment of independence.

Today, the process of decolonization is nearly complete. Nevertheless, the principle of self-determination retains vigor, manifestly having contributed to the decision by the leaders of the Soviet Union, beginning in 1989, to withdraw their military forces and political suzerainty from Eastern Europe and, more recently, from the Baltic States. Its pull prompted South Africa's decision to give independence to Namibia and Morocco's *volte-face* regarding Western Sahara. When another vestige of imperfect decolonization, the Angolan civil war, ended in 1991, it was on the basis of an agreement to hold free, internationally observed elections, which, *nunc pro tunc,* would give Angola the legitimate regime it had failed to acquire at the chaotic moment of its independence.[33] Another UN-supervised process of popular consultation was created by the Paris agreement ending the civil war in Cambodia.[34] As we shall discuss in detail, the idea of self-determination has evolved into a more general notion of internationally validated political consultation, one that is beginning to be applied even to independent (postcolonial) states like Nicaragua and Angola, albeit without implying the community's right to validate secessionist movements within sovereign states.

The story of self-determination, as the first building block in the creation of a democratic entitlement, may thus be seen as a remarkable saga that tells of a rule that gradually augments its compliance pull, overcomes resistance and ultimately brings about an incontestable, historic transformation. Rules that acquire this

---

Independence to Colonial Countries and Peoples, GA Res. 1514, 15 UN GAOR Supp. (No. 16) at 66, UN Doc. A/4684 (1960); and Declaration on Principles of International Law concerning Friendly Relations and Co-operation among States in accordance with the Charter of the United Nations, Annex to GA Res. 2625, 25 UN GAOR Supp. (No. 28) at 121, UN Doc. A/8028 (1970), *reprinted in* 9 ILM 1292 (1970) [hereinafter Friendly Relations Declaration]. Note also GA Res. 1654 of 1961, in which, without dissent, the Assembly expressed itself as "[d]eeply concerned that, contrary to the provisions of paragraph 6 of the Declaration, acts aimed at the partial or total disruption of national unity and territorial integrity are still being carried out in certain countries in the process of decolonization." 16 UN GAOR Supp. (No. 17) at 65, UN Doc. A/5100 (1961).

[32] *See* Franck, *The Stealing of the Sahara,* 70 AJIL 694 (1976).

[33] As part of the cease-fire package, UNAVEM, the UN observer mission in Angola, oversaw the withdrawal of Cuban troops. The mission will culminate in the observance of elections in 1992. *See* N.Y. Times, May 26, 1991, §1, at 9, col. 1; and *id.,* June 1, 1991, at A1, col. 3.

[34] Final Act of the Paris Conference on Cambodia, UN Doc. A/46/608–S/23177, Annex (1991).

kind of pedigree have a unique claim to legitimacy. Moreover, the deeply embedded roots of self-determination also anchor the legitimacy claims of other, more recent, components of the democratic entitlement.

V. Determinacy: Its Function in Bestowing Legitimacy

Thus we see that the democratic entitlement has roots in the conduct of states dating back at least to 1918. From this beginning, practice has proliferated. But practice is not enough to legitimate new norms. The dots of practice must be connected by lines of enunciated principle—conceptualized reasons for acting—if the shapes of legitimate rules are to emerge. The production of legitimate norms depends on a combination of persistent practice and enunciated concepts. In addition, to legitimate a rule, the underlying principles must be enunciated in a way that makes their content determinate. In this section, then, we will look at the determinacy of those principles that stake out the democratic entitlement. Just as an enunciated principle needs to be implemented in common practice before achieving recognition as a binding rule, so a common practice, to be accepted as establishing a norm, needs principled enunciation.

By determinacy we mean the literary property of a rule: that which makes its message clear.[35] The determinacy of a rule directly affects its legitimacy because it increases the rule's transparency and thus its capacity to pull members of the international community toward voluntary compliance. It is true that all written communications, including rule texts, suffer from some degree of elasticity of meaning. It is also true that "moderate indeterminacy does not undermine the law's legitimacy."[36] Nevertheless, the more opaque and elastic the rule text, the less compliance pull it is likely to exert. Obviously, a rule that cannot be understood is unlikely to be obeyed. A rule that is vague opens itself to creative misconstruction by those whose conduct it is intended to regulate. Perhaps most important, the indeterminacy of a rule undermines its compliance pull by reducing the contingent expectation of reciprocity that helps pull states toward compliance. States, like persons, often obey rules even when it is to their short-run advantage not to do so, in the expectation that by denying themselves the gain that would accrue from noncompliance they will reinforce the power of the rule to pull others toward compliance, to the states' future benefit. This deferred-gratification rationale for rule compliance falls away, however, when the rule text is so indeterminate as not to support a reasonable expectation that compliance in one instance will reinforce the pull toward compliance in future contingent situations. Reciprocity affords little inducement to voluntary rule compliance if the rule is so fuzzy that its applicability to future cases will be easy to dispute and hard to demonstrate.

While the determinacy of a rule may initially be judged by examining the clarity of its text, even a quite elastic text may be rendered more determinate if it is subjected regularly to case-by-case interpretation, utilizing administrative or adjudicatory procedures accepted as legitimate in the community to which the rule is addressed. For example, the International Court of Justice, in interpreting Article 83(1) of the Convention negotiated by the Third United Nations Conference on the Law of the Sea, has taken a highly indeterminate text—one that calls for "an equitable solution" in apportioning an undersea coastal shelf among neighboring

[35] T. Franck, *supra* note 12, at 52–55.

[36] Kress, *Legal Indeterminacy*, 77 Cal. L. Rev. 283 (1989).

states—and has rendered it increasingly determinate.[37] So, too, as a result of litigation between Finland and Denmark currently before the Court, will we "discover" whether a tall, self-propelled oil rig constitutes a "vessel" under the right of unimpeded passage through straits as established by the Law of the Sea Convention.[38] The determinacy of a rule may therefore depend not only on its text, but also on the work of legitimate institutions charged with reducing textual indeterminacy in specific disputes.

Thus understood, how fares the determinacy of a normative entitlement to democracy? Are there rule texts that convey principles that are specific, or capable of being rendered so, by persuasive case-by-case interpretation and application? We shall now examine the determinacy of existing and emerging rules that bear on the previously identified main historic components of the democratic entitlement: self-determination, freedom of expression and electoral rights.

Determinacy and Self-Determination

As noted, self-determination is legitimated by its long pedigree. Despite lacunae, it also has a large and precise textual canon, refined by a growing "jurisprudence" of interpretation. In addition to the role of self-determination among the purposes of the UN Charter and in the UN trusteeship system, under Article 73, members responsible for administering non-self-governing territories pledged to "develop self-government, to take due account of the political aspirations of the peoples, and to assist them in the progressive development of their free political institutions." These provisions not only were implemented zealously by the UN system, but also were augmented by additional normative texts that concerned two issues essential to the determinacy of self-determination: *to whom* does it apply and *how* is it to be implemented? If rule texts establishing rights do not provide answers to these basic questions, they lack determinacy and the rule's legitimacy is diminished.

To whom does self-determination apply? The first serious effort to enunciate the applicable principles was undertaken by the fifteenth General Assembly in the annex to Resolution 1541 of December 15, 1960. It attempts to stipulate the test for determining whether a territory is non-self-governing within the meaning of Article 73(e) of the Charter. Under Principle IV of the resolution, non-self-governing status exists *prima facie* "in respect of a territory which is geographically separate and is distinct ethnically and/or culturally from the country administering it." Once that test has been met, Principle V states, "other elements may then be brought into consideration," including those "of an administrative, political, juridical, economic or historical nature. If they affect the relationship between the metropolitan State and the territory concerned in a manner which arbitrarily places the latter in a position or status of subordination, they support the presumption" that the territory is non-self-governing.[39]

[37] United Nations Convention on the Law of the Sea, *opened for signature* Dec. 10, 1982, UN Doc. A/CONF.62/122, *reprinted in* UNITED NATIONS, OFFICIAL TEXT OF THE UNITED NATIONS CONVENTION ON THE LAW OF THE SEA WITH ANNEXES AND INDEX, UN Sales No. E.83.V.5 (1983), 21 ILM 1261 (1982). For the Court's interpretation of Article 83(1), see Continental Shelf (Tunisia/Libyan Arab Jamahiriya), 1982 ICJ REP. 18 (Judgment of Feb. 24); Continental Shelf (Libyan Arab Jamahiriya/Malta), 1985 ICJ REP. 13 (Judgment of June 3).

[38] *See* Passage through the Great Belt, 1991 ICJ REP. 12 (Order of July 29).

[39] GA Res. 1541, 15 UN GAOR Supp. (No. 16), *supra* note 31, at 29.

The 1970 Declaration on Friendly Relations elaborated the Charter "principle of equal rights and self-determination of peoples" by reiterating the duty to end colonialism and to permit each colonial territory to assume a "political status freely determined by" the inhabitants. More broadly, the declaration attributes to "all peoples"—not merely the inhabitants of colonies—"the right freely to determine, without external interference, their political status."[40]

This broader concept of a *universal* right of self-determination is further enunciated in Article 1 of the International Covenant on Civil and Political Rights.[41] This treaty, ratified or acceded to by 113 states as of November 1991, but probably binding on other states as customary law,[42] states categorically: "All peoples have the right of self-determination. By virtue of that right they freely determine their political status and freely pursue their economic, social and cultural development." This provision has been called the "most controversial" in a document created and steeped in considerable controversy.[43] Western powers, in particular, at first argued that the right was only a political principle, that it was ill-defined and unsuited to a treaty enumerating individual—as opposed to collective—rights and thus inappropriate to the unique quasi-judicial enforcement machinery envisaged by the Covenant. Nevertheless, its proponents insisted that the norm of self-determination was fundamental, and a precondition, to the enjoyment of all other enumerated individual rights and freedoms. As a result, "the tide of political opinion in favour of including a right of self-determination proved irresistible"[44] and the principle was given pride of place among the designated entitlements. More significantly for the long term, the majority—including states that had opposed inclusion of the right—utterly rejected the notion that the entitlement applied only to colonial "peoples," declaring, rather, that if included, it must apply to peoples anywhere, whether in a politically independent state or a dependent territory.[45]

The Covenant clearly intends to make the right of self-determination applicable to the citizens of all nations, entitling them to determine their collective political status through democratic means. It also makes an important distinction between that right of each nation's collective *polis* and the rights of minorities within each state, which the Covenant elucidates in Article 27. Under Article 27, "ethnic, religious or linguistic minorities . . . shall not be denied the right, in community with the other members of their group, to enjoy their own culture, to profess and practice their own religion, or to use their own language."

Notably, not included among the enumerated rights of these minorities as defined in Article 27 is any entitlement to secede.[46] When the Covenant came into force, the right of self-determination entered its third phase of enunciation: it ceased to be a rule applicable only to specific territories (at first, the defeated European powers; later, the overseas trust territories and colonies) and became a

[40] Annex to GA Res. 2625, *supra* note 31, principle 4.

[41] International Covenant on Civil and Political Rights, Dec. 16, 1966, 999 UNTS 171, *reprinted in* 6 ILM 368 (1967) (entered into force Mar. 23, 1976) [hereinafter ICCPR]. The same provision is stated as Article 1 of the International Covenant on Economic, Social and Cultural Rights, Dec. 16, 1966, 993 UNTS 3, *reprinted in* 6 ILM 360 (1967) (entered into force Jan. 3, 1976).

[42] T. Meron, Human Rights and Humanitarian Norms as Customary Law 80–81 (1989); Sohn, *Generally Accepted International Rules*, 61 Wash. L. Rev. 1073, 1077–78 (1986); Schachter, *International Law Implications of U.S. Human Rights Policies*, 24 N.Y.L. Sch. L. Rev. 63, 68 (1978).

[43] D. McGoldrick, The Human Rights Committee 14 (1991).

[44] *Id.*

[45] *Id.* at 15.

[46] For a different view as to the legal status of the right to secede, see Brilmayer, *supra* note 19.

right of everyone. It also, at least for now, stopped being a principle of exclusion (secession) and became one of inclusion: the right to participate. The right now entitles peoples in all states to free, fair and open participation in the democratic process of governance freely chosen by each state. When such participation is denied, when a people that, in the terms of the aforementioned 1960 General Assembly resolution, "is geographically separate and is distinct ethnically and/or culturally" has been placed "in a position or status of subordination,"[47] perhaps a secession option may reemerge as an international legal entitlement. That aspect of self-determination, however, is far less clear at present than the entitlement to democratic participation in governance.

How is self-determination to be implemented? Gradually, answers to this question have also emerged. During the first forty years of the United Nations, members responsible for trust territories and colonies were charged with making periodic reports on their progress; these reports were subjected to increasing scrutiny by various UN bodies. Since the coming into force of the Covenant, reporting and scrutiny have been formalized, depoliticized to an extent, and welded to the process of case-by-case norm application. This development will help shape the postcolonial concept of self-determination and give it more determinacy. The Covenant thus foresees a continuing, growing body of law made by means of the interpretation and application of its provisions by an expert, independent, quasi-judicial body.

As usual, this process begins with a form of monitoring. The 113 states parties to the Covenant are legally obliged to "undertake to submit reports on the measures they have adopted which give effect to the rights recognized herein and on the progress made in the enjoyment of those rights."[48] These reports are scrutinized by a Human Rights Committee of eighteen members elected by states parties to the Covenant, who serve in their personal capacities[49] for a term of four years.[50] While the Committee is not a court, it does have the right to question the reports submitted by members. It transmits its reviews and such general comments as it thinks appropriate to the states parties to the Covenant and to the UN Economic and Social Council.[51] Under an optional procedure, parties may also agree to permit other parties to allege violations in a formal complaint.[52] An Optional Protocol permits individuals to lodge complaints against accepting states.[53] As of November 1991, sixty-three of the parties to the Covenant had agreed to give the Committee the competence to consider petitions. A recent study concluded that the Committee members have succeeded in establishing a high degree of independence and judiciousness.[54]

Formally, all petitions brought under the Optional Protocol are drawn to the Committee's attention by the UN Secretary-General.[55] More than a hundred such

[47] GA Res. 1541, *supra* note 39.

[48] ICCPR, *supra* note 41, Art. 40(1).

[49] *Id.*, Arts. 28, 30.

[50] *Id.*, Art. 32.

[51] For a discussion of this procedure, see D. McGoldrick, *supra* note 43, at 62–119.

[52] ICCPR, *supra* note 41, Art. 41. For a discussion of this procedure, see D. McGoldrick, *supra* note 43, at 120–246.

[53] ICCPR, *supra* note 41, Optional Protocol, *opened for signature* Dec. 19, 1966, Art. 1, 999 UNTS 302; *see also* D. McGoldrick, *supra* note 43, at 127.

[54] D. McGoldrick, *supra* note 43, at 45.

[55] Human Rights Committee, Provisional Rules of Procedure, Rule 78(1), UN Doc. CCPR/C/3/Rev.2 (1989). *See* Report of the Human Rights Committee, 44 UN GAOR Supp. (No. 40) at 179–82, UN Doc. A/44/40 (1989).

"cases" have been taken up and fewer than twenty were dismissed for lack of evidence of a violation. Some 150 more petitions are pending.[56] Although the Covenant envisages the possibility of voting, the Committee's decisions to date have been taken by consensus.[57]

The Committee, so far, has not had much occasion to explain the content of the right of self-determination. Only one petition-based case has been heard. While it rejected as inadmissible a claim by a Grand Captain of the Mikmaq tribal society that Canada was denying his people their right of self-determination, the Committee based its rejection on the applicant's inability to demonstrate that he was authorized to represent the tribe or that he, personally, had been deprived of a right protected by the Covenant.[58] As noted, the Covenant validates free and equal political participation as well as the cultural rights of minorities, but not necessarily secession. The Committee's finding leaves open the possibility that another individual might succeed in bringing a comparable petition if he or she can demonstrate having the *bona fides* to act in a representative capacity and alleges a denial of cultural autonomy or free and equal political participation.

The Committee does not merely consider reports and complaints. Periodically, it also makes more general findings on the state of civil and political rights and prepares summaries of the developing normative expectations arising from the Covenant. In its general commentary on Article 1, the Committee has been rather cautious, merely reiterating the primacy of self-determination among the human rights enumerated in the Covenant. "In accordance with the purposes and principles of the Charter of the United Nations," the Committee has written, "article 1 . . . recognizes that all peoples have the right of self-determination. The right . . . is of particular importance because its realization is an essential condition for the effective guarantee and observance of individual human rights and for the promotion and strengthening of those rights."[59]

The right to self-determination, in sum, may be said to be poised to move toward still greater determinacy. Its general normative content already has been spelled out in General Assembly resolutions to which a large majority of the international community has assented, and in several widely ratified treaties, beginning with the UN Charter and culminating in the Covenant. Equally important to the determinacy of the right of self-determination is the institutional potential for applying and clarifying the emerging rules; while the Committee's accomplishments have been modest, a systemic basis has been laid for more solid results. Now that the inhibitions of Cold War politics have been lifted and the liberal democratic sensibility is widely shared by the membership, what began as review by politicized, anticolonial committees of the General Assembly and by the Trusteeship Council may be expected to become a judicious process of principled rule interpretation by independent experts.

[56] D. McGoldrick, *supra* note 43, at 127. [57] *Id.* at 48.

[58] A.D. v. Canada, Report of the Human Rights Committee, 39 UN GAOR Supp. (No. 40) at 200, UN Doc. A/39/40 (1984). *See also* Ominayak and Lubicon Lake Band v. Canada, Report of the Human Rights Committee, 45 UN GAOR Supp. (No. 40), vol. 2, App. A, UN Doc. A/45/40 (1990). See discussion in D. McGoldrick, *supra* note 43, at 254–56; and McGoldrick, *Canadian Indians, Cultural Rights and the Human Rights Committee*, 40 Int'l & Comp. L.Q. 658 (1991).

[59] General Comments of the Human Rights Committee, UN Doc. CCPR/C/21/Rev.1, at 10–11 (1989). *See also* D. McGoldrick, *supra* note 43, at 247–48.

Determinacy and Free Expression

The second building block in constructing a normative entitlement to democracy is the right of free political expression. This right originated conceptually in the antitotalitarianism born of World War II and was first enunciated normatively in the Universal Declaration of Human Rights, adopted by the General Assembly on December 10, 1948.[60] As a mere resolution, the Universal Declaration does not have the force of a treaty; yet it was passed with such overwhelming support, and such prestige has accrued to it in succeeding years, that it may be said to have become a customary rule of state obligation. More to the point, its text manifests considerable determinacy, specifically recognizing a universal right to freedom of opinion and expression (Article 19), as well as to peaceful assembly and association (Article 20).

These entitlements reappear with even greater specificity in the legally binding Covenant on Civil and Political Rights.[61] Spelled out in that treaty are specific rights to freedom of thought (Article 18) and freedom of association (Article 22). Article 19(2) is an especially important component of the democratic entitlement. It states: "Everyone shall have the right to freedom of expression; this right shall include freedom to seek, receive and impart information and ideas of all kinds, regardless of frontiers, either orally, in writing or in print, in the form of art, or through any other media of his choice." While Article 19(2) is subject to restriction by law where "necessary . . . [f]or the protection of . . . public order . . . , or of public health or morals,"[62] these restrictions, like the rule itself, are subject to case-by-case review and application by the Human Rights Committee.[63]

Rights to opinion, expression and association contained in Articles 18, 19 and 22 look both backward and forward. They are a refinement of an aspect of the older right of self-determination; they also constitute the essential preconditions for an open electoral process, which is the newest component of the democratic entitlement. First mooted in the Universal Declaration, they became explicit treaty-based entitlements by incorporation into the Covenant and are likely to be made even more explicitly determinate by the review and monitoring of required national reports on compliance and specific petitions by complainants. The Human Rights Committee, for example, has been critical, albeit in a circumspect manner, of the compliance of Uganda and Zanzibar under Tanzanian control.[64] The Committee has also posed searching questions to representatives of Mali[65] and Jamaica[66] regarding the openness of their marketplaces of ideas. Professor Dominic McGoldrick has commended

> the close, detailed and critical analysis undertaken by members under the reporting process. The dialogue between the [Committee] and the States parties, in so far as it has developed, has been both direct and constructive. [Committee] members have in a diplomatic but forthright way criticized or expressed strong doubts concerning the compatibility with article 19 of specific ideological conceptions of and wide restrictions on freedom of expression.[67]

[60] GA Res. 217A (III), UN Doc. A/810, at 71 (1948).

[61] ICCPR, *supra* note 41.

[62] *Id.*, Art. 19(3).

[63] *See* D. McGoldrick, *supra* note 43, at 461.

[64] Report of the Human Rights Committee, 36 UN GAOR Supp. (No. 40) at 42–43, UN Doc. A/36/40 (1981) [hereinafter 1981 Report].

[65] *Id.* at 50–51.

[66] *Id.* at 56–57.

[67] D. McGoldrick, *supra* note 43, at 469–70.

In their tough questioning of the representatives of reporting states, the Committee's members are now aided regularly, behind the scenes, by a network of nongovernmental organizations.

While most of these critiques have occurred under the aegis of the general reporting requirement, a few case-by-case reviews have taken place under the Optional Protocol. The Committee found Uruguay's military regime in violation of Article 19(2) of the Covenant when it denied a petitioner the right freely to engage in political and trade union activities.[68] In *Perdoma and DeLanza v. Uruguay*,[69] the complainants alleged that they had been detained on account of "subversive association" based on their political views and connections. The Committee concluded that there was no evidence to substantiate the authorities' charge and that the arrest, detention and trial of the petitioners had not been justified on any of the grounds permitted in Article 19(3).[70]

When rules are impartially applied, whether by judges, administrators or experts, the determinacy of those rules increases and so, also, their legitimacy. Thus far, the Human Rights Committee's review of complaints regarding restrictions on expressive rights has just begun to have an impact, but in view of the end of the Cold War, the prognosis is much better. Moreover, other avenues for international protection of these rights are opening up, as evidenced by the requests of the intergovernmental Human Rights Commission to the UN Secretary-General that he appoint special representatives to report on alleged gross violations by various governments. In this respect, a significant new role for the Secretary-General was recently agreed upon by both the Government and insurgents in El Salvador. Under UN auspices, the parties consented to the establishment of ONUSAL, the UN Observer Group in El Salvador, which is to be controlled by the Secretary-General and is to supervise, and thereby seek to ensure citizens' rights to, free expression and association as part of a plan to create the circumstances for civil peace.[71]

In addition to such activity at the global level, parallel and reinforcing norm building and defining is under way at the regional level. The European Convention for the Protection of Human Rights and Fundamental Freedoms, the best-established regional normative system, provides in Article 10, paragraph 1: "Everyone has the right to freedom of expression. This right shall include freedom to hold opinions and to receive and impart information and ideas without interference by public authority and regardless of frontiers."[72]

Paragraph 2 of Article 10 does permit derogation in the form of

> restrictions . . . necessary in a democratic society, in the interests of national security, territorial integrity or public safety, for the prevention of disorder or crime, for the protection of health or morals, for the protection of the

[68] Alba Pietroroia v. Uruguay, Communication R.10/44, 1981 Report, *supra* note 64, at 153–59.

[69] Report of the Human Rights Committee, 35 UN GAOR Supp. (No. 40) at 111, UN Doc. A/35/40 (1980) [hereinafter 1980 Report].

[70] *Id. See also* Grille Motta v. Uruguay, Communication R.2/11, 1980 Report, *supra* note 69, at 132; Weinberg Weisz v. Uruguay, Communication R.7/28, 1981 Report, *supra* note 64, at 114; Hertzberg v. Finland, Communication R.14/61, Report of the Human Rights Committee, 37 UN GAOR Supp. (No. 40) at 161, UN Doc. A/37/40 (1982).

[71] Central America: Efforts Towards Peace: Report of the Secretary-General, UN Doc. S/22494 and Corr.1 (1991); *see also* N.Y. Times, Aug. 13, 1991, at A8, col. 3.

[72] European Convention for the Protection of Human Rights and Fundamental Freedoms, Nov. 4, 1950, 213 UNTS 221, Europ. TS No. 5 (entered into force Sept. 3, 1953) [hereinafter European Convention].

reputation or rights of others, for preventing the disclosure of information received in confidence, or for maintaining the authority and impartiality of the judiciary.

The application of both the rule and its exceptions, however, is subject to review by a commission of experts and a European Human Rights Court.[73] These bodies have augmented the determinacy of the system. As in a mature regime, the European Commission and Court of Human Rights have made key decisions balancing the rights of individuals against specific exceptions. The Court has weighed freedom of the press against a defendant's right to an impartial trial.[74] It has drawn boundaries between free expression and obscenity[75] and sought a balance between a free press and the laws of libel and slander.[76] In so doing, it has made far more specific—hence legitimate—the Council of Europe's system of norms pertaining to expressive rights, just when it is rapidly expanding to include the newly freed nations of Eastern Europe.

Comparable progress is being made by the more recently established inter-American regional system. The 1969 American Convention on Human Rights[77] provides an elaborate textual basis for freedom of thought and expression (Article 13), the right of assembly (Article 15) and freedom of association (Article 16). Monitoring and enforcement is performed by two institutions created by the OAS Charter: the Inter-American Commission on Human Rights (Articles 34 and 64(1)) and the Inter-American Court of Human Rights (Articles 33, 62 and 64). The Court consists of seven judges elected by the states adhering to the Convention, who serve for a term of six years. As of May 1990, ten states—not including the United States—had accepted its jurisdiction.[78]

Determinacy and Electoral Rights

The third and newest building block in constructing the entitlement to democracy is the emerging normative requirement of a participatory *electoral* process. Despite its infancy, it, too, is rapidly evolving toward that determinacy which is essential to being perceived as legitimate. As early as 1948, the Universal Declaration of Human Rights, in Article 21, clearly enunciated the right of all persons to take part in government, as well as in "periodic and genuine elections which shall be by universal and equal suffrage and shall be held by secret vote or by equivalent free voting procedures." At the time, only UN members outside the socialist, Arab and Latin American blocs took this as a restatement of conditions already prevailing in their *polis.* With rapid decolonization, the proportion of UN members actually practicing free and open electoral democracy began to shrink further under the aegis of one-party modernizing authoritarianism in Africa and

[73] *Id.*, Art. 19, establishing the European Commission on Human Rights and the European Court of Human Rights. *See also* Arts. 20–55.

[74] The Sunday Times Case, 30 Eur. Ct. H.R. (ser. A) (1978).

[75] Handyside Case, 24 Eur. Ct. H.R. (ser. A) (1976); Case of Muller and Others, 133 Eur. Ct. H.R. (ser. A) (1988).

[76] Lingens Case, 103 Eur. Ct. H.R. (ser. A) (1986).

[77] American Convention on Human Rights, Nov. 22, 1969, OEA/Ser.K/XVI.1.1, doc. 70, rev.1, corr.1 (1970), *reprinted in* 1 THE INTER-AMERICAN SYSTEM, pt. II at 51 (F. V. García-Amador ed. 1983), 9 ILM 673 (1970) (entered into force July 18, 1978) [hereinafter American Convention].

[78] Argentina, Colombia, Costa Rica, Ecuador, Guatemala, Honduras, Peru, Suriname, Uruguay and Venezuela. *See* Current State of Conventions and Protocols on Human Rights, Annual Report of the Inter-American Commission on Human Rights, OEA/Ser.L/V.II.79, doc. 12, rev.1, Ann. A (1991).

Asia. Nevertheless, even in that relatively hostile atmosphere, few states were willing openly to block the textual evolution of a specific electoral entitlement, however many mental reservations their regimes may have harbored. Thus, two decades later, the Civil and Political Covenant was opened for signature,[79] entering into force in 1976 as a set of legal obligations now binding on more than two-thirds of all states. With the balance now heavily tilting toward the substantial new majority of states actually practicing a reasonably credible version of electoral democracy, the treaty-based legal entitlement also begins to approximate prevailing practice and thus may be said to be stating what is becoming a customary legal norm applicable to all.

Article 25 extends to every citizen the right:

> (*a*) To take part in the conduct of public affairs, directly or through freely chosen representatives;
>
> (*b*) To vote and to be elected at genuine periodic elections which shall be by universal and equal suffrage and shall be held by secret ballot, guaranteeing the free expression of the will of the electors.

Admirable as it is, this standard still needs greater specificity. Textual determinacy, once again, is gradually being augmented by process determinacy under the auspices of the Human Rights Committee, which is authorized to monitor compliance. That body has discussed the implications of Article 25 in connection with its review of national reports on implementation and a small number of petitions lodged under the Optional Protocol. In reviewing two citizens' complaints against the military regime of Uruguay, the Committee concluded that the complainants had been arbitrarily deprived of protected rights by decrees banning their political party and by being barred from running for office.[80]

During the Cold War, it was difficult to utilize the Human Rights Committee to hone the rule outlined in Article 25. Now the Committee is likely to perform that function more effectively as the members' ideological divisions narrow and citizens become more willing to risk submitting complaints. This evolution would be accelerated if, as seems likely, the United States ratified the Covenant. If, as seems *less* likely, the United States also ratified the Protocol permitting individual complaints,[81] the determinacy of the entitlement would be further legitimized, which, surely, must accord with our nation's interest and ethos.

The new climate has also permeated the General Assembly. At its forty-fifth session, that body adopted a resolution entitled Enhancing the effectiveness of the principle of periodic and genuine elections.[82] This nonbinding, yet important, document reaffirms and further specifies the electoral entitlement first outlined in the Universal Declaration of Human Rights and later embodied in Article 25 of the Covenant. It "stresses" the member nations'

> conviction that periodic and genuine elections are a necessary and indispensable element of sustained efforts to protect the rights and interests of the governed and that, as a matter of practical experience, the right of everyone to take part in the government of his or her country is a crucial factor in the effective enjoyment by all of a wide range of other human rights and fundamental freedoms, embracing political, economic, social and cultural rights.[83]

[79] ICCPR, *supra* note 41.

[80] Case 34/1979, 1981 Report, *supra* note 64, at 130; Case 44/1979, *id.*, Ann. XVI, at 153.

[81] *Supra* note 53.

[82] GA Res. 45/150 (Feb. 21, 1991).

[83] *Id.*, para. 2.

The resolution also declares "that determining the will of the people requires an electoral process that provides an equal opportunity for all citizens to become candidates and put forward their political views, individually and in co-operation with others, as provided in national constitutions and laws."[84] It commends "the value of the electoral assistance" the United Nations has provided member states at their request,[85] and asks the Secretary-General to seek the views of members and others on how the Organization can best respond to further such requests and to report his findings to the next Assembly, together with "an account of United Nations experience in election monitoring."[86]

At its next session the Assembly, with only four dissents, passed Resolution 46/137 of December 17, 1991, which declared that "periodic and genuine elections" are a "necessary and indispensable element" and a "crucial factor in the effective enjoyment . . . of a wide range of other human rights." The resolution established a procedure for authorizing the monitoring of national elections and endorsed the Secretary-General's decision to create an office, headed by a senior official, "to act as a focal point . . . in order to ensure consistency in the handling of requests of Member States organizing elections."

Parallel and reinforcing norm-generating activity occurring in regional frameworks has accelerated this evolution. The Charter of the Organization of American States, in Article 5, establishes the duty of members to promote "the effective exercise of representative democracy." The OAS Ministers of Foreign Affairs and the Organization's Permanent Council have issued a series of resolutions affirming this regional entitlement while censuring those committing apparent violations. For example, in June 1979, the Ministers demanded the "immediate and definitive replacement of the Somoza regime" in Nicaragua and the installation of a "democratic government" with the "holding of free elections as soon as possible."[87] Similarly, in December 1987, the Permanent Council took note of the "deplorable acts of violence and disorder" that had taken place in Haiti during that year's failed elections, expressed its "conviction that it is necessary to resume the democratic process" and urged the "Government of Haiti to adopt all necessary measures so that the people of Haiti may express their will through free elections."[88] In May 1989, the Ministers decided that "General Manuel Antonio Noriega . . . [had] abridged the right of the Panamanian people to freely elect their legitimate authorities" and thus had "seriously jeopardize[d]" an "essential purpose" of the OAS, which "is to promote and consolidate representative democracy." They further called for a "transfer of power in the shortest possible time" by means of "democratic mechanisms."[89]

On June 5, 1991, the Ministers adopted a crucial resolution on representative democracy. Its preamble states that the principles of the OAS Charter "require the political representation of [member] states to be based on effective exercise of representative democracy" and, in its operative sections, the resolution decides that the Secretary General shall

> call for the immediate convocation of a meeting of the Permanent Council in the event of any occurrences giving rise to the sudden or irregular interruption of the democratic political institutional process or of the legitimate exer-

[84] *Id.*, para. 3.

[85] *Id.*, para. 8.

[86] *Id.*, paras. 10, 11. The Secretary-General's report to the Assembly is UN Doc. A/46/609 (1991).

[87] OEA/Ser.F/II.17, doc. 40, rev.2 (1979).

[88] OEA/Ser.G/CP/RES.489, doc. 720 (1987).

[89] OEA/Ser.F/II.21, doc. 8, rev.2 (1989); *see also* OEA/Ser.F/II.21, doc. 45 (1989).

cise of power by the democratically elected government in any of the Organization's member states.[90]

Within ten days, the Ministers of Foreign Affairs or the OAS General Assembly must convene so as to "look into the events collectively and adopt any decisions deemed appropriate."[91] It was this procedure that was invoked to bring about sanctions against the regime established by the military coup in Haiti in September 1991.[92]

Alongside these quasi-legislative developments, a regional quasi jurisprudence is germinating. In 1990, the Inter-American Commission on Human Rights, in considering a complaint of electoral fraud and other impropriety against Mexico, began to spell out in some detail the right of access, under general conditions of equality, to a nation's public functions.[93]

Even more dramatic are recent efforts by the nations of Europe to make the electoral entitlement explicit and specific. Article 3 of Protocol 1 to the European Human Rights Convention obliges the parties to "undertake to hold free elections at reasonable intervals by secret ballot, under conditions which will ensure the free expression of the opinion of the people in the choice of the legislature."[94] Finding the Greek colonels' regime in violation, the European Court of Human Rights interpreted this Protocol to require "the existence of a representative legislature, elected at reasonable intervals."[95] The European Commission, meanwhile, has rejected the purist argument that the Protocol requires states to adopt a system of proportional representation.[96]

As members of the Conference on Security and Co-operation in Europe,[97] the same nations, augmented by Canada, the United States and the nations of Eastern Europe, recently joined unanimously in spelling out the contents of the new right to participate in free and open elections. At a meeting in Copenhagen in June 1990, they affirmed that "democracy is an inherent element of the rule of law" and recognized "the importance of pluralism with regard to political organizations."[98] Among the "inalienable rights of all human beings," they decided, is the democratic entitlement, including "free elections that will be held at reasonable intervals by secret ballot or by equivalent free voting procedure, under conditions which ensure in practice the free expression of the opinion of the electors in the choice of their representatives"; a government "representative in character, in which the executive is accountable to the elected legislature or the electorate"; and political parties that are clearly separate from the state.[99] The thirty-five

[90] Representative Democracy, OEA/Ser.P/AG/RES.1080 (XXI–0/91), para. 1.

[91] *Id.*, para. 2.

[92] Support to the Democratic Government of Haiti, *supra* note 2.

[93] Annual Report of the Inter-American Commission on Human Rights, OEA/Ser.L/V/II.77, doc. 7, rev.1, at 97 (1990) (Mexico Report).

[94] Protocol 1 to the European Convention, *supra* note 72, Mar. 20, 1952, 213 UNTS 262, entered into force May 18, 1954, and, as of June 1991, had been ratified by all but one party to the Convention (Liechtenstein).

[95] The Greek Case, 12 Y.B. EUR. CONV. ON HUM. RTS. 179 (1969); *see also* Case of Mathieu-Mohin, 113 Eur. Ct. H.R. (ser. A) at 22 (1987).

[96] Application 7140/75, 7 Eur. Comm'n H.R. 95, 97 (1977).

[97] Conference on Security and Co-operation in Europe, Final Act, Aug. 1, 1975, 73 DEP'T ST. BULL. 323 (1975), *reprinted in* 14 ILM 1292 (1975).

[98] Conference on Security and Co-operation in Europe, Document of the Copenhagen Meeting of the Conference on the Human Dimension, June 29, 1990, *reprinted in* 29 ILM 1305, 1308, para. 3 (1990) [hereinafter Copenhagen Document].

[99] *Id.*, para. 5.

CSCE participants also linked recognition of the democratic entitlement by governments to the validation of their right to govern: "the will of the people, freely and fairly expressed through periodic and genuine elections, is the basis of the authority and legitimacy of all government,"[100] they declared, implying the illegitimacy of regimes that deny their citizens basic democratic rights.

According to Professor Theodor Meron, one of the public members of the U.S. delegation, the "language of Copenhagen goes far beyond any existing human rights instruments."[101] The document is detailed to an unprecedented degree, establishing a standard that the UN General Assembly might profitably emulate in a resolution. Citizens have the right to expect "free elections at reasonable intervals, as established by law"; a national legislature in which at least one chamber's membership is "freely contested in a popular vote"; a system of universal and equal adult suffrage; a secret ballot or its equivalent; free, nondiscriminatory candidature for office; freedom to form political parties that compete "on a basis of equal treatment before the law and by the authorities"; fair and free campaigning; "no legal or administrative obstacle" to media access, which must be available "on a non-discriminatory basis for all political groupings and individuals wishing to participate in the electoral process"; and a guarantee that the "candidates who obtain the necessary number of votes required by law are duly installed in office and are permitted to remain in office until their term expires or is otherwise" terminated in accordance with law.[102]

This unprecedented North Atlantic and Europe-wide initiative to endorse and define a popular right of electoral democracy[103] went on to commend the growing practice of involving foreign observers in national elections. The participating states invited "observers from any other CSCE participating States and any appropriate private institutions and organizations who may wish to do so to observe the course of their national election proceedings, to the extent permitted by law," and pledged to "endeavour to facilitate similar access for election proceedings held below the national level."[104]

Later in 1990, the leaders of the thirty-four CSCE states joined in Paris to declare "a new era of democracy, peace and unity."[105] Unanimously, they endorsed an extraordinary Charter, which commits them "to build, consolidate and strengthen democracy as the only system of government of our nations."[106] The Charter restates the older entitlement to free expression but adds the right of every individual, without discrimination, "to participate in free and fair elections,"[107] backed by the leaders' pledge to "co-operate and support each other with the aim of making democratic gains irreversible."[108] Although the Charter is not a treaty, its language is weighted with the terminology of *opinio juris*. It is deliberately norm creating. In particular, the Charter builds on the assumption

[100] *Id.* at 1309, para. 6.

[101] Meron, *Democracy and the Rule of Law*, 153 WORLD AFF. 23, 24 (1990). *See also* Steiner, *Political Participation as a Human Right*, 1 HARV. HUM. RTS. Y.B. 77 (1988).

[102] Copenhagen Document, *supra* note 98, at 1310, para. 7.

[103] Buergenthal, *The Copenhagen CSCE Meeting: A New Public Order for Europe*, 11 HUM. RTS. L.J. 217, 221–22 (1990).

[104] Copenhagen Document, *supra* note 98, at 1310, para. 8.

[105] Conference on Security and Co-operation in Europe, Charter of Paris for a New Europe and Supplementary Document to Give Effect to Certain Provisions of the Charter, Nov. 21, 1990, Preamble, *reprinted in* 30 ILM 190, 193 (1991) [hereinafter Paris Charter].

[106] Paris Charter, *supra* note 105, at 193.

[107] *Id.* at 194.

[108] *Id.* at 195.

that electoral democracy is owed not only by each government to its own people, but also by each CSCE state to all the others. According to Judge Thomas Buergenthal, another U.S. participant in the Copenhagen meeting, today

> no domestic institution or norm, in theory, is beyond the jurisdictional reach of the CSCE. Here the traditional domestic jurisdiction doctrine, which has tended to shield the oppressive state practices and institutions from international scrutiny, has for all practical purposes lost its meaning. And this notwithstanding the fact that non-intervention in the domestic affairs of a state is a basic CSCE principle. Once the rule of law, human rights and democratic pluralism are made the subject of international commitments, there is little left in terms of governmental institutions that is domestic.[109]

In this connection, one should note that the United States *is* a party to this normative evolution of the CSCE process.

To safeguard the rights concerned, the Paris Charter establishes an institutionalized process for monitoring compliance with the electoral duties of states. It gives the CSCE several organs, including a secretariat at Prague[110] and an Office for Free Elections at Warsaw. The latter is to "facilitate contacts and the exchange of information on elections within participating States."[111] The Charter also envisages the eventual creation, after further consultations, of a "CSCE parliamentary assembly, involving members of parliaments from all participating States," to achieve "greater parliamentary involvement in the CSCE."[112]

The new Office for Free Elections and its functions are described in the "supplementary document" appended to the Charter.[113] The office is to "foster the implementation" of the provisions of the Copenhagen Document pertaining to electoral democracy and, to this end, is authorized to "compile information," including, but not limited to, reports by governments on elections and the electoral process in participating states, "as well as reports of election observations." It is also to "serve to facilitate contact among governments, parliaments or private organizations wishing to observe elections and competent authorities of the States in which elections are to take place."[114]

Most recently, in September to October 1991, these nations' representatives unanimously endorsed the Document of the Moscow Meeting of the Conference on the Human Dimension of the CSCE. It reaffirms "that issues relating to human rights, fundamental freedoms, democracy and the rule of law are of international concern, as respect for these rights and freedoms constitutes one of the foundations of the international order." The participating states "categorically and irrevocably declare[d] that the commitments undertaken in the field of the human dimension of the CSCE are matters of direct and legitimate concern to all participating States and do not belong exclusively to the internal affairs of the State concerned."[115] More important yet is the mechanism and procedure established in paragraphs 3–16, which envisages a "resource" of experts, up to three of whom may be named by a state requesting good offices or mediation services in connec-

[109] Buergenthal, *CSCE Human Dimension: The Birth of a System,* 1 COLLECTED COURSES OF THE ACADEMY OF EUROPEAN LAW, No. 2, at 3, 42–43 (forthcoming).

[110] Paris Charter, *supra* note 105, at 206.

[111] *Id.* at 207.

[112] *Id.*

[113] *Id.* at 214–15.

[114] *Id.* at 214.

[115] Conference on Security and Co-operation in Europe, Document of the Moscow Meeting of the Conference on the Human Dimension of the CSCE, Oct. 3, 1991, Preamble, at 2 (unofficial text of the U.S. delegation), *reprinted in* 30 ILM 1670 (1991). [hereinafter Moscow Document].

tion with any domestic dispute arising under the "human dimension." If a CSCE state poses a human dimension question to another member and that member does not itself invite such a mission of inquiry, the requesting state and five others may invoke the process, with one expert of the three-person panel to be selected from the "resource" list by the requesting state, one by the requested state, and the third by agreement between the other two or by the ranking official of the CSCE designated by its Council. These "rapporteurs" are to establish the facts and report on them, and they may give advice on possible solutions to the problems raised. Most important of all is part II of the Moscow Document, in which the members pledge that they

> will support vigorously, in accordance with the Charter of the United Nations, in case of overthrow or attempted overthrow of a legitimately elected government of a participating State by undemocratic means, the legitimate organs of that State upholding human rights, democracy and the rule of law, recognizing their common commitment to countering any attempt to curb these basic values.[116]

The evolution of textual determinacy with respect to the electoral entitlement is a relatively recent development. In practice, however, the monitoring component of the entitlement has a long history. The long record of UN election monitoring both in the former trusteeship territories and in some colonies immediately before they attained independence was already mentioned as instrumental in establishing pedigree. But that practice also honed the normative content of the entitlement. As early as May 1956, the Trusteeship Council sent monitors to the plebiscite in which the people of British Togoland chose to join Ghana.[117] Its monitors were involved in conducting the preindependence plebiscites in the British Cameroons in November 1959 and February 1961.[118] Similarly, following the November 1959 violence between the Hutu and Tutsi tribes in what was then Belgian-administered Ruanda-Urundi, the United Nations supervised a preindependence election and referendum that determined the separation of the linked indigenous kingdoms and the future of the monarchy.[119]

In 1961 the United Nations assisted New Zealand, the administering authority, in conducting a plebiscite in Western Samoa that endorsed a draft constitution and a form of association with the former trustee.[120] On June 17, 1975, the

[116] Moscow Document, *supra* note 115, para. 17, at 9.

[117] Report of the United Nations Plebiscite Commissioner for the Trust Territory of Togoland under British Administration, UN Doc. T/1258 and Add.1 (1956).

[118] *See* GA Res. 1350, 13 UN GAOR Supp. (No. 18A) at 2, UN Doc. A/4090/Add.1 (1959) (whether the Northern Cameroons wished "to be part of the Northern Region of Nigeria when the Federation of Nigeria becomes independent"); GA Res. 1352, 14 UN GAOR Supp. (No. 16) at 26, UN Doc. A/4354 (1959) (whether the Southern Cameroons wished to achieve independence by "joining the independent Federation of Nigeria [or] the independent Republic of Cameroons"); GA Res. 1473, *id.* at 38 (putting the questions posed in the GA Res. 1352 plebiscite before the Northern Cameroons); *see also* Report of United Nations Commissioner for the Supervision of the Plebiscites in the Southern and Northern Parts of the Trust Territory of the Cameroons under United Kingdom Administration, UN Doc. T/1556 and app. (1961).

[119] GA Res. 1579, 15 UN GAOR Supp. (No. 16), *supra* note 31, at 34 (elections); GA Res. 1605, 15 UN GAOR Supp. (No. 16A) at 8, UN Doc. A/4684/Add.1 (1961) (referendum).

[120] GA Res. 1569, 15 UN GAOR Supp. (No. 16), *supra* note 31, at 33 (whether the inhabitants of the territory accepted "the Constitution adopted by the Constitutional Convention on 28 October 1960" and endorsed "that on 1 January 1962 Western Samoa should become an independent State on the basis of that Constitution"); *see also* Report of United Nations Commissioner for the Supervision of the Plebiscite in Western Samoa, UN Doc. T/1564 and Add.1 (1961).

United Nations observed the vote in which residents of the Northern Mariana Islands endorsed a loose form of political confederation with the United States;[121] and, at various times in the 1980s, it supervised plebiscites in the rest of the U.S. Pacific Islands Trust that determined the future status of those several archipelagoes.[122]

The monitoring of political progress in trust territories led to the case-by-case enunciation of principles applicable to the democratic entitlement. Throughout the 1950s and 1960s, the Trusteeship Council and the General Assembly, on the basis of reports made by visiting missions, made recommendations to the states administering trust territories. These frequently specified the steps necessary to effect democratic participation by the inhabitants in choosing their political future. For example, in its 1959 report on Belgian administration of the Ruanda-Urundi Trust, the Council urged that the representation of inhabitants in the legislative body be increased and that it be given greater power. The Council also called for direct universal suffrage and an increase in the responsibilities of elected local authorities.[123] Such advice was influential both in determining the rate and direction of a territory's emancipation and in crystallizing a broadly shared expectation about the requirements of the democratic entitlement.

Although the United Nations had a specific legal ground for intervening in, and validating, the democratic process within trust territories, it also found bases for supervising colonial elections and referendums just prior to independence and this role gradually came to be an accepted element in legitimizing those crucial transitions. Thus, UN observers oversaw the referendum establishing a new constitution for the Cook Islands in 1965[124] and the preindependence referendum and elections in Spanish Equatorial Guinea in 1968.[125] The United Nations undertook similar monitoring of the referendum on the future status of West New Guinea (West Irian) from July 14 to August 2, 1969,[126] as well as of the November 1980 elections conducted in the New Hebrides under French and British administration, which led to the creation of independent Vanuatu.[127]

As the colonial era drew to a close, the significance of the UN election-monitoring role, instead of declining, appears to have increased, partly because the last

[121] Report of the United Nations Visiting Mission to Observe the Plebiscite in the Northern Mariana Islands, Trust Territory of the Pacific Islands, 43 UN TCOR Supp. (No. 2) at 24, UN Doc. T/1771 (1976).

[122] *See* Report of the United Nations Visiting Mission to Observe the Plebiscite in the Federated States of Micronesia, Trust Territory of the Pacific Islands, 51 UN TCOR Supp. (No. 1) at 14, UN Doc. T/1860 (1984) (June 21, 1983 plebiscite for the islands of Truk, Yap, Kosrae and Ponape); Report of the United Nations Visiting Mission to Observe the Plebiscite in the Marshall Islands, Trust Territory of the Pacific Islands, *id.* (No. 2) at 12–13, UN Doc. T/1865 (1984) (Sept. 7, 1983 plebiscite); Report of the United Nations Visiting Mission to Observe the Plebiscite in Palau, Trust Territory of the Pacific Islands, 53 UN TCOR Supp. (No. 2) at 14, UN Doc. T/1885 (1986) (Feb. 21, 1986 plebiscite).

[123] 24 UN TCOR Annex 1 (Agenda Item 3) at 21, UN Doc. T/L.928 (1959).

[124] GA Res. 2005, 19 UN GAOR Supp. (No. 15) at 7, UN Doc. A/5815 (1965); Report of the United Nations Representatives for the Supervision of the Elections in the Cook Islands, UN Doc. A/5962 and Corr.1 (1965).

[125] GA Res. 2355, 22 UN GAOR Supp. (No. 16) at 54, UN Doc. A/6716 (1967); United Nations Mission for the Supervision of the Referendum and the Elections in Equatorial Guinea, UN Doc. A/7200/Add.4, Anns. V, VI (1968). Independence was formally achieved on October 12, 1968.

[126] GA Res. 1752, 17 UN GAOR Supp. (No. 17) at 70, UN Doc. A/5217 (1962); Report of the Secretary-General regarding the Act of Self-determination in West Irian, UN Doc. A/7641 (1969).

[127] GA Res. 34/10, 34 UN GAOR Supp. (No. 46) at 199, UN Doc. A/34/46 (1979); Report of the United Nations Mission to Observe the Elections in the New Hebrides, UN Doc. A/34/852 (1979).

cases of decolonization were among the most difficult. In these, a UN "honest broker" role proved indispensable. A remarkable example is UNTAG, the UN transitional administration that acted as midwife in the birth of independent Namibia. Under South African administration since Germany's defeat in World War I, the territory was set on the road to independence first by the General Assembly's termination of South Africa's mandate in 1966, followed by a landmark advisory opinion by the International Court of Justice in 1971,[128] and by a decision of the Security Council in 1978 establishing the parameters for the territory's political development and democratic entitlement.[129] It took another decade, however, for the political climate in South Africa to change sufficiently to permit international implementation of self-determination through a UN-supervised vote. By that time, tribal and racial cleavages had become potential obstacles to a peaceful transition. Created by the Security Council precisely to prevent a preindependence civil conflict, UNTAG monitored the final months of South African administration and supervised the elections immediately prior to independence. But UNTAG did not merely monitor a vote. It took responsibility for maintaining peace, overseeing the South African military withdrawal and assisting in the drafting of a new constitution. It helped achieve the rapid repeal of discriminatory legislation, implementation of an amnesty and the return of political refugees; and it was instrumental in keeping the election peaceful and productive. Deploying more than seven thousand military and civilian personnel at a cost of $373 million, it prepared the November 1989 elections and conducted them so successfully that a risk-filled situation became, instead, a model of political transformation.[130]

The Security Council authorized a similarly complex role for the United Nations in a resolution of April 29, 1991, that established a United Nations Mission for the Referendum in the Western Sahara.[131] Under the plan negotiated by the Secretary-General with the Government of Morocco and the POLISARIO liberation movement, electoral monitoring is to be but one component of a project that gives the Organization predominant responsibility for governance of the territory in the period leading up to, and during, the crucial plebiscite. After almost two decades of war for control of the territory, the United Nations is to ensure security, facilitate large-scale repatriation of refugees, oversee the withdrawal of rival militias, and supervise the delicate process of determining who is eligible to vote.[132]

Even more remarkable than its monitoring in trust territories and colonies is the recent supervision by the United Nations of crucial votes in independent member states. In the first of these, the 1990 election in Nicaragua, UN monitoring was the culmination of the Secretary-General's far more extensive "good offices" negotiations, in cooperation with the OAS, aimed at ending the Central American regional conflict. This effort led, in August 1987, to the Esquipulas II agreement

[128] Legal Consequences for States of the Continued Presence of South Africa in Namibia (South West Africa) notwithstanding Security Council Resolution 276 (1970), 1971 ICJ REP. 16 (Advisory Opinion of June 21).

[129] SC Res. 435, 33 UN SCOR (Res. & Dec.) at 13, UN Doc. S/INF/34 (1978). It did not authorize the sending of UNTAG until 1989. SC Res. 628, 44 UN SCOR (Res. & Dec.) at 2, UN Doc. S/INF/45 (1989); SC Res. 629, *id.*

[130] *Namibia, Independence at Last,* UN CHRON., June 1990, at 4. Namibia formally achieved independence on March 21, 1990. *Id.*

[131] SC Res. 690 (Apr. 29, 1991).

[132] The Situation Concerning Western Sahara: Report by the Secretary-General, UN Doc. S/22464 (1991).

between five Central American Presidents, which established a blueprint for restoring peace and ensuring legitimacy in Nicaragua. In response to its call for free, internationally monitored elections, on March 3, 1989, the Nicaraguan Foreign Minister requested that the Secretary-General establish an observer mission.[133] The General Assembly had already authorized the Secretary-General to assist the Esquipulas process in appropriate ways,[134] but that resolution had made no mention of election monitoring. Nevertheless, the Secretary-General thought he had a "sufficient legislative basis" to comply with Nicaragua's request.[135] As a result, he established ONUVEN on July 6, 1989,[136] an initiative approved by the Security Council three weeks later.[137]

The active, far-reaching role of the UN observers in Nicaragua clearly illustrates how much the ground rules for international election monitoring had evolved in practice from the days of the missions to British Togoland and Ruanda-Urundi. The observers sent by the Secretary-General monitored the activities of the Supreme Electoral Council in drafting and implementing new laws applicable to nominating, campaigning and related activities. They were deployed throughout the electoral campaign and mediated disputes between candidates concerning access to funding, the media and even the streets. They oversaw the rights of political parties to organize and campaign, verified the campaigners' right of access to radio, television and newspapers, and investigated numerous charges of abuses and irregularities that might have undermined the legitimacy of the outcome.[138] At the final stage, ONUVEN observed the voting and established its own projection of the results.[139] Commenting on these varied functions, the head of ONUVEN, Elliot Richardson, noted that his group had decided early in its career "that responsibility for verification of the electoral process demanded more than merely recording the process, more than monitoring, and could not stop short of actively seeking to get corrected whatever substantial defects had been discovered."[140]

Creating a UN mandate for ONUVEH, the mission established on October 10, 1990, to oversee Haitian elections, was more controversial. The Haitian case—greeted by many but feared by others—was seen as a potential precedent for international monitoring in any independent state. While the same might have been said of ONUVEN, Nicaragua's long civil war could have been seen as sufficiently threatening to the peace to justify, exceptionally, a UN role in validating those national elections. In Haiti's case, however, there was no obvious threat to international peace and the elections did not constitute part of a regional program for internationally supervised postwar reconciliation. In fact, the UN monitoring role there resulted solely from a request in a letter to the Secretary-General from the Haitian Transitional Government.[141] In normative terms, Haiti may be understood as the first instance in which the United Nations, acting at the request of

[133] *See* The Situation in Central America: Threats to International Peace and Security and Peace Initiatives, UN Doc. A/44/642, at 2 (1989) [hereinafter First Nicaragua Report].

[134] GA Res. 43/24, 43 UN GAOR Supp. (No. 49) at 27, UN Doc. A/43/49 (1988).

[135] UN Doc. A/44/304, at 2 (1989).

[136] UN Doc. A/44/375 (1989).

[137] SC Res. 637, 44 UN SCOR, *supra* note 129, at 19.

[138] *See, e.g.*, The Situation in Central America: Threat to International Peace and Security and Peace Initiatives, UN Doc. A/44/927 (1990) [hereinafter Fifth Nicaragua Report]. *See also* First Nicaragua Report, *supra* note 133; UN Doc. A/44/834 (1990) (Second Report); UN Doc. A/44/917 (1990) (Third Report); UN Doc. A/44/921 (1990) (Fourth Report).

[139] Fifth Nicaragua Report, *supra* note 138.

[140] *Id.* at 3.

[141] UN Doc. A/44/965 (1990).

a national government, intervened in the electoral process solely to validate the legitimacy of the outcome.

Despite misgivings, ONUVEH secured the imprimatur of the General Assembly.[142] Once again, the monitors were authorized to do far more than oversee the ballot count. Their first report noted the lack of democratic traditions in Haiti and its long history of totalitarianism and violence, much of it government inspired and some of it quite recent.[143] In preemptive response to this problem, the Assembly had authorized the recruiting of observers "with solid experience in the public order field."[144] As ONUVEH soon discovered, the

> first task . . . was to help create a psychological climate conducive to the holding of democratic elections. . . . In this they were assisted by a radio and television campaign conducted by an ONUVEH information team. . . .
>
> . . . [They] inquired into difficulties encountered by the registration and polling stations in registering voters and into irregularities reported to them. They attended political meetings . . . and monitored radio and television broadcasts to make sure that all candidates had equal access to the mass media.[145]

Although the Secretary-General, in his final report on ONUVEH, expressed satisfaction with the fairness of the electoral process and the role played by the United Nations, he also noted the formidable obstacles that lay ahead for Haitian democracy and called for "launching a civil education campaign on the importance of the parliament and local authorities."[146] The Secretary-General rightly warned that, if electoral democracy is to be more than a one-time event in the history of a state with little experience in such matters, a far more sustained effort will have to be made under the auspices of the community of nations. This warning suggests the need for a long-term, preemptive assistance program. More, it at least implies the need for a longer-term international effort to create the grass roots elements of democratic political institutions and processes—a particularly challenging form of technical assistance—in nations without that tradition. This need, in turn, suggests an important future role for the nongovernmental, citizen-to-citizen organizations—at present, an underused, but invaluable, component of the UN system.

The military coup that ousted Haiti's elected Government on September 30, 1991, verified the Secretary-General's warning that elections are not necessarily a cure-all. The General Assembly responded less than two weeks later, passing by consensus a resolution that "[s]trongly condemns both the attempted illegal replacement of the constitutional President of Haiti and the use of violence, military coercion and the violation of human rights in that country" and "demands the immediate restoration of the legitimate Government." It also "[a]ppeals to the . . . Members" to "take measures in support" of action by the OAS to isolate Haiti diplomatically and economically.[147] By these provisions, the Assembly made clear its intention henceforth to regard the overthrow of a democratically elected

[142] GA Res. 45/2 (Oct. 12, 1990).

[143] First Report of the United Nations Observer Group for the Verification of the Elections in Haiti, UN Doc. A/45/870, at 9–10 (1990).

[144] GA Res. 45/2, *supra* note 142, para. 1(*d*).

[145] United Nations Electoral Assistance to Haiti, UN Doc. DPI/1120 (1991).

[146] Electoral Assistance to Haiti: Note by the Secretary-General, UN Doc. A/45/870/Add.1, at 23 (1991).

[147] GA Res. A/46/L.8/Rev.1, paras. 1, 2, 4 (Oct. 11, 1991) (italics omitted).

regime as an appropriate subject for censure and even for recommending collective measures.[148]

The Organization of American States has also engaged in election monitoring. Its members authorized the dispatch of a 435-person commission to Nicaragua in 1990 to observe 70 percent of the polling sites.[149] In addition, the OAS maintained a major presence during the Haitian elections,[150] not only to watch the polls, but also to assist in drafting the electoral law and organizing voter registration.[151] Over the past two years, OAS monitors have observed elections in Suriname, El Salvador, Paraguay and Panama as well.[152] As a result, in part, of such collective efforts,[153] the thirty-four OAS member states—with the lamentable exception of Haiti—all have governments chosen in accordance with the democratic entitlement.[154]

Monitoring by governmental and nongovernmental observers also became an important ad hoc part of the post-1989 transition from Communist to democratic regimes in Eastern Europe. These events foreshadowed the textual declarations regarding election standards and procedures in the Copenhagen and Paris documents. Once again, practice preceded the drafting of new principles. The United States sent an official mission to monitor Bulgaria's 1990 election, as did several other CSCE governments.[155] Several members of Congress observed the electoral campaigns in Bulgaria[156] and Czechoslovakia,[157] as did their counterparts from some Western European parliaments.

At the unofficial level, additional election monitoring has taken place in recent years. Emissaries of the Council of Freely Elected Heads of Government of the Carter Center observed the 1990 Nicaraguan and 1991 Zambian elections.[158] The (U.S.) National Democratic Institute for International Affairs has monitored elections in twelve countries since 1986.[159] At least half a dozen teams of foreign observers, including experts from the United States, the Philippines, Japan and the British Commonwealth, monitored parliamentary elections in Bangladesh on February 27, 1991.[160] International observers from Canada, France, Germany and the United States verified the propriety of elections held in Benin in March 1991.[161] Perhaps most remarkable was the authorized presence of sixty-five inter-

[148] The "secondary" role of the General Assembly in recommending collective measures by the members has been controversial, but was found to be justified by Article 17, paragraph 2 of the Charter. *See* Certain expenses of the United Nations (Article 17, paragraph 2, of the Charter), 1962 ICJ REP. 151, 163 (Advisory Opinion of July 20).

[149] N.Y. Times, Feb. 23, 1990, at A3, col. 4.

[150] OEA/Ser.G/CP/RES.537, doc. 805 (1990).

[151] Report of the Secretary General on the Assistance the Organization Is Giving to the Provisional Government of Haiti in its Electoral Process, OEA/Ser.G/CP/doc.2108/90, at 1.

[152] N.Y. Times, June 9, 1991, §4, at 2, col. 1.

[153] See, e.g., the OAS condemnation of General Manuel Noriega's usurpation of democratic electoral process in Panama's election of May 7, 1989, *supra* note 89. *See also* N.Y. Times, May 18, 1989, at A8, col. 3; *id.*, Aug. 16, 1989, at A9, col. 1.

[154] N.Y. Times, June 9, 1991, §4, at 2, col. 1. Cuba is not a member.

[155] N.Y. Times, June 6, 1990, at A10, col. 3.

[156] *See* Kahn, *Bulgaria's Different Pathway*, Christian Sci. Monitor, June 22, 1990, at 18. Helsinki Watch also sent monitors. N.Y. Times, June 11, 1990, at A1, col. 1.

[157] N.Y. Times, June 10, 1990, §1, at 31, col. 1.

[158] N.Y. Times, Aug. 9, 1989, at A13, col. 1; N.Y. Times, Nov. 1, 1991, at A3, col. 1.

[159] National Democratic Institute for International Affairs, Response to United Nations General Assembly Resolution 45/150: Developing a United Nations Elections Assistance Capability 2 (1991) (memorandum submitted to the Secretary-General).

[160] N.Y. Times, Feb. 28, 1991, at A5, col. 4.

[161] N.Y. Times, Mar. 12, 1991, at A11, col. 1.

national observers at the referendum on independence conducted in Latvia on March 3, 1991.[162]

Elliot Richardson, as head of the UN observers in Nicaragua, predicted that "the United Nations is likely in the future to be called upon for similar assignments in other countries."[163] "The results of such elections," as Professor Reisman recently observed, "serve as evidence of popular sovereignty and become the basis for international endorsement of the elected government."[164] Appropriately, President George Bush, in addressing the forty-fifth General Assembly, proposed the establishment of a standing UN electoral commission to assist nations, at their request, in guaranteeing that their elections will be free and fair.[165] A year later, as noted, the Assembly implemented that proposal.

Requesting international electoral monitoring thus will likely become an increasingly routine part of national practice, particularly useful whenever the democratic legitimacy of a regime is in question. Of course, there are still hard-core holdouts, such as the totalitarian governments of Myanmar, North Korea and China. Their number, however, is diminishing. The Government formed in Ethiopia in May 1991, after the end of the civil war, has undertaken to conduct "free, democratic and internationally monitored elections" within a year.[166] The insurgents who took power in Eritrea have committed themselves not to secede from Ethiopia until after a UN-monitored plebiscite, to be held within two years.[167]

A recent study by the UN Secretariat, noting the rising demand for monitoring, made a start at setting out the juridical, institutional, administrative and fiscal parameters of an expanded UN electoral monitoring service.[168] The OAS was authorized to prepare a similar study.[169] These begin the conceptually difficult task of sifting through the increasing body of practice to clarify the meaning of the normative concept signaled by the phrase "democratic entitlement." These data make it strikingly apparent that international election monitoring cannot be limited to guaranteeing citizens' right to vote, but rather must also ensure a far broader panoply of democratic rights of the sort enunciated in the Civil and Political Rights Covenant and the Charter of Paris. In case-by-case implementation and the distillation of that experience, greater determinacy will be achieved.

A study that seeks to connect the dots of practice with lines of enunciated principle must also look at the several instances when election monitoring was denied. For example, in 1990 the Secretary-General refused to monitor the Romanian elections on the ground that his participation had not been authorized by the General Assembly or Security Council. He added, perhaps even more persuasively, that he had not been invited to participate early enough in establishing the rules and methods to be used in conducting the election campaign.[170] In

[162] Fin. Times (London), Mar. 4, 1991, at 14.

[163] Fifth Nicaragua Report, *supra* note 138, at 3.

[164] Reisman, *Sovereignty and Human Rights in Contemporary International Law*, 84 AJIL 866, 868–69 (1990).

[165] N.Y. Times, Oct. 2, 1990, at A12, col. 1.

[166] N.Y. Times, May 29, 1991, at A6, col. 5.

[167] N.Y. Times, June 22, 1991, at 3, col. 1.

[168] Principles for United Nations Observance of Elections, Confidential Memorandum (June 6, 1989) (in the possession of the author).

[169] OEA/Ser.G/CP/RES.421, doc. 606 (1985).

[170] *See U.N. Says It Won't Monitor Romanian Elections* (NEXIS, CURRNT Library, Reuters, Jan. 25, 1990).

1991 the Office of the Secretary-General rejected requests for election monitoring made by Lesotho and Zambia, again on the ground that he felt he was unauthorized, in the absence of special circumstances, to monitor elections in sovereign states. The political organs of the United Nations may have been too cautious, so far, in giving the Secretary-General authority to respond favorably to a bona fide request by a member. On the other hand, the office of the Secretary-General may have been too cautious in denying requests for monitoring without even presenting them for approval to the Security Council or the General Assembly.

There is reason, nonetheless, for some caution. Commentators have rightly warned that the bare monitoring of the act of voting may place observers in the position of seeming to legitimate an electoral victory that was not fairly achieved. This reservation need not implicate fraud or repression but, more likely, concerns the effect on free choice of the normal operation of entrenched social and political institutions. In the words of a recent report to the General Assembly by the Secretary-General:

> [R]equests should pertain primarily to situations with a clear international dimension; the monitoring of an election or referendum should cover the entire electoral process in order to secure conditions of fairness and impartiality; . . . there must be broad public support in the State for the United Nations assuming such a role; and, finally, there should be approval by the competent organ of the United Nations.[171]

In future, in keeping with Assembly Resolution 46/137 of December 17, 1991, all requests for monitoring will be considered by the Council or Assembly, which will have the task of evolving standards for accepting or refusing.

While no observation process can reach back far enough into a nation's history to extirpate the impacted roots of social and cultural inequalities, observers can do—and already have done—more than simply watch tellers count ballots. To make citizens' rights to free and open elections a legitimate entitlement, its parameters need to be made clear and specific. To that end, a robust repertory of practice, a canon of enunciated principles and an institutional framework for implementation are developing that are capable of giving the entitlement increasing determinacy.

As the entitlement becomes an accepted norm, a drawn-out debate in international law will draw to a close. Do governments validate international law or does international law validate governments? It is becoming apparent that each legitimates the other.

The capacity of the international system to validate governments in this fashion is rapidly being accepted as an appropriate role of the United Nations, the regional systems and, supplementarily, the NGOs. A recent study conducted by the Netherlands Minister of Foreign Affairs gives expression to the new normative expectation. It asked: what can reasonably be expected of a European state seeking to join the European Communities and the Council of Europe? The study finds that applicant states "must be plural democracies; they must regularly hold free elections by secret ballot; they must respect the rule of law; [and] they must have signed the European Convention on Human Rights and Fundamental Free-

[171] Enhancing the Effectiveness of the Principle of Periodic and Genuine Elections, Report of the Secretary-General, UN Doc. A/46/609, para. 79, at 25 (1991). *See also* Gelb, *The Free Elections Trap*, N.Y. Times, May 29, 1991, at A23, col. 1.

doms."[172] Such a test for validation of governance and entry into a society of nations would have been unthinkable even a decade ago; it is considered unexceptionable in the new Europe. Some comparable rule in future should, and undoubtedly will, become the standard for participation in the multinational institutions of the global community.

As a step in this direction, the UN General Assembly might adopt and adapt the guidelines in the CSCE's Copenhagen Document and Paris Charter and declare these applicable to Article 25 of the Civil and Political Covenant. Such a resolution, among other things, would guide and assist the Human Rights Committee in more efficaciously carrying out its monitoring of compliance by the large majority of states parties to that global instrument. It would also help to make more determinate the content of the evolving customary law applicable to national political practices. Bringing the evolution of UN practice approximately into line with that of the CSCE would endow the emerging democratic entitlement with greater specificity and coherence.

VI. Coherence of the Democratic Entitlement

Pedigree and determinacy, as we have seen, give a rule the pull to compliance that we have identified as evidence of its perceived legitimacy. So also coherence. Coherence is that quality of a rule which permits it to be seen holistically: that is, as part of a rule context in which the parts gather compliance pull from the purpose and meaning of a larger whole. A rule that can plausibly lay claim to being part of such a skein exercises a greater compliance pull than one that cannot.[173]

Another way of understanding coherence is to examine the extent to which the compliance pull of a rule, invoked in one case, is augmented by evidence that it has connections that lead beyond the specifics of that dispute. Such augmentation may appear in several forms. First, it may become apparent that the rule being tested is so intimately connected with a larger regulatory scheme—for example, as one clause of an entire treaty—as to bring into play the weight and purpose of the larger whole. Second, the rule being tested may evince an important principle—English common law abounds in such "maxims": *nemo dat quod non habet*, for example—on which many distinct rules depend. Third, the issues in one instance may resemble those in others, creating a form of imperative to treat likes alike by applying the same rule.

How coherent, thus understood, is the normative canon of the democratic entitlement? Our examination of global and regional texts and processes will reveal that the rules pertaining to self-determination, freedom of expression and the right to participate in free and open elections are closely interwoven strands of a single fabric. These three generations of democratic entitlement, reinforced by regional systems, not only share many of the same or similar norms, but also have developed common or comparable kinds of institutions, procedures and customs. Each thread reinforces, and is reinforced by, the weave of the cloth.

When it comes to shared underlying principles, however, the connections are less straightforward. The democratic entitlement, after all, rests on the still-radi-

[172] Letter from the Minister for Foreign Affairs (H. van den Broek) to the Advisory Committee on Human Rights and Foreign Policy (June 20, 1990), *reprinted in* NETHERLANDS ADVISORY COMMITTEE ON HUMAN RIGHTS AND FOREIGN POLICY, DEMOCRACY AND HUMAN RIGHTS IN EASTERN EUROPE 30–31 (1990).

[173] *See* T. FRANCK, *supra* note 12, at 150–82.

cal principle that the community of states is empowered to compose and apply codes governing the comportment of governments toward their own citizens. No doubt, some such assumption long ago justified "enlightened" colonialism; its relic is still on view in Article 38(1)(c) of the International Court's Statute, which authorizes the judges to consult "general principles of law recognized by *civilized* nations" (italics mine). The term "civilized" may still be tainted by association with Cecil Rhodes, but the notion that governments can be graded for deportment is not. The Charter limits UN membership to states that are "peace-loving" (Article 4(1)) and enjoins governments to respect the "equal rights and self-determination of [their own] peoples" (Article 1(2)). The Genocide[174] and Racism Conventions[175] certainly do qualify as rules of deportment imposed on all states by the community of nations. Having become customary as well as treaty law—if not also rules of *jus cogens*—these Conventions may be said to exemplify the principle that states collectively have the authority to determine minimum standards of conduct from which none may long deviate without eventually endangering their membership in the club.

Nevertheless, the notion that the community can impose such standards, on which the democratic entitlement is based, has always been challenged by reference to another, embodied in Article 2(7) of the Charter. It provides, as formal recognition of the centuries-old principle of state sovereignty, that the Organization shall not interfere in matters "essentially within the domestic jurisdiction of states." While, as noted above, this conflict may have been resolved within the regional context of the CSCE with the recognition by the Copenhagen Document and the Paris Charter of the paramountcy of the democratic entitlement, the clear-cut supremacy of that entitlement is not yet apparent in the global context. Of course, state sovereignty, by operation of technological advances as much as of heightened humanistic sensitivity, is not what it used to be. Even those who defend the continued vitality of the principle would probably concede that genocide does not fall "essentially" within the ambit of protected "domestic" government activity. Nor, certainly, do egregious racism and, at least since the 1960s, denials of self-determination. Since the coming into force of the Civil and Political Rights Covenant, aggravated denials of the right to free speech and to free and open elections also have become generally acknowledged exceptions to the principle of noninterference in states' domestic jurisdiction. Nevertheless, a residual conflict of principles still troubles many states.

The problem is not so apparent in general theory as in application. To proclaim a general right to free elections is less intrusive than monitoring any particular election in an independent state. Effective monitoring is even more intrusive than the mere observation of balloting. And collective action to compel states to adhere to a standard is the most intrusive of all. Thus, the conflict of principles needs to be recognized, made explicit, and reconciled to the general satisfaction of the large preponderance of states before the democratic entitlement's global legitimacy is demonstrated by real, as opposed to formulaic, coherence. That will require action to meet the practical concerns of states that still regard the nonintervention principle as of overriding importance to their national well-being.

[174] Convention on the Prevention and Punishment of the Crime of Genocide, Dec. 9, 1948, 78 UNTS 277 (entered into force Jan. 12, 1951).

[175] International Convention on the Elimination of All Forms of Racial Discrimination, *opened for signature* Mar. 7, 1966, 660 UNTS 195, *reprinted in* 5 ILM 352 (1966) (entered into force Jan. 4, 1969) [hereinafter Racial Convention].

Also unclear is the extent to which the various parts of the democratic entitlement can yet claim the legitimacy that derives from "treating like cases alike." Are virtually all states, for example, ready to have their elections monitored by a credible global process? This and other issues need to be examined in detail before the democratic entitlement can be said to have achieved universal coherence.

Significance of the Human Rights Connection

A bright line links the three components of the democratic entitlement. The rules, and the processes for realizing self-determination, freedom of expression and electoral rights, have much in common and evidently aim at achieving a coherent purpose: creating the opportunity for all persons to assume responsibility for shaping the kind of civil society in which they live and work. There is a large normative canon for promoting that objective: the UN Charter, the Universal Declaration of Human Rights,[176] the International Covenant on Civil and Political Rights,[177] the International Convention on the Elimination of All Forms of Racial Discrimination,[178] the International Convention on the Suppression and Punishment of the Crime of *Apartheid*,[179] the Declaration on the Elimination of All Forms of Intolerance and of Discrimination Based on Religion or Belief,[180] and the Convention on the Elimination of All Forms of Discrimination against Women.[181] These universally based rights are supplemented by regional instruments such as the European Convention for the Protection of Human Rights and Fundamental Freedoms,[182] the American Convention on Human Rights,[183] the African Charter on Human and Peoples' Rights,[184] the Copenhagen Document[185] and the Paris Charter.[186]

Each of these instruments recognizes related specific entitlements as accruing to individual citizens. These constitute internationally mandated restraints on governments. As we have seen, they embody rights of free and equal participation in governance, a cluster within which electoral rights are a consistent and probably necessary segment. The result is a net of participatory entitlements. The various texts speak of similar goals and deploy, for the most part, a similar range of processes for monitoring compliance, several of which have already become common usage in connection with the democratic entitlement. One can convincingly argue that states which deny their citizens the right to free and open elections are violating a rule that is fast becoming an integral part of the elaborately woven human rights fabric. Thus, the democratic entitlement has acquired a degree of legitimacy by its association with a far broader panoply of laws pertaining to the rights of persons vis-à-vis their governments.

176 GA Res. 217A (III), *supra* note 60.

177 ICCPR, *supra* note 41.

178 Racial Convention, *supra* note 175.

179 GA Res. 3068, 28 UN GAOR Supp. (No. 30) at 75, UN Doc. A/9030 (1973), *reprinted in* 13 ILM 56 (1974) (entered into force July 18, 1976) [hereinafter Apartheid Convention].

180 GA Res. 36/55, 36 UN GAOR Supp. (No. 51) at 171, UN Doc. A/36/51 (1981), *reprinted in* 21 ILM 205 (1982).

181 GA Res. 34/180, 34 UN GAOR Supp. (No. 46) at 193, UN Doc. A/34/46 (1979), *reprinted in* 19 ILM 33 (1980) (entered into force Sept. 3, 1981).

182 European Convention, *supra* note 72.

183 American Convention, *supra* note 77.

184 African Charter on Human and Peoples' Rights, *adopted* June 27, 1981, OAU Doc. CAB/LEG/67/3/Rev.5, *reprinted in* 21 ILM 58 (1982) [hereinafter Banjul Charter].

185 Copenhagen Document, *supra* note 98.

186 Paris Charter, *supra* note 105.

Nevertheless, while we may well be moving in this direction, we may not have arrived. When, in November 1989, the UN Secretary-General was asked by the Nicaraguan Sandinista Government to monitor national elections, he felt compelled to link his acceptance not to the human rights framework but to older, perhaps better-established, norms of the international system. Indeed, he went out of his way to reassure the General Assembly that, while the United Nations had frequently supervised elections in the context of decolonization, "it has not been the practice to do so in respect of independent States." He even noted with pride that, "on a number of occasions over the years, we have declined invitations from Member States to that effect." Nevertheless, the Nicaraguan case could be distinguished because the request was not from "a single Member State, but one which has the support of the Presidents of Costa Rica, El Salvador, Guatemala, Honduras and Nicaragua," and thus "clearly belongs in the context of the Central American peace efforts."[187] The same effort to link the democratic entitlement and peacemaking is evident in the 1990 agreement negotiated by the Secretary-General between the Government of El Salvador and the insurgent Frente Farabundo Martí para la Liberación Nacional (FMLN).[188] It links the dispatch of UN monitors (ONUSAL) to observe human rights and the process leading up to Salvadoran elections with their larger role in ending the civil war.[189] Clearly, the content and scope of the democratic entitlement, in practice, will be shaped by whether it is connected to, and legitimized by, the relatively narrow *peacemaking*, or the much more expansive *human rights*, canon.

Coherence of Underlying Principles

So far, the Secretary-General's choice of the peacemaking linkage strategy has avoided a head-on conflict between proponents and opponents of election monitoring as a general normative democratic entitlement. Sooner or later, however, an unresolved conflict of deep-seated principles—the emerging right to free and fair elections and nonintervention in domestic affairs—is likely to generate a clash of political wills in the global and regional communities unless these dissonant principles are reconciled.

The very idea of general international monitoring of elections in sovereign states still arouses the most passionate ire, not only of the increasingly isolated residue of totalitarian regimes, but also of nations with long memories of humiliating interventions by states bent on "civilizing" missions. While they will accept occasional monitoring of elections to end a civil war or regional conflict, they consider it a necessary exception, not a normal manifestation of a universal democratic entitlement.

[187] UN Doc. A/44/210, at 2 (1989).

[188] Central America: Efforts Towards Peace, *supra* note 71.

[189] ONUSAL, the United Nations Observer Mission in El Salvador, will monitor the "release of individuals who have been imprisoned for political reasons . . . , the right of all persons to associate freely with others for ideological . . . political . . . or other purposes . . . , freedom of expression and of the press" and "freedom of movement." Agreement on Human Rights, Annex to Note verbale dated 14 August 1990 from the Charge d'affaires of the Permanent Mission of El Salvador to the United Nations addressed to the Secretary-General, UN Doc. A/44/971–S/21541, ann. at 4–5 (1990). For the March 1991 elections in El Salvador, however, the United Nations declined to mount an observer operation, dedicating its strained resources to other aspects of the peacemaking and monitoring process while letting the OAS take the lead, supported by nongovernmental organizations, in observing those elections. National Democratic Institute for International Affairs, *supra* note 159, at 14.

Conflict was clearly foreshadowed in 1990 when the General Assembly weighed the proposal to establish ONUVEH, the aforementioned observer group to monitor Haiti's elections. Since linkage between election monitoring and peace was much harder to demonstrate in the absence of armed hostilities, the creation of ONUVEH encountered significant opposition, notably from China, Cuba and Colombia.[190] The long specter of U.S. hemispheric interventions was invoked in the Assembly's corridors. Several months elapsed before suspicions could be assuaged by diplomatic assurances that the Haitian case, too, would set no general precedent. Cuba, in the debate prior to the vote authorizing ONUVEH, spoke emphatically against "any attempt to use this United Nations resolution or activity as a pretext for interfering in the internal affairs of Haiti"[191] and stressed that elections "can never be regarded as affecting international peace and security."[192] Mexico also went on record as denying any precedential value to the authorization of ONUVEH.[193] These states contended that UN election monitoring in an independent nation is unlawful *per se,* in the absence of exceptional peacemaking exigencies.

The International Court of Justice rebuffed this view indirectly in its 1986 *Nicaragua* decision. The majority stated, in connection with commitments binding a nation to electoral standards, that it could not

> discover, within the range of subjects open to international agreement, any obstacle or provision to hinder a State from making a commitment of this kind. A State, which is free to decide upon the principle and methods of popular consultation within its domestic order, is sovereign for the purpose of accepting a limitation of its sovereignty in this field. This is a conceivable situation for a State which is bound by institutional links to a confederation of States, or indeed to an international organization.[194]

There are thus no legal impediments to institutionalizing voluntary international election monitoring as one way to give effect to the emerging right of all peoples to free and open electoral democracy, but this is not to say that states as yet have a *duty* to submit their elections to international validation. Although the CSCE, in Europe, seems poised to pioneer a generalized duty to be monitored, even it has not made the duty mandatory for all. In the international community, while there may be a duty under Article 25 of the Civil and Political Rights Covenant and its regional and customary law analogues to permit free and open elections and review of national compliance by the Human Rights Committee, there is as yet no obligation to permit actual election monitoring by international or regional organizations. Indeed, one should expect resistance to any effort to transform an election-monitoring option, exercisable at the discretion of each government, into an obligation owed by each government to its own people and to the other states of the global community. Admittedly, however, a "rule" that only applies self-selectively has far less legitimacy than one of general application.

[190] The Security Council failed to reach consensus on the issue, with China threatening to veto. In the General Assembly, Cuba and Colombia argued that election monitoring in an independent state, unrelated to a threat to the peace, constituted a violation of Article 2(7) of the Charter. *See* UN Doc. A/45/PV.29 (1990).

[191] *Id.* at 62.

[192] *Id.* at 59–60.

[193] *Id.* at 64–65.

[194] Military and Paramilitary Activities in and against Nicaragua (Nicar. v. U.S.), 1986 ICJ Rep. 14, 131 (Judgment of June 27) [hereinafter *Nicaragua* opinion].

This deficiency was demonstrated by the General Assembly's incoherent tiptoeing around the democratic entitlement at its session in the fall of 1990. The members passed two seemingly incongruent resolutions on monitoring, which reflect the concern of Third World states as they contemplate the seemingly inexorable evolution of an entitlement to democracy, including free elections and resultant international supervision. We have already noted the first of these resolutions, in which the democratic entitlement was restated by the Assembly and election monitoring commended as one way to ensure its implementation.[195] Almost in the same breath, however—and over the opposition of only twenty-nine states, mostly European, but also including Australia, Canada, Israel, New Zealand, Turkey and the United States—the second resolution affirmed "that it is the concern solely of peoples [of each state] to determine methods and to establish institutions regarding the electoral process, as well as to determine the ways for its implementation according to their constitutional and national legislation";[196] and it urged all states "to respect the principle of non-interference in the internal affairs of States."[197] The vast preponderance of states voting for this resolution did not do so out of concern to protect dictatorships. Rather, they were worried about the underlying principle.

When underlying principles are coherent, the rules manifesting them assume increased legitimacy. When rules exemplify principles in collision, those rules are perceived as of low legitimacy. The principle underlying a universal democratic entitlement is that the participatory rights of persons in shaping their civil society may not be abridged arbitrarily by governments. This principle has powered the rights of self-determination and freedom of expression and, now, energizes the move to provide international protection for electoral rights.

There was a time when international efforts to implement the right of self-determination were vigorously opposed as trenching upon the right of governments, under Article 2(7) of the UN Charter, to administer their colonies without outside interference. That opposition gradually abated, as the principle of self-determination gained in determinacy. Efforts to monitor compliance with the right to freedom of expression have encountered similar expressions of outraged *amour-propre* by states called to task for arbitrarily silencing their own citizens. It is not surprising that passionate resentments should also arise in some quarters at the prospect of seeing the international community insinuate itself into the intimate political process by which governments are empowered by the citizenry.

The opponents are mostly motivated by fear that monitoring will be used to reimpose a form of neocolonialism under the banner of establishing democracy. That fear must be addressed, but it must also be put in perspective. History has warned, repeatedly, that the natural right of all people to liberty and democracy is too precious, and too vulnerable, to be entrusted entirely to those who govern. John Stuart Mill once observed that the moral fiber of a nation is weakened if the intervention of outsiders spares its people the trouble of liberating themselves.[198] In view of the technological edge dictators nowadays enjoy over their people, this proposition is no longer wholly defensible.\The opposite case was stated by Uganda's President Godfrey L. Binaisa, who, after the overthrow of Idi Amin's

[195] See *supra* text at and notes 82–86.

[196] GA Res. 45/151, para. 2 (Dec. 18, 1990).

[197] *Id.*, para. 4.

[198] 3 J. S. Mill, Dissertations and Discussions: Political, Philosophical and Historical 238–63 (1873).

bloody junta, went before the General Assembly to chide its delegates for their indifference to his people's plight. "In the light of the clear commitment set out in . . . provisions of the Charter," he said, "our people naturally looked to the United Nations for solidarity and support in their struggle against the Fascist dictatorship. For eight years they cried out in the wilderness for help; unfortunately, their cries seemed to have fallen on deaf ears." Acerbically, Binaisa observed that, "somehow, it is thought to be in bad taste or contrary to diplomatic etiquette to raise matters of violations of human rights by Member States within the forums of the United Nations."[199]

Where dictators can only be confronted effectively with the active support of the international community, inhibitions about interference in the "domestic jurisdiction" of states seem less compelling than they used to be. "We are arriving at the conclusion," then Soviet Foreign Minister Boris D. Pankin observed recently, "that national guarantees [of human rights] are not sufficient. So we have to review the principle of noninterference in affairs of other governments."[200] To this end, the Declaration of Human Rights and Freedoms, adopted by the Soviet Congress of People's Deputies on September 5, 1991, after the coup, states that "[e]very person possesses natural, inalienable and inviolable rights and freedoms. They are sealed in laws that must correspond to the universal declaration of human rights, the international covenants on human rights and other international norms and this declaration."[201] The OAS Foreign Ministers' 1991 resolution to the same effect has already been noted,[202] as have the CSCE heads' Paris Charter[203] and Moscow Document.[204]

It thus appears that support is increasing even—perhaps *particularly*—among former totalitarian states for the proposition that the democratic entitlement, enhanced by linkage with other basic human rights and the accompanying international monitoring of compliance, has trumped the principle of noninterference. Even the 1991 resolution of the General Assembly warning about outside "interference" in the electoral process[205] seemed to acknowledge this development, for it added an otherwise incongruous caveat,

> that only the total eradication of *apartheid* and the establishment of a non-racial, democratic society based on majority rule, through the full and free exercise of adult suffrage by all the people in a united and non-fragmented South Africa, can lead to a just and lasting solution to the explosive situation in South Africa.[206]

Surely, this assertion demonstrates not the supremacy of nonintervention but, rather, its opposite: that undemocratic electoral processes imposed upon a people by their government are now almost universally regarded as counternormative and not beyond the purview of the international community. In 1991 the UN Human Rights Commission further affirmed this view by voting unanimously to condemn the military Government of Myanmar for having failed to carry out its promise to return that country to democratic, civilian rule.[207] The junta's refusal to allow the elected legislature to meet and its arrest of many parliamentary

[199] UN Doc. A/34/PV.14, at 4–6 (1979).

[200] N.Y. Times, Sept. 10, 1991, at A13, col. 5.

[201] N.Y. Times, Sept. 7, 1991, at 5, col. 3.

[202] Resolution on Representative Democracy, *supra* note 90.

[203] Paris Charter, *supra* note 105.

[204] Moscow Document, *supra* note 116.

[205] *See supra* text at and notes 196–97.

[206] GA Res. 45/151, *supra* note 196, para. 7.

[207] N.Y. Times, Mar. 7, 1991, at A14, col. 1.

leaders were perceived as an international—not merely a domestic—issue, warranting a response from the community of nations.

Nevertheless, steps should be taken to meet the fear of some smaller states that election monitoring will lead to more Panama-style unilateral military interventions by the powerful, perhaps even for reasons less convincing than those which provoked the 1989 U.S. military strike against the Noriega dictatorship. That a new rule might authorize actions to enforce democracy still conjures up just such chilling images to weaker states, which see themselves as the potential objects of enforcement of dubious democratic norms under circumstances of doubtful probity. Of course, to give coherence to a general norm requiring free and open elections does not necessarily implicate military enforcement action.

If there is to be monitoring, some consequences could reasonably be expected to ensue for those who "fail the test." And if monitoring evolves into a systemwide obligation, perhaps some consequences will attach even to a refusal to be monitored. As Judge Buergenthal has observed about the effect of the Copenhagen Document and the Paris Charter, there is bound to evolve a "linkage of human rights to other questions (trade, security, environment, etc.). . . . Linkage permits the participating States . . . to condition their bilateral and multilateral relations in general upon progress in the human dimension sphere."[208] While perhaps true, today, only regarding the CSCE, this effect is likely to point the way toward the enforcement of the democratic entitlement in the global community, as well.

This prospect evokes hope, but also justified fears that must be abated. The coherence of the democratic entitlement ultimately will depend on whether most states, most of the time, freely agree to be monitored: whether, in short, the process is perceived as legitimate. To achieve this normative coherence, monitoring will have to be uncoupled, in the clearest fashion, from a long history of unilateral enforcement of a tainted, colonialist "civilizing" mission. If the duty to be monitored is to develop as customary law, it must be reconciled in the minds of governments with their residual sovereignty. This requires that all states unambiguously renounce the use of unilateral, or even regional, *military* force to compel compliance with the democratic entitlement in the absence of prior Security Council authorization under chapter VII of the Charter; such authorization, except for *regional* action under Article 53, would require a finding that the violation had risen to the level of a threat to the peace.[209] Such a pledge would merely reiterate the existing normative structure of the Charter, Articles 2(4), 51 and 53 in particular. Yet this reiteration is necessary, in view of the history of unilateral interventionism which has undermined that self-denying ordinance. Specifically, states must acknowledge that the evolution of a democratic entitlement cannot entitle a state or group of states to enforce the right by military action under the pretext of invoking Articles 51 or 53. *Ça va sans dire* is no answer to those demanding that assurance in the light of recent Soviet and U.S.-led unilateral or pseudoregional actions alleged to promote "democracy" in neighboring states and justified as "collective self-defense."

[208] Buergenthal, *supra* note 109, at 43.

[209] The General Assembly, in the case of the 1991 Haitian military coup, appears to have concluded that it is empowered to recommend action of an economic and diplomatic kind to its members. In approving regional military action under Article 53, the Security Council appears not to be limited to cases in which international peace has been threatened or breached.

A specific renunciation of unilateralism would obviously not obviate every possibility that some negative consequences might ensue for governments unwilling to be monitored or to hold free elections; nor should it. The international community long has asserted, in the case of South Africa, a right of all states to take hortatory, economic and—in extreme cases—even military action to enforce aspects of the democratic entitlement,[210] but only when duly authorized by the United Nations in accordance with its Charter. Article 2(7), in barring UN intervention "in matters which are essentially within the domestic jurisdiction of any state," stipulates that "this principle shall not prejudice the application of enforcement measures under Chapter VII." Rhodesia's Unilateral Declaration of Independence provoked a UN resolution permitting Britain to use military force.[211] It is no longer arguable that the United Nations cannot exert pressure against governments that oppress their own peoples by egregious racism, denials of self-determination and suppression of freedom of expression. That litany is being augmented by new sins: refusals to permit demonstrably free elections or to implement their results. However, if the sin is committed, the international community may only invoke collective enforcement measures such as sanctions, blockade or military intervention in limited circumstances—as when the Security Council finds that a threat or breach of the peace has occurred—or if it collectively determines that it is not engaging in enforcement *against* a member but is acting at the request of a legitimate government against a usurper. These prerequisite determinations, however, must be made by the appropriate collective machinery of the community and not by individual members.

This procedure is both legally required and politically essential. To obtain the general consent necessary to render the denial of democracy a cognizable violation of an international community standard, it must be understood that whatever countermeasures are taken must first be authorized collectively by the appropriate UN institutions. Collective action—so the tremulous must understand and the powerful aver—is not a substitute for, but the opposite of, unilateral enforcement. In this respect, as in many others, the principal enemy of the evolution of a new rule is fear of its vigilante enforcement.[212] For that reason, the entitlement to democracy can only be expected to flourish if it is coupled with a reiterated prohibition on such unilateral initiatives. Only then will the rule enjoy the degree of principled coherence necessary to the widespread perception of its legitimacy.

Treating Like Cases Alike

If voluntary acceptance of monitoring becomes the general practice of states, it will gradually evolve from an optional to a customary and, ultimately, mandatory means of satisfying the democratic entitlement. This transformation, surely, is to be encouraged, but it is unlikely to occur as a consequence of a global treaty. Too many states, especially smaller ones, still fear that it will erode the rule of nonintervention. It may occur, however, through gradual, incremental steps that make

[210] *See* Apartheid Convention, *supra* note 179. *See also* R. BISSELL, APARTHEID AND INTERNATIONAL ORGANIZATIONS 156–59 (1977).

[211] SC Res. 253, 23 UN SCOR (Res. & Dec.) at 5, UN Doc. S/INF/23/Rev.1 (1968).

[212] *See* Arend, *International Law and the Recourse to Force: A Shift in Paradigms*, 27 STAN. J. INT'L L. 1, 40–45 (1991).

voluntary submission an attractive option for most governments.[213] If the United Nations' concern to restore democracy in Haiti is grounded, in part, on the ousted government's having been legitimated by a monitored election, that constitutes a palpable inducement to governments to take up the option. When that option is generally taken, the international monitoring of an election will cease to be a special case and will have become normative, a rule that treats like cases alike.

We have already noted that the right of self-determination, as first enunciated and practiced at Versailles, lacked coherence because it applied only to the European territories of the former German, Austro-Hungarian and Turkish Empires. After the Second World War, the UN Charter, in Article 1(2), made "the principle of equal rights and self-determination of peoples" universally applicable. Nevertheless, for forty years thereafter, the right of self-determination was implemented only selectively, primarily in colonies and trusteeship territories. There may have been a reason it was applied to India but not to Hungary or Czechoslovakia, but, if so, no persuasive, principled distinction was advanced.[214]

Undoubtedly, this incoherence undermined its legitimacy. More recently, we have seen the right at last becoming—in theory and increasingly in practice—one of universal application as it merges with newer aspects of the democratic entitlement. Thus, we may conclude that self-determination is evolving from incoherence to coherence, which reinforces its legitimacy.

The same may be said of the right of free expression. We have already observed the work of the Human Rights Committee in implementing Article 19 of the Civil and Political Covenant and protecting citizens' expressive rights. In giving effect to the general reporting requirement, the Committee has begun to impart principled coherence to the textual provisions, in the sense of filling in the interstices and fitting the parts to the purposes of the whole.[215] With the end of the Cold War, the remnants of the "double standard" in applying expressive rights through international monitoring institutions will mostly wither away.

Coherence is being aided by parallel regional initiatives. These tend to monitor and implement the rules equally, regardless of "whose ox is gored." Notable in this respect is the aforementioned work of the European Court of Human Rights and the Inter-American Court of Human Rights, as well as the as-yet inchoate potential of the new African Human Rights Commission.[216] Equal application of the expressive entitlement is reinforced by the textual convergence regarding

[213] While it is true that General Assembly resolutions, state practice or even a subsequent treaty cannot vitiate a specific rule of the UN Charter, all three can affect a Charter rule's interpretation. *See* Czaplinski & Danilenko, *Conflicts of Norms in International Law*, 21 NETH. Y.B. INT'L L. 3, 35–41 (1990).

[214] *See* T. FRANCK, NATION AGAINST NATION 224–45 (1985).

[215] D. MCGOLDRICK, *supra* note 43, at 459–79. Under the procedure for review of country reports, the Committee has sought to

> examine, comment, and request clarification in respect of the different aspects of freedom of expression revealed in the State reports. This has involved, for example, such matters as general and specific banning or censorship, registration or notification requirements, governmental control and direction in its various forms, limitations applicable to particular groups, for example, armed forces, civil servants, prior restraints or subsequent penal responsibility for publications, rights of reply or correction, the applicable limitations embodied in the criminal law or penal codes for offences such as blasphemy or blasphemous libel, sedition, subversive propaganda, anti-State or anti-ideological propaganda, and the effective remedies demanded by . . . an individual who claims that his rights under article 19 have been violated.

Id. at 461.

[216] The Commission is established by part II of the Banjul Charter, *supra* note 184.

freedom of expression of the European Convention on Human Rights,[217] the American Convention on Human Rights,[218] and the African Charter on Human and Peoples' Rights.[219] The too-long failure of the United States to ratify the Civil and Political Rights Covenant and the American Convention nevertheless has detracted from this convergence and is only in part mitigated by the fact that the U.S. Constitution, as implemented by the courts and Congress, puts the United States essentially, if not wholly, in compliance with the international and regional standards.

So far, less uniformity of application, and thus less global coherence, can be ascribed to the emerging rule on citizens' right to participate in free and open elections. As we have observed, on-site monitoring remains voluntary and exceptional. If it is to become a more general obligation, likes must be treated alike, which means that the new majority of democratic states must submit to it. They, who have the least to fear and the most to gain, should want to participate in universalizing the practice, if only to help legitimize it. Few states are likely to volunteer as long as participation in international monitoring is tantamount to a government's admission that it does not have credibility with its own people. To induce a pull toward compliance in deviant and recalcitrant regimes—those that most need it—on-site monitoring must also be practiced by the states that least need it. It must become an unremarkable universal habit.

VII. Adherence and the Democratic Entitlement

Adherence refers to the vertical connection between a specific rule of obligation and other "higher" principles that define the objectives of the rule system or set out its normative standards. A particular rule ("cross on the green, stop on the red") is more likely to pull toward voluntary compliance if it is seen to be within the framework of a community's normative hierarchy than if it is a mere ad hoc arrangement.[220] The democratic entitlement also is more likely to be perceived as a legitimate rule if it can be seen as a necessary part of a normative hierarchy. As it happens, the right to democracy can readily be shown to be an important subsidiary of the community's most important norm: the right to peace.

With the exception of the principle *pacta sunt servanda*, no principle of international law has been more firmly established—first by the Kellogg-Briand Pact and, particularly since 1945, by the UN Charter—than that states "shall refrain in their international relations from the threat or use of force against the territorial integrity or political independence of any state."[221] Not only has this peace principle been featured in treaty law, but it has been resoundingly echoed in the jurisprudence of the International Court of Justice[222] and in *opinio juris* expressed in key UN resolutions.[223]

[217] European Convention, *supra* note 72, Arts. 9, 10, 11.

[218] American Convention, *supra* note 77, Arts. 13, 14, 15, 16.

[219] Banjul Charter, *supra* note 184, Arts. 8, 9, 10, 11.

[220] T. Franck, *supra* note 12, at 184.

[221] UN Charter, Art. 2(4). *See also* Treaty Providing for the Renunciation of War as an Instrument of National Policy, Aug. 27, 1928, Art. 1, 46 Stat. 2343, TS No. 796, 94 LNTS 57 (Kellogg-Briand Pact).

[222] *See Nicaragua* opinion, 1986 ICJ Rep. 14.

[223] The customary law is well summarized in the Court's *Nicaragua* opinion, *id.* at 98–105. *See, especially*, Friendly Relations Declaration, *supra* note 31; Definition of Aggression, GA Res. 3314, 29 UN GAOR Supp. (No. 31) at 142, UN Doc. A/9631 (1974), *reprinted in* 13 ILM 710 (1974).

Most recently, the Security Council, in its resolutions[224] and actions to reverse Iraq's attack on Kuwait, reiterated the primacy of the entitlement to peace and protection against aggression. More than thirty nations joined in liberating Kuwait because, at last, aggression against one has begun to be seen as a contingent violation of the common peace. Stopping aggression and maintaining the peace has become the central concern of a newly cohesive international community.

If that principle indeed stands at the apex of the global normative system, the democratic governance of states must be recognized as a necessary, although certainly not a sufficient, means to that end. Peace is the consequence of many circumstances: economic well-being, security, and the unimpeded movement of persons, ideas and goods. States' nonaggressiveness, however, depends fundamentally on domestic democracy. Although the argument is not entirely conclusive, historians have emphasized that, in the past 150 years, "no liberal democracies have ever fought against each other."[225] It has been argued persuasively that "a democratic society operating under a market economy has a strong predisposition towards peace."[226] This stands to reason: a society that makes its decisions democratically and openly will be reluctant to engage its members' lives and treasure in causes espoused by leaders deluded by fantasies of grievance or grandeur.

No one has stated this position more eloquently than the eighteenth-century German philosopher Immanuel Kant. He examined the correlation between democratic governance and nonaggressiveness in his essay *Perpetual Peace.*[227] There, he argued that democracy, leading to a "pacific union" among liberal states, would counteract the aggressive tendencies of absolutist monarchies by making government accountable to the majority. In contrast, a state of perpetual war would likely prevail between democracies and totalitarian states.[228] Moreover, Kant discerned a three-way linkage among democracy, peace and human rights.[229]

Neither Kant nor his modern interpreters make the argument that democracies will not fight: only that they are not disposed to fight each other. The historical record bears this out.[230] Consequently, one way to promote universal and perpetual nonaggression—probably the best and, perhaps, the only way—is to make democracy an entitlement of all peoples. This conclusion was eloquently and unanimously accepted as axiomatic by the CSCE representatives at their aforementioned 1990 Copenhagen meeting. Unanimously, they proclaimed "their conviction that . . . pluralistic democracy" is a prerequisite "for progress in setting up the lasting order of peace, security, justice and co-operation that they seek to establish in Europe."[231]

[224] SC Res. 660 (Aug. 2, 1990), *reprinted in* 29 ILM 1325 (1990), and subsequent resolutions. *See* Schachter, *United Nations Law in the Gulf Conflict*, 85 AJIL 452 (1991).

[225] Mearsheimer, *Why We Will Soon Miss the Cold War*, ATLANTIC MONTHLY, August 1990, at 35, 46.

[226] T. Smith, *Democracy Resurgent*, in SEA CHANGES 152, 157 (N. Rizopoulos ed. 1990).

[227] I. KANT, PERPETUAL PEACE 107–39 (T. Humphrey rev. ed. 1983) (1795).

[228] *See* Doyle, *Liberalism and World Politics*, 80 AM. POL. SCI. REV. 1151 (1986).

[229] Note, however, that the notion of human rights operates to limit not only totalitarian, but also democratic, excess. Thomas Jefferson underscored this with his oft-quoted observation that "an *elective despotism* was not the government we fought for." T. JEFFERSON, NOTES ON THE STATE OF VIRGINIA 120 (W. Peden ed. 1954).

[230] The point is well developed by Doyle, *An International Liberal Community*, in RETHINKING AMERICA'S SECURITY (G. Allison ed., forthcoming).

[231] Copenhagen Document, *supra* note 98, Preamble, at 1307.

The symbiotic linkage among democracy, human rights and peace is now widely recognized. Already in 1968, Security Council Resolution 253 invoked chapter VII of the Charter to impose military sanctions on Rhodesia. It expressly proceeded on the theory that gross denials of both human rights and the democratic entitlement can constitute "a threat to international peace and security."[232] At the regional level, the OAS Ministers of Foreign Affairs, in demanding the replacement of Nicaragua's Somoza dictatorship with a government chosen through free elections, declared in 1979 that democracy was the necessary precondition to "peace, freedom and justice." The dictatorship was characterized as "disrupting the peace of the Hemisphere."[233] A decade later, in condemning the fraudulent Panamanian elections staged by General Noriega, the OAS Ministers stated that this crisis of governmental legitimacy "involves internal and external factors . . . and could seriously endanger international peace and security."[234]

This understanding of the three-way linkage among democracy, human rights and peace is further illustrated by the recent cease-fire agreement negotiated by the UN Secretary-General between the Government of El Salvador and the FMLN.[235] As noted, it obliges the Government and the insurgents to work with yet another UN observer mission (ONUSAL), which is authorized to monitor and verify compliance with the basic human rights guaranteed by the signatories. The parties specifically recognized that compliance with human rights is a *sine qua non* to ending the war. They also accepted that the democratic entitlement must be guaranteed—and monitored by international observers—if peace is to be established.

Thus, it appears with increasing clarity, in normative text and practice, that compliance with the norms prohibiting war making is inextricably linked to observance of human rights and the democratic entitlement. The achievement of none of these basic objectives of the international community is possible, in any lasting sense, without the realization of them all. This interdependence suggests that the legitimacy of the democratic entitlement is augmented by its hierarchic relation to the peremptory norm of global peaceability.

A distinction needs to be noted here. As we have observed, some governments have argued that the international community's jurisdiction to intervene in the domestic affairs of states to secure compliance with the democratic entitlement is (or should be) limited to cases where its violation has given rise to breaches of the peace. Others have disagreed, claiming that the jurisdiction to intervene is also based on broader human rights law, which authorizes various intrusive forms of monitoring and even envisages sanctions against gross violators. One can prefer this latter view, while still agreeing that the democratic entitlement does have a connection to the United Nations' "peace" role, that the *legitimacy* of any collective international intervention to support a democratic entitlement is augmented by the entitlement's intimate link to peace. The substance of that link, however, is not merely the role of democracy in *making* or *restoring* peace after conflict has arisen but also—indeed preeminently—its role in *maintaining* peace and *preventing* conflict.

The World Court observed in the *Bernadotte* case that established rights and duties implicitly validate a penumbra of unenunciated, yet legitimate, means nec-

[232] SC Res. 253, *supra* note 211.

[233] OEA/Ser.F/II.17, doc. 40/79, rev.2.

[234] OEA/Ser.F/II.21, doc. 8/89, rev.2.

[235] Central America: Efforts Toward Peace, *supra* note 71.

essary to give them effect.[236] If the "end" of global peace demands the "means" of global democracy, a Charter-based system established to ensure peace must also be presumed to be authorized to ensure universal adherence to democratic political rights.

VIII. The Emergence of Democracy as a Global Normative Entitlement

The entitlement to democracy in international law has gone through both a normative and a customary evolution. It has evolved both as a system of rules and in the practice of states and organizations. This evolution has occurred in three phases. First came the normative entitlement to self-determination. Then came the normative entitlement to free expression as a human right. Now we see the emergence of a normative entitlement to a participatory electoral process.

The democratic entitlement, despite its newness, already enjoys a high degree of legitimacy, derived both from various texts and from the practice of global and regional organizations, supplemented by that of a significant number of nongovernmental organizations. These texts and practices have attained a surprising degree of specificity, given the newness of the entitlement and especially of its requirement for free and open elections.

It is easy to deconstruct this now commonly used set of textual formulations and the accompanying practice. The terms (e.g., elections, free, fair) inevitably convey different meanings in various political cultures but, remarkably, evoke an amply demonstrable degree of convergent expectations. They crisscross sociocultural and political boundaries. The entitlement now aborning is widely enough understood to be almost universally celebrated. It is welcomed from Malagache to Mongolia, in the streets, the universities and the legislatures, not only because it portends a new, global political culture supported by common rules and communitarian implementing institutions, but also because it opens the stagnant political economies of states to economic, social and cultural, as well as political, development. As the heads of European Community states and governments pointed out in the group's conclusions of June 1991, "suppression of individual freedoms impede[s] an individual from participating in and contributing" to "the process of development."[237] Economic development, as even the Chinese leadership must be discovering, is linked inextricably with political freedom. An economic free market cannot long flourish without creating pressure for a free market of ideas. At the same time, the problems of underdevelopment can only be addressed successfully in a world of stable, peaceable nations, which, in turn, also presupposes a world of open democracies.

The democratic entitlement's newness and recent rapid evolution make it understandable that important problems remain. We have considered these primarily under the rubric of coherence, indicating that this entitlement is not yet entirely coherent. The key to solving these residual problems is: (1) that the older democracies should be among the first to volunteer to be monitored in the hope that this will lead the way to near-universal voluntary compliance, thus gradually transforming a sovereign option into a customary legal obligation; (2) that a credible international monitoring service should be established with clearly defined

[236] Reparations for injuries suffered in the service of the United Nations, 1949 ICJ Rep. 174, 179–80 (Advisory Opinion of Apr. 11).

[237] European Council, Presidency Conclusions, Doc. SN 151/2/91 (Ann. V) at 27 (1991).

parameters and procedures covering all aspects of voting, from the time an election is called until the newly elected take office; (3) that each nation's duty to be monitored should be linked to a commensurate right to nonintervention by states acting unilaterally; and (4) that legitimate governments should be assured of protection from overthrow by totalitarian forces through concerted systemic action after—and *only* after—the community has recognized that such an exigency has arisen. In the longer term, compliance with the democratic entitlement should also be linked to a right of representation in international organs, to international fiscal, trade and development benefits, and to the protection of UN and regional collective security measures.[238]

Both textually and in practice, the international system is moving toward a clearly designated democratic entitlement, with national governance validated by international standards and systematic monitoring of compliance. The task is to perfect what has been so wondrously begun.

[238] To limit collective security measures to cases of attack against democratic states is a change in the system's rules that is unlikely to come about in the near future. Yet it is worth contemplating. Would it help Kuwait to establish a democratic internal order if its future protection by UN-authorized collective measures depended upon such a transformation?

[2]

DEMOCRACY AND INTERNATIONAL LAW*

By JAMES CRAWFORD[1]

I. AN OUTLINE OF THE PROBLEM

It is often said that democracies do not wage war on each other, and conflict researchers, looking at wars over the last 200 years, have confirmed that this is broadly true.[2] Admittedly, 'the clash of conflicting interests between States governed on democratic principles is not necessarily less serious than between those under less popular forms of government'.[3] Democracies seems able, however, to resolve such clashes by means other than war. Perhaps we might 'diminish . . . and finally . . . extinguish war between nations'[4] by developing international law and international institutions so as to reinforce democratic government, to deter attempts to overthrow it, and even to reinstate it in cases where it has been wrongfully overthrown. So far attempts at collective security have concentrated on the avoidance of international armed conflict, with rather limited concern for the internal conditions within States which are a major cause of war. Perhaps we need some form of collective democratic security?

An initial difficulty, no doubt, is that of definition. There can be different ideals or legitimate versions of democracy: is one particular ideal or version to be externally imposed? On the other hand, international law is already seeking to reach some agreement on an agreed minimum content of, or at least an agreed minimum standard for, democracy. The major human rights treaties spell out in some detail the essentials of democracy, understood as the right of all citizens to participate in the political life of their societies. The International Covenant on Civil and Political Rights pro-

* © Professor James Crawford, 1994.

[1] Whewell Professor of International Law, University of Cambridge; Fellow of Jesus College; Member, International Law Commission. This is the basis of an Inaugural Lecture delivered at the University of Cambridge on 5 March 1993. The author thanks Hugo Caminos, Maxwell Gaylard, Rein Mullerson, Matthew Neuhaus and Michael Reisman for their assistance in providing information.

[2] E. Weede, 'Some Simple Calculations on Democracy and War Involvement', *Journal of Peace Research*, 29 (1992), p. 377. The same is not true of covert action: D. P. Forsythe, 'Democracy, War and Covert Action', ibid., p. 385.

[3] A. Pearce Higgins, 'International Relations and International Law', in *Studies in International Law and Politics* (Cambridge, CUP, 1928), p. 1, at pp.10–11.

[4] To quote the terms of the bequest by William Whewell (1866) creating the Chair of International Law at Cambridge.

vides in Article 25 that every citizen has the right to take part in the conduct of public affairs, directly or through freely chosen representatives. This includes in particular 'the right to vote and to be elected at genuine periodic elections'. The elections must be by universal and equal suffrage, and must be held by secret ballot 'in circumstances which guarantee the free expression of the will of the electors'.[5] At the regional level, Article 25 has counterparts in Article 3 of Protocol 1 of the European Convention on Human Rights,[6] and in Article 23 of the American Convention on Human Rights.[7] It is also reflected, although to a lesser extent, in the African Charter on Human and Peoples' Rights.[8] The language of Article 25 goes back to Article 21 of the Universal Declaration of Human Rights of 1948, which adds the proposition that 'the will of the people shall be the basis of the authority of government'.[9]

That the will of the people is to be the basis of the authority of government is as good a summary as any of the basic democratic idea. But the idea of democracy reflected in the International Covenant, in the Universal Declaration and in other instruments is not a simple majoritarian one. It is a reflection of the idea that every person, whether a member of a majority or a minority, has basic rights, including rights to participate in public life. Thus the authority of a government, elected by a majority, to conduct for the time being the public affairs of the society is a *consequence* of the exercise of the rights of participation in public life of all citizens, whether they belong to the majority or the minority. The capacity of the government to limit or derogate from the rights of a minority is limited, even in times of public emergency.[10]

This is why human rights courts have not given much independent meaning to the qualifying phrase 'necessary in a democratic society', which

[5] *UN Treaty Series*, vol. 999, p. 171. There are more than 120 States parties to the ICCPR, a sharp increase since 1985, when there were 81.

[6] European Convention on Human Rights (ECHR), Protocol 1, 20 March 1952, *UN Treaty Series*, vol. 213, p. 262, Art. 3 (undertaking by States parties to hold free elections). Cf. ECHR, Art. 16 (restrictions on the political activity of aliens permitted).

[7] American Convention on Human Rights, 22 November 1969 (AMR), *International Legal Materials*, 9 (1970), p. 673.

[8] African Charter on Human and Peoples' Rights, 26 June 1981 (AFR), ibid. 21 (1982), p. 58, Art. 13 ('the right to freely participate in the government of his country, either directly or through freely chosen representatives in accordance with the provisions of the law'). It is not clear whether the qualifying phrase 'in accordance with the provisions of the law' applies only to the method of choice of representatives or to the right to participate itself.

[9] GA Res. 217A(III), 10 December 1948. Reisman regards Art. 21 as 'declaratory of customary international law' and as substituting for 'the sovereignty of the sovereign the sovereignty of the people': W. M. Reisman, 'Sovereignty and Human Rights in Contemporary International Law', *American Journal of International Law*, 84 (1990), p. 866 at p. 867.

[10] It should be noted that the right to participate is non-derogable under AMR (Art. 27(2)) and AFR (which has no derogation clause), but is derogable in time of public emergency under ICCPR (Art. 4) and ECHR (Art. 15). For discussion, see S. R. Chowdhury, *Rule of Law in a State of Emergency* (Pinter Publishers, London, 1989), at p. 250; J. Oraá, *Human Rights in States of Emergency* (Oxford, Clarendon Press, 1992), at p. 101.

occurs in the limitation article in the various human rights treaties.[11] That phrase might have been used as a way of relativizing human rights defined at the international level, of allowing local modifications deemed necessary in a given democratic society. No doubt the findings of human rights courts and commissions are context-dependent. It has been necessary to look carefully at the circumstances of the alleged breach in the circumstances of the society concerned. But in the end a democratic society, as envisaged in the human rights treaties, is one which respects the basic rights of its members.[12]

Some societies are tolerant, plural or relatively homogeneous, and have settled ideas of the proper limits of government. It may be appropriate in such societies to rely on majority institutions to protect individuals. That was Dicey's view of the protection of individual liberty in the United Kingdom.[13] For a long time his view was generally accepted, and it is still influential. It is one major reason why the United Kingdom still does not have an enforceable bill of rights.

Whatever the position may be in particular societies, the majoritarian theory is untenable in the context of the protection of human rights internationally. At the international level the point of human rights is not merely to relate the individual to public power, but to protect him or her from abuses of public power, including abuses supported by a majority. There is no international consensus on the values of tolerance and pluralism, or on the proper role of the State, which would secure individual liberty without express protection such as that contained in the various human rights treaties.

[11] That phrase occurs in the ICCPR in Arts. 14(1) (closed trials), 21 (peaceful assembly) and 22(2) (freedom of association). It is more frequently used in the ECHR: see Arts. 6(1) (closed trials), 8(2) (private and family life), 9(2) (manifestations of religion or beliefs), 10(2) (freedom of expression), 11(2) (peaceful assembly); Protocol 4, Art. 2(3) (right to leave a country). Cf. also AMR, Arts. 15 (peaceful assembly), 16(2) (freedom of association), 22(3) (freedom of movement and residence); 29(*c*) (savings clause for 'other rights or guarantees . . . derived from representative democracy as a form of government'). On the other hand the term does not appear at all in the AFR.

[12] On a number of occasions the European Court has held that laws with strong support within the relevant community (as manifested by elections or referenda) none the less violated the Convention, and has given little or no weight to the factor of local preference. See, e.g., *Open Door and Dublin Well Woman* v. *Ireland* (1992), ECHR, Series A, No. 249, p. 25, where the Court referred briefly to 'pluralism, tolerance and broadmindedness' as characteristics of a democratic society. Some of the dissenting judges pointed out that the law in question had recently been affirmed by national referendum ('eminently democratic process'): ibid., pp. 32 (Judge Cremona), 35 (Judge Matscher). For other examples of the reluctance to legitimate governmental conduct as 'necessary in a democratic society' see *Lingens* v. *Austria* (1986), ECHR, Series A, No. 103; *Oberschlick* v. *Austria* (1991), ECHR, Series A, No. 204; *Funke* v. *France* (1993), ECHR, Series A, No. 256–A; *Kokkinakis* v. *Greece* (1992), Series A, No. 260–A. Cases on the other side of the line (but equally lacking detailed analysis of the concept of a democratic society) include *Leander* v. *Sweden* (1987), ECHR, Series A, No. 116; *Hadjianastassiou* v. *Greece* (1992), Series A, No. 252.

[13] For analysis of Dicey's approach see T.R.S. Allan, 'Legislative Supremacy and the Rule of Law: Democracy and Constitutionalism', *Cambridge Law Journal*, 44 (1985), p. 111, esp. pp. 129–41; P. P. Craig, *Public Law and Democracy in the United Kingdom and the United States of America* (Oxford, Clarendon Press, 1990), ch. 2.

In addition to Article 25 of the International Covenant, the idea of democracy is also reflected in Article 1. Under Article 1, all peoples have the right of self-determination. By virtue of that right, it is said, 'they freely determine their political status and freely pursue their economic, social and cultural development'.[14] This suggests that self-determination is a continuing matter, not a once-for-all constitution of the State. Thus in addition to its familiar role in the decolonization process, Article 1 can be read as affirming the self-direction of each society by its people, and thus as affirming the principle of democracy at the collective level.[15] This is certainly the view taken by the United Nations Human Rights Committee. The Committee identifies as the beneficiaries of self-determination the people of existing States. It equates their right of self-determination with the existence within the State of a continuing system of democratic government based on public participation. It denies that self-determination involves a right to secede.[16]

Until recently, provisions such as Article 25, or Article 1 if it is understood as a sort of collective right to democratic institutions, were honoured more in the breach than in the observance. In the mid-1980s, only about a third of all the countries of the world could be described as democratic, and a still smaller proportion had long-standing and stable democratic structures. Moreover under the rights conception of democracy, it is not enough that the government of the day have been elected, in the comparatively recent past, at a general election. Democracy implies a range of rights to participate in public life, effective freedom of speech, the opportunity to organize political parties and other groups, and so on. In many countries, notoriously, such rights and opportunities have been lacking. A particular point is the denial of voting rights to women in many countries, and of an effective political voice to women in many more.

Thus it is hardly surprising that under international law (apart from treaties), there was no general endorsement of a principle of democracy.

[14] Among the regional human rights treaties, Art. 1 is reflected only in AFR, Art. 20.

[15] In this context the words of the Friendly Relations Declaration (GA Res. 2625 (XXV), 24 October 1970) are often cited. In elaborating the principle of equal rights and self-determination of peoples, the Declaration states that:

> 'Nothing in the foregoing paragraphs shall be construed as authorizing or encouraging any action which would dismember or impair, totally or in part, the territorial integrity or political unity of sovereign and independent States conducting themselves in compliance with the principle of equal rights and self-determination of people as described above and *thus possessed of a government representing the whole people belonging to the territory without distinction as to race, creed or colour*'. (Emphasis added.)

This certainly implies that the principle extends to internal self-determination so as to produce the result referred to in the words italicized: on the other hand the paragraph is a savings clause, and the 'foregoing paragraphs' do not, explicitly at least, so provide.

[16] See A. Cassese, 'The Self-Determination of Peoples', in L. Henkin (ed.) *The International Bill of Rights* (NY, Columbia UP, 1987), at pp. 92, 96–8, 101–2, 111–13; D. McGoldrick, *The Human Rights Committee* (Oxford, Clarendon Press, 1991), at pp. 247–58, for reviews of the Committee's approach to Art. 1. Generally on self-determination see J. Crawford, *The Creation of States in International Law* (Oxford, Clarendon Press, 1979), at pp. 84–106; T. Franck, 'The Emerging Right to Democratic Governance', *American Journal of International Law*, 86 (1992), p. 46, at pp. 52–63.

There was no requirement that the government of a State, to be a government, should have been democratically elected or even that it should have the general support of its people. As Oppenheim pointed out in 1905, the actual control of a government over the apparatus of the State has been treated as sufficient.[17] Jefferson's famous reference to the 'will of the people substantially declared' has not been taken literally.[18]

Moreover other features of classical international law were deeply undemocratic, or at least were capable of operating in a deeply undemocratic way. Six examples may be given.

First, international law assumes that the executive has comprehensive power in international affairs. Generally the head of State and the Minister for Foreign Affairs have plenary powers to make international commitments on behalf of the State, and to agree to and apply rules of international law which may affect the rights or claims of individuals without their consent, and even without their knowledge.[19]

Second, it is established that national law, no matter how democratically established, is not an excuse for failure to comply with international obligations.[20] At one level the rule is obvious, and would seem to have no adverse implications for democratic government. After all if an obligation exists at the international level, it cannot be the case that a law of one State can release that State from the obligation. At another level, however, the rule creates significant problems of democratic control. If an international obligation arises apart from a treaty, there may have been no direct process of commitment to the obligation either by Parliament or by elected leaders. In some countries treaties, or certain classes of treaties, require the approval of parliament, but many consensual obligations in international law (executive agreements, memoranda of understanding, to say nothing of less formal unilateral commitments) fall outside the scope of such procedures. In common law countries such as the United Kingdom there are no formal constutitional constraints at all on the Executive: the process of ratification of treaties is a purely executive act. Moreover if the executive enters into a treaty or commits the State in some other way, parliament may have little real choice but to enact the laws necessary to give effect to the obligation. It is true that practices of consultation have developed which seek to involve parliament at an early stage, or at least to keep it informed. But these are

[17] L. Oppenheim, *International Law* (1st edn., Longman, 1905), vol. 1, at pp. 403, 405.

[18] US recognition practice, in particular, has relied to some extent on the criterion of popular support for a new but unconstitutional government, but not consistently: see, e.g., M. Whiteman, *Digest of International Law* (Washington, US Government Printing Office, 1963), vol. 2, at pp. 4–6, 68–74, 261–2; L. T. Galloway, *Recognizing Foreign Governments. The Practice of the United States* (American Enterprise for Public Policy Research, Washington, 1978), at pp. 139–45.

[19] See, e.g., Vienna Convention on the Law of Treaties, 23 May 1969: *UN Treaty Series*, vol. 1155, p. 331, Art. 7(2)(*a*).

[20] The rule is enunciated in the context of treaty obligations by Art. 27 of the Vienna Convention on the Law of Treaties. For the equivalent rule in the context of non-treaty obligations, see ILC Draft Articles on States Responsibility, Part 1, Art. 4; Part 2, Art. 6, *bis*(3).

practices not laws, and do not eliminate the difficulty. Thus if the British Government had ratified the Maastricht Treaty despite the passage of an amendment relating to the Social Chapter, that might have presented problems of legality under United Kingdom law, but it would have been effective *vis-à-vis* the other members of the Community.[21]

The third potentially undemocratic rule relates to the important question of remedies. The executive government has virtually exclusive control over the availability of international remedies. The individual has no autonomous procedural rights in international law. In many cases rights of individual petition are based on an optional clause or an optional protocol, and may be to that extent precarious. This is true both of the right of individual communication under the International Covenant, and of the right of individual petition to the European Commission under the European Convention.

Fourth, the principle of non-intervention extends to protect even non-democratic regimes in relation to action taken to preserve their power against their own people. At least, that has been the traditional understanding.

Fifth, the principle of self-determination is not permitted to modify established territorial boundaries. Nor, on the whole, has it replaced the traditional rules for determining territorial disputes. Those rules are based largely on the political history of the territory concerned rather than on the current wishes of its inhabitants. The ninth edition of *Oppenheim's International Law* suggests that 'the injection of a legal principle of self-determination into the law about acquisition and loss of territorial sovereignty' amounts to a 'fundamental change'.[22] But it does not spell out what specific changes have been produced, outside the colonial context, and the recent cases involving territorial disputes in Africa and Central America have by-passed the principle of self-determination in the interests of stability.[23]

Sixth, the powers of a government to bind the State for the future seem to be virtually unlimited. International law recognizes the general authority of a government over the State as a continuing entity. That can be seen, for example, from the well-known *Tinoco* arbitration.[24] A military regime in Costa Rica seized power but was eventually overthrown and replaced by an elected government. The new government disputed its liability to pay for debts incurred by the military regime. The case went to arbitration, where

[21] *R* v. *Secretary of State for Foreign Affairs, ex parte Rees-Mogg* (QBD, 30 July 1993), noted *New Law Journal*, 143 (1993), p. 1153; cf. *Blackburn* v. *Attorney-General*, [1971] 2 All ER 1380.

[22] *Oppenheim's International Law* (9th edn., R. Y. Jennings and A. Watts, Longman, 1992), vol. 1, p. 715.

[23] *Burkina Faso/Mali Frontier Dispute*, *ICJ Reports*, 1986, p. 554, para. 25; *Land, Island and Maritime Frontier* case (*El Salvador/Honduras, Nicaragua intervening*), *ICJ Reports*, 1992.

[24] (1923), *Reports of International Aribtral Awards*, vol. 1, p. 369.

it was held that the successor government was bound by all the acts of its predecessor, on the basis that the predecessor regime was firmly established, and that its legitimacy or constitutionality were irrelevant.[25]

It is significant that that rule has rarely been challenged, even by successor governments with much to gain from a successful challenge and with no sympathy for their predecessor or its foreign supporters. The most important example of such a challenge was the rejection by the post-1917 Revolutionary Government of Russia of continuity with the pre-revolution Tsarist regime. That rejection was based on special grounds which did not challenge a general rule of governmental succession, and anyway was modified after a few years.[26] Not the least of the ironies surrounding the dissolution of the Soviet Union is the fact that the Russian Federation argued that it is the same legal person as the Soviet Union, and based that argument to some extent on the continuity of the Soviet Union with pre-revolutionary Russia.[27]

In its earlier manifestations, it is not surprising that international law had these six characteristics, since its own primary characteristic was as a law of co-ordination of the activities of potentates, principalities and powers. Before 1928, or perhaps 1945, international law made no final attempt to outlaw war, which was, as Lord McNair said in his inaugural lecture, 'extra-legal rather than illegal'.[28] Modern international law has changed in this crucial respect—that is to say, it now purports to protect the existence and territorial integrity of States. Earlier (pre-1945) international law could be defended, in a perhaps back-handed way, by the argument that it was, in a fundamental sense, *descriptive*. It did not underwrite regimes or even States; it merely accepted them while they continued. Not underwriting them, it could legitimately be argued that it did not assume any responsibility for quality control, any more than seismology exists to encourage 'good' earthquakes.

Formally, that position had changed by 1945, when the United Nations Charter prohibited the use of force in international relations except in self-defence or with the authorization of the Security Council. For example it

[25] For more recent applications of the principle that a government in control of the State can commit it internationally see, e.g., *Short* v. *Islamic Republic of Iran* (1987), 82 ILR 149; cf. *Yeager* v. *Islamic Republic of Iran* (1987), 82 ILR 179.

[26] T. A. Taracouzio, *The Soviet Union and International Law* (New York, Macmillan, 1935), at pp. 21–5; D. P. O'Connell, *State Succession in International Law and Municipal Law* (Cambridge, CUP, 1967), vol. 1, at pp. 19–20; Crawford, op. cit. above (n. 16), at pp. 405–6.

[27] The continuity of Russia with the former Soviet Union was asserted in the Agreement establishing the Commonwealth of Independent States, Alma Ata, 21 December 1991 (*International Legal Materials*, 31 (1992), p. 138) and has been accepted by UN organs and by foreign courts (see e.g. *The Kherson*, [1992] 2 Lloyd's Rep. 261). For discussion, see R. Mullerson, 'The Continuity and Succession of States by Reference to the Former USSR and Yugoslavia', *International and Comparative Law Quarterly*, 42 (1993), p. 473.

[28] A. D. McNair, 'Collective Security', this *Year Book*, 17 (1936), p. 150, at p. 152.

was on this basis that the Security Council took action to restore 'the sovereignty, independence and territorial integrity of Kuwait', and the authority of what it described as 'the legitimate Government of Kuwait'.[29] For a long time, however, the consequences of the change brought about by the United Nations Charter were limited. The six rules of international law referred to above remained essentially unchanged. Indeed some of them were reinforced.

This can be seen from the decision of the International Court in the *Nicaragua* case in 1986.[30] In that case, Nicaragua claimed that the assistance given by the United States to the *contras* was an unlawful use of force by the United States against Nicaragua, or at least an unlawful intervention in its internal affairs. The United States claimed that it was justified in supporting the *contras* for a number of reasons, including the breach by the Nicaraguan Government of commitments about the composition of the government and the installation 'of a truly democratic government that guarantees peace, freedom and justice'.[31]

In fact the Nicaraguan Government had been elected in 1984, in elections observed by a range of individuals and non-governmental organizations.[32] The major United States complaint against it related to the internal and external policies subsequently adopted by the Sandinista Government, although the State Department also rejected the 1984 elections as unfair. Rather than examining the question of compliance with the various commitments made by the Sandinistas as a condition of coming to power, the Court took another tack. It said:

> The assertion of the commitment raises the question of the possibility of the State binding itself by agreement in relation to a question of domestic policy, such as that relating to the holding of free elections on its territory. The Court cannot discover, within the range of subjects open to international agreement, any obstacle . . . to hinder a State from making a commitment of this kind. A State, which is free to decide upon the principle and methods of popular consultation within its domestic order, is sovereign for the purpose of accepting a limitation of its sovereignty in this field.[33]

It went on to point out that the OAS Charter referred to 'the effective exer-

[29] SC Res. 662 (1990) (adopted 15–0). See *International Legal Materials*, 29 (1990), p. 1325, for this and other Security Council resolutions on Kuwait.

[30] *ICJ Reports*, 1986, p. 14.

[31] The specific commitments on which the United States relied are set out in the dissenting opinion of Judge Schwebel: *ICJ Reports*, 1986, p. 14, at pp. 398–401. The majority opinion referred to them only in general terms: ibid., p. 130 ('questions such as the composition of the government, its political ideology and alignment, totalitarianism, human rights, militarization and aggression').

[32] On the 1984 elections in Nicaragua see *Keesing's Contemporary Archives*, 30 (1984), pp. 33269–72.

[33] *ICJ Reports*, 1986, p. 14, at p. 131.

cise of representative democracy' only as an aspect of 'solidarity' and as a 'high aim'. Given this unspecific language it rejected the view . . .

> that Nicaragua actually undertook a commitment to organise free elections, and that this commitment was of a legal nature . . . [T]he Court cannot find an instrument with legal force . . . whereby Nicaragua has committed itself in respect of the principle or methods of holding elections.[34]

This aspect of the Court's decision is rather unsatisfactory. Nicaragua was a party both to the International Covenant and to the American Convention, both of which contain clear commitments with respect to the principle of free elections and their regularity, although not with respect to precise issues of timing or method. The Court professed itself 'unable to find' such commitments: one can only say that it did not look very hard. To be fair, it was unaided in its search by any assistance from the United States, which did not appear at the stage of the merits and which did not rely either on the International Covenant or on the American Convention, no doubt because it was at that time a party to neither. The Court also made the point that any question of compliance with commitments made towards the OAS was not a matter for specific enforcement by the United States, and certainly not by way of forcible intervention.[35]

The Court's negative reaction even to the idea that Nicaragua was subject to international supervision or accountability in the conduct of elections reflects the emphasis of traditional international law on non-intervention in the internal affairs of States. The holding of free elections was treated still as essentially a matter of 'domestic policy'. Clearly, the Court was reluctant to accept that established international law might have changed. This is quite apart from the controversial question of the means used by the United States to enforce any commitment that might have been made.

In many other respects, however, international law has changed. It is increasingly concerned with issues which impinge on what were once considered matters of domestic policy. The potentially undemocratic aspects of the traditional international law rules are only heightened by this. Rules which draw lines between societies may be less problematic, from the point of view of democratic principle, than rules which deal with the internal life of those societies. International law is increasingly concerned with the second as well as the first.

Since 1986 the world has itself undergone vast changes. In particular there has been a significant change in the democratic balance. In the last decade the proportion of States with democratic systems, however fragile or tentative, has increased sharply—a process beginning in Southern Europe, extending to Latin America and Eastern Europe, the Soviet Union

[34] Ibid., pp. 131–2. But see the separate opinion of Judge Ago (ibid., pp. 186–7) for justified doubts on this point.

[35] Ibid., pp. 132–3.

and many of its former republics, and even to East Asia.[36] In Africa, according to one analysis, there were only 4 democracies, as against 40 States with apparently stable non-democratic regimes, in 1989. By 1992, the number of democracies had increased to 18, and the number of non-democracies was reduced to 12. Significantly, there had also been a great increase (from 3 to 22) in the number of regimes in a stage of transition to democracy.[37] No doubt this is all fragile and reversible, but it is also, in the words of the noted African commentator Ali Mazrui, an 'unmistakable' trend.[38]

With this change has come a new stress on democracy as a value, even a dominant value, in national and international affairs.[39] The same is true of the law regulating those affairs.[40] References to democracy, which a gener-

[36] There is now an enormous literature on these developments. See, e.g., G. A. O'Donnell and P. C. Schmitter, *Transitions from Authoritarian Rule* (Johns Hopkins, Baltimore, 1986); J. Higley and R. Gunther, *Elites and Democratic Consolidation in Latin America and Southern Europe* (CUP, Cambridge, 1991); S. D. Huntingdon, *The Third Wave: Democratization in the Late Twentieth Century* (Oklahoma, University of Oklahoma Press, 1991); G. Pridham, *Encouraging Democracy: The International Context of Regime Transition in Southern Europe* (Leicester UP, Leicester, 1991); A. Przeworski, *Democracy and the Market. Political and Economic Reforms in Eastern Europe and Latin America* (Cambridge, CUP, 1991); and the essays in D. Held (ed.), *Prospects for Democracy. North, South, East, West* (Polity Press, Cambridge, 1993), Part IV.

[37] See H. M. McFrerson, 'Democracy and Development in Africa', *Journal of Peace Research*, 29 (1992), p. 241, at p. 242. See also the annual Freedom House surveys: e.g., *Freedom in the World: Political Rights and Civil Liberties 1990–1* (New York, Freedom House, 1991).

[38] A. A. Mazrui, 'Planned Governance and the Liberal Revival in Africa: The Paradox of Anticipation', *Cornell International Law Journal*, 25 (1992), p. 541.

[39] A sample of the literature in political science and international relations includes: D. Held, *Models of Democracy* (Polity Press, Cambridge, 1987); G. Duncan (ed.), *Democracy and the Capitalist State* (Cambridge, CUP, 1989); D. Held, 'Democracy, the Nation State and the Global System', in D. Held (ed.), *Political Theory Today* (Polity Press, Cambridge, 1991), p. 197; F. Fukuyama, *The End of History and the Last Man* (Penguin, London, 1992); J. Dunn (ed.), *Democracy: The Unfinished Journey* (Oxford, OUP, 1992); E.–O. Czempiel, 'Governance and Democratization', in J. N. Rosenau and E.–O. Czempiel (eds.), *Governance without Government: Order and Change in World Politics* (Cambridge, CUP, 1992), p. 250; R. Bartley *et al.* (eds.), *Democracy and Capitalism: Asian and American Perspectives* (Institute of South-East Asian Studies, Singapore, 1993); Held (ed.), op. cit. above (n. 36). On democratic principles in different religious traditions see, e.g., A.Y. al-Hibri, 'Islamic Constitutionalism and the Concept of Democracy', *Case Western Reserve Journal of International Law*, 24 (1992), p. 1. For feminist perspectives see, e.g., S. Mendus, 'Losing the Faith: Feminism and Democracy', in Dunn, op. cit. above, p. 207; A. Phillips, 'Must Feminists Give up on Liberal Democracy?', in Held, op. cit. above (n. 36), p. 93. More-or-less sceptical accounts include N. Chomsky, *Deterring Democracy* (Vintage, London, 1992); O. M. Fiss, 'Capitalism and Democracy', *Michigan Journal of International Law*, 13 (1992), p. 908; B. Parekh, 'The Cultural Particularity of Liberal Democracy', in Held, op. cit. above (n. 36), p. 156.

[40] For international law perspectives (mostly North American), see esp. Franck, loc. cit. above (n. 16); G. H. Fox, 'The Right to Political Participation in International Law', *Yale Journal of International Law*, 17 (1992), p. 539. Other accounts include H. Steiner, 'Political Participation as a Human Right', *Harvard Human Rights Year Book*, 1 (1988), p. 77; Panel, 'The Human Right to Participate in Government: Towards an Operational Definition', *Proceedings of the American Society of International Law*, 82 (1988), p. 505; T. Meron, 'Democracy and the Rule of Law', *World Affairs*, 153 (1990), p. 23; Panel, 'National Sovereignty Revisited: Perspectives on the Emerging Norm of Democracy in International Law', *Proceedings of the American Society of International Law*, 86 (1992), p. 249; A. Rosas and J. Helgesen (eds.), *The Strength of Diversity: Human Rights and Pluralist Democracy* (Martinus Nijhoff, Dordrecht, 1992). For public law perspectives see, e.g., K. E. Klare, 'Legal Theory and Democratic Reconstruction: Reflections on 1989', *University of British Columbia Law Review*, 25 (1991), p. 69; R. F. and H. J. Taubenfeld, 'Some Thoughts on the Problems of Designing Stable

ation or even a decade ago would have been regarded as political and extra-legal, are entering into the justification of legal decision-making in a new way.

At the national level, two examples may be given. In 1992 the High Court of Australia invalidated a federal law prohibiting paid political advertising during election campaigns, on the basis that the constitutional requirement of parliamentary elections implied that the conditions for free elections, including freedom of speech and of the press, could not be infringed.[41] In February 1993 the House of Lords held that a local council could not sue for defamation, because to protect the reputation of public agencies such as councils by the law of defamation would unduly affect freedom of speech in a democratic society.[42] It is doubtful if either case would have been decided the same way fifteen years ago.[43] It is no accident that in both cases reference was made, alongside the idea of democracy, to international human rights treaties.

At the international level also, concern for democracy as a principle has deepened. This prompts the question to what extent international law may be moving in the direction of underpinning democracy, of taking seriously the democratic principles referred to in Articles 1 and 25 of the International Covenant, of giving effect to the proposition in Article 21 of the Universal Declaration that 'the will of the people shall be the basis of the authority of government'?

II. Developing International Law in Pro-democratic Directions

In one sense, there has been a great deal of development, as the following examples show:

(1) There is a developing practice of election monitoring by international organizations such as the UN and the OAS, as well as non-governmental organizations. This has occurred both in colonial territories and, more recently, in independent States.

The holding of plebiscites for elections to determine the future of a colonial or non-self-governing territory is a long established practice.[44] A recent and successful example was the pre-independence election in Namibia, where the role of non-governmental organizations was crucial in cre-

Democracies', *International Lawyer*, 24 (1990), p. 689; G. Ress, 'The Constitution and the Requirements of Democracy in Germany', in C. Starck (ed.), *New Challenges to the German Basic Law* (Nomos Verlag, Baden-Baden, 1991), p. 111.

[41] *Australian Capital Television Pty. Ltd.* v. *Commonwealth of Australia (No. 2)* (1992), 108 ALR 577. Cf. also *Nationwide News Pty. Ltd.* v. *Wills* (1992), 108 ALR 681.

[42] *Derbyshire County Council* v. *Times Newspapers Ltd.*, [1993] 1 All ER 1011 (HL), affirming [1992] 3 All ER 65.

[43] In the Australian case there is no doubt that the decision would have been different: see *Attorney-General for Australia, ex rel. McKinlay* v. *Commonwealth of Australia* (1975), 50 ALJR 279.

[44] Franck, loc. cit. above (n. 16), pp. 69–71.

ating an atmosphere in which 97% of the electors cast a vote.[45] It remains to be seen whether the same process will be allowed to occur in the Western Sahara,[46] or for that matter East Timor.[47]

Even more significant has been the development of election monitoring in independent States. The United Nations Observer Mission to Verify the Electoral Process in Nicaragua in 1989 was the first occasion where a public international organization monitored an election in an independent State.[48] It was followed in 1990 by the monitoring of the election in Haiti, though with less happy results.[49] The Commonwealth Secretariat has also played an active role in monitoring elections, and the preparations for elections, in independent Commonwealth countries.[50]

In some cases this involvement has extended to creating the conditions for free elections and for the establishment of democratic rule, as with the United Nations operation in Cambodia, the long-term success of which also remains to be seen.[51]

(2) There are moves to institutionalize these functions, for example the

[45] SC Res. 628 (1989). For the background see *Namibia* advisory opinion, *ICJ Reports*, 1971, p. 6; Fox, loc. cit. above (n. 40), pp. 576–9.

[46] As envisaged by SC Res. 690 (1991). For the background see *Western Sahara* advisory opinion, *ICJ Reports*, 1975, p. 12; T. M. Franck, 'The Stealing of the Sahara', *American Journal of International Law*, 70 (1976), p. 694.

[47] The issue of self-determination underlies proceedings brought by Portugal against Australia before the ICJ: see case concerning *East Timor*, *ICJ Reports*, 1991, p. 9; C. Chinkin, 'The Merits of Portugal's Claim Against Australia', *University of New South Wales Law Journal*, 15 (1992), p. 423. From the East Timorese perspective see J. Ramos-Horta, *Funu. The Unfinished Saga of East Timor* (Red Sea Press, New Jersey, 1987); J. G. Taylor, *Indonesia's Forgotten War* (Zed Books, London, 1991).

[48] See Fox, loc. cit. above (n. 40), pp. 597–83. Generally see Panel, 'International Observation of Elections', *Proceedings of the American Society of International Law*, 84 (1990), p. 375; J. M. Ebersole, 'The United Nations' Response to Requests for Assistance in Electoral Matters', *Virginia Journal of International Law*, 33 (1992), p. 91; W. M. Reisman, 'International Election Observation', *Pace University School of Law Year Book of International Law*, 4 (1992), p. 1; D. Stoelting, 'The Challenge of UN-Monitored Elections in Independent Nations', *Stanford Journal of International Law*, 28 (1992), p. 371.

[49] See OAS Res. MRE/RES 3/92, 17 May 1992; GA Res. 47/20B, 23 April 1993; SC Res. 841 (1993). It should be noted that the Security Council, though expressly acting under Chapter VII of the Charter in imposing a mandatory trade embargo on Haiti, did so on the combined basis that a request to that effect by the Haitian Permanent Representative and the action taken by the OAU and the General Assembly together defined 'a unique and exceptional situation warranting extraordinary measures'. No precedent was evidently intended to be created—but on the other hand the Council was clearly operating on the basis of a principle of legitimacy in taking action against what it described as a '*de facto* regime'. See Fox, loc. cit. above (n. 40), pp. 583–6; Franck, loc. cit. above (n. 16), pp. 72–4, and cf. below, n. 73.

[50] In the period 1990–3, Commonwealth Observer Groups have observed and reported on elections in the following countries: Malaysia (1990 general elections); Bangladesh (1991 Parliamentary elections); Zambia (1991 Presidential and National Assembly elections); Guyana (1992 general and regional elections); Kenya (1992 Presidential, parliamentary and civic elections); Seychelles (Constitutional Commission elections (July 1992), Constitutional referendum (November 1992), Presidential and National Assembly elections (July 1993)); Lesotho (1993 general election). In each case a report of the Observer Group was published by the Commonwealth Secretariat.

[51] For the Paris Agreement on Cambodia of 21 October 1991, see *International Legal Materials*, 31 (1992), p. 174.

Office of Fair Elections created by the Paris Charter of the Conference on Security and Co-operation in Europe in 1991 (CSCE),[52] and the Organization of American States Resolution on Representative Democracy of the same year.[53] In 1992 the United Nations General Assembly provisionally endorsed guidelines for election observation. Electoral assistance under the guidelines would be offered 'on a case-by-case basis . . . recognizing that the fundamental responsibility for ensuring free and fair elections lies with Governments'.[54]

(3) The various human rights courts and commissions have also begun to deal with these issues. For example the first case under Article 3 of Protocol 1 of the European Convention was decided by the European Court in 1986. That case involved complex arrangements for the decentralization of Belgium having regard to the interests of the different linguistic groups.[55] This follows the earlier action by the European Commission in the *Greek* case,[56] which signalled the departure of Greece from democratic standards, and which played a role in the suspension of Greece from the Council of Europe until those standards were reinstated. The Inter-American Commission on Human Rights has also been dealing with these issues, for example in a case involving a complaint by three Mexican citizens dealing with electoral

[52] Ibid., 30 (1991), p. 190. For the Report of the CSCE Seminar of Experts on Democratic Institutions (Oslo, November 1991) see ibid., 31 (1992), p. 374.

[53] OEA/Ser.P/AG/Res. 1080 (XXI–O/91); Franck, loc. cit. above (n. 16), pp. 65–6. In an exchange of correspondence with the UN Secretary-General concerning their respective competences in relation to the situation in Haiti, the Secretary-General of the OAS asserted that one of the 'unique features' of the OAS was 'the promotion and consolidation of democracy . . . yet another valuable contribution of the region to the development of international law, although this does not imply any claim of universal applicability for these distinctive features': OEA/Ser.F/V.1, MRE/INF.15/92, 25 July 1992.

[54] GA Res. 47/138, 18 December 1992 (adopted 141–0:20), paras. 4, 9. On the same day the General Assembly adopted a countervailing resolution on 'Respect for the principles of national sovereignty and non-interference in the internal affairs of States in their electoral processes': GA Res. 47/130 (99–45:16). Res. 47/130 reflects reservations on the part of many Third World States, who fear that the new emphasis on democratic standards will be used to justify or excuse interference in their affairs. It also reflects the older equation of self-determination with non-intervention in the case of independent States, as to which see Crawford, op. cit. above (n. 16), p. 102. On the other hand the level of support for these implicitly competing resolutions has been changing: cf. GA Res. 46/137 (134–4:13) and GA Res. 46/130 (102–40:13), both of 17 December 1991; GA Res. 45/150 (129–8:9) and 45/151 (111–29:11), both of 18 December 1990. For comment, see Fox, loc. cit. above (n. 40), p. 587; Franck, loc. cit. above (n. 16), p. 82.

[55] Case of *Mathieu-Mohin and Clerfayt* (1987), ECHR, Series A, No. 113. The Court held that, although Art. 3 was in form an inter-State undertaking, it vested rights in the citizens concerned (ibid., p. 15). It went on succinctly to outline its approach to Art. 3: on the positive side a universal right to vote and to stand for election on a basis of equality in any body which constitutes a 'legislature' under the constitutional structure of the State in question; on the negative side, a wide margin of appreciation in the legislature as to the system of representation and of voting, a system to be judged 'in the light of the political evolution of the country concerned', but subject to the overriding principle that the system must ensure 'the free expression of the opinion of the people in the choice of the legislature'. See ibid., pp. 16–17, and for comment, Merrills, this *Year Book*, 58 (1987), p. 466. For a review of the Commission's practice under Protocol 1, Art. 3, see Council of Europe, *Digest of Strasbourg Case-Law relating to the European Convention on Human Rights* (Carl Heymanns, Koln, 1985), vol. 5, pp. 829–67.

[56] *Yearbook of the European Convention on Human Rights*, 11 (1968), part 2, p. 690, at p. 730; ibid. 12 (1969), part 2, *passim*; *International Legal Materials*, 14 (1975), p. 313.

fraud.[57] In that case—in apparent contrast to the International Court in the *Nicaragua* case—the Commission refused to accept the argument that these matters were essentially domestic.

(4) At the universal level the Human Rights Committee has been dealing with a range of cases under the Optional Protocol involving restrictions on, and in most cases flagrant violations of, the political rights in Article 25.[58] The Committee is also drafting a general comment on Article 25: the draft comment points out that Article 25 is 'called to guarantee democratic political systems in States parties to the Covenant', stresses the close relationship between Articles 1 and 25, and notes that arbitrary deprivation of citizenship for the purposes of avoiding or diminishing the political rights of individuals would violate Article 25. The Committee doubts whether any form of one party State could comply with Article 25.[59]

There are a number of further elements in the debate. It is sometimes argued that a State may justifiably use armed force to overthrow a despotic government in another State. There were overtones of this idea in the so-called Reagan doctrine, and in the use of armed force by the United States in Grenada and Panama. The idea has found at least some support from commentators within and even outside the United States. For example it has been argued that the essential justification for the United States action in Panama was that it was taken 'in support of the democratic process', since it was directed against a regime which had been voted out of office but which refused to give up power, and since the intervention was followed by the holding of free elections after the American withdrawal.[60]

No-one can regret the fall of a Noriega, or for that matter a Pol Pot. But there are serious problems with the idea that democracy can be installed by the unilateral assertion of external force. The first problem, from the perspective of international law, is simply that the vast majority of governments, including the vast majority of democratic governments, do not accept that view. The Grenada and Panama interventions were roundly condemned by the United Nations and the Organization of American States respectively,[61] and it is significant that in its official justifications in each case the United States did not rely on the democratic argument, as dis-

[57] *Mexico Elections Decision* (Cases 9768, 9780, 9829) (1990), cited by Fox, loc. cit. above (n. 40), p. 594. And see D. Shelton, 'Representative Democracy and Human Rights in the Western Hemisphere', *Human Rights Law Journal*, 12 (1991), p. 353.

[58] e.g. *Mpandanjila* v. *Zaire* (No. 138/1983), reproduced in UN, *Selected Decisions of the Human Rights Committee under the Optional Protocol* (CCPR/C/OP/2), vol. 2, p. 164; *Mpaka-Nsusu* v. *Zaire* (No. 157/1983), ibid., p. 187.

[59] Draft General Comments (Article 25) (1993).

[60] E. Lauterpacht QC, *The Times*, 23 December 1989, p. 11. Similarly A. D'Amato, 'The Invasion of Panama was a Lawful Response to Tyranny', *American Journal of International Law*, 84 (1990), p. 516; D. W. Alberts, 'The United States Invasion of Panama: Unilateral Military Intervention to Effectuate a Change in Government: A Continuum of Lawfulness', *Transnational Law and Contemporary Problems*, 1 (1991), p. 259.

[61] As to Grenada: GA Res. 38/7, 2 November 1983 (108–9:27). As to Panama: OAS Resolution CP/Res. 534 (800/89), 22 December 1989.

tinct from a number of other arguments such as the protection of its nationals. Nor for that matter did Tanzania, when it took justified action against the Amin regime.[62]

There is also the problem that this asserted right to intervene has so far been exercised in a quite arbitrary way—in Panama but not elsewhere, in Nicaragua but not elsewhere. Moreover other countries taking action which might have seemed justified on similar grounds—Vietnam in Cambodia, to take one possible example[63]—have been subject to vigorous and sustained criticism, not least by the United States. As Bowett has pointed out, the 'nations of the world will not accept international rules that yield a different answer to the question of whether an action is legal depending on the identity of the actor'.[64] It was just such considerations that led the International Court to reject the idea that the United States had any 'special responsibility' to enforce any democratic commitments the Nicaraguan Government may have made to the OAS when it came to power. The Court refused to 'contemplate the creation of a new rule opening up a right of intervention by one State against another on the ground that the latter has opted for some particular ideology or political system'.[65]

This consideration is reinforced by the essential point that democracy is not something which can be installed by foreign force in a few days. It is not necessary to agree with the motives or programme of those carrying out a *coup d'état*—for example that in Fiji in 1987[66]—to see the potentially destabilizing effect of external intervention, or of the threat of such intervention. After the event, especially in cases where the intervention was on a major scale or lasted for a considerable time, it can be very difficult to re-establish local legitimacy.

No doubt the strength of the international reaction to interventions of this kind will vary, depending on the consequences. That point was made by W.V. Harcourt, in a discussion of the experience of intervention during the nineteenth century. He referred to intervention as 'a high and summary procedure which may sometimes snatch a remedy beyond the reach of law . . . [I]ts essence is illegality, and its justification is its success. Of all things, at once the most unjustifiable and the most impolitic is an unsuc-

[62] See J. Crawford, 'Self-Determination outside the Colonial Context', in W. J. A. Macartney (ed.), *Self-Determination in the Commonwealth* (Aberdeen University Press, Aberdeen, 1988), p. 1, at p. 10, and references there cited.

[63] e.g. GA Res. 34/22, 14 November 1979, and subsequent annual resolutions. See G. Klintworth, *Vietnam's Intervention in Cambodia in International Law* (AGPS, Canberra, 1989). On human rights violations under the post-1979 regime, see Lawyers' Committee for Human Rights, *Kampuchea: After the Worst* (New York, 1985).

[64] D. W. Bowett, 'International Incidents: New Genre or New Delusion?', *Yale Journal of International Law*, 12 (1987), p. 386, at p. 388.

[65] *ICJ Reports*, 1986, p. 133. Cf. also *Corfu Channel* case, *ICJ Reports*, 1949, p. 4, at p. 35.

[66] As to which see V. Lal, *Fiji: Coups in Paradise, Race, Politics and Military Intervention* (London, Zed Books, 1990); R. M. Kiwanuka, 'On Revolution and Legality in Fiji', *International and Comparative Law Quarterly*, 37 (1988), p. 961; M. R. Islam, 'The Proposed Constitutional Guarantee of Indigenous Governmental Power in Fiji: An International Legal Appraisal', *California Western Journal of International Law*, 19 (1988), p. 107.

cessful Intervention.'[67] Subsequent success, while it may mitigate, is not a test of legality. On the contrary a rule of legality for pro-democratic invasions would deny to the people concerned—the alleged beneficiaries of the rule—any opportunity to state their own views on the events.[68]

Despite this, there is scope for developing institutions at the international level which will reinforce democracy, and which may even, by mutual agreement, help to shore up democratic institutions against internal challenge. It is through international organizations, including regional organizations acting within the framework of Part VIII of the Charter, and not by unilateral intervention, that these problems should be tackled.

A second issue goes to the very existence of a clearly undemocratic government—existence in the sense of international capacity to represent the State. It has been argued that disputes over the credentials of a government to represent the State should be resolved by applying democratic standards rather than the standard of effective control, at least in cases where 'the results of a UN-monitored election are overturned and an incumbent regime refuses to yield power',[69] but possibly in other cases also.

This idea has some attraction, especially since its focus is on an organized collective response rather than unilateral military action. In particular it might be written into the procedures for United Nations supervision of elections, so that everyone has notice of the possible consequences—although there are so far no signs of this happening. But if the suggestion is that the continued recognition of a regime as a government should be made dependent on its continued acceptance of democratic standards, there are problems with it. In particular it leaves little or no room for manoeuvre, for nuance, in situations where manoeuvre and nuance may well be necessary. In many cases little is to be gained from denying the existence of a group actually in control in the institutions of State, whether or not they have recently won, or would ever win, an election. Of course there is no need to jump to the conclusion that mere occupation of the parliament building, or of the American embassy, is enough to make a government. A State may temporarily lack a government—as for example in Somalia.[70] If the consequence is that the extra-territorial property of the State is quarantined until a secure government emerges, so much the better. But transitional situations are one thing: the refusal to deal with established authorities is

[67] 'Neutrality or Intervention?', in *Letters by Historicus on Some Questions of International Law* (London, Macmillan, 1863), p. 41.

[68] See the debate between W. M. Reisman ('Coercion and Self-determination: Construing Charter Article 2(4)', *American Journal of International Law*, 78 (1984), p. 642) and O. Schachter ('The Legality of Pro-Democratic Invasion', ibid., p. 645). See also T. J. Farer, 'The United States as a Guarantor of Democracy in the Caribbean Basin: Is There a Legal Way?', *Human Rights Quarterly*, 10 (1988), p. 157; J. A. R. Nafziger, 'Self-Determination and Humanitarian Intervention in a Community of Power', *Denver Journal of International Law and Policy*, 20 (1991), p. 9; K. Ryan, 'Rights, Intervention and Self-Determination', ibid., p. 55.

[69] Fox, loc. cit. above (n. 40), p. 603.

[70] As Hobhouse J held in *Republic of Somalia* v. *Woodhouse, Drake & Carey (Suisse) SA*, [1992] 3 WLR 744, noted in *Cambridge Law Journal*, 52 (1993), p. 4.

another. No doubt there may be room for symbolic gestures—for example, the refusal of Hungarian credentials by the United Nations for some years after 1956.[71] On the other hand, failure to deal with established regimes may only harm the people whom it is intended to assist—as may have been the case in Haiti.[72]

This is not to suggest a mere capitulation to force, or even to power growing *slowly* out of the barrel of a gun. There are things that can be done. Philip Allott has remarked, in the context of his thorough-going critique of present international law, that the system lacks a principle or theory of representation.[73] That is perhaps not quite true. International law has a theory of representation. This is the theory that an established government stands for, and has responsibility for, the State and its people for all or virtually all purposes. The theory is simple, but not necessarily simple-minded. One underlying justification is that third parties, who are after all not supposed to intervene in the internal affairs of a State, are entitled to rely on whatever government is securely established in a State as being the entity with which they can deal.

But that justification goes only so far. Third parties are no doubt entitled to call on the established government of a given territory to respect the rights of those in the territory. Responsibility in this sense arises from control. But it is not intervention to deal with the government of a State on a consensual basis, even if the dealing—whether in the form of arms sales or bribes to officials to obtain some concession or special treatment—is in no sense in the interests of the people of the State, and even though this must be obvious to the participants. The difficulty with the all-or-nothing solution of non-recognition of an effective but undemocratic government is that it avoids holding those who have made the decisions responsible for their acts. Where there is power there should be responsibility, including legal responsibility.

This does not, however, end the argument. One possibility—which has had little or no consideration compared with either forcible intervention or blanket non-recognition—might be to develop a system under which third parties dealing with a grossly unrepresentative regime would be required to take the risk of doing so. This would apply both to States and to private parties, including corporations. It would put them on notice that if they wish to deal with a regime lacking any legitimacy or popular support, they would take the risk of the review of the transaction by a subsequent representative government.

No doubt the details would have to be worked out, including some provision for notice to third parties, some specification of the triggering con-

[71] R. Higgins, *The Development of International Law through the Political Organs of the United Nations* (OUP, London, 1963), at pp. 158–9.

[72] See M. Cerna, 'The Case of Haiti before the OAS', *Proceedings of the American Society of International Law*, 86 (1992), p. 378.

[73] P. Allott, *Eunomia. New Order for a New World* (Oxford, OUP, 1990), at pp. 306–10, 372–5.

ditions, and especially some provision for dispute settlement. There is a problem, increasingly common in international law, of the formulation of ever more complex rules in the absence of proper procedures for dispute settlement. This is one major reason for the attraction of simple rules, free of exceptions—idiot rules, as Franck calls them.[74] Such rules are determinate, even though they may not do justice in every case. By contrast the development of law in complex societies has seen a constantly increasing refinement, and international law has shared in this.

This suggestion—which, if the *Tinoco* case is right, does not represent the status quo—is not without some analogy in international law. Long-term transactions of a territorial trustee, or of a belligerent occupant, may be subject to this form of review. In the *Nauru* case the International Court seems to have accepted the principle of review of the acts of a trustee affecting the beneficiary prior to the independence of the territory concerned.[75]

At a deeper level, there is an analogy with the different rules relating to the competence of the State which are embedded in the law of treaties and State responsibility. State responsibility is dependent primarily on factual control.[76] On the other hand, the making of treaty commitments by a government is now dependent, to a limited but significant extent, on compliance with fundamental constitutional procedures. That rule is contained in Article 47 of the Vienna Convention on the Law of Treaties of 1969. When it was adopted it came as a surprise to many commentators, used to thinking of the primacy of international law over national law, or at least of their radical separation. But there is a common interest in the stability of treaties, and unconstitutional treaties are unlikely to be stable. The same could be said for unconscionable transactions with wholly undemocratic regimes.

III. Conclusions

This is only an initial survey of some of the issues that are raised by the question whether and to what extent international law endorses, or is even consistent with, democratic principle. Other issues relevant to this theme include:

(1) the problem of democratic accountability for the conduct of foreign policy;[77]

(2) the question whether individuals and groups are bound by as well as

[74] T. M. Franck, *The Power of Legitimacy among Nations* (OUP, New York, 1990), at p. 74.

[75] *ICJ Reports*, 1992, p. 240. The case was settled in August 1993 without giving the Court the opportunity finally to rule on this issue.

[76] I. Brownlie, *State Responsibility* (Oxford, Clarendon Press, 1983), at pp. 165–6, 175–6, 177–8, with references to the work of the ILC and to arbitral jurisprudence.

[77] See, e.g., A. Cassese (ed.), *Parliamentary Foreign Affairs Committees: The National Setting* (Oceana, NY, 1982); P. R. Trimble, 'Foreign Affairs Law and Democracy', *Michigan Law Review*, 91 (1990), p. 1371; Symposium, 'Parliamentary Participation in the Making and Operation of Treaties', *Chicago-Kent Law Review*, 67 (1991), p. 293.

beneficiaries of human rights law, and how that can be reconciled with democratic tenets.[78] In this context it is worth noting that even Sir Hersch Lauterpacht, the great early proponent of international human rights, accepted that the rule that individuals have no independent position in international law was a matter of 'moral principle'. Presumably the basis of this 'moral principle' is the fact that individuals have little or no role—and certainly no formal role—in making international law.[79] The problem has become all the more urgent in view of the revival of the idea of international criminal trials;[80]

(3) the relationship between democratic principle and respect for minority rights,[81] as well as the position of indigenous peoples in those countries where there are surviving indigenous societies;[82]

(4) the issue of democratization of international organizations, both global[83] and regional—in the European context, the issue of democratization of the European Community (the so-called democratic deficit),[84]

[78] See M. Forde, 'Non-governmental Interference with Human Rights', this *Year Book*, 56 (1985), p. 153; N. S. Rodley, 'Can Armed Opposition Groups Violate Human Rights?' in K. E. Mahoney and P. Mahoney, *Human Rights in the Twenty-first Century* (Martinus Nijhoff, Dordrecht, 1992), p. 297; C. M. Vázquez, 'Treaty-based Rights and Remedies of Individuals', *Columbia Law Review*, 92 (1992), p. 1082; J. J. Paust, 'The Other Side of Right: Private Duties under Human Rights Law', *Harvard Human Rights Journal*, 5 (1992), p. 51. The Inter-American Commission of Human Rights has on several occasions condemned violations of the American Convention by 'groups': Press Release No. 8/92, 22 July 1992 (Peru), Press Release No. 2/93, 17 February 1993 (Colombia).

[79] E. Lauterpacht (ed.), *International Law, being the Collected Papers of Hersch Lauterpacht* (CUP, Cambridge, 1970), vol. 1, p. 141. But Sir Hersch referred also to 'numerous exceptions which the practice of States has already grafted' on to that principle, and went on to argue that individuals are, and should be, 'the true subjects of international law' (ibid., p. 148)—although without addressing the question how they should contribute to its making.

[80] See International Law Commission, Revised Report of the Working Group on the Draft Statute for an International Criminal Court (A/CN.4/L.490 & Add.1, 19 July 1993); SC Res. 827, 25 May 1993.

[81] The Declaration on the Rights of Persons belonging to National or Ethnic, Religious and Linguistic Minorities, adopted by GA Res. 47/135, 18 December 1992, refers to the promotion of minority rights 'within a democratic framework based on the rule of law' (preambular para. 6), but does not expressly address this issue in the operative paragraphs. Cf. however Arts. 2(2) (right to participate effectively in public life), 8(4) (reservation of territorial integrity of States). For text see *International Legal Materials*, 32 (1993), p. 912. Cf. European Charter for Regional or Minority Languages, Strasbourg, 5 November 1992 (*European Treaty Series*, No. 148), which refers to 'the principles of democracy and cultural diversity within the framework of national sovereignty and territorial integrity' (Preamble, para. 6). See further P. Thornberry, *International Law and the Rights of Minorities* (Oxford, Clarendon Press, 1991), esp. Part IV.

[82] See, e.g., Australian Law Reform Commission 31, *The Recognition of Aboriginal Customary Laws* (AGPS, Canberra, 1986), vol. 2, ch. 39; I. Brownlie, *Treaties and Indigenous Peoples* (Oxford, Clarendon Press, 1992), esp. ch. 2, Thornberry, op. cit. above (n. 81), Part VI; M. E. Turpel, 'Indigenous Peoples' Rights of Political Participation and Self-determination', *Cornell International Law Journal*, 25 (1992), p. 579.

[83] See, e.g., D. Archibugi, 'The Reform of the UN and Cosmopolitan Democracy: A Critical Review', *Journal of Peace Research*, 30 (1993), p. 1.

[84] See, e.g., R. Beiber, 'Democratic Control of European Foreign Policy', *European Journal of International Law*, 1 (1991), p. 148, at p. 151. The European Court of Justice has made the most of its few opportunities in this field, and of the Parliament's limited role: e.g. *Roquette Frères* v. *Council of the European Communities*, [1984/4] ECR 3333 (failure to consult Parliament as required by Treaty invalidates measures adopted by the Council).

and the role of the democratic idea as a contested term in the Maastricht Treaty.[85]

Another and most important element concerns the growing role of non-governmental organizations in this field.[86]

Let me conclude with a few provisos. The first is, obviously, that democracy is not everything. It is a procedural principle which embodies a substantive value, and both the substantive value and the effectiveness of the procedures which are used to embody it remain under challenge. It is easy to overstate the depth or durability of the democratic revival, although we can be hopeful about it. Democratic regimes can violate rights, especially of minorities.[87] There is the problem of public alienation from political structures and political parties, evidenced for example by the declining membership of political parties in many countries. There are countervailing factors such as the growth of fundamentalism and of ethnic conflict. At a time of greater possibilities and expectations there are greater problems. These problems should put an end to the facile millenarianism that was an immediate product of 1989. Someone once asked the Chinese leader Chou En-Lai to assess the consequences of the French revolution of 1789. He said it was too soon to tell. Whether or not that is true of 1789, it is certainly true of 1989.

Obviously this is a difficult area, acutely difficult, and the role of international law in responding to it is correspondingly difficult. The difficulty was encapsulated by Sir Henry Maine, who asked how 'when the forces at work are so enormous . . . shall they be controlled, diminished, or reduced by a mere literary agency?'[88] If international law is a merely literary agency the question is unanswerable.

But international law in its relationship with practice is better described as an intellectual activity, carried out for practical purposes, though in more or less literary form. And an increasing proportion of our

[85] Treaty on European Union, Maastricht, 7 February 1992. The Treaty makes no essential change in the position of the European Parliament, although it is given a greater role in relation to grievances and maladministration, and there are changes to electoral arrangements (Arts. 137–138*e* as amended). The term 'democracy' is referred to in the preamble. Title 1, Art. A, describes the Treaty as regulating relations between member States and their peoples. Art. F stipulates that member States' governmental systems ('founded on the principles of democracy') are to be respected: this appears to be a declaratory, not a normative, provision. Title 2 inserts a new Part dealing with citizenship of the Union, but voting rights do not extend to voting for national as distinct from municipal elections. Art. 130*u* (Development Co-operation) provides that community policy should contribute 'to the general objectives of developing and consolidating democracy and the rule of law' (i.e. democracy for others). Similarly Title V, Art J.1(2). That is all.

[86] e.g. the Democratic Audit of the United Kingdom: see D. Beetham, *Auditing Democracy in Britain* (University of Essex Human Rights Centre, Democratic Audit Paper No. 1, London, 1993). Generally see A. M. Micon and B. Lindsnaes (eds.), *The Role of Voluntary Organizations in Emerging Democracies* (Danish Centre for Human Rights, Copenhagen, 1993).

[87] e.g. the Peruvian counter-insurgency: see A. Cornell and K. Roberts, 'Democracy, Counterinsurgency and Human Rights: The Case of Peru', *Human Rights Quarterly*, 12 (1990), p. 529.

[88] H. S. Maine, *International Law* (The Whewell Lectures, 1887; John Murray, London, 1888), at p. 7.

activity, our property, our social structures is intellectual rather than material. In his inaugural lecture, Sir Robert Jennings said: 'It is obvious today that a community of rival sovereignties, which claim to be above the law or which, while professing submission to it, in fact refuse to recognize its supremacy, cannot escape self-destruction. The only mechanism by which a viable international society of States can be reached is through effective submission to a developing international law.'[89] If that was obvious in 1958, it is even more obvious now.

And what should be noted is Sir Robert's reference to 'a developing international law'. Amid vast political change international law cannot but change. It is interesting to note that John Westlake—often viewed as the prototype of a positivist international lawyer—was not content with the definition of international law as 'the body of rules prevailing between States', but saw it also in broader terms, as 'human action not internal to a political body'.[90] He would have accepted that what was 'internal' or domestic to a particular political body could change with time, and is a relative matter. And this is because the emphasis of his definition was on 'rules of action' which develop and change. The difficulty is to envision appropriate forms of change, and at the same time to hold to those aspects of international law which embody the stable outcomes of the interaction between peoples, societies and their governments over many years.

[89] R. Y. Jennings, 'The Progress of International Law', this *Year Book*, 34 (1958), p. 334, at p. 355.

[90] Introductory Lecture' (17 October 1888) in L. Oppenheim (ed.), *The Collected Papers of John Westlake* (Cambridge, 1914), p. 393, at p. 393. It is true that in his 'Chapters on the Principles of International Law' (1894), in *Collected Papers*, vol. 1, p. 1, he gave the more conventional definition, but he immediately qualified it by saying that international law could also be described 'as the body of rules governing the relations of a State to all outside it', and his later discussion retains some of the more dynamic approach of his Introductory Lecture.

[3]

Democracy and international law

GREGORY H. FOX AND BRAD R. ROTH*

Abstract. The voluminous literature on recent transitions to democracy has generally lacked an analysis from the perspective of international law. This article explores four aspects of efforts to promote a normative 'democratic entitlement'. First, it reviews the ways in which notions of democratic legitimacy have infiltrated virtually every aspect of international legal discourse. Second, it explores how a normative legitimacy standard may alter foundational doctrines of international law, such as non-intervention and the recognition of states and governments. Third, it reviews arguments against the emergence of 'democratic entitlement'. These arguments both take issue with the sources of law relied upon by the entitlement's proponents, and ask whether the substantive and procedural aspects of democracy implicit in the democratic entitlement thesis are conceptually coherent. Finally, the article explores the ways in which a legal analysis of democratization confronts questions not addressed by the methodologies of other disciplines.

1. Introduction

Prior to the events of 1989–91, 'democracy' was a word rarely found in the writings of international lawyers.[1] Most legal scholars, and certainly most states, accepted the 1987 view of the American Law Institute that 'international law does not generally address domestic constitutional issues, such as how a national government is formed'.[2] Apart from its use in resolutions repudiating 'alien, colonial, and racist' domination, the term 'democratic' appeared in collective pronouncements as a mere platitude, so abstract as to encompass opposite interpretations. Although human rights instruments such as the International Covenant on Civil and Political Rights (ICCPR) had long provided for a right to political participation,[3] the diversity (and, in the case of Cold War participants, mutual hostility) of governmental systems in the international 'community' had precluded consensus on the specifications of this

* This article is adapted from the Introduction to *Democratic Governance and International Law* (Cambridge: Cambridge University Press, 2000), edited by the authors.

[1] For a discussion of doctrine and scholarship on this question prior to the end of the Cold War, see the essays in Gregory H. Fox and Brad R. Roth (eds.), *Democratic Governance and International Law* (Cambridge: Cambridge University Press, 2000).

[2] American Law Institute, *Restatement (Third) of the Foreign Relations Law of the United States*, sec. 203, comment e (1987).

[3] Article 25 of the ICCPR provides:

Every citizen shall have the right and the opportunity, without any of the distinctions mentioned in article 2 and without unreasonable restrictions:

(a) To take part in the conduct of public affairs, directly or through freely chosen representatives;

(b) To vote and to be elected at genuine periodic elections which shall be by universal and equal suffrage and shall be held by secret ballot, guaranteeing the free expression of the will of the electors;

(c) To have access, on general terms of equality, to public service in his country.

right.[4] Moreover, any assertion of a determinate 'right to democratic governance' would have suggested criteria of governmental legitimacy at odds with the 'effective control' doctrine that had long prevailed in the recognition practices of most states and intergovernmental organizations.

The United Nations, an organization founded on the principle of the sovereign equality of ideologically-diverse states, seemed an unlikely vehicle to further a specific mode of internal governance. Although the UN had an extensive history of monitoring elections and referenda in states emerging from colonialism, it did not send a monitoring mission to a sovereign state until the 1990 elections in Nicaragua.[5] Even after the UN Security Council began using its long-dormant Chapter VII powers to address humanitarian catastrophes arising from civil conflict, there seemed little prospect that the organization would get into the business of imposing solutions to internal power struggles, let alone that it would invoke liberal-democratic criteria in dictating outcomes. Regional intergovernmental organizations, despite occasional rhetorical commitments to political democracy[6], appeared scarcely more disposed to enter the fray.

Whatever one is to make of the developments in the 1990s, it is now clear that international law and international organizations are no longer indifferent to the internal character of regimes exercising effective control within sovereign states. In region after region, political change has swept through the former bastions of authoritarian and dictatorial rule, offering the promise, if not always the reality, of democratization, and this development has been reflected in international institutions. The status and determinacy of the right to political participation have been enhanced by pronouncements of the ICCPR Human Rights Committee,[7] the UN Human Rights Commission,[8] the European and Inter-American Commissions on Human Rights,[9] the Organization of American States (OAS),[10] the Organization for

[4] See generally Henry J. Steiner, 'Political Participation as a Human Right', *Harvard Human Rights Year Book* 1 (1988), p. 77. The impression that participatory rights could not transcend ideological conflict was reinforced by the US Government's invocations of that right in support of Cold War policies. See, for instance, Cynthia Brown (ed.), *With Friends Like These: The Americas Watch Report on Human Rights and US Policy in Latin America* (New York: Pantheon Books, 1985), pp. 3–23.

[5] See Yves Biegbeder, *International Monitoring of Plebiscites, Referenda and National Elections* (Dordrecht: Martinus Nijhoff, 1994), pp. 164–9.

[6] The 1948 Charter of the Organization of American States declares that 'representative democracy is an indispensable condition for the stability, peace and development of the region'. The 1950 European Convention for the Protection of Human Rights and Fundamental Freedoms states in its preamble that 'an effective political democracy is essential to the protection of fundamental freedoms'.

[7] Human Rights Committee, General Comment 25 (57), UN Doc. CCPR/C/21/Rev.1/Add.7 (1996) (elaborating the nature of the right to political participation in ICCPR, article 25); Bwalya v. Zambia, Commun. no. 314/1988, UN Doc. CCPR/C/48/D/314/1988 (1993), reprinted in *Human Rights Law Journal* 14 (1993), p. 408 (opining against the barring of electoral candidates who are not members of the ruling party).

[8] Promotion of the Right to Democracy, Commission on Human Rights Resolution 1999/57 (27 April 1999).

[9] See Greek Case, *1969 Yearbook of the European Convention in Human Rights* 179, 180 (Eur. Comm'n of HR); Case of the Socialist Party and Others v. Turkey, Case no. 20/1997/804/1007 (Eur. Ct. H. R. 1998); *Matthews v. United Kingdom*, App. No. 24833/94 (1999); *Mexico Elections Decision*, Cases 9768, 9780, 9828, Inter-American Commission on Human Rights 97, 108, OEA/Ser.L/V/11.77, doc. 7, rev. 1 (1990).

[10] See AG/RES. 1080 (XXI-0/91) (5th plen. sess., June 5, 1991) ('Representative Government' resolution coinciding with the 'Santiago Commitment to Democracy and the Renewal of the Inter-American System'); OEA/Ser.P/AG/doc.11 (XVI-E/92) (14 December 1992) (Charter amendment providing for suspension from participation in the OAS General Assembly of a state whose democratically-elected government is forcibly overthrown).

Security and Cooperation in Europe (OSCE),[11] and the UN General Assembly.[12] The UN and other intergovernmental organizations have invested heavily in the crafting and monitoring of electoral processes in many nations across the globe.[13] On two occasions, the international community has responded vigorously to military coups against elected governments, endorsing the use of external armed force to restore the deposed governments of Jean-Bertrand Aristide in Haiti in 1994 and Ahmad Tejan Kabbah in Sierra Leone in 1998.[14] So commonly espoused is the commitment to democratic institutions that the UN Secretary-General could assert in 1997 as 'an established norm' the view that 'military coups against democratically elected Governments by self-appointed juntas are not acceptable'.[15]

There can be little doubt that this unprecedented international attention to the internal governing structures of states has significant implications for the current content and future direction of international law. Legal scholars have only recently begun to assess these developments and to ask whether there can meaningfully be said to be, in Thomas Franck's pioneering words, a 'democratic entitlement' in international law.[16] Franck defines the democratic entitlement in words borrowed from the American Declaration of Independence: governments derive 'their just powers from the consent of the governed'.[17] To this traditional principle of contractarianism he adds a crucial second component, relating not to the legitimating authority of citizen consent but to the role of international actors in national processes of legitimation. Franck contends that the international community, acting through increasingly standardized legal mechanisms, now plays a crucial role in both the establishment and maintenance of national democratic institutions. Franck concludes, in the words of the Declaration, that each nation achieves 'separate and equal station' in the international community by demonstrating 'a decent respect to the opinions of mankind'.[18] Whether, and to what extent, that 'separate and equal station' is contingent on comportment with a determinate 'democratic' norm is, nonetheless, an intricate and controversial question.

It is the thesis of this article that the analytical tools of international law are now essential to a full understanding of collective initiatives in support of democratic governance. If these initiatives are to be fully understood, in other words, they must be conceptualized as having definable normative goals and as emerging within the larger body of international legal institutions. In the absence of a legal analysis, we

[11] See Conference on Security and Co-operation in Europe, Document of the Moscow Meeting, 3 October 1991, paras. 17.1, 17.2, 30, *International Legal Materials* (1991), pp. 1670, 1677 (condemning forces seeking to overthrow a freely and fairly elected government and pledging to 'support vigorously, in accordance with the Charter of the United Nations', the 'legitimate organs' of that State).

[12] See, for example, GA Res. 45/150 (1990) (on 'Enhancing the effectiveness of the principle of periodic and genuine elections').

[13] Biegbeder, *International Monitoring*.

[14] See SC Res. 940 (1994) (authorizing armed intervention in Haiti); UN Doc. S/PRST/1998/5 (Security Council Presidential Statement welcoming the removal of the Sierra Leonean junta); S.C. Res. 1162 (1998) (commending ECOWAS after the fact for its role in the Sierra Leonean transition).

[15] Annual Report of the Secretary-General on the Work of the Organization, UN Doc. A/52/1 (1997), para. 37.

[16] Thomas M. Franck, 'The Emerging Right to Democratic Governance', *American Journal of International Law*, 86 (1992), p. 46.

[17] Ibid. p. 46.

[18] Ibid.

will fail to understand both the systemic consequences and the inherent limitations of collective democratic initiatives.

2. Democratization and the international system

It once seemed incontrovertible that, given the range of ideologies and institutional structures of member states, the international system was, by its very nature, neutral on the subject of the internal character, let alone legitimacy, of domestic regimes. The recent wave of democratization, however, has had ramifications for the conduct of international organizations, and consequently for international law.

The end of the Cold War occasioned a challenging new role for international organizations as architects for the rebuilding of shattered states in the developing world. In countries from Nicaragua to El Salvador to Cambodia to Angola to Bosnia to Sierra Leone, it has become almost a given that international organizations will culminate their efforts at national reconciliation with the holding of democratic elections. Not once has the international community proposed that a new, post-conflict government be chosen in any other way.[19]

What began as an adjunct to conflict resolution has grown to a broader, institutionalized legitimating function. Many international organizations now maintain permanent electoral assistance divisions. From 1992 to August 1999, the United Nations Electoral Assistance Division provided various forms of electoral assistance to over 70 states, most of them in Africa, and most without the former predicate of a recently ended civil war.[20] Between 1990 and 1995 the European Union (EU) provided electoral assistance to forty-four different countries.[21] Similar statistics could be quoted for the OAS and the Office for Democratic Institutions and Human Rights of the OSCE. Many of these missions end with the organization determining whether the elections have been conducted according to criteria of fairness that have essentially achieved boilerplate status.[22] Necessarily, a determination as to whether an election was conducted properly speaks to the legitimacy of the purported victor's mandate to govern.

[19] See Edward Kofi Quashigah, 'Legitimate Governance in Africa: The Responsibility of the International Community,' in Edward Kofi Quashigah and Obicra Chinedu Okafor, (eds.), *Legitimate Governance in Africa* (The Hague: Kluwer 1999), pp. 461–85; Report of the Secretary-General, Support by the United Nations System of the Efforts of Governments to Promote and Consolidate New or Restored Democracies, UN Doc. A/53/554 and corr. 1 (1998); Luc Reychler, 'Democratic Peacebuilding and Conflict Prevention,' in Karel Wellens (ed.), *International Law: Theory and Practice – Essays in Honor of Eric Suy* (The Hague: Nijhoff, 1998); Sonia K. Han, Note: 'Building a Peace that Lasts: the United Nations and Post-Civil War Peace Building', *New York University Journal of International Law and Politics*, 26 (1994), pp. 837–92. Some may find contrary principles at work in the decision of the High Representative for Bosnia/Herzegovina to remove elected Bosnian Serb President Nikola Poplasen from office in March 1999. *OHR Press Release* (5 March 1999).

[20] *Main Types of Assistance Activities* (Electoral Assistance Division, United Nations Department of Political Affairs, 2000), p. 5, available at: www.un.crg/Depts/dpa/ead/Websites.htm.

[21] Report from the Commission on the Implementation of Measures Intended to Promote Observance of Human Rights and Democratic Principles, COM(96)672 (1997), p. 6.

[22] These are set out in detail in the UN Center for Human Rights' *Human Rights and Elections: A Handbook on the Legal, Technical and Human Rights Aspects of Elections* (Geneva: United Nations, 1994).

Such judgments sharply contradict the traditional international law maxim that the selection of national leaders is quintessentially a matter of exclusive domestic jurisdiction.[23] At the same time, such developments must be seen in context: international organizations are now involved in virtually every aspect of national policymaking, from budgeting priorities to labour issues to the eradication of official corruption. It is not self-evident that a great legal distance exists between weighing in on these important questions of policy and having a say in the selection of policymakers themselves.

The legal innovations related to democratic governance may be described as having both qualitative and quantitative aspects. The qualitative innovations involve defining various aspects of 'democracy'. No generally agreed definition has yet emerged, though most international actors using the term appear, at a minimum, to refer to the familiar pairing of free and fair elections and certain 'counter-majoritarian' political rights. Elections, as the procedural embodiment of 'popular sovereignty', are particularly emphasized,[24] though the UN Human Rights Commission recently included elections as only one of a long list of 'rights of democratic governance'.[25]

What has been made increasingly clear, at least in the jurisprudence of human rights bodies, is what democracy does *not* mean. Whereas the issue was off-limits during the Cold War years, several international institutions have expressly denied that the one-party state allows sufficient electoral choice to comport with treaty standards.[26] Similarly, these bodies have placed a heavy burden of justification on efforts to ban specific political parties as threats to national security or to the identity of the state.[27] With a drastic increase in their caseload, human rights bodies have developed an increasingly rich jurisprudence that has sought to bound the once open-ended debate over the nature of democratic institutions.

The quantitative changes relate to the infiltration of concerns for democratic legitimacy into virtually every aspect of international legal discourse. Pertinent developments include the following:

[23] As Oppenheim stated in the first edition of his influential treatise: 'The Law of Nations prescribes no rules as regards the kind of head a State may have. Every State is, naturally, independent regarding this point, possessing the faculty of adopting any Constitution according to its discretion'. *Lassa Oppenheim, International Law*, vol. 1 (London: Longmans Green, 1905), p. 403.

[24] Kurt Herndl, 'The Case-Law of the Commission as Regards the Right to Free Elections (Article 3 of protocol 1)', in *The Birth of European Human Rights Law*, Michele de Salvia and Marti E. Villiger (eds.) (Baden-Baden: Nomos Verlagsgesellschaft 1998): ('the right of an individual to take part in elections is quintessential for any democratic society and any democratic State'.)

[25] This non-exclusive list refers to (a) the rights to freedom of opinion and expression, of thought, conscience and religion, and of peaceful association and assembly; (b) the right to freedom to seek, receive and impart information and ideas through any media; (c) the rule of law; (d) the right of universal and equal suffrage, as well as free voting procedures and periodic and free elections; (e) the right to political participation; (f) transparent and accountable government institutions; (g) the right of citizens to choose their government system though constitutional or other democratic means; and (h) equal access to public service. Promotion of the Right to Democracy, Comm. HR Res. 1999/57 (27 April 1999) (approved by a vote of 51–0–2).

[26] See the discussion in Gregory H. Fox, 'The Right to Political Participation in International Law,' in Fox and Roth, *Democratic Governance*.

[27] Ibid., pp. 55–9.

- States and international lenders have started to withhold development assistance from states unwilling to pursue democratic reforms.[28]
- Military coups, once marginal events in the eyes of international law, are increasingly condemned as illegitimate exercises of state power.[29]
- States and international organizations that once professed either not to view recognition of new governments as a legal matter, or took the view that any regime in effective control of territory was entitled to recognition, have increasingly invoked democratic criteria in their recognition decisions.[30]
- The EU, the OAS and MERCOSUR now condition full membership on the maintenance of political democracy.[31]
- The EU now predicates its adherence to new treaty obligations on other parties' observance of democratic norms. All new EU treaties specify observance of democratic principles as an essential element of the accord, a material breach of which would permit the Union to suspend compliance with its treaty obligations.[32]
- The claim has been made, though it has yet to be generally accepted, that the transition to democratic rule is so profound as to constitute a 'fundamental

[28] Stephen Haggard and Steven B. Webb (eds.), *Voting for Reform: Democracy, Political Liberalization and Economic Adjustment* (New York: Oxford University Press, 1994); Leila L. Frischtak, *Governance Capacity and Economic Reform in Developing Countries*, World Bank Technical Paper no. 254 (1994).

[29] The African Commission on Human Rights has called upon 'incumbent military governments to hand over political power to democratically elected governments without prolonging their incumbencies and unnecessarily delaying the return to democratic civilian rule'. 'Resolution on the Military,' in *Eighth Annual Activity Report of the Commission on Human and Peoples' Rights*, 1994–5, Thirty-First Ordinary Session, 26–28 June 1995, Addis Ababa, Ethiopia 42 (1995). The Secretary-General of the Commonwealth stated in a June 1999 speech that 'no longer would the Commonwealth tolerate any one of its members slipping back into military rule or one-party dictatorship'. Cultures of Democracy: A Commonwealth Perspective (21 June 1999), available at: www.thecommonwealth.org/htm/info/info/speeches1997-1.htm. When Pakistan's elected government was ousted by the military on 12 October 1999, a Commonwealth Ministerial Action Group condemned the coup as 'a serious violation of the Commonwealth's fundamental political principles' and suspended Pakistan from all councils of the organization. Commonwealth News Release 99/60 (18 October 1999).

[30] Sean D. Murphy, 'Democratic Legitimacy and Recognition of States and Governments', *International and Comparative Law Quarterly*, 48 (1999), pp. 545–81.

[31] The Maastricht Treaty on European Union provides that democracy and respect for human rights, as set forth in the European Convention on Human Rights, shall be pre-conditions for membership in the European Union. Treaty on European Union, Title I(F), *International Legal Materials*, 31 (1992), p. 256. The Washington Protocol to the OAS Charter provides for the suspension from the General Assembly of any member state whose democratically constituted government has been overthrown by force. OAE/Ser.P, AG/doc.11 (XVI-E/92), rev. 1 (1992). MERCOSUR's 1996 Protocol of Ushuaia provides that any disruption of democracy in a member state may lead to the suspension of that state's right to participate in MERCOSUR organs and a suspension of its rights under the preferential trade instruments promulgated by the organization. *Protocol de Ushuaia Sobre Compromiso Democrático en el Mercosur, la Republica de Bolivia y la Republica de Chile*, arts. 4 and 5 (1996), available at *www.idrc.ca/lacro/investigacion/mercosur2.html*. The member states of MERCOSUR are Argentina, Brazil, Paraguay and Uruguay.

[32] *On the Inclusion of Respect for Democratic Principles and Human Rights in Agreements between the Community and Third Countries*, COM(95)215 (1995). Democratic principles are defined by reference to the Helsinki Final Act, Aug. 1, 1975, ILM 14, p. 1292, and the OSCE Charter of Paris, 21 Nov., 1990, ILM 30 (1991), p. 190. See Frank Hoffmeister, *Menschenrechts und Demokratie-Klauseln in den vertraglichen Aussenbeziehungen der Europäischen Gemeinschaft* (Berlin: Springer 1998); Barbara Brandtner and Allan Rosas, 'Human Rights and the External Relations of the European Community: an Analysis of Doctrine and Practice', *European Journal of International Law*, 9 (1998), pp. 473–77.

change in circumstances', permitting a newly democratic state to discard treaty obligations assumed by a previous, non-democratic regime.[33]

As notions of democratic legitimacy diffuse throughout the international legal system, one can identify at least four broad justifications for including democratization as a concern of the international law. A crucial feature of these justifications is that they do not simply repeat arguments about democracy found in political theory. While some overlapping with democratic political theory is certainly evident, these arguments address not only the well-being of citizens within democratic systems but the distinctive interests of the international community as well.

The first justification is a perceived connection between competitive multiparty elections and the range of other internationally protected human rights. For reasons of Cold War politics—relating primarily to the impossibility of agreement that free and fair elections were a human right on par with core norms such as the right against torture—these two categories have been consistently described in discrete terms: democracy *and* human rights.[34] Nonetheless, international organizations increasingly assert that a commitment to the principles of choice, transparency and pluralism that mark political democracy is essential to securing an institutionalized protection of other human rights.[35] This is hardly a new insight: the mutually reinforcing nature of broad political participation and individual freedom has been a major theme in Western political thought over the past two centuries.[36]

Second, democratization is increasingly regarded as a means of preventing internal armed conflict, which in the 1990s was unrivalled as the leading form of

[33] Gabcíkovo-Nagymaros Project (Hungary/Slovakia), 1997 ICJ 1, para.104 (International Court of Justice rejects Hungary's claim that 'profound changes of a political nature' in Eastern Europe, in combination with other factors, constituted a 'fundamental change in circumstances').

[34] See Vienna Declaration and Programme of Action, UN Doc. A/Conf. 157/23, para. 8 (1993) ('[t]he international community should support the strengthening and promoting of democracy, development and respect for human rights'); Annual Report of the Secretary-General on the Work of the Organization, UN Doc. A/52/1, para. 22 *et seq.* (section of report entitled 'Governance, Human Rights and Democratization'); Case C-268/94, Portugese Republic v. Council of the European Union, 1996–12 ECJ Rep. 6177, 6217 (1996) (article 130u(2) of the EC Treaty 'demonstrates the importance to be attached to respect for human rights and democratic principles'); Case 10.956, Inter-Am. CHR (Mexico), reprinted in *Annual Report of the Inter-American Commission on Human Rights 1993* (1994), p. 269 ('[t]he close relationship between representative democracy as a form of government and the exercise of the political rights so defined, also presupposes the exercise of other fundamental rights'); Final Declaration and Action Plan on Human Rights and Democracy of the Council of Europe's Second Summit Meeting of Heads of State and Governments 1997 (1997), reprinted in *International Human Rights Reports*, 5 (1998), p. 581 (reaffirming 'attachment to the fundamental principles of the Council of Europe—pluralist democracy, respect for human rights, the rule of law').

[35] Report of the Secretary-General: Supplement to Reports on Democratization, UN Doc. A/51/761 (Annex), para. 3 (1996) ('the practice of democracy is increasingly regarded as essential to progress on a wide range of human concerns and to the protection of human rights'); Inter-American Commission on Human Rights, *Ten Years of Activities 1971–1981* (1982), p. 337 ('the democratic context is the necessary element for the establishment of a political society where human rights can thrive to their fullest').

[36] See, for instance, James Madison, *The Federalist*, nos. 39, 51, in Michael Kammen (ed.), *The Origins of the American Constitution: A Documentary History* (New York: Penguin Books, 1986), pp. 180–86, 202–12; Benjamin Constant, 'The Liberty of the Ancients Compared With That of the Moderns', in Benjamin Constant, (trans.) Biancamaria Fontana, *Political Writings* (Cambridge: Cambridge University Press, 1988), p. 323; John Stuart Mill, 'Considerations on Representative Government', in *Utilitarianism, On Liberty, and Considerations on Representative Government* (London: J. M. Dent, 1972), p. 171.

deadly strife.[37] Democratization is said to address the exclusionary politics lying at the heart of civil conflicts. As UN Secretary-General Kofi Annan has stated, 'in the absence of genuinely democratic institutions, contending interests are likely to seek to settle their differences through conflict rather than through accommodation'.[38] In the Secretary-General's words, 'democratization gives people a stake in society. Its importance cannot be overstated, for unless people feel that they have a true stake in society lasting peace will not be possible.'[39]

Third, and relatedly, democratization has been asserted as a key to peace among states. The widely reported finding that democratic states do not go to war with one another, though not uncontroversial in its particulars,[40] has led many to link the international community's security interests to the promotion of democratic governance within states.

Finally, a range of emerging international norms, unrelated to democratization, have come to rely upon implementation through democratic processes. Three examples of this phenomenon can be found in the international efforts to protect the environment, to fight official corruption, and to promote the rights of indigenous peoples.[41] In each of these cases, instruments establishing the regimes provide for the maximum degree of popular participation in formulating strategies for implementing a state's international obligations. The 1992 Rio Declaration on Environment and Development, for example, in setting out a broad range of regulatory challenges, provides that '[e]nvironmental issues are best handled with the participation of all concerned citizens'.[42] The instruments also require the sort of transparent decision-making processes and free flow of information that are typical of democratic systems.[43] Indeed, it has been asserted more broadly that the increasingly complex demands of multilateral treaty regimes cannot easily be fulfilled by unrepresentative, non-transparent national institutions[44]—this quite apart from the

[37] In approving an electoral monitoring mission at the end of a long and brutal civil war in Liberia, for example, the Security Council declared 'that the holding of free and fair elections as scheduled is an essential phase of the peace process in Liberia.' SC Res. 1100 (1997). See also SC Res. 1116 (1997) (same).

[38] Report of the Secretary-General: *The Causes of Conflict and the Promotion of Durable Peace and Sustainable Development in Africa* (1998), para. 77.

[39] Ibid., para. 78.

[40] For a collection of scholarly articles on both sides of the 'democratic peace' controversy, see Michael E. Brown, Sean M. Lynn-Jones and Steven E. Miller (eds.), *Debating the Democratic Peace* (Cambridge, MA: MIT Press, 1996).

[41] For an extended discussion of these points, see Remarks of Gregory H. Fox, 'Implementing Democratization: What Role for International Organizations?' *Proceedings of the American Society of International Law*, 91 (1997), pp. 360–2.

[42] UN Doc. A/CONF. 151/PC/WG.III/L.33/Dev. 1 (1992). See also, Jonas Ebbesson, 'Public Participation in International Environmental Law', *Yearbook of International Environmental Law*, 8 (1997), pp. 51–97.

[43] The United Nations Economic Commission for Europe, for example, has devoted an entire treaty to the participatory aspects of environmental law-making. *Convention on Access to Information, Public Participation in Decision-Making and Access to Justice in Environmental Matters*, UN Doc. ECE/CEP/43 (1998). Article 1 provides that in order to protect the right of every person to live in a healthy environment, 'each Party shall guarantee the rights of access to information, public participation in decision-making, and access to justice in environmental matters in accordance with the provisions of this Convention'.

[44] Gregory H. Fox, 'Strengthening the State', *Indiana Journal of Global Legal Studies*, 7 (1999), pp. 35–77.

general question of whether democracies are more likely than other states to adhere to treaty commitments.[45]

In the *Tinoco* Arbitration, William Howard Taft famously held that non-recognition of governments on the ground of illegitimacy of origin was not a postulate of international law and did not secure general acquiescence.[46] Intervening events, however, have cast doubt on this conventional wisdom, and have raised the question of the emergence of a right to democratic governance in international law. Such an emergent right, if established, is so thoroughly at odds with traditional conceptions of state sovereignty as to augur a major transformation of the ground rules of the international system.

3. The 'democratic entitlement' thesis: scope and consequences

Because the assertion of a 'democratic entitlement' in international law is grounded in the right to political participation as established in Article 21 of the Universal Declaration of Human Rights (UDHR), Article 25 of the ICCPR, and the counterpart articles of regional human rights instruments, the questions posed by the thesis may, at first glance, appear confined to the human rights treaty system. As that system provides for only the most limited of remedies and notoriously lacks efficacious enforcement mechanisms, one might well imagine that the specification of its requirements in respect of political participation, as in respect of freedom of speech or religion or association, would be a development of limited significance to international law, organization, and relations overall.

Yet the right to political participation, at least as interpreted through the lens of the democratic entitlement, is unlike other human rights, for its individual enjoyment is inseparable from its collective effect. One participates in politics not solely (and usually not principally) for the fulfilment derived from the activity, but for the opportunity to affect the exercise of power in the polity. From the liberal-democratic perspective, to have the individual right to political participation is to have the collective right to oust a political leadership that fails to garner the support of at least a plurality of one's fellows. Article 21 of the UDHR, in a manner strikingly dissimilar to that of the document's other Articles and that of the ICCPR, speaks not merely of the individual right to take part in government, but also of the principle that '[t]he will of the people shall be the basis of the authority of government'.[47]

If the very basis of the authority of government can be said to rest, as a matter of international law, on the fulfilment of liberal-democratic participatory standards, the consequences will be wide-ranging. Indeed, if the sovereignty affirmed and protected by the international system is understood to be popular sovereignty, and popular sovereignty is understood to be predicated upon liberal democracy, the potential result is a revolutionary transformation of the full array of international norms,

45 Kurt Taylor Gaubatz, 'Democratic States and Commitment in International Relations', *International Organization*, 50 (1996), pp. 109–139.
46 Great Britain v. Costa Rica, 1923–24 Ann. Dig. Pub. Int'l L. Cas. 34, 37 (1923).
47 GA Res. 217 (III) (1948).

from norms governing recognition of states and governments to those governing the use of force. Thus, the most pointed interpretation of the democratic entitlement would permit unilateral armed intervention across state boundaries to depose a regime that has usurped an electoral mandate. In the words of W. Michael Reisman, the 'sovereignty' protected by contemporary international law 'is the people's sovereignty rather than the sovereign's sovereignty'.[48] From this, Reisman draws the conclusion that when the people's 'confirmed wishes are ignored by a local caudillo who either takes power himself or assigns it to a subordinate he controls, a jurist rooted in the late twentieth century can hardly say that the invasion by outside forces to remove the caudillo and install the elected government is a violation of national sovereignty'.[49]

It is by no means clear that the argument for a democratic entitlement need be taken to such a conclusion. Nonetheless, the democratic entitlement thesis generates a progression of path-breaking legal conclusions that has no clear stopping point. The progression can be elaborated as follows. The democratic entitlement thesis expressly embodies two assertions:

1. The right to political participation, however deliberately vague its specifications in human rights instruments that were adopted prior to the recent wave of liberal-democratic transitions, has now acquired a determinate content grounded in liberal-democratic institutional practices.
2. The right entails not merely the existence of appropriate participatory mechanisms, but also a determinate relationship between the mandated participatory mechanisms and the actual exercise of political power. As in the UDHR, but not the ICCPR, the individual right to cast a vote reflecting uncoerced choice is organically connected to the proposition that '[t]he will of the people shall be the basis of the authority of government'. The regime has a duty not merely to allow individuals 'to take part in government' through a consultative process, but also a duty to subject itself to the popular will — that is, to allow itself to be voted out of power.

From these two assertions, one can well infer a third:

3. The sovereignty affirmed by the international legal system belongs to the people, and can be cognizably asserted on the people's behalf only where the government conforms to the right to political participation; therefore, measures to implement democratic rights, undertaken by foreign states collectively and/or individually, need not respect the sovereign prerogatives of governments that violate those rights. This is especially so where a 'free and fair election' has actually taken place, and those elected have been denied, or ousted from, office by force of arms.

The third assertion is, of course, the critical one. The democratic entitlement literature is generally suggestive of this move, although the most often-cited works have

[48] W. Michael Reisman, 'Sovereignty and Human Rights in International Law', *American Journal of International Law*, 84 (1990), p. 869.

[49] Ibid., p. 871 (arguing for the legality of the US invasion of Panama).

avoided sweeping affirmations of it.[50] Acceptance of the third assertion is, perhaps, not compelled by acceptance of the first and second, but it is the logical next step.

The third assertion leaves open the practical question of how to further democratic development across borders. It does not necessarily mandate derecognition of regimes that fail to abide by international standards; proponents of the democratic entitlement neither assert as established law nor propose a mechanistic rule by which certificates of recognition, IGO delegation credentials, and diplomatic and trade relations are automatically to be denied to violators. Still less does the democratic entitlement thesis predict that measures will be taken to intervene in any particular state's internal affairs, whether by intrusive political or economic measures (for example, covert funding of opposition groups in violation of municipal law, or secondary boycotts to disrupt a state's trade relations) or by forcible measures (such as supply of insurgents or outright invasion).[51] Given the realities of international relations, none of these measures is likely to be used routinely against non-democratic governments.

What the democratic entitlement thesis does suggest, however, is that whereas intrusive political, economic, and military measures would previously have been excluded as violative of international law, they may now be included on the menu of lawful options for foreign powers seeking—collectively or perhaps even unilaterally—to implement democratization in a recalcitrant state. While limitations on aggressive promotion of democracy would continue to arise from considerations of efficacy and prudence, the bars traditionally posed by international law would be, at a minimum, open to question. In an international system that has repeatedly affirmed the sovereign right of each state to be free from the coercive interferences of others in its choice of political, economic, social, and cultural systems,[52] this alone is a revolutionary proposition.

Adherents of the democratic entitlement characterize it as an 'emerging' right. They understand full well that undemocratic regimes continue to be tolerated in the international community. They do not assert that state practice as yet manifests any legal *duties* of foreign states and intergovernmental organizations to adopt specific democracy-promoting measures. They are aware that expediency will ever under-

[50] See Thomas M. Franck, *The Empowered Self: Law and Society in the Age of Individualism* (New York: Oxford University Press, 2000), pp. 272–3 (asserting Security Council authority to licence 'military rescue of democracy', but insisting that international law does not 'permit any state, or any regional organization, to take enforcement of the democratic entitlement exclusively into its own hands'); Gregory H. Fox, 'The Right to Political Participation in International Law,' *Yale Journal of International Law*, 17 (1992), p. 595 ('regimes that thwart the will of the people lack legitimacy' to claim that the international community's insistence on participatory rights implementation violates national sovereignty, but 'it is still an open question as to how far this principle should be extended'); though see, for instance, Reisman, 'Sovereignty and Human Rights' (n. 48 above) advocating unilateral forcible measures; Lois Fielding, 'Taking the Next Step in the Development of New Human Rights: The Emerging Right of Humanitarian Assistance to Restore Democracy', *Duke Journal of Comparative and International Law*, 5 (1995), pp. 329–77; Malvina Halberstam, 'The Copenhagen Document: Intervention in Support of Democracy', *Harvard Journal of International Law*, 34 (1993), pp. 163–75; Anthony D'Amato, 'The Invasion of Panama Was a Lawful Response to Tyranny', *American Journal of International Law*, 84 (1990), pp. 516–24.

[51] In his seminal article, Thomas Franck warns that efforts to implement the democratic entitlement need 'to be uncoupled, in the clearest fashion, from a long history of unilateral enforcement of a tainted, colonialist "civilizing" mission'; he thus urges that 'all states unambiguously renounce the use of unilateral, or even regional, *military* force to compel compliance …' Franck, 'Emerging Right to Democratic Governance' (see n. 16 above) (emphasis in original).

[52] See GA Res 2625 (XXV) (1970) (the 'Friendly Relations Declaration').

mine consistency in efforts to promote democracy. They insist, however, that the legal door is now open to determined efforts to spur democratization, and that the failure to do good everywhere should not be seen as a bar to doing good anywhere.

4. Legal methodology and democratic norms

What can a legal analysis add to the already voluminous literature on democratization? This question implicates a much broader scholarly initiative to bring the tools of legal analysis to bear on the subject matter of international relations theory. One important insight of this scholarship is that interactions among international actors 'cannot be explained solely by the preferences and payoffs of the players; they are dependent in part on the *process* by which bargainers seek to resolve conflict or seek consensus'.[53] The emergence of a democratic entitlement has been marked precisely by innovations in normative and institutional processes. Since the end of the Cold War, the sources of international support for democratization have become increasingly multilateralized. Election monitoring, recognition decisions and even the use of military force in support of elected regimes have been undertaken pursuant to collective mandates issued by international organizations. If international support for democratization is indeed unfolding in a manner consistent with an emerging normative structure, then scholars must begin to employ analytical tools specifically designed to study these issues of process; that is, the tools of international law. A legal perspective on democratization initiatives promises a number of insights.

First, a legal analysis focuses attention on state consent to democratization initiatives, a consideration often missing from claims that these efforts represent the imposition of Western institutions on an unreceptive developing world. Developing states are long-standing members of the international organizations in which these initiatives originate. Frequently, as in the case of election monitoring, the initiatives begin with requests for assistance by a developing state. In other cases, when actions are taken over the objections of a target state, the organizations frequently act pursuant to specific legal mandates that permit the objections to be disregarded. Most of these initiatives, in other words, are taken pursuant to the consent of the developing state involved. The consent is either specific to the initiative or more general to the legal mandate permitting the organization to engage in certain types of coercive action.

International law endows such consensual acts with a presumptive legitimacy.[54] This process-based legitimacy stands apart from the truism that Western states wield

[53] Ann-Marie Slaughter, Andrew S. Tulumello and Stepan Wood, 'International Law and International Relations Theory: A New Generation of Interdisciplinary Scholarship', *American Journal of International Law*, 92 (1998), p. 387.

[54] See The Lotus Case (Fr. v. Turkey), 1927 PCIJ (ser. A) no. 10, p.18 ('[t]he rules of law binding upon States therefore emanate from their own free will as expressed in conventions or by usages generally accepted as expressing principles of law'). This presumption is embodied in the extraordinarily limited circumstances under which a State may opt out of a legal obligation binding under customary or treaty law. See *Vienna Convention on the Law of Treaties*, 23 May 1969, arts. 46–64, 1155 UNTS 331 (limited circumstances in which a treaty is deemed invalid, terminated or state performance is excused); Malcolm N. Shaw, *International Law*, 72 (4th edn., 1997) (newly created states, such as

substantial political power in bodies such as the UN Security Council. Powerful political actors influence legislative or quasi-legislative initiatives of all kinds, especially in domestic politics. In the absence of extraordinary circumstances, however, the political pressures and trade-offs surrounding passage of a legislative initiative are generally not taken as vitiating its legal legitimacy, assuming proper procedures have been followed.

If one nonetheless presses the critique that international legal processes are politicized to a degree rendering consent an empty formalism—masking exercises in Western cultural hegemony—that argument will have engaged issues of legal process generally absent from scholarship on democratization. Such a critique, for example, would need to address the substantial benefits developing states have derived from international law of the UN era: decolonization, the delegitimization of apartheid, the strengthening of norms against intervention, special dispensations in costly environmental regulatory schemes, and others. It is doubtful that any of these norms would have emerged in their present form without the multilateral institutions in which they were crafted. Developing states not only consented to these institutional processes but were active and vocal participants in creating the norms. In light of this confluence between means and ends, the focus on state consent afforded by a legal analysis assumes a central importance.

Second, a legal analysis confronts a paradox surrounding Cold War interventions by the United States (putatively) in support of democratic actors: how can law-based systems of government be installed by actions that are themselves, at best, of questionable legality? The prohibition on the unilateral use of force is generally considered to be the foundational norm of the postwar international legal order.[55] While some legal scholars find a right of unilateral intervention in customary international law,[56] an examination of 'pro-democratic' interventions in the UN era reveals that virtually none received substantial international support. Indeed, many were overwhelmingly condemned in the UN General Assembly. When the community of states reacts so negatively to unilateral actions, the acts are usually considered ineligible to serve as precedent for the emergence of a new customary norm. As a result, most legal scholars view unilateral 'pro-democratic' intervention with considerable suspicion.[57]

To avoid the paradox, one might argue that the use of extra-legal means to achieve law-based democratic ends entails no necessary contradiction, since any revolution by its nature subverts the pre-existing legal order. International law surely cannot be understood to outlaw revolution, especially pro-democratic revolution.

former colonies, are bound by all customary norms existing at the time of their independence); International Law Commission, *Draft Articles on State Responsibility*, UN Doc. A/CN.4/L.600 (2000), arts. 20–27 (limited circumstances excusing State acts otherwise deemed violative of legal obligations).

55 Article 2(4) of the United Nations Charter provides: 'All Members shall refrain in their international relations from the threat or use of force against the territorial integrity or political independence of any State, or in any other manner inconsistent with the Purposes of the United Nations'. The International Court of Justice has described the prohibition on unilateral force as a *jus cogens* norm - that is, one from which no derogation is permitted even by treaty. *Military and Paramilitary Activities in and against Nicaragua (Nicaragua v. United States), Merits*, 1986, ICJ 14, para. 190.

56 See, for example, D'Amato, 'The Invasion of Panama Was a Lawful Response to Tyranny', (see n. 50 above).

57 Michael Byers and Simon Chesterman, '"You the People": Pro-Democratic Intervention in International Law', in Fox and Roth, *Democratic Governance*.

But whatever the validity of this argument as a matter of domestic law, it has little relevance to the legality of external intervention. The corpus of international law prohibiting unilateral intervention is unaffected by subversions of any given domestic legal order, and indeed that law exists in large part to prevent domestic turmoil from becoming 'internationalized'. For many writers, the legally questionable nature of these unilateral interventions provided confirmation for arguments by John Stuart Mill, Michael Walzer and others that outside actors cannot (and should not) attempt to create democratic polities by fiat.[58]

But a legal analysis addresses the paradox by differentiating between unilateral intervention and pro-democratic intervention undertaken pursuant to multilateral deliberative processes. Acts authorized by the UN Security Council are the pre-eminent example. Since the early 1990s the Council has steadily expanded its understanding of events constituting a 'threat to the peace', the UN Charter's jurisdictional trigger for the Council to authorize forcible action against a member state.[59] In the cases of Haiti and Sierra Leone the Council deemed coups against elected regimes 'threats to the peace'.[60] No states voted against either resolution and both were supported by the target states' elected governments in exile.

A legal analysis would focus on whether such Council actions indeed resolve the paradox by bestowing an imprimatur of legality on pro-democratic intervention. Can an anti-democratic coup, without more, really be said to threaten the peace? What of the timing of Council actions? Interventions by the Economic Community of West African States in Liberia and Sierra Leone, for example, received Security Council approval after they occurred, not before, as is required by the Charter.[61] The questions can be broadened beyond the UN and acts of armed intervention. Can the World Bank consider the nature of a regime in making lending decisions? To what extent should organizations such as the OAS—which has adopted a collective commitment to oppose the ouster of democratic regimes—scrutinize the constitutional law and practice of member states to determine whether an 'anti-democratic' coup has taken place? An incongruity between extra-legal means and law-based ends may still be present in such cases, but the questions to be asked differ entirely from the case of unilateral action.

Third, the new democratic 'normativity' implicates the way in which law and politics are juxtaposed in the standard realist account of international relations. In describing international politics as almost wholly bereft of normative constraint, realists appear to assume that definable norms in fact address the specific aspects of state behaviour they describe. Otherwise their hypothesis could not be tested: without law one simply cannot postulate that law is either effective or ineffective in constraining state action. For most of the modern era, however, one could not make

[58] Michael Walzer, *Just and Unjust Wars* (New York: Basic Books, 1977), pp.86–108; Michael Walzer, 'The Moral Standing of States', Philosophy and Public Affairs, 9 (1980), pp. 209–29; John Stuart Mill, 'A Few Words on Non-Intervention', in J. S. Mill, *Dissertations and Discussions, III* (New York: Holt, 1874).

[59] UN Charter, Art. 39.

[60] S. C. Res. 841 (1993) (unanimous vote on Haiti economic sanctions); S.C. Res. 940 (1994) (12–0–2 vote on Haiti forcible measures); S.C. Res. 1132 (1997) (unanimous vote on Sierra Leone arms and oil embargo).

[61] Acts of regional organizations are governed by Chapter VIII of the Charter. On the Liberian intervention, see Georg Nolte, 'Restoring Peace by Regional Action: International Legal Aspects of the Liberian Conflict', *Zeitschrift für ausländisches öffentliches Recht und Völkerrecht*, 53 (1993), pp. 603–37.

this assumption about issues of democratic legitimacy. International law simply did not address the origin or nature of national governments. Because such questions were resolved in a legal vacuum, a theory postulating the impotence of law in this area would have been wholly without empirical grounding.

Now that international law pertaining to the internal character of domestic regimes has increased in scope and determinacy, the possibility of normative constraint has entered the picture. The initial denial to Croatia of membership in the Council of Europe, the ouster of General Cedras and his junta from Haiti, and the resolution of the 1997 UN accreditation crisis for Cambodia all implicated legal as well as political considerations and standards.[62] This is not to say that the outcomes of these and similar disputes are uniformly in accord with relevant legal standards. Realists may still conclude that law is not an explanatory variable in any of these circumstances. But they now must do so only after assessing a normative regime that did not exist even ten years ago.

Finally, a legal analysis provides a new perspective on the knotty definitional problems that attend promotion of 'democratic' governance. For writers starting from first principles, democracy is often seen as an 'essentially contested concept'.[63] Common definitions range from Joseph Schumpeter's procedural conception of democracy as the 'institutional arrangement for arriving at political discussions in which individuals acquire the power to decide by means of a competitive struggle for the people's vote', to substantive definitions phrased in consequentialist terms.[64]

But the emergence of legal structures has narrowed the range of democratic models potentially acceptable as multilateral initiatives. First, international legal instruments—for the most part human rights treaties—commonly avoid addressing 'democracy' as such. Instead, for better or worse, they treat the various component parts of most democratic models as discrete normative questions: political participation, freedoms of association, conscience and speech, self-determination, matters of economic subsistence, and the like are set out in separate articles, and each has become the subject of a rather detailed jurisprudence. By so disassembling broader conceptions of democracy, the instruments avoid—or evade—ideological disputes about the inter-relationship of these components. Each component involves a binding obligation under international law, and is properly the subject of multilateral protection.

Second, the memorialization of democratic or 'participatory' rights in binding legal instruments transforms definitional debates from purely philosophical discussions into, largely, exercises in legal exegesis. How, for example, should the international community assess leaders' appeals to the 'popular will' or 'popular sovereignty'? With the increased scope and determinacy of international law

[62] *The Guardian* (London), 14 May 1996, p.10 (Croatia); John C. Pierce, 'The Hatian Crisis and the Future of Collective Enforcement of Democratic Governance', *Law and Policy in International Business*, 27 (1996), pp. 477–512 (Haiti); Suellen Ratliff, 'UN Representation Disputes: a Case Study of Cambodia and a New Accreditation Proposal for the Twenty-First Century', *California Law Review*, 87 (1999), pp. 1259–63 (Cambodia).

[63] See William E. Connolly, *The Terms of Political Discourse* (Oxford: Blackwell, 3rd edn., 1993), pp. 29–35; W.B. Gallie, 'Essentially Contested Concepts', *Proceedings of the Aristotelian Society*, 56 (1956), pp. 107–98.

[64] Joseph A. Schumpeter, *Capitalism, Socialism and Democracy*, 2nd edn. (New York: Harper, 1947), p. 269. For a critical view of Schumpeterian proceduralism as neglectful of the substance of democracy, see for example, C. B. Macpherson, *The Life and Times of Liberal Democracy* (Oxford: Oxford University Press, 1977).

pertaining to the internal character of domestic regimes, this question cannot be answered without reference to instruments requiring states to hold periodic and genuine elections—employing a secret ballot and universal suffrage—in which opponents have a meaningful opportunity to participate. An answer must also at least acknowledge decisions of human rights treaty bodies, even where those bodies (as in the case of the Human Rights Committee set up under the International Covenant on Civil and Political Rights) do not have explicit authority to issue binding interpretations of the instruments. Finally, the now-substantial practice of international organizations in monitoring national elections, even though predicated on either host state invitation or exceptional circumstances, can scarcely be ignored, as monitors have developed criteria of electoral fairness that substantially parallel treaty-body interpretations of standards set forth in binding international instruments.

The democratic entitlement thesis, if accepted, would reduce the normative inquiry to the confines of a clearly bounded universe of relevant texts. Although this would not necessarily produce a common understanding of the norms themselves, the debate among international lawyers would be conducted within relatively clear points of doctrinal reference. Methodologically, contemporary debates in and around international institutions about the criteria for democracy and popular sovereignty are a far cry from the open-ended discussions that take place among political theorists.

The third reason for change in the definitional debate is the increasing availability of judicial and quasi-judicial bodies to resolve disputes. During the Cold War few international institutions were equipped to interpret or apply democratic norms. In the absence of such multinational bodies, the few treaty standards that existed were either ignored or interpreted unilaterally by the two contending camps, leading to such dubious categories as 'people's democracies' and 'authoritarian' (as opposed to 'totalitarian') regimes. Democratic standards without mediating institutions, in other words, were little better than no standards at all.[65]

Today, such questions are increasingly resolved in multilateral fora. Several human rights tribunals, both global and regional, have developed a jurisprudence elucidating various aspects of electoral fairness and other political rights.[66] Some international organizations limit membership to 'liberal democracies' and therefore inquire into the democratic *bona fides* of new state applicants.[67] The clearest application of democratic legitimacy criteria occurs in decisions to declare or refuse recognition of new states and governments, to open or break diplomatic relations, and to accord, withhold or suspend states' memberships in, or deny their governments' credentials to, intergovernmental organizations. On occasion, these measures may go so far as to express a collective *opinio juris* holding that the ruling apparatus lacks legal standing to assert rights, incur obligations, and confer immunities on behalf of the sovereign state entity—that is, legal, as distinct from merely political, non-recognition.[68] Not to recognize an undemocratic regime that nonetheless

[65] On this issue generally, see Thomas M. Franck, *The Power of Legitimacy Among Nations* (New York: Oxford University Press, 1990).
[66] Fox, 'The Right to Political Participation', (see n. 26 above).
[67] Murphy, 'Democratic Legitimacy and Recognition', (see n. 30 above).
[68] This phenomenon is the subject of Brad R. Roth, *Governmental Illegitimacy in International Law* (New York: Oxford University Press, 1999).

exercises effective control over the national territory represents (or at least affects) a profound affirmation of democratic principles. It affirms a willingness to forgo any sort of meaningful relationship with the state in the hope that 'legitimate' leaders might someday return to office.

Increasingly, intergovernmental bodies are taking decisions of this nature, the most dramatic being the UN measures of legal non-recognition against ruling military juntas in Haiti and Sierra Leone. The political organs of regional organizations, though having far less legal authority, have adopted legal or legalistic criteria and procedures to govern the adoption of political measures against 'undemocratic' regimes. For example, the European Union established an arbitral commission to determine whether the states of the former Yugoslavia met EU criteria for recognition.[69] The OSCE, OAS, MERCOSUR and the Commonwealth have adopted elaborate policies to ostracize regimes that depose elected governments.[70] The OAU has taken strong positions on an *ad hoc* basis in opposition to military takeovers in Sierra Leone and Côte D'Ivoire, using language that suggests broad disapproval of anti-democratic coups.[71] This practice suggests that the international community is not only elaborating clearer standards regarding democratic government, but also creating authoritative bodies to interpret and apply those standards to new and would-be democracies.

5. Misgivings about the democratic entitlement

Although there have been few scholarly efforts to examine the democratic entitlement sceptically at length,[72] many observers have expressed doubts about it. The case against the democratic entitlement rests in part on a more conservative juridical assessment of the instruments, practices, and pronouncements associated with democratization, with more emphasis accorded to the foundational presumption against derogations of the political independence of sovereign states. In equal part, however, the dissenting view is based upon an interpretation of the underlying political concept of popular sovereignty that is more open-textured than the one embraced by the entitlement's proponents.

To the extent that legal source materials are interpreted teleologically, in accordance with a set of basic ends attributed to the international legal system, interpretation of these underlying ends colours seemingly positivistic assessments. This teleological element is especially relevant where the claim at stake concerns an 'emerging', rather than fully established, norm, since the legal analyst is called upon

69 Opinions of the International Conference on the Former Yugoslavia Arbitration Commission, reprinted in *International Legal Materials*, 31 (1992), p.1497.

70 OSCE, Moscow Document (see n.11 above), OAS, Representative Government Resolution (see n. 10 above); MERCOSUR Protocol of Ushuaia (see n.1 above); Commonwealth, Cultures of Democracy (see n. 29 above).

71 *Agence France Presse*, 30 May 1997 (Sierra Leone); *Jane's Foreign Report*, 20 January 2000 (Cote D'Ivoire).

72 The most elaborate exception is the work of one of the authors of this article. Roth, *Governmental Illegitimacy in International Law* (see n. 68 above). For a detailed normative critique of the character of the democracy that the entitlement thesis embodies, see Susan Marks, *The Riddle of all Constitutions: International Law, Democracy and the Critique of Ideology* (Oxford: Clarendon Press, 2000).

not only to assess current developments but to project their future direction. Thus, while the controversy here is not merely a contest of subjectively-held ideas and aspirations, neither is it a matter of sterile application of competing legal 'methodologies' to source material.

The case against the democratic entitlement takes a sceptical reading of the source material cited as evidence of the 'emerging norm'. Given that states are presumptively free and equal, and that international institutions have no implicit licence to govern matters 'essentially within the domestic jurisdiction',[73] a heavy burden falls on proponents of the democratic norm to establish both its existence and its determinacy.[74] In the light of this burden, the evidence marshalled by democratic entitlement adherents, while impressive, is far from incontestable.

A sceptical approach highlights what relevant treaties and resolutions still do not say, and what agreements could not be reached. This scepticism need not go so far as to deny that norms pertaining to the internal character of domestic regimes have increased in scope and determinacy. But whereas the democratic entitlement's adherents see the international system as gradually establishing a set of determinate legal norms by which the whole of a state's internal politics can be authoritatively judged and—in principle—effectively regulated, the dissenting view sees legally-protected space for diversity and contingency, now and into the future.

Notwithstanding the recent proliferation of liberal-democratic electoral processes, their adoption has been by no means universal, and the depth of commitment to them is frequently uncertain. Moreover, adoption of such processes ordinarily entails neither a renunciation of a state's sovereign right to alter its constitutional system whenever and however it sees fit, nor any other affirmation relevant to external affairs.

Although the international community has, through UN electoral assistance projects and General Assembly pronouncements, manifested support for liberal-democratic electoral processes around the world, the assistance has been rendered only in cases where host states have requested it or where extraordinary measures have already been taken on independent grounds, and the pronouncements have been consistently two-sided. Even the more 'pro-democratic' resolutions, passed over the objections of the most recalcitrant states, include the pointed caveat that international electoral assistance 'should not call into question each State's sovereign right freely to choose and develop its political, social, economic, and cultural systems, whether or not they conform to the preferences of other States'.[75] These supportive resolutions are consistently accompanied by counterpart resolutions, passed by majority over the objection of the most strongly liberal-democratic states, that reaffirm 'respect for the principles of national sovereignty and non-interference in the internal affairs of States in their electoral processes', acknowledging the

[73] UN Charter, Art. 2 (7).

[74] To meet such a burden, one must demonstrate a consistent pattern of state practice, combined with manifestations of a generally-held subjective sense of legal obligation (*opinio juris*) on the part of state actors. Ian Brownlie, *Principles of Public International Law* (Oxford: Clarendon Press, 1990), 4th edn, pp. 4–11. Where treaty provisions are concerned, appeal must be made to the 'ordinary meaning' of the provisions in context, supplemented in case of ambiguity by the treaty's preparatory work and circumstances of conclusion, as well as by any state practice indicating subsequent agreement of the parties on interpretation. Vienna Convention on the Law of Treaties (1969), Arts. 31–32.

[75] GA Res. 45/150 (1990) (129–8–9).

plurality of approaches, reserving to the domestic jurisdiction control over implementation, and criticizing unwelcome external influences on local processes.[76]

It is true that UN electoral assistance, where sought by a host state, has come replete with exacting and non-negotiable standards of electoral fairness. Nonetheless, the General Assembly majority has maintained that there is 'no universal need' for such assistance,[77] and no definitive conclusions can be drawn from collective acquiescence in the Organization's attachment of these conditions, since even the states most protective of sovereign prerogative have no motivation or basis to question a host state's sovereign decision to accept those terms.

Regional organizations, especially in Europe and Latin America, have been less tepid in their assertions of a democratic norm, and have imposed liberal-democratic processes as a condition, variously, of declarations of recognition (for both states and governments), of membership in intergovernmental organizations, and of diplomatic courtesies.[78] It is important to note, however, that each of these political measures is a discretionary aspect of the foreign policies, unilateral and coordinated, of sovereign states. The use of these measures for putatively 'pro-democratic' purposes is a new and important political development—perhaps even a political development in support of legal standards—but it is not, without more, an assertion that a state's non-compliance licenses otherwise-inadmissible interferences in its internal affairs, let alone that a non-complying government generally lacks legal standing to assert the sovereign rights of its state. Only in the cases of Haiti and Sierra Leone, among the several cases of coups against elected governments in the 1990s, have intergovernmental organizations gone to such a length, and in those cases, the illegitimacy of the regimes in question was manifest in ways that went far beyond their disregard of an electoral mandate.

In the area of treaty law, which has addressed human rights obligations without any regard to externally-driven implementation, there is no question that a right to political participation exists both in the global and in regional human rights systems. The vagueness of the relevant provisions, especially in the ICCPR, as well as the Cold War-era inattention of most human rights bodies to this issue, can be attributed to efforts to appease unrepentant one-party states. The absence of such states in Western Europe was favourable to the development of an accepted international jurisprudence of democratic rights in that region, and this phenomenon has, for obvious reasons, now spread to East-Central Europe and Latin America. The global situation, however, is more complex. The ICCPR Human Rights Committee has lately ventured a more determinate interpretation of the political participation provisions—quite arguably, more determinate than can be attributed to

[76] GA Res. 45/151 (1990) (111–29–11); GA Res. 49/180 (97–57–14); GA Res. 54/168 (91–59–10). See also Boutros Boutros-Ghali, *An Agenda for Democratization* (New York: United Nations, 1996), pp. 1, 3 (the UN Secretary-General notes that 'individual states decide if and when to begin democratization' and that the new emphasis on democratization 'does not imply a change' in the traditional principle of non-intervention).

[77] GA Res. 49/180 (1994).

[78] See Stephen J. Schnably, 'Constitutionalism and Democratic Government in the Inter-American System," in Fox and Roth, *Democratic Governance*; Malvina Halberstam, 'The Copenhagen Declaration: Intervention in Support of Democracy', *Harvard International Law Journal* 34 (1993), p. 143; Francis G. Jacobs and Robin C. A. White, *The European Convention on Human Rights*, 2nd edn. (Oxford: Clarendon Press, 1996), pp. 269–76.

the consent of many of the member states at the time of ratification.[79] The Committee's interpretations of the Covenant are not, however, either by treaty provision or by established practice, binding on the states parties, and its 'activist' interpretation of some articles have raised questions as to the Committee's credibility with state actors.[80] There thus remains an onus to demonstrate acceptance by the community of states of democratic norms that go beyond the boilerplate abstractions of old.

In this regard, it is noteworthy that even in the course of approving without dissent a 1999 UN Human Rights Commission resolution affirming democratic values and related rights, a substantial portion of the international community went on record to question whether there exists anything that can meaningfully be termed an international 'right to democracy'.[81] The remarks of several states reflect, on the one hand, an unwillingness to repudiate either discrete participatory rights or democracy in the abstract, yet on the other hand, a deep concern about the implications of characterizing an entire and specific form of government as legally mandated.[82]

It is true that, in the absence of fixed standards specifying how much evidence is enough to substantiate the existence of a legal norm, a sceptic can always characterize the glass as half empty. The particular scepticism at work here, though, is not an insistence on endless formal criteria; it does not deny the need to read the source material generously in light of certain presumed purposes of a community of states. Nor does the scepticism rendered here deny that the UN Charter system's foundational norm of sovereign equality is predicated on the principle of the self-determination of peoples, and thus that the sovereignty upheld by international law is popular sovereignty, rather than the sovereignty of power holders *tout court*. Nonetheless, to read the source material teleologically is not necessarily to read it through a liberal-democratic lens, especially given the ideological pluralism that characterizes the international community's recent past and, to a non-trivial extent, its present and likely future.

One can acknowledge that sovereignty ultimately belongs to peoples and not to governments, and still question whether a liberal-democratic institutional structure

79 See n. 7 above.

80 See, for example, Toonen v. Australia, CCPR/C/50/D/488/1992 (31 March 1994), para. 8.7 ('the reference to 'sex' in Art. 2, para. 1, and Art. 26 is to be taken as including sexual orientation'); Human Rights Committee, General Comment 14 (1984), para. 6 (the right to life under Art. 6 entails that '[t]he production, testing, possession, deployment, and use of nuclear weapons should be prohibited and recognized as crimes against humanity'); Human Rights Committee, General Comment 24 (1994), para. 18 (a reservation determined by the Committee to be impermissible 'will generally be severable, in the sense that the Covenant will be operative for the reserving party without benefit of the reservation').

81 See n. 8 above. 25 out of 53 member states on the UN Human Rights Commission dissented or abstained on the 'right to democracy' language of Resolution 1999/57, though none dissented and only two (China and Cuba) abstained on the resolution as a whole. UN Doc. E/CN.4/1999/SR.57 (April 27, 1999).

82 The Indian representative commented that the 'right to democracy' language 'tended needlessly to politicize an essentially promotional concept, and raised questions and legal issues that found little support in international human rights instruments'. India affirmed that there was 'no prescriptive or single model of democracy, and that all peoples had the right freely to determine their own political and constitutional systems in accordance with their right of self-determination', adding that democracy, as a form of government that arises from the will of the people, cannot 'be imposed, especially from the outside'. Ibid.., paras. 8–9; see also ibid., paras. 15 (Pakistan), 20 (Mexico), 22–23 (Cuba), 29 (Russian Federation), 40 (Indonesia), 42 (China).

is the ultimate and indispensable vehicle of popular will. Indeed, in reducing popular will to the outcome of specified processes, adherents of the 'emerging right to democratic governance' neither worship empirical popular will nor own up to the consequences of an inherently ideological and controvertible enterprise.

On the one hand, no empirical account of popular satisfaction with an authoritarian system would satisfy the democratic entitlement. It would not be sufficient even for a dictatorship to hold a verifiably honest plebiscite on the continuation of dictatorial rule, since the 'proper conditions' for the exercise of popular will require a remaking of authoritarian institutions to allow for knowing, willing, and intelligent collective choice. Putting aside the problem that liberal-democratic structures alone may not establish the requisites of a collective choice that is genuinely knowing (based on good information), willing (not merely a choice among options imposed by the will of elites or by circumstance), and intelligent (taken in circumstances that allow for proper reflection, including widely available education, a robust societal market-place of ideas, and the absence of distortive economic pressures), the posited 'conditions of choice' require the very institutional transformation—perhaps an irreversible one—about which the populace was supposed to be empowered to choose. And even then, adherents of the democratic entitlement would not take no for an answer, on the ground that the present majority cannot legitimately vote to deny the democratic right to future instantiations of the polity.[83] Though justifiable from the standpoint of a particular comprehensive world-view, this is a rather presumptuous approach to popular self-determination.

On the other hand, the calculated effort to specify the democratic entitlement without express reference to wider social goals entails a contradiction. In defining democracy in essentially procedural terms, the democratic entitlement school follows the contemporary comparative politics literature in rejecting teleological definitions that render democratic performance inherently unmeasurable by social science techniques.[84] Yet political scientists justify this sterile definition, so much at odds with the term's role in both classical theory and popular morality, by purporting (perhaps not always ingenuously) to lighten the term's normative baggage—that is, by identifying democracy as, at most, one of many political virtues.[85] The democratic entitlement school restores to the term 'democracy' its former normative weight as the *sine qua non* of governmental legitimacy, but not its former complexity as a realization of substantive ends and, thus, as an object of ideological contestation.

Not only are there, as everyone concedes, other perceived first-order political virtues besides 'procedural democracy', but the many who have yet to adopt the whole of the liberal-democratic world-view (and, yet more troubling, even some of those who have) frequently perceive the former virtues to be achievable, in certain circumstances, only at the expense of the latter. Majorities occasionally choose—if, perhaps, unwisely—to eschew or to void liberal-democratic procedures where these appear to jeopardize other virtues.

On such occasions, one can always posit a 'higher' popular will, at odds with empirical manifestations, that embodies the 'objective' interests of the populace,

[83] Gregory H. Fox and Georg Nolte, 'Intolerant Democracies,' *Harvard International Law Journal*, 36 (1995), p. 1.

[84] Samuel Huntington, *The Third Wave: Democratization in the Late Twentieth Century* (Norman, OK: University of Oklahoma Press, 1991), pp. 5–13.

[85] Ibid., p. 10.

perhaps locating the 'true' collective decision in customary practice or an heroic revolutionary moment. Yet for the democratic entitlement to have recourse to such devices, it must take its place alongside every other variant of political messianism. It must accept the insight that what ultimately count as democratic are such acts as are calculated to bring about a 'truly' democratic social reality, the insight that inspires the bearers of a substantive political faith (liberal democrats included) to eschew procedural niceties as needed. Ultimately, we do not know what democracy *is* until we know what it is *for*, and although the proponents of the entitlement may themselves have a clear vision of democratic purposes, it is far more difficult to argue that a genuine international consensus has emerged on these.

For example, notwithstanding their vaunted fidelity to formal participatory mechanisms, many liberal democrats manifested sympathy with the coup in Algeria that pre-empted an Islamic fundamentalist landslide in 1992, the forcible dispersion of the supposedly pro-Communist Russian legislature in 1993, and the Dayton High Commissioner's removal of the Republika Srpska's elected ethno-nationalist President in 1999. This is a sign, not of hypocrisy, but of a teleological conception of democracy that permits only contingent loyalty to institutional forms. The attempt to give those forms a status that stands above ideology and politics is therefore problematic.

From the standpoint of those sceptical of the democratic entitlement, then, what remains is a partisan vision dressed up as international law, thereby to supply a rationale for meddling in the internal affairs of foreign political communities. When one affirms that the term 'democracy' demarcates the moral high ground in political struggle, one must also acknowledge that the word encompasses the universe of political virtues as variously perceived, at which point democracy's presence or absence largely ceases to be an empirical question. This acknowledgement should, arguably, lead the international actor to fall back on the principle of respect for the internal processes, however ragged, of countries not one's own.

To be sure, some consensus has emerged, at least, as to what democracy *is not*. One need only invoke 'Democratic Kampuchea' to point out that the existence of twilight does not refute the distinction between day and night.[86] But the 'democratic' merits of real-life political struggles in diverse lands are seldom so reliably judged from abroad, let alone reliably judged on the basis of a mechanistic application of procedural criteria. Or so an opponent of the democratic entitlement may contend.

6. Conclusion

Analysing democratic governance as an international legal entitlement involves substantially more than predicting the future of recent democratic transitions. To be sure, the contours of a democratic entitlement will be shaped by the same political

[86] The constitution of Democratic Kampuchea indeed dutifully provided for an elected legislature (Arts. 5–7), proclaimed 'complete equality among all Kampuchean people' (Art. 13) and described various aspects of Cambodian society as 'democratic' in three separate articles (Arts. 1, 13 and 21). Reprinted in François Ponchaud, Cambodia Year Zero (New York: Holt, Rhinehart & Winston, 1978), p. 199.

forces affecting every rule of international law.[87] But the democratic entitlement involves indeterminacy of an entirely different order, for the putative right embodies a marriage of law and politics that is in many ways unprecedented in international law. The entitlement is not simply law *affected by* politics. It is law that penetrates and regulates the very essence of political life, both domestically and internationally.

Domestically, the democratic entitlement sets out a theoretical blueprint for the proper allocation of national political power. In so doing it assumes a critical degree of trust and cooperation on the part of all factions participating in democratic institutions. While some argue that international law permits democracies to defend themselves against anti-democratic actors by restricting their participation in elections,[88] the uncertain record of democratic transitions in Africa, Central Europe, and Central Asia suggests that political actors determined to subvert democratic institutions will usually succeed in doing so. The democratic entitlement thus appears to envision, for its success, a change not only in political institutions but in political cultures as well.[89] It was for this reason that the 1990 UN Observer Mission to Haiti warned the General Assembly that 'there is no democratic tradition in Haitian politics ... [and] violence has always been the means of settling conflicts and choosing leaders'.[90] The governmental paralysis that followed 'restoration' of Haitian democracy in 1994 appeared to confirm the monitors' prescience. Such vagaries of domestic politics are usually relevant to international norms only to the extent that they facilitate or impede state compliance with their terms. In the case of the democratic entitlement, however, domestic politics and the terms of compliance are one and the same.

Internationally, the democratic blueprint translates into a legal standard of regime legitimacy. Where a regime is considered illegitimate according to democratic theory, other states face a stark choice. If they continue business as usual with an undemocratic regime, they implicitly affirm its capacity to act as agent for the state—that is, to serve as the state's legitimate government. In that case, the democratic entitlement will have failed to make normative inroads into the political dynamic of inter-state relations. The norm will likely suffer as a result, taking on more the hue of a political aspiration than a binding guideline.

Alternatively, states may incorporate democratic legitimacy criteria into their foreign policies and refuse to carry on relations with undemocratic regimes. This was the approach of many states toward the apartheid regime in South Africa: until majoritarian elections were held, any interaction with the regime was seen as an

[87] For a fascinating discussion of how customary norms are shaped by asymmetrical power structures, see Michael Byers, *Custom, Power and the Power of Rules: International Relations and Customary International Law* (Cambridge: Cambridge University Press, 1999).

[88] Fox and Nolte, 'Intolerant Democracies', (see n. 83 above).

[89] The Secretary-General has observed, 'democratization must begin with an effort to create a culture of democracy — a political culture, which is fundamentally non-violent and in which no one party or group expects to win or lose all the time'. *Support by the United Nations System of the Efforts of Governments to Promote and Consolidate New or Restored Democracies*, UN Doc. A/51/761 (Annex), at 7 (1996).

[90] *First Report of the United Nations Observer Group for the Verification of the Elections in Haiti*, UN Doc. A/45/870 (Annex), p. 9 (1990).

improper validation of its authority to act.[91] What if this were adopted as a global strategy toward all undemocratic regimes? As James Crawford, Michael Byers and Simon Chesterman have detailed,[92] the consequences of effectively disenfranchizing the world's non-democratic regimes would be almost unimaginable. International politics as it is now practiced would effectively halt. While proponents of a democratic entitlement would surely respond that no state (or the United Nations) is likely to adopt such a rigid legitimism, it is hard to dispute that a principle of non-recognition flows quite naturally from the internal logic of the democratic entitlement. Once again, political conflict is not exogenous to but inherent in the entitlement itself.

Two other aspects of the entitlement also bring political considerations to the fore. First, the view that democratic regimes are best able to implement a range of other international legal obligations[93] ties much of the case for the entitlement to realization of these other normative goals. But these other legal regimes may fail for a host of reasons unrelated to the democratic nature of participating states. Environmental norms, for example, while increasingly reliant on implementation strategies that utilize democratic political institutions, may be opposed by industry groups, may be perceived as inimical to appropriate rates of development, or may clash with other normative goals such as free trade. If these arguments succeed and schemes such as international environmental cooperation experience temporary or long-term failures, it will be the political power of those making the countervailing arguments that will contribute to undermining the case for the democratic entitlement.

Second, the democratic entitlement is often described as a necessary precondition to social progress in a wide range of other areas—protection of human rights, economic development, cultural diversity, and so on.[94] On this view, democratization sits atop a hierarchy of normative goals. But constructing such a hierarchy is as much an empirical statement of causation—a state must be democratic in order to achieve certain other normative objectives—as it is a ranking of values. And as an empirical statement it is susceptible to being proven false: Cuba has achieved remarkably high literacy rates; infant mortality in Singapore is among the world's lowest; ethnic conflict in Eastern and Central Europe was largely quiescent during the Communist era; and so on. While these counter-examples are clearly debatable, it is the very prospect of debate that contributes to politicizing the democratic entitlement. The value of enforcing the entitlement as a legal rule becomes subject to

[91] The myriad of international sanctions against the apartheid regime are detailed in I.E. Sagay, *The Southern African Situation and the Eventual Triumph of International Law* (Lagos, Nigeria: Nigerian Institute of Advanced Legal Studies, 1991), pp. 34–6. In a 1991 resolution the General Assembly set out the conditions for South Africa's re-entry into international society: 'only the total eradication of apartheid and the establishment of a non-racial, democratic society based on majority rule, through the full and free exercise of adult suffrage by all the people in a united and non-fragmented South Africa, can lead to a just and lasting solution to the situation in South Africa'. GA Res. 46/130 (1991).

[92] James Crawford, 'Democracy and the Body of International Law,' in Fox and Roth, *Democratic Governance*; Byers and Chesterman, 'You the People' (n. 57 above).

[93] See text accompanying notes 41–45.

[94] 'Because democratic Governments are freely chosen by their citizens and held accountable through periodic and genuine elections and other mechanisms, they are more likely to promote and respect the rule of law, respect individual and minority rights, cope effectively with social conflict, absorb migrant populations and respond to the needs of marginalized groups.' *Support by the United Nations System*, p. 6 (see n. 89 above).

the outcome of discussions involving highly complex issues of local culture, political economy and resource allocation. If democracy is thereby understood as a contingent value, then a legal rule embodying democratic principles will suffer from perpetual contingency as well.

Future analyses of a normative democratic entitlement will need to ask whether this extraordinary degree of politicization can be overcome. Will the broad community of states accept a Manichean rule that postulates a right way and a wrong way for governments to relate to their citizens and for states to relate to one another? This question cannot be answered simply by predicting a triumph of the democratic ideal—'liberal millenarianism' in Susan Marks' phraseology.[95] Reliance on political trends will not stand in for a rigorous legal analysis that investigates systemic consequences of a democratic norm.

An exercise in hindsight makes this point clear. In April 1917, former US Secretary of State Elihu Root gave an address to the American Society of International Law, of which he was then President, entitled 'The Effect of Democracy on International Law'.[96] Speaking only a few weeks after American entry into the First World War, and brimming with Wilsonian optimism, Root argued that the forward march of democracy then evident would remove the fundamental cause of international conflict—the territorial ambitions of dynastic rulers. To Root, the trajectory of history was clear, as he listed country after country in which democratic reforms were taking hold. These included Russia, which he described as 'engaged in establishing the new self-control of that vast Empire upon the basis of universal suffrage and republican institutions'.[97] Root argued that because 'democracies are absolutely dependent for their existence upon the preservation of law', respect for international law would arise as a natural corollary to the spread of democracy. The designs of autocracies, by contrast, could not be constrained by the consensual and self-enforcing tools of international society: 'The Congresses of Westphalia, of Vienna, of Berlin, and a multitude of others less conspicuous have sought to curb the evil through settings limits upon power by treaty. They have all failed.'[98] Only change at the national level would bring lasting peace between nations:

> The progress of democracy ... is dealing with the problem by destroying the type of government which has shown itself incapable of maintaining respect for law and justice and resisting the temptations of ambition, and by substituting a new form of government which in its nature is incapable of proceeding by the same methods, and necessarily responds to different motives and pursues different objects from the old autocratic offenders. Only when that task has been substantially accomplished will the advocates of law among nations be free from the inheritance of the former failure.[99]

This early articulation of the democratic peace thesis is as notable for its omissions as it is for the naiveté of its predictions. Root did not describe ways in which international law might encourage transitions to democracy. Nor did he assess

[95] Susan Marks, 'The End of History? Reflections on Some International Legal Theses', *European Journal of International Law*, 8 (1997), pp. 449–77.

[96] *Proceedings of the American Society of International Law*, 11 (1917), p. 2.

[97] Ibid. p. 5. Root also described China as 'throwing off the domination of the Manchu [and] striving to accustom her long-suffering and submissive millions to the idea of a constitutional right'. Ibid.

[98] Ibid., p. 7.

[99] Ibid.

the implications of its adopting political democracy as a normative goal. He appears to have assumed that the spread of democracy would portend little change in the direction or content of international rules. His focus was rather on the enhanced appeal and respect for existing international law that would come about once autocratic governments have given way to popularly elected regimes. The spread of democracy, in Root's view, was fundamentally a political question but one with important consequences for international law.

The time has come to address the democratic entitlement directly as a legal question. Politics, we have noted, is ever present. But only by understanding how political democracy can be conceived as a legal obligation, whether existing normative structures can accommodate a right to democratic governance, and, if not, what sort of reforms would be needed, will wholesale reliance on political factors be avoided. Root, speaking in the midst of war and at the dawn of a truly global American foreign policy, may be forgiven for his misplaced optimism. But it is imperative that contemporary international lawyers eschew reliance on pure politics and focus their unique analytical tools on the idea of a legal right to democratic governance. Their essential voice must be added to what has become a vigorous global debate.

The article indicates that it is a revised and expanded version of the Introduction to Democratic Governance and International Law (CUP 2000), which Brad R. Roth and Gregory H. Fox edited.

Part II
Definition(s) of Democracy in International Law

[4]

DEMOCRACY IN INTERNATIONAL LAW: A EUROPEAN PERSPECTIVE

STEVEN WHEATLEY*

I. INTRODUCTION

For lawyers in general, and international lawyers in particular, democracy is a neglected concept. Discourse is dominated by the ideas of human rights for individuals and minority or self-determination rights for groups. Those who seek greater protection for vulnerable members of a community argue for the recognition of new rights, or the more effective implementation of existing rights. They do not argue for more democracy. Indeed, given that claims for human and minority rights are not made only against authoritarian governments, but also democratic ones, there must exist an implied assumption that democracy is, by itself, not capable of protecting the interests of vulnerable minorities. Moreover, as the form of government which apparently venerates the will of the majority, democracy might be considered by some as being downright hostile to the interests of individuals and minorities.

This article examines the nature of democracy in European international law,[1] in doing so it makes clear that there is more to democratic government than the establishment of a mechanism for the election of the dictator every few years. This work examines, before rejecting, claims that international law should recognise a universal obligation for states to introduce and maintain democratic government. The paper does conclude however that such an obligation exists in Europe, and it considers the content of this obligation. It is shown that democratic government involves more than free and fair elections. Democracies must be tolerant of political debate and activity, except where harmful to democracy itself. Moreover, as will be seen, all concerned citizens must enjoy the right to participate in the decision-making processes in the state, and the state must take account of their interests.

* Law School, University of Liverpool. My thanks to Professor Dominic McGoldrick for his comments on an earlier draft. The usual caveats apply.

[1] 'Europe', in this context, is not the European Union, nor any particular geographical area. The term is defined broadly to include member states of the international institutions of 'Europe', viz. the Council of Europe, which has forty-four member states <http://www.coe.int>, the majority of which are party to the European Convention on Human Rights <http://conventions.co.int>, and the Organisation for Security and Co-operation in Europe (OSCE) (previously the Conference on Security and Co-operation in Europe (CSCE)), which has fifty-five participating states <http://www.osce.org/general/>. In this work, the organisation will be referred to throughout as the OSCE. Documents adopted when the organisation was the CSCE will be appropriately referenced.

II. THE APPEAL OF DEMOCRACY

Conflict between the interests of different individuals and groups is inevitable in all societies. It is then a requirement of internal, and indeed external, stability that every state develop institutions and mechanisms within which disagreements may be resolved without recourse to violence.[2] The collapse of authoritarian governments,[3] and the evident failings of socialist central planning, have resulted in a general recognition that democracy provides the best-known process through which the resolution of conflicts between different interests groups may be achieved. The Secretary General of the United Nations has argued that democratic institutions and processes, because they channel competing interests into arenas of discourse and provide means of compromise which can be respected by all participants in debates, minimise the risk that differences or disputes will erupt into armed conflict or confrontation.[4] Likewise, the European Court of Human Rights has observed that democratic government affords the possibility of resolving a country's problems through dialogue, without recourse to violence.[5]

The claims for democracy, though, extend beyond the establishment of peaceful relations within and between states.[6] The Bucharest Declaration, adopted at the Third International Conference of the New or Restored Democracies, asserts:

> [there exists] an almost universal recognition that a democratic system of government is the best model to ensure a framework of liberties for lasting solutions to the political, economic and social problems that our societies face.[7]

[2] See J Waldron, *Law and Disagreement* (1999), at 1–2.

[3] Authoritarian governments are those in which the people are totally excluded from the decision-making process and any control over it: see D Beetham, *Democracy and Human Rights* (1999), at 33. The UN Secretary General has argued that 'democratisation' is a process which leads to a more open, more participatory, less authoritarian society: 'Supplement to Reports on Democratization', UN Doc A/51/761, 20 Dec 1996, at para 1.

[4] 'Supplement to Reports on Democratization', ibid at para 17.

[5] *Socialist Party and others v Turkey*, Reports 1998-III, at para 45.

[6] The oft-repeated claim is that no two democratic countries have ever fought a war against each other: J Crawford, *Democracy in International Law* (1994) at 3, relying on E Weede, 'Some Simple Calculations on Democracy and War Involvement', 29 *Journal of Peace Research* (1992) 377.

[7] 'Progress Review and Recommendations', adopted by the Third International Conference of the New or Restored Democracies on Democracy and Development held at Bucharest from 2 to 4 Sept 1997, in which eighty states participated: UN Doc A/52/334, 11 Sept 1997.

See also the Inter-Parliamentary Union's (IPU) claim, in its Universal Declaration on Democracy (adopted without a vote by the Inter-Parliamentary Council at its 161st session (Cairo, 16 Sept 1997)), that democracy is a 'universally recognised ideal as well as a goal, which is based on common values shared by peoples throughout the world community irrespective of cultural, political, social and economic differences': at para 1 (repr 1 *Netherlands Quarterly of Human Rights* (2000) 127). The IPU, established in 1889, is the world organisation of parliaments of sovereign States. Over a hundred national parliaments are currently members: <http://www.ipu.org>.

Whatever the merits of democracy as a system of government, there have, in recent years, been calls for the recognition of a 'right to democratic governance' in international law. If this were accepted, the legitimacy of governments would be judged by international, as opposed to purely national standards.[8] Whilst it is not always clear from the writings on this issue who the holder of the right might be, and what legal interest other states might have in seeking to force compliance with the international norm, its recognition would clearly require all states to introduce and maintain a democratic system of government.[9]

III. A RIGHT TO DEMOCRATIC GOVERNMENT?

It is not difficult to adduce evidence that democracy forms one of the principles of the international legal system in general, and of the United Nations in particular. The idea of sovereign equality between states, for example, exactly replicates that of political equality within democratic systems of government (ie one person, one vote; one state, one vote). Moreover, in his report on *An Agenda for Democratization*, the Secretary-General of the United Nations has argued that the opening words of the Charter, 'We the Peoples', invoke the most fundamental principle of democracy, that of popular sovereignty. It roots the sovereign authority of Member states, and, consequently, the legitimacy of the United Nations itself, in the will of their peoples. The Charter, then, according to the Secretary General, 'offers a vision of democratic states and democracy among them'.[10] It is important however not to overemphasise the significance of the adoption of the expression 'We the peoples'. It may reflect that fact that certain founder members of the United Nations, Byelorussia and Ukraine, were not sovereign independent states. Or it may simply be regarded, and dismissed, as rhetoric. After all, 'democracy' does not appear in the Charter, and there is no breach of the obligations of membership by those states who are not democratic.

Even if we were to recognise democracy as a principle of the United Nations, that would not be the same as asserting that an obligation exists for states to introduce and maintain democratic systems of government. Arguments for this are grounded in the following rules of international law:

[8] Cf Nicaragua Case (Merits) ICJ Rep 1986, 14, at para 262.

[9] See, generally, T Franck, 'The Emerging Right to Democratic Governance', 86 *AJIL* (1992) 46. It is worth recognising that Franck does not himself assert that a right to democratic government exists, but that 'the international system is *moving toward* a clearly designated democratic entitlement, with national governance validated by international standards and systematic monitoring of compliance': ibid, at 91 (emphasis added).

[10] 'Supplement to Reports on Democratisation', above n 3, at para 28 (footnotes omitted). The General Assembly of the United Nations has repeatedly affirmed that democracy is one of the principles enshrined in the Charter of the United Nations: see, inter alia, GA Resolution 50/133, adopted 16 Feb 1996, 'Support by the United Nations system of the efforts of Governments to promote and consolidate new or restored democracies', preamble: A/RES/50/133.

self-determination; freedom of political activity; and the right to free and fair elections.[11] Freedom of political expression and association provide 'the essential preconditions for an open electoral process'.[12] Further, the universal and regional human rights instruments make clear the obligations of state parties to hold free and fair elections.[13] Although significant, these subsets of democratic norms do not provide the strongest grounds for recognising a right to democratic government. That privilege goes to the right to self-determination, and in particular the way in which understanding of the internal aspect of the right has developed in the last twenty years.

The nascent legal principle of self-determination makes two appearances in the Charter of the United Nations. The first provides a recognition of the 'equal rights and self-determination of peoples'.[14] The second, arguably more humanitarian, aspect is reflected in Chapters XI and XII of the Charter: those states responsible for the administration of Non-Self Governing Territories are required to 'develop self-government [in those territories]; and assist them in the progressive development of their free political institutions . . .';[15] whilst one of the objectives of the International Trusteeship System is to ensure the progressive development of the inhabitants of the trust territories 'to self-government or independence as may be appropriate to the particular circumstances of each territory and its peoples and the freely expressed wishes of the people concerned'.[16] Reference to a legal principle of self-determination is significant. It is, though, important to note that the Charter, as the basic document of the international legal system, continued to give pre-eminent importance to state rights.[17] The principle of self-determination, as originally conceived in the Charter, was not intended to be a threat to the principle of sovereignty. Yet, as Pomerance notes, upon these meagre and tentative foundations, 'the United Nations proceeded to construct an edifice of practice in which, increasingly, full 'external' self-determination . . . was viewed as an imperative and immediate goal for all peoples under colonial or alien domination'.[18] This position finds expression in General Assembly Resolution 1514: *Declaration on the Granting of Independence to Colonial Territories and Peoples*.[19] Where a majority of a non-self-governing population, whose

[11] Franck, above n 9 at 52. [12] Ibid, at 61. [13] Ibid, at 63–77.

[14] Art 1(2) provides that one of the purposes of the organisation is to 'develop friendly relations among nations based on respect for the principles of equal rights and self-determination of peoples'; whilst Art 55 determines that the UN shall promote, inter alia, universal respect for human rights with a view to the creation of 'conditions of stability and well-being which are necessary for peaceful and friendly relations among nations based on the respect for the principle of equal rights and self-determination of peoples'.

[15] Art 73(b). [16] Art 76(b).

[17] See for example the obligation to refrain from 'the threat or use of force against the territorial integrity or political independence of any state' (Art 2(4)), and the proscription of intervention by the United Nations in 'matters which are essentially within the domestic jurisdiction of any state' (Art 2(7)).

[18] M Pomerance, *Self-Determination in Law and Practice* (1982), at 10.

[19] General Assembly Resolution 1514 (XV) 14 Dec 1960, UN Doc A/4684 (1960). The rele-

members enjoyed equal status, voted for independence, association, integration or some other status, that view would be decisive. The decolonisation (external) aspect of self-determination then incorporates both elements of popular sovereignty and political equality for the inhabitants of a self-determining unit. These are the same principles which underpin the establishment of a democratic system of government.[20]

The recognition of a right of self-determination in Article 1 of the International Covenant on Civil and Political Rights (1966) was essential to the development of an 'internal' aspect of the right to self-determination. Article 1, which is both a Convention obligation and represents general international law,[21] provides, inter alia, that '(1) All peoples have the right of self-determination. By virtue of that right they freely determine their political status and freely pursue their economic, social and cultural development.' The right then extends beyond the colonial situation; it applies to all peoples,[22] and the term 'peoples' includes both those populations in non-self-governing territories, and the entire populations of a sovereign state.[23] This view is supported by a majority of state reports submitted to the Human Rights Committee under Article 40, and by the text and travaux of the International Covenant.[24] For the people of the state, the right to self-determination is not concerned with the determination of the international status of the territory (ie the 'external' aspect of the right), but with the choice by the people of the 'system of government and administration, and the substantive nature of the regime selected'.[25] This is the 'internal' aspect of the right of peoples to self-determination, and the Human Rights Committee has made clear, in its General Comment on Article 1, that it expects states to detail, in their reports, the constitutional and

vant peoples may choose between establishing a sovereign and independent state; free association, or integration with an independent state; or the emergence into any other political status freely determined by a people. It is clear, however, that resolution 1514, and UN practice in the General Assembly, 'are suffused with a strong bias in favour of one particular result, independence': Pomerance, ibid, 15.

20 See, below n 75, and accompanying text.

21 See, for the same formulation of the right of a people to self-determination, inter alia: Principle VIII, Helsinki Final Act (1975) 14 ILM 1292; Art 20, African Charter of Human and Peoples Rights (1981); Art 2, Vienna Declaration and Programme of Action (1993); Declaration on Principles of International Law concerning Friendly Relations and Co-operation among states in Accordance with the Charter of the United Nations, GA Res. 2625 (XXV) 24 Oct (1970).

22 See, eg, the Vienna Declaration and Programme of Action (1993), which provides that 'All peoples have the right to self-determination', but takes into account the '*particular* situation of peoples under colonial or other forms of alien domination or foreign occupation': Art 1 (emphasis added). Cf 'It is the position of the Government of Sri Lanka that the words "self-determination" appearing in this article apply only to people under alien and foreign domination and these words do not apply to sovereign independent states or to a section of a people or nation', Third periodic report (Sri Lanka) UN Doc CCPR/C/70/Add 6, para 2.

23 H Quane, 'The United Nations and the Evolving Right to Self-Determination', 47 *ICLQ* (1998) 537, 571.

24 P Thornberry, 'Self-Determination, Minorities, Human Rights: A Review of International Instruments', 38 *ICLQ* (1989) 867, 878.

25 E Daes, 'Explanatory note concerning the draft declaration on the rights of indigenous peoples', UN Doc E/CN 4/Sub 2/1993/26/Add 1, 19 July 1993, at para 17.

political processes which in practice allow the exercise of the right of the people of the state to self-determination.[26]

A democratic system of government is one in which the principles of popular sovereignty and political equality find expression in free and fair elections and popular participation in the political process. If these elements are present in the internal aspect of the right to self-determination then the right may be considered as coterminous with the right to democratic government.

It is clear that the right to self-determination allows the people to pursue freely their economic, social, and cultural development 'without outside interference'.[27] The clearest violation of this aspect of the right occurs when the people of the state are subject to foreign occupation or domination.[28] This right can though also be infringed by internal domination. Groups that seize power against the wishes of the people, notably in a military coup,[29] violate the right of the people to self-determination. Thus the right requires a recognition of the principle of popular sovereignty for the population of the state.[30] Authoritarian government is then difficult to reconcile with the principle of self-determination. The government is to be representative of the whole population (the 'people'). The point is made in the General Assembly's *Declaration on Principles of International Law concerning Friendly Relations*: state's conducting themselves in compliance with the principle of self-determination of peoples, will be 'possessed of a government representing the whole people belonging to territory without distinction as to race, creed or colour'.[31] Governments that represent only a minority of the population (or even a majority), most notoriously in the case of racist minority rule, cannot then be considered as acting in compliance with the right of the people to self-determination.[32]

[26] Human Rights Committee's General Comment 12, Art 1 (Twenty-first session, 1984), UN Doc. HRI\GEN\1\Rev 1 at 12 (1994), at paras 4.

[27] CERD General Recommendation (21) on the 'Right to Self-Determination', adopted 15 Mar 1996, at para 4. As has been noted, the principle of 'equal rights and self-determination of peoples' was introduced into the body of international law by the Charter of the United Nations in Arts 1(2) and 55. This principle guarantees the people of a state protection from interferences in their internal affairs by other peoples/states.

[28] This has been made clear in a number of General Assembly Resolutions on the *Universal Realisation of the Right of Peoples to Self-Determination*: see, inter alia, GA Res 54/155, 29 Feb 2000; and GA Res 55/85, 28 Feb 2001.

[29] See Fourth periodic report (Chile) UN Doc CCPR/C/95/Add 1, para 11.

[30] 'Stated broadly, popular sovereignty is the view that individual citizens bestow legitimacy upon a government through their implied or actual consent to its rule', G Fox, 'The Right to Political Participation in International Law', 17 *Yale Journal of International Law* (1992) 539, 550.

[31] GA Res 2625 (XXV) 24 Oct. Likewise, the Committee on the Elimination of Racial Discrimination has determined that the right of the people to self-determination requires the government 'to represent the whole population without discrimination as to race, colour, descent or national or ethnic origin', CERD General Recommendation (21) on the 'Right to Self-Determination', adopted 15 Mar 1996, at para 4.

[32] Declaration on Principles of International Law concerning Friendly Relations, above n 21. It might be noted that even if we could image a people 'choosing' such a regime, it is clear that its validity would not be recognised by the international community.

The right to self-determination is possessed by the people (the whole population of the state), it is not held by those who consider the territory to be the historical 'homeland' of their national, ethnic, linguistic, or religious group, or their 'nation', or their 'people'.[33] Nor is it held by particular minorities within the state, or even by a majority of the population (although the exercise of the right may well contain elements of majoritarianism).[34] The right to self-determination must be exercised in accordance with the principle of equality between the members of the political community. Moreover, it is established that the right to self-determination applies at all points in time; it is not exercised (and thus exhausted) at a single moment.[35] The people enjoy, on a continuing basis, the right to determine the system of government and administration, and the substantive nature of the regime selected. The state must then introduce some periodic mechanism for ensuring the ongoing exercise of the right to self-determination by the people of the state. Finally, Asbjørn Eide has claimed that 'the most basic principle of self-determination is that of the right of popular participation in the government of the State as an entity'.[36] We have then all the elements of democracy present in the internal aspect of self-determination. Does then a recognition of the internal aspect of the right to self-determination require the introduction and maintenance of democratic forms of government?

This understanding of the right contained in Article 1 of the International Covenant is reflected in the state reports to the Human Rights Committee of, inter alia, Bolivia,[37] Cameroon,[38] Croatia,[39] Ecuador,[40] Jamaica,[41] Republic

[33] Cf the report submitted by Slovakia which talks about the '1,000-year efforts of the Slovak nation [to achieve] its own self-determination [as an independent state]' (Initial report (Slovakia) UN Doc CCPR/C/81/Add 9, at para 1); the Macedonian report speaks of the 'historical, cultural, spiritual, and statehood heritage of the Macedonian people and their struggle over centuries for national and social freedom' (Initial report (The Former Yugoslav Republic of Macedonia) UN Doc CCPR/C/74/Add 4, at para 1). The report submitted by Germany talks of the problems of implementing the right to self-determination, as the result of the division imposed on the German people during the 40 years of the cold war, which 'prevented the German people from freely determining their own political status' (Fourth periodic report (Germany) UN Doc CCPR/C/84/Add 5, para 12).

[34] Thus for example it would be expected that constitutional change would receive the support of a majority of the population. It might be the case however that majority support in itself would not be sufficient, and constitutional amendments might require support from minority communities, or majorities above 50 per cent to be effected.

[35] See, Human Rights Committee's General 12, Art 1 (Twenty-first session, 1984), UN Doc HRI\GEN\1\Rev 1 at 12 (1994), at paras 3 and 4.

[36] UN Doc E/CN 4/Sub 2/1992/37, 33 para 165, quoted by A Rosas, 'Internal Self-Determination', in C Tomuschat (ed), *Modern Law of Self-Determination* (1993), 225, at 239. See also CERD General Recommendation (21) on the 'Right to Self-Determination', adopted 15 Mar 1996, at para 4.

[37] Second periodic report (Bolivia) UN Do. CCPR/C/63/Add 4, para 2.

[38] Second periodic report (Cameroon) UN Doc CCPR/C/63/Add 1, para 26.

[39] Initial report (Croatia) UN Doc CCPR/C/HRV/99/1, para 10.

[40] Fourth periodic report (Ecuador) UN Doc CCPR/C/84/Add 6, para 11.

[41] Second periodic report (Jamaica) UN Doc CCPR/C/42/Add 15, para 2.

of Korea,[42] Lebanon,[43] Lesotho,[44] Mauritius,[45] Nepal,[46] Peru,[47] Romania,[48] Sudan,[49] Trinidad and Tobago,[50] and Zambia.[51] All support the argument that the effective implementation of the (internal) right of the people to self-determination requires the introduction of democratic government. There might then be an argument that the only form of government compatible with the right to internal self-determination is a democratic one: a regime in which political power is based on the will of the people, and which provides all citizens the opportunity to participate equally in the political life of their societies.[52] The report submitted by India is clear on the matter:

> The internal aspects of self-determination, it is suggested, includes the right of people to choose their own form of government and the right to democracy. . . .[53]

Moreover, in many cases the state reports specifically link the right of the population of the state to democracy in general and to free and fair elections in particular. This is the view of the Republic of Korea,[54] the Lebanon,[55] and Sudan.[56] The report submitted by Germany makes an explicit connection between the right to self-determination, contained in Article 1 of the International Covenant on Civil and Political Rights, and the rights to take part in the conduct of public affairs, and to vote and to be elected at genuine periodic elections contained in Article 25.[57] A similar connection has been made by the Human Rights Committee.[58] Herein lies the problem: the International Covenant on Civil and Political Rights itself requires the introduction of democratic principles, including the right to vote and to be elected at genuine

42 Second periodic report (Republic of Korea) UN Doc CCPR/C/114/Add 1, para 18.

43 Second periodic report (Lebanon) UN Doc CCPR/C/42/Add 14, para 2.

44 Initial report (Lesotho) UN Doc CCPR/C/81/Add 14, paras 4–8.

45 Third periodic report (Mauritius) UN Doc CCPR/C/64/Add 12, para 5.

46 Initial report (Nepal) UN Doc CCPR/C/74/Add 2, para 1.

47 Fourth periodic report—Addendum (Peru) UN Doc CCPR/C/PER/98/4, para 3.

48 Fourth periodic report (Romania) UN Doc CCPR/C/95/Add 7, paras 6–7.

49 Second periodic report (Sudan) UN Doc CCPR/C/75/Add 2, para 22.

50 Third and Fourth periodic report (Trinidad and Tobago) UN Doc CCPR/C/TTO/99/3, paras 20–1.

51 Second periodic report (Zambia) UN Doc CCPR/C/63/Add 3, para 1.

52 J Crawford, *Democracy in International Law* (1994), at 4.

53 Third periodic report (India) UN Doc CCPR/C/76/Add 6, para 32.

54 'The Republic of Korea respects not only the right of self-determination . . . Nationals of the Republic of Korea hold the right to express their thoughts freely and determine their political status through voluntary, fair, universal and confidential voting', Second periodic report (Republic of Korea) UN Doc CCPR/C/114/Add 1, para 18.

55 'In accordance with . . . the people's right to self-determination, the Lebanese authorities are in the process of preparing the legislative elections', Second periodic report (Lebanon) UN Doc CCPR/C/42/Add 14, para 2.

56 Second periodic report (Sudan) UN Doc CCPR/C/75/Add 2, para 22

57 Fourth periodic report (Germany) UN Doc CCPR/C/84/Add 5, para 13.

58 The Human Rights Committee noted its 'concern that the Congolese people [had] been unable, owing to the postponement of general elections, to exercise their right to self-determination . . . [and called] on the state party to organise general elections as soon as possible in order to enable its citizens to exercise their rights under arts 1 and 25 of the Covenant . . .', concluding observations on the second periodic report of the Congo: UN Doc CCPR/C/79/Add 118, para 20.

periodic elections. For those states not party to the International Covenant it is not clear that an obligation to introduce democratic government exists; indeed it is possible to conceive, certainly in states with small populations, systems of government, other than democracy, in which the people may freely determine their political status and freely pursue their economic, social and cultural development in compliance with the right to self-determination.[59]

If an obligation to introduce and maintain democratic government did exist under general international law, it would have to have been generally adopted in the practice of states, and instances of state practice inconsistent with the rule should be considered as breaches of that rule. It is then worth noting that no evidence exists of the democratic credentials of a regime being relevant either in the recognition of states,[60] or in the international communities dealings with non-democratic governments. The Peoples Republic of China's non-democratic (communist) government, for example, is fully recognised within the international community, and indeed holds one of the five permanent seats on the Security Council of the United Nations.[61] Moreover, China is not alone in its failure to embrace democratic government. It is estimated that one-third of all states might be termed 'non-democratic'.[62] It is then difficult within the principles and practices of international law to identify an obligation to introduce democratic systems of government.[63]

In contrast to the absence of an obligation to introduce democracy, it is clear that any forcible repudiation of the democratically expressed will of the people, the clearest manifestation of the exercise of the right to internal self-determination, will not be accepted.[64] The report of Lesotho under Article 40

[59] That said, even where communities draw upon traditional social structures in the government of the state, they do so in conjunction with democratic structures (see, eg, the constitutional structures in the Marshall Islands, Palau, the Cook Islands, Vanuatu, and Fiji). The only alternative forms of government in praxis thus appear to be democratic and authoritarian.

[60] S Murphy, 'Democratic legitimacy and the recognition of states and governments', in G Fox and B Roth (eds), *Democratic Governance and International Law* (2000), 123, at 128.

[61] Ibid, at 143.

[62] The US state Department considers 117 states to be democratic <http://www.state.gov/g/drl/democ/>. This may be contrasted with the number of Member states of the United Nations: 189 <http://www.un.org/Overview/unmember.html>.

[63] See, on this point, General Assembly resolution 55/43, 'Support by the United Nations system of the efforts of Governments to promote and consolidate new or restored democracies', GA Res 55/43, 18 Jan 2001. In the Nicaragua Case, the International Court of Justice concluded that, in the absence of a specific legal obligation, there was no commitment on the part of the state to hold free and fair elections, Nicaragua Case (Merits), ICJ Rep 1986, 14, at para 261. The UN Secretary General has argued that 'individual societies decide if and when to begin democratisation', and if a state may choose to democratise or not, then logically, there can be no obligation for it to begin the process, 'Supplement to Reports on Democratisation', UN Doc A/51/761, 20 Dec 1996, at para 4.

[64] See, eg, the response of the African Commission on Human Rights to the removal of democratically elected Governments: Fox and Roth (eds), *Democratic Governance and International Law* (2000), 48, at 67–8. Consider, also, the international reaction to military coups in Haiti (Schnably, 'Constitutionalism and democratic government in the inter-American system', in ibid, 155, at 168–71), and Sierra Leone (M Reisman, 'Sovereignty and human rights in contemporary international law', in ibid, 239, at 252–3). Also, the response of the international community to

of the ICCPR, for example, talks about the 'infringement' of the people's right to self-determination' on occasions when the governing party annulled the result of an election which it had lost, and declared a state of emergency;[65] and when the democratically elected Government was overthrown in a royal coup.[66] Likewise, the declaration adopted at Warsaw in June 2000, at the Community of Democracies Ministerial Meeting, recognised the right of a democratically elected government to take office, and to not be removed from power.[67] The same point has been made by the participating states of the Organisation for Security and Co-operation in Europe.[68] Consequently, whilst it might not yet be possible to identify a general obligation on states to introduce democratic government, the evolving internal aspect of the right of a people to self-determination, the increasing numbers of states party to universal and regional human rights instruments (which all contain provisions on free and fair elections and political participation), and recognition that a democratic system of government may not legitimately be replaced by an authoritarian one, indicates a progressive and irreversible movement to a world community of democratic states.[69]

In Europe, this irreversible progress is complete. This is confirmed by all the major regional organisations: the Treaty on European Union provides in Article 6(1), that 'The Union is founded on the principles of liberty, democracy, respect for human rights and fundamental freedoms, and the rule of law,

the refusal of the military Government of Myanmar (Burma) to take 'all necessary steps towards the restoration of Democracy in accordance with the will of the people as expressed in the democratic elections held in 1990': UN General Assembly 49/197 'Situation of human rights in Myanmar': GA Res 49/197, 23 Dec 1994, at para 7. Cf reaction to the Pakistan coup (1999): I Bantekas and Z Ebrahim, 'International Law Implications of the 1999 Pakistan Coup d'etat', *ASIL Insights* (Nov 1999).

65 Initial Report (Lesotho) UN Doc CCPR/C/81/Add 14, para 4.

66 Ibid, at para 8.

67 'Warsaw Declaration: Towards a Community of Democracies,' 39(6) *ILM* (2000) 1306: 'The right of those duly elected to form a government, assume office and fulfil the term of office as legally established'. The foreign ministers and representatives from more than a hundred governments, who met in Warsaw, Poland, on 26–27 June, 2000, issued a 'Warsaw Declaration' that expressed their common aspiration and commitment to promote, strengthen and preserve democracy.

68 OSCE States have agreed to condemn unreservedly forces which seek to take power from a representative government against the will of the people as expressed in free and fair elections, Document of the Moscow Meeting of the Conference on the Human Dimension of the CSCE, at para 17.1. Further they agreed to support vigorously, in accordance with the Charter of the United Nations, in case of overthrow or attempted overthrow of a legitimately elected government of a participating state by undemocratic means, the legitimate organs of that state: ibid, at para 17.2.

69 The International Court of Justice has accepted that there is nothing within the body of international law to prevent a state from legally binding itself to adopt and maintain a particular form of government: Nicaragua Case (Merits), at para 259. For those 148 states (<htto://www.untreaty.un.org>) who are signatories to the International Covenant on Civil and Political Rights, it is arguable that their obligations to introduce democratic government (contained in Art 1 (self-determination), Art 19 (freedom of expression), Art 22 (freedom of association), and Art 25 (right to free elections)) are permanent and irreversible: see UN Doc CCPR/C/21/Rev/Add 8, General Comment No 26(61), adopted 19 Oct 1997, at para 5.

principles which are common to the Member states';[70] the Council of Europe's Court on Human Rights has concluded that '[d]emocracy . . . appears to be the only political model contemplated by the [European Convention on Human Rights] and, accordingly, the only one compatible with it';[71] and the participating states of the Organisation for Security and Co-operation in Europe have agreed to 'build, consolidate and strengthen democracy as the only system of government of our nations', and to 'co-operate and support each other with the aim of making democratic gains irreversible'.[72] If democracy is the only legitimate form of government in Europe, any state which is not 'democratic' is in breach of an international obligation. It is then important to be clear as to the scope and content of this (European) regional norm.[73] In considering this, the general principles adopted at the universal level will be considered initially, before any specific detailed elaboration of those principles within European institutions.[74]

IV. ON THE CONTENT OF THE RIGHT TO DEMOCRATIC GOVERNMENT

A democratic government is one in which political power is based on the will of the people, and which provides all citizens the opportunity to participate equally in the political life of their societies.[75] A regime may be termed 'democratic', then, if it embodies, within its institutions and mechanisms, the twin principles of political equality and popular sovereignty. It is important to recognise, in contrast to certain writings in political science, that the international legal community does not posit one paradigmatic conception of democracy;[76] it is, according to the UN Secretary General, 'not a model to be copied but a goal to be attained',[77] and democracy, and democratic government, can take many forms and evolve through many phases, depending on the particular

[70] Treaty of European Union 1992. The existence of a stable democracy is one of the criteria which must be met before new members may be considered for accession.

[71] United Communist Party of Turkey and others v Turkey, Reports 1998–I, at para 45.

[72] CSCE Charter of Paris for a New Europe (1990) 30 *ILM* 190 (1991).

[73] See also the position in the Americas following the adoption by the General Assembly of the Organisation of American States of the Santiago Commitment to Democracy and Renewal of the Inter-American System, June 4, 1991: S Schnably, in G Fox and B Roth (eds), *Democratic Governance and International Law* (2000), 155 at 162–4.

[74] It is worth repeating, above n 1, that this work is not concerned with developments in the European Union.

[75] Above n 52.

[76] The UN Commission on Human Rights has recognised the 'rich and diverse nature of the community of the world's democracies': 'Promotion of the right to democracy', UN Commission on Human Rights, E/CN 4/RES/1999/57, 28 Apr 1999.

[77] UN Secretary General, 'Support by the United Nations system of the efforts of Governments to promote and consolidate new or restored democracies', UN Doc A/52/513, 21 Oct 1997, at para 27. The Secretary General has argued that the imposition of foreign models of democracy on a society contravenes the Charter principle of non-intervention in internal affairs 'Supplement to Reports on Democratisation', above n 3, at para 10.

characteristics and circumstances of societies.[78] To associate democracy with particular institutions is to 'elevate a means into an end, [and] to confuse an instrument with its purpose'.[79] Democracy is defined primarily by reference its underlying principles (of popular sovereignty and political equality), and only secondarily in terms of the institutions which embody them. That does not mean that any given society may term itself democratic. Claims, for example, by Communist states in Eastern Europe that their regimes were 'democratic' are to be considered as nothing more than 'attempt[s] at semantic manipulation'.[80] A democratic state must conform with the internationally recognised principles, norms and standards on democratic government.[81] These provide the necessary components of a democratic government, and will be examined in turn.[82]

V. THE RIGHT TO FREE AND FAIR ELECTIONS

Democratic legitimacy depends upon the will of the people to their being governed by those in power.[83] Whilst we have characterised democracy as a system of government in which the principles of popular sovereignty and political equality are given effect, it would be impossible to conceive of a democratic state which did not seek to ascertain that will through free and fair elections.[84] Article 21(3) of the Universal Declaration on Human Rights provides the following:

[78] 'Supplement to Reports on Democratisation', above n 3, at para 4.

[79] D Beetham, above n 3, at 3.

[80] C Tomuschat, 'Democratic Pluralism: The Right to Political Opposition', in A Rosas and J Helgesen (eds), *The Strength of Diversity: Human Rights and Pluralist Democracy* (1992), 27 at 28. Cf Steiner's comment that the ICCPR had been born in a world where the term 'democracy' was employed by political systems that had little in common beyond the term itself: 'Liberal democracies stood beside socialist and people's democracies . . . [with the consequence that the term] "democratic" lost in descriptive power what it gained in popularity', Steiner, 'Political Participation as a Human Right', 1 *Harv Human Rights Yearbook* (1988) 77, 89.

[81] Universal Declaration on Democracy, above n 7, para 2.

[82] There is of course a counter argument to this thesis (that the obligation to introduce and maintain democratic forms of government creates a number of specific obligations for states): obligations to hold free and fair elections, to permit free political debate and activity and to allow political participation can be grouped together for convenience, and without significance, and termed 'obligations in respect of democracy'.

[83] See, eg, 'democracy is based on the freely expressed will of the people to determine their own political, economic, social and cultural systems', GA Res 52/18 Support by the United Nations system of the efforts of Governments to promote and consolidate new or restored democracies, adopted 2 Mar 1998, A/RES/52/18 (preamble).

[84] The traditional idea(l) of democracy is a system of decision-making in which all members of the polis meet together to reach decisions by aggregation (the will of the majority on a particular issue), and/or deliberation (that issues should be subject the fullest discussion, from all interests should be fully considered to come to the best outcome). Potentially, a state with a tiny population where all citizens might gather and make collective decisions might be termed 'democratic'. Niue has a total population of 2000. Even if only 1000 enjoyed the right to participate in the decision-making processes this would still be too great a number for any effective form of decision-making.

> The will of the people shall be the basis of the authority of government; this will shall be expressed in periodic and genuine elections which shall be by universal and equal suffrage and shall be held by secret vote or by equivalent free voting procedures.[85]

It is true that the Declaration was drafted at a time when 'the hegemony in the United Nations of the liberal democracies was unquestioned'.[86] It is clearly more influenced by the ideas of liberal democracy than the International Covenant.[87] Yet, this requirement, of electoral legitimacy for governments, is repeated in the Universal Declaration on Democracy;[88] in the Warsaw Declaration: Towards a Community of Democracies;[89] in the OSCE's Charter Of Paris For A New Europe,[90] and Copenhagen Document;[91]and in the work of the UN Commission on Human Rights.[92] Moreover, it is specifically required by both the International Covenant on Civil and Political Rights,[93] and the European Convention on Human Rights.[94] No particular electoral system need be introduced.[95] The system chosen must however provide for

[85] GA Resolution 217A (III). [86] Steiner, above n 80, 89. [87] Ibid, 87.

[88] 'The key element in the exercise of democracy is the holding of free and fair elections at regular intervals enabling the people's will to be expressed': above n 7, para 12.

[89] 'The will of the people shall be the basis of the authority of government, as expressed . . . through regular, free and fair elections', Warsaw Declaration: above n 67.

[90] 'Democratic government is based on the will of the people, expressed regularly through free and fair elections', CSCE Charter of Paris for a New Europe (1990) 30 *ILM* 190 (1991). There were thirty-four participating states.

[91] The thirty-five participating states declared that 'the will of the people, freely and fairly expressed through periodic and genuine elections, is the basis of the authority and legitimacy of all government', Document of the Copenhagen Meeting of the Conference on the Human Dimension of the CSCE, 29 *ILM* 1318 (1990), at para 6.

[92] See, UN Commission on Human Rights, 'Promoting and consolidating democracy', adopted 25 Apr 2000, CHR 2000/47, preamble and para 1(d).

[93] All citizens enjoy, without distinction, the right . . . (b) to vote and to be elected at genuine periodic elections which shall be by universal and equal suffrage and shall be held by secret ballot, guaranteeing the free expression of the will of the electors', Art 25, International Covenant on Civil and Political Rights (1966) (ICCPR).

[94] 'The High Contracting Parties undertake to hold free elections at reasonable intervals by secret ballot, under conditions which will ensure the free expression of the opinion of the people in the choice of the legislator': Art 3 of the First Protocol, of the European Convention on Human Rights (1952) (P1–3, ECHR). See also, All citizens enjoy, without distinction, the right '(a) to take part in the conduct of public affairs, directly or through freely chosen representatives; (b) to vote and to be elected in genuine periodic elections, which shall be by universal and equal suffrage and shall be held by secret ballot, guaranteeing the free expression of the will of the voters': Art 23(1), American Convention on Human Rights (1969) (AmCHR); 'Every citizen shall have the right to participate freely in the government of his country, either directly or through freely chosen representatives in accordance with the provisions of the law': Art 13(1), African Charter on Human and Peoples' Rights (1981) (AfCHPR).

[95] Electoral systems may, in the words of the European Court of Human Rights, legitimately vary 'from place to place and from time to time', Case of Mathieu-Mohin and Clerfayt, A 113 (1987) at para 54. Likewise, the drafters of Art 25, ICCPR, whilst making clear that each vote must count equally, were content to leave to states the question as to whether votes would have equal effect in the determination of the outcome of political power. Thus no preference is expressed in the travaux prepatoires of the Covenant for proportional or majority system of voting: Fox, above n 30, 556. Art 25, then, makes 'allowance for the coexistence of various types of democratic system': Steiner, above n 80, 91–2.

regular elections,[96] which are free and fair,[97] with universal and equal suffrage,[98] open to multiple parties, conducted by secret ballot,[99] monitored by independent electoral authorities, and free of fraud and intimidation. Beyond these minimum criteria, human rights law offers no guidelines for the selection of an electoral system in a given political and socio-economic context.[100] The key test for the validity of an electoral system, in the phraseology of the American Convention on Human Rights (1969), is that they must be 'genuine', in the sense that they reflect accurately the will of the people, and protect the electorate from government pressure and fraud.[101]

Elections within a democracy can be used for many things, and the election of many persons and officials. The primary purpose of elections is not though to provide the electorate with the direct power to determine which persons hold which positions of power within the state. Not all democracies provide for elections to determine the Head of State, Head of Government, or even directly the composition of the Government itself. The purpose of elections is, as the Universal Declaration on Human Rights makes clear, to ensure that the will of the people is the basis of the authority of government. Elections guarantee every citizen the right to participate in a system of collective decision-making that ultimately determines policy, leadership, and authority.[102] Consequently, any appointed, rather than elected, officials must in some way be responsible and accountable to elected officials.[103]

As a minimum however a democratic system of government must provide for free and fair elections for the legislative branch of government,[104] or in a bicameral system for one of the houses (which must be the dominant house in the legislature). The legislature must possess the requisite powers to legislate,

[96] See, Art 25(1), ICCPR; P1–3, ECHR; Art 23(1), AmCHR; Copenhagen Document above n 91 at para 7.1 and para 5.1.

[97] Art 25(1) ICCPR; Copenhagen Document above n 91 at para 7.4; see also GA Res 54/173, adopted 15 Feb 2000, 'Strengthening the role of the United Nations in enhancing the effectiveness of the principle of periodic and genuine elections and the promotion of democratisation', preamble: A/RES/54/173.

[98] Art 7, Convention on the Elimination of All Forms of Discrimination Against Women (1979); Art 23(1), AmCHR; Art 25(1), ICCPR; Copenhagen Document above n 91 at para 7.3.

[99] Art 23(1), AmCHR; Art 25(1) ICCPR; Copenhagen Document above n 91 at para 5.1.

[100] Steiner, above n 80.

[101] Fox, above n 30, at 557. See also the view of the Inter-American Commission on Human Rights, which concluded that an 'authentic' election occurs when there is 'some consistency between the will of the voters and the result of the election' (Mexico Elections Decision, Cases 9768, 9780, 9828, Inter-Am CHR 97, 108, OEA/ser L/V/11.77, doc 7, rev 1 (1990)): Fox, above n 30, 558. Fox concludes that an 'authentic' election, required by Art 23 of the AmCHR, 'is one in which no barriers, such as direct intimidation, fraud and harassment, come between the popular will and the elections result. . . The most important prerequisite to an authentic election is the absence of coercion or intimidation of voters', ibid, 567.

[102] J Waldron, above n 2, at 233.

[103] This position, Fox argues, is confirmed in Art 25, ICCPR: Fox, above n 30, 555.

[104] G Nodia, 'Nationalism and Democracy,' in L Diamond and M Plattner (eds), *Nationalism, Ethnic Conflict and Democracy* (1994), 3, at 5.

and the means to hold the executive to account.[105] The composition of the legislature(s) represents the clearest manifestation of the will of the people. Consequently, it is important that the members of the legislature, which will normally number many hundreds, as far as possible, represent the diversity of the society,[106] reflecting what the Canadian Supreme Court has called 'the diversity of [the] social mosaic'.[107] This ensures that the major interests within the society are represented within the legislature, and makes it more likely that enacted laws will enjoy widespread recognition and acceptance.[108] The extent to which a state adopts measures to promote more representative legislatures is a matter of discretion for the state,[109] as it seeks to balance the requirements of establishing a representative legislature and establishing mechanisms to ensure the emergence of a sufficiently clear and coherent political will.[110]

VI. POLITICS IN A DEMOCRACY

Having considered the right to participate in free and fair elections as one essential component of democratic government, the position of political parties and of political debate, and its limits, within a democratic system of government will be examined.

A. Freedom of Association: The Importance of Political Parties

Political parties are of central importance to a democracy as they provide organisational structures though which individuals can both seek to gain political office, and participate effectively in political debate.[111] Indeed, the Bucharest Declaration, adopted at the Third International Conference of the New or Restored Democracies, claims that political parties are not merely

[105] 'Democracy . . . requires the existence of . . . a Parliament in which all components of society are represented and which has the requisite powers and means to express the will of the people by legislating and overseeing government action', Universal Declaration on Democracy, above n 7 at para 11.

[106] Similarly, the UN Commission on Human Rights has recognised that 'freedom of opinion and expression is reflected in a democratic society through an electoral system which allows all tendencies, interests and feelings to obtain representation at the level of the executive and legislative power and, therefore, at all levels of power': 'Ways and means of overcoming obstacles to the establishment of a democratic society and requirements for the maintenance of democracy', adopted 7 Mar 1995, E/CN 4/RES/1995/60, preamble.

[107] [1991] 2 SCR. Reference re Prov. Electoral Boundaries (Sask.) 158. The Committee established under the Convention on the Elimination of Discrimination Against Women, in its General Comment (23) on 'Political and Public Life', notes 'Policies developed and decisions made by [one section of the community—in this case men] alone reflect only part of human experience and potential. The just and effective organisation of society demands the inclusion and participation of all its members', CEDAW, General Comment 23 on 'Political and Public Life', adopted 13 Jan 1997, at para 13.

[108] Waldron above n 2, at 10

[109] See, eg, CEDAW, General Comment 23 on 'Political and Public Life', above n 107, at para 15.

[110] *Case of Mathieu-Mohin and Clerfayt*, A 113 (1987) at para 54.

[111] *United Communist Party of Turkey and others v Turkey*, Reports 1998-I, at para 44.

important for democracy: they are essential to its effective functioning, with 'no single democratic system in the world able to dispense with their participation'.[112] The General Comment on Article 25 of the International Covenant on Civil and Political Rights, adopted by the Human Rights Committee, concluded that the right of citizens to vote presupposes a right to stand for election as members of a political party.[113] This ensures that the electorate has a free choice of candidates, allowing them to choose between a plurality of political ideas.[114] This is important, because, as the European Court of Human Rights has observed, 'there can be no democracy without pluralism'.[115]

Democratic government then requires that individuals enjoy the freedom to establish political parties, and that those organisations be provided with the necessary legal guarantees to enable them to compete with each other on a basis of equality.[116] The rights of political parties are guaranteed by the effective application of the human rights to free association and expression. Although not expressly mentioned in Article 11, on the right to freedom of association, the European Court of Human Rights has confirmed that, as a form of association essential to the proper functioning of democracy, political parties fall within its scope.[117] Moreover, in cases involving political parties, the exceptions to the general right to free association, set out in Article 11(2), are to be strictly construed.[118] It will then be difficult for the state to justify restrictions on the activities of political parties.

B. Freedom of Political Expression: The Importance of Political Discourse

Equally important, in a democratic system, to the right of freedom of association, is that of freedom of expression. Democracy, according to the European

[112] Bucharest Declaration, above n 7.

[113] General Comment 25 (57). Adopted by the Human Rights Committee. UN Doc CCPR/C/21/Rev 1/Add 7 (1996) at para 12. The right to stand for election is not absolute. See, in relation to P1–3, ECHR, *Ahmed and others v United Kingdom*, Reports 1998-VI, at para 75; generally, Mowbray, 'The Role of the European Court of Human Rights in the Promotion of Democracy', *PL* (1999) 703; on the International Covenant on Civil and Political Rights: see, Fox, 'The right to political participation in international law', in Fox and Roth (eds), *Democratic Governance and International Law* (2000), 48 at 54.

[114] Human Rights Committee's General Comment 25, ibid, para 15.

[115] *Socialist Party and others v Turkey*, Reports 1998-III at para 41. On the importance of pluralism in regard to political organisations, see, Document of the Moscow Meeting of the Conference on the Human Dimension of the CSCE at para 18; Copenhagen Document above n 91 at para 3. It is clear that the one party state is incompatible with the requirements of democracy: see, *Bwalya v Zambia*, UN HRCee, Comm No 314/1988, Decided 14 July 1993, 14 *HRLJ* (1993) 408 at para 6.6.

[116] Copenhagen Document above n 91 at para 7.6. The Document makes clear that the state must allow political campaigning to be conducted in a fair and free atmosphere in which neither administrative action, violence nor intimidation inhibits political parties from freely presenting their views, or prevents the voters from learning and discussing them or from casting their vote free of fear of retribution: ibid, at para 7.7.

[117] *Case of Refah Partisi (the Welfare Party) and Others v Turkey* App Nos 41340/98 and 41342–4/98, case decided 31 July 2001, at para 44.

[118] *United Communist Party of Turkey v Turkey*, Reports 1998-1, at para 46.

Court of Human Rights, 'thrives on freedom of expression'.[119] The essence of democracy, the German Federal Constitutional Court has pointed out, is the continuous free debate between opposing social forces, interests and ideas. Through this free debate, political goals become clarified, and a public opinion emerges which forms the beginnings of political intentions.[120] Informed participation in political debate is then an essential component of democratic government; without this, the UN Secretary General has argued, 'a true democracy cannot grow and prosper'.[121]

Although freedom of political debate is important for all citizens, the European Court of Human Rights has recognised that it is particularly important for political parties, elected officials and the media. Political parties and their active members, represent their electorate, draw attention to their preoccupations and defend their interests;[122] interferences with their freedom of expression call, in the words of the Court, 'for the closest scrutiny', particularly when the politician is a member of an opposition party.[123] The same may be said of elected representatives: they represent their electorate, draw attention to their preoccupations and defend their interests.[124] In the case of elected representatives, the Court has determined that '[v]ery weighty reasons' would be required to justify interfering with their freedom of expression exercised in Parliaments or comparable bodies.[125] In relation to the media, in *Lingens v Austria*, the Court concluded that the press has the right to impart political information and ideas, and 'the public . . . has a right to receive them':[126] freedom of the press, according to the Court, 'affords the public one of the best means of discovering and forming an opinion of the ideas and attitudes of political leaders'.[127]

This freedom of political expression applies not only ideas that are favourably received, but also those that offend, shock or disturb: 'such are the demands of that pluralism, tolerance and broadmindedness without which there is no "democratic society" '.[128] There must be open debate, with citizens able to express their ideas, including unpopular ones, free from government

[119] *Socialist Party and others v Turkey*, Reports 1998-III at para 45.

[120] *Brunner v European Union Treaty*, German Federal Constitutional Court [1994] 1 *CMLR* 57, at para 41 (footnotes omitted). Similarly, the UN Commission on Human Rights has noted: 'in a democracy the widest participation in the democratic dialogue by all sectors and actors in society must be promoted in order to come to agreements on appropriate solutions to the social, economic and cultural problems of a society': CHR 1995/60 above n 106. In a democratic system, debate can not be foreclosed. Democracy can not be used to introduce a regime that is not democratic: *Case of Refah Partisi*, above n 117, at para 43.

[121] UN Secretary-General, 'Support by the United Nations system of the efforts of Governments to promote and consolidate new or restored democracies', UN Doc A/53/554, 20 Oct 1998, at para 25.

[122] *Socialist Party and others v Turkey*, Reports 1998-III at para 41.

[123] *Incal v Turkey*, Reports 1998-IV, at para 46.

[124] *Jerusalem v Austria*, App No 26958/95, case decided 27 Feb 2001, at para 36.

[125] Ibid, at para 40.

[126] Ser A 103, at para 41.

[127] Ibid, at para 42.

[128] *Ahmed and others v United Kingdom*, Reports 1998-VI, at para 55.

interference.[129] There can be no justification for hindering a political group solely because it seeks to debate contentious issues or propose solutions to difficult problems:[130] there must exist 'tolerance for public debate'.[131] As the European Court of Human Rights has noted, in *Case of Freedom and Democracy Party*, 'it is of the essence of democracy to allow diverse political projects to be proposed and debated'.[132]

C. Limits on Political Activity and Expression

The European Court of Human Rights has accepted that the freedom to debate political ideas within a democracy is not unlimited.[133] There is though little scope for restrictions on political debate on issues of public interest.[134] Consequently, whilst restrictions may in principle be justified by reference to the exceptions listed in paragraph 2 of Articles 10 (freedom of expression) and 11 (freedom of association), in practice it is unlikely that limitations on freedom of political activity will be considered necessary, and therefore justified.[135] In both *Socialist Party and others v Turkey* and *United Communist Party of Turkey v Turkey*, the Court refused to accept the justifications advanced by the State for the proscription of the respective political parties. Both had been banned, in part, because of policies advocated by them in relation to the resolution of tensions between the State and the minority Kurdish population in Turkey. The Court accepted their proscription could be seen as pursuing at least one of the legitimate aims set out in Article 11(2): the protection of national security.[136] The actions were, however, 'disproportionate to the aim pursued and consequently unnecessary in a democratic society'.[137] Significantly, the Court determined:

> [The] fact that ... a political programme is considered incompatible with the current principles and structures ... does not make it incompatible with the rules of democracy. It is of the essence of democracy to allow diverse political programmes to be proposed and debated, even those that call into question the way a state is currently organised, *provided that they do not harm democracy itself.*[138]

[129] G Klosko, *Democratic Procedures and Liberal Consensus* (2000), at 43.

[130] *Socialist Party and others v Turkey*, Reports 1998-III at para 45. Also, *United Communist Party of Turkey and others v Turkey*, Reports 1998-I, at para 57.

[131] UN Secretary-General, 'Support by the United Nations system of the efforts of Governments to promote and consolidate new or restored democracies', UN Doc A/50/332 at para 105.

[132] *Case of Freedom and Democracy Party*, Reports 1999-VIII, para 41.

[133] *Incal v Turkey*, Reports 1998-IV, at para 53.

[134] *Wingrove v United Kingdom*, Reports 1996-V, at para 58.

[135] Legitimate political activity includes the freedom to debate public affairs, to hold peaceful demonstrations and meetings, to criticise and oppose, to publish political material, and to advertise political ideas: see Human Rights Committee's General Comment 25 (57) above at 79, at para 26.

[136] *Socialist Party and others v Turkey*, Reports 1998-III at para 36; *United Communist Party of Turkey and others v Turkey*, Reports 1998-I, at para 41.

[137] *Socialist Party and others v Turkey*, Reports 1998-III at para 54; *United Communist Party of Turkey and others v Turkey*, Reports 1998-I, at para 61.

[138] *Socialist Party and others v Turkey*, Reports 1998-III at para 47 (emphasis added). See also *Case of Freedom and Democracy Party*, Reports 1999-VIII, at para 41.

The only limits on the rights to freedom of political expression and association are then those that seek to protect democracy and the democratic system. The state may legitimately restrict the right of political participation where that facilitates a more effective democracy.[139] Further, it can limit freedom of political expression where that expression can be seen to incite violence against an individual or a public official or a sector of the population.[140] It is not however sufficient, to justify limitations on political expression, that the objectives of a political party coincide with those of a terrorist group waging an armed campaign. The state must distinguish between propaganda for terrorist activity and genuinely held political positions.[141] In the words of Michael Walzer, whilst it need not be tolerant of disruption,[142] the state must be tolerant of difference.[143]

These limitations seek to protect one cardinal principle of democracy, that of popular sovereignty. In *Case of Refah Partisi*, the European Court of Human Rights determined the following:

> The Court takes the view that a political party may campaign for a change in the law or the legal and constitutional basis of the state on two conditions: (1) the means used to that end must in every respect be legal and democratic; (2) the change proposed must itself be compatible with fundamental democratic principles. It necessarily follows that a political party whose leaders incite recourse to violence, or propose a policy which does not comply with one or more of the rules of democracy or is aimed at the destruction of democracy and infringement of the rights and freedoms afforded under democracy cannot lay claim to the protection of the Convention.[144]

Likewise, it is legitimate for the state to introduce measures restricting political activity which are intended to protect the second cardinal principle of democracy: political equality. Effective political equality demands that the political system accords equal value and respect to all individual members of the society in both law and fact. Thus, for example, the state might seek to limit the rights of political parties that promote hatred between the constituent groups of society. Hate propaganda, as the Canadian Supreme Court has noted,

[139] These may include for example a prohibition on local government officers participating in certain forms of political activity which could impair their impartiality. This restriction on the right to participate in political debate may be justified to protect the rights of others—the electorate—to an effective political democracy: *Ahmed and others v United Kingdom*, Reports 1998-VI, at para 54.

[140] *Baskaya and Okçuoglu v Turkey*, Reports 1999-IV, at para 62.

[141] *Incal v Turkey*, Reports 1998-IV, at para 58; see also *Sener v Turkey*, App. No. 26680/95, case decided 18 July 2000, at para 45. See generally on excluding undemocratic parties under international law, G Fox and G Nolte, 'Intolerant Democracies', 36 *Harvard International Law Journal* (1995) 1 at 38–43.

[142] Indeed the state may be obliged to be intolerant of anti-democratic forces, in order that the freely expressed will of the people may be protected against those that engage in or refuse to renounce terrorism or violence aimed at the overthrow of that order: Copenhagen Document above n 91 at para 6.

[143] M Walzer, 'The Politics of Difference: Statehood and Toleration in a Multicultural World', 10 *Ratio Juris* (1997) 165, 166.

[144] *Case of Refah Partisi and others v. Turkey*, above n 117, at para 47.

contributes little to the 'protection and fostering of a vibrant democracy where the participation of all individuals is accepted and encouraged'.[145] Democracy, then, can legitimately be intolerant of intolerance of the equal value of all with the political community. Support for this position may be found in a number of international human rights instruments.

The International Covenant on Civil and Political Rights, for example, requires that any advocacy of national, racial or religious hatred that constitutes incitement to discrimination, hostility or violence 'shall be prohibited by law'.[146] In relation to the politics of hatred, the UN Commission on Human Rights has made clear that 'political platforms based on racism, xenophobia or doctrines of racial superiority and related discrimination must be condemned as incompatible with democracy'.[147] Such political platforms have been 'resolutely condemned' by the General Assembly of the United Nations, which has urged states to 'take all available measures . . . to combat political platforms and activities based on doctrines of superiority which are based on racial discrimination or ethnic exclusiveness and xenophobia, including, in particular, neo-Nazism'.[148] In relation to Europe specifically, the Strasbourg authorities have repeatedly found inadmissible complaints from neo-Nazi organisations regarding limits on their freedom of expression. This limitations are justified by reference to the prohibition on the abuse of rights contained in Article 17 of the European Convention on Human Rights.[149]

VII. THE RIGHT TO SEEK TO INFLUENCE DECISIONS

Thus far, this analysis of the scope and content of democracy has concluded that a democratic system of government must, whatever its institutions and mechanisms, discern the will of the people through free and fair elections, and be tolerant of all political debate and activity—except that which threatens democracy or seeks to undermine the equal value accorded to all citizens. The final component of all democratic systems is the right of citizens, without distinction, to directly take part in the conduct of public affairs;[150] that is their individual right to political participation.[151]

145 [1990] 3 SCR r. v. Keegstra 697.

146 Art 20 (2).

147 'The incompatibility between democracy and racism', UN Commission on Human Rights, E/CN.4/2000/40, preamble. See also, the International Convention on the Elimination of All Forms of Racial Discrimination (1966).

148 GA Res 55/82, 'Measures to be taken against racial discrimination or ethnic exclusiveness and xenophobia, including, in particular, neo-Nazism', adopted 26 Feb 2001, A/RES/55/82, at para 3.

149 See, eg, *Glimmerveen and Hagenbeek v the Netherlands*, App Nos 8384/78 and 8406/78, 18 DR 187 (1979).

150 Art 25 (a), International Covenant on Civil and Political Rights (1966).

151 See, 'Promotion of the right to democracy', UN Commission on Human Rights, E/CN 4/1999/57, para 2. The Universal Declaration on Democracy makes clear, democracy is founded on the right of everyone to take part in the management of public affairs: above n 7 at para 11.

It is impracticable for all members of society to participate in the making of all decisions in an effective manner.[152] The modern democratic state is 'democratic' in the sense that laws are formulated and passed only by the peoples freely chosen elected representatives, or enacted with their express or implied consent. This is 'representative democracy', which, Held argues, offers the possibility of combining effective government with popular sovereignty.[153] It is important to be clear that representative democracy does not preclude the direct involvement of concerned citizens in the decisions making process: the right to participate in the decision-making process is not ceded exclusively to elected representatives. The 'great right of every man', as William Cobbett famously noted, is 'the right of having a share in the making of the laws, to which the good of the whole makes it his duty to submit.'[154]

In a democracy all concerned citizens enjoy the right to participate in, and seek to influence the outcomes of, the decision-making processes. For minorities this might appear of limited utility, as the governing majority might justify its indifference to their views by reference to its democratic mandate to govern according to its policies and ideologies. This would be a misunderstanding of the meaning and purpose of democracy. As the European Commission on Human Rights noted in the *Greek* case: the ultimate objective of the right to free elections and political participation is not democracy, but a democratic society, and in a 'democratic society' 'the majority has regard to the interests of all groups and people in the state, not merely those of its supporters.'[155] Likewise, the Court has determined that, 'democracy does not simply mean that the views of a majority must always prevail: a balance must be achieved which ensures the fair and proper treatment of minorities'.[156]

A democratic government is then obliged to listen and take into account the representations made to it on particular issues. Even if a person has a vote, they can hardly be expected to accept majority decisions as legitimate if they know that their interests are not taken seriously, or if established institutions evidence contempt or indifference towards them.[157] All voices must be heard and listened to, in particularly those of persons likely to be effected by particular policies and decisions.[158] Democratic government 'must be conceived as

[152] Above n 84.

[153] D Held, *Democracy and the Global Order: From the Modern state to Cosmopolitan Government* (1995), at 151.

[154] Cobbet, from *Advice to Young Men and Women, Advice to a Citizen* (1829), quoted in Maclarlane, *The Theory and Practice of Human Rights* (1985) at 141, in Waldron above n 2, at 232.

[155] D Harris, M O'Boyle, and C Warbrick, *Law of the European Convention on Human Rights* (1995), at 550—commenting on the findings of the Commission in the *Greek* case (12 YB (the *Greek* case) 1 at 179) on Art 3 of the First Protocol of the ECHR.

[156] *Chassagnou and Others v France*, Reports 1999-III, at para 112.

[157] Waldron above n 2 at 283–4.

[158] Where citizens are deprived of an equal voice in the government of a state, 'the chances are quite high that [their] interests will not be given the same attention as the interests of those who do have a voice', R Dahl, *On Democracy* (1998) at 76.

requiring that all citizens have the chance to participate in decision-making which affects them'.[159] The importance of this is highlighted by the United Nations' Commission on Human Rights:

> in a democracy the widest participation in the democratic dialogue by all sectors and actors of society must be promoted in order to come to agreements on appropriate solutions to the social, economic and cultural problems of a society.[160]

VIII. CONCLUSION

It is clear that democratic government, as conceived in (European) international law and institutions, involves more than a recognition that the government of the day should have been elécted, in the comparatively recent past, in free and fair elections.[161] Democracy is defined by reference to the cardinal principles of popular sovereignty and political equality. The state must be tolerant of all political debate and activity, unless it proposes harm to the democracy itself. Moreover, there must exist, as the Secretary General of the United Nations has pointed out,

> a political culture, which is fundamentally non-violent and in which no one party or group expects to win or lose all the time. Such a culture is built upon a societal consensus not about policy, but about the process and framework of democratic political life: that the will of the people is the basis of governmental authority that all individuals have a right to take part in government; that there shall be periodic and genuine elections; that power changes hands through popular suffrage rather than intimidation or force; that political opponents and minorities have a right to express their views; and that there can be loyal and legal opposition to the Government in power.[162]

A clearer understanding of democracy is important for two reasons. Where, as in Europe, a legal obligation exists to maintain effective forms of democratic government, failure by a state to comply with this international norm may permit other states to introduce non-forcible measures directed at the (re)introduction of democracy.[163] A clearer understanding of the interna-

[159] S Marks, *The Riddle of all Constitutions* (2000), at 60. Where individual human rights are involved, there may exist an obligation to consult: see, *Guerra v Italy*, Reports 1998-I, at para 60.

[160] E/CN 4/RES/1995/60, above n 106, preamble. Not only can institutions gain the allegiance of citizens by demonstrating procedural fairness, and better decision-making, and political stability, but they may, in the absence of agreement on certain contentious issues lead to an acceptance of the legitimacy of the decision or policy: see, Klosko, above n 129, at 210.

[161] Crawford, above n 6, at 7.

[162] 'Supplement to Reports on Democratisation', above n 3, at para 21; see also UN Secretary-General, 'Support by the United Nations system of the efforts of Governments to promote and consolidate new or restored democracies', UN Doc A/51/512, 18 Oct 1996.

[163] The September 2001 Belarus elections which gave President Lukashenko 75.6 per cent of

tional legal norms on democracy will then allow the identification of those states which are 'democratic' and those which are not. This may be of particular concern where formal sanctions mechanisms exist, as in the Commonwealth[164] and European Union,[165] in cases of breach. The elections aspects is relatively easy to determine: 'Elections either take place or they don't; they are or are not contested; fact finders can make judgments about [their] integrity; those elected do or do not take and hold office'.[166] It is more difficult to ascertain when the other aspects of democratic government (freedom of political activity and debate, and right to participation in the decision-making processes) have been violated, and when they have been violated to a sufficient degree to occasion a violation of the international obligation.[167]

The second reason for a clearer understanding of democracy is to ensure that vulnerable individuals and minorities, and indeed majorities, do not view democracy as government representing solely the will of the majority. A democratic system of government demands equal respect for all members of society, and as an ideal should ensure that all interests groups are represented in the legislature and/or decision-making processes. Further, a democratic system of government must be tolerant of the political expression and activity of minorities, and must take their interests into account when representations are made, or where decisions are likely to impact upon the minority. As the General Assembly of the United Nations has made clear, democracy is not promoted or consolidated by ensuring that the

the vote, were described by the head of the monitoring mission sent by the OSCE as not free and fair: 'There was an atmosphere of fear that made a fair election impossible', *The Times* (London) 11 Sept 2001. The response of the United States was to make clear that it would 'pursue measures designed to promote civil society and restore democracy to Belarus' (State Department Press Statement, 10 Sept 2001). This indicates a continuance of the policy of funding and support for anti-government parties and organisations, *The Times* (London), 3 Sept 2001. Belarus is a participating state of the OSCE, but not a member of the Council of Europe.

164 The Harare Declaration of 1991 provided the basis for Nigeria be suspended from the Commonwealth, and for Pakistan to be suspended from the Councils of the Commonwealth following military coups in those States.

165 The Treaty on European Union provides in Art 6(1), that 'The Union is founded on the principles of liberty, *democracy*, respect for human rights and fundamental freedoms, and the rule of law, principles which are common to the Member States' (emphasis added). Art 7 TEU sets out a procedure for the Council to determine the existence of a serious and persistent breach by a Member State of the principles on which the European Union is founded (as per Art 6(1)). Sanctions may go further than diplomatic shame. Alongside the determination of the existence of a serious breach, the Council acting by a qualified majority (disregarding the vote of the Member State in question) may suspend certain of the rights deriving from the application of the EU Treaty to the Member State in question (Art 7(2) TEU): see generally, N Neuwahl and S Wheatley, 'The EU and Democracy—Lawful and Legitimate Intervention in the Domestic Affairs of States?' in Arnull and Wincott (eds), *Legitimacy and Accountability in the European Union after Nice* (forthcoming).

166 Steiner, above n 80, 111.

167 In this context, the determinations of such bodies as the European Court of Human Rights on issues of freedom of expression and association may be particularly important.

will of the majority prevails, but by promoting pluralism, and maximising the participation of individuals in decision-making; promoting all human rights; and enhancing social cohesion and solidarity.[168] It might then be the case that the demand from vulnerable individuals and minorities should not be for greater and more elaborate rights, but for greater and more effective democracy.[169]

[168] GA Resolution 55/96, 'Promoting and consolidating democracy', adopted 28 Feb 2001, A/RES/55/96.

[169] The United Nations' Commission on Human Rights has concluded that the creation of the conditions for a democratic system of government are 'essential for the prevention of discrimination and for the protection of minorities', E/CN.4/RES/1995/60, above n 106, preamble.

[5]

Functional Democracy: Responding to Failures of Accountability

Molly Beutz*

I. Introduction

Since the end of the Cold War, the language of democracy has played an increasingly prominent role on the international level. Democracy has been identified as critical to the promotion and protection of human rights, as an essential factor in maintaining peace and stability between states, and as an emerging individual right. The Vienna Declaration and Programme of Action, adopted at the conclusion of the 1993 World Conference on Human Rights, states that "[d]emocracy, development and respect for human rights and fundamental freedoms are interdependent and mutually reinforcing."[1] International legal theorists, as well, have maintained "that a commitment to the principles of choice, transparency and pluralism that mark political democracy is essential to securing an institutionalized protection of other human rights."[2] Others have observed a growing global commitment, in theory if not in practice, to liberal democratic forms of government,[3] and have argued that democratic participation is "on the way to becoming a global entitlement."[4]

---

* Robert L. Bernstein Fellow in International Human Rights, Minnesota Advocates for Human Rights; B.A., Hamline University, 1996; J.D., Yale Law School, 2001. I am grateful to Professor W. Michael Reisman of Yale Law School for advising and providing valuable comments on an earlier draft of this Article.

1. World Conference on Human Rights, June 14–25, 1993, *Vienna Declaration and Programme of Action*, art. 1, ¶ 8, U.N. Doc. A/CONF.157/23 (1993), 32 I.L.M. 1661 (1993).

2. Gregory H. Fox & Brad R. Roth, *Introduction: The Spread of Liberal Democracy and Its Implications for International Law*, *in* DEMOCRATIC GOVERNANCE AND INTERNATIONAL LAW 1, 7 (Gregory H. Fox & Brad R. Roth eds., 2000).

3. *See, e.g.*, Thomas M. Franck, *The Emerging Right to Democratic Governance*, 86 AM. J. INT'L L. 46, 64 (1992).

4. *Id.* at 46. *See also* Reginald Ezetah, *The Right to Democracy: A Qualitative Inquiry*, 22 BROOK. J. INT'L L. 495, 513–15 (1997). Franck describes the human right of democratic participation as "the right of people to be consulted and to participate in the process by which political values are reconciled and choices made." Thomas M. Franck, *Legitimacy and the Democratic Entitlement*, *in* DEMOCRATIC GOVERNANCE AND INTERNATIONAL LAW, *supra* note 2, at 25, 25. Buergenthal, as well, has emphasized that "the absence of democracy in a state is today in itself a violation of the human rights of its population." Thomas Buergenthal, *The Normative and Institutional Evolution of International Human Rights*, 19 HUM. RTS. Q. 703, 715 (1997).

Yet despite a growing consensus about the importance of democracy, the definition of democracy and, correspondingly, the proper response to failures of democracy, have been deeply contested. For instance, when democracy is defined as a purely procedural norm, a failure of democracy can only be understood as the absence of such procedures and the proper response to such a failure as the establishment of democratic institutions. As many have argued, while democratic institutions are not without value, this logic does not satisfactorily capture other important issues, such as structural inequality or citizen empowerment to participate in political life.[5]

As democracy will continue to play an increasingly significant role in interstate relations, whether normatively or rhetorically, articulating a definition of democracy that can be used to identify and guide responses to failures of democracy is more critical than ever. Without such a definition, responses to failures of democracy will be determined "piecemeal, ad hoc, unilaterally, [and] opportunistically."[6] Such approaches risk undermining the legitimacy of the language of democracy, and thus its transformative power.

Part II of this Article seeks to articulate a definition of democracy that can guide such responses—a definition that neither reduces the concept to an institutional framework nor requires consensus about the particular ends to be achieved. Part II begins by discussing how the term "democracy" has been used on the international level and the connections that have been drawn between democratic forms of government and global peace and stability. It then examines a range of procedural and substantive approaches to democracy and the implications of these approaches for international responses to failures of democracy. This Part argues that the essential function of democracy is the creation and implementation of mechanisms that allow citizens to hold decision-makers accountable and thereby provide incentives for good governance and space for the resolution of disputes about power and resources. Building on this understanding of democracy, Part II concludes by outlining a functional vision of democracy as accountability that can help ensure that responses to failures of democracy promote good governance.

Part III of this Article uses the definition of democracy as accountability to articulate principles for identifying and responding to failures of democracy. Principally, responses can further accountability by strengthening domestic mechanisms where these are failing, or alternatively, by promoting institutional arrangements that vest citizens with effective sanctioning power.

---

5. *See, e.g.*, SUSAN MARKS, THE RIDDLE OF ALL CONSTITUTIONS: INTERNATIONAL LAW, DEMOCRACY, AND THE CRITIQUE OF IDEOLOGY 59 (2000); Martti Koskenniemi, *Whose Intolerance, Which Democracy?*, *in* DEMOCRATIC GOVERNANCE AND INTERNATIONAL LAW, *supra* note 2, at 436, 438; Brad R. Roth, *Evaluating Democratic Progress*, *in* DEMOCRATIC GOVERNANCE AND INTERNATIONAL LAW, *supra* note 2, at 493, 502–03.

6. Michael J. Glennon, *Sovereignty and Community After Haiti: Rethinking the Collective Use of Force*, 89 AM. J. INT'L L. 70, 73 (1995) (quoting T. C. Schelling, *The Global Dimension*, *in* RETHINKING AMERICA'S SECURITY: BEYOND COLD WAR TO NEW WORLD ORDER 196, 199 (Graham Allison & Gregory F. Treverton eds., 1992)).

This Part argues that responses should be tailored to target the incentives of elites and that the manner of response—i.e., who responds and how—may matter as much as the choice of response. Finally, Part III concludes by emphasizing that responses should promote the rule of law and transparency, two preconditions for accountability.

II. Democracy As Accountability

A. *The New Currency of Legitimacy*

The nation-state system has long been the dominant lens available for understanding the international order.[7] Within this system, control of people and territory is critical to the establishment and maintenance of internal stability, which, in turn, is the principal measurement of external legitimacy: "In the old order . . . the only test [of external legitimacy] was whether the authorities effectively controlled the state's population and territory and had the capacity to conduct foreign relations."[8] Over the last fifty years, however, the measure of state legitimacy has changed. While internal control remains a critical element of external legitimacy, such legitimacy is increasingly measured with reference to international norms. As Thomas Franck explains, "[w]e are witnessing a sea change in international law, as a result of which the legitimacy of each government someday will be measured definitively by international rules and processes."[9] One of these norms is "that those who seek the validation of their empowerment patently govern with the consent of the governed."[10] States are less willing to "accept at face value" a claim by an authoritarian or autocratic government that the legitimacy of its rule is based on "an unmanifested popular will or indigenous cultural norms . . . ."[11] The perceived legitimacy of a regime now depends, at least in part, on its ability to demonstrate that it rules with the consent of the governed. Interna-

---

7. *See, e.g.*, David Held, *The Transformation of Political Community: Rethinking Democracy in the Context of Globalization*, *in* DEMOCRACY'S EDGES 84, 86–98 (Ian Shapiro & Casiano Hacker-Cordón eds., 1999) (discussing the model of Westphalia).

8. Glennon, *supra* note 6, at 71. *See generally* Sean D. Murphy, *Democratic Legitimacy and the Recognition of States and Governments*, *in* DEMOCRATIC GOVERNANCE AND INTERNATIONAL LAW, *supra* note 2, at 123.

Control of territory and populations is also central to *internal* legitimacy. The ability to control organized violence, to "maintain order, to protect individuals in a physical sense, [and] to guarantee the operation of justice and the rule of law, are the primary functions of institutions from which [states] derive legitimacy." Mary Kaldor, *Governance, Legitimacy, and Security: Three Scenarios for the Twenty-First Century*, *in* PRINCIPLED WORLD POLITICS: THE CHALLENGE OF NORMATIVE INTERNATIONAL RELATIONS, 284, 285 (Paul Wapner & Lester Edwin J. Ruiz eds., 2000).

9. Franck, *supra* note 3, at 50.

10. *Id.* at 46. *See also, e.g.*, Ezetah, *supra* note 4, at 513–15; Thomas M. Franck, *Fairness in the International Legal and Institutional System*, 240 RECUEIL DES COURS D'ACADEMIE DE DROIT INTERNATIONAL 9, 102 (1993); Steven Wheatley, *Democracy in International Law: A European Perspective*, 51 INT'L & COMP. L.Q. 225, 236 (2002) ("Democratic legitimacy depends upon the will of the people to their being governed by those in power."). *Cf.* Western Sahara, Advisory Opinion, 1975 I.C.J. 12 (Oct. 16) (discussing self-determination as "the right of the population of Western Sahara to determine their future political status by their own freely expressed will").

11. Roth, *supra* note 5, at 507.

tional validation of a state's membership in the community of democratic states is increasingly "prized as evidence of a regime's legitimacy."[12]

This change is in accord with human rights and other international instruments.[13] The Universal Declaration of Human Rights,[14] the International Covenant on Civil and Political Rights (ICCPR),[15] the American Convention on Human Rights,[16] and the Banjul Charter on Human and Peoples' Rights[17] discuss the right to participate in government. The U.N. Human Rights Committee explains that Article 25 of the ICCPR creates rights that "are held by individuals and can therefore give rise to individual complaints if abrogated."[18] Article 3 of Protocol 1 of the European Convention on Human Rights requires signatories to hold elections.[19] Articles 2(b) and 3(d) of the Charter of the Organization of American States (OAS) affirm the OAS's commitment to representative democracy.[20]

These changes do not, however, suggest an abandonment of the importance of stability in interstate relations. The ability of a state to ensure stability in its territory continues to be the principal measure of state legitimacy. As Michael Ignatieff explains: "Western governments watching the slide of . . . regions into endemic civil war are only too likely to conclude that restoring stability—even if it is authoritarian and undemocratic—matters more than either democracy or human rights."[21] What has changed, however, is the extent to which effective control, by itself, can ensure the kind of stability needed by the world community.

Prior to the Second World War, as long as a state was in effective control of its people and territory, what occurred within its borders was by and large shielded from scrutiny by the principle of state sovereignty.[22] The develop-

---

12. Franck, *supra* note 4, at 29. *See also* MARKS, *supra* note 5, at 110 (observing that democratic governance "should be, and is arguably becoming, a criterion of international legal legitimacy").

13. *See* James Crawford, *Democracy and International Law*, 64 BRIT. Y.B. INT'L L. 113, 113–17 (1993) (discussing international human rights instruments); Tom J. Farer, *Collectively Defending Democracy in a World of Sovereign States: The Western Hemisphere's Prospect*, 15 HUM. RTS. Q. 716, 723 (1993) (same).

14. Universal Declaration of Human Rights, art. 21, G.A. Res. 217A, U.N. Doc. A/810, at 71 (1948).

15. INTERNATIONAL COVENANT ON CIVIL AND POLITICAL RIGHTS, Dec. 16, 1966, 999 U.N.T.S. 171.

16. Organization of American States, AMERICAN CONVENTION ON HUMAN RIGHTS, art. 23, Nov. 22, 1969, O.A.S. Treaty Series No. 36, 1144 U.N.T.S. 123.

17. Organization of African Unity, THE AFRICAN CHARTER ON HUMAN AND PEOPLES' RIGHTS, art. 13, June 27, 1981, O.A.U. Doc. CAB/LEG/67/3 rev. 5, 21 I.L.M. 58 (1982).

18. Margaret Satterthwaite, *Human Rights Monitoring, Elections Monitoring, and Electoral Assistance as Preventive Measures*, 30 N.Y.U. J. INT'L L. & POL. 709, 731 (1998).

19. Council of Europe, EUROPEAN CONVENTION FOR THE PROTECTION OF HUMAN RIGHTS AND FUNDAMENTAL FREEDOMS, art. 3, Nov. 4, 1950, ETS No. 155, 213 U.N.T.S. 221 ("The High Contracting Parties undertake to hold free elections at reasonable intervals by secret ballot, under conditions which will ensure the free expression of the opinion of the people in the choice of the legislature.").

20. CHARTER OF THE ORGANIZATION OF AMERICAN STATES, arts. 2(b), 3(d), 119 U.N.T.S. 3.

21. Michael Ignatieff, *Human Rights as Politics*, *in* HUMAN RIGHTS AS POLITICS AND IDOLATRY 3, 25 (Amy Gutmann ed., 2001).

22. *See generally* BRAD R. ROTH, GOVERNMENTAL ILLEGITIMACY IN INTERNATIONAL LAW 136–59 (1999) (discussing the evolution of effective control as a criterion for recognition and describing instances

ment and strengthening of international human rights norms have placed some limits on this principle. These limits, however, are consistent with, and to some extent a consequence of, a recognition that effective control is an increasingly inadequate means of ensuring global stability.[23] The articulation of the right to self-determination after the Second World War, for example, was not a radical norm shift, but rather was viewed as related to the prevention and reduction of conflict.[24] For a world emerging from a war caused in part by one of the most devastating failures of democracy,[25] the concepts of democracy, peace, and stability were vitally linked.

During the Cold War, the link between stability and democracy grew more attenuated because of the dominance of other stability-conferring mechanisms—namely, balance of power and deterrence. For example, no significant action was taken to denounce the abuses committed by the new regime in Chile after the coup in 1973 since "neither the Congress nor other international bodies seemed prepared to take measures that would have put genuine pressure on the Chilean regime."[26] As Stephen Garrett explains:

> [W]hatever his other unpleasant characteristics, Augusto Pinochet had brought considerable "order" to a Latin American country that was an important regional actor and whose destabilizing influence on the region . . . had been a matter of great concern under the [Salvador] Allende regime. . . . This acceptance of the Pinochet regime as a force for stability was accentuated by the first glimmerings of the so-called economic miracle that was to lead to very high growth rates for Chile in the latter 1970s . . . .[27]

The lack of widespread response to the Chilean coup was directly connected to the prevailing understanding that internal control and balance of power, not democracy, were the keys to ensuring stability and order. The language of democracy used during the Cold War did not refer to the responsiveness

---

in which the internal character of a regime was relevant to its international status).

23. As Fox and Nolte explain, the "idea that one state's commitment to democratic principles may also serve the collective interests of the international community predates the contemporary human right to political participation." Gregory H. Fox & Georg Nolte, *Intolerant Democracies*, 36 HARV. INT'L L.J. 1, 61 (1995).

24. *See, e.g.*, ANTONIO CASSESE, SELF-DETERMINATION OF PEOPLES: A LEGAL REAPPRAISAL 43 (1995) (explaining that the principle of self-determination, at the time of the creation of the U.N. Charter, "was considered to be a means of furthering the development of *friendly relations among States*: it would foster universal peace") (emphasis in original); Franck, *supra* note 3, at 54.

25. *Cf.* Susan Marks, *The European Convention on Human Rights and Its "Democratic Society,"* 66 BRIT. Y.B. INT'L L. 209, 222 (1996) (describing the connection between democracy and human rights articulated during the drafting of the European Convention on Human Rights and noting a drafter's concern about the importance of democracy in preventing "the re-establishment or establishment in some countries, of totalitarian dictatorships such as we saw in Italy and Germany before the war") (quoting *Collected Edition of the "Travaux Préparatoires" of the European Convention on Human Rights*, vol. 5, at 292–93 (Teitgen)).

26. STEPHEN A. GARRETT, DOING GOOD AND DOING WELL: AN EXAMINATION OF HUMANITARIAN INTERVENTION 104 (1999).

27. *Id.* at 105–06.

of a government or the political participation of its citizens, but rather served as a proxy for allegiance in ideological battles fought over spheres of influence. The balance of power that was based on these spheres of influence served, in turn, as the foundation of global political and economic stability.[28]

Balance of power, however, has been only one of many constructs that have supplemented effective control as a stability-conferring mechanism. The threat of destabilization after decolonization, for example, was the impetus behind the reliance on the principle of *uti possidetis*. This principle mandates that at decolonization, former colonial administrative boundaries become the international borders of the new state.[29] The principle of *uti possidetis* was adopted, in part, out of a belief that it would provide a clear and predictable resolution for disputes about borders, thus reducing the likelihood that competing factions would resort to armed conflict for territorial gain.[30] As the International Court of Justice has explained, the purpose of this principle is "to prevent the independence and stability of new States [from] being endangered by fratricidal struggles provoked by the challenging of frontiers following the withdrawal of the administering power."[31] Although the extent to which application of this principle contributes to long-term peace and stability is debatable,[32] its perceived stability-enhancing features led to its adoption in the context of decolonization.

With the end of the bipolar framework of the Cold War, balance of power, effective control, and the modern application of the principle of *uti possidetis*[33] are increasingly unable to satisfy the global community's need for stability. Increased transportation and communication across borders have undermined the ability of states to maintain effective control within their borders.[34] Intrastate conflicts, which undermine the ability of states to control

28. Richard Falk, *Re-framing the Legal Agenda of World Order in the Course of a Turbulent Century*, 9 TRANSNAT'L L. & CONTEMP. PROBS. 451, 464 n.45 (1999) ("The Cold War era was premised on a return to the central ideas of relying upon countervailing power and the readiness to use it as the foundation of international stability.").

29. Case Concerning the Frontier Dispute (Burk. Faso v. Mali), 1986 I.C.J. 554, ¶ 23 (Dec. 22).

30. Steven R. Ratner, *Drawing a Better Line:* Uti Possidetis *and the Borders of New States*, 90 AM. J. INT'L L. 590, 591 (1996).

31. Case Concerning the Frontier Dispute, *supra* note 29, ¶ 20. *See also* Murphy, *supra* note 8, at 127 (noting that retaining administrative borders helps promote "stability, by disfavoring unpredictable and excessive fragmentation").

32. *See, e.g.*, CASSESE, *supra* note 24, at 190–93; J. Klabbers & R. Lefeber, *Africa: Lost Between Self-Determination and* Uti Possidetis, *in* PEOPLES AND MINORITIES IN INTERNATIONAL LAW 37, 38 (Catherine Brölmann et al. eds., 1993); Ratner, *supra* note 30, at 591. Ratner explains that the "extension of *uti possidetis* to modern breakups leads to genuine injustices and instability by leaving significant populations both unsatisfied with their new status in new states and uncertain of political participation there." *Id.*

33. Murphy, *supra* note 8, at 153. The principle of *uti possidetis*, historically applied in the context of decolonization in Latin America and Africa, has been applied more recently, for example, to the breakup of the former Yugoslavia, where former internal administrative boundaries became the international borders of newly created states. *See* Ratner, *supra* note 30, at 596–97, 613–14.

34. Stephen D. Krasner, *Pervasive Not Perverse: Semi-Sovereigns as the Global Norm*, 30 CORNELL INT'L L.J. 651, 654 (1997) (explaining that "transborder flows ostensibly make it more difficult for states to exercise effective control within their own borders").

their borders, have become a dominant form of conflict in the world.[35] Further, market integration and weapons proliferation have made states more dependent on each others' stability: "[I]n the currently integrated international system, the travails of one society almost inevitably spill over into difficulties for others as well. . . . From this perspective, international instability is inherently infectious and is not likely to be as quarantined as in the past days."[36] Today, the increased instability that accompanies a regime's choice to continue or reinstitute a form of unchecked governance affects the international community. Simple, physical control of territory is increasingly insufficient to ensure international political and economic stability.

In light of the growing ineffectiveness of these existing mechanisms, democratic accountability is increasingly viewed as a highly effective alternative. As U.S. National Security Advisor Anthony Lake explained in a 1993 address, "[t]he addition of new democracies makes us feel more secure because democracies tend not to wage war on each other and tend not to sponsor terrorism. They are more trustworthy in diplomacy and they do a better job of respecting the human rights of their people . . . ."[37] States are often concerned about failures of democracy not because such failures deny citizens the right of political participation, but rather because the failure represents a threat to the global community.[38]

U.N. Security Council resolutions also reflect the understanding that failures of democracy, particularly failures represented by the overthrow of a legitimately elected government,[39] can threaten the international community as a whole. The threat to international peace and security caused by the overthrow of the elected government in Haiti, for example, was the basis for U.N. Security Council Resolution 940, authorizing intervention in Haiti under Chapter VII of the U.N. Charter.[40] Tom Farer notes that the U.N. Secu-

---

35. *See* Susan Marks, *International Law, Democracy and the End of History*, *in* DEMOCRATIC GOVERNANCE AND INTERNATIONAL LAW, *supra* note 2, at 532, 560.

36. GARRETT, *supra* note 26, at 6–7. *See also* Farer, *supra* note 13, at 726–27. The Security Council's response to the conflict in Somalia, for example, indicates that internal instability is increasingly understood as a threat to global security. *See* S.C. Res. 794, U.N. SCOR, 47th Sess., 3145th mtg., U.N. Doc. S/RES/794 (1992).

37. John Norton Moore, *Toward a New Paradigm: Enhanced Effectiveness in United Nations Peacekeeping, Collective Security, and War Avoidance*, 37 VA. J. INT'L L. 811, 825 (1997) (quoting Anthony Lake, Address Before the School of Advanced International Studies, Washington, D.C. (Sept. 21, 1993)).

38. *See* Stephen J. Schnably, *The Santiago Commitment as a Call to Democracy in the United States: Evaluating the OAS Role in Haiti, Peru, and Guatemala*, 25 U. MIAMI INTER-AM. L. REV. 393, 517 (1994) ("[G]overnments are more likely to feel threatened by and concerned about the possibility of disruption in the continuity of constitutional government than about disrespect for democracy and human rights per se.").

39. *Cf.* Malvina Halberstam, *The Copenhagen Document: Intervention in Support of Democracy*, 34 HARV. INT'L L.J. 163, 175 (1993) (arguing that intervention is permissible to restore a legitimate government deposed by force); Wheatley, *supra* note 10, at 234.

40. S.C. Res. 940, U.N. SCOR, 49th Sess., 3413th mtg., U.N. Doc. S/RES/940 (1994). *See generally* ROTH, *supra* note 22, at 366–93 (discussing the international responses to crises in Haiti, Angola and Cambodia); Douglas Lee Donoho, *The Complex Path to Peace and Democracy: Themes from the 2000 Goodwin Seminar*, 7 ILSA J. INT'L & COMP. L. 605, 610 (2001) (discussing the intervention in Haiti as justified by the threat to international peace and security posed by failures of democracy and human rights violations).

rity Council recognized the link between democracy and security as early as 1968, when it authorized economic sanctions against Rhodesia's white minority government pursuant to its Chapter VII powers.[41]

A number of scholars have argued that failures of democracy can in some contexts constitute such a threat to global stability as to justify military or other intervention. Under this view, intervention is necessary to restore the accountability mechanisms that are required for a stable world order. Gregory Fox and Georg Nolte argue, for example, that the international community may legitimately interfere with internal political processes because members of the community have a vested interest in and are affected by the outcomes of these processes.[42] Others have framed this argument for intervention in terms of the right to democratic participation. Given an individual human right to democracy, "the international community has the right . . . to concern itself with efforts designed to remove obstacles to [a state's] democratization."[43] According to this view, states that fail to ensure this right not only lose internal legitimacy, but external legitimacy as well.[44]

Regional organizations, as well, have identified threats to democracy, such as the overthrow of an elected government, as threats to regional peace and security, sufficient in some cases to justify intervention.[45] Under the Charter of Paris, for example, members of the Organization for Security and Cooperation in Europe (OSCE) commit to "co-operate and support each other with the aim of making democratic gains irreversible."[46] In the Moscow Document, the OSCE's commitment is even more explicit. Member states condemn "forces which seek to take power from a representative government of a participating State against the will of the people as expressed in free and fair elections" and agree, in the case of such overthrow, to support vigorously the legitimately elected government of that state.[47] The OSCE's Copenhagen Document provides that member states

---

Pursuant to Chapter VII of the U.N. Charter, the Security Council "shall determine the existence of any threat to the peace, breach of the peace, or act of aggression, or decide what measures shall be taken . . . to maintain or restore international peace and security." U.N. CHARTER art. 39.

41. Farer, *supra* note 13, at 726.

42. Fox & Nolte, *supra* note 23, at 61. *See also* David Luban, *Just War and Human Rights*, 9 PHIL. & PUB. AFF. 160, 164 (1980) (discussing the legality of intervention and arguing that "the duty of non-intervention exists only toward states which are legitimate").

43. Buergenthal, *supra* note 4, at 715. *See also, e.g.*, FERNANDO R. TESÓN, HUMANITARIAN INTERVENTION 15–16 (1985).

44. *See* Oscar Schachter, *The Legality of Pro-Democratic Invasion*, 78 AM. J. INT'L L. 645, 649–50 (1984).

45. *See, e.g.*, Buergenthal, *supra* note 4, at 727–39 (discussing actions undertaken by the OAS, particularly the OAS's response to the Somozas in Nicaragua); Marks, *supra* note 25, at 231–34 (discussing same in the European Community). In part, regional networks may place such an emphasis on democracy because the external effects of failures of democracy will be felt most immediately by neighboring states. The fact that the external effects of internal instability are felt first and most strongly within regional networks forms part of the rationale for response by local or regional organizations. *See infra* Part III.E.

46. Conference on Security and Co-operation in Europe, CHARTER OF PARIS FOR A NEW EUROPE, Nov. 21, 1990, 30 I.L.M. 190, 195 (1991).

47. Conference on Security and Co-operation in Europe, DOCUMENT OF THE MOSCOW MEETING OF THE CONFERENCE ON THE HUMAN DIMENSION OF THE CSCE, arts. 17.1, 17.2, Oct. 3, 1991, 30 I.L.M.

recognize their responsibility to defend and protect . . . the democratic order freely established through the will of the people against the activities of persons, groups or organizations that engage in or refuse to renounce terrorism or violence aimed at the overthrow of that order or of that of another participating State.[48]

Resolution 1080 of the OAS reflects similar concerns about threats to democracy within the region. In that resolution, the member states of the OAS resolved to instruct the Secretary-General "to call for the immediate convocation of a meeting of the Permanent Council in the event of any occurrences giving rise to the sudden or irregular interruption of the democratic political institutional process or of the legitimate exercise of power by a democratically elected government in any of the Organization's member states" so that appropriate action could be taken.[49] The OAS subsequently enacted the Protocol of Washington, which amended the OAS Charter to allow it to suspend from the organization a member state "whose democratically constituted government has been overthrown by force."[50]

Moreover, democratic accountability is increasingly viewed as critical to global economic stability. The conditional lending policies of the World Bank, for example, reflect this understanding. While the World Bank uses primarily "economic considerations" to determine a borrower's loan eligibility, it defines "economic" broadly to include such issues as fear on the part of foreign investors that "political instability of a non-democratic government might obstruct foreign investment."[51]

Because it promotes both internal and external political and economic stability, democracy as accountability "address[es] not only the well-being of those living within democratic systems, but the interests of outsiders as well."[52] As a result, the international community is, at the very least, "no longer indifferent to the internal character of regimes exercising effective control within

---

1670 (1991).

48. Conference on Security and Co-operation in Europe, DOCUMENT OF THE COPENHAGEN MEETING OF THE CONFERENCE ON THE HUMAN DIMENSION OF THE CSCE, art. 6, June 29, 1990, 29 I.L.M. 1305 (1990). *See also* Halberstam, *supra* note 39, at 175 (maintaining that the Copenhagen Document supports pro-democratic intervention).

49. Representative Democracy, ¶ 1, OAS G.A. Res. 1080, OAS Doc. AG/RES. 1080 (XXI-O 91) (June 5, 1991). *See generally* Farer, *supra* note 13, at 723 (discussing the evolution of the OAS's response to coups and other antidemocratic events in the region).

50. Organization of American States, PROTOCOL OF WASHINGTON, art. 9, OEA/Ser.A/2 Add. 3, 33 I.L.M. 1005 (1994). *See generally* Ellen L. Lutz, *Strengthening Core Values in the Americas: Regional Commitment to Democracy and the Protection of Human Rights*, 18 HOUS. J. INT'L L. 643, 650 (1997). In 2001, the OAS General Assembly adopted the Inter-American Democratic Charter, in which it affirmed that the Charter of the OAS "recognizes that representative democracy is indispensable for the stability, peace, and development of the region" and set forth democracy-strengthening procedures that can be followed by member states. INTER-AMERICAN DEMOCRATIC CHARTER, pmbl., OAS Doc. OEA/Ser.P/AG/RES.1 (XXVIII E/01) (Sept. 11, 2001).

51. Mark E. Wadrzyk, *Is It Appropriate for the World Bank to Promote Democratic Standards in a Borrower Country?*, 17 WIS. INT'L L.J. 553, 569–70 (1999).

52. Fox & Roth, *supra* note 2, at 6.

'sovereign' States."[53] Although concern about the threat to international security posed by terrorism has led to a renewed emphasis on control of borders and populations, failure to ensure that such control is paired with a commitment to principles of democratic accountability may ultimately undermine prospects for sustainable international peace and stability.[54] As a means of ensuring peace and stability, democratic accountability must be understood as an emerging obligation *erga omnes*—a duty owed not only "by all governments to their peoples," but also "by each government to all members of the international community."[55]

B. Approaches to Democracy

Although democracy has been identified as essential to both the protection of human rights and the furtherance of international peace and security, its definition is deeply contested. Current approaches to the definition of democracy often reference some procedural component or institutional political arrangement.[56] Yet theoretical approaches differ widely in the extent to which they articulate whether, and if so, what, substantive goals are or should be associated with those institutional arrangements.[57] At the same time, however, definitions that focus on institutional arrangements and those that focus on substantive concerns are not necessarily mutually exclusive. Rather, they embody a range of possibilities: "Substantive democracy is a maximal goal, relevant to normative evaluation of all regimes but susceptible only of incomplete realization in even the most highly developed polity. Popular sover-

53. *Id.* at 2.

54. *See* THOMAS L. FRIEDMAN, LONGITUDES & ATTITUDES 244–45 (2002).

55. Franck, *supra* note 3, at 54. Wheatley also observes:

> [While] it might not yet be possible to identify a general obligation on states to introduce democratic government, the evolving internal aspect of the right of a people to self-determination, the increasing numbers of states party to universal and regional human rights instruments . . ., and recognition that a democratic system of government may not legitimately be replaced by an authoritarian one, indicates [sic] a progressive and irreversible movement to a world community of democratic states.

Wheatley, *supra* note 10, at 234.

56. Participatory approaches to democracy, in contrast, emphasize not political arrangements, but the experience and transformative power of participation and deliberation. *See, e.g.*, BENJAMIN R. BARBER, STRONG DEMOCRACY: PARTICIPATORY POLITICS FOR A NEW AGE (1984); DAVID HELD, MODELS OF DEMOCRACY 264–73 (2d ed. 1996) (discussing the work of Carole Pateman and C.B. Macpherson). For discussions of the evolution and range of democratic theories and practices, see generally ROBERT A. DAHL, DEMOCRACY AND ITS CRITICS (1989); HELD, *supra*.

57. *Cf.* Robert A. Dahl, *Can International Organizations Be Democratic? A Skeptic's View*, *in* DEMOCRACY'S EDGES, *supra* note 7, at 19, 25 (describing a similar analysis with reference to political arrangements generally). Dahl notes that any distinction between substance and procedure is, to some extent, illusory: "Because substantive solutions are not self-enacting, they require procedures for determining the substantively best outcomes; and because procedures, including democratic procedures, are means to ends, not ends in themselves, their justification depends on more than purely procedural values." *Id. See also* Koskenniemi, *supra* note 5, at 437 (arguing that even those who posit an entirely procedural model of democracy "are automatically compelled to present an external ideal, or a principle, of the good life by reference to which their understanding of democracy may seem justified").

eignty is a minimal goal, requisite to the bare recognition of a government's legitimacy against the claims of rival contestants."[58]

Understood as a purely procedural norm, democratic institutions simply provide rules of decision for determining who is to govern. According to this view, as articulated by Joseph Schumpeter, democracy "is that institutional arrangement for arriving at political decisions in which individuals acquire the power to decide by means of a competitive struggle for the people's vote."[59] As James Allan explains, the essential distinction between this purely procedural model and more substantive visions of democracy "revolves around whether democracy involves or entails certain outcomes—certain right and just outcomes—or whether democracy is purely procedural—the procedure being that the views of the majority prevail."[60] This purely procedural view of democracy, i.e., the understanding of democracy as an "organizational form or checklist of procedures,"[61] has informed most democracy-promoting initiatives on the international level.[62] Because of the emphasis on institutional arrangements that generate political competition, democracy-promoting initiatives have focused almost exclusively on elections and other mechanisms that can foster such competition, such as multi-party systems and universal enfranchisement.[63]

A number of scholars, among them most recently Susan Marks, Martti Koskenniemi, and Brad Roth, have criticized exclusive reliance on democratic institutions, and in particular electoral processes, as inadequately attentive to issues such as structural inequality, human rights, and social justice. Roth explains that universal franchise

> merely allows all sectors of the society to select once every four years from among pre-packaged candidates that are, in the main, controlled by social élites (or worse, by neo-colonial interests). Such participation scarcely implies the rudiments of accountability, let alone popular empowerment. Popular prerogative to reject one given set of administrators of the social order in favor of another, while not a trivial devel-

---

58. Roth, *supra* note 5, at 512.

59. JOSEPH SCHUMPETER, CAPITALISM, SOCIALISM AND DEMOCRACY 269 (1942). *See also* HELD, *supra* note 56, at 177–98 (describing Schumpeter's theory of democracy). Generally, pluralist theories also focus primarily on institutional arrangements. Central to the "classic version" of pluralism is the non-hierarchical, non-competitive arrangement of power. Decisions are made and stability is achieved through a process of bargaining between a variety of interest groups. *Id.* at 201–02.

60. James Allan, *Liberalism, Democracy, and Hong Kong*, 28 H.K. L.J. 156, 164–65 (1998).

61. MARKS, *supra* note 5, at 59.

62. *Id.* at 52. For an overview and analysis of the United States' democracy-promoting initiatives, see generally THOMAS CAROTHERS, AIDING DEMOCRACY ABROAD: THE LEARNING CURVE (1999). Carothers explains that the United States' "core strategy" in providing democratization aid—what he calls the United States' "democracy template"—is focused on elections, state institutions, and civil society. *Id.* at 86. The U.S. democracy assistance program not only focuses on these three institutional components, but also assumes a model of democratization composed of a "natural sequence" of specific steps. *Id.* at 87.

63. *See, e.g.*, Tanja Hohe, *Totem Polls: Indigenous Concepts and "Free and Fair" Elections in East Timor*, 9 INT'L PEACEKEEPING 69, 69–70 (2002).

> opment, is very far from the power to make government responsive to popular initiatives, input, or needs.[64]

Drawing on scholarship that characterizes such systems as "low-intensity democracies,"[65] Marks argues that the focus on a purely procedural model of democracy "concentrate[s] attention on forms and events, and correspondingly . . . shift[s] the emphasis away from relationships and processes."[66] This preoccupation, Marks explains, obscures "more far-reaching objectives, such as enhancing respect for human rights, social justice, and civilian control of the military."[67] Koskenniemi similarly emphasizes that both procedural and participatory theories of democracy "leave aside powerful aspirations that are neither about procedural correctness nor about political participation, but that stress the primacy of spiritual and economic well-being to political rights and the quality of communal life to individual life-choices."[68] Henry Steiner, as well, has emphasized how focusing on electoral procedures can undermine citizen empowerment.[69] Although social and material inequalities affect the ability of individuals to exercise political power, the exclusive emphasis on procedures makes "the extent to which social and material conditions affect the opportunities for political participation . . . appear irrelevant."[70] This, in turn, further entrenches the status quo and undermines the chances for "transformative social and political change."[71] In essence, the minimalist definition of democracy becomes self-fulfilling by preempting inquiry into structural inequality and prospects for societal transformation.[72]

---

64. ROTH, *supra* note 22, at 106. As Diamond explains, this is the "fallacy of electoralism"—the error of "neglecting the degree to which multiparty elections may exclude significant sections of the population from the contest for power, allow for extensive human rights violations, or leave significant areas of state authority dominated by the military or other unelected figures." Larry Diamond, *Consolidating Democracy in the Americas*, 550 ANNALS AM. ACAD. POL. & SOC. SCI. 12, 13 (1997).

65. "Low-intensity democracies" are those in which

> [d]emocratization has been informed by a[n] . . . undemanding and highly formal conception of democracy, in which the holding of periodic multiparty elections is taken largely to suffice, and more far-reaching institutional changes are held to be optional extras. . . . [L]ow intensity democracy is largely a "cosmetic" model. It provides some of the forms associated with modern democracy, but leaves established centers of power substantially intact.

Susan Marks, *Guarding the Gate with Two Faces: International Law and Political Reconstruction*, 6 IND. J. GLOBAL LEGAL STUD. 457, 464–65 (1999).

66. MARKS, *supra* note 5, at 52.

67. *Id.* at 53. *See also, e.g.*, Farer, *supra* note 13, at 746; Koskenniemi, *supra* note 5, at 438; Marks, *supra* note 65, at 464–69; Roth, *supra* note 5, at 502–03; Gerry J. Simpson, *Imagined Consent: Democratic Liberalism in International Legal Theory*, 15 AUST. Y.B. INT'L L. 103 (1994); David Wippman, *Defending Democracy Through Foreign Intervention*, 19 HOUS. J. INT'L L. 659, 667 (1997).

68. Koskenniemi, *supra* note 5, at 438.

69. Henry Steiner, *Political Participation as a Human Right*, 1 HARV. HUM. RTS. Y.B. 77 (1988), *reprinted in* INTERNATIONAL HUMAN RIGHTS IN CONTEXT 890, 894 (Henry J. Steiner & Philip Alston eds., 2000) ("A nearly exclusive reliance on elections heightens the sense of powerlessness of the many to act other than passively by reacting to choices formulated by others.").

70. MARKS, *supra* note 5, at 61.

71. *Id.* at 74.

72. *Id.*

An exclusive focus on procedural democracy also renders international responses to failures of democracy vulnerable to manipulation. Such a focus allows governments to achieve international validation by implementing procedures, such as elections, while remaining unaccountable to their citizens. Although some procedures may be preferable to no procedures at all, Franck's observation remains apt:

> Increasingly, . . . governments whose legitimacy is questioned are turning to the international system for that validation which their national polis is as yet unable to give. They do so to avoid the alternative—persistent challenge to authority by coups, countercoups, instability and stasis—and to enable themselves to govern with essential societal acquiescence. What they seek is legitimization by a global standard monitored by processes of the international system.[73]

Haitian President Jean-Bertrand Aristide himself observed that "the forces of order wanted us to vote so that it would appear to the outside world that we were a happy, peaceful democracy, and then the exploitation and corruption could go on just as before."[74] Although democratic procedures are ostensibly intended to ensure legitimate authority, such procedures now themselves confer and measure legitimacy.

Finally, a purely procedural model of democracy provides no criteria for making normative assessments of the outcomes of the procedures because it merely "lists the institutional requisites without revealing the underlying logic of ends that generates the list."[75] Without such criteria, it is difficult to evaluate the usefulness of the institutions and procedures in different contexts. Working from such a model, responding actors may not be able to tailor their responses to the needs of a particular situation or adapt to changing circumstances.

Majoritarian democratic procedures, for example, may not adequately ensure the rights of minorities. The ideal of majoritarianism presupposes a "certain uniformity in basic political and social values such that no particular subset of the population is categorically relegated to minority status, and all members of the polity are able to participate in and influence the out-

---

73. Franck, *supra* note 3, at 50–51. As Franck explains, "the bare monitoring of the act of voting may place observers in the position of seeming to legitimate an electoral victory that was not fairly achieved." *Id.* at 76.

74. Schnably, *supra* note 38, at 523 (quoting JEAN-BERTRAND ARISTIDE, IN THE PARISH OF THE POOR: WRITINGS FROM HAITI 9–11 (Amy Wilentz trans., 1990)).

75. Roth, *supra* note 5, at 495. As Roth explains further, this understanding of democracy fails to provide criteria for evaluating outcomes in part precisely because it is a procedural norm. "[W]hat counts as democratic development . . . cannot be resolved by deduction from a procedural model, because whatever is deduced is ambiguous or incomplete without reference to the substantive social purposes for which one values the procedures." *Id.* at 496. *See also* DAVID BEETHAM, DEMOCRACY AND HUMAN RIGHTS 3 (1999) (emphasizing that associating "democracy with [particular institutions] is to 'elevate a means to an end, [and] to confuse an instrument with its purpose'") (citations omitted); C. DOUGLAS LUMMIS, RADICAL DEMOCRACY 111 (1996) ("[I]t is an error to refer to institutions as if they were synonymous with the conditions they are intended to promote.").

come of political decisions."[76] In reality, few states, if any, possess this level of homogeneity, and "majorities often willingly vote to maintain, reinforce, or even restore socioeconomic stratification."[77] Yet if the definition of democracy is purely procedural, majoritarian rule is no more or less appropriate than any other institutional arrangement, even when it results in the marginalization of one or more subsets of the population. If, on the other hand, the working definition of democracy includes some reference to ends—such as social and material equality—pure majoritarian rule may be less desirable. In other words, determining whether particular procedures are appropriate requires an analysis of the purposes those institutions are intended to promote.

In referencing the ends served by institutional arrangements, substantive visions of democracy avoid many of the problems posed by purely procedural definitions.[78] Some substantive approaches emphasize the extent to which democracy ensures the rights necessary for equal participation in communal life,[79] while others discuss democratic procedures as expressions or means of realizing other values, such as political equality and popular sovereignty.[80] Marks, for example, explains that democracy "must be understood as an ongoing process of enhancing the possibilities of self-rule and the prospects for political equality, against a background of changing historical circumstance."[81] Representative democracy, as well, has often been understood as a more substantive form of procedural democracy. The "key characteristic" of represen-

---

76. Chimène Keitner, *National Self-Determination: The Legacy of the French Revolution*, COLUM. INT'L AFF. ONLINE, ¶ 47 (Mar. 2000), http://www.ciaonet.org/isa/woc01/index.html. *See also* WILL KYMLICKA, MULTICULTURAL CITIZENSHIP 52 (1995) (explaining that Mill's understanding of democracy as government by the people "is only possible if 'the people' are 'a people'—a nation").

77. Roth, *supra* note 5, at 509. Roth explains that "[u]nder conditions where social hierarchy is locked in, such as non-polyarchy or sham democratization, the democratic perspective would not seem to favor legitimating the *status quo* and casting its disloyal opposition into a kind of international outlawry." *Id.* at 510.

78. *See, e.g.*, Allan, *supra* note 60, at 166 (explaining that Dworkin reconciled substantive and procedural democracy by equating "democracy with right outcomes (about equality and respect)" which then allowed him to justify the choice to "abandon majoritarian institutions when they do not respect these conditions (or, rather, to opt for procedures—like strong judicial review—that protect them better)").

79. *See, e.g.*, Diamond, *supra* note 64, at 13 (discussing Dahl's argument that "to be meaningful, competition and participation also require extensive civil liberties and true political pluralism and freedom") (quoting ROBERT DAHL, POLYARCHY: PARTICIPATION AND OPPOSITION 3 (1971)); Susan Marks, *The End of History? Reflections on Some International Legal Theses*, 8 EUR. J. INT'L L. 449, 471 (1997) (discussing substantive theories of democracy).

80. *See, e.g.*, Julie Mertus, *From Legal Transplants to Transformative Justice: Human Rights and the Promise of Transnational Civil Society*, 14 AM. U. INT'L L. REV. 1335, 1359 (1999) (explaining that democracy must "feature transparent and participatory decision-making and a government that is in constant dialogue with its citizens to shape and direct fundamental policies" and that "[i]t is pluralistic decision-making that is at the heart of democracy") (quoting Eric Dannenmaier, *Democracy in Development: Toward a Legal Framework for the Americas*, 11 TUL. ENVTL. L.J. 1, 3 (1997)); Wheatley, *supra* note 10, at 230 (defining democracy as a system of government "in which the principles of popular sovereignty and political equality find expression in free and fair elections and popular participation in the political process").

81. MARKS, *supra* note 5, at 59. *See also* Gregory H. Fox & Georg Nolte, *Intolerant Democracies*, *in* DEMOCRATIC GOVERNANCE AND INTERNATIONAL LAW, *supra* note 2, at 389, 401 ("Democratic procedure is not an end in itself but a means of creating a society in which citizens enjoy certain essential rights, primary among them the right to vote for their leaders.").

tative democracy is the attempt to construct a government "that is supposed to operate automatically to produce the result approximating what it would be if the people had political virtue, thereby making political virtue itself superfluous."[82]

Although the more substantive visions articulated by Marks, Koskenniemi, and Roth avoid the reductionist approach of purely procedural democracy, they, too, may be difficult to translate into principles for responding to failures of democracy. While guidelines are necessary to ensure consistent responses and avoid potentially "heavy-handed (and predatory) interventionism,"[83] substantive definitions of democracy may fail to yield such guidance because they are often "over- and under-inclusive at the same time, too general to provide political guidance and always suspect as a neocolonialist strategy."[84]

Substantive definitions of democracy are under-inclusive in that they often tend to presuppose a consensus on what constitutes just or fair outcomes and, thus, to impose particular substantive visions where they are neither appropriate nor useful. At the same time, however, the attempt to avoid this under-inclusiveness by describing the substance of democracy at a more general level presents the problem of over-inclusiveness. While true material and social equality among citizens is a worthy goal, it can be difficult to determine whether any particular response will ultimately further or undermine this goal. As Roth explains, in discussing the right to democratic governance, "[s]uch a 'right' either is indeterminate or entails the imposition of a specific liberal-democratic worldview that has yet to find general acceptance."[85]

Thus, despite the importance of more substantive visions of democracy as a counterweight to the purely procedural approach, substantive definitions are not easily put into practice. A vision of democracy that attends to questions of social and material equality and structural change may, however, be operationalized through a focus on the *function* of democracy: ensuring the accountability of decision-makers by providing those affected by the decisions with the power to sanction their leaders.

C. The Function of Democracy

A definition of democracy as accountability attends to substantive goals not by articulating the ends to be achieved, but by allocating power over deci-

82. LUMMIS, *supra* note 75, at 38. *See also* JAMES S. FISHKIN, DEMOCRACY AND DELIBERATION: NEW DIRECTIONS FOR DEMOCRATIC REFORM 44 (1991) (explaining that Madison's theory of government emphasized design of a system that would result in the election of governors who would speak with a "public voice" consonant with the greater public good, though not necessarily "what the people happen to think given their passions and lack of information"). *See generally* DAHL, *supra* note 56, at 28–30; Held, *supra* note 7, at 84, 89.

83. ROTH, *supra* note 22, at 149. *See also* Crawford, *supra* note 13, at 127 ("[T]he 'nations of the world will not accept international rules that yield a different answer to the question of whether an action is legal depending on the identity of the actor.'") (quoting D.W. Bowett, *International Incidents: New Genre or New Delusion?*, 12 YALE J. INT'L L. 386, 388 (1987)).

84. Koskenniemi, *supra* note 5, at 439–40.

85. ROTH, *supra* note 22, at 424.

sion-making to those who are affected by the decisions. Allocating power in this way fosters decision-making that is more responsive to the needs (i.e., the substantive goals) articulated by the populace because it requires leaders to bear the consequences of their decisions and provides space for dialogue within a society.

First, democratic structures prevent leaders from externalizing the costs of their bad decisions. As explained by the Chicago School approach to public choice theory,[86] leaders will be responsive to the needs and desires of the populace primarily when self-interest forces them to respond. Correspondingly, authoritarian regimes are unresponsive to citizens' needs because leaders of these regimes can insulate themselves from the consequences of their decisions. As Susan Gibson explains,

> without a voting public to tip the scales, the public choice concerns of a totalitarian leader are considerably different than those of a democratic leader. . . . [T]he public choice doctrine "operates off-the-scale within totalitarian and non-democratic regimes to produce what might be characterized as massive government failure in those systems."[87]

Accountability mechanisms, on the other hand, not only require leaders to face the consequences of their decisions, but place the power to sanction those leaders in the hands of those most affected by the decisions—the citizens. The ability of those affected by decisions to sanction the decision-makers functions as a powerful incentive for responsible and, more importantly, responsive decision-making. As Amartya Sen argues, "[g]overnmental response to the acute suffering of people often depends on the pressure that is put on the government, and this is where the exercise of political rights (voting, criticizing, protesting and so on) can make a real difference."[88] Accountability mechanisms are instrumental because of the incentive structures they impose on the decision-makers. Decision-makers have an incentive to respond effectively to the needs of the populace if they know they can be criticized and sanctioned by citizens.[89]

The clearest application of this understanding of democracy as accountability is represented by Immanuel Kant's theory of the "democratic peace."[90] According to this theory, democracies do not go to war with each other in

---

86. *See, e.g.*, Edward L. Rubin, *Public Choice, Phenomenology, and the Meaning of the Modern State: Keep the Bathwater, But Throw out That Baby*, 87 CORNELL L. REV. 309, 310–11 (2002).

87. Susan S. Gibson, *International Economic Sanctions: The Importance of Government Structures*, 13 EMORY INT'L L. REV. 161, 192 (1999) (quoting Moore, *supra* note 37, at 834).

88. AMARTYA SEN, DEVELOPMENT AS FREEDOM 151 (1999).

89. *See id.* at 152. *See also* Moore, *supra* note 37, at 831 ("The sense of distance between the ruler and the ruled—between 'us' and 'them'—is a crucial feature of famines.").

90. IMMANUEL KANT, PERPETUAL PEACE (Lewis White Beck ed., Liberal Arts Press 1957) (1795). *See also, e.g.*, Ezetah, *supra* note 4, at 517; John M. Owen IV, *International Law and the "Liberal Peace," in* DEMOCRATIC GOVERNANCE AND INTERNATIONAL LAW, *supra* note 2, at 343; Satterthwaite, *supra* note 18, at 764.

part because citizens would sanction a leader who decided to go to war despite popular opposition. Former U.N. Secretary-General Boutros Boutros-Ghali has explained that "accountability and transparency of democratic Governments to their own citizens, who understandably may be highly cautious about war, as it is they who will have to bear its risks and burdens, may help to restrain recourse to military conflict with other states."[91] Farer emphasizes, as well, that recent studies have tended to confirm the OAS founders' intuition "that the mutual possession of authentically democratic political orders vastly reduces the security dilemmas of states and correspondingly enhances their capacity for cooperation."[92] Although many have questioned whether democracies are inherently peaceful,[93] democratic peace theory does illustrate at least the potential stability-promoting aspects of systems that ensure accountability.

Second, accountability mechanisms can serve as a means by which various groups in a society can resolve disagreements about the proper allocation of resources and access to political power, which could otherwise be significant sources of societal conflict.[94] The accountability of the state to civil society, for example, helps ensure that "public power does not tread on private right, and . . . that no faction of civil society can capture enough of State power to disproportionately advantage itself at the expense of other interests."[95] Accountability mechanisms accomplish this principally by providing the power to sanction to citizens in all segments of the population. Ideally, providing sanctioning power to citizens can help ensure that they are consulted about their needs. Social programs, such as poverty alleviation, or shelter and food relief

91. Owen, *supra* note 90, at 347 (quoting The Secretary-General, Statement to the General Assembly ¶ 18, U.N. Doc. A/51/761 (Dec. 20, 1996)). *See also* Moore, *supra* note 37, at 824. Elsewhere, Boutros-Ghali emphasized that "[i]ndividual involvement in the political process enhances the accountability and responsiveness of governments. Governments which are responsive and accountable are likely to be stable and to promote peace." Fox & Nolte, *supra* note 23, at 4 (quoting Boutros Boutros-Ghali, *Maintaining International Peace and Security: The United Nations as Forum and Focal Point*, 16 LOY. L.A. INT'L & COMP. L. REV. 1, 2 (1993)).

92. Farer, *supra* note 13, at 724.

93. *See, e.g.*, MARKS, *supra* note 5, at 47 ("While liberal states are believed likely to avoid war with other liberal states, those states are not held to adopt an especially peaceful posture towards non-liberal states."); Koskenniemi, *supra* note 5, at 439 ("War has not been absent but has been externalized—wars by proxy. If so, then the causal link is not between democracy and peace but between imperialism, development, and peace—with the implication of underdevelopment and war *au delà*."); Fareed Zakaria, *The Rise of Illiberal Democracy*, FOREIGN AFF., Nov.–Dec. 1997, at 22, 36 (noting that in reality, democracies are "more warlike, going to war more often and with greater intensity than most states," and that "[i]t is only with other democracies that the peace holds").

94. As Wheatley explains, "[t]he collapse of authoritarian governments, and the evident failings of socialist central planning, have resulted in a general recognition that democracy provides the best-known process through which the resolution of conflicts between different interest groups may be achieved." Wheatley, *supra* note 10, at 226 (footnote omitted).

95. Roth, *supra* note 5, at 499–500. Stotzky similarly emphasizes that "to satisfy democratic values, the level of material satisfaction must be determined through a free process of deliberation among the people." Irwin P. Stotzky, *Establishing Deliberative Democracy: Moving from Misery to Poverty with Dignity*, 21 U. ARK. LITTLE ROCK L. REV. 79, 84 (1998). As discussed in Part III.C, *infra*, depending on the context, preventing any one faction from disproportionately advantaging itself at the expense of another may require unequal allocations of sanctioning power.

programs, will often be most effective when the communities that need them are involved in their selection, design, management, and delivery.[96] Accountability mechanisms may thus contribute to the reduction of systemic inequalities—and, correspondingly, intrastate conflict—because they ensure the participation of different groups in resolving conflicts about the allocation of resources.[97] Clearly, as Marks emphasizes, this function is not generally well-served in low-intensity democracies.[98] The prevalence of economic inequality in low-intensity democracies does not, however, indicate that accountability mechanisms do not contribute to the equitable distribution of resources; rather, it shows that low-intensity democracies may not be highly accountable.

In addition, constituencies defined by ethnic, religious, or other identities may come to agreements about power allocation through accountability mechanisms. For example, in Bosnia, the "fundamental source of dysfunction is the absence of a formula for governance acceptable to each of its ethnic constituencies."[99] Without structures that can be used to reach agreements about power, "contending interests are likely to seek to settle their differences through conflict rather than through accommodation."[100] Where, however, institutional arrangements give citizens the power to hold their leaders accountable and determine how and when that power may be exercised, the predictable governance created by such a system reduces the need for factions to resort to conflict to resolve disputes.[101]

---

96. *See, e.g.*, BEETHAM, *supra* note 75, at 107; LARRY DIAMOND, DEVELOPING DEMOCRACRY: TOWARD CONSOLIDATION 85 (1999). *See also* SEN, *supra* note 88, at 152 (arguing that no famine of substantial proportions "has ever occurred in any independent country with a democratic form of government and a relatively free press"). *But cf.* Michael Massing, *Does Democracy Avert Famine?*, N.Y. TIMES, Mar. 1, 2003, at B7 (discussing Sen's acknowledgment of the distinction between the "role of democracy in preventing famine and the comparative ineffectiveness of democracy in preventing regular undernourishment").

97. *Cf.* Russell Hardin, *Democracy and Collective Bads*, *in* DEMOCRACY'S EDGES, *supra* note 7, at 63, 63. Although democracies may be better at reducing the possibility that factions within a society will resort to conflict about disputes about resources, Hardin argues that they do not resolve distributional issues particularly well. *Id.*

98. MARKS, *supra* note 5, at 58.

99. Larry K. Wentz, *Bosnia—Setting the Stage*, *in* LESSONS FROM BOSNIA: THE IFOR EXPERIENCE 9, 12 (Larry K. Wentz ed., 1997).

100. Fox & Roth, *supra* note 2, at 7–8 (quoting *Report of the Secretary-General: Causes of Conflict and the Promotion of Durable Peace and Sustainable Development in Africa*, ¶ 77 (1998)). Zakaria articulates the correlation between democracy and the reduction in ethnic conflict as a distinction between liberal and illiberal democracies. "Mature liberal democracies can usually accommodate ethnic divisions without violence or terror and live in peace with other liberal democracies. But without a background in constitutional liberalism, the introduction of democracy in divided societies has actually fomented nationalism, ethnic conflict, and even war." Zakaria, *supra* note 93, at 35.

101. *See, e.g.*, Brad R. Roth, *The Illegality of "Pro-Democratic" Invasion Pacts*, *in* DEMOCRATIC GOVERNANCE AND INTERNATIONAL LAW, *supra* note 2, at 328, 335 ("Elections properly reflect, not transcendent principles of natural law, but historically contingent agreements among diverse political actors about how power may legitimately be exercised."). *See also* Satterthwaite, *supra* note 18, at 764 n.187 ("Democracy and development are linked . . . because democracy provides the only long-term basis for managing competing ethnic, religious, and cultural interests in a way that minimizes the risk of violent internal conflict."). *But cf.* Amy Chua, *Markets, Democracy, and Ethnicity: Toward a New Paradigm for Law and Devel-*

Finally, accountability mechanisms contribute to the resolution of intra-state conflicts by creating a space for public dialogue. The European Court of Human Rights, for example, has emphasized that "one of the principle characteristics of democracy is the possibility it offers of resolving a country's problems through dialogue, without recourse to violence."[102] Under this view, democracy is not complete unless it provides the space necessary to resolve disputes and come to agreements about the allocation of power and resources. Steven Ratner, for example, has described civil conflict as an indication of "the incompleteness of democracy in that people are not settling their disputes through democratic processes."[103] Accountability mechanisms create opportunities for public dialogue and engagement by providing formal rules and processes for the exercise of power. Where these mechanisms vest citizens with the power to influence decision-making, citizens will be more likely to seek such opportunities than resolve their disputes by other means.[104]

D. Defining Democracy

Focusing on accountability provides the basis for a functional vision of democracy that both attends to questions of social and material equality and structural change and can be applied in a variety of contexts. A vision of democracy as accountability is more robust than a purely procedural definition because it attends to important substantive goals.[105] At the same time, however, it avoids the necessity of a priori agreement on the substantive ends to be achieved by leaving those decisions in the hands of those who are in the best position to make them.[106]

---

opment, 108 YALE L.J. 1, 106 (arguing that in the presence of a market-dominant minority, the combination of markets and democracy can fuel ethnic conflict).

102. Gregory H. Fox, *The Right to Political Participation in International Law*, *in* DEMOCRATIC GOVERNANCE AND INTERNATIONAL LAW, *supra* note 2, at 48, 62 (quoting United Communist Party of Turkey v. Turkey, 26 Eur. Ct. H.R. 121, 153 (1998)).

103. Steven R. Ratner, *Democracy and Accountability: The Criss-Crossing Paths of Two Emerging Norms*, *in* DEMOCRATIC GOVERNANCE AND INTERNATIONAL LAW, *supra* note 2, at 449, 460. *Cf.* Satterthwaite, *supra* note 18, at 764 n.187 (emphasizing that democracy and development are linked "because people's participation in the decision-making processes which affect their lives is a basic tenet of development").

104. *See* Wheatley, *supra* note 10, at 226 (noting that former U.N. Secretary-General Boutros Boutros-Ghali has maintained that democratic processes minimize the risk of armed conflict "because they channel competing interests into arenas of discourse and provide means of compromise which can be respected by all participants in debates").

105. Schumpeter argued that the "notion of the common good is an unacceptable element of democratic theory" and thus excluded substantive ends from his definition of democracy. HELD, *supra* note 56, at 186 (citing SCHUMPETER, *supra* note 59, at 252). A definition of democracy as accountability, however, anticipates a role for the common good, but avoids defining its content.

106. Defining democracy as accountability does not necessarily mean that democracy and accountability are coextensive. A system labeled as "democratic" under this approach would be accountable; unaccountable "democratic" systems are the low-intensity democracies described and rejected by Marks and others. It is certainly possible, however, to imagine accountable systems that would be difficult to deem democratic; there are likely many values not adequately expressed within an understanding of democracy as accountability. The instant argument is not, however, an attempt to redefine the nature of democracy; indeed, accountability has been an important feature of many definitions of democracy. *See id.* at 3 (discussing a variety of possible interpretations of "rule" by "the people," a number of which cen-

A focus on the ability of citizens to sanction leaders thus avoids the problems of both over- and under-inclusiveness that are often associated with substantive visions of democracy. Democracy as accountability is specific enough to provide concrete political guidance; at the same time, however, it may be less "suspect as a neocolonialist strategy"[107] because it does not require agreement about the substantive ends to be achieved. Nor does democracy "entail[ ] the imposition of a specific liberal-democratic worldview that has yet to find general acceptance."[108] To the extent that such a worldview is defined by its emphasis on tolerance,[109] it is possible to imagine—at least, for example, in a state with a homogeneous citizenry—a government that is both accountable and intolerant.

Whether democracy as accountability necessarily requires the array of individual rights and freedoms often associated with liberal democracies[110] is a more difficult question. As Marks explains, "[t]he liberal preoccupation with rights and freedom from government control, and the democratic preoccupation with equal participation in, and accountability of, public power, may point in different directions."[111] Clearly, democratic accountability may require certain individual freedoms, such as freedom of expression, to function properly. As opposed to other substantive visions of democracy, democracy as accountability emphasizes the allocation of decision-making power instead of the decisions that are ultimately made. Thus, it may be compatible with a wider range of choices made by citizens about the array of rights they desire. At the very least, defining democracy as accountability may allow the international community to identify situations in which a response is required and to respond in appropriate ways without necessarily making assumptions about the choices that citizens would make with regard to any particular issue.[112]

Accountability can be understood as an institutional arrangement in which individuals affected by decisions have the power to hold the decision-makers responsible for their actions.[113] As John Dunn elaborates,

---

trally feature accountability). *See generally* Bernard Manin et al., *Introduction* to DEMOCRACY, ACCOUNTABILITY, AND REPRESENTATION 1, 10 (Adam Przeworski et al., 1999). Rather, this Article seeks to articulate an operational definition of democracy that can be used to identify and guide responses to failures of accountability at the international level.

107. Koskenniemi, *supra* note 5, at 440.

108. ROTH, *supra* note 22, at 424.

109. *See, e.g.*, Gerry Simpson, *Two Liberalisms*, 12 EUR. J. INT'L L. 537, 541 (2001). *See generally* Fox & Nolte, *supra* note 23, at 61 (discussing the problem of intolerant democracies).

110. *See, e.g.*, Roth, *supra* note 5, at 499.

111. Marks, *supra* note 79, at 456.

112. Some assumptions might reasonably be made about the rights citizens would likely choose in most situations. At the same time, however, a state may be accountable even if it does not necessarily guarantee the "comprehensive catalogue of social, political, economic, and religious rights" often associated with the ideal of liberal democracy. Zakaria, *supra* note 93, at 25. As Zakaria explains, "Sweden has an economic system that many argue curtails individual property rights, France until recently had a state monopoly on television, and England has an established religion." *Id.*

113. Beetham works from a similar definition, explaining that "a system of collective decision-making can be said to be democratic to the extent that it is subject to control by all members of the relevant

> the relation of accountability holds fully where persons exercising public powers are (1) liable for their actions in exercising those powers, (2) predictably identifiable as agents in the exercise of these powers to those to whom they are liable (in the democratic case, ultimately to the demos distributively), (3) effectively sanctionable for those acts once performed, and (4) knowably so sanctionable for them in advance.[114]

A political system that ensures accountability requires its leaders not only to face the consequences of their decisions, but also, more importantly, vests the power to sanction the leaders in those most affected by the decisions—the citizens.[115] Vesting citizens with effective power to sanction decision-makers is the most critical aspect of this approach. As Marks explains, "[h]owever effectively citizens may be able to hold their own governments accountable in connection with transgovernmental activities, democratic legitimacy depends on accountability to those affected by such activities."[116] In other words, democracy as accountability is premised on the assumption that "the people, with (or despite) their mix of abilities, education, and experience, will more often decide what is best for them than will aristocrats, autocrats, soi-disant philosopher kings, and sundry experts."[117]

Although citizens will often be in the best position to decide what course of action will be in their best interests, they may not always have the information necessary to make such decisions, either because this information is too costly for them to obtain or because only the government possesses it.[118]

association, or all those under its authority, considered as equals." BEETHAM, *supra* note 75, at 4–5. *See also* José Antonio Cheibub & Adam Przeworski, *Democracy, Elections, and Accountability for Economic Outcomes*, *in* DEMOCRACY, ACCOUNTABILITY, AND REPRESENTATION, *supra* note 106, at 222, 225 ("Governments are 'accountable' if citizens can discern whether governments are acting in their best interest and sanction them appropriately . . . ."); Jonathan A. Fox & L. David Brown, *Introduction* to THE STRUGGLE FOR ACCOUNTABILITY: THE WORLD BANK, NGOS, AND GRASSROOTS MOVEMENTS 1, 12 (Jonathan A. Fox & L. David Brown eds., 1998) (defining accountability of institutions).

114. John Dunn, *Situating Democratic Political Accountability*, *in* DEMOCRACY, ACCOUNTABILITY, AND REPRESENTATION, *supra* note 106, at 329, 335.

115. Because political systems operate within fixed geographical areas, even accountability within a system will not prevent leaders from externalizing the costs of their bad decisions on those outside state borders. *See* HELD, *supra* note 56, at 338 ("Territorial boundaries specify the basis on which individuals are included and excluded from participation in decisions affecting their lives (however limited the participation might be), but the outcomes of these decisions, and of the decisions of those in other political communities and agencies, often stretch beyond national frontiers."). *See also* MARKS, *supra* note 5, at 90.

116. *Id. Cf.* Ian Shapiro, *Group Aspirations and Democratic Politics*, *in* DEMOCRACY'S EDGES, *supra* note 7, at 210, 211 ("[T]here must be mechanisms through which those who are dissatisfied with a particular outcome can seek to produce change in the future, so long as they limit their opposition to producing a different decision rather than destroying the democratic order.").

117. W. Michael Reisman, *Stopping Wars and Making Peace: Reflections on the Ideology and Practice of Conflict Termination in Contemporary World Politics*, 6 TUL. J. INT'L & COMP. L. 5, 32 (1998). As such, democracy as accountability resembles Marks' "principle of democratic inclusion," which she defines as "the idea that all should have the right to a say in decision-making which affects them, and that systematic barriers to the exercise of that right should be acknowledged and removed." MARKS, *supra* note 5, at 119.

118. Manin et al., *supra* note 106, at 10–11. *Cf.* DAHL, *supra* note 56, at 337–38 (discussing objections to a guardianship approach to governance, under which decisions would be made by well-informed policy elites). For a discussion of some of the limits of accountability in a representative government, see generally Bernard Manin et al., *Elections and Representation*, *in* DEMOCRACY, ACCOUNTABILITY, AND REP-

In these situations, leaders might follow courses of action that are in the citizens' best interests, even when the citizens oppose such action.[119] Accountability mechanisms, however, promote information sharing and can therefore reduce the risk that conflicts will arise because of information asymmetries. By virtue of their power to sanction, citizens can demand access to the information necessary to evaluate their leaders' decisions. Further, the transparency necessary for the proper functioning of accountability mechanisms increases the likelihood that citizens will have access to such information and that information temporarily withheld will eventually be disclosed.

As others have noted in the context of efforts to increase the accountability of international institutions such as the World Trade Organization (WTO), applying a concept such as accountability

> is fraught with complications, starting with the politically and technically contested issue of assessing performance. Even if the measurement problem were solved, the factors explaining the process have received remarkably little research attention. . . . [P]olitical science . . . has not produced empirically grounded conceptual frameworks that can explain how public accountability is constructed across diverse institutions.[120]

Despite these measurement difficulties, it is important to discuss some of the indicators that may be relevant to an assessment of the accountability of a particular system. At the very least, such indicators may be a starting point for future evaluations; without indicators, however, there would be no basis for determining what constitutes a failure of accountability, and international responses would remain inconsistent and vulnerable to manipulation.

Although indicators may be relevant to assessing the degree of a regime's accountability, there is no clearly delineated line between "accountable" and "unaccountable" systems.[121] Rather, accountability should be viewed as a continuum, with highly accountable systems on one end and highly unaccountable systems on the other.[122] In addition, any list of indicators must be understood as non-exhaustive and context-specific. Such a list should not be allowed to obscure the logic behind its creation; the presence or absence of

---

RESENTATION, *supra* note 106, at 29.

119. Susan C. Stokes, *What Do Policy Switches Tell Us About Democracy?*, *in* DEMOCRACY, ACCOUNTABILITY, AND REPRESENTATION, *supra* note 106, at 98, 126.

120. Fox & Brown, *supra* note 113, at 12.

121. *See, e.g.*, BEETHAM, *supra* note 75, at 4 ("[J]udgements about whether given arrangements are democratic are typically judgements of degree, more or less, rather than absolutes."); MARKS, *supra* note 5, at 72 (arguing against an either-or definition of democracy and emphasizing the importance of evaluating the progress of both low-intensity and consolidated democracies); Wheatley, *supra* note 10, at 235 (cautioning against the adoption of any one definition of democracy).

122. Dahl, however, emphasizes the danger that an absence of a clear delineation between "democratic" and "undemocratic" might pose. He argues that if any kind of responsiveness to the opinions and needs of the governed "were sufficient to render a political system 'democratic' then I do not see how any political system could ever be non-democratic." Dahl, *supra* note 57, at 34.

an indicator is relevant to determining the extent to which a system is accountable and should not be interpreted formulaically.

Direct indicators of accountability include the institutional ability of citizens to sanction leaders, the de facto capacity of citizens to sanction leaders, and the government's responsiveness to the expressed will of the citizens.[123] First, an analysis of institutional arrangements should include an evaluation of whether citizens can, in fact, sanction their leaders. This analysis asks such questions as: Do the citizens have the power to sanction their governors? Can that power be frustrated by other actors within the political system?[124] Are decision-makers who cannot be sanctioned by the citizens accountable to ones who are? Is the sanction severe enough to provide a deterrent effect? Are citizens given the power to sanction but punished for its use? Are they encouraged or even allowed to disagree with the government?

A second indicator of accountability, the capacity of individual citizens to sanction leaders, requires an analysis of citizens' actual ability and willingness to sanction.[125] Are citizens informed about the government's decisions? Are they interested or otherwise engaged in the decisions of the government? Does each citizen hold sufficient sanctioning power to ensure that his or her voice is heard?[126] Do they have the economic ability to exercise this sanctioning power? How many citizens exercise sanctioning power, and how often? How do they exercise this power (e.g., individually, in groups, etc.)? Is there a belief that government policies can, and if so should, be changed?

A third significant indicator is the extent to which the government is responsive, i.e., the extent to which it "adopts policies that are signaled as preferred by citizens."[127] This indicator demonstrates whether the sanctioning power of the citizens has been internalized by decision-makers. If citizens are able to sanction leaders for bad decisions, leaders will eventually act in accordance with expressions of popular political will instead of waiting for sanctions.

---

123. Beetham has developed indicators for democracy that focus on elections, the continuous accountability of the government to the people and their representatives, guaranteed civil and political liberties, and civil society. BEETHAM, *supra* note 75, at 155–56.

124. Marks, for example, has criticized the use of the term "democracy" to characterize low-intensity democracies because such systems are "compatible with the maintenance, in practice, of a veto on the part of the military over legislative action." MARKS, *supra* note 5, at 53.

125. The second indicator—the capacity of citizens to sanction leaders—is informed by Held's critique of Schumpeter's theory as neglecting the fact that there may be many different reasons "for accepting or complying, consenting or agreeing to" political decisions or arrangements. HELD, *supra* note 56, at 195, 249. These reasons might include following orders or coercion, tradition, apathy, pragmatic acquiescence, instrumental acceptance or conditional agreement, normative agreement, and ideal normative agreement. *Id.*

126. Accountability requires equality of voice, even if that equality of voice is expressed through means other than elections. "Where citizens are deprived of an equal voice in the government of a state, 'the chances are quite high that [their] interests will not be given the same attention as those who do have a voice.'" Wheatley, *supra* note 10, at 245 (quoting ROBERT DAHL, ON DEMOCRACY 76 (1998)). As will be discussed later, *infra* Part III.C, equality of voice does not necessarily mean an equal allocation of sanctioning power.

127. Manin et al., *supra* note 106, at 9.

Although the objectives often embodied in substantive visions of democracy, such as respect for human rights or political, material, and social equality, do not necessarily provide sufficient guidance in identifying failures of democracy or determining appropriate responses, they remain extremely relevant considerations. While these objectives should not be regarded as litmus tests for accountability, they may serve as indirect indicators of government accountability and can inform an analysis of both the responsiveness of a regime and the success of the international response.

Whereas other substantive theories of democracy demand agreement on outcomes that may not be suitable in all contexts, an understanding of democracy as accountability allows the citizens themselves to determine the content of their democracy. At the same time, such an approach ensures that the goals of democracy—that the governors are held accountable to the governed—will not be circumvented by an exclusive focus on democratic procedures. Accountability thus balances the demand that democracy be more than a procedural formality, without dictating the political objectives that a given population should seek to achieve. A proper focus on accountability therefore allows for more flexible and appropriate responses where democracies have failed.

III. Responses to Failures of Democracy

The functional definition of democracy as accountability can guide international responses to failures of democracy by enabling states and international organizations to evaluate the success of a response without requiring a consensus on the substantive ends of democracy. As a result, this definition gives responding actors the flexibility to tailor their responses to a variety of situation- and context-specific needs.

A discussion of the principles that should guide responses to failures of accountability makes three crucial assumptions. First, it presupposes the appropriateness of distinguishing between states based on their internal composition. Such an assumption is contested and has been discussed extensively by others.[128] Second, this discussion presupposes the availability of intervention or other highly coercive actions[129] as potential responses, without dis-

128. *Compare, e.g.*, Simpson, *supra* note 109, at 541, *with* Tesón, *supra* note 43, at 15–16, *and* Franck, *supra* note 3, at 50. Simpson argues that theories that distinguish between states based on their internal composition—in particular, those that seek to distinguish between liberal and illiberal states—are in tension with the liberal principles embodied in the U.N. Charter. For example, these theories conflict with the principles that all states should be treated equally and guaranteed "the same rights afforded to individuals in a liberal society (i.e., domestic jurisdiction, equality, non-intervention)" and that the "diversity produced by these norms" should be at least tolerated, if not celebrated. Simpson, *supra* note 109, at 541. Tesón, in contrast, argues that "a government that engages in substantial violations of human rights betrays the very purpose for which it exists and so forfeits not only its domestic legitimacy, but its international legitimacy as well." Tesón, *supra* note 43, at 15–16. According to Simpson, because Franck's theory of the democratic entitlement "can be used to judge states," it also contradicts liberal principles of state equality. Simpson, *supra* note 109, at 561.

129. To some extent, even evaluating the extent of a democratic failure can be intrusive: "[J]udging

cussing the conditions under which such responses would be lawful or justified. The legality and justification of pro-democratic intervention[130] and intervention to enforce human rights[131] is highly controversial. Third, it assumes that international actors ideally would respond to all "failures" of accountability. In reality, however, the decision to respond will be dictated largely by the severity of the failure, as well as political considerations beyond the scope of this Article. Those situations that present the most significant threats to global security or involve the greatest violations of human rights will likely, and rightly so, be the primary focus of external responses.

Assuming the full range of possible responses, and without addressing the choice of when to respond, this Article will address only the question of what kinds of responses might best promote accountability at different levels of political control—local, national, and international. First, such responses should strengthen existing domestic accountability mechanisms when they are failing. Second, responses must work to foster accountability at the local level. Third, efforts to establish accountability mechanisms should replicate local structures and tailor them to the context and history of the community in question. Fourth, international responses must target the incentive structures of domestic elites at the national level. Fifth, the responding actors must operate within incentive structures that promote good governance and reduce possibilities for opportunism. Sixth, responses must also focus on the rule of law and transparency, the two elements without which accountability mechanisms cannot function.

---

whether an interruption of constitutional democracy has occurred requires far more detailed and potentially intrusive *international* interpretation of a country's constitution than one might expect." Stephen J. Schnably, *Constitutionalism and Democratic Government in the Inter-American System*, *in* DEMOCRATIC GOVERNANCE AND INTERNATIONAL LAW, *supra* note 2, at 155, 160 (emphasis in original). *See also, e.g.*, U.N. Econ. & Soc. Council, Sub-Comm. on the Promotion and Protection of Human Rights, *Working Paper: The Adverse Consequences of Economic Sanctions on the Enjoyment of Human Rights*, U.N. Doc. E/CN.4/Sub.2/2000/33 (June 21, 2000) (prepared by Mark Bossuyt) [hereinafter *Adverse Consequences of Economic Sanctions*]; W. Michael Reisman & Douglas L. Stevick, *The Applicability of International Law Standards to United Nations Economic Sanctions Programmes*, 9 EUR. J. INT'L L. 86 (1998).

130. *Compare, e.g.*, Lois E. Fielding, *Taking the Next Step in the Development of Human Rights: The Emerging Right of Humanitarian Assistance to Restore Democracy*, 5 DUKE J. COMP. & INT'L L. 329, 345–52 (1995), *and* W. Michael Reisman, *Humanitarian Intervention and Fledgling Democracies*, 18 FORDHAM INT'L L.J. 794, 804–05 (1995), *with* Schachter, *supra* note 44, at 649–50.

131. *Compare, e.g.*, W. Michael Reisman, *Sovereignty and Human Rights in Contemporary International Law*, 84 AM. J. INT'L L. 866, 875 (1990) ("Because rights without remedies are not rights at all, prohibiting the unilateral vindication of clear violations of rights when multilateral possibilities do not obtain is virtually to terminate those rights."), *and* Antonio Cassese, Ex Iniuria Ius Oritur: *Is International Legitimation of Forcible Humanitarian Countermeasures Taking Shape in the World Community?*, *in* INTERNATIONAL HUMAN RIGHTS IN CONTEXT, *supra* note 69, at 660, 660–61, *with* Michael Walzer, *The Moral Standing of States*, *in* INTERNATIONAL ETHICS 217, 234 (Charles Beitz ed., 1985) ("Rights are only enforceable within political communities where they have been collectively recognized, and the process by which they come to be recognized is a political process which requires a political arena. The globe is not, or not yet, such an arena.").

A. *Strengthen Existing Mechanisms of Accountability*

International responses should seek to strengthen internal accountability mechanisms when these are failing. Responses must therefore begin with an analysis of existing political arrangements—i.e., an evaluation of how power is exercised on the ground and whether this exercise of power corresponds to formal institutional structures, how these arrangements foster internal accountability, and whether and how accountability is frustrated. International actors must be aware that "a society is never left with a vacuum of political concepts, and is therefore not an uneducated mass without ideas about who should be their leaders and why."[132] Without such information, responses will be ineffective, or worse, may undermine accountability structures already in place.[133]

Where local mechanisms provide a foundation for accountability, the international community should tailor its response to address only those aspects of the mechanisms that are failing. If, for example, the democratic failure is a result of weak sanctioning power—that is, if accountability mechanisms are in place but the governed have no realistic way to sanction the governor—the international response will be most effective when it works to provide those citizens with such power. Thus, if a population has expressed its will by voting a governor out of office but the military intervenes to keep that governor in power, the international response should put pressure on the government to comply with the expressed will of the people. Similarly, if local mechanisms exist but the procedures are faulty, the international response should address only those particular defects. For example, where there are procedures in place to remove a governor, but the law allows the governor to circumvent these procedures, the intervening actor could pressure the government to ensure that these procedures are followed. Alternatively, domestic mechanisms may have failed because of an information problem, in which case the international response could facilitate the flow of information to citizens.[134]

International responses will be more effective when they identify, respect, and work within aspects of the existing system that already provide for the legitimate and accountable exercise of power. For example, strong kinship networks may ensure that leaders suffer the consequences of decisions that negatively affect the community, even in the absence of democratic proce-

---

132. Hohe, *supra* note 63, at 84.

133. *Cf.* Thomas Hammarberg & Patrick Gavigan, *Human Rights and Post-Conflict Institution Building*, *in* HONORING HUMAN RIGHTS FROM PEACE TO JUSTICE 167, 183 (Alice H. Henkin ed., 1998) ("Perhaps the most important operational lesson from the field mission experiences is the essential complementarity between human rights monitoring and institution building. Monitoring gave missions the ability to identify the sources and scope of human rights problems throughout the country. This information could then be used to design reform measures and training programs.").

134. *See* James D. Fearon, *Electoral Accountability and the Control of Politicians: Selecting Good Types Versus Sanctioning Poor Performance*, *in* DEMOCRACY, ACCOUNTABILITY, AND REPRESENTATION, *supra* note 106, at 55, 68–70 (discussing why elections may not be adequate accountability mechanisms).

dures. As Steven Wheatley explains, "it is possible to conceive, certainly in states with small populations, systems of government, other than democracy, in which people may freely determine their political status and freely pursue their economic, social and cultural development in compliance with the right to self-determination."[135] In addition, there may be indigenous mechanisms that provide for ways of selecting leaders; international responses should strengthen, support, and work within these paradigms, rather than impose an unfamiliar set of procedures.[136] In such cases, it can be useful to translate "[m]odern terminology . . . into local languages and contexts" to ensure that democratic concepts are understood and implemented in ways consistent with local beliefs and practices.[137]

Tanja Hohe, for example, emphasizes the tension between the Western-style elections held in East Timor and traditional Timorese governance structures. She explains that "[w]hat appeared superficially as a non-political environment was in fact highly politically charged in another way."[138] The local elections were not viewed by most Timorese as a way of choosing between different political agendas; rather, the elections were seen as an opportunity to replace illegitimate leaders with new local chiefs.[139] While the elections were based on a concept of competitive opposition, "[d]ecisions about political leadership" in Timorese societies are "taken through consensus among certain power holders."[140] Rather than imposing a set of procedures inconsistent with local practices and beliefs, these existing governance structures might have been viewed as a foundation for legitimate decision-making. Yet when international actors focus exclusively on Western-style liberal-democratic procedures, "such a controversy cannot even be engaged."[141]

Finally, focusing on existing mechanisms will help prevent displacement of pre-existing political arrangements that further accountability. Roth, for example, has noted that democratization in Eastern Europe "has so far sought to reverse those few features that, from the standpoint of substantive democracy, are favorable: relative social equality and the concentration of economic resources in the hands of a public sector that might potentially be held accountable to collective decision-making."[142] The internal and external emphasis on early privatization of the markets in Eastern Europe served to dis-

135. Wheatley, *supra* note 10, at 233.

136. *See* Hohe, *supra* note 63, at 81–83 (describing the inconsistency between the international response and local practices in East Timor). *See also* International Crisis Group, *Elections in Kosovo: Moving Toward Democracy?*, ICG Balkans Report No. 97, July 7, 2000, at 22 (arguing that holding municipal elections before Kosovo-wide elections was contrary to the way in which power was traditionally exercised in the region).

137. *See* Hohe, *supra* note 63, at 78. Hohe explains that "[o]nly if people can act from the perspective of their paradigm (which can nevertheless develop into a democracy), can they be genuinely empowered." *Id.* at 84.

138. *Id.* at 74.

139. *Id.*

140. *Id.* at 83.

141. Roth, *supra* note 5, at 496.

142. *Id.* at 504.

place a domestic arrangement—namely, the concentration of resources in the public sector—that could have provided a foundation for an accountability mechanism that may have better resolved disputes over resources.[143]

B. *Support Mechanisms at the Local Level*

Democracy is a means of ensuring participation and accountability, thereby guaranteeing that people have both "a voice and a stake in the functioning of their society."[144] Having a voice and a stake in governance fosters the sense of ownership that is critical to democratic consolidation, i.e., commitment to and internalization of democratic norms.[145] Democratic consolidation is, in turn, necessary to sustain any democratic transition. Unless democratic norms are internalized on a broad, grassroots level, newly implemented or reinstated accountability mechanisms will remain vulnerable to anti-democratic forces.[146]

Consolidation of the norm of accountability is intimately tied to the perceived legitimacy of the governance structures. A commitment to the rules and practices that define legitimate exercises of power enables accountability mechanisms to function properly; a shared and credible threat to sanction leaders for bad decisions is necessary to establish incentives for good governance. The credibility of the threat, in turn, helps governors internalize the belief that they will be sanctioned. As Diamond explains, "[o]nly when this commitment to the policing of state behavior is powerfully credible, because it is broadly shared by key alternative power groups, does a ruling party, president, or sovereign develop a clear self-interest in adhering to the rules of the game, which then makes those constitutional rules self-enforcing."[147] The

143. Displacing local with international mechanisms also carries with it the danger that governments will attempt to use international mechanisms to avoid local accountability—i.e., that they will "manipulate the internationally recognized symbols of legitimacy, so as to discredit militant (often armed) opposition and deflect international criticism that has impeded the flow of foreign (often military) aid." *Id.* at 503.

144. Satterthwaite, *supra* note 18, at 711.

145. Democratic consolidation can be defined as

> the process of achieving broad and deep legitimization, such that all significant political actors, at both the elite and mass levels, believe that the democratic regime is the most right and appropriate for their society, better than any other realistic alternative they can imagine . . . . [T]his legitimacy must be more than a commitment to democracy in the abstract; it must also involve a shared normative and behavioral commitment to the specific rules and practices of the country's constitutional system . . . .

Diamond, *supra* note 64, at 14. Consolidation thus involves "not just agreement on the rules for competing for power but fundamental and self-enforcing restraints on the exercise of power," regardless of who may be in power at any given time. *Id.* at 15. *See also* Mertus, *supra* note 80, at 1363 (discussing the fact that promotion of human rights norms, especially a norm like democratic participation, is only possible if internalized, and not forced according to pre-selected results); Roth, *supra* note 5, at 513 (describing a "constitutionalist order" as one in which governors acknowledge that decisions may be rendered only within the limits of their power and the governed "recognize that they must obey the final decision of those officeholders duly authorized to render it").

146. *See* Ezetah, *supra* note 4, at 523. *See also* Patrick Thornberry, *The Democratic or Internal Aspect of Self-Determination with Some Remarks on Federalism*, *in* MODERN LAW OF SELF-DETERMINATION 101, 120–21 (Christian Tomuschat ed., 1993).

147. Diamond, *supra* note 64, at 15.

legitimacy of these rules and practices is in turn further enhanced as accountability mechanisms successfully produce responsive governance.

One of the most effective ways to consolidate democracy is to implement accountability mechanisms on the local level.[148] Efforts at the local level can further consolidation in three ways. First, local political arrangements offer citizens more opportunities to participate in political affairs and greater control over the decision-making process.[149] Second, local government is often more flexible and responsive to the needs of a local community; if a government is more responsive, its decisions will be perceived with greater legitimacy.[150] Third, competing claims to resources—such as land or social benefits—are often resolved at the local level.[151] Consequently, more effective responses will be those that are "initiated, implemented, and conceptualized as a means toward the larger goal of creating vital, grassroots democracy, civil society, and accountable government."[152]

At the same time, however, efforts to increase local control may not always be appropriate. Direct control over the affairs of a national government can be difficult to achieve, particularly in a country without a tradition of democratic accountability or with a history of centralized control over decision-making. The mission in Kosovo, for example, made strengthening municipal government a top priority.[153] After decades of centralized decision-making, however, the emphasis on local control mechanisms was foreign and often counter-productive to the goal of consolidating accountability norms.[154]

---

148. *See* Franck, *supra* note 3, at 73 (emphasizing that the responses to the mission in Haiti "impl[y] the need for a longer-term international effort to create the grass roots elements of democratic political institutions and processes—a particularly challenging form of technical assistance—in nations without that tradition"). *See also* Diamond, *supra* note 64, at 33 ("Decentralized government reduces the scale of democracy as it is experienced by citizens in their daily lives. This means devolution of power: federalism and regional autonomy where the scale of the country calls for it and the culture and politics permit it; and, everywhere, elected local governments with meaningful autonomy and capacity to mobilize and spend resources."); Gro Hillestad Thune, *Lessons and Challenges*, *in* SOCIETIES IN CONFLICT: THE CONTRIBUTION OF LAW AND DEMOCRACY TO CONFLICT RESOLUTION 197, 207 (European Commission for Democracy Through Law ed., 2000) (noting that conference participants emphasized that international organizations must avoid a "top-down" approach that lacks "sufficient knowledge and respect for the underlying historical, cultural and ethnic factors" and emphasizing the importance of local initiatives).

149. *See* DIAMOND, *supra* note 96, at 123–24. Local arrangements also offer citizens "a direct say in the development of democracy programs for their country." CAROTHERS, *supra* note 62, at 266. Carothers also emphasizes the importance of the role of women in democratization. *See id.* at 345.

150. *See, e.g.*, Rita Falk Taubenfeld & Howard J. Taubenfeld, *Some Thoughts on the Problems of Designing Stable Democracies*, 24 INT'L LAW. 689, 693 (1990) (noting that the advantage of devolution of governmental tasks to lower levels of government is that the decisions are "likely to impose the minimum of coercion and potential loss on its citizenry").

151. *See, e.g.*, DIAMOND, *supra* note 96, at 123.

152. Satterthwaite, *supra* note 18, at 789.

153. International Crisis Group, *supra* note 136, at 2.

154. As the International Crisis Group has argued, holding municipal elections before Kosovo-wide elections ran "counter to the political traditions of Kosovo and the Balkans as a whole, where power in modern times has flowed from the centre to the regions or localities." International Crisis Group, *supra* note 136, at 22. The group warned that "[i]gnoring this aspect of the local political culture" could be divisive. *Id.* Other negative consequences of decentralization are discussed in DIAMOND, *supra* note 96, at 132–38.

C. *Tailor Mechanisms to Community Needs*

When reliance on local mechanisms is not feasible, either because existing arrangements are highly unaccountable or simply not viable, the international community should support mechanisms that vest citizens with the effective power to sanction leaders and are tailored to the needs of the community. In determining what mechanisms might be best in any given historical and cultural context, it is important to "emphasize social realities over formal structures."[155] In doing so, the appropriateness of each mechanism will depend on the incentives created and the functions served. Finally, whatever strategies are chosen, international actors should be able to modify them when necessary.

Although elections and other mechanisms for political competition are incomplete by themselves and, when viewed in isolation, serve as poor organizing principles for international responses,[156] they may be useful strategies in certain situations. In the absence of viable local mechanisms for ensuring accountability or measuring political will, such mechanisms—when tailored to the needs of the particular situation and located within a comprehensive strategy for furthering accountability—may be an important part of the response.[157]

For example, the ability to render decision-makers accountable to those affected by their decisions presupposes a way to measure political will, and elections are often the only way to do so: "In the absence of more reliable means of recording choice in complex societies, . . . it has become difficult to speak convincingly of democracy without reference to elections."[158] This inability to measure political will invites inappropriate responses:

> In decentralized systems whose members themselves perforce make the decisions, the more the number of constitutive appraisal norms, the more the number of cross-border appraisals and the greater the possibility of cross-border meddling by various actors. The problem is contained, to an extent, when internationally supervised "free and fair"

155. Roth, *supra* note 5, at 496.

156. Elections "may assist in the formation of a government responsive to the popular will, but they do not guarantee such a government. In many countries, systemic problems override the positive effects of free elections." Wippman, *supra* note 67, at 667. *See also* Gibson, *supra* note 87, at 215 (criticizing the administration as "too often . . . focused on the importance of elections, without the necessary attention to the concomitant details of a true liberal democracy").

157. As Fox and Nolte explain, while "[m]ost definitions of democracy are substantially broader than the mere holding of elections," that fact "does not render a focus on elections inappropriate." Fox & Nolte, *supra* note 81, at 396. Fox and Nolte explain further that "[w]hile the principle of popular sovereignty embodied in elections is analytically distinct from the notions of personal dignity and moral autonomy undergirding the protection of individual rights, in practice (according to this view) an elected regime has substantially greater incentives to respect the rights of citizen voters than a regime that need not seek a popular mandate." *Id.* at 397. If the international response includes elections, the responding actors must focus on the specific objectives to be achieved and guard against the tendency to equate elections with democracy.

158. Jan Knippers Black, *What Kind of Democracy Does the "Democratic Entitlement" Entail?*, *in* DEMOCRATIC GOVERNANCE AND INTERNATIONAL LAW, *supra* note 2, at 517, 517.

elections credibly and unequivocally indicate the wishes of a majority of the people.[159]

Thus, mechanisms like elections or referenda may be necessary to provide both the state and the international community with a quantifiable means of assessing local political will.

If electoral procedures are to play a role in the response, they must be tailored to the specific social realities of the situation. Pure majoritarian elections can be highly divisive, particularly where the polity is deeply divided along lines of ethnicity or other allegiance. For example, post-colonial Africa's "wholesale adoption of liberal democratic systems," without the inclusion of proportional representation, "accentuated the diversity inherent in the arbitrary colonial boundaries of Africa."[160] Majoritarian procedures may also be inappropriate in societies characterized by vast disparities in the distribution of resources, since such procedures often tolerate great inequality "in the ability of social groups to marshal the resources necessary to affect political decisions."[161]

Electoral systems can address these concerns by, for example, providing incentives for political leaders to consider the needs of multiple groups. Such tailoring may be particularly critical if there is a danger that leaders will draw on or foster ethnic divisions to gain power.[162] Ian Shapiro explains that in divided societies, well-tailored electoral processes can give leaders incentives to listen and attend to the needs of different communities; such incentives can be created by "requir[ing] politicians to compete for votes among ethnic groups other than their own."[163] Forms of proportional representation, as well, may help ensure that all segments of society are able to effectively exercise sanctioning power.[164] Thus, tailoring new procedures to the exigencies of the situation can help ensure that one segment of the community does not seek disproportionate political advantage to another's detriment.

---

159. W. Michael Reisman, *Sovereignty and Human Rights in Contemporary International Law*, 84 AM. J. INT'L L. 866, 875 (1990).

160. Ezetah, *supra* note 4, at 503.

161. Roth, *supra* note 5, at 497.

162. Shapiro, *supra* note 116, at 218.

163. *Id. See also* Donald L. Horowitz, *Constitutional Design: An Oxymoron?*, *in* DESIGNING DEMOCRATIC INSTITUTIONS 253, 269 (Ian Shapiro & Stephen Macedo eds., 2000) (discussing alternative voting, in which political groups are required to demonstrate a certain level of support from voters from other groups, as a system with "considerable power to foster intergroup accommodation").

164. Kymlicka notes that in designing a proportional representative system, "[t]he number of seats necessary for effective presentation of [minorities'] views . . . may exceed the number of seats required for proportional electoral representation." KYMLICKA, *supra* note 76, at 147. The timing of elections might also be tailored to the community's needs. As Murphy emphasizes, "the willingness to recognize a non-democratic government is not necessarily detrimental to the best interests of its people; respectable arguments are made . . . that a democratic form of government is not the best form for some States depending on their stage of economic and political development." Murphy, *supra* note 8, at 145. *See also* Chester A. Crocker, *The Varieties of Intervention: Conditions for Success*, *in* MANAGING GLOBAL CHAOS: SOURCES OF AND RESPONSES TO INTERNATIONAL CONFLICT, 183, 186 (Chester A. Crocker et al. eds., 1996).

Political competition, more generally, can also be an important, though not necessarily sufficient, accountability mechanism. The very existence of opposition parties, in fact, may ensure some measure of accountability. In discussing opposition movements in pre-democratic South Korea and Pinochet's Chile, Sen notes that "[m]any of the social programs that served these countries well were at least partly aimed at reducing the appeal of the opposition, and in this way, the opposition had some effectiveness even before coming to office."[165]

Yet a multiparty system is not the only means of ensuring political competition. Emphasizing "social realities over formal structures" might allow "a comparatively favorable view of a one-party State that does not allow organized opposition, but that is widely popular, incorporates public input in decision-making, and responds effectively to the needs of the vast majority."[166] Given the existence of other means of ensuring responsiveness, deciding not to create a multiparty system could be a legitimate choice. As originally drafted, even Article 25 of the ICCPR "did not prohibit one-party States per se."[167] Due mainly to efforts by the Chilean delegate during the drafting of Article 25, "[s]ingle-party elections would run afoul [of Article 25] only if (1) public opinion in a State were actually divided on important political issues, and (2) if a single party did not permit candidates representing each faction to stand for election."[168]

Although domestic prosecutions and truth commissions are likely to be employed on a case-by-case basis, they can be effective ways to promote accountability of governors for past abuses[169] and enhance the perception that the government is and can be held accountable. While other considerations—such as the potential effect on the country's prospects for transition—may counsel against the initiation of such proceedings,[170] the prospect of prosecution or disclosure of past abuses can have a deterrent effect on leaders and thereby foster consolidation of accountability norms.

An evaluation of potential responses must include not only an assessment of the incentive structures created by each response, but also the immediate needs of the populace. Unsuitable accountability mechanisms may undermine stability and order, thereby damaging the credibility of the response and increasing the appeal of non-democratic alternatives. As Roth notes, "[d]ictatorships have frequently in human history been seen by their subjects to secure very real benefits . . . that might be irretrievably lost by toler-

---

165. Sen, *supra* note 88, at 156.
166. Roth, *supra* note 5, at 496.
167. Fox, *supra* note 102, at 57.
168. *Id.*
169. Satterthwaite, *supra* note 18, at 786.
170. As Barnes notes, the ability to assure the leaders of the prior regime a position within the new system may be critical in ending a conflict. Samuel H. Barnes, *The Contribution of Democracy to Rebuilding Postconflict Societies*, 95 Am. J. Int'l L. 86, 88 (2001).

ating organized opposition."[171] Significant internal disorder or instability may similarly increase the appeal of non-democratic alternatives that appear to offer stability and an end to violence. Both Charles Taylor in Liberia and Alberto Fujimori in Peru were elected by overwhelming majorities, primarily because they were the only candidates who seemed able to achieve stability and peace. For example, Taylor seemed to be the "one person" in Liberia "willing to use all 'necessary' measures to ensure stability at long last for the beleaguered country."[172] Similarly, in Peru, business leaders and the population as a whole supported Fujimori because he was willing to implement the kind of measures needed to control the country's high levels of crime, terrorism, and corruption.[173]

Although order and accountability are not necessarily competing priorities, a minimum level of internal order must be established for accountability mechanisms to work and develop properly since weak or failing governments are as likely as authoritarian ones to be unaccountable to their citizens.[174] As a result, there may be many cases in which "strengthening the State to help create effective government is the necessary first step toward creating accountable government."[175] As James Fishkin explains, democratization itself can entail significant instability: "[T]he very notion of bringing 'power to the people'" can imply a lack of checks and balances, separation of powers, and the rule of law, all of which can be important for stability.[176] Indeed, the process of democratization can be particularly difficult when paired with a transition from a command to a market economy, primarily "because the economic dislocations for which the political system will be held accountable" during the economic transition will be severe.[177] In some circumstances, working sequentially toward the goals of economic reform and democratization might help ensure that political and economic transitions do not undermine each other.

D. *Target Responses to Incentives of Elites*

Although holding leaders accountable to the international community is a poor substitute for accountability to citizens, international responses can supplement local accountability mechanisms in a number of ways. Critical to the choice of response, however, is the extent to which the contemplated

171. Brad R. Roth, *Democratic Intolerance: Observations on Fox and Nolte*, *in* DEMOCRATIC GOVERNANCE AND INTERNATIONAL LAW, *supra* note 2, at 441, 443.

172. GARRETT, *supra* note 26, at 157.

173. Dawn Bennett-Ingold, *Latin American Democracy: Flourishing or Floundering?*, 28 GA. J. INT'L & COMP. L. 111, 114 (1999).

174. Anne-Marie Slaughter, *Government Networks: The Heart of the Liberal Democratic Order*, *in* DEMOCRATIC GOVERNANCE AND INTERNATIONAL LAW, *supra* note 2, at 199, 233 ("Lack of accountability is as likely to flow from a weak or failing government as an excessively strong one; liberal democracy is as threatened by anarchy as by autocracy.").

175. *Id.*

176. FISHKIN, *supra* note 82, at 76.

177. *Id.*

response targets the incentives of the country's elites and holds them accountable to citizens.[178] Conditional lending, sanctions, international prosecutions, truth commissions, and conditional recognition, for example, all accomplish this to different degrees and in different ways.[179]

Conditional lending and sanctions, for example, can be tailored to target the incentives of elites where the political system holds them at least minimally accountable. Critics argue that conditional lending policies punish citizens, not elites, and do not increase the accountability of these elites to the citizens: "[W]hen development is linked to austerity plans imposed by the [International Monetary Fund] and major donor countries, its effects can devastate the poor and the prospects for democracy."[180] Sanctions have also been criticized as punishing the wrong actors[181] and potentially undermining the long-term prospects for democratic consolidation.[182] Even "smart sanctions"[183] will be ineffective where the governors can insulate themselves from the consequences of their decisions and externalize the costs of the sanctions onto

---

178. As Moore explains, if their ability to externalize costs is what allows authoritarian elites to commit democide and engage in high-risk behavior, "then the most effective mode of deterrence will be to reimpose unacceptable costs on such elites." Moore, *supra* note 37, at 875.

179. The range of possible responses is unlimited and could also include, for example, the institution of professional standards of conduct, *see* Joseph S. Nye, Jr., *Globalization's Democratic Deficit: How to Make International Institutions More Accountable*, FOREIGN AFF., July–Aug. 2001, at 2, 5 (2001), civil suits by victims or disqualifying officials from office, *see* Ratner, *supra* note 103, at 457, and international aid to support democracy, *see generally* CAROTHERS, *supra* note 62.

Even refugee policies could theoretically be used to further accountability. Increasing the number of immigrants and refugees accepted from a particular country, for example, could increase pressure on that government to improve its decision-making. In such a situation, people would be "vot[ing] with their feet." Yoram Dinstein, *The Dilemmas of Democracy*, 26 ISR. Y.B. HUM. RTS. 1, 3 (1996). Borders isolate leaders of undemocratic regimes from the consequences of their decisions because they reduce the possibility of exit, primarily by increasing its cost. *See* James Tobin, *A Comment on Dahl's Skepticism*, *in* DEMOCRACY'S EDGES, *supra* note 7, at 37, 37 ("If membership is voluntary, if 'exit' is permissible and not terribly costly, then governance by 'voice' of members is not essential.") (relying on ALBERT O. HIRSCHMAN, EXIT, VOICE, AND LOYALTY: RESPONSES TO DECLINE IN FIRMS, ORGANIZATIONS, AND STATES (1970)). Additionally, allowing more people the right of entry would serve as an implicit symbol of condemnation.

180. Schnably, *supra* note 38, at 525.

181. Reisman, *supra* note 130, at 802–03 ("The bad news about economic sanctions for these violations is that, more often than not, they severely punish the victims while enriching the villains.").

182. Johansen notes, for example, that sanctions are inefficient in creating a "culture of compliance" because they may inflict heavy suffering on the populace and increase support for the government. Robert C. Johansen, *Enforcing Norms and Normalizing Enforcement for Humane Governance*, *in* PRINCIPLED WORLD POLITICS, *supra* note 8, at 209, 216–17.

183. For a discussion of "smart sanctions," see Craig Forcese, *Globalizing Decency: Responsible Engagement in an Era of Economic Integration*, 5 YALE HUM. RTS. & DEV. L.J. 1, 20 (2002) ("The essence of smart sanctions strategy is tailoring sanctions to meet specific objectives and focusing coercive pressure on particular groups and resources."). *See also Adverse Consequences of Economic Sanctions*, *supra* note 129, at ¶¶ 54–57 (explaining that smart sanctions could include, among other things, targeting personal foreign assets, limiting access to foreign markets, freezing business assets, banning luxury good imports); William H. Meyer & Boyka Stefanova, *Human Rights, the UN Global Compact, and Global Governance*, 34 CORNELL INT'L L.J. 501, 520 (2001) (discussing the ways in which smart sanctions create a bargaining environment for the imposition of penalties or rewards and emphasizing the need for monitoring to decrease the impact of the sanctions on third parties).

the population.[184] The inaccuracy of conditional lending and sanctions does not, however, necessarily mean that these approaches are always inappropriate; rather, the fact that they require a minimum level of accountability to affect the incentives of elites should inform the decision about when and where to use them.

Conditioning state recognition on democratic accountability is another potential response. As James Crawford emphasizes, democratic government is "one—not necessarily privileged—indicator of the existence of an established government in an existing State."[185] Such a response finds limited support in the precedents of Haiti and the former Yugoslavia.[186] At the same time, however, conditioning recognition on the internal character of a regime is far from established practice.[187] Further, a refusal to recognize an effective but unaccountable regime may insulate decision-makers from responsibility for their actions.[188] Despite these limitations, the threat of non-recognition can nonetheless put additional pressure on elites to institute reforms and increase their accountability to citizens.

Another approach that may increase pressure on elites is to modify the rule that a state's commercial commitments and legal obligations bind successor governments, even if the prior regime was illegitimate.[189] Crawford explains:

> One possibility . . . might be to develop a system under which third parties dealing with a grossly unrepresentative regime would be re-

---

184. *See* Eric S. O'Malley, *Destabilization Policy: Lessons from Reagan on International Law, Revolutions and Dealing with Pariah Nations*, 43 VA. J. INT'L L. 319, 341 (2003) ("[E]ven smart sanctions can be harmful and ineffective if they are not employed as part of a more comprehensive strategy, because governments frequently confiscate the aid and either sell it for profit or take credit for its distribution.").

185. James Crawford, *Democracy and the Body of International Law*, *in* DEMOCRATIC GOVERNANCE AND INTERNATIONAL LAW, *supra* note 2, at 91, 118.

186. *See* ROTH, *supra* note 22, at 370 (discussing the United Nations' refusal to recognize the government that overthrew the elected government in Haiti); Marc Weller, *The International Response to the Dissolution of the Socialist Federal Republic of Yugoslavia*, 86 AM. J. INT'L L. 569, 587–605 (1992) (discussing the European Community's conditions for recognition of the former Yugoslav republics, which included "respect for the provisions of the Charter of the United Nations and the commitments subscribed to in the Final Act of Helsinki and in the Charter of Paris, especially with regard to the rule of law, democracy and human rights," as well as renunciation of territorial claims and guarantees for the rights of minorities) (quoting European Community: Declaration on the Guidelines on the Recognition of New States in Eastern Europe and in the Soviet Union, Dec. 16, 1991, 31 I.L.M. 1485, 1486 (1992)).

187. *See* ROTH, *supra* note 22, at 318–19 (explaining that the principles of effective control and non-intervention are generally subject to only limited qualification); Weller, *supra* note 186, at 588 (noting that in imposing such an "extensive catalog of criteria, far in excess of traditional standards for recognition of statehood," the European Community "was not applying general international law in the determination of its position"); Wheatley, *supra* note 10, at 233 ("[N]o evidence exists of the democratic credentials of a regime being relevant either in the recognition of states, or in the international communities [sic] dealings with non-democratic governments.") (footnote omitted).

188. Crawford argues that refusing to recognize "an effective but undemocratic government . . . avoids holding those who have made the decisions responsible for their acts. Where there is power there should be responsibility, including legal responsibility." Crawford, *supra* note 185, at 109.

189. Tinoco Case (Gr. Brit. v. Costa Rica), 1 R. Int'l Arb. Awards 369, 376–84 (1923), *reprinted in* 18 AM. J. INT'L L. 147 (1924).

> quired to take the risk of doing so. This would apply both to States and to private parties, including corporations. It would put them on notice that if they wish to deal with a regime lacking in any legitimacy or popular support, they would take the risk of the review of the transaction by a subsequent representative government.[190]

Although this approach could undermine global economic stability, this would be due largely to the absence of standards for evaluating when a regime is grossly unrepresentative. Political risk assessment is a critical part of any investment decision.[191] Implementation of Crawford's policy would increase the risk that a contract would be voided by a subsequent regime and thus deter investment. This use of the term risk, however, relates to the increase or decrease in the probability that a particular outcome will occur.[192] To the extent that Crawford's policy did increase the probability that a subsequent regime would void a prior contract, it would accomplish its objective. Unaccountable governments would present a higher risk to investors, and thus would be pressured to reduce this risk by instituting reforms. Although citizens of the regime may also be hurt by policies that deter foreign investment, elites would likely experience the most substantial effects of reduced foreign investment.

A potentially more important question, however, is the extent to which Crawford's policy would increase uncertainty. In contrast to risk, "quantification of 'uncertainty' is far more difficult; indeed, the more heterogeneous the events, the less we know about the distribution of possible outcomes."[193] In the absence of rules—e.g., rules regarding when, how, and with what criteria a subsequent government could review a transaction—that would allow investors to more accurately predict outcomes, implementation of Crawford's policy could increase uncertainty and unnecessarily chill foreign investment. Such a chilling effect, however, would principally serve to increase pressure on unaccountable elites to adequately assure investors of the security of their transactions; in addition, the uncertainty that could be associated with this approach might be reduced through agreement on common standards.

---

190. Crawford, *supra* note 13, at 129. *See also* Farer, *supra* note 13, at 737 (arguing that the United States could have hastened the transition in Chile "by threatening to cut off access to the US market for Chilean producers (a principal constituency of Pinochet) and to collaborate with allies in blocking Chilean access to the facilities of international financial institutions").

191. P. Kenneth Kiplagat, *An Institutional and Structural Model for Successful Economic Integration in Developing Countries*, 29 TEX. INT'L L.J. 39, 53 (1994) (noting that "[i]nternational financial institutions dealing with private lenders factor risk into the cost of borrowing" and discussing "political instability, racial and religious disputes, and extreme economic hardships, which foreign investors fear may result in nationalization and expropriation" as forms of political risk) (footnotes omitted).

192. Accurate risk assessment thus requires homogeneity of events and knowledge of possible outcomes. Claire A. Hill, *How Investors React to Political Risk*, 8 DUKE J. COMP. & INT'L L. 283, 287 (1998) (relying on FRANK H. KNIGHT, RISK, UNCERTAINTY AND PROFIT (1921)). Hill argues that political risk is extremely difficult to estimate, mainly because of the level of heterogeneity and uncertainty associated with political events. *Id.* at 299.

193. *Id.* at 287–88.

Finally, international prosecutions and truth commissions have also been suggested as methods for holding leaders accountable.[194] Although prosecutions target elites, they have been criticized as insufficiently immediate to have a substantial deterrent effect.[195] While the extent to which the threat of prosecution actually affects the incentives of decision-makers is unclear, such proceedings may promote accountability in other ways. By subjecting leaders to a legal process and imposing sanctions for past abuses, prosecutions can strengthen the expectation that leaders can and should be held accountable for their decisions.[196] Truth commissions can foster transparency and accountability by exposing the decision-making process and bringing to light information that had been withheld from the public. In certain situations, retrospective accountability may even be an essential part of a transition to democracy.[197] Thus, by example and prescription, these processes can deepen popular commitment to the norm of accountability and promote democratic consolidation.

E. Ensure Accountability of the Responding Actor

The principle of democracy as accountability, founded on the premise that accountability mechanisms help ensure more responsive decision-making over time, should guide not only the choice of response, but also the manner of responding. Responding actors themselves must operate within incentive structures that promote good governance and long-term commitment to the stability of the region. To the extent that these responding actors influence the allocation of decision-making power, they must make sure that those holding power remain accountable to citizens. Ensuring that decision-making power is paired with accountability will foster both responsive governance and the consolidation of accountability norms.

International responses to failures of accountability must be undertaken by those actors who have most at stake in the success or failure of the response and who would benefit most from strengthening good governance and stability in the region. When the responding state is insulated from the

194. *See, e.g.*, Neil J. Kritz, *Coming to Terms with Atrocities: A Review of Accountability Mechanisms for Mass Violations of Human Rights*, 59 LAW & CONTEMP. PROB. 127 (1996); Schnably, *supra* note 38, at 546.

195. *See generally* Ratner, *supra* note 103.

196. Schnably examines the ways in which the OAS's response to coups could be improved both to "oust the instigators of the coup as quickly as possible" and to "ensure that the actions taken toward that end be done in such a way as to bolster the long-term prospects for democracy and human rights . . . ." Schnably, *supra* note 38, at 546. Toward this second goal, Schnably suggests that the OAS "give serious consideration to institutionalizing some form of a requirement that leaders of coups be brought to justice for the coup itself and for human rights violations committed during the period when constitutional government has been interrupted." *Id.* at 547.

197. Steven R. Ratner, *New Democracies, Old Atrocities: An Inquiry in International Law*, 87 GEO. L.J. 707, 736–37 (1999) (arguing that while accountability, when pursued without regard to the rights of the accused, can also undermine democratic prospects, prosecutions may well be necessary when "abusers are so thoroughly subverting democracy that only trial and punishment will remove them from [power] and bring an end to this behavior").

consequences of bad governance within the transition state, the interests of the responding state and the state in transition (and its citizens) may differ. The response must be designed to further the common interest of the responding state and the state in transition in strengthening mechanisms of accountability.

Responses by regional actors may enjoy greater legitimacy and confidence because these actors are more likely to be affected by the instability associated with failures of accountability and thus have a significant stake in the establishment and maintenance of good governance. Consequently, such actors may often be in a better position to take the lead in responding to failures of democracy than a state insulated from both the effects of such failures and the consequences of the response.[198] In addition, it may be easier for actors who are geographically, politically, and culturally closer to the government in question to exercise influence over that government's policies.[199]

In addition, a multilateral response will generally be preferable, in large part because multilateral frameworks can help prevent responding actors from pursuing interests unrelated to accountable governance.[200] In numerous cases, individual states have undertaken intervention "for ostensibly humanitarian reasons, but [their] real, less elevated motivations have not been hard to discern."[201] Farooq Hassan, for example, criticizes Tanzania's humanitarian justification for invading Uganda in 1979 as "simply a cloak of legality for the use of brute force by a powerful state against a weaker one, and experience has shown how readily more powerful states have used the pretext of a higher good to impose their own will and values on weaker

198. *See* Ruth Wedgwood, *Regional and Subregional Organizations in International Conflict Management*, *in* MANAGING GLOBAL CHAOS: SOURCES OF AND RESPONSES TO INTERNATIONAL CONFLICT, *supra* note 164, at 275, 276–77. Wedgwood describes a number of other benefits generated by reliance on regional structures, including the fact that regional structures offer a "local voice," "permit a multilateral voice when the Security Council is hobbled by superpower conflict," hold out the "promise of economy and rapid response," allow compartmentalization of the precedent of intervention, and "reduce[ ] the visibility of the debate." *Id.*

199. *See* L. David Brown & Jonathan A. Fox, *Accountability Within Transnational Coalitions*, *in* THE STRUGGLE FOR ACCOUNTABILITY: THE WORLD BANK, NGOS, AND GRASSROOTS MOVEMENTS, *supra* note 113, at 439, 469 ("Accountability is more difficult when the actors are separated by wide gulfs of physical, cultural, and political differences . . . .").

200. In some circumstances, a single actor with a substantial stake in the long-term outcome of the response (and thus incentives to promote accountable governance) may be more effective than a coalition of actors, each of whom would be relatively unaffected by the consequences of their decisions. *See, e.g.*, Jarat Chopra, *The UN's Kingdom of East Timor*, SURVIVAL, Autumn 2000, at 35 ("As with the use of force, perhaps coalition missions led by single countries may be more effective for temporary government."); Crocker, *supra* note 164, at 190 (noting that to be successful, a mission may require an intervenor with "the capacity for effective and prompt decision making"). Yet while many states may be "interested," few will have significant incentives to promote good governance; in addition, even states that had both such incentives and the political will to respond may not be sufficiently committed to promoting "the kinds of long-term structural reforms that would create more propitious conditions for democracy." Schnably, *supra* note 38, at 555.

201. GARRETT, *supra* note 26, at 16. As Chopra notes, "[i]nvariably, such missions will be criticised as vehicles for individual nations seeking regional hegemony." Chopra, *supra* note 200, at 35. Another observer has called the U.N. Transitional Administration in East Timor "an exercise in benevolent colonialism." James Traub, *Inventing East Timor*, FOREIGN AFF., July–Aug. 2000, at 74, 74.

states."[202] Others have raised similar criticisms of the United States' intervention in the Dominican Republic, Grenada, and Panama.[203] Garrett explains that the "evident hypocrisy found in these cases provides grist for the mill of those who question whether *any* intervention in the internal affairs of a state can ever be taken at face value, at least in terms of its supposed service to a basic moral purpose."[204]

Using a multilateral framework to respond to failures of democracy reduces the danger of opportunism by providing checks on decision-making. When the OAS rejected collective action against Manuel Noriega in Panama, for example, it also "lost the opportunity to dictate the timing, the dimensions and the goals of the intervention and to more deeply enmesh the United States in collective decision-making."[205] Because it incorporates a greater number of voices, collective decision-making tends to be more transparent than unilateral decision-making, frequently requires compromise, and often forces decision-makers to engage in debates with each other and with constituents about the proper course of action.[206]

Further, a multilateral response carries significant symbolic legitimacy and moral authority; it acknowledges that a failure of accountability anywhere is a threat everywhere.[207] A multilateral response based on the recognition of the threat posed by the failure of accountability avoids the appearance of self-interest and thus increases the likelihood of both international support and cooperation of the state and its citizens.[208] In particular, multilateral responses may be significantly more likely to foster the kind of long-term commitment necessary for an effective response.[209] Efforts to promote

---

202. Farooq Hassan, *Realpolitik in International Law: After Tanzanian-Ugandan Conflict "Humanitarian Intervention" Reexamined*, 17 WILLAMETTE L. REV. 859, 860 (1981) (quoted in GARRETT, *supra* note 26, at 52).

203. *See, e.g.*, Crawford, *supra* note 13, at 126–27; Karsten Nowrot & Emily W. Schabacker, *The Use of Force to Restore Democracy: International Legal Implications of the ECOWAS Intervention in Sierra Leone*, 14 AM. U. INT'L L. REV. 321, 382, 384–85 (1998).

204. GARRETT, *supra* note 26, at 16 (emphasis in original). *See also* Schachter, *supra* note 44, at 650 ("In the absence of an effective international mechanism to restrain force, individual governments would have wide latitude to decide on the 'reality' of democracy and self-determination in various countries.").

205. Farer, *supra* note 13, at 734 (footnote omitted).

206. *See, e.g.*, Fielding, *supra* note 130, at 374 (arguing in favor of a multilateral response, preferably through the U.N. Security Council or a regional organization, "because of the potential for abuse by individual states seeking political and territorial gain in the guise of assistance"); Ruth Wedgwood, *The Use of Force in Civil Disputes*, 26 ISR. Y.B. HUM. RTS. 239, 241 (1996) (arguing that in the context of the war in the former Yugoslavia, "[w]ithout public commitment to multilateral action, the demand for humanitarian intervention and unilateral rescue of *Landsmänner* might have been hard to resist in the domestic politics of one or more countries").

207. Held makes a related point when he calls for the internationalization of democratic law. Held maintains that "the implementation of . . . cosmopolitan democratic law and the establishment of a community of democratic communities—a cosmopolitan community—must become an obligation for democrats; an obligation to build a transnational, common structure of political action which alone, ultimately, can support the politics of self-determination." Held, *supra* note 7, at 106.

208. *See* Franck, *supra* note 3, at 85 (arguing that a multilateral response would be viewed as more legitimate by small states).

209. Johansen, in particular, argues that the response must not only be multilateral, but framed within the United Nations. He explains that a survey of the United Nations' experiences with interven-

accountability will have minimal chance of success unless they are supported by a sustained, long-term commitment on the part of the international community. Grounding the response in a multilateral framework, particularly one established under the auspices of an international institution such as the United Nations, can more effectively ensure international commitment and thus the continuity and longevity of the response.

Not only should the appropriateness of the responding actor be determined with reference to its stake in the outcome, but the responding actor itself must be accountable to the citizens of the failing democracy. The accountability of the responding actor to the polity is especially important when the response is highly coercive and involves the assumption of domestic administrative tasks. Interim administrations in peacekeeping missions, in particular, create problematic incentive structures by placing decision-making power in the hands of those outside accountability mechanisms.[210] To some extent, it may be necessary for the international mission to be the ultimate authority, particularly when a local administration is absent. Yet the international mission should, over time, attempt to revise power structures so that those who make decisions are evaluated and subject to sanctions by citizens.

In Kosovo, for example, the Kosovo Transition Council (KTC)—composed of political parties, religious leaders, and representatives from ethnic minorities—"largely function[ed] as a soapbox, allowing the international mission to hear the opinions of the Albanian representatives who dominate the KTC numerically but without giving them any real role in decision-making."[211] Similarly, despite its goal of strengthening local governance structures in Kosovo, the U.N. mission retained authority over the local police.[212] As interim measures, these arrangements may have been necessary; however, long-term efforts to enhance accountability should also foster increased citizen control over municipal institutions and authorities. Local police might be brought under the decision-making power of local administration, and local administration can be made accountable to the citizens (through, for example, procedures that allow for removal of administrators by citizens or citizen participation in the selection of officials).

Similar arguments about the importance of ensuring that those affected by decisions have the right to hold the decision-makers accountable have been advanced in connection with the activities of non-governmental and international institutions, such as the World Bank and the World Trade Or-

---

tion shows "a profound need for a *permanent* UN civilian police force that is . . . immediately available for deployment, and responsive only to the United Nations rather than to possibly confusing signals from national capitals." Johansen, *supra* note 182, at 223.

210. As illustrated by de Waal's discussion of humanitarian aid efforts, vesting decision-making power in the hands of international NGOs that are not necessarily accountable to citizens can be similarly ineffective and counterproductive. *See* Alex de Waal, *African Encounters*, 6 INDEX ON CENSORSHIP 14, 16, 31 (1994).

211. International Crisis Group, *Kosovo Report Card*, ICG Balkans Report No. 100, August 28, 2000, at 28.

212. International Crisis Group, *supra* note 136, at 2.

ganization. Critics claim that these institutions are not adequately responsive to the needs of those whom their decisions affect. Many proposed solutions have sought increased accountability, i.e., the establishment of mechanisms by which the institutions would be subject to a sanctioning power held by those affected by the decisions.[213] These calls for increased accountability led the World Bank to, among other things, create an independent appeals panel that would allow individuals adversely affected by a World Bank project to file a claim based on the World Bank's internal policies and procedures.[214]

Failure to ensure the accountability of responding actors not only alienates members of the local community, but also undermines the possibility of democratic consolidation. Jarat Chopra emphasizes that whether or not complete "governorship" assumed by the United Nations is a legitimate response, governorship requires "a judicious determination as to which parties are legitimate, and a concerted effort to prepare them, by example as well as by prescription, for sound representational government."[215] Democratic culture requires a commitment by both elites and the populace to the rules and procedures of democracy, but not necessarily to any particular outcome.[216] Over time, as individuals rely on their ability to hold leaders accountable, their commitment to the structures that empower them will increase.[217] Implementing mechanisms to ensure the accountability of international actors to the local population contributes to this process by strengthening the expectation of accountability.

Ensuring responsiveness might be accomplished, at least in part, through a sub-contracting model. An ideal transitional administration is one that could provide a "broad brokerage framework in which each ministry, department or office providing basic services is subcontracted to whatever international, national, non-governmental or private agency has the expertise and capacity to perform the function."[218] As long as contractors are accountable to the citizens, subcontracting allows for the efficient provision of services while ensuring that the decision-making capability rests with those affected by the decisions.

---

213. *See generally* de Waal, *supra* note 210, at 31 (calling for increased accountability of NGOs that distribute foreign aid); Fox & Brown, *supra* note 113, at 12–17 (describing efforts to increase the accountability of international institutions); Nye, *supra* note 179, at 3 (noting that "unlike self-appointed [NGOs], international institutions tend to be highly responsive to national governments and can thus claim some real, if indirect, democratic legitimacy").

214. Lori Udall, *The World Bank and Public Accountability: Has Anything Changed?*, *in* THE STRUGGLE FOR ACCOUNTABILITY: THE WORLD BANK, NGOS, AND GRASSROOTS MOVEMENTS, *supra* note 113, at 391, 392.

215. Chopra, *supra* note 200, at 36 (discussing the deficits of the mission in East Timor).

216. *See* Diamond, *supra* note 64, at 15. *See also* Johansen, *supra* note 182, at 212.

217. *Id.* at 227. *See generally* Ratner, *supra* note 103.

218. Chopra, *supra* note 200, at 36.

F. Promote Transparency and Rule of Law

While a number of conditions aid the proper functioning of democracy,[219] transparency and rule of law are preconditions of accountability. Together, transparency and the rule of law ensure that citizens' participation will be backed up by real authority and that efforts to hold leaders accountable will be effective.

Transparency and access to information facilitate accountability because citizens need information to know when to hold which leaders accountable for what decisions.[220] Access to information also implies some measure of freedom of expression; if critics of the government may not be heard, the information relevant to decision-making is limited. In addition, in order to hold their governors accountable, people need to be free to engage in dialogue.[221] Particularly when access to information is made more difficult by poverty and illiteracy, the cost of ensuring such access and transparency may be significant; nonetheless, these conditions are critical to the effective functioning of democratic accountability. If a lack of information effectively precludes individuals from participating in government and exercising sanctioning power, the government will not be responsive to their needs.

The rule of law is a necessary precondition for the proper functioning of accountability along four dimensions. First, it ensures that the power to sanction is enforceable. As Barnes notes, "[r]ational egoism's lesson is the importance of law in democratization. Without institutions to enforce the rule of law, political actors will ignore the public interest in favor of their private goals."[222] Corruption, whether related to manipulation of elections or bribery of officials charged with enforcing the law against the governors, allows the governors to externalize the costs of their decisions by circumventing the

219. Scholars of democratic theory have identified a number of elements as instrumental to the proper functioning of democracy, including respect for human rights, free political association and expression, periodic participatory elections, universal and equal suffrage, competition among political parties, an independent judiciary, rule of law, transparency and access to information, separation of powers, and an effective civil society. *See, e.g.*, Diamond, *supra* note 64, at 13; Ezetah, *supra* note 4, at 515–16; Franck, *supra* note 3, at 61, 63; Satterthwaite, *supra* note 18, at 791.

220. Fox and Roth call transparency and access to information "conditions of choice." The requisites of collective choice, they note, include that the choice is "genuinely knowing (based on good information), willing (not merely a choice among options imposed by the will of elites or by circumstances), and intelligent (taken in circumstances that allow for proper reflection, including widely available education, a robust societal marketplace of ideas, and the absence of distortive economic pressures)." Fox & Roth, *supra* note 2, at 14. They acknowledge that to some extent, true transparency and access to information "require the very institutional transformation—perhaps an irreversible one—about which the populace was supposed to be empowered to choose." *Id.*

221. *See* SEN, *supra* note 88, at 153 ("[W]e cannot, in general, take preferences as given independently of public discussion, that is, irrespective of whether open debates and interchanges are permitted or not."). *See also* Philippe Sands, *Turtles and Torturers: The Transformation of International Law*, 33 N.Y.U. J. INT'L L. & POL. 527, 540 (2001).

222. Barnes, *supra* note 170, at 92. *See also* Fox & Roth, *supra* note 2, at 11 (explaining that the democratic entitlement requires not only the "existence of appropriate participatory mechanisms, but also a determinate relationship between the mandated participatory mechanisms and the actual exercise of political power").

mechanisms by which they would be held accountable. Alternately, there may simply be such chaos or failures of the rule of law as to make implementation of accountability mechanisms impossible. In Kosovo, for example, one of the first tasks of the mission was to restore order, after which the civil administration would begin other tasks designed to foster greater accountability, such as training local civil administrators and raising awareness about possibilities for citizen involvement in political affairs.[223]

Second, the rule of law is relevant to the continuity of accountability. Latin American electoral systems, in particular, have historically been vulnerable to "delegative democracy," the approach of "'whoever wins election to the presidency is thereby entitled to govern as he or she sees fit, subject only by [sic] the hard facts of existing power relations and by a constitutionally limited term of office.'"[224] Horizontal accountability, like vertical accountability, can be achieved in a variety of ways—through checks and balances, separation of powers, or a strong judiciary. In some cases, even the "hard facts of existing power relations" will be enough to check the executive; in others, additional procedures will be required to assure horizontal accountability.

Third, rules provide the basis for determining when leaders are to be sanctioned and predictable methods for doing so. As Neil Kritz explains, as well,

> the rule of law does not simply provide yet one more vehicle by which government can wield and abuse its awesome power; to the contrary, it establishes principles that constrain the power of the government, oblige it to conduct itself according to a series of prescribed and publicly known rules, and, in the postconflict setting, enable wary former adversaries all to play a vital role in keeping the new order honest and trustworthy.[225]

Without rules, there would be no basis for determining whether the governors were being honest and trustworthy. Further, rules that define the legitimate exercise of government power not only provide predictable governance but may also be necessary "to protect those not in the majority."[226]

---

223. *See* S.C. Res. 1244, ¶ 9(a)–(d), U.N. SCOR, 4011th mtg., U.N. Doc. S/RES/1244 (1999). *See also Report of the Secretary-General on the United Nations Interim Administration in Kosovo*, ¶ 119, U.N. Doc. S/1999/799 (1999) (delivered to the Security Council) (noting that the interim administration will "endeavour to create conditions of normalcy in Kosovo under which all peoples can enjoy the benefits of democracy and self-governance"). Subsequent tasks included reestablishing the rule of law, training local civil administrators, and facilitating both the "awareness and involvement of citizens in social and political change" and "conditions that support pluralistic political party structures, political diversity and a healthy democratic political climate." *See id.* ¶¶ 80, 119, 121.

224. Schnably, *supra* note 129, at 165 (quoting Guillermo O'Donnell, *Delegative Democracy*, 5 J. DEMOC. 55, 59 (1994)). The problem of delegative democracy is compounded when "popular enthusiasm that leads to the election of such charismatic leaders is tempered by subsequent disillusion." Claudio Grossman, *Freedom of Expression in the Inter-American System for the Protection of Human Rights*, 7 ILSA J. INT'L & COMP. L. 619, 620 (2001).

225. Neil J. Kritz, *The Rule of Law in the Postconflict Phase: Building a Stable Peace*, *in* MANAGING GLOBAL CHAOS, *supra* note 164, at 588.

226. Ratner, *supra* note 197, at 707.

Fourth, rules are also partly the result of accountability mechanisms properly functioning over time. Roth distinguishes between "three normatively significant ends to which the establishment of competitive electoral mechanisms may to a greater or lesser extent be relevant."[227] These include:

> (1) the furtherance of broad popular empowerment with respect to the full range of social decisions that condition life in the society ("substantive democracy"); (2) the establishment of a government to which the populace may in some manner have been said to have manifested consent ("popular sovereignty"); and (3) the establishment of a broadly recognized basis for, and thereby limitation on, the legitimate exercise of power ("constitutionalism").[228]

The first two of these normatively significant ends—substantive democracy and popular sovereignty—describe the function of accountability. Citizens are empowered with respect to the decisions that shape their daily lives—such as decisions about the allocation and use of material resources[229]—because they can hold leaders accountable for those decisions. Correspondingly, the existence of accountability mechanisms implies to some extent that the populace consents to the government, because a lack of consent would ideally result in sanctions against the leaders.

Constitutionalism, however, adds an important element that is not fully articulated within a theory of accountability alone. According to Roth, democratic procedures can create a basis for the legitimate exercise of power, and thereby limit the exercise of that power. While accountability mechanisms themselves do not limit the exercise of power, they provide a vehicle for the creation of rules that do so and the establishment of a legitimate basis of power over time. Although a written constitution may represent rules that a society agrees will govern the legitimate exercise of power, the outer edges and nuances of these rules are developed through citizen responses to the exercise of power that are made possible through accountability mechanisms.

IV. Conclusion

Ultimately, democracy is about "creating the opportunity for all persons to assume responsibility for shaping the kind of civil society in which they live and work."[230] The international community increasingly recognizes that the purposes served by democracy are critical to internal stability as well as global and economic security. Yet the rhetoric of democracy has been used variously to signify procedures for electing leaders, to describe ideal deci-

227. Roth, *supra* note 5, at 494.

228. *Id.* Schnably also emphasizes the importance of "constitutional design," which he defines as the "set of institutional specifications that ensure that the State is accountable and governed by the rule of law." Schnably, *supra* note 129, at 166.

229. Roth, *supra* note 5, at 501.

230. Franck, *supra* note 3, at 79.

sion-making structures, and to connote particular ideological positions. For the term "democracy" to provide any meaningful criteria for guiding responses to failures of democracy, however, its content must be clear. The purpose of democracy is to ensure that those who are affected by decisions possess the power to sanction or reward decision-makers and to provide a framework for resolving disputes over resources and power.

Understanding democracy as accountability provides a framework for responses to failures of democracy that are appropriate to the given cultural and historical context and responsive to the needs of citizens. This conception of democracy directs a responding actor to strengthen domestic mechanisms, promote institutional arrangements that vest citizens with effective sanctioning power, and work toward consolidation of accountability norms. On the international level, the principle of accountability requires not only that responses target the incentives of elites and hold them accountable for their decisions, but also that the responding actors themselves operate within a structure that provides necessary checks and balances and appropriate incentives for good governance. Finally, this principle has at its foundation the rule of law and transparency, which are essential to the proper functioning of democracy. Using this understanding of democracy as accountability to guide international responses will not only foster long-term global peace and stability, but will also help ensure that all individuals are guaranteed the opportunity to shape the world in which they live.

[6]

THE RIGHT TO DEMOCRACY: A QUALITATIVE INQUIRY

Reginald Ezetah[*]

It is widely accepted that the end of the Cold War provided an opportunity for a new paradigm in the global search for peace and security. An examination of the old and persisting statist paradigm—which consists, at least partially, of mass murder by governments—belies the common assumption that most states possess a unity of identity, population, government, and territory. This assumption constitutes the moral and logical underpinnings of the statist model. However, new imperatives of justice, human rights, and self-determination have challenged the coercive order of the statist paradigm. Contrary to the statist model, it is becoming clear that enduring peace can be found only in order rooted in justice and human development, that is, in a *democratic peace*. However, the meaning of "democracy," especially as expounded in scholarly literature and state practice, remains a riddle of immense proportions.

Given the asymmetries that surround the notion and practice of democracy, the implanting of a democratic culture or the fortification of existing democratic ethos is an all-important project. We cannot afford to leave this to the fortunes of a slow and uncertain voyage of domestic political change. A firm and decisive measure is called for now—a positive, multilateral revaluation of the concept, process, and practice of democracy—with the primary purpose of restoring sovereignty to the

---

* Member, Nigerian Institute of International Affairs. I would like to thank Professor Maurice Copithorne, Q.C., Special Representative of the United Nations Human Rights Commission in Iran, and Obiorah Okafor (Killam pre-doctoral fellow) for valuable comments on initial drafts of this paper. I am also grateful to Professor Ivan L. Head, O.C., Q.C., for his intellectual support.

people.

Conceptually, democracy must be accepted as a context-dependent idea that has a core, unalterable, universal standard. It should be redefined as an instrument of human development in order to give the incentive to civil society for pulling together behind democracy. Put in simple terms, there has to be a material stake for the ordinary man on the street in the survival of democracy. Totalitarianism is often effective in a disenchanted, indifferent, or weak civil society, one that fails to demand accountability. Through a grudging withdrawal, such a society passively encourages the totalitarian state. The guarantee of welfare rights could be cultivated as a rallying point of democratic solidarity for the masses of civil society.

The tensions inherent in pluralism are not necessarily accommodated by the majoritarian ethic of democracy, which runs through all spheres of participation. Therefore, it is time to go beyond the "participatory" index of international instruments and reconciliatory devices of domestic institutions, and to internationally criminalize political oppression of minorities and the official looting of public resources. This is one way of ensuring that democratic institutions and devices for reconciling competing claims that flow from diversity are not undermined by corrupt leadership. It is yet another way of reassuring minorities and the voiceless, and of building a consensus of democratic commitment in lieu of a consensus of opinion.

Legitimacy of any administration is a function of the aggregate perception of the majority of the populace, and the process by which this popular will is expressed is of central importance to democracy. Therefore, elections—used in this context in a broad sense to include any systemic expression of popular mandate accepted and affordable by a people, but which ensures free and fair contest—could be further legitimized by the participation of a neutral, disinterested observer. This external participation should be multilateral and all-embracing, such that the sovereignty of all states and nations are equally affected and none is relatively disadvantaged.

I. INTRODUCTION

The primary purpose of the United Nations Organization (U.N.) as set out in Article 1 of the U.N. Charter (the Charter) is the maintenance of international peace and security.[1] Peace and security have maintained a prominent position in international relations since at least 1795, when Immanuel Kant proposed an international treaty on "Perpetual Peace" based on a guarantee of human rights in domestic laws.[2] Since Kant, the inter-connectedness of peace, security, human rights, and democracy has become axiomatic.[3] This has been matched with revolutionary laws, such as the Uniting for Peace Resolution of 1950 (giving the General Assembly extraordinary powers of intervention in the interest of international peace in the event of a deadlock at the Security Council),[4] and of more recent origin, an emergent norm of humanitarian intervention for the restoration of democracy. Since the inception of the Peace Resolution, activities of the United Nations have demonstrated that the Charter, through its focus on peace and security, presents a flexible instrument that could justify corrective measures to preserve democracy as long as those measures take place within a structured framework.[5] It is on this premise—in light of the international legal regime's reformation crisis—that this article is based.

Despite the near-global consensus on the right to democra-

---

1. U.N. CHARTER art. 1(1).

2. Immanuel Kant, *Perpetual Peace: A Philosophical Sketch*, *in* POLITICAL WRITINGS 93 (Hans Reiss ed., H.B. Nisbet trans., Cambridge Univ. Press 2d ed. 1991) (1795).

3. *See, e.g.*, Brian Urquhart, *The UN and International Security After the Cold War*, *in* UNITED NATIONS, DIVIDED WORLD 81, 97 (Adam Roberts & Benedict Kingsbury eds., 2d ed. 1993) ("The spread of democracy, and respect for human rights, are indispensable elements of a more stable, less violent human society, and are, as such, a legitimate—indeed an indispensable—international concern"); BOUTROS BOUTROS-GHALI, AN AGENDA FOR PEACE at 39, U.N. Doc. A/47/277-S/24111, U.N. Sales No. E.95.I.15 (2d ed. 1995), *reprinted in* UNITED NATIONS, DIVIDED WORLD, *supra*, at 468; *Interrelationship Between Human Rights and International Peace: Report of the Secretary-General*, U.N. ESCOR, 40th Sess., Provisional Agenda Item 4, at 4, ¶ 7, U.N. Doc. E/CN.4/Sub.2/1988/2 (1988) (discussing the United Nation's recognition of a "complex interrelationship between . . . human rights and fundamental freedoms, . . . peace and security, and . . . economic, social and cultural development"); *Alma Ata Declaration*, U.N. SCOR, 47th Sess., Annex II, at 4, U.N. Doc. A/47/60-S/23329 (1991).

4. G.A. Res. 377A, U.N. GAOR, 5th Sess., Supp. No. 20, 302d plen. mtg. at 10-12, U.N. Doc. A/1775 (1950); *see* Fernando R. Tesón, *Collective Humanitarian Intervention*, 17 MICH. J. INT'L L. 323, 331 (1996).

5. *See, e.g.*, G.A. Res. 1474, U.N. GAOR, 4th Emergency Special Sess., Supp. No. 1, 863d plen. mtg. at 1, U.N. Doc. A/4510 (1960) (requesting voluntary contributions and an arms embargo to restore peace in the Republic of the Congo).

cy, there remains a dearth of scholarly qualitative examination of the new international norm. This article, with the ultimate objective of unraveling all the contents of the right to democracy, will examine the liberal concept of democracy in the context of state practice. Part I of this article will demonstrate that liberal democracy, as we now know it, is not a universal phenomenon and is not the universal democracy envisioned when one speaks of "the right to democracy." Part II will further argue that because of philosophies stemming from international law and state practice, universal democracy must be based on a foundation of social welfare. Part III of the article will argue that the right to a democratic system of government should be considered a peremptory norm in international law. Part IV will describe the substantive, procedural, and structural content of the right to democracy. Part V will demonstrate that democracy suffers from an inherent weakness in its universal manifestation, and needs, therefore, to be reinforced through a convention. Finally, this paper proposes enhancing democracy by reinforcing *dēmokratia*, or "rule by the people," by means of a Convention on Democratic Governance, a proposed model of which is delineated in the Appendix.

II. THE MEANING OF DEMOCRACY

A. *Liberal Democracy*

"Democracy" was coined from the Greek word *dēmokratia* meaning "rule by the people."[6] Its philosophical underpinnings lie in the theories of the social contractarians, particularly in John Locke's theory of Civil Government,[7] which is founded on an initial presupposition of equality of all people.[8] These theories are the foundation of liberal democracy, which is identified as a western idea, and the main features of which are individual freedom and political equality.[9] The modern institutional

---

6. *See* Geraint Parry & George Moyser, *More Participation, More Democracy?*, *in* DEFINING AND MEASURING DEMOCRACY 44, 44 (David Beetham ed., 1994).

7. JOHN LOCKE, TWO TREATISES OF GOVERNMENT 137 (Peter Laslett ed., Cambridge Univ. Press 1988) (1690).

8. *See id.* at 269.

9. *See* Michael Saward, *Democratic Theory and Indices of Democratization*, *in* DEFINING AND MEASURING DEMOCRACY, *supra* note 6, at 6, 16-17; David Beetham, *Key Principles and Indices for a Democratic Audit*, *in* DEFINING AND MEASURING DEMOCRACY, *supra* note 6, at 25, 28.

framework of liberal democracy is based on the doctrines of separation of powers[10] and free market economy.[11] So authentic and influential has this "western idea" become that modern-day scholars describe the new norm of a right to democracy as the universal legitimization of a "western idea."[12]

Historically, liberal democratic theory has withstood a barrage of criticism. Its presumption of equality has been described as romantic nonsense,[13] and its individualism has been criticized for divesting the individual of his personality by divorcing him from his ontological bearings.[14] According to the critics of liberal democracy, the consequent emptiness[15] has observable political results, namely, a disorganized and fragmented public sphere.[16] Thus, according to its critics, liberal democracy is, by and large, undemocratic, and its conceptual pillars of "popular sovereignty" and "legitimate governance" are

---

10. *See* 1 BARON DE MONTESQUIEU, THE SPIRIT OF THE LAWS 151-62 (Franz Neumann ed., Thomas Nugent trans., 1949) (1748).

11. *See* JOHN RAWLS, A THEORY OF JUSTICE 270-74 (1971).

12. *See* Christina M. Cerna, *Universal Democracy: An International Legal Right or the Pipe Dream of the West?*, 27 N.Y.U. J. INT'L L. & POL. 289, 290 (1995); *see also* Thomas M. Franck, *The Emerging Right to Democratic Governance*, 86 AM. J. INT'L L. 46, 49 (1992).

13. *See generally* Lee Kuan Yew, *Democracy and Human Rights for the World*, 20 MEDIA ASIA 33 (1993). Yew draws an instructive analogy between the specious assumption that all humans are equal and the principle of "one nation, one vote" in the U.N. General Assembly. While the General Assembly organ of the United Nations appears equal, its resolutions do not carry the force of sanctions. True power in the U.N. is reserved for the permanent members of the Security Council. *See id.* at 38.

14. *See* Victor Segesvary, *Group Rights: The Definition of Group Rights in the Contemporary Legal Debate Based on Socio-Cultural Analysis*, 3 INT'L J. ON GROUP RTS. 89, 93 (1995). In this brilliant paper, the author demonstrates that the individual and his community are ontologically interdependent; i.e., the life and destiny of the individual and his community are inextricably intertwined. *See id.*; *see also* ERWIN SCHRÖDINGER, MY VIEW OF THE WORLD 54 (Cecily Hastings trans., Ox Bow Press 1983) (1961); CAROL GOULD, RETHINKING DEMOCRACY: FREEDOM AND SOCIAL COOPERATION IN POLITICS, ECONOMY, AND SOCIETY 93-94 (1988).

15. *See* John Golding, *Two Who Made a Revolution*, N.Y. REV. BOOKS, May 31, 1990, at 8 (offering the paintings of synthetic cubist Georges Braque as examples of objective detachment devoid of meaning). Here the consequence of isolationism is a meaningless existence depicted by Braque's mood toward the end of his life: "I no longer believe in anything. Objects don't exist for me except insofar as a rapport exists between them and myself." *Id.*

16. *See* JÜRGEN HABERMAS, THE STRUCTURAL TRANSFORMATION OF THE PUBLIC SPHERE: AN INQUIRY INTO A CATEGORY OF BOURGEOIS SOCIETY 142 (Thomas Burger & Frederick Lawrence trans., 1989); David Held, INTRODUCTION TO CRITICAL THEORY 223-59 (1980).

no more than fraudulent myths.[17]

The observable contradiction inherent in liberal theory and liberal practice[18] has undermined the liberal democratic system. The conceptual and practical problems of liberal theory are further entrenched by its laissez-faire economy, whose manifest aim of individual consumerism[19] combines with the isolationism of liberal theory to create a type of nominalism. As a result, "human dignity" and "subjective freedom" become mere by-products of a complex process of material relations.[20]

The reality of the foregoing is lost neither on the liberal politician[21] nor on the liberal scholar.[22] Indeed, contemporary definitions of democracy by liberal scholars manifest a tendency to look beyond empirical liberal structures, and toward liberal idealism.[23]

Liberal democratic theory has not survived this onslaught

---

17. *See* Yew, *supra* note 13, at 38.

18. Egalitarianism is the silver thread that runs throughout the bounds and fabric of the theories of social contractarians, and this can hardly be reconciled with the liberal philosophy of equality. For example, Hobbes' Leviathan was omnipotent, a mortal god having monopoly over all political wisdom. THOMAS HOBBES, LEVIATHAN (C.B. MacPherson ed., Penguin Books 1985) (1651).

19. *See* RAWLS, *supra* note 11, at 273-74.

20. The intractability of the dilemma posed by liberalism in the laissez-faire context is analogous to the scholastic debates over God's will, in which some philosophers argue that God is not free if His decisions are motivated by His knowledge, if that is independent of His will. Others counter that God is not wise if He goes against His better judgment. *See* Nikolai Biryukov & Victor Sergeyev, *The Idea of Democracy in the West and in the East*, *in* DEFINING AND MEASURING DEMOCRACY, *supra* note 6, at 182, 189.

21. In recognition of the foregoing, the United States in 1975 established a trilateral commission to reexamine the concept and practice of liberal democracy. *See* PHILIP K. LAWRENCE, DEMOCRACY AND THE LIBERAL STATE 2 (1989).

22. Liberal scholars are beginning to acknowledge the tension between liberal individualism and the notion of society. *See, e.g.*, JOHN RAWLS, POLITICAL LIBERALISM 190 (1993) (observing that while "[h]istorically one common theme of liberal thought is that the state must not favor any comprehensive doctrines and their associated conception of the good[,] . . . it is equally a common theme of critics of liberalism that it fails to do this and is, in fact, arbitrarily biased in favor of one or another form of individualism."). *See generally* RAWLS, *supra* note 11. Rawls, ostensibly battling with the fragmentary consequences of liberalism and the self consumerism of the free market economy, advocates social cooperation for the happiness of the "greatest number." In doing this, he undertakes the very difficult task of synthesizing seemingly conflicting concepts such as "liberty and equality," "individual self interest and toleration," and "social justice and free market capitalism." He ends up with an idealistic "well-ordered society" comprised of reasonable people. *See id.* at 453-62.

23. *See, e.g.*, SAMUEL BRITTAN, THE ECONOMIC CONSEQUENCES OF DEMOCRACY 274-77 (1977).

unscathed. Policies of social security, social welfare, and medical insurance are material evidence of a reversing trend, and ostensibly constitute a search for the social bonds that were undermined by laissez-faire liberalism. The capacity of these policies to uproot liberal theory's isolatory features remains to be seen.

However, the allure of certain aspects of liberal democracy has remained pervasive, such that some scholars hold the view that "[t]he liberal interpretation is not wrong. It just does not see the beam in its own eye."[24] While the liberal political formula offers a good doctrinal basis for fostering individual choice, liberty, and private property, its indisputable handicaps are its negation of social solidarity and its inability to provide the identity and meaning that are essential to the dignity and personality of the individual. The laissez-faire environment of liberal democracy is a perfect setting for eroding the public's freedom of opinion. Indeed, observable trends in liberal electoral processes point to a growing apathy, with less than fifty percent of eligible voters participating in the 1996 presidential elections in the United States.[25] As a necessary foundation for individual self-accomplishment, liberal free market democracy protects the privilege of a few at the expense of the majority

---

24. Jürgen Habermas, *What Does Socialism Mean Today? The Revolutions of Recuperation and the Need for New Thinking*, *in* AFTER THE FALL: THE FAILURE OF COMMUNISM AND THE FUTURE OF SOCIALISM 25, 31 (Robin Blackburn ed., Ben Morgan trans., 1991). Václav Havel construes liberal democracy's inability to gain universal acceptance as a consequence of its formulation as a pious doctrine, complete and unalterable, and its failure to come to terms with the harsh reality of a diverse and multicultural world. According to Havel, "[D]emocracy in its present Western form arouses skepticism and mistrust in many parts of the world." Václav Havel, *Democracy's Forgotten Dimension*, 31 STAN. J. INT'L L. 1, 10 (1995). Havel concludes:

> The effective expansion of democracy therefore presupposes a critical self-examination, a process that will lead to its internalization.
>
> . . . This internalization of democracy today can scarcely take the form of some doctrine, that is, a collection of dogmas and rituals. This probably would have exactly the opposite effect: To all the mutually distrustful cultural currents there would only be added others, ones that would be very artificial because they would not have grown out of the nourishing soil of myth-making eras. If a renaissance of spirituality does occur, it will far more likely be a multi-leveled and multi-cultural reflection, with a new political ethos . . . .

Id. at 12.

25. *See* R.W. Apple, Jr., *A Divided Government Remains, and with It the Prospect of Further Combat*, N.Y. TIMES, Nov. 7, 1996, at B6.

and in the face of widespread misery. Such a situation leaves much to be desired.

B. *Relativity of Democracy In Practice*

Democracy is a social theory, and thus has defied a universally accepted definition.[26] The appeal of its cardinal maxims, freedom and equality,

> makes it susceptible in different cultures and societies to its acceptance by degrees.
>
> Thus, in the biggest democracy of the world, India, the equality of people is thwarted by an extensive caste system and by religious divisions. In . . . the United States of America, the two top executives, the President and the Vice-President, are still elected by electoral colleges, not by popular vote.[27]

Further, in Asia, the Japanese model, which is widely endorsed as one of the most successful liberal democracies, has in fact retained the ideals of Confucianism, which dictate primacy of group interest as opposed to the individualism of liberal democracy, and this ideal has informed judicial attitude.[28] The new Russian democratic system simply classifies as "dissident" individual or minority dissent; thus, the people as individuals do not in reality exercise such independent franchise as liberalism would contemplate.[29] While some pre-colonial African societies were essentially democratic, as demonstrated

---

26. *See* ROBERT A. DAHL, A PREFACE TO DEMOCRATIC THEORY 1 (1956).

27. Filipe N. Bole, *Fiji's Chiefly System and its Pattern of Political Self-Reliance, in* CULTURE AND DEMOCRACY IN THE SOUTH PACIFIC 67, 69 (Ron Crocombe et al. eds., 1992). It is, however, important to note that in the recent history of U.S. democracy, the electoral college has in substance been a deadletter of the Constitution, as popular vote has been the decider of political contests for the presidency. Still, it is by no means insignificant that the non-populist and feudalistic philosophy of the electoral college has persisted as a constitutional principle in the world's foremost liberal democracy, and should the occasion arise, it would be the legal means for "electing" the president.

28. *See* Dean J. Gibbons, *Law and the Group Ethos in Japan*, 3 INT'L LEGAL PERSP. 98, 108-09 (1990). The normative traditional saying in Japan is: "*Deru kugi wa uteru*," which means, "The nail that sticks up gets hammered down." Rajendra Ramlogan, *The Human Rights Revolution in Japan: A Story of New Wine in Old Wine Skins?*, 8 EMORY INT'L L. REV. 127, 131 (1994).

29. *See* Nikolai Biryukov & Victor Sergeyev, *The Idea of Democracy in the West and in the East, in* DEFINING AND MEASURING DEMOCRACY, *supra* note 9, at 182, 194-95.

by the widely applied principle of public involvement in decision making,[30] post-colonial Africa attempted a wholesale adoption of liberal democratic systems without deference to cultural values. The most prominent models were the Westminster majoritarian model and the centralized executive model of Fifth Republic France. These models did not guarantee proportional representation, and thus accentuated the diversity inherent in the arbitrary colonial boundaries of Africa. Consequently, in contemporary Africa it is better to talk about "democratic impulses" than liberal democratic systems.[31]

So far, one may conclude that states' practice shows that the meaning of democracy is enriched by the culture in which it is examined. Accordingly, there is sufficient evidence that state practice does not endorse any particular political model as a universal democracy, nor has any one political model obtained legal status. In the U.N. forum, for example, countries whose systems hardly resemble liberal democracy but whose constitutions describe them as democratic, are nevertheless addressed as democracies, as is evinced by the use of terms such as "Republic," "Democratic Republic," "People," "Commonwealth," and "Federation" in U.N. instruments. However, it must be emphasized that the absence of a universal political model does not negate universal democracy.

III. THE LEGAL CONCEPT OF DEMOCRACY

A. *The Peremptory Norm of Self-Determination*

The norm of self-determination guarantees the right of a people or a nation freely to determine, without any outside interference, its political and legal status as a separate entity. Preferably, such self-determination will be effected through formation of an independent state; in addition, the people should have the right to choose their form of government, and their economic, social, and cultural systems.[32] So conceived,

30. *See* RICHARD HODDER-WILLIAMS, AN INTRODUCTION TO THE POLITICS OF TROPICAL AFRICA 13-14 (1984). A good example of pre-colonial democracy is the Ibo traditional society in Nigeria, depicted in CHINUA ACHEBE, THINGS FALL APART (Ballantine Books 1983) (1959).

31. *See* Naomi Chazan, *Democratic Fragments: Africa's Quest for Democracy*, *in* 4 DEMOCRACY AND MODERNITY 111, 112 (S.N. Eisenstadt ed., 1992).

32. *See* Frank Przetacznik, *The Basic Collective Human Right to Self-Determination of Peoples and Nations as a Prerequisite for Peace: Its Philosophical Back-*

self-determination is Janus-faced: On the one hand, it means political independence from alien domination or an already existing sovereign state, while on the other hand, it entails a people's democratic choice about its governance.[33] Self-determination has peremptory normative status (*jus cogens*) in international law[34] and can be set aside only by a subsequent peremptory norm of contrary effect.[35] Therefore, the right to democracy as an internal aspect of the right to self-determination of "all peoples"[36] and nations can properly be classified as an overriding customary international law.[37] Because the nationalist aspect of self-determination dominated the bipolar Cold War period as a result of the politically and ideologically sensitive question of colonies and non-self-governing territories,[38] the notion of internal self-determination as customary international law has suffered in obscurity.

---

ground and Practical Application, 69 REVUE DE DROIT INTERNATIONAL DE SCIENCES DIPLOMATIQUES ET POLITIQUES 259, 263 (1991).

33. *See* Jane E. Stromseth, *Self-Determination, Secession and Humanitarian Intervention by the United Nations*, 86 AM. SOC'Y OF INT'L L. PROC. 370, 370 (1992). Thomas Franck has defined the right of self-determination as the right of "a people organized in an established territory to determine its collective political destiny in a democratic fashion . . . ." Franck, *supra* note 12, at 52.

34. *See* HÉCTOR GROS ESPIELL, THE RIGHT TO SELF-DETERMINATION: IMPLEMENTATION OF UNITED NATIONS RESOLUTIONS at 11, U.N. Doc. E/CN.4/Sub.2/405/Rev.1, U.N. Sales No. E.79.XIV.5 (1980) (study prepared by Héctor Gros Espiell, Special Rapporteur of the Sub-Commission on Prevention of Discrimination and Protection of Minorities); IAN BROWNLIE, PRINCIPLES OF PUBLIC INTERNATIONAL LAW 515 (4th ed. 1990). Quite recently, the International Court of Justice has reaffirmed the erga omnes character of the right to self-determination as "irreproachable" in the case of East Timor (Port. v. Austl.), 1995 I.C.J. 90, 120 (June 30), *reprinted in* 34 I.L.M. 1583, 1589.

35. *See* BROWNLIE, *supra* note 34, at 515.

36. *Universal Realization of the Right of Peoples to Self-Determination*, G.A. Res. 93, U.N. GAOR, 48th Sess., 85th plen. mtg., Agenda Item 108(a), at 3, U.N. Doc. A/RES/48/93 (1994); *Right of Peoples to Self-Determination: Report of the Third Committee*, U.N. GAOR, 48th Sess., Agenda Item 108(a), at 10, U.N. Doc. A/48/626 (1993); *see* 1993 U.N.Y.B. 871, U.N. Sales No. E.94.I.1.

37. *See* Jean Salmon, *Internal Aspects of the Right to Self-Determination, in* MODERN LAW OF SELF-DETERMINATION: TOWARDS A DEMOCRATIC LEGITIMACY PRINCIPLE? 253, 277 (Christian Tomuschat ed., 1993).

38. *See* Patrick Thornberry, *The Democratic or Internal Aspect of Self-Determination with Some Remarks on Federalism, in* MODERN LAW OF SELF-DETERMINATION: TOWARDS A DEMOCRATIC LEGITIMACY PRINCIPLE?, *supra* note 37, at 101, 120.

B. The Right to Democracy

The issue of a right to democracy has been extensively commented on by scholars, especially some of "the most highly qualified [western] publicists,"[39] and there is a near consensus among these publicists on the existence of a right to democracy, as well as on the legitimacy of collective intervention for the restoration of democracy.[40] Though their thesis is of doubtful validity, Michael Reisman and Lois Fielding have gone further by endorsing unilateral intervention for the protection of democracy.[41] Whereas unilateralism is illegal under the terms of article 2 of the Charter,[42] and is contrary to the normative principle of collective security on which the U.N. system is founded,[43] scholars recognize that there is an inter-

39. Statute of the International Court of Justice, June 26, 1945, art. 38(1)(d), 59 Stat. 1055, 1060, 3 Bevans 1179, 1187 (in making judicial determinations, the International Court of Justice (I.C.J.) shall apply, inter alia, "the teachings of the most highly qualified publicists").

40. *See* Franck, *supra* note 12, at 90-91; Gregory H. Fox, *The Right to Political Participation in International Law*, 17 YALE J. INT'L L. 539, 552-70 (1992); Gregory H. Fox, *National Sovereignty Revisited: Perspectives on the Emerging Norm of Democracy in International Law*, *in* 86TH PROCEEDINGS OF THE ANNUAL MEETING OF THE AMERICAN SOCIETY OF INTERNATIONAL LAW 249 (1992); JAMES CRAWFORD, DEMOCRACY IN INTERNATIONAL LAW 4-7 (1994); Babacar Ndiaye, *International Co-operation to Promote Democracy and Human Rights: Principles and Programmes*, INT'L COMM'N JURISTS, Dec. 1992, at 23; Oscar Schachter, *The Legality of Pro-Democratic Invasion*, 78 AM. J. INT'L L. 645 (1984); Michael W. Doyle, *Liberalism and World Politics*, 80 AM. POL. SCI. REV. 1151, 1162 (1986); Lois E. Fielding, *Taking the Next Step in the Development of New Human Rights: The Emerging Right of Humanitarian Assistance to Restore Democracy*, 5 DUKE J. COMP. & INT'L L. 329, 332-38, 343-55 (1995).

41. W. Michael Reisman, *Humanitarian Intervention and Fledgling Democracies*, 18 FORDHAM INT'L L. J. 794, 804-05 (1995); Fielding, *supra* note 40, at 343. The International Court of Justice in the 1966 South West Africa cases decided that not even compelling grounds of necessity could justify an *actio popularis* in international law. South West Africa (Eth. v. S. Afr.; Liber. v. S. Afr.), 1966 I.C.J. 6, 47, para. 88 (July 18) (rejecting necessity argument as based on "extra-legal" considerations and concluding that although "an *actio popularis*, or right resident in any member of a community to take legal action in vindication of a public interest" is recognized in some municipal legal systems, it is not a general principle of international law). This decision was a judicial indictment of unilateralism in the multilateral context of the United Nations system.

42. U.N. CHARTER art. 2(4).

43. *See* Richard Falk, *The Haiti Intervention: A Dangerous World Order Precedent for the United Nations*, 36 HARV. INT'L L.J. 341, 357 (1995). According to Falk, it is imperative to be cautious in seeking further expansion of the frontiers of humanitarian intervention in a system where selective and discriminatory application of international law has become the rule. *Id.* at 345 n.23.

national right to democracy that could be protected by collective intervention. Moreover, global and regional human rights instruments also have endorsed the right to democracy.[44]

The Universal Declaration of Human Rights[45] (Universal Declaration) is the premier instrument on the right to democracy, and it contains the clearest statement on the issue of democracy.[46] While General Assembly resolutions are often regarded as not binding,[47] it must be noted that the Universal

44. *See* International Covenant on Civil and Political Rights, *adopted* Dec. 19, 1966, art. 25, S. EXEC. DOC. E, 95-2, at 23, 30-31 (1978), 999 U.N.T.S. 171, 179 (entered into force Mar. 23, 1976). Article 25 of the covenant provides that "every citizen shall have the right and the opportunity . . . without unreasonable restrictions . . . to vote and to be elected at genuine periodic elections which shall be by universal and equal suffrage and shall be held by secret ballot, guaranteeing the free expression of the will of the electors." *Id.* art. 25(b); *see also* Protocol to the European Convention for the Protection of Human Rights and Fundamental Freedoms, Mar. 20, 1952, art. 3, 213 U.N.T.S. 262, 264 (entered into force May 18, 1954) (acknowledging obligation of parties to "hold free elections . . . under conditions which will ensure the free expression of the opinion of the people in the choice of the legislature"); American Convention on Human Rights, *done* Nov. 22, 1969, preamble, 1144 U.N.T.S. 123, 144 (entered into force July 18, 1978) (reaffirming commitment of parties to protecting rights "within the framework of democratic institutions"); *id.* art. 23, 1144 U.N.T.S. at 151 (guaranteeing the right to participate in public affairs, vote, and to have access to public service); *id.* art. 29, 1144 U.N.T.S. at 153 (disavowing interpretations of the convention that would preclude other rights and guarantees "derived from representative democracy as a form of government"); Banjul Charter on Human and Peoples' Rights, *adopted* June 27, 1981, art. 13, 21 I.L.M. 58, 61 (entered into force Oct. 21, 1986); Conference on Security and Co-operation in Europe: Document of the Copenhagen Meeting of the Conference on the Human Dimension, June 29, 1990, art. 3, 29 I.L.M. 1305 (expressing agreement of participating states that "democracy is an element of the rule of law"); International Convention on the Elimination of All Forms of Racial Discrimination, *opened for signature* Mar. 7, 1966, art. 5(c), 660 U.N.T.S. 195, 220 (entered into force Jan. 4, 1969); Convention on the Political Rights of Women, *done* Mar. 31, 1953, arts. I-III, 27 U.S.T. 1909, 1911, 193 U.N.T.S. 135, 136-38; U.N. CHARTER arts. 2(1), 55-56.

45. Universal Declaration of Human Rights, G.A. Res. 217A, U.N. GAOR, 3d Sess., pt. 1, 183d plen. mtg. at 71, U.N. Doc. A/810 (1948) [hereinafter Universal Declaration].

46. *Id.* art. 21.

47. The conclusion that the resolutions are mere recommendations is based on narrow logic. If the fundamental principles of the United Nations are collectivism and sovereign equality, then one must concede at least that resolutions carry the moral force of the opinions of most sovereign states. Then again, there is no clear-cut distinction between morality and legality; both are overarching, mutually complementing.

The General Assembly's Uniting for Peace Resolution, G.A. Res. 377A, *supra* note 4, demonstrated the residual legal capacity of the General Assembly. *See* Legal Consequences for States of the Continued Presence of South Africa in Namibia (South West Africa) Notwithstanding Security Council Resolution 276

Declaration is not just another General Assembly Resolution. It has become an edifying referent for state constitutions, whose contents sometimes are a wholesale adoption of provisions of the Universal Declaration. Beyond state boundaries, the Universal Declaration has inspired regional and international agreements.[48] The Universal Declaration has effectively shed whatever stigma attended the circumstances of its birth because, according to the United Nations, the broadest legally binding human rights agreements—the International Covenant on Economic, Social and Cultural Rights[49] and the International Covenant on Civil and Political Rights[50]—have "take[n] the provisions of the Universal Declaration a step further by making them binding upon States parties."[51] Additionally, the universal acceptance of the Universal Declaration constitutes an *opinio juris* sufficient for a binding customary rule of international law. It is in this light that the Universal Declaration is seen as having "evolved into the Magna Carta of the international human rights movement and the premier normative international instrument on the subject."[52]

(1970), 1971 I.C.J. 16, 45-50 (June 21) (rendering opinion that General Assembly did not act beyond its powers in adopting resolution 2145, which terminated the Mandate for South Africa). See also Certain Expenses of the United Nations, 1962 I.C.J. 151, 163 (July 20), in which the I.C.J. held that the powers and responsibilities under article 24 of the Charter were only *primarily* those of the Security Council and were never intended to be exclusively vested in the Security Council; thus, article 24 did not exclude the General Assembly from assuming similar responsibilities.

In any event, there can be no better evidence of a general practice accepted as law than the resolutions of states reached in the most widely representative and democratic organ of the United Nations, and in the course of discussing issues under the Charter, which, juridically, is the constitution of the United Nations.

48. *See* Egon Schwelb & Philip Alston, *The Principal Institutions and Other Bodies Founded Under the Charter*, *in* 1 THE INTERNATIONAL DIMENSIONS OF HUMAN RIGHTS 231, 245 (Karel Vasak & Philip Alston eds., 1982).

49. International Covenant on Economic, Social and Cultural Rights, *adopted* Dec. 16, 1966, 993 U.N.T.S. 3.

50. International Covenant on Civil and Political Rights, *supra* note 44, S. EXEC. DOC. E, 95-2, at 23, 999 U.N.T.S. at 171.

51. *See* THE UNITED NATIONS AT 50: NOTES FOR SPEAKERS 52 (1995).

52. Thomas Buergenthal, *The Human Rights Revolution*, 23 ST. MARY'S L.J. 3, 7 (1991); *see also* Philip Alston, *The UN's Human Rights Record: From San Francisco to Vienna and Beyond*, 16 HUM. RTS. Q. 375, 376 (1994).

C. The Duty of Intervention

The right to a democratic governance is clearly borne out by article 21 of the Universal Declaration.[53] However, responsibility of States still must be determined. It is pertinent to note from the outset that "the traditional rule [is] that a State is not guilty of a breach of international law for injuring one of its own nationals."[54] By logical extension, a State that denies its citizens the right to democracy is protected from international scrutiny. The founders of the United Nations did attempt to entrench and widen this traditional sanctity of internal matters by substituting article 15, paragraph 8 of the League of Nations Covenant—which provided for non-interference in matters that according to international law are within the domestic jurisdictional sphere[55]—with article 2(7) of the Charter. Article 2(7) did not, on its own, leave the scope of internal matters to be determined by international law, but instead opted for the vague and expansive phrase "essentially within the domestic jurisdiction."[56] However, contemporary practice shows that international law has moved beyond this traditional constraint, and there are now several grounds for justifying multilateral protection of democracy. For example, where a denial of democracy is effected by violent repression, state practice indicates that there is a right of intervention based on humanitarian imperatives and the right to self-defense of the people.[57] United States intervention in Haiti stands out as a prominent example.[58]

Pursuant to international agreements, i.e., articles 55 and

---

53. Article 21 reads in full:

1. Everyone has the right to take part in the government of his country, directly or through freely chosen representatives.
2. Everyone has the right of equal access to public service in his country.
3. The will of the people shall be the basis of the authority of government; this will shall be expressed in periodic and genuine elections which shall be by universal and equal suffrage and shall be held by secret vote or by equivalent free voting procedures.

Universal Declaration, *supra* note 45, art. 21.

54. Barcelona Traction, Light and Power Co. (Belg. v. Spain), 1970 I.C.J. 3, 192 (Feb. 5) (separate opinion of Judge Jessup).

55. LEAGUE OF NATIONS COVENANT art. 15, para. 8.

56. U.N. CHARTER art. 2(7).

57. *See* Fielding, *supra* note 40, at 355-69.

58. *See id.* at 363-65.

56 of the Charter[59] and article 1 of the Covenant on Civil and Political Rights,[60] all states parties have a legal interest and a duty to ensure the protection of human rights and the right to self-determination within the boundaries of member states.[61] This interest, which would be useless without a remedy, could legitimize a multilateral measure.

Given that the right to democracy is an aspect of the peremptory norm of self-determination,[62] all states have a positive obligation *erga omnes*[63] (i.e., opposable to, and valid against, the whole world and all legal persons irrespective of consent) to protect the democratic character of member states.[64] The legality of a Chapter VII-type measure[65] for the protection of democracy may be justified under the positive obligation *erga omnes* of all states in international customary law to protect the internal self-determination of states. The normative status of this peremptory norm is now unquestionable, such that the usually passive International Court of Justice has, in one case, indicated its readiness to subsume the Charter or powers exercised under it to peremptory norms.[66] If, however, the measure must be forced into the pronouncements of Chapter VII, then the "domestic jurisdiction"[67] and "threat" to "international peace"[68] limitations in the Charter would be abridged by the overriding responsibility placed on states to protect democracy by the peremptory norm of self-

---

59. U.N. CHARTER arts. 55-56.

60. International Covenant on Civil and Political Rights, *supra* note 44, art. 1, S. EXEC. DOC. E, 95-2, at 23, 999 U.N.T.S. at 173.

61. *See* South West Africa (Eth. v. S. Afr.; Liber. v. S. Afr.), 1962 I.C.J. 6, 425-33 (Dec. 21) (separate opinion of Judge Jessup); *see also High Commissioner for the Promotion and Protection of All Human Rights*, G.A. Res. 141, U.N. GAOR, 48th Sess., 85th plen. mtg., Agenda Item 114(b), ¶ 3(a)-(b), U.N. Doc. A/RES/48/141 (1994).

62. *See* Barcelona Traction, Light and Power Co. (Belg. v. Spain), 1970 I.C.J. 3, 304 (Feb. 5) (separate opinion of Judge Ammoun).

63. *See id.* at 32. The court in *Barcelona Traction* comments on obligations *erga omnes*: "[A]ll states can be held to have a legal interest in their protection." *Id.*

64. *See South West Africa*, 1962 I.C.J. at 425, 428-29 (separate opinion of Judge Jessup).

65. *See* U.N. CHARTER arts. 39-51.

66. *See* Application of the Convention on the Prevention and Punishment of the Crime of Genocide (Bosn. & Herz. v. Yugo.), 1993 I.C.J. 325, 436-41 (Sept. 13) (separate opinion of Judge Lauterpacht).

67. U.N. CHARTER art. 2(7).

68. *Id.* art. 39.

determination.

The legality of an intervention may be sought in article 24 of the Charter, which has been interpreted as vesting general powers beyond the specific powers of Chapters VI, VII, VIII, and XII of the Charter.[69] However, there are limits on measures taken under Chapter V, article 24 inclusive. First, these limits dictate that the U.N. Security Council act in accordance with the purposes and principles of the Charter;[70] these purposes can validly be summarized as "humanism," and the principles of "collectivism." In other words, whatever action the Security Council takes must be informed by the overriding interest of the people of the target state. Second, intervention must be multilateral or collectively sanctioned under the aegis of the United Nations. Finally, the intervention must not violate the undefined domestic jurisdiction clause, which is permissible only when intervention is effected pursuant to Chapter VII.[71]

Since the end of the Cold War, state practice appears to have endorsed the principles of the rejected League of Nations Covenant, article 15, as the cornerstone of domestic jurisdiction; that is, what constitutes "internal matters" is increasingly an international law determination.[72] For example, it is no longer debatable that human rights issues are merely an item of domestic jurisdiction. In the same vein, the legitimacy of certain governments has acquired international relevancy. Given that they set a standard for legitimacy of government and internal sovereignty as the will of the people, international legal instruments[73] should be interpreted as validating international regulation and protection of that standard.[74] In addi-

69. *See* Legal Consequences for States of the Continued Presence of South Africa in Namibia (South West Africa) Notwithstanding Security Council Resolution 276 (1970), 1971 I.C.J. 16, 52-54 (June 21).

70. U.N. CHARTER art. 24(2).

71. *See id.* arts. 39, 48, 51.

72. Article 15 reads in pertinent part:

> If [a] dispute between . . . parties is claimed by one of them, and is found by the Council to arise out of a matter which *by international law* is solely within the domestic jurisdiction of that party, the Council shall so report and shall make no recommendation as to its settlement.

LEAGUE OF NATIONS COVENANT art. 15, para. 8 (emphasis added).

73. Particularly the Universal Declaration, *supra* note 45, art. 21, and the U.N. CHARTER arts. 55-56.

74. Former Secretary-General Javier Perez de Cuellar once observed that "[i]f

tion, the Declaration on Principles of International Law Concerning Friendly Relations[75]—which is widely accepted as customary international law[76]—expressly makes the territorial integrity of a state contingent on its possession of a consensual representative government.[77] The inescapable conclusion is that the legitimacy of a state government is no longer merely a concern of domestic jurisdiction.

D. Evidence of State Practice

While legal scholarship and international legal instruments do endorse the right to democracy, it is also important to examine the attitude of states in practice. Based on an annual survey in 1992, out of 183 states, six were communist, twelve were traditional monarchies, and eighteen were military regimes.[78] The remaining 147 states were either democratic or in transition to democracy.[79] Huntington has characterized this global phenomenon as the third wave of democratic expansion.[80] In Eastern Europe, the expansion was manifest in the disintegration of communist Russia, and the fall of the Berlin Wall.[81] Traditional hardliners, such as Hungary, Romania, Bulgaria, and Albania, are fast embracing democra-

---

the character, aims and standards of internal sovereignty are . . . internationally defined, the external manifestations of sovereignty are similarly regulated." Javier Perez de Cuellar, *Perez de Cuellar Discusses Sovereignty and International Responsibility*, INT'L COMM'N JURISTS, Dec. 1991, at 24, 25 (published text of Perez de Cuellar's November 21, 1991 address to the University of Florence).

75. *Declaration on Principles of International Law Concerning Friendly Relations and Co-operation Among States in Accordance with the Charter of the United Nations*, G.A. Res. 2625, U.N. GAOR, 25th Sess., 1883d plen. mtg., Supp. No. 28, at 121, U.N. Doc. A/8028 (1971).

76. *See* Frederic L. Kirgis, Jr., *The Degrees of Self-determination in the United Nations Era*, 88 AM. J. INT'L L. 304, 305 (1994) (citing BROWNLIE, *supra* note 34, at 513); *see also* Military and Paramilitary Activities in and Against Nicaragua (Nicar. v. U.S.), 1986 I.C.J. 14, 101 (June 27) (determining that the adoption of the Declaration on Principles of International Law Concerning Friendly Relations by states parties "affords an indication of their *opinio juris* as to customary international law" on the use of force).

77. *See* G.A. Res. 2625, *supra* note 75, princ. 4, para. 2(b), at 124.

78. *See* YVES BEIGBEDER, INTERNATIONAL MONITORING OF PLEBISCITES, REFERENDA AND NATIONAL ELECTIONS: SELF-DETERMINATION AND TRANSITION TO DEMOCRACY 2 (1994).

79. *See id.*

80. Samuel P. Huntington, *Democracy's Third Wave*, J. DEMOCRACY, Spring 1991, at 12, 12; *see also* BEIGBEDER, *supra* note 78, at 2.

81. *See* BEIGBEDER, *supra* note 78, at 3.

cy.[82] Honduras, Argentina, Grenada, Panama, Chile, Nicaragua, Haiti, and the Americas are aspirants to the democratic circle.[83] In Asia—although tyranny still reigns over the people of Myanmar, formerly Burma[84]—even China, one of the last bastions of communism, is said to be softening under intense international pressure.[85] Vietnam, Indonesia, Thailand, and Mongolia have demonstrated a resolve to join the train of democracy.[86] Nepal and Cambodia have moved towards democracy.[87] In Africa, the end of the Cold War signalled the death of totalitarianism.[88] African peoples have declared their preference for democracy in the Abuja Declaration of 1991[89] and the Dakar Declaration of 1992.[90] The European Union (EU) and the Organization of American States (OAS) have adopted measures that prioritize democratization of new states and the protection of member states' democratic character.[91]

The general embrace of democracy is also manifest in the operations of the United Nations, an organ that is perhaps the most credible index of consensus and collective will of states.

---

82. *See id.* at 3-4.

83. *See id.* at 5-6.

84. *See id.* at 6.

85. It is widely acknowledged that China is one of the fastest liberalizing market economies today. Underneath this liberalization lies a democratic ethic (at least of free enterprise) that should soon impact the political structure of China. While this point is debatable, it is unquestionable that the situation in China is far different than it has been in the past. A decade ago, no one would have anticipated China's warm reception of free enterprise in the 1990s.

86. *See* BEIGBEDER, *supra* note 78, at 6.

87. *See id.* at 6-7.

88. *See id.* at 7-8.

89. *Abuja Declaration on South Africa,* U.N. GAOR, 46th Sess., Annex II, Prov. Agenda Item 30, at 83-88, U.N. Doc. A/46/390 (1991) (indicating support for the abolition of apartheid and the institution of non-racial democracy in South Africa).

90. *Dakar/Ngor Declaration on Population, Family and Sustainable Development,* Recommendation 20, *in* U.N. DEP'T FOR ECONOMIC & SOCIAL INFORMATION AND POLICY ANALYSIS, POPULATION BULLETIN OF THE UNITED NATIONS at 37, 42, U.N. Doc. ST/ESA/SER.N/37-38, U.N. Sales No. E.94.XIII.16 (1994) (recommending democratization as a priority in the efforts to eliminate the underlying causes of the worldwide refugee problem); *see Africa: Population Conference Sets Ambitious Targets,* Inter Press Serv., Dec. 14, 1992, *available in* LEXIS, News Library, Arcnws File.

91. *See Declaration on the "Guidelines on the Recognition of New States in Eastern Europe and in the Soviet Union,"* U.N. SCOR, Extraordinary EPC Ministerial mtg., Annex II, at 4, U.N. Doc. S/23293 (1992); O.A.S. CHARTER preamble, *reprinted in* 33 I.L.M. 981, 981.

The United Nations has endorsed the monitoring of elections as an important activity by creating an office of Electoral Assistance in 1992.[92] It has assisted over forty-five states in conducting and financing elections.[93] In 1981, in a radical departure from its traditional passivism, the Human Rights Committee decided that Uruguay's military regime, by its curtailment of political freedom, was in violation of the International Covenant on Civil and Political Rights.[94] Hence, the normative status of the right to democracy is endorsed by state practice.

However, it must be restated that there is no evidence of a universally accepted model; indeed, there is overwhelming evidence to the contrary.[95] The Vienna Conference on Human Rights and Development expressly considered, and rejected, the more inclusive definition of democracy of "full participation of people in all aspects of their lives."[96] As Thomas Franck has noted, it is unnecessary to project any given model, for "the term 'democracy', as used in international rights parlance, is intended to connote the kind of governance which is legitimated by the consent of the governed. . . . [E]ssential to the legitimacy of governance is evidence of consent *to the process by which a populace is consulted* by its Government."[97] The

---

92. *See Enhancing the Effectiveness of the Principle of Periodic and Genuine Elections*, G.A. Res. 137, U.N. GAOR, 46th Sess., 75th plen. mtg., Agenda Item 98, U.N. Doc. A/RES/46/137 (1992); *Enhancing the Effectiveness of the Principle of Periodic and Genuine Elections: Report of the Secretary General*, U.N. GAOR, 46th Sess., Agenda Item 98(b), U.N. Doc. A/46/609 (1991); *Enhancing the Effectiveness of the Principle of Periodic and Genuine Elections: Report of the Secretary General*, U.N. GAOR, 47th Sess., Agenda Item 97(b), U.N. Doc. A/47/668 (1991); *see also* Tom J. Farer & Felice Gaer, *The UN and Human Rights: At the End of the Beginning*, *in* UNITED NATIONS, DIVIDED WORLD, *supra* note 3, at 240, 290-91 (discussing these resolutions).

93. *See* THE UNITED NATIONS AT 50: NOTES FOR SPEAKERS, *supra* note 51, at 70.

94. *Views of the Human Rights Committee under Article 5(4) of the Optional Protocol to the International Covenant on Civil and Political Rights (Concerning Communication No. R.10/44)*, U.N. GAOR Hum. Rts. Comm., 36th Sess., Supp. No. 40, at 153, ¶ 17, U.N. Doc. A/36/40 (1981).

95. *See supra* Part III.B.

96. *Vienna Declaration and Programme of Action*, U.N. GAOR World Conf. on Human Rts., 48th Sess., 22d plen. mtg. at 20, ¶ 8, U.N. Doc. A/CONF.157/24 (Part I) (1993) [hereinafter *Vienna Declaration*]; *see also* Susan Marks, *Nightmare and Noble Dream: The 1993 World Conference on Human Rights*, 53 CAMBRIDGE L.J. 54, 58 (1994).

97. Thomas M. Franck, *Fairness in the International Legal and Institutional*

position of the United Nations on this issue has been articulated by the former Secretary-General:

> When, like so many others before me, I stress the imperative of democratization, I do not mean that some states should imitate others slavishly, nor do I expect them to borrow political systems that are alien to them, much less to gratify certain Western States—in fact, just the opposite. Let us state, forcefully, that democracy is the private domain of no one. It can and ought to be assimilated by all cultures. It can take many forms in order to accommodate local realities more effectively. Democracy is not a model to copy from certain states, but a goal to be achieved by all peoples! *It is the political expression of our common heritage . . . .*[98]

IV. The Contents of the Right to Democracy

A. *The Substantive Content*

Our initial question—"What is Universal Democracy?"—still persists. What are the elements constituting the "common heritage" that in the view of the United Nations make up the minimum democratic heritage that has "a universal dimension?" Article 21 of the Universal Declaration emphasizes the overriding importance of the will of the people.[99] Therefore, a government that is not based on the consent of the governed is not democratic. In addition, the government must be substantially representative of all distinct groups in the country. This is a logical interpretation of the phrase "[e]veryone has the right to take part in the government" in article 21 of the Universal Declaration.[100] In order not to lose

---

System, 240 RECUEIL DES COURS D'ACADEMIE DE DROIT INTERNATIONAL [R.C.A.D.I.] 102 (1993-III).

98. Cerna, *supra* note 12, at 291-92 (quoting former Secretary-General Boutros Boutros-Ghali, from his address at the opening of the World Conference on Human Rights in 1993) (emphasis added). There are fundamental experiences shared by all beings despite geo-cultural diversities. *See* STANISLAV GROF & HAL ZINA BENNETT, THE HOLOTROPIC MIND 89-91 (1992).

The universal heritage of democracy should be seen as a sum total of global rational choice based on the shared human experience of class domination and exploitation. At the least, it is evident in the near-universal demystification of the concept of governance, and in a broader sense it manifests in popular calls for accountability in governments.

99. Universal Declaration, *supra* note 45, art. 21(3).

100. *Id.* art. 21(1).

the essence or undermine the ethics of the concept of representation, one must check the tendency to presume a representation in fact from a nominal representation.[101] Representation should be manifest in active participation such that "representation and participation [are] experienced as part of a continuum."[102] Article 21 of the Universal Declaration did, in fact, contemplate a solution to the question of representation by providing that everyone has the right to take part in government;[103] this provision denotes an active participation beyond the initial consent usually expressed through free elections. The United Nations has defined the right to popular participation as the "judicial and political structures [that] enable all citizens to participate, freely and actively, in laying the constitutional foundations of the political community, determining the scope and purpose of the various institutions, *choosing their leaders, and governing the State.*"[104] It would be frivolous to argue that because a people have voted in a government, every segment of the population must be deemed, *a fortiori*, to be participating. On the other hand, it is nonsensical to argue that a particular segment may choose to withdraw from participation in the government beyond exercising its voting rights. To be legitimate and democratic in international law, the emerging government must be based on the consent of the people and must be participatorily representative of all national and distinct political groups in the country. One assumption essential to this standard is that zero-sum politicking in international law is undemocratic and illegal. The consent of the governed and true representative quality of the government are the substantive components of universal democracy, to which everyone has a right; both components are necessary to preserve the sanctity and inviolability of a state's territorial integrity.

101. *See* WARWICK MCKEAN, EQUALITY AND DISCRIMINATION UNDER INTERNATIONAL LAW 12, 285 (1983).

102. Thornberry, *supra* note 38, at 116.

103. *See supra* note 53.

104. *Study by the Secretary-General*, U.N. ESCOR Hum. Rts. Comm'n, 41st Sess., Provisional Agenda Item 8(c), at 22, ¶ 94, U.N. Doc. E/CN.4/1985/10 (1985) (emphasis added).

B. The Procedural Content

Article 21 of the Universal Declaration provides for "periodic and genuine elections . . . by universal and equal suffrage and . . . by secret vote" as the only process by which democracy can be attained.[105] Government that gains or retains power by any other process is not democratic and is thus illegitimate in international law. Traditional monarchies apparently fail this test notwithstanding their acclaimed populist image. In short, the legitimacy of a government must be tested periodically by elections. There is no space for presumptions of consent.

C. The Structural Content

There is a third element—the structural element—which makes it mandatory for a state seeking to join the democratic circle to structure its government on a normative and institutional framework that provides for the welfare of the people.

1. Historical Perspective

History has portrayed the evolution of people from a natural, unorganized state to an organized civil society as being motivated by the necessity for collective security of both life and property.[106] In the 18th century, Immanuel Kant ob-

105. Universal Declaration, *supra* note 45, art. 21(3).

106. Even classical liberal thought, which professes to be averse to communitarianism, is paradoxically embedded in the logic of collectivism—the public good of the society. The social contractarians, notwithstanding their many differences, all recognized that from the inception of civil society, central authority has been a functional mechanism for the individual benefit of each and every member of society. John Locke theorized the central mechanism as follows: "Their power, in the utmost bounds of it, is limited to the public good of the society. It is a power that has no other end but preservation, and therefore can never have a right to destroy, enslave, or designedly to impoverish the subjects." LOCKE, *supra* note 7, at 160; *see also* JEAN-JACQUES ROUSSEAU, THE SOCIAL CONTRACT 49 (Maurice Cranston trans., Penguin Books 1968) (1762). Hobbes believed the very viability of a contract was dubious absent a central authority. As Hobbes put it:

> If a Covenant be made, wherein neither of the parties performe presently, but trust one another; in the condition of meer Nature, (which is a condition of Warre of every man against every man,) upon any reasonable suspicion, it is Voyd: But if there be a common Power set over them both, with right and force sufficient to compell performance; it is not Voyd.

HOBBES, *supra* note 18, at 196.

served the position of trust occupied by the institution of government and that position's connection with both internal and international peace which, according to Kant, must be rooted in a domestic institutional guarantee of human rights and social welfare.[107] Historical evidence shows that the reason for the dislodgement of the feudal system—which, in turn, dispersed political and economic powers among secular rulers, the church, and the feudal lords—was that a unification of powers of all three of those institutions in a unified national state was the best mechanism for furthering the interest of each individual institution.[108] In 1648, the Peace of Westphalia marked the birth of the modern state, which—though it was intended to effect total unity and progress of all individuals—has progressively vindicated Machiavelli's prediction[109] that the state would ultimately metamorphose into an entirely self-sufficing and non-moral entity.[110] The state is a unique sphere of human development, a functional instrument that, in isolation, has no inherent morality. The modern state, whether seen as a product of consensus, conflict or contrivance, evolved and was nurtured by people's search for security and social justice. Its moral justification should be measured by the extent to which it enhances the security and social welfare of its citizens. In other words, the primary purpose of the modern state should, as a basic norm, condition its functional framework, and this should necessarily translate into normative philosophy and material institutions.

2. Within the Framework of the Charter, By Necessary Implication

> [T]he U.N. Charter established an instrument for international cooperation[,] . . . an organism capable of life and growth . . . depending not simply on the written injunctions of the founding fathers but on the visions and wisdom of

107. *See* Immanuel Kant, *On the Relationship of Theory to Practice in Political Right*, *in* POLITICAL WRITINGS, *supra* note 2, at 73, 74.

108. *See* WILLIAM STUBBS, THE CONSTITUTIONAL HISTORY OF ENGLAND 85-87 (1979).

109. *See* NICCOLÒ MACHIAVELLI, THE PRINCE (George Bull ed., Penguin Books, 1961) (1513).

110. *See* J.L. BRIERLY, THE LAW OF NATIONS: AN INTRODUCTION TO THE INTERNATIONAL LAW OF PEACE 5-6 (Humphrey Waldock ed., 6th ed. 1963).

succeeding generations.[111]

The doctrine of necessity, which was applied in the *Expenses Case*,[112] has been the basis of much of U.N. activity falling outside the parameters of the Charter. The doctrine is perhaps at the root of the Uniting for Peace Resolution of 1950[113] and of the concepts of peacekeeping and humanitarian intervention. An authentic statement of the boundaries of "necessity" was set forth by Chief Justice John Marshall in *McCulloch v. Maryland*: "Let the end be legitimate, let it be within the scope of the constitution [in this case, the Charter], and all means which are appropriate, which are plainly adapted to that end, which are not prohibited, but consist with the letter and spirit of the constitution [the Charter]" are legitimate.[114]

---

111. BENJAMIN V. COHEN, THE UNITED NATIONS: CONSTITUTIONAL DEVELOPMENTS, GROWTH, AND POSSIBILITIES 2 (1961).

112. Certain Expenses of the United Nations, 1962 I.C.J. 151 (July 20). In this case, the court was faced with the difficult issue of the constitutional basis for the use of armed forces in the United Nations Emergency Force Operations in the Middle East (UNEF) and the United Nations operations in the Congo. The I.C.J., pursuing a policy of institutional effectiveness, decided that any action adjudged appropriate for the fulfillment of one of the stated purposes of the United Nations is presumed within the powers of the organization. *See id.* at 168; *see also* International Status of South-West Africa, 1950 I.C.J. 128, 136 (July 11) (court's advisory opinion on the international status of South-West Africa rested on the assumption of the necessity of international supervision); Corfu Channel (U.K. v. Alb.), 1949 I.C.J. 171, 183-85 (Apr. 9) (relying on the necessity of interpreting the legal personality of the U.N. as an objective international personality capable of bringing international claims against even non-signatories to the Charter).

113. G.A. Res. 377A, *supra* note 4 (adopted by a vote of 52-5 on November 3, 1950); S.C. Res. 119, U.N. SCOR, 11th Sess., 751st mtg. at 9, U.N. Doc. S/3721 (1956) (pursuant to the Uniting for Peace Resolution, Security Council's observation of "lack of unanimity" of permanent members necessitated an emergency special session of the General Assembly to make recommendations concerning the Suez Canal crisis); S.C. Res. 120, U.N. SCOR, 11th Sess., 754th mtg. at 8, U.N. Doc. S/3733 (1956) (necessity for emergency special session of the General Assembly to make recommendations concerning the Soviet suppression of "the efforts of the Hungarian people to reassert their rights"); S.C. Res. 129, U.N. SCOR, 13th Sess., 838th mtg. at 6, U.N. Doc. S/4083 (1958) (necessity for emergency special session of the General Assembly to make recommendations concerning complaints by Lebanon and Jordan of interference by the United Arab Republic in their domestic affairs); S.C. Res. 157, U.N. SCOR, 15th Sess., 906th mtg. at 8, U.N. Doc. S/4526, (1960) (necessity for emergency special session of the General Assembly to make recommendations concerning presence of Belgian troops in the Republic of the Congo).

114. McCulloch v. Maryland, 17 U.S. (4 Wheat.) 316, 421 (1819). To constitute a "necessity in the eyes of [international] law," the measure must be inherent in

A preliminary question arises: what are the ends of the Charter and who are the intended beneficiaries? Undoubtedly, states are the major actors in the U.N. system, but the interest of the people remains an overriding consideration. The opening phrase of the Charter, "We the peoples of the United Nations,"[115] clearly places government and states in a position of trust.[116] The ends for which the United Nations was established, as stated in the Preamble, are to forestall another world war; to reaffirm faith in fundamental human rights, in the dignity, worth and equality of all human beings; to establish favorable conditions for justice and respect for the rule of international law; and *"to promote social progress and better standards of life in larger freedom."*[117] Article 55 of the Charter identifies the well-being of the people as a necessary condition for peace,[118] while the primary function and purpose of the U.N. under article 1 of the Charter is the maintenance of

---

the U.N. system as it was originally conceived, and not merely because it is desirable. South West Africa (Eth. v. S. Afr.; Liber. v. S. Afr.), 1966 I.C.J. 6, 47, para. 89 (July 18).

115. U.N. CHARTER preamble.

116. *See* Richard Falk, *The Rights of Peoples (In Particular Indigenous Peoples)*, *in* THE RIGHTS OF PEOPLES 17, 25 (James Crawford ed., 1988); *see also* W. Michael Reisman, *Coercion and Self-Determination: Construing Charter Article 2(4)*, 78 AM. J. INT'L L. 642, 643-44 (1984).

117. U.N. CHARTER preamble (emphasis added). Article 31 of the Vienna Convention on the Law of Treaties provides that a treaty (to which judicial class the Charter belongs) shall be interpreted "in the light of its object and purpose." Vienna Convention on the Law of Treaties, May 23, 1969, art. 31(1), 1155 U.N.T.S. 331, 340 (entered into force Jan. 27, 1980). Article 31 classifies the preamble as part of the "context for purposes of interpretation," *id.* art. 31(2), and endorses a consideration of subsequent state practice, *id.* art. 31(3)(b). Hence, the Charter should be interpreted in the context of its preamble, and in the light of its stated objects, purposes, and contemporary state practice.

118. U.N. CHARTER art. 55. Article 55 reads in full:

> With a view to the creation of conditions of stability and well-being which are necessary for peaceful and friendly relations among nations based on respect for the principle of equal rights and self-determination of peoples, the United Nations shall promote:
>
> (a) higher standards of living, full employment, and conditions of economic and social progress and development;
>
> (b) solutions of international economic, social, health, and related problems; and international cultural and educational cooperation; and
>
> (c) universal respect for, and observance of, human rights and fundamental freedoms for all without distinction as to race, sex, language, or religion.

Id.

international peace and security.[119] These are legally binding international agreements that expressly stipulate certain obligations of a state to its citizens and the role of the United Nations in overseeing their implementation. Under article 56 each state accepts to take separate action for the achievement of the provisions of article 55. A literary interpretation of articles 55 and 56 imposes a legal obligation on the state and creates a populist responsibility for the United Nations. Any construction of state responsibility in this respect as lacking immediate obligation as a result of the United Nations' "promotional" role is bound to fail as it contradicts the letter and spirit of article 56. However, whatever interpretation is adopted should be contextualized. Within a socio-economic framework (where issues of social well-being are often displaced by the materialism of political power in most societies, and by individualism and liberal legalism in others), the externalization of social well-being from the reality of political power undermines any meaningful promotional activity. There must be a normative institutional framework providing empirical benchmarks for the evaluation of state performance, and also providing the leverage for internal enforcement.[120] Moreover, poverty is often rooted in the structure of a society. Thus, to be effective, any solution must be materially and normatively structural. If peace and social well-being are inseparable partners, then, in light of the duty assumed by states under article 56,[121] the right to democracy necessarily envisions a

119. *Id.* art. 1(1).

120. Commenting on the promotional activity of the United Nations Committee on Economic, Social and Cultural Rights, Asbjørn Eide observed that difficulties arose, inter alia, from the fact that within the state "the obligations—and neglect of them—are very difficult to pinpoint." Asbjørn Eide, *Realization of Social and Economic Rights: The Minimum Threshold Approach*, INT'L COMM'N JURISTS, Dec. 1989, at 40, 41.

121. U.N. CHARTER art. 56. Article 56 of the Charter states: "All Members pledge themselves to take joint and separate action in co-operation with the Organization for the achievement of the purposes set forth in Article 55." *Id.* The duty of states to take effective action to create reasonable living standards for their citizens under article 56 was reiterated by the General Assembly in a resolution of December 12, 1958. *See International Co-operation for Economic Development of Under-developed Countries*, G.A. Res. 1316, U.N. GAOR, 13th Sess., Agenda Item 28, U.N. Doc. A/RES/1316 (1958); *see also Permanent Sovereignty over Natural Resources*, G.A. Res. 2158, U.N. GAOR, 21st Sess., Agenda Item 45, U.N. Doc. A/RES/2158 (1966); *Charter of Economic Rights and Duties of States*, G.A. Res. 3281, U.N. GAOR, 29th Sess., Supp. No. 31, 2319th plen. mtg. at 50, U.N. Doc.

democratic system possessing the normative—that is, constitutional—and institutional guarantees of the people's social well-being.[122]

3. Within the Framework of the Universal Declaration of Human Rights

The Universal Declaration spells out civil, political, economic, social, and cultural rights of all beings. Specifically, the Universal Declaration provides, inter alia, for the right to democratic governance,[123] social security,[124] employment,[125] adequate standard of living, food, clothing, housing and medical care,[126] education,[127] and cultural development.[128] Article 28 states that "[e]veryone is entitled to a so-

---

A/9631 (1975); *Declaration on the Right to Development*, G.A. Res. 128, U.N. GAOR, 41st Sess., Supp. No. 53, 97th plen. mtg. at 186, U.N. Doc. A/41/53 (1987).

122. An African elder statesman once observed:

> What rights has our subsistence farmer? He scratches a bare living from the soil provided rains do not fail. His children work at his side without schooling, medical care or even good feeding. Certainly he has freedom to vote and speak as he wishes. But these freedoms are much less real to him than his freedom to be exploited. Only as his poverty is reduced will his existing political freedom become properly meaningful and his right to human dignity a fact.

Amos Wako, *The Rule of Law: Cornerstone of Economic Progress*, 23 INT'L BUS. LAW. 350, 353 (1995).

123. Universal Declaration, *supra* note 45, art. 21(3).

124. *Id.* art. 22. Article 22 states:

> Everyone, as a member of society, has the right to social security and is entitled to realization, through national effort and international co-operation and in accordance with the organization and resources of each State, of the economic, social and cultural rights indispensable for his dignity and the free development of his personality.

125. *Id.* art. 23(1). Article 23(1): "Everyone has the right to work, to free choice of employment, to just and favourable conditions of work and to protection against unemployment."

126. *Id.* art. 25(1). Article 25(1):

> Everyone has the right to a standard of living adequate for the health and well-being of himself and of his family, including food, clothing, housing and medical care and necessary social services, and the right to security in the event of unemployment, sickness, disability, widowhood, old age or lack of livelihood in circumstances beyond his control.

127. *Id.* art. 26(1). Article 26(1):

> Everyone has the right to education. Education shall be free, at least in the elementary and fundamental stages. Elementary education shall be compulsory. Technical and professional education shall be made generally available and higher education shall be equally accessible to all on the basis of merit.

128. *Id.* art. 27. Article 27(1): "Everyone has the right freely to participate in

cial and international order in which the rights and freedoms set forth in this Declaration can be fully realized."[129] It is clear from the integrative language of the preamble and article 28 that each article is to be interpreted in the context of the Universal Declaration and not in isolation. Thus, article 21 means a right to a democratic system that guarantees the rights set out in articles 22 to 27, as required by article 28. In short, articles 21 and 28 together define a democratic state in international law as one that possesses the requisite substantive content, procedural content, and structural content (i.e., a constitutional and institutional framework guaranteeing every individual the rights set forth in articles 22 through 27).[130]

4. Endorsement by United Nations Operations

More than 200 years after Immanuel Kant, the United Nations has programmatically endorsed his Republic. Indeed, "[Kant's] insight . . . anticipates and grounds Article 28 of the Universal Declaration of Human Rights . . . ."[131] The new emphasis on peace-building and development[132] is evidence of such endorsement, and the U.N. commitment to social progress was endorsed by 117 world leaders at the 1975 World Summit for Social Development.[133] The U.N. organizes and funds numerous conferences for critical assessment of national performance in the area of democracy, and takes positive steps to assist the uplifting of the welfare of peoples. The United Na-

---

the cultural life of the community, to enjoy the arts and to share in scientific advancement and its benefits."

129. *Id.* art. 28.

130. *See* John P. Humphrey, *The Just Requirements of Morality, Public Order and the General Welfare in a Democratic Society*, *in* THE PRACTICE OF FREEDOM 137, 147 (R. St. J. MacDonald & John P. Humphrey eds., 1979). Humphrey observes that "the General Assembly . . . meant by democratic society the kind of society in which the rights enunciated by the Universal Declaration of Human Rights are recognized and respected." *Id.*

131. Marilyn McMorrow, *Global Poverty, Subsistence Rights, and Consequent Obligations for Rich and Poor States*, *in* AFRICA, HUMAN RIGHTS, AND THE GLOBAL SYSTEM: THE POLITICAL ECONOMY OF HUMAN RIGHTS IN A CHANGING WORLD 37, 40 (Eileen McCarthy-Arnolds et al. eds., 1994).

132. *See* BOUTROS BOUTROS-GHALI, BUILDING PEACE AND DEVELOPMENT at 1, U.N. Sales No. E.95.I.3 (1994). The former Secretary-General noted that economic and social questions have long occupied the major part of U.N. efforts, and that the U.N. is "deepening its attention to the foundations of peace." *Id.*

133. *See* THE UNITED NATIONS AT 50: NOTES FOR SPEAKERS, *supra* note 51, at 32.

tions Children's Fund; Development Program; Population Fund; World Food Program; Food and Agriculture Organization; Educational Scientific and Cultural Organization; Industrial Development Organization; and Environment Program are all material evidence of such positive steps.[134] But beyond this, it is significant that while the U.N. budget does not normally exceed $3 billion,[135] the U.N. and the World Bank together disburse more than $30 billion on social and development programs ranging from irrigation systems to primary health and education networks.[136] The foregoing is itself an acknowledgement that every state (whether democratic or not) has an obligation of minimum welfare for its people.

However, the attainment of democratic status is different from its sustenance. In 1793-94, revolutionary France had a democratically elected government which succeeded in establishing and maintaining a state of bloody terror. And in the recent past, Panama, Grenada, and the Philippines have shown that the reinstatement of a democratically elected government is not necessarily an assurance of the emergence of a virile democracy. With the hindsight of fledgling democracies, the next and concluding sections seek to demonstrate that democracy has an internal morality that strengthens or weakens its structure and its functional harmony.

V. The Internal Morality of Democracy

The political ethic of a people is a product of the history and traditions of that people. It operates as a political instinct, informing and guiding political decisions, political relations, and political institutions. In the practical arena of politics, the personality of individuals and their acceptability for leadership are always preliminarily screened by this ethic and based on a wide range of cultural and traditional indices. For example, in most traditional African societies the public image of an indi-

---

134. *See generally id.*

135. *See, e.g., Programme Budget for the Biennium 1996-97*, G.A. Res. 215, U.N. GAOR, 50th Sess., Agenda Item 116, 100th plen. mtg. at 3, U.N. Doc. A/RES/50/215 (1996) (appropriating $2,608,274,000 for U.N. budget); *Programme Budget for the Biennium 1994-95*, G.A. Res. 220, U.N. GAOR, 49th Sess., Agenda Item 107, 95th plen. mtg. at 5, U.N. Doc. A/RES/49/220 (1995) (appropriating $2,608,274,400 for U.N. budget).

136. *See id.* at 34.

vidual is a reflection of the individual's ancestral antecedents. Evidence of some sacrilege or apostasy is an unspoken disqualification from public office; this disqualification may be reversed only by exceptional personal integrity and accomplishment. The political ethic could, in some cases, effectively perform the role of the unseen gatekeeper, filtering out the "unsuitable" from participating in leadership, thereby refining the quality of governance. It could constitute either an internal weakness or a pillar of strength of a democracy; for example, the mysticization of political leadership in some places is one surviving ethic that has consistently impeded the development of democracy. In some cases, the consequence of an extreme negative political ethic is a self-destructive democracy. Algeria's experience is instructive.[137] The importance of a people's democratic culture to the functioning of a democratic system was confirmed by the Report of the Conference on Security and Cooperation (CSCE) Seminar of Experts on Democratic Institutions made to the CSCE Council in Oslo in 1991.[138]

Often, a combination of external factors such as corruption, patrimonialism, and clientelism worsen an inherently weak democracy. In Haiti, for example, corrupt elected representatives conspired with the judiciary and the military to subvert the popular mandate of the people. In Nigeria, in the wake of the annulment of the June 1993 elections, corrupt

137. The 1991 election in Algeria was won by the Islamic Salvation Front (F.I.S.), but the election results were annulled by the military after the party declared its intention to uproot all democratic institutions and cancel periodic elections in order to enthrone the rule of Islam. *See Human Rights in Algeria Since the Halt of the Electoral Process*, 4 MIDDLE EAST WATCH, Feb. 1992, at 4-5.

However, it is submitted that the publicly declared intent of the F.I.S. to destroy democracy, which was the basis of its mandate, was a repudiation of the authority of its mandate. Since it would have been illegal for the F.I.S. to assume office without a mandate, the military intervention may be justified on grounds of a threat to national security. *See* Gregory H. Fox & Georg Nolte, *Intolerant Democracies*, 36 HARV. INT'L L. J. 1, 6-9 (1995) (discussing the Algerian question).

138. *See* Thornberry, *supra* note 38, at 102 n.2. Part I of the Report stated that a

> democratic culture was a necessary element for the functioning of all democratic governments, and required permanent encouragement. Where a democratic tradition of long duration has not had the chance to develop, or had been interrupted, it would be necessary to develop a democratic culture, on the local, regional and national level, in order to sustain new democratic institutions.

Id.

elected representatives betrayed their constituencies as they voted for the continuance of military dictatorship. In the Zairian "Kleptocracy," Mobutu Sesesoku amassed $6 billion as personal wealth,[139] whereas the 1994 per capita income of Zaire was barely $154 per annum.[140] The genocide that occurred in Rwanda, and is currently threatening Burundi, was partly due to non-representative and oppressive leadership.[141] There is force in the argument that the intractable problems of internal crisis and the oppression of minorities and indigenous peoples would be greatly reduced if the democratic audit is strengthened. The frightening consequences of criminal leadership and the challenge to international lawyers has been lucidly laid out by Stanley Hoffman as follows:

> [W]e face a world in which many States are "failed States," in a situation of chaos, anarchy or permanent strife, either because of disintegration along ethnic or religious lines, or because of the flimsiness and corruption of their institutions, or because of the artificiality both of their borders (arbitrarily traced by colonial rulers) and of the Western-based notion of the State when it is imposed on parts of Africa and Asia. . . . Both [Professor, and now Justice] Higgins and [Professor] Koskenniemi point out that the UN is simply not equipped to deal with collapsing States or with rulers who systematically violate human rights, and that "social transformation for the better might sometimes necessitate revolution."[142]

Perhaps disintegration of states can be reduced. Perhaps violent revolutions can be avoided.

VI. CONCLUSION

A. *Redefining Democracy*

This paper has attempted to situate the universal democracy within a universal heritage and away from any particular political model. It has used empirical data, the Universal Declaration of Human Rights, and international and regional in-

139. *See Why Bankroll Africa's Ceausescu?*, N.Y. TIMES, Apr. 21, 1990, at A22.
140. *See* 2 EUROPA WORLD YEAR BOOK 1996, at 3613 (1996).
141. *See* DIXON KAMUKAMA, RWANDA CONFLICT: ITS ROOTS AND REGIONAL IMPLICATIONS 20-24 (1993).
142. Stanley Hoffman, *Thoughts on the UN at Fifty*, 6 EUR. J. INT'L L. 317, 324 (1995).

struments to buttress the normative character and institutional/structural requirements of the universal democracy. It ended the inquiry by throwing some light into the internal aspects of democracy, its configuration by historical and cultural norms, values, and even myths. As a result, it has shown that an inherently undemocratic political culture germinates institutions that are easily appropriated to mask exploitation, illusion, or corruption. Given these asymmetries that surround the development of democracy (for the benefit of hindsight, the discussion on the internal morality of democracy showed how political integration of civil society often has to contend with centrifugal socio-cultural factors), the project of democratic peace should not be left to the fortunes of a slow and uncertain voyage of domestic political change. The human and material cost of unassisted change emphasize the immediate necessity for a positive multilateral measure. Such a measure must consist of a step towards realigning the dominant institutional definition of democracy to the supreme political power of civil society. In order to accomplish this it is necessary to conceptualize democracy in terms of human development. This calls for democracy's redefinition in the language and material of human welfare. This measure will serve as the foundation for building a democratic solidarity for a civil society that feels empowered to demand accountability from public institutions, to confront totalitarian governments, and, if necessary, to bear any sacrifice for democracy.

Second, as the discussion on the internal and external problems of democracy shows, tensions inherent in pluralism are visible in many societies. These tensions are not necessarily accommodated by the majoritarian ethos of democracy which undergirds all spheres of participation. It is thus time to fortify the participation index of international instruments and reconciliatory devices of domestic institutions. This can be done by internationally criminalizing political oppression of minorities and the looting of public resources. This step promises the additional benefit of reassuring minorities, and ensuring that democratic institutions and devices for reconciling competing claims that flow from diversity are not undermined by corrupt and inept leadership. It is yet another building block to the needed and attainable consensus of democratic commitment in lieu of consensus of opinion. Again, the statist version of legitimacy grounded on the logic of "defactoism" or effectiveness ought to be abandoned as it has masked the worst violations of civil and political rights. Legitimacy of any government should be a function of the aggregate perception of civil society. One way of materializing the populist expression of legitimacy is by neutralizing the capacity of any government to masquerade dictatorships as popular and accepted by the masses. With particular focus on democracy, the process by which civil society votes a government in or out (often the ultimate expression of popular sovereignty) presents a veritable means of realigning legitimacy to popular sovereignty. U.N. democratic activities around the world support the view that the participation of a neutral, disinterested observer is one means of protecting the sanctity of elections. Needless to say, such a principle of external involvement should be multilateral and of general application so that every state's sovereignty is equally affected.

B. A Role for International Law

In recent times the most authentic and stimulating intellectual effort to rediscover popular sovereignty and to subject political power to popular control is the work of the German philosopher Jürgen Habermas.[143] The major attraction of Habermas' work is that it demonstrates the capacity of positive law as an instrument of integration, and the building blocks of solidarity.[144] The challenge to international law is to

143. *See generally* JÜRGEN HABERMAS, BETWEEN FACTS AND NORMS: CONTRIBUTIONS TO A DISCOURSE THEORY OF LAW AND DEMOCRACY (William Rehg trans., MIT Press 1996) (1992). His theory of deliberative politics is an attempt to locate within the modern institutions of democracy a superior norm of deliberative public opinion. *Id.* at 274-75. Proceeding on the assumption of the existence of unavoidable factual complexities that make the ideals of uncoerced agreement and undistorted communication difficult to achieve, his theory offers a model that would overcome the tension between the "facts" of social complexities and the ideal "norms" of democracy. *Id.* at 430-36. The model emphasizes the use of law as an integrative instrument in guaranteeing a discursive lawmaking process in which all citizens reach an agreement. Furthermore, the model encourages open deliberations in both parliaments/congresses and in decisionmaking institutions, institutions in which all citizens can participate. *See id.* at 162-68. Habermas's stated objective is the transformation of "Communicative Power" into "Administrative Power." *See id.* at 187-88. In order to achieve this he seeks a new concept of normative legitimacy: "[O]nly those statutes may claim legitimacy that can meet with the assent (zustimmung) of all citizens in a discursive process of legislation that in turn has been legally constituted." *Id.* at 110.

144. Despite its logical appeal, the theory chooses a standard of democracy that is not practicable: *consensus*. *See id.* at 61. The theory therefore leaves many ques-

strengthen the internal morality of democracy by rediscovering popular sovereignty. Hence, international law must inject confidence and legitimacy to the electoral process by an institutionalized neutral observatory process, which should be applicable to all states without exception. Further, international law needs to serve as a deterrent to anti-democratic agents and to regulate the quality of representation in governments by clearly defining violations of a democratic mandate, in whatever form, as an international crime against the peace. International law needs to create a rallying point of solidarity for all citizens by fostering a sense of commitment and confidence in democracy. To accomplish this goal, however, the international legal regime must solidify its own view of democracy. When there is finally a clear-eyed view of democracy within the instruments of international law, the journey towards global peace and security may finally begin in earnest.

---

tions unanswered, in particular: 1) How can consensus be attained in an acknowledged context of diversity and pluralism?; 2) How practicable is it to create a forum or, indeed, multiple fora for all individuals to reach a consensus on multiple issues of governance?; 3) What is the basis for attributing requisite knowledge to all citizens, or is manipulation not more potent in uninformed participation?; and 4) Is mob governance not a real possibility in the model?

It is submitted that the very essence of democracy is the compromise between consensus and the pluralism-majoritarian principle. Indeed, if there were no differences in opinion there would be no need for democracy! In effect, a theory that seeks consensus can only be seeking an alternative to democracy.

Appendix

THE CONVENTION ON DEMOCRATIC GOVERNANCE

PREAMBLE

The States Parties to this Convention,

Determined to achieve international peace and security in accordance with the United Nations Charter;

Recognizing the need to ensure that States which are not signatories to this Convention act in accordance with its provisions and principles so far as may be necessary for the maintenance of international peace and security;

Reaffirming faith in fundamental human rights, in the dignity and worth of the human person;

Realizing that social and economic development of peoples founded on stable democratic systems of governance are the foundations of international peace and security;

Recognizing that the Universal Declaration of Human Rights is the normative standard of a democratic system;

Convinced that though democracy is susceptible to a people's culture and social economic reality, it has a core unalterable content as a result of a global cultural heritage which has been codified in Articles 21 to 28 of the Universal Declaration;

Have agreed as follows:

ARTICLE I

(1) All human beings have a right to democratic governance which shall consist of:

(a) a political system based on the free will of the people expressed in periodic and genuine elections which shall be by universal and equal suffrage and shall be by secret vote or by equivalent free voting procedures.

(b) a political system based on constitutional guarantees and institutional framework for the realization of the fundamental human rights and the rights to work, food, clothing, housing, medicare, unemployment, security and education.

(c) These rights shall be justiciable and enforceable by individual or group legal action in each State.

(2) It shall be the primary duty of every State to channel a substantial part of its resources into providing opportunities for the enjoyment of these rights, and an equivalent reduction in its defense budget. Therefore, the budget and expenditures of member States shall give priority to the realization of these rights.

(3) Member States agreeing that the national budget, and any other empirical measures and projects in their territories, shall constitute the indices for compliance assessment, hereby agree to the monitoring of the implementation of these rights by any organ chosen by the United Nations.

(4) All member States hereby accept international monitoring as a requisite part of the electoral process. The international monitoring team shall be made up of Non-Governmental Organizations accredited to the United Nations, and United Nations experts. The monitoring shall be carried out under the auspices of the United Nations.

(5) This article provides for the minimum of a democratic system and is without prejudice to any international instrument or national legislation which confers wider benefits on peoples in any material particular.

ARTICLE 2

(1) The democratic character of every State shall be unalterable, and no exceptional circumstance other than a state of war shall justify its modification in any form.

(2) Each State shall take effective legislative, administrative, judicial, or other measures to protect the democratic character of the political system as provided in Article 1.

(3) From the commencement of this convention no State party shall recognize any government that comes to power by an undemocratic means. The duty of non-recognition shall include a duty to refrain from any acts, dealings, diplomatic relationships, or any contacts which could imply a recognition of the legitimacy of the Government.

(4) By virtue of this Article, all States have the right and the duty to take collective measures to protect the democratic character of any State, provided such action is taken under the aegis of the United Nations and in accordance with its Charter.

(5) The duties of non-recognition and collective protection above shall be enforced simultaneously and in such a manner as not to inflict unintended hardship on the general public of the target State.

ARTICLE 3

(1) Each State shall ensure that all acts of overthrowing a democratic government by force of arms or threat of same or otherwise taking control of government by any other means not democratic within Article 1 herein are offenses under its criminal law. The same shall apply to an attempt to take over control of government in like manner and to an act by any person which constitutes complicity or participation by membership in the executive body of an undemocratic government.

(2) Each State, taking into account the grave nature of these offenses and their consequences, shall make provision for appropriate penalties which must not be less than 5 years imprisonment without option of fine.

ARTICLE 4

(1) Each State shall take effective legislative, administrative, judicial, or other measures to enforce the accountability and responsiveness of the government to the people, and the inde-

pendence of the judiciary.

(2) Each State shall ensure that all acts of official corruption are offenses under its criminal laws.

(3) Each State party shall provide a penalty for the offense of official corruption not less than five years imprisonment without option of fine.

(4) For the purposes of this Convention the term "Official Corruption" means any act by a member of the executive council of any government which amounts to an illegal enrichment of himself or other person(s) or group, or an abuse of public office for an unwarranted purpose which threatens or affects the democratic character of the State, and includes any misuse of official position for suppression or oppression of a minority or indigenous group.

ARTICLE 5

(1) The penalty for a conviction under Articles 3 and 4 shall include a forfeiture of all properties acquired by the accused during the commission of the offense, and any other property unlawfully acquired in connection with the commission of the offense to the benefit of any person whatsoever.

(2) Articles 3 and 4 are without prejudice to any international instrument or national legislation which does or may contain provisions of wider application.

ARTICLE 6

(1) Upon a formal notification of a criminal charge before a competent court of law by a democratic government accompanied with a copy of the charge sheet and proof of evidence, any State in whose territory a person alleged to have committed any offense of same nature as those referred to in Articles 3 and 4 shall take the individual into custody or take legal measures to ensure his or her presence, and shall take the interim measure of holding as disputed all his or her assets within its jurisdiction.

(2) Such a State shall immediately make a preliminary judicial

inquiry into the existence of a prima facie case based on the proof of evidence.

(3) Upon being satisfied with the evidence it shall extradite the alleged offender to the State of nationality pursuant to Article 7, otherwise it shall assume jurisdiction over the offenses and shall, on notifying the State of nationality, request for full record of evidence which shall be promptly dispatched.

(4) This Convention is without prejudice to the right of the alleged offender to a fair trial.

ARTICLE 7

(1) Every State shall deem offenses of the same nature as those in Articles 3 and 4 as extraditable offenses based on this Convention.

(2) The conditions for extradition under this Convention shall be:

(a) That the requesting government is democratic;

(b) That the proof of evidence disclose prima facie the commission of the act alleged by the alleged offender, or any circumstance linking the alleged offender with the act or its consequence.

ARTICLE 8

(1) Every State shall, upon reasonable notice of the criminal charge against the alleged offender, take effective measures to preserve the property in all the assets of the offender within its jurisdiction as "disputed property" for duration of trial.

(2) Each State shall to the extent possible enforce within its jurisdiction the judgment of a trial under this Convention and shall take measures to transfer legal ownership of properties forfeited under the trial law and by virtue of this convention to the State of nationality.

(3) The State of nationality shall be responsible for the expenses of member States incurred in the extradition, prosecution of

the offender, or execution of the judgment or implementation of any part of this Convention; and shall be solely liable for all actions, claims, and damages arising from the implementation of this Convention.

ARTICLE 9

(1) The International Court of Justice is hereby given the jurisdiction to review any decision or action taken pursuant to this Convention, on the application of the alleged offender, in any of the following cases:

(a) Where there is convincing evidence that the alleged offender was a victim of persecution by the government of his or her country; or

(b) Where there is a substantial miscarriage of justice in the trial.

(2) The court shall determine its jurisdiction to review based on the application of the alleged offender.

(3) The structure and procedure of the court for the proceedings shall be determined by the court in accordance with its statute.

(4) The decision of the court shall be binding.

Part III
Democracy and the International System

[7]

THE KANTIAN THEORY OF INTERNATIONAL LAW

*Fernando R. Tesón**

Introduction

This Article defends the view, first developed by Immanuel Kant, that international law and domestic justice are fundamentally connected.[1] Despite the recent prominence of the international law of human rights, the dominant discourse in international law fails to recognize the important normative status of the individual. Traditional international legal theory focuses upon the rights and duties of states and rejects the contention that the rights of states are merely derivative of the rights and interests of the individuals who reside within them. Accordingly, international legitimacy and sovereignty are a function of whether the government politically controls the population, rather than whether it justly represents its people. This statist conceptualization of international law argues for a dual paradigm for the ordering of individuals: one domestic, the other international. Justice and legitimacy are conceptually separate. It may well be that domestic systems strive to promote justice; but international systems only seek order and compliance.

International law thus conceived, however, is incapable of serving as the normative framework for present or future political realities.[2]

---

* Professor of Law, Arizona State University. J.D., University of Buenos Aires; Licencié en Droit International, Université Libre de Bruxelles; S.J.D., Northwestern University. This article is excerpted from my book The Philosophy of International Law (Westview Press, forthcoming). My thanks to Kirsten Spalding, David Kaye, and to the members of the Moral, Political, and Legal Philosophy Research Group here at Arizona State: Jeffrie Murphy, David Kader, Larry Winer, Peter de Marneffe, Joan McGregor, Richard Dagger, Jack Crittendon, Charles Dresser, and Al D'Amico. All these people contributed helpful comments and criticisms. My thanks also to Harold A. Neu from the Columbia Law Review for his excellent suggestions.

1. Immanuel Kant's most important work on international relations is Immanuel Kant, To Perpetual Peace: A Philosophical Sketch [1795], *in* Perpetual Peace and Other Essays 107 (Ted Humphrey trans., 1983) [hereinafter Kant, Perpetual Peace]. Kant elaborates on his international theory elsewhere, see Idea for a Universal History with a Cosmopolitan Intent [1784], *in* Perpetual Peace and Other Essays, supra, at 29, 34–39 [hereinafter Kant, Universal History]; On the Proverb: That May be True in Theory, But Is of No Practical Use [1793], *in* Perpetual Peace and Other Essays, supra, at 61, 85–89 [hereinafter Kant, Theory and Practice]. The best summary of Kant's moral theory by Kant himself is Immanuel Kant, Groundwork of the Metaphysic of Morals (H.J. Paton trans., Harper Torchbook ed. 1964) [hereinafter Kant, Groundwork]. A very useful secondary source for Kant's moral theory is Roger J. Sullivan, Immanuel Kant's Moral Theory (1989). This article relies extensively on Professor Sullivan's account.

2. I am referring to the liberal revolutionary changes in the last 20 years, including the Iberian Peninsula in the 1970s; Latin America (led by Argentina) in the middle 1980s; and Central Europe since 1989. See Dankwart A. Rustow, Democracy: A Global Revolution?, Foreign Aff., Fall 1990, at 75. On Latin America, see 4 Democracy In De-

While it is understandably hard for lawyers to forsake the statist assumptions of classic international legal discourse, new times call for a fresh conceptual and ethical language.[3] A liberal theory of international law can hardly be reconciled with the statist approach.[4] Liberal theory commits itself instead to *normative individualism*, to the premise that the primary normative unit is the individual, not the state.[5] The end of states and governments is to benefit, serve, and protect their components, human beings; and the end of international law must also be to benefit, serve, and protect human beings, and not its components, states and governments. Respect for states is merely derivative of respect for persons. In this way, the notion of state sovereignty is redefined: the sovereignty of the state is dependent upon the state's domestic legitimacy; and therefore the principles of international justice must be congruent with the principles of internal justice.[6]

Immanuel Kant was the first to defend this thesis,[7] and for that reason it will be called the Kantian theory of international law. This Article reconstructs and examines Kant's theory as put forth in his famous essay *Perpetual Peace*. Part I addresses the controversy regarding the essay's structure and organization, and argues that Kant developed a normative philosophy of international law, not merely a practical political program. Part II shows that Kant's reason for respecting states stemmed from concerns about individual freedom, not from holistic claims about the state as a moral person. Part III presents and defends

---

veloping Countries: Latin America (Larry Diamond, et al. eds., 1989); on Europe, see Vents D'Est: Vers l'Europe des Etats de droit (Pierre Grémion & Pierre Hassner eds., 1990).

3. The growing number of legal scholars who are challenging the statist paradigm include Anthony D'Amato, The Invasion of Panama Was a Lawful Response to Tyranny, 84 Am. J. Int'l L. 516 (1990); W. Michael Reisman, Sovereignty and Human Rights in Contemporary International Law, 84 Am. J. Int'l L. 866 (1990).

4. The word "liberal" is notorious for its multiple meanings in politics and political theory. I mean "liberal theory" here simply as a theory of politics founded upon individual freedom, respect for individual preferences, and individual autonomy. As such, it encompasses a broad spectrum of actual political positions, from social democrats to libertarians.

5. For a survey of the different meanings of "individualism," see Steven Lukes, Individualism (1973). The notion of individualism defended in this Article is both methodological and normative. Methodological individualism contends that social science explanations should only be made in terms of individuals, see id. at 110–22. Normative individualism insists that our moral concepts should be referred in the last analysis to individual rights and interests—this is *not* to be confused with ethical egoism, which is a substantive moral doctrine, see id. at 99–106.

6. I have elsewhere argued for the same thesis using a modified Rawlsian model. See Fernando R. Tesón, International Obligation and the Theory of Hypothetical Consent, 15 Yale J. Int'l L. 84, 109–18 (1990).

7. Kant was the first to suggest human rights as the basis of international law, but not the first to propose an international alliance or organization. In this latter sense, the pioneer work is C.I. Castel de Saint-Pierre, Selections from the Second Edition of the Abrégé du Projet de Paix Perpétuelle (H. Hale Bellot trans., 1927), reprinted in Peace Projects of the Eighteenth Century (Garland ed., 1974).

the two Kantian arguments for the international human rights imperative. First, an international community of just, democratic states is the best guarantee for international peace because internal freedom at home is causally related to peaceful behavior abroad. Second, international law requires respect for human rights because the just civic society is the ultimate goal of all political arrangements. The argument for human rights is universal since it is derived from the Kantian categorical imperative.[8] These two arguments link international law to human rights and individual autonomy, not to national interest, rights of governments, or other notions similarly rooted in the primacy of state sovereignty. Part IV examines the nature of the liberal alliance proposed by Kant. Kant's choice of a decentralized system of international authority and enforcement is discussed and defended. This Part also examines the place of war within the theory, showing an inconsistency in Kant's views on war, and proposing a modified version. Part V defends the Kantian theory of international law against recent challenges to the idea that justice should be a component of international legitimacy. This Part also sets forth some conclusions and suggestions for practical reforms in accordance with the theory.

While offering a modern reconstruction of Kant's thesis rather than a meticulously faithful account of what Kant meant, the interpretation of Kant suggested in this Article is accurate, whether one wants to confine oneself to the text of *Perpetual Peace*, or one views his discussion of international law against the backdrop provided by Kant's general moral theory. To be sure, this Article departs from Kant on a few important points,[9] but the main thrust of his account remains intact.

It is not surprising that Immanuel Kant's philosophy is cited with renewed frequency in many international fora. He is conventionally seen as the pioneering advocate of an international organization capable of securing a lasting peace. Commentators have justly praised Kant as the one philosopher who, in his effort to contest the prevailing views upholding the absolute right of governments to wage war, foreshadowed modern conceptions of international law associated with the United Nations.[10] The novelty of his proposals explains why Kant's contribution has been regarded as *avant la lettre* political advocacy for the United Nations and peaceful world order.[11] Nevertheless, Kant accomplished far more. He developed a subtle, rich, and innovative the-

---

8. For a discussion of Kant's categorical imperative, see infra notes 48–71 and accompanying text.

9. See notes 65–68, 167–170, 199–220 and accompanying text.

10. For a comparison between Kant's proposals and the precepts of the U.N. Charter, see Carl J. Friedrich, Inevitable Peace 33 (1948) (U.N. Charter in many respects mirrors Kant's conditions for world order); Wolfgang Schwarz, Kant's Philosophy of Law and International Peace, 23 Phil. & Phenomenological Res. 71, 76–78 (1962).

11. See A.C. Armstrong, Kant's Philosophy of Peace and War, 28 J. Phil. 197, 201–04 (1931) (Kant's proposals for world peace "run closely parallel to those of 20th century"); see also W.B. Gallie, Philosophers of Peace and War 11–12 (1978) (Kant's

ory of international law, one that was so much ahead of its time that even admirers were blind to its importance. Kant's originality stems not so much from predicting the rise of a global international organization, but from having been the first to show the strong links between international peace and personal freedom, and between arbitrary government at home and aggressive behavior abroad. Not only did he have the vision to predict modern international organization for the maintenance of peace; he also explained, for the first time, the connection between domestic freedom and the foundations of international law. In essence, he foresaw the human rights revolution of the twentieth century.

I. The Structure of *Perpetual Peace*

Perpetual Peace was published in 1795 and was one of Immanuel Kant's last philosophical works.[12] It is a relatively short essay that was meant for popular reading.[13] Kant was not very good at writing for the general public, however, and the essay suffers as a consequence: the arguments are at times too concise and the writing often obscure.[14] Nonetheless, Kant's genius pervades the essay.[15] It had immediate success, and Kant's authority has been invoked frequently by advocates of pacifism and internationalism throughout the nineteenth and twentieth centuries.[16] While there are many interpretations of *Perpetual Peace*, almost all commentators agree that in this short essay Kant made a subtle, rich, and lasting contribution both to the theory of international law and to the causes of justice and peace. The themes developed in *Perpetual Peace* have extraordinary contemporary relevance. It is no surprise that interest in the essay has been revived recently. Even the President of the former Soviet Union referred to Kant's work in his speech accepting the Nobel Peace Prize.[17]

Perpetual Peace contains six "Preliminary Articles," three "Definitive Articles," and two long "Addenda," the most important of which is "On the Guarantee of Perpetual Peace."[18] The structural organization

---

vision was both "original" and "unique"). Although I differ with Professor Gallie in important ways, I have benefitted greatly from reading his excellent discussion of Kant.

12. See supra note 1.

13. See Gallie, supra note 11, at 8–9.

14. For an account of Kant's background and the history of his interest in political philosophy, see Gallie, supra note 11, at 12–17.

15. In the words of Kenneth Waltz, Kant's mode of analysis is "rigorous and yet subtle, his style difficult but clear, his writing crabbed and still, as Goethe said, sometimes slyly ironic and even eloquent." Kenneth N. Waltz, Kant, Liberalism, and War, 56 Am. Pol. Sci. Rev. 331, 331 (1962).

16. See Armstrong, supra note 11, at 197–98.

17. See Gorbachev Skips Nobel Awards, Chi. Trib., Dec. 11, 1990, at 4.

18. The text of the Articles with their headings is as follows:

First Section Which Contains the Preliminary Articles for Perpetual Peace Among Nations

of *Perpetual Peace* raises two questions, the answer to which may provide insight into Kant's intent: Why is the essay put in the form of articles, like a treaty? What meaning, if any, should we ascribe to the categories of "preliminary" and "definitive" articles?

The selection of the format indicates that Kant intended to offer a programmatic formula for peace, rather than a philosophical analysis of the nature of international law and relations. Indeed, he wanted politicians to follow his advice—he specifically enjoins governments to take advice from philosophers.[19] Thus, the form of the essay, at least in part, suggests that Kant wanted to draft a model treaty of some sort,[20] with specific provisions to be honored by all signatories. However, he only partially succeeded: *Perpetual Peace*, as written, seems to suffer from a fundamental ambiguity. While the essay can be viewed as an unattainable moral ideal to which states ought to aspire in their international relations,[21] it is preferably treated as an attempt to explicate international moral principles—the principles that should underlie the

---

1) No treaty of peace that tacitly reserves issues for a future war shall be held valid.

2) No independent nation, be it large or small, may be acquired by another nation by inheritance, exchange, purchase, or gift.

3) Standing armies (*miles perpetus*) shall be gradually abolished.

4) No national debt shall be contracted in connection with the foreign affairs of the nation.

5) No nation shall forcibly interfere with the constitution and government of another.

6) No nation at war with another shall permit such acts of war as must make mutual trust impossible during some future time of peace: Such acts include the use of *Assassins* (*percussores*), *Poisoners* (*venefici*), *breach of surrender*, *instigation of treason* (*perduellio*) in the opposing nation, etc.

Second Section Which Contains the Definitive Articles for Perpetual Peace Among Nations

1) The civil constitution of every nation should be republican.

2) [International law] shall be based on a federation of free states.

3) Cosmopolitan [Law] shall be limited to conditions of universal *hospitality*.

Kant, Perpetual Peace, supra note 1, at 107–18. In the Second and Third Definitive Articles, I prefer to use the word "law" rather than Humphrey's "right." The word "*Recht*" used in the original is ambiguous (as are the words "*derecho*" in Spanish and "*droit*" in French) and it may be translated as "law" or as "right," depending on the context. It is clear from the context in Perpetual Peace that Kant is referring to the objective international order, the "law," and not to "right" in the subjective sense. The German word "Volkerrecht" is ordinarily translated as "international law," not "international right." A better translation is offered by Carl Friedrich in Immanuel Kant, The Philosophy of Kant 441 (Carl J. Friedrich ed., 1949) ("law of nations").

19. Kant, Perpetual Peace, supra note 1, at 126. But cf. Waltz, supra note 15, at 339–40 (Kant "was not engaged in the puerile task of telling men of affairs to stop behaving badly").

20. See F.H. Hinsley, Power and the Pursuit of Peace 66 (1963).

21. See Waltz, supra note 15, at 334, 339–40. This ambiguity is quite distinct from differences of interpretation about the essay's substantive content, discussed below. See infra notes 23–34 and accompanying text.

relations among nations. Kant was a philosopher, not a mere pamphleteer.[22] There is also a call for political action, to be sure: it is the one that flows naturally from his normative theory of international law. Thus, the essay is both conceptual and normative; it attempts to draw applied international legal principles from an understanding of the underlying philosophical nature of international relations.

The second organizational issue is what meaning to attribute to the categories "preliminary" and "definitive." Some commentators have interpreted the Preliminary Articles to be those which might have served as the legal foundation of international peace, or as a statement of international law as it ought to be; whereas the Definitive Articles are interpreted to be the political premises and safeguards, without which no state could be expected to comply with the earlier articles.[23] For these writers, the Preliminary Articles are the solution, not a statement of the necessary preconditions to establishing the framework for a lasting peace.[24]

The reader may think that this debate is highly formalistic, exegetic, and overly textual. On the contrary, the debate over the purpose of Kant's choice of structure for *Perpetual Peace* is critical to an analysis of the work itself. Commentators in the realist tradition, who emphasize the primacy of the state as the international actor, exalt the Preliminary Articles.[25] Indeed, the key pro-government rule, nonintervention, is embodied in one of the Preliminary Articles. In addition, Kant's commentary ostensibly relies on the analogy of the state as a moral person, which is a favorite theoretical device of realists.[26] In contrast, each of the three Definitive Articles enshrines in different ways the primacy of individual freedom and the logically consistent unity of purpose of international and domestic law.[27] Thus, a reading of *Perpetual Peace* that emphasizes the Preliminary Articles leads to a realist or statist interpretation that gives primacy to states and governments over individuals; whereas a reading that relies on the Definitive Articles leads to an interpretation that gives the priority to human rights over the power of the state as a foundation of international law.

---

22. See Karl Jaspers, Philosophy and the World 113–17 (E.B. Ashton trans., 1963) (Kant sets forth principles underlying international law, not political program). But see Waltz, supra note 15, at 334 ("Kant does set forth 'shoulds' and 'oughts' of state behavior.").

23. See Hinsley, supra note 20, at 69; Gallie, supra note 11, at 9–10.

24. See Hinsley, supra note 20, at 66–69.

25. See id. at 69 (arguing that Preliminary Articles are "a statement . . . of Kant's solution"). Hinsley flatly rejects the First Definitive Article—the requirement that all states be republican—by observing that "[i]t is impossible to overlook the lameness of [Kant's] conclusion [that republican states are more likely to be peaceful]." Id. at 71. His views are characteristic of the discomfort felt toward Kant's revolutionary humanism by those who cling to a statist world view and as a result adopt a statist reading of Kant.

26. For further discussion, see infra Part II.D.

27. See infra Parts II and III.

The realist interpretation seems dubious. According to Kant, no perpetual peace can be achieved unless states are internally free and agree on an alliance or federation;[28] therefore, it does not seem that adherence to the Preliminary Articles alone would have sufficed to maintain peace even among the 18th century European powers. The better interpretation of the Preliminary Articles is that they are those urgent agreements that should enter into force if the state of nature[29] among states is to progress toward the formation of a federation that mirrors the relation of men under a civil constitution. The Preliminary Articles describe the most pressing steps to be taken if we want subsequently to proceed toward the lasting solution.[30]

In contrast, the substantive solutions, the institutional features of an effective and just international organization, are contained in the Definitive Articles. When Kant wrote "definitive," he meant what the word implies—a structure providing the final and conclusive solution to the problem of international relations. The Preliminary Articles do not even provide for the everlasting peace that Kant envisioned, which is included in the Second Definitive Article. Moreover, the Definitive Articles—which, as conceded by one of the above mentioned realist commentators, contain "Kant's most original political thinking"[31]—are

28. See infra Part III.

29. Commentators have emphasized how much Kant owed to Rousseau. See Gallie, supra note 11, at 17. Yet, Kant's conception of the state of nature as the pre-civil state of human beings before the formation of the state is, in different ways, closer to that of Hobbes and Locke. There are striking similarities and contrasts between Kant's conception of the state of nature and that of each of the great English philosophers. Kant shares with Hobbes the belief in the evil propensities of men and their tendency to immoral social conduct. See, e.g., Kant, Universal History, supra note 1, at 31; see also Sullivan, supra note 1, at 238–39 (Kant believed that "everyone is infected by the tendency to evil"). But Kant did have tremendous faith in reason. See Kant, Universal History, supra note 1, at 31 ("[A]s a class of rational beings . . . [humanity] is destined to develop its capacities to perfection."). In contrast, Rousseau believed that man in the state of nature was ignorant of vice. See Jean-Jacques Rousseau, A Discourse on the Origin of Inequality, *in* The Social Contract and Discourse, 27, 66 (G.D.H. Cole trans., 1973). On the other hand, Kant shares with Locke the belief in morality *predating* the social contract (contrary to Hobbes). In Locke this takes the simple form of natural rights; whereas in Kant this innate morality is anchored in individual reason and autonomy. See Kant, Universal History, supra note 1, at 29–31. Finally, for both Kant and Locke, but not for Hobbes, the purpose of the state is to protect the citizen's freedom. See Thomas Hobbes, Leviathan 98–102 (Michael Oakeshott ed., 1962) (1651); David P. Gauthier, The Logic of Leviathan: The Moral and Political Theory of Thomas Hobbes 134–46 (1969); John Locke, Two Treatises of Government 350–53 (Peter Laslett ed., student ed. 1988) (1698). The analogy for the state of nature in international relations is qualified, however. The Kantian theory insists that *individual* morality, and therefore individual freedom, not "state" morality, predates the creation of international law.

30. See Schwarz, supra note 10, at 75; Thomas L. Carson, *Perpetual Peace*: What Kant Should Have Said, 14 Soc. Theory and Prac. 173, 174 (1988); Michael W. Doyle, Kant, Liberal Legacies, and Foreign Affairs (pt. 1), 12 Phil. & Pub. Aff. 205, 225–32 (1983).

31. See Gallie, supra note 11, at 10.

preceded by a very important paragraph in which Kant writes that the state of peace must be founded or established; hence the need for the federation or alliance proposed in the Second Definitive Article.[32]

The most natural interpretation, then, is that the Definitive Articles are the foundation of perpetual peace; they contain the institutional arrangements that directly reflect the precepts of international justice. They are the ones that are designed to eliminate war from the face of the earth for all time.[33]

The defining characteristics of the Preliminary Articles are that they are the first steps that governments must take to end international lawlessness; those points upon which they must agree first in order to agree subsequently on the definitive and fundamental principles of international law. Here, Kant is trying to lay down the preliminary conditions conducive to definitive peace. These norms are designed to govern the intermediate status of international relations after the lawless state of nature is ended, but before the definitive law of nations is established.[34] Yet, the important point to remember is that they are meant to be permanent; they are preliminary, but not provisional. Standing armies must disappear; peace treaties should not contain reservations for future wars; states should not intervene in other states' affairs; states should not be acquired by conquest; and abject means of conducting war should be permanently prohibited. The Preliminary Articles will not suffice to guarantee peace unless the Definitive Articles are agreed upon.

II. The Requirement That States Be Liberal Democracies

The first principle of international ethics, embodied in the First Definitive Article, is: "The civil constitution of every nation should be republican."[35] The requirement of a republican form of government must be read in conjunction with the Second Definitive Article: "The

---

32. Kant writes:

> The state of peace among men living in close proximity is not the natural state (*status naturalis*); instead, the natural state is one of war, which does not just consist in open hostilities, but also in the constant and enduring threat of them. The state of peace must therefore be *established*, for the suspension of hostilities does not provide the security of peace, and unless this security is pledged by one neighbor to another (which can happen only in a state of *lawfulness*), the latter, from whom such security has been requested, can treat the former as an enemy.

Kant, Perpetual Peace, supra note 1, at 111 (footnotes omitted).

33. The interpretation suggested by Gallie and Hinsley is not consistent with the meaning of the words "preliminary" and "definitive." See Webster's Third New International Dictionary 592, 1789 (1981). Hinsley tries to meet this objection by suggesting that the word "preliminary" is used in the sense of the law of treaties, see Hinsley, supra note 20, at 69; Gallie, supra note 11, at 9–10. Even if this is true, it does not provide or explain the contextual meaning of the word "definitive."

34. See Hinsley, supra note 20, at 69; Gallie, supra note 11, at 9–10.

35. Kant, Perpetual Peace, supra note 1, at 112.

law of nations shall be based on a federation of free states."[36] Together, these first two articles stipulate that international law should be based upon a union of republican states.[37] Kant asserts that adherence to these requirements will result in an alliance of free nations that will maintain itself, prevent wars, and steadily expand.[38] Contrary to the predominant belief of his time, and to conventional present legal thinking, international law and the peace it intends to secure can only be based upon a union or an alliance of participant states that protect freedom internally and whose governments are representative. Kant for the first time linked arbitrary government at home with aggressive foreign policies.

By "republican," Kant means what we would call today a liberal democracy, a form of political organization that provides full respect for human rights.[39] This is so notwithstanding Kant's assertion that a *pure* democracy is a form of despotism.[40] Kant's explanation of a republican constitution[41] strongly suggests the idea of a constitutional democracy, conceived as a participatory political process constrained by respect for rights. Kant correctly points out that a system of pure democracy, if unconstrained by rights, will result in the tyranny of the majority. Kant writes:

> Among the three forms of government, *democracy*, in the proper sense of the term, is necessarily a *despotism*, because it sets up an executive power in which all citizens make decisions about and, if need be, *against one (who therefore does not agree); consequently, all, who are not quite all, decide, so that the general will contradicts both itself and freedom*.[42]

Plainly, Kant wanted to set constraints upon majoritarian decisions.[43] So, only a *pure* democracy ("in the proper sense of the term") is despotic. In contrast, the republican constitution is a form of political organization that allows people to govern themselves and to legislate by majority vote, provided that the rights of everyone are

36. Id. at 115.

37. The word "free" in the Second Definitive Article may be a reiteration of the requirement of the republican constitution: a federation of *free* states. See Friedrich, supra note 10, at 45. However, it is possible also to interpret the word "free" in that article as meaning "politically independent," thus suggesting that states enter the alliance voluntarily. See infra part III. This second interpretation is suggested by Kant's commentary to this article. See Kant, Perpetual Peace, supra note 1, at 115–18.

38. See Kant, Perpetual Peace, supra note 1, at 117–18.

39. I wish to avoid terminological debate about the meaning of the words "liberal" and "democracy." The word "liberal," as used in this Article, is broad and refers to a political theory centered around the notion of individual autonomy, individual preferences, or individual rights. A liberal democracy is one in which individual rights are honored and rulers are appointed by the people.

40. See Kant, Perpetual Peace, supra note 1, at 114.

41. See infra notes 45–47, 72–73, 88 and accompanying text.

42. Kant, Perpetual Peace, supra note 1, at 114.

43. See infra notes 45–47, 72–73, 88 and accompanying text.

respected—in short, a *constitutional* democracy. Thus, the Kantian idea of republicanism is best understood as being in opposition to the idea of despotism, whether exercised by a minority (one person or a junta), or by the majority enforcing its decisions in violation of the rights of dissenters.[44] Kant envisions the republican state as one defined by a constitution based upon three principles: freedom, due process, and equality.[45]

A. *Freedom*

The principle of freedom[46] consists of the liberal principles of respect for individual autonomy and government neutrality of ends:

> No one can compel me (in accordance with his belief about the welfare of others) to be happy after his fashion; instead, every person may seek happiness in the way that seems best to him, if only he does not violate the freedom of others to strive toward such similar ends as are compatible with everyone's freedom under a possible universal law . . . .[47]

One can hardly overemphasize the importance of this highly innovative Kantian thesis. Kant includes freedom—respect for individual autonomy under the rule of law—as the first tenet of international ethics. He is not committing the fallacy of transposing the notion of individual freedom into the conceptual framework of nationalism: freedom here is not the right *to* a nation-state, but primarily claims *against* it, claims against fellow citizens and against the government established by a social contract to implement social cooperation.

In order to understand Kant's discussion of the principle of freedom in the republican constitution, it is necessary to analyze in some detail Kant's categorical imperative. In his writings on moral philosophy, Kant attempted to demonstrate the possibility of human freedom and autonomy in the face of the deterministic laws of nature.[48] Only a

---

44. See Kant, Perpetual Peace, supra note 1, at 114 ("government is either *republican* or *despotic*").

45. The requirements of a republican constitution, merely summarized in Perpetual Peace, are eloquently put forth in Kant, Theory and Practice, supra note 1, at 71–84.

46. See Kant, Perpetual Peace, supra note 1, at 112.

47. Kant, Theory and Practice, supra note 1, at 72. In his *Critique of Pure Reason*, Kant argues for the proposition that

> [a] constitution allowing the greatest possible human freedom in accordance with laws by which the freedom of each is made to be consistent with that of all others . . . is at any rate a necessary idea, which must be taken as fundamental not only in first projecting a constitution but in all its laws.

Immanuel Kant, Critique of Pure Reason 312 (B373) (Norman Kemp Smith trans., 1929) [hereinafter Kant, Critique of Pure Reason].

48. Within the general framework of Kant's Critical program, the categorical imperative constitutes the solution to the third antinomy of pure reason, to wit, the apparently irresolvable conflict between the ideas of freedom and causal determinism. Kant, Critique of Pure Reason, supra note 47, at 409–15. (A445/B473–A451/B479); Immanuel Kant, Critique of Practical Reason 3–8 (4–8) (Lewis W. Beck trans., 1956)

free and autonomous being is capable of acting morally and can be said to have dignity and be worthy of respect. Thus Kant's primary aim in the *Groundwork* was "to seek out and establish the supreme principle of morality."[49] This he calls the categorical imperative, a universal law that all rational beings can make and act upon for themselves as free, self-determining agents whose actions are morally good.[50] Kant offers three different formulae of the categorical imperative, yet contends that they are "at bottom merely so many formulations of precisely the same law."[51]

The first formula is the most abstract. It emphasizes the impartiality and universal nature that moral principles ought to exhibit: "Act only on that maxim through which you can at the same time will that it should become a universal law."[52] While initially this formula seems empty of content, there is good reason for that. Kant insists that moral philosophy must have an *a priori* foundation, which in turn necessarily must be formal.[53] In this way, the violation of the categorical imperative is not only morally reprehensible, but irrational and self-contradictory.[54] Additionally, while this maxim is formal, it is not entirely devoid of content, for it enjoins us to "act autonomously and respect the right and obligation of everyone else to do the same."[55] From the standpoint of a theory of international law, the first version of the cate-

[hereinafter Kant, Critique of Practical Reason]; Kant, Groundwork, supra note 1, at 123–29.

49. Kant, Groundwork, supra note 1, at 60. Kant defines the categorical imperative and explicates the complex ideas contained within it in the Groundwork. In his two later works on moral philosophy, Critique of Pure Reason and The Metaphysics of Morals, Kant demonstrates the binding force of the categorical imperative on human beings who are only imperfectly rational and employs the categorical imperative to derive the whole system of human duties. It is important to note that, for Kant, the categorical imperative cannot be proved but can be deduced from pure practical reason. In the Critique of Practical Reason, Kant presents this deduction and demonstrates "the unity of practical and theoretical reason in [the] common principle" that is the categorical imperative. Kant, Groundwork, supra note 1, at 59. See Kant, Critique of Practical Reason, supra note 48, at 43–51 (42–50).

50. Kant, Groundwork, supra note 1, at 98–103.

51. Id. at 103. Paton identifies five interrelated but distinct formulations of the categorical imperative in the Groundwork. H.J. Paton, The Categorical Imperative: A Study in Kant's Moral Philosophy 129–30, 133–98 (1971).

52. Id. at 88.

53. See Kant, Groundwork, supra note 1, at 55; Sullivan, supra note 1, at 151–53.

54. See Kant, Groundwork, supra note 1, at 90; Sullivan, supra note 1, at 151–53. Most philosophers agree that Kant has provided a *necessary* condition for the validity of moral judgment. See, e.g., Marcus G. Singer, Generalization in Ethics: An Essay in the Logic of Ethics, with the Rudiments of a System of Moral Philosophy 34 (1971) (explaining that generalization is presupposed in every genuine moral judgment). However, doubt has been expressed by commentators as to whether Kant has provided a *sufficient* condition for such validity. Indeed, many principles which we intuitively regard as unacceptable comply with the formal requirement of this first version of the categorical imperative.

55. See Sullivan, supra note 1, at 165–66.

gorical imperative provides crucial support for the universality of human rights.[56]

The emphasis on the agent's autonomy and the respect for the autonomy of others leads naturally to the second version, the formula of respect for the dignity of persons: "Act in such a way that you always treat humanity, whether in your own person or in the person of any other, never simply as a means, but always at the same time as an end."[57] This second formula is a specification of the first in that here Kant identifies the class of moral agents: all human beings. The term "humanity" denotes the "functional complex of abilities and characteristics that enables us to set ends and make rational choices."[58] Because rationality defines the moral agent and because the categorical imperative requires universalization, we must presuppose rationality in the persons on whom the agent's behavior impinges. Kant's crucial step in the argument is that this rationality makes persons objects that are worthy of respect, ends in themselves. Things are instrumental and have only extrinsic value. Human beings, on the other hand, have *intrinsic* value. In Kant's words:

> Now I say that man, and in general every rational being, *exists* as an end in himself, *not merely as means* for arbitrary use by this or that will: he must in all his actions, whether they are directed to himself or to other rational beings, always be viewed *at the same time as an end*.[59]

The consequences for *political* philosophy of this view of respect for the dignity of human beings as the ultimate basis for the moral justification of our conduct are self-evident. If in our everyday behavior we should never consider fellow human beings merely as means, it follows *a fortiori* that the constitution of the state, an artificial creation to serve human needs, must embody and incorporate a formula of respect for persons—a bill of human rights.[60] Thus, in the Kantian vision, mechanisms for guaranteeing traditional civil and political rights, which act as barriers against the abuse of state power, form the basis of a republican constitution because such mechanisms implement the respect for autonomy and dignity of persons. [61]

---

56. For a development of this argument, see infra Part III.B.

57. Kant, Groundwork, supra note 1, at 96 (footnotes omitted).

58. Sullivan, supra note 1, at 193; cf. Kant, Groundwork, supra note 1, at 105 ("So act in relation to every rational being (both to yourself and to others) that he may at the same time count in your maxim as an end in himself."). Kant here attempts to demonstrate how the second version is logically equivalent to the first.

59. Kant, Groundwork, supra note 1, at 95.

60. See supra note 47.

61. The second version of the categorical imperative is not just a logical equivalent of the first. Rather, it adds substantive content to the formal requirements for moral judgement. Cf. John Rawls, A Theory of Justice, 251 & n.29, 251–57 (1971) (arguing that one should avoid interpretation of Kant's writings as merely providing formal elements of moral theory). See generally Jeffrie G. Murphy, Kant: The Philosophy of Right 60–86 (1970) (arguing that Kant's moral point of view is not strictly formal but contains

It would be a serious mistake, however, to conclude that the Kantian notion of freedom entails only negative duties, the duties to leave others alone to pursue their own happiness in accordance with their ideal of individual excellence. While Kant was against what he called "paternal government,"[62] the second version of the categorical imperative entails positive duties as well.[63] We must go beyond negative duties to make human beings our end. This command leads both to the perfection of our virtues of character and to acting benevolently toward others.[64]

A modern reconstruction of Kantian political theory should make room for what we would today call positive socioeconomic rights alongside the traditional negative, civil and political rights.[65] Respect for the dignity of persons requires, in addition to respecting their moral space, doing our best to secure an adequate level of material well-being for every member of society. Two reasons militate in favor of requiring that socioeconomic rights be recognized by domestic and international law. First, socioeconomic rights allow individuals to flourish and fully develop their uniquely human potential.[66] Second, a certain material well-being is necessary for persons fully to enjoy their civil and political rights and thus value and take advantage of liberty to its full extent. In an ideal society individuals are not only free; for them, liberty has high and roughly equal worth.[67]

There are, of course, problems of priority between these two generations of rights. From the standpoint of Kantian theory, the focus should be respect for individual autonomy. Securing socioeconomic rights is necessary for individuals to flourish as autonomous persons. Indeed, a neglect of the less favored will result in a lesser possibility for many to lead meaningful and fulfilling lives in freedom. Yet, sometimes a legitimate government may enforce socioeconomic rights in such a way that it ends up thwarting, instead of stimulating, individual autonomy. The neglect of civil and political rights for the benefit of socioeconomic equality may result, as it has often done, in outright tyranny. The question of priority can be resolved by applying a Kantian

---

ends, purposes, and values); O. Nora Nell, Acting on Principle: An Essay on Kantian Ethics 59–93 (1975) (discussing practical application of categorical imperative). For a defense of the Rawlsian reading of Kant, see Arnold I. Davidson, Is Rawls a Kantian?, 66 Pac. Phil. Q. 48 (1985).

62. See Kant, Theory and Practice, supra note 1, at 73.

63. See Paton, supra note 51, at 171–72; Sullivan, supra note 1, at 194.

64. See Paton, supra note 51, at 171–72; Sullivan, supra note 1, at 194.

65. The best modern reconstruction of Kant in this sense is, of course, Rawls, A Theory of Justice, supra note 61, at 60–75.

66. For an analysis of the place of socioeconomic rights in Rawlsian theory, see Frank I. Michelman, Constitutional Welfare Rights and *A Theory of Justice*, *in* Reading Rawls: Critical Studies on Rawls' *A Theory of Justice* 319 (Norman Daniels ed., 1973) [hereinafter Reading Rawls].

67. See Norman Daniels, Equal Liberty and Unequal Worth of Liberty, *in* Reading Rawls, supra note 66, at 253, 256–57.

standard: the ideal combination of rights is the one that yields the maximum possible individual autonomy under the coercion presupposed by the social contract. This is the point of equilibrium, as it were: any move from that curve would result in a reduction of individual autonomy.[68]

The third version of the categorical imperative is also highly revealing for its justification of the republican constitution and international human rights: "So act as if your maxims had to serve at the same time as a universal law (for all rational beings)."[69] This formulation points to an ideal vision of a moral community, where each individual is his own judge and the members obey only laws they can rationally prescribe.[70] Such a moral community describes an ideal just state and, consistently with *Perpetual Peace*, a world community of just states.[71]

B. *Due Process*

The second basic principle of a republican system is the derivation of all legal acts from, or dependence of all subjects on, a single common legislation.[72] The legitimacy of a legal act therefore depends upon whether it is in harmony with the constitution, procedurally and substantively.[73] Kant's formulation resembles the juridical definition of a state developed by Hans Kelsen.[74] Kelsen's system provides a valuable counterpoint to Kant's understanding of a legitimate republican regime. For Kelsen, all legal acts must derive from a single basic norm which in turn legitimizes the first positive norm, the constitution. How-

68. These important questions of priority between positive and negative duties and between civil-political rights and socioeconomic rights are beyond the scope of this Article. However, I join Rawls in defending the priority of liberty. See Rawls, supra note 61, at 243–51. Civil and political rights are definitive of freedom and individual autonomy, whereas socioeconomic rights, on the Kantian conception, are instrumental to freedom.

69. Kant, Groundwork, supra note 1, at 106. In the *Groundwork*, Kant treats the first formulation of the categorical imperative as primary, while the third version is given the position of priority in the *Critique of Practical Reason*. See Kant, Critique of Practical Reason, supra note 48, at 30; Paton, supra note 51, at 130.

70. See Sullivan, supra note 1, at 214.

71. There are important differences, however, between an ethical commonwealth, in which individuals self-legislate by obedience to moral duty, and a state in which duties are imposed by statute. See Sullivan, supra note 1, at 214–18.

72. See Kant, Perpetual Peace, supra note 1, at 112; Kant, Theory and Practice, supra note 1, at 75–77.

73. The Kantian position is neutral toward different forms of constitutional government, the legitimacy of judicial review, and similar questions. As the diversity of solutions to these issues in actual liberal democracies shows, a republican constitution, in Kant's sense, is compatible with many different mechanisms for distributing political power within the state. For a useful survey of the different ways in which constitutionalism has been implemented, see Mauro Cappelletti, Judicial Review in the Contemporary World (1971).

74. See Hans Kelsen, General Theory of Law and State 181–92 (Anders Wedberg trans., 1946).

ever, such derivation provides only formal legitimacy because the basic norm has no *a priori*, or objective, status. For Kelsen, the basic norm is "presupposed to be valid . . . . It is this presupposition that enables us to distinguish between individuals who are legal authorities and other individuals whom we do not regard as such, between acts of human beings which create legal norms and acts which have no such effect."[75]

Kant's system also mandates obedience to law that depends upon a single constitution. However, Kant's constitution, unlike Kelsen's basic norm, is not presupposed to be valid, but rather is the result of a rational choice by free agents as expressed in the legitimate social contract which requires that every citizen be a co-legislator.[76] The validity of the constitution is based on the fact that it proceeds from the exercise of rational cognitive faculties by the members of the body politic. Individual members of the state will insist that the principles of the constitution comport with the categorical imperative. For Kant, the constitution ceases to be valid when it no longer reflects this aggregate rationality. Thus, allegiance to the state by individuals is based upon their rationally believing that such allegiance is right, and the fact that a rational individual will not adhere to an irrational constitution.

The requirement of a dependence of all upon a common constitution is yet another instance of Kant's strong reliance on, and reverence for, the idea of law.[77] For him, an institution is justified only insofar as it has legally protected status.[78] This means, domestically, that both freedom from, and subjection to, the power of the state must be legally regulated: freedom and coercion under law, or freedom and coercion according to reason.[79] In a lengthy footnote, Kant explains that external lawful freedom means "the privilege not to obey any external laws [i.e., laws prescribed by someone else] except those to which I have been able to give my consent."[80] In line with the commands of the categorical imperative,[81] the laws enacted by the legislature must pass the test of rational deliberation to be deserving of compliance. It follows that only in the *Rechtstaat*, that is, under the rule of law, is allegiance to the law rational.

Kant's political theory, however, has one weakness. His thesis of

75. Id. at 115.

76. See Kant, Theory and Practice, supra note 1, at 75–76.

77. See, e.g., Kant, Groundwork, supra note 1, at 71 ("[R]evernce is the assessment of a worth which far outweighs all the worth of what is commended by inclination, and the necessity for me to act out of *pure* reverence for the practical law is what constitutes duty, to which every other motive must give way because it is the condition of a will good *in itself*, whose value is above all else.").

78. See Kant, Perpetual Peace, supra note 1, at 127–31; see also Gallie, supra note 11, at 22 (explaining Kant's view that anything of value must have legally protected status).

79. See Sullivan, supra note 1, at 247–52; Waltz, supra note 15, at 331–33.

80. Kant, Perpetual Peace, supra note 1, at 112–13.

81. See supra notes 48–64 and accompanying text.

rational allegiance to the law is not easily reconciled with his strong opposition to a right to revolution.[82] The proposition that citizens may revolt as a last resort against arbitrary power, when the sovereign has broken the agency contract,[83] follows logically from any liberal political theory.[84] Perhaps Kant was trying to make a purely formal point, namely that for citizens to have a *legal right* to revolution is self-contradictory, because there can be no higher judge to resolve the dispute between the citizens and the government.[85] Nevertheless, Kant's views on civil disobedience and revolution are inconsistent with his own moral theory and with the common-sense judgments of ordinary morality.[86] If government breaches the social contract, then the people may dismiss the government, by violence if all other means have failed.

The recognition of the right to resist tyranny is extremely important in international law. Beyond the consequences for the law of international human rights itself, it is significant with respect to developing a theory of humanitarian intervention. If citizens did not have a right to revolt against their tyrants, foreigners *a fortiori* would not have a right to help them, even by noncoercive measures, in the struggle against despotism. Humanitarian intervention can be defended as a corollary to the right to revolution: victims of serious human rights deprivations, who have rationally decided to revolt against their oppressors, have a right to receive proportionate transboundary assistance, including forcible assistance.[87]

---

82. See Kant, Perpetual Peace, supra note 1, at 136; Kant, Theory and Practice, supra note 1, at 79–80; Sullivan, supra note 1, at 244–45; see also Lewis W. Beck, Kant and the Right of Revolution, 32 J. Hist. of Ideas 411, 413–15 (1971) (attempting to reconcile Kant's denial of right to revolution with his enthusiasm over French and American revolutions).

83. See infra note 100 and accompanying text.

84. See, e.g., John Locke, An Essay Concerning the True Origin, Extent, and End of Civil Government, *in* Social Contract 1, 122–43 (Sir Ernest Barker ed., 1962) (1690).

85. In Kant's own words:

> For suppose they had such a right, and, indeed, that they opposed the actual judgment of the nation's leader, then who would determine on which side the right lies? Neither of them can serve as judge in his own case. Thus, there would have to be still another head above the head to decide between the latter and the people—and that is contradictory.

Kant, Theory and Practice, supra note 1, at 79. This is not the only reason that Kant offers to explain his belief that citizens cannot have a legal right to revolution, however. The other reasons include his obsession with the danger of reverting to the "lawless state of nature" and the prudential reason that since revolution is violent, citizens living under an unjust regime must go to the furthest extent to achieve liberal reforms peacefully. See Sullivan, supra note 1, at 244–45.

86. See Sullivan, supra note 1, at 245.

87. See Fernando R. Tesón, Humanitarian Intervention: An Inquiry into Law and Morality 5, 87–88 (1988); D'Amato, supra note 3, at 519. A growing minority of writers shares this view. See, e.g., Robert M. Chilstron, Humanitarian Intervention Under Contemporary International Law, 1 Yale J. World Pub. Ord. 93, 121–26 (1974); Anthony D'Amato, Nicaragua and International Law, 77 Am. J. Int'l L. 657, 659 (1985), reprinted in International Law: Process and Prospect 223, 225 (1987); W. Michael Reisman, Coer-

C. *Equality*

The third principle that defines a republican system is the principle of equality of all as citizens, that is, equality before the law.[88] The requirement of equality follows analytically from Kant's definition of law. Law is universal in form,[89] therefore every person must have exactly the same rights as every other person.[90] In *Perpetual Peace*, Kant reaffirms his long-standing rejection of nobility or birth as a basis for assigning rights and duties under a republican constitution.[91] Despite the fact that his writings were hardly accessible to the public, Kant reveals himself, in an historical context, as a philosopher of the ordinary people. Indeed, as Sullivan argues, "Kant's entire moral philosophy can be understood as a protest against distinctions based on the far less important criteria of rank, wealth, and privilege, and perpetuated by religious and political force and fear."[92] Kant's vision of society based upon a republican constitution is one that combines respect for moral autonomy and the individual, with the need for social order. It applies equally to classical laissez-faire and welfare states in the modern European tradition.

Observance of human rights is a primary requirement to join the community of civilized nations under international law. It follows that there cannot be a federation or peace alliance with tyrannical states. Domestic freedom is a primary credential required of any state before it may become a legitimate member of the international community. Yet, an important qualification is necessary here with respect to the question of democratic representation. In principle, both respect for human rights and democratic representation are needed to fulfill the requirements of the Kantian theory of international law. The main requirement of the First Definitive Article, however, is that *domestic freedom* be observed within each state. Because domestic freedom encompasses the right to elect the government, normally respect for human rights entails, and results in, representative government of the kind found in

cion and Self-Determination: Construing Charter Article 2(4), 78 Am. J. Int'l L. 642, 645 (1984); M. Sornarajah, Internal Colonialism and Humanitarian Intervention, 11 Ga. J. Int'l & Comp. L. 45, 75–77 (1981). Among those opposed to the legality or wisdom of humanitarian intervention, see, e.g., Louis Henkin, The Use of Force: Law and U.S. Policy, *in* Right v. Might: International Law and the Use of Force 37, 41–42, 61 (1989); Oscar Schachter, In Defense of International Rules on the Use of Force, 53 U. Chi. L. Rev. 113, 117–19, 145 (1986). For a scathing critique of Henkin's article, see Anthony D'Amato, Book Review, 85 Am. J. Int'l L. 201, 202 (1991).

88. See Kant, Perpetual Peace, supra note 1, at 112; Kant, Theory and Practice, supra note 1, at 73–75.

89. See supra notes 52–56 and accompanying text.

90. This is not inconsistent with the sorts of inequalities in wealth and power that arise in every society from a combination of talent, industry, and luck. See Sullivan, supra note 1, at 256.

91. See Kant, Perpetual Peace, supra note 1, at 112–13 & n.*.

92. Sullivan, supra note 1, at 197; accord Kant, Perpetual Peace, supra note 1, at 113 & n.*.

liberal democracies.[93] Thus, for example, we may assume that an originally unrepresentative monarchy that nevertheless respects human rights will naturally mature into a constitutional monarchy, much like those found in Western Europe today. Therefore, for the purpose of international law, the central requirement is respect for human rights. Governments that respect those rights, even if they are not representative in form, are entitled to a *presumption* of agency. Individuals who are free are presumed to consent to their government, much as citizens in a liberal democracy are presumed to consent to the governance of the administration brought to power through the electoral system, even if they did not vote for that government. It follows that governments that fully respect human rights are deemed to represent their citizens internationally.[94]

D. *The Normative Status of Nations*

Kant's understanding of the normative status of the state proceeds logically from the three criteria he proposed as the organizing principles of just republican states. The state when viewed as a unit interacting with other states does not acquire moral value greater than its components. Kant's Second Preliminary Article demonstrates that the moral standing of the state must be anchored in individual freedom. It provides that "[n]o independent nation be it large or small, may be acquired by another nation by inheritance, exchange, purchase, or gift."[95] For Kant, a state is not a possession or a piece of property, and since, like a tree, the state has its own roots, "to incorporate it into another nation as a graft, denies its existence as a moral person, turns it into a thing, and thus contradicts the concept of the original contract, without which a people [*Volk*] has no rights."[96]

At first blush, Kant seems to conceive of the state in a holistic way as a moral person, with rights and duties above and beyond the individuals who make up the state.[97] Such a view would regard the state as deserving respect because it is an autonomous moral being and enjoys

93. Again, a rights-constrained, as opposed to a pure, democracy is intended here by "liberal democracy." As indicated above, Kant thought that the latter was a form of despotism. See supra notes 39–44 and accompanying text.

94. This is very different from Michael Walzer's assertion that *all* governments are presumed to represent their people unless they render themselves guilty of genocide or similar atrocious and widespread crimes. See Michael Walzer, The Moral Standing of States, 9 Phil. & Pub. Aff. 209 (1980).

95. Kant, Perpetual Peace, supra note 1, at 108.

96. Id.

97. See Hinsley, supra note 20, at 66–67; see also Carson, supra note 30, at 183–84 (discussing Kant's idea of world federation in which states have duty to "higher authority"); Sullivan, supra note 1, at 257 (describing Kant's characterization of states as "moral persons" in *Perpetual Peace*). But see Tesón, supra note 87, at 53–76 (criticizing "Hegelian myth," in which states are entitled to autonomy as "moral beings" making choices).

sovereignty in its own right. This interpretation misunderstands Kant's argument. Kant maintains that a state is not a piece of territory, but rather a civil society created by a social contract. The state as moral person is just an analogy, except insofar as violating the state "contradicts the concept of the original contract."[98] What is important for Kant, and is captured by this analogy, is that the normative value of the individual not be violated by another state. Indeed, he emphasizes several times in the same paragraph the nature of the state as a society of men and how acquisition of the state violates that association.[99] The dichotomy established is between the state as a moral-political entity created by autonomous persons and the state as a mere piece of territory that can be bought and sold, not between rights of the state and rights of individuals, in which the community would hold a preeminent position at the expense of the individual. The state, for Kant, has moral standing *qua* the creature of a social contract.

The distinction often drawn between the horizontal and vertical contracts nicely illustrates why Kant maintains that the fundamental unit and, at the same time, fundamental end of both domestic and international law is the individual human being. The horizontal contract is the social compact entered into by citizens among themselves. The vertical contract is the agency contract between the individual beings, who comprise the state and are bound together by the horizontal contract, and their government. The vertical contract exists at the sufferance of, and for the purpose of maintaining, a healthy horizontal contract.[100] If a community of individuals is founded upon a legitimate social contract—horizontal and vertical—then foreigners must respect that community and accept its rulers as the legitimate representatives of that community. This principle can be extended to hold that the reason international aggression should be condemned is that the aggressor is using citizens of the victim state as mere things; in Kant's words, "subjects are used and wasted as mere objects to be manipulated at will."[101] Kant is not thinking about protecting governments unless they are legitimately appointed by their people, that is, unless there is a legitimate vertical contract. In spite of his metaphorical description of the state as a moral person, Kant is no Hegel.

Kant's international ethics follow from the categorical imperative. Just as individuals may not use human beings as mere means to an end, so foreigners, and especially foreign governments, may not use the persons that form another state by disrupting their free civil association in order to pursue the foreigners' own ends such as national glory, exer-

98. Kant, Perpetual Peace, supra note 1, at 108.

99. See id.

100. See Hannah Arendt, Crises of the Republic 85–87 (1969); see also Tesón, supra note 6, at 99–107 (arguing that "vertical contract" theory requires that government hold no autonomous rights).

101. Kant, Perpetual Peace, supra note 1, at 108.

cise of political power, material enrichment, or the aggrandizement of territory. All communities freely constituted are deserving of respect because they come into existence as a result of the rational exercise of free choice by autonomous agents. Thus, a government is not deserving of respect *per se*, but only insofar as it is the agent empowered by free individuals to make the law (legislative power), apply the law (executive power), and adjudicate claims among citizens (judicial power).[102] The state is the institution created to implement social cooperation grounded on the inviolability of liberty and must be honored because failure to respect the freely constituted state would be to deny the validity of the categorical imperative.

Kant's emphasis on the individual rather than the state is also apparent in his commentary to the Third Definitive Article, where Kant writes that "originally no one had a greater right to any region of the earth than anyone else."[103] Such a statement is hardly compatible with the idea of the state as the primary moral unit. For Kant, national borders are contingent features of social life. Kant never loses sight of the second version of the categorical imperative: persons should always be treated as ends in themselves, not merely as means.[104] Here we have the outline of a liberal theory of self-determination—one that relies not on mystical properties of the state or the prerogatives of enlightened rulers but, properly, on the rational pursuit of freedom by autonomous agents.[105]

But why must states guarantee internal freedom in order to be legitimate members of the international community? One could argue that, provided international peace and stability are secured, the fundamental goal of international law according to Kant,[106] the internal organization of states is irrelevant. Certainly it ought not be the indispensable starting point of a theory of international law. This argument has been repeatedly made; indeed, it is one of the tenets of the statist or realist school of thought.[107] Some commentators even em-

---

102. See, e.g., Kant, Theory and Practice, supra note 1, at 71–84.

103. Kant, Perpetual Peace, supra note 1, at 118. Kant also suggests here, along the same lines, that all men have a "common ownership of the earth's surface." Id.

104. See supra notes 57–61 and accompanying text.

105. I return below to Kant's liberal defense of a world divided into separate states, as opposed to world government, see infra Part III.

106. See Kant, Perpetual Peace, supra note 1, at 111; supra notes 35–38 and accompanying text.

107. Statism and realism overlap but are not coextensive. Statism is the view that the basic unit of analysis is the nation-state, not the individual. Realism is the view that nation-states act in the international arena motivated by national interest. Thus, all realists are statists, but not all statists are realists. For example, the "legalists" would argue that international law *conceived in a statist way* is a major component of foreign policy, thus rejecting the realist emphasis on national interest. The targets of this Article are *both* statists, because their version of international law is morally impotent, and realists, because they tend to be moral skeptics and because their explanation of international behavior is flawed.

brace such a reading of Kant.[108] All we can aspire to, it is argued, is balance of power, or peace. Except as an occasional political tool, concern for freedom or human rights does not belong in the realm of international relations because there is no centralized authority or superstate that can guarantee the rights of subjects.[109] There are of course several variations on this theme. Subtle realists would not discard the importance of human rights and democracy altogether.[110] But, characteristically, realists regard such concerns as subordinate to the national interest.[111] National interest is seen as an interest of the state that endures regardless of political or socioeconomic changes within the state, and extends over and above individual interests and the internal organization of the state. Conventional political theory, realists argue, addresses relations between government and governed—usually centering around individuals and their claims against the state—and is therefore incapable of accounting for the national interest as the key component of foreign policy. Only an international theory built around the state as the primary actor can do the job. The consequence of this approach is to overlook or downplay human rights in the study, formulation, and implementation of international law and policy.

One can legitimately ask how the notion of national interest is different from the understanding reached by citizens in the horizontal social contract. Why is it that national interest persists over and above changes in the actual interests of the citizens? The idea of national interest in the realist sense is incompatible with a view of the state as a creation of men and women to serve their needs. The only enduring collective interest is the preservation of freedom; political issues are issues of how to establish a fair, efficient, and mutually beneficial system of social cooperation consistent with the protection of everyone's liberty interests.[112]

The connection between freedom and international peace, however, runs even deeper than these considerations suggest. The realist challenge can be met by arguments proving that the link between peace and freedom is genuine and indisputable. Kant showed for the first

108. Classic works in the realist tradition include Hedley Bull, The Anarchical Society: A Study of Order in World Politics (1977); Kenneth N. Waltz, Man, the State, and War (1959). For an extended critical discussion of the realist view, see Marshall Cohen, Moral Skepticism and International Relations, 13 Phil. & Pub. Aff. 299 (1984).

109. See infra notes 117–120 and accompanying text. Kant seems to make a similar argument in his discussion of the right to revolution. I have argued Kant's views on revolution ought to be rejected wholesale. See supra notes 82–87 and accompanying text.

110. See, e.g., Stanley Hoffmann, Duties Beyond Borders: On the Limits and Possibilities of Ethical International Politics 95–140 (1981).

111. See authorities cited supra note 108.

112. It is not surprising that many of the goals that pass as national interest are, when closely examined, morally dubious: for example, territorial gains, economic gains, national glory, national unity, and ethnic pride.

time that we cannot aspire to a lasting international peace if individual freedom is not secured within every state's borders.

III. Freedom and Peace

A. *The Empirical Argument*

Kant's work on international law begins with the premise that peace is the fundamental purpose of international law, and that under normal circumstances war is an intrinsic evil that must be avoided. Kant does not furnish separate arguments for this maxim,[113] and his views on war are indeed complicated.[114] Kant believed that an international order could be established only when governments freely abjured their right to make war on each other, despite his emphasis on the necessity of coercion to sustain the law within a state.[115] From the peace premise, he attempts to design international law so that peace will be forever secured.

Kant gives several reasons why peace is likely to be achieved when individual rights and political participation are secured. His central argument is that if people are self-governed, citizens on both sides of any dispute will be very cautious in bringing about a war whose consequences they themselves must bear.[116] Those who will be eventually exposed to the horrors of the conflagration will decide whether or not to go to war. This central theme can be expanded in several directions.

In a liberal state, the government is elected and rotates periodically. These two factors are crucial restrictions on the power of the government to initiate war, both for reasons of self-interest (incumbency) and outright political and logistical limitations. In contrast, it is relatively easy for a despot to start a war. As Kant points out, the tyrant does not suffer the consequences; his privileges and prerogatives remain intact.[117] Crucially, the despot does not have the benefit of objective advice and debate. He rules by force, which means that within his own *entourage* he is feared and vulnerable to adulation. Advisors are not likely to tell the tyrant the harsh truths, but rather only what he wants to hear. More generally, because a despotic regime does not tolerate free-

113. Kant writes that "reason absolutely condemns war as a means of determining the right and makes seeking the state of peace a matter of unmitigated duty." Kant, Perpetual Peace, supra note 1, at 116; cf. Gallie, supra note 11, at 9 (opening section of Perpetual Peace "a *tour de force*, without any preliminary discussion of why or in what circumstances war is an unacceptable evil").

114. As we shall see, Kant had peculiar views, not all negative, about the role that war has played in the "Design of Nature." See infra notes 199–220 and accompanying text.

115. See Gallie, supra note 11, at 20.

116. See Kant, Perpetual Peace, supra note 1, at 113.

117. See id. Kant contends that the ruler does not act here as a fellow citizen, but as the nation's owner. See id. Kant's prudential reasons are always permeated by the theme of the categorical imperative: never use persons simply as means, which of course applies with even more strength to the government.

dom of expression, public opinion has no significant impact on the government's decisions; consequently, there is no opportunity for public debate on the moral and prudential reasons to make war. Psychologically, insulation of tyrannical rulers from criticism and debate fuels in them a sense of megalomania. Tyrants acquire a feeling of invincibility. They become accustomed to getting away with murder (literally) internally and no doubt reach a point of self-delusion where they become convinced that they can get away with external aggression as well.[118]

From an institutional standpoint, the separation of powers inherent in a liberal democracy creates a system of mutual controls and relative diffusion of power that complicates and encumbers governmental decisions about war.[119] No all-powerful sovereign exists who can by himself initiate hostilities. For Kant, that a multiplicity of decision-makers will participate in decisions to make war is implicit in the notion of autonomy inherent in the republican form of government.[120] The law-maker does not administer the law. Thus, liberal constitutions attempt to impose institutional limits on power, including the power to conduct foreign relations, through the checks and balances inherent in the separation of powers and through freedom of speech—notably freedom of the press.[121]

Another reason Kant believes that there is an increased likelihood of an enduring peace among free republics is that in a liberal democracy citizens will be educated in the principles of right, and therefore war will appear to them as the evil that every rational person knows it is.[122] Kant had a rich and exciting theory of cosmopolitan education, the main theme of which is that we must cultivate universal virtues that will prevail over the bellicose instincts that we also have.[123] Similar to the authors of some of the modern peace-education projects,[124] Kant saw clearly that peace education aimed only at inculcating fear of war

---

118. I suggested this explanation of the Malvinas war, see Fernando Tesón, 81 Am. J. Int'l L. 556, 558 (1987) (reviewing Crisi Falkland-Malvina e Organizzazione Internationale (Laura Forlati & Francisco Leita eds., 1985)) ("Dictators inevitably become persuaded that they can get away with anything."). The continuing validity of this explanation to the conduct of the Iraqi ruler in the recent Gulf crisis is painfully obvious.

119. See Kant, Perpetual Peace, supra note 1, at 114; Doyle, supra note 30, at 228.

120. See supra notes 35–45 and accompanying text.

121. See Sullivan, supra note 1, at 244.

122. See id. at 258. Citizens in a liberal democracy would not necessarily oppose *all* war. Some wars waged for liberal causes will be recognized as just. See infra notes 199–220 and accompanying text.

123. See Sullivan, supra note 1, at 287; see also Joseph M. Knippenberg, Moving Beyond Fear: Rousseau and Kant on Cosmopolitan Education, 51 J. Pol. 809, 815–19 (1989) ("Kant's proposed education is avowedly 'cosmopolitan.' . . . He advocates a process aiming successfully, at four goals: discipline, the acquisition of a trade, 'cleverness,' and morality.").

124. See generally Education for Peace and Disarmament: Toward a Living World (Douglas Sloan ed., 1983) (arguing that modern peace movement ought not be "impelled solely by fear").

and its instrumentalities was insufficient. Fear alone is demoralizing and may lead people to surrender to a tyrant, rather than act on behalf of a morally good and peaceful world.[125] A proper moral education should include instruction on the principles that underlie a just constitution from a cosmopolitan perspective, that is, on the value of human rights generally, not only as they relate to *our* domestic constitution.[126] Because this kind of moral education emphasizes rationality as a universal trait of persons, it will induce citizens in a liberal democracy to see individuals in other nations as deserving equal respect, and thus treat them as ends in themselves, not as mere objects for the satisfaction of local preferences.[127]

The final reason why liberal states are likely to be peaceful is that liberal democracies foster free trade and a generous system of freedom of international movement that Kant calls the Cosmopolitan Law.[128] Kant remarks that by observing a rule of hospitality for foreigners facilitating commerce with indigenous peoples, "distant parts of the world can establish with one another peaceful relations that will eventually become matters of public law, and the human race can gradually be brought closer and closer to a cosmopolitan constitution."[129] Kant reaffirms this idea by observing that peoples' mutual interests unite them against violence and war, for "the spirit of trade cannot coexist with war."[130]

He was cognizant, of course, that "peace to do business"[131] is a nonmoral reason to want peace, but that such pecuniary interests provide an additional argument for requiring a liberalization of trade and freedom of movement. Free trade and freedom of movement[132] are sufficiently linked to the principles of a liberal constitution to make leaders in liberal democracies much more prone to weigh economic

125. See Knippenberg, supra note 123, at 810.

126. Kant maintains that cosmopolitan education is aimed at the universal good and the perfection for which humanity is destined. Immanuel Kant, Education 15 (Annette Churton trans., 1960); Knippenberg, supra note 123, at 815.

127. Indeed, Kant thought that the moral law, the categorical imperative, was already present in a sound moral understanding and required not so much to be taught but clarified. See Kant, Groundwork, supra note 1, at 71–72.

128. See Kant, Perpetual Peace, supra note 1, at 118–19, 125; see also Doyle, supra note 30, at 231–32 ("The cosmopolitan right to hospitality permits the 'spirit of commerce' sooner or later to take hold of every nation, thus impelling states to promote peace and to try to avert war" if only out of fear of jeopardizing the benefits of trade).

129. Kant, Perpetual Peace, supra note 1, at 118; see also Kant's remarkable condemnation of colonialism, id. at 119.

130. Id. at 125.

131. "For among all those powers (or means) that belong to a nation, financial power may be the most reliable in forcing nations to pursue the noble cause of peace (though not from moral motives) . . . ." Id. at 125.

132. The rule of hospitality requires that "an alien not . . . be treated as an enemy upon his arrival in another's country." Id. at 118.

costs before initiating a war.[133] There is no question that free trade is a strong, if not dispositive, influence over external behavior. Free trade inclines diplomacy toward peace because international business transactions require stability and predictability to be successful. Kant's views have been confirmed by the success of the European Economic Community and even by the global system of international trade regulated by GATT and similar institutions. It is not by coincidence that the European Economic Community requires democracy as a prerequisite for membership, as does the more recent Mercosur, the Argentine-Brazilian free market agreement.[134]

Recent research by Michael Doyle and R.J. Rummel bolsters Kant's argument for the causal link between domestic freedom and peace.[135] These modern versions of Kant's argument have shown that Kant's prediction of a gradual expansion of the liberal alliance has been confirmed by events of the last 200 years, and notably the last 45 years. These authors' research has demonstrated that Kant was essentially right. Events since the publication of these articles provide splendid supplementary confirmation of the Kantian thesis.[136]

Liberal states have shown a definite tendency to maintain peace among themselves, while nonliberal states have shown themselves to be generally prone to make war. The historical data since 1795 seems to indicate that even though liberal states have become involved in numerous wars with nonliberal states, liberal states have yet to engage in war with one another.[137]

Doyle concedes that liberal states have behaved aggressively toward nonliberal states, but he attributes this fact precisely to the difference in regimes.[138] Conversely, nonliberal states have frequently behaved aggressively among themselves. Therefore, only a community of liberal states has a chance of securing peace, as Kant thought. Should people ever fulfill the hope of creating such a liberal international community, the likelihood of war will be greatly reduced.

Alternative hypotheses have not been forthcoming to explain the

---

133. One could expand this theme by saying that liberal citizens tend to be more cosmopolitan and less nationalistic, except concerning the defense of freedom, precisely because they place the individual at the origin and end of political arrangements.

134. For the European Economic Community, see 1978 Bull. Eur. Communities, No. 3, at 5–6; for the Argentine-Brazilian free trade agreement, see Shirley Christian, Argentina and Brazil Sign Pacts, N.Y. Times, July 31, 1986, at D18.

135. See Doyle, supra note 30, at 213; Michael W. Doyle, Kant, Liberal Legacies, and Foreign Affairs (pt. 2), 12 Phil. & Pub. Aff. 323 (1983) [hereinafter Doyle, Liberal Legacies (pt. 2)]; Michael W. Doyle, Liberalism and World Politics, 80 Am. Pol. Sci. Rev. 1151, 1162 (1986) (reprinted in substantially the same form as Michael W. Doyle, Liberal Institutions and International Ethics, *in* Political Realism and International Morality 185, 190–91 (Kenneth Kipnis & Diana T. Meyers eds., 1987)); R.J. Rummel, Libertarianism and International Violence, 27 J. Conflict Resol. 27 (1983).

136. See supra note 2.

137. See Doyle, supra note 30, at 209–17.

138. See Doyle, Liberal Legacies (pt. 2), supra note 135, passim.

liberal peace. I have not seen serious challenge to the evidence provided by Doyle and Rummel. Doyle's assertion that constitutionally secure liberal states have never engaged in war with one another is indeed bold.[139] Writers who take issue with this view contest only the thesis—held by Rummel but not by Doyle—that liberal democracies are *generally* peace-prone, regardless of the nature of the other regimes.[140] Nevertheless, everyone concurs in the factual assertion that democratic states rarely go to war amongst one another.[141] To be sure, there are some difficult cases.[142] Yet, even if those cases are treated as genuine instances of war between liberal states, the correlation is still so strong that it begs explanation. The argument is not that war between liberal states is impossible, but that it is highly unlikely. Kant warns that there will be regressive wars and setbacks in the establishment of the liberal alliance. Nevertheless he was confident that the alliance would expand and solidify with time.[143]

Some commentators have challenged the plausibility of the causal connection between freedom and war. They have treated the correlation as spurious, either the result of pure coincidence or, more likely, of an underlying common factor unrelated to the nature of the domestic regimes. Professor Diana Meyers has taken such a position: while she agrees that liberal states by and large have maintained peaceful relations, she raises questions about the explanation offered by Kant and Doyle.[144] Meyers offers two considerations to deny the premise that liberal democracies provide mechanisms through which aggregated self-interest is translated into national policy.[145] First, state bureaucra-

139. See Doyle, supra note 30, at 213.

140. See Chan, Mirror, Mirror on the Wall: Are the Freer Countries More Pacific?, 7 Peace Res. Soc'y Papers 31 (1984); Melvin Small & J. David Singer, The War Proneness of Democratic Régimes, 1816–1965, 1 Jerusalem J. Int'l Rel. 50 (1976); Erich Weede, Democracy and War Involvement, 28 J. Conflict Resol. 649 (1984). As indicated above, Doyle concedes, and the evidence seems to show, that liberal states behave aggressively toward nonliberal states.

141. See David Garnham, War-Proneness, War-Weariness, and Régime Type: 1916–1980, 23 J. Peace Res. 279, 283–84 (1986); authorities cited supra note 140. For another challenge to Rummel's methodology, see Jack Vincent, Freedom and International Conflict: Another Look, 31 Int'l Stud. Q. 103, 103–05, 111–12 (1987). But see R.J. Rummel, On Vincent's View of Freedom and International Conflict, 31 Int'l Stud. Q. 113, 113–17 (1987).

142. Two hard cases are the 1812 war between England and the United States, and the First World War. As to the first, arguably the United States became a liberal republic only after 1865; as to the second, Doyle's explanation is that Imperial Germany, although largely a liberal republic for domestic issues, did not allow any popular participation in foreign affairs decisions. See Doyle, supra note 30, at 216–17, n.8.

143. See Kant, Perpetual Peace, supra note 1, at 118.

144. See Diana T. Meyers, Kant's Liberal Alliance: A Permanent Peace?, *in* Political Realism and International Morality, supra note 135, at 212, 219.

145. Id. at 215. Similarly, Professor Hinsley opines that "[i]t is impossible to overlook the lameness of th[e] conclusion" that republican forms of government are more likely to lead to international peace. Hinsley downplays Kant's emphasis on internal

cies often distort public opinion, and thus "liberal democracy does not in any straightforward way place state action under the control of majority interests."[146] Second, people are deceived about their self-interest, and therefore express preferences that may militate for or against peace.[147] Public opinion in a liberal democracy, it is argued, may also be bellicose. Neither a free press nor a constitutional system with checks and balances has prevented leaders of liberal democracies from waging aggressive wars for spurious liberal causes.[148]

This reply to Kant and Doyle is unconvincing. The general skeptical position that liberal democracies do not provide a true outlet to majority opinions and preferences proves too much. To accept the argument one must believe that there is no real difference, in any respect—not just in the formulation of foreign policy or the initiation of wars— between liberal democracies and despotisms. While threats to popular participation posed by bureaucracies should be a matter of concern, this does not equate all political systems in terms of the degree to which popular will is expressed. Liberal democracies provide better mechanisms for political participation, to put it mildly, than do tyrannies. While there are surely hard cases, free political systems and despotic ones can be distinguished. We draw the distinction precisely in terms of how human rights are protected, how the citizen's interests are served, and the degree of their participation in the political process.

More importantly, this objection misses Kant's central point: peace is likely to be maintained only among liberal societies and, consequently, the likelihood of world peace will increase as the liberal alliance expands. All the examples of liberal aggression involve confrontations against nonliberal states.[149] Yet, the Kantian theory insists that the difference in regimes is the cause of instability. Liberal states do engage in aggressive behavior against nonliberal states, but this fact cannot support the claim that official duplicity could serve just as well to rationalize an attack on a bothersome liberal state.[150]

The argument seems to be that the psychology of power is the same regardless of which political system is in place and, therefore, both tyrannical and democratic rulers are equally prone to deceiving the people and waging war for dishonorable reasons such as the ruler's self-aggrandizement. However, the Kantian hypothesis is precisely that

---

freedom and emphasizes instead the freedom of the state and the "design of Nature" as Kant's main causes of peace. See Hinsley, supra note 20, at 71. Professor Hinsley's view on this point is empirically implausible and unfaithful to Perpetual Peace and to Kant's philosophy generally.

146. Meyers, supra note 144, at 215.

147. See id.

148. See id. at 216 (using the Vietnam War as an example).

149. Plausible candidates are the force used in Vietnam, Grenada, and Panama by the United States, and in Chad and Congo by France and Belgium, and in Pakistan by India.

150. See Myers, supra note 144, at 216.

in a liberal democracy there are intrinsic limitations on the ability and discretion of governments to deceive and manipulate. It is not enough to say that democratic governments are also capable of deceit and manipulation; the very point of democratic institutions is to keep political power, with all its corrupting potential, under check.[151] While the psychology of power may be the same across political systems, there is little question that in liberal societies institutional constraints are more likely to prevent bad governments from doing too much damage, both at home and abroad.

Other commentators have accepted the evidence, but have nevertheless attempted to explain the liberal peace by different hypotheses. The realist school of thought in international relations has long maintained that war is caused by prudential reasons that affect all state actors equally in the international arena. These reasons are not related to the difference in regimes. Doyle summarizes the realist theory of war:

> Specific wars . . . arise from fear as a state seeking to avoid a surprise attack decides to attack first; from competitive emulation as states lacking an imposed international hierarchy of prestige struggle to establish their place; and from straightforward conflicts of interest that escalate into war because there is no global sovereign to prevent states from adopting that ultimate form of conflict resolution.[152]

Thus, the realist explains peace through purely prudential factors that motivate state decision-makers. Realists downplay the importance of the difference in domestic regimes and emphasize features of states and governments that derive from the condition of international anarchy.[153]

151. There are countless real and counterfactual examples to illustrate the Kantian hypothesis. My favorite one is: there would have been no Malvinas war between the United Kingdom and Argentina had there been a democratic government installed in Buenos Aires. While there is no indication that irredentist sentiments have subsided in Argentina, the two countries, with Argentina now a member of the liberal alliance, are pursuing peaceful means to solve the conflict. See, e.g., the UK-Argentine Joint Statement on Relations and a Formula on Sovereignty with Regard to Falkland Islands, South Georgia, and South Sandwich Islands, 29 I.L.M. 1291 (Sept. 1990); see also BBC Summary of World Broadcasts, The Monitoring Report, Part 4 (Dec. 29, 1990) (Argentine Foreign Minister downplaying British Prime Minister's comparison of Iraqi invasion of Kuwait with 1982 Argentine invasion of Malvinas).

152. Doyle, supra note 30, at 219. As Doyle notes, this tradition goes back to Thucydides and Hobbes. See id.; authorities cited supra note 108. Other realist explanations of the liberal peace discussed and rejected by Doyle are based on hegemony or equilibrium, along the lines suggested by Raymond Aron. In refuting Aron, Doyle notes that the liberal peace persisted in the inter-war period when there was no hegemony. Doyle, supra note 30, at 223. Doyle also points out that hegemonic control is overestimated in both the pre-war and post-war periods. It is argued that in a situation of international equilibrium aggressive attempts at hegemony will deter wars. However, bipolar equilibrium is insufficient because it only explains peace among the polar powers, not proxy or regional wars. See id. at 224.

153. See id.

Realists have failed to explain the undeniable peace that has reigned among liberal states for so long. To suggest that relations among states with similar domestic regimes, liberal or not, would be peaceful, conflicts with the evidence regarding relations among feudal, communist, and fascist societies.[154] To say that the liberal peace only reflects the absence of deep conflicts of interest among liberal states simply begs the question of why liberal states have fewer or less fundamental conflicts of interest with other liberal states than liberal states have with nonliberal states, or nonliberal states have among themselves.[155]

But let us concede, *gratia argumentandi*, that the real reason for peace is the similarity in regimes, so that a community of despotic states could equally maintain peace. In that case, since peace is our ultimate goal and since uniformity of regimes is the only guarantee for peace, we have a choice of designing a system of international law that would either require respect for human rights or require despotism. On any defensible theory of morality, if that is our choice, we would prefer an international legal system that required states to secure human rights and political representation and thus be uniform on the side of liberty.

There is a strong factual correlation between internal freedom and external peaceful behavior toward similarly free societies; the causal dynamics that underlie the correlation seem very plausible; and those who disagree with this explanation have failed to provide convincing alternative explanatory hypotheses. The conjecture that internal freedom is causally related to peaceful international behavior is as safe a generalization as one can make in the realm of political science. Kant's empirical argument therefore shows that, if only for prudential reasons, international law must require full respect for human rights.

B. *The Normative Argument*

The second Kantian argument for including a requirement of respect for human rights as a foundational principle of international law is even more straightforward: Governments should be required by international law to observe human rights because that is the right thing to do. Because international law is rooted in the categorical imperative, it must likewise require respect for human rights if it is to be universal.

Kant commentators have overlooked the fact that Kant expressly offers this argument along with the empirical one. In *Perpetual Peace*, Kant defends the universal requirement of human rights and democracy as grounded in "the purity of its origin, *a purity whose source is the pure concept of right*."[156] The empirical argument is then offered in addition to this normative one. Writers who felt uncomfortable with Kant's

---

154. See id. at 22.
155. See id. at 224.
156. Kant, Perpetual Peace, supra note 1, at 113 (emphasis added).

First Definitive Article have attacked the plausibility of the empirical argument,[157] without realizing that it was just a reason given to reinforce the main argument, which alone suffices: that a global requirement of a republican constitution logically follows from the categorical imperative.[158] Thus, Kant's complete argument for democracy and human rights as a requirement of international law is far stronger than many of his critics thought. The normative argument is addressed to those who rank justice over peace; the empirical argument, to those who rank peace over justice.

Protecting human rights is the reason why governments exist in the first place.[159] The reasons that support internal freedom are universal, they derive from the categorical imperative, therefore, they should be embodied in the law of nations which also purports to be universal. Because Kantianism relies on rationality as a universal trait of persons, it is incompatible with relativism. It is not possible to defend simultaneously Kant's theory of human nature and morality, and the view that liberal democracy and respect for persons is good only for certain societies. The categorical imperative is universal and holds for every civil society regardless of history and culture. Liberal democracies, ranging from laissez-faire states to welfare states, are the only ones that are likely to secure individual freedom, thereby allowing human beings to develop their potential fully. Therefore, the only way in which international law can be made fully compatible with the freedom of individuals to pursue and act upon rational life plans is if it contains a strong obligation for governments to respect human rights. International law must be congruent with individual autonomy; the trait, for Kant, that sets human beings apart from other species.

Kant insists that pure ethics, or pure duty, be separated from historical and cultural contingencies. The whole enterprise of moral philosophy, for Kant, is based on that part of practical knowledge that is pure, perceived by human beings *a priori*, that is, independent of their experiences and traditions.[160] The nonrelative character of Kantian philosophy is easy to see in the realm of *individual* or personal morality. Indeed, the examples that Kant gives are of this type.[161] Yet, there is every reason to extend Kant's moral universalism to *political* morality as well. The contingent division of the world into discrete nation-states

157. See, e.g., Hinsley, supra note 20, at 71.

158. See Kant, Perpetual Peace, supra note 1, at 112–15; Kant, Universal History, supra note 1, at 34–36. In addition, Kant's general moral theory logically leads to the proposition, see authorities cited supra note 1.

159. See Tesón, supra note 6, at 99–120.

160. See Kant, Groundwork, supra note 1, at 55–56. Kant asks: "Do we not think it a matter of the utmost necessity to work out for once a pure moral philosophy completely cleansed of everything that can only be empirical and appropriate to anthropology?" Id. at 57.

161. See id. at 84–86.

does not transform political freedom[162] from an ethical imperative into a mere accident of history. Just as rational, albeit fallible, beings are capable of selecting the morally correct action out of a pure sense of duty, so too are the same rational beings creating the law of nations capable of selecting the morally correct form of political organization.

International law is concerned, at least in part, with the incorporation of those rules and principles that are deemed just on a global scale. First among them is the principle of a republican constitution proposed by Kant. This is not generated by a desire to impose an idiosyncratic system of values upon groups in other parts of the globe who have different traditions. The republican constitution of the liberal-democratic society, far from being idiosyncratic, is *objectively* right; it is not tied to empirical circumstance or historical accident. The republican constitution derives from the categorical imperative, from the exercise of rational faculties by autonomous agents capable of articulating the pure concept of right, as Kant expressly says in *Perpetual Peace* on this very issue.[163] To be consistent with justice, therefore, international law must require that states respect human rights. An international legal system that authorizes individuals to exercise despotic political power is morally deficient in a fundamental way. It disregards ethics that are central to Kant's "kingdom of ends,"[164] in which humans are defined by their aptitude to become members of the same moral community, worthy of dignity and respect.[165] Such is the notion that the international law of human rights attempts to vindicate.[166] In the Kantian vision, human rights are not mere privileges graciously granted by individuals in power—for example, by signing an international human rights convention. They are constitutive of the international definition of a legitimate nation-state.

The Kantian normative argument for the primacy of human rights can be reconstructed or extended using modern social contract theory.[167] The just civic constitution is the one that would be agreed upon by parties in an original position of uncertainty. The just world order likewise is the one that would be agreed upon by rational individuals in an original position of uncertainty, that is, knowing neither which country they will be part of nor what socioeconomic position they will occupy in that country. Under this model, and contrary to what John

162. See supra part II.A.

163. See supra notes 38–46 and accompanying text.

164. See supra notes 69–71 and accompanying text.

165. See Kant, Groundwork, supra note 1, at 95–96.

166. State-oriented international lawyers persistently disregard the fact that the respect for human dignity was a major concern of the international community after 1945. See, e.g., U.N. Charter pmbl.

167. See Rawls, supra note 61, at 11–17 (developing modern Kantian-contractarian theory). The passage that follows summarizes the arguments made in Tesón, supra note 6, at 109–20, and in Tesón, supra note 87, at 58–71.

Rawls himself has suggested,[168] the parties in the original position are individuals, not governments. They will agree on, among other principles of global justice, an international bill of human rights and on strong mechanisms to protect them against their governments, such as international human rights courts and even humanitarian intervention in cases of extreme human rights deprivations. They will include the notion of just constitutions as the fundamental requirement for a just world order. The contractors, however, will agree on a world of separate nations, thus stopping short of creating a global super-state, for reasons discussed below.[169] The original contractors will not risk their liberty interests by gambling on a law of nations that would permit governments to adopt tyrannical methods, because they might end up as citizens of tyrannical states.[170] Thus, the very principles of rational choice suggested by Rawls exclude a purely statist conception of international law.

IV. The Problem of Authority and Enforcement

Kant's Second Definitive Article provides that international law must be based on a federation of free states. Kant refers first to international law. We have seen already how important the idea of law is for Kant.[171] Domestically, civil society, the just civic constitution, results, as in Hobbes and Locke, from citizens surrendering their unlimited freedom in the state of nature in order to create the rule of law, the *Rechtstaat*, which alone can rationally secure individual freedom. The moral and civilized nature in us thus overcomes our evil instincts of lawlessness and destruction. We accept coercion and the idea of law and order to secure freedom for all.[172] Only then can we pursue the higher forms of life which define our essential humanity.

The human propensity to master our evil nature with reason[173] and reliance on law holds internationally as well. Governments, even in times of Kant's international state of nature, want to see their actions, no matter how self-interested and destructive, as legally justified. Far from reaching a skeptical conclusion from this crude reality of world

168. See Rawls, supra note 61, at 378.

169. See infra notes 182–197 and accompanying text.

170. See Tesón, supra note 6, at 109–20; Tesón, supra note 87, at 58–71; see also Mark R. Wicclair, Rawls and the Principle of Nonintervention, *in* John Rawls, Theory of Social Justice 289, 299–301 (H. Gene Blocker & Elizabeth H. Smith eds., 1980) (parties to contract in original position would choose limited intervention rule over nonintervention rule).

171. See supra notes 77–81 and accompanying text.

172. See Kant, Perpetual Peace, supra note 1, at 111–12 & n.† ("For by entering into civil society, each person gives every other . . . the requisite security.").

173. See Gallie, supra note 11, at 16 ("The intensity of feeling which Kant focused upon this hope for Reason in human life is unparalleled in the history of political thought, anyhow since Plato.").

politics, Kant saw this reliance on legal discourse as evidence of rationality:

> The homage that every nation pays (at least in words) to the concept of [law] proves . . . that there is in man a still greater, though presently dormant moral aptitude to master the evil principle in himself (a principle he cannot deny) and to hope that others will also overcome it.[174]

Therefore, according to Kant, the international order logically ought to mirror the domestic order; just as individuals would choose to create a civic constitution to solve the problems posed by the ruthless state of nature, so too would the same individuals, organized in nation-states, agree upon a system of international law to solve the problems posed by the international state of nature.

The analogy to domestic ordering raises the question of whether a successful system of international law must also be centralized into a super-state with a world government. This question is, of course, an old acquaintance of international lawyers: the view that there cannot be international law without an international sovereign has long since been discredited in international legal circles.[175] In addition, the controversy over whether international law is "really" law seems to be primarily semantic.[176] Yet, the objection is still worth examining, for it could well be that critical philosophical reflection will lead us to reconsider world government as a better alternative.[177]

In order fully to understand Kant's proposed solution to this dilemma, one must remember that Kant was writing at a time when war was the main method of settling international disputes and when the right of princes to make war was not seriously in dispute.[178] Politicians, scholars, and other educated persons living in that climate of interna-

---

174. Kant, Perpetual Peace, supra note 1, at 116. The word "law" has been substituted for "right" in this Article; see supra note 18.

175. See, e.g., Anthony D'Amato, International Law: Process and Prospect 1–26 (1987) (rejecting idea that international law must be centrally enforced to be considered law); W. Michael Reisman, Sanctions and Enforcement, *in* International Law Essays 381, 386 (Myres S. McDougal ed., 1981) (discussing community and group sanctions as distinguished from state-imposed); see also Eiichi Fukatsu, Coercion and the Theory of Sanctions in International Law, *in* The Structure and Process of International Law 1187 (R. St.J. Macdonald & Douglas M. Johnston eds., 1983) (discussing diplomatic, economic, and military coercion by individual state as international law sanctions).

176. See Glanville L. Williams, International Law and the Controversy Concerning the Word "Law," 22 Brit. Y.B. Int'l L. 146, 158–62 (1945).

177. See Carson, supra note 30 at 184–91 (arguing that "ultra-minimal" world government could preserve world peace).

178. For an account of international law allowing the right of states to wage war prior to the United Nations Charter, see 2 L. Oppenheim, International Law 177–78 (H. Lauterpacht ed., 7th ed. 1952); see also Hubert Thierry et al., Droit International Public 538–41 (1975) (discussing development of ideas of pacifism and just war from early Christianity to absolute monarchies of the 18th century). Kant has numerous references in his writings to international lawlessness and the international state of nature. See, e.g., Kant, Perpetual Peace, supra note 1, at 115–16; Kant, Theory and Practice, supra

tional lawlessness were his audience. Therefore, the idea of an international legal system that would outlaw war was revolutionary. Of course, today the presumption is against the right to make war, not in favor of it, and so many of Kant's arguments and assumptions might seem to us outmoded or taken for granted.

Both Hobbes and Rousseau faced the problem of authority before Kant. Hobbes, of course, thought that international relations were the state of nature par excellence.[179] Some commentators of Kant's work followed his argument to its seemingly logical conclusion: they read "federation" in the modern sense, as meaning a federated republic with a unified sovereign.[180] These commentators mistakenly argued that just as a constitutional government is the answer to the problems of social cooperation, freedom, and order within civil society; so too, world government should be the answer to similar problems internationally. Others believed that world government is what Kant should have argued for and that anything less is either useless, because it does not solve the problem of the international state of nature, or logically inconsistent with Kant's own arguments in *Perpetual Peace* and elsewhere.[181]

Most modern commentators, however, agree that Kant did not support world government.[182] Not only does Kant expressly disavow the creation of a centralized world government,[183] but the Third Definitive Article, establishing the Cosmopolitan Law, or the rules of free trade and universal hospitality, is inexplicable outside the context of a world of independent nation-states.[184]

Kant's answer (or, rather, the best Kantian answer) to this problem is to propose instead *an alliance of separate free nations, united by their moral commitment to individual freedom, by their allegiance to the international rule of law, and by the mutual advantages derived from peaceful intercourse.* The global distribution of authority proposed by Kant is thus quite close to the modern international legal system: states have rights and duties under international law, because they represent autonomous moral beings. However, there is no sovereign to enforce them; enforcement is

---

note 1, at 67; see also Waltz, supra note 15, at 334 (discussing Kant's conception of states in international system).

179. See Thomas Hobbes, On Dominion, ch. XIII, cited by Hinsley, supra note 20, at 51. The problem of authority confounded Rousseau. Consequently his works contain some inconsistencies about the appropriate resolution. See Hinsley, supra note 20, at 46–51 (discussing Rousseau's works on international relations).

180. See, e.g., Friedrich, supra note 10, at 45.

181. See Carson, supra note 30, at 179–84.

182. See Hinsley, supra note 20, at 62–70; Gallie, supra note 11, at 20–21; Waltz, supra note 15, at 335–37; Jean-Michel Besnier, Le Droit International Chez Kant et Hegel, 32 Archives De Philosophie Du Droit: Le Droit International 85, 91 (1987).

183. See Kant, Perpetual Peace, supra note 1, at 117.

184. See id., at 118–19.

decentralized.[185] Kant was ahead of modern international law in requiring that states observe human rights as a precondition for joining the alliance.

Quite apart from textual evidence, and notwithstanding the serious problem of the lack of centralized enforcement, there are good reasons to prefer a loose organization of separate states subject to international law to a centralized world government. Kant defended separate states not only because he thought that in this way his proposal would be more realistic, but because he thought that such a loose system was morally justified.[186]

First, he decided that world government presents too great a threat to individual freedom. Liberty is better secured when political power is relatively diluted. Kant wrote:

> [A world consisting of separate nations] is rationally preferable to [its] being overrun by a superior power that melds them into a universal monarchy. For laws invariably lose their impact with the expansion of their domain of governance, and after it has uprooted the soul of good a soulless despotism finally degenerates into anarchy.[187]

Kant was aware that while world government may be an attractive idea in theory, it carries the danger of degenerating first into a world tyranny and ultimately back into international anarchy.[188] Under a centralized world government, resisting the tyranny of a corrupt leadership would present an overwhelming logistical problem for individuals struggling to reestablish human rights and representative democracy. Freedom fighters would not have safe refuge, nor the fiscal and political support of independent representative governments. Nor would free states exist to moderate the excesses of despots through diplomacy and coercive intervention when appropriate.[189]

Second, a system of separate states allows individuals to associate with those that share their same culture, customs, history, and language. Such a system is more likely to respect the individuals' "community" interests and contribute to the affirmation of their self-respect that ultimately leads to the flourishing of individual autonomy. From a practical standpoint, a decentralized system minimizes conflicts originating as a result of those cultural differences.

Kant supports his view with a curious argument, mixing a Hobbes-

---

185. See infra notes 187–197 and accompanying text.

186. See Hinsley, supra note 20, at 63.

187. Kant, Perpetual Peace, supra note 1, at 125.

188. After suggesting the possibility that nations might consider world government, Kant writes: "But they do not will to do this because it does not conform to their idea of the [law] of nations, and consequently they discard in *hypothesis* what is true in *thesis*." Id. at 117; see also Gallie, supra note 11, at 23–24 (discussing Kant's rejection of both peace-by-empire and peace-by-federation).

189. See Terry Nardin, Law, Morality, and The Relations of States 238–39 (1983).

ian perspective with a sort of evolutionary determinism.[190] He argues that nature has used war as an instrument to force people to live in all sections of the globe, and eventually to reach the situation of separate nations in a state of (potential) war. On the other hand, nature has used the same features that divide peoples—differences in language and religion—to create an "equilibrium of the liveliest competing powers" which alone can control the danger of the deceptive peace that despotism brings—as he writes, "in the graveyard of freedom."[191] Despite Kant's dubious deterministic parlance,[192] the argument is based on Kant's original theory of the "asocial sociability" of human beings.[193]

In the international arena, the Kantian analysis shows how decentralized enforcement can take the place of a world police force, and underscores the subtlety of international mechanisms to secure compliance.[194] Of course, the idea that communities with a strong sense of cultural identity should be allowed to be autonomous is a relative assessment. It springs from the empirical conjecture that if subject to world government, different groups and minorities would tend to see their claims for identity ignored by a huge bureaucracy, whereas local government might appear to be more responsive to such claims. Yet by no means must all cultures live under separate governments; there are a number of successful examples of multicultural states. Furthermore, cultural differences should not preclude nations from voluntarily merging into larger political units, such as the European Economic Community. Finally, principles of respect for individual human rights trump the right to self-determination.[195]

---

190. See Kant, Perpetual Peace, supra note 1, at 120–25.

191. Id. at 125.

192. Why should the champion of free will talk about the Laws of Nature forcing people to do things? Professor Besnier rightly criticizes Kant's abuse of the notion of the Design of Nature. See Besnier, supra note 182, at 93–94 (calling the argument "la ruse de la nature"); see also Robert K. Faulkner, Liberal Plans for the World: Locke, Kant, and World Ecology Theories, Int'l J. World Peace, March 1990, at 61, 77–79 (1990) (critiquing Kant's "strangely ruthless humanitarianism" that assumes war will eventually dictate progress toward a rational world).

193. See George Modelski, Is World Politics Evolutionary Learning?, 44 Int'l Org. 1, 2–6 (1990) (Kant's historicist argument confirmed by recent studies on nature of international cooperation); Hinsley, supra note 20, at 72 (Kant's international philosophy combined "the historical sense, the moral element in politics, and the irrational element in man"); Gallie, supra note 11, at 28–29 (for Kant, idea of human reason excludes use of war); see also Sullivan, supra note 1, at 235–41 (summarizing Kant's philosophy of history).

194. Gallie eloquently summarizes the Kantian tension between man's rational powers: Reason is "that tendency, in all human thought and conscious effort, towards, at one and the same time, ever greater unity, system and necessity, and *equally* towards ever sharper and more constant self-criticism and self-control." Gallie, supra note 11, at 14.

195. The question of the interplay between self-determination and individual human rights is an extremely complex one, and is beyond the scope of this Article. See

Kant argues for the maintenance of separate nation-states as a balance between the dangers to freedom posed by centralized world government and the state of nature.[196] An alliance of liberal democracies subject to international law will provide the exact point of equilibrium for world order. Compliance will hopefully be achieved gradually by operation of subtle decentralized systemic mechanisms.[197]

If a morally justified international law is the result of such a liberal alliance, the question arises as to the legal status of those states that are not liberal democracies. First, tyrannical governments are outlaws. However, they are not outside the law of nations. Like domestic criminals, they are still bound by elementary principles, such as the rules that prohibit crimes of aggression and war crimes. While outlaw governments do not benefit from the rights conferred by membership in the alliance, they retain some rights. For example, if they are accused of human rights violations or war crimes, they have a right to be tried by an independent and impartial tribunal in accordance with well-established international rules.[198]

Second, a liberal theory of international law seeks to protect individuals. Therefore, actions, even by legitimate governments, that violate the rights of individuals in tyrannical states are prohibited. Citizens in undemocratic states lack representation, but they have not lost their rights. It follows that agreements creating obligations that benefit individuals should be respected. Such agreements include conventions inspired by elementary considerations of humanity and, in some cases, treaties that establish boundaries. However, agreements that dictators enter into to benefit themselves are binding neither upon members of the alliance nor upon the citizens of the tyrannical state. Because dictators do not represent their people, they cannot create obligations for their subjects. Such agreements are not respected because of the traditional principle *pacta sunt servanda*, but rather for prudential reasons or because they protect oppressed individuals.

Similarly, a liberal theory of international law must account for the role of force and war. Force may be used in defense of persons and, derivatively, in defense of representative governments and states.[199] Because members of the liberal alliance are in compliance with the First

---

Avishai Margalis & Joseph Raz, National Self-Determination, 87 J. Phil. 439, 454–61 (1990).

196. According to Kant, the state of nature exists when states are at war or a threat of war exists. See Kant, Perpetual Peace, supra note 1, at 111. Yet, the establishment of the liberal alliance, while a dramatic improvement, will still harbor dangers of war *against nonmembers*, i.e., despotic states. See infra text accompanying notes 199–220. Perpetual peace will be finally achieved when all nations become democratic and join the alliance.

197. See supra note 175.

198. See, e.g., European Convention for the Protection of Human Rights and Fundamental Freedoms, art. 6, 213 U.N.T.S. 221, 228 (1955).

199. See Tesón, supra note 87, at 111–23 (arguing that intervention is appropriate only if (1) force is used to thwart human rights violations, (2) nonhumanitarian motives

Definitive Article, force will never need to be used to exact compliance with their international obligations. However, force will sometimes have to be used against nonliberal regimes as a last resort in self-defense or in defense of human rights. Liberal democracies must seek peace and use all possible alternatives to preserve it. In extreme circumstances, however, violence may be the only means to uphold the law and to defend the liberal alliance against outlaw dictators that remain nonmembers. Such, I believe, is the proper place of war in the Kantian theory.

However, Kant seems to disagree. In his commentary to the Sixth Preliminary Article, Kant dismisses the idea that there could be a just war. War, Kant writes, is "a sad necessity in the state of nature [where] the outcome of the conflict (as if . . . it were the so-called 'judgment of God') determines the side on which justice lies."[200] Kant was troubled by the impossibility of rationally making a judgment of right prior to the conflict itself, since in international relations there is "no tribunal empowered to make judgments supported by the power of law."[201] Kant returns to the theme of justice as identified with law and legal adjudication.[202] Because in the international arena there can be no courts backed by force, there can be no rational decision about the justice of a particular war.[203]

How can we reconcile the extreme pacifism voiced in these passages with Kant's acceptance of a decentralized law of nations[204] and with the analysis of the causes of war as intimately related to the difference in regimes?[205] As to the first point, Kant's argument for rejecting the possibility of a just war proves too much. For if the absence of international courts with compulsory jurisdiction means that no war can ever be just, then there can be no law of nations at all. There would be no courts to render enforceable judgments about *any* disputes among nations. There seems to be an inconsistency here. We saw that in the addendum entitled "On the Guarantee for Perpetual Peace," Kant accepted a definition of international law that did not require a sovereign power, courts, legislators, or police—in short, world government.[206] Perhaps Kant fell prey to his obsession with the definition of law in *civil society*, which indeed requires courts rendering decisions

---

do not detract from paramount human rights objective, (3) means used is rights-inspired, and (4) victims welcome intervention).

200. Kant, Perpetual Peace, supra note 1, at 110.

201. Id. Kant concludes that a war of extermination, which extinguishes all rights, is absolutely prohibited because it would achieve perpetual peace only "in the vast graveyard of humanity as a whole." Id.

202. See supra notes 77–81 and accompanying text.

203. Kant reiterates this point in his commentary to the Second Definitive Article. See Kant, Perpetual Peace, supra note 1, at 116–17.

204. See supra notes 182–185 and accompanying text.

205. See supra part III.A.

206. See Kant, Perpetual Peace, supra note 1, at 120–25.

backed by the power of the state. In his discussion of international authority, in contrast, Kant addressed the difficulty and dangers of creating world government by the incorporation of the notion of decentralized enforcement. Yet, decentralized enforcement means that, while war is absolutely banned within the alliance, force will sometimes need to be used by individual states or members of the alliance acting in concert against enemies of the alliance. Therefore, a war of self-defense by a democratic government and its allies against a despotic aggressor is a just war.[207]

The central difficulty with Kant's rejection of just war is the status of tyrannical regimes that have not yet joined the alliance. If the analysis in Part III is correct, the difference in domestic regimes will be a permanent threat to peace. Perhaps one could devise principles of political prudence designed to moderate the historical intolerance of liberal governments toward despots,[208] but there are at least two thorny problems with Kant's view. The first, already mentioned, concerns the reaction of liberal democracies against aggressive despots. There is no doubt that democratic governments should retain their inherent right of self-defense,[209] which in Kantian terms is nothing more than the defense of persons by their government against foreign attack.[210] Second, similar perplexities arise in the case of intervention to stop serious violations of human rights in other states. Kant's Fifth Preliminary Article provides that "no nation shall forcibly interfere with the constitution and government of another."[211] In a very succinct commentary, Kant justifies this precept by saying that "[g]enerally, the bad example that one free person furnishes for another . . . does not injure the latter."[212] For example, a tyrant who tortures his citizens does not injure citizens in neighboring nations.

Leaving aside for the moment the patent inconsistency of this view with the universalist thrust of Kant's thesis, there remains the question whether such an absolute rule of nonintervention can be reconciled with Kant's First Definitive Article, the requirement that states be lib-

---

207. In his commentary to the Third Preliminary Article, Kant seems to justify war in cases of self-defense. See id. at 108 (distinguishing between "paying men to kill or be killed," which Kant deems "inconsistent with the rights of humanity," and "the *voluntary*, periodic military training of citizens so that they can secure their homeland against external attack.") (emphasis added); see also Gallie, supra note 11, at 24 (discussing Kant's advocacy of a confederation of common defense against aggression).

208. See, e.g., Doyle, Liberal Legacies (pt. 2), supra note 135 at 343–49.

209. U.N. Charter art. 51 ("Nothing in the present Charter shall impair the inherent right of individual or collective self-defence [sic] if an armed attack occurs against a Member of the United Nations, until the Security Council has taken measures necessary to maintain international peace and security.").

210. See Kant, Perpetual Peace, supra note 1, at 108; cf. Michael Walzer, Just and Unjust Wars 21–32 (1977) (war is crime because it forces people to fight for their rights).

211. Kant, Perpetual Peace, supra note 1, at 109.

212. Id.

eral democracies. A possible answer would be that nations join the alliance voluntarily, not as a result of intervention, however benign, by liberal members of the alliance.[213] Voluntary adherence to the alliance means allowing citizens in nonliberal states to resolve their differences among themselves, through their own efforts. In this way, citizens of a nonliberal state could eventually upgrade their society, as it were, so it could become a liberal democracy and qualify as a member. Only through the unfolding of such a process of self-determination will a decision to join the liberal alliance be voluntary; and members of the alliance should patiently wait until that occurs spontaneously and not force the process by intervening.

This reading of Kant is certainly possible. A reading more consistent with the rest of Kant's views, however, is that the nonintervention principle is dependent upon compliance with the First Definitive Article. Internal legitimacy is what gives states the shield of sovereignty against foreign intervention. Since morally autonomous citizens hold rights to liberty, the states and governments that democratically represent them have a right to be politically independent and should be shielded by international law from foreign intervention.[214] The liberal version of nonintervention and self-determination thus emphasizes respect for human rights and true representation. Political legitimacy is thus seen as the proper foundation of state sovereignty.[215] The question of internal legitimacy must be resolved prior to the question of nonintervention.[216] Noninterventionism, therefore, follows from whatever theory of internal legitimacy one adopts. If the only just political arrangement is the republican constitution, state sovereignty reacquires its shielding power only in states that have adopted and implemented such a constitution. Sovereignty is to be respected only when it is justly exercised.[217]

213. See, e.g., id. at 115 ("[E]ach nation can and should demand that the others enter into a contract resembling the civil one and guaranteeing the rights of each.").

214. See Doyle, supra note 30, at 213.

215. The nonintervention principle seems to us a permanent feature of international law, and so it might seem peculiar to see it included by Kant among the Preliminary Articles. Unlike Woodrow Wilson, for example, Kant was indeed a noninterventionist liberal, but what commentators have failed to emphasize is that his being liberal is a precondition of his being noninterventionist. See Waltz, supra note 15, at 339–40.

216. Even Hinsley, who repeatedly underscores the importance of state sovereignty, writes: "Just as [Kant] derived the right to freedom of the individual from the dictates of a moral law, so he derived the right to freedom of the state—*the route to and the guarantee of the freedom of the individual*—from the same moral law." Hinsley, supra note 20, at 63 (emphasis added). The moral law mandates freedom of the individual and freedom of the state as but a means to that end. See Kant, Universal History, supra note 1, at 34 (problem of just civic constitution cannot be solved without solving international problem).

217. See, e.g., Tesón, supra note 87, at 82; Charles R. Beitz, Political Theory and International Relations 80–83 (1979).

This suggests that Kant's Fifth Preliminary Article (the prohibition of forcible intervention) might be misplaced. If the protection against intervention is a consequence of domestic legitimacy, then nonintervention holds *only* among liberal states, and therefore the nonintervention principle should be seen as a definitive precept that governs the liberal alliance, not as a step that must be taken before the alliance is formed.

It follows from these considerations that citizens in a liberal democracy should be free to argue that, in some admittedly rare cases, the only morally acceptable alternative is to intervene to help the victims of serious human rights deprivations.[218] However, even if Kant is correct on the issue of humanitarian intervention, his rejection of the possibility of just wars is not consistent with the normative individualism underlying the rest of his theory of international law.[219] While aggression by members against other members of the alliance will be banned forever, in some cases democratic nations must resort to self-help to enforce their rights against outsiders.[220] At the very least, Kant's view does not account for the case of aggression by despots against members of the alliance. More generally, Kant's reason for rejecting just wars—that there are no courts to determine the justice of the cause—is unconvincing. Kant himself advocates an international law among separate nations that entails a decentralized system of authority. Judgments on the legality of wars are no different from judgments of legality generally, so if there are no courts available for the former, there are no courts available for the latter. Yet, Kant's whole purpose is precisely to show that a law of nations, and judgments of legality in conformity with it, are possible notwithstanding such a decentralization of power.

V. Why Justice: The Neo-Positivist Theory of Legitimacy

The attempt to use theories of justice, such as Kantian or Rawlsian social contract theory, as the basis for international law has been recently criticized. Professor Thomas M. Franck argues that theories of justice should not be used as a springboard for determining the legiti-

---

218. See Tesón, supra note 87, at 111–23.

219. Kant's view here is also inconsistent with his own rejection of the right to revolution. See supra notes 82–87 and accompanying text. For it is often the case that the only way for a tyranny to become a liberal democracy, and thus qualify for the alliance, is for citizens violently to overthrow the tyrant. Of course, I have rejected Kant's views on revolution; someone may still salvage Kant's views on the nonintervention issue by disagreeing with him on the revolution issue. My own position is that the right of humanitarian intervention in appropriate cases is an extension of the right to revolution.

220. There is yet another case: the use of force by a nonliberal state against another nonliberal state. The justice of that will depend on whose rights are being violated. Even an illegitimate government may defend citizens against aggression by foreigners. However, despotic governments do not have any right to defend themselves against external force used to remove them from power, provided that such foreign help is welcomed by the victims themselves. See Tesón, supra note 87, at 119–23.

macy of international rules.[221] He maintains that an international rule is deemed legitimate if the governments upon which it operates accept the rule and agree that it accords with generally accepted principles of "right process."[222] Professor Franck's definition of "right process" is quite rich, a blend of traditional positivism, critical legal studies, and natural law *á la* Fuller. According to Franck, legitimacy has four components: determinacy, symbolic validation, coherence, and adherence.[223]

Franck rejects the inclusion of principles of justice as a component of legitimacy. He asserts an operational and a theoretical objection. The operational problem is that justice applies to individuals, while international law addresses states and governments. The theoretical problem with global justice raised by Franck is an old tenet of positivism, namely that the concepts of justice and legitimacy are conceptually distinct.[224] On this view, justice and legitimacy are two separate concepts which should be carefully kept apart, even though their normative commands may sometimes overlap.[225] That a rule is legitimate does not mean that it is just and, conversely, many just rules may not be legitimate. This is so even in domestic systems.[226] Under Franck's theory, the first task is for nations to comply with international law, even if many of its rules are unjust. An international legal system seeks compliance with the rules that participating governments have created, mostly through custom and treaty.[227]

There is much to commend in this account of legitimacy. Professor Franck should be applauded for tackling long-neglected foundational issues in international law. In particular, the notion of right process seems useful as a method for identifying legitimate norms when the international legal system as a whole is just. However, by and large, this view is an extension of the traditional positivist belief that international law is created exclusively by the acts of governments. As such, his theory of international legitimacy is open to a number of objections.[228]

---

221. See Thomas M. Franck, The Power of Legitimacy Among Nations 208–46 (1990).

222. Id. at 19.

223. Id. at 49. He develops each of these ideas in chapters four through twelve. Franck explains that "symbolic validation" only obtains once the "cues" or symbols that confer legitimacy are perceived to be true which occurs as a result of historical practice and custom.

224. See id. at 208–09.

225. See id. at 242.

226. See id. at 236. Regarding domestic organization, Franck confines his analysis to "secular democracies" maintaining that this bifurcation may not apply to nonwestern "moral communities," see id. at 235.

227. See id. at 210.

228. For a general critique of consent theory (or positivism), see Tesón, supra note 6, at 99–107.

The contention that international law emphasizes compliance, not justice, does not merely describe the way international law works, it states a normative proposition. The theory *recommends* that international lawyers emphasize compliance and order to the detriment of moral considerations.[229] By requiring that a legitimate norm satisfy the four part test of determinacy, symbolic validation, coherence, and adherence, Franck constructs his own principle of international justice that sacrifices morality and the primacy of respect for individual autonomy in favor of procedural regularity. The idea that order and compliance are a good in and of themselves and, consequently, a valid end of international law is insufficient. Franck's theory amounts to a normative decision that law deserves allegiance irrespective of its substantive content, who created the law, and the extent to which rulers represent their citizens. Franck substitutes political power as the basic determinant of international legitimacy without explanation; he does so at the expense of more important and basic values, such as respect for human rights and fair representation of members of the state.

Second, the operational objection that justice may work among individuals, but not among nations, presupposes the statist paradigm. Professor Franck is correct that the idea of justice among nations seems awkward, but because states are merely representatives, not persons, international justice must also focus on the rights of individuals—the central claim of the Kantian theory of international law. Take, for example, the question of human rights. Kant argued that a world order is just if, and only if, the governments themselves are legitimate, which can only be true if the state's constitution is republican. Despots, who by definition represent no one but themselves, should not play a role in forming international rules. There is no reason why dictatorships ought to be protected under international law and accorded the honorific label of legitimate governments for the purpose of participating in the international legal process.[230] The first precept of the Kantian theory of international justice is quite simple: international law should not sanction a rule that permits the exercise of tyrannical power. One would think this a basic precept of legitimacy, yet Franck's view claims that domestic rule is a matter of justice which is not, and should not, be addressed by the international system. Once one accepts normative individualism, not statism, Franck's premise must be rejected.

Professor Franck reveals his adherence to the statist paradigm in his discussion of Rawls' theory. Rawls argued that international principles of justice are the ones that would be agreed upon by representatives of nations. These representatives would adopt the principles of equality of nations, self-determination, and nonintervention.[231] Using the hypothetical example of a genocidal government, Franck correctly

229. See Franck, supra note 221, at 210.
230. See Tesón, supra note 6, at 99–103.
231. See supra notes 167–170 and accompanying text.

observes that the absolute principle of nonintervention suggested by Rawls leads to unacceptable results from the standpoint of justice.[232] However, he then reproduces Rawls' mistake of postulating governments as the original contractors and understandably concludes that such a model, which he believes is also supported by the practice of states, would yield the almost absolute nonintervention principle. Furthermore, because noninterventionism is incompatible with elementary notions of justice, at least in extreme cases, he argues that *justice*, not the absolute nonintervention rule, should be discarded as a component of legitimacy.

This is a rather stunning conclusion in Franck's own positivist terms, because reasoning from state practice yields an inconsistent rule on the question of humanitarian intervention.[233] Even within the positivist paradigm, in some instances state practice supports intervention.[234] It is obvious that governments interested in incumbency and preserving their power and privileges will agree on rules of international law that protect the political space in which they can do as they please. Examples of such rules that protect governments[235] are the principle of nonintervention, as opposed to humanitarian intervention, and the preservation of territorial integrity, as opposed to the right of secession.[236] Professor Franck, like several Rawls commentators before him,[237] acknowledges the problem with considering states and not individuals as the primary subjects of justice. However, he concludes that since rulers insist that international law be couched in statist terms, the precepts of justice should not count as components of international legitimacy. His conclusion does not follow logically.

The logical conclusion should be that current international law is wrongly conceptualized in terms of prerogatives of rulers, and that we should move toward a theory of international law that has the individual, not the state, as its subject and basic moral unit. The point that justice makes sense only among individuals not among states is correct, but the conclusion that we must discard justice is incorrect. Instead, the logical corollary should be that international law must be made con-

---

232. See Franck, supra note 221, at 221. The same point is argued at length in Tesón, supra note 87, at 58–71.

233. See Tesón, supra note 87, at 155–200.

234. See Richard Lillich, Humanitarian Intervention: A Reply to Ian Brownlie and Plea for Constructive Alternatives, *in* Law and Civil War in the Modern World 229, 235–37 (John N. Moore & Wolfgang G. Friedman eds., 1974).

235. Such rules serve to protect governments although they often use euphemistically collective nouns such as "the people" or "the state." See Fernando R. Tesón, Le Peuple, C'Est Moi! The World Court and Human Rights, 81 Am. J. Int'l L. 173, 181–82 (1987).

236. See the hypothetical example in Franck, supra note 221, at 226–30.

237. See Wicclair, supra note 170, at 297-98; Thomas Pogge, Rawls and Global Justice, 18 Can. J. Phil. 227, 238–39 (1988); Tesón, supra note 87, at 58–64.

gruent with justice, and thus be conceived in terms of individuals, not states or governments.

By modifying the Rawlsian model in which the contracting parties are individuals or representatives of individuals, not representatives of states, the logical problem of applying the requirements of justice to states is solved. Professor Franck, however, rejects such a model. He concludes that a social contract among individuals or their legitimate representatives,[238] far from eliminating the rules suggested by Rawls' model that conflict with our moral intuition, would yield an unjust system and fail to accord with reality because it requires that we "imagine two things at once: just nations making a just world."[239] Franck maintains that such a system could never appear just from the perspective of the individual because "[t]he priorities and sensibilities of rulers, not the people's shared (or intersecting) notions of justice, usually frame the contents of [international] rules and also have the most say in determining their compliance pull."[240] His reasoning misses the point. If the Rawlsian model with governments in the original position yields results incompatible with justice, such as precluding intervention in case of a genocidal government, then we should alter the model to accommodate our moral intuitions, rather than forsake justice.

The statist paradigm is precisely what is wrong. To say that a theory of international justice centered on the individual is unjust because current international law is created by and for governments begs the question of why justice should be a component of legitimacy. If part of what a normative theory of international law wants to do is evaluate the behavior of states in the light of what is right, then the standard cannot be the very behavior of states. What the Kantian thesis suggests is that domestic justice must be the first priority of the international system both because that is intrinsically right and because it is causally linked to peace and, by extension, to all other important global challenges.[241]

Franck's theory is also open to the objection raised by Kant's empirical argument.[242] If international law validates tyrannical governments as legitimate members of the international community, it interferes with the purpose of achieving peaceful cooperation needed to meet pressing global challenges. If Kant and Doyle are right that nonliberal governments are naturally prone to aggression, the chance of getting them to work for peace and mutual understanding is indeed

238. See supra note 195 and accompanying text; see also David A. J. Richards, International Distributive Justice, 24 Nomos 275, 282 (1982) (arguing for plausibility of contractarian theory to provide foundations for moral duties in international area).

239. Franck, supra note 221, at 226, 233.

240. Id.

241. Professor Franck includes among these challenges the control of arms, ozone depletion, desertification, hunger, and virulent disease. See id. at 210. One would think that all these tasks are instrumental in achieving the two most important global ends: freedom and peace.

242. See supra part III.A.

slim. The international community would be admitting a Trojan Horse in its midst. Franck's deceptively realistic approach, obsessed with compliance, will in the end result in the defeat of the very ends that international law was supposed to pursue.

The more natural approach is this: Insofar as international law addresses governments, it does so in their capacity as agents of persons, as representatives. This in turn raises the question of representation as an international matter. The agency relationship itself must be subject to international scrutiny. Individuals who claim to represent a nation but in fact have seized power by brute force should not be accepted as members of the community that makes the law. There is every reason to extend these common sense notions of justice to international relations and include them in a definition of international legitimacy.

State-oriented theories of international law like Franck's propose a double paradigm for the ordering of individuals: one for international law and the other for domestic law.[243] Justice and legitimacy are always conceptually separate,[244] but whereas in domestic law justice permeates legitimacy, in the international legal system the main goals are order and compliance. In contrast, the Kantian theory of international law rejects this dual paradigm and dual purpose, attempts to unify our theory of justice, and makes legitimacy depend on justice.[245] Thus, there is only one theory of justice, embracing both global and national institutional arrangements.[246]

Any theory of international or domestic justice attempts to put forward principles which amount to an ideal standard for adjudicating competing claims in a scheme of social cooperation. Thus, the Kantian theory of international law contends that a morally just world order comprises nation-states that are internally just and whose governments therefore represent individuals. The rights and interests of individuals form the ultimate touchstone of the theory. Along with this substantive thesis, the theory must provide a notion of formal justice or legitimacy not altogether different from the one Professor Franck suggests.

Once one leaves the domain of ideal theory, many rules enacted by

243. See Franck's discussion of *pacta sunt servanda*: for domestic law, in which justice reigns, he argues that principle is justified by moral sacredness of promises. For international law, in which order controls, the justification is stability. See Franck, supra note 221, at 234–36.

244. See id. at 242.

245. Franck does appreciate the importance of justice. He writes: "As the firm outlines of world order become readily apparent, and as that order increasingly focuses on the individual's place in global society, a keener understanding of the theory, function, and power of justice must surely move to the top of the agenda." Id. at 246. Yet, he settles for the statist paradigm and rejects the view that justice should be the basis of legitimacy and international law.

246. Cf. Lea Brilmayer, Justifying International Acts 157, 159 (1989) (agreeing with unity of domestic and international theory from methodological standpoint but rejecting notion that justice underlies theory of legitimacy).

governments, even representative governments that respect human rights, may be unjust. What is the role of ideal theory in those cases? First, international rules enacted through right process are legitimate provided that the system as a whole is just.[247] For example, if just governments agree by treaty to a uniform tax, which upon reflection is considered contrary to notions of distributive justice, the tax may be collected legitimately nonetheless, because the basic requirement of justice that the rule be agreed upon by representative governments that respect basic human rights has been fulfilled. The Kantian theory, far from rejecting right process, makes it a central feature of international law second only to the elementary precepts of justice.

The second function of an ideal theory, such as the Kantian theory, is to achieve determinacy of the rules of international law.[248] Treaties and custom should be interpreted in the light of appropriate principles of justice; there is no such thing as objective state practice. The behavior of governments cannot be normatively understood without presupposing a moral-political judgment.[249] In order to glean a normative pattern or a rule from diplomatic history, one must interpret that history and draw from it the best normative teachings. Thus, ideal theory, far from being "wishful thinking,"[250] performs the double role of being an impulse for reform in those cases in which the behavior of states conflicts with the theory's basic tenets; and, in hard cases, of providing standards of interpretation that will make international law consistent with the precepts of justice.

On the other hand, the Kantian theory of international law cannot be seen merely as a rational reconstruction of the actual rules and principles of international law. Some rules may be so much in conflict with the theory that all we can say is that they ought to be repealed or ignored. Yet in those cases in which the practice of states can be interpreted in accordance with the theory, justice becomes the major component of legitimacy.

CODA

The Kantian theory is not limited to a rarified philosophical domain. The theory yields practical solutions in many fields. First, the theory mandates the creation of compulsory judicial mechanisms to settle controversies arising from the three Definitive Articles: an Interna-

247. See Rawls, supra note 61, at 350–55 (discussing "the duty to comply with an unjust law").

248. See Tesón, supra note 87, at 6, 11, 200 (arguing that countries do not disagree on whether to follow international law, but rather on what that law dictates); Tesón, supra note 6, at 85–89 (same).

249. See sources cited supra note 248; Charles de Visscher, Theories et Realités en Droit International Public 171 (1970) (normative force of custom is result of lawyer "reconstituting" facts in light of moral imperatives).

250. See Franck, supra note 221, at 233.

tional Court of Human Rights, the International Court of Justice, and an International Court of Trade (roughly corresponding to Kant's three Definitive Articles respectively). Second, the Kantian theory also necessitates amendment of the conditions of admission and permanence in the United Nations. Articles 4 and 6 of the Charter of the United Nations should be amended to include the requirement that only democratic governments that respect human rights should be allowed to represent members, and that only democratic states will be accepted as new members.[251] Third, the law of treaties must undergo important changes. Representatives of dictators must be disenfranchised for the purposes of expressing the state's consent to be bound by the treaty.[252] Fourth, the law of diplomatic relations should be amended to deny diplomatic status to representatives of illegitimate governments.[253] Finally, the law of recognition should prohibit recognition of illegitimate governments, along the lines suggested by President Woodrow Wilson in the beginning of this century[254] and by the International Court of Justice for South Africa in the *Namibia* opinion.[255] These and other reforms will have to be worked out in detail, and many variations consistent with the Kantian theory are possible.

---

251. Article 4 of the U.N. Charter reads: "Membership in the United Nations is open to all other peace-loving states which accept the obligations contained in the present Charter and, in the judgment of the Organization, are able and willing to carry out these obligations." U.N. Charter art. 4, ¶ 1. While article 4 may conceivably be read as requiring respect for human rights from prospective members, the main organs of the United Nations have not interpreted it so. For a summary of the practice, see Guy Feuer, Article 4, *in* La Charte Des Nations Unies 171–72, 177–79 (Jean-Pierre Cot & Alain Pellet eds., 1985).

252. See, e.g., article 7 of the Vienna Convention on the Law of Treaties, in which the only requirement for considering a person as representing a state for the purposes of expressing the consent to be bound by a treaty is that such person produce "appropriate full powers." Vienna Convention on the Law of Treaties, art. 7, U.N. Doc. A/Conf. 39/27, 5, 8 I.L.M. 683 (1969).

253. Articles 2, 4 and 7 of the Vienna Convention on Diplomatic Relations give almost unlimited discretion to sending and receiving states, so in theory it allows for the receiving state either to refuse to establish diplomatic relations with a tyrannical government, or to deny *agrément* to representatives of illegitimate governments. Vienna Convention on Diplomatic Relations, Apr. 18, 1961, art. 2, 4, 7, 23 U.S.T. 3227, 500 U.N.T.S. 95. There is a difference between denying *agrément* to the individual because of his or her past or other circumstances, and denying the *agrément* because the envoy is not representative of the sending state. The practice of states, however, has not shown much concern for true representativeness, with one exception: South Africa. The General Assembly recommended members to sever diplomatic relations with South Africa as early as 1962. See Ludwik Dembinski, The Modern Law of Diplomacy 92 (1988). South Africa is a clear case of *internal* illegitimacy for lack of representativeness and serious human rights deprivations. The principle governing that case should be extended to other cases of tyranny.

254. See Wilson's famous Mobile statement, 7 Am. J. Int'l L. 331 (1913) (discussing United States' desire only to deal with just governments in Central and South America).

255. See *Namibia* Opinion, 1971 I.C.J. 16, 58, ¶ 133 (June 21) (obligation by states not to recognize South Africa's illegal occupation of Namibia because of South Africa's human rights violations in Namibia).

One of the most remarkable developments since the end of the Second World War has been the exponential growth of individual liberty—the impressive expansion of human rights and democracy to societies that had been excluded from the benefits of freedom. This extraordinary and, for many, unexpected development disproves the claim that human rights and democracy are just the luxury of industrial societies and lends credence to the assumption that every rational person, regardless of historical or cultural circumstance, is apt to value and pursue freedom both as an intrinsic good and as the necessary means to formulate and act upon rational plans of life.

This enlightened moral and political global reality is ill-served by the statist model of international law. The model promotes states and not individuals, governments and not persons, order and not rights, compliance and not justice. It insists that rulers be permitted to exercise whatever amount of coercion is necessary to politically control their subjects. Yet, the reasons to prefer a world of free nations are strong enough to place the burden of proof on international lawyers who cling to the traditional statist paradigm that privileges power-holders and ignores people. If some empirical confirmation is required, recent events in the Persian Gulf should teach us at least the lesson that things would have been very different had the states in the region been liberal democracies of the kind defended here.

Perhaps there is no necessary link between the political triumph of human rights and democracy and the theoretical foundations of international law and politics. Perhaps all we can say is that the wind is blowing now in the direction of individual freedom and that the historical cycle will before long see nations return to despotism and gross injustice. It is indeed possible that the optimism caused by the triumph of human rights is hasty and that the celebration is therefore premature.[256] Yet, if the tide is going to turn against individual freedom, it will be the product of human design, not of the forces of nature pushing us around. It follows that we have to construct and defend our global institutions if we want them to last.

International law can make an important contribution in this respect. We must rethink and reconstruct international law in a way that incorporates and recognizes that the ultimate aim of global institutional arrangements is to foster the development of each individual's full po-

256. Recall the warnings of former Soviet Foreign Minister Shevardnadze, who resigned in protest of Gorbachev's courtship of the hardliners which he felt would lead toward the reestablishment of totalitarianism in the U.S.S.R., Tom Wicker, An Ominous Warning, N.Y. Times, Dec. 23, 1990, at O11. These warnings proved to be accurate: in the last week in August 1991, a coup d'état in the Soviet Union succeeded in reestablishing a dictatorship for a couple of days. Freedom and democracy, however, re-emerged with renewed force after the restoration of the legitimate government. The adherence to the liberal alliance by the nations that succeeded the now extinct Soviet Union will be perhaps the most encouraging event of the century.

tential as an autonomous human being, to protect freedom. This is so even if pessimist forecasters are right that we should expect significant setbacks to freedom globally in the years to come. Moreover, international law does not merely describe international behavior, so that our conceptual model would be more or less statist depending on the progress or restriction of human rights around the world. Rather, international law purports to set standards of international behavior. Judgments of legality are evaluations of diplomatic history according to that standard. It is insufficient to verify that many governments ignore the precepts of justice and conclude that justice should be discarded. The better view includes moral analysis as an integral part of international law. The alternative positivist paradigm, by clinging to the deceptively simple notion of the unrestrained practice of states as the touchstone for legitimacy, ends up surrendering to tyranny and aggression, the evils that international law was intended to control in the first place.

Kant's accomplishment in the field of international theory and ethics is magnificent. Few other thinkers have successfully combined so many disparate elements of morality, politics, epistemology, and history in a theory of international law. The community of free nations envisioned by Kant will hopefully expand gradually and maintain itself, as it has done for the past two hundred years, and the aim of perpetual peace will be achieved the moment when the liberal alliance comprises every civil society. It is never too late to replace the grim view of a world order in which naked political power is the standard of legitimacy with Kant's inspired cosmopolitan vision of moral progress in which tribute is paid to the definitive traits of humanity—freedom and reason.

[8]

International Law in a World of Liberal States

Anne-Marie Slaughter *

International law and international politics cohabit the same conceptual space. Together they comprise the rules and the reality of 'the international system', an intellectual construct that lawyers, political scientists, and policymakers use to describe the world they study and seek to manipulate. As a distinguished group of international lawyers and a growing number of political scientists have recognized, it makes little sense to study one without the other.

In keeping with this tradition, this article seeks to develop an integrated theory of international law and international relations. Previous efforts in this vein fall into several categories. Myres McDougal and Harold Lasswell, progenitors of the New Haven school, used a theory of domestic politics and domestic law to rethink the nature and definition of international law. The international legal process school, pioneered by scholars such as Abram Chayes and Louis Henkin, sought to explore and take account of the actual impact of international legal rules on international political processes, from crises to routine decision-making. The task was to determine to what extent law shapes 'how nations behave'.[1]

Both of these approaches were developed in response to ongoing work in political science. The young discipline of international relations surged to respectability on the tide of Realism, proffering a hard-boiled code of conduct for the Cold War and disdaining the dangerous moralism of international law. International lawyers thus faced the 'Realist challenge': the claim that law was simply irrelevant to international politics. McDougal and his disciples offered a theoretical response; international legal process scholars sought to establish more

* Professor of Law, Harvard Law School. Formerly Anne-Marie Burley. I am grateful to Lea Brilmayer, Walter Mattli, Andrew Moravcsik, Robert Keohane, Joseph Weiler, and David Wippman for helpful comments. Sarah Fandell provided her customary excellent research assistance. Finally, thanks are due to the Russell Baker Scholars' Fund and the Herbert and Marjorie Fried Faculty Research Fund at the University of Chicago Law School. A more fully documented version of this essay will appear in a forthcoming volume of recent contributions to the *European Journal of International Law*.

1 For an overview of these earlier efforts to integrate international law and international relations, see Slaughter Burley, 'International Law and International Relations Theory: A Dual Agenda', 87 *AJIL* (1993) 205.

empirical connections between international legal rules and foreign policy decision-making.

A third approach – the one pursued here – turns back to the discipline of international relations itself for inspiration. It takes the 'law in context' injunction seriously and acknowledges the capacity of many international lawyers for nuanced political analysis. Nevertheless, instead of canvassing the political dimensions of various international legal problems, it looks first to the discipline charged with thinking and theorizing systematically about State behaviour in the international system. Neither law nor politics may be a science, but international relations theorists have a comparative advantage in formulating generalizable hypotheses about State behaviour and in conceptualizing the basic architecture of the international system.

This approach would look first to the congruence between the image or model of the international system that implicitly or explicitly informs international law and the models used by international relations theorists. As political scientists, these scholars are concerned with the empirical validation of these models. Who are the primary actors in the international system? What are the primary determinants of their behaviour? To the extent that the resulting evidence disconfirms assumptions embedded in the models used by international lawyers, international law and international politics will become increasingly divorced. If, for instance, the primary actors in the system are not States, but individuals and groups represented by State governments, and international law regulates States without regard for such individual and group activity, international legal rules will become increasingly irrelevant to State behaviour.

The inquiry in this essay thus begins not with classical international law, but with the dominant positive analytical framework shared by both international lawyers and political scientists – Realism. Part I outlines the basic tenets of Realism and introduces the principal alternative to Realism in international relations scholarship – Liberalism. Liberalism and Realism proceed from different fundamental assumptions about the international system: assumptions about the identity of the primary actors in that system, the relationship of those actors to State institutions, and the primary determinants of State relations with one another. International lawyers seeking to develop integrated theories of international law and international relations must take the Liberal critique seriously, examining the ways in which Liberal assumptions conflict with assumptions underlying traditional international law.

The most distinctive aspect of Liberal international relations theory is that it permits, indeed mandates, a distinction among different types of States based on their domestic political structure and ideology. In particular, a growing body of evidence highlights the distinctive quality of relations among liberal democracies, evidence collected in an effort to explain the documented empirical phenomenon that liberal democracies very rarely go to war with one another. The resulting behavioural distinctions between liberal democracies and other kinds of States, or more generally between liberal and non-liberal States, cannot be accommodated within the framework of classical international law.

The project here, consistent with an overall commitment to a new generation of interdisciplinary scholarship, is to reimagine international law based on an acceptance of this distinction and an extrapolation of its potential implications. Part II distills various factors that political scientists have correlated with the 'liberal peace', factors that can be translated into assumptions about political and economic relations among liberal States. Part III introduces the concept of a world of liberal States, acknowledging the distance between such a world and the present international system but arguing that the hypothesis may nevertheless describe an important dimension of the current system.

Part IV constructs a model of international law based on a hypothetical world of liberal States, integrating assumptions about relations among such States with the broader assumptions of Liberal international relations theory. It focuses first on relations among individuals and groups in transnational society, hypothesizing a set of voluntary norms selected by these actors but facilitated by States. The second level of law assumes the disaggregation of the State into its component political institutions – courts, legislatures, executives and administrative agencies – and examines the principles governing transnational interactions among these institutions. The third level examines the origin, form, negotiations and enforcement of inter-State agreements among liberal States. At each level the model seeks to define the relevant body of rules and doctrines that would be included in a definition of international law in a world of liberal States, and to introduce concepts and tools of analysis specific to relations among liberal States.

The model developed is advanced as a hypothetical positive model. To the extent it holds, however, it poses a set of normative challenges for international lawyers. Part V concludes with a preliminary effort in this vein, re-examining the norm of sovereignty in a world of liberal States. A central pillar of the positive model is the conceptualization of the State as a disaggregated entity composed of its component political institutions. Could the norm of sovereignty be similarly disaggregated? The discussion in this part sketches the potential form and substantive bases for complementary norms of judicial, legislative, and executive sovereignty in a world of liberal States.

The project in this essay is a thought experiment – a largely deductive effort supplemented with inductive illustrations – designed to generate a hypothetical model of international law based on a set of assumptions about the composition and behaviour of specific States. Its ultimate value must await empirical confirmation of specific hypotheses distilled from this model. At the same time, however, the explicit articulation of this model may cast a different light on current phenomena identified as exceptions to the classical model. Christoph Schreuer, for instance, has recently proposed a new paradigm for international law. He acknowledges, however, that in articulating his proposed paradigm he draws on examples from

Western Europe, the archetypal community of liberal States.[2] He may thus be proposing a paradigm that assumes underlying conditions prevailing only in those States.

The very idea of a division between liberal and non-liberal States may prove distasteful to many. It is likely to recall 19th century distinctions between 'civilized' and 'uncivilized' States, rewrapped in the rhetoric of Western political values and institutions. Such distinctions summon images of an exclusive club created by the powerful to justify their dominion over the weak. Whether a liberal/non-liberal distinction is used or abused for similar purposes depends on the normative system developed to govern a world of liberal and non-liberal States. Exclusionary norms are unlikely to be effective in regulating that world.

More generally, however, these concerns raise serious questions, questions that must and will be addressed if the insights generated by hypothesizing a world of liberal States prove capable of capturing significant aspects of actual relations among liberal States. For the moment, to the extent that a distinction is empirically supported, rather than normatively proclaimed, international lawyers have an obligation at least to assess its implications. A genuine commitment to interdisciplinary scholarship – to improving the conceptual fit between international law and politics – demands no less.

I. Liberalism and Realism in International Relations Theory

Scholars of international relations generate a wide range of theories to solve the problems and puzzles of State behaviour. Each 'theory' offers a causal account of a particular outcome or pattern of behaviour in inter-State relations in a form that isolates independent and dependent variables sufficiently precisely to generate testable hypotheses. At a higher level of generality, however, these theories can be grouped into different families or 'approaches' based on a set of positive assumptions about the international system as a whole.[3] From these very general assumptions spring a host of more specific theories seeking to explain specific international events or phenomena, from the causes of war to the dynamics of international negotiation. Each of these theories can be disputed on its own terms, on the basis of inaccurate empirical data or faulty logic. Alternatively, the entire family of theories can be challenged on the ground that the underlying assumptions about the international system are either wrong or unhelpful.

This part sets forth two of the most common approaches in international relations theory: Realism and Liberalism. Political scientists would find the versions

2 Schreuer, 'The Waning of the Sovereign State: Towards a New Paradigm for International Law?', 4 *EJIL* (1993) 447, 469.

3 The nature of these assumptions privileges the relative explanatory power of broad classes of causal factors, such as the distribution of power in the international system, international institutions, national ideology and domestic political structure.

presented here overly simplified and distilled. Yet as presented, each approach gives rise to a distinct 'mental map' of the international system, specifying the principal actors within it, the preferences (or motives) driving those actors, and the constraints imposed on those actors by the nature of the system itself. The following discussion presents Realism and Liberalism in terms of their competing assumptions along these three axes.

A. Realism

The dominant approach in international relations theory for virtually the past two millennia, from Thucydides to Machiavelli to Morgenthau, has been Realism, also known as Political Realism. Realists come in many stripes, but all typically share the following assumptions. First, they believe that States are the primary actors in the international system, rational unitary actors who are functionally identical. Second, they assume that State preferences, ranging from survival to aggrandizement, are exogenous and fixed. Third, they assume that the anarchic structure of the international system creates such a degree of either actual conflict or perceived uncertainty that States must constantly assume and prepare for the possibility of war. In this context, outcomes of State interactions are typically zero-sum and thus are determined by relative power. For Realists, power is the currency of the international system. States interact with one another within that system like billiard balls: hard, opaque, unitary actors colliding with one another.[4]

To grasp the defining characteristics and theoretical force of Realism, it is necessary to understand not only what it includes within its analytical framework, but also what it excludes: national ideologies, from nationalism to fascism to communism; domestic regime type, from democracies to dictatorships; and transnational actors, from multinational corporations to non-governmental organizations (NGOs). International norms serve only an instrumental purpose, and are likely to be enforced or enforceable only by a hegemon. The likelihood of positive-sum games in which all States will benefit from cooperation is relatively low.

B. Liberalism

A principal alternative to Realism among international relations theorists is Liberalism.[5] As in the domestic realm, Liberal international relations theories have

4 This is the classic Realist metaphor first used by Arnold Wolfers. A. Wolfers, *Discord and Collaboration: Essays on International Politics* (1962) 19-24.

5 I use 'Liberalism' here and throughout this paper as a term of art to refer to Liberal international relations theory. As Andrew Moravcsik has argued, the elements of this theory do indeed flow out of the political theory and philosophy that we call 'liberalism'. However, the transposition of liberal analytical assumptions from the domestic to the international realm is complicated. For present purposes it makes more sense to try and understand international Liberal theory on its own terms as a self-contained alternative to Realism. See A.M. Moravcsik, *Liberalism and*

been characterized repeatedly as normative rather than positive theories. The best known Liberal theory in this category is Wilsonian 'liberal internationalism', popularly understood as a program for world democracy. As used here, however, Liberalism denotes a family of positive theories about how States do behave rather than how they should behave. Efforts to reduce Liberalism to a set of core assumptions that can be stated as succinctly as their Realist counterparts are ongoing among a growing group of contemporary political scientists.[6] I draw here primarily on one particular version developed by Andrew Moravcsik.[7]

If Realists focus on States as monolithic entities in their interaction with other States within an anarchic international system, Liberals focus primarily on State-society relations. The first Liberal assumption is that the primary actors in the international system are individuals and groups acting in domestic and transnational civil society. Thus where Realists look for concentrations of State power, Liberals focus on the ways in which interdependence encourages and allows individuals and groups to exert different pressures on national governments.[8] Second, Liberals assume that the 'State' interacts with these actors in a complex process of both representation and regulation. Goverments are assumed to represent some subset of individual and group actors. The fact and process of representation, however, entails regulation of the activities of all social actors, both those represented and those that are not represented. Thus where Realists assume 'autonomous' national decision-makers, Liberals examine the 'nature of domestic representation ... [as] the decisive link between societal demands and state policy'.[9] Third, Liberals assume that the nature and intensity of State preferences, determined as the aggregation of the preferences of individual and group actors represented in a particular State, will determine the outcome of State interactions. Thus where Realists model patterns of strategic interaction based on fixed State preferences, Liberals seek first to establish the nature and strength of those preferences as a function of the interests and purposes of domestic and transnational actors.

International Relations Theory (Center for International Affairs, Harvard University, Working Paper No. 92-6, 1992).

6 See Moravcsik, *supra* note 5; See, e.g., Deudney, 'Binding Powers, Bound States: The Logica and Geopolitics of Negarchy', Paper presented at the International Studies Association. Washington, D.C., 28 March – 2 April 1994; Zacher, Matthew, 'Liberal International Theory: Common Threads, Divergent Strands', Paper presented at American Political Science Association, Chicago, IL, 3-6 September 1992; Keohane, 'International Liberalism Reconsidered', in J. Dunn (ed.), *The Economic Limits to Modern Politics* (1990) 155; Nye, 'Neorealism and Neoliberalism', 40 *World Politics* (1988) 235; Risse-Kappen, 'Ideas Do Not Float Freely: Transnational Coalitions, Domestic Structures, and the End of the Cold War', 48 *International Organization* (1994) 185; Powell, 'Anarchy in International Relations Theory: The Neorealist-Neoliberal Debate', 48 *International Organization* (1994) 313.

7 Moravcsik, *supra* note 5.

8 The phenomenon of 'interdependence', defined as a situation in which two or more nations each depend on the other, whether symmetrically or not, by virtue of trade and investment patterns, population flows, or even cultural and other social exchanges, can be analyzed from either a Realist or a Liberal perspective. Realists focus only on the impact of interdependence on the power differential between the nations concerned, whereas Liberals analyze it as an international social phenomenon.

9 Moravcsik, *supra* note 5, at 11.

II. Mapping the Attributes of the Liberal Peace

Liberal international relations theory applies to *all* States. Totalitarian governments, authoritarian dictatorships, and theocracies can all be depicted as representatives of some subset of actors in domestic and transnational society, even if it is a very small or particularistic slice. The preferences of such States are likely to differ from the preferences of States with more representative governments and more diverse and complex societies, but not necessarily and not on all issues. Thus, like Realism, Liberalism is a comprehensive theory of the international system.

Notwithstanding this universal applicability, however, Liberal theory explicitly takes domestic regime-type into account in its analysis of State behaviour. If the relevant universe for scholarly analysis is State-society relations, then the scope and density of domestic and transnational society, as well as the structure of government institutions and the mode and scope of popular representation, will be key variables. These variables will be interrelated: a strong civil society, for instance, is better able to support representative government institutions. Conversely, non-representative or oppressive governmental institutions can stunt the growth of domestic and transnational civil society. By taking account of these variables, in contrast to the uniform assumptions of State identity made by Realists, Liberal theory permits more general distinctions among different categories of States based on domestic regime-type.

The best-documented empirical distinction between different types of States by scholars working within the Liberal paradigm concerns the frequency of war among liberal States, as compared to war between liberal and non-liberal States or among non-liberal States alone. Liberal States are States with some form of representative democracy, a market economy based on private property rights, and constitutional protections of civil and political rights.[10] These States are far less likely to go to war with one another than they are to go to war with non-liberal States, giving rise to what some scholars have termed the 'liberal peace'.[11] The claim is not that liberal States are more pacific by nature, only that a variety of factors converge to reduce the likelihood of military conflict between them.[12]

To date, the phenomenon of the liberal peace is better documented than explained. Scholars have put forth a wide range of explanations focusing on variables related to the structure of liberal government and the nature and impact of

10 This is the definition used by Michael Doyle in his pioneering work on the phenomenon of peace among liberal States. See Doyle, 'Kant, Liberal Legacies, and Foreign Affairs', 12 *Philosphy and Public Affairs* (1983) 205, 207-208 (hereinafter Doyle, 'Liberal Legacies').

11 Scholars and policymakers use both the terms 'democratic peace' and 'liberal peace'. I use the term 'liberal peace', meaning the peace among liberal States, as a more accurate description of the empirical phenomenon.

12 The strongest form of the claim is that liberal States have never fought a war with one another. Many scholars, however, defining the criteria for both liberal State and war more broadly, would say 'hardly ever'. See B. Russett, *Grasping the Democratic Peace: Principles for a Post-Cold War World* (1993) 11-23.

liberal norms.[13] Other researchers argue that these are not causally relevant correlations, that the likelihood of peace and liberal government *both* correlate with other factors such as a high level of economic development, a high level of economic interdependence, a particular cultural tradition, or simply the presence of a common threat.[14] These scholars no longer deny that the liberal peace exists as an empirical phenomenon, but they dispute any causal analysis that posits a direct relationship between liberal governments and societies and the likelihood of war. Proponents of the liberal peace counter that factors such as economic interdependence have an *additional* impact on peace and may reinforce the beneficial influence of democracy.[15]

For present purposes, however, the precise mapping of cause and effect does not matter. That is a job for political scientists, who must determine whether democracy leads to peace, or economic prosperity leads to democracy and to peace, or peace leads to economic development which in turn strengthens democracy. In the meantime, international lawyers can canvass the available political science literature and note the presence of a set of attributes that correlate with regard to relations among a particular subset of States. These attributes provide a basis for a more generalized distinction between liberal and non-liberal States, a distinction that is positive rather than normative.

The following list of correlative attributes includes peace, liberal democratic government, a dense network of transnational transactions by social and economic actors; 'multiple channels' of communication and action that are both transnational and transgovernmental rather than formally inter-State; and a blurring of the distinction between domestic and foreign isssues. From both a Realist and a classical international legal perspective, it is jarring to mix descriptions of the domestic characteristics of the States that function within this system with descriptions of the general conditions under which such States interact with one another. But from the perspective of Liberal international relations theory, these various characteristics are all important dimensions of the relations between States and domestic and transnational society.

13 Explanations put forth include the following: 1) democratically elected leaders do not need to turn to democratic ambition as a means of legitimating their rule; 2) those who bear the costs of war are those who decide whether to go to war; 3) citizens in a democratic State will respect the political structure of other democratic States and be hesitant to go to war with them; 4) electoral process produces risk-averse elites and centrist policies – attributes militating against war; 5) States willing to submit to the rule of law and civil society domestically are more likely to submit to their analogues internationally; 6) democratic debate exposes policy to the marketplace of ideas, thereby allowing unsound ideas to be critically evaluated and challenged. This summary is borrowed from Kupchan, Kupchan, 'Concerts, Collective Security, and the Future of Europe', 16 *International Security* (1991) 114.

14 See K.T. Gaubatz, *Still Hazy After All These Years: Kant's Secret Plan of Nature and the Expansion of Democratic States in the International System* (1993) (unpublished manuscript, on file with author); Gowa, Mansfield, 'Power Politics and International Trade', 87 *American Political Science Review* (1993) 408.

15 J.R. Oneal, F.H. Oneal, Z. Maoz and B. Russett, *The Liberal Peace: Interdependence, Democracy, and International Conflict, 1950-1986* (1994) (unpublished manuscript, on file with author).

A. Peace

The assurance of peaceful relations is the assurance that conflict will not escalate into military conflict. It is important to recognize that this assumption does not posit automatic harmony of State interests. Far from it, conflicts of interest are an inevitable and important part of the international landscape. The posited difference affects only the means of resolving those conflicts. The assured choice of non-military means in turn establishes a different psychological and political context in which to interpret economic and political measures taken on either side of the conflict.

B. Liberal Democracy

Liberal democracy can be defined in many ways. As used here, it denotes some form of representative government secured by the separation of powers, constitutional guarantees of civil and political rights, juridical equality, and a functioning judicial system dedicated to the rule of law. These particular features of domestic political structure are important determinants of the interaction between the State and individual and group actors in domestic and transnational society.[16] Representative government assumes that the government must be responsive to a wide range of social actors; the guarantee of civil and political rights assures individuals and groups the opportunity to interact in 'civil society' free of undue interference from State organs;[17] and the existence of a judicial system independent of political direction makes available a neutral arbiter for private disputes arising in domestic and transnational society.[18]

16 A world of liberal democracies is particularly susceptible (and may indeed particularly require) Liberal analysis because it is among such States that domestic and hence transnational civil society should be most developed.

17 The causal links between liberal democracy and civil society are confused and contested. On the one hand, the civil and political rights that are the hallmark of liberal States are both the rights that protect the individual from the State sufficiently to demarcate the State from society, and the rights that permit and encourage voluntary associations among individuals. See R. Beddard, *Human Rights and Europe* (3d ed., 1993) 2-3. Liberal States are thus the States that allow maximum room for the development and flourishing of civil society, within and across territorial lines. On the other hand, both democracy and the prosperity needed to support it appear to require not only specific institutional forms, but also a measure of civic engagement. Haas, 'Beware the Slippery Slope: Notes toward the Definition of Justifiable Intervention', in L.W. Reed, C. Kaysen (eds), *Emerging Norms of Justified Intervention* (1993) 63, 79; R.D. Putnam, *Making Democracy Work: Civic Tradition in Modern Italy* (1993).

18 Judges are both agents and shapers of domestic and transnational civil society. They are the curbers of the State, creating the breathing space for individuals and groups to flourish; but they are also the agents of individuals, resolving disputes, stabilizing expectations. The definition of an 'independent judiciary' is a judiciary that is not the handmaiden of State power, that answers to law rather than to the individuals who make it. Such a judiciary can set itself against the State, but can also regulate a realm in which the State does not intrude. In civil law systems it operates self-consciously in a 'private law' sphere, applying codes designed to protect and foster private activity; in common-law systems it responds to and regulates such activity.

C. Market Economies

Market economies based on private property rights also assure at least the existence of an economic sphere distinct from the State, even if supported by State-created rights and subject to State regulation. The relatively unconstrained ability to pursue economic interest is an engine of social interaction, which in turn produces a climate of trust that facilitates economic expansion.[19] The pursuit of economic interest in a market economy is also a source of demand for legal rules and institutions, for the enforcement of property rights and the provision of the certainty and predictability necessary to minimize risk and permit calculation of future gain.

D. A Dense Network of Transnational Transactions

Another factor that has been correlated with a reluctance to use force among liberal democracies is a high level of transnational social and economic relations among individuals and groups. Karl Deutsch argued in the 1950s that the density and level of transnational contacts, to be measured through communication flows, was a reliable indicator of a 'pluralistic security community', a group of States whose members share a sense of common identity and who rule out the use of force in resolving disputes.[20] A second approach focuses more on economic contacts, particularly on levels of economic interdependence. These scholars seek empirical confirmation of claims dating back to Kant and the Manchester School about the pacific consequences of trade. Yet they must contend with those who note that interdependence can breed friction and suspicion as easily as harmony and trust.[21] The most promising recent scholarship in this debate suggests that economic interdependence does have a positive impact on the likelihood of military conflict among States, an impact independent from and in addition to the impact of republican constraints on executive decision-making and democratic norms of peaceful dispute resolution.[22]

Yet a third approach suggests that democratic norms and structures and economic interdependence reinforce one another in contributing to peaceful conflict resolution. In a book that has become a classic in the American international relations curriculum, Robert Keohane and Joseph Nye developed a model of

19 Again, the causal arrows here are unclear. Putnam argues that civic engagement permits economic expansion; the converse observation that economic interest generates social interaction is easily apparent from the expense budgets and golfing proclivities of business executives the world over. Compare Susan Strange's discussion of the 'international business civilization' in Strange, 'The Name of the Game', in N. Rizopoulos (ed.), *Sea-Changes* (1990) 238, 260-265.

20 K. Deutsch *et. al.*, *Political Community and the North Atlantic Area* (1957).

21 For a revival of the original Kantian argument, see Doyle, *supra* note 10, at 230-32; see also R. Cobden, *Political Writings* (1867). Many scholars have countered with the example, *inter alia*, of the high level of interdependence between Great Britain and Germany just prior to World War I. See, e.g., S. Hoffmann, *The State of War* (1965). Seeking to move past this debate, recent work has emphasized different *types* of interdependence. Art, 'A Defensible Defense: America's Grand Strategy after the Cold War', 15 *International Security* (Spring 1991) 5.

22 See Oneal *et. al*, *supra* note 15.

'complex interdependence' as an ideal-type of international relations.[23] This model correlated a reluctance to resort to the use of force among a group of States with 'multiple channels of contact connect[ing] societies'.[24] More recent work supports the proposition that

> [p]olitical and economic freedoms allow individuals to form transnational associations and to influence policy in light of the resulting interests, inhibiting their governments from acting violently toward one another.[25]

The point here is not the mutual vulnerability that economic interdependence implies, but rather the corollary network of transnational transactions and communications among individual and group actors in liberal States. This is the common denominator of all three schools.

E. Transgovernmental Communication

A subset of Keohane and Nye's model of complex interdependence is the phenomenon of 'transgovernmental communication', the existence of 'informal ties between governmental elites' and direct meetings and communications between bureaucrats from different countries.[26] These contacts coexist with 'formal foreign office arrangements'.[27] As they recognized, this dimension of inter-State relations cannot be accommodated within the traditional Realist conception of States as unitary actors.[28] It suggests instead an image of what I will call 'disaggregated sovereignty', the recognition of multiple actors exercising different types and modes of governmental authority. And when combined with the more general phenomenon of transnational communications among individuals and groups, it limits 'the ability of foreign offices tightly to control governments' foreign relations'.[29]

23 R.O. Keohane, J.S. Nye, *Power and Interdependence* (1977) 25.
24 Keohane, Nye, Jr., 'Power and Interdependence Revisited', 41 *International Organization* (1987) 725, 731. Russett characterizes an extension of this approach as 'transnationalism', the claim that 'individual autonomy and pluralism within democratic States foster the emergence of transnational linkages and institutions – among individuals, private groups, and governmental agencies'. He argues, however, that this factor cannot be isolated as a variable independent of democracy itself in explaining the liberal peace. Russett, *Grasping the Democratic Peace*, *supra*, note 12, at 26. Keohane and Nye themselves originally wrote before the phenomenon of the liberal peace had been identified, thus they made no effort to connect their model of complex interdependence to relations among liberal States *per se*. They did note, however, that the reluctance to use military force, a critical component of their model, was particularly observable 'among industrialized, pluralist countries'. *Power and Interdependence*, at 27. I have thus included aspects of their model as factors generally correlated with the liberal peace.
25 Oneal *et. al.*, *supra* note 15, at 4.
26 Keohane and Nye, *Power and Interdependence*, *supra* note 23, at 25-26.
27 Ibid., at 26.
28 Keohane and Nye, *Power and Interdependence Revisited*, *supra* note 24, at 740.
29 Ibid., at 738.

F. Collapse of the Foreign/Domestic Distinction

The final attribute of inter-State relations that political scientists have correlated with peaceful relations among a particular group of States is the absence of a hierarchy of foreign affairs issues, a hierarchy that traditionally ranked the 'high politics' of security above the 'low politics' of economics.[30] The relative parity of security with economic and environmental issues in turn breaks down the distinction between foreign and domestic politics, as many issues reach the foreign policy agenda that have a direct impact on domestic actors.[31] The ability of those actors to influence policy decisions further decreases the traditional insulation of foreign policy, a trend that is strengthened by the assurance of peace itself.

The standard equation of foreign policy with security policy is reflected in a host of legal and constitutional arguments for the autonomy of executive control of foreign relations, free of the normal political and legal constraints on policymaking. Arguments justifying an autonomous executive sphere are typically based on the need for secrecy, speed and flexibility in foreign policy, reflecting an underlying assumption that national security is at stake. Conversely, the factors underlying the disintegration of the foreign/domestic distinction in relations among liberal States suggest that these arguments are of decreasing relevance. Foreign policy among such States should be subject to the same constraints as domestic policy.

III. Hypothesizing a World of Liberal States

Taken together, the above six attributes describe a hypothetical world of liberal States, a world of peace, democracy, and human rights. By combining these attributes with the levels of analysis generated by Liberal international relations theory, we can generate a model of international law in such a world. This part will address the reasons for undertaking such an exercise and sketch the methodology for conducting a self-professed 'thought experiment'.

Why bother even hypothesizing a world of liberal States? It is manifestly not the world of traditional international law, a world that accepts many Realist assumptions about States as functionally identical unitary actors seeking primarily to preserve their own sovereignty. It is not the world of contemporary international politics, of Bosnia, Haiti, Rwanda or China. Nor is it a world likely soon to emerge. Do we then hypothesize such a world solely as a Utopia? Is the point simply to perform an abstract interdisciplinary exercise?

The answers are several. First, part of the world, a growing part, *is* composed of liberal States. The attributes listed above may be a more accurate description of relations among countries in this part of the world than the traditional model of the international system on which classical international law is based. If so, a model of

30 Keohane and Nye, *Power and Interdependence*, *supra* note 23, at 25.
31 Ibid., at 26-27.

international law derived from these attributes will capture more of the legal and political reality of relations among these countries. Legal relations among States such as the United States, Canada, the Member States of the European Union, Japan, Australia, and New Zealand are most likely to fit this model, but it could also at least provide a point of departure for conceptualizing the legal relations among Argentina, Chile, Brazil, Ecuador, and Mexico; Poland, Hungary, and the Czech Republic; Taiwan, South Korea, and the Philippines; India, Israel, and, with luck, South Africa.

Second, to the extent that this model shapes our expectations of how law operates among liberal States, it will also generate a corollary set of expectations concerning legal relations between liberal and non-liberal States. These twin sets of expectations will in turn provide the conceptual tools to grasp the differential significance of apparently universal phenomena. As a formal matter, for instance, all supranational tribunals are expected to wield the same authority. The judgments of the International Court of Justice and the European Court of Justice should thus have an equal impact on State behaviour. In practice, of course, our expectations of the effectiveness of these two tribunals vary considerably, but without justification or explanation in the language and conceptual framework of classical international law. A model of law among liberal States that analyzes the enforcement of international agreement in light of the underlying political configuration and the nature of individual and group interests in the States involved can instead generate a set of conditions in which we might expect supranational tribunals to be relatively more or less successful.

In both of the above categories, the model will provide a basis for empirical testing of specific hypotheses concerning legal relations among liberal States and between liberal and non-liberal States. If these hypotheses hold, the next step will be to develop a corresponding set of norms within each category. The positive model cannot itself give rise to normative propositions. Yet to the extent that the positive model gives rise to a different conceptualization of the principal actors engaged in legal relations and the nature of the relations between them, it will define the subjects of new norms and the type of activity such norms are designed to regulate. For instance, I will argue that legal relations among liberal States are characterized by 'disaggregated sovereignty', in which the 'State' is disaggregated into its component political institutions, each of which is bound to one another in a constitutionally determined set of relationships. This conceptualization would then require us to generate norms defining the content and limits of the sovereignty of each of these component institutions.

The third potential advantage of developing a hypothetical model of legal relations among liberal States flows from this normative project. We may find that in some instances it will be more attractive to use the model to generate a universal set of concepts and norms, applicable to liberal and non-liberal States alike. In many cases we are likely to find that relations between liberal and non-liberal States display some of the features of the model but not others. This congruity is to be expected to the extent that non-liberal States display some of the political, economic, and social attributes described above but not others. In such cases, it may be preferable to accept the necessary fiction inherent in applying a positive model and its corollary norms to States that only partially fit the model than to sacrifice the principle of universality.

Assume, then, a world of liberal States. Assume further that the vision of the international system developed by Liberal international relations theory is correct: that the primary actors in this system are individuals and groups operating in domestic and transnational society; that States seek to regulate these individuals and groups but simultaneously represent some aggregation of individual and group preferences; that the strength of State preferences determines the outcome of inter-State interactions. What would international law in such a world look like? What rules would we expect to govern transnational and inter-State transactions?

'International law', as defined here, comprises all the law that regulates activity across and between territorial boundaries. It can include the law of peoples and the law of nations, the *jus gentium* and the *jus inter gentes*. Existing categories and distinctions such as public and private, domestic, transnational and international are immaterial. The identifying element that qualifies a rule or set of rules for inclusion in this category is the potential for contribution to international order, whether by constraining domestic forces that might otherwise escalate international disputes into military or severe economic conflict, by strengthening or regulating transactions in transnational society, or by directly regulating inter-State relations. The resulting body of 'law' is defined not according to subject or source, but rather in terms of purpose and effect, in conformity with a particular body of international relations theory.

IV. International Law in a World of Liberal States

To develop a model of international law in a world of liberal States, I combine the levels of analysis generated by Liberal international relations theory with the political, economic, and social attributes of a world of liberal States. As discussed above, Liberal international relations theory offers a set of fundamental assumptions about the international system: about its primary and secondary actors, their preferences, and the constraints imposed by the system itself. In accordance with these assumptions, an effort to think about legal relations within the international system would focus first on relations among individuals and groups in transnational society; second on State institutions in relation to these social actors; and third on inter-State interactions where State preferences are a changing function of individual and group interests as those interests are themselves defined in domestic and transnational society. Within each of these categories, the social actors and State institutions involved are assumed to interact with one another as dictated by the ideological and structural principles of a liberal State.

The first level comprises a network of transnational relationships among individuals and groups governed largely by rules of their own choosing. These rules may not be 'law' per se, but rather voluntary norms adopted by a wide range of professional associations. Alternatively, individuals and groups may choose pre-existing bodies of national law to govern transnational contracts. They may also choose where they would like their disputes resolved, and by which tribunals, either arbitral or judicial. Individuals and groups are the primary actors within this network. State institutions are relevant primarily to the extent that they promote or hinder these voluntary choices, through doctrines governing personal jurisdiction, forum selection, parallel litigation, evidence-gathering, and enforcement of arbitral agreements and awards. States may also decide to codify voluntary norms. The policies underlying these doctrines and decisions bear directly on the depth and breadth of transnational society, with resulting impact on the pressures that social groups can exert on representative institutions, the transmission of knowledge about foreign legal systems, and the socialization of individuals and groups subject to multiple bodies of national regulation.

The second level is the level of domestic governmental institutions, primarily courts and legislatures, interacting directly with one another in the process of making, selecting and enforcing the law governing transnational transactions. The 'State' at this level is disaggregated into its component parts: legislative, executive, administrative and judicial. The assumption of liberal States permits further assumptions about the representativeness and relative independence of these institutions within their respective spheres, resting on a common foundation of core protection of individual rights. The legal relations among these institutions primarily comprise questions of overlapping national jurisdiction, embodied in doctrines governing choice of law and extraterritorial application of law. By departing from the traditional conception of States as unitary actors on the international stage, it is possible to understand these relations in the context of a transjudicial and trans-legislative dialogue, in which courts and legislatures acknowledge and evaluate foreign law. It also facilitates the conceptualization of a transnational legal process encompassing disaggregated judicial, legislative and executive interaction.

The third level is the level of inter-State interaction, in which States must present themselves as unitary actors at least to the extent of having a sole representative in international negotiations. The difference between the analysis presented here and traditional public international law is that the States involved are presumed to be embedded in transnational society. The unitary facade is thus in fact very porous, open to penetration by individuals and groups. Further, the 'aggregation' of the political institutions themselves for purposes of international negotiation will be quite loose. The executive, as negotiating representative, will be accountable to the legislature; acts of the legislature approving and implementing the results of executive negotiation will be enforceable by the courts. These conditions affect the origins, form, negotiation and enforcement of international agreements.

Before proceeding to a more detailed analysis within each of these categories, a final methodological note is in order. The methods used to imagine or conceptualize legal relations in a world of liberal States are both deductive and inductive. They are deductive to the extent that they follow logically from the various assumptions and attributes already discussed. They are inductive to the extent that they draw on anecdotal examples of relations among liberal States, such as the States of the European Union or the OECD. Whether these examples will in fact prove representative of the larger phenomena postulated here is a subject for empirical testing; I offer them here to add concrete form to abstract propositions and to stimulate further expansion of existing categories of thought.

A. The Voluntary Law of Individuals and Groups in Transnational Society

Much of the law governing relations among economic and social actors operating across borders is a decentralized network of self-selected and customized rules. These actors choose both the substantive law governing their association and the mode and forum for dispute resolution. Territorial boundaries impose no restrictions, but only delimit the menu of choices. Participants are free to choose the product of one legislature and the procedures and competence of another tribunal. A contract might thus specify that disputes will be tried in London under New York law. The resulting freedom and flexibility is particularly important for the efficient functioning of market economies.

1. Formal and Informal Voluntary Norms

The voluntary law governing transnational society divides into several categories. First is a category of proto-law generated by a wide range of business and professional organizations. In the domestic context, Robert Cooter has described these rules as the 'new law merchant', voluntary norms adopted by corporate networks, self-regulating professions, and business associations.[32] Many of these networks and associations extend transnationally as well, generating an accompanying network of transnational voluntary norms. These norms may not seem like law at all. Yet scholars and practitioners seeking to predict actual behaviour must take them into account as empirical facts that guide action. Further, as will be discussed below, these bodies of rules may be templates for future law.

A second category of rules governing transnational commerce is the law selected by individual actors to govern the interpretation and application of bilateral commercial agreements and the mode of resolving disputes arising out of those agreements. The actors enter into contractual relations. Their interaction is to be

32 Examples include rules promulgated by the VISA network, the American Bar Association ethical guidelines, and standards promulgated by the Association of Home Appliance Manufacturers. Cooter, 'Structural Adjudication and the New Law Merchant: A Model of Decentralized Law', *International Review of Law and Economics* (1994) 143, 144.

governed by the contract. But they also determine what law shall govern the contract and where and how disputes arising out of or related to the contract will be resolved. They can choose either a judicial or an arbitral forum. If they choose arbitration, they can also write their own rules of procedure governing the dispute resolution process.

Within international commercial arbitration, individuals and groups may find themselves, either by specification or not, governed by an independent body of law developed by international commercial arbitrators on the basis of customary transnational business practice. These rules have also been referred to as the 'new law merchant', or *lex mercatoria*. The arbitrators derive their authority from the arbitral agreement. They themselves form an informal network,[33] such that they can effectively draw on their collective experience in distilling and applying these rules. Formally, this body of law has no more status than voluntary norms developed and adopted by professional associations. It similarly evolves from social and economic practice in transnational society.

2. *State Facilitation of Individual Choice*

Thus far, the law of transnational society has been presented as essentially stateless. This is an accurate depiction in that individuals and groups are the primary actors; State functions are ancillary to individual choices. But the role of the State is nevertheless critical to the functioning of the system. It appears in several guises. First, of course, the State provides the bodies of rules available for selection by individual and group actors. State legislatures thus provide a public good. Second, States may ultimately adopt and codify the norms that individuals and groups have already developed through voluntary associations. Merchant custom, for instance, formed the basis for much of the common law. Today scholars from law and economics often urge the adoption of these voluntary codes by national legislatures. In this regard, developments in transnational society lay a foundation for subsequent State action.

Third, States determine to what extent bilateral commercial agreements will be enforced, thereby facilitating or blocking individual choice. This point has been most frequently recognized in the arbitral context; the availability of judicial enforcement – the coercive apparatus of the State – undergirds the entire system of international commercial arbitration. Thus States wishing to promote and facilitate commercial arbitration authorize their domestic courts both to compel arbitration at the request of one of the parties to the arbitral agreement and to enforce the ensuing award.[34] In the multilateral context, Michael Reisman observes that the New York

33 See Dezalay, Garth, 'Grand Old Men vs. Multinationals: The Routinization of Charismatic Arbitration into Off-Shore Litigation', Secs. IV, VI (American Bar Foundation Working Paper, No. 9317, 1994).

34 In the absence of State action, private trade associations can also provide enforcement mechanisms by enhancing reputation costs. This was the purpose of the associations arising out of the medieval 'champagne fairs'. Similar mechanisms, albeit less effective, are provided by Better Business

Convention[35] is effectively an agrceement whereby each State acknowledges the legitimacy of each other State's control of the arbitral process and thus agrees to enforce the results.[36]

Equally true, although less often observed, is the role of the State in facilitating individual choice in transnational litigation. The parallel is easiest to see in doctrines governing forum selection and choice of law where a particular forum and governing law is specified by agreement. Similarly, doctrines governing parallel litigation, such as the issuance of antisuit injunctions, often function to prevent one party in transnational litigation from circumventing the forum and law specified in a contract. Yet doctrines governing service of process, personal jurisdiction, *forum non conveniens,* transnational discovery of evidence, and enforcement of foreign judgments can also be analyzed from the perspective of facilitating or hindering dispute resolution in transnational society. The interpretation and application of these doctrines typically arise where one party to an international transaction chooses a forum to which another party objects. Party A seeks to invoke the power of the forum State to conduct the litigation on its terms; Party B may in turn assert the power of a foreign State as a counterweight. But the forum itself, in hearing and pronouncing on these arguments, is less an agent of one particular sovereign State than one of a number of multiple centres of authoritative dispute resolution available to actors in transnational society.

3. Theoretical Implications

From a traditional Realist 'billiard ball' perspective, all of the above doctrines ultimately pose questions of State power. The issue is whether a particular transaction or the parties to it fall within one or another sovereign sphere. In case of disagreement on this score, the only solution is to mediate conflicting claims of power by multiple competing sovereigns. Assuming a world of liberal States, however, a number of very different features emerge. First, transnational economic and social interactions are an important and enduring dimension of relations among liberal States. Second, all potential dispute resolution fora within the realm of liberal States, whether judicial or arbitral subject to judicial supervision, are assumed to be neutral and independent of direct political influences. Third, the core rights of individual litigants are assumed to be constitutionally protected in every potential forum. One such right is the right of a litigant not to be forced to defend in a forum with which she has no connection. Given these preconditions, participants in transnational transactions have multiple potential fora from which to choose. To the extent that the provision of dispute resolution mechanisms is regarded as a core function of a unitary State, the proliferation of such choices contributes to the

Bureaus. See generally Milgrom *et al.*, 'The Role of Institutions in the Revival of Trade: The Law Merchant, Private Judges, and the Champagne Fairs', 2 *Economics and Politics* (1990) 1.

35 Convention on the Recognition and Enforcement of Foreign Arbitral Awards, *opened for signature*, 10 June 1958, 21 UST 2517, TIAS No. 6997, 330 UNTS 38.

36 M. Reisman, *Systems of Control in International Adjudication and Arbitration* (1992) 139.

dispersal of the core functions of the State across a particular transnational community.

Even doctrines that appear to enforce one party's choice of forum over another party's objection look quite different in the context of transnational transactions among liberal States. Given the assumed procedural and substantive safeguards, the primary import of these doctrines is the translation of economic interdependence into a set of diagonal relationships between individuals and groups and States other than their home State for the limited sovereign function of dispute resolution.[37] The contacts with a foreign legal system that either give rise to an economic or social transaction in the first instance, or that flow from such a transaction undertaken for other reasons, become the basis for a limited relationship with a foreign sovereign, a sovereign that can be guaranteed to provide the same minimum safeguards in the performance of this sovereign function that the individual's home sovereign would provide.[38] The equation is not a straightforward transformation of economic power into legal power, but rather a decision in favour of one individual's choice of forum over another's based on an assessment of a relationship between the individuals involved and each of their connections with different States.

The density and velocity of transnational transactions among liberal States is related to the phenomenon of the 'liberal peace', although the precise causal relationships have not been mapped out. We may speculate that cross-fertilization among legal systems may play some role; knowledge of multiple legal means to similar ends in systems with similar safeguards might dampen perceptions of difference and 'otherness' so likely to escalate conflict; opportunities for transnational formulation of norms through business and professional associations may facilitate legal convergence. It may also be that subjection to multiple bodies of law has an important socializing dimension, transferring individual expectations to more than one source of sovereign power. Finally, the picture of transnational society presented here has an important self-governing dimension. Whether through professional associations or bilateral contracts, individuals and groups in transnational society are often able to make and enforce their own rules and to customize their own modes of dispute resolution, choosing among a number of disaggregated State 'products'. Power and responsibility are equally dispersed, laying the foundation for a hypothetical transnational polity with multiple centres of authority.

37 See L. Brilmayer, *Justifying International Acts* (1989) 55-57, 84-87 for a discussion of 'diagonal relationships' crossing the 'horizontal' relationships among States and the 'vertical' relationships between citizens and their home State.

38 In a similar vein, Lea Brilmayer uses jurisdictional analysis to determine when a sovereign owes the same duties to a foreign citizen as it does to its own. Brilmayer, *supra* note 37, Chapter I.

B. The Law of Transnational Governmental Institutions

If the first level of law among liberal States focuses on the rules encouraging and strengthening the formation and development of transnational society, the second level is the law governing relationships between governments and individual and group actors in transnational society. This law subdivides into two general categories: 1) the substantive law directly regulating these relationships, typically the domestic law of one or more States, and 2) the legal or quasi-legal principles regulating the interaction of governments themselves concerning the appropriate division of regulatory jurisdiction. At present, the relevant doctrines that would fit within these categories are an amalgam of private choice of law rules, public international law rules governing jurisdiction to prescribe and enforce, diverse domestic principles governing statutory interpretation, and various procedural rules governing the treatment of foreign governments in domestic court.

The traditional public international law doctrines governing State jurisdiction to prescribe and enforce conduct focus on the demarcation of horizontal relationships among competing sovereigns, relying on principles of territoriality and nationality as the legal corollaries of the physical limits of political power. Private international law doctrines, on the other hand, encompass a wide range of potential approaches, from territoriality to State interest-balancing to efforts to quantify and qualify the relationship between an individual or a dispute and a particular regulatory authority. Given its focus on State representation and regulation of individual interests, Liberal international relations theory would fit most comfortably with the amalgamated approach originally developed by Andreas Lowenfeld and adopted by the Third Restatement of American Foreign Relations Law, an approach combining links between the individual and her conduct and the States seeking to regulate that conduct, State interests, and individual expectations.[39]

The assumption of a world of liberal States would refine this analysis further by disaggregating the State itself. In such a world, each State is composed of roughly symmetrical and homogeneous domestic political institutions: representative legislatures, separate representative executives and administrative agencies,[40] and independent judiciaries. Each of these institutions, in turn, has a roughly similar relationship with individuals and groups in domestic society, performing the same functions within a broadly similar set of constraints designed to safeguard individual rights. It thus becomes possible to conceive of the State not as a unitary actor, but rather as a constellation of governmental institutions performing the three basic functions of law-making, execution, and enforcement, on the assurance that each State in our hypothetical world will replicate this structure.

39 See Lowenfeld, 'Public Law in the International Arena: Conflict of Laws, International Law, and Some Suggestions for their Interaction', 163 *Hague Academy of International Law* (1979-II) 311; *Restatement of Foreign Relations Law of the United States* (Third), paras. 402-403.

40 Even in parliamentary systems, the 'government' is distinct from the legislature; cabinet ministers in charge of different government departments often act on their own initiative.

Within each liberal State, these institutions form multiple centres of power, each reinforcing and checking the other. In international matters, however, the perceived threat to the State as a whole has often led legislatures and courts to line up behind the executive, the branch of government best equipped to engage in high-stakes international diplomacy. The assurance of peace in a world of liberal States, coupled with a presumption of stable and continuous relations with other liberal States, would be likely to remove these traditional impediments to independent judicial and legislative action. Executives and courts, legislatures and courts, legislatures and administrators could thus all interact across borders in multiple ways. Each would represent a facet of a particular State, but national allegiance would be counter-balanced by links to counterpart institutions performing the same functions in transnational society. The result would be a web of relations among multiple centres of State authority within and across borders.

Interactions among these institutions will typically be triggered by the interaction of individuals and groups in transnational society. Thus, for instance, a dispute between two citizens of different States regarding a transaction that took place in both States is likely to bring the courts of both States into contact with one another, directly or indirectly, to the extent that the two individuals involved each prefers to litigate the dispute in her home State. The same dispute may also bring the legislatures of the two States into contact with one another, directly or indirectly, to the extent that the two courts involved disagree over which legislature's prescriptions should apply to the conduct at issue. Alternatively, if only one court is involved, its disregard of a foreign legislature's prescriptions may invite a response from the foreign legislature itself or the foreign executive charged with implementing those prescriptions.[41]

The substantive legal rules applicable to a particular class of individuals or groups or of conduct in transnational society will thus be determined in the context of an interaction between the individuals and groups involved and two or more governmental institutions: courts, legislatures, executives and administrative agencies. The question then arises as to what principles should govern the interaction not of 'States', but of these specific institutions in interactions with one another in the larger context of regulating transnational society. To answer this question, it is helpful to begin first by analyzing actual and potential relations among like institutions across borders – court to court, legislature to legislature – in terms both of the principles that might govern an ongoing 'dialogue' between these institutions and the functions that such a dialogue might perform as part of a process of transnational governance. The final section examines interactions among all three institutions.

41 See Lowenfeld, *supra* note 39, at 330-331 (describing clashes of regulatory jurisdiction as involving two courts, one executive and one legislature).

1. A Transjudicial Dialogue

Courts in a world of liberal States would recognize each other as like units, dedicated to and legitimated by the same core principles of the rule of law: assumptions of impartiality in adjudication, of the separation of the political and judicial branches, and of the equality of all citizens before the law. They are likely to interact with and take account of one another in a form of transjudicial dialogue. This dialogue can be initiated by individuals, in the sense that the multiple transnational contacts of parties to a particular case raise choice of law questions. Alternatively, courts themselves can initiate the dialogue by seeking information as to how their counterparts in foreign countries resolve similar questions. This dialogue can take several forms, for several different purposes.[42]

First, the application of traditional choice of law rules can be conceptualized as a reciprocal dialogue in which courts of different States are engaged in a common endeavour to make transnational relations among individual and groups more certain and predictable while taking account of multiple State interests. Some conceptions of this dialogue would go further and envision a common effort to select and harmonize substantive rules. The significance of postulating a dialogue is that a court of one State may assume that its foreign counterpart will respond to signals of accommodation or confrontation in an ongoing conversation. Some conflicts-of-law scholarship has gone so far as to model this dialogue in game theoretic terms; other scholars argue that traditional notions of comity and reciprocity have long captured this phenomenon.[43]

The assumption of a world of liberal States means that this dialogue takes place in a setting in which national courts face fewer constraints on their application of foreign law. All courts can assume that a genuine 'choice of law' exists, in the sense of a choice between two rules arrived at by a process that both polities and societies would recognize as legitimate. The paradigm is set forth by a US court in the case *Bi v. Union Carbide Chemicals & Plastics Co.*,[44] in which the court recognized and gave effect to an Indian law on the ground that 'India is a democracy'.[45] The court looked only to affirm that the law in question had been 'passed by [India's] democratic parliament' subject to review by an independent judiciary.[46]

42 For a fuller exposition of different forms of transjudicial communication, see Slaughter, 'A Typology of Transjudicial Communication', *University of Richmond Law Review* (forthcoming 1995).

43 See, e.g., L. Brilmayer, *Conflict of Laws: Foundations and Future Directions* (1991) 155-167 (discussing game theoretical approaches in which actors have both common interests that they attain through cooperation and conflicting interests they realize at each other's expense); Larry Kramer, 'Rethinking Choice of Law', 90 *Colum. L. Rev.* (1990) 277, 339-344 (discussing choice of law in terms of prisoner's dilemma hypothetical); see also Weinberg, 'Against Comity', 80 *Georgia Law Journal* (1991) 53 (asserting that game theory as applied to conflicts of law reincarnates traditional notions of comity and reciprocity).

44 984 F.2d 582 (2d Cir. 1993).

45 Ibid., at 586.

46 Ibid.

Further, the process of choosing and applying a foreign law takes place within what I have called a 'zone of legitimate difference'.[47] Courts will presume the legitimacy of a wide range of different means to achieve similar ends.[48] Where they do refuse to apply an otherwise applicable foreign law, it is likely to be based on the perception that although the societies in question adhere to the same fundamental values, the potentially applicable laws reflect different choices as to which of those values should trump. Such a refusal is to be contrasted to a more general refusal even to assess the validity of the foreign law in cases in which the societies in question diverge not on specific choices between competing values, but on the identity and validity of the underlying values themselves.

Finally, in all of these instances the institutions involved can be expected to recognize, either implicitly or explicitly, a common core of political and economic values that will preserve roughly the same boundary between 'political' and 'legal' questions as would exist in purely domestic cases. In a world in which courts and lawmakers in one country can find no recognizable counterpart in another, or in which foreign policy concerns connected to a particular dispute might raise even the distant spectre of military conflict, courts may understandably cede the field to the political branches. But where such counterparts are readily ascertainable and peace is assured, disputes raising questions of international politics should be as amenable to judicial resolution as disputes raising questions of domestic politics. The degree of that amenability will vary by country, depending on the degree to which the judicial system in question recognizes some domestic variant of the American political question doctrine.

A second version of transjudicial dialogue may occur where the courts of liberal States seek to improve the quality of their decision-making on important public issues. Mary Ann Glendon has documented the increasing willingness of European constitutional courts to take account of the solutions crafted by their foreign counterparts on issues ranging from free speech to abortion.[49] The German constitutional court, for instance, maintains a library of constitutional decisions from courts around the world.[50] The presupposition here is of multiple societies, similarly structured and dedicated to the same basic values, grappling with the resolution of conflicts of those values. The institutions charged with the resolution of those conflicts communicate the fruits of their common experience to one another.

Third, courts may communicate with one another to protect or persuade their home governments. Joseph Weiler has documented this phenomenon among

47 Burley, 'Law among Liberal States: Liberal Internationalism and the Act of State Doctrine', 92 *Colum. L. Rev.* (1992) 1907, 1919, 1946.

48 The American judge (later Justice) Benjamin Cardozo put it best: 'We are not so provincial as to say that every solution of a problem is wrong because we deal with it otherwise at home...', *Loucks v. Standard Oil Co.*, 120 N.E. 198, 201 (N.Y. 1918).

49 M.A. Glendon, *Rights Talk* (1991) 158-159.

50 D. Kommers, *The Federal Constitutional Court* (American Institute for Contemporary German Studies, Key Institutions of German Democracy No. 2, 1994) 17.

national courts in the European Community, observing that in the context of common supranational obligations courts seek to ensure that acceptance of these obligations as a matter of national law will not disadvantage their governments relative to other governments. They thus canvass comparable decisions by their foreign counterparts. Alternatively, where a national court wants to urge compliance with a supranational obligation, it may argue that it is just keeping pace with the decisions of its foreign counterparts.[51] The result is a transjudicial dialogue that shapes domestic judicial conversations with national executives and legislatures.

2. A Transnational Legislative Dialogue

The assumption of a world of liberal States allows us to assume competing spheres of public regulation of represented individuals. Moreover, we assume a dense transnational society, such that laws passed by one legislature will inevitably have an impact on individuals and groups outside the national territory and citizenry. And we assume that those affected individuals and groups will have access to their own legislatures.

The upshot of these assumptions is that, like courts, national legislatures should also be presumed to be engaged in a reciprocal dialogue with their foreign counterparts. Legislative measures that adversely affect individuals and groups outside the national polity will invite retaliation where those individuals and groups have sufficient power in their home countries to secure a foreign legislative response.

These assumptions should inform judicial analysis of extraterritorial application of national legislation. This analysis includes an initial determination of legislative power to legislate extraterritorially and a secondary determination of whether in fact the legislature intended to exercise that power with regard to the statute before the court. The result may well be a reinforced presumption of 'legislative comity', the deference that one legislature gives to another.[52] At the very least, courts might be expected to adopt principles of statutory interpretation designed to ensure that a legislature has taken account of retaliatory possibilities.

In the normative realm, the conception of legislatures operating in dialogue with one another in a world of liberal States could be used to generate a set of principles that could function as an informal transnational constitution. Common principles of limited government, individual liberty, and the certainty and predictability inherent in the rule of law could be generalized across borders to mandate presumptions in

51 Weiler, 'A Quiet Revolution: The European Court of Justice and Its Interlocutors', 26 *Comparative Political Studies* (1994) 510, 521-522.

52 Compare Justice Scalia's distinction between legislative and judicial comity in *Hartford Fire Insurance Co. v. California*, 113 S.Ct. 2891, 2920 (1993) (Scalia, J., dissenting). Scalia distinguishes 'the comity of courts, whereby judges decline to exercise jurisdiction over matters more appropriately adjudged elsewhere' and '"rescriptive comity": the respect sovereign nations afford each other by limiting the reach of their law'. *Id.* Prescriptive comity is 'exercised by legislatures when they enact laws, and courts assume it has been exercised when they come to interpreting the scope of laws their legislatures have enacted'. *Id.*

favour of extraterritorial application of any statutes designed to limit the exercise of governmental authority and against the extraterritorial application of statutes restricting individual liberty where the individuals in question are demonstrably subject to competing regulation by their home legislatures. Further, common principles of representative government could lead to the adoption of principles designed to protect distortions of national legislative processes by rent-seekers trying to exploit transnational regulatory gaps.[53]

3. Disaggregated Transnational Judicial, Legislative, and Executive Interaction

A final aspect of this second level of law among liberal States is the interaction of the three domestic branches of government in each State transnationally with one another in much the same way that they would interact with their co-branches of government at home. Thus, for instance, executive branches have to take account not only of their own courts, but of the decisions of foreign courts as having an impact on the concerns and constraints of diplomacy.[54] They might choose to respond to a foreign judicial decision by pressuring a fellow executive to urge a reversal or reinterpretation. Alternatively, however, they can be expected to intervene directly in foreign litigation by presenting their views to the foreign court itself. Finally, a struggle between two national courts may require executive intervention on both sides.

Conversely, courts may choose to treat foreign executive branches in the same way that they relate to their own national executive. The United States Court of Appeals for the Seventh Circuit, for instance, chose to defer to a ruling by the French executive branch under the same US doctrine that requires deference to US administrative agencies.[55] In the process, it acknowledged the common function of the two entities rather than differentiating between them by drawing a line between foreign and domestic affairs and waiting for a communication from the branch of its own government charged with the conduct of foreign affairs.

With regard to executives and legislatures, executive branches can lobby foreign legislatures directly through national law firms. Legislatures can also conduct their own diplomacy through delegations of national legislators visiting foreign executives and consultations with foreign parliamentarians. Alternatively, a legislature might respond to the actions of a foreign court, such as the British and

53 See Turley, 'Dualistic Values in the Age of International Legisprudence', 44 *Hastings Law Journal* (1993) 185, 243-245 (arguing for the elimination of the presumption against extraterritoriality to prevent exploitation of legislative processes by multinational rent-seekers).

54 To take one recent example, the executive and legislative branches of the European Community found themselves waiting in suspense to see how the US Supreme Court would rule on the validity of a unitary corporate tax imposed by the State of California. *US Supreme Court to Hear Unitary Tax Case*, 5 *Eurecom 1* (No. 10, November 1993) (reporting the decision of the US Supreme Court to grant certiorari in *Barclays Bank Plc v. Franchise Tax Board of California* in accordance with 'EC and UK hopes, and disagreeing with the Clinton Administration').

55 *In the Matter of: Oil Spill by the Amoco Cadiz Off the Coast of France on March 16, 1978*, 954 F.2d 1279, 1312-1313 (7th Cir. 1990) (per curiam).

Australian legislatures did in enacting 'clawback' statutes to blunt US courts' extraterritorial application of US antitrust laws.[56] Finally, legislatures can pass resolutions requiring their executives to take a particular position in negotiations with foreign executives.

All of these interactions are sharply at variance with the classical 'billiard ball' image of inter-State relations. Each of the governmental institutions involved acts with a degree of autonomy determined as much by its specific function with regard to individuals and groups in domestic and transnational society as by its State allegiance. Moreover, each of these institutions acknowledges the autonomous functioning of counterpart and complementary functions. As discussed in Part V, the result challenges our conception of State sovereignty itself.

C. The Law of Inter-State Relations

The third level of law in a world of liberal States is the law governing inter-State relations, the traditional province of public international law. This body of law includes inter-governmental agreements, customary international law, and the law of international institutions. Liberal international relations theory combined with an assumption of liberal States generates insights and predictions in all three areas. The discussion here, however, will focus only on inter-governmental agreements.

Assuming a world of liberal States leads to predictions about the origins, nature, incidence, negotiation and enforcement of such agreements. The baseline assumption is that governments will interact with one another within a web of individual and group contacts in transnational civil society. This larger context will affect inter-governmental agreements in a variety of ways. For instance, the plethora of individual and group transactions will obviate the need for some kinds of agreements altogether, such as treaties providing for cultural and educational exchanges and certain kinds of economic assistance. On the other hand, a need for national regulation is likely quickly to become a need for transnational regulation. In addition, the negotiators to all inter-governmental agreements in this world will be responsible to national legislatures, which themselves must be responsive to domestic and transnational group pressure. Finally, all States parties to all inter-governmental agreements will have well-functioning domestic legal systems, with national courts accustomed to laying down the law.

1. Origins of Inter-Governmental Agreements among Liberal States

Regarding the origins of inter-governmental agreements, imagine an idealized spectrum running from a world composed only of non-liberal States on one end and only of liberal States on the other. In a world only of non-liberal States, the initiative

56 See G. Born, D. Westin, *International Civil Litigation in US Courts* (2d. ed., 1992) 600-603 for a discussion of various foreign responses to extraterritorial application of US antitrust laws.

for inter-State transactions should come from State actors, on the simplified assumption that they control all important aspects of the polity, economy and society.[57] In the middle of the spectrum are relations between liberal States and non-liberal States, in which individual and group actors within the liberal State might push for inter-governmental agreements to foster their interests with respect to the non-liberal State. Such interests might include family reunification and visitation, communications of various sorts, humanitarian aid, and targeted economic assistance. Individuals and groups in the non-liberal State might also encourage economic agreements with the non-liberal State designed to encourage that State to liberalize its economy so as to create opportunities for foreign investors and traders. Finally, at the far end of the spectrum, we would expect a dense network of individual and group activity. These actors do not require State intervention to spur or substitute for transnational activity, but only to regularize and channel it. Most agreements would be designed to address specific issues or problems arising out of ongoing activity.

Another important category of inter-governmental agreements among two or more liberal States should flow from transnational regulatory activity. Domestic regulators must follow the actors they seek to regulate. The assumption of a dense transnational society assumes that regulated activities will spill over borders, requiring regulators to interact with their foreign counterparts. Both conflict and informal cooperation are likely to result. In the case of regulatory conflict, an inter-governmental agreement may be necessary to coordinate or harmonize regulatory action. Where a range of informal cooperative practices develop, an agreement may be useful to institutionalize them as the basis for further cooperation.

In all cases involving liberal States, however, a fairly lengthy period of relatively decentralized transgovernmental interaction is likely to precede and shape the agreement. The parties involved can count on long-term, relatively stable relationships, and at least a presumption of trust and good faith. Counterpart agencies may proceed by trial and error as they grope for common formulae. Less cooperatively, multiple branches of government may become involved across boundaries, as in a confrontation between a court in one nation and the executive branch of another, or a stand-off between two legislatures. Even as the rhetoric heats up, however, all parties are likely to assume that the pulling and hauling will ultimately result in a stable informal equilibrium or a negotiated solution. Where an inter-governmental agreement results, it will be not the result of a deliberate 'foreign' policy decision, but rather of the evolution, coordination or harmonization of pre-existing domestic policy.

57 'Non-liberal' State here refers to a State that has neither a representative government nor a market economy.

2. Form of Agreements

Agreements among liberal States could be expected to come in three broad generic types. First are specific problem-solving agreements, in which a large number of private individual and group actors already have an interest. Such agreements are likely to be detailed and direct, intended either for direct judicial enforcement or immediate incorporation into domestic implementing legislation. Their specific provisions will probably be shaped in the halls of private firms as much as at the inter-State negotiating table, as lobbying groups pressure their respective governments to support particular interests.

Second are relatively vague and general agreements designed primarily to create a framework for further transgovernmental cooperation. The generality of such agreements is, paradoxically, an indicator of trust and cooperation. Increased interaction breeds mutual confidence, allowing further interaction to take place on the basis of imprecise and open-ended agreements, to be filled in in good faith. In some cases a formal and relatively specific agreement will help spark the process of regulatory cooperation, which will then develop in ways that will outstrip the agreement and make the specified procedures seem slow and cumbersome. Extradition treaties, for instance, typically concluded primarily between States confident of the quality of each other's judicial systems, were originally intended to create the possibility of rendition of fugitives where no such possibility previously existed. Over time, however, they have come to co-exist with a plethora of informal procedures. The initial agreement thus provides an umbrella for multiple modes of informal cooperation in the shadow of the treaty. At the same time, each renegotiation of the treaty becomes progressively more general in form, moving from a specification of crimes for which fugitives could be extradited to a general 'criminality' clause, assuming that any crime in one State would be recognized in the other.[58] Underlying such an evolution is an assumption of steadily increasing domestic convergence, and growing trust.

Another example, although with a different genesis, is the US-EC Memorandum of Understanding on Antitrust Enforcement. Here the intergovernmental agreement was the culmination of a long-simmering inter-governmental conflict, spurred by private actors. It is nevertheless very general in form, leaving it to the government agencies involved to fashion their own modes of working together. A similar example in the security field is the North Atlantic Treaty, the founding document of NATO.[59] The relatively few and sparse phrases of its founding treaty provided the framework for decades of effective cooperation.

A third category of agreements among liberal States are not actually agreements at all, but rather model codes designed to spur harmonization through convergence

58 See generally, M.C. Bassiouni, *International Extradition: United States Law and Practice* (1987) 329-333 (noting that the 'contemporary trend in extradition treaties is to designate extraditable offenses' purely on the basis that the penalty applied in both States meets 'an agreed degree of severity').

59 North Atlantic Treaty, 4 April 1949, 63 Stat. 2241, TIAS No. 1964, 401 UNTS 75.

toward a common focal point. Assuming States organized along similar economic and political lines, we could expect a variety of regulatory means adopted to achieve broadly similar aims. The resulting conflicts and contradictions would make all States worse off, notwithstanding their common goals. Such difficulties should once again be perceived by national regulators working informally with one another. Rather than a formal inter-governmental agreement, however, many such problems can be solved by decentralized harmonization, a process by which each State chooses independently to conform its domestic law to a model promulgated by a neutral third party, such as the OECD. This model is much closer to the 'model codes' promulgated for adoption by the States of the United States than to formal international agreements.

3. Negotiating Agreements

Much of the above analysis dissolves the traditional model of States negotiating agreements as unitary actors seeking to secure exogenous preferences through arms-length bargaining, substituting instead the image of communication among a network of national regulatory officials. Yet even where the more traditional model holds, negotiations among liberal States should be more likely to conform to Robert Putnam's 'two-level game' model than negotiations between liberal and non-liberal States.[60] Because each liberal State is relatively transparent and porous concerning its domestic political processes, legislative involvement will become increasingly important at the international level. Each treaty party should thus become increasingly familiar with its partners' domestic constraints; many should seek directly to influence each other's domestic legislative process. Members of the United States Congress have often been included in treaty delegations; in the Uruguay Round of the GATT negotiators for a number of States were in direct contact with US senators back in Washington.

Conversely, the host of political constraints on national executives in liberal States is likely to cast a favourable light on international agreements as a way of accomplishing goals through an international mechanism that, domestically, would be politically impossible. National executives, for instance, can use the arena of an international regime to achieve objectives that they can then sell to their domestic constituencies as internationally necessary, or as a disagreeable but indispensable part of an otherwise desirable international agreement. Challenges can always be deflected in part by the cloak of special executive expertise in foreign affairs and appeals to the need for a unified national voice in dealings with other nations. Over time, the force of these appeals should diminish in a world of entirely liberal States, in part because the assurance of peace blunts the spectre of war lurking in the background of such traditional executive arguments. Arguments for a unified

60 Putnam, 'Diplomacy and Domestic Politics', 42 *International Organization* (1988) 427; P.B. Evans *et al.* (eds), *Double-Edged Diplomacy: International Bargaining and Domestic Politics* (1993).

national position will remain, but will have less resonance in the face of divergent domestic interests and transnational coalitions of domestic interest groups.

4. Enforcing Agreements

Agreements concluded among liberal States are more likely to be concluded in an atmosphere of mutual trust, a precondition that will facilitate any kind of enforcement. In particular, however, the assumptions that these are agreements reached with the participation of a network of individuals and groups in the participating States, and that these States are committed to the rule of law enforced by national judiciaries should lead to more 'vertical' enforcement through domestic courts. This mode of enforcement contrasts with the traditional 'horizontal' mode involving State responsibility, reciprocity, and countermeasures.

Enforcement through the mechanism of a neutral tribunal backed by coercive force is an optimal way to ensure compliance with any agreement, whether between individuals or States. It is the mode of dispute resolution established where possible by societies the world over.[61] A system of horizontal counter-measures, by contrast, inevitably entails each party being judge in its own case, with the attendant illegitimacy of the resulting determination. International lawyers have long recognized the inferiority of this system, and thus have sought to rely on a general norm of enforcement of international obligations through domestic courts.[62] Yet horizontal enforcement remains prevalent. Why? One reason is that absent a minimum homogeneity of States, States cannot be certain that a treaty partner has the kind of domestic judicial system capable of or willing to enforce an international agreement against another branch of government.[63] Indeed, the risk averse position for all States in such a system is to assume that its treaty partners are subject to no domestic constraints.

The assumption of liberal States ameliorates these concerns in a number of ways. First, liberal States are States with governments of limited powers, powers limited by law enforced by courts. Such governments are thus accustomed to the application of a legal instrument to curtail asserted political power.[64] Second, the governments of liberal States are governments structured around a separation of powers. The courts of liberal States are thus governed by a constitution that specifies that they sit as a branch independent of the Executive. Third, liberal States

61 Martin Shapiro elegantly lays out the logic of such a system in his multi-country analysis of courts. M. Shapiro, *Courts: A Comparative and Political Analysis* (1981).

62 See Wyatt, 'New Legal Order, or Old?', 7 *EL Rev.* (1982) 147.

63 Based on this model, we should expect to find that tax treaties, extradition treaties and other types of treaties specifically negotiated on a *bilateral* basis are much more likely to be judicially enforceable than multilateral treaties. Each Member State could size up the domestic judicial system of its treaty partner, and design a mechanism of treaty enforcement accordingly.

64 Commenting on the power of the European Court of Justice's successful attempt to enlist national courts in the enforcement of the Treaty of Rome, Joseph Weiler writes: 'A state, in our Western democracies, cannot disobey its own courts'. Weiler, 'The Transformation of Europe', 100 *Yale Law Journal* (1991) 2403, 2421.

guarantee a host of individual rights against the government, to be enforced through legal action. Thus it is possible to imagine individuals as monitors of government compliance with agreed rules, whether arrived at through a domestic or an international legislative process. Fourth is a commitment to transparency as a key cog in the mechanism of liberal government. Treaty partners can thus be reassured that it will be relatively easy to monitor each other's political decisions. Fifth, liberal States are more likely to be monist than dualist, as evidenced by international 'override' provisions in domestic constitutions that mandate the supremacy of international over domestic law. These provisions are much more common in the constitutions of liberal States.[65]

In short, the domestic constraints on liberal governments are more likely to create the conditions in which States entering into an international agreement have reason to believe that their co-parties are equally constrained by domestic courts, such that domestic judicial enforcement would not handicap one party significantly more than another. If all States are similarly situated regarding this mode of enforcement, they will be prepared to acknowledge its relative efficiency in holding all parties to their initial bargain. Further, to the extent that the agreements concluded contain provisions of direct benefit to individuals and groups in circumstances in which the contents of such agreements are relatively well-publicized, private parties will have an incentive to use domestic courts to enforce these agreements. Indeed, in such circumstances, given representative legislatures, liberal governments may well need to hold out the prospect of domestic judicial enforcement to secure domestic ratification of the agreement.

Domestic judicial enforcement of international agreements can come in several modes. First is the requirement of domestic implementing legislation for an international agreement; legislation that will then be enforced by domestic courts as domestic law. The difficulty is monitoring comformity of the implementing legislation with the international agreement. Second is the self-executing treaty, in which the international agreement operates directly as law for domestic courts. Here the problem is likely to be variations in interpretation and application of the treaty provisions. In both these cases the possibility of having States be judge in their own cases remains, on the assumption that even an independent court is likely to be swayed more by the position of its executive versus that of a foreign executive. Thus a third mode of enforcement is to add an international tribunal to ensure impartiality and uniformity by deciding all questions of treaty law arising in cases brought to national courts that involve issues both of national law and treaty law. This type of system will give rise to a 'vertical dialogue' between national courts and the supranational court. Opportunities for this dialogue will be facilitated where members of the supranational tribunal are drawn from the ranks of well-respected domestic lawyers, such that the legitimacy and respect accorded members of the

65 See Stein, 'International Law in Internal Law: Toward Internationalization of Central-Eastern European Constitutions?', 88 *AJIL* (1994) 427, 428; Cassese, 'Modern Constitutions and International Law', 192 *RdC* (1985-II) 331, 352.

domestic bar in each country is transferred to the international tribunal. Finally, such a dialogue can be facilitated on a non-binding basis, in which domestic courts are instructed to 'take account' of the judgments of a supranational tribunal.

Vertical enforcement through domestic courts is not the only effective means of ensuring compliance with international agreements. It is also possible to bypass domestic courts altogether and rely on legislatures to take account of the judgments of a supranational tribunal. Yet this mechanism works best when embedded in domestic and transnational society, by empowering individuals and groups to bring cases in the first instance so that they can monitor and publicize the results as a means of pressuring domestic legislatures. Alternatively, a group of States can adopt procedural rules making the application of horizontal counter-measures dependent on the decision of a neutral third-party tribunal. Finally, a wide range of compliance measures and mechanisms exist that rely primarily on diplomatic suasion and informal dispute resolution. Nevertheless, the proposition here is that where available, vertical enforcement is the most secure means of assuring compliance with international agreements. And that means is most likely to be available in a community of liberal States.

V. The Disaggregation of Sovereignty

If the model of law among liberal States developed here holds as a positive model, it will present international lawyers with a new set of normative challenges. We will have to redefine existing principles of international law and develop new principles to govern actors and processes that remain obscured when viewed through the lenses developed by Realist international relations theory and traditional international law to view the international system. The *Grundnorm* of sovereignty is a natural point of departure for this normative project. I offer here some preliminary thoughts on how sovereignty might be redefined as a foundational norm in a world of liberal States.

According to the analysis above, a world of liberal States would be a world of disaggregated States. It would be a world with the following attributes:

- 'the State' is composed of multiple centres of political authority – legislative, administrative, executive, and judicial;
- each of these institutions operates in a dual regulatory and representative capacity with respect to individuals and groups in domestic society. Each is defined in terms of a specific set of functions it performs for the members of domestic society, a set of functions that structures its interaction with its coordinate branches as co-representatives of 'the people'.[66] At the same time,

66 Although it may seem odd to speak of courts 'representing' the individuals who appear before them in private disputes, a judge's conception of her duty to resolve such disputes as they are presented before her also reflects a wider conception of the need to represent the interests of an entire class of potential litigants

each of these institutions represents a facet of the exercise of State power – making, implementing, and enforcing regulations against individuals on behalf of the whole;
- the proliferation of transnational economic and social transactions creates links between each of these institutions and individuals and groups in transnational society. The development of links between individuals and groups in transnational society with the political institutions of multiple States in turn generates contacts among these institutions, either directly or indirectly;
- interactions among counterpart or coordinate institutions from different States – court to court, court to legislature, legislature to legislature, executive to court – are shaped by both an awareness of a common or complementary function transcending a particular national identity, and a simultaneous recognition of an obligation to defend and promote the interests of a particular subset of individuals and groups in transnational society.

The State is disaggregated, but remains the State: a constellation of political institutions bound together by territory, text, history and culture. What then of sovereignty? If the State is disaggregated as a positive matter, can sovereignty continue to attach to a unitary State as a normative principle designed to constitute that State as a unitary entity?

A world of liberal States could be conceptualized as a transnational polity. The organizing principle of this polity would mirror the organizing principle of liberal States: the limitation of State power by establishing multiple institutions designed both to overlap and complement one another. The resulting system of 'checks and balances' – competition and coordination, division and duplication – creates sufficient friction to curb the abuse of power. The result, to borrow a term coined by political theorist Daniel Deudney, is a 'negarchy', a liberal political order between anarchy and hierarchy in which power is checked horizontally rather than vertically.[67] These divisions and deliberately created frictions are further designed to create space for individuals and groups to interact with and influence State institutions, rather than being passive subjects of their rule.

Transposed to a transnational plane, the principle of negarchy would require the vigorous interaction of the governmental institutions of participating States with one another in as many combinations as possible. Assuming that 'sovereignty' is the principle that both constitutes States and defines their rights and duties in the international system consistent with an overarching principle of international order, the task is then to redefine sovereignty to conform to the ordering principle of negarchy. In practice, the norm of sovereignty would have to be constructed so as to constitute and protect the political institutions of liberal States in carrying out their individual functions and in checking and balancing one another.

The first element of such a redefined norm of sovereignty might thus be one of non-interference with basic legislative, judicial, and executive functions on the part

67 Deudney, 'The Philadelphian System: Sovereignty, Arms Control, and the Balance of Power in the American States-Union, circa 1781-1861', 49 *International Organization* (forthcoming 1995).

of the component institutions of each State in the system. Each institution could assert sovereignty both as a constitutive norm and as a shield to protect its ability to represent and regulate a subset of individuals and groups in transnational society – the individuals and groups principally associated with its State. If the flip side of the constitutive norm of sovereign Statehood is currently non-intervention in matters within a State's domestic jurisdiction, parallel norms of legislative, judicial, and executive sovereignty in a world of liberal States would dictate non-interference with the basic provision of legislative, judicial, and executive functions for the nationals or territorial residents of a particular State. Viewed from a transnational perspective, this norm of non-intervention as attached to these component institutions would protect the integrity of each institution sufficient to allow it to check and balance its counterpart and complementary institutions.

The second element of a redefined norm of sovereignty would concern the interaction of these disaggregated State institutions with one another as centres of authority in a transnational polity. Such interaction should be structured to achieve two functions: the representation and regulation of particular subsets of individuals and groups in transnational society. Each institution would thus encapsulate the dual dynamic of State-society relations in liberal States, simultaneously standing for the autonomous power of the State and the delegated authority of the people. As such, each institution must have the capacity not only to engage with other institutions, but also to receive communication from and to respond to the concerns of individual and group actors. Each must have the capacity to represent as well as to regulate.

A more concrete expression of this second element could be a right of equal participation in transnational legislative, judicial, executive and administrative processes. Such a right would ground claims on the part of component State institutions to be recognized and taken account of by fellow institutions involved in the negotiation of an international agreement, the regulation of transnational conduct, or the resolution of a transnational dispute. These claims would in turn rest not on abstract conceptions of national power, but on the capacity to represent and regulate a particular subset of individuals and groups in transnational society. Competing claims would be resolved by assessing the relative capacity of these institutions to perform the asserted function and the legitimacy of the claimed representation.[68]

Abram and Antonia Chayes have recently written of 'the new sovereignty', arguing that full membership in the international community no longer means the prerogative of splendid isolation, but rather requires engagement in a network of multilateral commitments.[69] Much current writing on the 'transformation of sovereignty' adopts a passive voice, emphasizing the extent to which State borders

68 This new conception of sovereignty would exist side by side with more traditional conceptions, which are still accurate and important in relations between liberal and non-liberal States. Where a government controls its people absolutely, its 'sovereignty' is still largely unitary and subject to violation primarily by coercive intervention. Sovereignty here is constrained less by individuals and groups in transnational society than by other States or by international institutions.

69 Abram and Antonia Chayes, *The New Sovereignty* (forthcoming 1995).

have become permeable to forces beyond a particular government's control. The Chayes and Chayes conception, by contrast, redefines the active component of sovereignty in relation to increased mechanisms and systems of global governance. Sovereignty becomes the capacity to participate in an international regulatory process. The redefinition of sovereignty in a world of liberal States pushes this redefinition one step further, devolving it onto the component institutions of individual States and giving it substantive content with regard to the relationship between these institutions and individuals and groups in transnational society.

VI. Conclusion

The purpose of this essay has been to reimagine international law from the perspective of Liberal international relations theory in a hypothetical world of liberal States. It has identified the relevant bodies of law governing different actors in this system – rules governing the voluntary interactions of individuals and groups in transnational society, rules selected and applied by national courts and legislatures, and inter-State agreements. It has mapped the interactions of the relevant actors and sketched new ways to interpret the results of those interactions.

The point of departure for this exercise was the proposition that international lawyers must be more explicit about their underlying political science. The 17th and 18th century fathers of classical international law internalized deep assumptions about the incidence of war and peace and the nature of States. These scholars lived in a world in which war was endemic and domestic governance structures diverse; a world in which furthering the domestic consolidation of power under an all-powerful sovereign and simultaneously delimiting that power in the international sphere offered the most promising hope of reducing violent conflict in both spheres.[70] The founding principle of the Westphalian system – *cujus regio, ejus religio* (look only to the prince and no farther) – was a formula for peace. A prohibition on taking account of domestic differences among States thus converged with an argument about the foundations of international security.

This convergence forged an analytical synthesis between classical international law and Realist international relations theory. Yet within political science, Liberal theorists consistently and successfully have challenged Realist assumptions about the nature of the international system. Their alternative framework assumes that how States behave depends on how they are internally constituted. Empirical research within this framework further suggests a fundamental difference in the nature of relations among liberal States as compared to relations between liberal and non-liberal States. My aim has been to consider this research and its underlying assumptions seriously and to explore its implications for international law.

70 See E.F. Hinsley, *Sovereignty* (1986) Chap. 5.

Imagining a world of liberal States is not a purely hypothetical exercise. The principles and postulates of classical international law have long been subject to numerous exceptions and modifications that reflect departures from the underlying positive assumptions of unitary and functionally identical States. Contemporary human rights law, for instance, was founded on the recognition that domestic political conditions have consequences for international security. To the extent that the existing catalogue of fundamental human rights expands to include a right of 'democratic governance', a right Thomas Franck proposes based in part on empirical evidence of peace among liberal States, international law will take the first step toward an explicit distinction among States based on domestic regime-type.[71]

Further, the record of bloodshed in the 20th century challenges the 18th century paradigm of the sources of international and domestic conflict. In many cases, strife appears to result more from the abuse than the absence of sovereign power. Representative political institutions, the protection of minority rights, and the furtherance of group autonomy short of Statehood appear more likely to further long-term domestic and international peace than the raising of new Leviathans. At the same time, the realm of peace and relative prosperity is no longer a condominium of all-powerful princes but rather a domain of representative governments embedded in a dense network of transnational economic and social transactions. The perception of such seismic shifts, to the extent they hold, could lead to the adoption of a new model of the international system, normatively applicable to all States even if positively descriptive of only some. Alternatively, the values of universalism could be sacrificed to the realism of recognizing that States in the international system inhabit very different worlds.

The world of liberal States, as hypothesized here, is a world of individual self-regulation facilitated by States; of transnational regulation enacted and implemented by disaggregated political institutions – courts, legislatures, executives and administrative agencies – enmeshed in transnational society and interacting in multiple configurations across borders; of double-edged diplomacy and inter-governmental agreements vertically enforced through domestic courts. Such a world is neither a utopia nor a panacea. It poses new problems and normative challenges, requiring the extension of domestic principles and safeguards to transnational and international governance processes. It requires a rethinking of the relationship between public and private international law, a reconceptualization of the rules that can be said to serve international order.

71 Franck, 'The Emerging Right to Democratic Governance', 86 *AJIL* (1992) 46.

[9]

INTERNATIONAL INTEGRATION AND DEMOCRACY: NO LOVE AT FIRST SIGHT

*By Eric Stein**

In this essay I suggest a correlation between the integration level of an international institution and the public discourse[1] about the lack of democracy and legitimacy in the institution's structure and functioning. This discourse includes ideas for remedial action at both the national and international levels; it also becomes inevitably intertwined with other reform proposals that may call for an incremental or—particularly in the case of a more integrated organization—a radical restructuring. Having originated in the highly integrated European Community, the debate on the "democracy-legitimacy deficit" has reached other institutions, particularly the World Trade Organization (WTO) and the international financial bodies, and has become one component of the backlash rhetoric against "globalization."

I first provide a glimpse of the ongoing mutations in the national and international systems and in the idea and practice of democracy. I next discuss the basic concepts including the process of integration. I offer a list of normative-institutional and empirical-social attributes germane to international organizations at discrete levels of integration. I then focus on public discourse regarding the democracy-legitimacy deficit in these organizations, with specific attention to two global organizations (the World Health Organization [WHO] and the WTO) and two regional groupings (the North American Free Trade Agreement [NAFTA] and the European Union [EU]). I conclude with some general observations and note the suggestions for possible reform, both modest and ambitious, reaching the heart of the international system.

I. THE FRAMEWORK—AN OUTLINE

Changes in the National and International Systems: Impact on the Discourse

Two trends. First, by one count the number of intergovernmental organizations (IGOs) and regimes has increased from 123 in 1951 to 251 in 1999 (although the numbers vary according to the different criteria employed).[2] The solution of vital problems, such as

* Of the Board of Editors. I wish to acknowledge with gratitude the very useful comments of Steve Charnovitz and Professors Frederick M. Abbott, Alfred F. Conard, William J. Davey, Daniel Halberstam, Robert Howse, John H. Jackson, Harold K. Jacobson, Petros C. Mavroidis, Bruno Simma, Joel P. Trachtman, and Michel Waelbroeck. The reference section of the University of Michigan Law School Library provided invaluable bibliographic service. Noah S. Leavitt, a student at the University of Michigan Law School, edited the draft with great skill.

[1] I use the term "discourse" in this essay to comprise a broad spectrum of communications, such as statements by academics, practitioners, and authoritative and civic-society spokespersons, as well as normative texts, including judicial opinions.

[2] The editors of the authoritative *Yearbook of International Organizations* "assume that an organization is intergovernmental if it is established by signature of an agreement engendering obligations between governments." [1999/2000] 4 Y.B. INT'L ORGS. 547, 549–50. "Regimes" are defined broadly as "sets of implicit or explicit principles, norms, rules and decision-making procedures around which actors' expectations converge in a given issue area of international relations." ROBERT O. KEOHANE, AFTER HEGEMONY: COOPERATION AND DISCORD IN THE WORLD POLITICAL ECONOMY 57 (1984). 2 UNITED NATIONS: LAW, POLICIES AND PRACTICE 928 (rev. Eng. ed., Rüdiger Wolfrum ed., 1999) estimates the current number of IGOs at "around 300." A "huge proportion" of the new IGOs were created not by governments but by other IGOs; "traditional IGOs" established by treaties declined from 394 in 1982 to 339 in 1992, while the "emanations" from other IGOs increased from 669 to 808. *See* DAVID HELD, DEMOCRACY AND THE GLOBAL ORDER: FROM THE MODERN STATE TO COSMOPOLITAN GOVERNANCE 108 (1995)

national security, protection of basic human rights, international trade and economic development, the surge of migration, environmental protection, and cross-border criminality, has moved beyond the reach of individual states and has called for institutionalized commitment and cooperation on global and regional levels.[3]

Second, the idea and practice of democratic government has received widening acceptance, particularly in the 1990s. According to the most recent Freedom House survey, the number of "electoral" democracies increased from 69 in 1988–1989 to 120 in 1999–2000, although not all trends have been positive.[4] Taking into account this growing acceptance and the commitment of most states under UN covenants and other global and regional treaties, as well as the extensive practice of states fostering democracy abroad, some commentators have argued that the rights to free elections and participation in public affairs are becoming—or have already become—part of the cluster of basic rights protected by general international law.[5]

The tension. These two trends, the internationalization of decision making in IGOs and the expansion of democracy, have led to a tension that underlies discourse on the democracy-legitimacy deficit in national and international arenas.

For one thing, internationalization "almost invariably means a loss of democracy."[6] A new level of normative activity superimposed on national democratic systems makes citizen participation more remote, and parliamentary control over the executive, notoriously loose in foreign affairs matters, becomes even less effective. This result can clearly be observed in parliamentary democracies and, perhaps less markedly, also in presidential systems where the chief executive, elected directly by the people, claims legitimacy independently of the parliament.[7] The problem becomes even more palpable when a member state is outvoted

(citing Krasner and others); Cheryl Shanks, Harold K. Jacobson, & Jeffrey H. Kaplan, *Inertia and Change in the Constellation of International Governmental Organizations, 1981–1992,* 50 INT'L ORG. 593, 594 (1996).

[3] On "internationalization" or "globalization" generally, see JEFFREY I. ANDERSON, REGIONAL INTEGRATION AND DEMOCRACY: EXPANDING ON THE EUROPEAN EXPERIENCE 5 (1999); DEIRDRE CURTIN, POSTNATIONAL DEMOCRACY: THE EUROPEAN UNION IN SEARCH OF POLITICAL PHILOSOPHY (1997); HELD, *supra* note 2; Boutros Boutros-Ghali, *Democracy: A Newly Recognized Imperative,* 1 GLOBAL GOVERNANCE 3 (1995); Robert O. Keohane, *International Relations and International Law,* 38 HARV. INT'L L.J. 487, 491–93 (1997).

[4] In 2000, 40.7% of the world's people were said to be living in "free societies" (the highest percentage in the history of the survey); 23.8% were "partly free" and 35.5% "not free." Freedom House, *Freedom in the World: Annual Survey of Political Rights and Civil Liberties 2000–2001,* Press Release (Dec. 20, 2000), *at* <http://freedomhouse.org/research/freeworld/2001>. *But see* Fareed Zakaria, *The Rise of Illiberal Democracies,* FOREIGN AFF. Nov./Dec. 1997, at 22. *See generally* THE RULE OF LAW AND THE UNDERPRIVILEGED IN LATIN AMERICA (Juan E. Méndez, Guillermo O'Donnell, & Paulo Sérgio Pinkeiro eds., 1999). On the effort to draw a sharp distinction between "liberal" and "illiberal" regimes' behavior in the international arena, see the exchange between Anne-Marie Slaughter and José E. Alvarez, *A Liberal Theory of International Law,* 94 ASIL PROC. 240 (2000). *See also* Harold H. Koh, *Why Nations Obey International Law,* 106 YALE L.J. 2599, 2650 (1995).

[5] For instance, more than a hundred states are party to the International Covenant on Civil and Political Rights, Dec. 16, 1966, Art. 25, 999 UNTS 171, which guarantees nondiscrimination, the right to free elections, and participation in public affairs. Gregory H. Fox, *The Right to Political Participation in International Law,* 17 YALE J. INT'L L. 539 (1992); Thomas M. Franck, *The Emerging Right to Democratic Governance,* 86 AJIL 46 (1992); *see also* Stephan Hobe, *Die Zukunft des Völkerrechts im Zeitalter der Globalisierung,* 37 ARCHIV DES VÖLKERRECHTS 253, 274 (1999) (noting the Moscow meeting of the Conference on Security and Co-operation in Europe, Oct. 3, 1991, and the Badinter Commission). On European regional law, see *infra* part V.

[6] Ralf Dahrendorf, *The Third Way and Liberty: An Authoritarian Streak in Europe's New Center,* FOREIGN AFF., Sept./Oct. 1999, at 13, 16; *see also* DIMITRIS N. CHRYSSOCHOOU, DEMOCRACY IN THE EUROPEAN UNION, pt. III, at 107 (1998); Robert O. Keohane, *International Institutions: Can Interdependence Work?* FOREIGN POL'Y, Spring 1998, at 82, 92; James N. Rosenau, *Governance and Democracy in a Globalizing World, in* RE-IMAGINING POLITICAL COMMUNITY: STUDIES IN COSMOPOLITAN DEMOCRACY 28 (Daniele Archibugi, David Held, & Martin Köhler eds., 1998) [hereinafter RE-IMAGINING]. Paradoxically, in the operational sense, the looser the parliamentary control over the executive in foreign affairs, the easier it is for the state to participate in IGOs.

[7] On the "neo-Brickerite" criticism of international institutions, see Thomas M. Franck, *Notes from the President,* ASIL NEWSL., Jan.–Feb. 1999, at 4. *See also* Detlev F. Vagts, *International Agreements, the Senate and the Constitution,* 36 COLUM. J. TRANSNAT'L L. 143, 153–54 (1997). *But see* Jack Kemp & Fred L. Smith, Jr., *Beware of the Kyoto Compromise,* N.Y. TIMES, Jan. 13, 1999, at A25.

in an IGO organ or when the law of the IGO is enforced directly in the domestic legal order without the national parliament's imprimatur (i.e., it is "self-executing," has "direct effect"). Again, the IGOs themselves are considered "undemocratic" since they operate with little transparency or public and parliamentary scrutiny. They are seen as being governed by an elite group of national officials who are instructed by their respective executives, and by international secretariats whose staffs at times act independently of the top IGO management.[8]

In the last decade, a "third force" has emerged in the shape of proliferating nongovernmental organizations (NGOs), which are founded both on grassroots and transborder links and take full advantage of the new information technology. Depending on the criteria employed, the number of NGOs is said to have risen from 832 in 1951 to 5825 or (for "total types of NGOs") 43,958 in 1999.[9] Some view these groups as emanations of an embryonic "international civil society" and as a possible substitute for representative democracy. Others see them as self-elected elite advocates of special causes, unrepresentative of the general public and engaged in an unholy alliance with international bureaucrats and "sympathetic states," "a romance" of questionable legitimacy.[10] At any rate, NGOs are justly credited both with raising national and international awareness and with opening the IGOs to the scrutiny of public opinion. They have left a deep imprint on a number of significant UN acts.

A caveat is in order. There is no assurance that the two trends noted above will continue in a linear mode, as shown by the rise of "illiberal democracies."[11] Moreover, the disputed impact of liberalization of trade and investment on developing economies, the environment, health, workers' rights, and human rights generally, as well as constraints on states' social policies, has stood at the core of the backlash movement against internationalization and globalization.[12]

[8] On the GATT Secretariat, see MICHAEL J. TREBILCOCK & ROBERT HOWSE, THE REGULATION OF INTERNATIONAL TRADE 57–58 (2d ed. 1999); Paul B. Stephan, *Accountability and International Lawmaking: Rules, Rents and Legitimacy*, 17 NW. J. INT'L L. & BUS. 681 (1997).

[9] Y.B. INT'L ORGS., *supra* note 2, at 550. The criteria employed are described at 547–48.

[10] Kenneth Anderson, *The Ottawa Convention Banning Landmines, the Role of International Non-Governmental Organizations and the Idea of International Civil Society*, 11 EUR. J. INT'L L. 91, 95, 104 (2000); *see also* James C. Hathaway, *America, Defender of Democratic Legitimacy? id.* at 121, 125 (replying to Anderson). *See generally* Richard Falk, *The United Nations and Cosmopolitan Democracy: Bad Dream, Utopian Fantasy, Political Project, in* RE-IMAGINING, *supra* note 6, at 308, 321–28. For a skeptical view of the ability of NGOs to provide accountability in the European Union, see Beate Kohler-Koch, *Organized Interests in European Integration: The Evolution of a New Type of Governance, in* PARTICIPATION AND POLICY-MAKING IN THE EUROPEAN UNION 50, 54–56 (H. Wallace & A. R. Young eds., 1997).

[11] Fareed Zakaria, *supra* note 4, points to the rise of "illiberal democracies" from Peru to the Philippines, in which free elections without constitutional liberalism produce centralized regimes, erosion of liberty, ethnic competition, and domestic conflict. Similar tendencies appear in some of the transitional regimes in the states of the former Soviet Union. Ricardo Housman, the chief economist for Latin America at the International Bank for Development, cites an inadequate regulatory environment, corruption, and—among political problems in Latin America—fragmentation of parties, volatility in voting patterns, low levels of popular participation, election of governments by a minority of voters, lack of transparency, and lack of cohesion between executive and legislative branches. IBD AMÉRICA, May–June 2000, at 21.

[12] DANIEL J. ELAZAR, CONSTITUTIONALIZING GLOBALIZATION: THE POSTMODERN REVIVAL OF CONFEDERAL ARRANGEMENTS (1998); Kenneth W. Abbott, *"Economic" Issues and Political Participation: The Evolving Boundaries of International Federalism*, 18 CARDOZO L. REV. 971 (1996). In particular, see CURTIN, *supra* note 3, with a historical survey at 1–25. Matthew Paterson, *Overview: Interpreting Trends in Global Environmental Governance*, 75 INT'L AFF. 793 (1999), describes two "contradictory accounts": a common interest of states, multinationals, and international agencies, which have the goal of organized capital accumulation and development; and a myriad of locally organized, but transnational groups, social movements, and NGOs, mobilized to resist the states, multinationals, etc. *See also* Judith Miller, *Globalization Widens Rich-Poor Gap, U.N. Report Says*, N.Y. TIMES, July 13, 1999, at A8 (describing a report by the United Nations Development Programme urging that the "rules of globalization" should be rewritten to prevent the sixty countries that are worse off now than they were in 1980 from falling even further behind). Czech Republic President Václav Havel said that globalization is leading to the "reckless destruction of the planet," to the spread of a "civilization based on pseudo-values, the swelling of organized crime and terrorism, and a short-sighted form of market economy that abuses poorer countries." *Czech President Criticizes Globalization*, RADIO FREE EUROPE/RADIO LIBERTY [RFE/RL], NEWSLINE, Jan. 3, 2000, pt. II, at 3, *at* <http: // www.rferl.org/newsline/2000/01/030100.html>.

More changes in democracy, the states, and the international system. What is the "democracy" which, it is argued, is not properly safeguarded in the structure and working of the IGOs? The idea and practice of democratic government has evolved over time. Direct democracy like that in Athens, the city-states of the Renaissance, and the Swiss cantons became impractical and obsolete with the rise of large states. Democracy was saved by the invention of representative government, but an ancient Athenian would hardly accept it as "democratic." Today, a variety of modern democratic governments can be found in which the individual citizen's voice is heard in varying ways and degrees: the parliamentary and republican-presidential systems, often marked by consensual variants and elements of communitarianism and authoritarianism.[13]

Modern democracy has developed within the nation-state and—because of the weakness of international institutions—still relies primarily on the state for its protection. In a state-based international system, sovereignty has served as a means of legitimating the distribution of power both within and among states. The state, however, has changed greatly from its original post-Westphalian form. Although it remains a privileged actor, the state's traditional "external sovereignty" has been eroded by the growing internationalization of decision making I described earlier, giving rise to new actors, including the IGOs and even individuals and legal persons (companies) with legal rights under the new international and regional human rights systems. At the same time, the state's "internal sovereignty" is undermined by public and private networks often extending across national frontiers. Thus, some argue that representative democracy no longer exists, that it has been replaced by the polyarchy of bureaucracy and organized interests in an administrative state, with massive official bodies, "independent" agencies, and central banks.[14]

The participants in the discourse naturally look to national democratic systems as models for an "international" or "cosmopolitan" democracy. Yet questions arise whether, particularly in light of the developments within modern democracies, the democratic deficit is a real issue and if so, whether representative democracy is a suitable model for international structures that will not impair their goals and efficiency. If it is not, what are the alternative, idiosyncratic patterns that could fill the democracy-legitimacy gap?[15] At this stage of the global, and even regionally defined, societies, can democracy—and for that matter fair social policy and interest mediation as well—be realized only within the state? Finally, if integration is inherently hostile to democracy, should any move toward the integration of states be made more difficult or, where private rights are affected, should it stop altogether?[16]

At the origin of the discourse are the clashing trends in domestic and international arenas and a genuine (and often not so genuine) concern for democratic values. From the viewpoint of domestic law, the issues raised concern limitations in national constitutions on the transfer of public power to international institutions; while from the international perspec-

[13] ROBERT A. DAHL, ON DEMOCRACY (1998); DAVID HELD, MODELS OF DEMOCRACY (1987); AREND LIJPHART, DEMOCRACIES: PATTERNS OF MAJORITARIAN AND CONSENSUS GOVERNMENT IN TWENTY-ONE COUNTRIES (1984); Derk Bienen, Volker Rittenberger, & Wolfgang Wagner, *Democracy in the United Nations System: Cosmopolitan and Communitarian Principles*, *in* RE-IMAGINING, *supra* note 6, at 291–92; Susan Marks, Democracy and International Governance 2 (unpublished manuscript, on file with author). For an interesting discussion of alternative models to representative democracy, "republican and institutional balance," and the Schumpeterian competitive elite model, see P. P. Craig, *Democracy and Rule-Making Within the EC: An Empirical and Normative Assessment*, 3 EUR. L.J. 105, 113–16 (1997).

[14] J. M. GUÉHENNO, LA FIN DE LA DÉMOCRATIE (1993). The problem of democratic control over such agencies has already arisen in a regional context: namely, the Central Bank in the European Union. It is argued, however, that these agencies can be made accountable to political institutions both *ex ante* and *ex post*. Conversation with Petros C. Mavroidis (Oct. 12, 2000).

[15] *See generally* Bienen, Rittenberger, & Wagner, *supra* note 13, at 287–93.

[16] Stephan, *supra* note 8, at 721, 734–35. There is a need for a "third transformation" of the definition of democracy. "[I]t is no longer possible for democratic states to be fully democratic in a non-democratic international system." Bienen, Rittenberger, & Wagner, *supra* note 13, at 288.

tive, the structure and working of a given IGO is the subject of criticism. The "de-parliamentization" of political processes in the member states combined with lack of democracy in IGOs' lawmaking is said to accentuate the progressive democracy-legitimacy deficit.[17] The intensity of the argument depends, I suggest, on the scope of the competence transferred to an IGO and the structure and impact of its institutions, that is, on the "level of its integration" as I explain in part IV below. Needless to say, little or none of this debate is waged within member states with authoritarian or Communist regimes, but it may flourish in the clandestine opposition.

Major concepts identified. Within the confines of this essay, I can do no more than offer some operational guides to the many-splendored basic concepts with which I deal.[18] As for *democracy*, I referred earlier to the minimalist scheme evolving in international law.[19] A modern liberal democratic state, however, requires not only free elections and majority rule but also constitutionalism (including the rule of law, protection of basic rights, and a measure of separation of powers between institutions), a space free of public power for individual and group action (civil society), and a free market sector. So-called participatory democracy, on the other hand, postulates open public debate in search of a consensus and includes access for individuals and groups to all levels of public institutions.[20] *Rule of law* is commonly defined in the procedural terms of a well-ordered legal system under an independent judiciary.[21] Although it is a source of legitimacy, the rule of law "is not self-sufficient . . . [without] institutions of governance that are a direct expression of democratic self-determination."[22] *Transparency* entails openness of proceedings and access to official documents. It supports democracy by facilitating access to information that enables citizens to participate in public life, hold public authority accountable to public opinion, counter "a capture" of public institutions by special interest groups, enhance citizens' confidence in

[17] Helmut Steinberger, *Der Verfassungsstaat als Glied einer europäischen Gemeinschaft*, 50 VERÖFFENTLICHUNGEN DER VEREINIGUNG DER DEUTSCHEN STAATSRECHTSLEHRER 9, 39 (1991) (report with reference to the European Union).

[18] *See* CURTIN, *supra* note 3, at 18–27.

[19] *See supra* text at note 5. Jon Elster, *Introduction* to CONSTITUTIONALISM AND DEMOCRACY 1 (Jon Elster & Rune Slagstad eds., 1998), offers the basic definition of democracy as "simple majority rule, based on the principle, 'One person one vote.' "

[20] See definitions in LIJPHART, *supra* note 13. *See also* CURTIN, *supra* note 3; ROBERT A. DAHL, DEMOCRACY AND ITS CRITICS (1989); ROBERT A. DAHL, ON DEMOCRACY (1998); DEMOCRATIZATION (David Potter, David Goldblatt, Margaret Kiloh, & Paul Lewis eds., 1997); DAVID HELD, MODELS OF DEMOCRACY (1987); James Crawford & Susan Marks, *The Global Democracy Deficit*, *in* RE-IMAGINING, *supra* note 6, at 72, 81 (noting a definition of representative democracy by the Inter-American Commission of Human Rights); Eric Stein, *Reflections on Democracy in the European Union*, *in* NEW DIRECTIONS IN INTERNATIONAL LAW: ESSAYS IN HONOR OF JOHN H. JACKSON 3 (Marco C.E.J. Bronckers & Reinhard Quick eds., 2000). According to Susan Marks, democracy is

> an *essentially* contested concept. In no setting is the meaning of democracy a technical issue, on which a scholar might hope authoritatively to pronounce. Rather, the significance attached to "rule by the people" is always and everywhere a political struggle, with winners and losers and exceptionally high stakes. It follows that democracy is defined and redefined not through scholarly *fiat*, but through the interplay of social forces.

Marks, *supra* note 13, at 30 (footnote omitted). On civic republican democracy, see Joanne Scott, *Law, Legitimacy and EC Governance: Prospects for Partnership*, 36 J. COMMON MKT. STUD. 175, 176–78 (1998) (citing Epstein, Pettit, Young, Selznick, and Sunstein). *See also* Craig, *supra* note 13.

[21] According to Philip Soper, the rule of law includes

> the largely formal or procedural properties of a well-ordered legal system. . . . : a prohibition of arbitrary power (the lawgiver is also subject to the laws); laws that are general, prospective, clear, and consistent (capable of guiding conduct); and tribunals (courts) that are reasonably accessible and fairly structured to hear and determine legal claims. Contemporary discussions of the rule of law focus on two major questions: (1) to what extent is conformity to the rule of law essential to the very idea of a legal system; and (2) what is the connection between the rule of law and the substantive moral value of a legal system?

THE CAMBRIDGE DICTIONARY OF PHILOSOPHY 699 (Robert Audi gen. ed., 1995).

[22] Robert Howse & Kalypso Nicolaidis, *Legitimacy and Global Governance: Why Constitutionalizing the WTO Is a Step Too Far*, *in* EFFICIENCY, EQUITY AND GOVERNANCE: THE MULTILATERAL TRADING SYSTEM AT THE MILLENNIUM (Pierre Sauvé & Arvind Subramanian eds., forthcoming) (manuscript at 25).

public authority, and improve the performance of public officials.[23] Democracy confers *legitimacy* on a system of governance. Claims of legitimacy, in the normative-institutional sense, are based on a system of determined rules administered by an "independent" expert body, or, in the empirical-social sense, on the acceptance of the citizens.[24]

Integration: a process. Karl Deutsch defined integration as a process of transforming "previously separate units into components of a coherent system."[25] Although this definition was drawn from the European experience, I do not read it as applicable only to the higher levels of integration. With this interpretation, the definition in its simplicity and comprehensiveness serves my design.[26]

I suggest that the level of integration of an international organization or regime is determined by two groups of factors:[27]

Normative-institutional

(1) the field (sector), scope of competence, and resources;

(2) the composition of organs (government-appointed representatives of states, appointed or elected individuals) and procedures (voting formula: positive or negative consensus, simple or qualified majority, required abstention, acceptance unless rejected);

(3) whether cooperative and non–rule directed: constituting a forum for exchange of information and views, studies, and assistance;

(4) whether rule oriented: authorized to propose rules and treaties, impose international obligations, and adopt rules without or with "direct effect" in member states' legal orders; and

(5) whether rule enforcing: providing reports on compliance, monitoring, publicity, dispute settlement (voluntary, obligatory), and adjudication by ad hoc or permanent tribunals.

Empirical-social

(1) the political, economic, and cultural impact of the measures adopted; and

(2) a level of common interest sufficient to overcome cultural differences between the component states, or a level of support or acquiescence by individual stakeholders and people in those states sufficient to uphold the transfer of national public power to a given international institution. States with the same or comparable political systems (democratic-undemocratic) are more likely to accept a higher level of integration than states with substantially different systems of governance. It is doubtful, however, that—even at a high level of integration—the existence of a single "people" must precede the

[23] Ronald B. Mitchell, *Sources of Transparency: Information Systems in International Regimes*, 42 INT'L STUD. Q. 109 (1998). The right to freedom of expression and *to receive and impart information* is guaranteed in Article 19 of the International Covenant on Civil and Political Rights, *supra* note 5, and Article 10 of the European Convention for the Protection of Human Rights and Fundamental Freedoms, Nov. 4, 1950, 213 UNTS 221.

[24] *See* THOMAS M. FRANCK, THE POWER OF LEGITIMACY AMONG NATIONS (1990); Thomas M. Franck, *Legitimacy in the International System*, 82 AJIL 705 (1988); José E. Alvarez, Book Review Essay, 24 N.Y.U. J. INT'L L. & POL. 199 (1991). Some human rights activists urge that undemocratic, oppressive regimes should be denied international recognition.

[25] KARL W. DEUTSCH, THE ANALYSIS OF INTERNATIONAL RELATIONS 198 (2d ed. 1978). "[T]he possibility for various internal decision processes [within an organization] makes the choice between integration and intergovernmentalism a choice along a continuum instead of a stark binary choice." *Id.* Another suggested scheme envisages four dimensions of integration: scope (range of issues), depth (extent of policy coordination and harmonization), institutionalization (decision making in organized, predictable way), and centralization. THE CHALLENGE OF INTEGRATION: EUROPE AND THE AMERICAS 5 (H. Peter Smith ed., 1993).

[26] For my purposes, I do not see the need to distinguish integration from "cooperation" on the basis of "intensity of relations between the participating states and the manner in which those relations are . . . managed" and the absence of intention "to impinge greatly on national sovereignty" since it remains under the control of states. BRIGID LAFFAN, INTEGRATION AND CO-OPERATION IN EUROPE 3 (1992). The yardstick appears uncertain and the intention to protect sovereignty may weaken in the process. *See generally* CHRYSSOCHOOU, *supra* note 6, at 6; Joel P. Trachtman, *The Theory of the Firm and the Theory of International Economic Organization: Toward Comparative Institutional Analysis*, 17 NW. J. INT'L L. & BUS. 470, 535 (1996/97).

[27] On the second group, the empirical-social group of factors, see J. H. H. WEILER, THE CONSTITUTION OF EUROPE—"DO THE NEW CLOTHES HAVE AN EMPEROR?" AND OTHER ESSAYS ON EUROPEAN INTEGRATION 84 (1999).

establishment of an international institution; such institution may advance, and even originate the process toward, a shared identity.[28]

Integration, marked by a significant transfer of national public powers, may reach a level high enough to speak appropriately about "constitutionalization" and a "constitutionalized" system. More often than not, these concepts are discussed with an eye on European integration. In this context a constitutionalized system may be defined, paraphrasing Joseph Weiler, as a legal order established by international treaties giving birth to an international organization that behaves as if its founding instrument were not a treaty governed by international law, but a constitutional charter governed by a form of constitutional law.[29]

An Experiment

Nobuo Kiriyama has placed six IGOs on an ascending line, indexing them according to the degree of "institutionalization" and "direction" toward closer institutionalization. He considered, however, only *selected* normative-institutional factors: dispute settlement mechanisms and procedures, "legislative organs" ("intergovernmental bodies"), secretariats, and their voting procedures and interrelationship. In this table, the Organisation for Economic Co-operation and Development (OECD) stands at the lowest level of institutionalization and direction, followed in ascending order by the North American Free Trade Agreement, the Association of Southeast Asian Nations (ASEAN), the World Trade Organization, and the North American Free Trade Agreement Chapter 19.[30] The European Union has attained the highest level. As interesting as the experiment may be, the omission of empirical-social factors, if nothing else, shows that any effort to rank IGOs in a hierarchical way is fraught with difficulties.[31] One may wonder, for instance, about placing the OECD at the bottom, particularly below ASEAN. Early in its existence, the OECD adopted by consensus various codes that legally bind its members, including the Code of Liberalization of Capital Movements, which is still of considerable importance. Its secretariat—in addition to undertaking wide-ranging studies—has established its authority to propose sometimes far-reaching conclusions and measures, including draft international treaties (such as the 1997 Convention on Combating Bribery of Foreign Public Officials), and to criticize policies of its members, a range of authority not wielded for instance by the director-general of the WTO. The OECD has had its failures (the proposed Multilateral Investment Agreement), but its voice represents 85 percent of world trade and 90 percent of world foreign investment, although its limited membership serves as both an advantage and a handicap in terms of its legitimacy.[32] ASEAN, on the other hand, a much smaller group, is long on ambitious design but short on accomplishment, if one considers additional normative-institutional and empirical-social factors. Riven by serious disputes among its members, this IGO has been unable to agree on sectors of the mandated liberalization and has failed to respond to the recent monetary crisis in the region. As a result, questions have been raised about "the very idea" of the organization.[33]

[28] *See infra* text at notes 203–07.

[29] WEILER, *supra* note 27, at 221.

[30] *See infra* text at note 120.

[31] Nobuo Kiriyama, *Institutional Evolution in Economic Integration: A Contribution to Comparative Institutional Analysis for International Economic Organization*, 19 U. PA. J. INT'L ECON. L. 53 (1998). James McCall Smith, *The Politics of Dispute Settlement Design: Explaining Legalism in Regional Trade Pacts*, 54 INT'L ORG. 137 (2000), provides an interesting study of some sixty regional IGOs that explores the relationships between the asymmetry of the economies of the members, the levels of integration, and "legalism" (judicialization). Focus is on formal procedures, not policy outcomes. The actual functioning of the IGOs is beyond the scope of the study. *Id.* at 172. *See also infra* text at notes 110–11.

[32] Conversation with an OECD staff member (fall 2000). *See generally* Convention on the Organization for Economic Cooperation and Development, Dec. 14, 1960, 12 UST 1728, 888 UNTS 179 (particularly Art. 5(a) authorizing binding decisions). Members may enter reservations and in some instances derogations regarding the codes. TREBILCOCK & HOWSE, *supra* note 8, at 277, 292.

[33] Zakaria Haji Ahmad & Baladas Ghoshal, *The Political Future of ASEAN After the Asian Crisis*, 75 INT'L AFF. 759 (1999).

II. The World Health Organization— A "Technical" Agency

The UN System

Most of the contemporary global IGOs originated in the halcyon days of the exuberant international institution building following World War II.[34] The "new world order," designed to replace the uncertain balance of power, autarchy, and protectionism of the 1930s, envisaged a global system of cooperation and standard setting on issues beyond the reach of individual states. It was to consist of "specialized agencies" of universal membership that would cover all major fields of human concern, including shipping, trade, health, labor, food supply, telecommunications, meteorology, development and finance, and education and culture. The United Nations would be the prime political, security, and coordinating body at the center, supported by major powers.[35]

The founders of the United Nations came from widely different systems of domestic governance. Not surprisingly, therefore, the word "democracy" appears nowhere in the UN Charter and democracy was not made a prerequisite for admission to the new structures.[36] Although the Charter provides for cooperation to advance basic human rights, it prohibits intervention into matters "essentially" within the domestic jurisdiction of states.[37] The UN Economic and Social Council is authorized to make arrangements for consultation with both national and international nongovernmental organizations—a Charter provision that has proved important in light of the proliferation of interest groups I mentioned earlier.[38] With this one exception, states were viewed as exclusive actors in the new institutions.[39] In contrast to the traditional realist theory, however, states were seen as pursuing not just power but also other goals, such as peace, stability, and welfare under international law. The original system has undergone meaningful changes, one of which has been the "invasion" by the NGOs of the UN-sponsored normative and policymaking conferences.[40] In another significant institutional development, the United Nations has created new functional agencies and programs, such as the United Nations Development Programme (UNDP), the United Nations Conference on Trade and Development (UNCTAD), and the United Nations High Commissioner for Human Rights (UNHCHR), and the many UN peacekeeping units.

With the exception of the IMF and the World Bank (two agencies that are organized on the basis of shareholder power, in the image of private corporations), the specialized agencies share three common features: (1) an assembly or conference composed of representatives of all members with a "one state, one vote" formula; (2) a council or board with

[34] David Held envisages three types of "international agencies and organizations":

- Global networks of coordination such as the Group of 7, with minimal institutions but considerable influence.
- Technical organizations such as the Universal Postal Union, which provide extension of services offered by individual states and are "nonpolitical" and uncontroversial.
- Organizations that deal with "more central questions of the management and allocation of rules and resources," such as the United Nations, the WTO, the International Monetary Fund (IMF), and the World Bank, which have become controversial and politicized. In the latter—or possibly in a separate fourth category—figures the European Union, a system combining an economic community with elements of a political community, which is a model for many regional organizations.

HELD, *supra* note 2, at 109, 111; *see also* Stephan, *supra* note 8, at 681.

[35] "Specialized agencies" have concluded standard agreements with the United Nations. For a list, see 1B INTERNATIONAL ORGANIZATION AND INTEGRATION, at xvi–xix (P. J. G. Kapteyn et al. eds., 1982).

[36] The UN Charter refers to "free political institutions" only in connection with non-self-governing territories. UN CHARTER Art. 73(b). On membership, see *id.*, Art. 4.

[37] *Id.*, Art. 2(7).

[38] *Id.*, Art. 71. A corresponding provision has been accepted by UN specialized agencies.

[39] On nonstate actors' participation in the International Labour Organization, see *infra* text at note 41.

[40] Richard Falk, *The United Nations and Cosmopolitan Democracy*, *in* RE-IMAGINING, *supra* note 6, at 309, 321–24.

a limited membership of state representatives elected by the assembly; and (3) a secretariat headed by a director who is appointed by the assembly.

Some structural and operational variants exist. For example, the principal organs of the International Labour Organization (ILO) include representatives of employers and workers as well as governments. When the ILO was established in 1919, this innovative feature was viewed as strengthening its legitimacy.[41] Again, the WHO relies heavily on its six regional and six liaison offices.

The competences of the specialized agencies are generally framed in broad terms covering a given field. Activities range from research and studies to technical and other assistance; forms of action include issuing recommendations, drafting treaties for acceptance by the member states, and adopting regulatory measures creating international obligations. Implementing procedures may take the form of obligations to report, monitoring, dispute settlement of variable stringency, and sanctions. The claim to legitimacy of these agencies is based on ratification by member parliaments of the constituent treaties, as well as on the expertise of standard-setting groups. The impact of these activities varies greatly, from normative changes in national standards to enhanced modernization and improvement of economic and social conditions in member states. The level of integration is generally low, and the corresponding discourse on the democracy-legitimacy deficit muted or altogether absent.

We now take a closer look at a specialized agency within the UN system, the WHO.

Normative-Institutional Factors

Of all the specialized agencies, the WHO has the largest budget (more than $842 million for two years) and—building on the heritage of international health activities dating back to 1857—probably the most expansive mandate of "directing and coordinating authority" for health work.[42] WHO institutions reflect the tripod structure. The Health Assembly is composed of representatives of all the member states, each with one vote. The Executive Board of limited membership decides in principle by majority vote. Both bodies generally meet in open session. A secretariat is headed by the director-general, who is appointed by the Health Assembly upon nomination by the Executive Board. The Health Assembly is authorized to adopt regulations on international health matters (e.g., sanitary requirements, public health practices, advertising, and labeling) that bind the members unless they opt out. The assembly may propose conventions by a two-thirds majority to be accepted domestically by the members, who must report on the acceptance or indicate reasons in case of nonacceptance; and it may also make recommendations. Thus, the WHO has a substantial potential for integration. In reality, however, the assembly has adopted only two regulations in its entire history.[43] Nor has it drawn on its authority to approve conventions, except in formal matters such as the headquarters agreement.[44]

[41] *See generally* Steve Charnovitz, *The International Labor Organization in Its Second Century*, 2000 MAX PLANCK Y.B. UN L. (forthcoming).

[42] WHO CONST., July 22, 1946, Art. 2, 62 Stat. 2679, 14 UNTS 185; David P. Fidler, *The Future of the World Health Organization: What Role for International Law?* 31 VAND. J. TRANSNAT'L L. 1079, 1084–86 (1998) [hereinafter Fidler, *Future*]. *See generally* YVES BEIGBEDER, MAHYAR NASHAT, MARIE-ANTOINETTE ORSINI, & J. F. TIERCY, THE WORLD HEALTH ORGANIZATION (1998) [hereinafter BEIGBEDER ET AL.]; DAVID P. FIDLER, INTERNATIONAL LAW AND PUBLIC HEALTH: MATERIALS ON AND ANALYSIS OF GLOBAL HEALTH JURISPRUDENCE (2000) [hereinafter FIDLER, INTERNATIONAL LAW]; *Reposturing the WHO: The World Health Organization Is About to Be Given a Much Needed Kick in the Backside*, ECONOMIST, May 9, 1998, at 79; *World Health Report 1999—Message from the Director-General, at* <http://www.who.int/whr/1999/en/dgmessage.htm> [hereinafter *Director-General's Message*] (visited July 16, 2001).

[43] Regulation No. 1, Unification of Statistical Classification of Morbidity and Mortality (1948, revised several times); and Regulation No. 2, International Sanitary Regulations (1951). BEIGBEDER ET AL., *supra* note 42, at 72.

[44] In 1996 the Health Assembly initiated work on an international framework convention for tobacco control. This would be the first convention to be adopted under Article 19 of the WHO Constitution. World Health Organization, Intergovernmental Negotiating Body, Chair's Text of a Framework Convention on Tobacco Control,

In theory, the assembly votes by majority, except on important questions, which require a two-thirds vote. In reality, WHO activities have been carried out primarily by consensus through nonbinding and less formal procedures such as recommendations, resolutions, and the promulgation of technical standards or guidelines drawn up by expert bodies.[45]

In one instance, the assembly framed its recommendation in the form of a "code." This effort catapulted the WHO into a clamorous political-scientific controversy, involving not only governments but also powerful commercial interests and NGOs.[46] After this unhappy experience, the assembly abandoned the code format.[47] Interestingly, as a significant, but questionable innovation, in 1979 the assembly invited certain NGOs that had not been admitted to official relations with the organization to attend its meetings on an equal basis with those that had been officially recognized. The methods of some of these NGOs have since been criticized and their representativity questioned.[48] As of 1999, in addition to regular contacts with fifty-nine IGOs and a number of joint bodies established by them, the WHO had granted official status to nearly two hundred NGOs.[49] As in other specialized agencies, the director-general and the secretariat, staffed by thirty-eight hundred health and other experts, play a significant role in making proposals and influencing the agenda and outcomes.

Empirical-Social Factors; the Discourse

The WHO's principal impact has been in fighting infectious diseases.[50] However, over time the narrowness of this focus has caused problems for the organization, and other bodies, such as the World Bank, have entered the health field.

Not surprisingly, considering the actual low level of integration, I found nothing in either the public or the academic discourse questioning the compatibility of WHO membership or any particular WHO measures with national constitutions, or the adequacy of parliamentary control over the executive-appointed national delegation. Instead, criticism centered on WHO substantive policies, the failure to cooperate with the private sector, excessive or—contrariwise—inadequate control of the six regional offices by the headquarters, weak leadership, cronyism, antiquated management structure, and lack of outreach:[51] "There is no press room—no phones, nowhere for governments or NGOs to put their press releases, no message board, . . . no computer. . . . [I]t is at the heart of the decline of WHO's influence . . . ."[52]

Doc. A/FCTC/INB2/2 (Jan. 9, 2001); BEIGBEDER ET AL., *supra* note 42, at 71; *Meeting Set to Establish Global Rules on Tobacco*, N.Y. TIMES, Oct. 15, 2000, at 4.

[45] BEIGBEDER ET AL., *supra* note 42, at 84.

[46] International Code of Marketing of Breast-milk Substitutes, May 21, 1981, Doc. WHO/MCH/NUT/90.1. Other issues that created controversy were the effort to regulate international drug commerce, the abusive sale of pharmaceuticals in the Third World, and also the response to the AIDS epidemic. FIDLER, INTERNATIONAL LAW, *supra* note 42, at 101, 103.

[47] BEIGBEDER ET AL., *supra* note 42, at 75–84.

[48] *Id.* at 81.

[49] Y.B. INT'L ORGS., *supra* note 2, at 2300, 2302–03.

[50] A major WHO success was the eradication of smallpox. According to a WHO spokesperson, health research focuses disproportionately on diseases of concern to high-income countries, with only 0.20% of research dollars spent on "the biggest killers," pneumonia and diarrheal diseases. Elizabeth Olson, *Switzerland: Health Spending*, N.Y. TIMES, May 2, 2000, at A10. The WHO has been criticized for not paying attention to AIDS. David P. Fidler, David L. Heymann, Stephen M. Ostroff, & Terry P. O'Brien, *Emerging and Reemerging Infectious Diseases: Challenges for International, National, and State Law*, 31 INT'L LAW. 773, 799 (1997) (asking whether the WHO's power in the field should be increased).

[51] *See, e.g.*, ECONOMIST, *supra* note 42, at 79; Jill Turner, *For WHO or For Whom? World Health Organization's Influence on Health Policy*, LANCET, June 7, 1997, at 1639.

[52] Turner, *supra* note 51, at 1640.

The current director-general appears to have addressed some policy and structural deficiencies. She has introduced a cabinet form of decision making in the hope of improving transparency through a more open process.[53] Yet major decisions, particularly in the personnel field, purportedly continue to be negotiated in secrecy between the headquarters, the member governments concerned, and the influential regional directors. National quotas are strictly applied in the appointment procedure; personal contacts play a major role and little regard is given to the qualifications of the officials. Some believe the management has become, if anything, even more complex and less transparent, and that some changes are introduced solely for the sake of change.[54]

One criticism of particular interest for this essay focuses on the WHO's failure to apply and develop the legal instrumentalities available in its "Constitution." Thus, the dispute settlement facilities, including recourse to the assembly and the International Court of Justice, have been used infrequently. In only two instances did the assembly take advantage of its authority to request an advisory opinion from the International Court. The global surveillance system under the International Health Regulations was allowed to break down.[55] Several reasons have been advanced for this phenomenon: the exclusive domination of the organization by conservative personnel who were trained in public health and medicine; the difficulties inherent in formalizing technical requirements in the rapidly changing health field; the cost of maintaining facilities for the administration of legally binding instruments; the preference of governments for recommendations and guidelines; the absence of an assurance of reciprocity; the reluctance to make "official science"; and the uneven development of member states in science and technology.[56] Some of these "anti-integrationist" reasons may apply to other IGOs as well. The 1991 Nordic UN project noted that the traditional roles of the major specialized agencies, including the WHO, had been downgraded and it recommended strengthening their normative role.[57]

Because of the low level of integration, any discourse is typically limited to a small elite mostly concerned with health care. In its assessments, this group emphasizes greater transparency and sound management. Occasionally, an issue such as the political-scientific controversies I mentioned above or a contested election of the director-general engages a broader audience.

III. REGULATING GLOBAL TRADE: THE WORLD TRADE ORGANIZATION

Normative-Institutional Factors

Heritage, structure, competence. Originally, the International Trade Organization (ITO) was supposed to form a vital component of the post–World War II scheme of global IGOs. However, in 1947 it foundered in the U.S. Congress. The United States, "the hegemon" of international trade at the time, was not prepared to accept an institutional discipline. Later, the international community designed the General Agreement on Tariffs and Trade (GATT) to assume the role originally intended for the ITO. The GATT was an international agreement whose scope was periodically broadened by successive "rounds" of multilateral negotiations. Finally, the Uruguay Round vested the governance of GATT in the World

[53] *Director-General's Message*, *supra* note 42.

[54] Private conversation with a WHO staff member (fall 2000).

[55] *See* WHO CONST. ch. VII; Fidler, *Future*, *supra* note 42, at 1079, 1090–91.

[56] BEIGBEDER ET AL., *supra* note 42, at 84–85; Fidler, *Future*, *supra* note 42, at 1099–1100.

[57] NORDIC UN PROJECT, THE UNITED NATIONS IN DEVELOPMENT: REFORM ISSUES IN THE ECONOMIC AND SOCIAL FIELDS: A NORDIC PERSPECTIVE 66–67 (Stockholm 1991), *cited in* BEIGBEDER ET AL., *supra* note 42, at 85. "The scientific progress of the antibiotic revolution . . . allowed public health officials to go directly after the pathogenic microbes rather than thinking about international legal regimes designed to control diseases." FIDLER, INTERNATIONAL LAW, *supra* note 42, at 121.

Trade Organization and at the same time extended the GATT's competence and discipline and also improved its text.[58]

The GATT's history left several marks on the WTO, distinguishing it from other components of the post–World War II system. First, as a condition for admission to membership in the WTO, a state must negotiate concessions with major trade powers. The mutual rights and obligations of member states may differ.[59]

Second, unlike that of other global IGOs, the WTO's competence extends across a broad spectrum of trade and trade-related activities.[60] One might say that, in theory, there are no formal limits to matters on which the WTO can make rules by consensus, particularly considering the breadth of purposes listed in the preamble to the WTO Agreement, such as sustainable development and higher standards of living. As Marco Bronckers points out, this wide range enables the member states to negotiate on rules by means of "package deals" encompassing more than a single area,[61] a process that facilitates agreement and advances integration, as the "neo-functionalists" (Ernst B. Haas, Leon N. Lindberg, and others) have demonstrated on the basis of the European Community experience. On the other hand, the linkage to nontrade issues has accentuated concern about a democracy-legitimacy deficit and strained the basic consensus.

A third distinguishing characteristic of the WTO is that it is not a "specialized agency" of the United Nations in the technical sense and its structure departs in significant ways from the standard "tripod." While the Ministerial Conference of all member states and the secretariat headed by the director-general fit the conventional pattern, the composition of the General Council, the body in charge of day-to-day decisions, is different. The council consists of representatives of all the members, testimony to the historical reluctance of states to delegate decision making on trade matters to any body of limited membership, which is clearly an "anti-integrationist" feature.[62] All members are also represented on the Trade

[58] The Agreement Establishing the World Trade Organization contains institutional and procedural provisions. It is a leading portion of the complex 26,000-page treaty, with four important annexes comprising most of the pages and all of the substance. Annex 1, for instance, contains twelve agreements on different subjects. Also included is a series of "understandings," "ministerial decisions," and "declarations." Marrakesh Agreement Establishing the World Trade Organization, Apr. 15, 1994, 1867 UNTS 3 [hereinafter WTO Agreement]; General Agreement on Tariffs and Trade 1994, Apr. 15, 1994, 1867 UNTS 190 [hereinafter GATT 1994]. *See generally* JACQUES H. J. BOURGEOIS, FREDERIQUE BERROD, & ERIC GIPPINI FOURNIER, THE URUGUAY ROUND RESULTS: A EUROPEAN LAWYERS' PERSPECTIVE (1995); MARCO C. E. J. BRONCKERS, A CROSS-SECTION OF WTO LAW (2000); ROBERT E. HUDEC, ENFORCING INTERNATIONAL TRADE LAW: THE EVOLUTION OF THE MODERN GATT LEGAL SYSTEM (1993); INTERNATIONAL TRADE LAW AND THE GATT/WTO DISPUTE SETTLEMENT SYSTEM (Ernst-Ulrich Petersmann ed., 1997); JOHN H. JACKSON, LEGAL PROBLEMS OF INTERNATIONAL ECONOMIC RELATIONS (3d ed. 1995); JOHN H. JACKSON, THE WORLD TRADE ORGANIZATION—CONSTITUTION AND JURISPRUDENCE 36–41 (1998) [hereinafter JACKSON, WORLD TRADE ORGANIZATION]; JOHN H. JACKSON, THE WORLD TRADING SYSTEM (2d ed. 1997); ERNST-ULRICH PETERSMANN, THE GATT/WTO DISPUTE SETTLEMENT SYSTEM—INTERNATIONAL LAW, INTERNATIONAL ORGANIZATIONS AND DISPUTE SETTLEMENT (1997); TREBILCOCK & HOWSE, *supra* note 8; Robert F. Housman, *Democratizing International Trade Decision-Making*, 27 CORNELL INT'L L.J. 699 (1994).

[59] At the time of publication, the WTO had 140 members and current applicants included China and Russia. For information about the WTO and dispute settlement reports, see the WTO Web site at <http://www.wto.org>.

[60] The liberalization commitments cover trade in goods (tariffs and nontariff barriers), services (including financial services and competition in telecommunications), aspects of agriculture, government procurement, sanitary and phytosanitary measures, antidumping, subsidies and countervailing measures, and intellectual property. TREBILCOCK & HOWSE, *supra* note 8, at 37–38. The WTO budget is only $80 million, an amount the IMF is said to spend on travel. *Washington*, EUROPE, Nov. 1999, at 11.

[61] Marco C. E. J. Bronckers, *Better Rules for a New Millennium: A Warning Against Undemocratic Developments in the WTO*, 1999 J. INT'L TRADE 547, 548.

[62] The General Council seems to have overall supervising authority. There is, however, in addition, a Council for Trade in Goods, a Council for Trade in Services, and a Council for Trade-Related Aspects of Intellectual Property Rights. For an informative table of the institutional scheme, see JACKSON, THE WORLD TRADING SYSTEM, *supra* note 58, at 66. *See generally* JACKSON, WORLD TRADE ORGANIZATION, *supra* note 58, at 41. The WTO Agreement does provide for authoritative interpretation of the broad general principles by the two all-member organs, but this provision has remained a dead letter. Bronckers, *supra* note 61, at 551. A three-fourths majority is required for such interpretation. A corresponding power has been used in the GATT by the Contracting Parties.

Policy Review Mechanism, which reviews the trade policies of each member on a regular basis, and on the important Dispute Settlement Body (DSB), to which I return later.

As for voting, the WTO charter provides for the continuation of the GATT practice of decision making by consensus for the two principal organs, but when consensus cannot be achieved, a simple majority is to prevail (except in specified cases where a qualified majority or unanimity is required). In reality, the members have resorted to voting in very limited instances.[63] Although in certain cases a decision could impose an international obligation on a dissenting member[64] (an important integrational factor), such a decision has not been taken thus far and voluntary acceptance has been the rule, a factor pointing to a lower level of integration.

Dispute settlement: judicialization. Although consensus prevails in rule-making practice, it has been significantly curtailed in the unified dispute settlement procedure. In the first place, a government claiming a violation of its rights in effect is entitled, after consultation, to the establishment of an impartial panel.[65] The panel's "recommendations" stand as final unless overturned in the DSB (the General Council acting as DSB) by a vote of all members, including the winning party, against the panel report ("reverse consensus"). Recourse to a permanent Appellate Body (appointed by the DSB) leads to a final decision, which again stands unless overturned in the DSB by reverse consensus. This procedure assures the finality of the decision. It means that the Appellate Body's report will come into force in practically every case. If the losing party does not comply with the report, the winning party, upon authorization by the DSB, may take retaliatory action by suspending its own obligations toward the loser, which in turn may challenge the magnitude of the retaliatory action. The loser may offer compensation to avoid retaliation.[66]

Several features of this system point to a higher coefficient of integration: fallback procedures and strict deadlines for the successive procedural steps; elimination of the possibility of blockage; the contribution of the international secretariat to the composition of the panels;[67] and "the negative consensus" vote in effect assuring the finality of the decision,

[63] Voting has been used in cases of waiver of certain obligations. "Consensus" is defined as a situation where no member present formally objects to the decision. WTO Agreement, *supra* note 58, Art. IX n.1; JACKSON, WORLD TRADE ORGANIZATION, *supra* note 58, at 68.

[64] In theory, new rules could be established by an amendment in accordance with Article X of the WTO Agreement, *supra* note 58; but the prerequisite of formal acceptance by members makes the process "very hard, if not impossible to use." Letter from Professor William J. Davey, to the author (Oct. 16, 2000) (on file with author). In principle, new rules are adopted at the end of the negotiating rounds, which add to, or amend, the constituent agreements; new provisions are created only sporadically between the negotiating rounds. Broncker, *supra* note 61, at 553. According to Article X, in negotiations for further evolution of the WTO conducted within a standing committee, changes may be adopted by a two-thirds majority. Thus, conceivably a party could be outvoted and therefore bound internationally without its consent. Some may view this possibility as raising questions of constitutionality and "sovereignty," while others may welcome it as facilitating desirable changes. *See* Housman, *supra* note 58, at 714.

[65] *See* John H. Jackson, *Dispute Settlement and the WTO: Emerging Problems*, 1 J. INT'L ECON. L. 329 (1998) [hereinafter Jackson, *Emerging Problems*]. *See generally* JACKSON, WORLD TRADE ORGANIZATION, *supra* note 58, at 75; DAVID PALMETER & PETROS C. MAVROIDIS, DISPUTE SETTLEMENT IN THE WORLD TRADE ORGANIZATION (1999); TREBILCOCK & HOWSE, *supra* note 8, at 61; Thomas Cottier, *Dispute Settlement in the World Trade Organization: Characteristics and Implications for the European Union*, 35 COMMON MKT. L. REV. 325 (1998); *Symposium on the First Three Years of the WTO Dispute Settlement System*, 32 INT'L LAW. 609 (1998). The secretariat proposes panelists from a roster of names. The parties usually agree on the selection of the panelists. If they fail to agree, the director-general decides. E. Vermulst & B. Driessen, *An Overview of the WTO Dispute Settlement System and Its Relationship with the Uruguay Round Agreements: Nice on Paper But Too Much Stress for the System*, *in* THE WORLD TRADING SYSTEM 415, 423–33 (Robert Howse ed., 1998). William J. Davey, *Supporting the World Trade Organization Dispute Settlement System*, J. WORLD TRADE, Feb. 2000, at 167, 169, recommends the creation of a "permanent body of some kind." *See also* Yong K. Kim, *The Beginnings of the Rule of Law in the International Trade System Despite U.S. Constitutional Constraints*, 17 MICH. J. INT'L L. 967, 978–81 (1996).

[66] TREBILCOCK & HOWSE, *supra* note 8, at 36–37. Some of the pressures for compliance include continuous monitoring and fallback procedures in case the parties do not agree on the composition of the panel or its terms. Joost Pauwelyn, *Enforcement and Countermeasures in the WTO: Rules Are Rules—Toward a More Collective Approach*, 94 AJIL 335 (2000); *see also infra* note 68.

[67] TREBILCOCK & HOWSE, *supra* note 8, at 63–64.

which may be considered as imposing an international law obligation on a member.[68] An appeal to the Appellate Body may be taken only on questions of law and the procedure provides limited quasi-judicial safeguards of "due process."[69] The scope of retaliatory sanctions is subject to central control. The sum of these provisions points strongly in the direction of "judicialization" and "depoliticization" of the system. This tendency is strengthened by the fact that in the absence of authoritative interpretation, the dispute settlement mechanism carries the burden of clarifying and applying the often vague treaty clauses, establishing a chain of precedents that other panels would be loath to ignore as a step toward legal certainty and the rule of law.[70]

WTO dispute settlement proceedings, however, in sharp conflict with the concept of a modern judiciary, remain closed.[71] This feature derives from the original GATT scheme, which viewed dispute settlement as a continuation of the diplomatic negotiations. Moreover, contrary to the EU system, the members of the Appellate Body serve on a part-time basis and its decisions are not enforceable in domestic courts.[72] Some 234 complaints have been notified and fifty-seven panel reports adopted in the GATT/WTO system with high compliance rates, albeit often after delays, and with relatively few instances of noncompliance and retaliation.[73]

One may conclude that, structurally, the GATT/WTO is a treaty-based, state-controlled intergovernmental organization (one state, one vote) governed by the treaty text and general international law without a direct link between its institutions and the citizens. In rule making it is essentially institutionalized diplomacy. Yet the adjudicatory system—an incipient rule-of-law scheme—works effectively, lifts the organization on the ascending integration line, strengthens the rule-oriented approach, and offers an element of legitimacy attached to the rule-of-law concept. There is no indication, however, that the dispute settlement organs will be able or willing to "constitutionalize" the basic agreements in the image of the crucial role that the European Court of Justice has played in European integration, which I discuss in part V below. If nothing else, the existential difference between the nature of the global system and the ideologically based regional European Union, and the balance between diversity and convergence that it implies, stand in the way of such a process today.[74]

[68] Jackson makes a strong case that an adopted panel/appellate report creates an international law obligation. JACKSON, WORLD TRADE ORGANIZATION, *supra* note 58, at 81–89; *see also* John H. Jackson, *The WTO Dispute Settlement Understanding—Misunderstandings on the Nature of Legal Obligation*, 91 AJIL 60 (1997); Petros C. Mavroidis, *Remedies in WTO Legal System: Between a Rock and Hard Place*, 11 EUR. J. INT'L L. 763, 778–88 (2000). But see the "contract theory" approach in Frieder Roessler, Warren F. Schwartz, & Alan O. Sykes, The Economic Structure and Dispute Resolution in the WTO/GATT System (unpublished paper for workshop at University of Michigan Law School). See further Judith Hippler Bello, *The WTO Dispute Settlement Understanding: Less Is More*, 90 AJIL 418 (1996).

[69] On conflict of interest and working procedure of the Appellate Body, see JACKSON, WORLD TRADE ORGANIZATION, *supra* note 58, at 18; Steven P. Croley & John H. Jackson, *WTO Dispute Procedures, Standard of Review, and Deference to National Governments*, 90 AJIL 193 (1996); David Palmeter & Petros C. Mavroidis, *The WTO Legal System: Sources of Law*, 92 AJIL 398 (1998).

[70] "Our function in this case is judicial. . . . We are guided . . . by the jurisprudence of the Appellate Body." United States—Sections 301–310 of the Trade Act of 1974, WTO Doc. WT/DS152/R, paras. 7.12, 7.14 (Dec. 22, 1999) [hereinafter U.S.—Trade Act]; *see* PETERSMANN, *supra* note 58, at 84–85 (citing HUDEC, *supra* note 58). *See generally* Frederick M. Abbott, *NAFTA and the Legalization of World Politics: A Case Study*, 54 INT'L ORG. 519 (Special Issue, Summer 2000); Judith Goldstein, Miles Kahler, Robert O. Keohane, & Anne-Marie Slaughter, *id.* (exploring the problems of legalization); Arie Reich, *From Diplomacy to Law—The Juridicization of International Trade Relations*, 17 NW. J. INT'L L. & BUS. 775 (1996/97). On the authoritative interpretation, see *supra* note 62.

[71] Housman, *supra* note 58, at 710–12. Oral hearings of the European Court of Justice are normally public. However, written pleadings are accessible only to parties or to third parties with a legitimate interest. Peter Dyrberg, *Current Issues in the Debate on Public Access to Documents*, 24 EUR. L. REV. 157 (1999).

[72] Piet Eeckhout, *The Domestic Legal Status of the WTO Agreement: Interconnecting Legal Systems*, 34 COMMON MKT. L. REV. 11 (1997). An individual may sue potential suppliers directly in national courts under the GATT Agreement on Government Procurement, *amended* Apr. 15, 1994, WTO Agreement, *supra* note 58, Annex 4(b).

[73] WTO Secretariat, *Overview of the State-of-Play of WTO Disputes*, Statistical Overview at 2 (July 13, 2001). *See generally* HUDEC, *supra* note 58.

[74] Howse & Nicolaidis, *supra* note 22, at 17, *passim. But see* Thomas Cottier, *Limits to International Trade: The Constitutional Challenge*, 94 ASIL PROC. 220 (2000); Petersmann, *infra* note 106.

In fact, a panel has recognized that, unlike the European Community, the GATT/WTO did not create a legal order that would comprise both the member states and their nationals and that it had only "indirect effect" on private operators. It added, however, that "the multilateral trading system is, per force, composed . . ., indeed mostly, of individual economic operators."[75]

Empirical-Social Factors; the Impact

Few observers doubt that GATT/WTO was one of the significant factors contributing to the massive reduction of trade barriers and the corresponding increase in international trade.[76] These achievements raise the level of WTO integration in terms of the social-empirical yardsticks. However, there is no agreement on the relative impact on individual countries or groups of countries.[77]

The Discourse

At the national level: constitutional objections. One significant aspect of the debate over the democracy-legitimacy deficit concerns the preservation of the integrity of national constitutions. As could be expected, it was the adjudicatory aspect of the trade agreements—the "outpost" of higher integration—that has raised the question of conformity with national constitutions. Emerging in connection with the Canada-U.S. Free Trade Agreement of 1988,[78] the problem resurfaced in the U.S. Congress in connection with the consideration of the WTO Agreements[79] and was then hotly debated during the negotiation and ratification proceedings of the North American Free Trade Agreement. The constitutional issue was raised in a number of other WTO member states as well, including Canada and the EC countries.[80] In the United States, the principal arguments against constitutionality rested on

[75] U.S.—Trade Act, *supra* note 70, paras. 7.76, 7.78. The panel indicated that, in considering whether one state has violated its treaty obligations, the adjudicatory body may consider not just the interests of the state, but also the impact on private actors. Steve Charnovitz, *The WTO and the Rights of the Individual,* INTERECONOMICS, Mar./Apr. 2001, at 98. In the United States and the European Community, the legislation implementing the WTO Agreement purports expressly to exclude direct effect in national law; in Canada and Australia, such exclusion is the result of both dualism practice and the implementing legislation; and in Switzerland, the denial of direct effect derives from rulings of the Federal Supreme Court. In Japan's monist system, the situation is unclear; it is up to the courts to decide which provisions of the WTO Agreement are to be applied directly, but it is unlikely that the courts would strike down an act of the legislature. For detailed treatment, including the practice in Belgium, Germany, Korea, Costa Rica, and Brazil, see IMPLEMENTING THE URUGUAY ROUND (John H. Jackson & Alan O. Sykes eds., 1997) [hereinafter URUGUAY ROUND]. The definitional problem of "direct effect" is noted in *id.* at 460–61. *See also* text after note 7 *supra.*

[76] Since the establishment of the GATT, tariffs have been cut by roughly 90%. In addition, the volume of international trade has increased fifteen times since 1960. Delegation of the Commission of the European Community, *Washington,* EUROPE, Nov. 1999, at 8.

[77] GARY C. HUFBAUER & BARBARA KOTSCHWAR, THE FUTURE COURSE OF TRADE LIBERALIZATION (Institute for International Economics, 1998); JOHN WHALLEY & COLLEEN HAMILTON, THE TRADING SYSTEM AFTER THE URUGUAY ROUND 59–76 (1996); Douglas A. Irwin, *The GATT in Historical Perspective,* 85 AM. ECON. REV. 323 (1995). They see "great uncertainty as to the quantifiable and non-quantifiable aspects." WHALLEY & HAMILTON, *supra,* at 75.

[78] Kim, *supra* note 65, at 975-78. For the treaty, see Free Trade Agreement, Jan. 2, 1988, Can.-U.S., 27 ILM 281 (1988).

[79] *E.g., Implementation of the Uruguay Round Trade Agreements and Establishment of the World Trade Organization: Hearings Before the Subcomm. on Trade of the House Comm. on Ways and Means,* 104th Cong. 5 (1996) (statement of Amb. Michael Kantor); Kim, *supra* note 65, at 979. The Uruguay Round Agreement Act states that federal law shall prevail over any conflicting provision of the Agreement. Pub. L. No. 103-465, 108 Stat. 4809 (1994).

[80] *See infra* text at notes 137–42; Kim, *supra* note 65, at 968 n.3. For the treaty, see North American Free Trade Agreement, Dec. 17, 1992, U.S.-Can.-Mex., 107 Stat. 2066, *reprinted in* 32 ILM 296 (1993). In the European Community, a constitutional issue arose over the division of treaty power between the member states and the Community. In Japan, the approval of the WTO Agreement by the Diet avoided a potential controversy over the authority of the executive to conclude treaties. In Canada, the key constitutional issue was which level of government—federal or provincial—had the authority to implement parts of the WTO Agreement. URUGUAY ROUND, *supra* note 75 (reporting also on constitutional issues in other states). On the constitutional challenge to congressional delegation of power, see DELEGATING STATE POWERS: THE EFFECT OF TREATY REGIMES ON DEMOCRACY AND SOVEREIGNTY

Article III of the Constitution, which vests the judicial power of the United States in a federal judiciary established by Congress with life tenure and salary protection; the use of a congressional-executive agreement rather than a treaty; the inadequacy of the due process guarantees; and, as John Jackson calls it, "the sovereignty argument."[81] With considerable hyperbole, the prominent leader of an American NGO called the WTO dispute settlement mechanism a "staggering rejection of our due process."[82] None of the challenges has prevailed.

At the international level: power, participation, transparency. The opposition to the working of the GATT/WTO system was first brought to national and worldwide public attention when a dispute settlement panel held that the United States had violated the Agreement by excluding the importation of Mexican tuna caught by fishing methods outlawed in the United States because of the damage to the dolphin population.[83] The ensuing campaign against the panel's holding signaled the emerging power of NGOs in the trade area. This power peaked in November 1999 in Seattle, where massive demonstrations, organized by a coalition of environmentalists, labor unionists, and advocates of "poor people," with a crowd of anarchists at the fringe, helped to abort the plans of WTO leaders to prepare another round of negotiations.[84]

Opponents specifically criticized both the way the GATT/WTO had used its power and the democratic deficit and lack of transparency and legitimacy. They claimed that the organization is dominated by business interests and major trading states and excludes the voices of other states and groups in both the trade negotiations and the dispute settlement "star chamber" process;[85] it operates behind closed doors (the "club model").[86] Moreover, the critics charged that the WTO elevates the value of free trade above, and in disregard of, other values such as environmental protection and the rights of workers, consumers, and poor people.

Remedies for the democracy-legitimacy deficit. The need to meet some of the criticisms has been widely recognized.[87] In addition to many NGOs, advocates for reforming the WTO include

(Thomas M. Franck ed., 2000); Michael C. Dorf & Charles F. Sabel, *A Constitution of Democratic Experimentalism*, 98 COLUM. L. REV. 267, 270–72 (1998). For more extensive discussion, see text following note 131 *infra*.

[81] John H. Jackson, *The Great 1994 Sovereignty Debate: United States Acceptance and Implementation of the Uruguay Round Results*, 36 COLUM. J. TRANSNAT'L L. 157, 187 (1997); *see also* JACKSON, WORLD TRADE ORGANIZATION, *supra* note 58, at 77; JACKSON, THE WORLD TRADING SYSTEM, *supra* note 58, at 99.

[82] Ralph Nader, *quoted in* G. R. Shell, *Trade Legalism and International Relations Theory: An Analysis of the World Trade Organization, in* 2 THE WORLD TRADING SYSTEM, *supra* note 65, at 333, 382 n.4; *see* Robert Howse, *Eyes Wide Shut in Seattle: The Legitimacy of the World Trade Organization, in* THE LEGITIMACY OF INTERNATIONAL INSTITUTIONS (V. Heiskanen & J.-M. Coicaud eds., 2001).

[83] United States—Restrictions on Imports of Tuna (GATT panel, unadopted, Aug. 16, 1991), 30 ILM 1594 (1991); *see also* Agreement for the Reduction of Dolphin Mortality in the Eastern Pacific Ocean (EPO), June 1992, 33 ILM 936 (1994). On another decision with the same result, of May 15, 1998, sharply criticized, see Robert Howse, *The Turtles Panel—Another Environmental Disaster in Geneva*, J. WORLD TRADE, Oct. 1998, at 73. United States—Import Prohibition of Certain Shrimp and Shrimp Products, WTO Doc. WT/DS58/R (May 15, 1998) [hereinafter U.S.—Shrimp/Turtle].

[84] *Seattle Is Under Curfew After Disruptions*, N.Y. TIMES, Dec. 1, 1999, at A1; *Seattle WTO Ministerial Conference*, HARMONIZATION ALERT, Nov.–Dec. 1999, at 1–4, *at*<http://www.harmonizationalert.org>. When President Clinton proposed that workers' rights and environmental protections be included in the negotiations, and mentioned sanctions for noncompliance with standards to be agreed upon, some developing countries, including Egypt, Brazil, and India, refused even to discuss it. *Shipwreck in Seattle*, N.Y. TIMES, Dec. 5, 1999, at 14; *Trade Ministers Sidestep a Sticky Issue: Secrecy*, N.Y. TIMES, Dec. 4, 1999, at A6; *U.S. Isolated on Key Issues at Trade Talks in Seattle*, *id.* Egypt's chief trade representative stated: "[W]e needed a decision to stop this process until we can figure out how to balance transparency and efficiency." *Impasse on Trade Delivers a Stinging Blow to Clinton*, N.Y. TIMES, Dec. 5, 1999, §1, at 1.

[85] Housman, *supra* note 58, at 711–13. In Public Citizen v. Office of United States Trade Representative, 804 F.Supp. 385 (D.D.C. 1992), the court held that GATT panel submissions and decisions must be released promptly upon receipt of a proper request under the Freedom of Information Act unless protected by a specific exemption.

[86] Robert O. Keohane & Joseph S. Nye, Jr., The Club Model of Multilateral Cooperation and the World Trade Organization: Problems of Democratic Legitimacy (rev. June 30, 2000) (paper presented at John F. Kennedy School of Government, Harvard University, June 1–2, 2000).

[87] On remedies for the democracy-legitimacy deficit, see Jan Aart Scholte, with Robert O'Brien & Marc Williams, *The WTO and Civil Society*, J. WORLD TRADE, Feb. 1999, at 107, 116–18.

then-President Clinton and spokespersons for other governments, some business interests, and academic "Gattologists" who fear for WTO legitimacy.[88] Here are some of their suggestions with pertinent comments:

— Documents of the WTO institutions, including the minutes of some meetings, should be published and private-group representatives should be given an opportunity to express their views prior to and during the negotiations. Some steps toward greater openness have in fact been taken.[89] Most of the dispute settlement documents appear on the World Wide Web, albeit at times with long delays due to a shortage of translators.

— The list of panelists proposed by the WTO members should be diversified beyond the elite group of trade lawyers and diplomats, and the role of the secretariat in the selection of panels should be reduced. However, others would increase the power of the "independent" secretariat at the expense of governments or replace the panel system by a standing tribunal of independent experts.[90]

— The Appellate Body's ruling that allows panels to admit amicus curiae briefs from NGOs has been welcomed, but viewed as not going far enough to assure adequate access. That body has also agreed to accept such briefs and to hear a private attorney, but only as a member of the government delegation.[91] Similarly, the establishment of a private Policy Dialogue on Trade and Environment to advise the WTO's Committee on Trade and Environment has been noted with approval.[92]

— In the adjudication process, when facing a claim that national legislation restricts trade contrary to the Agreement, the panel should reject the claim of illegality—so goes the suggestion—(1) when "the national measure reflects a deeply embedded value (which at times may be idiosyncratic)" and "enjoy[s] the clear support of [that country's] population"; and (2) "where the country imposing the measure bears the greater part of the cost" of any trade distortion the legislation has caused.[93] This standard-of-review test is to serve as "a useful screen to instances where democracy is invoked to question the appropriateness, if not the legitimacy, of an international trade dispute outcome."[94]

— A strongly held view to the contrary would allow the panels to ask one and only one question: Is the national measure under review protectionist, so that it constitutes arbitrary and unjustified discrimination?[95] All other value considerations, the argu-

[88] On President Clinton in 1998 in Davos, see *Clinton Shift on Trade: Wake-Up Call*, N.Y. TIMES, Jan. 31, 1998, at A6; and in Geneva, on the 50th anniversary of the GATT/WTO, WTO Doc. WT/FIFTY/H/ST/8 (1998). *See* TREBILCOCK & HOWSE, *supra* note 8, at 66–78. The WTO director-general advocated enlargement of the negotiating circle and improvement of the decision-making process. BULLETIN QUOTIDIEN EUROPE [BULL. QUOT. EUR.], Jan. 6, 2000, at 10.

[89] Acting under Article 5 of the WTO Agreement, *supra* note 58, which authorizes the council to make "appropriate arrangement" for consultation and cooperation with the NGOs concerned, the General Council agreed to de-restrict WTO documents more quickly and to make information more accessible. There was consensus, however, that any further NGO participation was inappropriate. GATT/WTO Agreements make no fewer than forty-one references to "transparency" in domestic legal systems, which is viewed as essential for enforcement. Kim, *supra* note 65, at 989–92; *see also* Whitney Debevoise, *Access to Documents and Panel and Appellate Body Sessions: Practice and Suggestions for Greater Transparency*, 32 INT'L LAW. 817 (1998).

[90] Bronckers, *supra* note 61, at 565 (discussing giving more power to the secretariat and other recommendations); Davey, *supra* note 65.

[91] United States—Import Prohibition of Certain Shrimp and Shrimp Products, WTO Doc. WT/DS58/AB/R, paras. 88–91, 187a (Oct. 12, 1998) (on briefs); *see also* United States—Imposition of Countervailing Duties on Certain Hot-Rolled Lead and Bismuth Carbon Steel Products Originating in the United Kingdom, WTO Doc. WT/DS138/AB/R (May 10, 2000); European Communities—Regime for the Importation, Sale and Distribution of Bananas, WTO Doc. WT/DS27/AB/R, paras. 10–12 (Sept. 27, 1997) (on private counsel); Indonesia—Certain Measures Affecting the Automobile Industry, WTO Doc. WT/DS54/R (July 9, 1998). On comparable power of arbitration tribunals under NAFTA, see Methanex Corp. v. United States, Petitions from Third Persons to Intervene as "Amici Curiae," paras. 47–53 (arb. under Ch. 11 of NAFTA & UNCITRAL Arb. Rules, 2001).

[92] Shell, *supra* note 82, at 378.

[93] Jeffery Atik, *Identifying Antidemocratic Outcomes: Authenticity, Self-Sacrifice and International Trade*, 19 U. PA. J. INT'L ECON. L. 229, 234, 261 (1998).

[94] *Id.* at 261–62.

[95] GATT 1994 Art. XX headnote.

ment goes, must be eschewed because the panels are not tribunals set in an established legal order, such as the European Court of Justice; hence, their decision would lack predictability. Nor can they legitimately engage in complex cost-benefit analysis. When faced with competing values, the dispute settlement organs, relying on the principle of "global subsidiarity," should defer to other international institutions with superior credentials (such as the ILO and special environmental protection bodies) and to the political process of negotiations; they should interpret the WTO Agreement in accordance with established rules of international law; and they should pay attention to due process values of transparency, fairness, nonarbitrariness, and prior deliberation with all affected interests.[96]

— Another suggestion in this vein calls for the panels to avoid deciding highly contested "trade and . . . " cases by resorting to jurisdictional and procedural devices such as standing and ripeness, which are widely employed in domestic legal systems and some international tribunals, including the European Court of Justice.[97]

— Courts of member states should interpret their own trade law in accordance with WTO law.[98]

— It is broadly agreed that basic workers' rights must be respected. However, how these rights are to be enforced is controversial. Advocates of workers' rights in industrial states press for strict standards to be enforced by the WTO, while the developing countries, fearing the loss of their comparative advantage of lower labor costs, prefer the less exacting forum of the ILO. It has been suggested that the IGOs concerned cooperate. At any rate, in view of the broad goals articulated in the preamble to the WTO Agreement (e.g., sustainable development, full employment, and reiterated concern for less developed states) and other comparable provisions, WTO bodies should include the core of fundamental human rights in their canon.[99]

As a broad generalization, one may note that when reviewing national legislation, the Appellate Body is more likely than the panels to adopt an interpretation that looks beyond the trade liberalization provisions to other clauses and purposes of the WTO Agreements, which reduces the grounds for some of the criticism I mentioned earlier.[100] The panels, however, do not consistently follow any single method of interpretation.[101]

[96] Steve Charnovitz, *Free Trade, Fair Trade, Green Trade: Defogging the Debate*, 27 CORNELL INT'L L.J. 459, 481–87 (1994); *see* Howse & Nicolaidis, *supra* note 22, at 27–35. As an interesting comparison with the European Community, the European Court of Justice reinterpreted the constituent treaty prohibition on protective legislation to reduce significantly the scope of the prohibition. With the Community discipline (and its own authority) firmly established, the Court loosened the strict review standard allowing the member states' lawmakers more leeway. Joined Cases C–267/91, C–268/91, Criminal Proceedings Against Bernhard Keck & Daniel Mithouard, 1993 ECR I–6097.

[97] Jeffrey L. Dunoff, *The Death of the Trade Regime*, 10 EUR. J. INT'L L. 733, 759–61 (1999); *see also* Lawrence R. Helfer & Anne-Marie Slaughter, *Toward a Theory of Effective Supranational Adjudication*, 107 YALE L.J. 273, 316 (1997).

[98] Some member states' constitutions might allow *some* WTO provisions in their national legal order to have direct effect, while others would not. Since WTO dispute settlement organs, unlike the European Court, lack the authority to impose a uniform rule on this issue that would bind all parties, the argument against granting direct effect is the absence of reciprocity, "a mercantilist argument." Thomas Cottier, William Davey, Petros Mavroidis, & Norio Komuro, *Is the WTO Dispute Settlement Mechanism Responsive to the Needs of the Traders: Would a System of Direct Action by Private Parties Yield Better Rules?* 32 J. WORLD TRADE 147, 154–63 (1998) [hereinafter Panel Discussion]. *But see* text at note 75 *supra*.

[99] TREBILCOCK & HOWSE, *supra* note 8, at 456–58, 462–63; Charnovitz, *supra* note 41, at 10–16, 22–30. *See generally* ROBERT HOWSE & MAKAU MUTUA, PROTECTING HUMAN RIGHTS IN A GLOBAL ECONOMY: CHALLENGES FOR THE WORLD TRADE ORGANIZATION (International Center for Human Rights and Democratic Development, Quebec, Canada 2000); Frank J. Garcia, *The Global Market and Human Rights: Trading away the Human Rights Principle*, 25 BROOK. J. INT'L L. 51 (1999); Christopher McCrudden, *International Economic Law and Pursuit of Human Rights: A Framework for Discussion of the Legality of 'Selective Purchasing' Laws Under the WTO Government Procurement Agreement*, 2 J. INT'L ECON. L. 3 (1999).

[100] See, for example, the Appellate Body report in the Shrimp/Turtle case, *supra* note 83, WTO Doc. WT/DS58/AB/R (Nov. 6, 1998); Petros C. Mavroidis & Damien J. Neven, *Some Reflections on Extraterritoriality in International Economic Law: A Law and Economic Analysis*, *in* MÉLANGE EN HOMMAGE À MICHEL WAELBROECK 1297, 1311–18 (1999).

[101] One recent panel report has been vigorously criticized for "failing to interpret the TRIPS Agreement in a manner that does justice to the delicate balance of social and economic interests reflected in the stated purposes

According to G. R. Shell, the reform steps suggested above are mere palliatives that do not obviate "the twin problems of the WTO legal system": "overreliance on states to represent public interests and overcommitment to economic theory as the foundation for a jurisprudence of world trade."[102] The first of the duo relates directly to the problem of democracy and legitimacy. Relying on the civic republican theory, Shell calls for a regime of open, explicit legislative and regulatory bargaining, which would encompass, in addition to states, private commercial parties and social and environmental interest groups.[103] The second problem—exclusive reliance on the free trade value—evokes the lively discussion of "linkage" with other noneconomic values that I reported earlier.[104] As for overreliance on states, to open the dispute settlement mechanics to private "stakeholders" would mean abandoning the inveterate system of diplomatic protection in which only a state government can press a private claim against another state government and enjoys absolute discretion as to which claim to press. Unlike a private claimant, a government presumably takes into account not only the private but also the "state interest," such as the general relations with the "defendant" country and its relative political strength. On the other hand, a government may select a "bad" case under pressure from special interests, while permitting a "good" case to languish.[105]

In terms of integration, the progressive expansion of GATT rules and its "judicialization" in the WTO have marked a distinct advance, not unlike—in a broad sense—the evolution from the European Coal and Steel Community to the European Union. Unlike the European Union, however, the WTO institutions do not make important decisions (except in dispute settlement) since, in principle, any substantive obligations must be independently accepted by the members, a factor pointing strongly to a lower level of integration.

The question would arise, for those not satisfied with civic republicanism and "participatory democracy," whether the WTO—enhanced by greater transparency, access for consultation at all levels for stakeholders and NGOs, and closer relations to national parliaments—would meet the standards of liberal, representative democracy. Another question to ask is whether the global commitment to free trade is strong enough to sustain a significant expansion of WTO competence to the full scope of trade-related environmental, social, and sustainable development issues, and eventually perhaps to aspects of armaments trade, monetary questions, and consumer interests. For both the "nationalists" concerned about state sovereignty, and the liberals concerned about democracy, the answer may be to "stop the integration" and allow other (less integrated) international agencies (e.g., the ILO and mechanisms established by environmental treaties) to deal with the other values. One hears an echo of the familiar discourse on the democracy-legitimacy deficit and state sovereignty

of that Agreement" and for adopting an interpretation "that unduly curbs the regulatory autonomy of Members and that will undermine the legitimacy of the WTO in the eyes of its critics at a difficult point in the Organization's history." Robert Howse, *The Canadian Generic Medicines Panel—A Dangerous Precedent in Dangerous Times*, 3 J. WORLD INTELL. PROP. 493, 506 (2000); *see* U.S.—Trade Act, *supra* note 70. *See generally* Jackson, *Emerging Problems, supra* note 65.

[102] Shell, *supra* note 82, at 378. A panel discussion concluded that private action possibly with direct effect "has some promise although it has some problems." Panel Discussion, *supra* note 98, at 165.

[103] Democracy and legitimacy require standing and enforcement rights of private parties. Andrea K. Schneider, *Democracy and Dispute Resolution: Individual Rights in International Trade Organizations*, 19 U. PA. J. INT'L ECON. L. 587, 589 (1998).

[104] Shell proposes such linkage, but Philip Nichols believes that it should be made primarily in domestic politics and that market-oriented rules should yield to conflicting maximal values. Philip M. Nichols, *Trade Without Values*, 90 NW. U. L. REV. 658 (1996), *cited in* Kenneth W. Abbott, *The Decline of the Nation State*, 18 CARDOZO L. REV. 971, 976 (1996); Daniel C. Esty, *Linkages and Governance*, 19 U. PA. J. INT'L ECON. L. 709 (1998); *see also* John O. McGinnis, *The Decline of the Western Nation State and the Rise of the Regime of International Federalism*, 18 CARDOZO L. REV. 903 (1996).

[105] Panel Discussion, *supra* note 98, at 148, 158–59 (Eleanor Fox). Consider the experience with the investment chapter in NAFTA, *infra* text at notes 145–47.

surrounding the European Union as its competence expands from the Common Market to economic-monetary and social policies and other fields. While many accept the WTO essentially as currently constituted, others find it increasingly difficult to conceive of a multilateral trade regime confined exclusively to promoting economic efficiency through trade liberalization, in isolation from other vital values.[106]

IV. REGIONAL ECONOMIC GROUPINGS: THE NAFTA

Using the GATT global regime as an umbrella[107] and the European Community as an ideal model, regional groupings have emerged in Latin and North America,[108] Asia, and Africa, as well as in Europe, aiming essentially at the elimination of barriers to intraregional trade, often with the added vision of further integration in a more or less distant future.[109]

James McCall Smith studied some sixty regional trade pacts to assess factors such as the interaction between market size and trade dependence of their members; and the competences, goals, and structures, which range from exchange of specific trade concessions, to free trade area, customs union, "common market," and economic and monetary union. He also analyzed the "judicialization" or "legalism" of the dispute settlement mechanisms, ranging from ad hoc panel review to adjudication by a permanent court with access by private parties.[110]

[106] Andrew L. Strauss, *The Case for Utilizing the World Trade Organization as a Forum for Global Environmental Regulation*, 3 WIDENER L. SYMP. J. 309 (1998); WTO, Singapore Ministerial Declaration, Doc. WT/MIN(96)/DEC (Dec. 18, 1996) (stating that trade and labor cases should be dealt with by the International Labour Organization); *see also* Trade and Environment in the New WTO Round, Doc. WT/GC/W/197 (June 1, 1999); Dunoff, *supra* note 97, at 756. Ernst-Ulrich Petersmann suggests that subjecting national policies such as those on trade and social matters to international supervision in different fora advances the principle of checks and balances. Ernst-Ulrich Petersmann, *Constitutionalism and International Organization*, 17 NW. J. INT'L L. & BUS. 398, 431 (1997). Petersmann, despairing of the opposition by the "trade politicians and trade diplomats" to a European-style constitutionalization, calls for the creation of a new constituency (beyond that of the export industry) and for national parliaments and civil society to press for inclusion in future WTO rounds of a new initiative to "strengthen individual rights, constitutional safeguards and more representative institutions." Of his many writings on this subject, see most recently Ernst-Ulrich Petersmann, *From 'Negative' to 'Positive Integration' in the WTO: Time for Mainstreaming Human Rights into WTO Law*, 37 COMMON MKT. L. REV. 1363, 1570, *passim* (2000). He also proposes the establishment of an advisory WTO Economic and Social Committee composed of civil-society representatives and an advisory "parliamentary body" to help keep national parliaments better informed, *id.* at 1373. For suggestions on how the WTO should cope generally with the linkage problems, see Kym Anderson, *Environmental and Labor Standards: What Role for the WTO? in* THE WTO AS AN INTERNATIONAL ORGANIZATION 231, 245–52 (Anne O. Krueger ed., 1998). *See also* Thomas J. Schoenbaum, *International Trade and Protection of the Environment: The Continuing Search for Reconciliation*, 91 AJIL 268 (1997); Richard H. Steinberg, *Trade-Environment Negotiations in the EU, NAFTA and WTO: Regional Trajectories of Rule Development*, 91 AJIL 231 (1997). Christopher McCrudden and Ann Davis, *A Perspective on Trade and Labor Rights*, 3 J. INT'L ECON. L. 43 (2000), foresee continuing pressure on the WTO to encompass labor issues, if for no other reason because it has more effective enforcement instruments than the ILO.

[107] According to GATT Art. XXIV, regional groupings have to request a waiver of the most-favored-nation rule.

[108] For the NAFTA, see *supra* note 80. *See generally* Smith, *supra* note 31.

[109] TREBILCOCK & HOWSE, *supra* note 8, at 24. Examples are the African Common Market, the Andean Community, Asia-Pacific Economic Cooperation (APEC), the Association of Southeast Asian States (ASEAN), the Caribbean (CARICOM), and Mercosur. NEW DIMENSIONS IN REGIONAL INTEGRATION (Jaime de Melo & Arvind Parnagariya eds., 1993) explores integration in sub-Saharan Africa, Latin America, western and eastern Europe, and East Asia, and its prospects in the Middle East. *See also* FREDERICK M. ABBOTT, LAW AND POLICY OF REGIONAL INTEGRATION: THE NAFTA AND WESTERN HEMISPHERIC INTEGRATION IN THE WORLD TRADE ORGANIZATION SYSTEM (1995); REGIONAL INTEGRATION AND DEMOCRACY: EXPANDING ON THE EUROPEAN EXPERIENCE (Jeffrey J. Anderson ed., 1999) [hereinafter REGIONAL INTEGRATION].

[110] In a regional grouping, the relatively large countries tend to prefer less judicialization than their smaller partners and they also tend to prevail in defining the lowest common denominator. Again, where economic asymmetry among members is high and the level of integration low, the judicialization of dispute settlement is invariably low. By focusing exclusively on third-party review, the study did not take into account dispute settlement modes and organs such as secretariats, commissions, and surveillance authorities. McCall Smith, *supra* note 31. In what was termed "naïve institutionalism," the inquiry did not purport to deal with the actual development and impact of the pacts. Robert O. Keohane, Comments, *in* MILES KAHLER, INTERNATIONAL INSTITUTIONS AND THE POLITICAL ECONOMY OF INTEGRATION, *cited in* McCall Smith, *supra*, at 172.

The institutions established by the respective treaties differ greatly both in the degree of purported integration and in their rates of success. In reality, many of the organizations have hardly begun to approach their goals and some even ended in outright failure.[111]

I will briefly discuss the NAFTA, which was concluded in 1992 and in large part extended the 1988 bilateral U.S.-Canada Free Trade Agreement to include Mexico.[112] I have two related reasons for this choice. First, the NAFTA represents a step beyond the integration level of the WTO in its substantive competences; and second, the public and academic discourse the NAFTA has elicited has been particularly revealing. In the United States, for instance, the NAFTA led to a court proceeding even before it had entered into force.[113]

Normative-Institutional Factors

Competence, structure, voting. The NAFTA's competence cuts across an even wider swath of trade and trade-related activities than the WTO's. Moreover, to assuage the strong opposition from private groups, the NAFTA negotiators, contrary to those of the WTO, expressly included many trade-related aspects of national environmental and labor policies in parallel agreements.[114]

Reflecting its limited membership, NAFTA's institutions deviate from the three-part pattern to an even greater extent than the WTO's. The NAFTA Free Trade Commission, comprising cabinet-level representatives of the three state parties, supervises implementation of the Agreement, "oversees its further elaboration," resolves disputes regarding interpretation of the Agreement, and plays a role in the dispute settlement process. It is supported by a full-time secretariat composed of three national sections and complemented by various trilateral working groups and committees.[115] In the implementation process, the commission acts generally by consensus but may agree by consensus on another formula. No provision is made for public participation or the publication of reports or other documents.[116] Unlike the European Commission, the NAFTA Commission is little more than a name given to meetings of high-ranking NAFTA trade officials, and the activities of the secretariat's sections have been quite limited.[117] New rules and changes in the Agreement are negotiated and approved by the three parties, signaling a low level of integration in rule making.

[111] Among those listed in the category of the highest judicialization (a permanent judicial tribunal), the East African Community and the West African Economic Community have been formally dissolved, the Court of Justice of the Economic Community of West African States awaits the realization of the treaty commitments, and the jurisdiction of the Economic Court of the Commonwealth of Independent States "appears to be severely restricted." Judicial bodies envisaged for the Central American Common Market, the Andean Pact, the European Free Trade Area, and the Common Market for Eastern and Southern Africa draw on the model of the European Court of Justice. McCall Smith, *supra* note 31, at 158; *see also* Maricel Sequeira, *Bilateral Bickering Stalls Regional Integration*, TICO TIMES, Mar. 3, 2000, at 9 (suggesting that Central America is in a strange process of simultaneous social integration and political disintegration). Is regionalism preferable to multilateralism? *See* Frederick M. Abbott, *Integration Without Institutions: The NAFTA Mutation of the EC Model and the Future of the GATT Regime*, 40 AM. J. COMP. L. 917 (1992).

[112] TREBILCOCK & HOWSE, *supra* note 8, at 39. *See generally* WILLIAM J. DAVEY, PINE AND SWINE: CANADA–UNITED STATES TRADE DISPUTE SETTLEMENT: THE FTA EXPERIENCE AND NAFTA PROSPECTS (1996); FREDERICK W. MAYER, INTERPRETING NAFTA: THE SCIENCE AND ART OF POLITICAL ANALYSIS (1998); NAFTA: A PROBLEM-ORIENTED COURSEBOOK (Ralph H. Folsom, Michael Wallace Gordon, & David Lopez eds., 2000).

[113] Public Citizen v. Office of United States Trade Representative, 782 F.Supp. 139 (D.D.C. 1992), *rev'd*, 5 F.3d 549 (D.C. Cir. 1993), *cert. denied*, 510 U.S. 1041 (1994). The NAFTA "package" did not need to be submitted to Congress before the U.S. government had prepared an environmental impact statement; NAFTA is not "final agency action" reviewable under the Administrative Procedure Act. For a related proceeding, see Public Citizen v. Office of United States Trade Representative, 822 F.Supp.2d 21 (D.D.C.), 5 F.3d 549 (D.C. Cir. 1993), *cert. denied*, 510 U.S. 1041 (1994). *See generally* David A. Gantz, *Principal Features of the North American Free Trade Agreement*, *in* MAKING FREE TRADE WORK IN THE AMERICAS 34 (Boris Kozolchyk ed., 1993).

[114] For a succinct enumeration, see Gantz, *supra* note 113, at 34–51. *See also* TREBILCOCK & HOWSE, *supra* note 8, at 39–42.

[115] NAFTA, *supra* note 80, Art. 2001(1)e4; ABBOTT, *supra* note 109, at 28; TREBILCOCK & HOWSE, *supra* note 8, at 43.

[116] Housman, *supra* note 58, at 722.

[117] E-mail from Professor William J. Davey to the author (Nov. 2, 2000) (on file with author).

Adjudication. Subject to several exceptions, a party to a dispute has the option to resort either to GATT or to NAFTA settlement procedures.[118] The general NAFTA system envisages a conciliation phase with the assistance of the tripartite commission. If no agreement is reached, a party has the right to the appointment (by the commission) of a five-member arbitration panel, chosen from a roster compiled "by consensus" of the three parties. The panel decides by majority vote and its decision is final. There is no permanent appellate body. As in the WTO, in cases of noncompliance with the panel's recommendations, the prevailing party has the right to suspend benefits of equivalent effect. If that measure is disputed, the commission establishes another panel to determine whether the level of suspended benefits is "manifestly excessive." Clear deadlines are set for the consecutive steps and the judicial nature of the panel proceeding is emphasized. While the NAFTA, like the WTO, provides for a final decision, the ultimate resolution of the dispute rests in the hands of the political representatives of the three parties on the commission.

The panel sessions, initial reports, and briefs are all confidential. A panel may seek information from outside sources or a scientific review board only if both parties agree. The final report is published after fifteen days unless the commission decides otherwise.[119] The picture is more complex than just described, however, because several areas have their own, distinct dispute settlement mechanisms.

Special procedures deal with antidumping and countervailing duties under NAFTA Chapter 19. They are particularly interesting because they reach into the domestic legal order in a unique way and thus may be viewed as raising the level of normative integration.[120] In these cases, private parties that would normally be entitled to judicial review of administrative determinations may demand, *as of right*, that their government proceed to establish a binational panel. This panel replaces national judicial review of final determinations by domestic authorities; it issues a binding decision on whether the final determination conforms to the domestic law of the importing country in question, but it must apply the standards of judicial review and the general principles that a court of that country would apply.[121] If the panel finds that the national determination does not accord with the NAFTA text, it refers the matter to the domestic agency for redetermination. The panel decision is binding on the two parties and is not reviewable by a domestic judicial procedure. If the exporter company concerned is dissatisfied with the redetermination by the domestic agency, it may have its government request another panel. The only recourse against the panel's ruling is the "Extraordinary Challenge" before a special committee on very limited grounds, such as gross misconduct and violation of fundamental rules of procedure, which may result in the taking of compensatory measures by the complaining party. A similar procedure applies in disputes over contested changes in national antidumping or countervailing legislation.[122] Many cases have arisen under this procedure.[123]

[118] Sections 3 and 4 of Article 2005 allow only the NAFTA procedures in environmental, conservancy, sanitary, and phytosanitary matters.

[119] NAFTA, *supra* note 80, Arts. 2012–18; ABBOTT, *supra* note 109, at 100–01; Abbott, *supra* note 70. The roster of prospective panelists is to consist "to the fullest extent practicable" of judges or former judges and the majority of the panel must be lawyers. NAFTA Annex 1901.2.1, .2.2. The process is to be based "on judicial rules of appellate procedure." NAFTA Art. 1904.14. It is argued that particularly in the light of textual and contextual differences between the WTO and the NAFTA, the final NAFTA reports under Chapter 20 are less likely to be viewed as imposing an international obligation on the losing party than on its counterpart in the WTO. The only obligation is to negotiate in good faith. This question apparently has not been widely explored. E-mail from Frederick M. Abbott to the author (May 22, 2001).

[120] The provisions of Chapter 19 encapsulate a laboriously negotiated compromise between Canada and the United States. Canada insisted on a change in what it viewed as protectionist American legislation and practice, and the United States peremptorily rejected any such change.

[121] TREBILCOCK & HOWSE, *supra* note 8, at 84.

[122] *Id.* at 43. In contrast with decisions under Chapter 20, discussed above, the decisions under Chapter 19 are likely to be considered as imposing international legal obligations. *See supra* note 119.

[123] Gustavo Vega-Cánovas, *NAFTA and the EU: Toward Convergence?* in REGIONAL INTEGRATION, *supra* note 109, at 225, 240–41. He reports that thirty-five antidumping cases have arisen since March 1992 in what appears to be a "recurring problem, causing deep frustration among businesses." *Id.* at 240.

Another special dispute procedure relevant to the subject of this essay pertains to investments and is outlined in Chapter 11 of the NAFTA. An individual investor who claims that a host government has breached an obligation under this chapter is entitled to invoke an arbitration tribunal with the possibility of obtaining an interpretation from the NAFTA Commission. The arbitration procedure may be based on rules of the International Centre for Settlement of Investment Disputes or the UN Commission on International Trade Law. The arbitral awards for monetary damages are directly enforceable in domestic courts as if they were domestic court judgments. This procedure raises NAFTA's level of normative integration. Although individual access to domestic courts or arbitral tribunals for the protection of investment has been an established international practice, private parties are given direct access to international dispute resolution mechanisms for the first time in an international trade treaty.[124] In fact, investors have filed nearly a dozen Chapter 11 cases, at least one of which prompted Canada to repeal a domestic environmental law and pay a multimillion-dollar compensation award.[125]

Side Agreements on Environment and Labor

Important "side agreements" on the environment and labor cooperation were negotiated primarily at the insistence of the United States in order to assuage NGO opposition and to assure the passage of the NAFTA in Congress. These accords contain separate sets of institutions. For the environment, they comprise the commission, the ministerial-level council, the secretariat, and the tripartite, fifteen-member Joint Public Advisory Committee. The council makes nonbinding recommendations by consensus.[126] The core obligation of the parties is to enforce their own environmental law effectively. The parties are held to this obligation by means of binding dispute settlement similar to general NAFTA procedures, but leading ultimately to a monetary assessment against the persistently noncomplying party. As an interesting feature, the assessment is paid to a fund administered by the NAFTA rather than to a party.[127] Although only party governments have access to dispute settlement, "interested persons" may ask a party's authorities to investigate an alleged instance of noncompliance. In addition, NGOs may submit a complaint to the secretariat, which may prepare a factual report on the charges if so authorized by the Environment Council. That report may be published—the only penalty for noncompliance—if the council authorizes it by a two-thirds vote. Of the fifteen NGO submissions received by the end of 1998, only one had led to a determination by the secretariat that a full factual report should be developed.[128]

The North American Agreement for Labor Cooperation,[129] like its counterpart for environmental issues, establishes an "umbrella" commission with a ministerial-level council, a

[124] TREBILCOCK & HOWSE, *supra* note 8, at 83.

[125] Laurence R. Helfer, *in* Forum, *Do the Lessons of EU Integration 'Travel'?* ECSA REV., Winter 2000, at 2, 4–5. In 1999 a Canadian company sued the U.S. government in an American court for violating Chapter 11 of NAFTA. HARMONIZATION ALERT, June–July 1999, at 1. *See generally* Pavel Šturma, *Commerce et investissement*, 52 REVUE HELLÉNIQUE DE DROIT INTERNATIONAL 39 (1999). A Mexican professor of international law considers Chapter 11 incompatible with the Mexican Constitution, particularly because it does not provide for exhaustion of local remedies (citing Arts. 133, 27, and 13 of the Constitution), and he advocates a reservation to NAFTA. Bernardo Sepúlveda Amor, *International Law and National Sovereignty: The NAFTA and the Claims of Mexican Jurisdiction*, 19 HOUS. J. INT'L L. 565, 573, 590–93 (1997). It is said that criticism of Chapter 11 "spilled over" into the debate on the proposed Multilateral Agreement on Investment and contributed to its defeat.

[126] North American Agreement on Environmental Cooperation, Sept. 14, 1993, Can.-Mex.-U.S., pt. V, Arts. 5, 6, 8, 12, 32 ILM 1480 (1993); TREBILCOCK & HOWSE, *supra* note 8, at 436; Frona M. Powell, *The North American Commission for Environmental Cooperation's San Pedro Report: A Case Study and Analysis of the CEC Process*, 6 ENVTL. LAW. 809 (2000).

[127] NAFTA, *supra* note 80, Annex 34, Art. 3. Withdrawal of NAFTA trade benefits is also available as a penalty.

[128] TREBILCOCK & HOWSE, *supra* note 8, at 438–39.

[129] Sept. 8, 9, 12, 14, 1993, Can.-Mex.-U.S., 32 ILM 1499 (1993); *The North American Agreement on Labor Cooperation: Linking Labor Standards and Rights to Trade Agreements: A Conference*, 12 AM. U. J. INT'L L. & POL'Y 815 (1997).

secretariat, and a similar dispute settlement procedure. In addition, each party is required to establish a national administrative office at the federal level with a variety of contact, study, and information functions. By early 1999, some twenty submissions alleging violations of the obligation to enforce national labor laws were submitted by NGOs to the respective national administrative offices in all three countries.[130]

Empirical-Social Factors; the Impact

The NAFTA was superimposed on large-scale movements of goods and services in the region. It is impossible to determine with any degree of accuracy its direct impact on trade flow, investment, and employment, but both its defenders and its opponents tend to exaggerate its effects. A Mexican scholar noted that the NAFTA's years of existence have been marked by a vigorous expansion of trade and investment: "NAFTA has also served as a vehicle for government cooperation on a variety of regulatory matters and has provided a valuable context for resolving several controversies."[131] But he also observed a number of problems, not least of which was the undiminished flow of antidumping-countervailing cases. Furthermore, some evidence suggests that the existence of the NAFTA has advanced the movement toward democracy in Mexican politics.

The Discourse

At the national level: constitutionality, identity. The question of NAFTA's constitutionality, and particularly that of the binational panels in the antidumping-countervailing chapter, has been raised in all three countries, but thus far has elicited lively debate and court action only in the United States. In the academic discourse of all three countries, the removal of the right of judicial review from national courts under the antidumping–countervailing duty provisions was viewed as arguably inconsistent with the constitutionally guaranteed right of access to national courts.[132] Moreover, in Canada the issue of federalism surfaced, particularly in light of the limits on federal power set by the provinces' competence regarding services, investment, and labor.[133]

In the United States the bitter exchange in Congress, the media, and the academy was accentuated by attacks on the "fast track" procedure employed in congressional approval of the NAFTA and the trade treaties.[134] In contrast to Canada and Mexico, the United States

[130] *See* Reba S. Koerner, *Pregnancy Discrimination in Mexico: Has Mexico Complied with the North American Agreement on Labor Cooperation?* 4 TEX. F. ON C.L. & C.R. 235 (1999). *See generally* Stephen F. Diamond, *Labor Rights in the Global Economy: A Case Study of the North American Free Trade Agreement, in* HUMAN RIGHTS, LABOR RIGHTS AND INTERNATIONAL TRADE 199, 212–21 (Lance A. Compa & Stephen F. Diamond eds., 1996); Robert E. Herzstein, *The Labor Cooperation Agreement Among Mexico, Canada and the United States: Its Negotiation and Prospects,* 3 U.S.-MEX. L.J. 121 (1995).

[131] Vega-Cánovas, *supra* note 123, at 241. Mexico has become the second largest market for U.S. exports. Anne O. Krueger, Trade Creation and Trade Diversion under NAFTA (Working Paper 7429, National Bureau of Economic Research, Dec. 1999), *at* <http://www.nber.org/papers/w7429>; *see* JOINING TOGETHER, STANDING APART: NATIONAL IDENTITIES AFTER NAFTA (Dorinda G. Dallmeyer ed., 1997) [hereinafter JOINING TOGETHER]. In particular, see Robert A. Pastor, *id.* at xi–xiv; Louis L. Ortmayer, *id.* at 25–34; and Alejandro Nadal, *id.* at 51–62. For a case study of the impact on the environment, see Powell, *supra* note 126.

[132] For Mexico, see CONST. Art. 27; *see also id.*, Art. 13. On incompatibility, see Sepúlveda, *supra* note 125, at 592. For Canada, see Constitutional Act §96 (1867); Avi Gesser, *Why NAFTA Violates the Canadian Constitution,* 27 DENV. J. INT'L L. & POL'Y 121, 130 (1998). *See also* Louis Manuel Perez de Acha, *Binational Panels: A Conflict of Idiosyncrasies,* 3 SW. J. L. & TRADE AM. 431, 434 (1996).

[133] Writers have considered judicial precedents limiting the powers of both the federal and the provincial authorities to delegate judicial authority to other than "section 96 courts," and the notorious 1937 ruling of the Privy Council striking down federal legislation aimed at implementing an ILO convention. Gesser, *supra* note 132, at 137–50 (citing case law). The disruption of domestic federalism and federal-state relations was raised in the United States as well. David A. Wirth, *Government by Trade Agreement, in* JOINING TOGETHER, *supra* note 131, at 111, 112–29.

[134] In that procedure, Congress delegates advance negotiating authority to the president on the understanding that it will approve or disapprove the resulting text without amendment. Harold H. Koh, *Congressional Controls on Presidential Trade Policy-Making After* I.N.S. v. Chadha, 18 N.Y.U. J. INT'L L. & POL. 1191 (1986). *See generally* Wirth, *supra* note 133.

has seen challenges to NAFTA's constitutionality—thus far unsuccessful—in the federal courts.[135] For example, the constitutionality of the NAFTA was contested on the ground that it had been approved as a congressional-executive agreement by a majority of both houses, rather than as a treaty under Article II of the Constitution by a two-thirds majority of the Senate. The court of appeals directed that the case be dismissed as involving "a political question."[136] A more credible challenge, explored in ample legal writings, concerns Article III and the principles of separation of powers, due process, and equal protection. The Appointment Clause has also been mentioned as grounds for a possible constitutional objection.[137]

The writers' conclusions have varied greatly.[138] The proponents of constitutionality of the binational panels rely on the similarity of these panels to congressionally established "legislative courts" (particularly the regulatory agencies), which wield quasi-judicial power and have been held constitutional;[139] "[t]he structure of the system prevents Congress and the executive from exerting control over the panels' judicial functions, thus, securing the values that underlie Article III."[140] Other supporting arguments rely on the federal foreign relations power and the fact that only public (congressionally created) rights are involved.[141] In its present form, the NAFTA would probably pass the constitutional barriers in the United States, as well as in Canada and Mexico, both of whose constitutions contain provisions equivalent to Article III of the U.S. Constitution. If, however, the judicial power is further projected directly onto the national legal orders, the challenge to constitutionality may become more serious. Finally, in English-speaking Canada, critics of free trade agreements with the United States have worried about the impact on Canada's "cultural sovereignty,"

[135] As a concession to NAFTA opponents, Congress included in the implementing legislation a provision for an accelerated appellate procedure for judicial review of the actions of the NAFTA binational panels, 19 U.S.C. §1516a(g)(4)(A) (Supp. V 1999). The first of the early cases before the federal courts, brought by an important trade association and arising out of the Extraordinary Challenge Committee's ruling, was withdrawn by voluntary motion to dismiss (Jan. 5, 1995). Coalition for Fair Lumber Imports v. United States, No. 94-1627 (D.C. Cir. filed Sept. 14, 1994). A second case was dismissed unanimously because of the plaintiff's lack of standing to sue the president and the U.S. government. Am. Coalition for Competitive Trade v. Clinton, 128 F.3d 761 (D.C. Cir. 1997). See the extensive provisions for consultation with the states and protection of their competence in the U.S. implementing legislation, 19 U.S.C. §3312(b)(1)(A) (Supp. II 1997).

[136] Made in USA Found. v. United States, 56 F.Supp.2d 1226 (N.D. Ala. 1999), *appeal dismissed*, 242 F.3d 1300 (11th Cir. 2001), 2001 U.S. App. LEXIS 2800; *see* Bruce Ackerman & David Golove, *Is NAFTA Constitutional?* 108 HARV. L. REV. 799 (1995); Laurence H. Tribe, *Taking Text and Structure Seriously: Reflections on Free-Form Method in Constitutional Interpretation*, 108 HARV. L. REV. 1221 (1995).

[137] William J. Davey, *The Appointments Clause and International Dispute Settlement Mechanisms: A False Conflict*, 49 WASH. & LEE L. REV. 1315 (1992); Kim, *supra* note 65, at 985–86.

[138] *E.g.*, Ethan Boyer, *Article III, the Foreign Relations Power, and the Binational Panel System of NAFTA*, 13 INT'L TAX & BUS. LAW. 101 (1996) (constitutional under the Schor balancing test); Denis J. Edwards, *NAFTA and Article III: Making a Drama out of a Crisis*, 1 NAFTA: L. & BUS. REV. AM. 69 (1995) (constitutional); Brian F. Havel, *The Constitution in an Era of Supranational Adjudication*, 78 N.C. L. REV. 257 (2000) (constitutional); Kim, *supra* note 65, at 967 (constitutional); Demetrios G. Metropoulos, *Constitutional Dimensions of the North American Free Trade Agreement*, 27 CORNELL INT'L L.J. 141 (1994) (unconstitutional); Patrick Tangney, *The New Internationalism: The Cession of Sovereign Competences to Supranational Organizations and Constitutional Change in the United States and Germany*, 21 YALE J. INT'L L. 395 (1996) (doubtful). In a 1997 address, the chief judge of the U.S. Court of International Trade, Gregory W. Carman, expressed serious doubts about the constitutionality of Chapter 19, calling it a "flawed system." He was particularly troubled by the presidential executive order implementing the NAFTA, which accepts "in advance all decisions of binational panels and the Extraordinary Challenge Committee." Gregory W. Carman, *Address: Resolution of Trade Disputes by Chapter 19 Panels: A Long-Term Solution or Interim Procedure of Dubious Constitutionality*, 21 FORDHAM INT'L L.J. 1, 9 (1997). Mexico omitted Chapter 19 from trade agreements with the Latin American countries, as did Canada and Chile. *Id.* at 10.

[139] *See* Boyer, *supra* note 138, at 115, 123; Kim, *supra* note 65, at 983 (citing the precedent of the U.S.-Canada Free Trade Agreement).

[140] Boyer, *supra* note 138, at 141. Even Chomsky's linguistic theory is enlisted to put a seal of constitutionality on the NAFTA. Havel, *supra* note 138, at 272.

[141] *See generally* LOUIS HENKIN, FOREIGN AFFAIRS AND THE UNITED STATES CONSTITUTION 26 (2d ed. 1996). The nondelegation doctrine does not apply with equal force to foreign affairs. *See* Harold H. Koh, *The Fast Track and United States Trade Policy*, 18 BROOK. J. INT'L L. 143, 168 (1992); *see also* Dames & Moore v. Regan, 453 U.S. 654 (1981); DELEGATING STATE POWERS, *supra* note 80; Kim, *supra* note 65, at 984. On the provisions of the Canadian and Mexican Constitutions, see *supra* note 132.

while "Quebec nationalists and sovereignists have welcomed NAFTA and endorsed its underlying globalizing and modernist force."[142]

At the international level: transparency, citizen participation. The other phase of the democratic-deficit discourse focuses on the working of the NAFTA institution. It concerns the lack of openness and citizen participation both in the negotiations creating the NAFTA and in its operation. Thus, the critics stress that NAFTA bodies meet in private and produce no transcript or public report. Citizens and NGOs are precluded from appearing before the panels and from independently supplying information to them. The dispute panels are open only to interested states, and the pleadings published only with the approval of the parties concerned. However, provision is made under the Agreement on Environmental Cooperation for a public component and the publication of decisions and reports. The Environment Council may meet in public at its discretion, but consideration of citizens' or NGOs' submissions is subject to strict control.[143] Although the environment secretariat may draw on outside information, the public may be denied access to its reports by a vote of the council. The process under the Agreement on Labor is said to be even less open, except for the authority of the Evaluation Committee of Experts to review disputes. This committee is composed of three independent members, unaffiliated with the parties or the labor secretariat.[144]

Judicialization, integration, democracy. Although some criticize the selection process and the status of the judges-panelists, others stress the legitimacy of the NAFTA regime that derives from the conformity of its quasi-judicial system with the essence of the rule-of-law requirement. The binational panel system and its exclusion of national judicial review in one category of disputes, the role of individuals and groups in the application of the side agreements, and the enforceability of money awards in domestic courts raise the NAFTA's integration level incrementally over that of the WTO. There is, however, no counterpart to the standing WTO Appellate Body in the NAFTA.

The direct access of private investors to international arbitration of their rights under Chapter 11 suggests an analogy, on a lower scale of integration, to the advanced European judicial system and—on its face—would be expected to provide a measure of legitimation to the NAFTA. Nevertheless, in a backlash, a variety of environmental, labor, and consumer protection NGOs have branded Chapter 11 plaintiffs as "corporate predators" who use a "secret tranche of international laws" to overturn national laws that obstruct their business activities.[145] Even some government officials are reported to view Chapter 11 as a threat to national sovereignty and to endorse proposals that would do away with private-party access.[146] Although Chapter 11 was originally intended to protect investors against expropriation and discrimination, by extensive interpretation—so goes the argument—these same investors have been able to use its provisions to challenge national laws of general application, particularly environmental regulations.[147] This quarrel suggests an ironic twist to the proposals discussed earlier to make individual stakeholders the principal actors in the WTO.

The NAFTA remains a state-based regime that, like the GATT/WTO, retains many features common to diplomacy. As in the WTO, rule making is strictly consensual. However, the dispute settlement process is heavily institutionalized, even though the NAFTA provides for greater use of "soft enforcement mechanisms" (e.g., consultation, negotiation) than the WTO. Reform toward more democracy might call for a more effective link with national

[142] Daniel Salée, *NAFTA, Quebec, and the Boundaries of Cultural Sovereignty: The Challenge of Identity in the Era of Globalization*, *in* JOINING TOGETHER, *supra* note 131, at 73, 88.

[143] Compare the problem of publicity in the WTO, *supra* text after note 88.

[144] Housman, *supra* note 58, at 722–27; Petros C. Mavroidis, *Trade and Environment After the* Shrimps-Turtles *Litigation*, J. WORLD TRADE, Feb. 2000, at 73.

[145] Helfer, *supra* note 125, at 5 (quoting Paul Kingsnorth, *A Very Happy Birthday for NAFTA*, ECOLOGIST, Jan. 1, 1999).

[146] Ian Jack, *Ottawa Pushes for Reform of NAFTA Lawsuit Provisions: $1 Billion in Claims*, FIN. POST (Can.), Apr. 20, 1999, *cited in id.*

[147] Helfer, *supra* note 125. See the discussion on state v. individual stakeholder, *supra* text after note 104.

parliaments, but a more promising avenue might be toward more transparency and public participation.[148] Commentators have suggested that diplomacy and politics tend to seep through the NAFTA panel process and that the WTO procedure would treat the weaker partners more impartially.[149]

V. Beyond Economic Integration: The European Union

Vive la Différence?

Three major features distinguish the European Union[150] from the traditional scheme of the UN specialized agencies and the regional groupings for which the Union has served as a model. These differences, striking as they may appear at first, do not, in my view, stand in the way of a meaningful comparison with other international structures. Nor do I agree with the argument that the evolution of the European Union and its law, particularly in its relation to nonmember states, is irrelevant to international law and the law of international organizations.[151]

The first and foremost distinguishing characteristic is the uncommonly high level of integration. I discuss this in the next section.

The second differentiating factor is the distinctive environment in post-World War II Europe. Whatever the status of the democracy requirement under general international law, it has doubtless become part of European regional law, as reflected in regional treaties and the behavior of the governments. Unlike, for instance, the United Nations, the "all European" Council of Europe requires acceptance by its members of democracy, the rule of law, and basic human rights protection, and provides for suspension and ultimately exclusion of any member that seriously violates these undertakings.[152] More specifically, Protocol No. 1 to the Council-sponsored European Convention for the Protection of Human Rights and Fundamental Freedoms obligates the parties "to hold free elections at reasonable intervals by secret ballot, under conditions which will ensure the free expression of the opinion of the people in the choice of the legislature."[153] The Organization for Security and Co-operation in Europe (OSCE) has embraced the same triad of principles.[154]

[148] *See* Housman, *supra* note 58, at 728–47 (with detailed suggestions).

[149] Vilaysoun Loungnarath & Céline Stehly, *The General Dispute Settlement Mechanism in the North American Free Trade Agreement and the World Trade Organization System—Is North American Regionalism Really Preferable to Multilateralism?* J. World Trade, Feb. 2000, at 39.

[150] Consolidated Treaty on European Union, Oct. 2, 1997, 1997 O.J. (C 340) 145 [hereinafter EU Treaty]; Consolidated EC Treaty, Oct. 2, 1997, 1997 O.J. (C 340) 173 [hereinafter EC Treaty]. A handy consolidated version including changes by the Treaty of Amsterdam was published by the Council of the European Union, General Secretariat, Intergovernmental Conference, Consolidated Versions, CONF 4005/97 & Adds. 1& 2.

For an introduction to the structure of the European Union, see, for example, P. J. G. Kapteyn & Pieter Verloren van Themaat, Introduction to the Law of the European Communities (L. W. Gormley ed., 3d rev. ed. 1998); Lawmaking in the European Union (Paul Craig & Carol Harlow eds., 1998); P. S. R. F. Mathijsen, A Guide to European Union Law (7th ed. 1999); Michael Newman, Democracy, Sovereignty and the European Union (1996); Weiler, *supra* note 27.

[151] *See generally* J. H. H. Weiler & Joel P. Trachtman, *European Constitutionalism and Its Discontents*, 17 Nw. J. Int'l L. & Bus. 354, 355 (1997).

[152] Council of Europe Statute pmbl., Art. 3, 87 UNTS 103. The Council of Europe has repeatedly rebuked Ukraine for failing to fulfill its obligation to abolish the death penalty and for harassing independent media. RFE/RL, Newsline, Oct. 19, 1999, pt. II, at 3. Additionally, EU institutions have often criticized central/eastern European states for their failure to respect principles of democracy and human rights.

[153] Optional Protocol No. 1 to the European Convention for the Protection of Human Rights and Fundamental Freedoms, Nov. 4, 1950, Art. 3, 213 UNTS 262.

[154] OSCE election commitments were established in the document on the Copenhagen meeting of the Conference on the Human Dimension of the CSCE, June 29, 1990, paras. 6, 7, 8, 29 ILM 1305 (1990). See most recently the Istanbul Summit Declaration, with a new Charter for Security, Nov. 19, 1999, secs. III, IV, 39 ILM 255 (2000). ASIL, International Law in Brief, Nov. 22–26, 1999, at 9–10, *at* <http://www.asil.org>; NATO Rev., Spring/Summer 2000, at 23–26.

The European Community was conceived as an essentially technocratic organization, and has moved gradually toward greater democracy.[155] Today, the EU Treaty enshrines the principles of democracy, human rights, and rule of law as specific obligations for both its internal and its external activities. It also lays down an elaborate procedure in case of a serious and persistent breach by a member state.[156] However, these broad principles, although made more specific in the European treaties, still do not provide more than a general guide in the discourse about reshaping EU institutions to make them more democratic and legitimate. As we explore the "living law" of the European Union, it might be useful to keep in mind the three-pronged paradigm of a modern liberal democracy I offered in part I.[157]

A third aspect that sets the European Union apart from other international institutions is the nature and intensity of the debate on the democracy-legitimacy deficit, which reached a high pitch at the time of the national ratification procedures of the EU Treaty in the early 1990s. That debate has quickly expanded, as I shall show, to include the more general issues of the Union's future configuration, with social concepts such as solidarity and identity coming to the fore. Paradoxically, the European Union, though composed exclusively of liberal democratic states seeking to advance democracy in other states,[158] and bound by the principles of democracy as a legal person within the texture of European regional law and even more emphatically by its own constituent treaties, has been subjected to more charges of sustaining a democratic deficit within its institutions than any other international structure. The paradox may be explained by the origin and evolutionary method of the Union, but above all by the general difficulty of injecting democracy into international institutions, which I discussed above and which in this case is exacerbated by the unprecedentedly high level of integration.

Normative-Institutional Factors

Competence, lawmaking process. The original competence of the European Union covered the building and policing of a common market with free movement for goods, workers, capital, services, and entrepreneurs, and common policies in agriculture, competition, transportation, and foreign commerce. The Union's powers have progressively grown, at first by interpretive processes and then by successive treaty amendments, to include the transition to a "single market," an Economic and Monetary Union with a common currency, common control of EU frontiers, judicial cooperation, aspects of environment and consumer protection, social, educational, and cultural policies, and a foundation for common foreign and security policies. The Union also stands at the center of an elaborate network of treaties with nonmember states.[159] In a limited number of areas the Union wields exclusive competence, while in others it shares competence with member states. However, the long-range tendency has been toward more integration in a complex pattern of shared governance.

[155] Federico Mancini & David T. Keeling, *Democracy and the European Court of Justice*, 57 MOD. L. REV. 175 (1994).

[156] EU TREATY pmbl., Art. 6 (ex-Art. F), Art. 7 (ex-Art. F.1). In the crucial vote on sanctions against a delinquent state, the vote of that state is not taken into account. EC TREATY Art. 11 (ex-Art. J.1), Art. 177 (ex-Art. 130u). An "early warning" procedure of a persistent breach of basic rights was introduced by the Nice Treaty of 2000, *infra* note 165. The EU member states went so far as to impose limitations on the contacts with one of the members (Austria) because that country included in its government representatives of a political party deemed opposed to EU principles, even though that party had emerged as the second most popular group in a free election. BULL. QUOT. EUR., Jan. 31/Feb. 1, 2000, at 5–6; Martti Ahtisaari, Jochen Frowein, & Marcelino Oreja, Report (adopted Sept. 8, 2000), *at* <http://www.austria.gv.at/e/> (visited July 16, 2000).

[157] *See supra* text at notes 18–24. *See generally* MARIO TELÓ, DÉMOCRATIE ET CONSTRUCTION EUROPÉENNE (1995).

[158] Council Regulation 975/1999, 1999 O.J. (L 120) 1 (setting as a general objective of cooperation policy toward developing countries, the advancement of democracy, the rule of law, and respect for human rights; and also setting forth the procedure for implementing this objective); Stein, *supra* note 20.

[159] ERIC STEIN, THOUGHTS FROM A BRIDGE: A RETROSPECTIVE OF WRITINGS ON NEW EUROPE AND AMERICAN FEDERALISM 220–43 (2000) [hereinafter STEIN, BRIDGE].

In Community lawmaking, the executive EC Commission ("the conscience and motor" of the Community and "guardian of the Treaty"), appointed by agreement of the member governments but presumed to be independent, proposes legislation and policy, and the Council of Ministers, composed of ministers in national governments, "disposes," originally with mere advice from the European Parliament.[160] The European Council is composed of the heads of member states or governments and provides general political direction. In contrast with voting procedure in the earlier stages of integration and largely as a result of the Single European Act of 1987, the current voting formula in the Council of Ministers calls for a qualified majority in most instances, although consensus is still required for sensitive sectors such as taxation, workers' rights, and generally foreign affairs. This aspect—which again contrasts with lawmaking in the specialized agencies—greatly raises the level of integration in the normative-institutional sense, since it eliminates the power of the veto as an ultimate protection of national "sovereignty."

The origins of the European Parliament (EP) hark back to the Common Assembly of the 1950s' European Coal and Steel Community. That body was composed of delegates appointed by the national parliaments of the member states and had a purely advisory function. Today the European Parliament is directly elected by universal suffrage within each member state; although the electoral systems now vary, a unified system is envisaged.[161] The Parliament commands a significant voice in the Union's budget; its assent is needed for major "constitutional" and foreign affairs decisions; and its voice in lawmaking nearly equals that of the Council, albeit still only in specified areas. Since adoption of the 1997 Amsterdam Treaty, the European Parliament must be consulted on the appointment of the president of the Commission; it approves the president and the Commission's members before they are appointed by the member governments; and it may dismiss the Commission by a vote of censure. In March 1999, when an inquiry instituted by the European Parliament brought forth charges of mismanagement, the entire Commission resigned. Thus, the Commission's claim to legitimacy, based originally on its expertise and independence from the political process, has been shifting to a new base of accountability to the Union's electorate represented by the European Parliament, with the consequent "politicization" of the Commission's role. At the same time, the Commission's political influence shows signs of weakening in its relation to the Council establishment, and the effectiveness of the European Parliament is questioned in some political and academic circles. As I shall illustrate below, it is this lawmaking process that bears the brunt of the charge of a lack of democracy.

"Adjudication": rule of law and protection of human rights. The rule of law and protection of basic rights are maintained in the EU institutions with some gaps that are generally not much wider than those in the legal orders of the member states.[162] Drawing on the innovative provisions in the constituent treaties and guided by its own vision of the Community, the European Court of Justice has developed an original design for "a new legal order in international law" based on direct effect and supremacy of Community law in the member states' legal orders and the principle of judicial review. The Court has employed a teleological method of interpretation of the constituent treaty, the concept of implied powers, and the need for uniform application of Community law throughout the Common Market. In a series of early cases the Court used this method to define the Community in the vocab-

[160] This procedure was called partial "de-parliamentarisation" and "de-democratisation" by Paul Kirchhof, *The Balance of Powers Between National and European Institutions*, 5 EUR. L.J. 225, 227, 238 (1999). *See generally* Georg Ress, *Democratic Decision-Making in the European Union and the Role of the European Parliament*, *in* 2 INSTITUTIONAL DYNAMICS OF EUROPEAN INTEGRATION: ESSAYS IN HONOUR OF HENRY G. SCHERMERS 153 (Deirdre Curtin & Ton Heukels eds., 1994).

[161] It is not organized by "government majority" and opposition.

[162] The Court of Justice has declared that the Community is "based on the rule of law." Case 294/83, Parti écologiste 'Les Verts,' 1986 ECR 1339, 1365, para. 23.

ulary of constitutional principles rather than the international law of treaty interpretation.[163] An American philosopher tells us: "It is changing the way we talk, and thereby changing what we want to do and what we think we are."[164]

Today individual rights, including basic human rights, are enforceable not only against Community institutions but also against member governments when Community law is involved. Since the constituent treaties do not contain a catalog of basic human rights to bind the Union's institutions, the Court of Justice has fashioned "general principles of Community law" based on the European Convention on Human Rights and the constitutional tradition common to the member states. However, this improvisation, later codified in the European Union (Maastricht) Treaty, has not been viewed as an adequate "constitutional" foundation. One proposal was for the Community itself to become a party to the European Convention, but the Court of Justice did not favor this option. As an alternative, an "indigenous" EU Charter of Fundamental Rights was proclaimed in the form of a nonbinding declaration whose definitive status remains to be determined.[165]

Despite manifold criticism directed at the Court of Justice (to which I shall return), the basic scaffolding of the rule of law cannot be questioned. In a qualitative sense it exceeds the dispute settlement procedures in any other global or regional international structure. Its existence provides the Union with a measure of legitimacy independent of the democracy requirement.[166] While some question "the rule of unelected, unaccountable judges," it is worth remembering that in the West, at any rate, the "impartial judge" predated modern democracy.[167]

[163] The Court transformed the preliminary ruling procedure of the original Article 177 of the EEC Treaty from a check on Community institutions into a device through which private litigants could challenge national measures as inconsistent with Community law. Parties have done so with a vengeance. Eric Stein, *Lawyers, Judges, and the Making of a Transnational Constitution*, 75 AJIL 1 (1981), *reprinted in* STEIN, BRIDGE, *supra* note 159, at 15.

[164] RICHARD RORTY, CONTINGENCY, IRONY, AND SOLIDARITY 20 (1989). Rorty speaks of Galileo's role in replacing Aristotelian vocabulary with "the words which were needed to fit the world properly." *Id.* at 19. In the end everybody except the Thomists agreed. For today's "Thomists," who challenge the Court's basic thinking, see Kirchhof, *supra* note 160, and FRANKFURTER ALLGEMEINE ZEITUNG, Apr. 12, 1996, at 11, *cited and effectively criticized in* Jochen A. Frowein, *Legitimation und Wirkung des Rechts der Europäischen Union/Gemeinschaft*, *in* PERSPEKTIVEN DES RECHTS IN DER EUROPÄISCHEN UNION 105 (Heidelberger Forum, C. F. Müller-Graff ed., 1998). Kirchhof was the reporting judge on the German Constitutional Court case mentioned in note 168 *infra*, and believes that the Community is just a run-of-the-mill association of states. *See* T. C. HARTLEY, CONSTITUTIONAL PROBLEMS OF THE EUROPEAN UNION 29 (1999) (arguing that the Community has no original authority independently of its member states). *Contra* W. T. Eijsbouts, *Review Essay: Classical and Baroque Constitutionalisms in the Face of Change*, 37 COMMON MKT. L. REV. 213, 216, 220 (2000). For a strained argument, see Ole Spiermann, *The Other Side of the Story: An Unpopular Essay on the Making of the European Community Legal Order*, 10 EUR. J. INT'L L. 763 (1999). On the relationship between language and governance, see Inger-Johanne Sand, *Understanding the New Forms of Governance: Mutually Interdependent, Reflexive, Destabilised and Competing Institutions*, 4 EUR. L.J. 271, 289–90 (1998).

[165] Treaty of Nice, Dec. 12, 2000, 2001 O.J. (C 80) 1. For the Charter of Fundamental Rights of the European Union, Dec. 7, 2000, see 2000 O.J. (C 364) 1, *reprinted in* 40 ILM 266 (2001). The European Court's practice was codified in Article 6 (ex- Art. F) of the European Union Treaty. *See also* Ernst Joachim Mestmäcker, *Über das Verhältnis der europäischen Wirtschaftsordnung zu den Mitgliedstaaten*, VERÖFF. JOACHIM JUNGIUS-GES. WISS. 149, 158 (1994). The Union activities in the human rights field have been partly in response to member states' constitutional courts (particularly Germany's), which made their approval of further transfers of powers to the Union conditional on an effective observance of basic rights by the Union institutions. See most recently the German Constitutional Court in the "Bananas case," BVerfG, 2 Bvl. 1/97 (June 7, 2000), relying on earlier precedents. Some are dissatisfied with "excessive reliance" on the courts in the application of human rights and they call for a comprehensive and coherent human rights policy with, among others, a separate commissioner and a Directorate General for Human Rights within the Commission and a special agency with a monitoring function. Philip Alston & J. H. H. Weiler, *An 'Ever Closer Union' in Need of a Human Rights Policy: The European Union and Human Rights*, *in* THE EU AND HUMAN RIGHTS 3, 21–22, & *passim* (Philip Alston ed., 1999); Philip Alston, *Leading by Example: A Human Rights Agenda for the European Union for the Year 2000*, *id.* at 919. Others argue that because of the important differences between the "negative" civil and political rights and the "positive" economic and social rights, such proposals are both unrealistic and overintrusive. Armin von Bogdandy, *The European Union as a Human Rights Organization? Human Rights and the Core of the European Union*, 37 COMMON MKT. L. REV. 1307, 1310–16 (2000).

[166] Karen J. Alter, *Who Are the 'Masters of the Treaty'?: European Governments at the European Court of Justice*, 52 INT'L ORG. 121 (1998).

[167] Zakaria, *supra* note 4, at 27; *see also* DAVID HUME, *Essay V on the Origin of Government*, *in* DAVID HUME: THE PHILOSOPHICAL WORKS 113, 113–14 (Thomas Hill Green & Thomas Hodge Grose eds., 1964) (stating that "[w]e are . . . to look upon all the best apparatus of our government, as having ultimately no other object or purpose but the distribution of justice, or in other words, the support of the twelve judges").

The Discourse

The debate over the role of the judiciary within the Union system has raised two sets of issues. One—a consequence of the declaration of supremacy of Community law—concerns the vertical, hierarchic relationship between the European Court, on the one hand, and the courts and political organs of the member states, on the other. It has been a part of the general debate on the compatibility of Community law with the national constitutions. The second set of issues—the horizontal level—involves the European Court's relation with other Union organs and falls within the concept of balance of institutional powers.

The "supremacy" issue. Although the issue of the supremacy of Community law in national legal orders arose early in the Community's history, it assumed central concern in the debate on ratifying the Maastricht Treaty, which transferred significant additional powers to the EU institutions, including the creation of a common currency.

When weighing the Maastricht Treaty's compatibility with a national constitution, high courts in some member states found it difficult to reconcile the supremacy of Union law and the role of the European Court as the final arbiter with what they perceived as the mandate of their national constitutions, particularly in the protection of human rights. In the end, the courts approved the Maastricht Treaty (in some instances subject to an amendment to the national constitution) despite its imposition of a critical restraint on national "sovereignty."[168] A confrontation has not taken place thus far because the national courts have found a variety of procedural and interpretive ways to elude one. While avoiding a challenge to the concept of supremacy of Community law over national constitutions, the obvious pragmatic approach would be sensible restraint on both sides.[169] This approach would also accord with the general mandate of the constituent treaty-constitution to "facilitate the achievement of the Community's tasks" and to "abstain from any measure which could jeopardise the attainment of the objectives of this Treaty."[170]

[168] In France, a popular referendum on the Maastricht Treaty was approved by a 51.04% majority. In Denmark, this process took two referenda (56.2% majority), while a proposal to join the common currency was defeated in a separate referendum. For some of the opinions of the highest courts, see German Constitutional Court, 2 BvR 2134, 2159/92, BVerfGE 89, 155; in Spain, Diego J. Liñán Nogueras & Javier Roldán Barbero, *The Judicial Application of Community Law in Spain*, 30 COMMON MKT. L. REV. 1135, 1139 (1993); Gil Carlos Rodríguez Iglesias & Alejandro Valle Gálvez, *El Derecho comunitario y las relaciones entre el Tribunal de Justicia de las Comunidades Europeas, el Tribunal Europeo de Derechos Humanos y los Tribunales Constitucionales nacionales*, 1 REVISTA DE DERECHO COMUNITARIO EUROPEO 329, 364 (1997); in France, Cons. Const., Apr. 9, 1992, J.O. 1992, 92-308; Florence Chaltiel, *La Constitution française et l'Union européenne, à propos de la révision constitutionelle du 25 janvier 1999*, REVUE DU MARCHÉ COMMUN ET DE L'UNION EUROPÉENNE, Apr. 1999, at 228; in Italy, Adelina Adinolfi, *The Judicial Application of Community Law in Italy 1981–1997*, 35 COMMON MKT. L. REV. 1313, 1322 (1998); in Greece, Emmanuel Maganaris, *The Principle of Supremacy of Community Law in Greece—from Direct Challenge to Non-Application*, 24 EUR. L. REV. 426 (1999); in Denmark, Katja Høegh, *Denmark: The Danish Maastricht Judgment*, 24 EUR. L. REV. 80 (1999); Fredrik Thomas, *Das Maastricht-Urteil des dänischen Obersten Gerichtshofs von 6 April 1998*, 58 ZEITSCHRIFT FÜR AUSLÄNDISCHES ÖFFENTLICHES RECHT UND VÖLKERRECHT [ZAÖRV] 879 (1998). From a veritable avalanche of literature, I cite Jochen A. Frowein, *Das Maastricht-Urteil und die Grenzen der Verfassungs-Gerichtsbarkeit*, 54 ZAÖRV 1 (1994); Kirchhof, *supra* note 160; N. MacCormick, *The Maastricht Urteil: Sovereignty Now*, 1 EUR. L.J. 259 (1995); J. H. H. Weiler, *Does Europe Need a Constitution? Demos, Telos and the German Maastricht Decision*, 2 EUR. L.J. 219 (1995); J. H. H. Weiler & Ulrich R. Haltern, *The Autonomy of the Community Legal Order: An Analysis of Possible Foundations or Through the Looking Glass?* 37 HARV. J. INT'L L. 411 (1996); Manfred Zuleeg, *The European Constitution Under Constitutional Constraints: The German Scenario*, 22 EUR. L. REV. 19 (1997).

[169] Weiler would jettison the insistence on supremacy in this context and finds it more realistic to think in confederal-consociational terms, envisaging "conversation of many actors in a constitutional interpretative community, ... constitutional conversation, not a constitutional *diktat*." Weiler & Haltern, *supra* note 168, at 447. His position deserves consideration. I wonder whether *in practice* his and my views would make a difference. For a criticism of the debate in Germany on the "Kompetenz-Kompetenz issue" as reminiscent of the controversy over Bismarck's federalism, see Stefan Oeter, *Souverenität und Demokratie als Probleme in der 'Verfassungs-entwicklung' der Europäischen Union*, 55 ZAÖRV 659 (1995). This is not the first time in history that a central power in a divided-power system has been challenged by a component unit and the system has survived. See the "doctrine of nullification" pressed by South Carolina against federal law. BERNARD BAILYN ET AL., THE GREAT REPUBLIC 501–02 (4th ed. 1992).

[170] EC TREATY Art. 10 (ex-Art. 5).

The Court and other organs. In one view of the relationship of the judiciary with other branches of government, the individual has entitlements (rights) that precede the political process since they are constitutionally guaranteed and do not need to be renegotiated; they need only to be registered, which takes place in the courts rather than in the political institutions. Benjamin Barber has coined the term "judicial democracy" for this doctrine.[171] The counterargument is that in a fully evolved modern system, excessive reliance on the judiciary may impair the necessary balance between courts and political institutions to the prejudice of representative democracy. In the first decades of Community life, when lawmaking was sparse and hampered by the broad unanimity requirement, the Court of Justice functioned as a motor of integration and felt compelled to "make law" by filling the gaps in the constituent treaty. Some accuse the Court of having transgressed its competence both by exceeding its own jurisdiction and by blessing excessive use of the "implied powers clause" and broad construction by the political organs.

Other critics claim that the Court has applied a stricter standard of review to member states' legislation than to measures of the Community's own institutions. In fact, although the Court has invalidated many Community acts on other grounds, until recently it avoided doing so on the ground of lack of Community competence. The Court was presumably inclined to save a Community act in view of the burdensome Community lawmaking process and also—aware of the limits to its own legitimacy—out of reluctance to guide the Community's substantive policies. Most recently, however, the Court enunciated a stricter standard of scrutiny of Community acts and actually struck down a significant directive on the ground of lack of competence.[172] Nevertheless, as lawmaking surged after the widening of majority voting by the Single European Act, the Court has become less activist.[173] With its authority established beyond question, the Court has tended to reduce its intrusion into the member states' legal orders.

Renaud Dehousse suggests that the primary safeguards against Community *ultra vires* action should rest within the political lawmaking process rather than the adversarial judicial proceeding,[174] and warns against backlash if national institutions and people should resent the Court's striking down strongly supported domestic measures.[175] Recent public reaction to certain decisions of WTO panels confirms this general concern.[176]

One persistent, and in my view, justified, criticism concerns the Court's excessively narrow interpretation of the citizen's *direct* access to it, which risks leaving the complainant against a Community measure without any remedy through either national or Community courts. That would constitute a denial of a basic right.[177]

[171] BENJAMIN R. BARBER, STRONG DEMOCRACY: PARTICIPATORY POLITICS FOR A NEW AGE 142–43 (1984), *cited in* Ulrich R. Haltern, Idolatry and Identity—Human Rights and Citizenship in the European Union 34 (1999) (unpublished manuscript, on file with author).

[172] Case C–376/98, Germany v. Parliament and Council (Oct. 5, 2000); von Bogdandy, *supra* note 165, at 1320–30. Recent decisions of the European Court of Justice and the Court of First Instance are available online at <http://europa.eu.int/en>.

[173] Thus, the Court reinterpreted the Community Treaty provision invalidating protective legislation of the member states so as to exclude a broad category of national measures from the reach of the prohibition. *See* Joined Cases C–267/91, C–268/91, *supra* note 96; Norbert Reich, *'The November Revolution' of the European Court of Justice: Keck, Meng and Audi Revisited,* 31 COMMON MKT. L. REV. 459 (1994). The Court is blamed for not being activist enough in gender antidiscrimination cases, while viewed by others as overactivist for holding provisions of the German Constitution and legislation that exclude women from weapons-related military service as contrary to Community law. Evelyn Ellis, *The Recent Jurisprudence of the Court of Justice in the Field of Sexual Equality,* 37 COMMON MKT. L. REV. 1402, 1425–26 (2000); *see also* Case C–285/98, Tanja Kreil v. Germany (Jan. 11, 2000), *discussed in id.* at 1433 n.2.

[174] EUROPE AFTER MAASTRICHT: AN EVER CLOSER UNION 124 (Renaud Dehousse ed., 1994). On the proper exercise of the power of judicial review of federal legislation, see JAMES BRADLEY THAYER, JOHN MARSHALL 104–10 (1901).

[175] RENAUD DEHOUSSE, EUROPEAN COURT OF JUSTICE 173 (1998). Regarding the criticism of the Court particularly from Germany, see Mancini & Keeling, *supra* note 155, at 185–86.

[176] *See supra* text at notes 83–84.

[177] If an individual seeks redress of a violation of Community law by one of its institutions, she must in principle file a complaint against the national measure implementing that Community law. The national court must ultimately refer the issue of Community law to the Community Court of First Instance, with the possibility of appeal

The Democracy-Legitimacy Issues

Much of the critical discourse on the European Union has focused on the inadequacy of democratic representation, accountability ("there is no way of turning the rascals out"), and citizen participation, as well as on the lack of institutional balance of powers and transparency with the consequent lack of legitimacy. Significantly, however, opinion polls disclose that the majority of citizens does not seem to be bothered by these issues, if indeed they have ever heard of them.[178]

In the discourse on these "failings," the democratic institutions of the member states have understandably been viewed as a model for possible remedies.[179] This line of thought, however, has met with two problems, and other organizations in an advanced state of integration are bound to face a comparable dilemma. First, as I suggested in part I of this essay, the general idea and practice of democracy has undergone a profound mutation from the direct to the representative system and its many modern variants. Today in Europe, democracy appears in a great variety of institutional forms in which the voice of an individual citizen is heard in varying ways and degrees. It ranges from the "omnipotent" Parliament in Westminster to the republican-presidential system in France where the parliament plays a secondary role; to the consensual (consociational) pattern in the Netherlands, Belgium, Austria, and Switzerland (with particular reliance on popular initiative); to the strong regionalism in Spain; and to the federal variants in Germany, Austria, Belgium, and Switzerland. In all member states direct parliamentary control has been weakened by the establishment of "independent" expert agencies, among other things. The constitutional principle of separation of powers between the legislative and the executive is blurred considerably, for instance in Britain and France; and the concept may not fit the Union institutions as currently structured: there is no "government" or "legislature" in the conventional sense and it may be more realistic to speak of "balancing" the principal organs. As for the second problem, a new situation has arisen for representative pluralist democracy and legitimacy, as Union institutions with extensive normative powers have been superimposed on national systems.[180]

Transparency: "more light." One obstacle to legitimacy is the secrecy of the proceedings in the Commission, and above all in the Council, which, with its pyramid of committees, has been dubbed "the Kremlin of the West."[181] It is estimated that nine-tenths of all decisions

to the Court of Justice. In certain instances the complainant may invoke the Community judiciary directly, thus avoiding a lengthy and costly procedure through national courts. *See* Eric Stein & Joseph G. Vining, *Citizen Access to Judicial Review of Administrative Action in a Transnational and Federal Context*, 70 AJIL 219 (1976), *reprinted and partially updated in* STEIN, BRIDGE, *supra* note 159, at 161. Understandably, the Court of Justice prefers the facts of the case to be collected by the domestic court, as well as an indication of that court's view on the law. My critique goes only to the few cases where the individual plaintiff is denied standing before the European judiciary by a formalistic and restrictive interpretation of the vague texts of the constituent treaty such as lack of "individual interest." See, most recently, Case T–69/96, Hamburger Hafen- und Lagerhaus AG v. Commission, para. 51 (CFI Mar. 21, 2001), in which the Court of First Instance considered the absence of an effective remedy "irrelevant" because that court cannot exceed the limits of its jurisdiction set forth in the EC Treaty. *But see* Gil Carlos Rodríguez Iglesias, *Judicial Protection of the Citizen Under European Law, in* THE CLIFFORD CHANCE MILLENNIUM LECTURES 195, 196 (Basil Markesinis ed., 2000).

[178] JEAN BLONDEL, RICHARD SINNOTT, & PALLE SVENSSON, PEOPLE AND PARLIAMENT IN THE EUROPEAN UNION: PARTICIPATION, DEMOCRACY, AND LEGITIMACY 71 (1998). This work is an effort to explain the low level of participation in the elections for the European Parliament.

[179] Karl Doehring, *Demokratiedefizit in der Europäischen Union*, DEUTSCHES VERWALTUNGSBLATT, No. 19, 1997, at 19–20, *cited in* STEIN, BRIDGE, *supra* note 159, at 335, 338.

[180] Majone considers the standards of representative democracy irrelevant to European integration: since voters insist on national sovereignty, there can be no political integration and the only answer is to keep economics separated from politics. The key issue for democratic theory concerns tasks that may be legitimately delegated to institutions insulated from politics and how they can be made independent and accountable (the "regulatory model" of the Community). Giandomenico Majone, *Europe's 'Democratic Deficit': The Question of Standards*, 4 EUR. L.J. 5 (1998). This view may have been more appropriate before the competence of the Union was broadened to embrace aspects of social, cultural, foreign, security, and other policies.

[181] Ress, *supra* note 160, at 166 n.49; *see also* Jan Beyers & Quido Dierickx, *The Working Groups of the Council of the European Union: Supranational or Intergovernmental Negotiations?* 36 J. COMMON MKT. STUD. 289 (1998).

are made in innumerable closed committees of national and Union bureaucrats and only rubber-stamped by the Council.[182] Actually, the conflicting and collusive interaction between Union officials, national civil servants, experts, and lobbyists in the image of the elite alliance we have encountered in other IGOs extends to practically all fields of public affairs and lies at the base of Union action. Secrecy, particularly at this high level of integration, feeds the tendency to shift the balance from the parliaments to executive power still further and facilitates privileging one interest group over another. As the modern administrative state can attest, transparency in the Union is essential not only to inform the national parliaments and the electorate, but also to help form an all-European debate and opinion. Consequently, it has been argued that the first step must be to lift the veil of secrecy beyond the indispensable confidential area.[183]

In the last twenty years, eight member states have adopted legislation or constitutional rules that confer on citizens a general right of access to documents held by their public authorities.[184] In contrast, the European Community functioned under the principle that everything is secret except what is expressly stated to be accessible.[185] This practice was consistent with the methodology of integration "by stealth" but became untenable when the Community's competences increased substantially to affect the position of individual citizens and firms. The turning point was the Maastricht Treaty of 1992, which required the Council to lay down general principles on the right of access to public documents. In response, in 1993 the Council adopted a code of conduct declaring that "[t]he public will have the widest possible access to documents held by the Commission and the Council," subject to specified exceptions designed to protect interests ranging from public security and international relations to confidentiality of the Council's proceedings. Those whose requests for information had been refused had to be informed of the possible recourse to the ombudsman or the Court of First Instance.[186]

[182] *Coreper, Europe's Managing Board,* ECONOMIST, Aug. 8, 1998, at 46. Generally, the proposals elaborated by committees are negotiated and approved in the powerful Committee of Permanent Representatives, which is composed of the member states' ambassadors to the European Union. They are then formally submitted to the Council (and—where so required—to the European Parliament). There is no public access or publicity in this phase. When the Council delegates certain powers to the Commission to "assist" it, the Commission is required to establish committees composed of representatives of member states and chaired by Commission staff, "comitology" in Brussels lingo. T. C. HARTLEY, THE FOUNDATION OF EUROPEAN COMMUNITY LAW 18 (3d ed. 1994). *See* Council Decision 1999/468/EC Establishing the Procedures for the Exercise of Implementing Powers Conferred on the Commission, 1999 O.J. (L 184) 23. According to Article 7, the European Parliament is to be informed "on a regular basis" and a list of the committees as well as an annual report on their working is to be published by the Commission. Some 300 such committees meet in secrecy. Helmut Kortenberg [pseudonym of an EC official], *Comitologie: le retour,* 34 REVUE TRIMESTRIELLE DE DROIT EUROPÉEN 317 (1998).

[183] OFFICE OF PRESS AND PUBLIC AFFAIRS, EUR. COMM'N, WASHINGTON, D.C., ACCESSING EUROPEAN UNION INFORMATION (1998). In addition to publicizing information on the Internet, the Commission holds briefings for the press and issues press releases on pending proposals. The need for publication in twelve languages causes delays.

[184] According to the documentation service of the Court of Justice, the following member states have adopted rules conferring a general right of access to "administrative" documents on individuals: Belgium, Spain, Finland, Portugal, Sweden, Austria, Denmark, and Greece. Case C–58/94, Netherlands v. Council, 1996 ECR I–2169, 2179 (opinion of advocate general); *see* Peter Dyrberg, *Current Issues in the Debate on Public Access to Documents,* 24 EUR. L. REV. 157 (1999); Michael O'Neil, *The Right of Access to Community-Held Documentation as a General Principle of the EC Law,* 4 EUR. PUB. L. 403 (1998); *see also Public Access to the Institutions' Documents,* 1993 O.J. (C 156) 5 (containing a list of specific EC provisions requiring publication and an overview of member states' legislation).

[185] *See generally* OPENNESS AND TRANSPARENCY IN THE EUROPEAN UNION (Veerle Deckmyn & Ian Thomson eds., 1998); Willem H. Buiter, *Alice in Euroland,* 37 J. COMMON MKT. STUD. 181 (1999) (dealing with lack of transparency in the Economic and Monetary Union arrangements, including the Central Bank); John Peterson, *Playing the Transparency Game,* 2 J. EUR. PUB. POL'Y 69 (1995); Bo Vesterdorf, *Transparency—Not Just a Vogue Word,* 22 FORDHAM INT'L L.J. 902 (1999); Roberto Viciano Pastor, *Publicité et accès aux documents officiels dans les institutions de l'Union européenne avant et après le Traité d'Amsterdam, in* 1 MÉLANGES EN HOMMAGE À MICHEL WAELBROECK 649 (Marianne Dony ed. with Aline De Walsche, 1999).

[186] Code of Conduct Concerning Public Access to Council and Commission Documents, 1993 O.J. (L 340) 41; *see also* Council Decision 93/731 on Public Access to Council Documents, 1993 O.J. (L 340) 43; EC TREATY Art. 255 (ex-Art. 191a), with Declaration 17 annexed to the Final Act. The Council exempted documents whose disclosure could undermine protection of the public interest (i.e., public security, international relations, monetary stability, court proceedings, inspections, and investigations), the individual and privacy, commercial and industrial

In its 1999 Rules of Procedure, although preserving "the obligation of professional secrecy" in its deliberations, the Council mandated the publication of results, explanations of votes, minutes, and statements entered in minutes when it acts in its *legislative* capacity. Finally, in March 2001, the Council adopted a decision introducing publication on the Internet of preparatory texts produced by the working groups. These measures represent progress from the complete secrecy of the Council as a forum for intimate negotiations.[187]

Since 1996, the Court of First Instance has entertained some dozen complaints against the denial of access to information. With only one exception,[188] the court reversed in full or in part the decisions denying access to documents, either on procedural grounds (such as the institution's failure to state reasons) or on substantive grounds, and it has strictly interpreted the exceptions from the duty to disclose.[189]

Regarding confidentiality in the interest of the institutions, only documents relating to current or possible court proceedings and internal legal opinions are viewed as "confidential," the latter on the ground that disclosure could give rise to uncertainty about the legality of a Community measure, impairing "the public interest in the stability of Community law and the proper functioning of the institutions." This sweeping exclusion of legal opinion has been criticized.[190]

Advocate General Giuseppe Tesauro observes that openness is directly linked with the democratic nature of the institutions and appropriate publicity is required for effective supervision, thus emphasizing that the right of access to official documents is part of the democratic principle.[191] Juliet Lodge suggests, however, that at the level of EU integration,

secrecy, the Community's financial interests, and the confidentiality requested by persons who supplied the information or required by legislation of the member state that supplied the information. Finally, access may be refused to protect "the confidentiality of the Council's proceeding." The code of conduct was also implemented by other organs of the Union. Commission Decision 94/90 on Public Access to Commission Documents, 1994 O.J. (L 46) 58. See, most recently, Council Decision 2001/320/EC on Making Certain Categories of Council Documents Available to the Public. 2001 O.J. (L 111) 29. The European Parliament pressed for greater openness at an early date, *e.g.*, Resolution on the Compulsory Publication of Information by the European Community, 1984 O.J. (C 172) 176. For an extensive list of writings, see Dyrberg, *supra* note 184, at 157 n.1. The Amsterdam Treaty reaffirmed the right of access to documents and called on the Council to implement it in a regulation. On January 26, 2000, the Commission adopted a proposal for a European Parliament and Council Regulation Regarding Public Access to Parliament, Council and Commission Documents, COM(2000)30. The exception of confidentiality has been criticized as too broad. BULL. QUOT. EUR., Jan. 28, 2000, at 11–12; Deirdre M. Curtin, *Democracy, Transparency and Political Participation: Some Progress Post-Amsterdam, in* OPENNESS AND TRANSPARENCY IN THE EUROPEAN UNION, *supra* note 185, at 115. The Commission uses the Internet to publicize its proposals.

[187] Council Decision 1999/385, adopting the Council's Rules of Procedure, Arts. 5-8, 1999 O.J. (L 147) 13; *EP/Transparency*, BULL. QUOT. EUR., Mar. 23, 2001, at 13; *see also* Council Decision 2000/23/EC on the Improvement of Information on the Council's Legislative Activities and the Public Register of Council Documents, 2000 O.J. (L 9) 22.

[188] Case T-309/97, Bavarian Lager Co. v. Commission, 3 COMMON MKT. L. REV. 544 (1999).

[189] On appeal, the Court of Justice affirmed the rulings of the Court of First Instance. It is noteworthy that, with the exception of the Netherlands and the Nordic states, France, Britain, and some other member states urged the Court to sustain the confidentiality of the requested documents. For the list of cases through April 1999, see Dyrberg, *supra* note 184, at 161–62. More recently, in Case T–188/97, Rothmans Int'l BV v. Commission (CFI July 19, 1999) and Case T–14/98, Hautala v. Council (CFI July 19, 1999), decisions refusing access to documents were struck down as unlawful. 22 EUR. C. MONITOR 17–20 (2d term 1999). It was disputed whether, prior to the Maastricht Treaty, the Court had established free access as a principle common to the constitutional tradition of member states, although it was clearly stated by the advocate general in Case C–58/94, Netherlands v. Council, 1996 ECR I–2169, 2182.

[190] Case T–610/97 R, Carlsen v. Council, 1998 ECR II–485, 505; Dyrberg, *supra* note 184, at 164, 166. In the area of "justice and home affairs," which was marked by endemic secrecy, the Council decided to make public a register of all unclassified documents. EC Justice and Home Affairs Council, Press Release 1998-03-26-6889/98 (Mar. 19, 1998); *see* Jochen Abr. Frowein & Nico Krisch, *Der Rechtsschutz gegen Europol*, 19 JURISTENZEITUNG 589 (1998). EU policies on border crossing and movement of people generally have been criticized as reducing standards on the rule of law in part because of the secrecy, restrictions on the competence of the Court of Justice, and the lack of accountability in determining refugee status. H. MEIJERS ET AL., DEMOCRACY, MIGRANTS AND POLICE IN THE EUROPEAN UNION (1997).

[191] Case C–58/94, *supra* note 184, at I–2180, 2182, *passim*. The advocate general cited, in addition to the Maastricht and Amsterdam Treaties, Article 10 of the European Convention for the Protection of Human Rights, *supra* note 23, and Article 19 of the International Covenant on Civil and Political Rights, *supra* note 5, which guarantees the rights to freedom of expression and to receive and impart information. The rationale for these rights is better knowledge on the part of citizens and more effective participation and supervision by public opinion. Dyrberg,

the transparency issue is a diversion from "the central problem of the Council's position."[192] At any rate, in institutions less integrated than the Union, reduction of secrecy may be a major, practical move toward legitimacy.

The complexity and incoherence of the Union Treaty magnify its lack of transparency. So does the "flexibility," which enables member states to "opt out" of Union activities (only eleven of the fifteen have accepted the common currency) and makes the legal and political situation even more convoluted.[193] Yet permitting the core states to advance integration among themselves, and the rest of the members to follow in due course, may be the only way to absorb the accession of the numerous current applicants.

I should mention in this context that the constituent treaty requires the Council to consult with the Economic and Social Committee, which is composed of government-selected, but "independent" representatives of the main socioeconomic sectors. Although its composition suggests a step up on the integration scale as an avenue for citizen participation, the committee has not been successful because of its limited influence. The Commission has systematically consulted with the Union-wide NGOs centered in Brussels, but it has been criticized for unequal access.[194]

Remedies

Via national parliaments. It has become clear that to remedy these shortcomings, the Union must develop its own version of democracy, just as it has already succeeded in designing its own original form of the rule of law and human rights protection. One step toward this goal, prominently featured in the discourse, has been to increase the control of national parliaments over Union institutions. In theory, ministers, as members of the national executives, are controlled by and accountable to their national parliaments, similarly to the national delegations to the central organs of other international organizations. This distribution of responsibility and the need for parliamentary approval of any transfer of national powers to the Union would appear to meet the representation and accountability requirement. The reality, however, has been different. In the first place, as I suggested in part I, in foreign affairs matters the national parliaments have played a notoriously limited role. Moreover, serious problems have emerged as regards the timely flow of information to and from the parliaments, a problem encountered by international organizations generally. Again, final decisions are made in the give-and-take, closed-door negotiations of the Council. Finally, since the Council in an increasing number of instances decides by a qualified majority, ministers may be outvoted, no matter what their national mandate may have been. Increased use of majority voting raises the level of integration but "exacerbates the democracy deficit by weakening national parliamentary control of the Council."[195] A more recent "complication," if one can use that word, has resulted from the substantially increased role of the European Parliament in lawmaking. To enhance control over their respective executives, most of the national parliaments have established special committees to deal with Union affairs. Only some, however, such as the Danish, British, and German committees, seem to be positioned to influence, if not control, their respective ministers.[196] The Euro-

supra note 184, at 158, suggests that the right of access is an efficient way to enhance citizens' confidence in public authorities and to improve the functioning of public officials.

[192] Juliet Lodge, *Transparency and Democratic Legitimacy*, 32 J. COMMON MKT. STUD. 343, 345 (1994).

[193] Deirdre M. Curtin, *The Constitutional Structure of the Union: A Europe of Bits and Pieces*, 30 COMMON MKT. L. REV. 17 (1993). For a suggested catalog of Union competences, see EUROPA '96—REFORM PROGRAMM FÜR DIE EUROPAISCHE UNION 18–31 (Werner Weidenfeld ed., 1994).

[194] European Commission, An Open and Structured Dialogue Between the Commission and Special Interest Groups, SEC(92)2272.

[195] WEILER, *supra* note 27, at 85.

[196] With a touch of irony, a German writer reports that the German parliamentary committee of sixty members meets *in secret*. Rudolf Lamprecht, *Untertan in Europa: Über den Mangel an Demokratie und Transparenz*, 1997 NEUE

pean Parliament is required to cooperate with these committees, provide information, and participate in "assizes" with national parliaments. This cooperation between parliaments reflects what Anne-Marie Slaughter sees as transgovernmentalism: a disaggregation of the state into its components—the legislature, the executive, the courts—and their cooperation across state lines as a crucial aspect of "the new world order."[197]

Via the European Parliament. An alternative way to fill the gaps in representative democracy can be found in the role of the European Parliament. Elected to represent the distinct "peoples" of the Union, the European Parliament—as I recounted earlier—shares in budgetary and legislative powers and holds the executive Commission accountable.[198] It also appoints an ombudsman who receives citizen complaints against Union institutions. An increasing number of complainants resort to this new organ as an alternative to the lengthy and expensive proceedings before the Court of Justice.[199] The Parliament may establish its own committees of inquiry, but it does not have the power to subpoena witnesses. Nevertheless, it grilled the first president-designate of the new European Central Bank for several hours.[200] In terms of the normative-institutional criteria, however, it still holds limited powers if one insists on a comparison with national parliaments. Thus, it has no taxing power; nor does it have the formal power of legislative initiative, which is reserved to the Commission. Its legislative competences, broad as they are, are still confined to specific instances, and more important, except for the legislative co-decision, it has no authority over the Council or any of its members. To address this last problem, which goes to the core of the democracy deficit, some want to turn the Council into an upper chamber of the European Parliament in the image of the original United States Senate or the German Bundesrat, whose members are appointed by the governments of the component states of the federation. As a corollary, former Commission President Jacques Delors made the intriguing suggestion that the president of the Commission be elected directly by the people in an all-European campaign—a move that would add to the "politicization" of the Commission, increase its legitimacy and accountability, recalibrate the institutional balance in the Union, and stimulate a European debate.[201] In the alternative, the European Parliament itself might be given the authority to elect the Commission's president.

Philippe Schmitter offers no less than sixteen reform suggestions, including changing the electoral systems and campaign funding, extending the time and improving facilities for EP voting, defining the control functions of EP standing committees, and finally—a radical proposal—eliminating current disparities in representation due to the existential differences in the size of the populations of the member states.[202]

JURISTISCHE WOCHENSCHRIFT 505. Claude Chesson, a former member of the EU Commission and French minister of foreign relations, believes that the European Parliament will have only symbolic importance and that the burden for democracy will fall on national parliaments. BULL. QUOT. EUR., Dec. 17, 1998, at 16.

[197] Anne-Marie Slaughter, *The Real New World Order*, FOREIGN AFF., Sept/Oct. 1997, at 183. José Alvarez, *Do Liberal States Behave Better?: A Critique of Slaughter's Liberal Theory*, 12 EUR. J. INT'L L. 183 (2001), questions the adequacy of the evidence offered to support this trend.

[198] CHRYSSOCHOOU, *supra* note 6, at 35. *See generally* FRANCIS JACOBS, RICHARD CORBETT, & MICHAEL SHACKLETON, THE EUROPEAN PARLIAMENT (2d ed. 1992); EIVIND SMITH, NATIONAL PARLIAMENTS AS CORNERSTONES OF EUROPEAN INTEGRATION (1996); THE EUROPEAN PARLIAMENT, THE NATIONAL PARLIAMENTS, AND EUROPEAN INTEGRATION (Richard S. Katz & Bernhard Wessels eds., 1999); PHILIPPE A. WEBER-PANARIELLO, NATIONALE PARLAMENTE IN DER EUROPÄISCHEN UNION (1995); Michael Shackleton, *The Internal Legitimacy Crisis of the European Union*, *in* EUROPE'S AMBIGUOUS UNITY 69, 73–75 (Alan W. Cafruny & Carl Lankowski eds., 1997).

[199] British Labor MEP Edward Newman said in the European Parliament that ten million people had signed over 6500 petitions "in the last five years." BULL. QUOT. EUR., Apr. 19/20, 1999, at 12.

[200] *Duisenberg Survives Grilling by MEPs*, EP NEWS, May 1998, at 1.

[201] BULL. QUOT. EUR. (n.s.), May 20, 1998, at 2–3; BULL. QUOT. EUR., May 27, 1998, Documents at 1, 3.

[202] Schmitter would replace the current EP composition with three "collegia" that contain representatives elected respectively from the largest, middle-sized, and small states; any decision would require a concurrent majority in all three collegia. The Council's president would be replaced by a "troika" elected by the three collegia. The same process would apply to appointments of the president and members of the Commission. PHILIPPE C. SCHMITTER, HOW TO DEMOCRATIZE THE EUROPEAN UNION—AND WHY BOTHER? 84–87 (2000). For other useful suggestions, see

Demos: a red herring? Some oppose approaching reform through the European Parliament. They deny its representative status[203] because there can be no democracy without "a people" and the Parliament cannot speak for "the European people." They argue that there is no European people (*demos*), only distinct "peoples" in the different member states; there are no European-wide political parties, no European public debate or opinion.[204]

One simple answer to this argument is that while there may be no "European people," the Union is not a state. It has not reached the integration level of a state, it does not need the underpinning of a single "people," and its institutions need not mirror the exacting democracy-legitimacy standards of a liberal democratic state. More important, however, Oeter questions the basic assumption of the critique,

> namely that any system of democracy needs a pre-existing people in an ethnic sense which then finds its expression in a system of democratic representation. . . . "People" in that traditional sense of Western constitutional theory does not presuppose ethnic, linguistic or cultural homogeneity: it merely requires the political will of its component groups to be organized in a common structure of public authority, a common system of political integration.
>
> The European Union undoubtedly already constitutes such a system of common political integration, although only partially supplied with the competence to exercise public authority.[205]

It is a sad irony, Oeter concludes, that the current debate on European integration obscures this insight "behind a smokescreen of false questions [based on the obsolete concept of sovereignty] . . . which are strongly reminiscent of the debate in Germany at the turn of the [nineteenth] century."[206]

Schmitter concurs in this view and reminds us that in history "constitutionalization" and constitutions of states came before the emergence of the demos within those states. In Great Britain, France, Spain, and Portugal (and one may add Canada and the United States), "the state was often established long before a 'feeling of belonging to a (single) community' [the demos] existed among its subjects and, indeed, played a significant role in bringing about such a feeling."[207]

Both these authors assume that the state-building experience is fully transferable to the building of international institutions by modern, established states. I see no reason why this should not be the case *mutatis mutandis*. Nevertheless, it is legitimate to point to the continuing linguistic and other cultural differences (eleven languages are now spoken in the Union) that divide "the peoples" of the Union and that in the past have had a way of

MICHAEL NEWMAN, DEMOCRACY, SOVEREIGNTY AND THE EUROPEAN UNION 179–85 (1996). The Commission has suggested limiting its own size, introducing a qualified majority as a general rule in the Council with limited use of unanimity, providing options for vote weighing in the Council, enlarging the Community's power in foreign commercial policy, etc. BULL. QUOT. EUR., Jan. 27, 2000, at 3–4.

[203] "[T]he European Assembly that calls itself 'Parliament.'" Kirchhof, *supra* note 160, at 238.

[204] *See* Weiler & Trachtman, *supra* note 151, at 377–85.

[205] Oeter, *supra* note 169, at 710 (quoted from the English summary).

[206] *Id.* at 711. *See generally* CULTURE AND IDENTITY IN EUROPE: PERCEPTIONS OF DIVERGENCE AND UNITY IN PAST AND PRESENT (Michael Wintle ed., 1996).

[207] SCHMITTER, *supra* note 202, at 118. Schmitter discusses Great Britain, where "there was no single-formal constitutional 'act of will,' just a lengthy accumulation of precedents." In regard to Germany, it "seems especially characteristic of German scholars who postulate a 'universalistic' sequence whereby an *ethnos* must precede a *demos*, and the latter can only be created by an explicit constitutional act whereby this *demos* or people 'submit itself to a political order of its own invention." *Id.* (quoting Claus Offe, The Democratic Welfare State: A European Regime Under the Strain of European Integration (unpublished essay, Humboldt University 1999)). Perhaps this was because of Germany's being "one of the few European states where a 'belief in commonality' . . . preceded the formation of its national state or because of the strength of legal formalism in its juridical tradition." *Id.* "[B]ut it seems reflective of a broader strand of German thinking that goes back to Jellinek, Weber, Habermas, and the contemporary German [Constitutional] Court judge, Dieter Grimm . . . ." *Id.* at 131 n.3. On the United States at the time of the Revolution, see Manfred Zuleeg, *What Holds a Nation Together? Cohesion and Democracy in the United States of America and in the European Union*, 45 AM. J. COMP. L. 505, 578–79 (1997), citing American historians.

turning into exclusionary, xenophobic nationalisms with catastrophic results. For better or worse, an interdependent economy, modern information technology, and the worldwide use of English in science and business have worked toward reducing these differences. Democracy and legitimacy—at the level of Union integration—do postulate a certain community of a common good and common expectations of the people that bridges the cultural differences *to the extent necessary* to sustain the common institutions as their powers increase. Yet even at a much lower level of integration, such as in the WTO, the question has arisen whether the commitment based on the benefits from free trade would prove strong enough, considering the diversity of the members, to sustain any expansion of its authority.

The Maastricht and Amsterdam Treaties, amending the original Community Treaties, contain rudiments of institutional arrangements designed specifically to advance the process of empirical-social integration. The Maastricht Treaty provides for Union "citizenship," superimposed on citizens of the member states, that engenders new, albeit still limited, citizen rights to be added to the significant "bundle of rights" derived from the constituent treaties.[208] These rights, Weiler believes, should be complemented by citizens' duties, such as paying Union taxes, and a definition of duties toward other human beings. He also proposes introducing a popular initiative that would enable voters to place on the Union-wide ballot specific proposals for Community legislation.[209]

In the same vein, and for the purpose of enhancing the sense of political cohesion, the two amending treaties anchor the recognition of Union-wide political parties in the text, and specifically call for closer cooperation between national parliaments and the European Parliament.[210] The common currency, a powerful stimulus for cohesion, is in effect the first project in which *all* Union people are called to participate. As a modest step toward decentralization, a regional advisory body is established to bring subnational voices into the Union process.[211] The "subsidiarity principle" was incorporated with a view to confining Union action to instances where the member states cannot act effectively. It is too soon to take stock of the impact of these provisions.

[208] The new citizenship includes the right of free movement and residence throughout the Union's territory; the right of a member state's national, resident in another member state, to vote and run for office in local elections of that state and also in elections for the European Parliament; the right to diplomatic protection by any member state; and the right to petition the European Parliament and to apply to the ombudsman. In addition, this citizenship "bundle" comprises significant rights to the free movement of goods, services, capital, and persons (economic rights already accorded in constituent treaties and protected within the rule-of-law system). *See generally* MASSIMO LA TORRE, EUROPEAN CITIZENSHIP: AN INSTITUTIONAL CHALLENGE (1998); ELIZABETH M. MEEHAN, CITIZENSHIP AND THE EUROPEAN COMMUNITY (1993); WEILER, *supra* note 27, at 344–49. There has been some criticism of the Union's citizenship provisions—mistakenly based on the concept of national citizenship—on the ground that they are so minimal as to debase the concept of political citizenship. I find this criticism difficult to understand, particularly in view of the clause specifically enabling the unanimous Council "to adopt provisions designed to strengthen or to add to the above rights," which it shall recommend to the member states for adoption in accordance with their respective constitutional requirements. EC TREATY Art. 22 (ex-Art. 8e).

[209] Weiler also suggests the establishment of a European constitutional council for resolving constitutional disputes with the highest national courts, an idea with unfortunate implications. WEILER, *supra* note 27, at 353–54. For an effective criticism of this proposal, see P. J. G. Kapteyn, *The Court of Justice of the European Communities After the Year 2000, in* INSTITUTIONAL DYNAMICS OF EUROPEAN INTEGRATION, *supra* note 160, at 135, 146–47 (citing other critics at 147 n.22). Prof. Kapteyn is a judge of the European Court of Justice. *See also* Neil Walker, *Sovereignty and Differentiated Integration in the European Union*, 4 EUR. L.J. 355, 387 (1998). For a series of modest, but useful, reform suggestions, see NEWMAN, *supra* note 202; Weidenfeld, *supra* note 193, at 37–48.

[210] SIMON HIX & CHRISTOPHER LORD, POLITICAL PARTIES IN THE EUROPEAN UNION (1997). Court of Justice President Rodríguez Iglesias warns that participation of national parliaments beyond a certain point might limit substantially "the possibilities of common action."Gil Carlos Rodríguez Iglesias, *Zur Verfassung der Europäischen Gemeinschaft*, 23 EUROPÄISCHE GRUNDRECHTE ZEITSCHRIFT 125, 131 (1996).

[211] The German Länder (states) succeeded in obtaining a constitutional amendment assuring their participation in the formulation and implementation of German government policies in relation to the Union. Martin A. Rogoff, *The European Union, Germany and the Länder: New Patterns of Political Relations in Europe*, 5 COLUM. J. EUR. L. 415 (1999). In Austria the Länder and the parliament were empowered to formulate bargaining mandates for the Austrian ministers in the Council. However, the Länder must present a unanimous point of view in order to bind the ministers. Gerda Falkner, *Effects of EU Membership on a New Member State*, 38 J. COMMON MKT. STUD. 223, 241 (2000).

Actually, some Union-wide parties now exist, albeit in embryonic form as alliances of national parties. The interplay between these emerging all-Union political parties, the political "groups" organized in the European Parliament on the traditional right-left pattern, and the corresponding national parties in the national parliaments promises to help politicize the working of the Union and reduce its image as a distant, technocratic monster in the eyes of its politicians and citizens. Although satellite television makes cross-boundary broadcasting possible, genuine all-Union mass media outlets do not exist. The plethora of languages accentuates the problem. At least 40 percent of the voters have no image of the Parliament, the turnout for the elections has been relatively low, and crucial matters of domestic politics, rather than all-Union issues, are invariably aired in the electoral campaigns.

As the powers of the European Parliament increase, so do lobbying efforts and general public interest. Current Union activities, such as the standardization of health and safety regulations, transcontinental transportation and communication projects, and the massive exchange of students, have promoted the same integrative objective.[212] The removal of internal frontiers advances a "border-crossing trust relationship."[213] Not surprisingly, a wealth of proposals for further action are on the table.

Some see the historical basis of national identity within the member states shifting from ethnicity and cultural heritage to respect for constitutional order and democratic tradition. Elements of what might emerge as a "European identity" may be in place, but if this evolves, it will differ from, and will coexist with, the discrete identities of the peoples in the individual member states. That, at any rate, is the hopeful vision.

A federal "superstate"? For some voices in the European discourse, all efforts and proposals to remedy the lack of democracy I have described amount to little more than ineffective palliatives. The respected late Judge Federico Mancini of the European Court of Justice launched an impassioned appeal for turning the Union into a European federal state as the only possible way to eliminate this deficiency.[214] Two lines of argument resonate in opposition to Mancini's idea. First, claims are heard in Germany that democracy can be achieved only within a national framework and that a European state is illusory and undesirable in the absence of "spiritual, social and political homogeneity."[215] For this and other reasons, some scholars oppose any further integration entailing more powers for "Brussels."[216] The Euro-skeptics everywhere would applaud.

Professor Weiler, who has produced seminal writing on the subject, opposes the Mancini proposal for a federal state on a different, more plausible ground and also offers different

[212] There are about 3000 special interest groups in Brussels, with up to 10,000 employees working in the lobbying sector; 50 offices of Länder, regional, and local authorities; 200 individual firms with their own representation; 100 consultant firms; and 100 law firms in Belgium specializing in Community law and many more in other member states. There are no Commission rules on accreditation. *See The Commission's Approach Towards Special Interest Groups, at* <http://europa.eu.int/index_en.htm> (visited July 16, 2001). In 1998, 200,000 students (5% of the entire EU student population) studied in another member state.

[213] Michael Zürn & Dieter Wolf, *European Law and International Regimes: The Features of Law Beyond the Nation State*, EUR. L.J. 272, 291 (1999).

[214] G. Federico Mancini, *Europe: The Case for Statehood*, 4 EUR. L.J. 29, 34–35 (1998). The German minister for foreign affairs (not speaking on behalf of the government) made a similar suggestion by advocating a federation with a directly elected president and a parliament with real powers. N.Y. TIMES, June 28, 2000, at A10. For a response by the French president and foreign minister, see *id.*; ECONOMIST, July 1, 2000, at 47–48; BULL. QUOT. EUR., Aug. 12, 2000, at 4 (citing French President Jacques Chirac as proposing "to work towards drafting a constitution . . . that would be submitted for future ratification by all the people" but reaffirming his hope for a "limited Europe of States rather than a United States of Europe" and opposition to a "European Superstate"). *See also* Joschka Fischer, *Von Staatenbund zur Föderation—Gedanken über die Finalität der europäischen Integration*, INTEGRATION, July 2000, at 149.

[215] Mancini, *supra* note 214, at 35 (quoting the decision of the German Constitutional Court, *supra* note 168, and the writings of Justices Grimm and Kirchhof, who participated in the decision). Although the writers explain their position by the absence of an indispensable European-wide political discourse, Mancini sees "the metaphysical concept of Volk" "hiding behind the demos." *Id.* at 34, 35.

[216] Fritz W. Scharpf, *Democratic Policy in Europe*, 2 EUR. L.J. 136 (1996).

medicine. He abhors the idea of a European "global superstate" with all the inevitable vices of a major nation-state, including its own brand of exclusionary nationalism resulting from an excessive aggregation of central power. He obviously discounts the chance that the modern state could become less centralized and less threatening as a result of what some see as a mutation in its nature and in the international system generally along the lines I discussed in part I. Nor does he consider the evidence that in the federal context the central organs have proved more hostile to exclusion than some component states. Instead, he prefers the "supranational" Community within the Union. He sees the Union as the very antithesis of a nation-state.[217]

Daniel J. Elazar prophesied a future proliferation of confederal-type regimes similar to the European Union both across issue-areas and in other geographic regions.[218] One pragmatic question to ask, however, is whether the Union, despite its uniqueness, will be able to resist the centralizing or, on the contrary, the centrifugal forces, and avoid the historical fate of loose confederal-type structures that invariably either break up or turn into a more or less centralized state of one shape or another (e.g., the American Confederacy, the German Bund, Belgium, Switzerland, and Tito's Yugoslavia). Some observe distinct forces toward renationalization that would turn the Union into a traditional intergovernmental organization. With the accession to membership of the central/eastern European and other states, one may ask whether a Union in its current, essentially decentralized form would be "governable" and, conversely, whether the increased diversity would sustain a more centralized structure.[219]

The success of the European integration enterprise has resided in the phased, consensual, elite-driven movement toward an "ever closer union among the peoples of Europe"—as the constituent treaties phrased it—the ultimate shape of this "union" remaining undefined. In the latest phase, after arduous negotiations in an intergovernmental conference, the member states adopted a plan for partial institutional reform required by the impending accession of as many as twelve new members. They also recognized "the need to improve and to monitor the democratic legitimacy and transparency of the Union and its institutions" and to conduct a wide-ranging discussion of the future of Europe, considering the serious differences of views on the subject.[220] After these items, the next course on the

[217] He views the constituent treaties "not only as an agreement among states (a Union of States) but as a 'social contract' among the nationals of those states"—ratified in accordance with the constitutional requirements in all member states—"that they will in the areas covered by the Treaty regard themselves as associating as citizens in this civic society." This society is based not on organic national-cultural identity but on a matrix of values including specific European values (such as the welfare state) and a discipline of decision-making procedures representing interests beyond those of the individual member state. The structure is supported not by a "European demos," which does not exist, but by multiple demoi. Weiler & Trachtman, *supra* note 151, at 384; *see also* Weiler, *supra* note 168. In a similar vein, see Timothy Garton Ash, *Europe's Endangered Liberal Order*, FOREIGN AFF., Mar./Apr. 1998, at 51; Neil MacCormick, *Democracy, Solidarity and Citizenship in the Context of the European Union*, 16 LAW & PHIL. 331 (1997); Fritz W. Scharpf, *Can There Be a Stable Federal Balance in Europe?* in JOACHIM JENS HESSE & VINCENT WRIGHT, FEDERALIZING EUROPE? 361 (1996).

[218] ELAZAR, *supra* note 12, at 63.

[219] Youri Devuyst, *The Community Method After Amsterdam*, 37 J. COMMON MKT. STUD. 109, 118 (1999). On decreasing support for a federation, see *Goodbye, Federal Europe*, ECONOMIST, Nov. 15, 1997, at 51. A skeptic would see two equally utopian contradictory visions: a European federation without the exclusionary, centralized features of a superstate, and a supranational/confederal/consociational Union resisting the destabilizing forces described above. *See generally* Zenon Bañkovski & Emilios Christodoulidis, *The European Union as an Essentially Contested Project*, 4 EUR. L.J. 341 (1998).

[220] Treaty of Nice, *supra* note 165, Declaration on the Future of the Union, 2001 O.J. (C 80) at 86, para. 6. The unanimity voting requirement will be reduced for thirty more kinds of decisions (but not for some important decisions such as on taxation, immigration, workers' rights, and the environment); the size of the European Parliament will be increased and minor new powers added; the number of votes allocated to each member in the Council will be reassigned and the qualified majority voting formula adjusted as of January 1, 2005; the number of Commission members will be reduced in an undefined rotation system "when the Union consists of 27 member states"; greater flexibility will be given to the core members to proceed with closer integration ahead of the others; a new Charter of Fundamental Rights was "proclaimed"; and provision was made for the quick approval of a rapid reaction force. *Id.*, Protocol on the Enlargement of the European Union, 2001 O.J. (C 80) at 49; *id.*, Declaration

integration menu is likely to include simplification, systematization, and clarification of the labyrinthine constituent treaties, together with steps to further democratization. One wonders whether this is the time to seek more democracy through radical proposals such as the adoption of a formal Union constitution (which may be in the cards for the future).

At this stage of integration, the institutions of the European Union are endowed with broad authority to make and implement norms with direct impact on its citizens, but they do not meet the current idea of representative democracy. The Union's judiciary, on the other hand, in a unique symbiosis with national courts, is accessible both to member governments and (with some limitations) to citizens while satisfying the legitimating exigencies of a modern rule-of-law order. In the worldwide context, the Union, like the WTO, faces problems arising from the trend toward globalization, which includes the extension of its rules to a growing number of new members, the specialization of international policies by sectors, growing interference of multilateral rules with its own policies and enforcement schemes, and the emergence of new actors claiming to represent a "global civic society."[221]

VI. Some Concluding Thoughts: On Reality and Utopia

On the Correlation

The review of the four IGOs confirms the correlation between the level of integration (normative-institutional and empirical-social), on the one hand, and the intensity of the discourse on the democracy-legitimacy deficit, on the other. In an organization where the rule of consensus prevails and the area of activity is essentially technical and relies on "independent" experts, the discourse does not arise or is muted. The debate about the WHO, confined generally to elites of experts and bureaucrats, is an appropriate example. At the point, however, where the member states become subject to majority vote and the organization's competence is broad enough to require the setting of priorities and mediation between conflicting interests and values, the level of discourse in democratic societies rises, and becomes linked to a more general debate on reforming the organization. This is what has happened in the evolving EU. In the WTO, the discourse originated in the use of the adjudicatory power of the institution.

Propelled by the search for assured reciprocity, adjudication procedures have formed the vanguard in the path toward closer integration, offering legitimacy as an aspect of the rule of law. In the WTO, the NAFTA, and the European Union, however, the transfer of judicial power to international institutions raises questions of conformity with the national constitutions of the member states. Moreover, the scope of review of national legislation by the adjudicatory organs points up the problem of linkages to spheres outside the specified competences of the organization and creates a potential conflict between the acts of the organization and the national law that reflects competing values. The potential for such conflict is enhanced markedly if the issue may be raised directly by a concerned individual or firm. Where, as illustrated by the European Community, some law of the international organization becomes directly applicable and enforceable in the domestic law of a member state, the rule of law (and legitimacy) is enhanced, but this system standing alone cannot cure the democracy gap without incorporating political institutions that fit the idea of

on the Future of the Union, 2001 O.J. (C 80) at 85; *id.*, Declaration on the European Security and Defence Policy, 2001 O.J. (C 80) at 77. For interesting ideas on improving the intergovernmental conference procedure, see George A. Berman, *The European Intergovernmental Conference: An American Perspective*, 25 SYRACUSE J. INT'L L. & COM. 61 (1998).

[221] EC Commission, White Paper on European Governance, Commission Staff Working Document, SEC(2000) 1547/7 final (Oct. 11, 2000).

democracy. More generally, where norm-making facilities are not keeping pace, disproportionate reliance on nonelected adjudicatory bodies fans the democracy-legitimacy discourse. This proved to be a problem in the early decades of the European Community and some see it as an emerging challenge in the WHO.

In Search of Remedies

In searching for remedies to the democracy-legitimacy deficit, one would logically look to the practice within the modern democratic states, as varied as this may be. Yet any such model of governance is obviously not transferable to the international level and idiosyncratic solutions are therefore required to fit a discrete organization. It has been suggested that the very idea of democracy needs to be redefined for this purpose, but to my knowledge no general theory has emerged so far. Richard Falk argues that

> the statist view of democratization (. . . within existing states) will itself not be viable unless reinforced by the extension of democracy to all arenas of authority, those of societal character (family, workplace, place of worship) and of an institutional character, including the family of organizations that constitute the United Nations itself.[222]

This vision is linked to the concept of a "cosmopolitan democracy" to which I return in the last section.

One controversial idea would eschew representative democracy in international institutions such as the WTO and instead pursue the civic republican ("participatory") approach based on institutional balance, broad deliberation, and consensus, bolstered by open access to policymaking for interest groups and individual standing to litigate claims before tribunals.[223] The question is—as the varied interests become increasingly affected—whether ultimately this system could perform the essential mediatory function of a representative democracy.

Remedies for the deficit are sought in the national procedures of the member states and/or at the international level in the structure and functioning of the particular organization. As demonstrated by the EU experience, those who see the member states not just as privileged actors but as "masters" of the organization would seek to improve representation and accountability through national parliaments.[224] This solution is likely to be the inclination of the "neo-realists," "neo-functionalists," and "intergovernmentalists" of diverse hues.[225] On the other hand, those who view the organization as a multilevel governance regime, in which the member states wield significant influence in a complex process with a wide range of participants, would emphasize the EP route. Thus, a dialectic tension exists, although both alternatives may be usefully pursued.

At the national level, experience has shown that the legitimacy of a state's adhesion to an IGO, grounded in the act of approval by an elected legislature, dissipates quickly as the national delegation, appointed and instructed by the national executive, often acts within the organization in alliance with other delegations and IGO staff, and finds itself with little actual supervision by, or accountability to, the legislature. Several suggestions to reduce this deficiency have been advanced in the discourse:

[222] Falk, *supra* note 10, at 326; *see also* Crawford & Marks, *supra* note 20, at 72.

[223] Shell, *supra* note 82, at 365, 373 (citing Symposium, *The Republican Civic Tradition*, 97 YALE L.J. 1493 (1988) (contributions of Mark Seidenfeld and Cass R. Sunstein)).

[224] *See supra* text following note 194.

[225] Andrew Moravcsik, *Preference and Power in the European Community: A Liberal Intergovernmentalist Approach*, *in* ECONOMIC AND POLITICAL INTEGRATION IN EUROPE: INTERNAL DYNAMICS AND GLOBAL CONTEXT 29 (Simon Bulmer & Andrew Scott eds., 1994), *criticized by* WEILER, *supra* note 27, at 227; *see also* MARCELL KAUFMANN, EUROPÄISCHE INTEGRATION UND DEMOKRATIEPRINZIP (1997) (insisting on continuing sovereignty of national parliaments against some federalist or functionalist mirage).

— Members of the legislature and representatives of the private sector should participate in the negotiations for the constituent treaty and any major amendments, allowing space for confidential bargaining by the executive alone. Similar representation should be assured in the process of domestic implementation of the constituent treaty and acts of the organization. National referenda on appropriate major issues before an international institution may be useful in democratic states.

— An ample flow of information from the national delegation to the legislature is a prerequisite to effective supervision. A special legislative committee should be charged with this task. Contacts between national legislatures and the all-membership organs of the organization should be encouraged, including common sessions ("assizes" in the European Union).

— Even in those national orders that do not confer direct effect on treaties, the domestic courts of the member state should interpret national law in accordance with the state's obligations under the constituent treaty and the rules adopted by the international organization.[226]

All of these ideas deserve serious consideration. Some have been adopted, such as the procedure for the implementation of NAFTA in the United States and the special legislative committees in some member states of the European Union. The referendum route may not be practicable if complex texts are to be put before poorly informed voters or deeply fractured constituencies. Care must be taken as well that intervention by national legislatures is not carried so far as to impair the working of the international institution.

Despite their usefulness, national procedures alone can hardly be expected to meet the democracy-legitimacy requirement appropriate to the integration level of an IGO. Measures must also be sought at the level of the organization:

— Most sessions of the institutions, particularly rule-making sessions, should be open to the public and documents, including draft proposals, should be placed on the Internet (Weiler).

— In organizations at higher levels of integration, a standing consultative body composed of members of national parliaments might be established to assure greater accountability.[227]

— Actual decision making should not be confined to major powers acting in a clublike setting (Keohane and Nye); the broad membership should have an opportunity for genuine participation.

— Nongovernmental organizations and interest groups should be given adequate and fair access to the institutions for exchange of data and consultation.[228] A normative framework should be devised for such participation.

— An inspection panel (such as that created by the World Bank) and an ombudsman should be appointed to receive citizen complaints of maladministration.

— At low integration levels such as that of the WHO, remedial measures should focus on transparency, openness to the outside world, accountable and effective management, and policy results that gain the constituency's acceptance in terms of empirical-social legitimacy.

— Some of the discrete features of the European Union may be transferable to international institutions, such as phased development, the vigorous use of institutional

[226] INTERNATIONAL TRADE LAW AND THE GATT/WTO DISPUTE SETTLEMENT SYSTEM, *supra* note 58, at 239–40; Davey, Remarks, Symposium, *supra* note 223, at 162.

[227] This proposal was approved unanimously for the WTO at the Seattle ministerial meeting in December 1999 by the parliamentarians of the WTO members present. BRIDGES WKLY. TRADE NEWS DIG., Oct. 31, 2000.

[228] "Indeed, some of the organizations that have pressed hardest for a democratization of the WTO have done little to secure democracy in their own operations." J. A. Scholte with Robert O'Brien & Marc Williams, *The WTO and Civil Society*, 33 J. WORLD TRADE 107, 122 (1999).

powers, the ombudsman mentioned above, the procedures and precedent building of the EU judiciary, the consultation system and advisory organs, measures to improve transparency, cooperation with national parliaments, and—depending on the level of integration—the efforts to advance the sense of common good and expectations.

— Particularly at a higher level of integration, dispersion of the organization's central power should be sought through reliance on regional and local authorities, and the principle of subsidiarity should be honored.[229]

— In the interest of legitimacy, if for no other reasons, IGOs and regimes should explore the ways of protecting the core of fundamental human rights within the confines of their competence.

Several observations regarding this list are in order. The new information technology, including the Internet, has already contributed to greater transparency and to enhancing the role of NGOs. A major problem has been finding a way to open the preparatory proceeding that precedes final action, while protecting genuinely confidential information and allowing space for confidential bargaining. The protesters against the WTO "club system" of decision making included not only NGOs but also government delegates from less developed countries—a signal to the WTO establishment. Generally, NGOs play a useful role, provided that they shun violence and are themselves democratic in their organization and transparent in respect of their constituency, internal proceedings, and sources of funding.

The institution of the ombudsman has proved highly popular in the European Union and should be considered for other international structures. In principle, however, the transfer of any feature of one organization to another succeeds only if the basic contexts of both are roughly comparable.

Regionalism has figured prominently, if not uncontroversially, in the WHO, but in the Union it appears only in the form of an advisory committee with limited influence. Both regionalism and subsidiarity should be kept in mind in connection with all international institutions since only those powers that are necessary to deal with international problems should be centralized in IGOs.

Some participants in the discourse see the currently feasible measures as palliatives. They believe that nothing short of a radical restructuring of the international and regional systems can cure the democracy-legitimacy gap. Thus, in the WTO, private individuals and firms are to replace the member governments as the principal actors. In the European Union, voices in the judiciary and high political circles call for a federation (often not meaningfully defined) based on a European constitution as the only effective remedy.

All of these "radical" measures are designed to inject the voice of individual citizens into the exclusively state-based structures. This could be accomplished in two major ways. First, individuals could be recognized as stakeholders with individual rights derived from the constituent treaty and broadly enforceable by the domestic or supranational judiciary. A less intrusive alternative would be to enable a private party to pursue a specific claim in an arbitration proceeding, as in the NAFTA chapter on investment. In this context, I have noted the vital differences between the European Union and the WTO, which at this stage of integration make transfers of the basic features of the European Union difficult to envision.

A second avenue toward broadening citizen participation would enlarge the structure by adding an assembly, elected directly by the people in the member states, with powers to recommend norms and policy; such an assembly would eventually replace the organs of general membership represented by states and obtain lawmaking powers. As globalization

[229] The principle of subsidiarity, as generalized from the amended European Community Treaty, may be defined as follows: an international institution should take action only if and insofar as the objective of the proposed action cannot be sufficiently achieved by the member states, and therefore, by reason of the scale or effects of the proposed action, can be better achieved by the international institution. *See* EC TREATY Art. 5 (ex-Art. 3b).

progresses and democracy spreads worldwide, a "cosmopolitan" democracy could make possible—so goes the argument—the direct election by universal suffrage of a Global Peoples Assembly, with general competence to legislate where worldwide action is called for and to coordinate the work of international institutions.[230]

History has taught us not to underestimate the power of utopia. Too often in the past it has proved difficult to foresee a systemic change that would turn a utopian vision into a "political project" (Falk).[231] But some of the ideas adumbrated in this section, especially the world legislature, postulate a radical transformation of the present international system. As international integration advances, new actors—intergovernmental, subgovernmental, and nongovernmental—have appeared on the international scene; their number and influence on the behavior of states have grown over the last few decades and hold "the potential [for] spillover of democratic practices."[232] However, in view of the enormous differences in the size, population, and powers of states (which are not about to fade away), as well as the persistent, deep-rooted differences in the peoples—cultural-ethnic, economic, and political—there is little evidence that the democracy-legitimacy gap can be filled by "Great and desperate Cures,"[233] at the global level at any rate. On the other hand, there is ample evidence that creative, idiosyncratic arrangements commensurate with the respective level of integration are called for in both the national and the international institutions.

[230] A "World Parliament," as a subsidiary organ of the UN General Assembly, should be elected directly by the people and should advise and report to the General Assembly. Japan Association for United Nations Studies, The Role of the United Nations in the Twenty-first Century World (Sept. 8, 1999); *see also* Richard Falk & Andrew Strauss, *On the Creation of a Global Peoples Assembly: Legitimacy and the Power of Popular Sovereignty*, 36 STAN. J. INT'L L. 191 (2000); Yozo Yokota, *A Charter for a New World Organization: Comments on Mr. Maurice Bertrand's Proposal*, *in* A NEW CHARTER FOR A WORLDWIDE ORGANISATION? 133 (Maurice Bertrand & Daniel Warner eds., 1997); *Citizens in the International Realm: The New Participatory Demands*, 95 ASIL PROC. 162 (forthcoming 2001) (remarks by Andrew L. Strauss, Richard Falk, Thomas M. Franck, & Jessica Tuchman Mathews).

[231] Falk, *supra* note 10.

[232] Harold K. Jacobson, *International Institutions and Systems Transformation*, 2000 ANN. REV. POL. SCI. 149, 161 (citing, among others, March, Olsen, and Slaughter).

[233] JOHN BUNYAN: GOOD NEWS FOR THE VILEST OF MEN, THE ADVOCATESHIP OF JESUS CHRIST 27 (Richard L. Greaves ed., 1985) (1668).

Part IV
International Institutions and the Promotion and Protection of Democracy

[10]

The United Nations and Democracy

Christopher C. Joyner

The UN has been maligned over the past decade for peacekeeping failures in Somalia and Bosnia and for being a bloated, inefficient, ineffective bureaucracy. Yet, at the same time, the organization has become increasingly active in promoting the democratic process around the world, particularly in developing countries. It is, in fact, not hyperbole to assert that the UN Secretariat has assumed the impressive role of international agent for democratization, as it has engaged the UN organization in various activities toward that end in more than seventy-five states and territories over the past decade. Unfortunately, this formidable UN effort at assisting the democratic process worldwide has gone largely neglected and unappreciated.

This study aims to remedy this neglect by pursuing three main purposes. First, I examine the concept of "democracy" as interpreted and applied by the UN so that a clearer picture can be derived of the particular political system envisioned, promoted, and supported by the UN Secretariat. I also offer an appraisal of the Secretariat's rationale for undertaking such efforts at promoting democracy and the special role, if any, that certain member states might play in these efforts.

Second, I examine the ways and means the UN has adopted for implementing assistance to states that have requested special help from the UN in the democratization process. This analysis provides insights into how the UN facilitates the democratic process and which states have been most active in seeking UN support. For the discussion, a clearer picture emerges of which facets of democracy are considered paramount by the UN and how the organization has contributed to institutionalizing those facets in various countries around the world.

A third purpose of the study is to gauge what success the UN has had in its efforts to promote democracy. I do this by examining certain key questions, among them: Have the UN's efforts been worthwhile? Where has the UN succeeded in promoting democracy, and where has it failed? Are there political, legal, and ideological lessons to be learned from the UN experience in promoting democracy? In sum, can the UN make a difference in promoting the acceptability of democracy worldwide? If so, how, and to what degree? Finally, the conclusion aims to draw lessons learned from the UN's experience for effecting democracy throughout the past decade.

At the outset, however, two important caveats are in order. First, this study focuses on the recent efforts of the UN to promote democratic practices around the world. The analysis does not mean to imply, though, that the UN is either the only or the most effective agent for doing so. Clearly, other bilateral and multilateral democratization efforts, such as the U.S. Agency for International Development, the Scandinavian donors, the Organization of American States, or even Mercosur, may be as important, if not more so, in promoting the ways and means of democracy around the world. My main aim is to explain how, where, and why the UN has taken up the challenge of promoting democracy after the Cold War and the legal, political, and economic implications those efforts hold for member states.

The second caveat deals with how the notion of democracy is treated throughout the study. Although the analysis concerns the UN and its role as an agent of democratization, it must be emphasized that democratization as a process comes down to people. Often international democracy is equated with the notion of sovereignty and equality of all states. That is not the meaning here. Rather, democracy refers to the practices of people in a national society that strive to provide free and fair elections, with respect for the civil and political rights of individuals, protected under the rule of law. This means that the concept of democracy at the global level must constantly give attention to the roles and actions of people in different countries. In sum, since 1990, the UN has acted openly to provide the ways and means for instituting democratic practices in various countries. This study examines those ways and means, along with their underlying philosophies, as articulated by the UN secretaries-general in documents and deeds over the past decade.

The Evolving UN Role

Since 1945, the meaning of democracy has changed markedly in international relations. During World War II, democracy was viewed as the political system that opposed fascism. During the Cold War, the notion of democracy was pulled in two different directions, East and West, mainly to appeal to developing countries in the Third World. On the one hand, Eastern socialist states espoused democracy in terms of economic, social, and cultural circumstances threatened by Western imperialism, with the overarching need that more egalitarian opportunities be given to all states. In these revolutionary efforts, the Eastern bloc often resorted to violent means to subvert legitimate governments. In the West, democracy was viewed as the political rights and civil liberties of a free, independent state that must be protected from global communism. Paradoxically, however,

Western governments often supported selected authoritarian, antidemocratic regimes that opposed communism. The end of the Cold War brought about a new, revised recognition of democracy—not only as a system of political rights and liberties, but also as a process through which economic and social development can be promoted toward the goal of securing peace and security. It is this view that undergirds the UN's strategy toward democratization.

During the late 1980s, the democratic process became recognized by the UN Secretariat (largely in the person of the secretary-general) as offering the means to respond to a wide range of human concerns and as being essential to the protection of human rights, broadly interpreted. As conceived by UN officials, democracy reflects a particular system of government that, through its laws and institutions, embodies the ideal of political power based on the will of the people.[1] Democratization is the gradual process that fosters a more participatory, less authoritarian society. In effect, then, democratization aims to attain a civil society based on the rule of law and pervasive respect for human rights.

Acknowledgment of the UN's potential for contributing to the process of democratization was indicated as early as 1988, when the General Assembly first adopted a resolution that advocated enhanced effectiveness of the principle of periodic and genuine elections.[2]

The initial UN-sponsored effort to concentrate attention on democratic values and political systems came in the First International Conference of New or Restored Democracies, held in Manila in June 1988, with thirteen states attending.[3] This summit was followed in July 1994 by the Second International Conference of New or Restored Democracies, which convened in Managua with seventy-four states participating.[4] Most recently, the Third International Conference of New or Restored Democracies was held in Bucharest in September 1997 and attracted the participation of eighty states;[5] and a Fourth International Conference of New or Restored Democracies on Democracy and Development is scheduled to be held in Benin early in the new millennium.[6]

Following the Second International Conference, in Managua, the General Assembly requested in late 1994 that the secretary-general prepare a report that studied "the ways and mechanisms in which the UN system could support the efforts of governments to promote and consolidate new or restored democracies."[7] Similarly, following receipt of a special report by the secretary-general in late 1995,[8] the General Assembly again requested that the secretary-general prepare a report that evaluated the efforts made by the Secretariat to respond to the goal of democratization, including "innovative ways and means" that permitted the UN to respond more effectively.[9] That respondent report was submitted to the General Assembly in October 1996,[10] and the General Assembly reiterated its call for another report by the secretary-general that assessed the ways and means through which the UN could respond most effectively to member states' requests for democratizing assistance.[11] In early 1998, the General Assembly considered in a special resolution[12] the third *Report of the Secretary-General,* in which special focus was directed on policies and principles shaping the emerging framework for intergovernmental action in democratization.[13] A fourth *Report of the Secretary-General* issued in October 1998 highlights the policies and principles advocated by the UN in fostering democracy worldwide, as it gives numerous examples of assistance activities by the UN system that contribute to an intergovernmental framework for promoting democratization.[14] These world conferences and the attendant reports of the UN secretary-general have given stronger momentum and clearer focus to the processes of global and regional democratization as viewed from the UN.

In approaching the concept of democracy, the UN Secretariat has endorsed the notion that democracy does not advocate the rights of the individual person over or at the expense of the community. Rather, it is through democracy that individual and collective rights can be reconciled, and here democratization can make a critical contribution. Democratic processes and institutions offer the ways, means, and opportunities for striking balances between the rights of the individual and the rights of the people.[15]

The UN's view asserts that, by providing legitimacy for a government and encouraging the people's participation in decisionmaking on issues that affect their lives, democratic processes can contribute to the effectiveness of adopting and implementing domestic laws and policies. Democratic institutions and practices foster greater governmental accountability and transparency to contend with domestic economic problems and social concerns. Without democratic institutions to channel popular pressures for social-economic development and political reform, unrest and instability might result. In this sense as well, democratic processes are seen by the UN Secretariat as providing relief from political pressures that otherwise might derail policies for international economic, social, and cultural development at home and abroad.[16]

UN Philosophy and Democratization

Philosophically, the UN is well conceived to justify assistance to governments and peoples who desire greater democratization of their societies. Indeed, the UN was founded on certain beliefs and ambitions supportive of democratic principles that remain salient today. Foremost among these are to guard against dangerous nationalism by advocating self-determination; to eliminate reliance on precarious balances of international power by providing for a system of collective security; to dissuade arms races through disarmament; and to do away with treaties, secretly arrived at, by sponsoring open, international diplomacy. Thus, as originally conceived, democratic processes within and among states would be the glue that would hold these aspirations together in the UN enterprise.

Under the UN's philosophy, interstate democracy preserves the cardinal principles of sovereignty and independence among states and promotes political participation by allowing peoples to exercise the right of self-determination. Democratic opportunities would permit states to participate in democratic international organizations and institutions, ostensibly guided by the principle of one nation, one vote. No less important, the acceptance of democracy also was intended to promote respect for the rule of law within and between states. Establishing democracy thus will lessen violence, dissuade aggression, and promote states as the sovereign guarantors of human rights.

In terms of moral objectives, the contemporary attitude of the UN embraces democracy as the pivotal principle for governing international relations, which is well expressed in three core UN documents. First, there is the UN Charter.[17] While the word *democracy* does not appear in the charter, the opening words of the preamble do assert the fundamental essence of democracy as they intone, "We the Peoples of the United Nations . . . "; this single phrase invokes the sovereign authority of each state and legitimizes the UN organization that they comprise in the will of their peoples.[18] The charter goes on to envision a democracy of states that emanates from the founders' "faith in fundamental human rights, in the dignity and worth of the human person, in the equal rights of men and women and of nations large and small."[19] The founders' commitment to democracy is revealed in the asserted Purposes of the United Nations, in particular to promote the principle of equal rights and self-determination of peoples[20] and human rights and fundamental freedoms for all without discrimination "as to race, sex, language or religion."[21] The charter asserts, moreover, that "the Organization is based on the principle of the sovereignty equality of all of its Members."[22] Not to be overlooked is that the UN Charter is an international treaty instrument, with full binding legal effect on its party states.

Second, the Universal Declaration of Human Rights, adopted without opposition by the General Assembly in 1948,[23] enshrines the UN's aspirations for liberal democracy, undergirded by fundamental political rights and civil liberties. All persons have the right to "take part in the government of [their] country, directly or through freely chosen representatives."[24] Moreover, "the will of the people shall be the basis of authority of government," which is to be expressed in periodic and genuine elections conducted by universal and equal suffrage and held by secret vote or equivalent voting procedures.[25] In addition, the universal declaration affirms that all persons are born "free and equal in dignity and rights,"[26] and that "everyone has the right to life, liberty and the security of person."[27]

Other rights fundamental to a liberal democracy are also asserted, among them the right to equality before the law (Article 7), freedom from arbitrary arrest, detention, or exile (Article 9), freedom of opinion and expression (Article 19), freedom of thought, conscience, and religion (Article 18), and the right to peaceful assembly and association (Article 20).[28]

Third, the Declaration on the Granting of Independence to Colonial Countries and Peoples,[29] adopted by the General Assembly in 1960, is viewed by the UN Secretariat as constituting another signal contribution to principles of democracy in the international realm, especially for newly independent states.[30] This instrument, which is nonbinding but is certainly presumed to reflect international public opinion,[31] strongly reaffirms the right of all peoples to self-determination and proclaims that, by virtue of that right, all peoples are free to determine their political status and to pursue their economic, social, and cultural development.[32] Toward that end, the declaration avers that "immediate steps" be taken to ensure that in all trust territories, non–self-governing territories, and other nonindependent territories powers be transferred "to the peoples of those territories, without any conditions or reservations, in accordance with their freely expressed will and desire, without any distinction as to race, creed, or colour, in order to enable them to enjoy complete independence and freedom."[33]

Taken as a package, these three documents—the UN Charter, the Universal Declaration of Human Rights, and the Declaration on the Granting of Independence to Colonial Countries and Peoples—furnish the normative framework for casting the UN's role in promoting democratization. They constitute, in essence, what can be called a UN's "Bill of Democratic Rights and Duties," which has found expression as binding legal obligations in subsequent international instruments.[34]

Challenges for Emerging Democracies

For developing societies to achieve a democratic culture, the UN Secretariat rightly observes that certain fundamental conditions must be attained. At base, there must be full respect for human rights, with emphasis on upholding the rights of minorities, children, women, and the elderly.[35] A modern democratic society must also have an independent, respected, and impartial judiciary that is professionally run and staffed. Judicial reform is essential for responsible government if it is to be transparent and operate as a fulcrum between legislative and executive branches that can hold politicians accountable for their actions.[36]

There exists too the critical need to stem corruption and organized crime in developing societies. Benefits must be increased to give incentives for being honest; greater transparency must be developed to detect corruption; and penalties must be increased on those facilitating corrupt practices and criminal practices such as drug trafficking and money laundering.[37]

New democracies also need to realize the criticality of decentralization as an asset for government. Local and regional governments should be given greater authority over resources, and citizens should be allocated greater influence over decisions. These situations would make it easier to exert political accountability by bringing the government closer to the people and the people closer to the government.[38] At the same time, a government can become more legitimized if the process is made more open and responsive to popular participation, especially through more opportunities for political groups to promote diverse policies. Such pluralism broadens considerations of views and needs in the formulation of national policies.[39]

Democracy functions better in a system of broad-based political parties. To give voice and vote to disparate interests, parties should be recognized and constituted as national organizations that also practice internal democracy. Strict control and transparency must be imposed over campaign finances.

An essential first step toward democratization is choosing political leadership through elections. These elections need to be free, fair, and sustained over time as a process that has as active participants functioning parties, a legislative framework, media coverage, and nongovernmental organizations.

Civic education is critical for ensuring the sustainability of the democratization process. Gender equality and equity must be recognized, accepted, and implemented by the political society. The government must promote civic education that creates awareness of democratic rights and responsibilities and serves to strengthen political parties, the judiciary, law enforcement, the accountability of elected officials, and local management capabilities.

Likewise, political accountability and transparency must be implanted by permitting the people to easily obtain information about the government and its policies—information that can be used to hold public officials accountable. The government should publish information about budgets, taxes collected, executive decisions made, and laws adopted. Public finances should be independently audited. Finally, publicity through the media should be used to engage the government and the people in a democratic dialogue. A free press operates as the vehicle for democratization, which in turn promotes an open society in which a free press can flourish.[40]

Finally, the UN Secretariat recognizes that the need exists to establish conditions that help the private sector to be competitive in the increasingly interdependent global market economy. To this end, governments of emerging democracies must provide a predictable legal framework that includes control of corruption, increased quality of public services, and the necessary regulatory systems for protecting the environment and the underprivileged in society.

Promoting Democratic Culture

Fundamental to democratic institutions and processes is the need to channel competing interests into a forum where they can be discussed, debated, compromised, and worked out to the mutual satisfaction of all participants. Such an international arena for debate and discussion can help to minimize differences and thus lessen the possibilities for interstate conflict or confrontation. The UN became that global forum for democratic institution building during the 1990s.

The UN also aims to promote the institutional ground in which democratization can take root and grow. Functional work in economic development and human rights involves preparing institutions for civil society. Institution building for democratization involves improving the means of accountability and transparency among the political elite, improving the civil service, promoting institutional support for the rule of law (especially in which UN departments, agencies, and programs assist states in reforming and strengthening legal and judicial systems), forging human rights institutions (including those supporting humanitarian law), training police and military forces to be more respectful of the rule of law and civil liberties, and depoliticizing military establishments. The UN can also help in creating independent trade unions and in promoting fuller integration of women into all aspects of the political, economic, social, and cultural life of a state's society.

Before the UN can assist a member state in democratization, it must receive a formal request from that government. The Office of the Under-Secretary-General for Political Affairs is the UN focal point for electoral requests and is responsible for coordinating UN units working in the electoral field. This office provides advice on requests for electoral assistance and aids in the publication of guidebooks on electoral assistance and the convening of workshops and seminars.

The administrative committee on coordination, which is chaired by the secretary-general and composed of all the executive heads of the UN programs and specialized agencies, coordinates efforts for economic and social development. At the country level, a UN resident coordinator system operates to administer UN-supported democratic activities.

The UN cannot establish democracy for a society or install democratic government in a polity. Rather, what the UN does is to help promote and consolidate democratic culture in a society in two fundamental contexts. First, there are the organizations's peacemaking, peacekeeping, and peace-building activities. Most of the cases in which the UN undertakes such activities today are internal conflicts. Their causes are complex but often involve political, economic, and social systems from which sectors of the population feel alienated, as was the case in Namibia, Mozambique, and South Africa. Often, agreed-on measures to set up more participatory opportunities are made part of negotiated peace settlements. Where conflict has more the character of a struggle for power between rival factions (for example, in Cambodia, Nicaragua, and El Salvador), democratic elections are made an essential part of the peace arrangement. In helping to consolidate the peace arrangement, the UN becomes an essential player in promoting a democratic culture.

The second context pertains to the organization's general efforts to promote human development by assisting member states to provide more equitable and effective governance by strengthening civil society.[41] Clearly, development and civil society reflect a symbiotic relationship. For social and economic development to go forward, there must be effective governance. At the same time, however, the functioning of a robust civil society is also indispensable for long-term social development.[42]

The UN view recognizes that democratization offers a new area for technical assistance to developing countries. Traditional concepts of technical assistance have focused on economic and social development, with principal interest being concentrated on constructing and strengthening physical infrastructure. During the post–Cold War era, requests for technical assistance from the UN have tended to come increasingly for issues related to democratization. Such UN efforts have included several key areas, including developing political parties, assisting in the conduct of national elections, assisting in media relations, instituting means of accountability and transparency for decisionmakers, and improving the national human rights situation.

Political Parties

Political parties are essential elements in the democratization process. The UN experience in fostering political parties has derived mainly from multinational peace operations. That is, on occasion armed rebel movements have been transformed into legitimate political parties, as evidenced by UN efforts in Cambodia, El Salvador, and Mozambique. UN efforts in Cambodia were successful in preparing the people for the elections and informing them about political choices, which prompted more than 4.5 million Cambodians to vote in 1993.[43] Some major factions were integrated into Cambodian parties; yet exclusion of the Khmer Rouge from the political party system proved to be a fatal flaw for undoing the results of that democratic experience, as Cambodia's coalition government disintegrated into civil conflict in 1997. In El Salvador, the UN Observer Mission in El

Salvador worked to transform the Frente Farabundo Marti para la Liberación Nacional (FMLN) into a political party, which participated in a national election in 1992. In Mozambique in 1994, support for political parties was facilitated through a trust fund for political parties established by the electoral division of the UN Operation in Mozambique (ONUMOZ). Special attention was focused on transformation of the rebel army Resistencia Nacional de Moçambique (RENAMO) into a legitimate political party as part of the process for creating a multiparty system. The UN political party monitoring program for election days in October 1994 included thirty thousand political party monitors assigned to polling stations.[44] In these three cases, the UN intended to move from the conditions of a prolonged civil war to peace and reconstruction.[45]

Nongovernmental organizations (NGOs) have become recognized by the UN as essential partners in the democratization process. NGOs serve as channels for developmental assistance and can be used to nurture the growth of civil society. For example, in 1995, the Joint Unit of the UN Mission for the Verification of Human Rights and Compliance with the Compliments of the Comprehensive Agreement on Human Rights (MINUGUA) and the UN Development Programme (UNDP) conducted a joint study on NGOs. Although the study's focus fell specifically on the situation in Guatemala, it also clarified which activities NGOs in general needed to pursue in order to improve their technical capability for filing lawsuits against human rights violators and to enhance their administrative and financial management.[46]

Member states have increasingly turned to the UN for support in facilitating democratization. Since 1989, more than 140 requests for electorial assistance have come from more than sixty states, nearly one-third of the entire UN membership.[47] UN peacekeeping mandates often include restoration of democracy and protection of human rights. UN departments, agencies, and programs are called on to help states draft constitutions, create and improve independent systems for the administration of justice, provide civil police forces that respect the rule of law, reign in the reach of military establishments, and establish national institutions that can promote and protect human rights. Toward these ends, UN agencies have also been asked by states striving for democratization to facilitate the participation of citizens in political processes and to integrate the communications media into a role that more responsibly contributes to democratization.

Electoral Assistance

For free and fair elections to go forward, the UN must successfully integrate several key actors—government officials, political leaders, parliamentarians, judicial officials, police and military forces, and individual citizens—into roles appropriate for election politics. In addition, the UN must be prepared to mediate or facilitate situations in the event a crisis threatens to disrupt the political process or derail the democratization process. The role of the UN can be critical for ensuring popular acceptance of election results as well as for encouraging respect for democratic practices.[48]

Since 1989, as Table 1 shows, the UN has provided several types of electoral assistance to countries. The type of assistance is determined on the basis of a needs assessment mission sent to the country.[49] This mission has two major tasks: (1) to conduct a realistic evaluation of the conditions for and possibility of viable elections; and (2) to assess the basic electoral needs of the country.[50] Several factors must be considered by the mission, including the provisions in the national constitution and election laws; the existence and capabilities of an independent election commission; the availability of voter registration; and the views of all parties, including the government, regarding UN assistance and a legitimate electoral process.[51] The following are types of assistance offered by the UN to facilitate fair and free national elections.

1. Organization and conduct of elections. The most extensive electoral assistance furnished by UN was to Cambodia, culminating in the election of 1993. An integral part of the peace agreements signed in Paris in 1991, the Cambodia experience marked the first time that the UN was given responsibility for organizing and conducting national elections in a state.[52] The UN also supervised the countrywide cease-fire, verified the withdrawal of foreign forces, and undertook an extensive landmine removal program. Civilian police of the UN Transitional Authority in Cambodia (UNTAC) assumed responsibility for controlling local police. The UN high commissioner for refugees was instrumental in repatriating some 365,000 Cambodian refugees between 30 March 1992 and 30 April 1993. Under UNTAC, nearly 5,000 Cambodians were trained as polling officers for fourteen hundred polling stations. Some nine hundred international polling station officials were enlisted from forty-four states and the Inter-parliamentary Union to assist in processing voters in election. Nearly 90 percent of voters turned out in what was declared by the UN in June 1993 to have been a free and fair election.[53]

2. Election supervision. Supervision involves coordination and support services and has been done most often in cases of decolonization, because the procedure is not deemed appropriate for use in sovereign states. The special representative of the secretary-general certifies not only the results of elections but also the steps taken in political and election processes. Although the UN provided at least twenty-five cases of coordination or support assistance to member states during 1989–1996, the most impressive example was the preparation of Namibia for independence from South Africa in 1994.[54]

The Namibia election was overseen by an administrator-general appointed by South Africa, but supervision was administered by the special representative of the secretary-general, who retained authority to approve

Table 1 Types of UN Electoral Assistance, 1989–1996

Types of Assistance	Number (comment)	Country
Organization and conduct	1 (provided)	Cambodia
	1 (in preparation)	Croatia (Eastern Slavonia)
	1 (in abeyance)	Western Sahara
Verification	7 (provided)	Angola, El Salvador, Eritrea, Haiti, Mozambique, Nicaragua, South Africa
	1 (in abeyance)	Liberia
Coordination and support	25 (provided)	Armenia, Azerbaijan, Benin, Burundi, Central African Republic, Chad, Comoros, Congo, Côte d'Ivoire, Djibouti (x2), Equatorial Guinea, Ethiopia, Guinea-Bissau, Kenya, Kyrgyzstan, Lesotho, Malawi (x2), Namibia, Nicaragua, Niger, Uganda, Sierra Leone, United Republic of Tanzania
Technical assistance	43 (provided or being provided)	Albania, Angola, Argentina, Bangladesh (x2), Comoros, El Salvador (x2), Equatorial Guinea, Eritrea, Ethiopia, Fiji, The Gambia, Guinea, Guinea-Bissau, Guyana (x2), Haiti (x2), Honduras, Kyrgyzstan, Lesotho, Liberia (x2), Madagascar, Malawi (x2), Mali, Mozambique, Nicaragua, Niger (x2), Panama, Paraguay, Peru, Philippines, Romania, Rwanda, Sierra Leone (x2), Togo, Uganda (x2)
Follow-up and report/observation	27 (provided)	Algeria, Cameroon, Central African Republic, Congo, Djibouti, Gabon, Guinea (x2), Kyrgyzstan, Madagascar, Mali, Netherlands (Antilles) (x2), Paraguay, Republic of Moldova, Romania, Russian Federation, São Tomé and Principe, Senegal, Seychelles (x2), the former Yugoslav Republic of Macedonia, Togo, Uganda, Ukraine (x2), Uzbekistan
Training of national observers	1 (provided)	Mexico

Source: UN Doc. A/51/512, *Report of the Secretary-General: Support by the United Nations System of the Efforts of Governments to Promote and Consolidate New or Restored Democracies.*

election procedures, including the registration of voters and tabulation of results. In addition, the special representative was responsible for ensuring that no intimidation or interference occurred with the electoral process.

The UN Transition Assistance Group (UNTAG) was a massive operation given a mandate not only to certify electoral process but also to ensure conditions conducive to free and fair election. The mission was composed of some eight thousand persons, including two thousand civilians, fifteen hundred civilian police monitors, and forty-five hundred military personnel. More than seven hundred thousand voters in Namibia were registered. Approximately eighteen hundred UNTAG electoral personnel supervised twenty-five hundred South African counterparts to conduct the polling stations. Certified fair and free by the special representative, these elections opened the door for a Constituent Assembly and earlier independence for Namibia.[55]

3. Verification of elections. This form of electoral assistance was provided between 1989 and 1996 by the UN to seven states: Angola, El Salvador, Eritrea, Haiti, Mozambique, Nicaragua, and South Africa.[56] Verification missions often are made part of larger peacekeeping missions, with international observers deployed throughout a country during an election period.

Mozambique offers an instructive case of the verification process. In late 1993, the UN helped the Mozambican National Assembly to appoint a national election commission. Further, the UN established for dispute settlement an electoral tribunal, on which sat three judges designated by the UN; it also trained some sixteen hundred voter registration teams and sixty thousand election-day poll workers.[57]

During the final phase of elections, some twenty-three hundred international observers worked throughout the country, including nationals of 113 states and representatives of intergovernmental organizations such as the European Union, the Organization of African Unity, and the Association of West European Parliamentarians Against Apartheid.[58] The results announced on 19 November 1994 were certified by the special representative as those of a free and fair election.

4. Coordination and support of international observers. A more standard form of election assistance is the coordination and support mission. This was first attempted in Ethiopia in 1992 and was subsequently applied more fully in twenty-four other states, among them Armenia, Djibouti, Lesotho, Malawi, Nicaragua, and Niger.[59] For this kind of assistance, the UN sets up a small secretariat in the requesting state to coordinate and support logistical operations for international election observers. The advantages of this type of assistance are twofold: the UN can maintain a low profile while supporting election-related processes; and the approach appears less intrusive into a state's national sovereignty while still providing for on-site observer presence.

5. Support for national election observers. This type of election assistance, done only for Mexico in 1994, places the emphasis on long-term national institution building for monitoring elections. A statewide observer network composed of national organizations must be established. Although the UN provides technical and material assistance to strengthen those organizations' capabilities to oversee and assess electoral process, a country's own NGOs must take on the responsibility to monitor elections.

6. Technical assistance. Technical assistance is the most frequently requested form of election aid. The UN electoral assistance division provides a variety of technical assistance in the form of training and education to improve civic and voter education, election organization, election budgets, district boundary identification, logistics, training of election administrators, and use of election materials. Between 1989 and 1996, forty-eight requests for such assistance were approved by the Secretariat for forty different states.[60]

The elections in Guinea-Bissau in 1994 provide a useful example of long-term technical support by the UN. A needs assessment mission was sent in December 1992. Using its findings, the UN chief technical adviser advised electoral authorities on how to reform Guinea-Bissau's election laws, compose its election commission, undertake logistics for voter registration, and construct the ballot, organize poll stations, and compute election results. The elections took place in July and August 1994.[61]

7. Observation. A final aspect of UN electoral assistance is election observation by a few official UN representatives. Although costs are low, this technique is not extensively used, simply because a few observers can exert only limited effects on the conduct of elections. Between 1989 and 1996, twenty-seven requests for UN observation missions were approved for elections held in twenty-four states.[62] The UN observer presence is largely symbolic, with little access to the election process itself.

Figure 1 shows the numbers and trends in various forms of electoral assistance provided by the UN between 1989 and 1996. The principal finding is that all forms of UN activity peaked in 1993, a fact attributable to the increasing popularity of democracy in the aftermath of the Cold War and an inordinate number of elections held in African states that year. Since then, trend lines indicate a falling off in all forms of UN electoral assistance. Although no clear explanation is evident, the inference might be drawn that this decline since 1993 in grants of UN electoral missions might be attributable to democratic electoral systems taking root in many of these emerging civil societies, with less need for UN support. That conclusion, however, would be too optimistic. A more likely explanation suggests that budgetary constraints throughout the UN Secretariat have inhibited more active response for such electoral assistance and that UN grants are being made on a more selective basis.

Figure 1 Types and Trends of UN Electoral Assistance Missions, 1989–1996

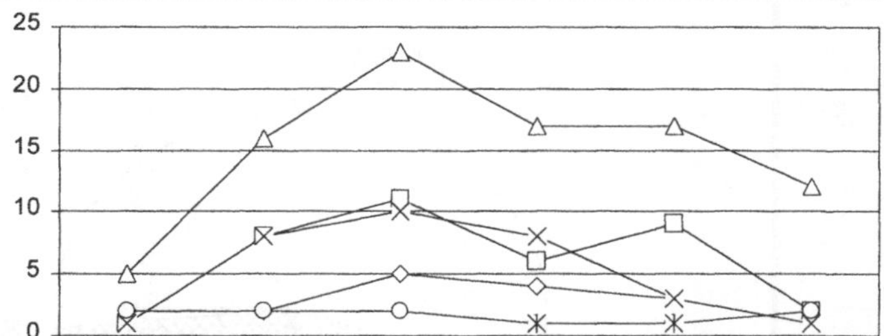

	1989-1991	1992	1993	1994	1995	1996
–◇– Verification	2	2	5	4	3	1
–□– Coord. & Support	1	8	11	6	9	2
–△– Technical Assistance	5	16	23	17	17	12
–×– Observation	1	8	10	8	3	1
–○– Org. & Conduct	2	2	2	1	1	2
–✱– Training Observers				1	1	

Source: UN Document A/51/512, Report of the Secretary-General on Support by the United Nations System of the Efforts of Governments to Promote and Consolidate New and Restored Democracies.

Figure 2 illustrates the regional apportionment of states receiving UN electoral assistance between 1989 and 1996. Interesting to note, of sixty-nine states receiving such aid, thirty-nine (or 56 percent) were African and eleven (or 16 percent) were former Soviet bloc states in Eastern Europe. In the Middle East, the only state receiving UN assistance was Yemen, for an election scheduled for 1997. Two nonmember regions, Palestine and Western Sahara, requested assistance, but neither received it. Palestine's request for observers to monitor its 1996 election was rejected because the observation function was coordinated by the European Union, although some logistical support was provided by the UN Relief and Works Agency for Palestine Refugees in the Near East (UNRWA).[63] The UN mission to organize and conduct an election for Western Sahara remains "in abeyance"[64] until negotiated arrangements can be finalized for an election in that territory.

In sum, the UN has functioned to create a network for information sharing, policy development, and cooperation in democratization in developing countries. Postelection needs missions, offered by the UN Electoral Assistance Division, are dispatched to election sites to recommend programs to local authorities for consolidating democratic approaches and joint initiatives with international actors.[65]

The UNDP has come to play an increasingly important role in providing technical assistance to electoral processes in close consultation with

Figure 2 States Receiving UN Electoral Assistance by Region, 1989–1996 (total number assisted or under consideration = 69)

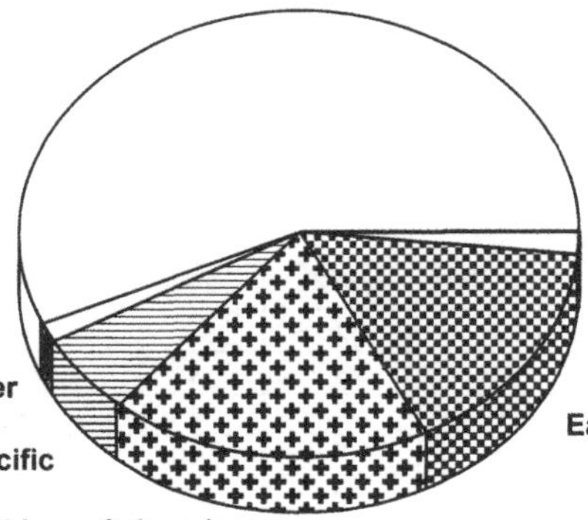

Source: UN Document A/51/512, Report of the Secretary-General on Support by the United Nations System of the Efforts of Governments to Promote and Consolidate New and Restored Democracies.

the Electoral Assistance Division. Similarly, the Office of UN High Commissioner for Human Rights (UNHCHR) has become more involved in election assistance, especially with regard to the legal and human rights aspects of elections through its technical assistance program. The focus here by UNHCHR falls on supplying legal analysis of election laws, recommendations concerning human rights and institutional needs, support for civic education programs, and training public officials for electioneering.[66]

The key purposes of UN election assistance over the long term are to build peoples' confidence in the democratic political processes in their states and to develop the national capacity to carry out periodic, genuinely free elections. The UN uses technology to construct a national electoral process and electoral infrastructure. In these ways, the organization aims to create a network for electoral observation that encourages participation of national political parties and nongovernmental organizations as a base of ongoing democratization.

Free and Independent Media

The UN promotes democratization through programs designed to educate people about the press media and its social-political role. The UN Department of Public Information serves as a key facility for encouraging the development of and respect for a free and responsible press in democratizing states. Five regional seminars have been organized since 1991 to discuss why pluralistic and independent media are so essential for effective democratization.[67] In addition, workshops sponsored by UNICEF's division of communication have been held to promote better standards of journalism and media reporting in several countries, among them India, Sri Lanka, Mozambique, Romania, Kenya, Malawi, Nepal, and Albania.[68]

Human Rights Monitoring

The transition from an authoritarian government to greater popular participation in making political decisions requires sustained efforts, especially with regard to the protection of human rights and civil liberties. UNHCHR has responsibility for giving technical assistance aimed at incorporating international human rights standards into national laws and policies and strengthening national institutions that are supposed to protect human rights and democracy under the rule of law; during 1997 and 1998, some forty-five technical cooperation projects were carried out by UNHCHR in more than twenty-five states.[69] These programs have included human rights training for domestic police and security forces, assistance in drafting constitutions, and support for parliamentarians. The UN, assisted by nongovernmental organizations, undertakes to verify reported human rights violations and to publicize respect for human rights as fundamental for democracy.

Accountability and Transparency

Key concerns for the process of institution building and governance are political legitimacy, accountability, and transparency between the people and the government. At the heart of democratic governance is the accountability of public officials. Free and fair periodic elections permit officials to be held accountable, but there is also the critical need to punish persons who abuse the public trust through corruption and violation of laws. This requires greater transparency of how and why decisions are made and who is responsible for authorizing which policies. Also in this regard, public sector management must be taken into consideration, as the administration of developmental programs can be a serious source of corruption for undermining public confidence in democratic institutions. The UNDP is now sponsoring several programs to assist governments in designing and executing long-term strategies to improve sector management.[70] Notable examples of countries participating in these programs include Bhutan, Nepal, Thailand, Papua New Guinea, Morocco, Georgia, Lesotho, Kuwait, Pakistan, Bangladesh, The Gambia, Burundi, Sierra Leone, and Mozambique.[71]

The Balance Sheet

The UN cannot offer a standard model for democratization in a particular society and has made no pretense of doing so. For democracy to take root in a society, the desire for democratization must derive from the people themselves. Imposition by the UN of its own or any foreign model of democracy has been recognized as impractical and foolish. Such a strategy smacks of arrogance and interference. More significantly, such factors undoubtedly could breed resentment both within the government and among the people and thereby encourage domestic forces that might oppose the adoption of democratic processes. The UN has opted instead for a more pragmatic course of assisting those governments that make specific requests, in order to provide the services needed to bolster democratic institutions and facilitate realization of the political benefits derived from a more liberal system of government.[72]

The UN does not promote any specific form of government. Democracy is not a political system to be copied but is to be regarded as a goal for attainment.[73] Consequently, in its formal documents and adopted policies, the UN has embraced no particular model or system of democracy for application to all societies. Rather, the people in each polity are expected to decide for themselves if and when democratization should occur and what its character and pace should be. Democratization must therefore remain an ongoing process of political renewal and development that takes into account the particular culture, political dynamics, and economic circumstances of each state's society.

That the UN is undertaking increased efforts to promote democracy worldwide should not be viewed as a disavowal of respect for state sovereignty nor a repudiation of Article 2(7) of the UN Charter, which upholds the principle of nonintervention in internal state affairs.[74] To the contrary, the UN endorsement of democracy reflects a commitment to popular self-rule, guided by the principle of self-determination.

It is because democratic governments are freely chosen by their citizens and held accountable through periodic and genuinely open elections and other means that they are more likely to respect and promote the rule of law, respect individual and minority rights, and mitigate social conflict through accepted political means. Truly democratic governments are less likely to abuse political power against their own people. The social contract thus forged is designed to foster a society at peace with itself and its government. In sum, "a culture of democracy is fundamentally a culture of peace."[75]

Over the past decade, the UN Secretariat has also bought into a version of the democratic peace theory. That is, securing democratic institutions and processes domestically can be translated into opportunities for ensuring peace and security internationally. As Boutros Boutros-Ghali observed in late 1996,

> Democratic institutions and processes within States may likewise be conducive to peace among States. The accountability and transparency of democratic governments to their own citizens, who understandably may be highly cautious about war, as it is they who will have to bear its risks and burdens, may help to restrain recourse to military conflict with other States. The legitimacy conferred upon democratically elected Governments commands the respect of the peoples of other democratic States and fosters expectations of negotiation, compromise and the rule of law in international relations. When states sharing a culture of democracy are involved in a dispute, the transparency of their regimes may help to prevent accidents, avoid reactions based on emotions or fear and reduce the likelihood of surprise.[76]

Absent the legitimacy and genuine public support offered by free elections, authoritative governments frequently resort to intimidation and violence to suppress internal dissent. They tend to reject institutions such as a free press and independent judiciary that can provide the transparency and accountability needed to dissuade such unwanted government interference. The resultant climate of political oppression and societal tensions, according to the UN Secretariat, can heighten the concern among other states that internal violence might spill over into international conflict. If threatened by their own domestic resentment, nondemocratic governments might be tempted to incite hostilities against other states in order to justify their suppression of internal dissent or consolidate national unity against a foreign enemy.

The practice of democracy is increasingly becoming regarded as essential for progress on a wide range of social-economic concerns and the protection of human rights. Hence, as posited by the UN Secretariat, certain preconditions or prerequisites must be in place if democracy is to take root in a national society. First, the political elite in a state must be genuinely willing and able to create and tolerate conditions for democracy. This is especially so as regards free and fair elections; but it is also true for the development and maintenance of institutions necessary to sustain the practice of democratic politics.[77]

Second, in the language of the UN Secretariat, "a culture of democracy" must be established to foster the processes of democratization.[78] This special political culture, which is essentially nonviolent, is built on the premise that no group or political party can expect to win all the time. Moreover, such a civic culture operates through a fundamental social consensus less concerned about policy and more directed by certain democratic political processes—namely, that the will of the people furnishes the basis of governmental authority; all individuals have the right to participate in government; there should be free and fair elections; political power changes through nonviolent popular suffrage rather than by intimidation or force; and political opposition groups and minorities have unfettered rights to express their views without fear of government retaliation.

Third, democratization must seek to obtain a balance between the government and a civil society. That is, support for democracy must be linked to support for development to ensure that social and economic, as well as civil and political, rights are respected. Sustainable development is more likely to be lasting if it is achieved and maintained through democratic processes.[79]

At this point, a note of caution is necessary. Efforts by the UN Secretariat in the late 1990s to link concepts of democracy and democratization to the processes of social-economic development hark back to notions during the 1970s suggesting the need for a New International Economic Order (NIEO). Today these same developmental aspirations are being presented by the UN Secretariat as greater opportunities needed in an era of democracy for all states. Admittedly, the ideological rhetoric and political tensions of North-South economic confrontation have waned over the past two decades, and no formal call has been made by the UN Secretariat for returning to the NIEO ideology as an intellectual justification for promoting democratization in developing states.

Even so, when UN perceptions of preconditions for democratization are presented by the Secretariat and discussed in the General Assembly,[80] certain impressions do suggest the need for reinvigorated transnational socialism and a process of "redistributive justice." The premise plainly suggested is that "a culture of democracy, marked by communication, dialogue and openness to the ideas and activities of the world, helps to foster a culture of development."[81] In line with this logic, then, the tenets of egalitarianism and equal political participation are fundamental to democracy. All states and all peoples are equal in a democratic international system. The implication, therefore, is that all states should strive to be equal in their social, economic, and cultural development. While perhaps noble aspirations, elevating democratic values and conditions to these planes poses serious questions of ways, means, and ends—especially with regard to the impact that such "equality" would portend for different cultures in different states. And, of course, there persists the critical question of who pays for the economic betterment of developing states that presumably would enhance their prospects for instituting democratic practices. That answer has not been formally addressed by the UN Secretariat in setting out its attitude toward promoting democratic processes. But if the suggestion is made that international democratization carries a bill for economic and social development in developing countries, there is little doubt that developed states, especially Western democracies, will balk at paying it.

Conclusion

This study reveals that since 1990 the UN has become more a salient than silent contributor to fostering the democratization process worldwide—a fact that substantiates the organization's value for promoting greater interstate cooperation in coming years. In the view of the UN Secretariat, the emergence of a civil society is tied to two symbiotic processes: the securing of more democratic, transparent, accountable governance; and the increasing preponderance of market-based approaches to national and regional economic management. Over the past decade, UN-sponsored activities for promoting civil society through greater democratization have focused on both processes.

UN assistance programs for creating a culture of democracy strive to create governance that is effective, participatory, transparent, accountable, equitable, and promotional of the rule of law. While the state leads processes toward democratization, there must also be collaboration between the private sector and civil society. It is the state that creates an environment conducive to political, economic, and political development. But the private sector generates employment opportunities and income, and civil society facilitates political and social interaction and mobilizes groups to participate in political and economic intercourse.

The UN can strengthen support for democratization through information gathering and awareness raising, as the organization offers member states a global forum for dialogue, debate, and consensus. Through the UN, multilateral agreements can be negotiated and arrived at—either as nonbinding "soft law," internationally recognized standards, or as binding international instruments—that contribute to defining a common legal and political framework for action. It is, in fact, through UN institutions that an international consensus on democracy has begun to take form.

Democratization must have indigenous support if it is to take root in a society. The UN contributes to fostering such support by helping to promote a culture of democracy. The UN retains a unique position in this regard in that it is seen by developing states as having ideological impartiality and universal legitimacy.

But the active presence and assistance of the UN is not, of course, sufficient for democracy to take hold and flourish in a national society. For the process of democratization to take place, certain conditions must be met. First, sufficient political will must be evident among the political elite and the people to make democratization happen. Second, the means must be made available for citizens to participate democratically in decision-making, including participation in fair and free elections, freedom to associate and form political parties, and full access to information furnished by independent media. The UN can assist states to establish the institutions and mechanisms of democracy. But no less critically needed is the government-supported action to institute and sustain a culture of democracy through a developed civil society and political culture of popular participation and consultation. The UN cannot make democracy work in a society. The people of that society must make democracy succeed as a political system and must organize and work to that end through their own social and political institutions. If the end of the Cold War offers prospects for a new age of democracy, securing this popular political will must be viewed as a fundamental international challenge for the UN and individual governments in the twenty-first century. ⊕

Important UN Documents Relating to Democracy

Boutros Boutros-Ghali, *Agenda for Democratization,* UN General Assembly, UN Doc. A/51/761 (20 December 1996).

The Managua Declaration, UN Doc. A/49/713 (6 July 1994) and Annex I. The conference's Plan of Action is in Annex II of the document.

UN General Assembly, *Progress Review and Recommendations, Adopted by the Third International Conference of the New or Restored Democracies on Democracy and Development Held at Bucharest from 2–4 September 1997,* UN Doc. A/52/334, attached as Appendix to *Support by the United Nations System of the Efforts of Governments to Promote and Consolidate New or Restored Democracies,* UN Doc. A/52/334 (11 September 1997), 3–15.

Report of the Secretary-General: Support by the United Nations System of the Efforts of Governments to Promote and Consolidate New or Restored Democracies, UN Doc. A/51/512 (18 October 1996).

Report of the Secretary-General: Support by the United Nations System of the Efforts of Governments to Promote and Consolidate New or Restored Democracies, UN Doc. A/52/513 (21 October 1997).

Report of the Secretary-General: Support by the United Nations System of the Efforts of Governments to Promote and Consolidate New or Restored Democracies, UN Doc. A/53/554 (29 October 1998).

UN General Assembly, Resolution A/RES/49/30 (7 December 1994).

UN General Assembly, Resolution A/RES/50/133 (20 December 1995).

UN General Assembly, Resolution A/RES/51/31 (6 December 1996).

UN General Assembly, Resolution A/RES/52/18 (21 November 1997).

Notes

Christopher C. Joyner is professor of international law and government at Georgetown University. This article is an elaboration of the ideas originally prepared in a paper for the Humanities Institute on Democracy, Community and Social Justice in an Era of Globalization, convened at the University of Denver, 23–25 April 1998.

1. Boutros Boutros-Ghali, *Agenda for Democratization*, UN General Assembly, UN Doc. A/51/761 (20 December 1996), at Annex: *Supplement to Reports on Democratization,* p. 2. (Hereinafter cited as *Agenda for Democratization*)

2. UN General Assembly, Resolution A/RES/43/157 (8 December 1988). This resolution reaffirmed that the will of the people, expressed in periodic and genuine elections, shall be the basis of authority for government and that "the right of everyone to take part in the government of his or her country is a crucial factor in the effective enjoyment of a wide range of other human rights and fundamental freedoms, embracing political, economic, social, and cultural rights."

3. See UN Doc. A/43/538 (6 June 1988).

4. See the Managua Declaration, UN Doc. A/49/713 (6 July 1994), Annex I, and the conference's Plan of Action, Annex II of the document.

5. See UN General Assembly, *Progress Review and Recommendations, Adopted by the Third International Conference of the New or Restored Democracies on Democracy and Development Held at Bucharest from 2–4 September 1997*, UN Doc. A/52/334, attached as Appendix to *Support by the United Nations System of the Efforts of Governments to Promote and Consolidate New or Restored Democracies*, UN Doc. A/52/334 (11 September 1997), pp. 3–15. (Hereinafter cited as *Democracy Progress Review and Recommendations*)

6. *Report of the Secretary-General: Support by the United Nations System of the Efforts of Governments to Promote and Consolidate New or Restored Democracies*, fifty-third session, UN Doc. A/53/554 (29 October 1998). (Hereinafter cited as *1998 Report of the Secretary-General*) In 1999, the First Conference of the Americas on New or Restored Democracies convened in Costa Rica, organized by Programa Centroamericano para la Sostenibilidad Democrática along with the UN University of Peace. *1998 Report of the Secretary-General*, p. 12.

7. See UN General Assembly, Resolution A/RES/49/30 (7 December 1994).

8. *Report of the Secretary-General: Support by the United Nations System of the Efforts of Governments to Promote and Consolidate New or Restored Democracies*, UN Doc. A/50/332 and Corr. 1 (7 August 1995). (Hereinafter cited as *1995 Report of the Secretary-General*)

9. UN General Assembly, Resolution A/RES/50/133 (20 December 1995).

10. *Report of the Secretary-General: Support by the United Nations System of the Efforts of Governments to Promote and Consolidate New or Restored Democracies*, UN Doc. A/51/512 (18 October 1996). (Hereinafter cited as *1996 Report of the Secretary-General*)

11. UN General Assembly, Resolution A/RES/51/31 (6 December 1996).

12. UN General Assembly, Resolution A/RES/52/18 (21 November 1997).

13. *Report of the Secretary-General: Support by the United Nations System of the Efforts of Governments to Promote and Consolidate New or Restored Democracies*, UN Doc. A/52/513 (21 October 1997). (Hereinafter cited as *1997 Report of the Secretary-General*)

14. See generally *1998 Report of the Secretary-General*.

15. *Agenda for Democratization*, p. 6; *1998 Report of the Secretary-General*, p. 3.

16. Ibid.

17. Done 26 June 1945, 59 Stat. 1031, T.S. No. 993, 3 Bevans 1153, entered into force 24 October 1945.

18. *Agenda for Democratization*, p. 7.

19. UN Charter, preamble.

20. Ibid., Article 1, par. 2, and Article 55.

21. Ibid., Article 1, par. 3, and Article 55.

22. Ibid., Article 2, par. 1.

23. Done 10 December 1948, UN General Assembly, Resolution 217 (III 1948), UN Doc. A/810, 71 (1948).

24. Ibid., Article 21, par. 1.

25. Ibid., Article 21, par. 3.

26. Ibid., Article 1.

27. Ibid., Article 3.

28. With respect to these rights, the most recent UN General Assembly resolution dealing with democracy asserts in its first preambular paragraph that "the

General Assembly, bearing in mind the indissoluble links between the principles enshrined in the Universal Declaration of Human rights and the foundations of any democratic society." UN General Assembly, Resolution A/RES/52/18 (15 January 1998).

29. UN General Assembly, Resolution 1514 (XV), 15 GAOR, Supp. 16, UN Doc. A/4684, p. 66 (1960).

30. *Agenda for Democratization*, p. 7.

31. See Christopher C. Joyner, "U.N. General Assembly and International Law: Rethinking the Contemporary Dynamics of Norm-Creation," *California Western International Law Journal* 11, no. 3 (summer 1981): 445–478.

32. UN General Assembly, Resolution 1514 (XV), Article 2.

33. Ibid., Article 5.

34. Most notably in this regard have been the International Covenant on Civil and Political Rights, done 16 December 1966, 999 U.N.T.S. 171, entered into force 23 March 1976, and the International Covenant on Economic, Social and Cultural Rights, done 16 December 1966, 993 U.N.T.S. 3, entered into force 3 January 1976.

35. *Democracy Progress Review and Recommendations*, p. 5.

36. Ibid.

37. Ibid., p. 6.

38. Ibid., p. 7.

39. Ibid., p. 8.

40. Ibid., p. 10.

41. See *Agenda for Development*, UN Doc. A/48/935 (1993).

42. This point was reinforced by the follow-up mechanism for the Third International Conference of New or Restored Democracies on Democracy and Development and its decision to create a special website on democracy and governance within the UN Development Programme's home page. See "Democratization and Governance: International Conferences on New or Restored Democracies" at <http://www.undp.org/undp/governance>.

43. *Report of the Secretary-General*, UN Doc. S/25124 (24 January 1993); UN Doc. S/25913 (10 June 1993).

44. *Report of the Secretary-General: Support by the United Nations System of the Efforts of Governments to Promote and Consolidate New or Restored Democracies*, UN Doc. A/50/332 (7 August 1995), par. 19, 21.

45. *1996 Report of the Secretary-General*, p. 5.

46. Ibid., pp. 5–6.

47. See *1998 Report of the Secretary-General*, p. 6; *Agenda for Democratization*, p. 2.

48. See *1998 Report of the Secretary-General*, pp. 6–7.

49. Often problems are revealed by a UN needs assessment mission, among them the lack of material resources to organize elections; lack of skilled human resources to run elections; lack of voter identification documents; high level of illiteracy; lack of reliable electoral register; lack of logistical and communications infrastructure. See *1995 Report of the Secretary-General*, par. 45.

50. *1995 Report of the Secretary-General*, par. 44.

51. Ibid., par. 44.

52. The UN has organized and conducted elections in only one country, Cambodia, but is also preparing to do so in Croatia and Western Sahara. *1996 Report of the Secretary-General*, p. 344.

53. See *Report of the Secretary-General*, UN Doc. S/25913 (10 June 1993).

54. *1996 Report of the Secretary-General*, p. 34.

55. *1995 Report of the Secretary-General*, par. 57.

56. *1996 Report of the Secretary-General*, p. 34.

57. *1998 Report of the Secretary-General,* p. 6.
58. *1995 Report of the Secretary-General,* par. 65.
59. *1996 Report of the Secretary-General,* p. 34.
60. Ibid.
61. *1995 Report of the Secretary-General,* par. 76.
62. *1996 Report of the Secretary-General,* p. 34.
63. Ibid., p. 27.
64. Ibid., p. 29.
65. See UN General Assembly, Resolution 48/131 (20 December 1993).
66. *1998 Report of the Secretary-General,* pp. 6–7.
67. These seminars are organized by Department of Public Information, in co-operation with the UN Educational, Scientific and Cultural Organization (UNESCO) supported by the UNDP. Seminars have been held for African, Asian, Latin American and Caribbean, Arab, and Central and Eastern European media. *1996 Report of the Secretary-General,* p. 8.
68. *1998 Report of the Secretary-General,* p. 7.
69. Ibid., p. 4. See the discussion on human rights in the report.
70. Ibid., pp. 8–11.
71. *1996 Report of the Secretary-General,* p. 10.
72. *Agenda for Democratization,* p. 3.
73. *1996 Report of the Secretary-General,* p. 3.
74. *Agenda for Democratization,* p. 3.
75. Ibid., p. 4.
76. Ibid., p. 5.
77. *1997 Report of the Secretary-General,* pp. 4–7.
78. *Agenda for Democratization,* p. 4.
79. Ibid., p. 5.
80. See, for example, UN press release, "General Assembly Encourages Active Follow Up to Bucharest Conference of New, Restored Democracies," UN Doc. GA/9512, 67th GA Plenary Meeting (23 November 1998).
81. *Agenda for Democratization,* pp. 5–6.

[11]

The Promotion and Protection of Democracy by Regional Organizations in Europe: The Case of Austria

Richard Burchill*

The inclusion into Austria's governing coalition of the far right Freedom Party has raised a great deal of controversy regarding democracy as a legal principle. At the centre of this controversy is the ability of an international organization to 'enforce' a legal concept of democracy. The EU has been at the forefront of condemning Austria, claiming that the inclusion of the Freedom Party violates the principles of democracy upon which Europe is founded. This condemnation has so far only remained rhetorical, as Austria has not in fact broken any of its obligations regarding democracy and human rights. This article examines the dilemmas faced by international organizations in promoting and protecting democracy in the absence of any clear agreement as to the content of a legal principle of democracy.

Introduction

The entry of the far-right Freedom Party into the governing coalition of Austria has raised a number of questions concerning the existence of democracy as a legal principle and the ability of international organizations to promote and protect principles of democracy. In reaction to the inclusion of the Freedom Party, led by the controversial figure Jörg Haider, numerous states have declared that they have downgraded their contacts with the Austrian Government on the basis that they

* Lecturer in Law, University of Hull.

cannot recognize the existence of the far-right party in the ruling coalition.[1] The other fourteen members of the European Union (EU) have joined together in downgrading bilateral relations with Austria and in the conduct of EU affairs offering at best a cold shoulder to Austrian representatives.

These measures have been justified on the basis that the inclusion of the Freedom Party is a threat to democracy and human rights in Austria and potentially a threat to wider Europe. This explanation is deemed legitimate even though the Austrian Government has not done anything that can be considered in violation of any accepted legal principles of democracy or human rights. The other Member States of the EU have justified the marginalizing of Austria on the basis that the EU is founded on principles of democracy and human rights and the Freedom Party does not conform to these principles. However, this position raises a serious issue concerning the ability of international organizations to promote and protect democracy as a legal principle. If, on the pressure from the other Member States of the EU, Austria were to exclude the Freedom Party from the ruling coalition, despite the fact that it achieved a significant percentage of the popular vote in a democratic election, would the EU itself be abiding by the principles of democracy and human rights upon which Europe is based? Much of the reaction against the inclusion of the Freedom Party in the Austrian Government is due to the statements made by its former leader Jörg Haider. Haider has been closely linked with the Nazi past and has publicly spoken of his approval of a number of aspects related to the Nazi regime. He has also taken a blatantly racist anti-foreigner stance in many of his policy statements as the governor of Carinthia.

Events in Austria have led to a fundamental dilemma in democracy – what to do when the democratic process produces an unfavourable result? This article will look at three regional organizations in Europe – the European Union (EU), the Council of Europe (COE) and the Organization for Security and Cooperation in Europe (OSCE) – and how they are able to promote and protect through legal means a principle of democracy upon which membership within each of the organizations is based. The situation in Austria will be used to demonstrate the inherent difficulties involved.

Democracy as a Legal Principle

The situation of Austria demonstrates the difficulties faced in transforming a contested political idea like democracy into an enforceable legal principle. The debate surrounding the idea of democracy as a legal principle took off in the 1990s with Thomas Franck's article on the existence of a right to democracy.[2] Much of the

1 Along with the other Member States of the EU, the USA and Israel have also officially downgraded their relations with Austria: *Keesing's Record of World Events* 43223, 43373.

2 T. Franck, 'The emerging right to democratic governance' (1992) 86 *American Journal of International Law* 46.

debate has concentrated on this idea of a right to democracy in general international law.[3] Less consideration has been given to the issues surrounding the promotion and protection, including the eventual 'enforcement', of democracy as a legal principle by international organizations. The three regional organizations of Europe being studied here all have membership requirements that include commitments to democracy and respect for human rights. The content and scope of the required commitment to democracy is not elaborated to a great degree by any of the organizations.

In the general literature of democracy, and the relevant works of international legal literature, there is a tendency to take a limited view of democracy confined to procedural aspects, most notably voting.[4] The favouring of this procedural view of democracy is attributable to the work of Joseph Schumpeter and has had a considerable influence on the bulk of subsequent writing on democracy.[5] A procedural view of what democracy is or should be is perhaps the easiest approach to the subject. When discussions of democracy deal with normative issues concerning ends and ideals, numerous complications arise when the theory presented contrasts with the reality in practice. Schumpeter and others have overcome this 'embarrassing situation' by limiting democracy to a verifiable event – elections.[6] By limiting democracy to a procedure, an understanding of what democracy is or should be not only becomes limited but also allows for claims that democracy exists when in reality the will of the people has no impact as individuals are not part of the processes surrounding their lives. In those situations a rhetorical form of democracy may exist but this does not mean that it is effective for the protection and development of the individual. If any theory of democracy 'seems intolerably remote from reality, it may be charged with utopianism'[7] which explains the emphasis on elections. Conversely, maintaining Schumpeter's idea of democracy only being the vote is easily criticized as an apology for exclusionary government power, as it creates legitimate obstacles preventing individuals and groups from effectively pursuing their self-determination.

For establishing a legal principle of democracy, a starting point may be found in

3 See C. Cerna. 'Universal Democracy: An International Legal Right or the Pipe Dream of the West?' (1995) 27 *New York University Journal of International Law and Politics* 290; M. Reisman. 'Sovereignty and Human Rights in Contemporary International Law' (1990) 84 *American Journal of International Law* 868; A.-M. Slaughter 'International law in a world of liberal states' (1995) 6 *European Journal of International Law* 514; S. Marks. 'The end of history? Reflections on some international legal theses' (1997) 8 *European Journal of International Law* 449.

4 For example, see the collection of essays in G. Fox and B. Roth. *Democratic Governance and International Law*, Cambridge University Press, Cambridge, 2000, with the exception of the concluding section dealing with critical approaches.

5 For the influence of Schumpeter on democratic theory, see D Ricci. 'Democracy attenuated: Schumpeter, the process theory. and American democratic thought' (1970) 32 *Journal of Politics* 239; C. Macpherson, *The Life and Times of Liberal Democracy*. Oxford University Press, Oxford. 1977. pp. 77–8.

6 Ricci, *op. cit.*, note 5. p. 255.

7 G. Duncan and S. Lukes. 'The new democracy' (1963) 11 *Political Studies* 165.

the Universal Declaration on Human Rights: 'the will of the people shall be the basis of the authority of government.'[8] This goal is accomplished through participation and autonomy allowing the individual and society continually to engage in the process of self-determination. It is essential to view democracy as existing beyond the act of voting. Democracy needs to be seen as integral to the social, economic and cultural spheres of society. Democracy cannot be merely a set of political practices but must consist of the ability of individuals to participate fully in society and governance and provide for the necessary protection of human dignity. At the UN World Conference in 1993, the Vienna Declaration defined democracy as being 'based on the freely expressed will of the people to determine their own political, economic, social and cultural systems and their full participation in all aspects of their lives'.[9] The inclusion of 'full participation in all aspects of [life]' shows that democracy is more than a political system or a method designed for choosing leaders but a set of practices and values based on the respect of human dignity.[10] Democracy exists to allow individuals to be part of the decisions and processes which affect their lives, it helps to create a better thinking about others in society, and provides non-violent means to settle differences in society.

Inherent in democracy is the paradox where democracy presents itself as inclusive, allowing all to participate regardless of position or status,[11] but it also allows for the legitimate domination of a group over the larger society. Effective democracy needs to strike a balance between individual aspirations and collective responsibilities to ensure the development of the individual and society.[12] The purpose of democracy is to provide a system where the individual is able to achieve personal self-determination while at the same time fostering communal development within society.[13] These two purposes are often seen as contradictory but there exists the possibility that they can be accommodated into a single conception of democracy.[14] This accommodation is achieved through two foundational elements – participation and autonomy – which have been identified as common ground in a majority of democratic theories.[15] Participation is necessary, for it allows individuals to be part of the processes impacting their lives. It is not confined to political acts but includes actions occurring in all aspects of society that are important to the individual.

8 Article 21(3) of the UDHR, GA Resolution 217A (III). GAOR. 3rd Session, Part I. Resolutions, p. 71.

9 Vienna Declaration and Programme of Action. 12 July 1993, UN Doc. A/CONF.157/23, para. 8.

10 L. Diamond, *The Democratic Revolution: Struggles for Freedom and Pluralism in the Developing World*, Freedom House, New York, 1992, p. xiii.

11 See D. Held, *Models of Democracy*. 2nd edn, Polity Press, Cambridge, 1996, pp. 2–3.

12 Council of Europe, *The Challenges of a Greater Europe: The Council of Europe and Democratic Society*, Council of Europe, Strasbourg, 1996, p. 168.

13 For an historical discussion, see I. Berlin, *Four Essays on Liberty*, Oxford University Press, Oxford, 1969, p. 118.

14 See the work of Held, *op. cit.*, note 11: and B. Fine, *Democracy and the Rule of Law: Liberal Ideas and Marxist Critiques*, Pluto, London, 1984.

15 Held, *op. cit.*, note 11, p. 300.

Participation allows for the pursuit of self-determination and ultimately fosters a greater sense of community.

Participation must occur within a specific framework so that the ability and right of an individual to participate does not infringe the rights of others and prevents abuse of the participatory process. It is known that strict personal autonomy – the ultimate and unfettered ability of the individual to exercise personal rights with no regards to others – is an unworkable concept.[16] The converse holds equally true in that the individual cannot be made subject to the will of the community with arbitrary limits on personal autonomy. Human rights and the rule of law are necessary to ensure that all can participate equally with the understanding that individual rights are not supreme but carry equal obligations of respect. To ensure the ability of participation and to secure against the excesses of power, Held has formulated a principle of autonomy, which states that:

> persons should enjoy equal rights and, accordingly, equal obligations in the specification of the political framework which generates and limits the opportunities available to them; that is, they should be free and equal in the determination of the conditions of their own lives, so long as they do not deploy this framework to negate the rights of others.[17]

Institutional and structural arrangements are necessary to the realization of the principle of autonomy, as they will provide rules and stability when agreed forms and methods are used in the process of governance instead of arbitrary behaviour. The purpose of these arrangements will be to promote discussion and debate among the divergent views of the society. Active participation will occur within an accepted framework that protects and nurtures the principle of autonomy. Stability depends upon the effective protection of human rights, maintenance of the rule of law, the ability to carry out effective social and economic policies and other areas of governance.[18] Respect for human rights alone cannot create democracy but does assist in ensuring the effective exercise of democracy by allowing for individuals to be active participants in society and ensuring the process is not abused.

The development of democracy as a legal principle is no easy task, as the actual forms of democracy will vary between societies in the international system, as the case of Austria has proven in the limited context of the EU membership. There can be no single model of democracy; democracy cannot be reduced to a structure of government or an act of society (elections) as it goes further to include the social, economic and cultural environments in which individuals exist. The interaction between society and the democratic structures and institutions it has

16 R. Harrison, *Democracy*, Routledge, London, 1993, p. 171.

17 Held, *op. cit.*, note 11, p. 301.

18 L. Diamond, *Promoting Democracy in the 1990s: Actors and Instruments, Issues and Imperatives*, Report to the Carnegie Commission, New York, 1995, p. 41.

created is important since the two work together.[19] A society will work to determine its democracy through institutions and structures that in turn will also react to the evolution of society.[20] This interaction means that the democratic structures and institutions of a society must uphold the underlying beliefs of the purposes of democracy. All democracies will have the same purpose 'to provide conditions for the full and free development of the essential human capacities of all members of the society'.[21] Most importantly, democracy is to be seen as a dynamic process that carries on through thought, practice, experiences and reflection.

Events in Austria

Austria held parliamentary elections on 3 October 1999 with the Social Democrat Party winning sixty-five seats in the 183-member parliament, the Freedom Party and the People's Party each taking fifty-two seats, and the Greens fourteen seats.[22] The Social Democrats were unable to form any sort of coalition so it was left to the Peoples Party and the Freedom Party to do so.[23] The new government was sworn in on 5 February 2000 with the two parties dividing the twelve government posts evenly, with Haider not taking up a government position.[24]

Following the elections and the creation of the new government, the Portuguese Presidency of the EU stated: 'If a party which has expressed xenophobic views, and which does not abide by the essential values of the European family, comes to power, naturally we won't be able to continue the same relations as in the past.'[25] The Portuguese Presidency went on to release an official statement on action to be taken concerning the bilateral relations between Austria and the other fourteen Member States. The actions taken include the refusal to promote or accept official bilateral contacts with Austria, Austrian ambassadors will only be received on a technical level and there will be no support given to Austrian candidates seeking positions in international organizations.[26] Portugal's foreign minister, Jaime Gama, stated that the EU 'cannot stand by passively when faced with the possibility of the participation in an EU government of a party whose election platform represents

19 See J. Anaya, 'A contemporary definition of the international norm of self-determination' (1993) 3 *Transnational Law and Contemporary Problems* 143.

20 With regard to Europe, see A.-M. Rieu, 'Introduction', in A.-M. Rieu and G. Duprat (eds.), *European Democratic Culture*, Routledge, London, 1993, p. 10.

21 C. Macpherson, *The Real World of Democracy*, Clarendon, Oxford, 1966, pp. 36–7.

22 For the full results of the election, see *Keesing's Record of World Events* 43223.

23 *Keesing's Record of World Events* 43373.

24 Haider remains the governor of Carinthia but has resigned as leader of the Freedom Party: see *Keesing's Record of World Events* 43419.

25 CNN, 'EU threatens to cut political ties with Austria', 31 January 2000.

26 'Statement from the Portuguese Presidency of the EU', www.portugal.ue-2000.pt/news.

a systematic attack on the democratic values of Europe'.[27] Belgium called for an unprecedented meeting of foreign ministers in order to defend the 'democratic values' on which the EU was founded.[28] The German Chancellor, Gerhard Schroeder, stated that any action taken with regard to Austria was not interfering with the domestic affairs of another state but that the position taken was an expression of the democratic values upon which Europe is based and to which Haider does not adhere.[29]

The reaction to the inclusion of a far-right political party in the government of Austria is primarily fuelled by past events. While Austria's history will give rise to concern over the inclusion of the Freedom Party in the government, concern over the presence of such a party in a government applies to any society. Statements based on emotion can be viewed as acceptable when presented by politicians and individuals. However, no international organization can legitimately apply legal rules based on the emotional impact of history. Austria is an equal member of the international system and of the organizations to which it belongs. There are no special conditions attached to its membership of any organization. Therefore, any action taken regarding the inclusion of a far-right party in the government needs to be based on the fundamental principles that are common to all members in a particular organization, not contextualized with regard to a particular history of a particular society.[30] To do so would make a mockery of any set of legal rules or legal system. If we were to stand by the logic that, due to Austria's history existent legal rules safeguarding against the abuses of far-right political agendas have to be applied in a more stringent sense, then it would hold that legal rules regarding race discrimination have to be applied more stringently to states such as Portugal and the UK due to their colonial past. Any suggestion that because of their past certain states are deserving of a greater degree of criticism and scrutiny than others would be rejected by these states, and rightly so.

The legal principles discussed below that have been developed by the regional organizations of Europe with the purpose of promoting and protecting democracy and human rights have their origin in Europe's past. The mechanisms in place have as their primary function the prevention of the destruction of democracy and the abuse of human rights; in other words, to prevent the history of Europe from repeating itself. If these mechanisms are to work and the legal rules involved are to be respected, then they must be applied to all members equally. Arguments calling

[27] 'Austria warned on coalition talks with far right', *Financial Times*, 2 January 2000.

[28] CNN, 'Belgium seeks EU meeting on possible Haider inclusion in Austria government', 28 January 2000.

[29] The USA has also stated that it will review its ties with Austria for the same reason: CNN, 'Austria shrugs off threats, will allow far-rightists into ruling coalition', 2 February 2000.

[30] The US Defence Secretary, William Cohen, stated that the inclusion of the Freedom Party in the Austrian Government 'might be a step back into a very dark past'. 'Riots as Austria's crisis deepens', *Guardian*, 5 February 2000, p. 1. Such statements assume that history will automatically repeat itself in Austria. A point upon which the USA itself is on dubious ground with regard to its own history.

for the application of legal rules based on a particular context are bound to fail if the overall system is to survive.

Democracy and the EU

From the outset it is important to note that the reaction of the Member States of the EU was taken collectively but implemented individually. The EU as an organization has not taken any official action against Austria. The ability of the individual Member States of the EU, or any other state, to declare its dissatisfaction with Austria complies with international practice where states may choose to recognize governments as they see fit.[31] This is in essence what the statement from the Portuguese Presidency of the EU is stating; it is the bilateral relations with Austria and not the EU itself that is affected.[32] Individually, states are free to do as they please in their bilateral relations relying on whatever criteria they choose to determine how another government is to be treated. International organizations, on the other hand, have to act within their constitutive treaties that set out the obligations of members and action to be taken when those obligations are not met.

The beginnings of the EU are found in the Treaty of Paris (1951) and the Treaty of Rome (1957). These treaties were economic in nature and did not contain any specifics concerning democracy with the belief that democracy in some form would exist through the eventual creation of an assembly.[33] At the 1972 Paris Summit, the Member States reaffirmed 'their resolve to base their Community's development on democracy, freedom of opinion, free movement of men and ideas and participation by the people through their freely elected representatives'.[34] In 1978 a 'Declaration on Democracy' was issued at the Copenhagen Summit[35] which stated that the application of the principles of representative democracy, social justice, the rule of law, and respect for human rights implies a political system of pluralist democracy guaranteeing freedom of expression and opinions within the constitutional organization of powers and the procedures necessary to protect human rights. It was further declared that the respect and maintenance of representative democracy and human rights are essential elements of membership of the EC, a point only recently institutionalized in a binding treaty provision. The Single European Act (1987) expressed the idea of democracy for the EU in a treaty-based document for

31 On recognition generally, see H. Lauterpacht, *Recognition in International Law*, Cambridge University Press, Cambridge, 1947; M. Peterson, *Recognition of Governments: Legal Doctrine and State Practice, 1815–1995*, Macmillan, Basingstoke, 1997; 'Symposium: Recent developments in the practice of state recognition' (1993) 4 *European Journal of International Law* 36.

32 European Commission, 'Statement on Austria', IP/00/93, Brussels, 1 February 2000.

33 C. Duparc, *The European Community and Human Rights*, COE, Luxembourg, 1993, pp. 11–12.

34 EC Bulletin 10-1972, p. 15.

35 EC Bulletin 3-1978, p. 5.

the first time. The signatories declared, in the preamble, their determination towards the promotion of democracy on the basis of fundamental rights, freedom, equality and social justice and confirmed the European Parliament as an indispensable means of expression for the democratic wishes of the individuals of the Member States.[36] The Treaty on European Union (TEU), signed in 1992, marked a continuing commitment to the idea of democracy as a guiding principle of the organization and was further developed by the changes implemented through the Treaty of Amsterdam signed in 1997.[37]

Article 6(1) of the TEU reads: 'The Union is founded on the principles of liberty, democracy, respect for human rights and fundamental freedoms, and the rule of law, principles which are common to the Member States.' The Council of the European Union is entrusted with the task of ensuring members meet these objectives and may suspend members if they fail to do so. Article 7(1) of the TEU and Article 309(1) of the EC Treaty set out that:

> The Council ... acting in unanimity on a proposal by one third of the Member States or by the Commission and after obtaining the assent of the European Parliament, may determine the existence of a serious and persistent breach by a Member State of principles mentioned in Article 6(1), after inviting the government of the Member State in question to submit its reservations.

If a serious and persistent breach is found to exist, the Council may suspend certain rights of the Member State in question and is able to vary or revoke suspension based on changing circumstances.[38] Naturally the requirement of unanimity will not include the state in question and the actions taken by the Council in this regard apply equally to the EC Treaty.[39] To date the procedures under Article 7 of the TEU and Article 309 of the EC Treaty have not been used.

Much of the debate surrounding democracy in the EU deals with the democratic nature of the workings of its own institutions.[40] The treatment of Austria is a new dimension where the issue of democracy is being raised as a constituent principle and a requirement of continuing membership in the organization. A number of difficulties have immediately arisen since there is no clear formulation of what the principles of democracy expressed in Article 6(1) actually are, leading to a fundamental contradiction in the treatment of Austria. The Freedom Party was brought into the coalition government through an accepted and legitimate

[36] See N. Neuwahl, 'The Treaty on European Union: A step forward in the protection of human rights?', in N. Neuwahl and A. Rosas (eds.), *The European Union and Human Rights*, Nijhoff, The Hague, 1995, p. 14.

[37] OJ 1997 No. C340/1.

[38] Article 7(2)–(3) of the TEU.

[39] Article 7(4) of the TEU and Article 309 of the EC Treaty.

[40] A point that will not be elaborated upon here. For further discussion, see P. Craig and G. de Búrca, *EU Law: Text, Cases and Materials*, 2nd edn, Oxford University Press, Oxford, 1998, pp. 155–62, who provide a concise account complete with references to the voluminous literature.

democratic process. The fourteen other Member States of the EU say that the Freedom Party's existence in the government is contrary to the democratic principles upon which the EU is founded. If the Freedom Party were denied a position in the government even though it received a considerable part of the popular vote, would this not be a denial of democracy and fundamental rights? The reaction of the EU brings to light the fact that the principle of democracy in Article 6(1) of the EC Treaty has no determinate meaning and that the organization itself has no coherent mechanism for addressing compliance with freedom, democracy and human rights.

There is no denying that democracy and human rights have evolved into important principles in the EU regime. The ECJ has established that principles of democracy and human rights are based on the common heritage and provisions of the Member States. The criticism of Austria is that they are going against the common understanding of democracy that exists within the Member States. Austria disagrees and says it must recognize the democratic choice expressed by its electorate. How then do we determine what is common to the Member States? The ECJ has explained that, when assessing the common constitutional provisions of the Member States, recourse cannot be made to the national legislation of a single Member State since that would undermine the Community order.[41] This was reiterated in the case of *Nold* where it was stated that the 'constitutions of Member States' determine the existence of fundamental rights.[42] However, the Advocate-General in *ICRA* stated that principles under a single constitutional tradition of a Member State should be upheld as part of the overall legal regime.[43] In *Grogan*, the ECJ held the constitutional traditions of one Member State to be indicative of fundamental rights at the Community level.[44] Finally, Article 6(3) of the TEU provides: 'The Union shall respect the national identities of its Member States.'

Austria has gone through an accepted democratic process that can be seen to be similar to the other Member States of the EU. It has held free and fair elections where the diverse views of society have been expressed and individuals have been allowed to make their own choices. This leads to the conclusion that in this respect Austria has conformed to the traditions of democracy common to the EU. Since all democratic systems differ, preferred results may be disputed. The other Member States appear to imply that their democratic process would never allow a right-wing party to enter into power and that this in turn is a fundamental principle of the EU. This raises a number of problems, for it implies that the other Member States are better able to control the expression of opinion by their societies. Either that or they are making a claim that far-right-wing groups do not exist. The denial of

41 Case 11/70, *Internationale Handelsgesellschaft* v. *Einfuhr-und Vorratsstelle Getreide* [1970] ECR 1125, paras. 3–4.

42 Case 4/73, *Nold* v. *Commission* [1974] ECR 491, para. 13.

43 Case 7/76, *ICRA* v. *Amministrazione delle Finanze dello Stato* [1976] ECR 1213.

44 Case 159/90, *SPUC* v. *Grogan* [1991] ECR I-4685.

representation due to differing views not shared by the majority would appear to be fundamentally in conflict with the principles of democracy in the EU.

It has been stated by the ECJ that democratic legitimacy depends upon the right of the people to participate in the law-making process through properly constituted representatives.[45] If the Freedom Party were to be denied its place in government, then the legitimacy of the Austrian political system would be in question for there would not be 'properly constituted representatives' for a large minority of the population. Furthermore, there is no basis to discard the democratic process due to subjective differences in ideology.[46] If Austria subsequently adopts any policies that run contrary to fundamental rights as established by the ECJ the individuals affected may be able to pursue their case through the appropriate Community procedures. The ECJ has actively interpreted the rights provisions of the treaties and has looked to the European Convention on Human Rights (ECHR) and other human rights treaties to which the Member States are party in order to determine the rights individuals possess and the obligations upon governments.[47] The ECJ has viewed the existence of rights as within the larger framework of a democratic society and any restriction must be 'necessary in a democratic society'.[48] The ECJ has not fully elaborated its conception of a democratic society but it has in general followed the approach of the European Court of Human Rights (see below). The denial of the results of a legitimate electoral process cannot be deemed to be 'necessary in a democratic society'. Furthermore, the Austrian Government will not be allowed to justify any policies that violate the rights of certain groups as being 'necessary in a democratic society'.

Alongside the protection of fundamental rights, a further source of protection against anti-democratic action taken by Austria may be found in Article 13 of the EC Treaty which states that: 'the Council, acting unanimously on a proposal from the Commission and after consulting the European Parliament, may take appropriate action to combat discrimination based on sex, racial or ethnic origin, religion or belief, disability, or sexual orientation.'[49] Action by the Council under Article 13 is not mandatory[50] and the requirement for unanimity might appear to be a major obstacle in taking any action. In the present situation, Austria is not

45 Case 26/62, *Van Gend en Loos* v. *Nederlandse Administratie der Belastingen* [1963] ECR 1.

46 At the Community level, the ECJ has held that it is necessary to follow democratic procedures in the decision-making process: see Case 138/79, *Roquette Freres* v. *Council* [1980] ECR 3333, para. 33. If this is the case, then there can be no basis for ignoring the democratic procedures at the national level.

47 Case 4/73, *Nold* v. *Commission* [1974] ECR 491, para. 12.

48 Case 36/75, *Rutili* v. *Minister for the Interior* [1975] ECR 1219, para. 32. See also Case 136/79, *National Panasonic* v. *Commission* [1980] ECR 2033.

49 For a more in-depth view of Article 13 of the EC Treaty, see T. Hervey, 'Putting Europe's house in order: Racism, race discrimination and xenophobia after the Treaty of Amsterdam': and C. Barnard, 'Article 13: Through the looking glass of Union citizenship', in P. Twomey and D. O'Keeffe, *Legal Issues of the Amsterdam Treaty*, Hart, Oxford, 1999, pp. 329 and 375.

50 See Hervey, *op. cit.*, note 49, p. 338. Individuals will not be able to rely directly on Article 13: see Barnard, *op. cit.*, note 49, p. 382.

preventing unanimous agreement as it has expressed a willingness to establish some form of monitoring or scrutiny regarding discrimination.[51] Furthermore, the European Monitoring Centre on Racism and Xenophobia has been established which has the task of studying and investigating racism and xenophobia throughout the EU.[52] Undoubtedly this body will be keeping a close eye on Austria, as well as the other Member States for none are immune from the problems of racism and xenophobia.

The situation of Austria has placed the other members of the EU in an awkward position. They are claiming that the Freedom Party is contrary to the principles of democracy and human rights as accepted in the treaties. At the same time the existence of the Freedom Party in government is a result of Austria respecting democracy and human rights. Until there is an actual occurrence where the democratic process is restricted or the rights of individuals and groups are actually violated the EU's ability to react is limited. Presently there are in place a number of mechanisms for ensuring that the people of Austria do not suffer from any negative consequences brought about by the Freedom Party. Beyond the political measures taken by the individual Member States, there has been no action taken at the institutional level. For Article 7 measures to be invoked, only five Member States need to act; this has yet to occur. Article 13 has not been brought into action either, and no action has been brought before any of the Community institutions alleging behaviour by Austria that violates any of the principles of democracy and fundamental rights set out in the treaties. For the 'enforcement' of democracy to be seen as legitimate, it would be more constructive for the EU to use the institutional measures that are in place rather than the other Member States acting collectively outside the EU regime but under its banner. The end result is that Austria has not acted in any way that would allow for the present mechanisms to be invoked, demonstrating the contentious nature of democracy as a legal principle.[53]

Democracy and the Council of Europe

All the members of the EU are also members of the Council of Europe (COE) and signatories to the ECHR.[54] As members they have obliged themselves to the Charter

[51] Haider and Wolfgang Schüssel, the leader of the People's Party, the other member of the governing coalition, took the unprecedented step of signing a document entitled 'Responsibility for Austria – A Future in the Heart of Europe'. *Keesing's Record of World Events* 43419.

[52] Council Regulation No 1335/97 OJ 1997 No. L151. 10 June 1997.

[53] Austria's president, Thomas Klestil, has called on the EU to change the arrangement concerning Article 7 to include a monitoring regime so that it may determine if democracy and human rights were actually being violated. 'Austria looks for end to political isolation in EU', *Financial Times*, 13 April 2000, p. 10.

[54] ETS No. 5, as amended by Protocol No. 11, ETS No. 155.

of the COE[55] which states in Article 3 that all members 'must accept the principles of the rule of law and the enjoyment of all person within its jurisdiction of human rights and fundamental freedoms'.[56] Article 8 of the Charter stipulates that any member which has seriously violated the terms of Article 3 may be suspended from the work of the organization until it complies with Article 3 or it may have its membership revoked. The Committee of Ministers declared in 1994 that it has the power to ensure Member States conform to their commitments to democracy, human rights and the rule of law as agreed to in the COE Statute, the ECHR and other legal instruments.[57] The Committee is able to take up the issue of compliance with commitments in situations referred to it by a Member State, the Secretary-General or the Parliamentary Assembly of the COE. Once a situation is before the Committee it will receive information on the matter and issue an opinion or recommendation or 'take any other decision within its statutory powers'. The COE Parliamentary Assembly also conducts monitoring activities on compliance with the Charter commitments for both existing states and potential members.[58]

The primary legal framework in the COE for the protection and promotion of democracy and human rights rests with the ECHR. Keeping in mind the past events in Europe, the ECHR was adopted with the purpose of protecting against the revival of aggressive and repressive dictatorships.[59] In the preamble states reaffirm their belief in human rights which are seen as a foundation for peace and justice and 'are best maintained ... by an effective political democracy and ... a common understanding and observance of the Human Rights upon which they depend'. Interpretation of the ECHR takes into account the aims of the COE, the need for effective representative democracy and the acknowledgment of a common heritage among members with respect for the rule of law.[60]

The ECHR framework assumes the existence of democracy in a signatory state through the membership criteria of the COE. The ECHR itself contains no provision

[55] ETS No. 1.

[56] This has been interpreted to included elections at reasonable intervals with secret ballot and universal suffrage, sovereign parliaments and free political parties: COE Parliamentary Assembly Resolution (800), 'Principles of democracy' (1983). The Consultative Assembly felt that democracy, individual freedoms, and the rule of law are three aspects of one reality and that they were inseparable, see COE, *Collected Edition of the 'Travaux Preparatoires' of the European Convention on Human Rights*, Nijhoff, The Hague, 1979, vol. 5, p. 288.

[57] 'Declaration on compliance with commitments accepted by Member States of the Council of Europe', 95th Session of the Committee of Ministers, 10 November 1994, reprinted in (1995) 2 *International Human Rights Reports* 250; 'Procedure for implementing the Declaration of 10 November 1994 on compliance with commitments accepted by Member States of the Council of Europe', 20 April 1995, reprinted in (1997) 4 *International Human Rights Reports* 244.

[58] The Monitoring Committee's website contains information on their activities: see stars.coe.fr/index_e.htm.

[59] A. Robertson and J. Merrils, *Human Rights in the World*, 3rd edn, Manchester University Press, Manchester, 1989, p. 82.

[60] *Kjeldsen, Busk Madsen and Pedersen* v. *Denmark*, Series A, No. 23 (1976), para. 53.

directly dealing with democracy, with obligations regarding voting being a later inclusion in Protocol No. 1. During the drafting of the ECHR there was disagreement as to whether there should be explicit protection of democratic institutions.[61] Some states favoured such an inclusion,[62] while others, like the UK, felt that it would be 'inappropriate' to include provisions concerned with democratic institutions.[63] The Consultative Assembly, which was charged with drafting the ECHR, felt strongly about including provisions on democracy as a necessary means to give practical effect to the protection of rights, as the only way to ensure rights are truly protected is through a democratic regime and democratic institutions.[64] In the end, the Committee of Ministers rejected the Assembly's proposals and there was no inclusion of measures for the protection of democracy within the ECHR regime.

The European Court of Human Rights has established that the ECHR is 'an instrument designed to maintain and promote the ideals and values of a democratic society'.[65] The belief of democracy underwriting the entire ECHR system was expressed by the Commission who stated that Article 3 of Protocol No. 1 'presupposes the existence of a representative legislature, elected at reasonable intervals, as the basis of a democratic society'.[66] The Court has expressed the view that, regardless of variations upon the right to vote, the 'free expression of the people' remains the core concept of democracy as well as 'one of the essential foundations' of a democratic society.[67] The Court has made it clear that a democratic society does not mean that the will of the majority shall prevail over the minority.[68] During its existence the Commission contributed to this idea by declaring the need for government to be accountable to society[69] and that the 'democratic process is dependent on the interplay of a wide variety of group interests'.[70] The Court has expressed the need to take into account 'pluralism, tolerance and broadmindedness' without which there is no 'democratic society'.[71] This was in the

61 For more on the drafting history, see S. Marks, 'The European Convention on Human Rights and its "democratic society"' (1996) 66 *British Yearbook of International Law* 209.

62 See the remarks by Ireland in *Collected Edition, op. cit.*, note 56, p. 60.

63 *Ibid.*, p. 70

64 *Ibid.*, p. 290.

65 *Kjeldsen, Busk Madsen and Pedersen* v. *Denmark*, Series A, No. 23 (1976), para. 53. The Court's translation of the original French text is found in *Soering* v. *UK*, Series A, No. 161 (1989), para. 87.

66 *The Greek Case*, Commission Report (1969), para. 416.

67 *Handyside* v. *UK*, Series A, No. 24 (1979–80), para. 49. Freedom of expression is also essential for each individual's self-fulfilment: *Vogt* v. *Germany*, Series A, No. 323 (1995), para. 52.

68 *Johnston* v. *Ireland*, Series A, No. 112 (1986). In the Separate Opinion of Judge De Meyer, 'democracy does not simply mean that the views of the majority must always prevail: a balance must be achieved which ensures the fair and proper treatment of minorities and avoids any abuse of the dominant position', para. 5.

69 *Barfod* v. *Denmark*, Series A, No. 149 (1989), para. 64.

70 *Markt Intern and Deerman* v. *Germany*, Series A, No. 165 (1990), para. 203.

71 *Handyside* v. *UK*, para. 49. *Young, James and Webster*, Series A, No. 44 (1981), para. 63; *Dudgeon* v. *UK*, Series A, No. 45 (1982), para. 53; *Jersild* v. *Denmark*, Series A, No. 298 (1994), para. 37.

context of freedom of expression with the same idea being applied to the freedoms of association and assembly[72] and religious freedom,[73] demonstrating that 'pluralism, tolerance and broadmindedness' are general principles of democracy for Europe.

In establishing the context of a 'democratic society' the European Court of Human Rights has usually taken the Member States of the COE as examples but has also allowed for the possibility of examining the situations and practices of other democratic societies.[74] The meaning and content of a 'democratic society' is not elaborated upon concerning its inclusion in Articles 8–11 of the ECHR. The result, in the view of some commentators, is 'a phrase heavy with uncertainty'.[75] The approach to the idea of a democratic society by the organs of the ECHR demonstrates the difficulty of giving a political concept legal elaboration, for, even if the members of the COE possess a common heritage, the intricacies of their democratic systems do differ.[76] To accommodate the essential differences of the democratic societies of the members states there has developed the concept of 'margin of appreciation' used by the Court to acknowledge the variations that exist in the different domestic systems.[77] In utilizing the margin of appreciation, the existence of a 'democratic society' creates the basis by which the actions of governments are judged.[78] With democratic governments there is the assumption that human rights are generally adhered to and any action taken to limit rights, as with assembly, expression, etc., is justified since the elected representatives imposing the limitations possess a legitimate mandate from society. Within the ECHR framework there is the need to balance the popular mandate upon which government action is based, while at the same time ensuring that power is not arbitrarily abused or sectors of society are disadvantaged by the tyranny of the majority.[79] The margin of appreciation provides the Court with a legal tool

[72] *Plattfrom 'Arzte für das Leben'*, Series A, No. 139 (1988), para. 32.

[73] *Kokkinakis* v. *Greece*, Series A, No. 260-A (1993), para. 31. *Buscarini* v. *San Marino*, No. 24645/94, judgment of the Court, 18 February 1999, para. 34.

[74] See L. Loucaidis, 'Restrictions or limitations on the rights guaranteed by the European Convention on Human Rights' (1993) 4 *Finnish Yearbook of International Law* 350.

[75] D. Harris *et al.*, *Law of the European Convention on Human Rights*, Butterworths, London, 1995, p. 291. One author has come up with a non-exhaustive list of the elements of a democratic society based on the statements of the Court; it includes participation, accountability, representation, pluralism, tolerance, broadmindedness, freedom of expression for public discussion and the protection of minorities. A. Clapham, *Human Rights in the Private Sphere*, Clarendon, Oxford, 1993, p. 147.

[76] The Court recognized this in *Mathieu-Mohin and Clerfayt* v. *Belgium*, Series A, No. 113 (1987): 'any electoral system must be assessed in the light of the political evolution of the country concerned: features that would be unacceptable in the context of one system may accordingly be justified in the context of another', para. 54.

[77] See generally 'The doctrine of the margin of appreciation under the European Convention on Human Rights: Its legitimacy in theory and application in practice' (1998) 19 *Human Rights Law Journal* 1.

[78] P. van Dijk and G. van Hoof, *Theory and Practice of the European Convention on Human Rights*, 3rd edn, Kluwer, The Hague, 1998, pp. 772 3.

[79] See the Court's opinion in *Young, James and Webster*, Series A, No. 44 (1981), para. 63.

allowing it to agree that the limitations upon certain human rights as defined by the government are necessary.[80]

For the Court democracy is 'a fundamental feature of the European public order'[81] and the ECHR generally has the purpose of upholding democracy. 'Democracy ... appears to be the only political model contemplated by the Convention and, accordingly, the only one compatible with it.'[82] The Court does not feel it necessary to lay out the specifics of a democratic society as it 'considers one of the principal characteristics of democracy to be the possibility it offers of resolving a country's problems through dialogue, without recourse to violence'.[83] This implies that European societies have a wide 'margin' to establish the democratic structures best fitting for their circumstances with the role of the Court making determinations regarding conflict over the exercise or limitations of rights within a democratic society. As stated above, the Austrian Government will not be allowed to exploit this margin of appreciation by adopting policies that violate the rights of certain groups or individuals. Nor will the Court be likely to allow the destruction of the democratic process through actions justified by the margin of appreciation.

In addition to the ECHR framework, the 1993 Vienna Summit created the European Commission against Racism and Intolerance (ECRI). The ECRI consists of independent experts who have the purpose of examining 'the effectiveness of the range of measures (legal, policy and other) taken by member States to combat racism, xenophobia, anti-semitism and intolerance and propose further action in this field' through a country-by-country approach. The ECRI has found that discrimination continues to persist throughout Europe at multiple levels of society, a situation exacerbated by the lack of anti-discrimination legislation at the domestic level. The ECRI places a great deal of importance upon legal measures for combating racism and intolerance as a means of offering the individual a remedy and shaping the attitudes of a society to see that racism is wrong.[84] As with the EU's Monitoring Centre on Racism and Xenophobia there is in place a monitoring system to ensure that Austria does not eventually begin to act in a discriminatory way towards certain targeted groups. The ECRI has yet to release any official statements regarding Austria.[85]

To date the institutions of the COE have not taken any legal action regarding Austria and its commitments to democracy under Article 3 of the COE Charter. The reason for this has already been discussed above – by including the Freedom Party in the government, Austria has only recognized the democratic process; it has not

[80] *Mathieu-Mohin and Clerfayt* v. *Belgium*, Series A. No. 113 (1987), para. 52.

[81] *Loizidou* v. *Turkey*, Series A, No. 310 (1995), para. 75.

[82] *United Communist Party* v. *Turkey*, para. 45. *Kjeldsen, Busk Madsen and Pedersen* v. *Denmark*, Series A, No. 23 (1976), para. 53.

[83] *United Communist Party* v. *Turkey*, para. 57.

[84] ECRI General Recommendation No. 1 (1997), 'Combating racism, xenophobia, anti-semitism and intolerance'.

[85] See their website at www.ecr.coe.int.

violated it. Both the Parliamentary Assembly and the Committee of Ministers have expressed concern over the inclusion of the Freedom Party in the Austrian Government. The Secretary General of the COE, Walter Schwimmer, recognized the concern of states over the situation in Austria and reiterated the COE's commitment to democracy, the rule of law and human rights.[86] He pointed out that to respect these principles 'governments are formed strictly according to the constitution and are responsible to a parliament elected in free and fair elections'. Furthermore, governments must continually respect the rights of all which means rejecting racist or xenophobic attitudes. He rightly concluded that *if* Austria violated any of these principles the COE would take action. The President of the Parliamentary Assembly, Lord Russell-Johnston, used stronger terms that appear to contradict the Court's position to say that pluralism is to be respected but not when it extends to racist or xenophobic practices.[87] So far no practice has occurred that can be deemed to be racist or xenophobic. Until that determination may be made the official position of the COE is that the policies and practices of the Austrian Government will be closely watched along with the attitudes it encourages among the citizens of Austria.[88]

Democracy and the Organization for Security and Cooperation in Europe

The OSCE (formerly the CSCE) has had a long-standing commitment to democracy and human rights in Europe. Its effectiveness in this area has been limited as the organization itself has been restricted by Cold War politics. The OSCE has been actively involved in the process of democracy and human rights in the former communist states but its principles apply to all members, which includes the rest of Europe. Unlike the EU and the COE, the OSCE contains no binding obligations to democracy or human rights, or any type of enforcement action in this area.[89] It has, however, elaborated at great length on the importance of democracy and human rights and all Member States have expressed a commitment to these principles.[90]

86 COE Secretary General, 'On the political situation in Austria'. Press Release. Strasbourg, 3 February 2000.

87 From the COE Parliamentary Assembly President. 'Our belief in pluralism cannot extend beyond our values of tolerance and anti-racism'. Press Release. Strasbourg, 2 February 2000.

88 'Council of Europe sends clear signal to new Austrian government', Press Release, Strasbourg, 4 February 2000.

89 There is no binding legal framework with which the participants in the process have to comply. However, it is commonly held that many of its principles and declarations do have some binding force: see O. Schachter, 'The twilight existence of non-binding legal instruments' (1977) 71 *American Journal of International Law* 296; T. Buergenthal, 'The CSCE rights system' (1991) 25 *George Washington Journal of International Law and Economy* 340; and *OSCE Handbook*, 3rd edn, 1999, P. 3.

90 The primary documents are the Helsinki Final Act; the Copenhagen Concluding Document; and the Charter of Paris. See A. Bloed (ed.), *The Conference on Security and Co-operation in Europe: Analysis and Basic Documents, 1972–1993*, Kluwer, Dordrecht, 1993.

In 1990 the OSCE adopted the Copenhagen Concluding Document, one of the first international instruments adopted by an organization that explicitly sets out the importance of democracy for its members.[91] Participants committed themselves to multi-party democracy based on free, periodic and genuine elections, the rule of law and equal protection under the law for all based on respect for human rights and effective, accessible and just legal systems. The Document states that 'pluralistic democracy and the rule of law are essential for ensuring respect for all human rights and fundamental freedoms' and recognizes the need for the active involvement of all persons, groups, organizations and institutions to ensure the continual progress of the democratization process. The Concluding Document outlines a number of specific ingredients that are necessary for a society based on democracy and the rule of law with the underlying belief that the protection and promotion of human rights and fundamental freedoms is a basic purpose of government.[92]

The primary work of the OSCE for the promotion and protection of democracy and human rights rests with the Office for Democratic Institutions and Human Rights (ODIHR).[93] The focus of the ODIHR is to assist the participating states of the OSCE in building and strengthening democratic institutions and the implementation of commitments related to human rights. The priorities for the ODIHR are the promotion of elections based on OSCE commitments and the building of civil society and democratic institutions. In their work of strengthening civil society and democratic institutions the ODIHR works closely with the media and NGOs, for the free flow of information is seen as an essential element of the democratic process.[94] Within the OSCE there is also a High Commissioner for National Minorities.[95] The High Commissioner's responsibility is to identify, and seek early resolution of, ethnic tensions that might endanger peace, stability or friendly relations between the participating states of the OSCE. The High Commissioner operates independently of all parties concerned conducting on-site missions, engaging in preventive diplomacy and providing reports and recommendations. The primary goal of the High Commissioner is to promote dialogue, confidence and cooperation between conflicting parties.

If a participating state of the OSCE engages in 'clear, gross and uncorrected'

91 See T. Buergenthal, 'The Copenhagen CSCE meeting: A new public order for Europe' (1990) 11 *Human Rights Law Journal* 221; and M. Halberstam, 'The Copenhagen Document: Intervention in support of democracy' (1993) 34 *Harvard International Law Journal* 164.

92 Copenhagen Concluding Document, paras. 5–15.

93 On the activities of the ODIHR, see A. Glover, 'The human dimension of the Organization on Security and Co-operation in Europe – The ODIHR in Warsaw' (1997) 2 *European Human Rights Law Review* 553.

94 See R. Brett, 'A new role for NGOs in the CSCE', in A. Bloed (ed.), *The Challenges of Change: The Helsinki Summit of the CSCE and Its Aftermath*, Nijhoff, Dordrecht, 1994, p. 359.

95 See R. Zaagman and H. Zaal, 'The CSCE High Commissioner on national minorities: Prehistory and negotiations', and R. Zaagman, 'The CSCE High Commissioner on national minorities: An analysis of the mandate and the institutional context', in Bloed, *op. cit.*, note 94, pp. 95 and 113.

violations of these commitments they may be suspended by the organization.[96] The ODIHR could easily keep track of events in Austria through its cooperative relationships with NGOs and the media. If Austria begins to discriminate or in any other way violates the rights of minorities then the High Commissioner for Minorities will be able to act within the terms of his mandate. Presently Austria holds the Chairman in Office of the OSCE and there has been no official calls for it to stand down. As Chair in Office Austria has been active in supporting OSCE efforts in democracy and human rights where the OSCE is involved and it appears the other participants, including the members of the EU, have not taken any action against Austria in the workings of the organization.

The Selective Enforcement of Democracy in Europe

The reaction of the individual Member States of the EU to the inclusion of the Freedom Party in the Austrian Government indicates that they do not believe Austria's form of democracy in this instance is acceptable, even though Austria has yet to contravene any of its obligations. They are further denying any acceptance of diversity, pluralism, tolerance or broadmindedness based on their own subjective determinations of the situation within Austria. Of greater concern for the future of democracy in Europe is that they are demonstrating a lack of faith in the current systems of protection provided by the regional organizations that will ensure that the Austrian Government does not engage in any form of illegal behaviour. Inclusion of a far-right-wing party in a government is a worry. Considering what has occurred in the recent past, Europe's voicing concern over the policies of the party and the statements of its former leader is only right. However, calling for action to be taken based on the past and automatically assuming those same events are possible in the future has put the Member States of the EU in a position they will find difficult to get out of.[97]

Traditionally international law has only required a minimum of conditions for recognizing the legitimate existence of a state.[98] Beyond these minimum conditions individual states are free to recognize as legitimate any government that meets their own subjective criteria. In the past, states such as the USA and the UK have changed their criteria for recognition, sometimes requiring elements of democracy, sometimes not.[99] Leaving it up to individual states to 'enforce' democracy on their own terms

96 As was done in 1992 with the former Yugoslavia: see *OSCE Handbook*, *op. cit*., note 89, p. 29.

97 See P. Ludlow, 'Europe's righteous indignation', *Financial Times*, 7 February 2000, p. 24.

98 These minimum conditions are a permanent population, a defined territory, a government, and a capacity to enter into international relations. They were originally set out in the Montevideo Convention on Rights and Duties of States, (1933) 165 LNTS 19.

99 See Lauterpacht, *op. cit.*, note 31, pp. 115–40; and P.K. Menon, *The Law of Recognition in International Law*, Lewiston, Lampeter, 1994, pp. 221–54.

hinders the development of a legal principle of democracy, as adherence will continue to be based on subjective political choices cloaked in legal terms.[100] Confusion regarding the existence of a legal principle of democracy is compounded when individual states act under the guise of an international organization.

International organizations that possess an obligatory principle of democracy are not allowed the subjective leeway that individual states have in the process of recognition under international law. International organizations must possess clear standards of democracy established in the constituent documents that apply equally to all members. Furthermore, there needs to be specific machinery that is able to react when standards of democracy or human rights are not met. The major issue that Austria has raised is how international organizations are able to react to what are perceived by individual members to be violations of principles of democracy and human rights based on political preferences. To place the reaction of individual states and the organizations of Europe into perspective it is worth examining how they are responding to current events in Russia. specifically with regard to Russia's actions in Chechnya.

Russia is a member of the COE and the OSCE and is a signatory to the ECHR. Russia is not a member of the EU but the EU does have a strong interest in developments there.[101] In its actions in the Chechen Republic Russia has been accused of

(1) the total and wanton destruction of the city of Grozny, the most striking example of indiscriminate and disproportionate military action which has cost hundreds, if not thousands, of civilian lives;
(2) continued attacks on the civilian population, ranging from the use of aerial bombardments and other heavy weaponry in densely populated areas to the committal of war crimes by federal troops, including the murder and rape of civilians;
(3) rape -- a cruel means of war – perpetrated on Chechen women and girls;
(4) the alleged arbitrary arrest and detention of non-combatants, and their reported subsequent ill-treatment in detention; and
(5) the continued use of young conscripts in the military campaign in the Chechen Republic.[102]

[100] Lauterpacht felt that some form of collective recognition by an international organization would help in overcoming the problems of individual recognition. He also noted that states are unlikely to give up this sovereign prerogative, as demonstrated by the members of the EU. See Lauterpacht, *op. cit.*, note 31, pp. 401–2.

[101] The following statement demonstrates this importance: 'The Council underlines Russia's importance as a major partner of the EU. The EU would like to continue to build and develop this long-term strategic partnership with a view to enhancing security and stability in Europe and beyond. To this end, it is ready to continue its political dialogue with Russia in order to address questions of mutual interest, including issues of disagreement and concern such as the conflict in Chechnya.' Council of the EU, 2239th Council Meeting, Brussels, 24 January 2000.

[102] Recommendation 1456 (2000), 'Conflict in the Chechen Republic – Implementation by Russia of Recommendation 1444 (2000)'.

These accusations are not speculation as to what might happen in the future, in the same way the Austrian Government is being chastised, but real and verifiable events that are clear violations of international obligations ranging from democracy to humanitarian law to human rights. The COE Parliamentary Assembly has revoked Russia's right to vote in the Assembly. It has further called for the Committee of Ministers to begin the process of revoking Russia's membership of the COE due to its actions and for other signatories to the ECHR to bring action against Russia under Article 33.[103] So far no action has been taken on either point by the Committee of Ministers, who in turn have tried to emphasize the positive steps taken by Russia and only agreeing to keep the issue under consideration.[104] The OSCE has had an Assistance Group of only five individuals in Chechnya since 1995 that has relied on the power of persuasion to resolve the conflict.[105] The ODIHR has also been involved in discussions with Russia with the hope of contributing to a solution to the conflict.[106]

The Council of the EU has also only limited itself to persuasion, calling on Russia to respect human rights and to live up to 'the standards expected from all members of the community of free and democratic nations'.[107] Chris Patten, the European Commissioner responsible for external relations, has also condemned Russia but then concluded the only way to a solution was through understanding and dialogue between the EU and Russia.[108] One may try to explain the difference in treatment by the EU as due to the difference in membership status of Austria and Russia with regard to that particular organization. However, this does not change the fact that Austria has not violated any obligations under the EU treaties nor under any other international convention. Russia on the other hand has been taken to task for its actions by the COE Parliamentary Assembly and by the United Nations, but the EU feels that dialogue and understanding are the most appropriate way of approaching the situation.[109] Calls for more forceful action to be taken against Russia have fallen on deaf ears as leaders who express deep concern regarding the possible future for democracy and human rights in Austria are not so concerned with the presently reality in Russia.[110]

[103] *Ibid.* Article 33 of the ECHR allows for inter-state complaints regarding violations of the Convention.

[104] Press Communiqué of the 106th Session of the Committee of Ministers, 10–11 May 2000.

[105] *OSCE Handbook*, *op. cit.*, note 89, pp. 60–2.

[106] Most recently the Director of the ODIHR met with the Russian Presidential Special Representative for Human Rights in Chechnya, OSCE/ODIHR Press Release, 24 March 2000.

[107] 2239th Council Meeting, Brussels, 24 January 2000.

[108] SPEECH/99/166, The Rt Hon. Christopher Patten, Member of the European Commission Responsible for External Relations Declaration on Chechnya, European Parliament, Strasbourg, 17 November 1999.

[109] The United Nations High Commissioner for Human Rights visited Russia in March and reported widespread allegations of human rights abuses that warranted international attention and concern. See Commission on Human Rights, 56th Session, 5 April 2000.

[110] US President Clinton, speaking before the Russian Parliament, demonstrated a degree of support for democracy and Russia while at the same time recognizing Russia's past. 'Clinton backs democracy in Russia', *Financial Times*, 6 June 2000, p. 10.

Obviously Russia and Austria rate very differently in importance in the international political scene. However, this should not prevent the equal application of principles of democracy and human rights. It further harms the legitimacy of any idea of democracy as a legal principle if Austria is ostracized for allegedly contradicting shared fundamental principles by recognizing the democratic process but Russia is only given the most delicate of rhetorical condemnation in the face of outright violations of democracy and human rights. The politicians provide plenty of excuses to explain the difference in treatment – the need to improve trade and business relations,[111] the desire to avoid basing relationships on single issues and the necessity of establishing good relations with an important world leader.[112] Such selective use of the importance of principles of democracy and human rights does not help the development of legal principles.

Conclusion

The treatment of Austria, especially by the EU, demonstrates that democracy, as a legal principle, is highly indeterminate and subject to a wide degree of controversy. Any definition of democracy depends upon who is providing the definition and the context in which they are speaking, making democracy an 'essentially contested concept'.[113] In the present case the statements being made show how contentious democracy is, especially when one's own system is questioned. In response to criticisms of the Austrian political system, Wolfgang Schüessel, leader of the People's Party, stated: 'Austria does not need lessons in democracy. We are not a developing country as far as human rights are concerned.'[114] Mr Schüessel misses the point; no one's democracy is perfect and that in all cases it needs to be kept under observation. However, those observations need to be based on a recognition of difference and with a good deal of tolerance and faith in monitoring systems. Even though democracy in both meaning and practice is essentially elastic in nature allowing for numerous forms, this does not preclude efforts at establishing foundations for an effective democracy.[115]

The Austrian example shows that there is no acceptable definition of democracy that may be enforced through purely legal means. Even when legal regimes contain built-in elements that recognize diversity and difference as to how a democratic society develops, political differences of opinion will carry a great deal of weight. All

[111] 'Putin announces investigation into Chechnya "abuse"', *Financial Times*, 18 April 2000, p. 2.

[112] 'Putin greeted by London protests', BBC Online, 17 April 2000.

[113] T. Ball and R. Dagger, *Political Ideologies and the Democratic Ideal*, Harper Collins, New York, 1991, pp. 22–3. See also K. Bollen, 'Political democracy: Conceptual and measurement traps', in D. Beetham, *Defining and Measuring Democracy*, Sage, London, 1994, p. 5, who observes that providing a definition of democracy that everyone finds acceptable is impossible.

[114] 'Austria is risking isolation over far rights, EU warns', *International Herald Tribune*, 1 February 2000.

[115] R. Harrison, *Democracy*, Routledge, London, 1993, p. 134.

Austria has done is recognize the results of a democratic election. Elimination of the Freedom Party from the government would be a refusal of the expressed will of the people by the Austrian Government and would have to be seen as a serious violation of human rights as stated in Article 6(1) of the TEU. Attempts by the EU to ensure the expressed will of 27 per cent of the Austrian population is not adhered to would be a contradiction of its own expressed principles. If the Freedom Party works to exclude others from the process of governance or acts in a discriminatory fashion, then it may be held to be violating legal principles of democracy; the EU and the COE can then take action at the intergovernmental level and individuals will be able to utilize the ECHR protection system.

The overwhelming majority of individuals in Europe and the world do not subscribe to the ideas of Haider and his political platform.[116] The Freedom Party, along with other right-wing parties, has been part of European politics for a good period of time. Their presence has usually been minimal raising few reactions. As one commentator notes, we are able to handle far-right political parties in society so long as their share of the vote remains low, but once that share begins to rise to about 10–15 per cent then anxieties arise.[117] It is feared that Haider will follow the path of Hitler and use the democratic process in order to gain power and destroy Austrian democracy.[118] To prevent the possible destruction of democracy in Austria based on past events, undemocratic action by a certain group of states acting under the banner of an international organization suddenly becomes acceptable.

The UK MEP, Glyn Ford, has expressed the belief that it is legitimate to intervene in the Austrian political process and not recognize the outcome of elections.[119] This would set an extremely dangerous precedent especially since Austria has not violated any accepted obligations. Admittedly there is the potential for violations, but it would be better left to the international organizations involved to deal with these when they arise and not for individual states to demand action based on their own political preferences. If democracy is to be accepted as a legitimate legal principle, it must be applied equally. It cannot be applied as a single model for all states that will guarantee the same results. It must be a process that recognizes the freely expressed will of a society and provides for peaceful mechanisms of conflict resolution when differences arise. Anything less based on subjective political differences of opinion would be a significant obstruction to the long-term development of democracy as an effective legal principle.

[116] It is interesting to note that one of the Freedom Party members who was a potential candidate for finance minister was a strong believer in the economic policies of Margaret Thatcher: see 'Haider set to call the shots from power base', *Financial Times*, 3 February 2000, p. 8.

[117] 'The far right: A nationalist international?', BBC Online, www.bbc.co.uk/worldservice/ theneweurope/ wk19.htm.

[118] The President of the European Parliament has stated that the concern over the inclusion of the Freedom Party in the Austrian Government is based on 'an observable fact and an indelible memory': 'Austria looks for end to political isolation in EU', *Financial Times*, 13 April 2000, p. 10.

[119] BBC Online, 'MEPs Threaten Sanctions against Austria', 3 March 2000.

The most worrying aspect of the treatment of Austria is the 'righteous indignation'[120] and closedmindedness of those critical of the regime, the so-called defenders of democracy. Democracy is about diversity and debate where differences are resolved through peaceful discussion. However, those that say they are concerned about the future of democracy in Austria refuse to engage in any sort of debate and discussion. The EU declared in 1978 that democracy depended upon pluralism and respect for freedom of expression and opinion. The European Court of Human Rights has stated that respect for freedom of expression and opinion is central to democracy, that the majority cannot impose its views on the minority, that wider group interests and needs have to be taken into account and, most importantly, that pluralism, tolerance and broadmindedness are the core of the democratic process. There is no doubt that the ideas of the Freedom Party are dangerous, even more so now that they have been legitimated to a degree by being part of the government of Austria. Of greater danger though is the belief that we can override the democratic process in order to save what we feel to be the appropriate form of democracy.

[120] Term used by Ludlow, *op. cit.*, note 97.

[12]

Is There a Democratic Norm in the Americas? An Analysis of the Organization of American States

Dexter S. Boniface

The preamble of the Organization of American States (OAS) Charter is explicit about a commitment to representative democracy as "an indispensable condition for the stability, peace and development of the region."[1] However, in the four decades after its inception in 1948, the OAS failed to develop a consistent policy regarding the promotion of democracy in the hemisphere. For instance, while the Cuban government was suspended from the OAS in 1962 for its incompatibility with inter-American "principles and objectives," the (anticommunist) authoritarian regimes that emerged in South America in the 1960s and 1970s were passively condoned. Many observers came to view the OAS as a facile extension of the Cold War security interests of its most powerful member, the United States.

With the end of the Cold War, however, the OAS has come to play an increasingly significant role in Western-hemispheric relations.[2] With the approval in June 1991 of the "Commitment to Democracy and the Renewal of the Inter-American System" and the adoption of OAS Resolution 1080, the organization renewed its pledge to protect democracy in the region and established the institutional mechanisms for doing so. In particular, Resolution 1080 pledges the OAS secretary-general to convene an immediate emergency meeting of the OAS Permanent Council following any "sudden or irregular interruption of the democratic political institutional process."[3] It is then the task of the Permanent Council to examine the situation and recommend whether or not a special meeting of the ministers of foreign affairs or of the General Assembly is warranted—all within ten days of the democratic crisis. In amending the charter through the adoption of the Washington protocol, the organization established that the General Assembly could, with a two-thirds vote, suspend any member state from the OAS in the event that "its democratically constituted government has been overthrown by force."[4] The OAS also created a specific organization arm, the Unit for the Promotion of Democracy (UPD), to develop programs reinforcing the hemispheric trend toward democracy. Moreover, with the recent adoption of the Inter-American Democratic Charter on 11 September 2001, the OAS broadened its conception of what constitutes a democratic crisis to include any "unconstitutional alteration of the constitutional regime."[5]

In short, the OAS now appears to spearhead a vigorous international regime for the defense of democratic rule in the hemisphere. Indeed, Heraldo Muñoz, a former chairman of the OAS Permanent Council, recently claimed that "there is now a right to democracy in the Americas in the sense that a concern for the promotion and defense of democracy in the inter-American system has evolved into a normative obligation and, most important, is being implemented through collective action."[6] This new commitment by the OAS, in turn, raises several key questions for the study of international politics. First and foremost, is OAS action in relation to the defense of democracy motivated primarily by strategic or by normative factors? Second, under what conditions would the OAS actually intercede to protect and/or restore democracy in a member state? Finally, what *type* of OAS action would we expect to see if the OAS were to intervene?

Two competing theories in international relations, realism and normativism, offer different explanations for the existence and behavior of international organizations (IOs). Realists view IOs as reflections of the underlying balance of power within the international system; as such, IOs are thought to have no real autonomy of their own. Normativists, in contrast, see IOs as reflections of a normative consensus shared by member states and the wider population of epistemic communities. IOs, for normativists, may develop considerable autonomy from member states. In order to assess the purported normative obligation to democracy in the Western Hemisphere, this essay examines the predictions that realist and normativist theories make regarding IOs and evaluates them against the evidence of OAS practice since the Santiago declaration.

I have organized the essay into three sections. First, I review existing theoretical contributions on the behavior of international organizations, highlighting the distinctions between realist and normativist thought. In the second section, I analyze the behavior of the OAS in response to democratic crises in Haiti (1991), Peru (1992), Guatemala (1993), and Paraguay (1996). In the third and final section, I analyze all four cases in comparative perspective. Overall, the evidence lends conflicting support to both realist and normativist explanations of OAS behavior: while normative factors explain *why* the OAS intervenes, strategic interests account for *how* the OAS intervenes.

Competing Explanations of International Organizations: Realism and Normativism

Realists and normativists differ substantially as to why IOs exist and what interests they represent (see Figure 1).[7] For realists, states are the dominant actors in the international system. Given international anarchy and the ubiquity of security threats, moreover, the main imperative that states confront is survival. States, in turn, mind their own interests and pursue gains relative to other states. As a consequence of these assumptions, realists view international organizations in an instrumental fashion: IOs are created merely to pursue selfish state interests—often under the legitimating (but false) guise of neutrality.[8] IOs (and other international institutions), thus, are merely a reflection of the balance of state power in the world. Great-power states, in particular, dominate IOs through their control of financial resources, leadership appointments, and informal influence. It would be naive, realists argue, to treat IOs as autonomous or even semiautonomous since states would never voluntarily cede sovereignty to a supranational institution.[9]

In contrast to the state-centric and inherently anarchic world of the realists, normativists start with an entirely different set of assumptions about the nature of international relations.[10] For normativists, a focus on states as the central actors in international relations is misleading. Instead, these scholars regard states as embedded within a larger "inter-

Figure 1 International Organizations' Interests and Autonomy

Theories of International Organizations

Theoretical Tenets		Realism	Normativism
	Central actors	States.	States and nonstate actors, including supranational and epistemic communities.
	Interests and autonomy	IOs reflect the balance of military power among states; IOs have no autonomy from member states.	IOs reflect a normative consensus on international rules and values; IOs have considerable autonomy from member states.

national society" of shared values, norms, and purposes. States are a significant part of the world society, but so too are international institutions, ideas, and epistemic communities. Norms, for these scholars, do not operate merely as constraints on state behavior, but shape (and are therefore constitutive of) state interests themselves. In this manner, normativists argue that international-organizational behavior is driven, in part, by the underlying patterns of normative consensus in a given community (including, for example, international regimes). IOs can thus act with considerable autonomy and causal significance.[11]

In important respects the OAS represents an ideal test case for assessing these broad theoretical claims about international organizations and international politics. To begin, the OAS is clearly dominated by a regional hegemon, the United States. In addition to being the hemisphere's most commanding military and economic power, the United States contributes approximately 60 percent of the $80 million in the regular OAS budget (excluding some $11 million in voluntary funds, of which the United States contributes approximately $7 million).[12] U.S. hegemony, nevertheless, is coupled with a clear normative commitment to democracy in the hemisphere, made explicit in the mandate of Resolution 1080. The OAS thus offers a compelling test case for assessing realist and normativist propositions about hegemonic power and IO behavior.

Hypotheses

Realism and normativism each generate different hypotheses to explain the conditions under which the OAS would intercede to protect and/or restore democracy in a member state (see Figure 2). Realists, for instance, would expect the OAS to intervene only in cases that clearly advance the strategic interests of the regional hegemon, the United States. A realist would furthermore expect the United States to dictate the terms under which intervention would take place—even if the final outcome were multilateral in nature. For normativists, on the other hand, international values can lead states to act against their own narrow interests and on behalf of a greater normative good. As Thomas M. Franck argues, "Both textually and in practice, the international system is moving toward a clearly designated democratic entitlement, with national governance validated by international standards and systematic monitoring of compliance."[13] Normative scholars thus emphasize the power of the democratic ideal and would expect a strong and unified OAS response to any democratic crisis.

Figure 2 The OAS: Behavioral Hypotheses

	Theories of International Organizations	
	Realism	Normativism
Conditions Under Which the OAS Would Intervene to Protect Democracy	Response is case-specific: OAS intervenes only when U.S. strategic interests are advanced.	Response is norm-induced: OAS intervenes whenever the democracy "regime" is threatened.
Nature of OAS Intervention	U.S.-dominated response.	Multilateral consensus among member states.

Case Studies

To adjudicate between these competing hypotheses, I analyze all of the existing democratic crises that have induced an OAS response pursuant to Resolution 1080. In chronological order, the cases include coups in Haiti (1991), Peru (1992), and Guatemala (1993) as well as the civil-military crisis in Paraguay (1996).[14] While these four countries are relatively small and economically undeveloped in relation to the larger states of the Americas, the response of the OAS to each of these crises varied considerably; the sample of cases thus provides substantial variation in the dependent variable of interest (that is, the nature of OAS intervention).[15] In assessing each case, I adopt the approach formulated by Audie Klotz in her study of norms of racial equality; namely, I regard material self-interest (in particular, that of the United States) as a baseline from which to assess *how much* international norms impact IO behavior.[16]

Haiti 1991: Intervention Without Interest

The resolve of the OAS to protect democracy in the Americas was put to the test just four months after the Santiago meeting. On 30 September 1991, the Haitian military, led by General Raoul Cédras, overthrew Haiti's first elected president, Jean-Bertrand Aristide. The situation was critical as the military not only forced Aristide into exile but also gunned down pro-Aristide demonstrators in Port-au-Prince.

Within days of the coup, OAS foreign ministers met pursuant to Resolution 1080 and swiftly decided to recognize Aristide as the only legitimate leader of Haiti. The ministers also recommended that Haiti be diplomatically and economically isolated. After brief and failed negotiations with the Haitian military, the OAS imposed a trade embargo on Haiti (beginning 8 October 1991) and later recommended the freezing of Haitian assets. The ruling junta nevertheless remained obstinate and refused to recognize Aristide. In December 1992, OAS ministers began discussing tougher measures, including the possibility of taking the case to the United Nations (UN) to achieve a universal embargo and possibly initiate military intervention. Later, in June 1993, the UN Security Council passed Resolution 841, which imposed a global oil and arms embargo on Haiti and declared the country a threat to international peace.

The strong resolve of the OAS and the UN brought the Haitian military to sign a compromise pact, the Governor's Island Accord of 3 July 1993.[17] Yet the Haitian military again faltered as an angry mob turned away the U.S.-Canadian mission aboard the USS *Harlan County*. The UN responded with renewed sanctions, including a naval blockade. Later, in a landmark resolution in July 1994 (UN SC Res. 940), the United Nations Security Council authorized the use of a multinational force to intervene in Haiti to restore Aristide using "all necessary means."[18] On 19 September 1994, some 20,000 U.S. troops landed in Haiti. The Haitian military finally capitulated and Aristide was peacefully restored to power in October 1994; the embargo was at last lifted. A presidential decree by Aristide in March 1995 later disbanded 7,000 soldiers of the Haitian armed forces. At the conclusion of Aristide's term, Prime Minister Rene Préval was elected for a five-year term, starting in early February 1996.[19]

From a theoretical perspective, intervention in Haiti begs two important questions: were there strategic interests at stake in Haiti for the United States, and was action costly? The high costs of intervention and the low strategic interests at stake suggest that a normative commitment to democracy may have been the driving force behind OAS action. Indeed, being the poorest state in the hemisphere, with a per capita GNP well below $1,000, Haiti's democratic crisis did not pose any serious strategic threat to any of the major powers in the Americas, not least the United States.[20] U.S. trade interests in Haiti were likewise minuscule. Furthermore, U.S. intervention on behalf of Haiti was all the more unlikely given Aristide's anti-imperialist rhetoric and promulgation of liberation theology. One might argue, however, that strategic interests were at stake with respect to the reputation of the United States; failure to act would profoundly delegitimate the Santiago commitment to democracy and, ultimately, undermine U.S. policy toward nondemocratic Cuba. However, it is unclear to what extent U.S. reputation was really at stake in Haiti; in relation to U.S. policy toward Cuba, there was already a widespread view in the United Nations that the U.S. trade embargo toward Cuba was in fact *not* legitimate.[21] One might furthermore argue that the United States intervened on behalf of strategic *domestic* interests, namely preventing thousands of Haitian "boat people" from flooding U.S. shores. While this point cannot be easily dismissed, one must question whether OAS (and later UN) action was truly commensurate with the supposed threat of economic migration; U.S. intervention, after all, merely dampened—but did not stop—the flow of migrants from Haiti to the United States.[22] In summary, following the premises of realist theory, there is scant evidence to suggest that intervening in Haiti advanced vital U.S. interests.

One must furthermore ask whether or not the actions implemented by the OAS (and made global by the UN) were truly costly to the United States. The answer is clearly yes. Besides the costs of implementing an embargo, the United States committed some 20,000 soldiers to a potentially unstable and risky intervention. Moreover, the OAS and UN missions bore a significant price tag—on the order of $400 million.[23] In short, the high costs of intervention and the low strategic interests at stake suggest that a normative commitment to democracy was a driving force behind IO action.

Nevertheless, can one conclude that normative factors were indeed decisive and that the OAS initiated action only in the name of democracy? Ultimately, the lack of consensus among member states and the actual nature of OAS actions indicate several limitations to a strictly normative interpretation of events. In particular, OAS policies were undermined by a lack of consensus among member states, including the region's largest powers. First, U.S. policy of repatriating Haitian boat people as economic (as opposed to political) migrants undermined the normative claim made by the OAS that the Haitian military regime was indeed politically repressive.[24] Equally significant, Brazil registered its disapproval when ministers within the OAS sought to take the case to the United Nations Security Council and sanction intervention under Chapter VII of the UN Charter. Brazil, arguably, was not willing to treat Haiti's democratic breakdown as if it were a security threat because of the possible implications of such a move for human rights and environmental policies in the hemisphere.[25] Brazil awkwardly joined China in abstaining from the vote on UN Resolution 940. National interests thus undermined OAS resolve in defending the democratic norm. A normative interpretation of Haitian intervention is also contradicted by the nature of the intervention itself. In particular, the United States played a dominant role, single-handedly directing the military occupation of Haiti. In accord with realist predictions, the problem of collective action (intervention) was solved through U.S. hegemony rather than through broad hemispheric cooperation. What is most challenging from a realist perspective, however, is that the United States intervened at all.

Peru 1992: Intervention Against Interest

On 5 April 1992, Peruvian president Alberto Fujimori nullified Congress, displaced the judiciary, and announced the suspension of key civil liberties. Several opposition leaders were arrested. As in the case of Haiti, OAS ministers met within days to discuss the situation and on 13 April passed a resolution urging the restoration of democratic institutions in Peru. In addition, the OAS appointed a special mission to travel to Peru and mediate between Fujimori and opposition forces. The mission was also instructed to report back to the OAS by 23 May as to whether further action, including human rights monitoring, was necessary. Although there was no forceful call for a general trade embargo, many countries cut aid to Peru. The United States, for example, suspended nonhumanitarian economic aid to Peru and successfully lobbied to suspend some $2.5 billion in pending loans to Peru.

The next month Fujimori surprised his opponents when he made a personal appearance at the second ad hoc meeting of OAS foreign ministers on Peru, held in Nassau, Bahamas. Fearing international isolation, Fujimori announced a compromise path: he would hold parliamentary elections instead of a personal plebiscite. The OAS ultimately endorsed this plan (called the Bahamas Resolution) on 18 May 1992 and later monitored the constituent elections on 22 November 1992. In early 1993, Peru was returned to good standing in the OAS.[26] But despite Peru's return to good standing, the OAS did not fundamentally alter Fujimori's usurpation of power. With the compromise solution presented at Nassau, Fujimori prevented the suspension of critical international credits while simultaneously positioning himself to control the constitution-writing process.[27] Relying on his domestic popularity, Fujimori resisted making concessions to the opposition even though he was accused of frequent human rights abuses.

As in the Haitian case, a theoretical analysis of OAS intervention in Peru requires an evaluation of the strategic interests at stake and the costs of intervention. Unlike the Haitian case, important security issues *were* at stake in Peru. In the first place, Peru is a key producer of raw coca in the hemispheric drug trade—accounting for a significant portion of the raw coca that makes it to the United States after being processed in Colombia. U.S. security interests were thus directly tied to the Peruvian regime. Moreover, Fujimori had shown strong resolve in combating drug production and countering the guerrilla threat posed by the Maoist

Sendero Luminoso (Shining Path). Realist theory would thus predict a more cautious OAS policy, since U.S. drug enforcement efforts were of greater strategic interest to the United States than Peruvian democracy per se.[28] A second strategic factor is that Peru is located within a zone of geopolitical conflict; border skirmishes between Peru and Ecuador posed a potential threat to the stability of disputed areas in Chile and along the vast Amazonian border of Brazil.

Security factors may have restrained the OAS's response toward Peru, but the fact that the OAS intervened at all lends credibility to the notion of a growing hemispheric obligation to defend democracy. Indeed, while the United States had no intention of breaking diplomatic relations with Peru, U.S. economic influence was decisive in pushing Fujimori toward a compromise solution. In other words, the United States appeared willing to initiate potentially costly action *even though its strategic interests would have dictated otherwise*—that is, even at the risk of alienating an important (and indeed effective) partner in the war against drugs. Clearly normative factors shaped the U.S. perception that Fujimori's threat to democracy was no less important than his cooperation in the hemispheric drug war. As in the case of Haiti, then, the evidence lends credibility to a normative explanation of *why* the OAS intervenes. However, underscoring the importance of hegemonic power as regards *how* the OAS intervenes, the United States once again played a dominant role in bringing Fujimori to the bargaining table.

Guatemala 1993 and Paraguay 1996: Intervention Without Cost?

On 25 May 1993, President Jorge Serrano Elías of Guatemala attempted to replicate Fujimori's self-coup experiment. Serrano dissolved Congress, dismissed the courts, and announced the suspension of the constitution. In contrast to Peru, however, Serrano's acts were answered with strong domestic opposition—as well as clear indications from the international community that Guatemala would face political isolation and economic sanctions if a democratic solution to the crisis were not found. Actors within the government and Guatemalan civil society openly defied Serrano's mandates. The Supreme Electoral Tribunal, the Court of Constitutionality, and the Office of the Human Rights Ombudsman refused to cooperate, and the Guatemalan media mocked Serrano's calls for state censorship.

Moreover, the international community reacted with firm opposition to Serrano's conduct. The OAS Permanent Council met immediately and called for an emergency meeting of foreign ministers. An OAS mission to Guatemala led by Secretary-General João Baena Soares of Brazil also made it clear that the Serrano regime would confront serious international repercussions, including economic sanctions, if democracy were not restored through institutional means. Baena met not only with opposition groups but also with the military high command. Meanwhile, the United States reacted by unilaterally suspending aid; a day after the coup, the U.S. State Department warned that a $67 million aid package for Guatemala might be withheld. Moreover, U.S. trade representative Mickey Kantor suggested that Guatemala's critical duty-free privileges under the Generalized System of Preferences might be suspended.[29]

Spurred on by the posture of the international community, Guatemalan civil leaders organized the Instancia Nacional de Consenso to coordinate their support for a democratic solution to the crisis. Responding to the threat of lost trade privileges and a falling currency, many Guatemalan business elites joined the prodemocracy movement. With the final withdrawal of the military's support, Serrano fled into exile on 1 June. The Instancia not only rejected Serrano's self-coup but also attempts by his vice-president, Gustavo Espína, to assume office. Ultimately, the movement succeeded in catapulting the attorney general for human rights, Ramiro de León Carpio, into the presidency (by vote of a constitutionally mandated congressional election). The crisis was all but over by the expiration of the ten-day mandate provided for by Resolution 1080.

In several ways, the case of Paraguay in 1996 parallels that of Guatemala in 1993. In February 1989, military strongman General Alfredo Stroessner was ousted by an army coup that eventually ushered in a liberalization of the long-standing authoritarian regime. In 1993, Juan Carlos Wasmosy became Paraguay's first-ever civilian president selected in a free and fair election (monitored by the OAS). However, on 22 April 1996, when Wasmosy called for the resignation of army commander General Lino César Oviedo, the general refused to comply. Heading Paraguay's most powerful branch of the armed forces and commanding considerable influence in Paraguay's Colorado Party, Oviedo threatened to invade the presidential palace.

Within hours of the crisis, OAS secretary-general César Gaviria Trujillo traveled to Paraguay where he encouraged Wasmosy not to back down to Oviedo's threats. At the same time, Lawrence Chewning Fábrega, Panamanian ambassador and president of the OAS Permanent Council, called for the exercise of Resolution 1080, even though there had been no forcible seizure of power. Within twenty-four hours of the crisis, the OAS unanimously resolved to condemn Oviedo's behavior in accord with the Santiago commitment. International pressure outside the

OAS also played an important role. The U.S. embassy in Asunción was quick to condemn the crisis, and the United States made it clear that it was willing to suspend military aid (and possibly economic aid) if the crisis was not resolved in a democratic fashion. The Brazilian minister, speaking on behalf of the other member states of Mercosur (the Southern Cone Common Market), likewise denounced Oviedo's behavior; Paraguay was threatened with suspension from the trade group.[30]

Initially, President Wasmosy caved in to Oviedo's threats, offering him a position as minister of defense if he would retire his post as army commander. Wasmosy's compromise agreement, however, encountered stiff opposition from Paraguayan civil society as well as from the international community.[31] Emboldened by strong support for a democratic solution to the crisis, Wasmosy withdrew his offer; Oviedo in turn retired his post without a fight. Wasmosy, in short, had successfully reasserted his authority as president. As in Guatemala, then, the crisis in Paraguay ended rapidly and within the ten-day period mandated by Resolution 1080. Oviedo, for his part, was imprisoned and later given a ten-year sentence by a military tribunal.

However, the crisis in Paraguay did not end there. In 1998, an Oviedo-supporter, Raúl Cubas, was elected president and swiftly commuted Oviedo's ten-year sentence to three months. More ominously, in March 1999, Oviedo's main rival within the governing Colorado Party, Vice-President Luis María Argaña, was assassinated. Fearing impeachment and prosecution for orchestrating the assassination, President Cubas and ex-general Oviedo fled the country, and Luis Ángel González Macchi, the head of the senate, assumed the vacated presidency. In a dramatic turn of events one year later (on 18 May 2000), loyalists to Oviedo orchestrated a military coup to depose González: the coup ultimately failed for reasons largely reminiscent of 1996. The OAS Permanent Council "vehemently" condemned the coup, and the representatives of the United States and Brazil warned Paraguay's military high command that they would face "ruinous isolation" (including expulsion from Mercosur) if González were overthrown; the Paraguayan military, after some hesitation, quickly put down the rebellion.[32]

The swiftness and coherence of OAS action in both Guatemala and Paraguay suggests that the organization was indeed motivated by a normative concern for democracy and that the Permanent Council was highly effective in working behind the scenes—perhaps exercising limited autonomy in support of the democratic norm. The OAS clearly played an important role in signaling to domestic actors in both Guatemala and Paraguay that antidemocratic actions would not be tolerated. Moreover, even with few strategic interests at stake, the United States and other regional powers exerted significant economic pressure on each of these countries to fulfill their obligations as OAS member states to uphold representative democracy.

At the same time, however, the actions of the OAS do not seriously challenge a realist interpretation for the basic reason that they did not entail serious costs. In Guatemala, Serrano's unpopular self-coup did little to alter the strategic interests of the United States (except perhaps to worsen them marginally by raising the specter of civil-military conflict in Central America). Condemnation of the regime and suspension of aid were thus low-cost actions with a potential payoff. Similarly, in Paraguay, OAS actions were more symbolic than material, imposing no significant costs on the United States or other regional powers. In both Guatemala and Paraguay, the conflict was ultimately over before OAS resolve was fundamentally challenged.

Theoretical Conclusions

The OAS response to democratic crises in Haiti, Peru, Guatemala, and Paraguay lends partial support to the idea of a strong democratic norm in the Americas.[33] A normativist perspective is especially appealing when one examines Resolution 1080 in historical perspective. OAS practice in the 1990s clearly departs from that of the 1970s and 1980s when authoritarian regimes were not only widespread but also passively condoned. Consider, for example, how the organization responded to the democratic crisis in Panama, just two years before the Santiago declaration. In the spring of 1989, there simply were no explicit guidelines for the OAS to follow in the event of a democratic crisis such as General Manuel Antonio Noriega's violent nullification of democratic elections (clearly won by his opposition). The OAS, in short, had no clear plan. Impatient with the lack of OAS resolve to take stronger actions, the United States bypassed the organization and unilaterally invaded Panama in December 1989. Two years later, the Haitian case would prove to be different.

In this new democratic era, the OAS has clearly played a significant role in signaling support for democracy to domestic actors. OAS actions in all four cases legitimated domestic opposition movements and delegitimated authoritarian leaders. The OAS Permanent Council also appears to have exercised some institutional autonomy, at least in establishing a clear agenda for action. Even in a poor and strategically insignificant Caribbean state like Haiti, the OAS intervened on behalf of democracy, working to restore a president with strong anti-imperialist views. Moreover, whereas in Haiti the OAS intervened in the absence of vital U.S. interests, in Peru the OAS intervened *in spite of* such a threat. In short, a normative commitment to democracy appears to be a compelling explanation for *why* the OAS has intervened in recent democratic crises.

On the other hand, a realist perspective appears better equipped to explain *how* the OAS intervenes. In particular, the regional hegemon, the United States, clearly dominated the agenda when costly actions were deemed necessary. Instead of the type of OAS intervention one would expect from a strictly normative perspective (that is, multilateral coordination among regional powers), it was U.S. hegemony that solved the collective action problem of coordinating political, economic, and especially military resources. Furthermore, OAS actions have often inspired significant dissent among regional powers, particularly Brazil and Mexico (and, more recently, Venezuela).[34]

Finally, as regards *when* the OAS intervenes, a critical caveat must be added to the argument that the OAS is guided by a strong normative commitment to "democracy." While the language of Resolution 1080 and the Washington protocol is explicit when one considers the sudden overthrow of a democratic government by force, the OAS's mandate is less clear as regards more subtle threats to the democratic process, such as constitutional irregularities or electoral fraud. Dubious measures taken by Ecuador's congress to remove President Abdala Bucaram in February 1997 and threats made by Venezuela's President Hugo Chávez to dissolve congress in April 1999 prompted scant reaction by the OAS. In recent elections in Peru (April–May 2000) and Haiti (May 2000), moreover, OAS election monitors noted significant irregularities—but the Permanent Council failed to invoke Resolution 1080 or contemplate significant sanctions against either country (although the United States in each case exerted unilateral pressure by withholding aid).[35] Moreover, while the recent adoption of the Inter-American Democratic Charter aims to surmount some of these ambiguities by calling for OAS action in the event of an "unconstitutional alteration of the constitutional regime," it remains to be seen what this contentious statement will mean in practice. As the recent cases of Peru and Haiti ultimately suggest, there is limited consensus among member states as to how the OAS's democratic mandate should be applied to democratic crises that are beyond the scope of coups and self-coups. ⊕

Notes

Dexter S. Boniface is an advanced Ph.D. candidate in political science at the University of Illinois at Urbana-Champaign. Earlier versions of this paper were presented at the International Studies Association, February 1999, in Washington, D.C., and at the International Studies Association–Midwest, November 1998, Chicago.

1. Organization of American States Charter as amended by the Protocol of Managua, adopted on 10 June 1993.

2. The move toward greater hemispheric cooperation in the 1990s was also reinforced by the gradual democratization and economic liberalization of Latin America and by concomitant changes in policy outlook; for a persuasive account of these changes, see especially Javier Corrales and Richard E. Feinberg, "Regimes of Cooperation in the Western Hemisphere: Power, Interests, and Intellectual Traditions," *International Studies Quarterly* 43 (March 1999): 1–36, especially 26–28.

3. OAS General Assembly Resolution 1080: Representative Democracy, AG/RES. 1080 (XXI-0/91), adopted by the OAS General Assembly at the fifth plenary session, Washington, D.C., 5 June 1991.

4. The Protocol of Washington, adopted by the 16th Special Session of the OAS General Assembly on 14 December 1992.

5. The Democratic Charter was largely an outgrowth of the Third Summit of the Americas held in Quebec in April 2001. During the summit, the institutional scope of the hemispheric commitment to democracy was significantly extended: a democracy clause was established, making democracy a conditional prerequisite to a state's participation in the summit process and in the proposed Free Trade Area of the Americas (FTAA).

6. Heraldo Muñoz, "Collective Action for Democracy in the Americas," in Heraldo Muñoz and Joseph S. Tulchin, eds., *Latin American Nations in World Politics* (Boulder: Westview, 1996), pp. 17–34.

7. While these two theoretical perspectives are not exhaustive of all possible explanations of IO behavior, the predictions of realism and normativism bring into sharp focus the central issue of interest here: whether OAS action is motivated primarily by strategic or by normative factors. For a similar (but not equivalent) theoretical distinction, see Robert Keohane, "International Institutions: Two Approaches," in Friedrich Kratochwil and Edward Mansfield, eds., *International Organization: A Reader* (New York: Harper Collins, 1994), pp. 44–61.

8. Perceived neutrality arguably allows for greater efficiency in serving selfish interests through enhanced legitimacy. See Kenneth W. Abbott and Duncan Snidal, "Why States Act through Formal International Organizations," *Journal of Conflict Resolution* 42, no. 1 (1998): 3–32.

9. See John Mearsheimer, "The False Promise of International Institutions," *International Security* 19, no. 2 (1994–1995): 5–49.

10. On the role of norms in international relations, see especially Audie Klotz, *Norms in International Relations: The Struggle Against Apartheid* (Ithaca: Cornell University Press, 1995); Andreas Hasenclever, Peter Mayer, and Volker Rittberger, *Theories of International Regimes* (Cambridge: Cambridge University Press, 1997), chap. 5; and Jeffrey T. Checkel, "The Constructivist Turn in International Relations Theory," *World Politics* 50, no. 2 (January 1998): 324–348.

11. See, for example, Klotz, *Norms in International Relations*; and Martha Finnemore, *National Interests in International Society* (Ithaca: Cornell University Press, 1996).

12. The four other regional powers—Argentina, Brazil, Canada, and Mexico—account for just over 30 percent of the remaining contributions.

13. Thomas M. Frank, "The Emerging Right to Democratic Governance," *American Journal of International Law* 86, no. 1 (January 1992): 46–91.

14. This is not to imply that other countries have not experienced significant democratic crises since the Santiago declaration. For instance, a short-lived coup overthrew the democratically elected president of Ecuador in January 2000 and was unanimously condemned by the OAS in Permanent Council Resolution 763 (1220/00). Venezuela (first under President Carlos Andrés Pérez in 1992 and, later, under former coup-plotter President Hugo Chávez) was also beset by executive crises of varying severity. Among the cases of OAS intervention, moreover, Haiti, Peru, and Paraguay have all experienced renewed threats to democracy, as discussed below.

15. Still, as discussed below, the Guatemalan and Paraguayan cases exhibit important similarities.

16. Klotz, *Norms in International Relations*, pp. 13–14.

17. According to the accord, Aristide would be returned to power on 30 October 1993, and a prime minister designated by Aristide, Robert Malval, would assume office. Additionally, Cédras would resign from the army and a UN mission would be established to modernize the Haitian military and police. In return, the sanctions would be lifted.

18. It is worth emphasizing that there is a clear connection between the earlier actions of the OAS and the later actions of the UN. Former U.S. secretary of state Madeleine Albright recently remarked that "if the OAS had not acted, we would never have gained UN Security Council approval for a multinational force" (quoted in *OAS News*, March–April 2001, p. 2). The interplay between OAS and UN policy is discussed in greater detail in David Malone, *Decision-Making in the UN Security Council: The Case of Haiti, 1990–1997* (Oxford: Clarendon Press, 1998).

19. Aristide succeeded Préval in February 2001 after a landslide electoral victory in November 2000. While ostensibly a victory for Haitian democracy, local and presidential elections in the year 2000 were marred by irregularities (see conclusion below).

20. Most Americans agreed; a *Washington Post/ABC News* poll in 1994 found that only 38 percent felt vital national interests were at stake in Haiti. See "Public Support for U.S. Action in Haiti Appears Malleable," *Christian Science Monitor*, 1 August 1994, p. 19.

21. Moreover, the significance of such reputational interests lends equal credibility to the normativist thesis that legitimacy and norms affect the perceptions of state interests and, ultimately, guide IO action.

22. Additionally, if we suppose that domestic politics were ultimately driving U.S. behavior, this clearly undermines realist suppositions that international structure drives foreign policy.

23. More recent figures put the total price tag to the United States at $2.2 billion (see "Aristide Once Again, in Haiti," *The Economist*, 30 December 2000, p. 39).

24. President Bush's repatriation policy was made effective 24 May 1992. President Clinton, after campaigning against this stance, later continued it. U.S. policy in this case arguably reflects domestic political considerations (given the electoral significance of Florida).

25. See Richard J. Bloomfield, "Making the Western Hemisphere Safe for Democracy? The OAS Defense-of-Democracy Regime," *Washington Quarterly* 17 (1994): 157–169.

26. Peru's good standing in the OAS unraveled in 1999 and 2000, starting with Fujimori's rejection of the compulsory jurisdiction of the Inter-American Court of Human Rights in 1999, the election fiasco of April/May 2000 (see conclusion below), and the ensuing corruption scandal involving Fujimori's spy chief, Vladimiro Montesinos.

27. In elections for the Constituent Congress (November 1992), Fujimori's party won forty-four of the eighty seats; two established Peruvian political parties, the Popular Action (AP) Party and the American Popular Revolutionary Party (APRA), refused to participate in the elections. The new constitution was ratified by popular referendum the following October.

28. This policy preference had already been demonstrated by the passage of President George Bush's 1989 "Andean Initiative," which authorized the disbursement of substantial military aid to Peru despite questions about democracy and human rights practices.

29. "Guatemalans and U.S. Put Pressure on President to Restore Democracy," *Christian Science Monitor,* 28 May 1993, p. 7.

30. At the time, Mercosur did not contain an explicit provision regarding the maintenance of democracy and membership; however, such a clause was added some two months after the Paraguayan crisis.

31. Arturo Valenzuela, "Paraguay: The Coup that Didn't Happen," *Journal of Democracy* 8, no. 1 (1997): 43–55.

32. See OAS Permanent Council Resolution 770 (1235/00), 19 May 2000; "Paraguay Renegades Get Stern Warnings," *The Gazette* (Montreal), 20 May 2000, p. A26; and "Paraguay: Cavalry Charge," *The Economist,* 25 May 2000, p. 38.

33. This normative commitment to democracy, it bears emphasizing, reflects two distinct but related processes. On the one hand, there has been a genuine normative shift in the policy preferences of the United States (and in varying degrees, the other member states of the OAS) in support of democracy. On the other hand, the consensually adopted procedures of the OAS have increased the institutional autonomy of the Permanent Council and other OAS bodies (such as the UPD) to initiate action on behalf of the democratic norm.

34. On the conflicting roles played by the "intermediate" regional powers in the OAS, see especially Andrew F. Cooper and Thomas Legler, "The OAS Democratic Solidarity Paradigm: Questions of Collective and National Leadership," *Latin American Politics and Society* 43, no. 1 (spring 2001): 103–126, especially 113–119.

35. In the case of Haiti, the Permanent Council, on 15 March 2001, issued a resolution expressing concern but did not take more aggressive action. In the case of Peru, U.S. ambassador Luis Lauredo initially called on the OAS to invoke Resolution 1080, but he withdrew the idea once it became clear it would

not pass (see "OAS Opposes Condemning Peru Election; U.S. Fails to Muster Support Against Vote," *Washington Post,* 1 June 2000, p. A15). For a more detailed discussion of the OAS mission to Peru, see Andrew Cooper and Thomas F. Legler, "A Model for the Future? OAS in Peru," *Journal of Democracy* 12, no. 4 (October 2001): 123–136.

[13]

THE OAU AND THE RECOGNITION OF GOVERNMENTS IN AFRICA: ANALYZING ITS PRACTICE AND PROPOSALS FOR THE FUTURE

KOFI OTENG KUFUOR*

INTRODUCTION 369
I. GHANA 372
II. UGANDA 378
III. LIBERIA 1980 379
IV. CHAD 382
V. LIBERIA 1990 386
VI. SIERRA LEONE 388
VII. THE OAU DECLARATION ON THE RECOGNITION OF GOVERNMENTS 389
VIII. PROPOSALS FOR THE REFORM OF THE LAW RELATING TO THE RECOGNITION OF UNCONSTITUTIONAL REGIMES 393
CONCLUSION 400

INTRODUCTION

One of the consistent features of politics in Africa, since the collapse of the colonial system, is the rarity of constitutional change in governments.[1] Since the first coup d'etat in 1952,[2] a series of military

---

* Associate Fellow, Royal Institute of International Affairs, and Research Fellow, School of Law, University of East London.

1. *See infra* notes 2-3 (discussing the various methods by which different African governments have changed, the majority of which do not include constitutional change).

2. *See* ERIC CARLTON, THE STATE AGAINST THE STATE, 160-71 (1997) (describing the coup that overthrew King Faruq in Egypt on July 23, 1952).

revolts and civil wars have instigated change in the governments of a majority of African states.[3] In the wake of this method of political change, more than one political or military faction has claimed to be the government of a particular State at numerous times.[4] Although the charter of the Organization of African Unity ("OAU") expressly prohibits interference in a Member's internal affairs,[5] this provision has been ignored on occasion and, as a result, a delegation's claim to be the representative of a state has caused considerable controversy at OAU summit meetings.[6] Also, in some instances, even though there has been no dispute over who should represent a particular state at OAU meetings, the OAU has still barred representatives from its deliberations.[7] As demonstrated in this paper, the OAU's reaction to such situations has depended on the interplay of legal, social, and political factors surrounding the delegation's volatility, which shapes its responses to particular situations.

Moreover, the OAU has begun to develop a policy on constitutional change that has as its crux the non-recognition of coups.[8] This

3. *See* Adebayo Adedeji, *Comprehending African Conflicts*, *in* COMPREHENDING AND MASTERING AFRICAN CONFLICTS: THE SEARCH FOR SUSTAINABLE PEACE AND GOOD GOVERNANCE 1, 1-10 (Adebayo Adedeji ed., 1999) [hereinafter COMPREHENDING AND MASTERING AFRICAN CONFLICTS] (examining the violence plaguing the Sub-Saharan African continent, especially as it relates to changes in government). By the end of 1998, thirty-three out of the forty-eight Sub-Saharan countries had undergone periods of "political tumults, violence, and brutalization." *Id.* at 5. Since 1998, there has been a coup in Cote d'Ivoire. *Id.* Only a few countries, including Botswana, Gabon, Mauritius, Sao Tome & Principe, Swaziland, Tanzania, and Zimbabwe, have been spared violent changes of government since their independence. *Id.*

4. *See* Segun Odunuga, *Nigeria: A Victim of its Own Success*, *in* COMPREHENDING AND MASTERING CONFLICTS 221, 221-28 (describing the events leading up to a thirty month long Civil War with different factions claiming control of different areas of the country).

5. *See* OAU CHARTER AND RULES OF PROCEDURE, art. 3, para. 2 [hereinafter OAU CHARTER] (indicating the member states' adherence to the principle of non-interference in the internal affairs of other states).

6. *See infra* notes 12-34 and accompanying text (describing the controversy surrounding the seating of the Ghanaian delegation in the wake of the coup that overthrew Nkrumah).

7. *See infra* notes 56-68 and accompanying text (discussing the OAU's refusal to recognize the new regime of Liberia after a violent coup in 1980).

8. *See infra* Part VII (examining the OAU's recognition practices with regards to coups and other non-democratically initiated changes of government).

coincides with the link between democracy and socio-economic development recently stressed by international organizations[9] and states.[10] Given Africa's debilitating social and economic problems, if

9. *See* UNITED NATIONS GENERAL ASSEMBLY, THE CAUSES OF CONFLICT AND THE PROMOTION OF DURABLE PEACE AND SUSTAINABLE DEVELOPMENT IN AFRICA; TEXT PRESENTED TO THE UNITED NATIONS SECURITY COUNCIL BY THE SECRETARY-GENERAL, U.N. Doc. A/52/871-S/1998/318 (1998) (expressing the current UN Secretary-General, Kofi Annan's opinion of the importance of democracy for development). The report states:

> Democratic government helps to guarantee political rights, protect economic freedoms, and foster an environment where peace and development can flourish. Today, as never before, countries around the world are seeking to establish pluralistic systems of government in which political leaders are elected by the will of the majority to fixed terms of office and exercise their authority within legal limits. This is a very hopeful trend for Africa's future because in the absence of genuinely democratic institutions contending interests are likely to seek to settle their differences through conflict rather than through accommodation.

Id. at 18. Annan's predecessor as Secretary-General, Boutros Boutros-Ghali, also emphasized the interrelationship between human rights and socio-political stability when he wrote:

> Democracy within nations requires respect for human rights and fundamental freedoms, as set forth in the Charter. It requires as well a deeper understanding and respect for the rights of minorities and respect for the needs of the more vulnerable groups of society, especially women and children. This is not only a political matter. The social stability needed for productive growth is nurtured by conditions in which people can readily express their will. For this, strong domestic institutions of participation are essential.

BOUTROS BOUTROS-GHALI, AN AGENDA FOR PEACE, 70-71 (1995).

10. *See* TONY SMITH, AMERICA'S MISSION: THE UNITED STATES AND THE WORLDWIDE STRUGGLE FOR DEMOCRACY IN THE TWENTIETH CENTURY, 85 (1994) (arguing that the foundation for American twentieth century foreign policy, including the belief that democracy is the most peace-loving and only legitimate form of government, and that the United States has a self-interested, as well as moral, obligation to further its prospects abroad, was laid by President Wilson at the beginning of the twentieth century). In particular, a resurgence of Wilson's liberal democratic internationalism in America's foreign policy is evident in the both President Bush I and President Clinton's policies. *Id.* at 312-45; *see also* Edward N. Muller, *Democracy, Economic Development, and Income Inequality*, 53 AM. SOC. REV. 50 (1988) (demonstrating that scholars, in addition to international organizations and states, note the link between democracy and income inequality by presenting the causal relationship between income inequality and democratic experience within a country); Michael W. Doyle, *Liberalism and World Politics*, 80 AM. POL. SCI. REV. 1151 (1986) (claiming a close relationship between democracy and political stability); R.J. RUMMEL, POWER KILLS:

the OAU acts constructively on the recognition of democratic governments it can emerge from its current dysfunctional state and start to serve as a tool for the enhancement of economic prosperity and political stability on the continent.[11] Notwithstanding its current measures, however, this paper argues that the OAU's policy on recognition does not go far enough and needs to be elaborated further with rules that bind it to adhere to articulated and transparent procedures.

This paper is thus an analysis of the recognition practice of the OAU. Parts I through VI of the paper are case studies of the OAU's recognition policy in practice. These studies examine instances when the OAU has adhered to the international law principle of non-interference in the internal affairs of its members. The case studies also discuss instances when the OAU has departed from its position of non-interference. Insights into domestic and regional politics, the security perceptions of some African states, and the OAU's internal organization are examined to better understand how the OAU policy has evolved. Part VII is an introduction to the OAU's recent declaration on unconstitutional change of governments. Part VIII explores methods to reinforce the substantive and procedural dimensions of the declaration. The conclusion comments on the impact of the OAU's new position on its future significance.

I. GHANA

The OAU's first major recognition problem involved the seating of the Ghanaian delegation sent to the sixth ordinary session of the OAU

DEMOCRACY AS A METHOD OF NONVIOLENCE, 85-89 (1997) (arguing that democracy also contributes to domestic peace within a country).

11. *See* GEORGE B. AYITTEY, AFRICA IN CHAOS, 346 (1998) (describing the irrelevance of the OAU by noting that although the mandate of the OAU includes conflict resolution, the OAU has achieved the "unenviable distinction of being the most useless organization on the African continent"). Ayittey describes the delegates to the OAU as "a den of unrepentant despots" and notes that the organization itself is known for "its glitzy annual jamborees, where rabid autocrats click champagne glasses to celebrate longevity in office." *Id.* In addition, Ayittey argues that they "use the OAU summit to extort aid from the international community instead of taking the initiative to solve the continent's problems themselves." *Id.*

Council of Ministers[12] by the then newly-established military junta in Ghana, the National Liberation Council ("NLC").[13] Kwame Nkrumah, one of the main architects behind the creation of the OAU,[14] had been overthrown in a coup in 1966.[15] The arrival of the NLC's delegation led to controversy among the OAU Members, some of whom attempted to prevent it from participating in the Council of Ministers' meeting.[16]

The deliberations over the NLC's delegation revealed the emergence of two clear positions on the issue of recognition.[17] One group in the Council maintained that as the NLC was now the de facto government of Ghana, there should be no question about seating its delegates at the meeting.[18] Although, ostensibly, this claim was based on the OAU's principle of non-intervention in its Members' internal affairs and the fact that the NLC had secured effective control of Ghana, there was

12. *See* OAU CHARTER, *supra* note 5, art. 7(2) (creating the Council of Ministers as one of the organs of the OAU).

13. *But see* A. Bolaji Akinyemi, *The Organization of African Unity and the Concept of Non-Interference in Internal Affairs of Member-States*, *in* 46 THE BRITISH YEARBOOK OF INT'L LAW 391, 399 (1975) (indicating that the issue of recognition of governments actually first arose in 1963 as a result of the overthrow and assassination of President Olympio of Togo). Although this took place before the OAU was established, Togo's delegates were prevented from attending the OAU's inaugural conference because of opposition from some states. *Id.* By July of that year, however, the Togolese delegation was allowed to participate in OAU meetings. *See Costly Claims in Togo*, W. AFR., July 27, 1963, at 832. (noting the recognition by all African states of the new government of Togo).

14. *See* DAVID ROONEY, KWAME NKRUMAH: THE POLITICAL KINGDOM IN THE THIRD WORLD, 203-36 (1988) (describing the role Nkrumah played in the creation of the OAU).

15. *See President Nkrumah Deposed by the Armed Forces and Police*, 3 AFR. RES. BULL. 462, 465 (1966) (reporting about the coup d'etat by the Armed Forces and an instance in which the police overthrew Nkrumah).

16. *See* C. O. C. AMATE, INSIDE THE OAU: PAN-AFRICANISM IN PRACTICE, 423 (1986) (describing the events surrounding the NLC delegation's arrival to the sixth ordinary session of the OAU Council of Ministers).

17. *See id.* at 424 (describing the difference between the opposing sides of the debate over the validity of the NLC delegation); *see also infra* notes 31-39 (analyzing the arguments of each side of the debate over the NLC delegation).

18. *See id.* at 423 (describing the states that recognized the NLC as the de facto government).

probably a subtler underlying factor.[19] Nkrumah had been accused of supporting attempts to overthrow certain African regimes[20] as a means of gaining influence and shaping the course of African unity on lines he deemed appropriate.[21] Hence, his demise was seen by some of the Members as an event that would improve their prospects of survival.[22]

On the other hand, other OAU Members[23] tried to prevent the NLC's delegation from taking its seat.[24] These Members argued that foreign governments, bent on eliminating Nkrumah because of his ideological position and his radical Pan-Africanism, backed the NLC's coup.[25] The opposition members therefore believed that the NLC's delegation represented a puppet regime whose existence was at odds with the aspirations of the OAU, as articulated in its preamble.[26] The argument, therefore, was not that the NLC had not yet exercised effective control over Ghana.[27] Instead, the challenge to the NLC's delegation was based

19. *See id.* (noting that the same states that recognized the NLC as the de facto government of Ghana were also the states that in the past had accused the ousted Ghanaian leader of masterminding subversive efforts against their governments).

20. *See African Unity and Political Alignments*, 2 AFR. RES. BULL. 311 (1965) (describing some of the allegations of subversion measured against Ghana).

21. *See* KWAME NKRUMAH, AFRICA MUST UNITE, 216-23 (1985) (arguing for a continental government for Africa). Nkrumah believed in a surrender of state sovereignty with economic planning on a continent-wide basis. *Id.* In addition, he argued for a unified military and defense strategy capable of defending Africa from an external attack as well as a unified foreign policy. *Id.* He was also a proponent of a continental constitution implying a single government for all of Africa. *Id.*

22. *See* Amate, *supra* note 16, at 423 (stating that the coup in Ghana ended the dispute between Ghana and those countries that had been accusing Ghana of subversive efforts against them).

23. *See The Seating of Ghana*, W. AFR., Mar. 5, 1966, at 281 (naming Guinea, Mali, and Tanzania as the main advocates for non-recognition of the credentials of the NLC's delegation).

24. *See id.* (reporting about the heated debate over the recognition of the NCL delegation).

25. *See* Amate, *supra* note 16, at 423 (describing that the opponents to the recognition of the NLC delegation believed that the overthrow of Nkrumah was the work of international imperialism, which they condemned).

26. *See* OAU CHARTER, *supra* note 5, pmbl. (stating that the member-states of the OAU are committees, among other things, to fight against neo-colonialism in all its forms).

27. *See* JOSEPH G. AMAMOO, THE GHANAIAN REVOLUTION, 45-46, (1988) (noting that by the time the OAU Council of Ministers meeting had begun, the

on perceptions of neo-colonialism, considerations of Pan-Africanism, and Nkrumah's role in the struggle to dismantle the colonial system.[28] At the end of the discussions, the faction that supported the NLC prevailed and the Council decided to seat the Ghanaian delegation.[29] In response, some of the anti-NLC delegation withdrew from the meeting in protest.[30]

The reaction to the coup in Ghana and the seating of the NLC delegation amounted to a triumph of legalism in the OAU. It was obvious, that at this stage, the OAU had accepted the international law principle of effective control as one of the primary conditions for recognition of governments. Also, the seating of the Ghanaian delegation was indicative of the OAU's reaffirmation of the principles of Article 3(2) of its Charter on non-interference.[31]

In addition, apart from the commitment to legalism, a number of political factors influenced the OAU's decision to accept the new Ghanaian delegation. First, the anti-colonial tenets and utterances,

---

effective control of the NLC was not in doubt since all resistance to the coup ended on the same day it was executed).

28. *See* Amate, *supra* note 16, at 423-24 (discussing the arguments for and against the recognition of the NLC delegation).

29. *See* AMAMOO, *supra* note 27, at 48 (describing the events surrounding Nkrumah's Foreign Minister's failure to appear at the summit). Nkrumah thus lost the opportunity to persuade the Council of Ministers to bar the NLC's delegation form the meeting. *Id.* Perhaps the absence of Nkrumah's foreign minister tilted the majority opinion in the Council towards the NLC. *See also The Seating of Ghana*, *supra* note 23, at 281. In handling this dispute, the OAU may have taken guidance from the United Nations. *See Recognition by the United Nations of the Representation of a Member State*, G.A. Res. 396(V), U.N. GAOR, 5th Sess., Supp. No. 20 at 24, U.N. Doc. A/1775 (1950) (adopting a resolution that asserted that whenever there is a dispute between more than one authority claiming to represent a government in the UN that becomes a subject of controversy, the issue should be considered in the light of the Purposes and Principles of the Charter and the circumstances of each case). Even if the UN model, which presupposes competing claims, was used for guidance in this case, the OAU has demonstrated its willingness to expel a delegation without hearing claims of a rival faction claiming to be the government of a given state. *See infra* notes 54-68 and accompanying text (discussing the case of Liberia in 1980).

30. *See* Amate, *supra* note 16, at 424 (identifying Algeria, Egypt, Guinea, Kenya, Mali, Tanzania, and Somalia as the countries that left the OAU meeting in protest).

31. *See* OAU CHARTER, *supra* note 5, art. 3(2) (indicating the member states' adherence to the principle of non-interference in the internal affairs of other states).

typical of the OAU in its beginning, were no longer influential because 1966 marked the end of the dynamic period of the OAU's first two years. The small group of so-called radical states,[32] such as Algeria, Egypt, Ghana, Guinea, Mali, Tanzania, and Uganda, which had considerable influence when the OAU was established, saw its fortunes decline when two of its leaders, Ben Bella of Algeria,[33] and Nkrumah were overthrown.[34] By 1966, the moderates, with their focus on economic cooperation, dominated the debates and shaped opinion in the OAU.[35] With the moderates in control, the radical's justification for expulsion—that the government had been unstable with the aid of imperialist powers—was not going to win much support.[36]

Second, the founders of the OAU had deliberately created a weak

---

32. *See* Zdenek Cervenka, *Major Policy Shifts in the Organization of African Unity, 1963-1973*, *in* FOREIGN RELATIONS OF AFRICAN STATES 323, 333 (K. Ingham ed., 1974) (identifying the radical states that dominated the OAU during its first couple of years).

33. *See id.* (stating that the radical group of the OAU lost one of its major leaders with the death of Ben Bella); *see also* ARSLAN HUMBARACI, ALGERIA: A REVOLUTION THAT FAILED, 263 (1966) (quoting a member of the military junta that ousted Bella as saying, "The era of noisy speeches, of vulgar catchwords and of impulsive frenzy is over," indicating Algeria's more sober foreign policy). Ben Bella was overthrown in a coup in 1965. *See A Person Again*, ECONOMIST, Nov. 8, 1980, at 42. His replacement as head of state, Houari Boumedienne, shifted from Ben Bella's fiery radicalism to a more practical approach. *See* Humbaraci, *supra* at 263. Although the new government continued to support "radical African causes" such as aid for guerrilla movements seeking to topple colonial regimes, the amount of aid was limited to a smaller number of groups and was given with much less brazenness than was the case under Ben Bella. *Id.*

34. *See* Cervenka, *supra* note 32 at, 333 (describing the loss of the radical group's leadership). The radicals' cause was further damaged when the NLC restored links with Britain, which had been broken by Nkrumah in the wake of the Rhodesia affair. *See* ANTON BEBLER, MILITARY RULE IN AFRICA: DAHOMEY, GHANA, SIERRA LEONE AND MALI, 40-41 (1973). The NLC also consolidated links with other Western countries such as the United States. *Id.* In addition, the NLC made a point of shutting down camps established by Nkrumah to train freedom fighters. *See* KWAME NKRUMAH, DARK DAYS IN GHANA, 139-40 (1968).

35. *See* Cervenka, *supra* note 32, at 333 (discussing the influence wielded by the moderate states in the OAU since 1966 and their focus on economic cooperation); *see also* JON WORONOFF, ORGANIZING AFRICAN UNITY, 592-97 (1970) (detailing the rise of the moderates in the OAU).

36. *See The Seating of Ghana*, *supra* note 23 (reporting that the radical's argument lost its force and the Ghana delegation was seated without further questioning of their credentials).

organization.[37] The Charter forbade member states from interfering in the affairs of the other member states and declared sovereign equality of all members.[38] Hence, the very thinking of its Members, coupled with the powers given to it, made the OAU virtually powerless to deal with coups, even if they resulted in the overthrow of governments that were staunchly committed to its goals.[39]

The emergence of differences among the Members and the role of rival African organizations further diluted the OAU's effectiveness. The OAU had to confront rival African organizations, some of which had similar goals and were capable of attracting a lot of its Members.[40] Thus, this contest for dominance on the continent made any radical decisions about Article 3(2) virtually impossible. If the OAU was seen as asserting too much influence this could have easily set off a defection by some of its Members to rival African organizations.[41]

Moreover, the Members of the OAU may have based their decision to seat the Ghanaian delegation after a cost-benefit analysis. Continuing to seat delegates of ousted regimes would probably be too burdensome for it in its formative years. After all, what role would the outside regime play since they would not be in a position to implement OAU resolutions or the provisions of the Charter? Would such a move result in a situation where the majority of OAU Members were governments-in-exile?[42] In addition, how could the OAU collect

---

37. *See* Woronoff, *supra* note 35, at 331 (stating that the OAU charter was strangely silent on ways and means for the organization to maintain order in Africa).

38. *See* OAU CHARTER, *supra* note 5, art. 3(1) and (2) (declaring each member-state's adherence to the principle of sovereign equality and non-interference in the internal affairs of states).

39. *See* Woronoff, *supra* note 35, at 331-33 (discussing the OAU's difficulty in resolving disputes between member-states, and especially within member-states).

40. *See* BOUTROS BOUTROS-GHALI, THE ADDIS ABABA CHARTER 50 (1964) (questioning whether the larger grouping of African nations provided by the OAU will help in unification, or whether smaller focused regional organizations will be more affective on the African continent).

41. *See id.* (presenting the issues associated with the competition between the OAU as a single continental organization and smaller, regional associations of states in terms of reaching African unification).

42. *See supra* notes 1-3 and accompanying text (discussing the frequency of violent governmental change). The possibility of an organization consisting in a majority of governments-in-exile's delegations was quite possible given the

contributions from non-recognized regimes and what implications would this have for its financial health and survival? Hence, the decision taken to accept coups (and other forms of unconstitutional political change), as a fait accompli was most likely based on institutional self-interest as well as legal and political considerations.

II. UGANDA

The issue of the recognition of a new military regime again became a matter of intra-OAU controversy when Idi Amin overthrew the government of Milton Obote in Uganda in 1971.[43] Amin and the deposed government sent rival delegations to the OAU's sixteenth session of the Council of Ministers. Again this clash of factions resulted in the polarization of opinions on recognition.[44] The faction opposing Amin's delegation argued that it was not certain whether the new junta had effective control over Uganda.[45] Opposition to Amin's delegation probably stemmed from his declaration that he intended to remain in the British Commonwealth, notwithstanding Britain's sale of arms to South Africa, while Obote had indicated his inclination to withdraw Uganda from the organization on this issue.[46] Amin's position was thus unacceptable to some of the OAU's Members. Other factors adding grist to the mill of the pro-Obote faction included the participation of six Israeli advisors in Amin's delegation and some African countries growing animosity toward Israel.[47]

---

number of coups that had already occurred and the likelihood of more to come. *Id.*

43. *See Uganda: Coup d'etat*, 8 AFR. RES. BULL. 1993 (1971) (describing the coup d'etat against the government of Milton Obote).

44. *See Session Postponed*, W. AFR., Mar. 12, 1971, at 290 (stating that support for Obote's regime principally came from Guinea, Somalia, Sudan, Tanzania, and Zambia, while Members such as Ghana, Liberia, and Nigeria supported the seating of Amin's delegation).

45. *See id.* (citing no clear indications that Amin controlled the entire country).

46. *See* James H. Mittleman, *The Anatomy of a Coup: Uganda, 1971*, XI AFR. QUARTERLY 184, 187 (1971) (detailing the circumstances surrounding Obote's threat and his role in refusing student protests). Obote's threat to withdraw the Commonwealth over British arms sales to South Africa in 1971, the very month in which Amin overthrew his government, was surprising, since he had been criticized in October of 1970 for refusing to permit students to march to the British High Commission in Kampala in protest against the arms to South Africa policy.

47. *See* JOEL PETERS, ISRAEL AND AFRICA: THE PROBLEMATIC FRIENDSHIP 51-54 (1992) (surveying the deterioration of the relationship between Israel and

The group that supported the seating of Amin's delegation noted that delegates from the new government had already participated in a meeting of the United Nations Economic Commission for Africa.[48] Thus, in effect, the new regime had already been "recognized" as the government of Uganda. In addition, as was the case with the overthrow of Nkrumah, a number of African governments saw Uganda under Obote as a threat to their security.[49] His removal therefore meant there was one less subversive state to worry about.

The impasse at the OAU continued and neither delegation was seated.[50] This was due to the role played by Members in key positions within the OAU at the time.[51] These States provided the necessary support for Tanzania's concerns about the coup and, consequently, made it possible to prevent the seating of Amin's delegation.[52] However, at the Council's session in June of that same year, Amin's delegation was seated without any controversy.[53]

III. LIBERIA 1980

Another recognition controversy at the OAU arose as a result of the 1980 coup in Liberia.[54] Measures adopted by some OAU Members and

---

African countries).

48. *See Session Postponed*, supra note 44, at 290 (stating that Ghana's delegation pointed out the pro-Amin delegation's participation).

49. *See id.* (explaining that although there was support for the seating of Amin's delegation, the countries that opposed the seating focused on the confusion and uncertainty facing Uganda as the reasons for insecurity).

50. *See* Amadu Sesay, *The OAU and Regime Recognition: Politics of Discord and Collaboration in Africa*, 4 SCANDINAVIAN J. OF DEV. ALTERNATIVES 25 (1985) (describing the sequence of events that prevented either delegation from being seated).

51. *See id.* at 33 (identifying that Guinea, Somalia and Zambia, all regarded as radicals and close to Obote, held the positions of OAU Secretary-General, Chairman of the Council of Ministers, and Chairman of the OAU, respectively.).

52. *Id.*

53. *See id.* (explaining how Zambia and Somalia's loss of their positions equated to the removal of an obstacle which allowed Amin's delegation to be seated).

54. *See Liberia: Coup Topples Tolbert*, 17 AFR. RES. BULL. 5645, 5645-50 (1980) (including the assassination of the President William Tolbert and the execution of thirteen of his senior government officials as consequences of the military coup).

implicitly supported by the others amounted to the non-recognition of the new Liberian regime. Nigeria, for example, refused permission for Liberia's new Foreign Minister to attend the OAU economic summit in Lagos.[55]

Although this measure was a unilateral decision, it received the tacit approval of the summit's participants.[56] This decision was later justified by the OAU on the ground that since the summit was exclusively for heads of state, a mere foreign minister could not attend.[57] Another theory suggests that the real basis for the OAU's concern was that it had scheduled an extraordinary summit in Nigeria on the economic problems of Africa during which Tolbert, in his capacity as the OAU Chairman, would preside.[58] Consequently, Tolbert's death raised the issue of whether Samuel Doe, the coup leader, would assume the chairmanship of the OAU and preside over the meeting.[59]

These factors alone, however, do not explain the OAU's reaction. They were probably secondary and possibly irrelevant considerations that merely cloaked the OAU Members' underlying fears. The real concern lay in the composition of the forces that had deposed Tolbert's administration. The coup had been planned and executed by Non-Commissioned Officers ("NCOs") in the Liberian army.[60] The conspirator with the highest rank was Doe himself; he was a master sergeant.[61] The fear now was that a new class of coup-makers had burst

55. *Id.* at 5650.

56. *See id.* (noting no dissent among representatives of the fifty-member organization).

57. *See id.* (undermining this explanation was the fact that only half of the OAU heads of states attended and that numerous foreign ministers also participated).

58. *See* Edward Kannyo, *The Banjul Charter on Human and People's Rights: Genesis and Political Background*, *in* HUMAN RIGHTS AND DEVELOPMENT IN AFRICA 128, 135-36 (Claude E. Welch, Jr. & Ronald I. Meltzer eds., 1984) (forcing the OAU to confront the issue of succession to power in Liberia).

59. *Id.* at 136.

60. *Liberia: Coup Topples Tolbert*, supra note 54, at 5645 (1980).

61. *Liberia: PRC Members Named*, 17 AFR. RES. BULL. 5637 (1980) (listing other members of the People's Redemption Council, the military junta established after the coup, which included two staff sergeants, four sergeants, eight corporals, and one soldier first-class).

onto the scene in Africa. The loyalty and control of the relatively small number of majors and generals no longer sufficiently guaranteed the survival of a regime; the larger mass of NCOs also had to be contended with. This further jeopardized the already precarious security situation existing in almost all African countries. Therefore, if only to deter other NCO's, condemnation of Doe's coup was necessary. The reaction of some African states in the past illustrates this point. For example, in 1979 reaction to events in Ghana in which junior officers of the armed forces seized power,[62] with the overwhelming support of NCOs demonstrates fear of coups.[63] They established a junta with NCOs making up half of the membership[64] and proceeded to execute eight senior officers of the armed forces. Nigeria's reaction resulted from its concern that their junior officers and NCOs would follow suit.[65]

Consequently, the actual execution of Tolbert and other members of his government did not constitute the real source of the OAU's outrage; the identity of those that had not only planned but performed the killings truly fueled the OAU's outrage.[66] However, once the Doe administration indicated that executions would cease,[67] his government was seated at the next OAU annual summit.[68] The implication of the

62. *See Ghana: Military Coup*, 16 AFR. RES. BULL. 5306 (1979) (following fighting on June 4, 1979, a new military administration called the Armed Forced Revolutionary Council seized power in Ghana).

63. *See* Amamoo, *supra* note 27, at 190 (depicting the massive support of NCO's).

64. *See Ghana: Military Coup*, *supra* note 62, at 5306 (1979) (including a warrant officer, private, corporal, lance corporal, and staff sergeant). The new ten-member military administration was called the Armed Forces Revolutionary Council. It included a Warrant Officer, Private, Corporal, Lance Corporal and Staff Sergeant. *Id.*

65. *See* BARBARA E. OKEKE, 4 JUNE: A REVOLUTION BETRAYED 55, 55-56 (1982) (stating that Rawling's popularity and the approval of the objectives of the Ghanian revolution constituted threats to all corrupt governments, including Nigeria)

66. *See Liberia: Coup Topples Tolbert*, *supra* note 54, at 5648-49 (pronouncing the feelings of the OAU in light of the upcoming summit conference).

67. *See id.* at 5650 (announcing that Liberia would halt the execution of political prisoners on April 29, 1980).

68. *See OAU: Summit Conference*, 17 AFR. RES. BULL. 5730 (1980) (describing the seventeenth summit conference of the OAU, which occurred in July 1980). Doe's delegation was seated at the OAU's Seventeenth Annual Summit. *Id.*

Liberia controversy for the OAU was that legalism, so clearly upheld in the question over the seating of the NLC delegation from Ghana, had been ignored, albeit temporarily. This also demonstrated that under certain circumstances legalism would have to yield to political expediency and/or moral outrage.

IV. CHAD

In 1982, two delegations claiming to represent Chad arrived at the OAU's meeting of Foreign Ministers in Libya.[69] One delegation, representing the faction led by Hussein Habre, insisted on participating in the meeting since it was in effective control of Chad.[70] This claim was correct. As a result of a civil war, Habre had overthrown President Goukhouni Oueddei earlier in the year[71] and meaningful resistance ended when Oueddei fled to Cameroon.[72] However, another delegation representing Oueddei arrived at the meeting also demanding to be seated as the official Chadian delegation.[73] Libya, the host government, led the countries that supported this delegation's claim.[74]

Libya argued that Habre's government was not the true representative government of Chad.[75] This was based on the claim that

69. *See* Eddie Momoh, *A Time for Compromise*, W. AFR., Nov. 22, 1982, at 3006 (documenting the disagreement among OAU Foreign Ministers as to which delegation should be recognized as the legitimate representatives of Chad).

70. *See id.* (stating that the moderate countries supported this contention).

71. *Chad: Habre Comes Back*, 19 AFR. RES. BULL. 6489 (1982).

72. *Id.*

73. Momoh, *supra* note 69, at 3006.

74. *Id.*; *see* Mario J. Azevedo & Emmanuel U. Nnadozie, CHAD: A NATION IN SEARCH OF ITS FUTURE 114-24 (1998) (analyzing the factors influencing Libya's anxiety about the regime in control of Chad, such as Libya's territorial claims to the Chad's Aouzou Strip, as well as Colonel Gadaffi's view that Libya should unite the Arab states since he had always viewed Chad as an Arab country); *see also* Sam Nolutshungu, LIMITS OF ANARCHY: INTERVENTION AND STATE FORMATION IN CHAD 147 (1996) (concluding that Gadaffi also wanted to avoid a situation whereby Chad's government would have close links with foreign powers opposing him, like France, and that Habre posed such a threat since he had long declared himself an enemy of Libya and an alliance between him, France, and Sudan was viewed as a threat).

75. *See* Momoh, *supra* note 69, at 3006 (claiming that Habre represents only a fraction of Chad, not the entire country).

Oueddei was organizing resistance to Habre in Chad's northern radical region and, therefore, Habre lacked popular support.[76] Moreover, if the OAU gave its support to Habre's delegation by seating it, rebels could construe this to mean that it supported the overthrow of its Members.[77] In Libya's view, the OAU the should demonstrate its support for ex-president Oueddei, as a number of African countries faced similar civil rebellions.[78] Libya also alleged that Habre's government would serve as a pawn for imperialist powers in Africa by turning Chad into an "imperialist base," with the possibility that Chad would become the source of instability not only in Africa, but particularly in the six countries on its borders.[79]

Libya's contention was wrong. If the claim that Habre's government lacked a popular base were to apply to all delegations sent to the OAU, virtually all of them would be denied the right to participate in that organization's meetings. By 1982, few truly representative governments existed in Africa. Military dictators or civilian presidents-for-life ruled the overwhelming number of OAU member states.[80] Assumption of power and change of government through the ballot box was an extremely rare occurrence.[81] Nevertheless, these unrepresentative governments participated freely in OAU meetings. Thus, the Libyan claim concerning the representative nature of Habre's

---

76. *Id.*

77. *See OAU: Second Summit Failure*, 19 AFR. RES. BULL. 6640, 6641 (1982) ("if we were to recognize the usurpation of authority in N'Djamena, then we would have to recognize all those usurpations . . . It would be a serious precedent to recognize a rebel minister of defense.") (quoting Colonel Gadaffi's perspective on Chad).

78. *Id.*

79. *See id.* (quoting Colonel Gadaffi as saying, "All the African states neighboring Chad will pay the price of their recognition of Habre when Chad turns into an imperialist base. We can never allow a regime in the heart of Africa to become an imperialist base.")

80. *See generally* Yusuf Bangura, *Authoritarian Rule and Democracy in Africa: A Theoretical Discussion* 1991 UN Res. Inst. for Soc. Dev. § 2.3 (explaining that military and one-party regimes eventually came under pressure to adopt programs to shift the countries to multi-party rule).

81. *See generally id.* at § 2 (reflecting that the attitudes of Africa's ruling elite toward the multi-party system of government and free elections became clear as soon as they won independence because the general consensus was that Africa could not afford the socio-political cost of such a system).

delegation could not be supported in light of the OAU's practice. Even if the Libyan position stated that the consent of the people meant their acquiescence to the new government and not necessarily their enthusiastic and voluntary support,[82] neither the facts, nor an analysis of the OAU charter, would support this argument. As noted above, Oueddei had been defeated and had fled the country. As a result, all meaningful resistance to the rebellion had ended. Therefore, that crucial act of acquiescence had occurred in the minds of the bulk of Chadians. Moreover, even if the later attempts by Oueddei to establish a foothold in the northern part of Chad were significant, Habre's administration did not have any ground for non-recognition of because of a lack of acquiescence. Prior to the Chad recognition controversy, some well-established African governments, such as Angola and Mozambique, in effective control of a greater part of their territories, faced rebel uprisings. However, these rebel uprisings had never been used to question their claim to represent their states at OAU meetings.

Moreover, the OAU has never claimed seating delegations from usurpers implicitly supported such means of political change in Africa. The OAU believes that the change of government is an internal affair.[83] As noted above, attempts to prevent participation by rebel governments from Ghana and Liberia in OAU meetings represented a departure, albeit a failed one in the long run, from the norm. The change of government falls within the scope of Article 3(2) of the OAU's

82. Policy makers have found that in many coups the concept of actual consent expressed through popular support for the overthrow of a government is meaningless. As one US State Department memorandum noted:

> Most coups occur in less developed countries which have predominantly illiterate and politically dormant populations. The coup is usually quick, bloodless, and effective. Moreover, such changes in government usually occur in one-party states, and take the form of one elite replacing another elite, political, or military. In such circumstances the popular will remains largely irrelevant. In the absence of popular revolution or a clear division of allegiance within the country, the consent or acquiescence of the population must, as a practical matter, be taken for granted.

See L. Thomas Galloway, *Recognizing Foreign Governments: The Practice of the United States* 7 (1978) (quoting Memorandum dated June 1, 1971, from the US Department of State, Office of the Legal Adviser).

83. *See* OAU CHARTER, *supra* note 5, art. 3(3) (demanding respect for the sovereignty and territorial integrity of each State and for its inalienable right to independent existence).

Charter.[84]

It is unclear whether Habre became a puppet of imperialism and therefore lent his active support to external forces bent on destabilizing Africa. However, it did not provide a good reason for excluding a delegation from an OAU meeting. Although the OAU's Charter mentions the defeat of colonialism as an objective,[85] being a tool of imperialism has never been a barrier to membership. The OAU membership rules clearly state that the organization invites the participation of independent, sovereign African States.[86] Nothing in the OAU's charter precludes a government of a Member State from participating in OAU summits because of its foreign relations.

Furthermore, the Members of the OAU finally agreed on a compromise solution on the issue of Chad's representation.[87] This agreement recognized the right of Habre's delegation to participate in the summit meeting over Oueddei's claims.[88] However, the concession requested, but not granted was that Habre himself voluntarily stay away from the Summit.[89]

The de facto amendment to the OAU Charter frustrated the Habre delegation. This amendment created the position of OAU Chairman, even though the OAU Charter itself does not provide for such position.[90] A merely ceremonial position, the Chairman lacks any

---

84. *See* OAU CHARTER, *supra* note 5, art. 3(2) (making it an intention of the OAU to refrain from interfering in the internal affairs of member states).

85. *See* OAU CHARTER, *supra* note 5, art. 2(1)(d) ("To eradicate all forms of colonialism from Africa").

86. *See* OAU CHARTER, *supra* note 5, art. 4 ("Each independent sovereign African State shall be entitled to become a Member of the Organization").

87. *See OAU: Second Summit Failure*, 19 AFR. RES. BULL. 6640, 6641 (1982) (explaining that the members of the OAU formulated a compromise, but it was rejected by the Chadian Foreign Minister).

88. *See id.* (pointing out that the compromise allowed for the recognition of Habre's delegation, but called for him to voluntarily abstain from being seated at the summit).

89. *See id.* (recognizing that the compromise suggested that Habre reffrain from attending the summit, therefore, leaving the Chad seat empty and preventing the required thirty-one members for a quorum to hold an effective meeting).

90. *See* GINO J. NALDI, THE ORGANIZATION OF AFRICAN UNITY: AN ANALYSIS OF ITS ROLE 14 (1989) (providing for practices and procedures that are not actually outlined in the OAU Charter).

executive powers. However, over the years the position has gained prestige[91] as the Chairman emerged as the official spokesman of the OAU. The parties exploited this role and the influence surrounding it during the negotiations on the representation of Chad.

V. LIBERIA 1990

In 1989 a rebel army, the National Patriotic Front of Liberia ("NPFL") took up arms against the regime of Samuel Doe.[92] The NPFL effectively destroyed the Doe administration and by June of 1990, it had nearly eradicated all meaningful resistance by government forces to its military offensive.[93] The Economic Community of West African States ("ECOWAS") decided to intervene in the Liberian conflict at this late stage.[94] ECOWAS' measures made it possible to create Liberia's Interim Government of National Unity ("IGNU").[95] The IGNU was installed in the capital, Monrovia, under the protection of the ECOWAS expeditionary force, the ECOWAS Ceasefire Monitoring Group ("ECOMOG").[96] For the three years that it existed the IGNU had no army or police force of its own and ECOMOG was responsible for its safety.[97] Moreover, the ECOWAS-IGNU alliance never controlled any territory beyond Monrovia, and its immediate

---

91. *See id.* (institutionalizing the practice of placing the host Head of State as chairman of OAU until subsequent summit).

92. *See* ABIODUN ALAO, ET AL., PEACEKEEPERS, POLITICANS, AND WARLORDS: THE LIBERIAN PEACE PROCESS 20-24 (1999) (explaining the event that started the Liberian civil war).

93. *See* ABIODUN ALAO, THE BURDEN OF COLLECTIVE GOODWILL (1998) (providing a general history of the Liberian civil war).

94. *See* ALAO, *supra* note 92, at 28 (citing inaction by the United States and the international community as the reason why the ECOWAS chose to intervene in the Liberian civil war).

95. *See* Peter da Costa, *Interim Leaders Emerge*, W. AFR., Sept. 10, 1990, at 2438 (reporting that in Gambia, in August 1990, ECOWAS organized a conference, attended by over fifty delegates from Liberian political parties, interest groups, and concerned citizens, after the election of Amos Sawyer, President of Liberia). The assembly also agreed on an interim national legislative assembly consisting of thirty-five members. *Id.*

96. *See* ALAO, *supra* note 93, at 65-66 (1998) (discussing the success of ECOMOG's mission for peace in Liberia).

97. *Id.*

outskirts.[98]

Thus, the important question is why did the OAU seat the IGNU? The OAU's recognition of IGNU is particularly perplexing because the IGNU was not the de jure government of Liberia when the NPFL launched its uprising. If the IGNU had been the de jure government it could have argued for the presumption of recognition until the NPFL dealt the coup de grace.[99] However, as noted above, the IGNU was installed and was being protected by a foreign force-ECOMOG. In effect, the IGNU was a rebel faction in the conflict relying on an outside force to help it assert its claims. Its status as a rebel faction is supported by the fact that it too, like the NPFL, laid a claim to power when Doe and the rump of his government still occupied the presidential mansion.[100] Hence, consistent with the rule of international law that hasty recognition of rebels should be avoided until they have consolidated their hold over a State, the OAU's recognition of IGNU was obviously wrong.[101]

Therefore, the answer to why the OAU recognized INGU as the government of Liberia lies, arguably, in an examination of the political interests of key players in the Liberian crisis. Most Members of ECOWAS wanted to see the NPFL's rebellion fail. If the rebels, essentially a civilian army, had succeeded in their undertaking this could provoke similar uprisings in the other West African countries.[102]

---

98. *See* Kofi Oteng Kufuor, *Developments in the Resolution of the Liberian Conflict*, 10 AM. U.J. INT'L L. & POL'Y 373, 374 (1994) (providing the boundaries of territory controlled by the ECOWAS-IGNU alliance). Although ECOMOG did succeed in pushing the NPFL out of Monrovia, the only real threat to the NPFL's power came from the numerous guerilla movements that sprang up over Liberia during the conflict.

99. *See* HERSCH LAUTERPACHT, RECOGNITION IN INTERNATIONAL LAW, 93-94 (Cambridge, University Press, 1947).

100. *See* da Costa, *supra* note 95, at 2438 (reporting that NPFL occupied Monrovia but failed to occupy the presidential mansion).

101. *See* Lauterpacht, *supra* note 99, at 92 (claming that premature recognition of a rebellious group is essentially a tort committed against the lawful government).

102. *See* Gilbert da Costa, *Fresh Impetus for Peace*, W. AFR., Nov. 16, 1992, at 1968 (reporting the events of a meeting in Nigeria on the Liberian crisis). At a meeting of ECOWAS President Babangida and the Nigerian Head of State emphasized the self-defense aspect of the intervention when they asserted possible future effects of Taylor's uprising, stating, "Today it is Liberia; tomorrow it could

In effect, African leaders' concerns regarding the 1980 Liberian recognition question were played out as civilian armies were compromising regional security. The OAU obviously bowed to pressure from ECOWAS when it accepted the IGNU as the delegation from Liberia. It was clear that the OAU sacrificed the rule of law in order to assuage the misgivings of some of its members.

VI. SIERRA LEONE

The recognition practice of the OAU underwent a radical transformation in the wake of events in Sierra Leone during 1997. Army officers overthrew the democratically elected civilian government of Sierra Leone, with Tejan Kabbah as president, after it had been in power for aproximately a year.[103] The OAU condemned the coup and refused to recognize the Armed Forces Revolutionary Council ("AFRC") as the de facto government of Sierra Leone. The OAU justified its position on the basis of Kabbah being a popularly elected president.[104] Although preserving democracy in Africa had never been a raison d'être for non-recognition of a revolutionary government, the AFRC coup occurred at a time when elected civilian governments were starting to re-emerge as the norm.[105] In effect, this was the beginning of the OAU's policy of not recognizing regimes that overthrow constitutional democracies.

---

be any one of the countries represented here. Indeed the canker we are fighting against is already showing itself in Sierra Leone and in other parts of the sub-region." *Id.*

103. *See Sierra Leone: A New Democratic Era*, 33 AFR. RES. BULL. 12,191 (1996) (reporting the election results and potential conflicts resulting from those results). Sierra Leone elected Tejan Kabbah president in March 1996. *See Sierra Leone: A Coup in Freetown?*, W. AFR., June 2, 1997, at 887 (describing the coup that attempted to bring military rule back to Sierra Leone after a year of civilian rule).

104. *See Sierra Leone: A New Democratic Era*, *supra* note 103 (providing that Kabbah was elected with 60% of the vote and his party will have a controlling interest in the National Assembly, holding 51 of 80 seats).

105. *See generally* JOHN A. WISEMAN, THE NEW STRUGGLE FOR DEMOCRACY IN AFRICA (Ashgate Publishing Company, Avery 1996) (discussing the movement towards democracy in Africa). *But see* Richard Joseph, *Africa, 1990-1997: From Arbetura to Closure*, 9 J. OF DEMOCRACY, 1998, at 3-17; Letitia Lawson, *External Democracy Promotion in Africa: Another False Start?* 37 COMMONWEALTH & COMP. POL., 1-30 (1999) (arguing that the transition to democracy has not been that successful).

Further, it was doubtful if the AFRC could claim that the bulk of the population had consented to its assumption of power.[106] Moreover, the AFRC did not have effective control over Sierra Leone as ECOMOG, and the Kamajors, a militia loyal to the ousted president, competed with it for control of the country.[107] ECOMOG's role was also driven by Nigeria's desire to expand its importance in West Africa[108] and to cloak its then military government, seen by the international community as a pariah regime, with some form of legitimacy.[109] This would have enabled the Nigerian junta to justify its claim, though patently spurious, that it was committed to liberal democracy.[110]

VII. THE OAU DECLARATION ON THE RECOGNITION OF GOVERNMENTS

The above analysis demonstrates that illegality, inconsistency, and a lack of transparency characterize the OAU's recognition process. This lack of transparency is visible in a number of ways. First, the OAU recognition deliberations are not open to the public and recorded minutes for such deliberations are unavailable.[111] Second, the OAU's Charter makes no provision for the recognition of governments.[112] It also does not permit the suspension or expulsion of governments.[113] Article 3(2) further prohibits the OAU from interfering in the internal affairs of its Members, and yet the recognition controversies have

106. *See* John Bankole, *A Country on Trial*, W. AFR., July 6, 1998, at 576; *Sierre Leone: Koroma Pleads*, W. AFR., June 16, 1997, at 952 (reporting on popular resistance to the AFRC by civilians in Sierra Leone).

107. *See* Yusef Bangura, *Security in ECOWAS*, W. AFR., June 30, 1997, at 1038 (reporting on the popular resistance to the AFRC by civilians in Sierra Leone); *see also Sierra Leone: Nigerian Intervention Fails*, 34 AFR. RES. BULL. 12,711, 12,735 (1997) (reporting that the Kamajors controlled most of the south and east of the country in 1997).

108. *See generally* http://news1.thdo.bbc.co.uk/hi/english/world/analysis/newsid_55000/55993.stm (last visited May 13, 2001).

109. *Id.*

110. *Id.*

111. *See generally* OAU CHARTER, *supra* note 5 (providing no requirements for the recording of deliberations).

112. *See id.* (making no mention of new government recognition).

113. *Id.* (requiring respect for the independence of each nation).

amounted to a disregard for Article 3(2). Also, effective control has not always been a deciding factor in the seating of delegations at OAU meetings.[114]

Third, recognition has been swayed by the influence of various OAU chairmen or regional powers. Thus, as we have seen, in the wake of the overthrow of Milton Obote, Goukhouni Oueddei, and William Tolbert, the OAU chairman, host countries managed to exert considerable influence on deliberations over recognition.[115] In effect, the process has been more the rule of personality then the rule of law and each incident has seen the OAU lurch from one position to another.[116] Consequently, this lack of consistency has produced a situation where the OAU refused to recognize the AFRC as the government of Sierra Leone, while welcoming Denis Sassou-Nguesso at OAU meetings after he had subverted democracy in Congo Brazzaville.[117]

As noted above, however, the OAU has placed the question of recognition of governments on its agenda. At the OAU Summit in Algiers a decision was taken to reactivate the OAU sub-committee on unconstitutional change in order to finalize work with regard to the overthrow of elected regimes in its Member states.[118] An OAU

114. *See supra* notes 43-47 (discussing the matter of effective control with regard to the recognition of a delegation from Uganda); *see also supra* notes 75-80 (reiterating the controversy surrounding the seating of the delegation from Chad, where effective control did not result in automatic acceptance by the OAU).

115. *See* OAU CHARTER, *supra* note 5, art. 3(2) (pointing out that this influence violates the Charter because it demands that the OAU refrain from interfering in internal affairs of its Member States).

116. *See supra*, note 43 (discussing the politics behind the non-recognition of the Ugandan coup).

117. *See The Congo: Fighting Breaks Out*, W. AFR., June 16, 1997, at 953 (reporting clashes between supporters of Sassou-Nguesso and supporters of Lissouba); *Congo Brazzaville*, W. AFR., Oct. 20, 1997, at 1655 (announcing the planned swearing in of Sassou-Nguesso). In 1997, Denis Sassou-Nguesso challenged the authority of the elected president of Congo-Brazzaville, Pascal Lissouba. For thirteen years Congo-Brazzaville had been a one-party state under Sassou-Nguesso. However, bending to pressure for political change, Sassou-Nguesso agreed to multiparty elections. This resulted in his defeat by Lissouba in 1992. However, rivalry between the two led to a civil war in June of 1997 and the victory of Sassou-Nguesso's forces in October of that year. Given the zeal with which the OAU supported Kabbah in Sierra Leone, it was surprising that the OAU never condemned Sassou-Nguesso. *Id.*

118. *See* Joe Branford Nyinah, *Coups Out, Democracy In*, W. AFR., July 24,

Declaration adopted after a meeting in Lome followed this decision.[119] The Lome Declaration noted that coups were a disturbing trend and contributed to the erosion of democracy in Africa.[120] The OAU Members also agreed on a set of principles as the basis for the articulation of common values and principles for democratic governance. Included in these principles are respect for the constitution of a Member,[121] democratic change, the recognition of a role for the opposition,[122] and the organization of free and regular elections.[123]

The Declaration considers unconstitutional change of government to occur where a democratically elected government is overthrown either through a coup d' etat,[124] by mercenaries,[125] by armed dissident groups and rebel movements,[126] or when there is the refusal by an incumbent government to relinquish power to the winning party after free, fair, and regular elections.[127] The Declaration also states that illegal regimes will be given six months to restore constitutional order.[128] After the expiration of this six-month period, during which the illegal regime will be suspended from the policy-making organs of the OAU,[129] a range of sanctions will be instituted against it.[130] Sanctions could include denial of visas for members of the government in question, restriction of government-to-government contacts, or trade

---

2000, at 12 (focusing on the OAU's attempt to maintain more influence over unconstitutional changes in control in its member countries).

119. *See* DECLARATION OF THE FRAMEWORK FOR AN OAU RESPONSE TO UNCONSTITUTIONAL CHANGES OF GOVERNMENT, AHG/DECL.5 (XXXVI) (July 2000) [hereinafter DECLARATION] (condemning any unconstitutional change of government in OAU states).

120. *See id.* at pmbl. (expressing concerns about recent coups in Africa).

121. *Id.* at 3.

122. *Id.* at 4.

123. *Id.* at 4.

124. DECLARATION, *supra* note 119, at 4.

125. *Id.*

126. *Id.*

127. *Id.* at 5.

128. *Id.* at 5-6.

129. DECLARATION, *supra* note 119, at 5.

130. *Id.* at 6-7.

restrictions.[131]

The Declaration gives the Secretary-General the duty of gathering facts relevant to an unconstitutional change of government.[132] The Secretary-General should also establish appropriate contacts with the perpetrators in order to ascertain their intentions with regard to restoring constitutional rule.[133] African leaders and personalities may also be consulted by the Secretary-General in the discharge of his duties under the Declaration.[134] African leaders and personalities should be asked to help put pressure on the perpetrators to cooperate with the OAU.

In order to give effect to the Declaration, the OAU has decided that existing OAU mechanisms, particularly the Central Organ of the OAU Mechanism for Conflict Prevention, Management, and Resolution ("the Central Organ")[135] will be the instrument for its implementation.[136] The Secretary-General should determine the best way to enhance the role of the Central Organ to enable it to implement the Declaration.[137] The OAU's Members agreed to establish a Central Organ sanctions sub-committee responsible for monitoring compliance with decisions with respect to situations of unconstitutional changes.[138] The sub-committee should also recommend appropriate review measures to the OAU's Policy Organs.[139]

On its face, the Declaration is a meaningful step towards promoting

---

131. *Id.*

132. *Id.* at 6.

133. *Id.*

134. *See* DECLARATION, *supra* note 119, at 6.

135. *See Mechanism for Conflict Prevention, Management and Resolution*, 6 AFR. J. INT'L & COMP. L. 149, 158-160 (1994) (establishing the Mechanism for Conflict Prevention, Management and Resolution as a means of anticipating and preventing conflicts in Africa). The Mechanism is "built around the Central Organ with the Secretary General and the Secretariat serving as its operational arm." *Id.* at 160. The Central Organ is "composed of the States members of the Bureau of the Assembly of Heads of State and Government." *Id.*

136. *See* DECLARATION, *supra* note 119, at 7 (giving the Central Organ the authority to implement OAU responses to unconstitutional changes in Africa.)

137. *Id.*

138. *Id.*

139. *Id.*

constitutional democracy and the rule of law in Africa. However, the Declaration's underlying theme should be reinforced by expanding on the preconditions for the non-recognition of an unconstitutional regime. To achieve its objective, the OAU should set basic rules with regard to non-recognition of governments that come to power by overthrowing constitutional regimes.

VIII. PROPOSALS FOR THE REFORM OF THE LAW RELATING TO THE RECOGNITION OF UNCONSTITUTIONAL REGIMES

First, as noted above, a government that has been installed as a result of a free and fair election and that respects its citizens' fundamental human rights will be recognized by the OAU as the government of its country, even if it is overthrown by armed forces and the new regime is in effective control.[140] It is interesting to note that the Declaration has guarded against so-called illiberal democracies exploiting the OAU's new position to entrench themselves in power.[141] An illiberal democracy occurs in a situation in which elected democratic regimes regularly disregard the constitutional restraints on their authority and, as a consequence, violate their citizens' fundamental human rights.[142] This is the case in many states that have supposedly swung from totalitarianism and authoritarianism towards constitutional rule and liberal democracy.[143]

Realizing this potential problem, the Declaration lists a number of values and principles deemed to underpin democratic government in

140. *See id.* at 2-5 (outlining the situations that could be considered unconstitutional change of government and the actions the OAU will take in response to those unconstitutional changes).

141. *See id.* at 1-4 (introducing values and principles to promote democratic institutions and reduce risks of unconstitutional change).

142. *See* Fareed Zakaria, *The Rise of Illiberal Democracy*, 76 FOREIGN AFF. 22, 22 (1997) (observing a growing phenomenon of illiberal democracies around the world).

143. *See id.* at 28 (introducing examples of countries in Africa, Asia, and Latin America where rapid democratisation without liberal governance have lead to illiberal regimes).

Africa.[144] The values include the adoption of a democratic constitution; respect for the Constitution and parliamentary legislation; the separation of powers and judicial independence; the promotion of political pluralism and acknowledging the role of civil society; the principle of democratic change with a clear role of political opposition; free and regular elections; freedom of expression and freedom of the press; constitutional recognition of fundamental human rights in conformity with the Universal Declaration of Human Rights and the African Charter on Human and Peoples' Rights (the Banjul Charter); and the guarantee and promotion of human rights.[145]

Implicitly, reference to the Banjul Charter indicates that to enjoy recognition as the legitimate government, an ousted administration should have a consistent record of respect for, and compliance with, decisions of its domestic courts.[146] In addition, the government should also have demonstrated its commitment to the protection of the rights of its citizens. Thus, for example, it should not just be a party to the Banjul Charter, as envisaged in the Declaration.[147] Rather, the government claiming legitimacy from the OAU should have regularly complied with the Charter's provisions on the submission of periodic reports to the African Commission on Human and Peoples' Rights.[148] It should also have accepted in good faith the determinations of the African Commission regarding communications filed before it.

In addition, the OAU should stress that under no circumstances should the overthrown government have denied access to a human rights fact-finding mission or on-site study by the African Commission, United Nations, or where applicable, the Commonwealth or a similar

144. *See* DECLARATION, *supra* note 119, at 3-4.

145. *Id.*

146. The African Charter on Human and Peoples' Rights, OAU DOC. CAB/LEG/67/3 REV. 5 (1981), *reprinted in* 21 I.L.M. 58 (1982).

147. DECLARATION, *supra* note 119, at 4.

148. *See* African Charter on Human and Peoples' Rights, *supra* note 146, at 63, 68 (establishing that under Articles 30 and 62 each state party must submit a report every two years that consists of legislative or other material that "give effect to the rights and freedoms recognized and guaranteed by the present Charter" to the African Commission on Human and Peoples' Rights). *But see* EVELYN A. ANKUMAH, THE AFRICAN COMMISSION ON HUMAN AND PEOPLES' RIGHTS: PRACTICE AND PROCEDURES, 108-09 (1996) (discussing the problems of non-compliance in the submission of reports and overdue reports).

inter-governmental organization.[149] Also, the regime should ratify or accede to the newly established African Court on Human and Peoples' Rights,[150] and through a declaration, it should accept the competence of the Court to receive non-state petitions.

The OAU's new policy applies only to democratically elected governments.[151] This principle should be extended to current undemocratic regimes. There are still a number of countries where the government is not accountable to its people through periodic elections. If there is a coup d'etat or successful civil war in such a country, the OAU's policy on recognition should come into play. Here, the OAU should grant provisional recognition to the new regime and insist on a transfer of power to an elected civilian administration within a time frame acceptable to the OAU.[152] However, if any member of the new military administration wins the presidency while the junta still holds office, then the OAU policy should be that unless the electoral process is declared to be fair by international observers it will not grant recognition to the new government because it would be a continuation of the military junta.[153]

---

149. *See* Ankumah, *id.* at 114-15 (describing the difficulties of the African Commission in conducting fact-finding missions due to obstacles erected by African governments such as Malawi under president Banda and Zaire under Mobutu).

150. *See* Draft Protocol to the African Charter on Human and Peoples' Rights on the Establishment of an African Court on Human and Peoples' Rights, *reprinted in* 9 AFR. J. OF INT'L & COMP. L. 593 (1997) (memorializing an agreement between African nations to protect the human rights of their citizens).

151. *See* Declaration, *supra* note 119, at 1-7 (setting forth the principals on democratic governance).

152. On many occasions military regimes have drawn out the return to constitutional rule. For instance Nigeria's transition to democracy after the coup of 1983 dragged on until 1999.

153. The tendency of incumbent coup-makers to contest or try to contest elections is well known in Africa. *See* Ronald Allen, *Strasser Ousted in Palace Coup,* W. AFR., Jan. 22, 1996, at 102 (describing the removal of Captain Valentine Stresser due to "his attempt to impede the democratic process" in Sierra Leone); *Gambia: Jammeh Elected President*, W. AFR., Sept. 30, 1996, at 1540 (reporting the opposition leader, Ousainou Darboe's flight to take refuge in the Senegalese Embassy in order to avoid the unrest following the elections). This practice is not limited to the 1980's and 1990's. *See Ghana: General Ankrah's Resignation*, 6 AFR. RES. BULL. 1376 (1969) (describing General Ankrah's resignation resulting from the collection of illegal funds).

The OAU's criteria should also be procedurally transparent, especially in the instance of a coup leader seeking recognition after the overthrow of a supposedly democratic government. As we have seen, OAU deliberations on recognition have been held in camera.[154] Thus, there should also be a provision for oral statements and any counter-claims by organizations with observer status at the OAU, the deposed regime, or the new government seeking recognition. The OAU should also be obliged to consider the reports of the African Commission on Human and Peoples' Rights concerning any state-sponsored human rights abuses by the ousted applicant-government. Reports on the government's compliance with judgments of the African Court (whenever it becomes operative) should also be considered in deciding whether to withhold or grant recognition.

During the Chad controversy, an attempt to create a credentials committee to deal with the question of competing delegations failed.[155] The rules of procedure of the Council of Ministers state that each Member must provide a list of its accredited delegates in advance of a Council meeting.[156] The rules, however, fail to state what should happen if there is more than one list due to rival claims from different factions. Accordingly, a credentials committee should be empowered to make recommendations to the OAU on the issue of recognition. The Council of Ministers or the Assembly of Heads of State and Government[157] should act on the report submitted by the credentials committee. A two-thirds majority vote should be required if either of these institutions chooses to ignore the credentials committee's report. The report of the credentials committee and the reasons for any rejection of a claim by the AHSG or Council of Ministers should be made public.

Furthermore, the credentials committee should be able to consult any

154. *See* OAU CHARTER, *supra* note 5, arts. 7, 9 (stating that the Council of Ministers and the Assembly of Heads of State and Government deliberations are to be held in camera).

155. *See Twelve Days that Shook the OAU*, W. AFR., Dec. 6, 1982, at 3127 (detailing the events that led to the attempt and failure of the credentials committee during the Nineteenth summit of the OAU).

156. *See* OAU CHARTER, *supra* note 5, rule 5 (providing that each Member State communicate to the Council of Ministers a list of its duly accredited delegation).

157. *See* OAU CHARTER, *supra* note 5, art. 7 (setting forth the principal institutions of the OAU including the Assembly of Heads of State).

individual, national organization, government, as well as any regional or international organizations as part of its recommendation process. The power of consultation, therefore, should not be left to the OAU Secretary-General as provided for in the Declaration.[158] When necessary, the credentials committee should also have the power to conduct a fact-finding mission on its own volition to help it arrive at a fair and impartial determination on recognition. Additionally, the importance of the Chairman of the OAU or Council of Ministers should be diminished. As we have seen in the case of Chad, the Chairman can exert considerable influence on the recognition of a delegation.[159] Therefore, reducing the role of the Chairman of both institutions in specific relation to the issue of recognition could result in a more equitable conclusion by the credentials committee.[160]

Thomas Franck argues that the entitlement to democracy in international law has undergone a normative and customary evolution.[161] It has evolved both as a system of rules in the practice of States and organizations.[162] Franck identifies three distinct phases of change.[163] The first stage had as its essence the normative entitlement to self-determination.[164] The normative entitlement to free expression as a human right marked the second stage.[165] Franck argues that the advent of a normative right to a participatory electoral process is the

---

158. *But see* Declaration, *supra* note 119, at 6 (providing that the Secretary-General should obtain the contribution of African leaders and personalities as part of the process of pressurizing the illegitimate government to restore constitutional order).

159. *See supra* part IV (discussing the case of Chad and the seating of their delegation).

160. *But see* Declaration, *supra* note 119, at 5 (empowering the Current Chairman of the OAU and the Secretary General to condemn any unconstitutional change of government, warn perpetrators that such change is unacceptable, and request a meeting of the Central Organ to consider situations that could be construed as an unconstitutional change of government).

161. *See* Thomas M. Franck, *The Emerging Right to Democratic Governance*, 86 AM. J. INT'L L. 46 (1992) (explaining that while the ideas that seemed radical at the time of signing the Declaration of Independence in this country remain radical notions at the international level, they are quickly becoming more normative).

162. *Id.*

163. *Id.* at 90.

164. *Id.*

165. *Id.*

pillar of the third stage.[166] African organizations have in recent times acknowledged this entitlement.[167] Hence, in 1990 the OAU issued a Declaration entitled "The Political and Socio-Economic Situation in Africa and the Fundamental Changes Taking Place in the World."[168] This Declaration acknowledged the importance of democracy and its link with development,[169] attaching the proviso, however, that African countries were entitled to determine their own systems of democracy based on their socio-cultural values.[170]

In addition, other African regional organizations have issued declarations on democracy. In a series of resolutions, the African Commission on Human and Peoples' Rights asserted that the right to democratic governance applies to Africa. The Commission issued further resolutions on the Military,[171] Nigeria,[172] Gambia,[173] and the Human Rights Situation in Africa, stating that the military overthrow of an elected government threatens human rights and the rule of law in Africa.[174]

---

166. *Id.*

167. *See Organization of African Unity: Annual Summit (Addis Ababa)*, 27 AFR. RES. BULL. 9747 (1990) (stating the recognition of the relationship between democracy and development amongst heads of state and government participating the 26th OAU Summit).

168. *Id.*

169. *Id.*

170. *Id.* at 9748.

171. *See* Sixteenth Ordinary Session of the African Commission on Human and Peoples' Rights, Banjul, The Gambia, 83 (1994) (stating in the Preamble the declarations of the Commission regarding governments of African countries). The Commission encourages military governments to instill power in the hands of a democratic government. *Id.*

172. *See id.* at 84-85 (calling upon the Nigerian military government to respect the right of free participation in government and the right to self-determination and hand over the government to duly elected representatives of the people without unnecessary delay).

173. *See id.* at 86-87 (resolving that the military coup in Gambia is a flagrant and grave violation of the right of the Gambian people to freely choose their government and requesting the Armed Forces Provisional Ruling Council to transfer power to freely elected representatives of the people).

174. *See id.* at 87-88 (stating that the Commission condemns the planning or execution of Coups d'Etat and any attempt to seize power by undemocratic means, and calls upon all African governments to ensure that elections and electoral processes are transparent and fair).

The OAU's emerging practice is consistent with historical and contemporary trends regarding the recognition of governments. Although constitutional legitimacy of a government is not a condition for recognition,[175] as noted in the Tinoco Arbitration, recent and past practice of states point to the fact that the right of rebellion has never been fully accepted. The Conference on Security and Co-operation in Europe's support for democracy at its Copenhagen Meeting in 1990 and the Tobar Doctrine are examples of states committing themselves to actively work towards the support and protection of liberal democratic regimes.[176] Further, it shows that such regimes deny recognition to extra-constitutional governments.[177] The United Nations support for the restoration of Jean Bertrand Aristede to power in Haiti after the overthrow of his constitutional regime by the armed forces is another indication of the fact that constitutional legitimacy is emerging as an important pre-condition for recognition.[178]

---

175. *See* Convention Between the British Government and the Government of Cost Rica for the Submission to Arbitration of Certain Claims Against the Government of Costa Rica, Jan. 12, 1922, 1 REP. INT'L. ARB. AWARDS 371, 381 (arguing that a de facto government should be recognized if it "maintains a peaceful administration, with the acquiescence of the people for a substantial period of time. . ." and should not have to follow the previous constitution).

176. *See generally* Conference on Security and Co-operation in Europe: Document of the Copenhagen Meeting of the Conference of the Human Dimension, 29 I.L.M. 1305-21 (1990) [hereinafter Copenhagen Document] (laying out the participating States' commitment and recognition of democracy and political pluralism).

177. *See generally* Additional Treaty to the Treaty of Peace Concluded at the Central American Conference, Dec. 20, 1907, S. Treaty Doc. No. 357 (1776-1909) (rejecting any government that comes into power through a coup d'etat or a revolution against the recognized government). After a period of serious instability in Central America, the Central American nations adopted in 1907 an agreement, among others, in which they agree not to recognize new unconstitutional regimes in Central America. The signatories to this agreement stated that before recognition is granted there should be a collective or multilateral appraisal of the constitutional validity of a new regime. This doctrine, called the Tobar Doctrine, named for Carlos R. Tobar, a former foreign minister of Ecuador introduced a principle of collective recognition. *See* Donald Marquand Dozer, *Recognition in Contemporary Inter-American Relations,* 8 J. INTER-AM. STUD. 318, 321 (1966) (explaining the origins of the Tobar doctrine).

178. *See generally* S. Res. 875, U.N. SCOR, 3293th Sess., U.N. Doc. S/RES 875; S. Res. 917, U.N. SCOR, 3376th Sess., U.N. Doc. S/RES 917; S. Res. 940, U.N. SCOR, 3413th Sess., U.N. Doc. S/RES 940 (setting forth the United Nation's stance on the illegal de facto regime in Haiti and the goal in restoring democracy in

Some observers might argue that the OAU cannot act decisively on the recognition of democratic governments, as most of its Members are either undemocratic (i.e. they have not been elected through universal adult suffrage in the context of a multi-party system) or the government's commitment to democracy is spurious. While this observation may be true, it is also a fact that recent political change in Africa has resulted in a situation in which, as noted above, a number of genuine democracies are emerging as a result of democratic elections. Thus countries such as Benin[179] and Madagascar[180] are joining the already established democracies of Mauritius and Botswana. These states can form the core of a group within the OAU committed to the promotion of democracy and the non-recognition of governments that overthrow elected regimes.

Also, the non-recognition of governments could result in the OAU becoming an organization that is dominated by governments-in-exile. If, however, the OAU is firm on its policy of recognition, this could serve as a deterrent to future coup makers and thus eliminate the fear of the OAU becoming an organization with Members that are not de facto governments. Moreover, to encourage liberal democratic regimes, it should be possible for international organizations and States that have insisted on democracy in Africa to compensate the OAU for any income lost as a result of the continued recognition of an ousted democratic regime.

CONCLUSION

The recent coup attempt in Burundi,[181] the overthrow of Pascal Lissouba's government in Congo Brazzaville, and the coup that

Haiti by returning the legitimately elected President, Jean-Bertrand Aristid).

179. *See* Themon Djaksam, *Kérékou is Back,* W. AFR., Apr. 15, 1996, at 584 (detailing democratic practice in Benin under the leadership of President Mathieu Kérékou); Kate Whiteman, *The Chameleon Returns*, W. AFR., Apr. 1, 1996. at 498 (reporting the return of Mathieu Kérékou as President of Benin).

180. *See Madagascar: Ratsirika Comeback*, 34 AFR. RES. BULL. 12,559 (1977) (describing the outcome of the national elections and Admiral Didier Ratrsiraka's victory as President).

181. *See* http://www.cnn.com/2001/WORLD/africa/04/18/burundi.unrest.o2/ (last visited May 13, 2001).

deposed Henri Bedie's regime in Côte d'Ivoire[182] are indicative of the fact that the phenomenon of coups, something observers of African politics thought had ended, is still a feature of that continent's political landscape.[183] Moreover, there was no response by the OAU to the overthrow of Lissouba and so far only a condemnation of the coup in Côte d'Ivoire.[184]

The analysis and proposals in this paper seek to contribute to the discussion on how the OAU can deal with the overthrow of constitutional regimes. For the OAU to be a meaningful institution that contributes to political stability and development in Africa, and thus help to arrest the progressively debilitating conditions on the continent, it must be an engine of democracy on the continent. It can be that engine if it adheres to and constructively reinforces its emerging position on the recognition of governments.

182. *See Côte D'Ivoire: Is it Africa's 'Good Coup'?*, NEW AFR., Feb. 2000, at 10 (commentating on the OAU's reaction to the coup in Côte D'Ivoire after making the recent announcement of outlawing all coups); *see also Côte D'Ivoire: Ecowas' Somersault,* NEW AFR., Feb. 2000, at 13 (reporting on ECOWAS' justifications in its failure to act as it had done in Sierra Leone in 1997 on the grounds that forcibly reinstating the government would have been unpopular with Ivorians).

183. *See Banjul, Gambia,* W. AFR., Jan. 24, 2000, at 37 (describing efforts of the Gambia government to squash a planned coup by the Gambia state guards).

184. *See supra* note 182.

[14]

Good Governance and Aid Effectiveness: The World Bank and Conditionality

CARLOS SANTISO
Paul H. Nitze School of Advanced International Studies
Johns Hopkins University

Prompted by concerns over the effectiveness of aid, the World Bank has significantly stretched its policy frontiers by endorsing "good governance" as a core element of its development strategy. Governance, which captures the manner in which power is exercised in the management of a country's economic and social resources for development, is a multifaceted concept. Limited by its restrictive mandate and institutional ethos, the Bank has adopted a restrictive approach, confining itself to the economic dimensions of governance. While democracy tends to refer to the legitimacy of government, good governance refers to the effectiveness of government. This article assesses the Bank's approach for promoting good governance in developing countries. It argues that the quality of governance is ultimately attributable to its democratic content. Neither democracy nor good governance is sustainable without the other. Therefore, for the Bank to substantially improve good governance in developing countries, it needs to explicitly address issues of power, politics and democracy. The article further argues that aid conditionality is not the most appropriate approach to strengthen good governance in developing countries. What is needed is a more radical approach in which donors cede control to the recipient country, within the framework of agreed-upon objectives.

Introduction: Good Governance and Development Assistance

"Justice without strength is helpless, strength without justice is tyrannical. Unable to make what is just strong, we have made what is strong just." –Pascal, *Pensées* (1670)

Aid strategies are undergoing fundamental reassessment. In recent years, the strengthening of good governance in developing countries has become both an *objective* of and a *condition* for development assistance. However, combining these two aims in aid policies represents a daunting challenge for development institutions.

This article sets out to examine the World Bank's efforts at strengthening good governance in developing countries and improving the effectiveness of aid. It focuses on the relationship

AUTHOR'S NOTE: Earlier versions of this paper were presented at a World Bank conference on development economics (ABCDE) in Paris in June 2000 and at a summer workshop of the Academic Council of the United Nations System (ACUNS) in Warwick, United Kingdom, in August 2000. The author gratefully acknowledges the support and assistance of Anja Linder, John Williamson, Arne Dish, Morten Bøås, Jan Aart Scholte, Monique Bergeron, Massimo Tomassoli, and the editorial staff of The Georgetown Public Policy Review, particularly Brian Harrigan and Mwihaki Kimura.

between good governance and aid effectiveness in providing a critical assessment of the Bank's approach to governance reform in developing countries. This paper scrutinizes the shifts in policies and strategies of the Bank during the 1990s as well as the research it generated to support them.

The wide array of issues under "governance" occupies center stage in the development debate and the agenda of the international financial institutions (IFIs). The concept of governance captures "the manner in which power is exercised in the management of a country's economic and social resources for development" (World Bank 1992, 1). Devesh Kapur and Richard Webb attest: "For the IFIs, the new mandate is a boost to their importance, but one fraught with peril. The new mission arrived at a moment when growing doubts regarding the purpose and effectiveness of the IFIs seemed to threaten their funding, and even their continued existence" (2000, 18).

However, the approaches used to strengthen good governance in developing countries remain strikingly similar to those used to promote economic reform. Aid conditionality, i.e. conditioning aid on a number of prerequisites and promises of reform, has been extended from the economic realm to the political arena. During the 1980s and 1990s, the scope of these conditionalities both widened and deepened as IFIs attempted governmental and social re-engineering.

The Bank has significantly stretched its policy frontiers by endorsing "good governance" as a core element of its development strategy. Since 1996 the Bank has begun more than 600 governance related programs and initiatives in 95 countries and is involved in supporting significant programs of governance and public sector reform in 50 countries (Development Committee 2000). Some argue the new governance agenda is a smorgasbord of economic and political prescriptions for development and a "fig leaf" hiding renewed conditionalities. Nevertheless, introducing the concept of good governance has resulted in a broadened understanding of development and has significantly altered the agenda of IFIs. More fundamentally, it has affected what they do and how they do it. In "The World Bank at the Millennium," former Bank chief economist Joseph Stiglitz asserts: "Views about development have changed in the World Bank, as they have in the development community. Today there is concern about broader objectives, entailing more instruments, than was the case earlier" (1999, F587).

The introduction of the concept of governance in the development agenda reflects growing concerns over the effectiveness of aid whose ultimate aim is to reduce poverty and human suffering. Confronted with declining aid budgets and increased scrutiny by civil society, the Bank has given greater consideration to the pervasive effects of mismanagement and endemic corruption. Furthermore, the Bank's involvement in governance work has also upset the traditional division of labor between the United Nations (UN) agencies and the IFIs, questioning their respective roles in global governance. This has resulted in considerable encroachment on other organizations' traditional institutional territory (a trend commonly referred to as "mission creep"). The reform of multilateral development finance is thus an integral component of current efforts at reforming the international financial architecture.

The governance agenda promoted by the Bank represents an ambivalent enterprise plagued with both promises and dilemmas. Reforming the systems of governance is a politically sensitive endeavor that has traditionally been considered outside its core mandate. The Bank's founding charter prohibits it from taking into account political considerations when designing aid programs. A remnant of the bipolar confrontation of the Cold War, this legal restriction is antiquated and should be revised.

Furthermore, the mainstreaming of good governance has been fragmented, leading to multiple understandings of the concept, as it originated within the neo-liberal economic development paradigm. This approach tends to give governance a false sense of political neutrality, as it portrays development without politics. The Bank's understanding of good governance continues to reflect a concern over the effectiveness of the state rather than the equity of the economic system and the legitimacy of the power structure.

Openly criticized by nongovernmental organizations (NGOs), its main stakeholder the United States and its most respected economists, the Bank is at a critical juncture in its history. It plays a central role in global governance, and its leverage in the aid regime remains important. The Bank has significantly shaped development thinking and "has acquired a quasi-monopoly on institutional knowledge in the field of economic development" (Hiboux 2000, 3). "The Bank does not just lend money and produce ideas: it packages the ideas and the money together," combining lending with conditionality (Gilbert, Powell and Vines 1999, F610). These considerations command a critical look at the Banks' intellectual ethos and modes of operation.

This article argues that the quality of governance is ultimately attributable to its democratic content. Therefore, for the Bank to substantially improve good governance in borrowing countries and reinvent itself, it will need to explicitly address issues of power, politics and democracy. The article further argues that aid conditionality is not the most appropriate approach for strengthening good governance in developing countries. What is needed is a more radical approach in which donors cede control to the recipient country, within the framework of agreed-upon objectives.

Origins of a Controversial Concept

Although the concept of good governance is increasingly being used, its contours remain uncertain. Aid practitioners have not yet been able to articulate a clear and operational definition of the concept. A variety of definitions, greatly differing in scope, rationale and objectives, has been advanced. This multitude of definitions has generated an increasing confusion regarding the boundaries of the concept.

An Innovative Concept

The notion of good governance is relatively new. It surfaced in 1989 in the World Bank's report on Sub-Saharan Africa, which characterized the crisis in the region as a "crisis of governance" (World Bank 1989). It then represented an important departure from previous policy, prompted in large part by the experience in Africa. The main thrust behind its introduction in the Bank's corporate policies resides in the continuing lack of effectiveness of aid, the feeble commitment to reform of recipient governments and the persistence of endemic corruption in developing countries. In addressing governance, the Bank calls into question the ability, capacity and willingness of political authorities to govern effectively in the common interest. There is heightened awareness that the *qual-*

ity of a country's governance system is a key determinant of the ability to pursue sustainable economic and social development.

According to the Bank's own definition, governance encompasses the form of political regime; the process by which authority is exercised in the management of a country's economic and social resources for development; and the capacity of governments to design, formulate and implement policies and discharge functions (World Bank 1991 1992 1994; World Bank 2000a). However, while recognizing the importance of the political dimensions of governance, the Bank interprets the concept restrictively, arguing that the first aspect–whether a government is democratic or not–falls outside its mandate. As a result, it focuses on the economic dimensions of good governance, which has been equated with "sound development management."[1] Consequently, the main thrust of governance-related activities has been public sector management, financial management, the modernization of public administration and the privatization of state-owned enterprises.

However, the shift from the notion of governance to *good* governance introduces a normative dimension. A good governance system puts further requirements on the process of decisionmaking and public policy formulation. It extends beyond the capacity of the public sector to the rules that create a legitimate, effective and efficient framework for the conduct of public policy. It implies managing public affairs in a transparent, accountable, participatory and equitable manner. It entails effective participation in public policymaking, the prevalence of the rule of law and an independent judiciary, institutional checks and balances through horizontal and vertical separation of powers, and effective oversight agencies. Researchers at the World Bank Institute have distinguished six main dimensions of good governance:

- Voice and accountability, which includes civil liberties and political stability;
- Government effectiveness, which includes the quality of policymaking and public service delivery;
- The lack of regulatory burden;
- The rule of law, which includes protection of property rights;
- Independence of the judiciary; and
- Control of corruption.

(Kaufmann, Kraay and Zoido-Lobaton 1999)

There are understandable justifications for such a restraint. The pressure by donor governments to address endemic corruption, bureaucratic ineptness and economic mismanagement had to be accommodated by the Bank. Framing governance as a technical question has permitted the Bank to justify its involvement in governance issues while remaining within the boundaries of its mandate. Conceptualizing governance in functional terms has enabled the Bank to address governance failures in developing countries and smooth resistance from its varied constituency. Nevertheless, this compromise has been fragile and constantly questioned in the course of the 1990s, either as inadequate or unacceptable.

Limits of Technocratic Consensus

There are limits to what Morten Bøås calls the "technocratic consensus." "Governance is a difficult concept for the multilateral development banks that do not want to be seen as political and have always advocated a doctrine of political neutrality. They have embraced the functionalist logic that technical and economic questions can be separated from politics" (2001, 2). The functionalist approach gives the illusion that technical solutions can solve political problems: "Politics is treated as a negative input into policy decision-making" (Grindle 2001, 370), as the politics of self-interest and rent-seeking negatively distort policy choices. This approach echoes the consensus of rational choice theory according to which policy is created in a fairly orderly sequence of stages. However, this model fails to capture "the essence of policy making in political communities: the struggle over ideas" (Stone 1989, 7). It circumvents politics by negating it.

For economists who dominate the Bank's ethos, policy is essentially a sphere of rational analysis, whereas politics is the sphere of irrational analysis. Their approach to governance is thus aimed at extricating policy from politics, assuming that analysis and politics can be separated in the process of public policymaking. This continues to guide the Bank's approach to governance reform. Political contexts offer both constraints and opportunities for change. Indeed, the shortcomings of the market-oriented economic reforms of the late 1980s and 1990s reside in their insufficient consideration of the political economy of policy reform.

Despite its legal limitations, the Bank struggles to separate the economic and political aspects of good governance. This tension surfaced as early as 1991 when the Bank recognized that the reasons for underdevelopment and mismanaged government are "sometimes attributable to weak institutions, lack of an adequate legal framework, damaging discretionary interventions, uncertain and variable policy frameworks and a closed decision-making process which increases risks of corruption and waste" (World Bank 1991, i). These concerns do not refer only to the soundness of economic management but also to the overall quality of the political system and ultimately to the nature of the political regime. A similar tension between the economic and political dimensions of good governance can be found in the International Monetary Fund (IMF 1997; James 1998).

As Moises Naím asserts, the IFIs "have to reconcile their political character with their technical vocation"(1994, 4). The inherent tension between the economic and political dimensions of good governance appears to be the most contentious conceptual issue. While democracy tends to refer to the *legitimacy* of government, good governance refers to its *effectiveness*. Consequently, one could in theory be strengthened and promoted independently from the other, as each has value in its own right. Nevertheless, as the legitimacy and effectiveness of government are not always congruent in reality, the relationship between democracy and good governance is laden with controversy. There are still no clear or settled ideas about how effective governance and democratic consolidation should be suitably defined, let alone how they could be supported from abroad. Good governance, although theoretically distinct from democracy, often substantially overlaps with it in practice. Incorporating the promotion of democracy and the strengthening of good governance in aid policies is a permanent challenge and aid agencies have difficulty in advancing these intertwined agendas.

Governance and Economic Development

Recent research on the political

economy of policy reform suggests that the influence of political context on economic performance is paramount. If political systems can be held responsible for slow economic development, it is because of fundamental weaknesses in governance institutions. Institutional economics maintains that economic reform and poverty-reduction strategies will not succeed without effective democratic institutions. David Dollar and Jacob Svensson (1998) found several political and institutional features associated with successful reform programs. They suggest that the success of adjustment loans can largely be predicted by a country's underlying institutional and political features, including whether the government was democratically elected and how long it has been in power. In general, newly elected governments have a higher rate of success with reform than authoritarian governments in power for a long time. The election of a new government opens a window of opportunity enabling it to launch audacious reforms.

Well-institutionalized democracies are more likely to produce, over the long run, effective, efficient and sustainable economic and social policies, because they provide effective and stable institutional and procedural mechanisms to represent interests, arbitrate disputes, provide checks and balances and negotiate change. According to Dani Rodrik (2000), political institutions matter for economic development because of the propensity of democracies to moderate social conflict and induce compromise. Jonathan Isham, Daniel Kaufman and Lant Pritchett (1997) find that effective citizen voice and public accountability often lead to greater efficacy in government action and a more efficient allocation of resources. More fundamentally, open governance systems are more likely to generate responsible and responsive government and thus adopt public policies that favor the poor. Daniel Kaufmann, Aart Kraay and Pablo Zoido-Lobaton (1999) show that these various aspects of good governance are significantly associated with income levels in the expected manner. *Effective* democratic institutions, rather than their mere formal existence, are key.

The quality of democratic institutions determines the ability of governments to respond to financial crises. Examining the response of Southeast Asian countries to the 1997 financial crisis, Rodrik argues: "Adjustment to shocks will tend to be worse in countries with deep latent social conflicts and with poor institutions of conflict management" (1999, 28). Indeed, democratic institutions provide mechanisms of regulation to ease out economic crises and respond to them more effectively. Elections provide a mechanism for rebuilding the legitimacy and authority of government, and consequently the credibility of the economic reforms needed to address the financial crisis.

The comparison between South Korea and Indonesia from 1997 to1999 is particularly striking. As Stephan Haggard argues, political factors are crucial to understanding the East Asian crisis and the different ways in which democracies and authoritarian regimes responded to it. Unlike Indonesia under the authoritarian rule of President Suharto, South Korea was able to use the elections of December 1997 to restore confidence in government and lend credibility to structural reforms. The events of late 1997 exposed the structural weaknesses of authoritarian rule in Indonesia, ultimately leading to the breakdown of the regime and collapse of the country. In South Korea, a new reform-oriented government came into office, and Kim Dae Jung was able to initiate important policy reforms and spur recovery.

The quality of democratic institutions is also believed to influence the effectiveness of aid by providing accountability mechanisms in the management of external resources. In a recent study, Svensson finds that "in the long-run growth impact of aid is conditional on the degree of political and civil liberties in the recipient country. Aid has a positive impact on growth in countries with institutionalized and well functioning checks on governmental power" (1999, 275).

Conditionality and Aid Effectiveness

The Failure of Conditionality

The Bank's use of traditional approaches to strengthen good governance in developing countries is misguided. The introduction of governance concerns in aid policies resulted from the failure of past strategies to promote specific policies and induce policy changes in developing countries. In particular, the notion and practice of conditionality have spawned an intense controversy. Tony Killick defines aid conditionality as "a mutual arrangement by which a government takes, or promises to take, certain policy actions, in support of which an international financial institution or other agency will provide specified amounts of financial assistance" (1998, 6). This represents an attempt by donors to use aid as an incentive for reforming the policies and institutions of developing countries.[2]

The Bank's policy-based lending and structural adjustment programs include a wide array of policy and structural conditions. Aid without some sort of conditionality is unthinkable and politically impossible, as donor governments must account for the use of their taxpayers' money. Nevertheless, while the principle of conditionality has some legitimizing arguments, it is open to criticism as to the way it is applied and its ultimate effectiveness in achieving its intended objectives. Reviewing the experience in Southeast Asia and Latin America with structural adjustment lending, Killick (1998) demonstrates the inability of conditionality to act as a credible mechanism to induce policy reform.

The failure of conditionality to attain its desired objectives and bring about sustained policy reforms is widely recognized. Catherine Gwin and Joan Nelson (1997) argue that "aid is only effective in promoting growth in a good policy environment, and on the whole, it has not succeeded in leveraging good policies." Killick dismisses the belief that aid tied to conditionality can buy better policies, at least in a sustainable way, or anchor sound governance institutions. The failings of conditionality reside in its inability "to create an incentive system sufficient to induce recipient governments to implement policy reforms they otherwise would not undertake, or would undertake more gradually" (Killick 1998, 163). In the general case, conditionality is not a credible commitment mechanism.

Conditionality cannot substitute or circumvent domestic ownership of and commitment to reform. Evaluating aid conditionality in the African context, Paul Collier, director of research at the World Bank, asserts: "The IFIs have radically overestimated their own power in attempting to induce reform in very poor policy environments. They have, in effect, ignored domestic politics" (1999, 325-326). Furthermore, the fungibility argument questions the extent to which policy-based lending can contribute to its intended objectives. Aid is said to be fungible because the marginal increase in public expenditure in response to an aid inflow is not the expenditure toward which the aid was targeted. Aid tends to free-up resources (World Bank 1998). As a result, it becomes critical to assess and influence the quality of overall government spending, rather than focus on sectoral spending. The Bank now regularly conducts public expenditure reviews (PER).

Overall, aid agencies have had limited influence on the decisions to embark on economic reforms and their successful implementation. Indeed, a study by Paul Mosley, Jane Harrigan and John Toye (1991) finds no clear association between the intensity of conditionality and success in implementation of promised reforms. In order to alleviate the "credibility problem," Collier (1999) argues the IFIs must radically redesign their lending policies, revisit their traditional assumptions and adopt a more selective approach rewarding good behavior and performance.

Conditionality has had perverse effects. It undermines the domestic democratic processes by supplanting public policymaking. Collier warns against the abuse of conditionality: "The extension of the practice of conditionality from the occasional circumstances of crisis management to the continuous process of general economic policy-making has implied a transfer of sovereignty which is not only unprecedented but is often dysfunctional" (1999,319).

The Centrality of Ownership

Using conditionality to induce governance reform results in a fundamental paradox. It tends to make improvements in governance *both* a condition and a goal of development aid. Since these dual objectives can hardly be met in practice, the tension becomes a contradiction in operational terms. Furthermore, governance-related conditionality is confronted with the traditional dilemma of external assistance: loans or grants will not yield the desired results unless the recipients are credibly committed to reform. External support to policy change has all too often failed to offset a lack of local commitment and ownership of reform. The use of financial leverage is not a substitute for weak domestic institutions or feeble political will. Some Bank researchers suggest that aid dependence can even undermine the quality of governance. For instance, Stephen Knack (2000) finds that over the period 1982 to 1995, aid has been associated with an increase in corruption, deterioration in the quality of the bureaucracy and a weakening of the rule of law. Without going to such extremes, it appears clear that aid policies are in dire need of reform.

Ownership of and commitment to economic and political reform have progressively been identified as major determinants of aid effectiveness. Miles Kahler (1992) shows a positive association between government commitment to reform and program implementation: in nine out of 16 programs with high implementation levels prior government commitment to reform was strong; in eight of 11 poorly executed programs government commitment was low. Broadly, external agencies were less important than domestic political forces in determining the timing and scope of adjustment decisions. Conditionality tends to undermine countries' ownership of the reforms and delay their implementation. However, while it is now widely recognized that ownership matters for development and aid effectiveness, fostering a sense of partnership remains an elusive quest.

Toward Greater Selectivity

It is now believed that the effect of aid on growth tends to increase with the quality of policy. As a consequence, aid would be more effective if it were either more systematically targeted to poor countries with sound economic reform programs or used to promote good policies. The influential research by World Bank economists Craig Burnside and David Dollar (1997, 1998) on the impact of aid, policy and growth shows that aid has been highly successful in reducing poverty and promoting growth in countries with sound economic management and robust government institutions. These authors found no evidence that the amount of aid systematically affected policy. This finding is substantiated by a recent case study on Sub Saharan African countries (Devarajan, Dollar and Holgren 2001), which shows that aid cannot buy reform and that the conditionality attached to adjustment loans did not successfully induce policy change. However, when reforms have been initiated, foreign assistance helped accompany reform and assuaged the social costs of adjustment. For example, in Ghana, balance of payment support provided the government with the breathing space it required to contain domestic opposition to market-based reforms.

Furthermore, the pervasive effects of corruption on economic management and aid effectiveness have been a major source of concern for the Bank since the early 1990s, as foreign finance tends to become a source of rents. "Aid allocation needs to take corruption into account because, even if aid cannot significantly reduce corruption, corruption can significantly impair aid effectiveness" (Collier and Dollar 2001, 21).

The Bank's 1998 report *Assessing Aid: What Works, What Doesn't and Why* recommends a more systematic targeting of aid to poor countries with sound policies and effective institutions. The objective of this system is to increase the effectiveness of aid by concentrating it on those countries showing a genuine commitment to improving governance.This strategy creates a performance-based allocation system that links the allocation of aid to the government's success in promoting sustainable development and reducing poverty.It encourages the aid community to link aid to performance and not to promises.

As a result, aid is increasingly being determined not only by the objective needs of the recipient country but also by its performance in implementing reforms. As Anne Krueger, former Bank vice president and current deputy managing director of the IMF, points out: "For the World Bank, it will need to differentiate carefully between countries where reforms are serious and stand a reasonable prospect of success and those in which window dressing is used as a means of seeking additional funding" (Krueger 1998, 31).

The Bank has amended its operational guidelines to give good governance greater importance in adjustment and investment lending operations (Santiso 2000). The Bank's Country Assistance Strategies and the World Bank/IMF Poverty Reduction Strategy Papers (PRSP) now integrate considerations regarding the quality of governance, and since 1999 the Bank has been conducting Institutional and Governance Reviews. Similarly, the 12th replenishment of International Development Association (IDA) resources has introduced a performance-based allocation system. IDA, which provides highly concessional resources to low-income countries to address poverty, amended its guidelines to better assess governance reform in recipient countries. Aid allocations now take into account the efforts made to improve governance. The joint World Bank/IMF Highly Indebted Poor Country Initiative (HIPC) is aimed at relieving the debt burden of least developed countries and links debt relief to policy reform.

Donor governments have been instrumental in advocating greater selectivity. Regime features are increasingly used as criteria for selecting the main recipients of aid as well as the scope and amount of the assistance provided through bilateral aid. Donors have significantly influenced Bank lending, in particular its IDA component, which greatly depends on grants from donor governments.

The Pitfalls of Selectivity

The practice of selectivity has often contradicted the evidence, suggesting that political considerations remain important in determining aid flows, especially for large donors and multilateral institutions. Research on aid policy has found that there is no direct relationship between development aid flows and policy reform (Burnside and Dollar, 1997). In general, donors have not effectively tailored their assistance to the specific country and phase of the reform process (Devarajan, Dollar and Holgren, 2001). Better policies and improving performance all too often lead to decreasing levels of development aid (Collier and Dollar, 1998), sending the wrong signal. These researchers argue good performance should not become a pretext for a reduction of development aid.

Aid selectivity is subject to a number of pitfalls. 1) Despite these research findings, the use of conditionality has expanded in scope and depth in the course of the 1990s. As the IMF itself recognizes, both the share of programs with structural conditions and the average number of conditions per program have increased significantly during the past decade: from 1989 to 1999, the share of programs with structural conditions increased from 60 percent to 100 percent and the average number of structural conditions per program increased from three to 12. Figures 1 and 2 summarize the burden of conditionality.

Most governance-related conditionalities are related to transparency and accountability issues in the fiscal sector (IMF, 2001c). However, quantitative measures of conditionality are rendered difficult by the ambiguity of the concept. Using a broader definition of conditionality, Kapur and Webb note that, "even if conditionality is interpreted narrowly, its burden on borrowers has grown significantly. The average number of criteria for a sample of 25 countries having a program with the IMF in 1999, with programs initiated between 1997 and 1999, is 26. This compares to about six in the 1970s and ten in the 1980s" (2000, 4). For example, the 1997 IMF program for Indonesia contained 81 conditions, of which 48 were governance related. As Table 1 shows, governance-related conditionalities represent the bulk of the conditions imposed by the IFIs. The question then becomes whether poor countries have the capacity to simultaneously manage a wide variety of reforms, some of which have dubious urgency. As a result, upon assuming office in 2000, the IMF's managing director, Hans Köhler, launched an effort to streamline and focus structural conditionality (IMF 2000).

2) Selectivity is difficult to implement in practice, as high levels of poverty are often associated with weak governance. Reducing poverty remains the core mission of the Bank. It is extremely difficult to devise and apply consistent and even-handed

Figure 1: Share of Programs with Structural Conditions (1989-1999)

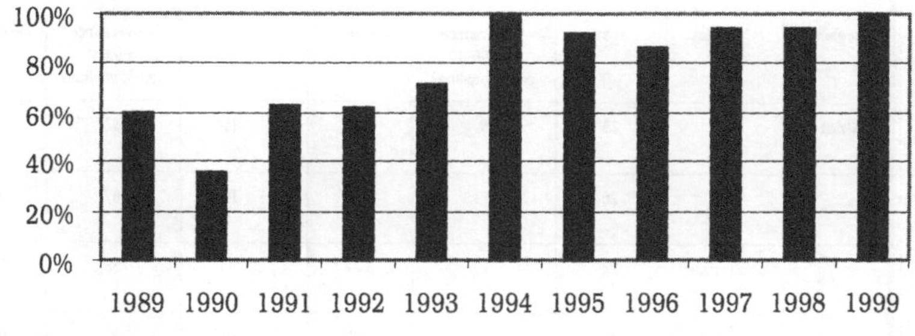

Source: IMF 2001a, 25

Figure 2: Average Number of Structural Conditions (per program per year, 1989-1999)

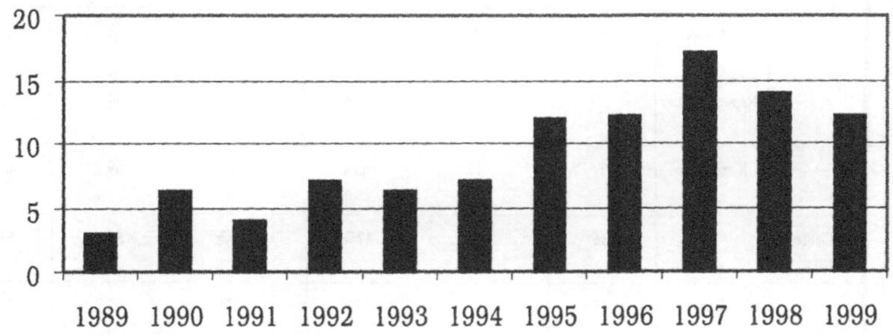

Source: IMF 2001b, 10

criteria to measure country performance in terms of governance. In reality, few countries exist that can be classified as either good or bad performers. Most lie somewhere in between. Individual country circumstances make judgmental approaches inescapable. Furthermore, why good policies come about in one country and not in another remains a mystery. Poor performance is not always voluntary but may be caused by a wide variety of factors affecting a developing country's capacity to implement reforms. This form of ex-post conditionality should not penalize least developed countries by concentrating aid exclusively on good performers, most of which are middle-income countries. The poor in poorly performing countries already have to bear the burden of inept governments and authoritarian regimes.

3) The underlying analysis and consequent policy conclusions of Bank research have not gone unchallenged. The effectiveness of aid on policy reform and on economic growth and poverty reduction are two distinct things. While aid might be ineffective

12 The Georgetown Public Policy Review, 7:1 (Fall 2001)

Table 1. Examples of the Burden of Conditionality

		Conditionality Strictly Defined				Conditionality Loosely Defined		
Region	**Countries**	**Total**	**Governance related conditionalities**	**Percentage**		**Total**	**Governance related conditionalities**	**Percentage**
Africa		**23**	**9**	**39%**		**114**	**82**	**72%**
	Mali	26	13	50%		105	67	64%
	Mozambique	22	12	55%		74	58	78%
	Senegal	27	9	33%		165	99	60%
	Zambia	18	6	33%		87	59	68%
Asia		**17**	**4**	**24%**		**84**	**49**	**58%**
	Cambodia	30	9	30%		83	65	78%
	Indonesia	18	8	44%		81	48	59%
	Rep. of Korea	10	4	40%		114	44	39%
	Kazakhstan	27	17	63%		114	69	61%
East/Central Europe		**36**	**24**	**67%**		**93**	**55**	**59%**
	Albania	43	33	77%		72	47	65%
	Latvia	28	20	71%		65	28	43%
	Romania	43	25	58%		82	34	41%
Latin America		**33**	**13**	**39%**		**78**	**41**	**53%**
	Brazil	38	21	55%		89	45	51%
	Bolivia	32	21	66%		95	44	46%
	Nicaragua	29	18	62%		50	34	68%

Source: Kapur and Webb 2000, 5-7

*Note: Data for the continents represent the average of all of the countries in the continent, not just the independently referenced countries. For example, the Africa total includes more data than just that shown for Mali, Mozambique, Senagal and Zambia.

in inducing and sustaining policy reform, it is effective in stimulating growth. Recent research discussed at a seminar of the Organization for Economic Cooperation and Development (OECD) in January 2001 shows that there may be a positive relationship between aid and growth even in countries hampered by an unfavorable policy environment (Hansen and Tarp 2000a,b). Aid can affect poverty through channels other than economic growth by increasing aggregate savings and investment. "Growth is not the only route to poverty reduction, nor is growth the only benefit of aid" (Beynon 2001, 2). This research argues that the performance-based aid reallocation system implied in *Assessing Aid* is an unreliable guide to policy. It suggests that the latest fad in development thinking–aid selectivity–has created a dangerous exaggeration, that aid *only* works in an environment of sound policy (Beynon, 2001).

4) There remain many contested areas of debate. "Using past performance as an indicator of future performance is especially dubious in this environment, given the existing limited understanding of the interplay between aid, macroeconomic policy and political economy variables. In sum, the unresolved issue in assessing aid effectiveness is not whether aid works, but how and whether we can make the different kinds of aid instruments at hand work better in varying country circumstances" (Hansen and Tarp 2000b, 22). Concentrating aid on "good performing" poor countries begs the original concern that spurred the current shift in policies: how can external agencies *promote* development in poor performing countries? How can external agencies deal with poor performers and unreliable governments headed by despotic rulers that repeatedly renege on their commitments? How can these agencies deal with Afghanistan, Kenya, Zimbabwe, Nicaragua, Kyrgyzstan or Belarus? Aid selectivity experts also remain silent on how to improve policies, institutions and governance in poorly performing countries and how to support large numbers of poor people in middle-income countries such as China, India, Mexico or Brazil (Beynon 2001). The policies of aid selectivity circumvent these questions by pushing them aside.

Furthermore, the elegance of the approach masks an important caveat, namely that aid works in a "sound policy environment" which has largely been defined in the context of the neoliberal economic policy model. The proxy for assessing the quality of economic policies and institutional settings is derived from the Bank's own Country Policy and Institutional Assessment which is composed of 20 components that are grouped into the following categories: macroeconomic policies, structural policies, public sector management and social inclusion.

The debate on aid effectiveness is likely to remain imbued with controversy. Pragmatic observers argue that the adoption of performance-based aid allocation policies merely constitutes an *a posteriori* justification for *de facto* cuts in aid budgets, which had reached dangerously low levels by the end of the 1990s. Nevertheless, the fact that aid works *better* in good policy environments appears undisputed (Tarp 2000).

Beyond the Washington Consensus

The recognition of the centrality of good governance introduces important innovations to the global aid regime. It compels the development community to revisit the economic orthodoxy of the "Washington consensus" that has dominated economic development thinking since the 1980s. The consensus' policy prescriptions include opening trade, fiscal restraint, prudent macroeconomic management, deregulation and privatization (Williamson 1990). They advocate significantly reducing the size and prerogatives of the state. These views have informed political conditionalities imposed on developing countries, through policy-based lending.

The governance agenda challenges the conceptual foundations of the Washington consensus in a number of ways. Its emergence has given rise to what some analysts describe as a "post-Washington consensus" (Burki and Perry 1998).

Recognizing the Role of Politics

An important dimension of the post-Washington consensus is the recognition that politics matters for development. It suggests that sustaining development requires reforming not only the policies but also the institutional framework in which policies are formulated. It has become apparent that effective democratic institutions are urgently needed to complement macroeconomic policy changes, provide safety nets and assuage the adverse social consequences of structural adjustment programs.

Effective reform requires building the capacity to pursue it. However, as Gerald Caiden points out, "Countries most in need of state reform are least able to implement it" (1994, 111). Developing countries must strengthen their effective capacity to govern. As a consequence, the issue of state capacity and autonomy is being revisited in the context of market reform and democratic consolidation.

There is increasing recognition that consolidating democracy beyond elections and sustaining economic reform beyond structural adjustment requires strengthening the institutions of governance, enhancing the rule of law and enhancing accountability and transparency. Because the Bank realizes that getting the macroeconomic fundamentals right is not enough, it is gradually reforming institutions and in some instances political systems. Between 1987 and 1998, the Bank financed 169 civil service reform programs in 80 countries. Since the early 1990s, it has supported legal and judicial reform and decentralization programs around the developing world. In 1996, the fight against corruption became a priority, and the Bank began supporting programs aimed at strengthening other accountability institutions such as ombudspersons and parliamentary oversight bodies (World Bank 2000b).[3]

Reforming the State

Another important dimension of the post-Washington consensus concerns the state. This view holds that changes in the institutions and modes of governance are required to sustain market reforms and to consolidate democracy *simultaneously*. A major thrust of the structural adjustment programs of the 1980s and 1990s has focused on balancing public finances and reducing the size of the bureaucracy. However, while "first generation" economic reforms aim to stabilize and liberalize the economy, "second generation" economic reforms seek to deepen the economy by reforming the state and strengthening governing institutions (Naím 1995).

These second generation reforms entail improving the efficiency and effectiveness of governing institutions (in particular the judiciary and parliaments), developing sound financial markets with appropriate regulations and supervision, enhancing legal and regulatory environments, improving the quality of the public sector and building social capital and cohesion.

This stage requires structural changes within the political institutions in charge of economic policy formulation, implementation and oversight. The *World Development Report* has focused on the changing role of the state and marked a stepping-stone in the mainstreaming of good governance. It revealed that many of the difficulties facing developing countries stem not from excessive executive power but from institutionally weak states.

The first requisite for both sustainable development and democracy is an effective state governed by the rule of law. During the 1990s, the international donor community tended to avoid the state, circumventing it by strengthening non-state actors and promoting decentralization and local governance.

For good governance to be enhanced, the state must be strengthened. Experience shows that shrinking the state's prerogatives and capacities may have perverse effects, causing a dramatic reduction in public service delivery and eroding the authority of government. While the state is expected to withdraw from policy interventions and become leaner, the transition usually requires both nimble and robust political institutions that can implement and enforce policy reform and a responsive bureaucracy.

The recognition of the crucial role of the state in economic management and in the regulation and supervision of financial markets has conferred acute significance on the strengthening of good governance. Markets require a legal and regulatory framework that only governments can provide, appropriate legal and financial institutions and regulations ensuring competition and contract enforcement, the guarantee of property rights, the assurance of sound financial and banking regulations and the establishment of oversight bodies and regulatory agencies.

Strengthening Public Institutions

The post-Washington consensus also relates to the need to strengthen governing institutions, defined as "formal and informal rules and their enforcement mechanisms that shape the behavior of individuals and organizations in society" (Burki and Perry 1998, 11). More fundamentally, good governance entails altering the incentive structure in which people operate. The need for institutional reform has been neglected in the practice of policy reform. The Washington consensus policies often disregarded the analysis of institutions and failed to assess how state institutions can be reformed effectively to make public policies more responsive to people's needs. The post-Washington consensus focuses on improving public sector institutions and the performance of public policies. Problems of governance involve fundamental institutional weaknesses combined with inappropriate policies and un-enforced legal frameworks.

While the importance of institutions is now widely recognized, definite approaches on how to devise and implement institutional reform are sorely lacking. How do institutions emerge, develop and consolidate? How do they change? Rodrik (1999) argues that the question should be "which institutions matter and how to acquire them?" Consensus on this subject remains elusive when the discussion moves from general goals to the specific means of achieving them. The lack of clear prescriptions for the successful implementation of institutional reform leads to a politically difficult agenda. Institutional reform is indeed the subject of the recent *World Development Report 2002: Building Insti-*

tutions for Markets.

However, while the governance agenda amends the dominant neo-liberal economic policy model, it does not repudiate it. Market reform thus remains a precondition for institutional reform (Williamson 1999; Naím 2000). The IFIs tend to view sustaining economic reform and anchoring the market-based strategies as the ultimate objectives of governance and institutional reform. Indeed, almost all statements about the policy priorities of the post-Washington consensus include a strong preface clarifying that sound macroeconomic fundamentals are indispensable. Sound macroeconomic policy has thus progressively become not only an objective, but also a precondition for sustainable development. Certainly, as the reform agenda broadens, it is also becoming more complex. "The difficult paradox, is that any country that is capable of meeting such stringent requirements is already a developed country" (Naím 2000, 9).

A Return to Democratic Institutions

Even in the narrow economic sense, good governance puts further requirements on the process of public policy formulation and implementation. Good governance requires an efficient executive, a functioning legislature, an independent judiciary and the effective balance and separation of powers, all constituent elements of a democratic regime. Consequently, good governance is not sustainable without *effective* democratic institutions.

Strengthening Accountability

At the core of the governance agenda is the fight against corruption and the corresponding need to enhance accountability and strengthen transparency in public policymaking. Indeed, the fight against corruption, which was formally integrated into the Bank's mandate in 1996, constitutes the core of the governance agenda that has been forcefully advocated by World Bank President James Wolfensohn. Agencies of restraint anchored in core state institutions such as autonomous oversight bodies and independent judiciaries are vital foundations for effective anti-corruption strategies. Although the Bank emphasizes financial accountability, strengthening accountability entails a systemic reform of the state and modes of governance (administrative, parliamentary, legislative and judicial reform). In particular, enforcing political accountability requires strengthening the mechanisms both of "vertical accountability" (between the governed and the governing through periodic and fair elections) and "horizontal accountability" (between the different branches of government, including executive-legislative relations and an independent judiciary). It entails the effective independence of state powers and the existence of institutionalized checks and balances, as found in pluralist democracies. It also requires the depoliticization of public administration and the existence of an effective opposition enabling the parliament to control the executive and enact legislation that is credible and impartial.

Enhancing the Rule of Law

Rule-based, predictable legal regimes are of the utmost importance in the new market order. As a consequence, the strengthening of the rule of law constitutes a central element of the Bank's strategies to fight rampant corruption. Legal and judicial reforms have become core components of the Bank's governance portfolio, which is primarily motivated by the Bank's concern with the regulation of economic activity and private sector development. It thus focuses mainly on ensuring the stability and predictability of the legal framework, focusing on private law to secure property rights and enforce contracts. However, the reliability of the rule of law is determined by the political context. A judiciary independent of executive meddling is vital to ensure that the legislative and executive branches remain accountable under the law and to interpret and enforce the terms of the consitution.

Enhancing good governance entails ensuring the effective separation of powers. It thus requires addressing the factors underpinning the political independence of the judiciary, guaranteeing the impartial administration of justice and reducing "the opportunities for corruption by cutting back on discretionary authority" (World Bank 1997, 8).

Promoting Participation

Good governance also concerns facilitating effective participation. Originally, the Bank conceptualized participation in the narrow perspective of the effectiveness of the projects it supports (Isham, Narayan and Pritchett 1995). However, the consideration of local ownership of development projects subsequently led the Bank to broaden its approach and address the central issue of participation in public policymaking. Participation helps to build coalitions supporting policy reform, while the involvement of civil society helps build social capital. Restricting participation in policymaking often weakens the legitimacy, accountability and the quality of decisions made. The Comprehensive Development Framework, introduced in the Bank's corporate policies in 1999 by Wolfensohn, reflects the recognition of the importance of effective participation for sustainable development. *The World Development Report of 2000/2001: Attacking Poverty* introduces the notion of empowerment as an integral part of development.

Participation and representation are more likely to lead to public policies that are more responsive to the needs of the poor. They require regular, free and fair elections and a genuine choice between alternative government policies. Participation also occurs beyond and between elections. It calls for a continuous consultation in the formulation, monitoring and implementation of public policies in order to reach a sufficient agreement to sustain reform. Effective participation is inextricably linked to the existence of legitimate and representative parliamentary procedures, which are a constituent part of a democratic regime. Participation in the formulation of public policies and representation in the parliament are impossible without a sufficient level of civil liberties and political rights as well as a functioning multiparty system.

Furthermore, the current efforts at reforming and modernizing the state focus on the devolution of power to lower levels of government. Decentralization, which carries the promise of local self-government, has become a major component of the Bank's reform strategies (World Bank 1999).

Some multilateral development banks are already promoting political reform. For example, the Inter-American Development Bank has interpreted its mandate more broadly and adopted a clear political stance (Santiso 2001). The European Bank for Reconstruction and Development (EBRD), created in 1990, is obligated by its founding charter to lend only to multiparty democracies.[4] Ultimately, the approach adopted by each specific multilateral organization depends on its respective constituency rather than its legal framework.

Conclusion: Reforming the Governance of Aid

The time has come again to revisit and amend the Bank's founding charter, its Articles of Agreement. The World Bank has radically changed over the course of the 1990s. The introduction of governance concerns in development assistance signals an increased willingness to take the political dimensions of development into account. These concerns reflect a shift in economic development thinking and lead the IFIs to induce political reform in recipient countries. New policy should focus on state reform by strengthening governance systems and enhancing governing institutions. The modernization of the state, the fight against corruption, the reform of the judiciary, the strengthening of legislatures and the decentralization of government are now integral parts of the Bank's public sector work.

Reform of governance systems in recipient countries should be matched by corresponding reform in the governance of aid and, in particular, the aid delivery system. As Marco Feroni (2000) underlines, reforming foreign aid requires crafting genuine partnerships and processes for reaching agreement on priorities, procedures and reciprocal obligations toward specified objectives. In particular, the governance agenda compels development institutions and aid agencies to link economic assistance and political aid. So far, these two agendas have evolved independently of each other, leading to fragmented aid policies.

Furthermore, there is increasing recognition that international assistance for strengthening good governance can only have limited impact unless the country's society and particularly its leaders have a genuine political commitment to democracy. Traditionally, development assistance has ignored the realities of power and the intricacies of politics. It has relied on technical solutions to address political problems, often adopting a mechanistic application of a standardized package of reform.

This approach faces significant hurdles when applied to the reform of institutions of governance, in particular judicial systems and parliamentary structures. Without addressing the underlying distribution of power, parliaments will likely remain passive and judiciaries dominated by the will of powerful executives. A fundamental lesson learned is that "if donors wish to make a real difference, they will need to focus more explicitly and more rigorously on issues of power, politics and interest groups, [than] they have tried to do in the past – messy and difficult though these things often are" (Riddell 1999, 333). Consequently, the Bank ought to broaden its understanding of good governance by "bringing politics back in" and systematically integrating considerations concerning the quality of government and the nature of the political regimes in its lending practices.

The extent to which good governance has influenced the operations on the ground will likely affect its overall relevance. The renewed emphasis on democracy and good governance raises questions about whether recipient states will have sufficient liberty to articulate their own development strategies and political development models. The governance agenda introduces a tension in the policies of institutions mandated not to meddle in politics, and upsets the traditional division of labor and the economic-political divide of the global aid regime.

Ultimately, the concept of good governance questions the legitimacy of the IFIs as institutions of global governance. As Kapur and Webb rightfully stress: "Well applied, [governance-related conditionality] could help to empower people and nations. But if applied in an ad hoc manner, in response to the short-run foreign policy problems of large shareholders, and with a high degree of discretion rather than commonly agreed rules, the outcome is unlikely to be fair or significantly pro-poor" (2000, 18).

The governance agenda does not only question *what* the Bank does, but more fundamentally *how* it does it. Conditionality is not the appropriate approach to strengthening good governance in developing countries. What is needed is a more radical approach in which external agencies cede developing countries greater control over the use of aid, within the framework of agreed-upon objectives. Reforming the oversight of aid should lead to radically new approaches to development assistance in which donors cede greater control over the use of aid. Genuine development partnerships will most likely enhance the effectiveness of aid and influence the prospects for sustained reform. These development partnerships should, however, be embedded in "pacts for governance reform." They must enshrine the shared political objectives of cooperation, mutual obligations and reciprocal commitments for donors and recipients.[5] Nevertheless, in particularly adverse circumstances, aid is likely to be ineffective and can easily be diverted from its intended purposes. In such situations, a democratic conditionality should be applied. Official aid to the government should be suspended, in order to prevent autocrats from holding on to power and mercilessly exploiting their citizens.

Notes

[1] The Institute on Governance defines governance as "comprising the traditions, institutions and processes that determine how power is exercised, how citizens are given a voice, and how decisions are made on issues of public concern" (http://www.iog.ca/about.html).

[2] Various forms of conditionality exist, including preconditions or prior actions as well as trigger actions, which determine continued access to development financing and the next outstanding installment of credit.

[3] The World Bank's 2000 governance strategy does not envision the Bank becoming involved in some areas of public service reform such as police reform, criminal justice systems (including prosecutorial and prison reform), general parliamentary processes and political governance (including election processes or the structure and financing of political parties) .

[4] The EBRD is the only multilateral development bank to include a commitment to multiparty democracy in its founding charter. However, it has progressively adopted a more conservative approach to the political dimensions of its mandate.

[5] Indeed, it could be argued that such a pact for governance reform, either explicit or implicit, should constitute the bedrock of current debt relief efforts. To ensure that the funds freed by the HIPC of the World Bank and the IMF are most efficiently used, debt relief should be linked to a commitment to strengthen democratic governance.

References

Beynon, J. 2001. *Policy Implications for Aid Allocation of Recent Research on Aid Effectiveness and Selectivity*, paper presented at the joint Development Center and Development Assistance Committee Seminar on Aid Effectiveness, Selectivity and Poor Performers, Paris, OECD, January 17.

Bøås, M. 2001. *Multilateral Development Banks and Sustainable Development· The Limits of Technocratic Consensus*, paper presented at the Annual Meeting of the Academic Council of the United Nations System (ACUNS), Puebla, Mexico, 15-17 June.

______. 1998. "Governance as Multilateral Development Bank Policy: The Cases of the African Development Bank and the Asian Development Bank," *European Journal of Development Research* 10(2): 116-117.

Burki, S.J. and G. Perry. 1998. *Beyond the Washington Consensus. Institutions Matter.* Washington, DC: World Bank.

Burnside, C. and D. Dollar. 1998. *Aid, the Incentive Regime, and Poverty Reduction.* Washington, DC: The World Bank, Policy Research Working Paper 1937.

______. 1997. *Aid, Policies and Growth.* Washington, DC: The World Bank, Policy Research Working Paper 1777.

Caiden, G. 1994. "Administrative Reform," In *Comparative Public Management: Putting US Public Policy and Implementation in Context,* ed. Randall Baker. Westport: Praeger.

Collier, P. 1999. "Learning from Failure: The International Financial Institutions as Agencies of Restraint in Africa," In *The Self-Restraining State: Power and Accountability in New Democracies*, A. Schedler, L. Diamond and M. Plattner. Boulder and London: Lynne Rienner.

Collier, P. and D. Dollar. 2001. *Development Effectiveness: What Have We Learnt?* Washington, DC: World Bank.

______. 1998, October. *Aid Allocation and Poverty Reduction.* Washington, DC: World Bank, Research Paper.

Devarajan, S., D. Dollar and T. Holgren. 2001. *Aid and Reform in Africa: Lessons from Ten Case Studies.* Washington, DC: World Bank.

Development Committee of the World Bank. 2000, September 18. *Note from the President of the World Bank*. Prague, Czech Republic: DC2000-21.

Dollar, D. and J. Svensson. 1998. *What Explains the Success or Failure of Structural Adjustment Programs?* Washington, DC: The World Bank, Policy Research Working Paper 1938.

Easterly, W. 2001. *The Elusive Quest for Growth: Economists' Adventures and Misadventures in the Tropics.* Cambridge, MA: MIT Press.

Ferroni, M. 2000. *Reforming Foreign Aid: The Role of International Public Goods.* The World Bank Operations Evaluation Department, OED Working Paper Series, no.4.

Gilbert, C., A. Powell and D. Vines. 1999. "Positioning the World Bank," *Economic Journal* 109: F-598-633.

Grindle, M. 2001. "In Quest of the Political: The Political Economy of Development Policymaking," In *Frontiers in Development Economics: The Future in Perspective,* eds. G. Meier and J. Sticglitz. New York: Oxford University Press.

Gwin, C. and J. Nelson, eds. 1997. *Perspectives on Aid and Development.* Washington, DC: Overseas Development Council.

Haggard, S. 2000. *The Political Economy of the Asian Financial Crisis.* Washington, DC: Institute for International Economics.

Hansen, H. and F. Tarp. 2000a. *Aid and Growth Regressions*, paper presented at the joint Development Center and Development Assistance Committee Seminar on Aid Effectiveness, Selectivity and Poor Performers. Paris, OECD, 17 January 2001.

______. 2000b. "Aid Effectiveness Disputed," *Journal of International Development* 12(3): 375-398.

Hiboux, B. 2000, February. *The Political Economy of the World Bank's Discourse: from Economic Catechism to Missionary Deeds and Misdeeds.* Paris: Etudes du CERI: 39.

International Monetary Fund. 2001a, February 16. *Structural Conditionality in Fund-Supported Programs–Policy Issues*. Washington, DC: IMF PDRD.

______. 2001b, February 16. *Structural Conditionality in Fund-Supported Program*. Washington, DC: IMF PDRD.

______. 2001c, March 28. *Review of the Fund's Experience in Governance Issues*. Washington, DC: IMF PDRD, March 28.

______. 2000. *Streamlining Structural Conditionality in Fund-Supported Programs. Interim Guidance Note*. Washington, DC: IMF.

______. 1997. IMF, *Good Governance. The IMF's Role*. Washington, DC: IMF.

Isham, J., D. Kaufman and L. Pritchett. 1997. "Civil Liberties, Democracy and the Performance of Government Projects," *The World Bank Economic Review* 11(2): 219-242.

Isham, J., D. Narayan and L. Pritchett. 1995. "Does Participation Improve Performance? Establishing Causality with Subjective Data," *World Bank Economic Review* 9(2).

James, H. 1998. "From Grandmotherliness to Governance: The Evolution of IMF Conditionality," *Finance and Development* 35(4).

Kapur, D. and R. Webb. 2000. *Governance-Related Conditionalities of the International Financial Institutions*. New York and Geneva: UNCTAD, G-24 Discussion Paper Series 6.

Kaufmann, D., A. Kraay and P. Zoido-Lobaton. 1999, October. *Governance Matters*. Washington: The World Bank, Policy Research Working Paper 2196.

Killick, T. 1998. *Aid and the Political Economy of Policy Change*. London: Overseas Development Institute.

Knack, S. 2000. *Aid Dependence and the Quality of Governance: A Cross-Country Empirical Analysis*. Washington, DC: World Bank, Policy Research Working Paper 2396.

Krueger, A. 1998, December. "Whither the World Bank and the IMF?" *Journal of Economic Literature* (XXXVI): 1983-2020.

Lensink, R. and H. White. 2000. "Aid Allocation, Poverty Reduction and the *Assessing Aid* Report," *Journal of International Development* 12(3): 399-412.

Mosley, P., J. Harrigan and J. Toye. 1991. *Aid and Power: The World Bank and Policy-Based Lending*. London: Routledge.

Naím, M. 2000. "Washington Consensus or Washington Confusion?" *Foreign Policy* (Spring): 87-103.

______. 1995. "Latin America: The Second Stage of Reform," In *Economic Reform and Democracy,* eds. L. Diamond and M.F. Plattner. Baltimore: The John Hopkins University Press.

______. 1994. "The World Bank: Its Role, Governance and Organizational Culture," *Bretton Woods: Looking to the Future*. Washington, DC: Bretton Woods Commission.

Riddell, R. 1999. "The End of Foreign Aid to Africa? Concerns about Donor Policies," *African Affairs:* 98.

Rodrik, D. 2000, February. *Participatory Politics, Social Cooperation and Economic Stability*. Cambridge: Harvard University, CID.

______. 1999. *Institutions for High-Quality Growth: What they Are and How to Acquire Them?* paper presented at the IMF Conference on Second Generation Reforms. Washington, DC, 8-9 November.

Santiso, C. 2000. "Towards Democratic Governance: The Contribution of the Multilateral Development Banks in Latin America," In *Democracy Assistance: International Co-operation for Democratization, ed.* P. Burnell. London: Frank Cass Publishers, 150-190.

______. 2001. "International Co-operation for Democracy and Good Governance: Moving Toward a Second Generation?" *European Journal of*

Development Research 13(1):154-180.

Stiglitz, J. 1999. "The World Bank at the Millennium," *The Economic Journal* 109 (November): F577-597.

Stone, D. 1989. *Policy Paradox and Political Reason*. London: Scott, Foresman, and Co.

Svensson, J. "Aid and Growth: Does Democracy Matter?" *Economics & Politics* 11(3).

Tarp, F., ed. 2000. *Foreign Aid and Development: Lessons Learnt and Directions for the Future*. London: Routledge.

Williamson, J. 1999. *What Should the Bank Think about the Washington Consensus?* Washington, DC: International Institute of Economics.

______. 1990. "What Washington Means by Policy Reform," in *Latin American Adjustment: How Much Has Happened?* ed. J. Williamson. Washington, DC: Institute of International Economics.

World Bank. 2001. *World Development Report 2002: Building Institutions for Markets*. Washington, DC: OUP for World Bank.

______. 2000a. *The Quality of Growth*. New York: Oxford University Press.

______. 2000b, November. *Reforming Public Institutions and Strengthening Governance: A World Bank Strategy*. World Bank: Public Sector Group, PREM Network.

______. 2000c. *World Development Report of 2000/2001: Attacking Poverty*. Washington, DC: OUP for World Bank.

______. 1999. *Beyond the Center: Decentralizing the State*. Washington, DC: World Bank Latin American and Caribbean Studies.

______. 1998. *Assessing Aid. What Works, What Doesn't, and Why*. New York: Oxford University Press.

______. 1997. *World Development Report 1997: The State in a Changing World*. Washington, DC: OUP for World Bank.

______. 1994. *Governance: The World Bank Experience*. Washington, DC: The World Bank.

______. 1992. *Governance and Development*. Washington, DC: The World Bank.

______. 1991, June 25. *Managing Development: The Governance Dimension*. Washington, DC: The World Bank, Discussion Paper.

______. 1989. *Sub-Saharan Africa: From Crisis to Sustainable Development*. Washington, DC: World Bank.

Carlos Santiso is a doctoral candidate at the Paul H. Nitze School of Advanced International Studies at the Johns Hopkins University in Washington, DC, working on democratization and governance reform in emerging markets, particularly the reform of the state and the rule of law. He previously served at the International Institute for Democracy and Electoral Assistance (1996-2000) and with the Cabinet of the French Prime Minister (1995-1996). He is a consultant for various international organizations and aid agencies.

Part V
Critical/Sceptical Voices on Democracy and International Law

[15]

The End of History? Reflections on Some International Legal Theses

*Susan Marks**

Democracy used to be a word that international legal commentators preferred to avoid. At least by the second half of the present century, this was not because too few governments identified themselves as democratic. It was rather because too many did so. The world's most repressive regimes joined their more representative counterparts in claiming a title that had become synonymous with praiseworthy and justified politics. In some cases modifying adjectives were used ('one-party democracy', 'people's democracy', etc.); in other cases the appropriation was unmodified. Either way, observers found normative inferences difficult to draw, for democracy appeared to mean everything, and therefore nothing.

What put an end to the commentators' reticence was, of course, the demise of communism and the turn in all regions of the world to multi-party electoral politics. For many, these events confirmed both that democracy was the foundation of political legitimacy, and that repressive regimes, whatever they chose to call themselves, lacked that legitimacy. Influential international legal scholars felt able to declare that a 'right of democratic governance' was now 'emerging',[1] and that international law was, or at any rate should now be, beginning to take in the lessons of 'liberal internationalism'.[2]

* Fellow, Emmanuel College, Cambridge, CB2 3AP, United Kingdom. I would like to thank Professor James Crawford for his invaluable assistance and support in the writing of the PhD dissertation on which this article draws.

1 The leading exponent of this is Thomas Franck. See, esp., 'United Nations Based Prospects for a New Global Order', 22 *NYUJ. Int'l L. & Pol.* (1990) 601; 'The Emerging Right to Democratic Governance', 86 *AJIL* (1992) 46 (hereinafter Franck 1992); 'Democracy as a Human Right', in L. Henkin and J. Hargrove (eds.), *Human Rights: An Agenda for the Next Century* (1994) 73 (hereinafter Franck 1994); and *Fairness in International Law and Institutions* (1995) (hereinafter Franck 1995), Ch. 4 (largely reproducing Franck 1992).

2 See esp. Slaughter (Burley), 'Revolution of the Spirit', 3 *Harv. Hum. Rts J.* (1990) 1 (hereinafter Slaughter 1990); 'Towards an Age of Liberal Nations', 33 *Harv. Int'l L.J.* (1992) 393 (hereinafter Slaughter 1992a); 'Law Among Liberal States: Liberal Internationalism and the Act of State Doctrine', 92 *Columbia L.R.* (1992) 1907 (hereinafter Slaughter 1992b); 'Law and the Liberal Paradigm in International Relations Theory', *Proc. ASIL* (1993) 180 (hereinafter Slaughter 1993); and 'International Law in a World of Liberal States', 6 *EJIL* (1995) 503 (hereinafter Slaughter 1995). For a related theme, see Tesón, 'The Kantian Theory of International Law', 92 *Columbia L.R.* (1992) 53 (hereinafter Tesón 1992).

Susan Marks

This article examines these claims.[3] The concern here is not to affirm or deny that state practice and *opinio juris* square with an emerging right of democratic governance. The evidence relevant to deciding that doctrinal question will not be presented, and no conclusion will be offered with respect to it. Nor does this article seek to maintain that democracy is a Western artefact, with limited relevance outside the West. On the contrary, the premise of what follows is that, *provided* it is understood to refer to a general concept or ideal of self-rule on a footing of equality among citizens,[4] rather than to particular conceptions of democratic politics and their institutional manifestations, democracy is an idea of potentially universal pertinence. Its historical roots may be localized. But the worldwide struggles being waged in democracy's name leave little room for doubt that democracy has today become globalized.

The previous paragraph's proviso is, however, a very large one, and points to the central question addressed in this article. What is the understanding of democracy that informs the claims concerning the right of democratic governance and liberal internationalism? The argument advanced here is that the international legal scholars who put forward these claims precisely *do not* identify democracy with a concept or ideal of self-rule on a footing of equality among citizens. Rather, they, along with many of their critics, for the most part elide democracy with certain liberal institutions. This serves, in ways to be highlighted, to attenuate the emancipatory and critical force that democracy might have. In doing so, it limits the contribution that international law (should it develop along the lines the scholars suggest) might make with respect to anti-authoritarian politics, whether in countries yet to embrace democracy, in countries newly embracing democracy, in countries of long-standing democratic commitment, or indeed in the innumerable other non-national settings of contemporary political life.

The elision of democracy with certain liberal institutions can be linked to a more general perspective evinced in the claims concerning the norm of democratic governance and liberal internationalism. This perspective will be referred to as 'liberal millenarianism' (an expression which hopefully makes up in salience for what it

3 For elaboration of these claims, see also Fox, 'The Right to Political Participation in International Law', 17 *Yale Int'l L.J.* (1992) 539; Fox and Nolte, 'Intolerant Democracies', 36 *Harv. Int'l L.J.* (1995) 1; and Cerna, 'Universal Democracy: An International Legal Right or a Pipe Dream of the West?', 27 *N.Y.U. J. Int'l L. & Pol.* (1995) 289. For arguments refuting the claims, see Carothers, 'Empirical Perspectives on the Emerging Norm of Democratic Governance', *Proc. ASIL* (1992) 261; Koskenniemi, '"Intolerant Democracies": A Reaction', 37 *Harv. Int'l L. J.* (1996) 231; and Roth, 'Democratic Intolerance: Observations on Fox and Nolte', 37 *Harv. Int'l L.J.* (1996) 235. For discussion of the claims, see Panel 'National Sovereignty Revisited: Perspectives on the Emerging Norm of Democracy in International Law', *Proc. ASIL* (1992) 249–71.

4 Amongst the vast literature on the subject of democracy, D. Held, *Models of Democracy* (2nd ed., 1996) and J. Dunn (ed.), *Democracy: The Unfinished Journey 508 BC to AD 1993* (1992) provide exceptionally valuable overviews of the roots and vicissitudes of this ideal. In evoking the ideal, this article seeks not to define democracy (the contestability of which resists definition), but rather to associate itself with a venerable and powerful strand of democratic thought. For an exemplary distillation of that strand, see Beetham, 'Key Principles and Indices for a Democratic Audit', in D. Beetham (ed.), *Defining and Measuring Democracy* (1994) 25.

lacks in euphony). Liberal millenarianism is the analytical framework adopted in this article, and the first section sketches the key features that are here associated with it. The second section then reviews the international legal scholarship in which the claims under discussion are elaborated. The final section considers to what extent, and with what consequences, that scholarship exhibits a liberal millenarian perspective. This article's conclusion is that, if international law is to lend its support to ongoing efforts to extend and deepen democracy's purchase, the emerging norm of democratic governance and liberal internationalism offer, at best, a partial agenda.

I. Liberal Millenarianism

Liberal millenarianism finds its most extreme, and certainly its best known, expression in the work of Francis Fukuyama in the late 1980s and early 1990s.[5] Fukuyama undoubtedly set out to provoke, and this he very effectively did. His work of this period attracted many critics and few unqualified supporters.[6] One is tempted to dismiss him as isolated, a passing gadfly not to be taken too seriously. To do that would, however, be to ignore his many qualified supporters. It would be to overlook that his premises and argument found resonance – and continue to find resonance – in the work of a broad spectrum of commentators, including many whose outlooks are considerably more moderate than his. Liberal millenarianism refers to this whole spectrum. That said, precisely because he articulates in bold, telegraphic fashion, and even at times rhetorically overstates, that which others more delicately bury or hedge, Fukuyama's work offers an excellent vantage point for surveying the shared terrain.

A. Fukuyama and the End of History

Fukuyama's central thesis is that the end of the Cold War confirms a worldwide consensus in favour of liberalism, including not just capitalism but liberal democracy as well. As he sees it, liberalism has conquered all rival ideologies, most recently communism, and liberal democracy is now the sole legitimate system of gov-

5 Fukuyama's thesis, discussed below, was first advanced in an article published in 1989, and then elaborated in a further article and in a book published three years later. See Fukuyama, 'The End of History', *The National Interest* (Summer 1989) 16 (hereinafter Fukuyama 1989); 'A Reply to My Critics', *The National Interest* (Winter, 1989/90) 18; and *The End of History and the Last Man* (1992) (hereinafter Fukuyama 1992).

6 For a sampling of critiques, see Huntington, 'No Exit: The Errors of Endism', *The National Interest* (Fall, 1989) 3; Holmes, 'The Scowl of Minerva', *New Republic* (March 23, 1992) 27; Macey and Miller, 'The End of History and the New World Order: The Triumph of Capitalism and the Competition between Liberalism and Democracy', 25 *Cornell Int'l L.J.* (1992) 277; and Held, 'Liberalism, Marxism and Democracy', 22 *Theory and Society* (1993) 249 and 'Anything But A Dog's Life? Further Comments on Fukuyama, Callinicos and Giddens', 22 *Theory and Society* (1993) 293.

ernment. This marks the 'triumph of the West'.[7] More than that, it heralds – he proposes – the 'end of history'.

> What we may be witnessing is not just the end of the Cold War, or the passing of a particular period of postwar history, but the end of history as such; that is, the end point of mankind's ideological evolution and the universalisation of Western liberal democracy as the final form of human government.[8]

This claim obviously relies on a distinctive notion of 'history'. If most scholars today conceive history as without grand design, Fukuyama considers this an understandable response to the abominations of the first half of the twentieth century. But he holds that this conception now requires rethinking. In the events of the century's closing decades he finds warrant for returning to the teleological notion of history that can be found in the work of Hegel and Marx, their secular reworkings of the pre-modern deterministic understanding. According to this perspective, history is purposive, directional, progressive, and oriented towards a particular goal. Fukuyama endorses the view, which he identifies especially with Hegel,[9] that the goal towards which history is oriented is rationality and freedom, and that human societies progress towards it dialectically, through the clash of ideologies. The culmination – or 'end' – of history is eventually reached when perfect freedom and rationality are attained, and the clash of ideologies is resolved. This is what Fukuyama argues may now have occurred. Ideological competition appears to be over. Whereas Marx thought democracy in the shape of communism was our final destiny, it turns out – so Fukuyama holds – to be liberal democracy that has emerged from the fray, to await us at the end of history. It turns out to be liberal democracy that overcomes all the defects, irrationalities and contradictions of earlier forms of government, and promises to bring the historical dialectic to a close.

Fukuyama recognizes, of course, that not all countries of the world have embraced liberal democracy, and that those which have done so face continuing challenges. His point, he insists, is that history may have ended in the sense that the *ideology* of liberal democracy represents the final stage of political evolution. By this he means that the idea of liberal democracy cannot be improved upon. Ideology and ideas are one thing; practice is quite another, and in this case lags far behind. Thus, the end of history does not entail that there may, or will, be no further events and no further conflict. Nationalism and religion, in particular, appear to Fukuyama likely to remain sources of violence. Many societies have not yet begun, or have scarcely begun, to realize liberal democracy, and will face turbulent times before they do. In particular, he remarks, 'the vast bulk of the Third World remains very much mired in history'.[10] Even 'post-historical', Western societies have incom-

7 Fukuyama 1989, at 3.
8 Fukuyama 1989, at 4.
9 A consideration of whether this is accurate is beyond the scope of this article. Fukuyama acknowledges, in any event, that his understanding of Hegel is strongly influenced by the interpretation of French philosopher Alexandre Kojève (himself introduced in English translation by Allan Bloom).
10 Fukuyama 1989, at 15.

pletely implemented liberal democratic principles. For this reason they are likely to experience continuing internal strife. In their relations with one another, however, war has – so Fukuyama holds – become 'unthinkable'.[11] In this connection, he argues that the post-historical West should actively defend its gains through a 'league of democratic nations', 'capable of forceful action to protect its collective security from threats arising from the non-democratic part of the world', and 'inclined also to expand the sphere of democracy, where possible and prudent'.[12]

Why is it that liberal democracy has achieved such a victory, at least at the level of ideas or consciousness? On what basis does Fukuyama claim that liberal democracy embodies perfect rationality and freedom? He takes the view that the main engine of progress in the modern world is what he terms the 'logic of modern natural science'.[13] By this he means instrumental rationality, especially calculations of economic cost and benefit. According to Fukuyama the logic of modern natural science accounts for the triumph of capitalism and the establishment of a 'universal consumer culture'. It also accounts for the decline of traditional forms of social organization and the profound worldwide impact of technological innovation. But of itself this logic cannot account for liberal democracy's privileged place in history. While liberal democratic countries generally fare best economically, and while economic modernization may help create the material conditions for liberal democracy, such as urbanization and education, economic efficiency may in some contexts militate in favour of authoritarian-bureaucratic government, rather than liberal democracy. Economics alone cannot explain liberal democracy's consummate status. In his words, the logic of modern natural science 'gets us to the gates of the Promised Land of liberal democracy, but does not quite deliver us to the other side'.[14]

Fukuyama believes that liberal democracy may represent the ultimate form of government because it satisfies certain fundamental human psychological needs. These he refers to (drawing again on Hegel) as the desire for 'recognition', a desire he takes to be manifested in such feelings as self-respect, self-esteem, dignity, ambition, pride and concern for prestige. For Fukuyama 'the problem of human history can be seen ... as the search for a way to satisfy the desire of both masters and slaves for recognition on a mutual and equal basis; history ends with the victory of a societal order that accomplishes that goal'.[15] As he sees it, liberal democracy is that order; it offers a framework for mutual and equal recognition of all citizens.

11 Fukuyama 1992, at 283.

12 Fukuyama links this idea with Kant and the tradition of liberal internationalism, as to which see *infra*, sections II and III. He considers that the league of democratic nations he recommends – a 'Kantian liberal international order' (Fukuyama 1992, at 283) – already exists to an degree under the umbrella of organizations such as NATO, EC, OECD, Group of Seven and GATT. He contrasts such a league with other organizations and alliances, such as the UN, which are not limited to liberal democratic nations. See Fukuyama 1992, at 276–284 (quotations are at 283 and 280 respectively).

13 This is explained further in Fukuyama 1992, ch. 6.

14 Fukuyama 1992, at 134.

15 Fukuyama 1992, at 152.

And yet, if liberal democracy awaits us at history's end, there is another sense in which, according to Fukuyama, the human desire for recognition will be left profoundly unfulfilled, even debilitated. There is an aspect of that desire that can only find fulfilment in the context of ideological competition. Whereas those – he refers to them as the 'first men' – who began the struggle for liberal democracy had to exhibit courage, take risks, and aim high, the 'last men' at the end of history will have no further need of heroism.[16] Indeed, they will be encouraged not to stand out. Fukuyama worries about the mediocrity, ignobility and materialism of liberal democracy's 'last men'. Following in the tradition of Tocqueville and others,[17] his enthusiasm for democracy is tinged with regret for the decline of aristocracy, and a belief that too much equality, rather than too little, may pose liberal democracy's greatest challenge.

B. Liberal Millenarianism

This thesis was widely interpreted – and Fukuyama himself confirms that it was intended – as an attempt to provide an antidote to the prevailing 'declinist' mood of American political analysis in the 1980s.[18] Those 'pessimists' who were continuing to assert that the power and influence of the United States were in decline had failed to notice the 'good news'[19] that a 'liberal revolution' was underway worldwide. Those 'intellectuals who believe they grasp the world in all its complexity and tragedy'[20] had failed to see that history has a pattern, and that, posturing aside, '[t]oday ... we have trouble imagining a world that is radically better than our own'.[21]

Patently, Fukuyama's antidote was strong stuff. Though not without ambivalences, his work makes few concessions to those who do not share his outlook, and is almost ostentatious in its disdain for those he takes to be left-liberal or, perhaps, un-American. And yet, his themes are not confined to what has been called the New Right. Rather, they appear, as noted at the outset, to exemplify a more widely held perspective. It is this perspective to which liberal millenarianism refers. Its key features may be summarized as follows.

In the first place there is the notion that history has a *telos*. This involves a view of historical change as directional, linear and evolutionary, with identifiable developmental stages and an end-point that can be known, and potentially reached. Secondly, there is the supposition that history's *telos* is liberalism, or at any rate liberal

16 Concerning the 'last man', see F. Nietzsche (R. Hollingdale, trans.), *Thus Spoke Zarathustra* (1969) 45–47.
17 See A. de Tocqueville (G. Lawrence trans.; J. Mayer. ed.), 2 *Democracy in America* (1994) 690–95. Fukuyama's contemporary influences are conservative-elitist thinkers, Leo Strauss and Allan Bloom.
18 See, e.g., R. Keohane, *After Hegemony* (1984) and P. Kennedy, *The Rise and Fall of Great Powers* (1988).
19 Fukuyama 1992, at xiii.
20 Fukuyama 1992, at 69.
21 Fukuyama 1992, at 46.

democracy in association with a market-oriented economy. This is based both on an empirical assertion that all alternatives to liberalism have been eliminated, and on a normative assertion that liberalism is superior to all alternatives. A third feature is a distinctive voice, a 'we' who (fine tuning aside) *have* liberal democracy and experience no serious – or, at any rate, no intractable – problems, in contradistinction to a non-liberal 'they' (in the Third World and elsewhere) for whom things will necessarily remain more complicated and more unpleasant. Finally, there is a distinctive tone, a call to celebrate the present, tempered perhaps by nostalgia for the past, but nonetheless optimistic, confident and flushed with a sense of victory over the forces of regression.

Millenarianism refers in Christian doctrine to the belief that Christ will return to reign on earth for a thousand years. More generally, it is applied to premonitions of global futures of diverse kinds, but especially redemptive ones.[22] Liberal millenarianism's *millenarianism* thus consists in its perception that the world may stand on the brink of an unprecedented era of peace and good government, a perception which is millenarian also in the more literal sense that it pertains to the millennium about to begin.[23] Reinforcing the millenarian character of this vision in Fukuyama's work is the annunciatory, exalted, sometimes even ecstatic, language in which it is expressed, and the evocation of eschatological, especially evangelical,[24] themes. The *liberal* character of liberal millenarianism derives obviously from the fact that this is presented as a vision of a liberal world. But what sort of liberal world? To pursue this question, and also to explore further liberal millenarianism's implications for the meaning of democracy, it is helpful to draw into the discussion some of Fukuyama's critics.[25]

22 Fredric Jameson contrasts this with 'inverse millenarianism' – claims about 'the end of this or that' – which he associates with postmodernism. See F. Jameson, *Postmodernism, or The Cultural Logic of Late Capitalism* (1991), at 1. The difference between millenarianism and 'inverse millenarianism' appears to be principally one of emphasis, however, for both look at once backwards and forwards. Liberal millenarianism, in any event, has this ambivalence.

23 James Crawford refers to 'the facile millenarianism that was an immediate product of 1989'. See J. Crawford, *Democracy and International Law: Inaugural Lecture* (1994) 25.

24 Jacques Derrida finds a specifically Christian resonance in Fukuyama's work, thus buttressing the present characterization of Fukuyama as 'millenarian'. When Fukuyama says that economics takes us 'to the gates of the promised land but does not quite deliver us to the other side', and when he finds a spiritual basis for his 'good news' concerning liberal democracy in the human desire for recognition, Derrida suggests that Fukuyama is not only choosing Hegel in preference to Marx, but is also (in so doing) choosing a Christian account in place of a Jewish one. The other great religion of the 'promised land', Islam, does not feature in Fukuyama's allusive repertoire; he observes that the Islamic world falls outside the consensus he finds in favour of liberalism. See J. Derrida (P. Kamuf, trans.), *Specters of Marx* (1994), at 59–61 and 66.

25 The following discussion draws mainly on Held, *supra* note 6; Macey and Miller, *supra* note 6; Huntington, *supra* note 6; and Derrida, *supra* note 24. These critiques proceed, it should be noted, from widely divergent standpoints and reach widely divergent conclusions from their analysis of Fukuyama.

C. Liberal Millenarianism and Democracy

One striking feature of Fukuyama's argument is that it largely proceeds as if there is, and can be, only one liberalism, one democracy and one liberal democracy. While recognizing a certain diversity of institutional arrangements, Fukuyama fails to consider the diversity of values and beliefs that contributes to producing divergent understandings of the meaning of liberalism and democracy, and of their interrelation. Liberal democracy cannot spell the end of ideological struggle because it is itself the subject of ideological contestation, and will continue to be so.

What, then, of Fukuyama's own understanding of liberalism, democracy and liberal democracy? A number of critics highlight Fukuyama's failure to address the tension between liberalism and democracy. The liberal preoccupation with rights and freedom from government control, and the democratic preoccupation with equal participation in, and accountability of, public power, may point in different directions. Rights and freedoms justified by reference to liberalism may compromise the extent to which all citizens are equally enabled to participate in politics; political decisions justified by reference to democracy may compromise individuals' rights and freedoms. On this point David Held observes that Fukuyama endorses economic liberalism, without examining the extent to which the 'free market' constrains democratic processes, by generating and sustaining systematic inequalities of wealth that involve systematic inequalities of power.[26] Thus, without addressing the implications of doing so, Fukuyama effectively resolves the tension between liberalism and democracy in favour of liberalism (especially in its neo-liberal economic aspect). This leads him, Jonathan Macey and Geoffrey Miller remark, to proclaim a victory for liberal democracy wherever he sees economic liberalism.[27]

Also of concern is Fukuyama's 'uncritical affirmation'[28] of liberal democracy. He neglects to investigate alternatives to prevailing liberal democratic practices, and gives little sign of grasping the limitations of those practices. Indeed he leaves largely unexplained the basis on which an evaluation might be made. His celebration of liberal democracy, thus ungrounded, overlooks the obvious failures of liberal democracy, its omissions with respect to the historic promise of self-rule on the basis of equality among citizens. These omissions find reflection in the pervasiveness of unaccountable power and the persistence of asymmetrical life chances between sexes, ethnic groups and classes.[29] At the same time, Fukuyama's celebration

26 Held, *supra* note 6, at 257–58.

27 Macey and Miller, *supra* note 6, at 282. This comment finds support in Fukuyama's inclusion, in a list of countries he characterizes as liberal democratic, of Singapore, South Korea, Honduras and Mexico. See Fukuyama 1992, at 49–50. (But see also his later discussion of, e.g., Singapore's authoritarianism, Fukuyama 1992, at 241.)

28 Held, *supra* note 6, at 295.

29 An illustrative summary of democracy's 'broken promises' and 'unforeseen obstacles' can be found in N. Bobbio (R. Griffin, trans.; R. Bellamy, ed.), *The Future of Democracy* (1987), at 27–39. (The conclusions Bobbio draws are, however, at variance with the position adopted in the present article.)

also overlooks that liberal democracy has never been under so much strain. He considers the challenges posed to liberal democracy by nationalist and religious movements. But, as Held and others observe, he fails to address the far-reaching challenges posed by the diffusion of decision-making power and political activity in the contemporary world.[30] This arises from a wide range of developments, among them innovations in the media and communications and information technology, economic globalization, and the rising importance of social movements (the environmental and women's movements, etc.).[31] In profound and diverse ways, these developments put in doubt the tenability of an account of liberal democratic politics that focuses solely on national governments, and treats periodic elections, the rule of law and civil and political rights as not just necessary but largely sufficient. Yet this is the account that informs Fukuyama's claims.

Fukuyama's uncritical approach to liberal democracy is accompanied by a portrayal of the world that is hard to locate in actuality. Like Voltaire's Pangloss, he insists on an account of this 'best of all possible worlds' that defies, rather than attends to, contemporary realities. Jacques Derrida puts this point starkly:

> [N]ever have violence, inequality, exclusion, famine, and thus economic oppression affected as many human beings in the history of the earth and humanity. Instead of singing the advent of the ideal of liberal democracy and of the capitalist market in the euphoria of the end of history, ... let us never neglect this macroscopic fact, made up of innumerable singular sites of suffering: no degree of progress allows one to ignore that never before, in absolute figures, have so many men, women and children been subjugated, starved or exterminated.[32]

These sites of suffering, of course, cross-cut the distinction Fukuyama draws between 'historical' and 'post-historical' states, and serve to assure the continuance of ideological divergences in both categories of countries.

A further problematic element in Fukuyama's argument is his premise that a 'liberal revolution' is underway. He acknowledges that the Islamic world stands outside the consensus that he takes to be forming concerning liberal democracy, but discounts the significance of resistance there and elsewhere. Commentators have countered that, while few profess to reject the basic ideas associated with democracy and while some form of capitalism characterizes most economies, there is little evidence of support in many countries for liberal values more generally. Fukuyama exaggerates the scope of the consensus by finding liberal democracy almost – though not invariably – wherever he locates some variant of capitalism.

Fukuyama's defence is that his thesis about the end of history posits the end of *ideological* contestation, and is not an empirical claim. Thus it is not falsifed by the

30 For a wide-ranging and instructive discussion of the implications of globalization for democracy, see D. Held, *Democracy and the Global Order* (1995).

31 Amongst the many accounts of globalization and associated developments, from diverse perspectives, M. Waters, *Globalization* (1995) is especially instructive. A valuable corrective to over-enthusiastic accounts of globalization, especially economic globalization, can be found in P. Hirst and G. Thompson, *Globalization in Question* (1996).

32 Derrida, *supra* note 24, at 85.

obvious fact that not all societies have embraced liberal democracy. But does this thesis not presuppose compelling evidence as regards aspirations, even if not as regards political practices and institutions? What precisely is Fukuyama's 'good news'? Derrida calls attention to the way Fukuyama characterizes liberal democracy both as an ideal and as an occurrence, alternating between the two to suit his argument.[33] On the one hand, Fukuyama refutes evidence that contradicts his thesis, insisting that he is speaking of an ideal that transcends events. On the other hand, he maintains that events have occurred – the death of communism, the establishment of liberal democracy and capitalism as ideologies of near-universal choice, the recognition accorded by Western liberal democracies to their citizens – which represent the realization of this ideal. Fukuyama's 'good news' thus intends to refer, Derrida shows, both to an accomplished fact and to a vision of the future.

This leads to a final observation. Inasmuch as Fukuyama's linear conception of history admits of only one future, it reduces and oversimplifies the processes of historical change. While Fukuyama acknowledges that reversals are possible, he assumes that the trends he identifies will broadly continue. In this, Samuel Huntington observes, Fukuyama overstates the predictability of history and the permanence of the moment. Current trends may continue, but experience suggests that they may well not.[34] The historical record to date offers little support for Fukuyama's notion of progress. Held too finds that Fukuyama has failed to appreciate the contingency of events and the complexity of social processes. Held highlights that Fukuyama's essentialized conception of 'man' and his two master engines of modernity (instrumental rationality and the desire for recognition) cannot adequately explain such central historical phenomena as classes, gender inequalities and the international division of labour.[35] If this is the case, then the predictive value of his conceptual framework must likewise be open to question.

To summarize, it can be argued that the thesis of the end of history – as the ideological triumph of capitalist economics and liberal democracy – attaches insufficient importance to a number of matters which render ideological divergences inescapable and, indeed, vital. These include the following points: the meaning ascribed to the terms involved is itself at least partly a matter of ideology; the enduring tension between liberalism and democracy invites continuing contestation concerning liberal democracy; liberal democracy is subject to profound – increasingly profound – challenge; at the end of the twentieth century progress is far from obvious; the scope of support for any version of liberal democracy, even at the level of ideas, is not clear; history follows not a single path but multiple and diverse trajectories that proceed and interact in complex and imponderable ways.

Critics draw diverse conclusions from their analyses of Fukuyama's thesis, though almost all find in it a dangerous inducement to complacency. Huntington's worry is that it may encourage Americans to underestimate the contemporary sources of

33 *Ibid*, at 62–63.
34 Huntington, *supra* note 6, at 10.
35 Held, *supra* note 6, at 296–97.

political instability, and on this basis to relax their vigilance in foreign relations. Declinism, in Huntington's view, was, in contrast, a useful warning and goad to action.[36] Held has a different concern. Only fifty years after nazism, fascism and Stalinism almost eclipsed liberal democracy, Fukuyama prematurely pronounces a secure future for liberal democracy, and glosses over the most serious challenges that currently confront it.[37] Derrida shares this anxiety that Fukuyama masks the fragility of liberal democracy, and thus reduces the possibilities for strengthening and improving it. In this regard Derrida expresses particular disquiet at the way Fukuyama seeks to deny (while himself, however, in key respects exemplifying)[38] the continuing relevance of ideas and critical practices that draw inspiration from Marx.[39] Like a number of other scholars,[40] Derrida takes the view that these ideas and practices are rendered more, not less, pertinent by liberalism's gains.

The points discussed here arise in relation to Fukuyama's writings. But most apply with equal force to liberal millenarianism generally. This is because most stem from the features of Fukuyama's work that have been characterized as, more broadly, liberal millenarian: the progressivist notion of history; the identification of liberal democracy as history's *telos* ; the distinctive 'post-historical' voice; the celebratory tone. Indeed, the critical perspectives just reviewed highlight the extent to which these features are interrelated and mutually reinforcing. With respect to the progressivist conception of history that is a central pillar of liberal millenarianism, Fukuyama's critics echo insights that can be found in the work of many other scholars. Among these, Michel Foucault's well-known account of history and genealogy is worth briefly recalling at this point.[41] Foucault shows how progressivist history

36 Huntington, *supra* note 6, at 4.

37 Held, *supra* note 6, at 296.

38 A number of commentators make this argument on the basis, e.g., of Fukuyama's teleological notion of history and his turn to 'grand theory'. See, e.g., Huntington, *supra* note 6, at 9–10. Others, however, disagree. See, e.g., A. Callinicos, *Theories and Narratives* (1995), ch. 1.

39 Derrida, *supra* note 24, at 68–69 and 86–94. Derrida has an intriguing explanation for why Fukuyama does this. He proposes that, in advancing the thesis of the end of history, Fukuyama is engaging in a kind of 'mourning work' following the death of 'actually existing socialism'. Out of fear and 'bereavement' as Marx's unacknowledged heir (for, Derrida insists, we are all Marx's heirs, whether we wish it or not), Fukuyama is denying the continued relevance of socialist critique. As Derrida puts it, adapting Marx and Engels' own immortal image, Fukuyama is attempting to 'conjure away' the 'spectre of Marx' that has long haunted liberalism. Yet, Derrida maintains, this work of mourning cannot succeed. It can displace, but it cannot efface, the spectre of Marx, for that spectre is liberalism's necessary accompaniment. In this regard Derrida refers not only to Marx and Marxian thought. He evokes the spectre – or, as he prefers to say, spectres (for he stresses the extent to which Marx's legacy is plural and diverse) – of Marx *metonymically* to stand for *all* the forms of critique that can help to evaluate ideals, grasp realities, and reduce the gap between them. In view of the importance of these forms of critique, Derrida urges instead a 'counter-conjuration', a strategy of active engagement, rather than disavowal. In this, he contends, scholars have a particular role. Quoting (at 176) a line in connection with another famous ghost, Derrida recalls Hamlet's injunction: 'Thou art a scholar; speak to it, Horatio.' See Derrida, *supra* note 24, at 61 and 68–75.

40 See, e.g., the essays in R. Blackburn (ed.), *After the Fall* (1991).

41 M. Foucault (P. Rabinow, ed.), 'Nietzsche, Genealogy, History', in *The Foucault Reader* (1984) 76. I am grateful to Professor Gerald Frug, Harvard Law School, for calling my attention to this text, and for an illuminating discussion of it.

confirms rather than unsettles established power relations. It represses dissension, struggle, and domination, rather than articulating and addressing them. It presents the world comfortingly, as simple, coherent and ordered, rather than challengingly, as complex, heterogeneous and contingent. In seeking to hold onto things as they are, it asserts blithely, but also impotently, that things must be as they are. What this puts in relief is the sense in which liberal millenarianism, for all its professed optimism, is ultimately pessimistic, not – as Fukuyama suggests – because it envisions a world of excessive equality, but because it evokes a world of enduring and immutable inequalities.

II. The 'Norm of Democratic Governance' and Other Theses

Insofar as the thesis of the emerging norm of democratic governance and related claims share the liberal millenarianism of Fukuyama's end of history narrative, the foregoing discussion is rich in implications. Before addressing the issue of these theses' liberal millenarianism, however, it is necessary to set out the arguments involved. For this purpose a distinction may be drawn between those which discuss democracy primarily as a right and those which discuss democracy primarily in more instrumental liberal internationalist terms.

A. Democracy as a Right

The right-oriented theses involve the claim – first advanced by Thomas Franck,[42] but subsequently taken up and developed by others as well[43] – that international law is beginning to embrace a 'norm of democratic governance' or 'global democratic entitlement'. Such a norm or entitlement would mean three things. First, it would entail that the legitimacy of governments is judged by international, rather than purely national, rules and processes. Second, it would connote that those international rules and processes stipulate democracy; that is to say, only democratic governments are legitimate. And third, it would establish that democracy is an internationally guaranteed human right, in respect of which international procedures of monitoring and enforcement are justified and, indeed, required.

How has this norm or right come to 'emerge'? Franck offers the fullest explanation. He traces the normative and customary evolution of the global democratic entitlement by reference to three overlapping phases or 'generations'[44] of international rule-making and implementation. The first generation, born after the First

42 See the references cited at note 1. The thesis has earlier roots, which can be found, e.g., in Steiner, 'Political Participation as a Human Right', 1 *Harv. Hum. Rts Ybk* (1988) 77.

43 See *supra* note 3.

44 Franck 1992, at 52. Franck is not referring to the three-generational scheme used (and debated) in human rights commentary, according to which civil and political rights are the first generation; economic, social and cultural rights are the second; and peoples' rights are the third.

World War (but with older antecedents), is the right of self-determination. The plebiscites, popular consultations and commissions of inquiry that were mandated at the Versailles Peace Conference in connection with the redrawing of European boundaries gave rise to the idea that 'a people organised in established territory [has the right] to determine its collective political destiny in a democratic fashion'.[45] At the same time, a body of practice concerning plebiscite-holding and international supervision was initiated. This was further developed when self-determination was applied outside Europe in the context of decolonization.

The second generation, born after the Second World War, is the international legal recognition of human rights. With this the idea was established that all human beings have the right to freedoms of expression, thought, assembly and association (among other rights). Procedures for holding governments to their obligations in this regard, and for clarifying the scope of the rights and correlative obligations, were also elaborated. The third generation, still in its infancy, is the right to free and open elections. This was effectively born with the transformations of the late 1980s. While the right to vote and stand for election had been recognized in key human rights instruments decades before, it was not until those transformations occurred that this right began to be taken seriously as a norm of universal application. It was not until those transformations occurred, in other words, that it became possible to consider this right an emerging norm of customary international law. That it has begun to be taken seriously is reflected in the fact that a substantial majority of states now actually practise 'a reasonably credible version of electoral democracy'.[46] This is also reflected in international efforts to establish and define the 'principle of genuine and periodic elections'; in the increasingly common provision of 'technical assistance' by the UN and other organizations and agencies to governments holding democratic elections for the first time; and in the expanding practice of international and regional election monitoring. Varying his metaphor so as to emphasize the way that the right to free and open elections extends, and depends on, international legal developments with respect to self-determination and human rights, Franck sometimes refers to these as three 'building stones'[47] in the edifice that is the global democratic entitlement.

Other scholars likewise hold that, while the global democratic entitlement has had a basis for decades in international human rights instruments, and before that in the principle of self-determination of peoples, it has only recently begun to be respected, monitored and enforced to a significant extent.[48] Thus, it has only recently begun to acquire the status of a norm of customary international law. In addition to the evidence of this to which Franck calls attention, Christina Cerna notes the procedures elaborated in the 1990s within the framework of the Council of Europe and the Or-

45 Franck 1992, at 52.
46 Franck 1992, at 64.
47 Franck 1992; Franck 1995, ch. 4; and Franck 1994, *passim*.
48 See, e.g., Fox, *supra* note 3 and Cerna, *supra* note 3.

ganisation of American States for conditioning admission or continued participation on democratic government.[49]

As this suggests, these scholars take free and fair elections to be the decisive criterion of democracy, though they in no way underestimate the extent to which the right to such elections presupposes other rights, especially freedoms of expression, thought, assembly and association. Elections are in this perspective decisive because they legitimate governance. Thus, the expressions 'democratic entitlement', 'right to democracy', 'norm of democratic governance', 'entitlement to a participatory electoral process', 'right to political participation', 'electoral rights', and the 'right to free and open elections' are employed with relative interchangeability. Franck explains:

> The term 'democracy', as used in international rights parlance, is intended to connote the kind of governance that is legitimated by the consent of the governed. Essential to the legitimacy of governance is evidence of *consent to the process by which a populace is consulted* by its government.[50]

Franck acknowledges that this is a limited conception of democracy. 'This definition', he observes, 'is not ambitious, it is not necessarily unambiguous, and it is almost certainly not the one Americans would prefer'.[51] But given the diversity of polities and traditions in the world, and given the inbuilt resistance of the states system to the international regulation of national affairs, he considers that this conception or something like it 'probably represents the limit of what the still frail global system of states can be expected to accept and promote as a right of peoples assertable against their own, and other, governments'.[52]

Gregory Fox and Georg Nolte, while sharing the view that elections are the central issue in a norm of democratic governance, have highlighted that holding regular elections which are free and fair may not always be sufficient to protect the democratic entitlement.[53] Where candidates are opposed to liberal democracy, and are committed to the establishment in its place of, for instance, a theocratic political order, the question arises whether those candidates should be allowed to stand.

49 Cerna, *supra* note 3. In connection with applications for membership from Central and Eastern European States, the Council of Europe has begun to require evidence of commitment to democracy. See, e.g., 'Report on the Legal Order of the Russian Federation', Council of Europe Doc. AS/Bur/Russia 7 (1994), reprinted at 15 *Hum. Rts L. J.* (1994) 249. The Organisation of American States has long had this as a formal – though, for much of the OAS's life, unenforced – requirement for OAS member states. See the Declaration of Santiago, adopted at the Fifth Meeting of Consultation of Ministers of Foreign Affairs, August 1959, reprinted in T. Buergenthal and R. Norris (eds.), *Human Rights: The Inter-American System* (hereinafter Buergenthal and Norris), Binder 1, Booklet 6, 134. More recently, the OAS has sanctioned the further step of engaging in collective action to secure the installation, or reinstatement, of democratic government in the event that a coup occurs. See OAS General Assembly Resolution 1080 (adopted 5 June 1991) reprinted in Buergenthal and Norris, Binder 2, Booklet 7.6, 43; and Protocol of Amendments to the Charter of the OAS ('Protocol of Washington') (adopted 14 December 1992), OAS AG/DOC.11 (XVI-E/92).

50 Franck 1994, at 75.

51 Franck 1994, at 75.

52 Franck 1994, at 75.

53 Fox and Nolte, *supra* note 3. They have in mind particularly the case of Algeria.

Based on a survey of constitutional laws and traditions of diverse democratic states, Fox and Nolte contend that in customary international law the exclusion of such candidates is warranted, and perhaps even required. This reflects, they observe, a conception of democracy as not simply a set of procedures for ascertaining majority preferences, but rather as a means by which citizens are enabled to enjoy basic rights. Thus, Fox and Nolte find support in customary international law for an account of democracy that tolerates only the tolerant, and that in this respect insists on the value of 'political liberalism'.[54] More generally, they find support for an account of democracy that rests on the liberal notion that government is legitimated not just procedurally but also to the extent that it fulfils its side of the social contract and protects citizens' rights.

Those who advance the thesis of the emerging norm of democratic governance give close attention to the question of how compliance might be monitored and enforced. As noted, existing election-monitoring efforts and innovations with respect to participation in regional organizations are among the developments which persuaded the scholars that the norm was emerging in the first place. They consider a number of possible ways of strengthening enforcement. Franck proposes that the 'older democracies' might volunteer to have their elections monitored, so as to encourage a custom of election-observation that might eventually evolve into an obligation.[55] In the longer term, he proposes that democratic government might be set as a precondition to participation in all international organizations, including the United Nations, a proposal also developed by Fox.[56] Franck suggests additionally that democratic government might be made a precondition for fiscal, trade and development benefits, and for the protection of UN and regional collective security measures. He strongly rejects as a means of enforcement unilateral intervention to install or reinstate elected governments, though he finds acceptable collective action at UN or regional level, even, in extreme cases, involving the use of force. Franck considers that, while the question of the scope and incidents of the norm of democratic governance is likely to remain on the international law agenda, the more pressing problem is the monitoring and enforcement of compliance. He urges that the future emphasis of international efforts should be laid accordingly.[57]

B. International Law and the 'Liberal Peace'

The writers so far considered base their case for the emerging democratic entitlement on, above all, developments with respect to the holding of elections, international and regional election monitoring, and democratic conditionality in regional organizations. Those whose work will now be reviewed are also impressed with these developments. What strikes them as even more significant, however, is the

54 See J. Rawls, *Political Liberalism* (1993).
55 Concerning this and the other proposals considered here, see Franck 1992.
56 Fox, *supra* note 3.
57 Franck 1994.

correlation between liberal democracy and peace.[58] This forms the basis of an argument that there should be a norm of democratic governance, and that the signs that it is emerging confirm this. The theorists of the right to democratic governance also draw support from the correlation between liberal democracy and peace to help explain and vindicate the right.[59] Thus, the difference between the two sets of theses is largely one of emphasis. Both sets are at once empirically-based claims that a norm is emerging, speculations concerning its future as *lex lata*, explanations of why it is emerging, and justifications for its recognition in international law. And in both sets the so-called 'liberal' or 'democratic' 'peace' plays a part.

Among the leading proponents of theses of this second type are Fernando Tesón[60] and Anne-Marie Slaughter.[61] In presenting the correlation between liberal democracy and peace, they take account of both speculative and empirical literature. With respect to the former, the key figure is Kant. These scholars, like the international relations analysts on whose work they draw, look to Kant for the insight that liberal states are likely to maintain peaceful relations with one another. As is well known, Kant held that 'perpetual peace' would depend on three things: every state having a 'republican' constitution; a 'pacific federation' being established among states, in the shape of an agreement to refrain from war against one another; and extensive international commerce, underpinned by 'cosmopolitan law'. Republican government would discourage warfare, he believed, because, if government was accountable to citizens, the fact that citizens would suffer the consequences of war – as soldiers, bereaved civilians, taxpayers, etc. – would serve to engender caution in waging it.[62]

Internationalists have long attended to the points about the pacific federation and extensive international commerce. Particularly compelling in the aftermath of the twentieth century's two World Wars, these ideas are reflected in the League of Nations, the Kellogg-Briand Pact, the United Nations, and the General Agreement on Tariffs and Trade. Indeed, they inform the whole enterprise of modern international law and institution-building. But what, according to Tesón, Slaughter and the international relations analysts, has *not* received sufficient attention is Kant's insight about republican government. For these scholars the sort of 'republican' state Kant had in mind corresponds in contemporary terms to a liberal democratic state.[63] The

58 The scope of the correlation that is claimed to exist will be discussed below.

59 See, e.g., Franck 1995, at 134–137, and Fox and Nolte, *supra* note 3 , at 61–63.

60 See esp. Tesón 1992.

61 See the references to Slaughter's work cited at note 2. Slaughter 1995 develops a more general 'Liberal model' of international law. 'Liberalism' is presented as an account of how some – liberal – states 'do behave rather than how they should behave' (at 508). But 'Liberal' theory appears to be envisaged as serving a normative function as well, inasmuch as Slaughter evokes the possibility that this theory might become 'normatively applicable to all States even if positively descriptive of only some' (at 538). See further *infra*, section III.

62 See I. Kant (H. Nisbet, trans.), 'Perpetual Peace: A Philosophical Sketch' (1795), in H. Reiss (ed.), *Kant: Political Writings* (1991), at 93 *et seq.*

63 If Kant himself drew a sharp distinction between a republican constitution and a democratic one, this was because his conception of democracy was a pre-modern one. His frequently quoted definition of a 'republican' constitution entails three principles: 'firstly, the principle of *freedom* for all

Second World War, along with the bitter ideological rivalries of the Cold War, fuelled a realist outlook which got in the way of a proper appreciation of Kant's idea. Now that many countries of the world have embraced this liberal model, a fresh appraisal is called for. The notion that the prospects for peace may be greatest among liberal states should, these scholars maintain, no longer be ignored.

Slaughter and Tesón observe that international relations scholars have presented evidence which appears to back up this notion. Based on analysis of international wars since 1817, Michael Doyle, among others, has argued that a separate 'zone of peace' does indeed exist among liberal states.[64] This zone has steadily expanded as the number of liberal states has increased. Doyle has reported that throughout this period liberal states, while they have engaged in wars with non-liberal states, have remained at peace with one another. From this he has drawn the inference that liberal states are likely to be more pacific than non-liberal ones, not in general, but at least in their relations with other liberal states. The scope of this claim, the precise character of the link it posits, and the reasons for that link, remain the subject of debate. In its broad lines, however, the 'democratic' or 'liberal' 'peace' is spoken of as a 'fact'[65] and 'as close as anything we have to an empirical law in international relations'.[66] It is an empirical law that, according to Slaughter and Tesón, has profound implications for international law.

The first implication is that international law should place the question of the legitimacy of governments on its agenda. It should abandon the idea that this is an exclusively national issue. The second implication is that international law should accept as legitimate only liberal democratic governments. It should stipulate that a legitimate government – one that has a right to exercise sovereign authority – is not just any government that wields factual power; it is a liberal democratic one. Tesón calls this a 'Kantian theory of international law'. Slaughter employs the name given by international relations scholars, 'liberal internationalism'.[67] *Internationalism* evokes the second and third dimensions of Kant's formula for perpetual peace noted above, those that find reflection in international cooperation; *liberal* internationalism includes also the first dimension, 'republican government'. Against an international law that is in thrall to realism and power politics, Slaughter counterposes a vision of an international law that takes seriously the connection between national political

members of society (as men); secondly, the principle of *dependence* of everyone upon a single common legislation (as subjects); and thirdly, the principle of legal *equality* for everyone (as citizens)'. He wrote that 'republicanism [is] that political principle whereby the executive power . . . is separated from the legislative power', and that 'republican' government is, in principle, 'representative'. *Ibid*, at 99–102.

64 Doyle, 'Kant, Liberal Legacies and Foreign Affairs', 12 *Philosophy & Public Affairs* (1983) 205 (Part 1) and 323 (Part 2). For a survey of relevant empirical literature, see B. Russett, *Grasping the Democratic Peace* (1993), ch. 1.

65 Russett, *supra* note 64 (Ch.1: 'The Fact of Democratic Peace').

66 Levy, 'Domestic Politics and War', 18 *J. Interdisciplinary History* (1988) 653, 662.

67 For her general 'model' of international law, developed in recent work, Slaughter prefers the term 'Liberal', and distinguishes a 'Liberal' theory of international relations from 'Wilsonian liberal internationalism'. See Slaughter 1995, at 508 *et seq.* for her definition of 'Liberal' in this context.

ideology and international relations, and in this way dedicates itself to (in the phrase of one international relations scholar) 'grasping the democratic peace'.[68]

In effect this is a vision of a norm of democratic governance along the lines proposed in the first category of theses considered, though without the same emphasis on the notion of democracy as a human right.[69] Slaughter thus finds signs that her vision is beginning to materialize in the developments to which Franck and others call attention. She also finds signs that the 'zone of peace' is accompanied and reinforced by a 'zone of law', in that transnational disputes involving only liberal states are more readily resolved through judicial procedures than is the case where non-liberal states are involved. She presents evidence that courts of liberal states cooperate with one another, and take into account each other's national interests, in a way that courts of non-liberal states do not, and in a way that courts of liberal states themselves do not where a dispute involving a non-liberal state is at issue.[70]

On the question of how this norm might be enforced, Tesón concurs with Franck and Fox that the UN and other international organizations might change their rules to admit only states with liberal democratic governments, and to allow only such governments to participate. In his view the unilateral use of force might even be justified in some circumstances, especially where violation of the norm is associated with gross abuses of human rights. Tesón also proposes that the law of treaties might be made to reflect the illegitimacy of non-liberal governments; such governments might, for instance, be deprived of the competence to create binding obligations in their own favour. Diplomatic law too might be changed so as to deny diplomatic status to representatives of non-liberal regimes.[71] Slaughter differs in rejecting the right of unilateral intervention, and generally distances herself from Tesón's professed anti-statism. Nonetheless, she shares the view that liberal democracies have a 'leadership' role to play in relation to liberal internationalist international law.[72]

As this discussion indicates, these claims revolve around a distinction between 'liberal' or 'liberal democratic' states and 'non-liberal' states. It is worth pausing at this point to note more fully how the theorists understand this distinction. Slaughter defines a liberal state as, in broad terms, a state with 'juridical equality, constitutional protections of individual rights, representative republican governments, and market economies based on private property rights'.[73] This uncontroversial defini-

68 Russett, *supra* note 64.

69 Tesón does, however, argue that international law should accord legitimacy only to liberal democratic states not just for prudential reasons but also because this is morally justified. His 'Kantian theory' includes the idea that governments should be required to respect liberal rights because this is the right thing to do. See Tesón 1992, esp. 81–84.

70 Slaughter 1992b. See Slaughter 1995 for further development of this argument. Slaughter claims, for instance, that interaction between the executive and legislative branches of government is also greater among liberal states than among non-liberal states or between liberal and non-liberal states.

71 Tesón 1992, at 100.

72 Slaughter 1992a, at 404 and 394. Doyle for this reason expresses concern at what he takes to be the decline of the United States from hegemonic status. See Doyle, *supra* note 64, at 233–235.

73 Slaughter, 1992b, at 1909. This is largely reiterated, though the need for market economies based on private property rights is separately stated, in Slaughter 1995, at 511–152.

tion corresponds closely to that used by Doyle and other international relations analysts in their work on the 'liberal peace'.[74] Tesón adopts a similar approach, variously referring to the legitimate state of his 'Kantian theory of international law' as a 'democratic state', 'free state', 'liberal democracy' and 'form of political organisation that provides full respect for human rights'.[75] For both scholars the key feature of a liberal state, which explains its irenic character (at least *vis-à-vis* other liberal states), is the fact that there are powerful checks on the exercise of public power – constraints that operate principally through the periodic recall of legislators, the separation of powers and the protection of civil and political rights.

III. Liberal Millenarianism and International Law

It is now possible to return to the question of the relationship between these international legal theses and liberal millenarianism. In this context, the implications for the understanding of democracy that underpins these claims can be brought into view. It will be valuable at the end of this discussion to take stock of the fact that, if these international legal scholars are right, democracy has, will have, or at any rate ought to have, far-reaching significance in international law, as determinant of the legitimacy of governments.

A. Liberal Millenarian Perspectives

Most likely, all the international legal scholars discussed in this article would locate themselves at some considerable distance from Fukuyama on almost every issue. Certainly, none shares the narrow, elitist outlook that pervades his account of the 'end of history'. A number explicitly dissociate themselves from that account. Franck, for instance, states that he does not consider that '[exulting] in smug satisfaction at the "end of history"' is an appropriate response to the post-Cold War juncture, which he sees rather as an occasion for 'seizing the moment to rethink the basic structure and processes of the international system'.[76] Slaughter explains that liberal internationalism promises a result that is 'neither utopia nor the end of history, but holds out the hope of at least a small measure of progress toward individual rights and the global rule of law'.[77] There are some grounds for believing that liberal millenarianism may, nonetheless, be built into the form and structure of these scholars' arguments. As discussed earlier, liberal millenarianism includes, but extends beyond, Fukuyama. It is characterized by a progressivist notion of history, coupled with a conceptualization of history's *telos* in terms of liberalism, and a distinctive voice and tone. On what basis, and to what extent, can it be said that the international legal theses considered here exhibit these features?

74 See, e.g., Doyle, *supra* note 64, at 206.
75 Tesón 1992, *passim*.
76 Franck 1990, 601. See also Franck 1995, at 141.
77 Slaughter 1992a, at 405.

A progressivist view of historical change is evident in Franck's history of the development of the norm of democratic governance. His account is divided into developmental phases, beginning with the principle of self-determination and culminating in the right of free and open elections, now evolving from lip service into widely respected normative commitment. 'The transformation of the democratic entitlement from moral obligation to prescription has evolved gradually', he explains, but 'in the past decade the tendency has accelerated'.[78] Each phase pushes further along the course to eventual prescription. The fact that the phases overlap does not detract from, but rather reinforces, the impression of progress and directionality, as do the metaphors of generations and building blocks. The norm of democratic governance appears to be growing out of, or building on, earlier developments. This evolutionary logic also informs the work of scholars who put forward liberal internationalist and Kantian theses. Slaughter, for instance, in seeking to connect international law with developments in international relations, offers an unmistakeably progressivist account of the history of international relations. This account starts with Wilsonian internationalism (or idealism, in the phraseology of those who later called themselves realists), passes through the stage of realism, and reaches its conclusion with liberal internationalism, which is said to combine the strengths, but also to overcome the shortcomings, of both its forerunners. Since these forerunners are presented as the only alternatives, liberal internationalism is made naturally to appear as an advance.[79] The notion of the 'liberal peace', liberal internationalism's central premise, likewise posits that historical change is incremental and directional. The image is one of an expanding zone of peace among liberal states that will reach the end of its expansion when all are included within it.

The second aspect of liberal millenarianism is that history's *telos* is taken to be liberal democracy, along with a market-oriented economy. It hardly needs restating that this is indeed the goal envisaged in the international legal theses examined here. That this should be so is believed, in the liberal millenarian perspective described earlier, to be supported empirically by the elimination of all ideological alternatives. And it is also believed to be supported normatively. That is to say, these ideological alternatives have been eliminated because they were flawed, as democracy and capitalism – at least in principle, if not in current practice – are not. Both points are alluded to in a memorable passage by Franck:

> [T]he [global democratic] entitlement now aborning is widely enough understood to be almost universally celebrated. It is welcomed from Malagache to Mongolia, in the streets, the universities and the legislatures, not only because it portends a new, global political culture supported by common rules and communitarian implementing institutions, but also because it opens the stagnant political economies of states to economic, social and cultural, as well as political, development.[80]

78 Franck 1992, at 47.
79 See, e.g., Slaughter 1993. For a further narrowing of alternatives to 'Realism' and 'Liberalism', see Slaughter 1995.
80 Franck 1992, at 90.

For Slaughter, 'the geopolitical framework for the millennium is ... liberal internationalism'.[81] An eventual 'world of liberal states' is the sole alternative to '[sacrificing] the values of universalism ... to the realism of recognising that States in the international system inhabit very different worlds'.[82] The choice, in her account, is either liberal universalism or realist difference, either grasping the liberal-democratic peace or living perpetually on the edge of war. The embrace of liberal democracy in every country thus appears as humanity's ultimate salvation.[83]

Liberal millenarianism involves, thirdly, a 'post-historical' voice or standpoint that figures the non-liberal world, still mired in 'history', as radically 'other'. Progress towards the full achievement of liberal democracy is taken to be more or less straightforward in liberal societies, while elsewhere the almost total transformation of prevailing realities will be required. This is, again, apparent in the thesis of the emerging norm of democratic governance. Such governance is portrayed as something some largely have, and the rest almost entirely lack. Thus, Franck writes that for the citizens of some states this norm will 'merely embellish rights already protected by their existing domestic constitutional order. For others it could be the realization of a cherished dream'.[84] A similar standpoint orients the liberal internationalist and neo-Kantian approaches. Slaughter envisions that her model of international law for a one-world order of liberal states might be 'normatively applicable to all States even if positively descriptive of only some'.[85] In practice, she observes, the distinction between liberal and non-liberal states may be difficult to apply, especially in the context of 'quasi-liberal' and 'transitional states'. Certainly, it cannot be treated as an 'absolute divide'.[86] But the point of the 'liberal peace', around which her argument turns, is that, as Doyle explains, liberal states are not just relatively but 'fundamentally different' from non-liberal states. Hence the 'separate peace' among them.[87] If this is the reason for the 'separate peace', it is, of course, also the consequence. In any event, the claim of liberal internationalism, as of the norm of democratic governance, is that this fundamental difference should, and is beginning to, be reflected in international law.

There is, finally, the issue of liberal millenarianism's distinctive tone, its momentous, celebratory, and apparently optimistic, key. Liberal millenarianism seeks

81 Slaughter 1992a, at 393. (emphasis omitted)

82 Slaughter 1995, at 538.

83 It also appears as *international law's* salvation, inasmuch as liberal universalism also represents an option in favour of law, rather than politics. Liberal internationalism thus seems to rescue international law from realist irrelevance. Fukuyama suggests this too, arguing that, while 'international law in general' (Fukuyama 1992, at 281) became discredited owing to the failure of the League of Nations and the United Nations, the 'states making ... up [the "league of democratic nations" which he proposes] would be able to live according to the rules of international law in their mutual dealings' (Fukuyama 1992, at 283).

84 Franck 1992, at 50.

85 Slaughter 1995, at 538.

86 Slaughter 1992b, at 1988–89.

87 Doyle, *supra* note 64, at 235. Slaughter takes up Doyle's phraseology, noting the 'fundamental difference in the nature of relations among liberal States as compared to relations between liberal and non-liberal States'. Slaughter 1995, at 537.

to call attention to events which augur that history's destination may finally be in sight. The discussion in the previous section gave only a slight indication of the tone of these international legal arguments. The quotation from Franck above is, however, typical of the terms in which his claims, and those of some of the other international legal scholars, are expressed.[88] Thus, for instance, Franck goes on to speak of a 'cosmic but unmysterious change' in which governments, 'no longer blinded by the totalitarian miasma' have come to recognize the advantages of democracy.[89] Slaughter likewise writes emphatically of revolutions that 'liberated millions. *Millions* ...', and occasioned a 'human rights victory on an unprecedented scale, a triumph of human dignity and the human spirit'.[90] On the basis of those events she proposes liberal internationalism as a new vision of peace and good government for a new age.

If the thesis of the emerging norm of democratic governance and related claims share key features of liberal millenarianism, they also give rise to a number of the concerns raised by Fukuyama's critics. In accounts of the norm of democratic governance and the order of liberal states envisioned by the liberal internationalist and Kantian theories, liberal democracy is presented largely as an identifiable, coherent and stable system. It is stressed that a great variety of practices and institutions is consistent with liberal democracy, but little attention is drawn to the diversity of the values, ideas and principles that might animate those practices and institutions. In particular, little attention is given to the enduring tensions within liberal democracy between liberal and democratic preoccupations, and to the implications for that tension of different models of liberal democracy. While the international legal theorists are less apt than Fukuyama to mistake capitalism for liberal democracy, their arguments nonetheless tend, like his, towards an attenuation of the democratic dimension.

The democratic component of liberal democracy comes to revolve, principally, around elections. That what is denoted is a particular method of producing governments is made particularly clear in the thesis of the emerging norm of democratic governance. Democracy's part there is adjectival; it is a procedure for securing the acquiescence of citizens in their governance by others.[91] The same holds, however, whether democracy is understood in these terms, or in terms of a social contract to protect citizens' rights (as by Fox and Nolte), a mechanism to ensure that government acts not just in its own interests but in the interests of society as a whole (as by Slaughter) or a system of government that is not just prudentially but also morally justified (as by Tesón). The shared assumption is that democracy refers to the 'process by which the people choose those they entrust with the exercise of power',[92] the

88 But not all express themselves in this way. Cf. the more cautious tone of, e.g., Fox and Nolte, *supra* note 3.
89 Franck 1995, at 85–86.
90 Slaughter 1990, at 1.
91 Franck 1992, at 51 and *passim*.
92 Franck 1992, at 50.

right 'to participate in the selection of one's own national government'.[93] Yet, according to some political theorists, democracy entails not just the right to participate in the selection of national governments, but also the right to participate directly in decision-making affecting one.[94] For other theorists, democracy involves not just the process of selecting governments, but also the process of connecting people with their governments through civil society.[95] Still other theorists emphasize that democracy requires not just the right to vote and stand for election and associated civil liberties, but also the whole range of further rights that actually enable participation in public life on a footing of equality.[96] While Franck, Fox and Nolte take their position to be dictated by that which customary international law will support,[97] what is being suggested here is that it is also embedded in the structure of their argument. Inasmuch as elections stand at the narrative's climax, democracy is made to appear to have nowhere further to go. Issues of citizenship, accountability and equality, and their respective significance and relative importance – along with other issues at the heart of democratic debate – are thus removed from view.

An additional, related concern is these theses' uncritical, affirmative approach towards liberal democracy. Franck's reference, cited above, to the embellishment of rights in existing liberal states suggests a perception that such states are already satisfactory; the rest is ornament. Depicting democratic political practice as entailing a 'genuine [openness] to meaningful political choice'[98] and a 'free market in ideas',[99] Franck puts to one side the many grounds for doubting the meaningfulness of political choice and the freedom of the market in ideas. Slaughter attaches much importance to what she refers to as the 'paradox of liberal states'. By this she intends that 'as a factual rather than a legal matter, liberal states are likely to have a lesser capacity for autonomous economic and political action than non-liberal states'.[100] But she too neglects to consider how well these constraints on power work, whether they work better for some social groups than others, and whether further constraints might be valuable. With liberal democracy the pinnacle of political development – and with dictatorship, communism and 'forced march modernization' the only alter-

93 Fox, *supra* note 3, at 542.

94 See, e.g., B. Barber, *Strong Democracy* (1984).

95 See, e.g., J. Cohen and A. Arato, *Civil Society and Political Theory* (1992).

96 Amongst the innumerable different ways and contexts in which this argument has been advanced, see, e.g., A. Phillips, *Engendering Democracy* (1991) and *Democracy and Difference* (1993).

97 Fox also emphasizes that his position is dictated by that which is feasible, elections being the most readily monitored dimension of democratic politics. See Fox, concluding comments in panel 'National Sovereignty Revisited: Perspectives on the Emerging Norm of Democracy in International Law', *Proc. ASIL* (1992) 249, 270–71, and *infra* text at note 121 for discussion of this point.

98 Franck 1995, at 86. Franck lists 130 states which as of late 1994 were 'legally committed to permit open, multiparty, secret-ballot elections with a universal franchise'. Of these he remarks that '[w]hile a few may arguably be democracies in form rather than substance, most are, or are in the process of becoming, genuinely open to meaningful political choice'. Franck 1995, at 85–6.

99 *Ibid*, at 138.

100 Slaughter 1992a, at 395–96 (emphasis omitted). The sense in which this is a paradox is unclear. If the thought is that the freedom associated with liberal states entails in another sense greater constraint than is the case with non-liberal states, then the paradox remains obscure, inasmuch as the freedom is that of citizens and the constraint is that of the state.

natives ever mentioned[101] – questions concerning liberal democracy's limitations can scarcely arise, let alone be addressed. It is not only issues of the kind just noted that are left out of account, however. The whole matter of liberal democracy's tenability in a world of intensified globalization is largely passed over. While globalizing processes are certainly registered,[102] the ways in which they are putting democracy under strain receive limited attention.[103] These scholars evoke a liberal democracy that is triumphant, vigorous, redemptive.

They also evoke a liberal democracy that provides the key to expanded prospects for peace. In this respect too, however, limitations are glossed over. The 'peace', which some international relations analysts claim is now a 'fact', is a '*liberal* peace'; it is said to hold *among liberal states*. Relations between liberal and non-liberal states are not claimed to be especially pacific, and may, according to the analysts, even be especially aggressive.[104] In finding warrant in this for a norm of democratic governance, the international legal scholars give little attention to the implications of the fact that democratic governance does not appear to induce pacific relations with non-liberal states.

But there is also a much larger limitation of which these writers take insufficient cognizance. The *'peace'* that is postulated among liberal states is an absence of armed conflict between them. Yet the Clausewitzean paradigm of war between nation-states to which this refers today fits only a minority of violent conflicts, even large-scale ones. Mary Kaldor highlights that much contemporary conflict arises out of the break-up of states, and centres on issues of 'identity politics' (ranging from religious communalism, to ethnic nationalism, to 'tribalism').[105] Support frequently comes from overseas diasporas, along with foreign governments and 'experts'. State actors are often hard to distinguish from non-state actors. Fighting is commonly sporadic, scattered within and across borders, and focused to a large extent on civilian targets.[106] Is this peace or war? Civil war or international war? The boundaries between these categories – like those between violent crime and armed conflict, public aims and private aims, combatants and civilians – are becoming blurred. She concludes that

> the prognosis is grim. The breakdown of the distinction between war and peace, the re-privatisation of violence, implies more or less continuous and geographically pervasive low-level violence, ranging from individual criminality to organised warfare.[107]

101 See, e.g., Franck 1995, at 86.
102 See, esp. Slaughter 1995.
103 A rare example of such attention can be found in the final eight pages of Franck's 484-page study of 'fairness' in international law and institutions. Franck 1995, at 477–484.
104 See Doyle, *supra* note 64, at 323 *et seq.*
105 Kaldor, 'Introduction', in M. Kaldor (ed.), *New Wars* (forthcoming).
106 For a similar account of war in the 1990s, see *Supplement to an Agenda for Peace: Position Paper of the Secretary-General on the Occasion of the Fiftieth Anniversary of the United Nations*, UN Doc. A/50/60; S/1995/1 (1995), esp. para. 10 *et seq.*
107 Kaldor, *supra* note 105.

Alongside these considerations concerning the character of war are further questions concerning the character of peace. There is, for instance, the question of whether peace can be held to prevail where certain forms of non-forcible coercion are occurring, arising (*inter alia*) from the exploitation of relations of dependency. There is also the broader issue of whether systemic inequalities of power, resources and opportunities, between and within nation-states, may in themselves constitute a type of ongoing 'structural violence'.[108] The identification of peace with an absence of armed conflict leaves out of account the possibility that peace may entail more than the failure to resort to arms.

It follows that the scope of the claims associated with the 'liberal peace' is highly circumscribed. Even assuming those claims are justified on their own terms, they miss important contemporary sources of violence, and important questions that arise in connection with that violence.

Moreover, Derrida's 'macroscopic fact, made up of innumerable singular sites of suffering' cited earlier finds scarcely greater resonance in these arguments than does Kaldor's 'grim prognosis'. These international lawyers are undoubtedly no Panglosses. Yet the progressivist premises of their claims, buttressed by the celebratory tone and 'post-historical' voice, do tend to shift attention away from the scale, character and sources of deprivation, oppression and conflict in the contemporary world. To read this international legal literature is to be filled with enthusiasm about the state of, or at any rate prospects for, human flourishing.

Also arguably overestimated is the extent to which there is evidence to support an emerging norm of democratic governance. For Franck and the other theorists of the emerging norm, this empirical issue – raised by some of Franck's critics[109] – has a different significance than it does for Fukuyama. While Fukuyama might shift between the empirical and the ideal, the international legal commentators cannot avoid confronting state practice if they are to make good their claim that the norm is emerging in international law. Or maybe Fukuyama's move, or something like it, is precisely what they intend. Perhaps characterizing the norm as 'emerging' allows it to remain poised between occurrence and prediction.

Finally, the international legal arguments are inclined to overstate the significance of the present moment, as an indication of the future. While the possibility of setbacks is certainly acknowledged, the evolutionary logic of the arguments tends to signal that contemporary trends will continue in a more or less linear fashion. As Fukuyama's critics highlight, the processes of historical change appear to be far more complex and contingent than this logic allows.

The observations made by Fukuyama's critics are also worth recalling as regards the consequences of these concerns. There is a danger of inducing complacency, and of prematurely pronouncing liberal democracy's future secure. In masking the limi-

108 The notion of 'structural violence' is elaborated in the work of Johan Galtung. See, e.g., 'Violence, Peace and Peace Research', 1 *Essays in Peace Research* (1975), ch. 4.

109 See, e.g., Carothers, *supra* note 3.

tations of liberal democracy, the prospects that those limitations might be addressed are correspondingly reduced. Inequalities may be made to seem, and to become, unalterable. And, to the extent that Kaldor's 'grim prognosis' is inadequately heeded, there is a danger of attaching insufficient importance and urgency to the medicine she prescribes. This entails re-establishing legitimate control of violence at a transnational level.[110]

To these points might be added further misgivings expressed by international legal commentators. Thomas Carothers argues that '[a]dvocacy of a democratic norm actually highlights [the] West versus non-West division and the tension in international law concerning the fact that it is at root a Western system that Western countries are seeking to apply to the whole world'.[111] He worries, furthermore, about the harm that might be done, via sanctions or armed intervention, in the 'implementation' of such a norm. Is the way opened up for the waging of 'just wars' or neo-colonial adventures? All the international legal scholars whose work is discussed here recognize the force of this concern.[112] With the exception of Tesón, none accepts unilateral intervention as a legitimate means of enforcing the norm, though each does appear to accept collective action by regional organizations and the United Nations.

Carothers here echoes a widely shared apprehension as regards the division of the world into liberal democratic and non-liberal democratic states. This is an apprehension that cannot forget all the other notorious divisions of history: between civilized and barbarian, Christian and heathen, European and oriental, developed and underdeveloped. Given the historical record, there is a case to be answered that a norm of democratic governance, like Fukuyama's 'league of democratic nations', would express a 'new ideology of imperialism'.[113] This article's premise is that democracy's universal relevance can indeed be defended.[114] The question is whether it is likely to be defensible within the framework of liberal millenarianism.

That it is not is highlighted in some observations by Martti Koskenniemi.[115] Like Carothers, Koskenniemi warns that a universal norm of democracy will 'always be suspect as a neocolonialist strategy'. 'The nation-State and its democratic forms may not be for export as pure form', he suggests. 'They may equally well constitute a specific product of Western history, culture and, especially, economy.'[116] What Koskenniemi appears to have in mind here is the sort of liberal world envisioned in liberal millenarianism. He seems to confirm this when he voices the further concern that a universal norm of democracy is 'too easily used against revolutionary politics

110 Kaldor, *supra* note 105.
111 Carothers, *supra* note 3, at 264. Derrida likewise discerns the outlines of a renewed European Christian alliance. Derrida, *supra* note 24, at 60–61.
112 See, e.g., Franck 1992, at 84.
113 F. Füredi, *The New Ideology of Imperialism* (1994). Franck and others acknowledge the concern. See, e.g., Franck 1992, at 80, 82.
114 See text at *supra* note 4.
115 Koskenniemi, *supra* note 3.
116 *Ibid*, at 234.

that aim at the roots of the existing distributional system and it domesticates cultural and political specificity in an overall (Western) culture of moral agnosticism and rule by the market'.[117]

If Koskenniemi's objections are informed by the same vision of democracy as that of the commentators he criticizes, then perhaps the source of his disquiet is not democracy *per se* but that particular (liberal millenarian) vision of it.[118] At any rate, his objections are unlikely to be refuted by arguments appealing to such a vision. However, from this it does not follow that those objections are unlikely to be refuted by *any* arguments. The simple point which this article has sought to recall is that the vision of democracy on which Koskenniemi (in common with Franck, Slaughter and others) relies is not the only one conceivable. Defenders of democracy's universal relevance have a wide range of *alternative* democratic possibilities upon which to draw. Among these are many that are substantially more congenial to redistribution and difference, and substantially less subordinate to the market and its mangers, than is liberal millenarianism.

B. Conclusion

The thesis of the emerging norm of democratic governance, and the liberal internationalist and neo-Kantian perspectives considered here, grapple with the significance for international law of profound transformations. They call attention to important normative and institutional developments, and connect subject matters more commonly treated in isolation from one another: international law and international relations; self-determination, human rights, and electoral assistance; political theory and international law. In doing so, however, they adopt a narrow understanding of democracy, largely equating it with certain liberal institutions. Franck expresses regret that this is all customary international law will currently support.[119] Fox recognizes that democracy entails much more than periodic national elections, but considers that elections, being easier for international organizations to monitor than other facets of democratic life, are international law's most appropriate starting point. 'It is much more difficult', he observes, 'to stay in a country after elections, for the long haul, to monitor all institutions of government and attempt to secure key elements of democracy ... Elections ... must not end the push to a democratic society, but they are an essential first step'.[120]

Yet it is not self-evident either that elections are democracy's first step or that ease of monitoring by international organisations should determine international

117 *Ibid.*

118 *Ibid.* Koskenniemi appears to recognize this, inasmuch as his 'most fundamental problem' is that these international legal commentators position themselves 'as possessing a transparent view of the essential meaning of democracy. . .'.

119 This is what Franck appears to suggest when defending a conception which, he acknowledges, is 'not ambitious, not unambiguous, and . . . almost certainly not the one Americans would prefer'. Franck 1994, at 75.

120 Fox, *supra* note 97, at 270–71.

law's priorities. Democracy involves no necessary order of events, and difficulties of monitoring have all too frequently served in international law to make chosen priorities seem unavoidable.[121] This is not to suggest that periodic elections and related institutions lack value.[122] It is just to highlight the way democracy's further dimensions may be eclipsed. This article has sought to show that, whatever may be the constraints of the international legal system, they are not the only constraints in operation here. The scholars' liberal millenarian standpoint also plays a part in shaping the account of democracy that informs their claims.

At the same time, the theses provide powerful reasons for being concerned about this. If a norm of democratic governance indeed 'emerges', this will entail – to reiterate earlier discussion – that international law lays down criteria of governmental legitimacy, and that those criteria require democracy. It may also entail that individuals can claim a human right to democracy. The international legal scholars suggest that the norm should be enforced by making admission to, and participation in, international organizations conditional on democratic government (as is currently the case with some regional organizations). Franck proposes that financial and trade benefits and development assistance, and even the protection of UN and regional collective security measures in the event of an invasion, might likewise be made conditional on democratic government. Tesón advocates modifications of treaty and diplomatic law that would place further pressure on governments which do not meet the criteria of liberal democracy. Though Tesón alone would be prepared to sanction unilateral intervention, the other scholars appear to support collective enforcement.

Dire consequences could thus follow where legitimacy is denied. From the perspective of citizens, dire – perhaps even direr – consequences could also follow where legitimacy is accorded. This latter danger is easy to overlook. Yet if, in line with the international legal scholarship discussed in this article, liberal millenarianism shapes the criteria used, international law may find itself according legitimacy for what may in some circumstances be the most cosmetic democracy. In so doing, the law may undercut efforts to deepen democracy's purchase in the countries concerned. To the objection that any step in the direction of democracy is better than unmitigated repression, it may be replied that this is not necessarily so if the conditions upon which power is exercised remain essentially unchanged. Where international law confers on a repressive regime a legitimacy that it formerly lacked, the regime is strengthened and counter-authoritarian forces correspondingly debilitated.

According to former United Nations Secretary-General Boutros Boutros-Ghali, democracy is today an 'ideal that belongs to all humanity'.[123] To characterize de-

121 An example is the case of economic, social and cultural rights, and the way their relative deemphasis is routinely linked to undeniable, but exaggerated, difficulties of monitoring and enforcement.

122 However, for an intriguing critique of the 'reality' of elections, see J. Baudrillard (P. Foss *et al.*, trans.), *In the Shadow of Silent Majorities, or The End of the Social and Other Essays* (1983).

123 'Democracy: A Newly Recognized Imperative', 1 *Global Governance* (1995) 3, 4. See further B. Boutros-Ghali, *An Agenda for Democratization* (1996).

mocracy as an ideal is to highlight that it is an engine of criticism and change, necessarily at odds with prevailing realities. To label it as the property of all humanity is to recall, amongst other things, that its institutional complements necessarily reflect the huge diversity of social circumstances to which it is applied. Should international law seek to vindicate efforts animated by such an ideal, then a framework of ideas that posits liberal institutions as history's end scarcely seems an adequate basis on which to proceed.

[16]

Imagined Consent: Democratic Liberalism in International Legal Theory

*Gerry J Simpson**

Certain forms of consensus are so essential to community life that they reestablish themselves despite every attempt to shake them. At most they are reestablished in a more dogmatic or, I would say, more fanatical way... the majority (to defend the ideological bases of consent) would become fanatical...

(Umberto Eco, *Travels in Hyperreality* (1987), p 177)

I. Introduction

The idea of an imaginary social contract has animated liberal thinkers for centuries. From places as mythical and disparate as the state of nature and the original position, humans have been projected into compacts in the name of justice, democracy or order.[1] In international law too, consent is imagined in order to provide normative justification for the projects of three distinct, yet distinctively, liberal schools. These I call secular or classical[2] liberalism (mostly associated with positivism) and, its more recent radical variants, Kantian liberalism and democratic governance. In this article I want to focus on the latter

---

* Senior Lecturer in International Law and Legal Theory, University of Melbourne, SJD Candidate, University of Michigan at Ann Arbor. Melbourne University's Current International Legal Problems class of 1994 contributed greatly to the development of many of the ideas contained in this article. Philip Alston and Deborah Cass also made some very useful comments on earlier drafts of this essay. A version of this article was delivered as a paper at the Second Annual Meeting of the Australia and New Zealand Society of International Law in 1994.

1 See eg Rawls J, *A Theory of Justice* (1971); Rousseau JJ, *The Social Contract* (1762); Hobbes T, *Leviathan* (1651).

2 I have used the term "classical" to describe what has been the prevailing statist creed in international law. However, there is some confusion over the meaning of this term. James Watson contrasts the classical position with the modern view which he criticises for adopting "autonomous modes of reasoning and sources" when, for example, suggesting that the General Assembly can create international law or that States can be bound without their consent. See Watson, "State Consent and the Sources of International Obligation" (1992) 86 *American Society of International Law Proceedings* 108. On the other hand, Martti Koskenniemi associates modernism with statism and positivism, and the classical approach with natural law. See Koskenniemi, "The Normative Force of Habit: International Custom and Social Theory" (1990) 1 *Finnish Yearbook of International Law* 77 at 77–89. Finally, Nigel Purvis uses the term classical to describe all pre-Charter reasoning about international law and claims that this classical period is characterised by a dialogue between positivism and naturalism. See Purvis, "Critical Legal Studies in Public International Law" (1991) 32 *Harvard International Law Journal* 81.

two movements but place all three in the context of wider trends in international legal theory.

To this end, I first suggest a typology for understanding the various theoretical accounts of the nature of international law (Section II). The purpose of this section is to show how alternative theories of international law might have prompted or motivated the attempt to reshape liberalism through democracy. As part of this typology, I then describe, in more detail, the familiar classical liberal approach to international law and some of its principal failings (Section III). Finally, I consider two versions of the democratic liberal approach: Kantian liberalism represented here by Ferdinand Tesón, and democratic governance represented by Thomas Franck and reflect, fairly broadly, on some difficulties with these schools (Section III and IV). I will argue that neither enterprise is capable of sustaining a universal or coherent vision of normative renewal. Kantian liberalism fails to convince that its elevation of the individual as the primary normative actor in international law is any more than a romanticised preference for the current, flawed constitutional forms of liberal government. Thomas Frank's idea of democratic governance is a bold synthesis of the democratic and classical traditions in a norm which restates the Kantian position that individual consent is a prerequisite for State legitimacy, but argues that this principle of legitimacy will be enforced though the emergence of a community expectation that States should be democratic. However, the dynamics of individual consent imagined in the democratic component of his work are insubstantial and excessively technical while the principles of international law from which it is derived are incomplete and illusory.

....

When the world is in flux, theory excites the critical mind. The end of the Cold War and the onset of the various postmodern disorders have brought in their wake a renaissance in thinking about the role of international law and lawyers in shaping a new normative order for global society.[3] The imminence of the 21st century has given these thoughts a millennial significance. Some legal scholars, notably Richard Falk, have suggested that the State system itself is crumbling and that changes of revolutionary magnitude are occurring.[4] Falk goes on to argue that legal scholarship must undergo a comparable transformation to maintain its dynamism and relevance in these times.[5]

Whether the international system born at Westphalia survives the present convulsions is inevitably questionable. Nevertheless, this latter argument of Falk's at least has some merit and certainly in recent years the traditional

---

3 Most notable in this regard have been the book length studies by Allott P, *Eunomia: New Order for New World* (1990); and Koskenniemi M, *From Apology to Utopia: The Structure of International Legal Argument* (1989). For a general bibliography of these self-styled new approaches see Kennedy and Tennant, "New Approaches to International Law: A Bibliography" (1994) 35 *Harvard International Law Journal* 417 at 431–60.

4 See Falk R, *Revitalizing International Law* (1989).

5 Ibid, at 21–26.

debates about the nature of international law have given way to a series of new challenges from cognate disciplines. Poststructuralism, for example, has found the perfect host in the ascending and descending rhetorical patterns of international lawyering and the self-contradictions of international law.[6] Drawing on poststructural methodology, the rhetorical school (or new stream) has invented an historiography of international law in which scholars vie to provide the most convincing demolition of traditional histories of the discipline.[7]

Some feminists have suggested accounts of international law which critique its basic premises[8] as well as question the distribution of primary goods in the international system and the exclusion of women from leading roles within it.[9] Even international relations theorists, long disdainful,[10] have renewed their interest in the legal regime.[11] Meanwhile, writers adopting more traditional or classical approaches are being forced to respond to these sharp incursions into their territories.[12] This has had the beneficial effect of introducing into international law more vigorous debates and engendering a livelier intellectual environment. Ultimately, however, the dominant descriptive theories of international law remain liberal in character and, while some of the new approaches mentioned so far will be discussed here, the focus of this article is three peculiarly liberal explanations of international law.

---

6 See particularly Koskenniemi, n 3 above: a book-length analysis of these ultimately self-refuting patterns of argumentation.

7 The most readable exponent of this school is Nigel Purvis. See Purvis, n 2 above. See also Kennedy, "Primitive Legal Scholarship" (1986) 27 *Harvard International Law Journal* 1.

8 See eg Charlesworth, "The Public/Private Distinction and the Right to Development in International Law" (1992) 12 *Aust YBIL* 190; Charlesworth and Chinkin, "The Gender of Jus Cogens" (1993) 15(1) *Human Rights Quarterly* 63; Knop, "Re/Statements: Feminism and State Sovereignty in International Law" (1993) 3 *Transnational Law and Contemporary Problems* 293.

9 Charlesworth, Chinkin and Wright, "Feminist Approaches to International Law" (1991) 85 *American Journal of International Law* 613.

10 I refer here to the dominant realist tradition in international relations (see n 17 below). Much of the alternative international relations literature is relevant to international legal theory and has remained relatively untapped by international legal scholars. These approaches range from regime theory (notably Keohane R, *After Hegemony* (1984)) to work on the institutional socialisation of rules (Haas E, *When Knowledge is Power* (1990)) to Hedley Bull's study of justice and order (Bull H, *The Anarchical Society* (1977)).

11 The most notable contribution to this debate has come from Anne-Marie Slaughter Burley. See Slaughter Burley, "International Law and International Relations Theory: A Dual Agenda" (1993) 87 *American Journal of International Law* 205. See also Abbot, "International Law and International Relations Theory: Building Bridges" (1992) 86 *American Society of International Law Proceedings* 167.

12 See eg Tesón, "Feminism and International Law: A Reply" (1993) 33 *Virginia Journal of International Law* 647; Higgins R, *Problems and Process* (1993); McDougal, "McDougal's Jurisprudence: Utility, Influence, Controversy" (1985) 79 *American Society of International Law Proceedings* 266 at 283–86, 288.

II. A Typology

In summary, there appears to be at least five plausible, contemporary approaches to an understanding of international law.[13] However, these five categories I have sketched below should be approached with some caution for three obvious and interrelated reasons. First, the brevity of the descriptions necessarily militates against complete understanding of the various perspectives. Second, there are the inevitable overlappings, contradictions and simplifications that are the mark of all attempted categorisations. Third, most international lawyers fit rather uneasily (if at all) into categories. Indeed one might say that the predominant view of international law today is an open-textured, quasi-sociological, eclectic, interdependence approach which complicates and leavens the statism with which it cannot entirely break.

(a) Democratic liberalism: Kantian liberalism and democratic governance

This school provides a focus for the rest of this essay so these comments, necessarily, will be brief. According to Ferdinand Tesón, the philosophical roots of democratic liberalism can be traced back to Kant who first envisaged an international society of democratic States acting in the interests of their citizenries.[14] On this view of international law, only democratic States belong to the society of nations while the rest are consigned to the state of nature. The cosmopolitan society of nations is thus, in evolutionary terms, a moral improvement on the Hobbesian State of international relations. In this society there is the possibility of constructing more than simply a law of minimum world order.

The liberalism of Thomas Franck also belongs to this school but represents a more conservative, consensual approach to the construction of norms premised on some version of democracy. The statecraft of American Presidents Woodrow Wilson (especially) and Jimmy Carter is an example of the practice of democratic liberalism in international politics emphasising the possibilities of universal humanitarian progress and the institutional implementation of common values and principles by like-minded democratic States.[15]

---

13 This list merely provides a framework for understanding recent movements and should not be taken to be either definitive or exhaustive. It excludes some views of international law eg, the description of international relations that denies international law's existence altogether or the sharp objections to the current system made by scholars from the developing world or from indigenous perspectives (see eg Sathirathai, "An Understanding of the Relationship Between Legal Discourse and Third World Countries" (1984) 25 (2) *Harvard International Law Journal* at 395). Equally, the Marxist contribution to international legal theory, while small, should not be dismissed (see eg Chimni B, *International Law and World Order: A Critique of Contemporary Approaches* (1993), p 211).

14 Tesón, "The Kantian Theory of International Law" (1992) 92 *Columbia Law Review* 53 at 54–55.

15 Both Wilson and Carter became disillusioned of the possibilities of upholding these values on a global scale and both became infected with realist tendencies by the end of their presidencies.

(b) The Grotian or solidarist school

The Grotian approach to international law assumes the existence of a more inclusive international society of States, individuals and non-State communities each contributing to, and sharing in, global governance.[16] The idea of international society has been elaborated on by a number of scholars and there is a great deal of disagreement as to what exactly such a society entails.[17] The Grotian school has occasionally encompassed theoretical positions ranging from harsh pragmatism to visionary idealism.[18] However, while acknowledging the unstable nature of this category, it appears that it can be contrasted with the Kantian approach to international law in the sense that individuals are not considered the sole or even primary subjects of law, and with the realist perspective in that Grotians reject secret diplomacy, the balance of power and unbridled national egotism.

Grotians posit an international civil society in which there is moral solidarity among a wide variety of actors and institutions and a willingness to take action against those that threaten these values and interests. Accordingly, the United Nations collective security model, the objective treaty regime and the notion of universalisable values (*jus cogens, erga omnes*) are features of the Grotian model at work in the present international system.[19]

However, the Grotian approach (and here we do diverge considerably from Grotius himself) has also been described as revolutionary since several of its central premises issue radical challenges to the current system. According to Martin Wight, the Grotians also argue that the international system is inadequate and illegitimate and that it must inevitably be dismantled in a revolutionary transformation.[20] It is this latter aspect of the Grotian system that provides the animus for much of Richard Falk's work and purports to accommodate the various radical critiques of the existing framework.

---

16 The most significant recent volume on Grotian approaches to international law and international relations is Bull H, Kingsbury B and Roberts A, *Hugo Grotius and International Relations* (1990). See also Yasuaki O (ed), *A Normative Approach to War* (1993); especially Yasuaki, "Introduction", p 1; and Tadashi, "Grotius's Method", p 32. Grotius's own great contribution to international law is, of course, *De jure belli ac pacis* (1625). For a general account of Grotian international law see Lauterpacht, "The Grotian Tradition in International Law" (1946) *British Year Book of International Law* 15.

17 Some scholars argue, for example, that Grotius excluded institutions from his view of international law. See Lauterpacht, ibid.

18 It is remarkable that Richard Falk and Hedley Bull can belong to the same school of international law/relations. See Bull, n 10 above; Falk, n 4 above. Perhaps the most visionary of the idealists is the English scholar Philip Allott whose *Eunomia* (n 3 above) is a dense but ambitious work of imagination.

19 See eg Security Council Resolutions: 660 SC Res 660, UN SCOR, 45th Sess, 2932d mtg, UN Doc SC Res 660 (1990) and SC Res 678, SC Res 678, UN SCOR, 45th Sess, 2963d mtg, UN Doc SC Res 678 (1990) 689; Vienna Convention on the Law of Treaties, article 63.

20 See Wight, "An Anatomy of International Thought" (1987) 13 *Review of International Studies* 221.

Finally, of course, Grotius has long been associated with the natural law movement in international law.[21] For Grotians belonging to this naturalist stream, the values of the international system can (or should) be found in the conscience of humankind or the deeper values of universal reason. It is this form of solidarism which found expression at Nuremburg and was revived in the just war debate over the Gulf Crisis. Indeed, implicit in this system of values is the idea of individual responsibility for international crimes which is again enjoying community support.[22]

(c) Feminist currents in international legal theory

International law has proved curiously impervious to feminist theory until relatively recently. While other disciplines and indeed other areas of the law have been subjected to feminist critique for many years, the first major feminist contribution to international law occurred fairly belatedly. Interestingly, much of the writing from this perspective has had an Australian provenance.[23]

The self-declared agenda of this Australian school is to expose the ideological underpinnings of an international legal system holding itself out as rational, objective and neutral. In this sense, at least, the feminist project has much in common with that of the rhetorical school.[24] However, there are two important differences between feminist and poststructural critiques of international law. The first is methodological. While the new stream seeks to reveal the rhetorical manoeuvrings behind international legal scholarship and law-making by focusing on these writings and instruments and the dualities contained within them, feminists are concerned to show the absence of (women's) voices and experiences from these texts and institutions of international law. Second, and more significantly, there is within the feminist movement a commitment to moral value which distinguishes it from most of the poststructural writings and certainly from the statist orientation of contemporary positivism. This value is, of course, universal gender equality. Feminist writings

---

21 Though perhaps Vitoria is regarded as the truer exponent of natural law thinking in international legal theory. See Vitoria F, *De indis et de jure belli reflectiones* (1557).

22 The differences between positivists and Grotians on these issues and the question of *jus cogens* are sharply delineated in Weil, "Towards a Relative Normativity in International Law?" (1983) 77 *American Journal of International Law* 413.

23 This particular feminist approach is the focus of this section. See eg Chinkin, "A Gendered Perspective to the International Use of Force" (1992) 12 *Aust YBIL* 279; Gardham, " A Feminist Analysis of Certain Aspects of International Humanitarian Law" (1992) 12 *Aust YBIL* 265. Charlesworth, "Subversive Trends in the Jurisprudence of International Law" (1992) *Proceedings, International Law Weekend ANU* 80. Note, however, that feminist international jurisprudence is beginning to fracture into a number of different and not always compatible approaches. These are not necessarily represented in this discussion. For a fuller treatment of these varying strategies see the work of Karen Engle eg, Engle, "After the Collapse of the Public/Private Distinction: Strategising Women's Rights" in Dallmeyer D (ed), *Reconceiving Reality: Women and International Law* (1993), p 143.

24 See Charlesworth, ibid, p 86.

in international law thus possess an explicitly prescriptive, political and moral dimension. This attachment to value is at odds with a great deal of scholarship which seeks comfort in analyses of a descriptive or relativistic nature.

Thus the early feminist writings in this area have possessed a distinctly Grotian flavour.[25] They have been somewhat revolutionary and have assumed certain shared values that are deserving of protection in international law but are not being nurtured within the current system. This is not to say that feminist universalism has not been challenged by other feminisms nor that it has not been acknowledged in these early writings. Nonetheless, the feminist contribution to international law is likely to be perceived as an attempt to redeem the international legal process through global normative change.

Where feminism differs from solidarism (apart from the difference in values) is in the different methodologies employed. While Grotian scholars tend to think in abstractions, historical transformations and international societies, much feminist theory is committed to building a normative regime from below. This would, in contrast to the Grotian project, involve by-passing the State altogether (seen as patriarchal) and deriving principles and rules (at least partly) from the lived experiences of women.[26] The fundamental difficulty facing feminist readings of international law would seem to lie in reconciling the apparent particularism of this focus on experience with the implicit universalism of international law itself.[27]

(d) The new stream (or rhetorical) school

David Kennedy introduced the term "new stream" into the vocabulary of international law as a way of describing a group of scholars who had absorbed the lessons of the critical legal studies movement and applied the stratagems and

---

25 Martin Wight categorises international thought as consisting of realists, rationalists and revolutionists. It seems clear that feminists writing as international lawyers belong to this latter group. See Wight, n 20 above, at 221.

26 Marilyn Waring makes the point that treaty action is unlikely to help given that treaties tend to be made by the brothers and uncles of the leaders of nation-States. The patriarchal State remains unrepresentative and there is no real consent. Waring, "Gender and International Law: Women and the Right to Development" (1992) 12 *Aust YBIL* 177; Hilary Charlesworth and Christine Chinkin, meanwhile assert, that:

> [T]he utter failure of the "liberal" international legal system in responding to the global phenomenon of oppression of women should indeed make us question its foundations. Patriarchy is not a temporary imperfection in an otherwise adequate system; it is part of the structure of that system and is constantly reinforced by it.

Charlesworth and Chinkin, "Introduction to Symposium on Feminist Inquiries into International Law" (1993) 3(2) *Transnational Law and Contemporary Problems* i at iv. Karen Knop adopts a slightly different approach suggesting that the State can be conceived or personified in a number of different ways not all of which are necessarily prejudicial to women. See Knop, n 8 above, at 332–44.

27 This problem is likely to remain acute because feminists are sceptical about deriving norms from notions of individualism. Tesón's normative individualism evades (but does not avoid) this apparent dichotomy by presupposing the existence of a universal individual.

insights of poststructuralist theory to the discipline of international law.[28] The leading new stream scholars are Martti Koskenniemi,[29] Kennedy[30] and Anthony Carty.[31] Recently, their views have come under criticism from fellow sceptics such as Scobbie,[32] feminists such as Charlesworth[33] and from those who wish to recuperate the liberal project (for example, Dencho Georgiev).[34]

The problem with defining this school is that one seems doomed to invoke a raft of fashionable phrases and ideas which collectively give the impression of progressive or radical activity, but hardly suggests a persuasive methodology or distinctive analytical approach. Thus, new stream tends towards critiques that are variously (self) characterised as postcolonial, non-hierarchical, transdisciplinary, anti-foundational or subaltern.

Three features seem salient for the purpose of this discussion. First, there is a fascination with the rhetoric or form of international law; for example, how its history is presented, what this says about the discipline, how its categories of argument are constructed and what is left out and why? Second, there is a rejection of simple theories of consent but usually a refusal to discover or propose another single social phenomenon as the essential basis of social life in the postmodern world. Kennedy seems typical of this school though Koskenniemi less so because of his continued commitment to the liberal State system despite his scepticism about the explanatory force of theories based on consent.[35] Third, there is a concern for the redistributive consequences of the flight from politics implicit in the partial autonomy of international legal argument. Koskenniemi's postmodernism lies in his argument for contextualised decision-making, more open politics and individualised rather than rule-based solutions.

Kennedy and Koskenniemi are two of the best-known members though each pursues a different line of inquiry. Kennedy examines the formal sources and internal logic of international law (its rhetoric and structure) and suggests that legal scholarship is at best, self-referential. For Kennedy, the whole intellectual enterprise is philosophically unstable and therefore defensive, stylised and repetitive. International law survives, not because of its coherence or its capacity

---

28 Kennedy, "A New Stream of International Law Scholarship" (1988) 7 *Wisconsin International Law Journal* 1; Landauer, "International Legal Structures" (Book Review) (1989) 30 *Harvard International Law Journal* 1.

29 Koskenniemi, n 3 above; Koskenniemi, n 2 above.

30 Kennedy, "The Sources of International Law" (1987) 2 *American University Journal of International Law and Policy* 1.

31 Carty A, *The Decay of International Law* (1986).

32 Scobbie, "Towards the Elimination of International Law: Some Radical Scepticism About Sceptical Radicalism" (1990) *British Year Book of International Law* 346.

33 Charlesworth, n 23 above.

34 Georgiev, "Politics or Rule Law: Deconstruction and Legitimacy in International Law" (1993) 4 *European Journal of International Law* 1.

35 See Koskenniemi, "The Future of Statehood" (1991) 32 *Harvard Journal of Law and Politics* 397.

to resolve disputes but simply because sufficient numbers of commentators and practitioners accept its existence.[36] It is rich in (and as) rhetoric.

According to Koskenniemi, international legal argument is structured around a series of endlessly deferred and irresolvable oppositions.[37] These are themselves dependent on a deeper contradiction underlying international law itself. International law must satisfy the realist demand for concreteness (that is, rules with legitimacy dependent on State support) and the naturalist demand for a normative system that regulates State behaviour from above. These two tendencies manifest themselves as apologetic (the creation of rules that simply countenance and reflect State practice and do not seek to modify it) or utopian (the drafting of principles and ideals which reflect scholarly or non-State prejudices but have little hope of gaining State support). In common with the critical legal studies project generally, the deconstruction of these patterns of argument is designed to prove that international law cannot escape international politics and retreat into objectivity. The rule of law cannot exist in international politics despite the best intentions of international lawyers. International law is either too close to State practice (therefore reflecting exactly the political predilections of States) or too far from State practice (therefore reliant on the politicised foundations of subjective natural justices).

For Koskenniemi, the answer is to make explicit the political nature of international legal argument instead of resolving disputes using the self-defeating and inappropriate language of rules and principles.[38] This would have the merit of contextualising legal argument and opening it up to previously excluded voices.

The new stream, then, share a commitment to developing a social theory of international law. Accordingly, the autonomy, stability and uniqueness of international law is denied and its social and historical embeddedness is emphasised. In this vein, Anthony Carty advocates a cultural anthropology of international law in order to confront the crisis of identity currently suffered by the discipline.[39] On a more ambitious note, some critical scholars condemn the amoral and detached nature of international society as presently constituted and would have it replaced by a more engaged, porous and "boundaryless" community.[40] Perhaps most importantly for present purposes, the new stream critique of classical liberalism has, to an extent, inspired the democratic liberal response that is the subject of much of this article.

---

36 Kennedy, n 28 above, at 4–7, 47.

37 Koskenniemi, n 3 above.

38 Famously, Koskenniemi makes the point in ibid, p 48, that "International law is singularly useless as a means of justifying or criticising international behaviour".

39 See Carty, "Social Theory and the 'Vanishing' of International Law: A Review Article" (1992) 41 *International and Comparative Law Quarterly* 930.

40 Philip Allott is probably a critical scholar in this regard. Indeed feminists like Jean Elshtain and Grotians like Richard Falk must surely be represented on this spectrum. See Elshtain, "Sovereign God, Sovereign State, Sovereign Self" (1991) 66 *Notre Dame Law Review* 1355 at 1375–78 (though also, like Koskenniemi, warning against abandoning the State altogether and allowing a collapse into authoritarianism). See Falk, n 4 above.

(e) Classical liberalism(s)

Of the five schools described here, the dominant theory of international society was, until recently, classical liberalism. This school is hospitable to both the Lockean strand of liberal thought,[41] (the focus of this section) and the Hobbesian realism of a pre-contractual state of nature or minimal world order. Its preferred methodology in international law was positivism.[42] Traditionally, most international lawyers were, by definition, Lockeans, emphasising the possibilities of international diplomatic intercourse and the creation of rules through the extended practice of all or most States in the international community.

Realists, on the other hand, assume that international relations is marked by the unmediated pursuit of national self-interest.[43] For some realists,[44] international relations is in a permanent state of deferred warfare in which there can be no such thing as international society because there are no shared values and few shared long-term interests. International law has a negligible role in this realist universe.[45] Machiavelli inaugurated this scholarly tradition with "The Prince"[46] while latter-day statesmen, such as Henry Kissinger and Richard Nixon, vigorously practised it in the international arena. Significantly, Nixon,

41 Emphasising the notions of consent and social contract and premised on the assumption that humans are social and cooperative. See Locke J, *The Second Treatise of Government* (ed Carpenter 1924).

42 See Oppenheim, "The Science of International Law: It's Task and Method" (1908) 2 *American Journal of International Law* 313. See also Kelsen H, *General Theory of Law and State* (1945). See also Danilenko G, *Law-Making in the International Community* (1993) for a contemporary defence of positivism in international law. For a modified classicism see D'Amato A, *The Concept of Custom in International Law* (1971). For a critique of Daninlenko's position see Alvarez, "Nihilism Postponed, Positivism Regained" (1994) 15 *Michigan Journal of International Law* 747 at 784.

43 These references are to the classical realists rather than the alter structural and institutional neo-realists. For a fuller examination of these sub-categories see Slaughter Burley, n 11 above, pp 216–20.

44 This realism should be distinguished from the self-styled "realistic jurisprudence" of international legal positivists such as James Watson. This is really more accurately characterised as voluntarism. While positivism/voluntarism and realism are by no means incompatible, positivism is a theory of sources while realism is a theory of behaviour. See Watson, "A Realistic Jurisprudence of International Law" (1980) 30 *Year Book of World Affairs* 265.

45 See eg Dean Acheson's comment that "the second rule is...to keep our own purposes perfectly straight...and not get them mixed up with legal quibbles": Acheson, "Crisis in Asia—An Examination of US Foreign Policy" in Morgenthau H, *In Defence of National Interest* (1951), p 262. For a more modified realism see Morgenthau H, *Politics Among Nations: The Struggle for Power and Peace*, 1st ed (1946). Morgenthau, "Positivism, Functionalism and International Law" (1940) 34 *American Journal of International Law* 260. Morgenthau, in common with many realists, was particularly concerned with international law's inability to restrain or regulate power—the key phenomenon in international relations.

46 Machiavelli N, *The Prince* (ed 1985).

with Hobbesian candour, titled his book about the long peace following the World War II, "The Real War".[47]

Ultimately classical liberalism appears to be simply one form of liberal theory mapped onto international society. International legal regulation is based on the ideas of consent (representativeness), liberty and equality. However, where domestic liberal theory appeals to a conception of the individual as a bearer of rights and a democratic actor, classical liberalism substitutes the State for the individual and posits the nation-State as the free and equal object and subject of international law.

The parallels are instructive. The State, like the individual in liberal theory, possesses a zone of private action into which the law cannot intervene. The right to privacy of individuals is converted into a State's immunity from interference (that is, domestic jurisdiction).[48] The controversy surrounding official involvement in domestic or family matters in local jurisdictions is mirrored in international law by the ambivalence felt by most States about increased United Nations involvement in States' internal affairs.

Similarly, the taboo on violence in domestic law is replicated by use of force jurisprudence in international law. Even in the most libertarian of international orders, harm to the independent State is regarded as intolerable just as the prevention of harm to the autonomous individual has been the first rationale of most liberal States and conceptions of the State from Hobbes to Hart.[49]

At the level of moral theory, the most revealing parallel between the liberal theory of the individual and that of the State in international relations occurs in the discussion and construction of origins. "Man" in the state of nature is replaced by States in a state of nature. In both constructions, the individual State or human is vulnerable, aggressive and free. Societies, international and national, are designed to mitigate the vulnerability, restrain violence and maintain freedom. This is a particular view of the state of nature and the nature of States which has been accepted as complete and remains highly influential.[50]

However, perhaps the defining political, as opposed to moral, idea of liberalism is that of the consensual or representative polity. This is the institution which embodies the various claims of the individual and which

---

47 Nixon RM, *The Real War* (1980).

48 See article 2(7) of the United Nations Charter.

49 According to Hart, a major purpose of the State is to prevent human beings inflicting arbitrary violence on one another. See Hart HLA, *The Concept of Law* (1961). For liberal international lawyers, one of the primary purposes of the State system is to prevent illegal uses of force. However, in both cases, these rationales are incomplete. Both the municipal and international legal systems regularly apply sanctions against violence that threatens the legal order but not against violence *per se*. Feminists have suggested that the private/public division in international law replicates and reinforces the division of public and private life in domestic law. See eg Charlesworth, n 8 above.

50 The classic expression of this doctrine is found in the *Lotus* case where the PCIJ stated that "[T]he rules of law binding upon States therefore emanate from their own free will...restrictions upon the independence of States cannot therefore be presumed." (1932) PCIJ, Series A, No 10.

mediates between the impossible desirability of unanimity and the undesirable possibility of anarchy. The notion of the consensual polity rests on the ideal of representativeness in the domestic life of nations. Responsible government, parliamentary sovereignty and the distribution of powers are manifestations of this political creed. In the international society of nations, consent replaces representativeness as the prevailing liberal metaphor. Classical liberals are committed to the idea that international law is a creation of the general will of States expressed through their collective consent.[51] Indeed for positivists, the formation of norms can only occur through more or less unanimous State consent.[52] Paradoxically, the most anarchical of societies (the international one) is also the society in which law can only be created through near unanimity.

Where liberal theorists suggest a fictitious social contract between citizenry and State in constitutional theory, classical liberals demand an actual covenant between the law and the States in international society. The classical liberals seem to have escaped reliance on metaphor. For positivists, the empirical fact of State behaviour is a reliable indicator of law and provides a complete normative basis for that law.

Critique

The classical liberal theory of international law has been severely deflated by four critiques. These are the moral, social, doctrinal and democratic critiques. Democratic liberalism has arisen as a response to this final set of objections to classical liberalism.

The social and moral critiques have been described (though not accepted as valid) by Koskenniemi.[53] The social critique of classical State-centred liberalism derives its force from the sociological fact of interdependence and the withering away of the State. According to this view, States no longer exist in their pure form. They have either devolved political sovereignty to supra-national institutions (North American Free Trade Agreement, the European Community), lost political sovereignty to sub-State groups (self-determination, regionalism, devolution) or witnessed the disappearance of their economic sovereignty into the transnational corporate markets. In addition to all this, the social critique notes that States are incapable of meeting their own environmental, ecological and security needs without a level of cooperation that threatens the whole notion of autonomous statehood upon which classical liberalism is premised.

The moral critique focuses on the oppressive nature of States and draws on the growing human rights field to argue that States have suffered an ethical disengagement from human beings and cultural communities. On this view State egotism is a morally indefensible foundation for international society because it appears to sanction some forms of inter-State violence and is neglectful of intra-

51 Ibid.
52 See Watson, n 2 above, and Weil, n 22 above.
53 See Koskenniemi, n 35 above.

State abuses of human rights and community values. For these reasons, the State must be either abandoned or heavily modified.[54]

Doctrinally, too, there are many difficulties with the raw positivism or voluntarism of classical international legal theory not least its cripplingly self-referential and circular theory of sources.[55] However, as a liberal theory of consent, it suffers from a single major failing. The consent of States is real enough in practice (though extremely difficult to decipher at times) but the States themselves, as conduits of representativeness, are largely imagined. This critique of both the current State system and classical liberalism, questions the democratic credentials of the large majority of States which make up the international order.

III. Democratic Liberalism

Democratic liberalism in international legal theory is an attempt to meet this important objection to classical liberal theory by transplanting a richer and more substantive liberalism onto international society. In the process, the individual assumes her place as a primary actor in international legal life. Consent in this way works at two levels. States remain primary in the sphere of international law-making. Their consent is vital to the creation of international law.[56] However, the link between State and individual is reasserted through the democratic process. Individuals must give consent to governments in order that they can possess the formal credentials of statehood. Consent thus becomes a threshold requirement for law-making at the two levels of inter-State and intra-State legitimacy.[57] This rhetorical manoeuvre has obvious attractions. It appears to combine the stability and predictability of classical liberalism or voluntarism (State consent) with a new source of State legitimacy based on a deeper democratic or individualistic tradition (popular consent).

To varying degrees, the "New Haven" approach, the Kantian model and the democratic governance standard are all variations on this theme of democratic liberalism. They each share in common a desire to reposition the individual in international law as subject. Each draws on a vein of democratic theory and justification stretching back to Kant and recalling the decisive motifs of American constitutionalism. In each case, a self-conscious response to the aridities of positivism and classical liberalism, has resulted in an appeal to the international legal community to discard formalism and relativism by developing a political morality of international law with liberal democracy at the apex. To this extent, these schools represent an attempt to revive the liberal project.

---

54 This position is the inspiration for recent works by Carty, n 31 above; and esp Allott, n 3 above.

55 See eg Koskenniemi, n 2 above, at 1.

56 Though there are important differences between various strands of democratic liberalism with Franck emphasising the State and Tesón the individual. See generally below.

57 There are stronger (more individualistic) (Tesón) and weaker (more statist) (Franck) versions of this approach discussed in the remainder of the essay.

The "New Haven" model (or Yale school) has been discussed and critiqued at great length elsewhere.[58] Its practitioners are a group of men and women who wish to invest the international legal process with an interdisciplinary mentality. First phase, New Haven originated by Harold Lasswell and Myres McDougal was a curious mixture of American legal realism and European psycho-social theory.[59] Its more recent versions have featured scholars like Michael Reisman and Richard Falk who have expunged most of the arcane language of the McDougal/Lasswell school and have sought to bring these ideas into the mainstream.[60] They have mostly succeeded to the extent that the New Haven approach is widely regarded as the second school of international legal jurisprudence in the US and the most significant antithesis to classical liberalism. The New Haven approach is marked by its anti-positivism. International law is to be judged by its ability to meet the demands of a general right to human dignity and not according to its general acceptance by States.

However the New Haven ground has now been captured by the two approaches I wish to focus on for the purpose of this article. These are Kantian liberalism and democratic liberalism.[61]

(a) A Kantian view: Tesón

Ferdinand Tesón has developed his idea of a Kantian[62] international law over a number of articles and critiques.[63] The major philosophical premise of Kantian liberalism is normative individualism. On this conception of law, the protection of individual human rights is regarded as the central aspiration of a normative regime.[64] In Tesón's view, justice is not just possible in the international legal system but mandated. The just community, whether international or domestic, is the purpose of all social life and juridical arrangement. A just community is one in which individual human flourishing is valued above stability or order. For

---

58 See eg Trimble, "International Law, World Order and Critical Legal Studies" (1990) 42 *Stanford Law Review* 811.

59 See eg McDougal M and Associates, *Studies in World Public Order* (1960); McDougal, Lasswell and Reisman, "Theories About International Law: Prologue to a Configurative Jurisprudence" (1968) 8 *Virginia Journal of International Law* 188.

60 See eg Falk, "The Status of Law in International Society", n 4 above. The leading British scholar associated with this approach is Rosalyn Higgins whose concern with process, choices and authoritative decision-making, in her recently published book, place her firmly in the Yale camp. Interestingly, she also provides something of a rejoinder to the new stream critique in the first chapter of her book. See Higgins, n 12 above, at 1–16, esp 7–11.

61 It is quite clear that W Michael Reisman occupies positions across this spectrum. His article, "Sovereignty and Human Rights in Contemporary International Law" (1990) 84 *American Journal of International Law* 866, is really an embryonic attempt to develop a theory of democratic liberalism.

62 This approach is associated variously with the cosmopolitan and humanitarian approach to international law.

63 Tesón, n 14 above; n 12 above; Tesón F, *Humanitarian Intervention: An Enquiry into Law and Morality* (1988).

64 See Tesón, n 14 above, at 54.

Tesón, as for Kant, the liberal-democratic State is the only polity capable of advancing this conception of justice.[65]

Closely associated with this assumption is the belief that liberal-democratic States are peace-loving and committed to the rule of law. The prescription arising from this is the principle that only liberal-democratic States should be admitted to the family of nations.

Tesón credits Kant with enormous prescience. In various places throughout his article, Kant is described as the theoretical inspiration for the system of international institutions,[66] the visionary who predicted the ascendancy of human rights[67] and the first philosopher to perceive a link between "arbitrary government at home and aggressive behaviour abroad".[68] Kant's moral theory of international rights is set out in "Perpetual Peace", a pamphlet designed to influence international diplomacy of the 18th Century. In this study, Kant outlines the conditions for a liberal-cosmopolitan world community dedicated to peace and underwritten by a commitment to individual liberty.[69] Accordingly, the basic principles of international governance are as follows:

(1) The civil Constitution of every nation should be republican.[70]

(2) [International Law] shall be based on a federation of free States.[71]

There is a necessary connection between the requirements of peace and the maintenance of a system which guarantees individual liberty. This is because representative democracies ("republican States") are most likely to observe human rights standards and least inclined to engage in hostilities.

Tesón offers an explanation for this and a great deal of empirical evidence. Representative democracies are founded on the consent of individuals. There is, therefore, presumed consent between the government and the people. In common with other contractarian theorists, Tesón argues that humans are rational, free and peaceable. When these traits are reflected in the formation of the Constitution, governments will inherit or derive these attributes from the citizenry. When governments are despotic, autocratic or authoritarian the State will display contempt for individual autonomy in the domestic sphere and will act in an irrational manner internationally. The key to restraint in the international sphere is the moderating influence of public opinion. The force of public opinion is supplemented by a free press and protected by a Bill of Rights while the separation of powers ensures that a system of checks and balances mitigates the tendency of executive government to act rashly, unilaterally or

---

65 This can be compared with the similar position adopted by Rawls in his essay, "The Law of Peoples" in Shute S and Hurley S (eds), *On Human Rights*, Amnesty Oxford Lectures (1993).

66 Tesón, n 14 above, at 100

67 Ibid, at 102.

68 Ibid, at 56.

69 Kant, "To Perpetual Peace: A Philosophical Sketch" [1795] in Reiss H (ed), *Kant: Political Writings* (1970).

70 Tesón, n 14 above, at 62. As Tesón remarks we would, today, describe these polities as constitutional democracies.

71 Ibid, at 57.

belligerently. Self-governing States are disinclined to go to war because the effects of war are felt by the people who when represented in the decision-making process will seek to avoid the privations associated with their role in the war. Finally, liberal States, in favouring a global free market, have invested too much in peace to risk it all in war. For Tesón, the free exchange of goods and persons has the dual effect of spreading common ideas and pacifying the international culture though rational communication.

(b) The right to democratic governance: Franck

Democratic liberals of the non-Kantian persuasion have a slightly different agenda. Liberated by the end of the Cold War and emboldened by the liberal triumphalism of commentators such as Francis Fukuyama,[72] the new democratic liberals have sought to encapsulate the *zeitgeist* in the phrase "a right to democratic governance". The containment strategies of classical liberalism have been replaced by a series of evangelical flourishes in the name of universal democracy. The old positivism based on the consent of States has been replaced and extended by a theory of international law based on the dual consent of States *and* individuals.

In modern international law the idea of a right to democratic governance can be traced back to Woodrow Wilson's idealism at the end of the Great War in 1918. The failure of Wilson's system and the onset of the hot and cold wars of the latter half of the 20th Century effectively entombed the idea of universal democracy until 1991. In its place came the harsh realism of international politics reflected in Machiavellian statecraft from Dulles to Kissinger, and given theoretical underpinning by thinkers such as Hans Morgenthau[73] and Kenneth Waltz.[74] International lawyers faced with a choice between the rock of irrelevant idealism and the hard place of a realistic jurisprudence based on positivism and statism, tended to choose the latter.

The internal lives of States were not the concern of these scholars who, with the exception of a few human rights experts, were instead busy constructing a minimum world order with stability at the centre. International law, in this period of classical liberalism, was the law *between* States. It regulated their extra-territorial affairs, prohibited transborder use of force and provided for a process of diplomatic intercourse. The authority and legitimacy of international law was derivable from State consent. What States agreed to was law, what they refused to agree to was not law. The legitimacy of law was based on consent but the legitimacy of the States themselves was founded on effectiveness. In this way, governments represented regardless of representativeness. A social contract existed between States and the system, but this was not extended to a compact between the State and its citizens despite the best efforts of human rights lawyers. Indeed, it is arguable that the single most important legal text extant in this period was article 2(7) of the United Nations Charter.

72 Fukuyama F, *The End of History and the Last Man* (1992).

73 See Morgenthau references, n 45 above.

74 Waltz K, *Man, the State and War* (1959).

Those who support a norm of democratic governance ask us to envisage international law as the law *of*, as well as between, States. This would be an international standard of internal governance which would have direct effect *within* States.

Professor Thomas Franck was the first international lawyer to fully explicate the idea of democratic governance in a provocative and engaging article for the *American Journal of International Law* entitled "The Emerging Right to Democratic Governance", and this article will remain the focus of these comments.[75] It was Franck who, three years before, had argued in another article that justice could play no role in international law because States were the relevant actors in international relations and States were not and could not be just.[76] Franck's conversion seems to have arisen out of a number of developments.

First, there had been the conclusion of the Cold War and the greater receptiveness of the States of Eastern and Central Europe to Western liberalism. Second, there was the self-belief and exceptionalism manifested in the United States during the Reagan and Bush years. This exceptionalism encouraged the belief that United States democratic values were universal values or at the very least that the American democratic tradition could be exported. Third, there was the news of "the end of history" conveyed to us by Francis Fukuyama and accompanied by a considerable amount of empirical evidence to suggest that democratic liberalism was on the point of eliminating all its ideological competitors.[77]

Drawing inspiration from these developments, Frank argued that State consent had been supplemented by the need for individual or democratic consent in international law.[78] The social contract is revived and a theory of dual consent is propounded. In this way, legitimacy is no longer a matter of effectiveness but rather of democratic will.

Ultimately, Franck seems to want it both ways. Unlike Tesón, he is unprepared to renounce the commitment to State consent completely and focus

75 See eg Franck, "The Emerging Right to Democratic Governance" (1992) 86 *American Journal of International Law* 46. The themes in Franck's work have been adopted and expanded in a number of articles. See eg Halperin, "Guaranteeing Democracy" (1993) 91 *Foreign Policy* 105 (arguing that a series of constitutional guarantees should be put in place within the UN system to ensure support for States willing to hold democratic elections. Further arguing that this international guarantee clause should include a promise to defend republican government); Fox, "The Right to Political Participation in International Law" (1992) 17(2) *Yale Journal of International Law* 539 (arguing that a series of treaties have now created a human right to participate in the political process and that international law is now based on the sovereignty of States and people). See Fox, "The Right to Political Participation in International Law" (1992) 86 *American Society of International Law Proceedings* 249; Steiner, "Political Participation as a Human Right" (1988) 1 *Harvard Human Rights Yearbook* 77.

76 Franck, "Is Justice Relevant to the International Legal System?" (1989) 64 *Notre Dame Law Review* 945.

77 Fukuyama, n 72 above.

78 Franck, n 75 above, at 46–49.

exclusively on normative individualism. How, then, does he reconcile the apparent conflict between a system based on State consent and one based on individual consent? In essence, Franck merges the two ideas of consent and imagines a world in which States *themselves* consent to a new norm of international law that demands the consent of the citizens for State legitimacy. In his words, "increasingly, governments recognise that their legitimacy depends on meeting a normative expectation of the community of states".[79] Democratic entitlement becomes foundational not because individuals are central actors (Tesón) but because States deem them to be so (Franck). It appears that there would be no individual consent without prior State consent. Therefore, the pragmatics of classical positivism remain prior to any moral theory of individual liberty. Franck's democratic entitlement is reliant on a happy and global coincidence between governed and government. Tesón's normative individualism is the basis of international law regardless of whether States possess this democratic tendency or not. Tesón's liberalism has therefore abrogated the covenant between States and international law much more thoroughly than Franck's.

IV. Imagined Consent: Some Reflections

There are some significant difficulties with both the Kantian and democratic liberal approaches.

(a) Kantian liberalism revisited

Tesón's more radical Kantianism is often characterised as cosmopolitanism.[80] However, the term cosmopolitan must surely be a misnomer in this context implying as it does a plurality of values, cultures and systems. This is the antithesis of Tesón's position which imposes a pattern of conformity on all the States of the world. The community of nations as it now stands, revels in its heterogeneity. There is no test for membership at the United Nations.[81] All States, no matter what their internal constitutions, are equal members of the

79 Ibid, at 46.

80 See eg Nardin, "Realism, Cosmopolitanism and the Rule of Law" (1987) 81 *American Society of International Law Proceedings* 415 at 416; Tesón, n 14 above, at 102.

81 Article 4(1) of the UN Charter states:

> Membership in the United Nations is open to all other peace-loving States which accept the obligations contained in the present Charter, and, in the judgement of the Organization, are willing and able to carry out these obligations.

However, this condition has never consistently been applied by the two bodies invested with determining membership, ie the Security Council and the General Assembly. Indeed in the *Conditions of Admission of a State to Membership in the United Nations* case the ICJ made it clear that a member State was "not juridically entitled to make its consent to the admission dependent on conditions not expressly provided [by article 4(1)] ICJ Rep 1948, p 56. Tesón, of course, advocates an amendment to this provision to bring it in line with the Kantian prescriptions, ibid, at 100.

United Nations.[82] The exclusion of States for failing to meet democratic standards might be regarded as a retrograde step by relatively new nation-States whose independence was achieved recently. The Kantian theory in effect trades in one liberal ideal (the equality of States) for another (the representativeness of government).

Over 30 years ago, Martin Wight offered us an historical reminder that:

> the principle that members of international society should be doctrinally uniform can be used by ideologists of more than one kind.[83]

Wight was discussing Kant's "Perpetual Peace" but he noted that there are a number of ways to perpetuate peace. Metternich's "Holy Alliance" is one, and nuclear deterrence, another.

Exporting democracy too, has a habit of proving counter-productive or, worse, can be a disguise for action in pursuit of suspect ideological ends. Tesón's idea of an exclusive company of democratic States finds expression in the term "rogue State" which has been used to justify interventions in Nicaragua, Panama, Grenada, Libya, Iran, Iraq and Chile. North Korea is the latest in a line of these enemies of international society. The ease with which States are demonised by opposing them to an idealised international society must stand as a warning to Kantians as well as Grotians.[84]

The mechanics of exclusion, too, may prove beyond the United Nations and/or world community should the Kantian view prevail. Terms such as minimum world order, democratic governance and general respect for human rights lack even a core meaning in the international order. There is certainly no supranational body capable of making the sort of determinations and authoritative interpretations that such a norm would surely require. The United Nations has on several occasions debated a resolution calling for expulsion of a member. On none of these occasions was there any attempt to infuse the

---

82 See eg article 2(1), United Nations Charter.

83 Wight, n 20 above, at 225. Tesón diverges from Frank *et al* here. For Tesón, States can be divided into two categories depending on their capacity to conform to the liberal ideal. It is remarkable how similar this taxonomy is to the one developed by James Lorimer, the Scottish commonsense international law jurist, who described a world composed of civilised States, semi-savage States and savage States. Indeed both Lorimer and Tesón would seek to exclude the vast majority of nations from the international community on the basis of their inability to meet certain moral postulates. See Lorimer J, *The Institutes of the Law of Nations* (1883), vol 1, pp 101–02 where he states:

> as a political phenomenon, humanity, in its present condition, divides itself into concentric zones...that of civilized humanity, that of barbarous humanity, and that of savage humanity.

Those not belonging to the first two groups are described as "the residue of mankind" and are not entitled to jural recognition in Lorimer's system. See further similarities between Lorimer, Tesón and Rawls, in Rawls, n 65 above.

84 See eg D'Amato, "The Invasion of Panama was a Lawful Response to Tyranny" (1990) 84 *American Journal of International Law* 516.

admission process with a standardised, principled approach to membership.[85] There is no reason to suggest that politicised, *ad hoc* decisions would not also be the mark of a new admissions procedure to exclude undemocratic States.

At an empirical level, the Kantian theory is unsatisfactory. Norman Angell said in 1910 that a major world war between States was impossible given the global conditions of capitalism and democracy.[86] There is something of this optimism in Tesón's work. Certainly both he and Kant share the unproven assumption that democratic nations do not go to war but I would like to focus on the reasons Tesón gives for this apparent tendency because it seems to be the key to Tesón's understanding about how democratic States are actually governed.

For Tesón, a democracy is a political system in which "individual rights are honoured and rulers are appointed by the people".[87] What Tesón never specifies is how these two standards inevitably give rise to full participatory democracy that is the continuing involvement of an informed electorate in the decision-making of their elected representatives. Instead there is excessive reliance on the form of representative democracy over the substance of participatory democracy. This is most clearly reflected in Tesón's arguments about the tendency of democracies to abjure war.

According to Tesón, the two constitutional principles promoting this tendency are the separation of powers and freedom of the press. The first ensures that decisions to go to war cannot be made by an "all-powerful sovereign" with scant regard for the effects on his people. The second permits the citizenry a voice in the foreign and domestic policy of the nation. Together they "create a system of mutual controls and relative diffusion of power that complicates and encumbers governmental decisions about war".[88]

There are of course severe shortcomings in such a theory of democracy because it neglects two important features of life in the post-liberal State. One is the concentration of power, the other is the concentration of information. Governmental decisions about war are the very decisions which are often *not* encumbered by reference to public opinion in constitutional democracies. In relatively few of the major constitutional democracies does the legislature have a substantial role in making war. The executive has accrued more and more power through the years by recourse to national security arguments. Even in cases where elected representatives are given a role in the Constitution, methods are found to circumvent these checks and balances.[89] The history of the 20th Century is in some respects a narrative in which young men and women are sent to their deaths by often democratic governments either against their will (for

85 The work of the Badinter Commission can hardly be regarded as a success in this area given its confused jurisprudence and rather formal requirements for the "observance" of human rights.

86 Angell N, *The Great Illusion: A Study of the Relation of Military Power to National Advantage* (1910).

87 Tesón, n 14 above, at 61.

88 Ibid, at 75.

89 See eg Walsh L, *Iran-Contra: The Final Report* (1994).

example, the Vietnam War) or under the spell of the crudest of propaganda (for example, World War I).

Meanwhile, the role of the free press in such cases has been well-documented in several studies arising out of the Gulf War.[90] It is now generally accepted that in the Gulf War, the media were denied access to important material about the conduct of the war and were reluctant to explore alternative political strategies during the war. Tesón's blithe promise of a fully-educated, involved citizenry acting as a check on governmental action is not borne out from the experience of the Vietnam War or the Gulf War far less the vicious colonial wars fought by republican governments from Algeria to Malaysia during the era of decolonisation. Indeed, even if citizens in democracies were given a true republican education it is doubtful if "therefore war will appear to them as the evil that every rational person knows it is".[91] Noam Chomksy, for example, has cast doubt on the presupposition that there is any connection between higher education and critical thinking arguing that education can be an inculcation of ideological values rather than critical faculties.[92] There are further unsupported assumptions (for example, that individuals themselves are not warlike) that seem to contradict a great deal of psychological evidence.

In conclusion, Tesón seems to have placed too much faith in the constitutional forms of liberal governance while averting his critical gaze from the political and social contexts in which these forms are given meaning.

(b) The right to democratic governance: Some problems

The difficulties with Professor Frank's right to democratic governance can be grouped into two. These relate first, to the substantive, political problems with the whole notion of democratic governance and second, to his use of a series of largely indeterminate and formless international legal principles to support an argument for the emergence of the right to democratic governance and to provide sources for the right.

The first group of objections question the legitimacy, both legal and political, of the norm. These have been considered in great detail elsewhere and so will be mentioned only briefly here.[93] In this category, there are three significant problems with the idea of democratic governance.

---

90 See eg MacArthur J, *Second Front: Censorship and Propaganda in the Gulf War* (1992); Draper, "The True History of the Gulf War", *New York Times Review of Books* (30 January 1992); Dennis EE et al, *The Media at War: The Press and the Persian Gulf Conflict* (1991).

91 Tesón, n 14 above, at 75.

92 See eg Chomsky N, *Necessary Illusions* (1987). There are further unsupported assumptions (eg that individuals themselves are not warlike) that seem to contradict a great deal of historical evidence. See Ignatieff M, *Blood and Belonging: Journeys into the New Nationalism* (1994), for a contrary perspective on the "rationality" of war.

93 For a series of reservations as to the durability and sustainability of the norm on the ground see eg Carothers, "Empirical Perspectives on the Emerging Norm of Democracy" (1992) 86 *American Society of International Law Proceedings* 261. For a more conceptual critique see Otto, "Challenging the 'New World Order':

First, there is the inadequacy of the empirical evidence for the purported ascendancy of the democratic impulse. This evidence has come mostly from Central America, Central Europe and South America as well as the Iberian Peninsula. Leaving aside the issue of whether democracy has really been entrenched in some of these regions, there is the additional failing of the norm that it has not taken root in large parts of Asia and Africa.[94] This is different from saying that States in this region are undemocratic (though this may be the case). Rather the problem is that the whole notion of electoral and contractual democracy is alien to some of these cultures who may well practice their own forms of participation that are not recognisably democratic. This is equally a problem with indigenous societies and minorities. The democratic norm imposed on indigenous cultures is often perceived by them as a form of neo-colonialism.

A second, associated, problem lies in excessively formalistic and narrow conception of the right as elaborated by Franck. There is little consideration of the economic conditions and cultural contexts which make democracy meaningful. Nor is there any regard for the savage effects decades of repression have had on the democratic consciousness. One wonders whether traumatised electorates in El Salvador, Angola, Mozambique, Guatemala, Argentina and Nicaragua are capable of enjoying the norm of democratic governance to any realistic extent.[95]

Third, there is the conflict between this norm of legitimacy and other more basic and disposative values within the international system with the concomitant impossibility of enforcing this right to democracy while remaining committed to the current international legal regime. Ultimately, democratic liberalism comes into serious conflict with the fundaments of international law. The 1970 Declaration on Friendly Relations, for example, contains the following provision: "Every state has an inalienable right to choose its political, economic, social and cultural systems, without interference in any form by any other state".[96] The norm of democracy, while not as exclusive or monotheistic as Kantian republicanism, nevertheless carries with it the beginnings of a world community in which some States are more formally equal than others.

International Law, Global Governance and the Possibilities for Women" (1993) 3 *Transnational Law and Contemporary Problems* 371; Otto, "Popular Perspectives on the Global Promotion of Democracy and the Role of International Law" (1994) *Australian and New Zealand Society of International Law Proceedings* 159.

94 Indeed the most progressive African leaders are beginning to question whether democracy is worth aspiring to on the continent. See, "Southern Africa's old front line ponders it's future in mainstream", *New York Times* (21 November 1994), p 1; where President Chiluba of Zambia is quoted as saying "Maybe Africa was not cut out for Western-style democracy…maybe the one-party state is the way to go after all".

95 See Farer, "Elections, Democracy and Human Rights: Towards Union" (1989) *Human Rights Quarterly* 504.

96 General Assembly Declaration on Principles of International Law Concerning Friendly Relations and Co-operation Among States in Accordance with the Charter of the United Nations, GA Res 2625 (XXV), 24 October 1970.

However, a more serious set of objections to the norm is that it relies on a pair of international legal principles which lack the determinacy and content that Franck himself regards as threshold requirements for the emergence of new norms.[97] These are the right to self-determination and the right to free expression.

Any potential role self-determination may have had in promoting a norm of democratic governance has been diminished by two interpretive trends. The first trend has been towards conservative and statist definitions of the principle.[98] This process reached its apogee during the period when self-determination came to be identified exclusively with decolonisation. In effect, self-determination has most assiduously served the same State system it pretends to assail. A more recent, second, trend has involved the misappropriation of the label. The elasticity of self-determination, throughout history, has both ensured its longevity but diminished its legitimacy.[99] It has had to be capable of surviving inconsistent application, absorbing anomalies and, ultimately, satisfying powerful strategic and political interests and realities without compromising its revolutionary appeal. In this latter role, it has frequently flattered to deceive and in the process has evolved into an open-textured, highly manipulable, and indiscriminately employed slogan. It vests a tainted respectability in all those who use it, but is (at the same time) deprived of clarity and the possibility of legal content.[100] The most startling recent examples of this are the claims to self-determination and a white homeland or *volkstadt* made by elements of the white minority in South Africa and the comparably disingenuous assertions of a right to self-determination by the Bosnian Serbs. Meanwhile, the various attempts by the European Community and United Nations to give substance to the norm have been exercises in practical futility and theoretical inconsistency.[101]

---

97 Franck T, *The Power of Legitimacy Among Nations* (1990); Franck, "Legitimacy in the International System" (1988) 82 *American Journal of International Law* 705.

98 For example, the salt-water or blue-water test which limited the application of the norm to those entities which had been colonised by European powers.

99 See eg Pomerance M, *Self-Determination in Law and Practice* (1982).

100 One scholar even argues that self-determination is "unworthy of the appellation of a rule of law"; Verzjil, *International Law in Historical Perspective* (1968), p 325: quoted in Hannum, "Rethinking Self-Determination" (1993) 34 *Virginia Journal of International Law* 1 at 31.

101 See eg, a book length critique of UN practice by Pomerance, n 99 above. See also, *Conference on Yugoslavia Arbitration Commissions*, Opinions on Questions arising from the dissolution of Yugoslavia, 11 January, 4 July, (1992) 31 ILM 1488. See especially, Opinion No 1 at 1494, and Opinion No 2 at 1497. For a general overview of theoretical problems associated with self-determination see Berman, "Sovereignty in Abeyance: Self-Determination and International Law" (1988) *Wisconsin International Law Journal* 7(1) at 51.

Clearly then, self-determination at present lacks both definition and applicability,[102] and has yet to be salvaged from "its descent into incoherence".[103]

Free speech doctrine in international law is in a similar state lacking the determinacy and coherence that Franck deems necessary for founding a legitimate and mature rule of international law.[104] The incoherence of free speech stems from the extremely open-textured and heavily qualified nature of the right as laid out in article 19 of the International Covenant on Civil and Political Rights (ICCPR).[105] Here we have a rather illiberal and potentially anti-democratic enunciation of the free speech principle. The core right to speak freely on political matters is hedged to such an extent that it ceases to exist in any meaningful sense.[106] The right guaranteed in article 19 bears little resemblance to the libertarian version of free expression prevalent in many Western States, notably the United States.

Problems related to the indeterminacy of the rule spring from the absence of any authoritative pronouncements on what article 19 actually protects. Indeed, the protection of free expression is disappointingly weak in international human rights law being less well-developed internationally than in many domestic systems. This lacuna is hardly filled by reference to the work of the Human Rights Committee.[107] Dominic McGoldrick, whom Franck quotes in support of his thesis,[108] stated at the conclusion of his analysis of article 19:

> The fundamental norms within article 19 remain undefined and largely undeveloped. It appears unlikely that the work of the Human Rights Committee will redress the disappointing record of the United Nations concerning freedom of expression.[109]

Even if one agrees with Franck that a right to free expression is crystallising in international law it is unlikely to be one as closely linked to the democratic process as he imagines. The conceptual leap from free expression as the human right to criticise government without suffering harm to free expression as the right to participate fully in the democratic affairs of the State is not one the international community seems inclined to make. Indeed while the first, much

---

102 See Simpson, "New Developments in the Law of Self-Determination" (1991) *Proceedings, International Law Weekend ANU* 69. This is not to deny its talismanic appeal to National Liberation Movements and unrepresented people.

103 See Franck, "Legitimacy in the International System", n 75 above.

104 Ibid.

105 ICCPR (16 December 1966), 999 UNTS 171, (1967) 6 ILM 368.

106 Article 19(3) reads, in part:

> It [the right to free expression] may therefore be subject to certain restrictions, but these shall only be such as are provided by law and as necessary:
> (a) For respect of the right or reputation of others;
> (b) For the protection of national security...of public order (ordre public), or of public health or morals.

107 Franck, n 75 above, at 62–63.

108 Ibid, at 61.

109 McGoldrick D, *The Human Rights Committee: Its Role in the Development of the International Covenant on Civil and Political Rights* (1991), p 471.

weaker and diluted, version of the right remains controversial, it is unlikely that the more sophisticated and deeper right will attain normative standing in international law. The examples given by Franck, again from the work of the Human Rights Committee, seem almost forlorn in their isolation.[110] The Committee has never been a staunch advocate of free expression preferring to give States a margin of appreciation when evaluating the effect of speech. This approach is perhaps exemplified in the *Hertzberg* case[111] where the Committee found that the Finnish Broadcasting Authority could invoke parts of article 19 as a justification for banning the transmission of homosexual ideas and material on radio and television.[112]

Ultimately, Professor Franck has provided us with a stimulating and challenging account of the possibilities of universalising democratic governance. However, his claim that this norm is now a global entitlement cannot be maintained in the face of the inchoate and ambiguous nature of the legal standards upon which it is said to rest namely: the principle of free expression and the norm of self-determination.

V. Conclusion

This article has examined some of the ways in which consent (of States and individuals) is deployed in liberal international legal reasoning. Consent in the case of classical positivism is imagined in at least two senses. First, States often do not actively consent to the formation of norms but are, in the vast majority of cases, deemed to have consented.[113] This is particularly so for new States and in the case of norms of *jus cogens*. Second, this consent is not derived from the consent of the individuals on whose behalf governments rule and States purport to act since the majority of States remain unrepresentative.

In an attempt to cure this defect in classical theory, democratic liberals have proposed either reinstating the individual at the centre of international society (Tesón) or have suggested a democratic entitlement norm (Franck). Normative individualism, the basis of Kantian liberalism, is an attractive idea but the relationship between the constitutional mechanics that undergird it and the world order outcomes sought is a tenuous and underdeveloped one. In addition to this, Kantian liberalism proposes an unequal international society of outsiders and insiders in which those citizens on the peripheries of the republican society are condemned to exist in a lawless state of nature.

Meanwhile, the norm of democratic governance rests on the consent of States and the consent of individuals, but depends on a theory of legitimacy which continues to implicitly prioritise the State. The purported existence of a

110 Franck, n 75 above, at 60.

111 *Hertzberg and others v Finland*, UN Doc A/35 40, 176.

112 When the committee charged with drafting the ICCPR convened to write article 19 they originally published a list that included no less than 26 possible limitations on the right to free expression. See Bossuyt MJ, *Guide to the "Travaux Préparatoires" of the International Covenant on Civil and Political Rights* (1987), p 375.

113 This particular critique is not the focus of this article.

democratic governance norm is not evidence of a renewed commitment to the individual in the doctrine of international law, but is a product of historical and potentially ephemeral forces in the ideology of consent.

In at least two senses, consent is imagined to provide a foundation for the norm. First, the vast majority of States have not consented to the establishment of this norm in their practice. The principles from which the norm is derived are themselves either inconsistent or indeterminate. Second, and most critically, the consent of the governed in the prevailing theories of democratic entitlement is a predominantly artificial and formalistic construct. The conditions of economic choice and fully realised civil society based on genuine consent are neither required nor mandated by the democratic entitlement norm. Instead, it is satisfied to rely on the rhetorical forms (representation, imagined consent) and technical contingencies (elections, qualified free speech rights) of a highly specific, partial and superficial notion of democracy.

[17]

Challenging the 'New World Order': International Law, Global Democracy and the Possibilities for Women

*Dianne Otto**

I. Introduction 372

II. The Construction of Democracy in International Law 374

- A. Developments in Democratic Discourse Since 1945 374
- B. Democracy as a Means to Peace 376
- C. Democracy as Human Right 379
- D. Democracy as a Measure of State Legitimacy 382
- E. The Potential for Change 385

III. The Effects of Democratization on Women in Eastern Europe and the Former Soviet Union 386

- A. The Absence of Women from the Main Agenda 387
- B. Exclusion by Suffrage 388
- C. Exclusion by Equality 389
- D. Control by the Denial of Liberty 391
- E. The Distinction Between Private and Public 393
- F. Resistances 394

IV. The Alternative of Emancipatory Democracies 396

- A. Alternative Democratic Traditions 396
- B. Deepening Democracy 399
- C. Exposing Neutrality 400
- D. Embracing Diversity 402
- E. Redefining Political 404
- F. The Possibility of Transformation 405

V. The Role of International Law in Promoting Democratic Diversity 406

- A. The Power of Legal Discourse 406
- B. Law Making Processes 407
- C. Decentering the State 410
- D. Relinquishing Western and Patriarchal Loyalties 412
- E. Fundamental Reform 413

VI. Conclusion 414

---

* Amnesty International. B.A., University of Adelaide; L.L.B., University of Melbourne.
I would like to thank two teacher-friends: Professor Hilary Charlesworth for her continuing support and inspirational guidance and Dr. Adrian Howe for her challenging comments and thoughtful suggestions.

I. INTRODUCTION

Both George Bush and Mikhail Gorbachev greeted the end of the Cold War as the dawning of a new world order. From Bush's expansive North American viewpoint, this was the birth of an international consensus embracing the great U.S. ideal of freedom for all.[1] Australia's Foreign Minister, Gareth Evans, approvingly identified the components of this global metamorphosis as "the promotion of democratic practices; the consolidation of free market economies; collective resistance to aggression; and the upholding of 'universal values.'"[2] While acknowledging the interdependence of these elements in the scheme of the new world order, this paper focuses on the possibilities for women associated with democratization, and explores the role the international legal system could play in the realization of these possibilities.

The new world order, according to President Bush and other commentators, is the triumph of liberal democracy over communism[3] or, in more extreme views, the arrival of the end of history.[4] Such universalist claims, characteristic of Enlightenment perspectives, sweep aside contention and ignore radical dissent as if they did not exist. As a result, the diversity of the democratic tradition is erased by these totalizing assertions of unanimity and final truth.

The new world order discourse of democracy lies at the restrictive or protective end of the liberal democratic spectrum.[5] Democracy is constructed as a representative rather than participatory political process. The existence of a capitalist market economy is assumed as a democratic prerequisite, and universalist, masculinist, Eurocentric assumptions are employed in constructing the citizen. The result is an emphasis on democratic form rather than substance and the protection of the inequities of the political status quo from radical democratic challenge.

---

1. *See* George Bush, *The Possibility of a New World Order: Unlocking the Promise of Freedom*, 57 VITAL SPEECHES OF THE DAY 450, 452 (1991).

2. Gareth Evans, *The New World Order and The United Nations*, *in* WHOSE NEW WORLD ORDER: WHAT ROLE FOR THE UNITED NATIONS? 1 (Mara Bustelo & Philip Alston eds., 1991).

3. *See* James Kurth, *Things to Come: The Shape of the New World Order*, THE NATIONAL INTEREST, Summer 1991, at 3, 4.

4. Francis Fukuyama, *The End of History?*, THE NATIONAL INTEREST, Summer 1989, at 4.

5. The origins of the "protective" democratic tradition may be associated with John Locke. *See* CAROLE PATEMAN, THE DISORDER OF WOMEN: DEMOCRACY, FEMINISM AND POLITICAL THEORY 94-95 (1989); NOAM CHOMSKY, DETERRING DEMOCRACY 359 (1991).

Among those excluded by the grand narrative of global liberal democracy are women. As Carole Pateman explains:

> The most serious failure of contemporary democratic theory and its language of freedom, equality and consent and of the individual, is that women are so easily and inconspicuously excluded from reference to the "individual."[6]

The promotion of gender-bound liberal democracy as the pinnacle of world emancipation is a retrograde turn of events for women. It has the potential to entrench liberal forms of male domination universally as natural, rational, and indeed, democratic.

This article sets out to reveal the gendered and restrictive form of democracy supported by the discourse of the new world order. I explore the potential of the international legal system to provide a forum for unmasking the interests served by this type of democracy, for contesting its claim to democratic supremacy, and for recognizing instead what Chantal Mouffe describes as "the composite, heterogeneous, open and ultimately indeterminate character of the democratic tradition."[7]

Section I examines how the concept of democracy has been constructed by international legal processes since World War II. This examination makes apparent a potential for acknowledging democractic diversity, but this potential is confined by the liberal roots of the international legal system, by an imperative not to threaten world power arrangements, and by a preoccupation with the enforcement and control of democratic processes.

Section II illustrates the gendered allegiances and effects of new world order democracy by exploring its initial impact on women in Eastern Europe and the former Soviet Union. I show how the mainspring liberal discourses of respresentative democracy, equality, and liberty support a version of freedom that marginalizes and controls women.

The third section outlines alternative discourses of global democracy that value diversity and communality and reject gendered individualism. Finally, section IV suggests fundamental change in the international legal system necessary for contesting the Western and patriarchal interests served by the new world democratic order.

---

6. PATEMAN, *supra* note 5, at 218.

7. Chantal Mouffe, *Radical Democracy: Modern or Postmodern?*, *in* UNIVERSAL ABANDON? THE POLITICS OF POSTMODERNISM 31, 41 (A. Ross ed., 1988).

II. THE CONSTRUCTION OF DEMOCRACY IN INTERNATIONAL LAW

Examining how post-World War II ideas of democracy have been constructed in international law reveals two competing versions of democratic entitlement. On the one hand, theoretical conceptions of democracy, developed by way of treaties and General Assembly Resolutions, are notably open textured despite, or perhaps because of, the Cold War polarization of democratic forms. On the other hand, the version of democracy that emerges from the *practice* of international law is narrow and restrictive. The post-Cold War claim that liberal democracy lays the foundation for a new world order strengthens the restrictive practice of democracy and threatens the tenuous juridical recognition of democratic heterogeneity. The new world order democratic discourse promotes conservative and protective forms of liberal democracy hostile to the evolution of popular and participatory democratic processes. Even the more participatory forms of the liberal democratic tradition are submerged by a preoccupation with establishing international norms and mechanisms in order to monitor electoral standards.

A. Developments in Democratic Discourse Since 1945

In 1945, democracy was an ideal shared by the victors of World War II. The West emphasized individualism, self-interest and liberty, and the East stressed collectivism and equality.[8] These different accounts of democracy became polarized with the advent of the Cold War.[9] The resulting duality of dominant democratic discourses is still evident in the language of the new world order which aligns democracy with the Western emphasis on civil and political rights, and largely excludes economic, social, and cultural rights from its agenda.[10]

Democratic developments since World War II have not, however, been confined to the terms set by the superpowers, although Western history would often have it this way.[11] In the shadow of the East/West divide, democratic principles have provided the framework for diverse popular movements producing many different accounts of

---

8. Yoshikazu Sakamoto, *Introduction: The Global Context of Democratization*, 16 ALTERNATIVES 119, 119 (1991).

9. Theodor Meron, *Democracy and the Rule of Law*, 153 WORLD AFF. 23, 24 (1990).

10. C. Muzaffar, *The New World Order: Gold or God?*, *in* 24 HOURS SUPPLEMENT: WHATEVER HAPPENED TO THE NEW WORLD ORDER 28, 31 (ABC Radio, Feb. 1992) (on file with author).

11. CHOMSKY, *supra* note 5, at 20.

democracy. Included are movements seeking decolonization and self-determination, the liberation of women, freedom from racial discrimination, indigenous peoples' rights, environmental democracy, and emancipation from economic domination and political repression. These developments reveal the breadth of the emancipatory potential of democracy. These democratic movements share two characteristics: first, their grass roots base; and second, their advocacy of the extension of democracy to include universal suffrage,[12] to operate in the private/domestic sphere of social life,[13] to counter institutionalized racism,[14] to restructure workforce relationships,[15] and to reorganize the global marketplace. [16]

The form of democracy that emerges from these democratic movements is dynamic and heterogeneous. Collectivism rather than individualism is the foundational principle and substantive equality is a principle goal. The political is redefined and political participation becomes integral to everyday life.

Although the international legal system's post-World War II construction of democracy has not excluded this diversity, it has not encouraged diversity nor has the discourse of diversity been dominant. The superpower dualization of democractic values has functioned to prevent any single narrative of democracy from assuming international dominance. Cold War polarization led to relatively open-ended pronouncements in international legal instruments that may be read to support democracy in many different forms.

The theoretical potential for democratic diversity within the discourses of international law is illustrated by international legal formulations of democracy. I focus on democratic conceptions that have evolved in three different contexts: first, the application of the principles of the U.N. Charter linking democratic ideas with international peace and security; second, the development of human rights law that identifies participation in government as a human right; and third, the recent discourses about the criteria required for a state to be recognized as a subject of international law.

---

12. Sakamoto, *supra* note 8, at 119. Even the achievement of the fundamental liberal democratic right of everyone to vote was due to popular struggle. *Id.*

13. PATEMAN, *supra* note 5, at 118.

14. *See, e.g.*, THE STRUGGLE FOR SOUTH AFRICA (Rob Davies et al. eds., new ed. 1984).

15. CAROL C. GOULD, RETHINKING DEMOCRACY: FREEDOM AND SOCIAL COOPERATION IN POLITICS, ECONOMY, AND SOCIETY 84 (1988); CAROLE PATEMAN, PARTICIPATION AND DEMOCRATIC THEORY 45-102 (1970).

16. THE NEW INTERNATIONAL ECONOMIC ORDER (Karl P. Sauvant & Hajo Hasenpflug eds., 1977).

B. Democracy as a Means to Peace

Many facets of the U.N. Charter are associated with democratic ideas. Of particular importance are the Charter's recognition of the sovereign equality of member states of the United Nations,[17] and its commitment to the self-determination of peoples.[18] Closer examination reveals that these two ideals are considerably qualified by the practice of the United Nations.

Consider the principle of the sovereign equality of U.N. member states. Despite proclaiming its importance, the Charter does not reflect this democratic principle in the structure it prescribes for the operation of the United Nations. The Charter vests the ultimate decision-making power about international peace and security in the Security Council which is controlled by the five most powerful post-war victor nations.[19] Further, the 1970 Declaration on Friendly Relations, which spells out the principle of sovereign equality of states in more detail, is conspicuously silent on the implications of sovereign equality for democratic world governance.[20] Clearly, the democratic spirit of the United Nations does not extend to sharing decision-making power, not least because it would disrupt the unequal balance of world power. The United Nations' own decision-making structures reveal a concern to preserve the political status quo rather than to promote democratic practice.

The undemocratic structures of the United Nations rely on the assumption that peace is more likely to result from the consolidation of world power arrangements than from deepening democracy[21] which would involve challenging global inequalities. Other international organizations and processes such as the hierarchical and Western-dominated structure of the international economic system reflect this assumption. The financial institutions of the World Bank, the International Monetary Fund, and the General Agreement on Tariffs and Trade mirror, rather than redress, the

17. U.N. CHARTER art. 2, ¶1.

18. *Id.* art. 1, ¶2.

19. *Id.* at ch. 5 (setting out the membership and role of the Security Council). Article 23(1) nominates the Republic of China, France, the Union of Soviet Socialist Republics, the United Kingdom of Great Britain and Northern Ireland, and the United States of America as permanent members. *Id.* Article 27(3) requires that an affirmative vote of the Council must include the votes of the permanent members. *Id.*

20. *Declaration on Principles of International Law Concerning Friendly Relations and Cooperation Among States in Accordance with the Charter of the United Nations*, G.A. Res. 2625, U.N. GAOR, 25th Sess., Annex at 121, U.N. Doc. A/8028 (1971) [hereinafter *Declaration on Friendly Relations*].

21. Sakamoto, *supra* note 8, at 121 (using the term "deepening democracy" to refer to popular democratization or "democratization from below" rather than "from above").

unequal global distribution of economic power.[22] The absence of women from most international decision-making positions and forums also reflects the failure of the United Nations system to remedy worldwide patterns of male domination.[23] These examples show that, in practice, the goal of democracy in international relations is compromised by the United Nations' deference to the current distribution of world power among states, and between women and men.

The U.N. Charter's commitment to the principle of self-determination of peoples also illustrates the selective application of democratic principles in U.N. practice. The General Assembly has enunciated the principle of self-determination on various occasions. Its 1960 Declaration on the Independence of Colonial Peoples stressed that

> [a]ll peoples have the right to self-determination; by virtue of that right they freely determine their political status and freely pursue their economic, social and cultural development. [24]

This view was strongly reaffirmed in 1970 when the right of "all peoples...freely to determine, without external interference, their political status" was reiterated. [25] This broad approach was again reflected in the 1980 resolution responding to the Soviet invasion of Afghanistan, in which the General Assembly stated that it

> reaffirmed the inalienable right of all peoples to determine their own future and...to determine their own form of government and choose their economic, political and social systems free from outside interference, subversion, coercion or constraint of any kind whatsoever. [26]

While making no specific references to democracy in these restatements of the right to self-determination, it is clear that the General Assembly, at least in principle, has consistently promoted the involvement of citizens in their own government. In doing so, the

---

22. Susan George, *Who Gives the Orders in the New World Order?*, *in* 24 HOURS SUPPLEMENT:WHATEVER HAPPENED TO THE NEW WORLD ORDER 22, 23 (ABC Radio, Feb. 1992) (transcript on file with author); Peter J. Opitz, *The United Nations and the Emancipation of the Third World*, 35 LAW & ST. 7, 16 (1987).

23. Hilary Charlesworth, Christine Chinkin, & Shelley Wright, *Feminist Approaches to International Law*, 85 AM. J. INT'L L. 613, 621-25 (1991).

24. *Declaration on the Granting of Independence to Colonial Territories and Peoples*, G.A. Res. 1514, U.N. GAOR, 15th Sess., Supp. No. 16, at 42, U.N. Doc. A/4684 (1960).

25. *Declaration on Friendly Relations, supra* note 20.

26. G.A. Res. ES-6/2, U.N. GAOR, 6th Emergency Special Sess., Supp. No. 18, at 470, U.N. Doc. ES-6/2 (1980).

General Assembly has asserted a conception of national democracy that is not aligned with any particular democratic tradition.

The International Court of Justice has referred approvingly to these views of the General Assembly in its advisory opinions in the *Western Sahara* and *Namibia* cases.[27] This broad approach is also supported by both of the international human rights covenants which state:

> All peoples have the right to self-determination. By virtue of that right they freely determine their political status and freely pursue their economic, social and cultural development. [28]

These legal sources can be read as manifesting a commitment to promoting and legitimating democratic diversity in the attainment of self-determination.

Like the previous example of sovereign equality, the principle of self-determination has been severely restricted in its practice. It has never been a right belonging to everyone. Rather, the principle has generally been applied narrowly to "peoples" of European colonies.[29] By selective application of the principle, self-determination has been constructed to exclude any relation to women,[30] to indigenous peoples,[31] to those colonized by non-Europeans,[32] and until recently,[33] to secessionist claims.[34] The intention apparent from these limitations is, again, to leave the status quo essentially undisturbed

27. Namibia (South West Africa) Advisory Opinion, 1971 I.C.J. 16 (Jan. 26); Western Sahara Advisory Opinion, 1975 I.C.J. 12 (Oct. 16).

28. *International Covenant on Civil and Political Rights*, G.A. Res. 2200, U.N. GAOR, 21st Sess., Supp. No.16, art. 1, U.N. Doc. A/6316 (1966); *International Covenant on Economic, Social and Cultural Rights*, G.A. Res. 2200A, U.N. GAOR, 21st Sess., Supp. No. 16, art. 1, U.N. Doc. A/6316 (1966).

29. Rhodesia, South Africa and the Palestinians are notably exceptions to the rule.

30. Christine Chinkin, *A Gendered Perspective to the International Use of Force*, 12 AUSTL. Y.B. INT'L L. 279, 289 (1992).

31. Russel L. Barsh, *Revision of ILO Convention No. 107*, 81 AM. J. INT'L L. 756 (1987).

32. For example, West Irian and Eritrea. On the other hand, the International Court of Justice upheld the right of the Western Sahara people to self-determination in the face of claims by the would-be colonizers Mauritania and Morocco. Western Sahara Advisory Opinion, *supra* note 27.

33. Marc Weller, *The International Response to the Dissolution of the Socialist Federal Republic of Yugoslavia*, 86 AM. J. INT'L L. 569, 606 (1992).

34. M. G. Kaladharan Nayar, *Self-Determination Beyond the Colonial Context: Biafra in Retrospect*, 10 TEX. INT'L L.J. 321 (1975). United Nations responses to the Biafrans and Eritreans are examples of U.N. policies that chose to preserve territorial integrity (i.e. colonial boundaries) rather than recognize self-determination claims that would result in secession.

by confining the democratic entitlement of self-determination to narrow circumstances. Broader application of the principle, to allow secession for example, has usually been rejected on two grounds. First, that it would pose a potential threat to international peace and security, and second, that territorial integrity would be violated. This is, in effect, a thinly disguised rationale for U.N. protection of the status quo of states' boundaries.

The qualified application of the United Nations' democractic principles of sovereign equality and self-determination is associated with the liberal tradition of protective democracy. The discourse of protective democracy developed in order to protect the status quo from the challenge of more radical democracies.[35] The effect of supporting such a limited form of democracy, in practice, aligns the international legal system with existing arrangements of power and results in the promotion of a dominant world view that accepts global inequalities as inevitable. This view prevents the identification of the undemocratic nature of the international community as an impediment to world peace. As a result, the international legal system is divested of any role in the redistribution of world power.[36] The potential of the legal system to provide a forum for challenge to undemocratic practices is thus severely restricted. The international legal system emerges as an unlikely mechanism for the promotion of deepening and emancipatory democracies.[37]

C. Democracy as Human Right

A second context in which international legal discourse has developed democratic conceptions is in human rights law. As with the democratic principles of the U.N. Charter just discussed, some support for expansive versions of democracy may be found in human rights instruments. This support is confined in practice, however, by an overriding emphasis on policing formal electoral and voting processes rather than on promoting more flexible and participatory forms of democracy.

The development of human rights law has been dominated by liberalism which conceives of human rights in universal and essentialist terms. This conception has resulted in a Eurocentric domination of human rights discourse. From a critical legal studies perspective, the emphasis in liberal rights discourse on individualized and formalistic rights results in indeterminate and

35. PATEMAN, *supra* note 5, at 94-95; CHOMSKY, *supra* note 5, at 358.

36. Surakiart Sathirathai, *An Understanding of the Relationship Between International Legal Discourse and Third World Countries*, 25 HARV. INT'L L.J. 395, 398 (1984).

37. *See supra* notes 12-16.

malleable constructions of human rights that create impediments to progressive social change by abstracting and atomizing human experience.[38] From a feminist perspective, liberal human rights are uncertain and qualified in relation to women because they are based on a male standard, focusing attention on individual instances of inequality rather than on the systemic socio-economic structures that subordinate women.[39]

The right to political participation illustrates these criticisms. The right is expressed in human rights law in two ways: as a broad right to "take part in government" and "public affairs," and as a more specific right to "participate in elections." [40] Article 25 of the International Covenant on Civil and Political Rights (ICCPR) sets out these two formulations of the right:

> Every citizen shall have the right and the opportunity...
>
> (a) To take part in the conduct of public affairs, directly or through freely chosen representatives;
>
> (b) To vote and be elected at genuine periodic elections which shall be by universal and equal suffrage and shall be held by secret ballot, guaranteeing the free expression of the will of the electors.... [41]

The *travaux preparatoire* of the Covenant note that paragraph (a) is the general rule and that paragraph (b) can be considered an application of it.[42] Both paragraphs are restrictive despite the generality of the first. The general rule confines the idea of democracy to the narrow arena of public affairs of the state. The specification of elections as its application in paragraph (b) further limits the general rule by orienting implementation towards a concern with democratic form rather than substance.

The 1954 U.N. Convention on the Political Rights of Women is even narrower.[43] According to that instrument the sum total of women's political entitlement is (on equal terms with men) to vote, to

---

38. Mark Tushnet, *An Essay on Rights*, 62 TEX. L. REV. 1363 (1984).

39. Charlotte Bunch, *Women's Rights as Human Rights,* 12 HUM. RTS. Q. 486, 488 (1990).

40. Henry J. Steiner, *Political Participation as a Human Right,* 1 HARV. HUM. RTS. Y.B. 77, 78 (1988).

41. *International Covenant on Civil and Political Rights*, *supra* note 28, art. 25.

42.*Travaux Preparatoire for the International Convention on Civil and Political Rights*, G.A. Res. 2200, U.N. GAOR, 21st Sess., Supp. No.16, art. 1, U.N. Doc. A/6316 (1966).

43. Convention on the Political Rights of Women, July 7, 1954, T.I.A.S. No. 8289, 193 U.N.T.S. 135.

be eligible for election, and to hold public office.[44] The more recent 1980 Convention on the Elimination of All Forms of Discrimination Against Women is only slightly broader, adding the right to participate in the formulation of government policy and in public political non-governmental organizations.[45] Clearly these human rights instruments construct women's political rights as formal, public, individual, and the same as men's. Such rights do not alter the systematic exclusion of women from political participation and from holding positions of power, either within states or within the international community.

The Declaration from the 1993 World Conference on Human Rights does nothing to expand the idea of democracy at international law. In the context of the dominant discourse of the new world order, this failure is hardly surprising. On the one hand the Declaration affirms that:

> Democracy is based on the freely expressed will of the people to determine their own political, economic, social and cultural systems and their full participation in all aspects of their lives.[46]

On the other hand, in spelling out a program of action, the Declaration places "particular importance" on the provision of electoral assistance to governments wishing to strengthen their democratic processes.[47] Again we see a broadly stated commitment to democratic diversity compromised in its implementation by defining its practice in terms of electoral processes.

At the same time, it is important to explore the boundaries of the more open-textured aspects of these statements of political rights, including the wording of their precursor in the Universal Declaration of Human Rights.[48] There is room to assert, as Henry Steiner does in his reading of the ICCPR, that

44. *Id.* arts 1, 2 and 3 respectively.

45. Convention on the Elimination of All Forms of Discrimination Against Women, G.A. Res. 34/180, U.N. GAOR, 34th Sess., 10th plen. mtg., Supp. No. 46, Annex at 194, U.N. Doc. A/34/830 (1979).

46. *Vienna Declaration and Programme of Action*, 25 June 1993, ¶ 5.

47. *Id.* section III, ¶ 2.

48. *Universal Declaration of Human Rights*, G.A. Res. 217A, U.N. GAOR, 3rd Sess., art. 21, U.N. Doc. A/810 (1948) (unanimously approved by the General Assembly and signed Dec. 10, 1948).

> neither through the preamble nor through its enumeration of rights does the Covenant [ICCPR] invoke a single political tradition to the necessary exclusion of others....the Covenant does not by its terms distinguish among such political systems as liberal democracy, democratic socialism, corporatism, or communism.[49]

In this view, human rights law leaves open the form of governance whereby states fulfill their obligations to provide participatory political mechanisms. From this perspective, the capacity of international law to uphold democratic diversity is not completely infeasible.

However, the attendant insistence by all international human rights instruments that voting in periodic elections constitutes the essence of political rights compromises this apparent flexibility. The electoral focus exposes the protective liberal bias of these formulations of political rights. The emphasis is on individuals voting rather than on relational political processes, on formal rather than substantive democracy, and on the public sphere of social life as distinct from the private.

The conservative liberal underpinnings of international human rights law–its positivistic emphasis on formality and individualism and its division of life into public and private spheres–account for the electoral focus of democratic human rights formulations. As a result, human rights law can support patriarchal and Western interests by promoting universally a minimalist electoral approach to democracy. Thus although alternative democratic traditions are not specifically precluded by human rights instruments, they have not been legitimated in the application of human rights law.

D. Democracy as a Measure of State Legitimacy

International law has also envisaged democracy as a foundation for the legitimacy of a state. According to Michael Reisman, this conception of democracy goes back as far as 1945 when "popular sovereignty was firmly rooted as one of the fundamental postulates of political legitimacy."[50] But the legal obligations of states created by this democratic requirement have only recently been explored with any rigor, spurred by advocates of the new world order.

Article 21 of the Universal Declaration of Human Rights declares that "the will of the people shall be the basis of the authority of

---

49. Steiner, *supra* note 40, at 87-88.

50. W. Michael Reisman, *Sovereignty and Human Rights in Contemporary International Law*, 84 AM. J. INT'L L. 866, 867 (1990).

government."[51] This requirement has been largely ignored because the alternative, according to Tom Farer, would be "to disqualify the great majority of delegates [to the United Nations] on the grounds that they represent illegitimate governments."[52] This inaction may not operate for much longer. The proselytizing climate of the new world order is prompting a growing number of international legal scholars to assert that democratic governance is emerging as an international customary norm upon which a state's legitimacy *must* be founded.[53] They point to recent decisions by the European Community made in response to the unprecedented number of claims to recognition from secessionist movements within former communist states. Although the Community's response has been contradictory and confused,[54] the requirement that intending states constitute themselves on a democratic basis has emerged as a consistent theme.[55] This requirement seems to be satisfied by holding a referendum in which majority support for secession is expressed, accompanied by assurances of human rights guarantees associated with ethnic minorities.[56] Such requirements are minimalist in terms of democratic possibilities and are consistent with protective liberal democratic indicators which look to form rather than substance as evidence of democracy.

The implications of imposing protective Western democratic forms as a condition of the recognition of a state at international law are far-reaching. It creates new opportunities for Western imperialism, despite the bold claim made by Thomas Franck that

> people almost everywhere now demand that government be validated by a western-style parliamentary, multiparty, democratic process...Very few argue that parliamentary democracy is a western illusion and a neocolonialist trap for unwary Third World peoples.[57]

---

51. *Universal Declaration of Human Rights*, *supra* note 48.

52. Tom J. Farer, *The United States as Guarantor of Democracy in the Caribbean Basin: Is There a Legal Way?*, 10 HUM. RTS. Q. 157, 157 (1988).

53. This was the subject of a forum at the American Society of International Law. National Sovereignty Revisited: Perspectives on the Emerging Norm of Democracy in International Law, 86th ann. mtg., Apr. 1-4, 1992. (The speakers were Thomas Carrothers, Karen Engle, Gregory Fox & Claudio Grossman) (transcript on file with author).

54. Weller, *supra* note 33, at 606.

55. European Community, *Declaration on the "Guidelines on the Recognition of New States in Eastern Europe and in the Soviet Union"* (Dec. 16, 1991).

56. Weller, *supra* note 33, at 592-96.

57. Thomas M. Franck, *The Emerging Right to Democratic Governance*, 86 AM. J. INT'L L. 46, 49 (1992).

Franck assumes a world consensus about the liberal democratic form. Further, he asserts that the foundation for this global development lies in the U.S. Declaration of Independence.[58] He is not alone in making such a claim.[59] Such assertions generalize democratic experience and silence the knowledge produced by the many democratic movements which would decry such origins and associations.[60]

In the post-Cold War environment, efforts to define the content of the obligation of democratic governance are dominated by concerns with the mechanics of enforcement rather than with the substance of the duty.[61] Franck, for example, envisages the identification of universal democratic standards to which states will be compelled to adhere,[62] and proposes that states be obliged to submit their elections to a global monitoring process.[63] This reveals a protective preoccupation with electoral mechanics rather than with substantive democratic principles, and an emphasis on procedure rather than on outcomes.[64]

Proposals like Franck's for standardizing and centrally monitoring the procedures of global democratic change constitute an attempt to control and homogenize democratic developments. This need to control is consistent with protective forms of liberal democracy.[65] It is a defensive response to developments that have the potential to alter the inequitable global distribution of power and to involve people, as collectives and individuals, in processes of self-determination within and beyond the boundaries of states.

Notwithstanding the protective democratic proclamations and action plans emerging in the new world order context, the General

58. *Id.* at 46.

59. *See* Carl Gersham, *Freedom Remains the Touchstone*, 19 NAT'L INTEREST 83, 86 (1989); GREGORY A. FOSSEDAL, THE DEMOCRATIC IMPERATIVE: EXPORTING THE AMERICAN REVOLUTION (1989); Reisman, *supra* note 50, at 867.

60. *E.g.*, many feminist, decolonization and indigenous peoples' democratic movements are highly critical of U.S. forms and practices of democracy.

61. *See generally* Franck, *supra* note 57; Fox, *supra* note 53.

62. *Id.* at 78.

63. *Id.* at 79.

64. Ted G. Carpenter, *The New World Disorder*, 84 FOREIGN POL'Y 24, 37 (1991).

65. In Noam Chomsky's view:

> The success of the popular movements of Eastern and Central Europe are a historic achievement in the unending struggle for freedom and democracy throughout the world. Throughout history, such successes have elicited efforts to institute order and docility and thus to contain and deter the threat to privilege.

CHOMSKY, *supra* note 5, at 6.

Assembly is evidently proceeding cautiously. Two recent resolutions, which refer to the monitoring of democratic elections, bear this out.[66] The first resolution supports international monitoring of elections and stresses the indispensability of "periodic and genuine elections" to ensure protection of the governed, and identifies "the right of everyone to take part in the government of his or her country."[67] The second resolution does not support the international monitoring of elections but states:

> that it is the concern solely of peoples [of each state] to determine methods and to establish institutions regarding the electoral process, as well as to determine the ways for its implementation according to their constitutional and national legislation...[urging all states] to respect the principle of non-interference in the internal affairs of States.[68]

The incongruity of these resolutions reconfirms the presence of two versions of democratic entitlement at international law: one that is restrictive and controlling, and another that tentatively takes a stance of openness to different democratic forms.

Thus, despite the claims by proponents of the new world order, it is possible to conclude that the international legal system is not yet fully committed to conservative liberal democracy as the universal democratic form upon which a state's legitimacy is founded. However, the grounds for defending such a conclusion are diminishing rapidly. The growing emphasis on democratic standardization and enforcement is shifting the balance strongly towards the primacy of protective liberal democracy and away from any possibility of the legal recognition of democratic diversity.

E. The Potential for Change

The end of the Cold War marks a moment in history from which diverse democratic forms could emerge.[69] The cumbersome law-making processes of the international legal system are reeling with the unaccustomed pace of change and global democratization is a central theme in these developments.

Co-opting the international legal system to serve the new world

---

66. Franck, *supra* note 57, at 82.

67. G.A. Res. 45/150, U.N. GAOR, 45th Sess., at 255 (1990).

68. G.A. Res. 45/151, U.N. GAOR, 45th Sess., at 256 (1990).

69. Radmila Nakarada, *Democratic Alternatives: A Perspective from Eastern Europe*, 16 ALTERNATIVES 129, 141 (1991).

order agenda of the globalization of protective liberal democracy effectively amounts to Western expansionism in the guise of democracy and the promotion of human rights.[70] Unfortunately, many aspects of the liberal form of international law make it well-placed to support this endeavour of "subvert[ing] democracy in the name of democracy."[71]

The operation of international law as an apology for Western interests is, however, not an automatic outcome. Martti Koskenniemi, from a deconstructionist perspective argues that international law emerges as a site for contesting "objective" social realities.[72] In this view, the international legal system is a forum for challenging positivistic and conservative meanings of democracy which opens the possibility for the emergence of alternative democratic alternatives. The potential for radical intervention by way of open-textured expressions of the democratic entitlement that I have identified provides one example. Those who are marginalized and silenced by the restrictive and disciplining effects of liberal democracy associated with the new world order must understand the power of their agency in the international legal context, and develop ways to utilize it.

III. THE EFFECTS OF DEMOCRATIZATION ON WOMEN IN EASTERN EUROPE AND THE FORMER SOVIET UNION

This section surveys the initial impact of post-Cold War democratization on women in the former communist states, and provides some insights into how and why gender issues have been submerged. The discussion focuses on themes identified in the first section, particularly liberal democracy's preoccupation with democratic form rather than substance, its privileging of civil and political rights, its control over the meaning and reach of democracy and its exclusionary and silencing effects. What emerges are the contradictions for women that inhere in the change from collective to individualist systems, and from state-controlled to market-regulated economies. Male domination underpins both communist and liberal

70. Gerry Simpson, *False Harmonies and Tragic Ironies: Human Rights in the New World Order*, INT'L L. NEWS 5, 6 (1991).

71. This highlights the need for change in the form of international law which will be discussed further in section IV of this article. *See also* Farer, *supra* note 50, at 174.

72. "[T]he language of international law...conveys to us a certain interpretation of the social reality to which it is addressed, under the veil of objectivity, or naturalness. Deconstruction...shows that legal argument cannot produce the kinds of objective resolutions it claims to produce....Thus it opens up a possibility for alternative descriptive–and simultaneously normative–characterizations of the world in which States live. MARTTI KOSKENNIEMI, FROM APOLOGY TO UTOPIA xxiii (1989).

political traditions and, as a conseqence, neither is concerned with building a democracy that includes women as subjects, rather than objects, of democratic discourse.

A. The Absence of Women from the Main Agenda

The almost complete absence of women's participation in the official post-Cold War democratization agenda contrasts starkly with the prominence of nationalist and ethnic concerns. Although women played a significant role in the development of the popular democratic movements in Eastern Europe[73], their mass presence at the forefront of initial change has not translated into an ongoing political presence.[74] To date, only controversy over abortion rights has briefly propelled women's issues onto the main agenda, particularly in Poland and the reunited Germany.[75]

Rapid change continues in the former communist states,[76] and the situations of women are not homogeneous.[77] Acknowledgement of these multiplicities is crucial, not least because liberalism denies them, but also because this denial is a tool of Western imperialism.[78] I examine how the discourse of new world order liberal democracy contributes to women's subordination by looking first at the exclusionary effects of the liberal concept of suffrage; second, at the gendered effects of the liberal ideal of equality; third, at the disciplinary effects of the denial of reproductive liberty to women; and finally at the underlying form of liberal democracy which makes

---

73. Doroty J. Rosenberg, *Shock Therapy: GDR Women in Transition from a Socialist Welfare State to a Social Market Economy*, 17 SIGNS 129, 139 (1991).

74. This is similar to the experience of self-determination movements in which women often play a large initial role but become increasingly marginalized as the movement gains power. See Chinkin, *supra* note 30, at 283.

75. Sally Low, *Polish Women Confront Church and Union*, GREEN LEFT (Melbourne), June 26, 1991, at 16; Rosenberg, *supra* note 73, at 135.

76. S. Bassnett, *Crossing Cultural Boundaries: Or How I Became an Expert on Eastern European Woman Overnight*, 15 WOMEN'S STUDIES INT'L F. 11 (1992); Julia Szalai, *Some Aspects of the Changing Situation of Women in Hungary*, 17 SIGNS 152 (1991).

77. Maxine Molyneux's 1990 survey of feminist political activity in Eastern Europe bears this out in her finding of differing political priorities influenced by regional conditions and circumstances. Molyneux also found broadly shared concern with abortion, contraception, social equality, violence and sexuality. This points to aspects of women's experience of subjugation which have their genesis in the gendered political and legal discourses which structure social experience. Maxine Molyneux, *The "Women Question" in the Age of Perestroika*, 183 NEW LEFT REV. 23, 28 (1990).

78. Chandra Mohanty, *Under Western Eyes: Feminist Scholarship and Colonial Discourses*, 30 FEMINIST REV. 61 (1988); Annie Bunting, THEORIZING WOMEN'S CULTURAL DIVERSITY IN FEMINIST INTERNATIONAL HUMAN RIGHTS STRATEGIES (1993).

this possible–the public/private distinction.

B. Exclusion by Suffrage

The right to vote for political candidates who represent the interests of geographically defined electorates is one of the cornerstones of liberal democracy. This tradition assigns a disproportionate prominence to electoral processes, as evidenced by the preoccupations of new world order protagonists. This concern with democratic form rather than substance diverts attention from the goal of democratic *outcomes*.

Historically, liberal democracy is founded upon the exclusion of women from politics.[79] By constructing women's nature as equipped only for domestic life and as incapable of developing a sense of justice, liberalism initially barred women from public life altogether.[80] Only after prolonged and bitter struggles was formal voting equality extended to women.[81] Enfranchisement has not, however, led to substantial formal political participation by women because the gendered form of liberal democracy was left intact. Women occupy two to ten per cent of national political positions in Western liberal democracies.[82] The only exception to this pattern is a recent shift in Nordic countries as a result of the introduction of quota systems which ensure women's representation.[83]

A replica of the Western pattern of women's insignificant formal political involvement is emerging in Eastern Europe as a result of democratic elections. Quota systems, which previously guaranteed women a certain number of positions, have been dismantled and a dramatic drop in women's representation has resulted.[84] Generally, the percentage of women elected in national elections has fallen by over half, dropping eighty per cent in Hungary and ninety per cent in Romania.[85]

---

79. Pateman describes how liberal political forms were formulated as a defense against the "subversiveness" and "disorder" of women. PATEMAN, *supra* note 5, at 18.

80. *Id.* at 21.

81. ANNE PHILLIPS, ENGENDERING DEMOCRACY 60 (1991). Swiss women won the right to vote only in 1971.

82. *Id.* at 60.

83. *Id.* at 85.

84. *Women Today–The Facts,* 227 NEW INTERNATIONALIST 18, 19 (1992).

85. Molyneux, *supra* note 77, at 35. In the March 1989 elections to the Congress of Peoples Deputies [in the Soviet Union] the percentage of women fell by over half, from 34.5 % to 15.6%...In Poland in January 1988, the number of women holding parliamentary seats fell from 20.2 % to 13.3%; and after 1989 similar drops were registered in Romania [from one third of all seats to only 3.5 %; in Czechoslovakia

The earlier record of communist systems' integration of women into political processes left much to be desired: although high levels of local participation by women were achieved, the more influential positions of political and economic power were still occupied by men.[86] But despite this already unsatisfactory situation, liberal democratization has further diminished women's scant formal political power. Clearly, access to liberal political rights does not lead to substantive improvement in the participation of women in political processes.

C. Exclusion by Equality

Equality, like democracy, is an ideal embraced by both communist and liberal political traditions. It is a comparative measure which has been revealed by Western feminists to construct gender equality according to a standard that is male.[87] This paradigm produces a tenuous and questionable equality for women, achievable only to the extent that women are able to emulate a male standard or alternatively, to prove a worth that is comparable with measures of male worth. Most women, in most situations, fall completely outside the calculation of equality in these terms since they are involved with work or social functions that are different from men's, and therefore not comparable.

Communist notions of equality appear to have suffered these same structural shortcomings. Despite the communist commitment to achieving the emancipation of women through workforce participation, gender inequality in the segmentation and valuation of the labor force remained–women's wages were lower than men's, the workforce was largely segregated along gender lines, more women than men had part-time jobs, and domestic labor and childcare continued to be seen as women's work.[88]

But the already disadvantaged economic position of women is worsening in the former communist bloc, as women bear the brunt

---

[from 29.5 % to 6 %]; in Hungary [from 20% to 7 %]. *Id.*

86. Rosenberg, *supra* note 73, at 141; Molyneux, *supra* note 77, at 29.

87. *See* Patricia A. Cain, *Feminism and the Limits of Equality*, 24 GA. L. REV. 803 (1990); Hilary Charlesworth, *A Law of One's Own? Feminist Perspectives on Equality and the Law*, 51 MEANJIN 67 (1992); Kathleen A. Lahey, *Feminist Theories of (In)Equality*, 3 WIS. WOMEN'S L.J. 5 (1987); Christine A. Littleton, *Reconstructing Sexual Equality*, 75 CAL. L. REV. 1279 (1987).

88. Elizabeth Waters, *Restructuring the 'Woman Question' Perestroika and Prostitution*, 33 FEMINIST REV., Autumn 1989, at 3, 4; Rosenberg, *supra* note 73, at 138-39; Michelle Royer, *Women in a Changing Europe*, 15 AUSTL. FEMINIST STUD. 99, 100 (1992); Kathleen T. Bailey, *Soviet Social Scientists Talking: An Official Debate About Women*, 9 WOMEN'S STUD. INT'L F. 240 (1986) (reviewing Mary Buckley, 1986).

of the rationalizations of economic liberalization. Disproportionately high levels of unemployment among women is resulting from labor market reorganization.[89] In dramatic contrast to the previous full employment guaranteed by the state, the unemployment rate for women in the former East Germany reached fifty-seven per cent in 1991 as many were forced to give up paid work outside the home to provide jobs for men.[90] Cuts in childcare services are also forcing many women to return to the domestic sphere.[91] The programs of leave and wage entitlements designed to support maternity in the previous system are adding to women's unequal bargaining position in the new conditions. Maternity entitlements, rather than supporting women's employment, are proving to be insurmountable obstacles to employment for many women as employers avoid these obligations by employing males.[92] The loss of a job may have extremely wide ramifications.[93]

Women's decreasing workforce participation in the former communist states is resulting in the feminization of poverty.[94] The burdens of the transition to a free market economy were distributed unevenly because liberalism, based on self-interest, autonomy and the male standard, seeks equality by encouraging competition which has highly gendered effects. State intervention cannot be relied upon to promote more socially just outcomes because conservative liberalism rejects such intervention as interference with market forces.[95] Because of liberalism's promotion of self-interest, liberal constructs of equality operate in a way that deepens gendered divisions in post-communist states and further extends the global

---

89. Rosenberg, *supra* note 73, at 132.

90. Frauke Lenkos et al., *Interview with Terry Lane* (ABC Radio, July 26, 1991) (transcript on file with author).

91. Rosenberg, *supra* note 73, at 133.

92. Susan Magary, *Perestroika Has Been Bad for Women*, 15 AUSTL. FEMINIST STUD. 105, 107 (1992).

93. As Susan Magary explains with reference to the Soviet Union:

> [t]he enterprises order food and clothing for their workers, and furniture, things virtually unavailable through shops. Losing your job means losing your ability to place orders...It can mean losing your place in a queue for housing, for a car, for a garden plot...Losing your job means losing the whole fabric of your links with the world.

Id.

94. Ruth Ellen Boetcher Joeres & Barbara Laslett, *Introduction to Forum*, 17 SIGNS 112, 115 (1991); Szalai, *supra* note 76, at 169-70.

95. Nigel Purvis summarizes the new effect as follows: "Liberalism itself makes no room for a theory of material justice in the world because it imagines the pursuit of liberty as the only legitimate substantive objective." Nigel Purvis, *Critical Legal Studies in Public International Law*, 32 HARV. INT'L L.J. 98 (1991).

pattern of women's poverty.[96] Liberal democracy has opened new channels for exploitation, rather than progresssively revaluing women's labor.

D. Control by the Denial of Liberty

In the context of liberal democracy, the concept of liberty seeks to protect individual freedom of action and autonomy of thought from encroachment by the state.[97] For women, reproductive control is fundamental to liberty.[98] Yet reproductive freedom has been the most contentious women's rights issue in the transitions from communism to liberal democracy.[99]

The liberty championed by liberal democracy does not include women's unfettered access to abortion. The issue of abortion was so divisive that it almost derailed Germany's reunification treaty in 1991.[100] The less restrictive abortion laws of East Germany were unacceptable to those who held power in the West. A compromise was eventually reached which narrows the former East German law and slightly relaxes the West German regulation.[101] In Poland too, serious threats to women's access to abortion have accompanied democratic developments.[102] The pressure to restrict the availability of abortion is also mounting in the independent states of the former Soviet Union.[103] Malgorzata Fuszara notes the double standards involved:

---

96. Cynthia Enloe, *Silicon Tricks and the Two Dollar Woman*, 227 NEW INTERNATIONALIST 12 (1992).

97. *See* Purvis, *supra* note 95, at 94.

98. As Zillah Eisenstein reasons: "if democracy is, in part, based on human rights and the individual freedom of choice to determine the decisions that affect one's life, then abortion and the broader concern of reproductive rights are crucial to the practice of democracy." Zillah Eisenstein, *Privatizing the State: Reproductive Rights, Affirmative Action and the Problem of Democracy*, 12 FRONTIERS 98, 117 (1990).

99. The United States itself, the standard bearer of the liberal democratic revolution, has placed further limits on women's abortion rights over this same period. In 1991, the U.S. Supreme Court upheld federal regulations that prohibited government funded family planning centers from making any reference to abortion as a possible choice for pregnant women. Rust v. Sullivan, __U.S.___, 111 S. Ct. 1759 (1991). In 1992, the Court further ruled that states were lawfully able to impose retrictions on a woman's right to abortion, thereby removing the flimsy constitutional protection that the right had hitherto received. Planned Parenthood v. Casey, __U.S.___, 112 S. Ct. 2791 (1992).

100. Rosenberg, *supra* note 73, at 135.

101. *German MPs Vote to Ease Abortion Laws*, AGE , June 27, 1992, at 7.

102. Low, *supra* note 75, at 16.

103. Maxine Molyneux refers to the increasingly common characterization as another symptom of communism's "corrupted feminity." Molyneux, *supra* note 77, at 44.

> The fall of communist governments in the countries of Central and Eastern Europe has generally been followed by more tolerant, less punitive approaches to social issues. Despite this, with respect to abortion a quite contrary trend is evident.[104]

These restrictions on women's reproductive freedom may be understood in the broader context of patriarchal control of women by the "*maternalization* of the female body."[105] This occurs when legal and political discourses result in the primary association of women's identities and purposes with motherhood. This restrictive social construction of women justifies limiting their access to childcare, contraception, and workforce participation, and identifying domestic responsibilities as primarily women's work.[106]

The ascendancy of these views corresponded with the emergence of support for a return to a family wage for male workers in Poland.[107] The same issue was debated by Gorbachev's advisers in the Soviet Union in 1989, during the period of *perestroika* which marked an initial reorientation of Soviet policy towards redomesticating women.[108] Democratization is entrenching this further by imposing conservative liberal ideas of women's biological and natural predilections.

The maternalization of women is becoming an important focus for feminist organizations.[109] It is apparent that the liberty of liberal democracy operates to protect the freedom and autonomy of men, which depends to a large degree upon the circumscription of women's liberty. This denial of liberty to women is achieved through legal and political processes which maternalize women and deny them reproductive rights.

---

104. Malgorzata Fuszara, *Legal Regulation of Abortion in Poland,* 17 SIGNS 117, 117 (1991).

105. Mary Joe Frug, *A Postmodern Feminist Legal Manifesto (An Unfinished Draft)*, 105 HARV. L. REV. 1045, 1050 (1992).

106. Krystyna Politacha, a former member of the Polish Women's Committee of Solidarity, described this process of maternalization after many of Solidarity's leaders had moved into government: "My [male] colleagues started to speak of women's role as mother and wife in the home and claim that women do not want to be active in the union." *See* Low, *supra* note 75, at 16.

107. *Id.*

108. Molyneux, *supra* note 77, at 38.

109. Cynthia Cockburn observes that: "Feminism in Eastern countries is increasingly clarifying its identity as a movement of women seeking to resist the move to return women to their 'natural functions,' aiming to extend rights to safe contraception and to defend a woman's right to choose against intensifying attacks on abortion rights." Cynthia Cockburn, *The European Forum of Socialist Feminists: Talking on the Volcano,* 15 WOMEN'S STUD. INT'L F. 53, 55 (1992).

E. The Distinction Between Private and Public

The liberal democraticization of former Communist countries is resulting in a decrease of women's formal political power, the feminization of poverty and the increasing maternalization of women's bodies. These gendered effects are not just short-term or unintended by-products of rapid social change, but are inherent in the form of liberal democracy which structures social relations so as to normalize gendered inequities.

Western feminists have identified the conceptual mechanism that provides the foundation for gendered inequalities as the dichotomy drawn between private and public or political spheres of social life. In liberal discourse, a corresponding dualism between women and men justifies the attribution of different social status on the basis of gender. The separation between public and private normalizes the male preponderance in the public sphere of politics, the higher value placed on male workforce participation, and the controls placed on women's bodies by the male dominated state. Women are positioned in the private sphere as secondary and associated with a natural or biological predisposition to domesticity, altruism, and dependence. This conceptual dualism shapes women's actual experiences and operates to mystify the patriarchal operation of liberal discourse. [110]

Because the rights valued and protected by liberal democracy are those associated with the public realm, liberal discourse privileges civil and political rights (narrowly defined) and constructs them in dichotomous relation with social and economic rights.[111] The impact of this dualism is apparent in the former communist states where liberal democratization is resulting in an expansion of civil and political rights, but a corresponding contraction of rights in the so-called private sphere .[112]

---

110. Pateman observes, "[t]he separation of the private and public is both part of [women's] actual lives and an ideological mystification of liberal-patriarchal reality." PATEMAN, *supra* note 5, at 131.

111. *See* Tom J. Farer, *Elections, Democracy and Human Rights: Towards Union,* 11 HUM. RTS. Q. 504, 504 (1989). Farer reports that:

> The Reagan administration would not pursue economic and social rights it declared, because there were, in fact, no such rights to pursue. Improvement in the condition of the poor was, no doubt, a desirable end; but translating that end into a "right," that is a claim on government, was inconsistent with liberal theory and values.

Id.

112. Dorothy Rosenberg points out that the unification of Germany "cancelled an array of economic rights rarely found in Western market economies–guarantees of employment and affordable housing, free medical care and education, paid parental

The theoretical framework of the public/private dichotomy reveals its differential impact on women. The increase in economic vulnerability and social isolation experienced by women in a capitalist liberal democracy compounds their susceptibility to other forms of gendered abuse.[113] For instance, rape and other types of male violence against women have increased in some states of the former Soviet Union.[114]

By way of the public/private dichotomy, liberalism institutes and protects male domination as the status quo. In theory, liberalism delineates the private as an area that is free from state regulation and control. But in practice, political and legal systems construct this private realm directly as well as indirectly by non-intervention.[115] Consequently, the private sphere provides a state-sanctioned area of liberty for men which includes the liberty to dominate women.[116] It is evident that the structures and processes of liberal democracy are built upon foundations of gendered differences, which commit this type of democracy to the promotion of male domination as a fundamental principle of social organization.

F. Resistances

Patriarchal discourses are deeply embedded in liberal democracy. Fundamental liberal tenets such as universal suffrage, equality, and liberty function to exclude and control women. Liberalism's claims to neutrality and objectivity serve to disguise its gendered operation and cloak its inconsistencies.[117] The international ascendancy of liberal democracy has the potential to globalize liberal forms of male domination. This potential is enhanced by liberalism's allegiance to self-interested individualism

---

leave and day care, and a variety of other benefits, transfer payments and subsidized services." Rosenberg, *supra* note 73, at 129.

113. Bunch, *supra* note 39, at 488.

114. Molyneux, *supra* note 77, at 45.

115. KATHERINE O'DONOVAN, SEXUAL DIVISIONS IN LAW 14 (1985).

116. As Shelley Wright asserts: "[T]he very creation of liberal democratic bourgeois society, in which individual civil and political rights are protected, presupposes, and indeed relies upon, the subjugation of women to this untouchable 'private' sphere." Shelley Wright, *Economic Rights and Social Justice: A Feminist Analysis of Some International Human Rights Convention*, 12 AUSTL. Y. B. INT'L L. 241, 250-51 (1992).

117. In the widely quoted words of Catherine MacKinnon, "male dominance is perhaps the most pervasive and tenacious system of power in history...it is metaphysically nearly perfect. Its point of view is the standard for point-of-viewlessness, its particularity the meaning of universality." *See* Catherine A. MacKinnon, *Feminism, Marxism, Method and the State: Toward Feminist Jurisprudence*, 8 SIGNS 635, 638 (1983).

and the absence of a substantive notion of justice within liberalism, which leaves it bereft of a value system able to envisage social justice.[118]

Paradoxically, liberal democracy also creates more opportunities for the organization of women's movements, for critique, and for the promotion of change.[119] Alongside the promotion of new forms of male domination, new possibilities for feminist resistance are developing in Eastern Europe and the former Soviet republics. Prior to democratization, governments had barred autonomous feminisms on the grounds that they were bourgeois. Developments since the end of the Cold War have been dramatic. Women's movements and organizations have emerged in the former East Germany, Poland, Czechoslovakia, and Hungary. ZEST, a feminist political party, was formed in Yugoslavia before its disintegration as a state, and the first national autonomous women's conference was organized in the Soviet Union in early 1991.[120]

These new forms of political participation are countered by new and more insidious disciplinary measures which closely control participation.[121] One such mechanism of control is the maternalization of women already referred to. The striking ascendancy of conservative forces over the more progressive democratic discourses in Eastern Europe and the former Soviet Union are evidence of the paradox that new forms of social control are accompanying the liberalization of political and economic systems.[122]

Pursuing the interests of women lies in the transformation of both communist and liberal democratic systems. Although the former communist states provided certain guarantees for women by way of electoral quota systems, full employment, and abortion rights, women's social position was still secondary. With the coming of protective democratization, women are losing many of these guarantees while gaining space for women's rights movements.

118. Purvis, *supra* note 95, at 94-95.

119. Ruth Ellen Boetcher Joeres and Barbara Laslett observe that: "the issue of gender relations and gender inequalities, and of partriarchy and its contestation, are being openly debated in ways that we have not seen before in Eastern Europe." Boetcher Joeres & Laslett, *supra* note 94, 116.

120. Cockburn, *supra* note 109, at 55.

121. In Chomsky's view, rather than controlling through force, as despotic states do, governments that claim to be "free and popular" use control of thought in order to produce a sedated and compliant general population. CHOMSKY, *supra* note 5, at 357.

122. Radmila Nakarada observes: "The paradox of the present global situation is that we are simultaneously witnessing an almost universal upsurge of movements and democratic institutions and the expansion and modification of power as a force of subjugation, control, and exclusion." Nakarada, *supra* note 69, at 129.

Whether the freedom to organize outweighs the loss of economic and social rights is a question beyond the scope of this article.[123] But is it clear that neither system is committed to the emancipation of women.

IV. THE ALTERNATIVE OF EMANCIPATORY DEMOCRACIES

This section surveys the popular accounts of democracy which have developed since World War II and identifies the dominant themes that have emerged, with an emphasis on feminist discourses. I examine four major ways in which emancipatory democratic movements present a challenge to the form and rhetoric of liberal democracy: first, the extension and deepening of democracy to spheres other than the formal public processes of the nation state; second, the rejection of neutrality as a viewpoint and the assertion of values that enhance community well-being over individual self-interest; third, the recognition of multiplicity and diversity in ways that empower rather than control people; and fourth, the redefinition of "political" so as to overcome the inequalities of the private/public distinction.

Democratization is envisaged by these movements as an ongoing and dynamic process with radical and transformative potential. These approaches contrast starkly with the liberal democratic concern with preservation of the status quo and the silencing of diversity.

A. Alternative Democratic Traditions

Democracy is not just about the right to vote in elections and the establishment of institutional safeguards to prevent the autocratic abuse of official power. The idea of democracy constitutes fundamental values upon which social interrelationships are predicated. Democratic discourses provide a foundation for human identities and for the possibility of social justice. The notion of democracy has implications at the everyday local level as well as nationally and globally; and in gendered sexual relationships as well as in the public spheres of workplace and government.

Democracy is a framework that organizes the holding and the exercising of power in particular ways. [124] There is much at issue in

123. Carol Bacchi, *Women: Left, Right and Centre,* AUSTL. LEFT REV. 34 (1992).

124. In Philip Allott's view the power at stake includes "a power over consciousness itself, through its control of society's reality-forming, as well as the power to embody the values derived from such reality-forming in legal relations and to interpret and apply those legal relations authoritatively." PHILIP ALLOTT, EUNOMIA: NEW ORDER FOR

struggles for democracy, and the process of democratization creates dual possibilities of reinforcing or challenging the distribution of power in a society. The orientation of protective democracy towards formalism and positivism, which confines democratic potential, becomes explicable when the power of democratic discourses to threaten the status quo is recognized. Protective democracy's minimalist approach to democratic participation promotes and relies upon widespread apathy as a stabilizing force which neutralizes resistance and dissent.[125]

Liberal democracy constructs citizens as homogeneous, autonomous, abstract, male individuals motivated by private self-interest, and conceptualizes each in a relation of formal equality with the next.[126] As Pateman aptly asks, "what [then] is the collective, political interest of citizens who are bound together by only a formal status?"[127] Manfred Halpern's answer is instructive:

> [l]iberal democracy [is] where people believe that their ego and its self-interest constitute the only ultimate ground of existence.... [T]his way of life lacks any ultimate grounds for valuing justice or compassion more highly than, say, power and profit.[128]

The absence of a substantive egalitarian value system enables liberal democracy to turn the rhetoric of freedom and equality to serve the agendas of those who are most powerful.[129]

In contrast, emancipatory democracies speak with many different voices.[130] Emancipatory democracies are founded on participation rather than apathy and exclusion.[131] They arise from

---

A NEW WORLD 210 (1990).

125. CHOMSKY, *supra* note 5, at 368; Manfred Halpern, *Choosing Between Ways of Life and Death and Between Forms of Democracy: An Archetypal Analysis*, 12 ALTERNATIVES 5, 22 (1987).

126. Lester Edwin J. Ruiz, *After National Democracy: Radical Democratic Politics at the Edge of Modernity*, 16 ALTERNATIVES 161, 171-73 (1991).

127. PATEMAN, *supra* note 5, at 104.

128. Halpern, *supra* note 125, at 12, 21.

129. As Tom Carrothers observes: "in international politics this often results in 'a stated concern for promoting democracy shaded into political interference or outright interventionism' in the affairs of less powerful states." TOM CARROTHERS, IN THE NAME OF DEMOCRACY: U.S. POLICY TOWARDS LATIN AMERICA IN THE REAGAN YEARS (1991).

130. Robert Bernasconi notes that "the language of democracy is not so much one language, as a multiplicity of languages; it is its own form of the rule of many." Robert Bernasconi, *Rousseau and the Supplement to the Social Contract: Deconstruction and the Possibility of Democracy*, 11 CARDOZO L. REV. 1539, 1539 (1990).

131. Arguably liberal and communist notions of democracy could claim the same foundations. However, this is no longer where they find their base.

grass roots experiences of oppression, and seek to change the liberal prioritization of pursuing self-interest to counter gendered and racial marginalization and exploitation.[132]

Perhaps contrasting most starkly with protective liberalism are the efforts of emancipatory movements to enunciate values which seek to ensure egalitarian democratic ideals.[133] This concern is apparent in the languages of these movements that speak of "social justice,"[134] "solidarity,"[135] and "care and connection."[136] These movements construct social relationships on a foundation of relational obligations rather than on individual self-interest.[137] Liberationist discourses associated with decolonization and broadly defined self-determination present fundamental challenges to the dominant liberal discourse on democracy.

Feminist movements form an essential part of these oppositions to the global expansion of liberal democracy. Feminism is committed to grass roots political participation and concerned in particular to democratize the so-called private sphere of everyday life, a major locus of women's oppression.[138] The insights of feminism reveal the deeply gendered form of liberal democracy and contribute to the formulation of alternative emancipatory goals: of deepening democracy, of uncovering the biases of the liberal standard of neutrality, of embracing diversity, and of redefining the political. I discuss these radical democratic goals in turn.

---

132. These alternate struggles for democracy are described by Lester Ruiz as a "question of community and identity." Ruiz, *supra* note 126, at 189.

133. *See supra* notes 12-16.

134. *See, e.g.*, ALLOTT, *supra* note 124, at 85.

135. MOHAMMED BEDJAOUI, TOWARDS A NEW INTERNATIONAL ECONOMIC ORDER 261 (1979).

136. Pauline Johnson, *Feminism and Liberalism*, 14 AUSTL. FEMINIST STUD. 57, 65 (1991); *see* REGINA GRAYCAR & JENNY MORGAN, THE HIDDEN GENDER OF LAW 50-55 (1990).

137. As Manfred Halpern explains, in this view

> 'democracy' does not mean rule of the people. It means power of the people. It refers to a persistent dramatic problem: the persistent reopening of the process of the participation by the people as they discover new grounds and new capacity to reshape their life together and as they join in nourishing what they hold to be good.

Halpern, *supra* note 125, at 10.

138. As Ann Phillips describes: "In contemporary feminist politics, democracy is usually presented as something that should enter the fabric of all social relations, and certainly not be restricted to the way governments come about. Wherever there are decisions, there is an issue of democracy." PHILLIPS, *supra* note 81, at 158.

B. Deepening Democracy

Deepening democracy refers to the extension of democratic social organization to loci other than the formal processes of the nation state. Concern with deepening democracy requires going beyond the procedural motions of democracy, such as universal suffrage, to the realization of democracy in substance. While formal mechanisms may constitute necessary components of a democratic society, they fall far short of being sufficient in achieving the substance of democracy, as the women's suffrage shows. Deepening movements aim for the realization of democracy as an integral aspect of individual identity and of all social interrelationships.

Yoshikazu Sakamoto identifies two forms of deepening democracy: democratization from above where democratic processes are initiated by those who hold power; and democratization from below where the impetus for change comes from grass roots movements.[139] The *imposition* of democracy from above, no matter how well-intentioned, will not result in emancipatory outcomes. As we have seen, democratic institutions do not, in themselves, guarantee the fulfillment of substantive democratic goals[140] despite the claims of international legal scholars like Franck.[141] Unless grass roots democratic discourses construct and sustain national and global democratic institutions, these structures are democratic in name only.

The issue of global democracy seems far from the local roots of many of the contemporary emancipatory struggles which seek empowerment through participation in everyday life.[142] Yet global concerns have been consistently enunciated by feminist, environmental, and human rights movements, and by movements in the developing world.[143] A world-wide perspective becomes unavoidable because of the interdependence of the local and the global.[144]

---

139. While recognizing perestroika as a possible example of the former (although President Gorbachev was clearly responding to grass roots pressures), Sakamoto cautions, "however important democratic leadership may be, it is only when 'democratization from below' has gained ground that the dynamics of *truly democratic* democratization are set in motion." *See* Sakamoto, *supra* note 8, at 120-21.

140. Angela Cornell & Kenneth Roberts, *Democracy, Counterinsurgency and Human Rights: The Case of Peru*, 12 HUM. RTS. Q. 529, 552 (1990).

141. Franck, *supra* note 57.

142. Robin Leidner, *Stretching the Boundaries of Liberalism: Democratic Innovation in a Feminist Organization*, 16 SIGNS 263, 281 (1991).

143. *See generally* Richard K. Ashley & R.B.J. Walker, *Speaking the Language of Exile: Dissident Thought in International Studies*, 34 INT'L STUD. Q. 259 (1990).

144. Beverly Harrison refers to this as the "interstructuation of domination" meaning

The everyday discourses of social ordering according to class, race and gender domination are integral to legitimating and maintaining international inequalities. The hierarchical global economic system[145] and the masculine domination of the international legal system[146] provide but two examples of such social ordering.

The interdependence of the local and the global means that deepening democracy involves "the creation of a global perspective and values in the depths of people's hearts and minds, establishing the idea of a global civil society."[147] The growing interconnectedness of states' economic, military, and communications systems make this task simultaneously more urgent and more possible.[148] These movements to deepen democracy world-wide must be distinguished, however, from the creeping globalization of Western liberalism. Deepening democracy is committed to the ongoing evolution of democratic discourses, not to a particular static and controlling democratic form.

C. Exposing Neutrality

Liberalism's claim to international supremacy relies heavily upon its self-characterization as objective, rational, neutral "truth." The task of revealing the biases inherent in liberalism has been an important focus for emancipatory movements. Feminist movements have exposed liberalism's gendered operation;[149] movements in the developing world have highlighted its Eurocentrism;[150] human rights movements have decried its blindness to economic inequalities;[151] and self-determination movements have exposed many democratization processes associated with decolonization as

---

"the irreducibility of history to forces, factors, elements and variables that can be and need to be isolated in order to be understood." *See* BEVERLY HARRISON, MAKING THE CONNECTIONS: ESSAYS IN FEMINIST SOCIAL ETHICS 3-80 (1985).

145. Peter J. Opitz, *The United Nations and the Emancipation of the Third World,* 35 LAW. & ST. 7, 16 (1987).

146. Charlesworth, *supra* note 23, at 621-34.

147. Sakamoto, *supra* note 8, at 122.

148. David Held, *Democracy and Globalization*, 16 ALTERNATIVES 201, 203 (1991).

149. PATEMAN, *supra* note 5.

150. *See, e.g.,* RAM P. ANAND, CONFRONTATION OR COOPERATION? INTERNATIONAL LAW AND THE DEVELOPING COUNTRIES 106 (1987).

151. Adamantia Pollis & Peter Schwab, *Human Rights: A Western Construct with Limited Application*, *in* HUMAN RIGHTS 1 (Adamantia Pollis & Peter Schwab eds., 1979); Bunch, *supra* note 39.

merely the installation of local elites, loyal to the colonizing power.[152] Further, the double standards of U.S. promotion of liberal democracy in Latin America have been widely condemned for consistently targeting left-wing governments and ignoring right-wing authoritarian regimes.[153] The recent popular democratic movements in Eastern European countries have been similarly hijacked by conservative liberal forces.[154] These revelations leave liberalism's claim of neutrality in tatters.

These challenges to liberalism construct a consistent picture of liberal democracy's ideological allegiance to the interests of Western privilege. Unlike communist approaches to democracy which *declare* their loyalty to the interests of the working classes, liberal democracy claims objective universality and constructs social reality upon this premise. The claim to universality gives liberal discourse a strong grip on the power to construct social meaning and makes it difficult to imagine alternatives.

A first step taken by popular democratic movements is to dispense with the possibility of neutrality and seek to enunciate a framework of values or ethics. Unlike foundations which identify the ultimate source of power and good in a god or in nature, this process involves the evolution of new epistemologies arising from the collective experience of those constructed as "other" by the discourses of liberal democracy–those excluded, silenced, marginalized, exploited, injured and dominated by the prevailing status quo. From these knowledges new principles of human association will emerge, not from universal judgments made from alleged neutral viewpoints.[155]

Seeking to affirm emancipatory democracies involves overcoming the polarization of the liberal construction of the individual and the collective, and "substitut[ing]...full human capacity for self-interested power."[156] Such a goal is not, and does not claim to be, neutral. It pursues social justice rather than liberty.[157] It connects democracy with an ethic of sexual, racial, and economic egalitarianism, with the needs of the global community and polity, and with the organization of domestic relationships within states *and* households.[158]

---

152. Sakamoto, *supra* note 8, at 125.

153. Farer, *supra* note 52, at 158; CARROTHERS, *supra* note 129; CHOMSKY, *supra* note 5, at 385.

154. Boetcher Joeres & Laslett, *supra* note 94, at 115; Nakarada, *supra* note 69, at 138.

155. Mouffe, *supra* note 7, at 37.

156. Halpern, *supra* note 125, at 33.

157. Purvis, *supra* note 95, at 98.

158. It is interesting to note that the theme of the 1994 U.N. Population Conference is

D. Embracing Diversity

Liberal democracy constructs its universal citizen, the European middle-class male, in dichotomous relationship with "others." Being female, non-European, poor, communist, or having one of an array of other non-standard attributes results in the social construction of one's identity as "different." This categorization enables the systematic exclusion of those possessing attributes of difference from the enjoyment of liberal democratic promises like equality and liberty,[159] as I have illustrated earlier in relation to women.[160]

Within the dualisms of liberalism is a hierarchy of legitimacy and value which consistently positions one side as dominant and the other as subordinate.[161] Dualisms opposing public and private, objective and ethical, autonomous and relational, civil and political rights with social and economic rights extend beyond the characterization of male/female as a duality to include all those who are "different" in the "female" side of the dichotomy. Those who fall within the second side of the dualism are homogenized as "other" and subordinate.[162] Not suprisingly, in this liberal paradigm every characteristic of emancipatory democratic movements is constructed as other.

Rather than simply reversing these dichotomies, popular democratic struggles seek ways in which multiplicity and diversity can be valued non-hierarchically. Rather than fearing the disorder of difference,[163] emancipatory movements emphasize democracy's potential to build an inclusive society that values difference and seeks equality of outcomes rather than of form. Diversity is encouraged and empowered rather than controlled.[164]

Constructing a social framework which values diversity requires conceiving new formulations of rights which evolve from difference

---

"The Family as the World's Smallest Democracy." These words do not reveal whether the intention is to promote an emancipatory or restrictive democratic agenda.

159. Clare Dalton, *The Faithful Liberal and the Question of Diversity*, 12 HARV. WOMEN'S L.J. 1, 7 (1989).

160. *See supra* notes 86-109 and accompanying text.

161. Ruiz, *supra* note 126, at 173.

162. Joan Scott, *Deconstructing Equality-Versus-Difference: Or, the Uses of Poststructuralist Theory for Feminism*, 14 FEMINIST STUD. 33, 46 (1988).

163. PATEMAN, *supra* note 5, at 18.

164. A commitment to diversity is not true of all popular movements, notably the popular contributions to the ethnic and national conflicts that have erupted throughout the former communist states. Such struggles maintain the dualism of ethnic self and other, with tragic consequences. *See, e.g.*, Nakarada, *supra* note 69.

rather than from falsely claimed commonality.[165] Zillah Eisenstein uses the example of reproductive rights to illustrate this reformulation.[166] She starts from the observation that since pregnancy is not a possibility for males, the pregnant body has not hitherto been the subject of human rights attention because of its difference. In Eisenstein's view, the use of women's bodies (rather than men's) as the starting point for articulating reproductive rights "particularizes *and* destabilizes the discourse of rights in terms of their original meaning."[167] She develops this idea with reference to "the pregnant woman of color" as an even more useful starting point because it includes the specificities of race as well as gender differences, while acknowledging pregnancy as a universal female experience.[168] Eisenstein locates radical egalitarianism somewhere "*between* our difference and our sameness."[169]

In seeking to acknowledge differences, Ruiz draws attention to the distinction between political pluralism, which involves the *recognition* of differences, and democratic pluralism, which involves the *practice* of difference.[170] The elimination of the dualisms of liberal democracy is central to liberatory democratic transformation. Until democracy is reconstructed to welcome multiplicity, the international community will remain polarized and hierarchically organized around difference, despite the eclipse of the particular East/West dualisms of the Cold War.

E. Redefining Political

Liberalism locates politics in the public sphere of civil society and postulates its separation from law, market forces, and sexual relationships. The idea of politics is thus confined to the formal political processes of the state and, in the view of many, does not extend beyond the machinations between and within official political parties. By circumscribing the political, liberal democracy confines

165. As Chantal Mouffe explains: "Radical democracy demands that we acknowledge difference–the particular, the multiple, the heterogeneous–in effect, everything that had been excluded by the concept of Man in the abstract. Universalism is not rejected but particularized; what is needed is a new kind of articulation between the universal and the particular." Mouffe, *supra* note 7, at 36.

166. Eisenstein, *supra* note 98, at 117.

167. *Id.* at 121.

168. *Id.*

169. *Id.* at 122.

170. Ruiz, *supra* note 127, at 183 (emphasis added). Ruiz further asserts that "democratic pluralism is more than its political expression; it must include not only the recognition of differences, such as the differences within a community of women and men, but the celebration and practice of these differences." *Id.*

the application of democratic ideals to the narrow segment of social relations which is classified as "political."[171]

Emancipatory democratic movements contest liberal boundaries to the political as yet another mechanism of social exclusion and control which serves the interests of those with privilege. As we have seen, the delimitation of public and private spheres institutes and protects male domination as the status quo. In relations between states, the parallel distinction drawn between the public sphere of international politics and the domestic sphere, where a state's power is paramount, largely insulates states' internal activities from international scrutiny and accountability.[172] While this separation may be useful as a defense against Western neocolonialism, it also prevents radical developments in international values and norms.

The narrow liberal view of the political justifies establishing a hierarchy of human rights so as to give primary importance to those associated with formal political processes. Further down the hierarchy, in order of importance, are the social and economic rights prioritized by communism, the collective and development rights claimed particularly by those in developing countries, and the rights of indigenous peoples. The coincidence of the ranking of these rights with the relative power of the groups they primarily affect exposes the allegiance of liberal discourse to the existing unequal distribution of world power.

Liberation movements seek a vastly expanded conception of democratic discussion and accountability. As encapsulated by the feminist claim that "the personal is political,"[173] politics becomes the hub of social life. In these emancipatory projects "democracy" becomes the narrative of an entire society rather than the description of a form of government.

F. The Possibility of Transformation

In this discussion, I have not distinguished between those who would describe their project as radicalizing or reconstructing liberal

---

171. As Anne Phillips charges: "The great crime of liberalism was that it turned the activities of citizenship to the service of private interest or desires, and emptied politics of its public importance. The solution is...to re-establish the political as what makes us human and free." *See* PHILLIPS, *supra* note 81, at 16.

172. U.N. CHARTER art. 2, ¶ 7.

173. Halpern states a parallel formulation: "politics is all we can do and need to do." *See* Halpern, *supra* note 126, at 8.

democracy,[174] and those who aspire to nothing short of transformation or revolution.[175] This distinction risks falsely dichotomizing political views that are as diverse as their origins. Polarization between "reform" and "revolution" can divide liberatory social movements and risk repeating the liberal maneuver of dualizing difference and erasing commonalities. Rather, a dialectical process is involved as power shifts, as inequalities are contested and as democracy deepens.[176] As a conservative force, protective forms of democracy serve undemocratic agendas[177] and conceal subordination. But as a liberationist force, democratic change has the potential to forge more egalitarian social relations.[178]

In the post-Cold War context, the dominant discourse of protective liberal democracy is ripe for challenge. Some, like Karl Klare, are optimistic:

> 1989 reopens all of the enduring questions about the meaning and institutional structure of democracy. Eastern Europe is living through a "metaconstitutional moment" when it is possible to imagine that everything can be changed, that political, social and economic institutions can be fundamentally transformed, a moment in which democracy can be "reinvented." There is a chance–if perhaps not a likelihood then at least an authentic opportunity–to imagine and put into place a new, "postliberal" form of democracy, one more egalitarian, participatory and environmentally sensitive, one that is feminist in inspiration and design.[179]

Others, like Nakarada, hold the more pessimistic view that these possibilities have been thwarted by liberal democratic processes which "have proved adept at absorbing critical initiatives and adapting just enough to preserve existing forms of domination."[180]

The alternatives are clear. In the context of the widespread

---

174. *See, e.g.*, Agnes Heller, *Rights, Modernity, Democracy*, 11 CARDOZO L. REV. 1377 (1990); Mouffe, *supra* note 7; PHILLIPS, *supra* note 81; Eisenstein, *supra* note 99; Johnson, *supra* note 137.

175. *See, e.g.*, Halpern, *supra* note 126; Dalton, *supra* note 160; PATEMAN, *supra* note 5; Ruiz, *supra* note 127.

176. Sakamoto, *supra* note 8, at 126.

177. Farer, *supra* note 52, at 169.

178. Chantal Mouffe envisages such a society as "the outcome of the articulation of the greatest possible number of democratic struggles." Mouffe, *supra* note 7, at 41.

179. Karl E. Klare, *Legal Theory and Democratic Reconstruction: Reflections on 1989*, 25 U. BRIT. COLUM. L. REV. 69, 71 (1991).

180. Nakarada, *supra* note 69, at 130.

emergence of grass roots democratic movements, the international legal system *could* play a facilitative role by providing a forum for the promotion of emancipatory forms of democracy. But liberal legal constructs could also stymie this development by assisting protective forms of liberal democracy to claim the vast terrain of democracy movements as their own.

V. The Role of International Law in Promoting Democratic Diversity

This final section returns to the suggestion that international law, in its current form, is highly susceptible to being utilized by proponents of the new world order to "subvert democracy in the name of democracy."[181] Following a general discussion of the role of the legal system in constructing international realities, I look critically at several aspects of international law: its sources, its sovereign-centrism and separation of international and domestic spheres, its professed neutrality, and its preoccupation with control rather than participation. I conclude that the international legal system is in need of fundamental reform if it is to assist in global democratic emancipation, rather than frustrate it.

A. The Power of Legal Discourse

The international legal system can legitimate the existing distribution of world power, but at the same time it is a site for contesting the ways in which social arrangements of power are understood and organized. Legal discourse has the power to universalize certain knowledges and experiences and to disqualify others.[182] Clearly, international law plays a part in constructing Eurocentric and gendered social realities and possibilities.

The liberal legal tradition seldom expressly recognizes the constitutive power of law. Recognizing the power of law in constituting the social order is not to equate law with politics, but rather to say that law is also political.[183] As a result, legal processes,

---

181. Farer, *supra* note 52, at 174.

182. Carol Smart, Feminism and the Power of the Law 11 (1989). I illustrated this power with examples of the restriction of the principle of self-determination to certain peoples, and the denial of reproductive freedom to women. *See supra* text pp. 11-14 and 32-35.

183. As Karl Klare explains, such a recognition:

> does not mean that legal argument is indistinguishable from political argument or that it has no unique content, accumulated tradition, or constraining conventions. Rather, the notion is that legal argument

while marginalizing certain discourses, simultaneously create important opportunities for contesting these exclusions.

The construction of democracy by international law is thus a critical component of democratic change. Currently, two versions of democracy are discernible in international legal instruments and practice.[184] One construct is open-textured and unaligned to any particular democratic tradition while the other is conservative and associated with the tradition of protective liberalism. While there is some scope for the international legal system to acknowledge and promote democratic diversity, this scope is diminishing with the increasing influence of the discourse of the new world order.

Protagonists of the new world order claim that liberal democracy has now triumphed over all alternative traditions of social organization and are seeking legitimation for this view from the international legal system.[185] Their efforts to establish liberal democracy as an international norm have the potential to engage the law in *controlling* the developments of democratization rather than facilitating them. These efforts create new and urgent opportunities to contest and develop the ideas of democracy in international law. The form of international law, however, presents some structural impediments to recognizing diverse accounts of democracy.

B. Law Making Processes

The Statute of the International Court of Justice (ICJ), recognizes four sources of international law: expressly agreed rules set out in international treaties and conventions, customary rules evidenced by states' practice and acceptance, legal principles recognized by "civilized" nations, and subsidiary sources in judicial decision-making and the teachings of publicists.[186] Many have argued that to restrict law-making to these static and positivist sources has "a strong element of absurdity."[187]

184. *Id.*

185. *See, e.g.*, Franck, *supra* note 57; Fukuyama, *supra* note 4.

186. Statute of the International Court of Justice, Oct. 24, 1945, art. 38, 59 Stat. 1031.

187. Robert Y. Jennings, *The Identification of International Law*, *in* INTERNATIONAL LAW: TEACHING AND PRACTICE 9 (Bin Cheng ed., 1982).

Customary law in particular is highly resistant to change.[188] For example, customary law, which relies on consistent state action and opinion over a considerable period of time,[189] would no doubt affirm the subordination of women and confirm other inequalities in the global distribution of power and resources. In tandem with the conservative effects of customary law, legal principles "recognized by "civilized' nations" predispose international law towards affirming Western and patriarchal domination. The one area of primary law-making where fluidity is possible is treaty law, which usually results from extensive consultation and negotiation. These participatory aspects make treaties the most democratic source of international law. Treaty law, however, binds only those states which are parties to the agreement.

To date, treaty law and General Assembly resolutions (GARs) have provided the primary means for developing legal democratic discourses.[190] GARs are not recognized in the Statute of the ICJ as a source of law[191] and fall within a controversial grouping of international written instruments that are referred to as "soft law." Legal positivists argue that soft law blurs the normative threshold of international law and threatens the solid foundations of the international legal system.[192] Progressive legal scholars, on the other hand, argue that the instruments of soft law offer opportunities for change and challenges that are otherwise absent from the international arena:

---

188. Mohammed Bedjaoui has trenchantly argued: "Backward looking, conservative because static, iniquitous in its content, ponderous in its formation, custom as traditionally conceived cannot be of use in the development of new rules, and could actually be an obstacle to any attempt at change." BEDJAOUI, *supra* note 136, at 59.

189. *See* North Sea Continental Shelf Cases (F.R.G. v. Den., & F.R.G. v. Neth.), 1969 I.C.J. 3 (Feb. 20). The Court set out the elements of customary international law as: (1) virtually uniform and consistent practice over a period of time; and (2) evidence of *opinio juris* that the practice in question is considered virtually obligatory by states.

190. U.N.CHARTER; *Universal Declaration of Human Rights*, G.A. Res. 217A, U.N. GAOR, 3rd Sess., at 7, U.N. Doc. A/810 (1948); *International Covenant on Civil and Political Rights*, G.A. Res. 2200, U.N. GAOR, 21st Sess., Supp. No. 16, at 52, U.N.Doc. A/6316 (1966); *Declaration on the Granting of Independence to Colonial Countries and Peoples*, G.A. Res. 1514, U.N. GAOR, 15th Sess., Supp. No. 16, at 66, U.N. Doc. A/4684 (1960); *Declaration on Principles Concerning Friendly Relations*, G.A. Res. 2625, U.N. GAOR, 25th Sess., Supp. No. 28, at 121, U.N.Doc. A/8028 (1970); G.A. Res. 45/151, U.N. GAOR, 45 Sess., U.N. Doc. A/Res/45/151 (1990); G.A. Res. 45/150, U.N. GAOR, 45 Sess., U.N. Doc. A/Res/45/150 (1991).

191. There are a limited number of ways in which GARs may be recognized as law. For example, they may crystallize customary law.

192. *See, e.g.*, Prosper Weil, *Towards Relative Normativity in International Law*, 77 AM. J. INT'L L. 413 (1983).

> They provide for the shaping and sharing of values and so create expectations as to the restraints States will accept upon their own behaviour and will urge or impose upon others within their jurisdiction.[193]

The promotion of democratic diversity by way of the international legal system cannot rely on the traditional law-making processes for support. Instead, progressive change will be heavily dependent on the utilization of soft law mechanisms.

The importance of soft law to global change has been recognized before. During the 1970s and 1980s, the developing world united in an attempt to promote a New International Economic Order (NIEO), which sought to carve out a strategic role for GARs in international law-making. The democratic basis of the General Assembly was one of NIEO lobby's rationales for promoting it as a law-making forum.[194] At the high point of this process, Wang Tieya claimed that "[t]he Third World in both name and reality has become a new creator of international law...both its new subjects and its new masters [sic]."[195]

The response of legal positivists to elevating GARs to a source of law was, predictably, outrage.[196] Such responses reveal the high levels of resistance to change within the liberal establishment of international law. This bears witness to the strength of liberalism's opposition to law-making processes which may connect with radical democratic forces for change. Although the attempt to establish a NIEO is now regarded as a failure,[197] the challenge that was presented to the traditional sources of international law remains. The protagonists of the NIEO introduced notions of law-making as participatory, flexible, dynamic and indeed, democratic. Those who seek radical democratic change need to build upon this groundwork to include not only developing countries in law-making processes, but also women, indigenous peoples, and ethnic minorities. Such a

---

193. Christine M. Chinkin, *The Challenge of Soft Law: Development and Change in International Law,* 38 INT'L & COMP. L.Q. 850, 865 (1989).

194. "Through its [the General Assembly's] egalitarian character, its majority basis and hence its democratic origins, the resolution seems...to present sufficient guarantees as a method for the elaboration of international norms responding to today's needs." BEDJAOUI, *supra* note 135, at 140.

195. Wang Tieya, *The Third World and International Law, in* THE STRUCTURE AND PROCESS OF INTERNATIONAL LAW: ESSAYS IN LEGAL PHILOSOPHY, DOCTRINE AND THEORY 955, 965 (Ronald St. John MacDonald & Douglas M. Johnston eds., 1986).

196. Weil, *supra* note 192, at 415.

197. Thomas M. Franck, Lessons of the Failure of NIEO, Address Before the Canadian Council on International Law Annual Conference (Oct. 17, 1986); Russel L. Barsh, *Current Developments: A Special Session of the UN General Assembly Rethinks the Economic Rights and Duties of States,* 85 AM. J. INT'L L. 192 (1991).

broadening would make it possible, for the first time, for international law to be universally conceived.

C. Decentering the State

Sovereign states are the subjects and objects of international law. Because of its liberal foundations, the international legal system conceives states in much the same way as liberalism conceives citizens in domestic law: as homogeneous atomistic individual units motivated by self-interest, standing in a relation of formal equality with each other. The goal of international law, as constructed by its sovereign-centered liberal framework, is "the pursuit of a world order (or lack thereof) that maximizes sovereign liberty."[198] This formula enables the international legal structure, resting upon the autonomy of states, to militate against the evolution of a democratic world order because community values exist only as an amalgam of states' self-interest.[199] As Phillip Allott observes, this structure confines "reality-forming" to the jurisdiction of separated states, which prevents society from being conceived internationally. This scheme perpetuates "interstatal unsociety"[200] which serves the interests of the ruling classes of the all states.

In addition, the sovereign-centrism of international law constructs democracy as *national* democracy.[201] This construction at least partially accounts for the nationalist conflicts erupting in the wake of post-Cold War democratization. By narrowing democracy to the government of states, international law creates a double obstruction for movements that seek to "deepen" democracy. First, it insulates the undemocratic international order from legal challenge by these movements because only states are recognized as subjects of law. Second, the sovereign-centrism of international law precludes popular democratic movements by confining democracy to the public realm of official government within states. Elections thus emerge as the major signification of a state's democratic credentials and civil and political (i.e. public) rights gain priority over economic and social rights. Further, international law's sovereign-centrism applies progressive principles, such as self-determination, only to the population of a state as an entirety. Non-state-based groupings, like women, who seek self-determination are excluded from the reach of international law.

The separation of international public affairs from the internal

---

198. Purvis, *supra* note 95, at 95.

199. *Id.* at 93-94.

200. ALLOTT, *supra* note 124, at 248-49.

201. Sakamoto, *supra* note 8, at 125.

domestic affairs of states underlines the liberty of states as the central organizing principle of international law, but this separation is becoming increasingly controversial. Human rights law has contested this separation with some success.[202] Paradoxically, new world order lobbyists have also argued that sovereignty should be lawfully violated in order to promote democratic goals.[203] The issue is double-edged. On the one hand, many women and ethnic minority groups argue that sovereign immunity from international scrutiny helps to perpetuate their oppression.[204] But from the perspective of the developing world, sovereignty provides a bulwark against imperialist encroachment by the West.[205] Despite the persuasiveness of this view, there is a strong imperative to develop alternative defenses against Western domination which recognize groupings other than states at international law.

Purvis argues that liberal ideas "[m]aintain such a tight grip on our consciousness that has become difficult to imagine a world order built on some principle other than sovereignty."[206] Despite this difficulty, many emancipatory democratic movements argue that the interdependence of the international community must eventually erode state sovereignty. Surakiart Sathirathai argues, from the perspective of developing countries, that it is necessary to develop

> a participation approach [which] begins with an alternative vision of the relationship among states...[which] will push at social, national and cultural boundaries, and lead to the acceptance and sharing of different beliefs and concepts.[207]

The nation state must be understood as only one locus of democracy and power. Further, the idea of democracy itself must be reconstructed as a process "from below," with its base in popular movements, rather than "from above" and confined to a state's formal political processes. These changes would diminish, if not eliminate, the dualism of international and domestic spheres and allay well-founded fears of Western neocolonialism.

---

202. Steiner, *supra* note 40, at 129; *Optional Protocol to the International Covenant on Civil and Political Rights,* G.A. Res. 2200A, U.N. GAOR, 21st Sess., Supp. No. 16, at 59, U.N. Doc. A/6316 (1967).

203. Carpenter, *supra* note 64, at 25.

204. CHARLOTTE BUNCH, *Prospects for Global Feminism,* in PASSIONATE POLITICS: FEMINIST THEORY IN ACTION 301-05 (1987).

205. As Wang Tieya explains: "It is only by tenaciously upholding sovereignty that the new nations can preserve real self-government; protect their legitimate rights and interests on the basis of equality; eliminate colonial oppression and exploitation; and avoid having to suffer from them again." *See* Tieya, *supra* note 195, at 969.

206. Purvis, *supra* note 95, at 101.

207. Sathirathai, *supra* note 36, at 416.

D. Relinquishing Western and Patriarchal Loyalties

International law originated in regulating relations between European states "reflecting their Christian, capitalistic, imperialistic interests."[208] The post-World War II reconstruction of international law transformed it from a European law to "a law of the great powers."[209] Only the form of Western domination changed, not its substance. The ending of the Cold War has increased the leverage of Western liberal thought within the international legal system.[210] This development is illustrated by assertions that liberal democracy is attaining the status of an international legal norm and by heightened confidence with which liberal forms are being promoted as being universal in application and meaning.

Further, the new world order preoccupation with monitoring and standardizing global democracy shows a concern to protect, rather than to challenge, the unequal distribution of world power. A strategy that coerces states into a standardized Western democratic framework fundamentally undermines democracy as a dynamic and grass roots evolution. Not surprisingly, only protective liberal forms of democracy lend themselves to this classification, and herein lies the liberal agenda. Because the multiplicities of emancipatory democracies cannot be standardized, they stand to become constructed by law as outside acceptable democratic development and thus to be denied legal legitimacy. This coercive approach indicates that from a conservative liberal viewpoint, law is an instrument of social control rather than a forum for social development. In this view the legal system is rightfully engaged in defending discourses that protect social privilege rather than promote social justice.

This colonization of legal discourse by conservative liberal forces is controversial, contestable and undemocratic.[211] The co-optation of the United Nations by the discourse of the new world order is not to

---

208. LOUIS HENKIN, HOW NATIONS BEHAVE: LAW AND FOREIGN POLICY 121 (1979).

209. BEDJAOUI, *supra* note 135, at 59-60.

210. George, *supra* note 22, at 23; Kurth, *supra* note 3.

211. As Phillip Allott points out,

> [i]n generating...the idea and the ideal of democracy, a society seeks the means to enable the people, the members of society, to embrace law as their own, not merely because they may conceive of themselves as its authorizing source but because they may will and act the law in their participation in the total social process which forms it.

ALLOTT, *supra* note 124, at 256.

be mistaken for the globalization of democracy.[212] The many voices of dissent and knowledge of resistance must unite to contest the international legal system's allegiance to the West and to male domination. Alternative democratic movements must expose law's professed neutrality which both furthers and disguises gendered and Eurocentric global imbalances of power. In solidarity, grass roots movements can reveal law's link with politics and thus its potential to transform liberalism.

From emancipatory democratic movements, affirmative visions of a socially just and egalitarian international community are emerging. Law's role as a "prominent conversation"[213] in international relations may provide an arena for these visions to assist in processes of empowerment rather than of control. However, the international legal system will not fulfill this function unless its allegiances to liberalism, male-domination, and the West are acknowledged and rejected.

E. Fundamental Reform

The international legal system needs fundamental reform if it is to provide a forum for advancing deepening democracy. The static and conservative sources of international law are antagonistic to change. Its sovereign-centrism confines the focus of democracy to national democracy, repressing alternative visions of diverse and egalitarian local and international communities. The professed neutrality of international law disguises its gendered and Western loyalties which disqualify emancipatory visions of change. Its preoccupation with control distorts democracy to protect the interests of the undemocratic status quo. As a result, international law's liberal origins and form make it highly susceptible to co-optation by the protective liberalism of the new world order.

Alternatively, law as a dynamic and political process, rather than as a mechanism for social control, opens opportunities for contesting its construction of social reality. This contestation must challenge the form of the legal system, not just its content. As feminists have discovered through their efforts at domestic legal reform, liberalism structures legal method to appear impervious to feminist challenge.[214] By extension, leaving the form of international law unchanged severely restricts its potential to contribute to emancipatory democratic change.

---

212. Sakamoto, *supra* note 8, at 123.

213. Purvis, *supra* note 95, at 118.

214. Mary Jane Mossman, *Feminism and Legal Method: The Difference it Makes*, 3 AUSTL. J. L. & SOC'Y 30, 45 (1986).

VI. CONCLUSION

The ending of the Cold War marks an opportunity for the globalization of patriarchal and liberal forms of democracy under the banner of a new world order. The international legal system is in danger of being coopted to assist this agenda of Western expansionism in the guise of promoting democracy and human rights. Pressure is mounting for the international legal system to legitimate these developments, specifically by taking a role in standardizing and enforcing world-wide protective liberal democratic forms.

The new world order heralds an intensification of patriarchal domination. The experiences of women resulting from the democratization of Eastern Europe and the former Soviet Union attest to this development. Discourses which control and subordinate women are increasing in influence. Women are being excluded from formal political processes, expelled from the paid workforce, and denied reproductive freedom as their bodies and identities are maternalized and domesticated. In addition, women are bearing the brunt of the economic liberalization which is increasing the global spread of the feminization of poverty.

Contesting the meanings of democracy and the fundamental values upon which social relationships are predicated is an urgent task. New instruments of power are emerging in the wake of the Cold War as global economic and technological systems grow beyond the reach of existing political forms. New systems of value and meaning are accompanying these changes. As a result, social relationships are increasingly shaped by market forces which rely upon a divided, unequal, and subjugated international "unsociety."[215]

At the same time, this new world brings new possibilities for radical change. Emancipatory democratic movements may emerge more coherently and forcefully in resisting these mechanisms of control. There is "an authentic opportunity"[216] to create post-liberal and post-communist forms of democracy inspired by feminist and communitarian values. Contemporary grass roots movements envisage democracy as participatory and empowering, founded on an ethic of sexual, racial, and economic egalitarianism and directed towards achieving social justice. The impetus of these popular democractic movements is, however, in danger of being coopted by the West to serve its global designs.

In the wake of the Cold War human rights have catapulted from

215. *See* ALLOTT, *supra* note 124, at 248.

216. Klare, *supra* note 179, at 71.

the fringes of mainstream international legal discourse onto center stage as an adjunct of liberal democracy.[217] The defense of democracy has been claimed as a lawful rationale for the use of force by one state against another, throwing into question previously fundamental principles of territorial integrity and peaceful resolution of disputes.[218] And most recently the World Conference on Human Rights has proclaimed democracy to be interdependent with economic development and respect for human rights.[219] These developments present many opportunities for radical democratic advancement.

International law is at a crossroads. Will it assist in developing socially just and sexually egalitarian global relations, or will it remain loyal to its roots in Western history? The form and content of international law present major barriers to the evolution of an emancipatory vision of international society. Yet law's role in contesting international discourse positions it well to contribute to progressive change. There is some basis for arguing that international law contains the seeds of an affirmative vision of democratic diversity in its open-textured versions of the democratic entitlement.

The restrictive liberal orientation of the international legal system and its disciplinary ordering of human relations must change. We must extend the discourse of international law beyond the interests of states to hear the many voices currently excluded. Opportunities for dialogue between the local and the global must be forged. We need to expand and collectivize the limited opportunities already provided by human rights law. Ways of celebrating difference must be developed so that difference no longer legitimates inequality. The time is ripe for radical challenge to global patterns of inequality. The international legal system *could* be a site for contesting the Western and patriarchal interests served by the "New World" democratic order, and for promoting alternative discourses of global democracy that value diversity and communality and reject gendered individualism. The challenge is before us.

---

217. Irving Kristol, *'Human Rights': The Hidden Agenda*, THE NATIONAL INTEREST, Winter 1986-87, at 5 (illustrating the previously suspect nature of the concept of human rights in conservative liberal thinking).

218. Carpenter, *supra* note 64, at 26 (referring to the U.S. invasion of Panama in 1989).

219. *Vienna Declaration and Programme of Action*, *supra* note 46, at 5.

[18]

Human Rights and Governance: The Asia Debate

*Yash Ghai**

I. The International Context of Human Rights and Democracy

The history of human rights is ancient but its contemporary salience can be traced to the establishment of the United Nations and the proclamation by its General Assembly of the Universal Declaration of Human Rights in 1948. Since then the United Nations and related agencies have concluded a number of conventions to implement the provisions of the Universal Declaration by elaborating detailed formulations of specific rights and establishing some machinery for their supervision. Much of this work was done in committees of officials and did not, for the most part, attract much public attention. There were undoubtedly differences among groups of countries on the scope of particular rights, the priorities among them, and the extent of their enforceability. These were resolved within the committees and did not engage great public interest (even in the highly controversial instance of the right to development). However, in the last few years questions of human rights have achieved a high salience. This has revealed considerable differences among governments and intellectuals on the understanding, scope and importance of human rights.

There is broad agreement that a key purpose of society is to ensure the dignity of the human person. For many people, human dignity is to be secured through the protection of human rights. Others have different views on how to achieve this aim, but all would concede some role for human rights. However, there is no general agreement on the nature of human rights. The conception of

---

* Sir YK Pao Professor of Public Law, University of Hong Kong. This paper draws upon my two previous papers, "Asian Perspectives on Human Rights" (1992) and "Human Rights and Governance in Asia" (1994). The first paper was presented at a conference on Human Rights of Migrant Workers organised by the Scalabrini Migration Centre in Manila. It was also tabled at a workshop on Human Rights and Governance in Asia organised by the Asia Foundation in Manila in March 1993. The second paper was written at the request of the Asia Foundation as a record of my reflections on the discussions at the workshop. It was subsequently used as a background paper for an Asian Foundation sponsored dialogue on the same subject between Asia scholars and senior officers of the Clinton Administration and the United States Congress in Washington in June 1994. The present paper reflects also on the Washington discussions. I am grateful to the participants of all these meetings for their thoughtful and stimulating contributions. An earlier version of this paper appeared as an occaisional paper of the Asia Foundation. The author is grateful to the Hong Kong Research Grants Council for support of his work on human rights.

the basis of human rights has varied from time to time, and from place to place. For a long time in the West, the belief that rights were derived from a divine ordering held sway, but it gradually gave way to the notion that rights originated from and were a response to the very nature of man. In that sense they are inherent and inalienable. This secularisation of the source of human rights arose under certain social and economic conditions which are said to mark the rise of market economic systems and consequently to emphasis individualism. In one way, it could be argued that basing human rights on the nature of man (and these days we must concede, woman) should lay the foundations for a universal regime. Unfortunately, this has not been the consequence—for a variety of reasons, it would seem. At first the attacks came from those who believed that these rights, associated with the market, served merely to strengthen the dominance of one social class over others, and to result in the misery of the general public. It was also perceived that the "man" of the market system is acculturated in its peculiar values and dynamics, "disembodied" from the community. In societies where the dominance of the market over culture and community has not taken place or is incomplete, this view of human rights does not command universal acceptance. Similarly where the sway of religion or tradition is strong, the secular basis of human rights affects their acceptability, for which they must draw from the orientation of a particular religion or tradition. The difficulties of establishing political order and political authority in several regions of the world have also brought into question the utility of norms that detract from the power of the government.

Differences over perceptions and status of human rights are not new. After the somewhat uneasy consensus over the Universal Declaration of Human Rights, serious conflicts emerged which were responsible for protracted negotiations over the instruments that were to implement the Declaration as well as for the fact that a truce was possible only through the bifurcation of rights into civil and political on the one hand, and economic, cultural and social on the other—with separate Covenants for each. The West conceived of rights largely as political, while the socialist States provided the impetus for economic and social rights. At the heart of the controversy was the role of the market in the organisation of the economy and the distribution of resources. The interesting point about contemporary controversies about human rights is that all the major contestants are committed to the market (the opponents of the market get little hearing now). The basis of differences has changed—an aim of this Paper is to explore what that is.

These contemporary differences have been highlighted by the context in which human rights have now achieved salience. An important aspect of that context is the collapse of the communist regimes in Europe, which removed the Cold War agenda and introduced space for discussions of liberty and freedom. The West took the opportunity to develop another agenda centring around human rights and democracy. This interest coincided with the growth of highly visible international non-governmental organisations (NGOs) which assumed a major responsibility for the scrutiny of the record of individual countries on human rights. The link of human rights to democracy was established through the work of international aid agencies, particularly the World Bank and the United States Agency for International Development, which made "governance" a central feature of their development assistance. Good governance was largely equated with democratic institutions and practices (including transparency of policy-making and administration).

There are other aspects of the post-Cold War context which bear upon human rights. The collapse of the communist systems was attributed largely to the inefficiencies of command economies, and while a few years previously there was much talk of the crisis in capitalism, there was now a surge in the legitimacy of markets. Much effort has gone into the establishment of markets in Eastern Europe and formerly communist States in Asia; indeed a veritable and diverse profession has developed around this enterprise. In some respects these efforts represent an extension of privatisation and structural adjustment policies that had been adopted by or imposed on various States in Africa, Asia and Latin America, the effect of which was to diminish the economic role of the State. The marketisation of domestic economies was paralleled by the globalisation of capital, markets and services, as national barriers to investments and trade were removed (under pressure from world economic institutions). The thrust of globalisation came largely from the West, and served to increase its economic influence and hegemony over the rest of the world.[1] But it was presented, instead, principally in terms of the virtues of entrepreneurship, economic rationality and an efficient legal regime marked by security, predictability and transparency. The links of these developments to human rights were sought to be established through claims of increased choices for investors, consumers and workers, the restrictions on State power and the emergence or strengthening of civil society. So democracy, marketisation of economies, the promotion of human rights and the emergence of civil society were declared to be all of a piece.

The result of the approach of the West was to bring out clearly the implications of the human rights work steadily (and indeed sometimes obscurely, as with the Convention on the Rights of Migrants) developed through the United Nations and its agencies. It brought to the fore the responsibility of the international community for the protection of human rights everywhere, and thereby highlighted the ways in which national sovereignty has been qualified by the UN Charter and the human rights conventions. Relations between a State and its nationals were no longer a matter merely for that State; some fundamental norms of that relationship (enacted at an exponential rate, some claimed) were now defined in international law, and subject not only to the scrutiny of the international community but also to its sanctions. International relations themselves are increasingly mediated through human rights discourse and practice. Aid conditionalities, unthinkable a decade ago, have become

1 The globalisation of capital and markets should minimise rather than increase tensions between the West and the successful economies of East Asia. They enhance the interests and stakes of each side in the success of the other, and alliances are forged increasingly on transnational class lines than national. The international rhetoric of confrontation hides this emerging transnational identity.

common place. The legitimacy of international involvement was heightened not only by the moral authority of human rights and the collapse of political regimes associated in many minds with their denial, but also by the willingness of several countries to accept international assistance for establishing human rights and democracy (for example, Eastern Europe, Russia, Nepal, Cambodia, and South Africa) and considerable public support in many countries for such intervention in their own case. Further support for the emphasis on human rights and good governance was secured through arguments about their link to sustained economic and social development. However, not all governments have taken kindly to the internationalisation of human rights and democracy, although many of them are unable to carry their opposition to it to international fora because of their fragile political and economic systems and the dependence on external donors. Several Asian countries, particularly in South-East and East Asia, have offered a spirited rebuttal of this internationalisation.[2] They resent the interposition of the international community (and particularly the hegemony of particular countries within it) in their relations with their citizens, in an ever increasing number of areas. They also resent the leverage it has given these other countries (and international institutions) over their policies, and see the new approach as attempts to undermine their moral authority, disrupt their political stability, and retard their economic progress. Rather than, as in some other regions, withdraw from the debate, they have sought to provide an alternative framework for the discourse of human rights and democracy.[3]

Secure in the economic success of their policies which owe little to democracy or human rights, they contest the claims of the positive links between democracy (and human rights) and economic development. Another plank in their argument is that most of the rights which the West is purveying are "Western" in origin, oriented towards an individualistic society and therefore inappropriate to Asia where the values of communal action are highly prized. Furthermore, the priorities as between different human rights vary from country

---

2 In this paper I sometimes refer indiscriminately to "Asian governments". Clearly not all governments subscribe to views that I attribute to "governments". So that my position is not misunderstood, I should say that my paper does not deal with the Middle East. It is also useful to try to make distinctions as among clusters of Asian governments. Issues and politics in South Asia (India, Pakistan, Nepal, Sri Lanka and Bangladesh) are often different from that in East Asia (China, Japan, North and South Korea, Taiwan, and Vietnam). The former are more plural with specific parliamentary traditions underpinned by ethnic politics, while the latter are influenced by Confucianism and a measure of authoritarianism. But even this broad generalisation needs to be qualified, since Japan may be said to have shed authoritarianism some decades ago, while Singapore could be included for this classification with East Asia, and Malaysia with South Asia. See Richard Cullen, "Protecting Individual Rights: East Meets West" (mimeo, 1994).

The politicisation of the discourse of human rights, along the North-South divide, has nevertheless resulted in a certain closing of ranks, and the more vocal of the governments are able in regional and international meetings to muster a show of solidarity on the basis of their own doctrines, as was demonstrated in the pre-Vienna regional meeting in Bangkok in 1993.

3 Perhaps the most articulate statement of this position is Kausikan, "Asia's Different Standard" (1993) 92 *Foreign Policy* 24.

to country, and certainly in their own States, the priority must be given to economic and social rights. On a more doctrinal but basic level, they challenge the legitimacy of international involvement in human rights and national political systems on the argument that the fundamental principle of international law and relations is State sovereignty (to which belong these questions). They also accuse the West of hypocrisy, since it has long been engaged in violations of human rights, from slavery to colonialism, and the current decline of moral authority and public order in its own States.

The politicisation of human rights that has followed their internationalisation raises acute questions of theory and practice. What is the basis for international action on human rights? What justifies political and economic conditionalities? What abuses are inherent in conditionalities? How does one check these abuses, particularly those of "double standards" and "double speak"? Why should a State's competence to deal with its citizens be circumscribed by reference to human rights or governance? At the heart of this debate lies the nature of human rights and the source of their authority. Are human rights determined by the culture or economic development of a country, contingent on history, or do they represent universal values true for all time and places? Stemming from considerations of theory and strategies, are some rights more basic than others? How do civil and political issues relate to economic and cultural rights? Is there a sequence in the development and achievement of human rights? How do human rights, the rule of law, and democracy relate to each other? How are human rights and democracy linked to economic and social development? What is the role of civil society? These are in fact extraordinarily hard questions, to which political theory does not provide ready answers. Yet some resolution of these questions is essential to place current international debates within a more rational, objective and consensual framework. The Vienna World Conference on Human Rights failed to resolve these issues, despite a "consensus" document. Consensus was achieved by genuflections to a series of contradictory positions, rather than an engagement with and the reconciliation of issues that divided them. The politicised environment of human rights discourse is not particularly conducive to a productive discussion of these issues. It is important to recall that these issues pre-date the North-South divide; and for a long time have been the basis of great controversy in Western political and social thought.

II. Asian Perspectives on Human Rights

As a backdrop to an exploration of some of these issues, I review the principal perspectives on human rights in Asia. In contemporary debates, it is generally assumed that there is one Asian view of human rights, and that it is opposed to the traditions of individual human rights that first developed in the West. It is easy to believe that there is a distinct Asian approach to human rights because some government leaders speak as if they represent the whole continent when they make their pronouncements on human rights. This view is reinforced because they claim that their views are based on perspectives which emerge from the Asian culture or religion or Asian realities. The gist of their position is that human rights as propounded in the West are founded on individualism and therefore have no relevance to Asia which is based on the primacy of the community. It is also sometimes argued that economic underdevelopment renders most of the political and civil rights (emphasised in the West) irrelevant in Asia. Indeed, it is sometimes alleged that such rights are dangerous in view of fragmented nationalism and fragile Statehood.

It would be surprising if there were indeed one Asian perspective, since neither Asian culture nor Asian realities are homogenous throughout the continent. All the world's major religions are represented in Asia, and are in one place or another State religions (or enjoy a comparable status: Christianity in the Philippines, Islam in Malaysia, Hinduism in Nepal and Buddhism in Sri Lanka and Thailand). To this list we may add political ideologies like socialism, democracy or feudalism which animate peoples and governments of the region. Even apart from religious differences, there are other factors which have produced a rich diversity of cultures. A culture, moreover, is not static and many accounts given of Asian culture are probably true of an age long ago. Nor are the economic circumstances of all the Asian countries similar. Japan, Singapore and Hong Kong are among the world's most prosperous countries, while there is grinding poverty in Bangladesh, India and the Philippines. The economic and political systems in Asia likewise show a remarkable diversity, ranging from semi-feudal kingdoms in Kuwait and Saudi Arabia, through military dictatorships in Burma and formerly Cambodia, effectively one party regimes in Singapore and Indonesia, communist regimes in China and Vietnam, ambiguous democracies in Malaysia and Sri Lanka, to well established democracies like India. There are similarly differences in their economic systems, ranging from tribal subsistence economies in parts of Indonesia through highly developed market economies of Singapore, Hong Kong and Taiwan and the mixed economy model of India to the planned economies of China and Vietnam. Perceptions of human rights are undoubtedly reflective of these conditions, and suggest that they would vary from country to country.

The official view

Perceptions of human rights are reflective of social and class positions in society. What conveys an apparent picture of a uniform Asian perspective on human rights is that it is the perspective of a particular group, that of the ruling elites, which gets international attention. What unites these elites is their notion of governance and the expediency of their rule. For the most part, the political systems they represent are not open or democratic, and their publicly expressed views on human rights are an emanation of these systems, of the need to justify authoritarianism and occasional repression. It is their views which are given wide publicity domestically and internationally.

The unity of governments is more apparent than real. Although the Bangkok Declaration[4] was endorsed by all the Asian governments at the April 1993 Asian regional preparatory meeting for the Vienna World Conference on Human

4 The Declaration has been published in the (1993) 57(3) *Law and Society Trust Fortnightly Review* 1 (1 May 1993).

Rights, some of them have a firm commitment to human rights and their record is better than one might expect from their endorsement of the Declaration. India is one example. Along with some other States, it is committed to human rights by its constitutional instruments, has a strong and independent judiciary, and despite problems and setbacks tries hard to maintain human rights. Nor is their adherence to traditional values and rules absolute; the Indian Constitution prohibits many traditional and religious practices like the discriminatory and degrading treatment of lower castes and provides for an equal treatment of women with men.[5] The reason for presenting a united front is not unconnected with a perceived North-South confrontation (as is evident from the Bangkok Governmental Declaration, which stressed the need to avoid the application of "double standards" in the implementation of human rights and its "politicisation").[6] Asian governments feel that since the end of the Cold War, the West has focused its attention on what it perceives to be the "undemocratic" nature of Third World polities. In Africa and Latin America the concern with human rights is seen to be an instrument for the establishment or strengthening of the market, in an attempt to restrict the interventions of the State in economic relations. In Asia, however, the key economies are heavily market oriented, and for the most part are successful. Even China is now turning to the market, which is widely credited for China's economic success. So the emphasis on human rights is not necessary as a spur to the market (and indeed, as I explore later, the relationship between the market and human rights is problematic).

Some Asian governments consider that the Western pressure on them for an improvement in human rights is connected with the project of Western global hegemony. This is to be achieved partly through the universalisation of Western values and aspirations, and partly through the disorientation of Asian State and political systems (and the consequent negative effect on their burgeoning economies). They have fashioned their response accordingly.

I turn first to "official" views of human rights of a number of influential Asian countries (Singapore, China, Malaysia, Indonesia). These views have developed primarily in response to two contingencies: the imperatives of control, and confrontation with Western pretensions. They are therefore formulated somewhat defensively. It also means, because they arise in the context of an engagement and a debate with the West, that they are formulated in universalistic terms, in the usual discourse of human rights. Several ingredients constitute the official view I am discussing. One which flows directly from both the contingencies is the assertion of "domestic jurisdiction" over human rights. Human rights are encapsulated within State sovereignty; the national treatment of human rights is no concern of other States or the international community. Self-determination, a concept which has been used to advance claims of human rights, is regarded as irrelevant to independent States.

5 Indian Constitution, see articles 14 and 17, and the Directive Principles of State Policy (particularly articles 42, and 46) which set a wide agenda of social reform consisting largely of attacks on traditional values and practices.

6 Note 2 above, para 7. These differences dominated the World Conference on Human Rights in Vienna, June 1993.

In its "White Paper" *Human Rights in China* (1991), the Chinese Government stated that "Despite its international aspect, the issue of human rights falls by and large within the sovereignty of each state".[7] The Chinese delegation to the UN Commission on Human Rights at its meeting in February 1993 urged that the World Conference in Vienna should

> reiterate the principle of State sovereignty contained in the UN Charter and international law which is basis for the realisation of human rights. Only when the state sovereignty is fully respected can the implementation of human rights be really ensured.[8]

This is also pre-eminently the position of the other countries mentioned above.

Another element in the official view is the relativity of rights, determined by the economic, political and cultural circumstances of each country. The Bangkok Governmental Declaration "recognises that while human rights are universal in nature, they must be considered in the context of a dynamic and evolving process of international norm-setting, bearing in mind the significance of national and regional peculiarities and various historical, cultural and religious backgrounds".[9] This stance reflects the position in the Chinese White Paper which states that "the evolution of the situation in regard to human rights is circumscribed by the historical, social, economic and cultural conditions of various nations, and involves a process of historical development. Owing to tremendous differences in historical background, social system, cultural tradition and economic development, countries differ in their understanding and practice of human rights.[10] "The Chinese use this framework to establish the priority of social and economic rights in their country, and much of the Paper is taken up with an account of the ending of pre-Communist regime practices of feudalism and other forms of human exploitation and the steady progress since in nutrition, education, health, the position of women and the disabled. Other countries too have used the state of national economic development as explanations for the failure fully to guarantee the complete range of human rights ("to eat their fill and dress warmly were the fundamental demands of the Chinese people who had long suffered cold and hunger").[11]

There are two major implications of this relativist position on human rights. The first relates to the conditions for political stability, and the other to the primacy of economic development. The implications of the first represent restrictions on civil and political rights. A forthright statement of this position is to be found in pronouncements of the Singapore Government following the detention of various social workers and activists in May 1987. I quote here from one such statement (dated 24 June 1987, and addressed by the then Minister for

---

7 *Human Rights in China* (1991). The Paper was published by the State Council to refute the charges of human rights violations in China. The quotation occurs ibid, p 11.

8 Statement by Mr Zhang Yishan, UN Doc E/CN. 4/1993/ SR 25, p 2 (17 Febuary 1993).

9 Note 7 above, para 8 at n 1.

10 Ibid, p 2 at n 2.

11 Ibid, pp 4–5 at n 5.

Home Affairs, Mr Jayakumar, to United States Congressmen who had written to complain about the detentions). It contrasted the "resilience and cohesiveness" and shared values of the nation of the United States (which presumably makes possible the tolerance of human rights) to the fragility and heterogeneity of Singapore.

> We are vulnerable to powerful centrifugal forces and volatile emotional tides. Like many other developing countries, Singapore's major problem of nationhood is simply to stay united as one viable nation. ...In our short history, Singapore has repeatedly encountered subversive threats from within and without. ...To combat these threats to the nation, the usual procedures of court trials, which apply in Singapore to most criminal cases, have proved totally inadequate. The very secrecy of covert operations precludes garnering evidence to meet the standards of the criminal law for conviction. In many cases of racial agitation, the process of trial itself will provide further opportunity for inflammatory rabble rousing. ...Singapore cannot be ruled in any other way...Preventive detention is not a blemish marring our record: it is a necessary power underpinning our freedom.

(Another aspect of the Singapore by-passing the formal legal system, with its guarantees of openness and fairness, not discussed in the Minister's statement, is the taped and doctored "confessions" extracted from the detainees under coercion, and then shown on the national television as proof of guilt and calculated to destroy their credibility and dignity.) These remarks were directed at a justification of administrative powers of detention without any kind of trial, but similar arguments have been used to justify other curtailments of civil rights, like the right to associate and assemble, of peaceful marches, of speech and expression. The Chinese Paper says that the people's right to subsistence will be threatened in the event of social turmoil or other disasters, and that it is the fundamental wish and demand of the Chinese people and a long-term, urgent task of the Chinese Government to maintain national stability and concentrate their efforts on developing productive forces.[12]

The economic backwardness of Asia has been used to establish the primacy of economic development over human rights. The argument is, in part, that civil and political rights are neither meaningful nor feasible in conditions of want or poverty. Therefore the first priority of State policy must be to promote economic development. It is implied that economic development may well require restrictions on human rights, both to provide a secure political framework in which it can be pursued and to remove obstacles in its way (for example, through forced movement of people from lands required for "development"). Economic backwardness is also used to establish the priority as between different kinds of rights, in which civil and political rights occupy a lowly position (in part a response to an argument that human rights are indivisible, and all of them enjoy an equal status).

---

12 Ibid, p 8. There is of course no easy way to find out what the people of China want since there are no truly representative bodies or a free press—a point I return to later to establish the link between political rights and social rights.

The emphasis these governments purportedly place on economic development has led them to support the right to development. This right is a matter of considerable contention internationally, with developing countries arraigned on the side supporting it, and most developed countries united in their opposition to it. It certainly does not have the quality of other kinds of rights, which inhere in individuals or groups and for the most part are entitlements against the State. Nevertheless, the General Assembly of the United Nations adopted, in the face of abstentions by most Western States, a Declaration on the Right to Development on 4 December 1986.[13] The Declaration ties the realisation of human rights in the developing countries to international economic aid for them and gives to "peoples" (presumably meaning "States") the right to "participate in, contribute to, and enjoy economic, social, cultural and political development, in which all human rights and fundamental freedoms can be fully realised". In return for these, several concessions are made in emphasising the indivisibility of rights and the claims of individuals to full participation in development and in the fair distribution of the benefits resulting from it.

The Declaration is a fuzzy document, trying to be all things to all persons. So while there are sections of it which can be used to advance the (more traditional) cause of human rights, the gist of it seeks to establish reason for the failure of the realisation of human rights in the international economic and political systems (including encroachments on the principle and practice of self-determination), while affirming that the primary responsibility for human rights are vested in States as part of their sovereignty. In other words, the rich countries must provide economic assistance to the poor countries, but must not question their human rights situation. (The Western riposte to the Declaration has been a massive imposition of political conditionalities on economic assistance and indeed, in the case of China, on economic relations and cooperation).

The Declaration is also an attempt to provide an alternative framework for the international discourse on human rights. It shifts the focus from domestic arenas (where most violations of human rights take place) to the international, and takes attention away from specific rights, for example, speech, assembly, social welfare to an ambiguous portmanteau right of development, for which in the nature of Third World affairs, the State must take the responsibility in defining and implementing it. Through the Declaration, Asian governments seek to promote the ideology of developmentalism which justifies repression at home and the evasion of responsibility abroad.

Another Asian initiative in changing the framework for the discourse on human rights is even more fundamental. The approaches discussed so far have taken the Western discourse as the main framework and have advanced qualifications to it or provided justifications for derogation from its values. Some governments have put forward the argument that the cultural matrix,

13 The Declaration is reprinted in, United Nations, *Human Rights: A Compilation of International Human Rights Instruments*, vol 1 (1994), p 548. I have criticised the Declaration in Ghai, *Whose Human Right to Development?* (1989).

within which relations between individuals and the State are embedded, is fundamentally different in Asia from that in the West. This matrix governs the nature and salience of human rights. This approach has been taken up aggressively in Singapore and Malaysia (less so in China, where the government's residual loyalty to Marxist thought is inconsistent with the adoption of this cultural approach, especially since so much of it is based on semi-feudal thought in Asia).[14]

I take as the basis of my discussion of this point an official 1991 statement of the Government of Singapore, *Shared Values*.[15] The context of this White Paper is a concern of the Government that the cultural values of its people are under attack from foreign ideas and values. It poses the rhetorical question, "Can we build a nation of Singaporeans, in South-East Asia, on the basis of values and concepts native to other peoples, living in other environments?" It goes on, "If we are not to lose our bearings, we should preserve the cultural heritage of each of our communities, and uphold certain common values which capture the essence of being a Singaporean".[16] It then finds certain perceptions and values which are common to the different ethnic communities of Singapore and which also distinguish them from society in the West. The key section of the Paper is devoted to a discussion of the relationship between the individual and society. Disputing the proposition that values are universal and common to all mankind, it states that there is a major difference between Asian and Western values in the balance each strikes between the individual and the community; Asian societies emphasise the interests of the community, while Western societies stress the rights of the individual. The Singapore society has always weighted group interests more heavily than individual ones. "This balance has strengthened social cohesion, and enabled Singaporeans to pull together to surmount difficult challenges collectively, more successfully than other societies. An emphasis on the community has been a key survival value for Singapore".[17] The core values of the Asian society are identified as placing society above self, upholding the family as building block of society, and resolving major issues through consensus instead of contention. There is a strong element of Confucianism in this elaboration, although the Government denies that the values it propagates are purely Confucian. It, however, picks up an element of Confucian teaching as particularly relevant to Singapore. "The concept of government by honourable men (*junzi*), who have a duty to do right for the people, and who have the trust and respect of the population, fits us better than the Western idea that a government should be given as limited powers as possible, and should always be treated with suspicion unless proven

14 This sentence was written in 1993. As I revise it, today's *People's Daily*, 19 September 1994, (Beijing) starts the rehabilitation of Confucius, in several articles extolling the virtues of Confucianism as an aid to political stability and economic development.

15 Singapore Government, *Shared Values*, Cmd 1 of 1991 (Government Printers).

16 Both these quotations appear at ibid, p 1, and are taken from a presidential address to Parliament, January 1989.

17 Ibid, p 5 at para 26.

otherwise".[18] The supremacy of political authorities is emphasised by the first of the Shared Values, "Nation before Community". Another aspect of Asian values, implicit though not explicit in the Paper, is the importance of duty as a counterpoint to right. The cohesion of society as well as the fulfilment of the individual is secured through a chain and hierarchy of duties. (The primacy of the notion of duty is emphasised elaborately both in the Chinese and Indian Constitutions.)[19]

The individual does not disappear altogether as a bearer of rights in the Singapore Paper. However, characteristically the concern with the individual is expressed more in terms of the obligations of the community to look after its less advantaged members. (In Singapore there is a twist to this, in that the "community" in question is the ethnic community of the individual, not the State, "to avoid the dependent mentality and severe social problems of a welfare state as experienced in many developed states",[20] laying the foundations of a kind of community corporatism in the wake of declining popularity of the ruling party, showing how much these questions are viewed in that country from the perspectives of governance and management).

Cultural "embededdiness" is not the only justification for this view of the relationship between the individual and the community and the interposition of the family. It is said to be also rooted in more pragmatic considerations. The White Paper hints at this, but it has been developed elsewhere. In at least South-East Asia, there is a strongly held view that an authoritarian political system is the secret of its economic success, and the frequent Singaporean mocking of the democratic efforts of the Philippines (with a rather inefficient economy) is advanced as proof of it. But there is also the belief that it is not the individual but the family (tied into a network of clan associations and relationships) which has been at the forefront of the phenomenal economic success of the region. There appears to be the view of a significant number of people (primarily but

---

18 Ibid, p 8 at para 41.

19 Chapter 2 of the Chinese Constitution is entitled "The Fundamental Rights and Duties of Citizens". Article 42 states that Chinese citizens have the right as well as the duty to work and article 46 says that they have the duty as well as the right to receive education. Other duties include safeguarding the "unification of the country and the unity of all its nationalities" (article 52); abiding by the Constitution and the law, keeping of State secrets, protection of public property, observing labour discipline and public order, and respecting social ethics (article 53); safeguarding the security, honour and interests of the motherland and a prohibition against acts detrimental to the security, honour and interests of the mother land (article 54); and to pay taxes (article 56). Article 55 states "the sacred duty of every citizen of the People's Republic of China to defend the motherland and to resist aggression" as well as to "perform military service and join the militia in accordance with the law".

The Indian Constitution requires citizens, *inter alia*, to abide by the Constitution, protect the sovereignty, unity and integrity of India, to promote harmony and the spirit of common brotherhood amongst all the people of India, and to renounce practices derogatory to the dignity of women, and to safeguard public property and abjure violence (article 51-A).

20 Ibid, p 7 at para 38.

not only, among the business community as is well evidenced in the debates in Hong Kong) that this combination of authoritarian rule and family and kinship networks lies at the root of economic success.[21] This model (which reverses the normal understanding of the relationship between the market, individualism and the rule of law) is seen to be threatened by democracy and human rights. Hence democracy and human rights are not high on many people's agenda.

Other voices

There are other Asian voices as well. There are, admittedly somewhat muted or censored, the voices of the oppressed and the marginalised. There are the passionate voices of indigenous peoples whose cultures are destroyed by governments which claim to be the custodians of Asian cultures; they speak in a language which finds few resonances even in the West (because their language is threatening to the system of the market). There is the voice, rising in density, of the middle classes, with a stake in affluence whose new found prosperity and economic enterprise shows to them the virtues of the legal protection of property and the rule of law. There are the strident voices of ethnic minorities who seek collective autonomies which challenge the governments' claims of political monopoly and State sovereignty. An important and articulate group are intellectuals who are alienated from the State, and for the most part are not apologists for the regime. Intellectuals respond to and engage in international debates; and like the NGOs they form networks with their counterparts in other parts of the world.[22] Like the NGOs they have a commitment to human rights and democracy (even in China there is a growing and vibrant academic community with a keen interest in human rights and constitutionalism).[23] They are less ready to accept Western conceptions in totality, and attempt to relate questions of human rights to specific national conditions.

I have space only to discuss the views of the NGOs which provide the most consistent and coherent alternative view of human rights to that of governments. An authoritative statement of the position of Asian NGOs was issued on 27 March 1993 on the occasion of the Asian intergovernmental conference on human rights preceding the Vienna World Conference.[24] It endorsed the view that human rights are universal, and are equally rooted in different cultures. While it supported cultural pluralism, it condemned those cultural practices which derogate from universally accepted human rights. Since in its view human

21 I have reviewed this literature (and examined its implications for the centrality or otherwise of the rule of law) in "Capitalism and the Rule of Law: Reflections on the Basic Law" in Wacks RI (ed), *Legal Theory: China, Hong Kong and 1997* (1993), p 343.

22 For a view of leading Indian intellectuals see Baxi, "The Right to be Human" (1986) 13(3) *India International Centre Quarterly*; Kothari S and Sethi H (eds), *Rethinking Human Rights: Challenges for Theory and Action* (1989); Baxi U, *Inhuman Wrongs and Human Rights* (1994), p 123.

23 For a succinct summary see Chen, "Developing Theories of Rights and Human Rights in China" in Wacks RI (ed), *Hong Kong, China and 1997: Essays in Legal Theory* (1993).

24 Note 4 above.

rights are of universal concern and universal value, it does not regard the advocacy of human rights as an encroachment upon national sovereignty. Indeed it recommends international cooperation and solidarity for the promotion of human rights, as a refutation of claims of national sovereignty over human rights issues. The NGOs signatories of the statement support the principle of the indivisibility and interdependence of human rights.

If in these perspectives the views of the NGOs are at variance with those of governments, there is some common ground on other points. The NGOs attribute the poor state of human rights to the international economic order, whose reform through structural changes as well as the adoption of a Convention on the Right to Development, they urge. Unlike the governments, they see a much closer connection with domestic oppression and international exploitation, in the collaboration of local economic and political elites with multinational corporations and aid agencies. Unlike the governments, they are critical of the consequences of the market system. They share with governments the desire to establish a broad framework for the analysis of human rights, but their framework (unlike that of governments which is informed by a statist view of development) is suffused with notions of social justice, eradication of poverty through equitable distribution of resources and the empowerment of people, especially women and other disadvantaged communities. The NGOs also part company from governments in their assessment of the state of human rights, which they find marked by massive and terrible violations of these rights and pervasive lawlessness on the part of State authorities. They deplore the militarisation of their governments and societies which is a primary cause of these violations. Their prescription for the ills of their countries is thorough going democracy and an unambiguous recognition and enforcement of human rights

III. A Critique of Governmental Perspectives

Asian governments are right to insist that human rights must be located within the social and economic conditions of specific societies. So called universal human rights of the West have evolved over a long period of European history, responding to the changing configurations of power and the tasks of each epoch of history. Claims of universality and indivisibility of rights are hard to sustain in the face of the West's history of the oppression of its own people and of others, with slavery which once enjoyed religious approbation, abuse of child labour, the exploitation of colonies and the other depredations of imperialism and racism. Nor is the process of the development of rights complete. Social welfare rights were acknowledged only in this century, and the appalling degradation of the environment has now set the stage for a new conception of rights and responsibilities, in which the community will have to be accorded a key position as a bearer of rights as well as duties. There is no reason why contemporary concerns and fads in the West should define the parameters of international discourse in, and aspirations, of human rights.

That is, however, not to say that the framework adopted by Asian governments is justifiable. I start with one element of that framework, religion, which has played a less important part in East Asia than in South and West Asia, but which is nevertheless supposed to give a uniform and distinctive character to Asian perspectives on human rights (although the invocation of religion is somewhat ambiguous since it is also argued that all religions are based on essentially the same values, and provide a common foundation for the primacy of human rights).

Religion

An immediate difficulty facing an exploration of the question whether a distinctive Asian perspective on human rights emerges from the religion of its people is that there are numerous religions in Asia, including all the world's major ones. Assuming that religion does indeed influence a people's perception of human rights, then one would have to concede that there would be a plurality of perspectives, not one. Even if we concede that for our inquiry what matters are "Asian" religions (Hinduism, Islam and Buddhism plus the influential set of beliefs represented by Confucianism), as reflecting more accurately Asian predispositions, they too vary in their beliefs and values. Nor does the same religion manifest itself uniformly in its discourse about human rights at all times and in all countries. Buddhism is militant and aggressive in Sri Lanka, asserting ethnic and religious superiority of one section of the population, while elsewhere, as in Cambodia, it has been a force for peace and the protection of the rights of all communities. Hinduism was once seen as tolerant and non-proselytising, providing a constitutional basis for secularism in India; today many of its adherents are militant and attack beliefs and institutions of other religions. The Hinduism of Nepal is more syncretised than of modern India, able to co-exist and even assimilate with other religions. In many East Asian countries, all religions seem to be mediated through Confucian thought and values. detracting from the specificity of the religion.

In many places religion takes its coloration from politics, woven into the apparatus of the State or claiming a special eminence in its affairs. While Western States separated State and religion (whatever the influence of religion on human rights), the contemporary tendency in many parts of Asia (particularly South Asia) is to connect religion with State. In some instances this has served to diminish the scope for human rights. Sometimes religion acts as a conservative force, at other times it is a major factor for change (and the same religion can play these opposite roles if we compare Christianity in Latin America with that in Europe).[25]

---

25 A strategic question is how far one should use religion to legitimise rights. Religions can lend themselves to alternative propositions. Texts of most religions can be mined for contradictory interpretations. In the circumstances, is it best to separate the discourse of human rights from religion? One answer is no, on the assumption that since Asian people rely on religion for spiritual sustenance and sometimes political authority, rights should be anchored in religion. This may also counter the argument that human rights are foreign constructs by providing an autochthonous base for them in Asian beliefs and values.

As to whether religions can provide a basis for a universal or pan-Asian regime of rights, it is always hard to say what the essence of a particular religion is, but it would seem that different values are enshrined in different religions. Some like Hinduism have sanctified social and caste distinctions, and others like Confucianism, established a social and political hierarchy. Nor is equality the hallmark of Islam, for despite its ideals, its practices cleaved to a tribal and unequal society of its origin. Christianity justified slavery for centuries, and Christian-based Western political systems did not accommodate the equal rights of blacks and women until this century. Not all Asian States (including the largest of them) encourage the holding or the exercise of religious beliefs (preferring, as in China, to base the source of rights in popular sovereignty). Religions would not appear, therefore, to hold the key to universalism. Indeed most religions in some sense deny the claims of equality: traditionally, Hindus found people of other religion polluting, and most other religions have a notion of the "non-believer" to whom an inferior status is accorded in both religious and secular systems. Nor does religion provide a basis for a distinctive Asian perspective on human rights.

Culture

If an interest in religion is frequently motivated by the wish to find common roots for human rights, culture is explored to explain diversity and specificity. As noted above, some Asian governments claim that their societies place a higher value on the community than in the West, that individuals find fulfilment in their participation in communal life and community tasks, and that this factor constitutes a primary distinction in the approach to human rights. The Western pre-occupation with individualism is explained by the alienation resulting from its economic system which has sapped the vitality of the community, and forced introspection on individuals as a means towards their identity. This argument is advanced as an instance of the general proposition that rights are culture specific.

The "communitarian" argument is Janus-faced. It is used against the claim of universal human rights to distinguish the allegedly Western, individual-oriented approaches to rights from the community centred values of the East. Yet it is also used to deny the claims and assertions of communities in the name of "national unity and stability". It suffers from at least two further weaknesses. First, it overstates the "individualism" of Western society and traditions of thought. Even within Western liberalism, there are strands of analysis which assert claims of the community (for example, Rousseau); and most Western human rights instruments allow limitations on and derogations from human rights in the public interest, or for reasons of State. Western courts regularly engage in the task of balancing the respective interests of the individual and the community.[26] Within liberal societies there are nuances in the approach to and the primacy of human rights, as becomes evident when one examines the differences among the United States, Canada, France and the United Kingdom.

26 See for example, Kymlicka W, *Liberalism, Community, and Culture* (1989).

Furthermore, liberalism does not exhaust Western political thought or practice. There is social democracy, which emphasises collective and economic rights, and Marxism, which elevates the community to a high moral order, is also reflective of an important school of Western thought. There is much celebration in Western political thought of "civil society".[27]

Secondly, Asian governments (notwithstanding the attempt in the Singapore Paper to distinguish the "nation" and the community) fall into the easy but wrong assumption that they or the State are the "community".[28] (A similar conflation occurs in the African Charter of Human and Peoples' Rights.)[29] Nothing can be more destructive of the community than this conflation. The community and State are different institutions and to some extent in a contrary juxtaposition. The community, for the most part, depends on popular norms developed through forms of consensus and enforced through mediation and persuasion. The State is an imposition on society, and unless humanised and democratised (as it has not been in most of Asia), it relies on edicts, the military, coercion and sanctions. It is the tension between them which has elsewhere underpinned human rights. In the name of the community, most Asian governments have stifled social and political initiatives of private groups. Most of them have draconian legislation along the lines of the British colonially inspired Societies Act[30] which gives the government pervasive control over civil society. Similarly rights to assemble and march peacefully have been mortgaged to the government. Governments have destroyed many communities in the name of development or State stability, and the consistent refusal of most of them to recognise that there are indigenous peoples among their population (who have a right to preserve their traditional culture, economy and beliefs) is but a demonstration of their lack of commitment to the real community. The vitality of the community comes from the exercise of the rights to organise, meet, debate and protest, dismissed as "liberal" rights by these governments.

---

27 See Cohen J and Arato A, *Civil Society and Political Theory* (1992).

28 Although, as I argue that the lip service to the "community" is hypocritical, the real "community" which motivates politicians is parochial and clannish, pursuing its selfish interest at the expense of other communities, and is the basis of public corruption and graft—and therefore nothing to be proud of. An interesting light on "community" occurred in Hong Kong in April 1994, when two shoppers beat up a shop assistant, while her colleagues watched but did nothing to defend her. However, she bore no grudge against them saying, "Even though I have known them for a long time what difference does it make? You cannot expect someone to help you. I am not their relative". (*Eastern Express*, 11–12 June 1994).

See Siu-kai Lau, "Utilitarianistic Familism: The Basis of Political Stability" in King A and Lee R (eds), *Social Life and Development in Hong Kong* (1981).

29 The African Charter was adopted in Nairobi in June 1981. Its preamble refers to the "values of their historical tradition and the values of African civilisation which should inspire and characterise their reflection on the concept of human rights and peoples' rights".

30 Typically such legislation provides that a society has to be registered before it can operate. The government has the discretion to refuse to register a society and to de-register it. It has the power to seek information from the society about its membership, finances and other affairs, and to control or prohibit political links with outside bodies.

Nor is the tight regulation of society as in China and Singapore particularly Confucian. Confucius argued against reliance on law or coercion, and advocated a government of limited powers and functions.[31]

Another attack on the community comes from the economic, market oriented policies of the governments. Although Asian capitalism appears to rely on the family and clan associations, there is little doubt that it weakens the community and its cohesion. The organising matrix of the market is not the same as that of the community. Nor are its values or methods particularly "communitarian". The moving frontier of the market, seeking new resources, has been particularly disruptive of communities which have managed to preserve intact a great deal of their culture and organisation during the colonial and post-colonial periods. The emphasis on the market, and with it individual rights of property are also at odds with communal organisation and enjoyment of property (and a further irony is that Asian leaders who allege their allegiance to communal supremacy and values are among the most ardent opponents of a Marxism that espouses the moral worth and authority of the community). Market policies have relied greatly on multi-national capital and corporations, which have brought new values and tastes, and are increasingly integrating their economies and elites into a global economy and culture. Indeed, it is these very considerations which prompted the Singapore White Paper, but the contradictions of official policies largely escaped its authors. It totally ignored the impact, indeed the onslaught, of modern technologies on traditional communities.

A final point is the contradiction between claims of a consensus and harmonious society, and the extensive arming of the state apparatus. The pervasive use of draconian legislation like administrative detention, disestablishment of societies, press censorship, and sedition, belies claims to respect alternative views, promote a dialogue, and seek consensus. The contemporary State intolerance of opposition is inconsistent with traditional communal values and processes. Contemporary State processes in Asia are less hospitable to community politics than the much derided adversarial processes of the West, which at least ensure a hearing for all parties.

Thoughtful Asians, who concede many of the above criticisms of a "communitarian" approach, nevertheless hold on to some important distinctions between the West and Asia, which they consider are rooted in culture. There is first the distinction between duties and rights. An aspect of this is the tendency in the West towards formalism, the transformation of values as legal rights, and the consequent emphasis on the rights and prerogatives of an individual. Based on a theory of competition and suspicion of authority, this leads to demands rather than concessions, to confrontation rather than reciprocity and accommodation. An emphasis on duties on the other hand leads to honour and

---

31 As with religion, Confucianism has been used for political purposes so that its essence has become somewhat obscure. It is undisputed, however, that Confucius was against tough laws and strong punishments, believing in the virtue of rulers and their sense of duty. See Rubin V, *Individual and State in Ancient China* (1976), and Van der Sprenkel S, *Legal Institutions in Manchu China* (1962), esp Chapters 2 and 3.

peace, as well as stability. It is argued that the rights-based emphasis leads to the impoverishment of society, so that in the search for the protection of the citizen against the State, the community collapses and non-State actors become the principal source of oppression and insecurity (making it unsafe to be on the streets of major metropolises after sunset). There is also the danger in formalisation of values as "rights" that the form may elude substance (so that the satisfaction of formal criteria hides realities that deny the values; as Professor Mazrui once said, the West may have abolished child marriages, but the number of teenage pregnancies and one parent families has vastly increased).

However, in the hands of an intolerant government, the concept of duties can become a justification as well as an instrument of authoritarianism. This is perhaps not inherent in the notion of duties because duties are also laid upon rulers (in the best Islamic and Confucian traditions), and indeed the notion of duty can be truly revolutionary. In practice, however, this is not how it often is, duties vary from person to person (persons at the top of the hierarchy having rights and those at the lower reaches, duties), reminiscent of feudalism. The emphasis on the fulfilment of duties, frequently betokening social, economic or political subordination, tends towards conservatism and the perpetuation of inequalities—antithetical to the claims of equitable development advanced by many Asian governments. Furthermore, the conflation between the State and community serves to strengthen the tentacles of the government over society. The notion of duties transferred from the community to the State changes its nature from inter-citizen obligations and responsibilities to the much more problematic case of State-citizen relations. The West has, to some extent, separated civil society from the State, creating a "neutral" public area and space for communities (from which of course the commanding heights of the State may be controlled), while in Asia the tendency is towards the convergence of the two, regarded perhaps as necessary for the legitimacy of the State[32] but ultimately destructive of the community.

Even if we were to concede that Asian cultures or religions are distinctive and that these colour the perception and reality of rights, it is not clear why the global debate has taken the opposition of political and civil rights ("Western") versus economic and social rights ("Asian"). Why should the communitarian approach suggest that economic and social rights are more important than political? It may be argued that traditionally, communities were hierarchically organised and that its cohesion depended on duties. But the communities were even less concerned with "development" which is undoubtedly more of a foreign concept than fair or accountable administration or harmony within the community. If human rights do not follow from Asian cultures, then neither does economic development. The same can be said of "Asian" religions, which are stereotyped as other worldly (like most religions), more concerned with

32 The argument here is that in non-Western States, legitimacy does not come from the rule of law, constitutionalism and the neutrality of State institutions, but from their association with religion and culture—which in the mostly heterogenous States, means the culture and religion of the majority community. See for example, Tiruchelvam, "Development and the Protection of Human Rights" (mimeo, 1993).

salvation in the next world than economic prosperity in this. Ethics are more important than power, and asceticism and austerity are values approved by most of these religions. Apart from the somewhat ambiguous position of Confucianism (which is mistakenly today regarded as development oriented rather than as preserving the status quo as traditionally regarded), there is little in "Asian" religions to support a privileged position for economic development. It is interesting that the most influential Christian church in Asia is Catholicism rather than the Weberian, development driven Calvinism or a variant of it! Asian governments are therefore on shaky ground when they invoke tradition to justify the primacy of development. If economic rights are seen to flow from "communal" or "collective rights" there is a misapprehension, for these rights are normally attributed to individuals, not groups (collective rights being associated with "solidarity" rights to a clean environment, property as commons, and a measure of equity, which are anathema to at least some Asian prime ministers).

If there is no substantial basis in community, culture or religion for economic and social rights, then why do Asian governments place such rhetorical emphasis on them? They sometimes say that civil and political rights are meaningless if the people are poor and illiterate. There is of course considerable truth in this, but there is reason to be sceptical about the sincerity of the governments for they have done little to establish economic rights or promote civil rights in countries which have achieved great economic success. The more plausible reason is that the talk of economic and social rights is diversionary, an attack on civil and political rights. Governments are anxious to minimise challenges to their authority or legitimacy, which means (as it seems to them) the suppression or emasculation of political opposition. A preference for economic rights might also arise from the consideration that it is much harder to hold governments accountable for them. They are for the most part, matters more of standards than precise rules and entitlements, their enforceability is problematic and they are widely regarded as contingent on resources. In fact these governments dislike talk of economic and social rights, except when engaged in global debates (many of them do not like talk of any rights). It is not easy to establish how civil and political rights threaten economic and social rights. The juxtaposition these governments play upon domestically is not between these different rights, but between civil and political rights and *economic development*. It is economic development, not economic rights, that they emphasis. They are, however, content to seek economic rights of *States*, the so-called developing States (as in their advocacy of the right to development). It is of course easy to understand why governments want economic development; it increases State resources, enables governments to establish larger armies, enhances the status of their leaders, and secures the support of the populace.

I conclude this section by reference to another distinction that is seen to flow from cultural differences—the role of the family (as that suggests an appropriate approach to study of human rights). It is frequently said that the bedrock of Asian societies is the family, and it has become fashionable to ascribe social problems in the West to the breakdown of family life. It is claimed for Asia that mutual responsibilities within the family provide for the welfare of its members, ensure traditions of respect and rectitude, and promote social stability and economic development. The conversion of values into individual rights undermines the basis of family solidarity. However, countries which are not known for their practice of individual rights have found that the family may well be weakening under the pressure of other social and economic changes. A particular irony is that a legislator in Singapore, known to enjoy government support, recently introduced a bill to give parents the right to sue their children for maintenance (and the children the defence that the parents mistreated them when they were young!). It is hard to imagine that such a bill would achieve its objective of maintaining family solidarity!

The concern with the erosion of family values is instructive in a number of ways. At one level, it minimises the Asian claim for cultural distinctiveness and therefore relativity of rights. At another level, it provides another basis for relativity. Societies are constantly changing, and with economic and social changes, there are also changes in the perception of what is important and valuable to a community or a group. In other words, an assessment of the priorities in human rights alters with the underlying economic transformations. The West too has had its "communitarian" phase (and the community is still important there) and the family is even now cherished, even if old solidarities are beginning to dissolve under economic pressures. Asian governments which cheerfully and sometimes aggressively espouse "Western" notions of development and the market, find that they can no longer ward off its child, human rights.

The above analysis suggests that a useful perspective on human rights is drawn from history: the (dialectical) unfolding of rights, and representing social achievements. This in turn suggests that the development and understandings of rights are contingent on a variety of factors, moral ideas as well as material conditions, and that differences in their perception are attributable to them rather than to any inherent ideas of culture or community. This approach does indeed provide a basis for reconciling so called "Western" and "Eastern" perceptions of human rights. In my view this provides a better basis for global debates on this subject. The notion that distinct "Western" and "Asian' perspectives exist is inaccurate, ahistorical, and leads to unfruitful polarities (ignoring, for example, that the West also has a notion of duty (limitations on rights/freedoms)). Equally it distorts the debates on human rights, by suggesting that the key conflict is between the East and the West, rather than that it is within each. It detracts from the relevance and urgency of human rights discourse in Asia, the keen debates on the appropriate models for representation, governance and accountability, and equity. Asian intellectuals and activists need to rescue the debate from the present sterile phase to place it at the centre of national and regional politics.

If human rights have to be located in their social and economic contexts, what are the appropriate features that constitute the context for them in Asia? If one may generalise (keeping in mind the simplification that this may involve), the following specifics of the Asian situation stand out. The first point is that the function of human rights (and discourse on them) in Asia is quite different from that in the West. Human rights in the West have responded to the configurations of power and economic relationships as they have evolved over a long period. They are consequently consistent with the patterns and structures of authority, and people's aspirations as well as expectations. There are no serious competing paradigms of political organisation. The role of human rights is to fine tune the administrative and judicial system and fortify rights and freedoms that are largely uncontroversial. In Asia, on the other hand, human rights have a transformative potential. They are a constant challenge to vested interests and authority in societies riven by enormous disparities of wealth and power, with traditions of authoritarianism and the helplessness of disadvantaged communities, of militarisation and the conjunction of corrupt politicians and predatory domestic and international capital. Human rights are therefore a terrain for struggle for power and the conceptions of good society. It is for this precise reason that Asian governments have engaged in the debate with the West; the real audience are their own people.

The second point is that there are massive violations of human rights in Asia, of the rights of women and children, of lower castes and otherwise disadvantaged communities, of ethnic minorities, and of workers. Violations range over the whole conspectus of human rights; civil and political rights, as well as cultural, social and economic; there are mass killings and widespread disappearances; torture; wide displacements of communities from their traditional abode; arbitrary detentions and extensive censorship of thought and expression. The State is a major culprit, brutalising whole populations, but massive violations also take place in and through civil society, sometimes with the connivance of the State, and frequently reflecting feudalistic and patriarchal dimensions of culture. Social conflicts, particularly those stemming from ethnic or caste differences, have politicised and militarised civil society in many States. These developments should caution us against over-romanticisation of civil society (which in India, for example, is a major source of the oppression of millions of people, through murder and rape, bonded labour, and a web of discriminatory and punitive customs and practices).[33]

The third point is that despite these violations, human rights consciousness is low. Explanations for this paradox may lie in the weight of oppression over centuries, a fatalistic acceptance of one's miseries, and obstacles placed in the way of those who would seek to make explicit to the downtrodden the causes of their oppression. It certainly lies in the ethnic divisions of societies; ethnic consciousness can dull human rights consciousness, distinguishing us from

---

33 The framers of the Indian Constitution were well aware of these problems of civil society. Article 15 declared illegal discriminations on ground, *inter alia*, of caste, in, for example, access to wells, tanks, bathing ghats, roads and other places of public resort. Article 17 abolished untouchability and its practice in any form. Article 23 prohibited traffic in human beings and forced labour, particularly the traditional form of bonded labour known as "begar". There are various laws at the central and State levels to implement these provisions, particularly the Civil Rights Act 1955 (expanded and renamed as the Scheduled Castes and Scheduled Tribes (Prevention of Atrocities) Act in 1989). Despite these attempts, the social and economic position of these disadvantaged communities shows little improvement.

"others" and facilitating justifications for their oppression. A major challenge to human rights workers is undoubtedly this ethnic consciousness which compels a perception of outsiders as less than human. Another cause of low human rights consciousness may be widespread poverty. Poverty is a great cause of the denial of human rights. The international system refuses to accept this reality—for largely political reasons. It refuses to acknowledge that poverty destroys human dignity; and without human dignity there can be no human rights; or indeed the capacity to challenge the system of oppression.

Thus economic development is undoubtedly important. But not just any kind of economic development. Economic growth must be accompanied by a wide measure of egalitarianism, the protection of the rights of workers, particularly migrant workers, and democratic practices at work places. Nor must economic growth be undertaken at the expense of land, customs and autonomy of long settled communities. Unless these and other community concerns are safeguarded in the process of economic growth, development is perverse and adds to the violation of human rights and dignity.

A further point about human rights in Asia is that challenges to their violations are not individual based, but group or class based. This is particularly the case in multi-ethnic States. The protection of human rights is therefore pursued through the group. This fact, and the fact that the State is a major violator of human rights, suggests strategies that are different from the traditional Western approaches which are legalistic and court centred. Asian strategies cannot realistically be court centred, however favourably the judiciaries may be disposed towards human rights (and for the most part they are not). Human rights conscientisation and mobilisation based on connections between them and their oppression are a fundamental starting point (connections which neither local governments or the West are anxious should be made).

Nor must the terrain of struggle be purely domestic. Despite the resistance of governments, the realisation of human rights in each country is intimately tied to wider global forces (particularly in the contemporary world wide pursuit of marketisation). Even today many governments in the Third World are surrogates for external economic and political interests, and it is necessary to take the battle to the homelands of these interests, just as it is necessary to recruit foreign interests to put pressure on domestic governments which deny their people the right to participate in decisions affecting their own destiny.

For Asians concerned with the welfare and dignity of their fellow citizens, the right strategy should embrace the universalism and indivisibility of human rights. The implication of universalism and indivisibility is that human rights can no longer be seen in national terms or responsibility or as contingent on particular economic systems. They raise global issues which highlight the responsibility of people in one State to peoples in others. They imply that consumers in the rich Western countries owe a duty to present generations in other parts of the world and to future generations everywhere. They necessitate the closure of the armaments industry. They require a more equitable international economic system. They import a more democratic international system. Consistent with the dominant role of human rights in history, they raise a truly revolutionary agenda, sufficient to discomfort the West.

IV. Theoretical Issues

The polemics between the "West" and "Asia" on human rights has stimulated the search for a consensus on the importance as well as the scope of rights. One strategy has been to find agreement on the source of rights, but as pointed out above, this has not been promising. Another is to see if there can be a consensus on the purpose of human rights, at least at a very general level. One aspect of this approach has been to try to identify rights which form a "core" that all cultures and jurisdictions would subscribe to—the obvious candidates are the right to life, the prohibition of slavery, and the prohibition of torture—but beyond that, lists tend to diverge.[34] Equally, while every one would subscribe to the view that a primary purpose is to ensure the "inherent dignity" of a person, dissent starts with attempts to draw out its implications. Since it is assumed that the West regards civil and political rights as central to human dignity and Asia accords economic and social rights that primacy, much effort has been expended on the reconciliation of these types of rights. The Vienna Conference formulation was that "rights are indivisible"—but the riders that followed it demonstrated that priorities may need to be established and that these varied from place to place. I discuss this issue later in this section, for in my view it shows not only the scope of disagreement, but also a certain kind of consensus. Indeed I would argue that there is a measure of hypocrisy in the polemics between the West and the part of Asia I am discussing. The United States has cordial relations with the States which are the most outspoken proponents of the Asian position (and also some of them with a poor record of human rights)—Indonesia, Malaysia, Singapore, and occasionally and in the past, Thailand and South Korea. The United States provides security for them both through its own troops and the sale of arms (there are willing donors and willing recipients). There are extensive economic and trade relations between them. There is, in practical terms, very little disagreement on the agenda of the government of these States. The sincerity of the commitment of both parties to human rights has to be judged in this context of cordiality and fundamental common purpose.

(a) Conditionalities

How far should (in this instance) Western countries specify conditionalities on their aid or economic relations with other (in this instance) Asian countries? What is the justification for conditionalities? What are the dangers in conditionality? How effective are they?

The justification goes to the nature of the responsibilities of the international community for human rights, and here we have a confrontation between those who argue that contemporary international law has brought human rights within

34 Even the avoidance of pain, which one might suppose is a basic human instinct, does not hold in all cultures—forms of self-immolation or self-injury are practised as expressions of dissent or mourning, etc.

the jurisdiction of the international community, and those (which includes most Asian States) believing that they remain securely within national sovereignty. From these perspectives, one difficulty is that conditionalities are rarely imposed by the international community. They are imposed by a State or an association of like minded States, which clearly affects their legitimacy. As national or regional initiatives they do not of course require to be justified by a rule of international law on human rights; they are within the sovereignty of the donor/trading State.

The justification for conditionalities weakens if there is no agreement on the universality of rights. To those who believe in relativities, this may seem merely another form of cultural imperialism. They may also be seen as economic imperialism, for they have frequently embodied requirements of privatisation and de-regulation, and the general strengthening of the market mechanism, generally under the rubric of good governance. If conditionalities are not controlled by generally accepted norms, there is the danger of "reverse" conditionalities, instances of which are provided by economic boycotts or threats of them by Malaysia against the United Kingdom and Australia (if the latter did not curb the freedom of the press in their countries to criticise the policies of Malaysia or to make allegation of corruption against its leaders). Indonesia too has practised similar conditionalities in its relations with Australia (and recently against the Philippines in relation to the 1994 Manila conference on East Timor).

Justification may also depend on the kind of conditionalities. The earlier instances of conditionalities, particularly in Africa, related to the restructuring of the economies of the recipient States which involved privatisation, liberalisation and the reduction or elimination of the State provision of welfare services. Subsequent conditionalities related to the respect for human rights and the establishment of democratic practices. Political conditionalities may be easier to justify in that they reinforce internationally agreed norms of governance—human rights and self-determination. They also increase the options and self-expression of the people of the recipient States, and for that reason one welcomes them. Economic conditionalities, however, represent a more fundamental invasion of State sovereignty (for there are no international norms on how an economy should be organised) and they also close options for governments and people—and hence are undemocratic. There is thus a basic contradiction between political and economic conditionalities.

Conditionalities raise other kinds of problems as well. There is the danger of "double standards" in a dual sense; the standards or human rights practices of the "donor" may be little better than that of the recipient, and the donor may pick and choose States for conditionalities, further politicising the practice of conditionality. The United States, "the mother of all conditionors", is particularly vulnerable to these temptations; its record of connivance in the massive violations of the rights of the Palestinian people by Israel, and its active engagement in the destabilisation of democratic orders in many parts of the Third World being particularly despicable. Political conditionalities (for example, regarding good governance) are particularly offensive when the "donor" engages in activities in the recipient country which are inconsistent with the conditionalities (forcing the recipient into a kind of schizophrenia)—a ready example (of widespread practice of Western States and corporations) is the deal made by the United Kingdom Government for the financing of a dam in Malaysia if Malaysia would purchase arms from the United Kingdom (not only is this corruption but also forcing the purchase of arms runs counter to the policy of the West to penalise such purchases).[35] Conditionality may threaten consistency in another sense; a State may decide that its national interests no longer lie in maintaining conditionality, and may abandon it after having initiated it (as with the recent United States decision on the Most Favoured Nation status for China). A country's foreign policy is determined by many considerations, largely of its own self-interest, and therefore human rights are unlikely to be an important or consistent factor. A change of policy may raise a particular moral problem; an important casualty of this change may well be human rights activists in the "recipient" country who have staked a great deal (personally and otherwise) on continued support from abroad.

For the above reasons, conditionalities are not often effective—even if they lead to some temporary improvements. Those who impose and those on whom conditionalities are imposed are generally anxious to return to normal relations, and are therefore astute to find an improvement even if such a conclusion cannot be supported by the evidence. Conditionality can also backfire if the local government decides to whip up anti-foreign sentiments on its basis—as it may frequently suit its purposes. They engage the State and civil society institutions in a human rights dialogue with the donors, rather than with their own people. They may also sharpen polarities which are unlikely to be productive (and which may weaken the capacity of the imposing State to achieve progress through other means).[36] Smaller and weaker countries are more likely to be subjected to conditionalities (as the reversal of United States policy towards China demonstrates).

Although sometimes conditionalities may be necessary (especially if a government, with a poor human rights, is particularly intransigent, there is

---

35 See the resolutions of the European Community and the Council of Europe reprinted in DANIDA, *Human Rights and Democracy: Perspectives for Development Co-operation* (1993).

36 Mr John Shattuck, the Assistant Secretary of State and the highest ranking United States official with responsibility for human rights, described human rights conditionality as a "blunt weapon" in his defence of the reversal of the United States position on China, at an Asia Foundation Washington meeting (June 1994). He explained that it prevented the United States from having normal relations with China and precluded the use of other methods and instruments for change in China's human rights pressure. However many people have interpreted the reversal of the United States policy as kowtowing to American business, and regard with distaste the unseemly haste with which Secretary for Commerce Ron Brown rushed to China with a coterie of business people to sign up several lucrative contracts.

The episode illustrates another danger with conditionalities: the reversal caused much confusion and was widely seen as a signal to human rights activists in China and elsewhere not to depend on the United States for support.

evidence of widespread dissatisfaction with the regime by the public, and there is multi-lateral support for the conditionalities), dialogue or other forms of "constructive engagement" are preferable—at least in the initial stages.

(b) Political and civil rights versus economic and social rights

The controversy over the priority of these two types of rights is not new. Representing a clash between "liberalism" and "Marxism", it dominated the drafting of the International Bill of Rights, and resulted in a bifurcation of rights into two covenants (the International Covenant on Civil and Political Rights, and the International Covenant on Economic, Social and Cultural Rights). The ideological context of the controversy has, however, changed. By and large the market provides the matrix for the proponents on both sides. For example, while the Soviet Union was firmly opposed to the right to property (which does not feature in the Covenants), Asian governments (including China now) are wedded to it. The difference between the two sides lies in the vision of the market. In Western theory the market is autonomous, and the safeguarding of that autonomy requires a number of civil and political rights (property, freedom of movement, association and organisation, expression and an independent and rational legal order). The control of the State (which provides the legal and administrative framework for the market) by the ruling group comes from its prior dominance in civil society (emphasising yet again the importance of civil rights). Asian markets are organised in a much more authoritarian and rapacious manner; there is wide scale corruption; the State, more autonomous of social forces than in the West, is a means to control over economic resources and civil society; and many are still at the "primitive accumulation" stage. Administration is more important than the law; and the imperatives of control override those of economic rationality.

Although both the West and the Asian States are committed to the market, there is competition between them for the national or regional dominance of world markets. Just how the market is organised may affect the interests of the States differently. The West has an interest in equalising the conditions of competition and in the opening up of markets, while Asian States are concerned with twin objectives—of increasing competitive edge and political control. It is thus easy to understand why the West would want to emphasise transparency, accountability, functioning legal codes and courts and a narrowing of the role of the State. It is equally easy to see why Asian States would resist these, using the shibboleths of economic, social and cultural rights. Culture becomes particularly functional as both providing a moral and popular mode of differentiating the East from the West, as well as in slowing down political mobilisation at home. But since the market remains the operating matrix, the process, as I have pointed out above, is not without deep contradictions.

Ideological justifications for the success of the markets in Asia, harping upon the Confucian values of authority, obedience and the salience of the family in economic affairs, are used not to establish the irrelevance of civil and political rights but their destructive qualities. Economic and social rights attempt to mediate between the market and the community, to soften the impact of market forces, to act as a safety net. Nothing in the present conjuncture enhances economic, social and cultural rights. On the contrary, the general acceptance of the market means that propertied and entrepreneurial classes have gained new salience, and that fresh restrictions on social and economic rights (including those of workers and in regard to the environment) are placed in the name of global competitiveness. Asian governments may have some justification to see the emphasis on workers rights and the environment as attempts by the West to reduce the competitiveness of Asian economies, but the restrictions nevertheless point to the shallowness of their commitment to economic rights. It is therefore unlikely that we shall get useful purchase on the question of economic and social versus political and civil rights by examining the stance of Asian governments.

If these inquires are unproductive, what then might be other approaches to the question? Here I must point to the negative consequences of the domination by lawyers of human rights questions. Armed with a number of international conventions, they have excessively juridified the debate, relying more on the text than the purpose of rights. Questions of justiciability have narrowed the range of rights that it is the responsibility of the State to protect. The focus on the State as the source of violations has tended to obscure the power (and the practice) of private groups to inflict massive denial of rights on individuals and communities, and to have led to a somewhat uncritical praise of civil society. Textual and legal analyses (which emphasise universalism) have also ignored the underlying social and economic circumstances which condition attitudes towards and the practice of human rights. I believe that it is in the examination of these circumstances that we can establish a link between political and economic rights.

Economic, social and cultural rights are particularly valuable in uncovering the rationale for human rights. Human rights were part of the post-war agenda of the United Nations which emphasised their close connection with peace, development and human dignity. Unlike the "negative" liberties of political rights, these other rights raise a different framework and pose larger questions—that of the purpose of society and State, of social responsibility and social justice, of equity, and the potential of the human person. They suggest that a person is born full of potentialities—potentialities which find fulfilment through civil and political rights, that of expression, association, and participation, but that these potentialities do not materialise without appropriate social and economic circumstances.[37] Undoubtedly poverty, as I have already argued, is the single most important cause of the violation of rights.

It is therefore necessary to move away from the polarities of civil and political rights on the one hand, and social and economic on the other. Each has a bundle of rights which vary in their impact on the State and citizens and not all are individually oriented (for example, the right of association serves political, economic and cultural functions). Their disaggregation and the purpose each

37 Fields and Narr, "Human Rights as a Holistic Concept" (1992) 14 *Human Rights Quarterly* 1.

serves may suggest different and more productive categorisations. The right of property is regarded as a civil right, yet it is pregnant with economic functions.

The better view is that rights are equal and indeed indivisible. Since one's perception of rights is governed by the state of one's belly, it could be argued that a certain level of literacy and economic security are essential for the exercise and enjoyment of civil and political rights. Equally, economic prosperity and high literacy without the freedom of expression or the right of association fail to develop the full potential of the human person, and the denial of these rights can be humiliating and degrading[38] (this position is increasingly being taken in recent international instruments on the rights of special groups—women, children and indigenous peoples, which have broken away from the bifurcation of the Covenants, being based on the understanding that real equality for women or indigenous people or the real protection of children's rights cannot be secured without major social transformations in their social and economic conditions).[39]

A variation of this position is to acknowledge that both sets of rights are important and even that they are indivisible, but to concede that it may not be possible to achieve them all at once (the reform of the legal system to ensure civil rights of fair and speedy trial, for example, can be as expensive as

---

38 The case of migrants provides an illustration. A large number of people migrate from the relatively democratic Philippines to work in States which are less protective of human rights, like Singapore, Malaysia and the Middle East, suggesting that they value economic advancement over rights. On the other hand, professionals from Singapore are emigrating to countries in the West where personal and artistic freedoms are more highly valued, suggesting that economic wellbeing is not sufficient for human happiness and fulfilment.

This example also illustrates another theme of my paper, that one's view of human rights is coloured by one's economic and social status.

39 For example, the Convention on the Elimination of All Forms of Discrimination Against Women (CEDAW) (1979) guarantees not only the traditional political and civil rights and the general entitlement to equality before the law, but sanctions affirmative action, and requires States parties to:

> take all appropriate measures (a) to modify the social and cultural patterns of conduct of men and women, with a view to achieving the elimination of prejudices and customary and other practices which are based on the idea of the inferiority or the superiority of either of the sexes or on the stereotyped roles for men and women; (b) to ensure that family education includes a proper understanding of maternity as a social function and the recognition of the common responsibility of men and women in the upbringing and development of their children...(article 5).

States have to take all steps to suppress all forms of traffic in women and exploitation of prostitution of women (article 6). Special responsibilities have been imposed on States in respect of rural women; in particular they are to ensure that rural women participate and benefit from rural development; participate in the elaboration and implementation of planning; have access to adequate health facilities, including information, counselling and services in family planning; obtain all types of training and education, formal and non-formal; access to agricultural credit and loans, and marketing facilities and appropriate technologies; and enjoy adequate living conditions, particularly in relation to housing, sanitation, electricity and water supply, transport and communications.

providing water supply to rural areas). This stance raises the question of the instrumentality and sequencing of rights. Professor Amaryta Sen has argued, for example, that a society that proclaims the urgency of basic needs, has first to have a democratic framework so that the society can decide what the basic needs are. He has also suggested that basic needs can probably not be met in a society which is not responsive to public pressures or public accountability.[40] One might add that the transformative potential of human rights (and that must be their role in many authoritarian and unequal societies in Asia) lies in the rights of association, speech and other trade union rights. One can turn to history for guidance on sequencing, but that might be another device to assert the priority of civil and political rights which may not be warranted in contemporary times. These issues are also raised in discussions on democratisation as it implies a process. They are therefore best explored in the section on governance below.

(c) Democratisation and governance

The context of this discussion is two-fold, one domestic and the other international. The domestic is the growing constitutionalisation of the political orders of several Asian countries—for example, Thailand, Taiwan, Pakistan, Cambodia, Bangladesh, the Philippines, South Korea, Hong Kong, Mongolia and Nepal. The international is the pressure for, or assistance towards, democratic and accountable political orders from Western donors and international economic institutions, particularly the World Bank (often expressed in the form of conditionalities). Sometimes domestic and international pressures coincide, but not always. Sometimes foreign pressures are towards marketisation (with the emphasis on clear legal regimes, transparency and level playing fields) as with the World Bank. At other times the stress is on democratisation as such.

The process towards better governance and democracy is extraordinarily complicated (even if governance and democracy had similar pre-conditions, which they may not), for it involves issues which, although they are often regarded as of a piece, have different dynamics and consequences—the development of civil rights, the rule of law and a liberal culture, democratic reforms through the extension of the franchise and other political rights, the securing of economic and social rights, and fair and transparent governance (to which in some instances we should add marketisation). One problem is that in contemporary constitutionalisation all these goals are being sought simultaneously. In any circumstances such a task would be daunting, but it becomes even more problematic because there may well, at least in the short

40 He illustrates his argument by a study of famines and shows that it was only when there was no freedom of expression or criticism that the governments were unable to anticipate shortages. He contrasts the relatively better position of immigrants in Britain, most of whom have the vote, with those in Germany, who do not. But he points to failures of democracy when preventing injuries or injustices in instances where it is not so easy to evoke human sympathy for them, unlike that in the case of major disasters. Sen, "Freedoms and Needs", *The New Republic* (10–17 January 1994), p 31.

run, be a conflict between them. In the 19th century, for example, the rule of law was considered to be under threat from democratisation. Many countries in the transition to democracy in this century have built in a deliberate "democracy deficit", in part to placate its former enemies, but also to create the capacity to absorb the social and political consequences of democratisation. It could be argued in historical terms that as democracy was preceded by civil rights and the rule of law, it was acceptable to the ruling group (because the economic and social rights of the bourgeoisie would be protected) and feasible (because of the importance attached to values and procedures which would moderate the consequences of popular demands), while democracy itself set the stage for economic and social rights. The relevance of this analysis in today's conditions may be questioned, although a plausible case can be made out that the fragility of democracy in many developing countries is due to the lack of traditions of civil liberties and the rule of law.

Democratic theory does not provide clear answers to a number of issues that require an instrumental solution—does economic liberalisation lead to political freedoms or vice versa (the Russia-China debate), is it more important to concentrate on the strengthening of civil society or the reform of State structures, can purely secular organisation of public power command legitimacy, what are the pre-conditions of democracy, what is the link between marketisation and human rights, and indeed the connection between different kinds of rights.

There is space only for some general comments. Let me first take the relationship between democracy and the market. The supporters of the market argue that it inevitably leads to democracy. The argument might be made on both logical and historical grounds. The market is a system of private economy, in which there is a massive decentralisation of decision-making and a wide scope for choice. Central to the market are private property, which ensures a measure of autonomy for individuals and groups, and the freedom of contract, which enhances choice and secures rights (and limits the powers of the State). Predictability and legal security, which are also essential to the market, lead to an expert and independent judiciary, and thus to the separation of powers. The market gives rise to or strengthens civil society, and provides a countervailing force to that of the State. In this analysis, the market is more dependent on rights than on democracy.

The historical case, however, is that the development of democracy in the West followed the rise of the market, and that parallel processes are underway in East Asia (in particular Taiwan and Korea). It would be argued that the market leads to certain forms of social formations which stimulate pressures for democracy. In particular it undermines traditional forms of economy and their corresponding forms of political authority, and frees labour from its previous constraints ("from status to contract"). It gives rise to a middle class with its specific interests, connected with rights and democracy, and the economic and political clout to protect them. It also facilitates the organisation of labour, leading to a competitive and pluralistic political order.

However, neither the logical or the historical evidence is conclusive. Drawing from a model of consumption, the former disregards the process of production (where economic coercion prevails and the mode of organisation is hierarchical). It also assumes a false dichotomy between the State and the market, ignoring their inter-penetration. The market favours a few and does not universalise rights, except perhaps at a formal level. The market oriented civil society substitutes economic pressures for direct political authority, but by that very fact removes accountability, and introduces a different mode of subordination. Similarly, the historical process may be no guide, since it was the market which shaped the State in the West, but it is the State which has shaped the market in Asia. Nor is the globalisation of capital and markets likely to be conducive to rights or democracy. Freed from a territorial nexus, capital may become even more irresponsible and less accountable—less responsive to public opinion and more accommodating of State restrictive practices in its pursuit of profit (as is demonstrated by the way in which both Murdoch and Turner have bent their communication empires to the censorship by China). The growing global dominance of the power of capital over political authority and structures diminishes rather than increases prospects of rights and democracy. The progress in rights and democracy has been achieved by the struggles of the workers and other disadvantaged communities, and not by the advocacy of capitalists.

Another problematic area is civil society, which has become something of a *deus ex machina* in the prescriptions for rights and democracy. The notions of civil society in contemporary discourse are hazy. Sometimes (as in Eastern Europe), it is used to refer to the marketisation of the economy—which I have argued is no reason for optimism. Other times it refers to non-State values and institutions outside the area of economy. But I have also tried to demonstrate that in most parts of Asia civil society so defined is responsible for great injustice and oppression, and is itself in much need of reform. Other times it is used to refer to civic organisations of professionals, workers, women and others, which not only lobby the State but also seek to humanise society. A particular species of them, the NGOs, have achieved much prominence in recent years, seen as champions of rights and democracy, and giving voice to the underprivileged. It is no time to enter into the debate on NGOs (whose positive contributions are numerous), except to sound a note of caution, as they proliferate under encouragement of or incentives from foreign donors, operate increasingly as consulting firms, and lose touch with, or accountability to, their local constituencies.

Let me finally explore some conflicts between human rights and democracy. (I do not refer to the older debates as to whether an entrenched bill of rights interpreted by non-elected judiciaries is compatible with democracy and whether it weakens the political process by its "legalisation" consequences, for it seems to me that the political process might be enriched, rather than impoverished, by rights in most developing countries and that the executive and the legislature have frequently few claims to democratic legitimacy). The formalisation and juridification of rights have thrust courts and tribunals at the centre of their definitions and enforcement and their discourse has become increasingly specialised. This detracts both from the responsibility and capacity of elected bodies for human rights. The globalisation of human rights detaches specific rights from the national context and relevance. The transformative consequences of economic and social rights (for example, the revolution in the position of women or the shift of power from one caste to another in rural Nepal) may be threatening to an infant democracy because of the interests of incumbent leaders and influential groups.

It is true that certain kinds of rights may be pre-requisites to democracy—franchise, expression, and association. It is also true that certain rights may be better protected in a democracy than in other political systems. But the logic of rights is different from the logic of democracy. The former are individual centred (even when they concern social rights), while democracy is majority-centred. The scope of rights is drawn from the nature of the human person, the scope of democracy from the general will. Rights serve to limit State power, while democracy justifies its expansion. Rights may be said to be "rational" and purposive, but democracy is frequently messy and manipulative.

When there are conflicts, rights are likely to give into democracy.[41] Although rights are now prescribed in considerable detail, and democracy is still nebulous (no international instrument defines or protects it), democracy seems to command greater legitimacy, at least in Asia. Rights are harder to enforce than democracy, in part because of the differing precision of definitions. It may also threaten existing power structures. For that reason, democracy may be used to suppress human rights. Politics are viewed largely as a formal business of professional politicians, as a kind of joust (to the finish) rather than as discourse, questioning the legitimacy of academics, journalists, and social workers, who wish to express opinions on policies (even in their areas of their own expertise). Democracy, seen largely as an electoral process, becomes plebiscitary. Democracy, seen as the access to State power, becomes manipulative and corrupting. Yet it is presented as the voice of the people, a talisman to ward off domestic and foreign pressures for rights and equity.[42] But for that very reason it increasingly relies on, and caters to, sectional interests.

In the South Asian context, ethnicity has frequently provided that sectional interest. Ethnicity, linked to the democratic or at least the electoral process, has had, for the most part, negative effect on governance and human rights. Political parties have aggregated and articulated ethnic demands, the majority community

41 The inability of the United States Government to maintain a consistent policy regarding human rights conditionalities, especially in relation to China, is itself the result of United States democracy, as the administration feels compelled, for electoral reasons, to take into account views of corporations and workers who benefit from investments in and trade with China.

42 Consider the following statement of Dr Mahathir, Prime Minister of Malaysia, in an attack on the power of judges to interpret and decide on the validity of laws, "If the people want the Government to be restricted so as not to be able to draft certain laws, the people will cause the downfall of the Government..." quoted in Hickling and Wishart, "Malaysia: Dr Mahathir's Thinking on Constitutional Issues" [1988–89] *Lawasia* 47 at 57.

has imposed its cultural forms on the State, and the rights of minorities have been trampled upon. The result has often been the militarisation of both the State and civil society and the application of oppressive legislation which has denied a whole array of political, civil, economic and social rights. And yet democracy of a sort has flourished and fed the process of the attrition of democratic values.

The time has come to forge and strengthen links between democracy and rights. Democracy, in all its dimensions, not merely electoral, has to be rehabilitated. The values of democracy provide the link to human rights. The strengthening of human rights would then mean strengthening democracy. But democracy, to validate and legitimise human rights, has to respond to the cultural and moral impulses of the society. Western forms of democracy (by which I mean the forms of former metropolitan powers) have not been appropriate for Asia (any more than for Africa). This may seem a route back to relativism. But it is the relativism of forms, not substance, and may be necessary for some sort of regime of universal values underpinning the dignity of women and men.

[19]

AL-LA NIDAM: AN ARAB VIEW OF THE NEW WORLD (DIS)ORDER

Larbi Sadiki

RECOGNITION OF THE NEED FOR GLOBAL ORDER coexists with the specter of global disorder in the post-Cold War world. A prime function of global order would be to balance the North's ever-growing scramble for profits, markets and military superiority with the demands of various peoples in the South for political, cultural, economic, spiritual, and environmental relevance and self-determination. This essay shows that the Middle East, especially its Arab component, represents a microcosm of unfolding global disorder. It identifies trends specific to that disorder and suggests options for its arrest.

> Out of these troubled times. . . a new world order can emerge. . . free from the threat of terror, stronger in the pursuit of justice, and more secure in the quest for peace. (George Bush, speech to the US Congress, 9 September 1990)[1]

THE SEARCH FOR WORLD ORDER: FROM THE BALANCE OF TERROR TO THE TERROR OF IMBALANCE

Humanity's search for order[2] — norms and structures conducive to more or less harmonious co-existence — is not new. The search for order in the Middle East is attested to by the deluge of divine revelations in the Holy Land. The Judaic, Christian and Islamic messages are all quintessential attempts and quests for universal peace, justice and order. Expounders of Christian and Islamic orthodoxies continue to be the bearers of the universalistic ideals inherent in both faiths. St. Thomas Aquinas' idea of a universal community bound together by Christianity is one example. Similar universalistic ideals are articulated in the Qur'an: "Humankind, we have created you from a single pair of a male and female and we made you into tribes and peoples (communities) that you might get to know one another."[3]

Larbi Sadiki teaches Arabic Studies and the Politics of the Middle East at the Australian National University, Canberra.

Yet for all their unrelenting and perennial search for order, Middle Easterners, perhaps more than most other peoples, have historically tended to experience more disorder than order. Even ideals and beliefs which Middle Easterners exported to Europe (via Christianity) where used against them in the Crusades and then the consecutive European colonial expeditions of the 19th Century under the guise of *missions civilisatrices*. The kernel of the problem is that:

(i) However sound their supporting ideologies may have been, most, if not all, past international orders have been structurally flawed owing to lingering and inveterate parochialisms — national, cultural, economic and ideological. This is also true of the post-W.W.I international order which established the sanctity of what Richard Falk calls the "Westphalian template of sovereign states"[4] (which was boosted by President Wilson's support for colonized peoples' rights for self-determination), and of the post-World War II order with its East-West ideological split. Any past order can be said to have been, by definition and by practice, nothing less than the universalization of hegemonic particularisms.

(ii) The movement toward universalistic ideals, norms, structures and codes of behavior has been vitiated by the inherently lingering and unfettered particularisms of competing nation-states. Nation-states, aided by international law and transnational agencies, have proliferated since the 1950s, a date coeval with decolonization, becoming the universalistic norm of social organization.

(iii) Whatever the outward permutations of the distribution of power ratios, consecutive international orders have also carried a degree of disorder, at least in the eyes of the dissatisfied. The imposition of a hegemonic particularistic order, usually masked by universalistic norms and structures, remains, by dint of marginalization of the powerless actors, wanting with regard to legitimacy, justice, equality, peace and universalism. In the Arab and Islamic Middle East, the crises of legitimacy, justice, equality and peace are closely associated with the notion of global disorder.

(iv) As in previous orders, power continues to be understood in a cultist sense. The guardians and guarantors of order have been those actors who dispose of quantitative and qualitative military superiority, although economic might is fast becoming a significant variable.

What are the characteristics of the unfolding global disorder or of the so-called "New World Order"? Although the notion of global disorder is generally associated with the waning and eventual collapse of the former Soviet Union, for Arabs it is coeval with Iraq's invasion of Kuwait and the subsequent UN-mandated, mostly Arab-funded, US-led forces' 43-day sustained and devastating bombing campaign that led to the "liberation" of Kuwait.

Two mutually reinforcing factors are at the core of the unfolding global disorder. Firstly, the former Soviet Union's disintegration has left a power vacuum, the corollary of which has been a movement from bipolarity to unipolarity. In other words, the asymmetries resulting from the absence of the former Soviet Union's balancing role can be said to have, *inter alia*, spawned a situation akin to a terror of imbalance. If bipolarity found equality in power balance and, later on, in its balance of terror variant (MAD), the post-Cold War world is lacking in such a balance. Not only is unipolarity undesirable, but also continuous blind faith in military means to maintain a modicum of world peace defeats the very purpose of peace. Secondly, the dissolution of the former Soviet Union has led to a greater US preponderance in world affairs, giving her a freer hand to meddle in the South and within the United Nations.

ILLUSIONS OF A NEW WORLD ORDER

From the outset George Bush's proclamation of a "New World Order" has, in the eyes of many Arabs, portended adversity. The historical divide following the second Gulf War could not have been wider. What is hailed in the West as a victory is by most Arab accounts a defeat, or what Mohamed Hasanayn Heikal calls "illusions of triumph".[5] The US has finally cast aside the "Vietnam syndrome", and since the Soviet Union's dissolution the American Right has declared "the end of history"[6] and the triumph of capitalism and liberalism. While many Arabs find consolation in Kuwait's restored sovereignty, they are still pained by the devastation, the divisiveness, and the moral, material and environmental[7] defeat brought about by the war. Arab-American scholar, Naseer Aruri, sees the war effort leading to the Coalition's victory in terms of a "recolonization of the Arab world".[8] Hence,

> The justification for the Gulf war was self-evident to most Americans and Britons, but less so to Arabs, including many in countries which supported the Coalition. President Bush emerged with his image enhanced, but most Arabs found it hard to share the West's euphoria.[9]

In the same vein, for many Arabs, the West's notion of world order leaves much to be desired. Disorder, akin to a kind of ordered chaos, is the order as far as they are concerned. The Arab term *al-la nidam*[10] conveys absence of order and imparts the idea of *al-fawda* (disorder, chaos). The Arab perspective tends toward disowning the "New World Order" for two interconnected reasons. Firstly, Arabs, like many other peoples, yet again find themselves on the periphery of such an order. As such the "New Order", being like its predecessors designed in Western chancelleries and presidential palaces, is not expected to be more favorable. Former Arab League observer at the UN, Clovis Maksoud notes:

> This new global order was basically an order defined and determined by the Western part of the globe. The Southern part of the globe, whose input, aspirations and rights are not yet factored into this new order . . . began to sense that perhaps the globe is solely defined as the North. But the South, which

> represents the majority of mankind . . . began to sense its disenfranchisement and potential dispossession.[11]

Secondly, disorder is associated with unpredictability, paralysis and inefficiency. Thus little or no confidence is held in the existing global system, especially with regard to solving unresolved Arab problems:

> In the light of this disorder, it is impossible to forecast either the future of world peace or of the global system. By disorder it is meant the explosion of problems that the institutional and organizational apparatuses of the existing international system are unable to solve.[12]

It is generally accepted that George Bush's proclaimed New World Order is little more than a reincarnation of the old order. What is new in Southern Lebanon, the Golan Heights, Gaza and the West Bank? What is new in the regional imbalance of power where nuclear Israel *conquers and rules*? Even with such historical developments started by the Madrid Peace talks, through to the Oslo-Cairo agreements between Israel and the Palestinians, the Israeli-Jordanian Peace Treaty, and the Israeli-Syrian negotiations over the Golan Heights, much remains unchanged. What about the imbalances associated with wealth and deprivation? Arabs cannot understand how a New World Order can be prefaced by the disorder unleashed by high-tech violence on an ancient Arab center of civilization (Babylonian and Abbasid). The promised "principles of justice and fair play"[13] of the New World Order are yet to materialize. Accordingly, Arab contempt and suspicion persist.

TRENDS OF DISORDER

If balance is a correlate of order, then imbalance and contradiction are correlates of disorder. The second Gulf War has not only heralded a new stage of uncertainty in the Middle East, but has also acted as a harbinger of trends antithetical to the highly-principled proclamations associated with the New World Order, and to international trends of democratization and disarmament. In this section four major contradictory trends are examined.

> Contradiction 1: *The persistence of Western direct and indirect support of authoritarianism in the Arab Middle East betrays the democratic claims and practices of the guardians of the New World Order.*

The Gulf War was not fought under the banner of democracy. Yet the Bush administration was quick to demonize Saddam Hussein and the authoritarian practices of his *mukhabarat* (police) state. Like Nasser during the 1956 Suez crisis,[14] Hussein was likened to Hitler. Such a comparison is far-fetched and would not pass the test of objectivity. Hussein's technologically-dependent Iraq cannot be compared to Hitler's industrialized Germany. While it is certain that the latter's actions were motivated by imperialist ambitions, racism and notions of Aryan supremacy, it cannot be safely assumed that the former was driven by illusions of Babylonian grandeur or ethnic superiority.[15] And Hussein's murderous record is no match to Hitler's calculated genocide. While the leader of Iraq was not a Hitler, he certainly was a leader with megalomaniac instincts, and a dictator that the West originally supported against a "bigger evil" — Iran — conveniently choosing to overlook his regime's human rights violations. And again, in 1990, it was only for the sake of convenience that the West chose to take notice of Halbaja and the gassing of Kurds and other atrocities against the Iraqi people. This point has not been missed by Noam Chomsky:

> The US is one of the major violators of the principles now grandly proclaimed . . . . George Bush warns of appeasing aggressors and clutches to his heart the Amnesty International (AI) report on Iraqi atrocities (after 2 August), but not AI reports on El Salvador, Turkey, Indonesia, and the Israeli Occupied Territories.[16]

More than four years have passed since the West's "triumph" in the Gulf. Yet as far as human rights and democratization are concerned there has been nothing to celebrate for either Arabs or the guardians of the proclaimed New World Order. In fact, despite encouraging democratic gains in Jordan and Yemen,[17] the trend has generally been one of persistent authoritarianism — a trend which is antithetical to the so-called global democratic revolution. Many Arabs have pinned high hopes on this global transformative process, and many among the intelligentsia have been crying for a response to it.[18] However, the Western response to Arab democratization has been less than enthusiastic.

A number of crucial points explain why the West would rather put the question of Arab democratization on the backburner:

(i) The West will not tolerate the fall or overthrow of friendly Arab regimes, especially those sitting on vast oil reserves. One shah's fall is one too many. The West will, in accordance with its interests, guarantee the survival of friendly regimes even when they are unelected and autocratic. Such protégé regimes, being almost invariably representatives of international capitalism and ruling without the input of a democratic opposition and virtually free from societal and constitutional restraints, engage unhindered in concessionary (military facilities and low oil prices) and beneficial deals with the West (subsidization of the Western military industrial complex and petrodollar recycling).[19] The West is no beacon of democracy in the Middle East.[20] The nonchalance toward democracy, which besmirched the U.S. messianic role and international reputation, led many Arabs to conclude that the U.S. commitment is not to democracy or human rights but to the *status quo*. Pro-Western authoritarian Arab regimes permit the US far more leverage and patronage than would be possible through Arab democratic regimes.[21] The Arab members of the U.S.-led coalition were no democratic models, and were motivated by self-interest.[22] Arab (and non-Arab) conspiratorial theorizing regards oil as the motivating factor for the Western members of the coalition.[23]

(ii) The execution of a war with devastating human,[24] financial and environmental[25] consequences resulted in the restoration of a Kuwaiti autocratic oligarchy. This stands in sharp contrast with the West's tough stance against despots elsewhere (such as in Haiti). A sense of *dejà vu* is strong with regard to this double standard, expressed in Jeanne Kirkpatrick's distinction between "bad" and "good" dictators.[26] The October 1992 elections restored parliamentary life in Kuwait. Yet women and *badw* (stateless Arabs) remained excluded. By excluding them, the patriarchal Sabahs have in fact reneged on the promise to increase political freedoms made in the Kuwait Popular Congress held in October 1990 in Jeddah, Saudi Arabia.[27] This exclusion is unconstitutional. Article 29 of Kuwait's constitution insists on the "equality of citizens before the law", according all "rights and duties" regardless of sex, race or religion. The witch-hunt that took place after Kuwaiti independence was restored went almost unnoticed in the corridors of power in Western capitals. Thousands of Arabs were made to pay for a minority's collaboration with the Iraqi invaders. State torture, killing, deportation and confiscation of property were committed against innocent workers who helped develop Kuwait. Many of the victims were Kuwaiti-born. Similarly, human rights violations by key Western allies (Egypt, Tunisia, Morocco) drew little criticism except for the perfunctory treatment given in the U.S. State Department's annual country reports.[28] In these countries, the personalized nature of Arab politics has made democratic initiatives inherently tentative or retractable, especially when the rules, procedures and ends of the democratic game clash with the rulers' interests.[29]

A classic case of Western confusion and disinterest with regard to Arab democratization was the U.S. response to the cancellation in January 1992 of the results of Algeria's first multiparty parliamentary elections. The initial response, read on 13 January by White House spokesperson Margaret Tutwiler, was clearly supportive of the coup, describing it as "constitutional". The following day, seeking to alleviate the damage and embarrassment caused by the previous statement, Tutwiler announced to a startled media that the U.S. would not comment further on the constitutionality, or lack thereof, of the Algerian military takeover.[30] Western governments know where their interests and sympathies lie — certainly not with Arab democratization. According to one Western commentator, "by neither criticizing nor approving the Algerian army's action, Western countries cloak their real attitude — that democracy is fine up to a certain point."[31] The idea is that "sovereign" Algerians cannot be allowed to elect Islamists (supposedly anti-democratic) who appeared on the verge of winning a majority. It is, however, quite acceptable for Western citizens to vote into office leaders (supposedly democratic) who, if need be, are prepared to go to war and bomb cities back to the Stone Age in the name of the national interest. A clear case of this double standard is the vigor with which U.S. leaders have pursued the restoration of democracy in Haiti. As Edward Said puts it:

> For two generations the United States has sided in the Middle East mostly with tyranny and injustice. No struggle for democracy, or women's rights, or secularism and the rights of minorities has the United States officially supported.[32]

(iii) Not only is democracy perennially quarantined when dealing with Arab autocracies, but also with the United Nations. The convenient "hijacking" of the UN Security Council[33] by a minority of powerful interests goes against the majoritarian democratic principle. As a result, the credibility of both the UN and the proposed New World Order are at stake. Malaysia's Prime Minister, a vociferous critic of the inequitable international system, expresses disillusionment with the international body. He questions the logic of the global push for democracy within national units but not among them:

> In the United Nations we are equal, but five are more equal than the rest . . . . Seven countries on their own lay down the laws which affect adversely the economies of others. A few nations on their own have taken it upon themselves to determine the New World Order.[34]

This is the sort of democratic deficiency that facilitates belligerence. Were it not for such deficiency, Western powers would not, as Richard Falk observes, have been able to "turn the [UN] . . . into an instrument legitimizing a war that could and should have been avoided".[35] Responsibility for the fact that the war was not avoided lies equally with the totalitarian nature of Ba'athism and Hussein's personalist rule. The Iraqi dictator placed himself in the difficult position whereby his endeavors for conditional withdrawal from Kuwait could not be reconciled with the coalition's demand for an unconditional withdrawal. Even if Hussein is to be assumed "insane" as was proclaimed in many Western circles, it was impossible for him not to have foreseen the consequential destruction to his country by the formidable firepower arrayed against Iraq. Accordingly, Iraq's search for a way out must not be overlooked. David Campbell cites the myriad of Iraqi proposals, made both directly and through third parties, to avoid a military confrontation.[36] However, the desire of the U.S. and its allies to avoid war must be questioned. Ramsey Clark showed that the destruction of the Iraqi military machine was one of three definite goals motivating the coalition's pursuit of the military option.[37] What logical explanation exists for the U.S. rejection of the Soviet initiative which finally secured Iraq's agreement to an unconditional withdrawal? Confusion about this did not even escape the American military:

"As one of Schwarzkopf's officers observed, 'the Soviets [were] talking about getting us exactly what we asked for, and we summarily turned them down.'"[38]

> Contradiction 2: *The international community's juggling of double standards stands in contrast to the New World Order's "principles of justice and fair play".*[39]

In the Middle East, the underdogs (Kurds, Palestinians. . .) of the embattled and stillborn New World Order balk at any suggestion of justice. The bitter experiences of the past have not been encouraging. They have become the "football" of high diplomacy. The September 1993 Israeli *blitzkrieg* into Southern Lebanon has only reinforced their cynicism. Arabs, and the Lebanese in particular, wondered how could such repeated flagrant transgression of international law and the UN Charter, which caused so much dislocation (nearly 300,000 Muslim Shiites fled their homes) and death (more than 100 civilians), go unpunished?[40] In short, many of them still ask: Why has the international system that many Arabs supported in 1991 against one fellow Arab country (Iraq) on behalf of another (Kuwait) consistently failed to support them?

The "victim syndrome" is deeply entrenched. Arabs almost invariably view themselves to be first in line when punishment is meted out and last when justice is distributed. The examples are numerous. Crippling embargoes are in place against Libya and Iraq. Libya is punished (UN Resolution 731 of January 1992) for failing to hand over two of her nationals to stand trial in Europe or the U.S. for their alleged role in the December 1988 Lockerbie Pan Am airliner disaster, and her alleged bombing in 1989 of a French UTA plane over Niger. Iraq is punished (through a series of UN resolutions, with 678 — which sanctioned the use of force — being still the most controversial) for continuous violation of UN resolutions, including suspected partial non-compliance with those concerning the destruction of all her chemical and nuclear weaponry capabilities and installations.

Inconsistencies with regard to conflict resolution are conspicuous, for little or no distributive justice has been forthcoming. Resolutions 242 and 338, the terms of reference most commonly cited, yet least important,[41] for addressing the Palestinian question, remain unfulfilled. Although much hope has, in certain circles, been pinned on the 13 September 1993 Israeli-PLO mutual recognition and Declaration of Principles (DOP) and the subsequent peace talks, thus far little progress has been made as evidenced by the difficulties surrounding many aspects of Palestinian self-rule in Gaza and Jericho.[42] Many Palestinians reject the DOP on the grounds that it lends itself to manipulation by the U.S. and Israel and is designed to serve their interests rather than those of the Palestinians. They assert that a genuine peace can only be achieved through recognition of their rights as stipulated in the UN Charter and various UN resolutions. Resolution 425, the legal framework for Israeli withdrawal from Southern Lebanon, remains only ink on paper.[43]

Inversion of international norms and values is exemplified in the lack of political will to respond with the same zeal toward anti-Arab aggression. No punitive action or compensation was ever considered when in February 1973 Israel shot down the Libyan Arab Airlines Boeing 727 over occupied Sinai, killing all 104 passengers on board.[44] Former U.S. President Reagan described as legitimate the Israeli raid on the Tunis PLO headquarters in October 1985. That Tunisian sovereignty was violated and more than 70 people were killed did not seem to matter much. America's April 1986 bombing of Tripoli and Benghazi from British bases was not without wide sympathy amongst Western governments.

Most recently, the bombing of Iraq for her alleged plot to assassinate former U.S. President George Bush has baffled many Arabs. First, Kuwait, which investigated the alleged plot, has a credibility problem. John Macarthur's *Second Front*[45] is living testimony. Second, Bush has not been killed. Third, why should the attempt on the life of a private American citizen spur state action by excessive means against another? A covert operation to kill Saddam Hussein is known to have been contemplated as one American option for ridding Iraq of her tyrannical leader. Arabs could not help noticing how the case of fellow Arab League member, Somalia, in which swift retaliation by the U.S. followed warlord General Aideed's killing of Pakistani troops, presented a stark contrast to UN and U.S. inaction in Bosnia.[46]

> Contradiction 3: *Continuous increases in armaments and violence do not bode well for the proclaimed peace of the embattled New World Order.*

The end of the Cold War is least conspicuous in the Middle East where historical protagonists still view one another with suspicion. This situation has not been helped by the Western arms suppliers who scramble continuously for petrodollars in the lucrative Middle Eastern arms bazaar.[47] Recently, for instance, the British Tornado Company has been saved from closure by a Saudi contract to purchase 70 of its jet fighters. In general, the trend in the Middle East to arm and rearm is antithetical to the more or less downward global trend of military expenditures.[48] While total Middle Eastern military expenditures have fallen slightly, mostly because of the UN embargo on Iraq, the oil-rich states have increased theirs. Two factors are central to this increase: ". . . costs accrued in the war against Iraq [and paid to the Coalition — especially the U.S.] . . . and new arms purchases."[49] The Saudi increase is staggering: It jumped from nearly U.S. $15 billion in 1990 to more than 26 billion in 1992 — an 80 per cent increase.[50] The irony is, as the Gulf experience shows, that the billions squandered by the conservative monarchy and the other Gulf quasi-states have not enhanced their security or their self-defense capabilities. Nor will the Saudi's attempt to build a small but fast "high tech" army[51] spare them dependence on the American protective umbrella, which accords with Washington's strategy "to build shared security arrangements in the Gulf".[52] Kuwait entered into a bilateral security agreement with the U.S. in 1991.[53] The other Gulf Cooperation Council (GCC) members, except Saudi Arabia, have since followed suit. The Saudis have, however, openly welcomed U.S. involvement in the Arab peninsula as vital for "international trade, balance of power, and oil flow".[54] U.S. involvement in the area will entail "the prepositioning of heavy military equipment in Kuwait".[55]

Simply put, the Arab World cannot be expected to be immune to the heightened state of militarization that characterizes international relations despite "peace-speak". The strategic connectedness between liberal democracy, with its inherently materialistic ethos, and military industrial complexes paradoxically stands to defeat any notion of peace that challenges the West's own notion of self-serving peace equated with outright cultural, economic and military preponderance. Hence, it is no surprise that "the liberal democratic 'peace' may be tied to the very tendency of hegemonic leadership to successfully organize and incorporate, above all, liberal democratic states in a strategic-military order."[56]

Arabs are very suspicious of the American military entrenchment in the region. *Haymanah* (hegemony) over Arabs and their oil resources are thought to be the coveted prize of the U.S. strategy.[57] It is hard to presage how the proclaimed New World Order could be "more secure in the quest for peace" with such grand-scale militarization, and narrow and mono-dimensional understandings of security. The tragedy in all of this is the probability that millions of Arab petrodollars will be invested to produce more arms to maim and kill human beings, many of whom will happen to be Middle Eastern children.

> Money inserted at one end generates technopower that inflicts one-sided destruction on the other. . . . The "New World Order" will attempt to deepen the vulnerability of the entire non-Western world to Nintendo war, both by widening the technological gap . . . and by increasing the control and surveillance over Third World acquisitions of any weapons that threaten the invulnerability of the West.[58]

In fact it is this kind of Nintendo war that Arab analysts believe has left the Arab World at a critical three-way disadvantage. The destruction of Iraqi capabilities is believed to have tilted the regional balance of power in favor of i) Iran, ii) Turkey, and iii) Israel, with the latter further widening her competitive edge.[59] According to this analysis, Arabs are left vulnerable to external threats to their water and oil resources, and remain divested of any bargaining power with regard to the resolution of the Arab-Israeli conflict.[60]

One aim of the U.S. four-part strategy is to stem the proliferation of chemical, biological and nuclear weapons. The destruction of Iraqi capabilities has thus far been the only undertaking in this regard. Arabs lament this as favorable to Israel. Despite arms control being on the Arab-Israeli peace talks agenda there is no expectation amongst Arab observers that Israel will freeze its nuclear program, as Egypt has done since 1986,[61] or destroy her nuclear arsenal.

While Iraq is forced to destroy its mass destruction capabilities, no safeguards have yet been put in place to compel an Israeli non-use of her nuclear weapons against Arabs in future confrontations. For Arabs the leeway given to Israel in this respect is hypocritical. In the early 1970s the U.S. knew of, but chose to ignore, Israel's acquisition of an atomic bomb.[62]

In the Middle East more arms has always meant more violence. This is reflected in the upward spiral of violence and counter-violence visible today within and between national units. The impasse of liberalizing Arab authoritarianism accounts for state violence and Islamist counter-violence in Egypt and Algeria.[63] The latter has increasingly moved toward a praetorian polity reversing the early trend of the state's shrinkage and society's expansion. In both Iran and Turkey, the Kurdish minorities are exposed to high forms of state brutality and cultural suppression. This has been met by violent resistance from a number of Kurdish groups. In northern and southern Iraq, Kurds and Shiites respectively continue to suffer from state reprisals against what is seen by the ruling clique in Baghdad as Western-instigated treason in the aftermath of the second Gulf War. In Israel the "iron fist" policy continues to be employed against Palestinians. Violence between Jewish settlers and Palestinians in the West Bank and Gaza has not subsided despite the DOP. An unabated war of attrition goes on between the Muslim north and the Christian-animist south in the Sudan,[64] and between Moroccan troops and separatist Sahrawis in the Western Sahara.

Violence, or the potential for it, between states in the region persists. In the Arabian peninsula, Saudi Arabia has recently advanced a territorial claim against Yemen.[65] This claim is seen as expressive of the monarchy's displeasure with both Yemen's anti-war stance (which is translated in Riyadh as a pro-Iraqi stance), and her incipient democratization which is feared for its future contagious spill-over effects throughout the traditionally authoritarian monarchies. Relations between Saudi Arabia and another oildom, Qatar, a fellow GCC member, have ebbed to their lowest point because of a border dispute. Further fissures in Arab ranks are evident in the "cold" response in the GCC capitals to Iran's renewed designs on the United Arab Emirates-owned islands of Abu Musa and the Greater and Lesser Tumbs, whose final status has remained inconclusive since 1971. In 1993 Iran unilaterally canceled the 1971 agreement that stipulated future joint exploitation of the islands' gas and oil resources.[66] Israel's recent incursion into Lebanon and its occupation of a "security zone" in the country's south and other Arab territories does not bode well for sustainable peace in the area. Hamas[67] and Hizballah (Party of God) remain committed to armed struggle against Israel. Nor has the Iraq-Kuwait border dispute been settled even with Baghdad renouncing territorial claims inside Kuwait. The promise of new peace, like that of a New World Order,[68] looks at this juncture to be "phoney".[69]

Contradiction 4: *The open proclamations of the "worldliness" and "universality" of the New World Order contradict its hidden ethnocentric and racist underpinnings.*

Arrogance is at the heart of this contradiction. It is the kind of arrogance that finds expression in jingoism. The visionaries of the New World Order are no doubt mostly, if not all, men. And their vision seems to have been largely informed by what feminists have referred to as "militarized masculinity", with its emphasis on violence as the primary means of ensuring order.[70] As noted by one feminist analyst, "The military is the distilled embodiment of patriarchy."[71] Their arrogance is, to a great measure, the by-product of the military victory in the Gulf. Such arrogance was not visible after the Vietnam war. And the messages of "grandeur" stem from the glory of that victory, a Christian God, and His self-assigned "missionaries" of peace and order with their superior scientific-technological culture. Falk captures the essence of these messages pointing out the inherent racism in them, which is evident in: i) "the assumption that God is on the side of the better technology"; ii) the wide belief that "military technology is the real test of civilization"; and iii) the tendency "to associate the evil 'other' with non-white, non-Christian peoples".[72]

The monopoly over claims to Godliness and civilization have produced xenophobic reactions in both East and West. There is a wide perception amongst Muslims that with the death of communism, Islam is being demonized, unnecessarily making it the West's new ideological foe.[73] For Muslims in general, and Islamists in particular, this directly threatens their cultural relevance and freedom. Cultural relevance is equated with identity and existence. Muslims and Arabs have been historically vulnerable to territorial and political division. They have not, however, been divided culturally, owing to Islam's relative resilience to cultural hegemony. Prominent Islamist leader Rachid al-Ghannouchi defines this resilience as the "acceptance of modernity but within the framework of the values of Islam."[74] Islamists oppose wholesale modernization. This stems from lingering suspicion of a process Muslims first encountered through colonial and neo-colonial experiences. For Islamist analysts, the West fears Islam's stand against oppression and for social justice, and its rejection of the *laissez faire* ethos that condones pillaging and exploiting the resources and disrespecting the cultures of the powerless.

Muslim concern with cultural relevance in the context of the New World Order is tremendous. Western media domination and a one-way flow of Western information to the Islamic world through sophisticated communication technologies is seen as a kind of cultural "tele-crusade". Islamists fear this media domination propagates "social norms, ways of life, and behaviors in a way that renders the indigenous culture inferior and second-class".[75] The five Western media giants (Time Warner Inc., USA; Bertelsman, Germany; Murdoch's News Corporation Ltd, Australia-USA; Hachette-SA, France; and Capitol Cities/ABC, Inc., USA)[76] have spread their tentacles worldwide. A similar flow from East to

West is absent. This media monopoly and the lack of a two-way information flow, combined with the frequently negative portrayal of Islam and Muslims by the Western media, has, in the eyes of many Islamists, helped "tarnish the image of Islam,"[77] and largely packaged it as inherently anti-democratic.

The association of Islam with violence is one example of such negative imagery — the "green peril scenario".[78] Robin Wright speaks of the return of "*jihad*" (holy war).[79] This is unhelpful reductionism. Jihad is a legally, politically and socially complex concept, a thorough explanation of which is beyond the scope of this paper.[80] Broadly speaking, however, holy war is one of two forms of jihad. *Al-jihad al-asghar* (lesser jihad), holy war, is not as important as *al-jihad al-akbar* (greater jihad) — spiritual, political, social, economic and intellectual forms of struggle. Islamists engage in one or both struggles. Electoral politics as forms of greater jihad have given way in Algeria to lesser jihad where the state and the outlawed Islamists engage one another violently. In Egypt, *al-Jama'a al-Islamiyyah* (the Islamic Group), being excluded from politics, is visibly engaged in lesser jihad, and without the moderate Muslim Brotherhood's legalization as a political party, things could get worse. In Lebanon, Hizballah has abstained from anti-state/society lesser jihad except against Israel, but engaged in greater jihad through the domestic political process. Hamas does the same in occupied Palestine. In Tunisia, although the banned *Harakat al-Nahdha* (Renaissance Movement) is coming under increasing pressure to engage in lesser jihad against Ben Ali's regime, its exiled leader, Rachid al-Ghannouchi, remains committed to greater jihad.[81]

There is a growing feeling amongst Islamists that the wide crackdown on Islamist movements throughout the Middle East aims at combating Islam as a political ideology and a medium of liberation from dependent authoritarianism. Western governments certainly appear to condone the crackdown. Western governments, their protégé Arab regimes, and Israel are all accused of forming an anti-Islamic power triangle.[82] An Israeli Defense Force-authored document, available at the Israeli Embassy in Canberra, lends credence to this scenario. The 13-page document, entitled "The Danger of Islamic Fundamentalism: Background Material", is a good example of the negative imagery cited in Islamist circles. Amongst many things, it claims that "the most prominent assassination in 1992 was that of the Copt spiritual leader, Faraj Foudah, who was considered to be one of the leading opponents of the extremists in Egypt." Faraj Foudah was never a Copt. He was a Muslim and his full name was Mohamed Faraj Foudah. Foudah was a leading secularist, hardly a "spiritual" leader. The document also fails to point out that Islam is not a monolith: Islamic movements are neither homogeneous nor are they united. While some engage in anti-Copt, anti-tourist, anti-West violence, they engage in anti-Muslim violence, too. The warring Islamists of Afghanistan are instructive in this regard. Other Islamists reject violence. The ballot, not the bullet, is their preferred *modus operandi*. Thus:

> To ignore these facts and claim that all Islamic movements are "fundamentalist". . . [and] against the West, is a gross misrepresentation of reality. Those who insist on it are either misguided or prisoners of a Cold War mentality.[83]

LOOKING AHEAD

The trends and imbalances of disorder are clearly manifest in the Middle East. Arresting and redressing them requires such vital human traits as trust, care, tolerance, mutuality, reciprocity, equality, honesty and reconciliation. For this, human beings do not need a New World Order. Rather, the New World Order requires these qualities in human beings for it to be orderly. As regards the trends identified above they can be dealt with through:

i) *Stressing the importance of democratic values and procedures for state-society relations, and state-state relations.* This has relevance for minorities, for gender relations, for civil society, for governance, and for power (a positive sum game as distinct from a zero sum game) in the Middle East. It also has relevance for the UN and genuine representation and operation. Societies, not just states, should be involved in the UN.[84] Any gains for democracy are gains for peace. However, it should also be noted that no democracy is complete without economic democracy, which has relevance for equity and justice. Australia, the aspiring "clever country", could play a role by promoting, while not imposing, democracy and human rights abroad. The "clever country's" potential is not limited to sheep and wheat.

ii) *Distributing justice to the dispossessed Palestinians and other aggrieved peoples in the region through peaceful means.* This has relevance for self-determination which is in essence a democratic norm. Strength and impartiality of the UN are essential if justice is to take hold.

iii) *Demilitarizing the Middle East.* This has internal and external relevance. Internally, many Middle Eastern polities cry for demilitarization. The military belongs in the barracks and not in government. Regional authoritarianisms are closely linked to militarized polities. Externally, demilitarization would mean confidence-building measures between historical protagonists. The civil economies would benefit from the freeing of huge and badly-needed financial and human resources currently monopolized by the military. Demilitarization also has relevance for non-violence. A reconceptualization of security is needed so as to encompass economic, environmental and spiritual dimensions. One proposal for lasting security is the emphasis of "community-sponsored and guaranteed security" and its indigenization to make it the shared business and enterprise of Middle Easterners, not outsiders.[85] Another possibility is a Conference on Security and Cooperation in the Mediterranean/Middle East.[86]

iv) "*Delinking Islam and terrorism,*"[87] and concentrating on the common bonds that connect peoples of various faiths and backgrounds, and accepting cultural differences. And no bond is greater than the human one. This has humanist relevance. For human beings happen to be Muslim, Christian, Jewish, or Hindu. They are not Muslim, Christian, Jewish and Hindu who happen to be human beings.

However desirable the above vision may be, the reality is one of persistent disorder. Unless self-determination, democracy, and a culture of non-violence and accommodation between and within communities and states are fostered, the gap between what *should* be and what *could* be will remain too wide to warrant optimism about deconstructing the foundations of disorder and reconstructing the foundations of order in the Middle East.

NOTES

---

1. As quoted in Thomas H. Henriksen, *The New World Order: War, Peace and Military Preparedness* (Stanford: Hoover Institution, Stanford University, 1992), p. 1.

2. The notion of "World Order" — globalism, worldism, universalism — is a conceptualization that has gained both comprehensiveness and wide circulation since World War I and II, the bloodiest chronicles in human history. The notion, however, appears to have had roots in ancient sacred and secular thinking. The Marxist ideal of an internationally-united proletariat transcending eventually-withering nationalism and nation-states is one example. Hedley Bull cites many others, such as the Kantian universalistic tradition and the Grotian/internationalist tradition. See *The Anarchical Society: A Study of Order in World Politics* (London: Macmillan, 1990), chapter 2.

3. Qur'an, 49:13. Universalistic sentiments are also articulated by, for instance, the medieval Arab poet, Abu al-'Ala al-Ma'arri, who deems religion to be divisive. Another, Muhi al-Din Ibn Arabi, expresses more or less identical views intimating that love for humankind is his religion.

4. Richard Falk, "World Order Conception and the Peace Process", in Elise Boulding, ed., *Building Peace in the Middle East: Challenges for States and Civil Society* (Boulder and London: Lynne Rienner, 1994), p. 190.

5. Mohammed Heikal, *Illusions of Triumph: An Arab View of the Gulf War* (London: Harper Collins Publishers, 1992). See also Earl H. Tilford, Jr., "The Meaning of Victory in Operation Desert Storm: A Review Essay", in *Political Science Quarterly*, 108, 2 (Summer 1993), pp. 327-331.

6. See, for instance, Francis Fukuyama, *The End of History and the Last Man* (London: Penguin Books, 1992).

7. See "*Tchernubeel al-Khaleej*" [The Gulf's Chernobyl], in *Al-Hawadith*, 5 April 1991, pp. 14-15.

8. Naseer Aruri, "The Recolonisation of the Arab World", in *Middle East International*, no. 385, 12 October 1990, pp. 18-19.

9. Heikal, *Illusions of Triumph*, p. 7.

10. See, for instance, "*Usuliat fi kulli makan. . . Limada?*" [Fundamentalisms everywhere. . . Why?], in *Al-Shuruq*, no. 54, 15-21 April 1993, pp. 12-21.

11. Clovis Maksoud, "The Healing Process Begins", in *American-Arab Affairs*, no. 35 (Winter 1990-91), p. 56.

12. Muhammad al-Sayyid Sa'id, *Mustaqbil al-Nidam al-'Arabi Ba'da Azmati al-Khaleej* [The Future of the Arab Regional System in the Aftermath of the Gulf Crisis] (Kuwait: Alim al-Ma'rifa, 1992), p. 242.

13. Richard K. Herrmann, "The Middle East and the New World Order", in *International Security*, 16, 2 (Fall 1991), p. 42.

14. Eden changed his mind and "wrote to Eisenhower that he [did] not think Nasser a Hitler, but that the parallel with Mussolini [was] close". See Ritchie Ovendale, *The Middle East Since 1914* (London: Longman, 1992), p. 75.

15. See Robert Springborg's criticism of the Hitler thesis, "Selling War in the Gulf", in St. John Kettle and Stephanie Dowrick, eds., *After the Gulf War: For Peace in the Middle East* (Leichardt, Sydney: Pluto Press, 1991), pp. 26-43.

16. Noam Chomsky, "The U.S. and the Gulf Crisis", in Haim Bresheeth and Nira Yuval-Davis, eds., *The Gulf War and the New World Order* (London and New Jersey: Zed Books, 1991), p. 19.

17. Since reunification in 1990, Yemen has slowly but progressively liberalized polity and society. Jordan's incipient democratization was inaugurated in the November 1989 elections. Further democratization initiatives saw the introduction of the National Charter, a supplement to the constitution, enshrining rights for both the citizenry and the Crown. In 1993, party politics were resumed with the legalization of political parties for the first time in nearly 30 years. The November 1993 elections produced a pluralist parliament.

18. Suad al-Sabah, "*al-Thawrat al-Thalatha*" [The Three Revolutions], in *Ash-shiraa'*, no. 421, 16 April 1990, p. 32.

19. Saudi Arabia is a classic example. The stationing of the Coalition troops on her soil contrasts with the Kingdom's long-standing reluctance to grant such concessions. In the mid-1950s and the early 1960s the U.S. deployed strategic bombers at Dhahran to deter Soviet and Egyptian aggression scenarios. See C. Madison, "Mastering the Game", in *National Journal*, 3 November 1990, p. 251. The U.S. had no problem securing funds from the Saudis for "Desert Shield", with King Fahd reported to have told visiting James Baker that "his government [would] pay all the monthly in-country costs of the U.S. troops. . . ." See details in W. Mossberg and P. Truell, "Arab Allies of the U.S. Promise Billions to Help Cover Pentagon's Expenses", in *The Wall Street Journal*, 10

September 1990. The pliancy of the Saudis encouraged U. S. legislators to make further requests through George Bush — namely, the reduction of oil prices (whatever happened to market forces?!). See "Senators Call on Saudis to Reduce Oil prices", in *East Asia/Pacific Wireless File 193*, (U.S. Information Service) 4 October 1990, p. 19.

20. Recall that the U.S. was behind the overthrow of the Mossadeq Government in August 1953.

21. For instance, Jordan suffered greatly, with her U.S. aid suspended, as a result of her anti-U.S.-led forces' deployment stance, and her favoring of a diplomatic solution to the crisis. These stances were, in great measure, influenced by a democratically-elected Lower House and an anti-war public opinion. Tim Niblock observes that Arab states which opposed the coalition forces' deployment were those in which democratic initiatives were being taken (Jordan, Yemen, Algeria). See his article, "The Need for a New Western Arab Order", in *Middle East International*, no. 385, 12 October 1990, p. 17.

22. Dina Haseeb and Malak S. Rouchdy illustrate this, pointing out the pecuniary motives of Egypt (which also applied to Syria). See "Egypt's Speculations in the Gulf Crisis: The Government's Policies and the Opposition Movements", in Bresheeth and Yuval-Davis, eds., *The Gulf War*, pp. 70-79.

23. Sami Yousif, "The Iraqi-US War: A Conspiracy Theory", *ibid.*, pp. 51-69. Still on the subject of conspiracy, according to Mohamed Heikal Libya's strongman, Qaddafi, believed in a conspiracy telling former Algerian leader, Chadli Benjedid, "I am haunted by a feeling that it's all arranged." (I.e., Saddam Hussein was implementing a U.S. plan). See *Illusions of Triumph,* p. 21.

24. See, for instance, Ramsey Clark, *The Fire this Time: U.S. War Crimes in the Gulf* (New York: Thunder's Mouth Press, 1992). See also *Needless Deaths in the Gulf War: Civilian Casualties During the Air Campaign and Violations of the Laws of War* (New York: Human Rights Watch, 1991).

25. For a detailed report on environmental damage associated with the Gulf War, particularly concerning the use of chemical weapons, see Sue Mayer and Paul Johnson, *Chemical Weapons and Their Effects on the Environment*, Greenpeace Environment Briefing (London: Greenpeace, February 1991). See also Andrew R. G. Price, *Possible Environmental Threats from the Current Gulf War* (York: University of York, 1991).

26. Noam Chomsky, referring to a similar convenient distinction, notes: "It is fashionable to distinguish between 'authoritarian' and 'totalitarian' regimes.... A regime is 'totalitarian', hence the essence of evil, if it restricts 'economic freedom', a term that does not refer to the freedom of workers or communities to control production, but rather to the freedom for private business . . . to conduct its affairs without constraint. If it does not restrict the freedom to invest and exploit, a state is at worst 'authoritarian'. This distinction has little relation to the concern of the regime for the welfare of the population." See his *Towards A New Cold War* (London: Sinclair Browne Ltd, 1982), p. 6.

27. A popular joke underscores the rulers' slowness to respond to Kuwaiti women's demands for enfranchisement. It states that the quickest decision the amir has ever made was to escape Kuwait on the eve of the Iraqi invasion.

28. For details of human rights violations in these countries, see country reports in *Huquq al-Insan fi al-Watan al-'Arabi* [Human Rights in the Arab Homeland] (Cairo: Arab Human Rights Organization, 1992 and 1993).

29. For examples of Arab democratic reversals and breakdowns see Larbi Sadiki, *Progress and Retrogression in Arab Democatization* (East Jerusalem: PASSIA, 1992). A shorter version of this monograph can also be found in *Journal of Arabic, Islamic and Middle Eastern Studies*, 1, 1 (September 1993), pp. 80-103.

30. *East Asia/Pacific Wireless File 009*, 14 January 1992, pp. 14-15.

31. Jim Hoagland, "Washington's Algerian Dilemma", in *The Washington Post*, 6 February 1992. Another excellent article is by David Ignatius, "Islam in the West's Sights: The Wrong Crusade?", in *The Washington Post*, 8 March 1992. For the U.S. response with regard to the restoration of democracy in Haiti, see "Restoring Democracy in Haiti: Persistence and Patience", *State Dispatch*, 3, 8 (24 February 1992), pp. 132-133.

32. Edward Said, *Culture and Imperialism* (London: Chatto & Windus, 1993), p. 363.

33. For details of how the Security Council was manipulated to secure resolutions to use force against Iraq, see Keith Suter, "The United Nations and the Gulf Conflict", in Kettle and Dowrick, eds., *After the Gulf War*, pp. 56-66. Arab suspicion of, and frustration with, the UN are articulated by 'Abd al-'Alim Mohamed Abd al-'Alim, "*Al-Umam al-Muttahida wa Harb al-Khaleej*" [The United Nations and the Gulf War], in *Qira'at Siyasiyyah*, 2, 2 (Spring 1992), pp. 101-119.

34. In *UN Chronicle* (March 1992), p. 29.

35. Richard Falk, "Reflections on Democracy and the Gulf War", in *Alternatives*, 16 (1991), p. 267.

36. David Campbell, *Politics Without Principle: Sovereignty, Ethics, and the Narratives of the Gulf War* (Boulder and London: Lynne Rienner, 1993), pp. 62-64. See also Michael McKinley, ed., *The Gulf War: Critical Perspectives* (Sydney: Allen and Unwin, 1994).

37. Clark, *The Fire This Time*, p. 61.

38. Campbell, *Politics Without Principle,* p. 63.

39. Richard K. Herrmann, "The Middle East and the New World Order", in *International Security*, 16, 2 (Fall 1991) p. 42.

40. From author's interview with visiting Lebanese Parliament Speaker, Nabih Birri, 27 September 1993, Canberra.

41. For instance, what ever happened to such resolutions by the General Assembly such as 181 (November 1947) which recommends "a plan of partition with economic union"; 194 (December 1948) which, *inter alia*, resolves the right

of return for Palestinians; 273 (May 1949), which in deciding Israel's admission to the UN, calls on the Jewish state to "unreservedly . . . undertake to honor" Resolutions 181 and 194 "from the day it becomes a Member of the United Nations"; 3236 (November 1974) which "reaffirms the inalienable rights of the Palestinian people in Palestine, including: a) the right to self-determination . . . . b) the right to national independence and sovereignty"; and "reaffirms also the inalienable right of the Palestinians to return. . ."? What is the fate, for instance, of Security Council resolutions 298 (September 1971) confirming the illegality of Israel's actions "to change the status of the City of Jerusalem, including expropriation of land and properties [and] transfer of populations and legislation aimed at the incorporation of the occupied section. . ."; 605 (December 1987) and 607 (January 1988) which deplore Israel's human rights violations in the Palestinian and Arab lands it occupies reaffirming the applicability of the Geneva Convention's provisions under the section on the "Protection of Civilian Persons in Time of War, of 12 August 1949" to those occupied lands?

42. For instance, Dr. Nabil Sha'ath, Minister for Planning and Economic Cooperation in the Interim Palestinian Authority (Gaza/Jericho), and chief Palestinian negotiator with Israel, projects an optimistic view that downplays the difficulties in the implementation of the agreements resulting from the DOP. This stands in contrast with the cynicism expressed by Dr. Raji Sourani, Director of the Gaza Centre for Rights and Law, the Gaza Affiliate of the International Commission of Jurists, and by Yosef Ben-Aharon, former Director-General of the Israeli Prime Minister's Office and Head of Israel's Delegation to the Peace Talks with Syria. The author spoke with all three men who gave seminars at the Australian National University on 20 September 1994, 15 November 1994, and 30 November 1994 respectively.

43. For a critical view of Western double standards regarding ignored UN resolutions on Arab questions see Abderrahmane Bensid, "The Maghreb and the Gulf Crisis", in *American-Arab Affairs*, no. 35 (Winter 1990-91), pp. 27-32.

44. Muhammad Amin Bwisir, son of the late Libyan Foreign Minister who was killed in that incident, has since 1992 begun legal proceedings through Egyptian courts to seek compensation from Israel. His argument is that a just world order should deal with and punish Israel the way it has Libya. See Tareq Hassan, "*Al-Irhab al-Israili Amam Mahkamat Janoub al-Qahira*" [Israeli Terrorism Before South Cairo's Court], in *Rose El-Youssef*, 3 March 1992, pp. 12-13.

45. John R. Macarthur, *Second Front: Censorship and Propaganda in the Gulf War* (New York: Hill & Wang, 1992).

46. Arabs have their inconsistencies too. While most Arabs, bar those from the Gulf states, opposed the U.S.-led involvement in the Gulf, today they would like to see similar involvement in Bosnia. It is also ironic that the most prominent "fundamentalist" leader, the blind cleric Shaikh 'Umar Abd al-Rahman,

sought exile in the United States, of all places, where he resided in Brooklyn. This constitutes a major contradiction with his anti-Western and anti-American stances.

47. The fallout from the revelations of Western arms transfers to Iraq continues. For an insight into the British example, see Richard Norton-Taylor, "Waldegrave Blamed for Iraqgate", in *Guardian Weekly*, week ending 19 December 1993, p. 1; pp. 10-11.

48. According to the Stockholm International Peace Research Centre (SIPRI), this downward trend is due to major cutbacks by the USA, the former USSR, and countries in Central and Eastern Europe. See *SIPRI Yearbook 1992* (Oxford: Oxford University Press, 1992), p. 189. See also Yahya M. Sadowski, *Scuds or Butter? The Political Economy of Arms Control in the Middle East* (Washington, D.C.: The Brookings Institution, 1993).

49. Refer to *SIPRI Yearbook, 1993,* p. 189.

50. *Ibid.* See table of world military expenditure, p. 260. See also William D. Hartung, "Relighting the Middle East", *The New York Times*, 20 September 1991. For details of American-Saudi arms deals from which the U.S. was expected to reap some U.S.$20 billion for the 1991-92 period alone, see *The Military Balance: 1991-92* (London: Brassey's, 1992). An excellent contribution to this debate is made by Said K. Aburish. He ably establishes the nexus between oil and power in the arch-conservative monarchy, observing, for instance, that the only two sectors that have enjoyed budgetary increases over the past five years have been the Ministry for Defence and the Royal Household. See his *The Rise, Corruption and Coming Fall of the House of Saud* (London: Bloomsbury, 1994), especially chapter 1.

51. Patrick E. Tyler, "Gulf Security Talks Stall Over Plan for Saudi Army", *The New York Times*, 13 October 1991.

52. Herrmann, *The Middle East and the New World Order*, p. 47.

53. Eric Schmitt, "US and Kuwait Sign Pact on Troops", *New York Times*, 20 September 1991. For details of Arab reaction to the Kuwait-US pact, see Joseph A. Kechichian, *Political Dynamics and Security in the Arabian Peninsula through the 1990s* (Santa Monica: RAND, 1993), pp. 86-88.

54. See *Qira"at Siyasiyyah*, 3, 3-4 (Summer/Fall 1993), p. 192.

55. Kechichian, *Political Dynamics and Security*, p. 86.

56. Robert Latham, "Democracy and War-making: Locating the International Liberal Context," *Millenium: Journal of International Studies* 22 (Summer 1993), p. 164.

57. Munir Shafiq, "*Al-Istratijiyyah al-Amirikiyyah wa Atharu al-Nidam al-'Alami al-Jadid 'ala al-'Alim al-'Arabi*" [The U.S. Strategy and the Effects of the New World Order on the Arab World], in *Qira'at Siyasiyyah*, 2, 1 (Winter 1992), pp. 5-24.

58. Falk, "Reflections on Democracy and the Gulf War", pp. 270-271.

59. Abd al-Fattah al-Rashdan, "*Al-Nidam al-Duwali al-Jadid wa Atharuhu 'ala al-Nidam al-'Arabi*" [The New World Order and its Effects on the Arab System], in *Qira'at Siyasiyyah*, 3, 1 (Winter 1993), p. 108.

60. *Ibid.*

61. Ali E. Hillal Dessouki, "Strategic Balance and Disarmament in the *Middle East*", in E. Boulding, ed., *Building Peace in the Middle East*, p. 201. At a meeting in Cairo in early February, the Damascus Declaration States (Egypt, Syria and the six Arab Gulf states) criticized Israel's exemption from nuclear inspections, arguing that this is incompatible with the quest for peace in the region. They want international pressure to be brought to bear on Israel to sign the Nuclear Non-Proliferation Treaty. Israel has never declared her nuclear status, although she is reported to possess installations for the manufacture and storage of some 300 nuclear weapons.

62. For further details on this point, and the "unraveling of the nonproliferation regime in the Middle East" see Samuel S. Kim, *The Quest for a Just World Order* (Boulder, Colorado: Westview Press, 1984), pp. 124-126.

63. See Larbi Sadiki, "Islamists Fight the Secular State", *The Canberra Times*, 3 August 1993.

64. See Larbi Sadiki, "Sudan Seeks Help", in *The Observer*, 1, 3 (December 1994), p. 21.

65. See Larbi Sadiki, "Why Yemen is at War", in *Current Affairs Bulletin*, 71, 3 (October/November 1994), pp. 41-43. Also by the same author, see "Why Yemen Matters", in *Asia-Pacific Defence Reporter*, 21, 4/5 (October/November 1994), p. 18; p. 27.

66. For a summary of these conflicts, see "The Fire Next Time", in *The Middle East* (January 1993), pp. 9-10.

67. Author's interview with Ibrahim Ghosha, Hamas spokesman, 5 June 1994, Amman, Jordan.

68. Joseph S. Nye, Jr., "What New World Order?", in *Foreign Affairs*, 71, 2 (Spring 1992), pp. 83-96.

69. Paul Hirst, "The World Order, The Phoney Peace", in *New Statesman and Society*, 3, 117 (7 September 1990), pp. 12-14.

70. See Simona Sharoni, "Gender Issues in Democracy: Rethinking Middle East Peace and Security from a Feminist Perspective", in E. Boulding, ed., *Building Peace in the Middle East*, pp. 99-109. See also Carol Cohn, "Sex and Death in the Rational World of Defense Intellectuals", in Linda Rennie Forcey, ed., *Peace: Meanings, Politics, Strategies* (New York: Praeger, 1989), pp. 39-72. Feminist discourses present alternative visions and conceptions for a more just and harmonious world order. Some contributions to these discourses include V. Spike Peterson, ed., *Feminist (Re)Visions of International Relations* (Boulder: Lynne Rienner, 1992); Nira Yuval Davis and Floya Anthias, eds., *Woman-Nation-State* (London: Macmillan, 1988); Anne Tickner, *Gender in International Relations* (New York: Columbia University Press, 1992); and Cynthia Enloe, *Bananas,*

Bases and Beaches: Making Feminist Sense of International Politics (London: Pandora, 1990). Also Evelyne Accad, *Sexuality and War: Literary Masks of the Middle East* (New York: New York Univ. Press, 1990), especially pp. 160-164.

71. Rita Whalstrom, "The Challenge of Peace Education: Replacing Cultures", in Elise Boulding (ed.), *New Agendas for Peace Research: Conflict and Security Reexamined* (Boulder, Colorado: Lynne Rienner, 1992), p. 173.

72. Falk, "Reflections on Democracy and the Gulf War", pp. 268-272.

73. Adel Mahdi, "*Al-Nidam al-Duwali al-Jadid wa Aatharuhu 'ala al-Wath' al-'Arabi al-Islami*" [The New World Order and its Impact on the Arabo-Islamic State of Affairs], in *Qira'at Siyasiyyah*, 1, 2-3 (Spring/Summer 1991), pp. 5-25.

74. Rachid al-Ghannouchi, "Islam and the West: Realities and Prospects", translated by Azzam Tamimi, unpublished paper delivered at Westminster University, London, 1993.

75. Hassan Elhag Ali, "The New World Order and the Islamic World", in *The Journal of Islamic Social Sciences*, 8, 3 (1991), p. 465.

76. *Ibid.*

77. Al-Ghannouchi, "Islam and the West", p. 4.

78. A fine article criticizing Western Islamophobia is by Leon T. Hadar, "What Green Peril?", in *Foreign Affairs*, 72, 2 (Spring 1993).

79. Robin Wright, "Islam, Democracy and the West", in *Foreign Affairs*, 71, 3 (Summer 1992).

80. One of the best references for explaining the different meanings of *jihad* can be found in M. Mazzahim Mohideen, "Islam, Nonviolence, and Interfaith Relations", in Glenn D. Paige, Chaiwat Satha-Anand and Sarah Gilliatt (eds.), *Islam and Nonviolence* (Honolulu: Matsunaga Institute for Peace, University of Hawaii, 1993), pp. 137-143. Also see Fazlur Rahman, *Islam* (Chicago and London: University of Chicago Press, 1979), p. 37, and John L. Esposito, *The Islamic Threat: Myth or Reality?* (New York and Oxford: Oxford University Press, 1992), pp. 32-33.

81. Interview with Rachid al-Ghannouchi, 15 April 1993, London.

82. *Ibid.*

83. Amin Saikal, "Islamic Fundamentalists, 'Now Under Every Bed'", *The Canberra Times*, 9 March 1992, p. 9.

84. See, for instance, Paul Ekins, *A New World Order: Grassroots Movements for Global Change* (London: Routledge, 1992). See also Keith Hindell, "Reform of the United Nations", in *The World Today*, 48, 2 (February 1992), pp. 30-33.

85. See "The Commission Document on Peace Building in the Middle East" in E. Boulding, ed., *Building Peace in the Middle East*, p. 49.

86. *Ibid.*

87. Fred Halliday, "International Relations: Is There a New Agenda?", in *Millenium*, 20, 1 (1991), pp. 57-72.

Name Index

Aideed, Mohamed Farah 615
Allan, James 133
Allende, Salvador 127
Allott, Philip 65, 566
Alvarez, Jose xv, xviii
Amin, Idi 39, 63, 422–3
Angell, Norman 520
Annan, Kofi 78
Aquinas, St.Thomas 607
Argaña, Luis María 405
Aristide, Jean-Bertrand 4, 73, 135, 399, 400, 443
Aruri, Naseer 609
Austin, J. 5

Baena Soares, João 404
Baker III, James A. 3
Barber, Benjamin 328
Barnes, Samuel H. 164
Bedie, Henri 445
Ben Ali, Zine El Abidine 619
Ben Bella, Ahmed 420
Beutz, Molly xiv, 123–67
Beynon, J. 459
Binaisa, Godfrey L. 39–40
Bøås, Morten 450
Boniface, Dexter S. xvii, xix, 395–411
Boutros-Ghali, Boutros 139, 362, 366, 498
Bowett, D.W. 63
Briand, Aristide B. 44, 486
Bronckers, Marco 308
Bucaram, Abdala 407
Buergenthal, Thomas 25, 41
Burchill, Richard xvii, xviii, xxiv, 371–94
Burki, S.J. 460–61
Burnside, Craig 455–6
Bush, George W. 32, 517, 528, 607, 609–11, 615
Byers, Michael 94

Caiden, Gerald 460
Campbell, David 613
Carothers, Thomas 496
Carpio, Ramiro de León 404
Carter, Jimmy 504
Carty, Anthony 508–9
Cédras, Raoul 85, 399
Cerna, Christina xii, xx, 483
Charlesworth, Hilary 508
Chávez, Hugo 407
Chayes, Abram 261, 294–5
Chayes, Antonia 294–5
Chesterman, Simon 94
Chewning Fábrega, Lawrence 404
Chomksy, Noam 521, 611
Chopra, Jarat 163
Chou, En-Lai 68
Clark, Ramsey 613
Clemenceau, Georges 10
Clinton, Bill 313
Cobbett, William 119
Collier, Paul 453–4, 455–6
Cooter, Robert 276
Crawford, James xiv, 49–69, 94, 157–8
Cromwell, Oliver 6
Cubas, Raúl 405

Dehousse, Renaud 328
Delors, Jacques 333
Derrida, Jacques 479–81, 495
Deudney, Daniel 293
Deutsch, Karl 270, 302
Devarajan, S. 455–6
Diamond, Larry 150
Dicey, A. 51
Doe, Samuel 424–5, 430–31
Dollar, David 452, 455–6
Doyle, Michael 235–8, 255, 487, 489, 491
Dulles, Allen 516
Dunn, John 142

Eco, Umberto 501
Eide, Asbjørn 105
Eisenstein, Zillah 559
Elazar, Daniel J. 337
Espína, Gustavo 404
Evans, Gareth 528
Ezetah, Reginald xiv, 169–208

Falk, Richard 339, 342, 502, 505, 514, 608, 613, 618
Farer, Tom 129, 139, 539
Feroni, Marco 464
Fielding, Lois 179
Fishkin, James 155
Ford, Glyn 393
Foucault, Michel 481
Foudah, Mohamed Faraj 619
Fox, Gregory H. xii, xiii, xv, xxiii, 71–96, 130, 484–5, 488, 492–3, 497
Franck, Thomas M. xii, xiii, xx, xxi, 3–48, 66, 73, 125, 135, 187, 251–6, 296, 372, 398, 441, 482–5, 488–93, 495, 497–8, 502, 504, 516–18, 521–5, 539–40, 555
Fujimori, Alberto 155, 402–3
Fukuyama, Francis 473–82, 489, 492, 495–6, 516–17
Fuller, Lon 252
Fuszara, Malgorzata 547

Gama, Jaime 376
Garrett, Stephen 127, 161
Georgiev, Dencho 508
Ghai, Yash xxiv, 573–606
Ghannouchi, al-, Rachid 618, 619
Gibson, Susan 138
Gilbert, C. 449
Glendon, Mary Ann 283
González Macchi, Luis Ángel 405
Gorbachev, Mikhail 528, 548
Grindle, M. 451
Grotius, Hugo 505–6
Gwin, Catherine 453

Haas, Ernst B. 308
Habermas, Jürgen 201
Habre, Hussein 426–9
Haggard, Stephan 452
Haider, Jörg 371–2, 376–7, 393
Halpern, Manfred 553
Hansen, H. 459
Harcourt, W.V. 63
Harrigan, Jane 454
Hart, H.L.A. 511
Hassan, Farooq 160
Hegel, Georg W.F. 229, 474–5
Heikal, Mohamed Hasanayn 609
Held, D. 119, 478–81
Henkin, Louis 261
Hiboux, B. 449
Higgins, Rosalyn 199
Hitler, Adolf 393, 611
Hobbes, Thomas 242, 244, 511
Hoffman, Stanley 199
Hohe, Tanja 149
Holgren, T. 455–6
Hume, David 6
Huntington, Samuel P. 185, 480–81
Hussein, Saddam 610–11, 613, 615

Ignatieff, Michael 126
Isham, Jonathan 452, 463

Jackson, John 312
James, H. 451
Jayakumar, S. 581
Jefferson, Thomas 6, 53
Jennings, Robert 69
Joyner, Christopher C. xviii, 345–69

Kabbah, Ahmad Tejan 73, 432
Kahler, Miles 454
Kaldor, Mary 494–6
Kant, Immanuel xv, xvi, 45, 138, 171, 190–91, 196, 211–37, 239–51, 253, 255, 258, 260, 270, 486–7, 504, 513, 515, 519–20
Kantor, Mickey 404
Kapur, Devesh 448, 456, 458, 464
Kaufman, Daniel 452
Kaufmann, D. 450, 452
Kellogg, Frank B. 44, 486
Kelsen, Hans 224–5
Kennedy, David 507–8
Keohane, Robert 270–71, 340
Killick, Tony 453
Kim, Dae Jung 453
Kiriyama, Nobuo 303
Kirkpatrick, Jeanne 612
Kissinger, Henry 510, 516
Klare, Karl 561
Klein, Pierre xvii
Klotz, Audie 399
Knack, Stephen 454
Köhler, Hans 456
Koskenniemi, Martti 133–4, 137, 199, 496–7, 508–9, 512, 542
Kraay, Aart 450, 452
Kritz, Neil 165
Krueger, Anne 455
Kufuor, Kofi Oteng xix, 413–45

Lake, Anthony 129
Lansing, Robert 10
Lasswell, Harold 261, 514
Lauterpacht, Hersch 67
Lindberg, Leon N. 308
Lissouba, Pascal 444–5
Locke, John 6, 172, 242
Lodge, Juliet 331
Lowenfeld, Andreas 280

Macarthur, John 615
McCall Smith, James 316
McDougal, Myres 261, 514
Macey, Jonathan 478
McGoldrick, Dominic 18, 524
Machiavelli, Niccolò 191, 265, 510
McNair, A.D. 55
Madison, James 6
Maine, Henry 68
Maksoud, Clovis 609
Mancini, Federico 336
Marcos, Ferdinand 6
Marks, Susan xiii, xx, xxi, xxiii, 95, 133–4, 136–7, 140, 142–3, 471–99
Marshall, John 192
Marx, Karl 474, 481
Mazrui, Ali 58, 591
McNair, A.D. 55
Meron, Theodor 24
Metternich, Clemens 519
Meyers, Diana 236
Mill, John Stuart 39, 84
Miller, Geoffrey 478
Moravcsik, Andrew 266
Morgenthau, Hans 265, 516
Mosley, Paul 454
Mouffe, Chantal 529
Muñoz, Heraldo 396
Murdoch, Rupert 604
Mussolini, Benito 6

Naím, Moises 451, 460, 462
Nakarada, Radmila 561
Narayan, D. 463
Nasser, Gamal Abdel 610
Nelson, Joan 453
Nixon, Richard 510
Nkrumah, Kwame 417–20, 423
Nolte, Georg 130, 484–5, 492–3
Noriega, Manuel Antonio 22, 41, 46, 62, 161, 406
Nye, Joseph 270–71, 340

Obote, Milton 422–3, 434
Oeter, Stefan 334
Oppenheim, L. 53–54
Otto, Dianne xxi, 527–71
Oueddei, Goukhouni 426–9, 434
Oviedo, Lino César 404–5

Pankin, Boris D. 40
Pascal, Blaise 447
Pateman, Carole 529, 553
Patten, Chris 391
Perry, G. 460–61
Pinochet, Augusto 127, 154
Plato 6
Pol Pot, 62
Powell, A. 449
Préval, Rene 400
Pritchett, Lant 452, 463
Purvis, Nigel 567
Putnam, Robert 289

Ratner, Steven 141
Rawls, John 241–2, 253–5
Reagan, Ronald 17, 615
Reisman, W. Michael xx, 9, 32, 80, 179, 277, 514, 538
Rhodes, Cecil 35
Richardson, Elliot 29, 32
Riddell, R. 464
Rodrik, Dani 452, 461
Root, Elihu xi, xiii, 95–6
Roth, Brad R. xii, xiii, xv, xxiii, 71–96, 133, 137, 149, 154, 166
Rousseau, Jean Jacques 244, 588
Ruiz, Lester 559
Rummel, R.J. 235–6
Russell-Johnston, David 387

Sadiki, Larbi xxii, xxiii, 607–28
Said, Edward 613
Sakamoto, Yoshikazu 555
Sands, Philippe xvii
Santiso, Carlos xx, 447–68, 455, 463
Sassou-Nguesso, Denis 434
Sathirathai, Surakiart 567
Schmitter, Philippe 333–4
Schreuer, Christoph 263
Schroeder, Gerhard 377

Schüessel, Wolfgang 392
Schumpeter, Joseph 85, 133, 373
Schwarzkopf, Norman 614
Schwimmer, Walter 387
Scobbie, Iain 508
Sen, Amartya 138, 154, 602
Serrano Elías, Jorge 403–4, 406
Sesesoku, Mobutu 199
Shapiro, Ian 153
Shell, G.R. 315
Simpson, Gerry J. xxi, 501–26
Slaughter, Anne-Marie xvi, 261–296, 333, 486–93, 497
Stein, Eric xvi, xvii, 297–342
Steiner, Henry 134, 537
Stiglitz, Joseph 448
Stone, D. 451
Stroessner, Alfredo 404
Suharto, President 452
Sullivan, Roger J. 227
Svensson, Jacob 452–3

Taft, William Howard 79
Tarp, F. 459
Taylor, Charles 155
Tesauro, Giuseppe 331
Tesón, Fernando R. xv–xvi, xxi, 211–60, 486–9, 492, 496, 498, 502, 504, 514–21, 525
Thucydides 265
Tieya, Wang 565
Tocqueville, A. de 476
Tolbert, William 424–5, 434
Toye, John 454
Trujillo, César Gaviria 404
Turner, Ted 604
Tutwiler, Margaret 612

Vines, D. 449

Waltz, Kenneth 516
Walzer, Michael 84, 117
Wasmosy, Juan Carlos 404–5
Webb, Richard 448, 456, 458, 464
Weiler, Joseph 283, 303, 335–6, 340
Westlake, John 69
Wheatley, Steven xiii, xiv, xvii, 99–122, 149
Wight, Martin 505, 519
Williamson, J. 460, 462
Wilson, Woodrow 10–11, 258, 504, 516, 608
Wolfensohn, James 462–3
Wright, Robin 619

Yeltsin, Boris 3

Zakaria, Fareed xv
Zoido-Lobaton, Pablo 450, 452